COASTAL CALIFORNIA

STUART THORNTON

SOUTHERN CALIFORNIA

Santa Cruz
Gilroy
Watsonville
101
152
Los Banos
152
Chowchilla
Oakhurst
41

Hollister
Monterey
Salinas
25
5
Madera
145
180
Millerton Lake
168
Shaver Lake
Sierra National Forest

Carmel
33
Fresno
99
Selma
180

Point Sur
Los Padres National Forest
King City
101
Coalinga
269
Kingsburg
Hanford
198
Visalia
245

Big Sur
198
Lemoore
41
Tulare

Cambria
1
Avenal
Kettleman City
43
99
190
Porterville

Paso Robles
Cholame
65
Delano

46
46
46
5
155

Morro Bay
41
Wasco
33
178

Point Buchon
San Luis Obispo
58
Buttonwillow
58
Bakersfield

101
119
99
223

Santa Maria
Los Padres National Forest
166
Maricopa
166

Point Arguello
Lompoc
1
Solvang
33
138

Point Conception
101
154
Santa Barbara
5

Ojai
Angeles National Forest

150
126

Ventura
Santa Paula

San Miguel Island
Channel Islands National Park
Oxnard
101

PACIFIC OCEAN

Santa Rosa Island
Santa Cruz Island
Point Dume
1
Glendale

Santa Monica

San Nicolas Island
Santa Catalina Island

San Clemente Island

0   25 mi
0   25 km

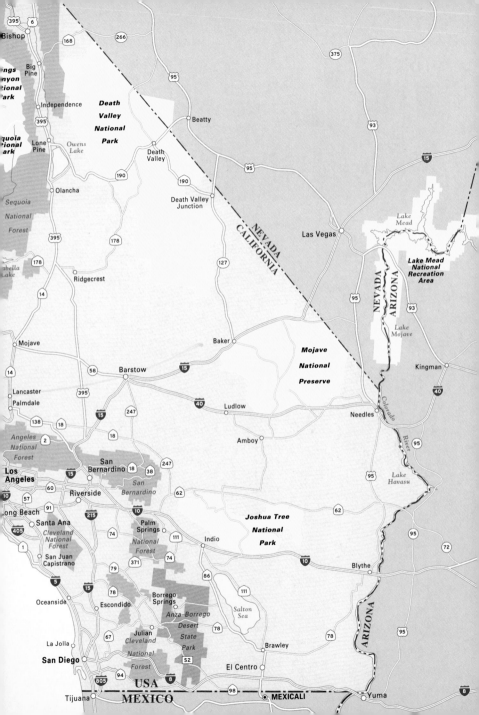

Contents

Discover
Coastal California

California exists on the edge of the continent, where land and sea collide. This primal collision is the source of stunning beauty and singular geological phenomena like the volcanic dome of Morro Rock, the honeycombs of sea caves along the La Jolla headlands, and sheer walls of rock falling to the ocean at Big Sur. Waterfalls decorate cliff faces like ribbons and spring wildflowers paint the hillsides above the blue-green ocean.

This land- and seascape can push you to your physical limits. Catch your first wave in the surf at Santa Cruz. Dive into a Monterey kelp forest. Explore deep into a Channel Islands sea cave by kayak. Trek the wild Lost Coast Trail. You might spot condors swirling in the night sky like embers, elk appearing out of the fog on secluded beaches, or migrating gray whales sounding offshore. You'll never get closer to the natural world than you can here.

Along the more placid sections of the coastline, the crashing surf smooths out into gentle waves lapping soft sands. This is the California coast that people all over the world know through popular culture, where surfers and sun worshippers share the shoreline with movie stars. Warm sunshine, colorful boardwalks, and easy access attract visitors seeking pleasure and relaxation.

California is also on the cutting edge of art, entertainment, and cuisine. Trends are born here before spreading to the rest of the country and the world. It's where we first heard the music of the Doors, the Grateful Dead, Dr. Dre, and Beck. You can still catch performances of up-and-coming bands of all stripes at venues like The Fillmore in San Francisco or The Troubadour in Los Angeles. Or see the art of the avant-garde at world-class museums and galleries. California gave the United States its first taste of sushi and its first native-born wines, and it still offers one-of-a-kind culinary experiences. Enjoy authentic dim sum in San Francisco, or sample Mexican street tacos topped with kimchi in Los Angeles. Head to Napa, Sonoma, Carmel Valley, or Paso Robles to discover your new favorite wine. Or visit one of the North Coast's many microbreweries for your first sip of oatmeal stout or tangerine wheat ale.

Drink it all in. You'll return from your adventures on the edge of the continent with stories at the tip of your tongue.

Planning Your Trip

▶ WHERE TO GO

San Francisco and the Bay Area

The politics, the culture, the food—these are what make San Francisco world famous. Dine on cutting-edge cuisine at high-end restaurants and off-beat food-trucks, tour classical and avant-garde museums, bike through Golden Gate Park and stroll along Fisherman's Wharf, where barking sea-lions and boisterous street performers compete for attention. The surrounding region is as diverse as the city itself. To the north, Marin offers wilderness seekers a quick reprieve from the city, while ethnic diversity and intellectual curiosity give the East Bay a hip urban edge. Meanwhile, Coastside's beaches are a quick drive away.

Wine Country

Wine Country is famous for a reason. This is the place to pamper yourself with excellent wines, fantastic food, and luxurious spas.

Napa offers all of the above in spades, while Sonoma boasts a bit of history and a mellower atmosphere. The Russian River adds redwoods and river rafting to the mix.

North Coast

For deserted beaches, towering redwoods, and scenic coastal towns, cruise north along the Redwood Coast. Explore Russian history at Fort Ross on the grassy bluffs of the Sonoma Coast, and fall in love with Mendocino's small-town charm and nearby wineries. Detour west to the Lost Coast to experience coastline barely touched by human development.

Monterey Bay

Go surfing and wine-tasting in Santa Cruz. Witness gray whales and sea lions off rugged Monterey Bay, and then explore their environment at the world-class Monterey Bay

Butterfly Beach in Santa Barbara

Aquarium. Wander around in the art galleries of Carmel-by-the-Sea and then take a stroll on the light sands of Carmel Beach. If you are a wine lover, be sure to head out to Carmel Valley to taste some of the region's best wines.

Big Sur and the Central Coast

Some of the most beautiful and most adventurous coastline in the world is along this section of the Pacific Coast Highway. Camp and hike the unspoiled wilderness of Big Sur, and then tour grandiose Hearst Castle in San Simeon. For a relaxing getaway, head to one of the region's beach towns: Cambria, Cayucos, Morro Bay or Pismo Beach.

Santa Barbara and Ventura

Take in the picturesque Santa Barbara Mission and then stroll down the city's State Street, which is lined with shops, restaurants, and bars. Enjoy the lonely coastline of Jalama Beach or, to truly get away from it all, take a boat ride out to Channel Islands National Park. Bask in Santa Barbara's abundant sunshine at nearby Refugio State Beach on the Gaviota Coast or visit the wine tasting rooms of downtown Santa Barbara and the nearby Santa Maria Valley. Farther south, Ventura offers visitors a historic mission, a vibrant downtown, and a reliable surf break.

Los Angeles and Orange Country

For a taste of the iconic California dream, you can't beat Los Angeles. From the glitz and glamour of Hollywood and Beverly Hills to the camp and kitsch of Santa Monica's Pier, L.A. is

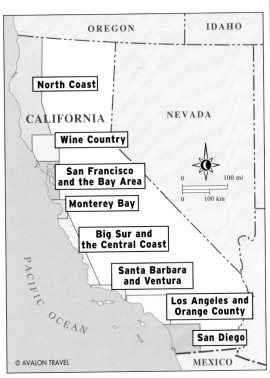

all California culture, all the time. Kids of all ages come to visit Walt's original Disneyland, while sun and surf worshippers ride the waves or relax on the sugar-sand beaches.

San Diego

For the sun-drenched, sugar-sand California beach experience portrayed in endless films and TV shows, come to San Diego. Maritime museums ring the downtown harbor, while, across the bay, Coronado's vibrant and historic Hotel del Coronado creates a centerpiece for visitors to the city. Gorgeous beaches stretch from Point Loma north to La Jolla and the North County coast, begging surfers, swimmers, strollers, and sunbathers to ply their sands.

fog over the Golden Gate Bridge

▶ WHEN TO GO

California's best feature is its all-season appeal. "The coldest winter I ever spent was a summer in San Francisco," a quote falsely attributed to Mark Twain, still holds true as the wind and fog that blows through the city June-August surprises unsuspecting visitors. Regardless, summer remains the coast's travel season; expect crowds at popular attractions, wineries, beaches, and campgrounds. In fall, the summer crowds have left but the weather is still warm. It is also the time when some of the best waves occur along the coast for surfers. Winter is the rainy season, with lots more precipitation falling on the northern section of the coastline than in the south.

▶ BEFORE YOU GO

The easiest airports to fly into are San Francisco (SFO) and Los Angeles (LAX). If you're flying into San Francisco, you can avoid some of the hassle by flying into nearby Oakland or San Jose. Similarly, Los Angeles offers several suburban airports—Burbank, Long Beach, and Ontario—which are less congested. Visiting the United States from abroad, you'll need your passport and possibly a visa.

Book hotels early and buy tickets for big-name attractions in advance. Purchase tickets to Alcatraz in San Francisco at least two weeks in advance. Save money buying advance tickets for Disneyland online as well. Make early reservations for big-name restaurants. Lodging and campground reservations are essential in Big Sur.

Summer fog is likely along the coast, and guaranteed in San Francisco. Bring layered clothing, especially a wind-resistant coat and a warm sweater. Expect warm temperatures and even desert heat in Los Angeles and San Diego in the summer. Bring sunscreen; that coastal fog doesn't stop UV rays.

Explore Coastal California

► PACIFIC COAST ROAD TRIP

The ideal way to experience the California coast is to hit the road. Following this legendary road trip will take you through California's bustling cosmopolitan cities, small beach towns, redwood forests, and lots and lots of sandy beaches.

For the most part, you'll cover this stunning 850 miles by following the legendary Pacific Coast Highway (Highway 1) and U.S. 101. You can switch back and forth between the two routes depending on your pace and your interests. Highway 1 is generally more scenic; U.S. 101 is usually faster. A few diversions onto other routes are necessary to cover the entire coast (for example, you'll be driving I-5 between San Diego and Los Angeles).

The day-by-day route below begins in San Diego, but you can just as easily start in Los Angeles or San Francisco, or reverse the route from driving north to driving south if that works better for you. You can also break out any section of the coast as its own 2-4 day getaway.

San Diego

DAY 1

Easygoing San Diego is a great place to start any vacation. Upon arrival, orientate yourself by driving to the top of Mt. Soledad Veterans Memorial, a small mountain that has views of the whole city. After that, head down to La Jolla Cove to go kayaking or snorkeling; or just lie on the beach.

In the afternoon, visit Balboa Park, where you'll spend most of your time at the San Diego Zoo. End your day with a meal in the Gaslamp Quarter. Try the historic Grant Grill or new favorite Café Chloe.

DAY 2

Take I-5 out of San Diego a half hour north to the North County beach towns of Encinitas, Carlsbad and Oceanside. The drive from Encinitas to Oceanside is just half an hour along a coastal road that changes names in

a seabird in San Diego

Santa Monica Pier

each city; make sure to stop for a surf or a swim since the ocean temperatures will get cooler and cooler as you head up the coast. Continue on Highway 1 rather than inland U.S. 101 to visit Huntington Beach before turning off towards Long Beach for a nighttime ghost tour on The Queen Mary, an ocean liner that is now home to restaurants, a hotel, shops, and a museum. If you are daring enough, book a room for the night in the haunted ocean liner.

Los Angeles
DAY 3
Jump on I-405 to save some time and drive about 30 miles north, exiting towards Venice Beach. Park your vehicle and take a stroll along the Venice Beach Boardwalk to take in the local wildlife that includes bodybuilders, street performers, and alternative-culture types. Without getting back on the highway, take the local roads paralleling the beach 10 minutes north to Santa Monica. Enjoy the amusement park rides of the Santa Monica Pier or just take a break on Santa Monica Beach. For dinner, get a taste of the

Caribbean at Santa Monica's causal but popular Cha Cha Chicken or backtrack to Venice for a hearty Italian meal at C&O Trattoria.

DAY 4
Consider heading inland for a day of culture (and pop culture) sights. For aesthetic stimulation, visit the world famous Getty Center or the Los Angeles County Museum of Art. Less rigorous on the mind is a walk down the star-studded Hollywood Walk of Fame and a stop at the historic Grauman's Chinese Theatre, where you can find the handprints of your favorite movie stars. End the day with a cocktail at Sunset Boulevard's Rainbow Bar & Grill. There might even be a grizzled, past-his-prime rocker sitting in the booth next to you.

DAY 5
Take the Pacific Coast Highway (Highway 1) out of Santa Monica west as it heads away from sprawling Los Angeles and into Malibu. Stop at Malibu's Surfriders Beach to watch the surfers compete for its famously peeling waves (or catch one yourself). After a morning outdoors, feed your

Malibu's Getty Villa

Santa Cruz Island

mind with ancient art at The Getty Villa in Malibu. (Admission is free, but you'll need to reserve a ticket in advance.) Finish the day by watching the sun slide into the Pacific from the outdoor deck of Neptune's Net, while enjoying fresh seafood.

If you want to spend more time in the Los Angeles area, you can easily fill a couple of days enjoying Disneyland Resort.

Santa Barbara and Ventura

DAY 6

Wake up early and drive north on the scenic Pacific Coast Highway. Thirty-five miles from Malibu, at Oxnard, merge onto U.S. 101. Once on U.S. 101, take the exit towards Ventura Harbor to catch a boat out to the Channel Islands National Park for a day of hiking, snorkeling, or kayaking on Santa Cruz Island. (Make boat reservations in advance.) Return to Ventura Harbor and eat dinner at one of the harbor's seafood restaurants, such as Brophy Brothers or Andria's Seafood Restaurant & Market. Or head to downtown Ventura for a vegan dinner at Mary's Secret Garden or an Italian meal and cocktail at hip Café Fiore.

DAY 7

Take U.S. 101 north just a half hour (28 miles) to Santa Barbara. Get a history fix at the Santa Barbara Mission, which might be the most beautiful of the 21 Spanish missions in California. Then taste some of Santa Barbara's wines on the Urban Wine Trail, six tasting rooms on lower State Street, or head north for a day at palm-lined Refugio State Beach, 20 miles west of Santa Barbara on U.S. 101.

If your schedule is flexible, you might consider another full day in Santa Barbara, another day of wine-tasting in nearby Santa Maria Valley, or a day on the Gaviota Coast. Whatever you do, stop at Santa Barbara's State Street for a fine meal or cocktail at a restaurant like the local favorite Opal. Or head off State Street for superb Mexican food at La Super-Rica Taqueria.

Hang gliders take flight over Morro Bay.

Big Sur and the Central Coast
DAY 8

Drive 1.75 hours (92 miles) north of Santa Barbara on U.S. 101 to San Luis Obispo's Madonna Inn, where you can take in its kitschy decor during a restroom and stretch-the-legs break.

Outdoor enthusiasts will want to head off the highway and go west on Los Osos Valley Road just 20 minutes (12 miles) to Montana de Oro State Park, one of the state's best coastal parks. Picnic at Spooner's Cove or hike to the top of 1,347-foot-high Valencia Peak. Then head back to U.S. 101 North, but be sure to turn onto Highway 1 north to take in sunset over Morro Rock, known as the "Gibraltar of the Pacific."

Another option is to drive an hour north (44 miles) to opulent Hearst Castle. Tours of this "ranch" built for newspaper magnate William Randolph Hearst offer insight into the lifestyle of the rich and famous.

However you spend your day, end it with a meal in one of the Central Coast's unassuming beach towns: Morro Bay, Cayucos or Cambria.

DAY 9

Head north on Highway 1 for what might be the most scenic day of driving on your whole trip. The two-lane highway here winds along the mountains of Big Sur with plentiful views of the ocean. From Cambria to the heart of Big Sur is 75 miles, but the scenery, winding roadway, and frequent road construction can make the drive last well over two hours. Be sure to make multiple stops to take in the scenery at places like Salmon Creek Falls, Sand Dollar Beach, and Julia Pfeiffer Burns State Park. Catch sunset at Pfeiffer Beach before spending the night camping in the redwoods of Pfeiffer Big Sur State Park or in the meadow at Andrew Molera State Park. Or splurge with a once-in-a-lifetime stay at the Post Ranch Inn or Ventana resort.

Monterey Bay
DAY 10

Continue up Highway 1 for 45 minutes (less than 30 miles) through the northern section of Big Sur to the Monterey Peninsula.

CALL OF THE WILD

Pier 39's resident California sea lions

California's ecosystems host a wide range of wildlife. Here are some spots where you can view animals that are truly wild in their natural surroundings.

SAN FRANCISCO AND THE BAY AREA

- **San Francisco's Pier 39** has shops, restaurants, an aquarium...and its own colony of **California sea lions.**

- **Point Reyes National Seashore** is rich in wildlife from giant **elephant seals** to tiny, endangered **Myrtle's silverspot butterflies.**

- The **Farallon Islands** off San Francisco are home to a quarter-million **seabirds** and one of the world's largest **great white shark** populations.

NORTH COAST

- **Elk Prairie** and **Elk Meadow,** in Prairie Creek Redwood State Park, are named after their inhabitants. A transplanted **herd of elk** also roams **Sinkyone Wilderness State Park.**

- **Bodega Head** offers views of migrating **gray whales** January-May.

MONTEREY BAY

- The eucalyptus grove at **Natural Bridges State Park** hosts thousands of migrating **monarch butterflies** mid-October and mid-February. They also stop at Pacific Grove's **Monarch Grove Sanctuary.**

- Marshy reserve **Elkhorn Slough** hosts 340 **bird species,** including brown pelicans and snowy plovers.

- Paddle up **Elkhorn Slough** to spot **sea lions, harbor seals,** and **sea otters,** as well as fish species like **bat rays** and **leopard sharks.**

- In the tide pools at **Natural Bridges State Park,** you can find **sea stars** and **sea anemones.**

BIG SUR AND THE CENTRAL COAST

- Keep your eyes peeled along **Big Sur's Highway 1** to spot **California condors,** North America's largest land birds.

- **Piedras Blancas Elephant Seal Rookery,** north of San Simeon, is a great place to see the beasts up close.

SANTA BARBARA AND VENTURA

- Unique native species like **island scrub jays** and **island foxes** are prevalent all over **Santa Cruz Island,** especially in the **Scorpion Ranch Campground.**

LOS ANGELES AND ORANGE COUNTY

- A **herd of bison** were introduced to **Catalina Island** in the 1920s for the filming of a movie, and have thrived in the years since.

- Take a snorkel or a scuba dive at the **Avalon Underwater Park** to view fish, including **garibaldi** and **gobies.**

SAN DIEGO

- A little underwater park right off **La Jolla Cove** is home to **sardines, garibaldi,** and **leopard sharks.**

- Book a trip on one of San Diego's **whale- and dolphin-watching** cruises; you might also spot **sea lions** and **harbor seals.**

Point Lobos State Reserve

Take a walk in Carmel's Point Lobos State Reserve or head to scenic Carmel Beach. Then drive a few miles north into Monterey to spend the afternoon at the Monterey Bay Aquarium.

Dine on fresh seafood at Pacific Grove's Passionfish, Monterey's Fish House in Monterey, or Phil's Fish Market up Highway 1 in Moss Landing.

If you want to spend another day in this area, consider heading inland to Carmel Valley for wine-tasting, wandering the galleries in Carmel-by-the-Sea, or golfing at Pebble Beach.

DAY 11

Getting to Santa Cruz is an easy 50-minute drive (44 miles) up Highway 1 from the Monterey Peninsula. The eclectic beach city is an ideal place for recreation whether you are surfing, stand up paddleboarding, or hiking redwood-filled Forest of Nisene Marks State Park or the coastal bluffs of Wilder Ranch State Park. End the day with thrill rides at the Santa Cruz Beach Boardwalk.

If your adrenaline is still racing from the Boardwalk rides, calm down with a drink at Red Restaurant & Bar or The Crepe Place.

San Francisco
DAY 12

Wake up early for a drive on Highway 1 from Santa Cruz less than two hours (80 miles) to San Francisco. In the city, spend a few hours in the hands-on science museum The Exploratorium. As the sun goes down, make sure to head out for dinner, whether it's seafood at the Tadich Grill, modern Vietnamese at The Slanted Door, or pizza at Tony's Pizza Napoletena. If you still have energy, make sure to check out some of San Francisco's vibrant nightlife or a concert at a venue like The Fillmore.

DAY 13

Head out on the San Francisco Bay to take a fascinating tour of the island prison Alcatraz. Or secure passage on a ferry to Angel Island, which has hiking trails that offer up some of the finest views of the city.

In the afternoon, shop the used clothing

CATCH OF THE DAY

Some of the state's best seafood can be found in unpretentious eateries just footsteps from the ocean.

SAN FRANCISCO AND THE BAY AREA

- A highlight of the seafood-heavy menu at **San Francisco** institution **Tadich Grill** (page 105) is the amazing seafood cioppino, chock full of prawns, scallops and shellfish.

- Sit at the long marble bar at **Swan Oyster Depot** (page 110) to dine on seafood that was swimming in the ocean just hours earlier.

- Enjoy a decadent Dungeness crab roll or a superbly spicy salmon sandwich at **Fish** (page 127), right on **Sausalito**'s harbor.

- At **Sam's Chowder House** (page 170), enjoy both daily fresh catches and a great view of **Half Moon Bay.**

NORTH COAST

- The smoked wild salmon at tiny **Katy's Smokehouse** (page 316) in **Trinidad** may be the best you've ever eaten.

- **Tomo Japanese Restaurant** (page 313) in **Arcata** serves creative sushi rolls with local ingredients like smoked albacore.

MONTEREY BAY

- **Abalonetti** (page 363) on **Monterey**'s Fisherman's Wharf is known for its spicy Buffalo calamari.

- Get a taste of local Sicilian fishermen's recipes like squid pasta at **Monterey's Fish House** (page 363).

- Tucked between the harbor and the ocean in **Moss Landing, Phil's Fish Market** (page 351) serves up hearty and tasty cioppino and sea scallops.

BIG SUR AND THE CENTRAL COAST

- Just off **Cayucos Beach, Rudell's Smokehouse** (page 415) serves seafood tacos with big flavors, including smoked salmon, smoked albacore, and an unexpected topping: chopped apples.

- People line up at **Splash Café** (page 438) in **Pismo Beach** for a taste of rich, buttery clam chowder.

- Right on **Morro Bay**'s Embarcadero, **Tognazzini's Dockside Restaurant** (page 421) is the place for fresh barbecued oysters in garlic butter.

SANTA BARBARA AND VENTURA

- **Andria's Seafood Restaurant & Market** (page 468), right by **Ventura**'s harbor, is known for its fish and chips.

- Expect salmon, ahi, and swordfish at local favorite **Brophy Brothers** (page 458), with locations on both the **Santa Barbara** and **Ventura** harbors.

LOS ANGELES AND ORANGE COUNTY

- Enjoy crispy shrimp tacos topped with a pineapple salsa at local hangout **Neptune's Net** (page 531), overlooking a **Malibu** surf break.

- **The Lobster Trap** (page 562) on **Catalina Island** is all about tasty crustaceans, with options like lobster stuffed with bay shrimp.

SAN DIEGO

- Choose between 13 varieties of fish tacos, including ahi and shark, at San Diego's **Blue Water Seafood Market & Grill** (page 617).

- Tattooed surfers serve up tasty rolls and microbrews at **The Fish Joint,** (page 625) a tiny sushi bar in **Oceanside.**

the view from Angel Island's Mount Livermore

stores of Haight-Ashbury or the department stores of Union Square. Or browse the books at North Beach's City Lights.

You'll quickly fall in love with San Francisco; you can easily extend your romance to three or four days if you have the time.

The North Coast
DAY 14
Your journey north begins with a drive on U.S. 101 over San Francisco's iconic Golden Gate Bridge. Then after five miles turn off U.S. 101 to Highway 1 at Mill Valley. On the slow, over-four-hour drive up the coast (around 160 miles), make time to stop at places like the tiny but unique Sea Ranch Chapel, which is just feet off Highway 1, and the Point Arena Cove, a mile drive off the highway to a scenic little bay popular for fishing and other recreation.

End the day in the community of Mendocino with a view of the sunset at Mendocino Headlands State Park or a pint at the lively Patterson's Pub.

DAY 15
Drive Highway 1 north of Fort Bragg until the road turns inland to connect with U.S. 101 after about an hour of driving. Opt for the Avenue of the Giants, a 31-mile drive through redwoods by the Eel River. Even though it's only 31 miles, the drive could take a few hours if you decide to get out of your car and ponder the trees.

Get back on U.S. 101 North and head an hour north (60 miles) to Eureka. Stop to wander the city's Old Town and Waterfront.

Continue on U.S. 101 another 10 minutes or so to charming Arcata. Wander through the redwoods of the Arcata Community Forest before sundown. Dine at one of the restaurants surrounding the lively Arcata Plaza.

DAY 16
Start your morning with a tasty crepe from Arcata's Renata's Creperie and Espresso before hitting U.S. 101 North on your final day. About 20 minutes north (15 miles), exit to the scenic coastal city of Trinidad. Have your camera handy for photos of Trinidad Memorial Lighthouse, Trinidad Head and Trinidad State Beach.

Another half hour up U.S. 101 (26 miles), turn onto Newton B. Drury Scenic Drive to explore Prairie Creek Redwoods State Park. If you have the energy, drive out Davison Road to Gold Bluffs Beach, where Roosevelt elk roam the sands, and continue on the dirt drive to hike the one-mile round-trip Fern Canyon Trail, which passes through a steep canyon draped in bright green ferns.

Head back out to U.S. 101 to drive the 45 minutes (38 miles) to Crescent City, where you can get a hotel room and a full night's sleep.

▶ BEST BEACHES

Wide, golden beaches with abundant sunshine and legendary surf breaks. Lonely stretches of sand framed by coast redwoods and jagged cliffs. Boardwalks crowded with kids, cotton candy, and roller coasters. California has any kind of beach you could possibly want.

San Francisco and the Bay Area

The Bay Area is one of California's largest urban centers, but sand seekers can still find beaches within—or just outside of—city limits.

OCEAN BEACH

Best for Sunsets, Strolls

Ocean Beach runs for miles along the western edge of San Francisco, offering a break from busy streets and popular tourist attractions (page 87).

BAKER BEACH

Best for Scenery, Photo-Ops, Sunbathing

On the northern tip of San Francisco, this mile-long swath of sand is your best bet for stunning views of the Golden Gate Bridge and San Francisco Bay. Its northernmost end is known for its nude sunbathers (page 87).

MUIR BEACH

Best for Scenery, Wildlife, Sunbathing

Wildlife enthusiasts flock to Muir Beach. It's a great place to spot migrating whales

Baker Beach

the overlook at Muir Beach

during the winter, while fall brings monarch butterflies. The stream that runs into the ocean at Muir Beach provides a habitat for shorebirds, salmon, trout, and amphibians. Meanwhile, the relatively secluded north side provides a habitat for nude sunbathers (page 133).

STINSON BEACH
Best for Families
In the summers, Stinson has lifeguards, a snack bar, picnic areas, and restrooms that are ideal for a family day at the beach. Surfers, kayakers, and paddleboarders test their skills in the surf (page 137).

AÑO NUEVO STATE RESERVE
Best for Wildlife
At Año Nuevo, gigantic elephant seals turn the beach into a battleground. You can also catch a glimpse of eerie, abandoned light station buildings right offshore (page 172).

North Coast
These beaches showcase the wild rugged beauty that happens when the land meets the sea with little or no human intervention. On these beaches, there is frequently more wildlife than people. The coast up here is perfect for long contemplative walks, as long as you remember to bundle up. Opportunities for recreation include surfing, diving, kayaking, and stand up paddleboarding—without the crowds typical of beaches to the south.

MANCHESTER STATE PARK
Best for Beachcombing, Solitude
The long, debris-strewn beach at Manchester State Park is ideal for beachcombers and offers views of the Point Arena Lighthouse in the distance (page 258).

BIG RIVER
Best for Kayaking, Stand Up Paddleboarding, Beginners' Surfing
Big River, just south of Mendocino Village, has a range of recreational opportunities. Surf the beach break, launch a kayak to explore the nearby headlands, or paddleboard the river before steering your board into the ocean (page 268).

SURF AND TURF

surfing in Santa Cruz

With great weather year-round, lots of ocean access, and a bounty of beaches, the California coast has a plethora of recreational opportunities.

SURFING

After Hawaiians introduced surfing to California, it became an essential part of the state's culture. California offers up waves for every level of surfer. Iconic surf breaks like San Diego's **Black's Beach,** San Onofre State Beach's **Trestles,** Santa Barbara's **Rincon,** and Santa Cruz's **Steamer Lane** make surfers from around the world drool with anticipation. Beginners can attempt their first waves at the gentle peeling waves of Santa Cruz's **Cowell's Beach** or Malibu's **Surfriders Beach.**

STAND UP PADDLEBOARDING

California's many bays, inlets, and protected areas offer the perfect places to get started paddleboarding, which is the coast's fastest growing sport. Hit the water at Orange County's **Dana Point Harbor,** the Central Coast's **Cayucos Beach, Santa Cruz Harbor,** and Mendocino's **Big River.**

SCUBA DIVING AND SNORKELING

The best way to see the multitude of sea life, kelp forests, and reefs off the California shoreline is to put on some snorkeling or scuba gear. The clear waters and swaying kelp forests of the **Monterey Peninsula** make it one of the biggest dive destinations in the state. **Santa Catalina Island** offers pristine underwater habitats for the adventurous, while San Diego's **La Jolla Cove** provides easy access to the undersea world.

BACKPACKING

To get away from the crowds, strap on a backpack and head to the state's more remote areas. The North Coast's **Lost Coast Trail** is a three-day backpacking trip along a 24-mile stretch of rugged coastline. Big Sur's **Ventana Wilderness** offers multiday excursions to hot springs and peaks with fabulous coast views. Get away from it all at backcountry camps on **Santa Cruz Island** and **Santa Rosa Island** in Channel Islands National Park.

Santa Cruz Beach Boardwalk

USAL BEACH
Best for Wildlife, Solitude

Follow the mountainous dirt road to Usal Beach, where you may spot Roosevelt elk. Even if you don't spot these giant animals, you can bask in the solitude (page 301).

BLACK SAND BEACH
Best for Scenery

An easier way to take in the rugged beauty of the Lost Coast is to marvel at Shelter Cove's Black Sand Beach, framed by the towering King Range (page 298).

EEL RIVER
Best for Swimming

Not all great beaches are on the ocean; beaches line the Eel River as it winds beside the popular Avenue of the Giants, offering motorists a cool dip and a sit in the sun (page 292).

TRINIDAD STATE BEACH
Best for Scenery, Picnics

This scenic stretch of shore under the rounded knob of Trinidad Head is ideal for a family picnic—especially if you pick up some smoked salmon from nearby Katy's Smokehouse (page 314).

GOLD BLUFFS BEACH
Best for Wildlife, Solitude

Back in 1850, prospectors found gold flakes on Gold Bluffs Beach, but now the treasures of this coastal area within Prairie Creek Redwoods State Park are its remote beauty and its wildlife (page 322).

SOUTH BEACH
Best for Surfing

Crescent City's South Beach offers one of the state's northernmost surf breaks, where surfers of all abilities can catch easy peeling waves (page 328).

Monterey Bay

Monterey Bay, a National Marine Sanctuary known for its wildlife, has relatively pristine waters and a handful of worthy beaches.

COWELL'S BEACH
Best for Surfing

Santa Cruz's Cowell's Beach has slow rolling

waves perfect for beginners. Even though it gets crowded, the surfers here are usually friendly (page 342).

SANTA CRUZ BEACH BOARDWALK
Best for Families
Just feet away from Cowell's, the Santa Cruz Beach Boardwalk makes families happy with its rides, games, and entertainment. The boardwalk's Giant Dipper roller coaster has been thrilling riders since 1924 (page 336).

MOSS LANDING
Best for Beachcombing, Solitude
Usually uncrowded except for a handful of surfers and anglers, Moss Landing State Beach and Zmudowski State Beach offer long stretches of lonesome sand (page 350).

CARMEL BEACH
Best for Scenery, Sunsets, Dog Lovers
With its pale sand and contrasting blue-green ocean water, Carmel Beach is a jewel of the Monterey Bay. It's also one of the friendliest beaches for dogs in the state. (page 371).

Big Sur and the Central Coast
The Big Sur coastline is rugged, but there are several places to access the beach and it's almost always worth the effort. As the mountains of Big Sur level out to the south, Cayucos, Morro Bay, and Pismo Beach have some of the finest swaths of sand north of the Los Angeles County line.

PFEIFFER BEACH
Best for Photo-Ops, Sunsets
Make sure that your camera has fully charged batteries for a trip to Big Sur's windswept Pfeiffer Beach, with picture-perfect rock formations offshore (page 389).

SAND DOLLAR BEACH
Best for Picnics
Protected by cliffs on windy days, crescent-shaped Sand Dollar Beach is a great spot for a picnic (page 391).

MOONSTONE BEACH
Best for Beachcombing
Hunt for the eponymous moonstones on

Big Sur's coastline

DOG DAYS

frolicking in the waves at Carmel Beach

Dog owners will have a lot more fun on the California coast with their furry friends along for the ride. Luckily, there are lots of options for people who want to bring their pets.

ACCOMMODATIONS

Kimpton Hotels, a luxury boutique hotel chain with 15 properties along the California coast, goes out of its way to welcome pets. It offers pet beds, food bowls, water bowls, and information about all the pet-friendly attractions and businesses in the area. Some of Kimpton's properties include San Diego's **Hotel Palomar,** Santa Barbara's **Canary Hotel** and San Francisco's **The Argonaut** and **Hotel Triton.**

In Del Mar, north of San Diego, **Les Artistes** has some pet-friendly rooms. Up the coast, the **Crowne Plaza Ventura Beach** has a whole floor of them.

In San Francisco's Pacific Heights neighborhood, the **Laurel Inn**'s rooms are all pet friendly, with a two-pet limit.

Wine Country is surprisingly pro-pet with Napa's **Napa Inn,** Saint Helena's **El Bonita Motel,** and Guerneville's **Sonoma Orchid Inn** all catering to canines.

On the North Coast, Fort Bragg's **Beachcomber Motel** offers pet-friendly hot tub suites. In nearby Anderson Valley, both the **Anderson Valley Inn** and the **Boonville Hotel** reserve a couple of rooms for families with dogs.

BEACHES

A few California beaches permit and even encourage dog visitation. One of the best is **Carmel Beach** located in Carmel-by-the-Sea. On any given day, more dogs roam this beach than people – and they can roam leash-free.

The north end of San Diego's **Ocean Beach** calls itself "The Original Dog Beach." It's also leash-free. **Del Mar City Beach** has a dog section that extends from 29th Street to Solano Beach.

Known as "Surf City USA," Orange County's **Huntington Beach** might as well be called "Dog City USA." The north end between Seapoint Avenue and 21st Street allows pets.

Santa Barbara's **Arroyo Burro Beach** permits pets to be off leash past the slough, while **Montara State Beach** in the Bay Area's Coastside invites dogs as long as they're leashed.

PARKS

The second largest park in San Francisco, **McLaren Park** has dog play areas. The **Coastside Trail** is a paved dog-friendly path that connects various Half Moon Bay beaches and the adjacent shoreline. One of the Monterey Peninsula's best places to hike with your dog is Carmel Valley's **Garland Ranch Regional Park.** The park has off-leash areas and water fountains designed to hydrate both you and your pet.

The **California State Parks** on the coast generally allow leashed dogs dogs in the day use areas but not on the trails. Contact the specific state park that you will be visiting to confirm where your pet is permitted.

McWay Falls on Pfeiffer Beach

this Cambria beach. Its impressive drift-wood structures are also worthy discoveries (page 409).

MORRO ROCK BEACH
Best for Photo-Ops, Surfing
Take a photo in front of 576-foot-high Morro Rock. The beach to its south is popular with surfers of all skill levels (page 420).

SPOONER'S COVE
Best for Scenery, Picnics
Soak up the natural beauty of Spooner's Cove, in Montana de Oro State Park. A scenic arch decorates the bluffs on the south end of the cove (page 416).

PISMO BEACH
Best for Families
Studded with volleyball courts and lifeguard stands, Pismo Beach feels like a Southern California beach without the massive development. It's ideal for a day with the family (page 435).

Santa Barbara and Ventura
The last strand of relatively undeveloped coastline before Southern California is north of Santa Barbara. Ventura draws surfers from throughout the Southland.

JALAMA BEACH COUNTY PARK
Best for Camping, Solitude
This beach park in the middle of nowhere is a refuge for surfers, anglers, beachcombers, and families who want to unplug from modern life (page 461).

REFUGIO STATE BEACH
Best for Swimming, Families
The best beach on the Gaviota Coast is on this protected cove lined with palm trees. Its ocean waters are calm enough for wading children and beginning kayakers (page 460).

ARROYO BURRO BEACH
Best for Dog Lovers
If you have a dog in tow, head to Santa Barbara's Arroyo Burro Beach. Past the slough, dogs are allowed off leash (page 449).

Leo Carrillo State Park

RINCON
Best for Surfing
Ranked 49th in *Surfer Magazine*'s list of the 100 best waves in the world, Rincon can produce a long peeling right with the right swell (page 451).

CALIFORNIA STREET BEACH
Best for Surfing, Sightseeing
To catch some hot surfing action, head to Ventura's California Street Beach, known locally as "C Street" (page 466).

Los Angeles and Orange County
Los Angeles and neighboring Orange County share a wealth of superb beaches, known to the world from decades of movies and television shows: broad, sandy, and packed with people during the summer months. The best of the best have a little something that sets them apart.

LEO CARRILLO STATE PARK
Best for Scenery, Camping, Dog Lovers
At the northern end of L.A. County, Leo Carrillo feels a world away from bustling Los Angeles. This 1.5-mile-long beach has tide pools, caves, and reefs. The northern section is also a perfect place to take your leashed pooch (page 512).

MALIBU SURFRIDERS BEACH
Best for Surfing
Surfers flock to Malibu Surfriders Beach to catch one of California's greatest peeling waves or to soak up the vibe of the surf culture that was born here in the early 1960s (page 512).

SANTA MONICA STATE BEACH
Best for Families, Sunbathing
Take in the plentiful Southern California sunshine and the amusements available at the Santa Monica Pier (page 513).

VENICE BEACH
Best for People-Watching
Venice Beach is a people-watcher's paradise, with a boardwalk filled with weightlifters, skateboarders, musicians, dancers, and vendors hawking their wares (page 498).

Hotel del Coronado, adjacent to Coronado Main Beach

HERMOSA BEACH
Best for Volleyball, Families

Hermosa Beach has the feel and attitude of a small beach town, even though it's surrounded by metropolitan Los Angeles. Volleyball nets are available for pickup games and "The Strand" is ideal for a jog or bike ride (page 550).

HUNTINGTON CITY BEACH
Best for Surfing, Sunbathing

Orange County's Huntington City Beach offers multiple recreation options, including surfing the waves that break on either side of the pier (page 564).

San Diego

With warmer ocean temperatures and year-round sunshine, San Diego's beaches are the most welcoming in the state.

CORONADO MAIN BEACH
Best for Families, Sunsets

Spread out, catch some sun, and take in views of the nearby Hotel del Coronado (page 601).

OCEAN BEACH
Best for People-Watching, Dog Lovers

Lying at the end of an eclectic hippie community, this beach is popular with dogs (and their people) (page 600).

LA JOLLA COVE
Best for Sunbathing, Snorkeling, Kayaking

La Jolla Cove is a pocket beach between two cliffs. Sunbathers take up most of the real estate on crowded weekends. An underwater park with sea caves right offshore is perfect for snorkelers and kayakers (page 586).

BLACK'S BEACH
Best for Advanced Surfing, Sunbathing

Black's Beach is a legendary surf spot and also a nudist beach. Getting here involves an adventurous hiking path down 300-foot-high cliffs (page 600).

▶ ROMANTIC GETAWAYS

Crashing waves, breathtaking views, gourmet restaurants, and luxury hotels make the California coast perfect for romance.

San Francisco and the Bay Area

Have a wonderful meal together at a fine San Francisco restaurant like Fleur de Lys or Michael Mina and then take in an opera at the War Memorial Opera House. End the night by sipping a cocktail and looking at the lights of the City from Harry Denton's Starlight Room. If you can really splurge, check into a room at the high-rise Mandarin Oriental San Francisco.

Just north of San Francisco, the Cavallo Point Lodge feels a world away from the city but still has all the amenities for a romantic evening, including a fine restaurant, a spa, a pampering staff, and stunning views of the Golden Gate Bridge and the Bay.

Down the coast, the Half Moon Bay area offers nice romantic retreats. Spend the night at the castle-like Ritz-Carlton Half Moon Bay or the comfy Pescadero Creekside Barn.

Wine Country

Wineries, superb restaurants, and a multitude of spas all conspire to make Wine Country a romantic environment. Spend a few hours tasting sparkling wine at Sonoma's Gloria Ferrer or Rutherford's Mumm winery, then splurge for a couples massage at Spa Terra. Treat your loved one to a meal at the revered French Laundry or Auberge du Soleil, with its wonderful views of Napa Valley.

North Coast

Pack up a bottle of wine and a blanket for a long walk on a secluded beach. Towards the upper end of the North Coast, Trinidad State Beach is a picturesque place to picnic. Farther south, Manchester State Park's beach offers miles of uncrowded coastline and large beached logs perfect for watching the sunset.

Rent one of the four private Victorian cottages at Eureka's Carter House Inns. Or spend a night at the lovely Elk Cove Inn, where you

Napa Valley vineyard at sunset

can walk down to a beautiful cove. Another option is the Sea Ranch Lodge, where every room has a view of the serene Sonoma Coast. The village of Mendocino has a variety of romantic bed-and-breakfasts including the Glendeven Inn and the Blue Door Inn.

Monterey Bay

Romance can blossom on a sunset walk on Carmel Beach, followed by a lovely French meal at La Bicyclette. Stay the night in one of Carmel's luxurious accommodations, like the coast-side Colonial Terrace Inn By The Sea or the East-meets-West-themed Tradewinds Carmel. Or drive a few miles north to Pacific Grove to spend an evening at the Seven Gables Inn, an ornate Victorian bed-and-breakfast with a view of the aptly named Lover's Point protruding into the bay.

Detour inland to Carmel Valley to visit one of the valley's many wine tasting rooms at the luxurious Bernardus Winery or the unassuming Heller Estate Organic Vineyards with its outdoor sculpture garden. Then relax together at Refuge Spa, a collection of hot, warm, and cool water tubs nestled under the Santa Lucia Mountains.

Big Sur and the Central Coast

Big Sur is a great place for romantic walks, whether to Pfeiffer Beach or to see Julia Pfeiffer Burns State Park's McWay Waterfall plunge into the Pacific. Post hike, a posh night at the Post Ranch Inn or Ventana resort will definitely impress your significant other. A less pricey but cozy alternative is Deetjen's Big Sur Inn.

South of Big Sur and inland, visit Paso Robles for wine-tasting and a growing foodie scene. Taste the fine wines at Eberle Winery and then have a fine meal at Artisan. Spend a night at the boutique Hotel Cheval or the Paso Robles Inn, where you can snuggle in a private hot springs mineral pool on the deck of your room.

Back on the coast, a romantic evening will come easy with a night at the historic Cass House Inn, a luxury bed-and-breakfast in the tiny beach town of Cayucos. Another option is to reserve one of the rooms with a

Avalon Harbor on Catalina Island

sunset on the beach in La Jolla

natural hot springs water tub on the deck at the Sycamore Mineral Springs Resort.

Santa Barbara and Ventura

Filled with fragrant flowers and beautiful Spanish-influenced architecture, Santa Barbara is one of the coast's finest spots for romance. Take the Urban Wine Trail to wine-taste within the city and then have dinner at fancy French restaurant Bouchon or enjoy Middle Eastern food on the garden patio at Zaytoon.

The Canary Hotel is a luxury hotel with a rooftop deck and a fireplace for a romantic evening under the stars. Another option is the elegant Cheshire Cat Inn, a Victorian bed-and-breakfast; some rooms have soaking tubs.

Los Angeles and Orange County

Is there anything more romantic than heading out to an island together off the coast? Find out on a trip to Catalina Island, where you'll spend the night in the small harbor city of Avalon. Once there, enjoy a romantic dinner at Avalon Grille or Ristorante Villa Portofino. Then splurge for a night's stay at the Pavilion Hotel or Villa Portofino.

In Orange County, Dana Point's Blue Lantern Inn has luxurious rooms and a deck out front to take in the sunset over the scenic harbor below. In nearby San Clemente, South of Nick's serves up creative upscale Mexican food and cocktails.

San Diego

San Diego is a great place for relaxing, re-charging, and romance. After enjoying the sun on one of the city's many fine beaches, head to the scenic coastal community of La Jolla for an afternoon of shopping. If you get hungry, enjoy a meal with ocean views inside George's at the Cove.

End the day with cocktails and seaside views at the historic Hotel del Coronado. Or opt for a drink at the Grant Grill, a restaurant and bar within the historic US Grant Hotel, located in the city's Gaslamp Quarter.

SAN FRANCISCO AND THE BAY AREA

Famed for its ethnic diversity, liberal politics, and chilling dense fog, the San Francisco Bay Area manages somehow both to embody and to defy the stereotypes heaped on it. Street-corner protests and leather stores are certainly part of the landscape, but family farms and friendly communities also abound. English blends with languages from around the world in an occasionally frustrating, often joyful cacophony. Those who've chosen to live here often refuse to live anyplace else, despite the infamous cost of housing and the occasional violent earthquake.

San Francisco perches restlessly on an uneven spit of land overlooking the Bay on one side and the Pacific Ocean on the other. Refer to the City as "San Fran," or worse, "Frisco," and you'll be pegged as a tourist immediately. To locals, the City is the City, and that's that.

Urban travelers can enjoy San Francisco's great art, world-class music, unique theater and comedy, and a laid-back club scene. Many visitors come to the City solely for the food; San Francisco functions as a culinary trendsetter that competes with the likes of Paris for innovation and prestige.

The Golden Gate Bridge leads into the North Bay, with its reputation for fertile farmland, intense material wealth, windswept coasts, and towering redwoods. An adventure here can be urban and touristy or rural and outdoorsy. The far more locally used Bay Bridge leads to the East Bay and the city of Oakland. The one-time hard-scrabble working-class town has entered a new phase of its evolution. Thanks to an influx of artists, creative chefs, and local entrepreneurs, the media,

HIGHLIGHTS

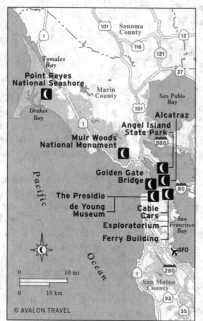

LOOK FOR **◖** TO FIND RECOMMENDED SIGHTS, ACTIVITIES, DINING, AND LODGING.

◖ Cable Cars: Get a taste of free-spirited San Francisco – not to mention great views of Alcatraz and the Bay – via open-air public transit (page 39).

◖ Ferry Building: The 1898 Ferry Building has been renovated and reimagined as the foodie mecca of San Francisco. The Tuesday and Saturday Farmers Market is not to be missed (page 42).

◖ Alcatraz: Spend the day in prison...at the famous former maximum security penitentiary in the middle of the Bay (page 46).

◖ Exploratorium: Explore San Francisco's innovative and interactive science museum in its new bayside location. The exhibits here are meant to be touched, heard, and felt (page 51).

◖ The Presidio: The original 1776 El Presidio de San Francisco is now a dormant military installation and national park. Tour the historic buildings that formerly housed a military hospital, barracks, and fort – all amid a peaceful and verdant setting (page 53).

◖ Golden Gate Bridge: Nothing beats the view from one of the most famous and fascinating bridges in the country. Pick a fogless day for a stroll or bike ride across the 1.7-mile span (page 53).

◖ de Young Museum: The revamped de Young has become the showpiece of Golden Gate Park. A mixed collection of media and regions is highlighted by the 360-degree view from the museum's tower (page 61).

◖ Angel Island State Park: While it once served as a waystation for immigrants, today this island in the Bay offers casual and serious hiking trails, and amazing views of the City, Alcatraz, and the Golden Gate Bridge (page 127).

◖ Muir Woods National Monument: Wander more than six miles of trails winding through redwoods – some of the most stunning and accessible of the big trees in the Bay Area (page 132).

◖ Point Reyes National Seashore: Point Reyes provides acres of hiking, biking, and birdwatching at the tip of the Marin coast. Brave the 300 steps to check out the 1870 lighthouse with its original Fresnel lens (page 139).

including *The New York Times*, have discovered Oakland and declared it a hip destination. The East Bay is also home to erudite, progressive (and sometimes aggravating) Berkeley—the birthplace of many liberal political movements from the 1960s all the way up to today.

The original University of California sits in Berkeley, offering protest groups for liberals and top-flight technical educations to multitudinous engineers.

South of the City, Silicon Valley is all about the technology. With the likes of

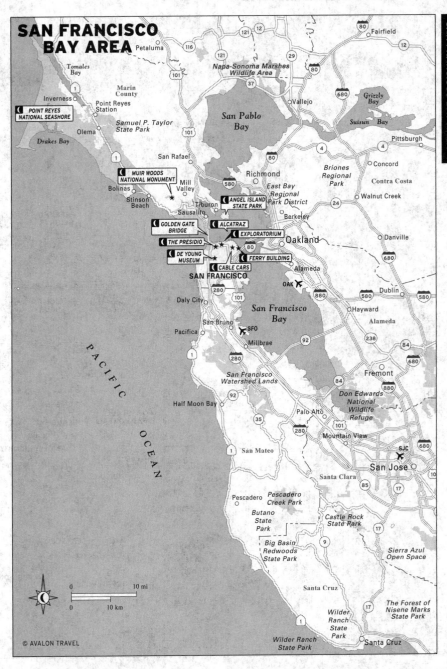

SAN FRANCISCO BAY AREA

POINT REYES NATIONAL SEASHORE

MUIR WOODS NATIONAL MONUMENT

ANGEL ISLAND STATE PARK

GOLDEN GATE BRIDGE

ALCATRAZ

THE PRESIDIO

EXPLORATORIUM

DE YOUNG MUSEUM

FERRY BUILDING

CABLE CARS

SAN FRANCISCO

Tomales Bay

Marin County

Inverness

Point Reyes Station

Petaluma

Samuel P. Taylor State Park

Olema

Drakes Bay

Bolinas

San Rafael

Stinson Beach

Mill Valley

Tiburon

Sausalito

Richmond

San Pablo Bay

Napa-Sonoma Marshes Wildlife Area

Vallejo

Grizzly Bay

Suisun Bay

Pittsburgh

Concord

Contra Costa

Walnut Creek

Briones Regional Park

East Bay Regional Park District

Berkeley

Oakland

Alameda

Danville

Daly City

San Bruno

Pacifica

Millbrae

SFO

San Francisco Bay

OAK

Hayward

Alameda

Dublin

San Francisco Watershed Lands

Half Moon Bay

Palo Alto

Don Edwards National Wildlife Refuge

Fremont

Mountain View

Santa Clara

San Jose

SJC

Pescadero

Pescadero Creek Park

Butano State Park

Big Basin Redwoods State Park

Castle Rock State Park

Sierra Azul Open Space

Santa Cruz

Wilder Ranch State Park

The Forest of Nisene Marks State Park

Santa Cruz

PACIFIC OCEAN

Fairfield

Petaluma

0   10 mi
0   10 km

© AVALON TRAVEL

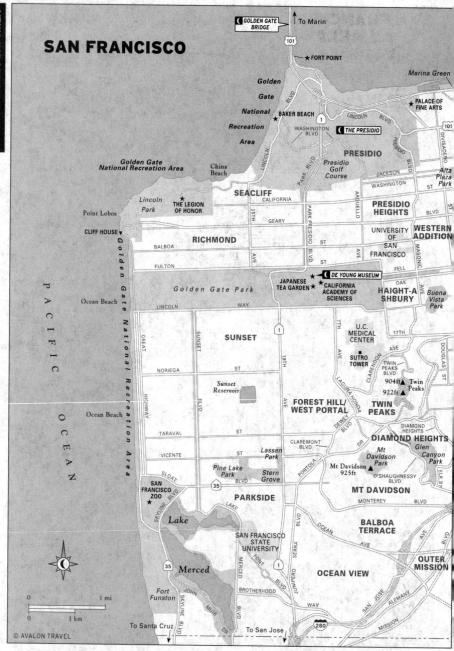

SAN FRANCISCO

GOLDEN GATE BRIDGE
To Marin
101
★ FORT POINT

Golden Gate National Recreation Area

Marina Green

★ PALACE OF FINE ARTS

★ BAKER BEACH

WASHINGTON BLVD

LINCOLN BLVD

THE PRESIDIO

PRESIDIO

101

DIVISADERO

Golden Gate National Recreation Area

China Beach

Presidio Golf Course

JACKSON

WASHINGTON ST

Alta Plaza Park

Lincoln Park

★ THE LEGION OF HONOR

SEACLIFF

CALIFORNIA

PRESIDIO HEIGHTS

BLVD

Point Lobos

GEARY

UNIVERSITY OF SAN FRANCISCO

WESTERN ADDITION

CLIFF HOUSE ▼

RICHMOND

BALBOA

MASONIC

FULTON

FELL

DE YOUNG MUSEUM

OAK

Golden Gate Park

JAPANESE TEA GARDEN ★

CALIFORNIA ACADEMY OF SCIENCES

HAIGHT-ASHBURY

Buena Vista Park

Ocean Beach

LINCOLN

WAY

7TH

U.C. MEDICAL CENTER

17TH

DOUGLAS

GREAT HIGHWAY

SUNSET

NORIEGA ST

SUNSET BLVD

19TH AVE

1

SUTRO TOWER

TWIN PEAKS BLVD

904ft ▲

922ft ▲ Twin Peaks

P A C I F I C

Sunset Reservoir

FOREST HILL/ WEST PORTAL

TWIN PEAKS

TARAVAL

O C E A N

Ocean Beach

VICENTE ST

Lassen Park

CLAREMONT BLVD

DEWEY BLVD

DIAMOND HEIGHTS

Mt Davidson Park

Glen Canyon Park

DIAMOND HEIGHTS

SLOAT

Pine Lake Park

Stern Grove

PORTOLA

Mt Davidson 925ft ▲

O'SHAUGHNESSY BLVD

ELK ST

SKYLINE BLVD

35

SAN FRANCISCO ZOO

PARKSIDE

LAKE

MT DAVIDSON

MONTEREY BLVD

Lake

OCEAN

BALBOA TERRACE

AVE

Merced

35

SAN FRANCISCO STATE UNIVERSITY

MERCED

SERRA

1

JUNIPERO

OCEAN VIEW

OUTER MISSION

SAN JOSE AVE

ALEMANY

Fort Funston

JOHN MUIR DR

SKYLINE BLVD

BROTHERHOOD

FONT BLVD

WAY

280

MISSION

To Santa Cruz

To San Jose

0   1 mi

0   1 km

© AVALON TRAVEL

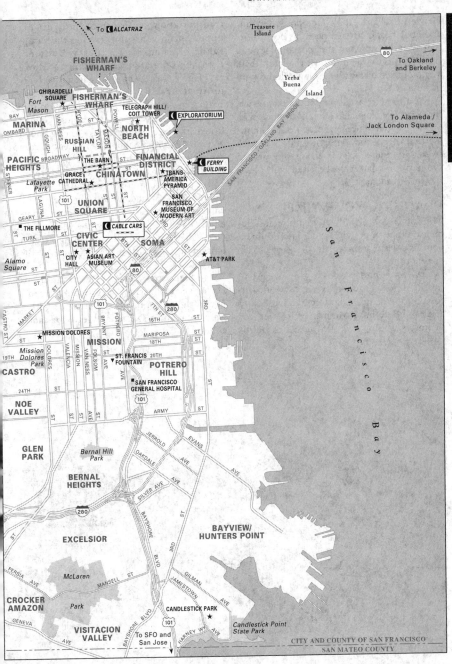

To **ALCATRAZ**

Treasure
Island

**FISHERMAN'S
WHARF**

80
To Oakland
and Berkeley

Yerba
Buena
Island

GHIRARDELLI
SQUARE **FISHERMAN'S
WHARF**

Fort
Mason

TELEGRAPH HILL/
COIT TOWER

EXPLORATORIUM

To Alameda /
Jack London Square

MARINA
LOMBARD

VAN NESS ST

POWELL

**NORTH
BEACH**

**RUSSIAN
HILL**

HYDE MASON ST

TAYLOR ST

**PACIFIC
HEIGHTS**
BROADWAY

THE BARN

**FINANCIAL
DISTRICT**

**FERRY
BUILDING**

SAN FRANCISCO OAKLAND BAY BRIDGE

STEINER

GRACE
CATHEDRAL **CHINATOWN**

Lafayette
Park

TRANS-
AMERICA
PYRAMID

101

LAGUNA

**UNION
SQUARE**

**SAN
FRANCISCO
MUSEUM OF
MODERN ART**

GEARY

THE FILLMORE

CABLE CARS

ST

TURK

**CIVIC
CENTER**

SOMA

Alamo
Square ST

**CITY
HALL** **ASIAN ART
MUSEUM**

80

AT&T PARK

San

101

7TH ST

280

3RD ST

F

MARKET

16TH

r

CASTRO ST

ST

MISSION DOLORES

MISSION

POTRERO

BRYANT

MARIPOSA

18TH ST

a

n

19TH

*Mission
Dolores
Park*

DOLORES

VALENCIA

MISSION

VAN NESS

FOLSOM

ST

**ST. FRANCIS
FOUNTAIN**

20TH

ST

c

CASTRO

AVE

**POTRERO
HILL**

**SAN FRANCISCO
GENERAL HOSPITAL**

ST

i

24TH ST

101

ARMY ST

s

**NOE
VALLEY**

ST

c

JERROLD

EVANS

o

**GLEN
PARK**

*Bernal Hill
Park*

OAKDALE AVE

AVE

B

**BERNAL
HEIGHTS**

SILVER AVE

ST

AVE

a

280

BAYSHORE

y

EXCELSIOR

**BAYVIEW/
HUNTERS POINT**

3RD ST

PERSIA AVE

McLaren

MANSELL ST

GILMAN AVE

JAMESTOWN AVE

**CROCKER
AMAZON**

Park

GENEVA

CANDLESTICK PARK

*Candlestick Point
State Park*

AVE

BAYSHORE BLVD

HARNEY WY

AVE

**VISITACION
VALLEY**

101

To SFO and
San Jose

CITY AND COUNTY OF SAN FRANCISCO
SAN MATEO COUNTY

Hewlett-Packard, Apple Computer, Google, and eBay headquartered here, it's no surprise that even the museums run to technology and the residents all seem to own the latest iPad. Visitors gravitate toward the multicultural wonderland of San Jose.

For a more relaxed, outdoorsy experience, the Coastside region has a small-town feel with big-time extreme ocean sports. Locals, knowing that this is not Southern California, pack sweatshirts and parkas as well as swimsuits and sun hats for a day at the beach in Half Moon Bay or Pescadero.

PLANNING YOUR TIME

San Francisco's rich, diverse culture and immense range of activities and entertainment make it a destination worthy of a day, a week, or a month.

Try to spend at least one weekend in the City, focusing your time downtown. Downtown's Union Square makes a great home base, thanks to its plethora of hotels, shops, and easy access to public transportation, but it can be fairly dead at night. Spend your time grazing the sumptuous offerings at the **Ferry Building,** then hop onto a crowded **cable car** down to Fisherman's Wharf to catch the ferry to **Alcatraz.** At night, relax at one of San Francisco's many well-regarded restaurants.

With a full week, you can explore Golden Gate Park's excellent museums—the **de Young** and the **California Academy of Sciences.** You can easily spend another full day exploring **The Presidio,** visiting the nearby **Exploratorium,** and taking a scenic, foggy stroll across the **Golden Gate Bridge.** With a few more days, you can explore less tourist-focused neighborhoods like Haight-Ashbury, the Mission, or Noe Valley. Or spend a day exploring a region outside the City, such as Marin County or the East Bay.

San Francisco's weather tends toward blanket fog and chilly windy days with bright spots of sun the exception. Come prepared with a warm coat and a sweater and leave the shorts at home.

Alcatraz, on the San Francisco Bay

© STUART THORNTON

Sights

UNION SQUARE AND NOB HILL

Wealth and style mark these areas near the center of San Francisco. Known for their lavish shopping areas, cable cars, and mansions, Union Square and Nob Hill draw both local and visiting crowds all year long. Sadly, the stunning 19th-century mansions built by the robber barons on Nob Hill are almost all gone—shaken then burned in the 1906 earthquake and fire. But the area still exudes a certain elegance, and restaurants are particularly good on Nob Hill.

If you shop in only one part of San Francisco, make it Union Square. Even if you don't like chain stores, you can just climb up to the top of the Square itself, grab a bench, and enjoy the views and the live entertainment on the small informal stage.

◖ Cable Cars

Perhaps the most recognizable symbol of San Francisco is the **cable car** (www.sfcablecar.com), originally conceived by Andrew Smith Hallidie as a safe mode for traveling the steep, often slick hills of San Francisco. Cable cars ran as regular mass transit from 1873 into the 1940s, when buses and electric streetcars began to dominate the landscape. Dedicated citizens, especially "Cable Car Lady" Friedel Klussmann, saved the cable car system from extinction, and the cable cars have become a rolling national landmark.

Today, you can ride the cable cars from one tourist destination to another throughout the City for $5 per ride. A full day "passport" ticket (which also grants access to streetcars and buses) costs $13 and is totally worth it if you want to run around the City all day. Cable car routes can take you up Nob Hill, through Union Square, down Powell Street, out to Fisherman's Wharf, and through Chinatown. Take a seat, or grab one of the exterior poles and hang on! Just be aware that cable cars have

San Francisco's iconic cable car

© STUART THORNTON

open-air seating only, making the ride chilly on foggy days.

Because everybody loves the cable cars, they get stuffed to capacity with tourists on weekends and with local commuters at rush hours. Expect to wait an hour or more for a ride from any of the turnaround points on a weekend or holiday. But a ride on a cable car from Union Square down to the Wharf is more than worth the wait. The views from the hills down to the Bay inspire wonder even in local residents. A ride through Chinatown feels long on bustle but in fact reveals the lifestyle in a place that is unique.

For aficionados, a ride on the cars can take you to **The Barn** (1201 Mason St., 415/474-1887, www.cablecarmuseum.org, Apr.-Sept. daily 10am-6pm, Oct.-Mar. daily 10am-5pm, free), a museum depicting the life and times of the San Francisco cable cars.

Grace Cathedral

Local icon **Grace Cathedral** (1100 California St., 415/749-6300, www.gracecathedral.org, Mon.-Fri. 7am-6pm, Sat. 8am-6pm, Sun. 8am-7pm) is many things to many people. The French Gothic-style edifice, completed in 1964, attracts architecture and Beaux-Arts lovers by the thousands with its facade, stained glass, and furnishings. It has been photographed by Ansel Adams and was the site of a 1965 speech by Dr. Martin Luther King. The labyrinths—replicas of the Chartres Cathedral labyrinth in France—appeal to meditative walkers seeking spiritual solace. Concerts featuring world music, sacred music, and modern classical ensembles draw audiences from around the Bay and farther afield.

But most of all, Grace Cathedral opens its doors to the community as a vibrant, active Episcopal church. The doctrine of exploration and tolerance matches well with the San Francisco community, of which the church remains an important part.

FINANCIAL DISTRICT AND SOMA

The skyscrapers of the Financial District create most of the San Francisco skyline, which extends out to the waterfront, locally called the Embarcadero. It's here that the major players of the San Francisco business world make and spend their money. The Stock Exchange sits in the middle of the action, making San Francisco not just rich but important on the international financial scene. But even businesspeople have to eat, and they certainly like to drink, so the Financial District offers a wealth of restaurants and bars. Hotels tend toward expensive tall towers, and the shopping here caters to folks with plenty of green.

SoMa (local shorthand for the area south of Market Street) was once a run-down postindustrial mess that rented warehouses to artists. Urban renewal and the ballpark have turned it into *the* neighborhood of the 21st century, complete with upscale restaurants and chichi wine bars.

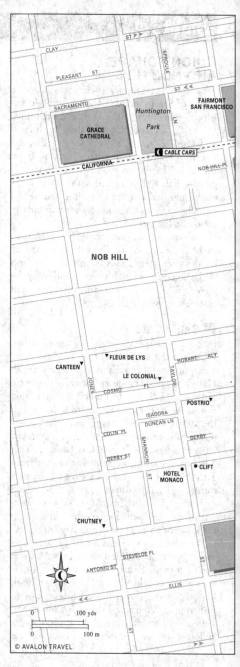

© AVALON TRAVEL

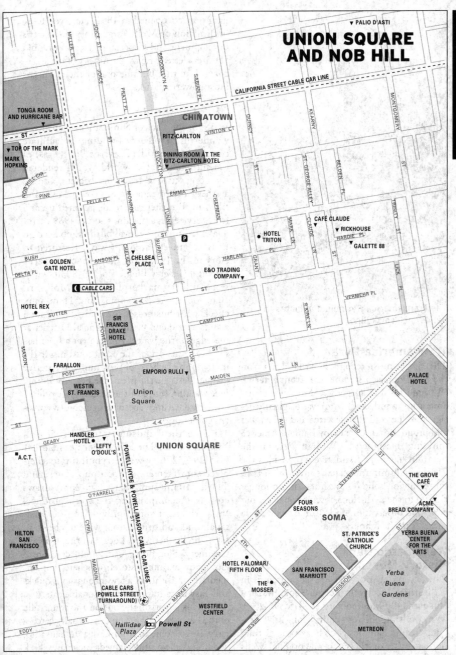

UNION SQUARE AND NOB HILL

▼ PALIO D'ASTI

CALIFORNIA STREET CABLE CAR LINE

TONGA ROOM AND HURRICANE BAR ▼

CHINATOWN

RITZ CARLTON
VINTON CT

▼ TOP OF THE MARK
MARK HOPKINS

DINING ROOM AT THE RITZ-CARLTON HOTEL

EMMA ST

CAFÉ CLAUDE ●
▼ RICKHOUSE
HARDIE PL
▼ GALETTE 88

HOTEL TRITON ■

PINE

● P

BUSH
● GOLDEN GATE HOTEL
DELTA PL
ANSON PL
CHELSEA PLACE

HARLAN

E&O TRADING COMPANY ▼

VERMEHR PL

● CABLE CARS

HOTEL REX ●
SUTTER
CAMPTON PL

SIR FRANCIS DRAKE HOTEL

FARALLON ▼
POST

EMPORIO RULLI ▼
MAIDEN

PALACE HOTEL

WESTIN ST. FRANCIS

Union Square

HANDLER HOTEL ●
● LEFTY O'DOUL'S

GEARY

UNION SQUARE

THE GROVE CAFÉ

■ A.C.T.

O'FARRELL

FOUR SEASONS

ACME BREAD COMPANY ▼

SOMA

ST. PATRICK'S CATHOLIC CHURCH

YERBA BUENA CENTER FOR THE ARTS

HILTON SAN FRANCISCO

HOTEL PALOMAR/ FIFTH FLOOR ●

SAN FRANCISCO MARRIOTT

THE ● MOSSER

Yerba Buena Gardens

CABLE CARS (POWELL STREET TURNAROUND) ✪

POWELL/HYDE & POWELL/MASON CABLE CAR LINES

WESTFIELD CENTER

Hallidie 🚏 *Powell St*
Plaza

METREON

The Transamerica Pyramid dominates the San Francisco skyline.

Transamerica Pyramid

The single most recognizable landmark on the San Francisco skyline, the **Transamerica Pyramid** (600 Montgomery St., www.transamericapyramidcenter.com) was originally designed to look a little like a tree and to be taller and prouder than the nearby Bank of America building. Designed by William Pereira, the pyramid has four distinctive wings, plus the 212-foot aluminum-plated spire, which is lit up for major holidays. Visitors can no longer ride up to the 27th-floor observation deck, but a "virtual observation deck" can be viewed via cameras in the lobby.

Wells Fargo Bank History Museum

One of a number of Wells Fargo museums in California, the **Wells Fargo Bank History Museum** (420 Montgomery St., 415/396-2619, www.wellsfargohistory.com, Mon.-Fri. 9am-5pm, free) in San Francisco boasts the distinction of sitting on the site of the original Wells

Fargo office, opened in 1852. Here you'll see information on Wells Fargo's role in the city's development and a special collection of Gold Rush-era letters. Enjoy the history of the stagecoach line that became one of the country's most powerful banks.

◖ Ferry Building

In 1898, the City of San Francisco created a wonderful new Ferry Building to facilitate commuting from the East Bay. But the rise of the automobile after World War II rendered the gorgeous construction obsolete, and its aesthetic ornamentation was covered over and filled in. But then the roads jammed up and ferry service began again, and the 1989 earthquake led to the removal of the Embarcadero Eyesore (an elevated freeway). Restored to glory in the 1990s, the **San Francisco Ferry Building** (1 Ferry Bldg., 415/983-8030, www.ferrybuildingmarketplace.com, Mon.-Fri. 10am-6pm, Sat. 9am-6pm, Sun. 11am-5pm, check with businesses for individual hours) stands at the end of the Financial District at the edge of the water. You can get a brief lesson in the history of the edifice just inside the main lobby, where photos and interpretive plaques describe the life of the Ferry Building. Free **walking tours** of the building are offered on Saturdays and Tuesdays at noon (www.sfcityguides.org).

Inside the handsome structure, it's all about the food. The famous **Farmers Market** (415/291-3276, www.ferrybuildingmarketplace.com/farmers_market.php, Tues. and Thurs. 10am-2pm, Sat. 8am-2pm) draws crowds. Accompanying the fresh produce, the permanent shops provide top-tier artisanal food and drink, from wine to cheese to high-end kitchenware. Local favorites Cowgirl Creamery, Blue Bottle Café, and Acme Bread Company maintain storefronts here. For immediate gratification, a few incongruous quick-and-easy restaurants offer reasonable eats.

Perhaps surprisingly, out on the water side of the Ferry Building, you can actually catch a ferry. Boats come in from Larkspur, Sausalito, Tiburon, Vallejo, and Alameda each day. Check with the **Blue and Gold Fleet** (www.blueand-goldfleet.com), **Golden Gate Ferry** (www.gold-engateferry.org), and **Bay Link Ferries** (www.baylinkferry.com) for information about service, times, and fares.

AT&T Park

The name changes every few years, but the place remains the same. **AT&T Park** (24 Willie Mays Plaza, 415/972-2000, http://sanfrancisco.giants.mlb.com) is home to the San Francisco Giants, endless special events, several great restaurants, and arguably California's best garlic fries. From the ballpark, you can look right out onto the Bay. During baseball games, a motley collection of boats float beside the stadium, hoping that an out-of-the-park fly ball will come sailing their way.

Cartoon Art Museum

The **Cartoon Art Museum** (655 Mission St., 415/227-8666, http://cartoonart.org, Tues.-Sun. 11am-5pm, adults $7, seniors and students $5, children $3) offers a fun and funny outing for the whole family. The 20-year-old museum displays both permanent and traveling exhibits of original cartoon art, including international newspaper cartoons, high-quality comics, and Pixar Studios' big-screen animated wonders. Even young children are captivated by the beauty and creativity found here.

San Francisco Museum of Modern Art

Longtime favorite **SFMOMA** (151 3rd St., 415/357-4000, www.sfmoma.org, Mon.-Tues 11am-5:45pm, Thurs. 11am-8:45pm, Fri.-Sat. 11am-5:45pm adults $18, seniors $13, students $11, children under 12 free) closed temporarily in June 2013 for a renovation that may take as long as three years. But the museum is still part of the artistic life of the city, sponsoring traveling exhibits and outdoor commissions during construction. With a wonderful array of pieces to suit every taste, its permanent collections include works by Ansel Adams, Henri Matisse, and Shiro Kuramata. Paintings, sculptures, and photographs are complemented by funky modern furniture, and some truly bizarre installation art.

CHINATOWN

The massive Chinese migration to California began almost as soon as the news of easy gold in the mountain streams made it to East Asia. And despite rampant prejudice and increasingly desperate attempts on the part of "good" Americans to rid their pristine country of these immigrants, the Chinese not only stayed but also persevered and eventually prospered. Many never made it to the gold fields, preferring instead to remain in bustling San Francisco to open shops and begin the business of commerce in their new home. They were basically segregated to a small area beneath Nob Hill, where they created a motley collection of wooden shacks that served as homes, restaurants, shops, and more. This neighborhood quickly became known as Chinatown. Along with much of San Francisco, the neighborhood was destroyed in the 1906 earthquake and fire. Despite xenophobic attempts to relocate Chinatown as far away from downtown San Francisco as possible ("back to China" was one suggestion), the Chinese prevailed, and the neighborhood was rebuilt where it originally stood.

Today, visitors see the post-1906 visitor-friendly Chinatown that was built after the quake. But small alleyways wend between the broad touristy avenues, entry points into the old Chinatown that still remains. Beautiful Asian architecture mixes with more mundane blocky city buildings to create a unique skyscape.

Chinatown Gate

Visible from the streets leading into Union Square, the **Chinatown Gate** (Grant Ave. and Bush St.) perches at the southern "entrance" to the famous Chinatown neighborhood. The gate, built in 1970, is a relatively recent addition to this history-filled neighborhood. The design features Chinese dragons, pagodas, and other charming details. The inscription reads, "All under heaven is for the good of the people," a quote from Dr. Sun Yat-sen. Its gaudy,

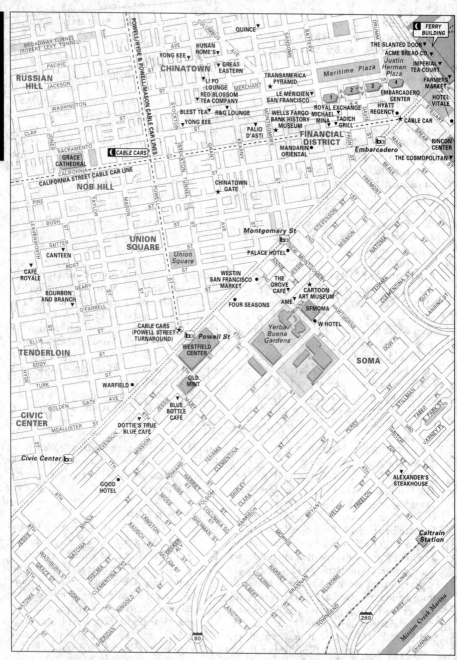

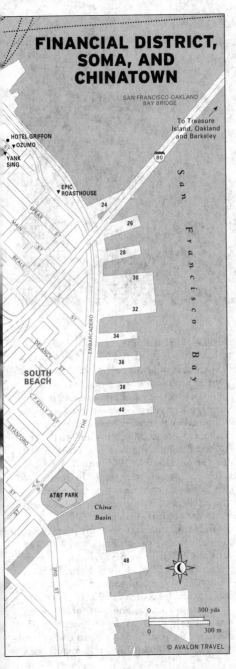

colorful splendor draws droves of visitors with cameras each day; on weekends it can be tough to find a quick moment to get your own picture taken at the gate.

Chinatown truly is a sight in and of itself. Visitors stroll the streets, exploring the tiny alleys and peeking into the temples, admiring the wonderful Asian architecture on occasionally unlikely buildings. Among the best known of these is the **Bank of America Building** (701 Grant Ave.)—an impressive edifice with a Chinese tiled roof and 60 dragon medallions decorating the facade. The **East West Bank** (743 Washington St.) is even more traditional in its look. The small, beautiful building that acted as the Chinatown Telephone Exchange was constructed in this ultra-Chinese style just after 1906, when the Great Earthquake demolished the original structure. The Bank of Canton purchased the derelict building in 1960 and rehabilitated it; like many banks, it has changed hands since then. The **Sing Chong Building** (601 Grant Ave. at California St.) was another 1906 quick-rebuild, the reconstruction beginning shortly after the ground stopped shuddering and the smoke cleared.

NORTH BEACH AND FISHERMAN'S WHARF

The Fisherman's Wharf and North Beach areas are an odd amalgam of old-school residential neighborhood and total tourist mecca. North Beach has long served as the Italian district of San Francisco, reflected in the restaurants in the area. Fisherman's Wharf was the spot where 19th-century Italians came to work; they were a big part of the fishing fleet that provided San Francisco with its legendary supply of fresh seafood.

In the 1950s, North Beach became one of the hubs of the Beat Generation, a group of groundbreaking writers that included Lawrence Ferlinghetti, Jack Kerouac, and Allen Ginsberg. Traces of the Beats remain in the area whether it's in The Beat Museum, down Jack Kerouac Alley, or in the famous City Lights Bookstore, which was co-founded by Ferlinghetti back in 1953.

San Francisco's vibrant Chinatown

© STUART THORNTON

Today, Fisherman's Wharf is *the* spot where visitors to San Francisco come to visit and snap photos. If you're not into crowds, avoid the area in the summer. For visitors who can cope with a ton of other people, some of the best views of the air show during Fleet Week and the fireworks on the Fourth of July can be found down on the Wharf.

◀ Alcatraz

Going to **Alcatraz** (www.nps.gov/alcatraz), one of the most famous landmarks in the City, feels a bit like going to purgatory; this military fortress turned maximum-security prison, nicknamed "The Rock," has little warmth or welcome on its craggy forbidding shores. The fortress became a prison in the 19th century while it still belonged to the military, which used it to house Civil War prisoners. The isolation of the island in the Bay, the frigid waters, and the nasty currents surrounding Alcatraz made it a perfect spot to keep prisoners contained with little hope of escape and near-certain death if the attempt was ever made.

In 1934, after the military closed down their prison and handed the island over to the Department of Justice, construction began to turn Alcatraz into a new style of prison ready to house a new style of prisoner: Depression-era gangsters. A few of the honored guests of this maximum-security penitentiary were Al Capone, George "Machine Gun" Kelly, and Robert Stroud, "the Birdman of Alcatraz." The prison closed in 1963, and in 1964 and 1969 occupations were staged by Indians of All Tribes, an exercise that eventually led to the privilege of self-determination for North America's original inhabitants.

Today, Alcatraz acts primarily as an attraction for visitors to San Francisco. **Alcatraz Cruises** (Pier 33, 415/981-7625, www.alcatrazcruises.com, daily 9:10am-3:55pm, 6:10pm, and 6:45pm, adults $28-35, seniors $26.25-32.25, children $17-20.50) offers ferry rides out to Alcatraz and tours of the island and the prison. Tours depart from Pier 33. Once on the island, most visitors embark on the **Cellhouse Audio Tour,** a 45-minute walk

SAN FRANCISCO WEEKEND

San Francisco may only be roughly seven miles long and seven miles wide, but it packs in historic neighborhoods, one of the West Coast's most iconic landmarks, and dozens of stomach-dropping inclines within its small area. Exploring all its hills and valleys takes some planning.

DAY 1

Start your day at the **Ferry Building** (page 42). Graze from the many vendors, including **Blue Bottle Café, Cowgirl Creamery,** and **Acme Bread Company.**

After touring the gourmet shops, catch the Muni F line (Steuart St. and Market St., $2) to Jefferson Street and take a stroll along **Fisherman's Wharf** (page 50). Be sure to stop into the **Musée Mécanique** to play a few coin-operated antique arcade games. Near Pier 39, buy tickets for the ferry to **Alcatraz** (page 46) or opt for a ride to **Angel Island** (page 127) at Pier 41. Alcatraz will fill your mind with amazing stories from the legendary island prison, while hiking around Angel Island will clear your mind and offer up scenic views of the Bay.

After you escape from Alcatraz or return from Angel Island, make your way back to the foot of Beach and Hyde Streets and board the Powell-Hyde **cable car** ($6). Watch for gorgeous Bay views as the cable car crests Russian Hill around Filbert Street. Hop off at Sutter Street and walk three blocks east past **Union Square** to lunch at **Café Claude** (page 103), a classic French brasserie. After lunch, window-shop around Union Square, meandering down to the Powell Street Muni station at Market Street.

Take the N Judah line ($2) to 9th Avenue and Irving Street, then follow 9th Avenue north into **Golden Gate Park** (page 57). The fabulous **de Young Museum** (page 61) is directly across from the **California Academy of Sciences** (page 62). Art lovers and science geeks can part ways here – or squeeze in a trip to enjoy both!

Leave Golden Gate Park by walking east along John F. Kennedy Drive to the **Haight,** the hippie enclave made famous in the 1960s. Enjoy the finely crafted cocktails and nibbles at **Alembic** (page 68). Or catch a cab to the **Tadich Grill** (page 105), where the tasty cocktails and extensive seafood menu will be a per-

fect ending to your day. Consider starting the night with a martini at the swank **Top of the Mark** (page 65), with its view of the SF skyline.

DAY 2

Head to North Beach for brunch at **Mama's on Washington Square** (page 108), whose specialty "m'omelettes" have made this joint a local favorite for decades. Then explore the neighborhood. Be sure to stop in **City Lights** (page 81), the legendary Beat Generation bookstore, and then head across the street to check out the **The Beat Museum** (page 52). Then further your tour of Beat haunts with a cappuccino at **Caffé Trieste** (page 107) or a cocktail at **Vesuvio** (page 66). You might also want to climb to the top of **Coit Tower** (page 52) to catch a great view of the city skyline – look west to find crooked **Lombard Street** (page 52).

Drive or take a cab to the Mission district for the afternoon. If you're hungry, enjoy an authentic Mission burrito at **Papalote Mexican Grill** (page 113). For something sweeter, try **Tartine Bakery** (page 112) or **Bi-Rite Creamery & Bakeshop** (page 112). History buffs will want to visit 18th-century **Mission Dolores** (page 57). Or check out the quirky Mission stores **826 Valencia** (page 83) and its neighbor **Paxton Gate** (page 84).

Then head out to see some live music at one of San Francisco's great music venues like **The Fillmore** (page 72), the **Great American Music Hall** (page 73), or **Yoshi's** (page 73).

DAY 3

Start your day with dim sum at **Great Eastern** (page 107) before exploring **Chinatown** (page 43). If you'd rather get an early start, try breakfast at **Dottie's True Blue Café** (page 111).

Then head north out of the city to experience some of the Bay Area's impressive outdoors. Travel on U.S. 101 over the **Golden Gate Bridge** (page 53) to explore **Marin** (page 119), including **Muir Woods** (page 132), **Mount Tamalpais** (page 134), and **Muir Beach** (page 133). Stay the night at the English countryside inspired **Pelican Inn** (page 134) or the luxurious **Cavallo Point Lodge** (page 124).

SAN FRANCISCO BAY AREA

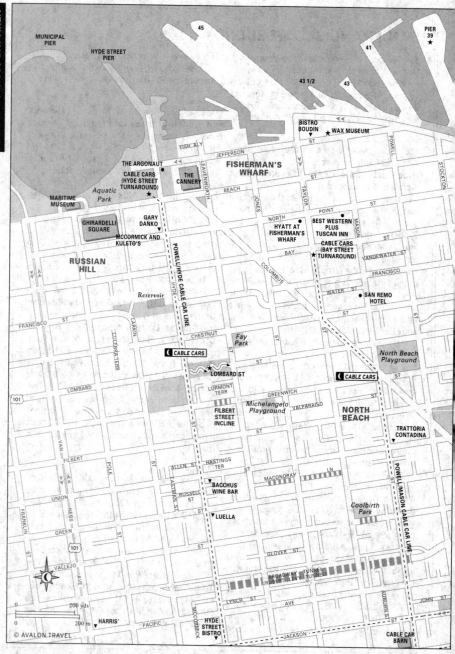

MUNICIPAL PIER

HYDE STREET PIER

45

PIER 39 ★

41

43 1/2   43

BISTRO BOUDIN ▼   ★ WAX MUSEUM

FISH ALY

JEFFERSON ST

FISHERMAN'S WHARF

THE ARGONAUT
CABLE CARS (HYDE STREET TURNAROUND) ★

THE CANNERY

BEACH ST

LEAVENWORTH

JONES ST

TAYLOR ST

MASON ST

POWELL ST

STOCKTON ST

MARITIME MUSEUM

Aquatic Park

GHIRARDELLI SQUARE

GARY DANKO ▼

McCORMICK AND KULETO'S

RUSSIAN HILL

Reservoir

NORTH POINT ST

HYATT AT FISHERMAN'S WHARF ●

BEST WESTERN PLUS TUSCAN INN ●
CABLE CARS (BAY STREET TURNAROUND)

VANDEWATER ST

BAY ST

FRANCISCO ST

COLUMBUS

WATER ST

● SAN REMO HOTEL

FRANCISCO ST

POWELL/HYDE CABLE CAR LINE

HYDE ST

LARKIN ST

CHESTNUT ST

Fay Park

☾ CABLE CARS

★ LOMBARD ST

North Beach Playground

☾ CABLE CARS

LURMONT TERR

Michelangelo Playground

GREENWICH ST

VALPARAISO

NORTH BEACH

FILBERT STREET INCLINE

TRATTORIA CONTADINA ▼

FRANCISCO ST

CULEBRA TERR

VAN NESS AVE

POLK ST

LARKIN ST

HYDE ST

EASTMAN ST

RUSSELL ST

ALLEN ST

HASTINGS TER

FILBERT ST

MACONDRAY LN

▼ BACCHUS WINE BAR

▼ LUELLA

Coolbirth Park

POWELL/MASON CABLE CAR LINE

UNION ST

GREEN ST

101

FRANKLIN ST

VALLEJO ST

☾

GLOVER ST

BROADWAY TUNNEL

AUBURN ST

JOHN ST

0   200 yds
0   200 m

© AVALON TRAVEL

HARRIS' ▼

PACIFIC AVE

McCORMICK

HYDE STREET BISTRO ▼

LYNCH ST

AVE

JACKSON ST

CABLE CAR BARN

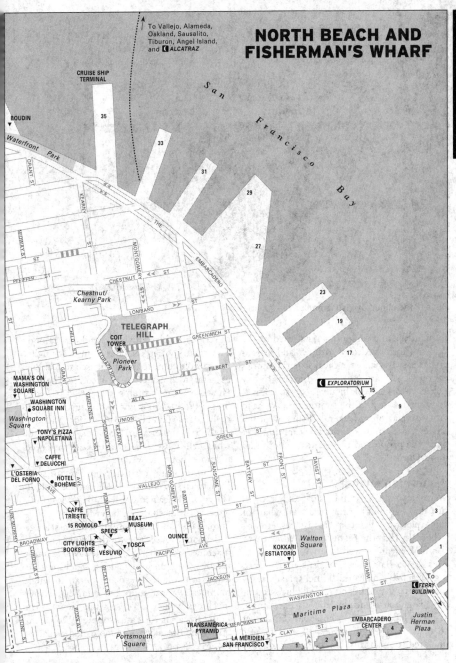

To Vallejo, Alameda, Oakland, Sausalito, Tiburon, Angel Island, and **C** ALCATRAZ

NORTH BEACH AND FISHERMAN'S WHARF

San Francisco Bay

CRUISE SHIP TERMINAL

BOUDIN

Waterfront Park

35
33
31
29
27
23
19
17
15
9
3
1

MIDWAY ST
GRANT ST
KEARNY ST
MONTGOMERY ST
THE EMBARCADERO

PFEIFFER ST

CHESTNUT ST

Chestnut/Kearny Park

LOMBARD

TELEGRAPH HILL

COIT TOWER

Pioneer Park

TELEGRAPH HILL BLVD

GREENWICH ST

FILBERT ST

C EXPLORATORIUM

MAMA'S ON WASHINGTON SQUARE

WASHINGTON SQUARE INN

Washington Square

TONY'S PIZZA NAPOLETANA

CAFFE DELUCCHI

L'OSTERIA DEL FORNO

HOTEL BOHÈME

CAFFÉ TRIESTE

15 ROMOLO

SPECS

CITY LIGHTS BOOKSTORE

TOSCA

VESUVIO

BEAT MUSEUM

QUINCE

KOKKARI ESTIATORIO

ALTA

GRANT AVE

TAVERNES

SONOMA ST

KEARNY ST

UNION ST

CASTLE ST

GREEN ST

MONTGOMERY ST

SANSOME ST

BATTERY ST

FRONT ST

DAVIST ST

Walton Square

VALLEJO

BATTOL ST

OSGOOD PL

BROADWAY

TURK/MURPHY

CORDELIA ST

BECKETT ST

ROMOLO ST

PACIFIC

JACKSON

DRUMM ST

To **C** FERRY BUILDING

WASHINGTON

Maritime Plaza

Justin Herman Plaza

STONE ST

ROSS ALY

Portsmouth Square

TRANSAMERICA PYRAMID

MERCHANT ST

CLAY

LA MÉRIDIEN SAN FRANCISCO

EMBARCADERO CENTER

1 2 3 4

© STUART THORNTON

Musée Mécanique at Fisherman's Wharf

through the imposing prison, narrated by the voices of former Alcatraz officers and prisoners. It's easy to get lost in the fascinating stories as you wander around. A good idea is to buy tickets at least a week in advance, especially if you'll be in town in the summer and want to visit Alcatraz on a weekend. Tours often sell out, especially in the evening. Be carefully after dark; the prison and the island are both said to be haunted!

Fisherman's Wharf

Welcome to the tourist mecca of San Francisco! Just don't go looking for an actual wharf or single pier when you come to visit Fisherman's Wharf. In fact, the **Fisherman's Wharf area** (Beach St. from Powell St. to Van Ness Ave., backs onto Bay St., www.fishermanswharf. org), reachable by Muni F line, sprawls along the waterfront and inland several blocks, creating a large tourist neighborhood. The Wharf, as it's called by locals, who avoid the area at all costs, features all crowds, all the time. Be prepared to push through a sea of humanity

to see sights, buy souvenirs, and eat seafood. Fisherman's Wharf includes many of the sights that people come to San Francisco to see: Pier 39, Ghirardelli Square, and, of course, **The Wax Museum of Fisherman's Wharf** (145 Jefferson St., 800/439-4305, www.waxmuseum.com, daily 10am-9pm, adults $16, seniors and ages 12-17 $12, under age 12 $8), the presence of which tells most serious travelers all they need to know about the Wharf.

One of the quirkier attractions in Fishermen's Wharf is the **Musée Mécanique** (Pier 45, Fishermen's Wharf, 415/346-2000, www.museemechanique.org, Mon.-Fri. 10am-7pm, Sat.-Sun. 10am-8pm, free), a strange collection of over 200 working coin-operated machines from the 1800s to today. The most famous is "Laughing Sal," a machine that causes a giant red headed woman to laugh maniacally for a couple of quarters. Other machines include a 3-D picture show of San Francisco after the catastrophic 1906 earthquake and fire, along with more modern games like Ms. Pac-Man.

Pier 39

One of the most-visited spots in San Francisco, **Pier 39** (Beach St. and The Embarcadero, www.pier39.com) hosts a wealth of restaurants and shops. If you've come down to the pier to see the sea life, start with the unusual **Aquarium of the Bay** (415/623-5300, www.aquariumofthebay.com, summer daily 9am-8pm, call for winter hours, adults $18, seniors and children $10). This 300-foot clear-walled tunnel lets visitors see thousands of species native to the San Francisco Bay, including sharks, rays, and plenty of fish. For a special treat, take the Behind the Scenes Tour.

Farther down the pier, get personal (but not *too* close) to the local colony of **sea lions.** These big, loud mammals tend to congregate at K-Dock in the West Marina. The best time to see the sea lions is winter, when the population grows into the hundreds.

A perennial family favorite, the **San Francisco Carousel** ($3 per ride) is painted with beautiful scenes of San Francisco. Riders on the moving horses, carriages, and seats can look at the paintings or out onto the pier. Kids also love the daily shows by local street performers. Depending on when you're on the pier, you might see jugglers, magicians, or stand-up comedians on the **Alpine Spring Water Center Stage** (show times vary, free).

◖ Exploratorium

Kids around the Bay Area have loved the **Exploratorium** (Pier 15, 415/561-0360, www.exploratorium.edu, Tues.-Sun. 10am-5pm, Wed. nights all ages 5pm-10pm, Thurs. nights 18 and up 6pm-10pm, adults $25, children $19) for decades. They will love it even more in its new location on the San Francisco Bay. This innovative museum makes science the most fun thing ever for kids; adults are welcome to enjoy the interactive exhibits too. The Exploratorium seeks to be true to its name and encourages exploration into all aspects of science. Learn about everything from frogs to the physics of baseball. Expect lots of mirrors, coiled wires, blowing air, lights, magnets, and motors. An expansion of exhibits includes a glass and steel bay observatory and a wind-activated installation between Pier 15 and Pier 17 that records atmospheric measurements.

Maritime Museum

The **San Francisco Maritime Historical Park** (900 Beach St., 415/561-7000, www.nps.gov/safr, daily 10am-4pm, adults $5, children free) comprises two parts—the visitors center museum on the bottom floor of the Argonaut Hotel and the ships at permanent dock across the street at the Hyde Street Pier. While the visitors center museum presents some of the long and amazing maritime history of San Francisco, the fun comes from puttering up the Pier and climbing aboard the historic ships. The shiniest jewel of the Museum's collection is the 1886 square-rigged *Balclutha,* a three-masted schooner that recalls times gone by. There are also several steamboats, including the workhorse ferry *Eureka* and a cool old steam paddle-wheel tugboat called the *Eppleton Hall.* Be careful if you're tall—as with most ships, these all have very short doorways and sometimes low ceilings. Ranger-led tours and programs, included in the price of a ticket, make this inexpensive museum more than worthwhile. Check the website for the fall concert series.

Ghirardelli Square

Jammed in with Fisherman's Wharf and Pier 39, **Ghirardelli Square** (900 North Point St., www.ghirardellisq.com), pronounced "GEAR-ah-DEL-ee," has recently reinvented itself as an upscale shopping, dining, and living area. Its namesake, the famous **Ghirardelli Chocolate Factory** (900 North Point St., 415/775-5500, www.ghirardelli.com, Sun.-Thurs. 9am-11pm, Fri.-Sat. 9am-midnight) sits at the corner of the square. Here you can browse the rambling shop and pick up truffles, wafers, candies, and sauces for all your friends back home. Finally, get in line at the ice cream counter to order a hot-fudge sundae. These don't travel well, so you'll have to enjoy it here. Once you've finished gorging on chocolate, you can wander out into the square to enjoy more shopping (there's even a cupcake shop if your teeth haven't dissolved yet) and the sight of an unbelievably swank condo complex overlooking the Bay.

Lombard Street

You've no doubt seen it in movies, on TV, and on postcards: **Lombard Street,** otherwise known as "the crookedest street in the world." So why bother braving the bumper-to-bumper cars navigating its zigzag turns? For one, you can't beat the view from the top. With its 27 percent grade and eight tight hairpin curves, Lombard Street offers unobstructed vistas of San Francisco Bay, Alcatraz Island, Fisherman's Wharf, Coit Tower, and the City.

The section that visitors flock to spans only a block, from Hyde Street at the top to Leavenworth Street at the bottom. Lombard was originally created to keep people from rolling uncontrolled down the treacherously steep grade. Brave pedestrians can walk up and down the sides of the brick-paved street, enjoying the hydrangeas and Victorian mansions that line the roadway. For convenience during the peak summer months, take a cable car directly to the top of Lombard Street and walk down the noncurvy stairs on either side.

Coit Tower

It's big, it's phallic, and it may or may not have been designed to look like a fire-hose nozzle or a power station. But since 1933, **Coit Tower** (1 Telegraph Hill Blvd., 415/362-0808, Mar.-Sept. daily 10am-5:30pm, Oct.-Feb. daily 9am-4:30pm, elevator ride adults $7, seniors and ages 12-17 $5, under age 12 $1.50) has beautified the City just as benefactor Lillie Hitchcock Coit intended when she willed San Francisco one-third of her monumental estate. Inside, murals depicting city life and works of the 1930s cover the walls. From the top of the tower on a clear day, you can see the whole of the City and the Bay. Part of what makes Coit Tower special is the walks up to it. Rather than contributing to the acute congestion in the area, consider taking public transit to the area and walking up the Filbert Steps to the tower. It's steep, but there's no other way to see the lovely little cottages and gardens that

mark the path up from the streets to the top of Telegraph Hill.

The Beat Museum

To some people, North Beach is still the old stomping grounds of the Beat Generation, a gang of 1950s writers that included Jack Kerouac, Allen Ginsberg, and Lawrence Ferlinghetti. Only a block or so from Ferlinghetti's famed City Lights Bookstore, **The Beat Museum** (540 Broadway, 415/399-9626, www.kerouac.com, adults $8, students and seniors $5) is as rambling and occasionally fascinating as the Beat writers' work. The displays here explain how the term "Beatnik" was coined and go into detail about the obscenity trial that followed the publication of Beat poet Allen Ginsberg's *Howl and Other Poems.* Beat Generation fans can stare at Jack Kerouac's jacket and Neal Cassady's striped black and white shirt, which he wore while driving the bus trip chronicled in Tom Wolfe's *The Electric Kool-Aid Acid Test.* Displays illuminate the lives of lesser-known Beat characters like Gregory Corso and Lew Welch, a poet who disappeared in the mountains of California in 1971. An on-site bookstore sells iconic Beat works like Kerouac's *On the Road* and William S. Burroughs' *Naked Lunch.*

MARINA AND PACIFIC HEIGHTS

The Marina and Pacific Heights shelter some of the amazing amount of money that flows in the City by the Bay. The Marina is one of the San Francisco neighborhoods constructed on landfill (sand dredged up from the bottom of the ocean and piled in what was once a marsh). It was badly damaged in the 1989 Loma Prieta earthquake, but you won't see any of that damage today. Instead, you'll find a wealthy neighborhood, a couple of yacht harbors, and lots of good museums, dining, and shopping.

Palace of Fine Arts

The Palace of Fine Arts (3301 Lyon St., 415/567-6642, www.palaceoffinearts.org, daily 6am-9pm) was originally meant to be nothing but a temporary structure—part of the Panama Pacific Exposition in 1915. But the lovely building won the hearts of San Franciscans, and a fund was started to preserve the Palace beyond the Exposition. Through the first half of the 20th century, efforts could not keep it from crumbling, but in the 1960s and 1970s, serious rebuilding work took place, and today the Palace of Fine Arts stands proud and strong and beautiful. It houses the Palace of Fine Arts Theater, which hosts events nearly every day, from beauty pageants to conferences on the future of artificial intelligence.

Fort Mason

Once the Port of Embarkation from which the United States waged World War II in the Pacific, **Fort Mason Center** (Buchanan St. and Marina Blvd., 415/345-7500, www.fortmason. org, daily 9am-8pm, parking up to $10) now acts as home to numerous nonprofit, multicultural, and artistic organizations. Where soldiers and guns departed to fight the Japanese, visitors now find dance performances, independent theatrical productions, and art galleries. At any time of year, a number of great shows go on in the renovated historic white and red buildings of the complex; check the online calendar to see what is coming up during your visit.

Other fun features include installations of the **Outdoor Exploratorium** (www.exploratorium.edu/outdoor, daily dawn-dusk). Ranging all over Fort Mason, the Exploratorium exhibits appeal to all five senses (yes, even taste) and teach visitors about the world around them—right there around them, in fact. You'll taste salt in local water supplies, hear a foghorn, and see what causes the parking lot to crack and sink. It's free, and it's fascinating—download a map from the website, or grab a guide from installation 5, Portable Observatories.

C The Presidio

It seems strange to think of progressive, peace-loving San Francisco as a town with tremendous military history, yet the City's warlike past is nowhere more evident than at **The Presidio** (Montgomery St. and Lincoln Blvd., 415/561-4323, www.nps.gov/prsf, visitors center Thurs.-Sun. 10am-4pm, trails daily dawn-dusk, free). This sweeping stretch of land running along the San Francisco Headlands down to the Golden Gate has been a military installation since 1776, when the Spanish created their El Presidio del San Francisco fort on the site. In 1846 the United States army took over the site (peacefully), and in 1848 the American Presidio military installation formally opened. It was finally abandoned by the military and became a national park in 1994. The Presidio had a role in every Pacific-related war from the Civil War through Desert Storm.

To orient yourself among the more than 800 buildings that make up the Presidio, start at the visitors center or the **Warming Hut Bookstore & Café** (983 Marine Dr., 415/561-3040, daily 9am-5pm). As you explore the huge park, you can visit the pioneering aviation area **Crissy Field**, Civil War-era fortifications at **Fort Point**, and the **Letterman Digital Arts Center** (Chestnut St. and Lyon St., www.lucasfilm. com), built on the site of the Letterman Army Hospital, which served as a top-notch care facility for returning wounded soldiers over more than a century's worth of wars. Newer additions to The Presidio include art installations by Andy Goldsworthy, who works with natural materials. The most renowned is *Spire*, a sculpture that rises 90 feet into the air, utilizing 35 cypress tree trunks.

C Golden Gate Bridge

People come from the world over to see and walk the **Golden Gate Bridge** (U.S. 101/Hwy. 1 at Lincoln Blvd., 415/455-2000, http://goldengatebridge.org, cars $6, pedestrians free). A marvel of human engineering constructed in 1936 and 1937, the suspension bridge spans the narrow "gate" from which the Pacific Ocean enters the San Francisco Bay. On a clear day, pedestrians can see the whole Bay from the east sidewalk, then turn around to see the Pacific Ocean spreading out on the other side. Or take in the stunning bridge

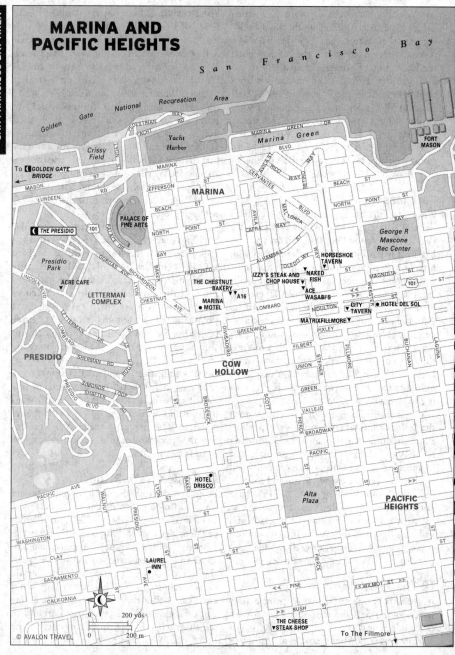

MARINA AND PACIFIC HEIGHTS

San Francisco Bay

Golden Gate National Recreation Area

FORT MASON

To GOLDEN GATE BRIDGE

THE PRESIDIO

Presidio Park

ACRE CAFE

LETTERMAN COMPLEX

PRESIDIO

Crissy Field

PALACE OF FINE ARTS

Yacht Harbor

Marina Green

MARINA GREEN DR

MARINA BLVD

MARINA

George R Mascone Rec Center

HORSESHOE TAVERN

THE CHESTNUT BAKERY

IZZY'S STEAK AND CHOP HOUSE

NAKED FISH

A16

MARINA MOTEL

ACE WASABI'S

CITY TAVERN

HOTEL DEL SOL

MATRIXFILLMORE

COW HOLLOW

HOTEL DRISCO

Alta Plaza

PACIFIC HEIGHTS

LAUREL INN

THE CHEESE STEAK SHOP

To The Fillmore

0   200 yds

0   200 m

© AVALON TRAVEL

view from the Marin Headlands barracks, looking down from the northwest and in toward the City skyline.

The bridge itself is not golden, but a rich orange color called "international orange" that shines like gold when the sun sets behind it on a clear evening. But newcomers to the City beware—not all days and precious few evenings at the bridge are clear. One of the most beautiful sights in San Francisco is the fog blowing in over the Golden Gate late in the afternoon. Unfortunately, once the fog stops blowing and settles in, the bridge is cold, damp, and viewless, so plan to come early in the morning, or pick spring or autumn for your best chance of a clear sight of this most famous and beautiful of artificial structures.

The Golden Gate National Parks Conservancy has begun offering **Golden Gate Bridge Tours** (day tour: May-Oct. daily 10:30am, 11:45am, 1pm, 2:15pm, 3:30pm, 4:45pm; evening tour: May-Oct. Fri.-Sun. 8:15pm; adults day tour $13, adults evening tour $22, seniors day tour $10, seniors evening tour $19, kids free) for those who want a guide to impart the history of the San Francisco landmark.

CIVIC CENTER AND HAYES VALLEY

Some of the most interesting neighborhoods in the City cluster toward its center. The Civic Center functions as the heart of San Francisco; the beautiful building actually houses the mayor's office and much of San Francisco's government. Visitors who last visited San Francisco a decade or more ago will notice that the Civic Center has been cleaned up quite a lot in the last few years. It's now safe to walk here—at least in the daytime.

As the Civic Center melts toward Hayes Valley, the high culture of San Francisco appears. Near the border you'll find Davies Symphony Hall, home of the world-famous San Francisco Symphony, and the War Memorial Opera House. And serving these, you'll find fabulous Hayes Valley hotels and restaurants.

© STUART THORNTON

Palace of Fine Arts

City Hall

Look at San Francisco's **City Hall** (1 Dr. Carlton B. Goodlett Place, 415/554-6139, www.sfgov.org, Mon.-Fri. 8am-8pm, free) and you'll think you've somehow been transported to Europe. The stately building with the gilded dome is the pride of the City and houses much of its government. (The dome is the world's fifth largest.) Complimentary 45-minute tours of City Hall are available daily at 10am, noon and 2pm. The inside has been extensively renovated after being damaged in the 1989 Loma Prieta earthquake. You'll find a combination of historical grandeur and modern accessibility and convenience as you tour the Arthur Brown Jr.-designed edifice. The park-like square in front of City Hall is also enjoyable (though this area can get a bit sketchy after dark).

Asian Art Museum

Across from City Hall is the **Asian Art Museum** (200 Larkin St., 415/581-3500, www.asianart.org, Tues.-Wed. 10am-5pm, Thurs. Oct.-Dec. 10am-5pm, Thurs. Jan.-Sept.

10am-9pm, Fri.-Sat. 10am-5pm, adults $12, seniors $8, ages 13-17 $7, under age 12 free). Yup, that's it right there with the enormous Ionic columns and Eurocentric facade. But inside you'll have an amazing metaphorical window into the Asian cultures that have shaped and defined San Francisco and the Bay Area. The second and third floors of this intense museum are packed with great art from all across Asia, including a Chinese gilded Buddha dating from AD 338, the oldest known dated Chinese Buddha in the world. Sit down on a padded bench to admire paintings, sculpture, lacquered jade, textiles, jewels, and every type of art object imaginable. The breadth and diversity of Asian culture may stagger you; the museum's displays come from Japan and Vietnam, Buddhist Tibet, and ancient China. Special exhibitions cost extra—check the website to see what will be displayed on the ground floor galleries when you're in town. Even if you've been to the museum in the past, come back for a browse. The curators regularly rotate items from the permanent collection, so

the foggy Golden Gate Bridge

© STUART THORNTON

Halloween party you've heard about—the City has cracked down, and Halloween has become sedate in this otherwise party-happy neighborhood.

With its mix of Latino immigrants, working artists, hipsters, and SUV-driving professionals, the Mission is a neighborhood bursting at the seams with idiosyncratic energy. Changing from block to block, the zone manages to be blue-collar, edgy, and gentrified all at once. The heart of the neighborhood is still very much Latin American, with delicious burritos and *pupusas* around every corner. It's a haven for international restaurants and real bargains in thrift shops, along with the hippest (and most self-conscious) clubs in the City.

Mission Dolores

Formally named Mission San Francisco de Asís, **Mission Dolores** (3321 16th St., 415/621-8203, www.missiondolores.org, May-Oct. daily 9am-4:30pm, Nov.-Apr. daily 9am-4pm, donation adults $5, seniors and children $3) was founded in 1776. Today, the Mission is the oldest intact building in the City, survivor of the 1906 earthquake and fire, the 1989 Loma Prieta quake, and more than 200 years of use. You can attend Roman Catholic services here each Sunday, or you can visit the Old Mission Museum and the Basilica, which house artifacts from the Native Americans and Spanish of the 18th century. The beauty and grandeur of the Mission recall the heyday of the Spanish empire in California, so important to the history of the state.

you'll probably encounter new beauty every time you visit.

Alamo Square

Possibly the most photographed neighborhood in San Francisco, **Alamo Square** (Hayes St. and Steiner St.) is home to the "painted ladies" on "postcard row." This is a row of stately Victorian mansions, all painted brilliant colors and immaculately maintained, that appear in many images of the City including the opening sequence of the late 1980s, early 1990s sitcom *Full House*. Stroll in Alamo Square's green park and enjoy the serenity of this charming residential neighborhood.

MISSION AND CASTRO

Perhaps the most famous, or infamous, neighborhoods in the City are the Mission district and the Castro district. The Castro is the heart of gay San Francisco, with the nightlife, festivals, and street-level activism centered around the LGBT community (not to mention leather bars and naughty shops). Just don't expect the

GOLDEN GATE PARK AND THE HAIGHT

At 3.5 miles long and 0.5 miles wide, **Golden Gate Park** (main entrance at Stanyan St. at Fell St., McLaren Lodge Visitors Center, 501 Stanyan St., 415/831-2700, www.golden-gate-park.com, daily 5am-midnight, free) is a huge urban oasis even larger than New York's Central Park. Golden Gate is home to some of the city's finest attractions including the de Young Museum, the Japanese Tea Garden, and the California Academy of Sciences. There

CIVIC CENTER, HAYES VALLEY, MISSION, AND CASTRO

United Nations Plaza

Civic Center

★ ASIAN ART MUSEUM

MAIN LIBRARY

CIVIC CENTER

Civic Center Plaza

CITY HALL

POLK ST (DR CARLTON B GOODLETT PL)

VAN ● NESS ● AVE

FRANKLIN

REDWOOD

GATE

GOLDEN

Jefferson Square

LAGUNA

WESTERN ADDITION

CHATEAU TIVOLI ●

PAINTED LADIES ★

THE GROVE INN ●

Alamo Square ★

★ NOPA

INN AT THE OPERA

WAR MEMORIAL OPERA HOUSE ■

DAVIES SYMPHONY HALL

JARDINIERE ●

SMUGGLER'S COVE ●

► ABSINTHE

BIERGARTEN ►

PLACE PIGALLE ►

SUPPENKUCHE ►

GOUGH

OCTAVIA

BIRCH

LINDEN

IVY

HICKORY

LILY

BUCHANAN

HAYES VALLEY

WEBSTER

FILLMORE

HAYES

FELL

OAK

PAGE

STEINER

HAIGHT

PIERCE

SCOTT

DIVISADERO

GROVE

BRODERICK

FULTON

McALLISTER

MCCOPPIN

YIELD AND PAUSE WINE BAR ►

ZEITGEIST

VALENCIA

ELGIN PARK

PEARL ST

PARK

CLINTON

CHURCH

RESERVOIR ST

LANDERS

RAMONA ST

14TH

To The Fillmore

TURK

THE PARSONAGE ●

ROSE

WALLER ST

GERMANIA

HERMANN

DUBOCE

POTOMAC ST

Duboce Park

WALTER ST

SANCHEZ ST

BELCHER ST

WILLOWS INN B&B ●

DUBOCE TRIANGLE

CARMELITA

DAVIES MEDICAL CENTER

CASTRO

LLOYD ST

DIVISADERO

ALPINE

TERR

HENRY

15TH

BUENA VISTA TERR

PARK HILL AVE

SOMA

WASHBURN

GRACE ST

8TH ST

9TH

10TH

11TH

12TH ST

MINNA

NATOMA

LAFAYETTE

SOUTH VAN NESS

PLUM

OTIS

JESSIE

STEVENSON

COLTON

BRADY

MARKET

NORFOLK ST

KISSLING ST

FOLSOM

HARRISON

ERIE ST

NATOMA ST

MINNA ST

WIESE

JULIAN AVE

CALEDONIA

LITTLE STAR PIZZA ►

ALBION

MISSION

NOE VALLEY

CASTRO

Dolores Park

TREAT

FOLSOM

SHOTWELL

SOUTH

VAN NESS AVE

CAPP

MISSION

SAN CARLOS

LEXINGTON

VALENCIA

ALBION ST

GUERRERO

LAPIDGE ST

LINDA

DEARBORN

CLARION ALY

SYCAMORE

HOFF ST

DALVA ▼
▲ BAR TARTINE

16th St

▲ BI-RITE CREAMERY AND BAKESHOP

▼ DELFINA ▲ TARTINE BAKERY

OAKWOOD

CUMBERLAND

★ MISSION DOLORES

DOLORES

CHULA

17TH

CHURCH

DORLAND ST

18TH

HANCOCK

19TH

CUMBERLAND

20TH

LIBERTY

20TH

▼ DINOSAURS

PROSPER ST

POND ST

NOE

FRANCES ▼

MARKET

HARTFORD

CASTRO

COLLINGWOOD

DIAMOND

EUREKA

DOUGLASS

21ST

ANCHOR OYSTER BAR ▼

LA MEDITERRANÉE ▼

● INN ON CASTRO

BEAVER ST

STATES ST

FLINT ST

MUSEUM WY

RANDALL MUSEUM

RANGE ▲

AMNESIA ▼

AMES

QUANE

FAIR OAKS

MERSEY

CHATTANOOGA

NELLIE

VICKSBURG

SANCHEZ

HILL

22ND

ALVARADO

ELIZABETH

JERSEY

BARTLETT

BERETTA ▼

SAN JOSE AVE

ALVARADO AVE

PAPALOTE MEXICAN GRILL ▼

POPLAR ST

ORANGE ALY

OSAGE ▶▶

LILAC ▶▶ ▲ LA TAQUERIA

LUCKY ◀◀

FAROLITO TAQUERIA ▼

CYPRESS

24th St

25TH

26TH

24TH

23RD

300 yds

300 m

© AVALON TRAVEL

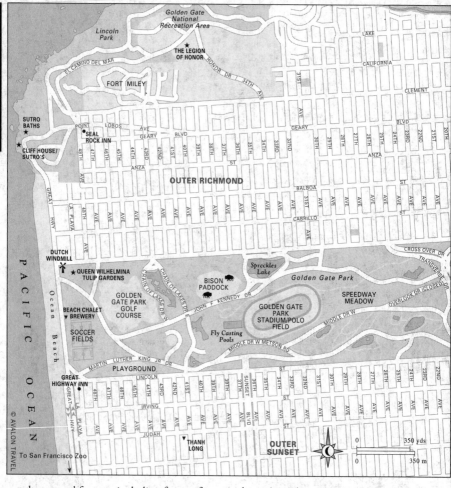

are also natural features including forests, formal gardens, and a buffalo pasture. In addition to its many sights, Golden Gate Park is also where San Francisco's Outside Lands and Hardly Strictly Bluegrass music festivals take place.

Haight-Ashbury

The neighborhood surrounding the intersection of **Haight and Ashbury Streets** (known locally as "the Haight") is best known for the wave of countercultural energy that broke out

in the 1960s. The area initially was a magnet for drifters, dropouts, and visionaries who preached and practiced a heady blend of peace, love, and psychedelic drugs. It reached a fever pitch during 1967's Summer of Love, when pioneering music acts the Grateful Dead, Jefferson Airplane, and Janis Joplin resided in the area.

The door to the promised new consciousness never swung fully open, and then it swung shut with a resounding bang. Today, thousands of visitors stand at the iconic intersection, and what they see is Ben & Jerry's. The district is

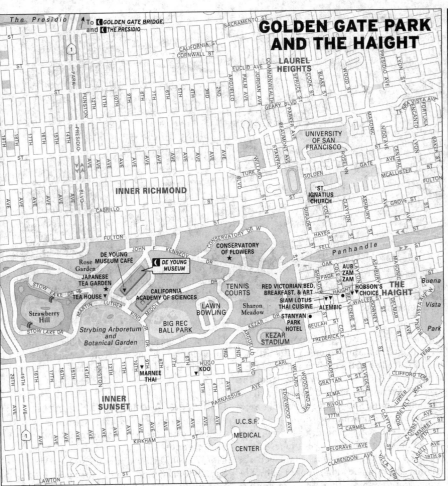

GOLDEN GATE PARK AND THE HAIGHT

still home to plenty of independent businesses, including vintage stores, lots of places to get pierced and tattooed, and, of course, head shops. Plenty of chain stores are interspersed with the indies, reminding visitors that the power of capitalism can intrude anywhere—even in a countercultural center.

A prettier aspect of local gentrification appears in the form of restored Victorian houses in the Haight. You can actually stay in a bright, funky Red Victorian, or check out the private homes on Page Street and throughout the

neighborhood. To learn more about the history of the Haight and to walk past the famed homes of the Grateful Dead and Jefferson Airplane, take the **Flower Power Walking Tour** (starts at intersection of Stanyan St. and Waller St., 415/863-1621, www.hippygourmet.com, Tues. and Sat. 9:30am, Fri. 11am, $20).

◖ de Young Museum

Haven't been to the City in a while? Take some time out to visit the **de Young Museum** (50 Hagiwara Tea Garden Dr., 415/750-3600,

© STUART THORNTON

the intersection of the counterculture: Haight-Ashbury

http://deyoung.famsf.org, Tues.-Sun. 9:30am-5:15pm, Fri. 9:30am-8:45pm, adults $10, seniors $7, students $6, children under 12 free) in Golden Gate Park. Everything from the striking exterior to the art collections and exhibitions and the 360-degree panoramic view of San Francisco from the top of the tower has been renewed, replaced, or newly recreated. The reason for the recent renewal was the 1989 earthquake, which damaged the original de Young beyond simple repair. The renovation took more than 10 years, and the results are a smashing success. For a special treat, brave the lines and grab a meal at the museum's café.

The collections at the de Young include works in various media: painting, sculpture, textiles, ceramics, and more modern graphic designs and "contemporary crafts." Some collections focus on artists from the United States, while many others contain art from around the world. The exhibitions that come through the de Young range from the work of fashion designer Jean Paul Gaultier to one focusing on Dutch 17th century paintings. There's something for just about everyone—even classic art purists will find a gallery to love inside the de Young.

California Academy of Sciences

A triumph of the sustainable scientific principles it exhibits, the **California Academy of Sciences** (55 Music Concourse Dr., 415/379-8000, www.calacademy.org, Mon.-Sat. 9:30am-5pm, Sun. 11am-5pm, adults $30, children 4-11 $20, students and seniors $25) drips with ecological perfection. From its grass-covered roof to its underground aquarium, visitors can explore every part of the universe. Wander through a steamy endangered rainforest contained inside a giant glass bubble, or travel through an all-digital outer space in the high-tech planetarium. More studious nature lovers can spend days examining every inch of the Kimball Natural History Museum, including favorite exhibits like the 87-foot-long blue whale skeleton, from the older incarnation of the Academy of

Science. Though it might look and sound like an adult destination, in fact the new Academy of Sciences takes pains to make itself kid-friendly, with interactive exhibits, thousands of live animals, and endless opportunities for learning. How could kids not love a museum where the guards by the elevators have butterfly nets to catch the occasional "exhibit" that's trying to escape?

Japanese Tea Garden

The **Japanese Tea Garden** (7 Hagiwara Tea Garden Dr., 415/752-4227, http://japaneseteagardensf.com, Mar.-Oct. daily 9am-6pm, Nov.-Feb. daily 9am-4:45pm, adults $7, seniors $5, children $2) is a haven of peace and tranquility that's a local favorite within the park. The planting and design of the garden began in 1894 for the California Exposition. Today, the flourishing garden displays a wealth of beautiful flora, including stunning examples of rare Chinese and Japanese plants, some quite old. As you stroll along the paths, you'll come upon sculptures, bridges, ponds, and even traditional *tsukubai* (a tea ceremony sink). You can visit the teahouse, the brilliant pagoda and temple, and the gift shop as well.

San Francisco Botanical Gardens

Take a bucolic walk in the middle of Golden Gate Park by visiting the **San Francisco Botanical Gardens** (1199 9th Ave. at Lincoln Way, 415/661-1316, www.sfbotanicalgarden.org, Apr.-Oct. daily 9am-6pm, Nov.-Mar. daily 9am-5pm, adults $7, students and seniors $5, ages 5-11 $2, families $15, under age 5 and city residents with ID free). The 55-acre gardens play home to more than 8,000 species of plants from around the world, including a California Natives garden and a shady redwood forest. Fountains, ponds, meadows, and lawns are interwoven with the flowers and trees to create a peaceful, serene setting in the middle of the crowded city. The Botanical Gardens are a great place to kick back with a book and a snack; the plants will keep you in quiet company as you rev up to tackle another round of touring.

Conservatory of Flowers

Lying at the northeastern entrance to Golden Gate Park, the **Conservatory of Flowers** (100 John F. Kennedy Dr., 415/831-2090, www.conservatoryofflowers.org, Tues.-Sun. 10am-4:30pm, adults $7, students and seniors $5, ages 5-11 $2) blooms year-round. The exotic flowers grow in several "galleries" within the enormous glassy white Victorian-style greenhouse. Rare, slightly scary orchids twine around rainforest trees, eight-foot lily pads float serenely on still waters, and cheerful seasonal flowers spill out of containers in the potted plant gallery.

If you're traveling with small kids, be aware that strollers are not permitted inside the conservatory; wheelchairs and power chairs are.

The Legion of Honor

Passing a full size bronze cast of Rodin's *The Thinker* on the way into the **Legion of Honor** (100 34th Ave. at Clement St., 415/750-3600, http://legionofhonor.famsf.org, Tues.-Sun. 9:30am-5:15pm, adults $10, seniors $7, students and ages 13-17 $6, children 12 and under free) is a sign that this ornate building sitting on its lonely promontory in Lincoln Park is going to house some serious art. A gift to the City from philanthropist Alma Spreckels in 1924, this French Beaux-Arts-style building was built to honor the memory of California soldiers who died in World War I. From its beginning, the Legion of Honor was a museum dedicated to bringing European art to the population of San Francisco. Today, visitors can view the second finest collection of sculptor August Rodin's works as well as gorgeous collections of European paintings, decorative arts, ancient artifacts from around the Mediterranean, thousands of paper drawings by great artists, and much more. Special exhibitions come from the Legion's own collections and museums of the world. If you love the living arts and music, visit the Florence Gould Theater or come to the museum on a Sunday for a free organ concert on the immense Skinner Organ, which is integral to the building's structure. Their rotating temporary exhibits sometimes include

SAN FRANCISCO BAY AREA

HONNEUR ET PATRIE

© STUART THORNTON

the Legion of Honor

fascinating looks into more modern artists like Man Ray and Marcel Duchamp.

San Francisco Zoo

Lions, tigers, bears, lemurs, meerkats, and penguins reside in the **San Francisco Zoo** (Sloat Blvd. at 47th Ave., 415/753-7080, www.sfzoo. org, summer daily 10am-5pm, winter daily 10am-4pm, adults $15, seniors $12, ages 4-14 $9), making it a favorite excursion for locals and visitors all year long. Over the last several years the zoo has undergone a transformation, becoming an example for naturalized habitats and conservatory zoo practices. Today, animal lovers can enjoy the native plants and funny faces in the lemur habitat, the families of meerkats, and the bird sanctuary. Families come to check out the wealth of interactive children's exhibits as well as the various exotic animals. However, it's wise to bring your own picnic as the food offerings at the zoo have not improved as much as the habitats. But watch out for seagulls—they fly low and love to steal snacks.

Note that the official address is 1 Zoo Boulevard, but if you put that address into a GPS system, it will take you to the zoo's service entrance. Go to the gate at the corner of Sloat Boulevard and 47th Avenue instead.

Entertainment and Events

NIGHTLIFE
Bars
UNION SQUARE AND NOB HILL

These ritzy areas are better known for their shopping than their nightlife, but a few bars hang in there, plying weary shoppers with good drinks. Most tend toward the upscale. Some inhabit upper floors of the major hotels, like the **Tonga Room and Hurricane Bar** (950 Mason St., 415/772-5278, www.fairmont. com, www.tongaroom.com, Wed.-Thurs. and Sun. 6pm-10pm, Fri.-Sat. 6pm-11pm), where an over-the-top tiki theme adds a whimsical touch to the stately Fairmont Hotel on Nob Hill. Enjoy the tropical atmosphere with a fruity rum drink topped with a classic paper umbrella. Be prepared for the bar's virtual tropical storms that roll in every once and a while.

Just outside the Union Square area in the sketchy Tenderloin neighborhood, brave souls can find a gem: **Café Royale** (800 Post St., 415/441-4099, www.caferoyale-sf.com, daily 3pm-2am) isn't a typical watering hole by any city's standards, but its intense focus on art fits perfectly with the endlessly eclectic ethos of San Francisco. Local artists exhibit their work in Café Royale on a monthly basis, and plenty of live performers grace the space. The primary intoxicants are lesser known microbrews and small batch beers.

Part live-music venue, part elegant bar, **Top of the Mark** (InterContinental Mark Hopkins, 999 California St., 415/616-6940, www.intercontinentalmarkhopkins.com, Sun. 5pm-11:30pm, Mon.-Thurs. 2:30pm-11:30pm, Fri.-Sat. 2:30pm-12:30am) has something for every discerning taste in nighttime entertainment. Since World War II, the views and drinks in this wonderful lounge at the top of the InterContinental Mark Hopkins Hotel have drawn visitors from around the world. The lounge doubles as a restaurant that serves breakfast and lunch, but the best time for cocktails is, of course, at night. That's when live bands play almost every night of the week. The dress code is business casual or better and is enforced, so leave the jeans in your room. Have a top-shelf martini, and let your toes tap along.

A less formal bar off Union Square, **Lefty O'Doul's Restaurant & Cocktail Lounge** (333 Geary St., 415/982-8900, www.leftyodouls.biz, daily 7am-2am) is named after the San Francisco native major league baseball player. This informal sports bar with 12 TVs serves up hearty fare like hand-carved roast beef or roasted turkey dinners that'll soak up any alcohol you've consumed at the bar.

Another place where you don't need to wear a suit in the Union Square area is the dive bar **Chelsea Place** (641 Bush St., 415/989-2524,

daily 1pm-2am). Dive-bar aficionados will appreciate its dinginess, as well as the friendly bartenders and clientele who are willing to talk or play a dice game over a beer or shot.

FINANCIAL DISTRICT AND SOMA

All those high-powered business suit-clad executive types working in the Financial District need places to drink too. One of these is the **Royal Exchange** (301 Sacramento St., 415/956-1710, http://royalexchange.com, Mon.-Fri. 11am-11pm). This classic pub-style bar has a green-painted exterior, big windows overlooking the street, and a long, narrow barroom. The Royal Exchange serves a full lunch and dinner menu, a small wine list, and a full complement of top-shelf spirits. But most of all, the Exchange serves beer. With 73 taps pouring out 32 different types of beer, the hardest problem will be choosing one. This business people's watering hole is open to the public only on weekdays; on weekends they host private parties.

The Cosmopolitan (121 Spear St., Suite B8, 415/543-4001, http://cosmopolitansf.com, Mon.-Tues. 3:30pm-midnight, Wed.-Fri. 11:30am-2am, Sat. 5:30pm-2am) offers the best of both worlds: a bar and piano lounge serving top-shelf liquors and reasonably priced well drinks, and a large dining room serving an ever-changing menu of California cuisine. You're more than welcome to enjoy drinks only at the bar, or make a reservation for a complete upscale dinner in the restaurant. If you're lucky, you might even get some live entertainment from a local musician plying the lounge piano.

In urban-renewed SoMa (South of Market), upscale wine bars have become an evening institution. Among the trendiest you'll find is **District** (216 Townsend St., 415/896-2120, http://districtsf.com, Mon.-Thurs. 4pm-1am, Fri. 4pm-2am, Sat. 5pm-2am). A perfect example of its kind, District features bare brick walls, simple wooden furniture, and a big U-shaped bar at the center of the room with wine glasses hanging above it. While you can get a cocktail or even a beer here, the point of coming to District is to sip the finest wines from California, Europe, and beyond. With more than 30 wines available by the glass each night, it's easy to find a favorite, or enjoy a flight of three similar wines to compare. While you can't quite get a full dinner at District, you will find a lovely lounge menu filled with small portions of delicacies to enhance your tasting experience (and perhaps soak up some of the alcohol).

Secret passwords, a hidden library, and an art deco vibe make **Bourbon and Branch** (505 Jones St., 415/346-1735, www.bourbonand-branch.com, Mon.-Sat. 6pm-2am, reservations suggested) a must for lovers of the brown stuff. Tucked behind a nameless brown door, this resurrected 1920s-era speakeasy evokes its prohibition-era past with passwords and secret passages. A business-class elite sips rare bourbon and scotch in dark secluded booths while those without reservations step into the hidden library.

The **Rickhouse** (246 Kearney St., 415/398-2827, www.rickhousesf.com, Tues.-Fri. 3pm-2am, Sat. and Mon. 5pm-2am) feels like a country shack plopped down in the midst of the Financial District. The artisan cocktail bar draws in the City's plentiful young urban hipsters. It's dimly lit, the walls and floors are wood, and stacks of barrels and old bottles line the mantle. There's also live music on Saturday and Monday nights.

CHINATOWN

Nightlife in Chinatown runs to dark, quiet dive bars filled with locals. Perhaps the perfect Chinatown dive, **Li Po Lounge** (916 Grant Ave., 415/982-0072, daily 2pm-2am, cash only) has an appropriately dark and slightly spooky atmosphere that recalls the opium dens of another century. Cheap drinks and Chinese dice games attract locals, and it's definitely helpful to speak Cantonese. But even an English-speaking out-of-town visitor can get a good, cheap (and strong!) mai tai or beer. The hanging lantern and Buddha statue behind the bar complete the picture. Another great local hangout worth checking out is the **Buddha Cocktail Lounge** (901 Grant Ave., 415/362-1792, daily 1pm-2am, cash only).

NORTH BEACH AND FISHERMAN'S WHARF

One of the oldest and most celebrated bars in the City, **Tosca** (242 Columbus Ave., 415/986-9651, http://toscacafesf.com, Tues.-Sun. 5pm-2am) has an unpretentious yet glam 1940s style. Hunter S. Thompson once tended bar here when the owner was out at the dentist. The jukebox plays grand opera to the patrons clustered in the big red booths. Locals love the lack of trendiness, the classic cocktails, and the occasional star sightings.

Almost across the street from Tosca is **Vesuvio** (255 Columbus Ave., 415/362-3370, www.vesuvio.com, daily 6am-2am). Jack Kerouac loved Vesuvio, which is why it's probably North Beach's most famous saloon. This cozy, eclectic bi-level hideout is an easy place to spend the afternoon with a pint of Anchor Steam.

Dress up a little for a night out at **15 Romolo** (15 Romolo Pl., 415/398-1359, www.15romolo.com, daily 5:30pm-2am). You'll have to hike up the steep little alley (Fresno St. crosses Romolo Pl., which can be a little hard to find) to this hotel bar, but once you're here you'll love the creative cocktails, edgy jukebox music, and often mellow crowd. The bar is smallish and can get crowded on the weekend, so come on a weeknight if you prefer a quiet drink. 15 Romolo also serves brunch (Sat.-Sun. 11:30am-3:30pm).

Known for its colorful clientele and cluttered decor, **Specs** (12 William Saroyan Pl., 415/421-4112, daily 4:30pm-2am, cash only) is a dive bar located in a North Beach alley.

MARINA AND PACIFIC HEIGHTS

Marina and Pacific Heights denizens enjoy a good glass of vino, and the wine bars in the area cater to local tastes. The **Bacchus Wine Bar** (1954 Hyde St., 415/928-2633, daily 5:30pm-midnight) is a tiny local watering hole that offers an array of wines, sake cocktails, and craft beers.

Another favorite bar is the **City Tavern** (3200 Fillmore St., 415/567-0918, www.city-tavernsf.com, Mon.-Fri. 3pm-2am, Sat.-Sun.

11am-2am). Here you'll get a mix of sports, drinks, and good company. Good solid American food comes at reasonable prices, while weekend brunch features an array of tasty classics as well as some health-conscious fare. The full bar pours an array of beers, wines, liquors, and cocktails. On weekdays, save money at The Tavern's happy hour (3pm-7pm).

All that's really left of the original Matrix is the ground you stand on, but the **MatrixFillmore** (3138 Fillmore St., 415/563-4180, www.matrixfillmore.com, daily 8pm-2am) does claim huge mid-20th-century musical fame. The Matrix, then a live music venue, was opened by Marty Balin in 1965 so that his freshly named band, Jefferson Airplane, would have a place to play. Subsequent acts included the Grateful Dead, Janis Joplin, and the Doors. Today, the MatrixFillmore is known for its dance music and bottle service.

The Marina District's Chestnut Street is known for its high-end restaurants and swanky clientele. The **Horseshoe Tavern** (2024 Chestnut St., 415/346-1430, daily 10am-2am) is a place for people to let their hair down, shoot pool, and drink without pretension.

CIVIC CENTER AND HAYES VALLEY

Hayes Valley bleeds into Lower Haight (Haight St. between Divisadero St. and Octavia Blvd.) and supplies most of the neighborhood bars. For proof that the independent spirit of the Haight lives on in spite of encroaching commercialism, stop in and have a drink at the **Toronado** (547 Haight St., 415/863-2276, www.toronado.com, daily 11:30am-2am). This dimly lit haven maintains one of the finest beer selections in the nation, with a changing roster of several dozen microbrews on tap, including many hard-to-find Belgian ales. These are more potent than typical domestic beers and may have an alcohol content as high as 12 percent.

The bar scene heads upscale with the **Yield and Pause Wine Bar** (1666 Market St., 415/241-9463, www.yieldandpause.com, Mon.-Sat. 4:30pm-midnight). The focus is on the food as much as the wine—the small plates menu is pleasantly diverse, and the items are

fit to complement the wines. The bar closes at midnight, encouraging an earlier night for a slightly older crowd.

Longtime classic bar Jade has given way to the hipster-tiki-cocktail stylings of **Smuggler's Cove** (650 Gough St., 415/869-1900, http://smugglerscovesf.com, daily 5pm-2am). Yes, it's all about the rum.

If what you really want is a dive bar, **Place Pigalle** (520 Hayes St., 415/552-2671, http://placepigallesf.com, Wed.-Sun. 2pm-2am, Mon.-Tues. 5pm-2am) is the place for you. This hidden gem in Hayes Valley offers 15 beer and wine taps. It also has a pool table, lots of sofas for lounging, and an uncrowded, genuinely laid-back vibe on weeknights and even sometimes on weekends. The too-cool-for-school hipster vibe somehow missed this place, which manages to maintain its friendly neighborhood feel.

MISSION

These neighborhoods seem to hold a whole city's worth of bars. The Mission, despite a recent upswing in its economy, still has plenty of no-frills bars, many with a Latino theme. And, of course, men seeking men flock to the Castro's endless array of gay bars. For lesbians, the Mission might be a better bet.

A red-lit bar and hipster hangout, **Amnesia** (853 Valencia St., 415/970-0012, http://amnesiathebar.com, daily 6pm-2am) has entertainment every night of the week. Among the most popular are the ongoing Monday bluegrass nights and Wednesday jazz nights.

Dalva (3121 16th St., 415/252-7740, daily 4pm-2am) is a small but sophisticated oasis in an ocean of overcrowded Mission hipster hangouts. You'll find dramatic high ceilings, modern paintings, and a jukebox stuffed with indie rock and electronica. Way back in the depths of the club, the Hideaway bar serves up a delectable array of cocktails poured by a rotating staff of local celebrity mixologists.

Excellent draft beers, tasty barbecue plates, and a motorcycle-inclined crowd give **Zeitgeist** (199 Valencia St., 415/255-7505, http://zeitgeistsf.com, daily 9am-2am)

Beretta

a punk-rock edge. This Mission favorite, though, endears itself to all sorts, thanks to its spacious outdoor beer garden, 40 beers on tap, and popular Bloody Marys.

The cocktails at **Beretta** (1199 Valencia St., 415/695-1199, www.berettasf.com, Mon.-Fri. 5:30pm-1am, Sat.-Sun. 11am-1am) consistently win raves from locals and visitors alike. Order a Rattlesnake—and a pizza to suck up the venom of that bite.

GOLDEN GATE PARK AND THE HAIGHT

Haight Street crowds head out in droves to the **Alembic** (1725 Haight St., 415/666-0822, www.alembicbar.com, daily noon-2am) for artisanal cocktails laced with American spirits. On par with the whiskey and bourbon menu is the cuisine: Wash down the pork belly sliders or chicken liver mousse with a Sazerac.

If rum is your favorite intoxicant, head to **Hobson's Choice** (1601 Haight St., 415/621-5859, http://hobsonschoice.com, Mon.-Fri. 2pm-2am, Sat.-Sun. noon-2am), which claims to have the largest selection of rums in the country. Try your rum in everything from a Brazilian caipirinha to a Cuban mojito or in one of Hobson's famous rum punches.

Featured in an episode of Anthony Bourdain's travel show *No Reservations,* **Aub Zam Zam** (1633 Haight St., 415/861-2545, daily 1pm-2am) is an old school bar with an Arabian feel. Zam Zam doesn't take credit cards, but it does have an Arabian mural behind the U-shaped bar, where an interesting mix of locals and tourists congregate for the cheap drinks.

The **Beach Chalet Brewery** (1000 Great Hwy., 415/386-8439, www.beachchalet.com, Sun. 8am-10pm, Mon.-Thurs. 9am-10pm, Fri. 9am-11pm, Sat. 8am-11pm) is an attractive brewpub and restaurant directly across the street from Ocean Beach. Sip a pale ale while watching the sunset, and check out the historic murals downstairs.

Clubs

Some folks are surprised at the smallish list of San Francisco clubs. The truth is, San

Francisco just isn't a see-and-be-seen, hip-new-club-every-week kind of town. In the City, you'll find gay clubs, vintage dance clubs, Goth clubs, and the occasional underground Burner rave mixed in with the more standard dance floor and DJ fare.

If you're up for a full night of club hopping and don't want to deal with transit headaches, several bus services can ferry your party from club to club. Many of these offer VIP entrance to clubs and will stop wherever you want to go. **Think Escape** (800/823-7249, www.thinkescape.com) has buses and limos with drivers and guides to get you to the hottest spots with ease.

UNION SQUARE AND NOB HILL

Defying San Francisco expectation, **Ruby Skye** (420 Mason St., 415/693-0777, www.rubyskye. com, Thurs. 7pm-2am, Fri.-Sat. 9pm-2am, cover charge, dress code enforced) books top DJs and occasional live acts into a big, crowded dance club. The building, built in 1890, was originally the Stage Door Theatre, but it has been redone to create dance floors, bars, DJ booths, and VIP spaces. Crowds can get big on the weekend, and the patrons tend to be young and pretty and looking for action. The sound system rocks, so conversation isn't happening, and the drinks tend toward overpriced vodka and Red Bull.

For a chic New York-style club experience, check out **Vessel** (85 Campton Pl., 415/433-8585, www.vesselsf.com, Wed.-Thurs. and Sat. 10pm-2am, Fri. 9:30pm-2am, cover $10-30). With old-school bottle service at some tables, Vessel caters to an upscale crowd that likes postmodern decor, top-shelf liquors, and a bit of dancing to round out the evening. Dress up if you plan to get in.

Down the brightly lit staircase in the aptly named **The Cellar** (685 Sutter St., 415/441-5678, http://cellarsf.com, Mon.-Fri. 5pm-2am, Sat.-Sun. 10pm-2am, cover from $25), you'll find two dance clubs, three bars, and bottle service booths.

Harry Denton's Starlight Room (450 Powell St., 21st Fl., 415/395-8595, www.harrydenton.com, Tues.-Sat. 6pm-2am, cover

up to $20) brings the flamboyant side of San Francisco downtown. Enjoy a cocktail in the early evening or a nightcap and a bite of dessert after the theater in this truly old-school nightclub. Dress in your best to match the glitzy red-and-gold decor and mirrors. Whoop it up at "Sunday's a Drag" shows (noon and 2:30pm Sun.). Reservations are recommended.

FINANCIAL DISTRICT AND SOMA

111 Minna Street Gallery (111 Minna St., 415/974-1719, www.111minnagallery.com, Wed. noon-11pm, Thurs.-Fri. noon-2am, Sat. 5pm-2am, cover $5) really is an art gallery, but it's also one of the hottest dance clubs in SoMa. Art lovers who come to 111 Minna to enjoy the changing exhibitions of new art in peace and quiet do so during the day. After 5pm the gallery transforms into a nightclub, opening the full bar and bringing in DJs who spin late into the weekend nights. While it may sound pretentious, the mix of modern art and lots of liquor really feels just right. Check the website for special events, including 1980s dance parties and art-show openings. Guests must be 21 and older due to the liquor license and because they often showcase explicit artworks.

It's dark, it's dank, and it's very, very Goth. The **Cat Club** (1190 Folsom St., 415/703-8964, www.sfcatclub.com, Tues.-Sat. 9pm-3am, cover $6-10) gets pretty energetic on 1980s dance nights, but it's still a great place to go after you've donned your best down-rent black attire and painted your face deathly pale, especially on Goth-industrial-electronica nights. In fact, there's no dress code at the Cat Club, unlike many local nightspots, which makes it great for travelers who live in their jeans. You'll find a friendly crowd, decent bartenders, strong drinks, and easy access to smoking areas. Each of the two rooms has its own DJ, which somehow works perfectly even though they're only a wall apart from each other. Check the website to find the right party night for you, and expect the crowd to heat up after 11pm.

Looking for *the* DJs and dance parties? You'll find them at the **DNA Lounge** (375 11th St., 415/626-1409, www.dnalounge.com, Mon.

SoMa's Cat Club

© DOMINI DRAGOONE

9:30pm-2:30am, Thurs. 9:30pm-3am, Fri.-Sat. 9pm-3am, cover varies). With Bootie (dance night) twice a month, 1980s parties, and live music, the DNA Lounge has been one of the City's perpetual hot nightspots for decades (it even has its own entry in Wikipedia). It's also one of the few clubs that's open after hours.

NORTH BEACH AND FISHERMAN'S WHARF
The North Beach neighborhood has long been San Francisco's best-known red-light district. To this day, Broadway Avenue is lined with the neon signs of strip clubs and adult stores, all promising grown-up good times. Do be aware that cover charges at most of the strip clubs tend to be on the high side, and lone women should approach this area with extreme caution after dark.

If you're just looking for a good time at a PG-rated (OK, maybe R-rated if you get lucky) dance club, check out the **Bamboo Hut** (479 Broadway, 415/989-8555, www.maximum-productions.com, Mon. 8pm-2am, Wed.-Fri.

5pm-2am, Sat. 7pm-2am). It's part tacky tiki bar, part impromptu dance club, and has a cheerful vibe and friendly scene that can be hard to come by in this part of town. You'll see the tiki god, the bamboo decor, and the fun umbrella-clad fruity rum drinks. The house specialty is the Flaming Volcano Bowl—yes, it's really on fire, and it's probably a good idea to share one with a friend or three. DJs spin on weekends at the Bamboo Hut; they might not be the hippest in town, but regulars have a great time dancing anyhow.

MARINA AND PACIFIC HEIGHTS
Clubs in the Marina are all about the trendy and the spendy. The **Hi-Fi Lounge** (2125 Lombard St., 415/345-8663, www.maxi-mumproductions.com, Wed.-Thurs. and Sat. 7pm-2am, Fri 5pm-2am, cover $5 Fri.-Sat.) personifies the fun that can be had in smaller San Francisco venues. This one-floor wonder with a tiny dance floor gets incredibly crowded. Yet even the locals have a good time when they come out to the Hi-Fi. The decor is funky and

fun, and the patrons are young and affluent. Most visitors find the staff friendly and the bartenders attentive. It being the Marina, come early to get decent parking and to avoid the cover charge. On Thursday and Friday, early birds get $1 draft beer.

CIVIC CENTER AND HAYES VALLEY

Not your slick, shiny nightclub, the **Rickshaw Stop** (155 Fell St., 415/861-2011, www.rickshawstop.com, Wed.-Thurs. 5pm-midnight, Fri.-Sat. 5pm-2am, cover $5-18) in the Hayes Valley neighborhood welcomes one and all with a cavernous lower bar, stage area, and dance floor, and a quirky balcony area complete with comfy old sofas. Up-and-coming live acts play here, DJs spin, and special events and parties add to the action almost every week. Have a drink, enjoy the music, and get comfortable! You'll feel almost as though you're in a friendly neighborhood coffee shop (albeit a really big one) than in some fancy nightspot. Check the website for events and club hours—the schedule varies widely.

MISSION AND CASTRO

The Mission and the Castro are popular clubbing districts in San Francisco, and as the urban renewal continues, SoMa is making its own play to create a hot nightlife rep. Naturally the biggest concentration of gay clubs is in the Castro.

Fans of the hipster lounge scene flock to the **Fluid Ultra Lounge** (662 Mission St., 415/385-2547, www.fluidsf.com, Thurs.-Sat. 9pm-2am, cover varies). The second you walk in, you'll probably feel you're not chic enough for this David Oldroyd-designed postmodern wonderland. Gleaming metal meets fascinating floralesque accessories in a series of rooms that boast really uncomfortable white chairs. If you're not up for lots of young and ultra-cool clubsters, you may find the decor to be the best part of Fluid. You can definitely dance on an interestingly lit floor, though it can be tough to pry a drink out of the bartenders at times. Big name DJs, including Jazzy Jeff and Mark Ronson, have performed here.

GOLDEN GATE PARK AND THE HAIGHT

In the infamous Haight, the club scene is actually an eclectic mix of everything from trendy to retro. **Milk** (1840 Haight St., 415/387-6455, www.milksf.com, Mon.-Sat. 9pm-2am, Sun. from 3pm, cover up to $5) counts itself among the trendy. It's tiny, and it's often empty on weekdays and packed solid on weekends. The music ranges from reggae to hip-hop to 1980s, depending on the night and the DJ. Milk attracts more locals than out-of-towners, but if that's what you're looking for in your visit to the City, a night of Milk might be just what the doctor ordered.

Gay and Lesbian

San Francisco's gay nightlife has earned a worldwide rep for both the quantity and quality of options. In fact, the gay club scene totally outdoes the straight club scene for frolicsome fabulous fun. While the City's queer nightlife caters more to gay men than to lesbians, there's plenty of space available for partiers of all persuasions. For a more comprehensive list of San Francisco's queer bars and clubs, visit http://sanfrancisco.gaycities.com/bars.

You'll have no trouble finding a gay bar in the Castro. One of the best is called simply **Q Bar** (456 Castro St., 415/864-2877, www.qbarsf.com, Mon.-Fri. 4pm-2am, Sat.-Sun. 2pm-2am). Just look for the red neon "Bar" sign set in steel out front. Inside, expect to find the fabulous red decor known as "retro-glam," delicious top-shelf cocktails, and thrumming beats spun by popular DJs almost every night of the week. Unlike many Castro establishments, the Bar caters to pretty much everybody: gay men, gay women, and gay-friendly straight folks. You'll find a coat check and adequate restroom facilities, and the strength of the drinks will make you want to take off your jacket and stay awhile.

Looking for a stylin' gay bar turned club, Castro style? Head for **Badlands** (4121 18th St., 415/626-9320, www.sfbadlands.com, daily 2pm-2am). This Castro icon was once an old-school bar with pool tables on the floor and license plates on the walls. Now you'll find an always-crowded dance floor, au courant peppy pop music, ever-changing video screens, and plenty of gay men out for a good time. Any number of local straight women count themselves among the regulars at this friendly establishment, which attracts a youngish but mixed-age crowd. Do be aware that Badlands gets incredibly crowded, complete with a hot and packed dance floor, especially on weekend nights. There's a coat check on the bottom level.

The **Lexington Club** (3464 19th St., 415/863-2052, www.lexingtonclub.com, Mon.-Thurs. 5pm-2am, Fri.-Sun. 3pm-2am) calls itself "your friendly neighborhood dyke bar." In truth, the Lex offers a neighborhood dive environment and cheap drinks—think $3 sake bombs on Wednesdays. Friendly? Depends on how dyke you are—tats, piercings, short hair, and tank tops make for a better Lex experience.

Unlike some of the harder-core Castro gay clubs, **Truck** (1900 Folsom St., 415/252-0306, www.trucksf.com, Mon.-Fri. 4pm-2am, Sat.-Sun. 2pm-2am) offers a friendly neighborhood

© DOMINI DRAGOONE
the Lexington Club

vibe. Truck lures in patrons with cheap drinks, friendly bartenders, and theme nights every week. When it rains outside, they offer two-for-one cocktails. Oh, and yes, that's a shower. Stop by late on Friday night for the Truck Wash to see it in action.

The Lookout (3600 16th St., 415/431-0306, www.lookoutsf.com, Mon.-Fri. 3:30pm-2am, Sat.-Sun. 12:30pm-2am, cover $2-5) gets its name and much of its rep from its balcony overlooking the iconic Castro neighborhood. Get up there for some primo people watching as you sip your industrial-strength alcoholic concoctions and nibble on surprisingly edible bar snacks and pizza. Do be aware that the Lookout hosts quite a few "events" that come complete with a cover charge.

Yes, there's a Western-themed gay bar in San Francisco. **The Cinch Saloon** (1723 Polk St., 415/776-4162, http://cinchsf.com, Mon.-Fri. 9am-2am, Sat.-Sun. 6am-2am) has a laid-back (no pun intended), friendly, male-oriented vibe that's all but lost in the once gay, now gentrified Polk Street hood. Expect fewer females and strong drinks to go with the unpretentious decor and atmosphere.

Live Music
ROCK AND POP
San Francisco is one of the best cities in the country to take in live music. Almost any act touring the nation stops here, and there are lots of great Bay Area bands including Metallica, Santana, and newcomers like Thee Oh Sees and The Fresh & Onlys.

Opened in the late 1960s, **The Fillmore** (1805 Geary Blvd., 415/346-6000, www.thefillmore.com, prices vary) became legendary by hosting performances by rock acts like the Grateful Dead, Jefferson Airplane, and Carlos Santana. These days, all sorts of national touring acts stop by, sometimes for multiple nights. The Fillmore is also known for their distinctive poster art: Attendees to certain sold-out shows are given commemorative posters.

Started by rock veteran Boz Scaggs in 1988, **Slim's** (333 11th St., 415/255-0333, www.

slims-sf.com, prices vary) showcases everything from the Subhumans to Billy Bob Thornton. Dinner tickets are the only way to score an actual seat.

The **Warfield** (982 Market St., 415/345-0900, http://thewarfieldtheatre.com, prices vary) is one of the older rock venues in the City. It started out as a vaudeville palace in the early 1900s, booking major jazz acts as well as variety shows. The Warfield's configuration is that of a traditional theater, with a raised stage, an open orchestra section below it, and two balconies rising up and facing the stage. There's limited table seating on the lowest level (mostly by reservation), reserved seats in the balconies, and open standing in the orchestra below the stage. The Warfield books all sorts of big name acts from Adele to Bob Dylan to Prince. The downsides include the total lack of parking—you'll need to hunt for a spot at one of the local public parking structures, and you'll pay for the privilege.

With its marble columns and ornate balconies, the **Great American Music Hall** (859 O'Farrell St., 415/885-0750, www.slimspresents.com, prices vary) is one of the nicest places to see a nationally touring act in the City. The venue has the bragging rights of hosting Arcade Fire and Patti Smith a few years back.

With little decor and no seats, **The Independent** (628 Divisadero St., 415/771-1421, www.theindependentsf.com, prices vary) has emerged as one of the best venues to see live music in San Francisco. Beck, Bon Ivor, and LCD Soundsystem have all graced The Independent's stage.

BLUES AND JAZZ

The neighborhood surrounding Union Square is one of the most fertile areas in San Francisco for live music. Whether you're into blues, rock, or even country, you'll find a spot to have a drink and listen to some wonderful live tunes.

Both a restaurant and live music venue, **Yoshi's** (1330 Fillmore St., 415/655-5600, www.yoshis.com, Tues.-Wed. 5:30pm-9pm, Thurs. 5:30pm-10pm, Fri.-Sat. 5:30pm-10:30pm, Sun. 5pm-9pm) attracts some big

names—Pat Metheney, Terence Blanchard, and the Bad Plus—as well as Fillmore locals for drinks and sushi in the stunning lounge.

In the same neighborhood is the **Boom Boom Room** (1601 Fillmore St., 415/673-8000, www.boomboomblues.com, Tues.-Thurs. 4pm-2am, Fri. 4pm-2:30am, Sat. 3pm-2:30am, Sun. 3pm-1:30am), where you'll find the latest in a legacy of live blues, boogie, groove, soul, and funk music. The Boom Boom Room is just across from The Fillmore so you can stop in before or after the bigger shows across the road.

Biscuits and Blues (401 Mason St., 415/292-2583, www.biscuitsandblues.com, Tues.-Sat. 6pm-2am) is a local musicians' favorite. Just around the corner from the big live drama theaters, this house dedicates itself to jazz and blues. Headliners have included Joe Louis Walker, Jimmy Thackery, and Jim Kimo. One of the best things about this club is that you can, in fact, get biscuits as well as blues. Dinner is served nightly and features a surprisingly varied and upscale menu combining California cuisine with the mystical flavors of New Orleans. Yum! So when you plan for your night of blues, consider showing up early to enjoy a jam session and a meal, then stay on for the main acts and headliners (and, of course, cocktails).

Comedy

San Francisco's oldest comedy club, the **Punch Line** (444 Battery St., 415/397-7573, www.punchlinecomedyclub.com, shows Tues.-Sun. 8pm and 10pm, cover varies) is an elegant and intimate venue that earned its top-notch reputation with stellar headliners such as Robin Williams, Ellen DeGeneres, and Dave Chappelle. An on-site bar keeps the audience primed.

Cobb's Comedy Club (915 Columbus Ave., 415/928-4320, www.cobbscomedy.com, show times vary, cover varies, two-drink minimum) has played host to star comedians such as Jerry Seinfeld, Sarah Silverman, and Margaret Cho since 1982. The 425-seat venue offers a full dinner menu and a bar to slake your thirst. Be sure to check your show's start time—some comics don't follow the usual Cobb's schedule.

THE ARTS
Theater

For a great way to grab last-minute theater tickets, walk right up to the **Union Square TIX** booth (350 Powell St., Union Square, 415/430-1140, www.tixbayarea.com, daily 10am-6pm). TIX sells same-day, half-price, no-refund tickets to all kinds of shows across the City. If you've got your heart set on a specific musical or play in a big theater, get to the booth early in the day and steel yourself for possible disappointment—especially on weekends, when many top-shelf shows sell out. If you're flexible, you'll almost certainly find something available at a reasonable price. It might be lesbian stand-up comedy, Beach Blanket Babylon, or the San Francisco Vampire Tour, but it'll be cheap and it'll be fun. TIX also sells half-price tickets to same-day shows online—check the website at 11am daily for up-to-date deals.

If you really, really need to see a major musical while you're in San Francisco, check out **SHN** (www.shnsf.com). SHN operates the Orpheum, the Curran, and the Golden Gate Theater—the three venues where big Broadway productions land when they come to town.

UNION SQUARE AND NOB HILL

Just up from Union Square, on Geary Street, the traditional San Francisco theater district continues to entertain crowds almost every day of the week. The old Geary Theater is now the permanent home of **A.C.T.** (415 Geary St., 415/749-2228, www.act-sf.org, prices vary). A.C.T. puts on a season filled with big-name, big-budget productions. Each season sees an array of high-production-value musicals such as *Urinetown,* American classics by the likes of Sam Shepard and Somerset Maugham, and intriguing new works; you might even get to see a world premiere. Don't expect to find street parking on Geary. Discount parking is available with a ticket stub from A.C.T. at the Mason-O'Farrell garage around the corner. Tickets can be

reasonably priced, especially on weeknights, but do be aware that the second balcony seats are truly high altitude—expect to look nearly straight down to the stage, and take care if you're prone to vertigo.

The **Curran Theater** (445 Geary St., 888/746-1799, www.curran-theater.com, prices vary), next door to A.C.T., has a state-of-the-art stage for high-budget productions. Audiences have watched *Les Misérables* and *War Horse* from the plush red velvet seats. Expect to pay a premium for tickets to these shows, which can sometimes run at the Curran for months or even years. Check the schedule for current shows, and leave children under age five at home—they won't be permitted in the Curran.

At the **EXIT Theatre** (156 Eddy St., 415/931-1094, www.theexit.org), down in the Tenderloin, you'll see plenty of unusual experimental plays, many by local playwrights. The EXIT also participates in the annual San Francisco Fringe Festival (www.sffringe.org).

NORTH BEACH AND FISHERMAN'S WHARF

There's one live show that is always different, yet it's been running continuously for over three decades. This musical revue is crazy, wacky, and offbeat, and it pretty much defines live theater in San Francisco. It's **Beach Blanket Babylon** (678 Green St., 415/421-4222, www. beachblanketbabylon.com, shows Wed.-Thurs. 8pm, Fri.-Sat. 6:30pm and 9:30pm, Sun. 2pm and 5pm, prices vary). Even if you saw *Beach Blanket Babylon* 10 years ago, you should come to see it again. Because it mocks current pop culture, the show evolves almost continuously to take advantage of tabloid treasures. And the hats! You'll never forget the hats. While minors are welcome at the Sunday matinees, evening shows can get pretty racy, and liquor is involved, so these are restricted to attendees 21 and over.

MARINA AND PACIFIC HEIGHTS

Beyond the bright lights of Geary and Market Streets lie any number of tiny up-and-coming (or down-and-going, depending) theaters, many of which produce new plays by local playwrights. One of the best known of the "small" theaters, the **Magic Theatre** (Fort Mason Center, Bldg. D, 415/441-8822, http://magictheatre.org, prices vary) produced Sam Shepard's new works back before he was anyone special. They're still committed to new works, so when you go to a show at the Magic you're taking a chance or having an adventure, depending on how you look at it.

At the **Palace of Fine Arts Theatre** (3301 Lyon St., 415/567-6642, www.palaceoffinearts.org, cover varies) you'll find accessible avant-garde performing arts pieces, live music performance, dance recitals, and the occasional children's musical recital or black-and-white film.

CIVIC CENTER AND HAYES VALLEY

Down on Market Street, the **Orpheum Theater** (1192 Market St., 888/746-1799, www.shnsf.com, prices vary) runs touring productions of popular Broadway musicals.

MISSION AND CASTRO

Take care getting to **Theatre Rhinoceros** (2926 16th St., 415/552-4100, www.therhino.org, $15-35), as it's in a less-than-ritzy part of town. But it's worth it: The Rhino puts on a wonderfully entertaining set of gay and lesbian plays and has branched out to explore the whole spectrum of human sexuality, especially as it's expressed in anything-goes (even conservative Republicans!) San Francisco.

Focusing on short works by new writers, **Three Wise Monkeys** (www.bayoneacts.org, $25-45) puts on productions at the **Boxcar Theatre** (505 Natoma St., 415/967-2227). Each year Three Wise Monkeys hosts the Bay One Acts (BOAs).

Classical Music and Opera

Right around the Civic Center, music takes a turn for the upscale. This is the neighborhood where the ultra-rich and not-so-rich classics lovers come to enjoy a night out. Acoustically renovated in 1992, **Davies Symphony Hall** (Grove St. between Van Ness Ave. and Franklin St., 415/864-6000, www.sfsymphony.org) is home to Michael Tilson Thomas's world-renowned San Francisco Symphony. Loyal patrons flock to performances that range from the classic to the avant-garde. Whether you love Mozart or Mahler, or you want to hear classic rock blended with major symphony orchestra, the San Francisco Symphony does it.

The **War Memorial Opera House** (301 Van Ness Ave., 415/621-6600, www.sfwmpac.org, performances Tues.-Sun.), a Beaux-Arts-style building designed by Coit Tower and City Hall architect Arthur Brown Jr., houses the **San Francisco Opera** (415/861-4008, http://sfopera.com) and **San Francisco Ballet** (415/865-2000, www.sfballet.org). Tours are available (415/552-8338, Mon. 10am-2pm).

Cinema

A grand movie palace from the 1920s, the **Castro Theatre** (429 Castro St., 415/621-6120, www.castrotheatre.com, adults $11, children and seniors $8.50, matinees $8.50) has enchanted San Francisco audiences for almost a century. The Castro Theatre hosts everything from revival double features (from black-and-white through 1980s classics) to musical movie sing-alongs, live shows, and even the occasional book signing. Naturally, the Castro also screens current releases and documentaries about queer life in San Francisco and beyond. Check the calendar online to figure out what's going to be playing when you're in town before buying tickets. Then plan your Muni route to the theater, which doesn't have a dedicated parking lot. Once inside, be sure to admire the lavish interior decor.

Expect an upscale movie-going experience at the **Sundance Kabuki Theater** (1881 Post St., 415/346-3243, www.sundancecinemas.com/kabuki.html, adults $9-17, seniors $9-15, children $8.25-15). The "amenity fee" pays for reserved seating, film shorts rather than commercials, and bits of bamboo decor. The Kabuki has eight screens, all of which show mostly big blockbuster Hollywood films, plus a smattering of independents and the occasional

© DOMINI DRAGOONE

War Memorial Opera House

filmed opera performance. The Over 21 shows, in the four theaters connected to the full bars, encompass the most compelling reason to see a typical first-run movie for several dollars extra.

FESTIVALS AND EVENTS

If you're in town for a big event, prepare to check your inhibitions at the airport. No town does a festival, holiday, or parade like San Francisco. Oddity abounds. Nudity and sex displays are possibilities, and even the "tame" festivals include things like fireworks and skeletons.

Gay Pride

Pride parades and events celebrating queer life have sprung up all over the country, spreading joy and love across the land. But the grand-daddy of all Pride events still reigns in San Francisco. **San Francisco Pride Celebration** (Market St., 415/864-0831, www.sfpride.org) officially lasts for a weekend—the last weekend of June. But in truth, the fun and festivities surrounding Pride go on for weeks. The rainbow

flags go up all over the City at the beginning of June, and the excitement slowly builds, culminating in the fabulous parade and festival. Everyone is welcome to join the wall-to-wall crowds out in the streets, to stroll the vendor booths, and pack in to see the Dykes on Bikes and cadres of magnificent drag queens.

Bay to Breakers

Are those naked people you see trotting through the fog? Yes! But why? It must be **Bay to Breakers** (http://zazzlebaytobreakers.com)! On the third Sunday of May every year since 1912, San Franciscans have gotten up early to get to the starting line of the legendary 12K race. But Bay to Breakers is like no other race in the world. Sure, there are plenty of serious runners who enter the race to win it or to challenge themselves and their abilities. And then there are the other racers...San Franciscans and visitors who turn out by the thousands wearing astonishing outfits, pulling carts and wagons, and stripping down to the buff as they make their way along the course without any care for their pace. A huge audience packs the racecourse, eager to see costumes and conveyances that may well be recycled for Pride the following month. If you want to participate in B2B, or just scope out the course location and best spots for spectators, check the website for all the details.

Chinese New Year

When Chinese immigrants began pouring into San Francisco in the 19th century, they brought their culture with them. One of the most important (and most fun) traditions the Chinese brought is the **Southwest Chinese New Year Festival and Parade** (www.chinese-parade.com, $30 parade bleacher seating). Cast off the weariness and bad luck of the old year, and come party with the dragons to celebrate the new! Chinese New Year is a major cultural event in San Francisco—schoolchildren of all races are taught the significance of the dancing dragons and the little red envelopes. The parade, with its costumed fan dancers and stunning handmade multicolored dragons' heads, is one of the most beautiful in the world. It's got more history than almost any other California celebration; the parades and festival events began in the 1860s, helping to bring a few days of joy to a Chinese population feeling the hardships of a life thousands of miles from home. Today, crowds in the tens of thousands join to help bring in the new year towards the end of January all the way to the end of February (on the Western calendar).

Dia de los Muertos

The latino community turns out into the San Francisco streets each autumn to celebrate their ancestors. The **Dia de los Muertos Procession and Festival of Altars** (www.dayofthedeadsf.org) takes place as close as possible to All Saint's Day (also Halloween, Samhain, and other cultures' harvest festivals) in the Mission District. Walkers are encouraged to bring flowers, candles, and special items to create altars in honor of their deceased loved ones, and artists create beautiful murals and signs to celebrate those who have

come and gone. You'll note a distinct theme to the artwork: skulls and bones, mostly, though roses also tend to twine through the scenes. This is not a funereal event, but a true celebration. Expect music, dancing, and a genuine sense of joy for the lives of the dead, rather than somber mourning.

Folsom Street Fair

Celebrating the uninhibited side of San Francisco each year, the **Folsom Street Fair** (www.folsomstreetfair.com) brings sex out of the bedroom and into the streets. Literally. This fair pays homage to the fetishes of consenting adults. You can watch a live BDSM show, shop for sex toys, get something pierced, or just listen to the top alternative bands rocking out on the main stage. The fair takes place at the end of September each year on Folsom Street between 7th and 12th Streets. It goes without saying that this major leather event is appropriate for adults only.

Outside Lands

Finally San Francisco has a music festival to rival Chicago's Lollapalooza and southern California's Coachella. In August, the world's biggest acts and lots of breakout Bay Area bands converge at the city's Golden Gate Park for three days of music during **Outside Lands** (www.sfoutsidelands.com). The 2012 edition saw Metallica, Stevie Wonder, Neil Young, and Jack White performing on the fest's mainstage. This being San Francisco, Outside Lands also has gourmet food vendors and top notch wines to enjoy along with the music.

Hardly Strictly Bluegrass

A gift to the City from wealthy philanthropist Warren Hellman, **Hardly Strictly Bluegrass** (www.strictlybluegrass.com) is a free, three-day music festival in Golden Gate Park featuring the best roots music acts in the world. Regular performers at the early October fest include Emmylou Harris, Steve Earle, and Gillian Welch. Though Hellman passed away in 2011, Hardly Strictly Bluegrass continues, and has become one of the City's most beloved events.

SAN FRANCISCO BAY AREA

Shopping

UNION SQUARE AND NOB HILL

For the biggest variety of chain and department stores, plus a few select designer boutiques, locals and visitors alike flock to Union Square (bounded by Geary St., Stockton St., Post St., and Powell St.). The shopping area includes more than just the square proper: More designer and brand name stores cluster for several blocks in all directions.

Department Stores

Several big high-end department stores call Union Square home. **Macy's** (170 O'Farrell St., 415/397-3333, Mon.-Sat. 10am-9pm, Sun. 11am-7pm) has two immense locations, one for women's clothing and another for the men's store and housewares. **Neiman Marcus** (150 Stockton St., 415/362-3900, www.neimanmarcus.com, Mon.-Wed. and Fri.-Sat. 10am-7pm, Thurs. 10am-8pm, Sun. noon-6pm) is a favorite among high-budget shoppers and PETA fur protesters, while **Saks Fifth Avenue** (384 Post St., 415/986-4300, Mon.-Wed. and Fri.-Sat. 10am-7pm, Thurs. 10am-8pm, Sun. noon-6pm) adds a touch of New York style to funky-but-wealthy San Francisco.

Clothing and Shoes

Levi's (300 Post St., 415/501-0100, www.levi.com, Mon.-Sat. 10am-9pm, Sun. 11am-8pm) may be a household name, but this three-floor fashion emporium offers incredible customization services while featuring new music and emerging art. Guys should head to the outpost of **Ben Sherman** (55 Stockton St., 415/593-0671, www.bensherman.com, Mon.-Tues. and Thurs.-Sat. 10am-8pm, Wed. 10am-9pm, Sun. 11am-7pm) for stylish threads from the British-based outfitter that has been dressing cool mods for almost five decades.

Macy's on Union Square

© DOMINI DRAGOONE

A gem of a boutique is the original shop of the San Francisco designer **Margaret O'Leary** (1 Claude Lane, 415/391-1010, www.margaretoleary.com, Tues.-Sat. 10am-5pm), who launched a knitwear-inspired line in her name. Women's fine sweaters—from sleeveless to cardigans—and chic fabric designs are featured in the cozy, European-inspired space.

An elegant space on boutiquey Maiden Lane houses **Wolford** (115 Maiden Lane, 415/391-6727, www.wolford.com, Mon.-Sat. 10am-6pm), the top name in hosiery. Stockings laced with elegant seams and zigzag patterns usually run $65, but sales can offer bargain prices. Upscale and inventive lingerie at **Agent Provocateur** (54 Geary St., 415/421-0229, www.agentprovocateur.com, Mon.-Sat. 11am-7pm, Sun. noon-5pm) promises a most unique and memorable souvenir to go with those Wolford stockings.

Fluevogers unite! There's an outpost of the popular **John Fluevog Shoes** (253 Grant Ave., 415/296-7900, www.fluevog.com, Mon.-Thurs. 10am-6pm, Fri.-Sat. 10am-7pm, Sun. noon-6pm) here. The Canadian designer's artistic creations have appeared on the pages of *Vogue* and on the feet of notable celebrities like Scarlett Johansson.

Gift and Home

Britex Fabrics (146 Geary St., 415/392-2910, www.britexfabrics.com, Mon.-Sat. 10am-6pm) draws fashion designers, quilters, DIYers, and costume geeks from all over the Bay Area to its legendary monument to fabric. If you're into any sort of textile crafting, a visit to Britex has the qualities of a religious experience. All four floors are crammed floor-to-ceiling with bolts of fabric, swaths of lace, and rolls of ribbon. From $1-per-yard grosgrain ribbons to $95-per-yard French silk jacquard and $125-per-yard Italian wool coating, Britex has it all. It's the place to shop if you're planning to hand-create an all-silk wedding gown with beaded lace trim and a matching cathedral-length veil. Or if you're very, very serious about your Renaissance fair outfit.

Health and Beauty

Another thing the elite of the City do down at Union Square is attend to their hair, faces, nails, and general beauty. One of the most rarified salons in Union Square is the **Elizabeth Arden Red Door** (126 Post St., Suite 4, 415/989-4888, Sun.-Mon. 10am-6pm, Tues. and Fri.-Sat. 9am-7pm, Wed.-Thurs. 9am-8pm). You'll definitely need an appointment to get a trim or a color touch-up here.

FINANCIAL DISTRICT AND SOMA

Is there any place in San Francisco where you *can't* shop? Even the Financial District has plenty of retail opportunities. Antiques, art, and design lovers come down to **Jackson Square** (Jackson St. and Montgomery St.) for the plethora of high-end shops and galleries. Don't expect to find much in the way of cheap tchotchkes—the objects d'art and interior accessories find places in the exquisite homes of the wealthy buyers who can afford such luxuries. But as always, it's free to look, to imagine, and to dream.

Kathleen Taylor–The Lotus Collection (445 Jackson St., 415/398-8115, www.ktaylor-lotus.com, Mon.-Fri. 10:30am-5pm, Sat. by appointment) specializes in antique textiles from around the world. Whether you fancy a medieval tapestry for your wall or an ancient Asian table runner, this is the place to find it. A more classic but intensely high-end and well-known gallery sells works of fine art to the cream of West Coast society.

The **Montgomery Gallery** (406 Jackson St., 415/788-8300, www.montgomerygallery.com, Tues.-Fri. 10am-5:30pm, Sat. 11am-5pm) seems like a museum, displaying works of the old masters as well as the top tier of more modern artists.

For tea, visit the **Imperial Tea Court** (1 Ferry Plaza, Suite 27, 415/544-9830, www.imperialtea.com, Mon.-Fri. 10am-6pm, Sat. 9am-6:30pm, Sun. 10:30am-6pm) at the Ferry Building. This Chinese teashop sells black teas in bulk, beautiful Asian tea ware, and, of course, serves hot tea at its six Chinese rosewood tables. If you want to get into the tea experience, consider signing up for a class with owner Ray Fong, who is a published author and tea consultant. You'll learn about the traditions of tea from plant to cup, including the Chinese ceremonial modes of serving.

CHINATOWN

Chinatown is one of the most popular shopping districts in San Francisco. Shopping in Chinatown isn't about seeking out a specific store; instead, it's an experience of strolling from shop to endless shop. It can take hours just to get a few blocks up Grant Street, and a thorough perusal of all the side streets might take days. Narrow, cluttered T-shirt and tchotchke shops stand between jewelry stores offering genuine gems and antiques shops crammed with treasures. Clothing boutiques run to slippery silks, while home-decor stores offer table linens made out of real linen as well as statuary, art, tea sets—everything a dedicated shopper could dream of and more.

Good ideas for shoppers who want to bring home gifts and souvenirs that cost less than $10 and fit easily in a carry-on bag include small China silk brocade items like wallets and jewelry pouches, colorful paper lanterns, small hand-painted china planters, chopsticks, and the good old Chinese waving cats. Be aware that in Chinatown shops, you're not just allowed to ask for discounts—haggling is expected and is part of the fun of shopping here. No matter what you're buying, ask for the special discount. You'll actually get it!

If you've only got a short time to shop, the epic **China Bazaar** (667 Grant Ave., 415/391-6369, daily 10am-9:30pm) has pretty much everything you can imagine coming from Chinatown and a lot of things beyond imagination. They've got some of the best prices in the district for pottery items, Chinese and Buddhist-inspired statuary, chopsticks, tea sets, and much more. Prices for small, pretty items run $2-10.

Gourmet Goodies

For a sense (and a scent) of the more local side of Chinatown, head off the main drag to Stockton Street and seek out the local food markets. Or visit the **Red Blossom Tea Company** (831 Grant Ave., 415/395-0868, www.redblossomtea.com, Mon.-Sat. 10am-6:30pm, Sun. 10am-6pm). You'll find top-quality teas of every type you can think of and probably some you've never heard of. Red Blossom has been in business for more than 25 years importing the best teas available from all over Asia. For the tea adventurous, the blossoming teas, specific varieties of oolong, and *pu-erh* teas make great souvenirs to bring home and share with friends. And if you fall in love, never fear; Red Blossom takes advantage of Bay Area technology to offer all their loose teas on the Internet. (Sadly, their website isn't scratch-and-sniff, or they'd probably run out.)

The **Golden Gate Fortune Cookie Company** (56 Ross Alley, 415/781-3956, daily 9am-6pm) makes a great stop, especially if you've brought the kids along. Heck, even if you're alone, the delicious aromas wafting from the building as you pass the alley on Jackson Street may draw you inside. Expect to have a tray of sample cookies pressed on you as soon as you enter. Inside the factory, you'll see the cookies being folded into their traditional shapes by workers, but the best part is checking out all the different types of fortune cookies. Yes, there are lots of kinds you'll never see on the tablecloth at a restaurant: chocolate and strawberry flavors, funky shapes, various sizes, and don't forget the cookies with the X-rated fortunes, perfect to bring home and share with friends. Bags of cookies cost only $3-4, making them attractive souvenirs to pick up—although with their lovely scent, they might not make it all the way home.

NORTH BEACH AND FISHERMAN'S WHARF

The best thing about the 40 zillion souvenir stores in the Fisherman's Wharf area is that they know what tourists to San Francisco really *need:* sweatshirts, hats, gloves, and fuzzy socks. For last-minute warm clothes on foggy days, you don't need a specific store. Just take

© STUART THORNTON

City Lights Bookstore, in North Beach

a walk from the cable car turnaround down Hyde Street to Jefferson Street and then over to Mason Street. You'll find the heavy sweatshirt you need or cheap-and-cheesy gifts for friends—fridge magnets, snow globes, and pewter replicas of cable cars. For more unusual souvenirs, try Pier 39. Funky boutiques crowd both sides and both stories of the buildings that line the pier.

Books

The North Beach district is filled with fun, beauty, and great Italian restaurants and cafés. The Italian district also boasts some of the hippest shops in the City, so it's a great place for shoppers who eschew chains to seek out thrift shops and funky independents. One of the most famous independent bookshops in a city famous for its literary bent is **City Lights Bookstore** (261 Columbus Ave., 415/362-8193, www.citylights.com, daily 10am-midnight). It was opened in 1953 by famous Beat poet Lawrence Ferlinghetti as an all-paperback bookstore with a decidedly Beat aesthetic,

focused on selling modern literary fiction and progressive political tomes. As the Beats flocked to San Francisco and to City Lights, the shop put on another hat—that of publisher. Allen Ginsberg's *Howl* was published by the erstwhile independent, which never looked back. Today, they're still selling and publishing the best of cutting-edge fiction and nonfiction. The store is still in its original location on the point of Columbus Avenue, though it's expanded somewhat since the 1950s. Expect to find your favorite genre paperbacks along with the latest intriguing new works. The nonfiction selections can really make you take a step back and think about your world in a new way, which is just what the founders of City Lights wanted.

Clothing

For hip dressers who prefer classic style to the latest stuff fresh out of the sweatshops, **Old Vogue** (1412 Grant Ave., 415/392-1522, Mon.-Thurs. 11am-7pm, Fri.-Sat. 11am-9pm, Sun. noon-7pm) is the perfect North Beach destination. Stop in at the funky little storefront and plan to spend a little while browsing through the racks of vintage apparel mostly for men: one floor dedicated to comfy old jeans and pants, the other to coats, blouses, dresses, and accessories. Old Vogue can provide you with just the perfect hat to top off your favorite clubbing outfit.

Eye-catching **Alla Prima** (1420 Grant Ave., 415/397-4077, www.allaprimalingerie.com, Tues.-Sat. 11am-7pm, Sun. 12:30pm-5pm) sells nothing but lingerie from the likes of Sarda, La Perla, and Andres Sarda. Pieces range from delicate and frilly to sturdy and functional. Hayes Valley boasts a second location of Alla Prima (539 Hayes St., 415/864-8180, Mon.-Sat. 11am-7pm, Sun. noon-5pm).

Music
For the ultimate hip North Beach shopping trip, stop in at **101 Music** (1414 Grant Ave., 415/392-6369, daily 10am-7pm). This independent shop is short on copies of the latest pop CDs and long on vintage vinyl and secondhand instruments and musical equipment. The vinyl collection hides downstairs. The organization of the records and CDs could be better, but isn't browsing for treasure in the bins part of the fun at such a shop? Customer service, much of it provided by the owner, keeps locals coming back.

MARINA AND PACIFIC HEIGHTS
Pacific Heights and its neighbor Presidio Heights, two quiet residential areas, are connected by Sacramento Street, home to interior design and clothing boutiques that display high-end wares that appeal to the well-heeled residents of this area. With 12 blocks' worth of shops, galleries, salons, and eateries, the main trouble folks have is getting through all of it in one shopping session.

Clothing
There are plenty of high-end boutiques to choose from. If you prefer fashions from earlier decades, browse through **GoodByes**

Consignment Shop (3483 Sacramento St., 415/674-0151, www.goodbyessf.com, Mon.-Wed. and Fri.-Sat. 10am-6pm, Thurs. 10am-8pm, Sun. 11am-5pm). GoodByes also has a men's store (3464 Sacramento St., 415/346-6388, www.goodbyessf.com) just across the street.

Gift and Home
It takes a ritzy San Francisco neighborhood to support a six-days-a-week orchid store. **Beautiful Orchids** (3319 Sacramento St., 415/567-2443, www.beautifulorchids.com, Mon.-Sat. 11am-5pm) specializes in rarified live orchid plants. Every color of the rainbow, amazing shapes, and waterfall figures spill from elegant planters. Expect to pay a premium for these rare hand-tended flowers, and to spend even more to ship them home. You can also find elegant home accessories here, most picked to complement the orchids rather than the other way around.

CIVIC CENTER AND HAYES VALLEY
In the Hayes Valley neighborhood adjacent to the Civic Center, shopping goes uptown, but the unique scent of counterculture creativity somehow makes it in. This is a fun neighborhood to get your stroll on, checking out the art galleries and peeking into the boutiques for clothing and upscale housewares, and then stopping at one of the lovely cafés for a restorative bite to eat.

Clothing and Shoes
Ver Unica (437B Hayes St. and 526 Hayes St., 415/431-0688, www.verunicasf.com, Mon.-Sat. 11am-7pm, Sun. noon-6pm) is a vintage boutique that attracts locals and celebrities with high-quality men's and women's clothing and accessories dating from the 1920s to the 1980s, along with a small selection of new apparel by up-and-coming designers.

The corset takes center stage at unique **Dark Garden** (321 Linden St., 415/431-7684, www.darkgarden.net, open daily, call for hours). Custom fitting and design doesn't come cheap, but you'll get quality. An assortment of lingerie is also sold here.

Paolo Iantorno's boutique **Paolo Shoes** (524 Hayes St., 415/552-4580, http://paoloshoes. com, Mon.-Sat. 11am-7pm, Sun. 11am-6pm) showcases his collection of handcrafted shoes, for which all leather and textiles are conscientiously selected and then inspected to ensure top quality.

On the same street is **Bulo** (418 Hayes St., 877/746-3790, http://buloshoes.com, Mon.- Sat. 11am-7pm, Sun. noon-6pm). Italian for hip, fresh, and attractive, Bulo caters to the fashion- and quality-conscious foot fetishist.

Gourmet Goodies

Those with a sweet tooth flock to **Miette** (449 Octavia St., 415/626-6221, www.miettecakes. com, Sun.-Fri. noon-7pm, Sat. 11am-7pm), a cheery European-inspired candy shop, sister store to the Ferry Plaza bakery (415/837-0300). From double-salted licorice to handmade English toffee, the quality confections include imports from England, Italy, and France.

MISSION AND CASTRO

In the 21st century, the closest you can come to the old-school Haight Street shopping experience is in the Mission. The big shopping street with the coolest selections is definitely Valencia Street, which has all the best thrift shops and funky stuff.

On Castro Street, shopping is sexy. Whether you want leather or lace, or just a pair of fabulous spike-heeled boots, you can find it in one of the racy shops found in the City's notoriously "everything goes" district.

Books

There's a **Books Inc.** (2275 Market St., 415/864-6777, www.booksinc.net, daily 10am-10pm) in the Castro. This small independent Bay Area bookseller's chain hosts numerous author events and stocks plenty of local authors. You can also find your favorite paperbacks. In keeping with the neighborhood of this location, the managers stock lots of great gay fiction and nonfiction. You're welcome to stay as long as you like, browsing through the books.

Clothing and Shoes

A local favorite vintage and secondhand clothing store in the Mission is **Schauplatz** (791 Valencia St., 415/864-5665, Mon. and Wed.- Sat. 1pm-7pm, Sun. 1pm-6pm). It might be a bit more expensive than your average Goodwill, but you'll be wowed by the fabulous and unusual apparel. Surf the racks for everything from 1940s dresses to vintage sunglasses.

At quirky designer boutique **Dema** (1038 Valencia St., 415/206-0500, www.godemago. com, Mon.-Fri 11am-7pm, Sat. noon-7pm, Sun. noon-6pm), you'll find a range of cotton goodies that include Velvet, Blended, and Orla Kiely as well as fine cashmere blends and silk dresses.

Sunhee Moon (3167 16th St., 415/355-1800, www.sunheemoon.com, Mon.-Fri. noon-7pm, Sat.-Sun. noon-6pm) showcases San Francisco designer Sunhee's own line of classic separates with a twist, which fit petite gals perfectly. Her boutique also carries jewelry, bags, sunglasses, and other accessories from local designers.

Therapy (545 Valencia St., 415/865-0981, www.shopattherapy.com, Mon.-Thurs. 11:30am-9:30pm, Fri.-Sat. 10:30am-11pm, Sun. 10:30am-9:30pm) surpasses the nearby competition with its well-priced mix of clothing, accessories, and goofy gifts.

Need shoes? One of the few honest-to-goodness local family-owned shoe stores, **De La Sole** (549 Castro St., 415/255-3140, www.delasole. com, Mon.-Sat. 10am-8pm, Sun. 11am-7pm) in the Castro proffers both men's and women's foot fashions. The shoes shine with the latest fashions, from sneakers to formals. Even the shop's interior carries on the theme of fun, fashionable modernity, making visitors feel hip just by walking in the door.

Gift and Home

Author Dave Eggers's tongue-in-cheek storefront at **826 Valencia** (826 Valencia St., 415/642-5905 Ext. 201, www.826valencia.org/ store, daily noon-6pm) doubles as a youth literacy center and pirate supply shop. Underneath

© DOMINI DRAGOONE

Schauplatz offers a well-curated selection of vintage clothes and accessories.

the hanging ropes and hooks, you'll find drawers that open to reveal shackles or fake mustaches for sale. You'll also find a good stock of literary journals and magazines, including *McSweeney's, The Believer,* and the DVD magazine *Wholphin,* all published by Eggers himself.

Need a bat skeleton or a freeze-dried frog carcass? Visit **Paxton Gate** (824 Valencia St., 415/824-1872, www.paxtongate.com, daily 11am-7pm) next door to 826 Valencia. In addition to the fossilized creatures, this quirky spot sells garden supplies, books, and candles.

Five and Diamond (510 Valencia St., 415/255-9747, www.fiveanddiamond.com, Mon.-Thurs. noon-8pm, Fri.-Sat. 1pm-9pm, Sun. noon-7pm) can bring you every aspect of the stereotypical San Francisco experience all in one storefront. Inside this unique space, you'll find off-the-wall art, unusual clothing, and downright scary jewelry. Those who make an appointment in advance can also get a tattoo here, or purchase some keen body jewelry. A trip inside Five and Diamond can be an exciting adventure for the bold, but might be a bit much for the faint of heart. Decide for yourself whether you dare to take the plunge.

Cliff's Variety (479 Castro St., 415/431-5365, www.cliffsvariety.com, Mon.-Fri. 8:30am-8pm, Sat. 9:30am-8pm, Sun. 11am-6pm) is no ordinary hardware store, though it does carry jigsaws and wrenches. Check out its delightful array of bric-a-brac, including toys, wigs, and lava lamps.

GOLDEN GATE PARK AND THE HAIGHT

In Golden Gate Park, the Museum Stores at the de Young and the Academy of Sciences sell high-priced but beautiful and unusual souvenirs—true remembrances of a visit to San Francisco. The Haight-Ashbury shopping district isn't what it used to be, but if you're willing to poke around a bit, you can still find a few bargains in the remaining thrift shops.

Counterculture

One relic of the 1960s counterculture still thrives on the Haight: head shops. Items from

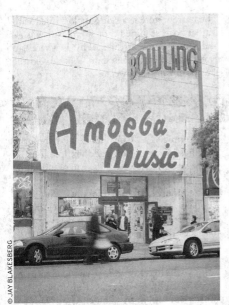

© JAY BLAKESBERG

Amoeba Music, on Haight Street

these shops will delight any teenagers on your gift list—their parents may be somewhat less delighted by the hemp clothing, Bob Marley T-shirts, and lava lamps. All pipes, water pipes, and other paraphernalia are *strictly for use in smoking legal tobacco*, you understand. For legal reasons, be sure not to mention anything else when you're browsing in shops like **Ashbury Tobacco Center** (1524 Haight St., 415/552-5556, daily 10am-9:30pm).

Want to get yourself a new tattoo, a split tongue, or a Prince Albert as a unique souvenir of your trip to San Francisco? Head down to **Mom's Body Shop** (1408 Haight St., 415/864-6667, www.momsbodyshop.com, daily noon-close).

Books and Music

Music has always been a part of the Haight. To this day you'll find homeless folks pounding out rhythms on *doumbeks* and congas on the sidewalks. Located in an old bowling alley, **Amoeba Music** (1855 Haight St., 415/831-1200, www.amoeba.com, Mon.-Sat.

10:30am-10pm, Sun. 11am-9pm) is a larger-than-life record store that promotes every type of music imaginable. Amoeba's staff, many of whom are musicians themselves, are among the most knowledgeable in the business. They also host free, live, in-store performances. Check the website for upcoming shows.

The award-winning **Booksmith** (1644 Haight St., 800/493-7323, www.booksmith. com, Mon.-Sat. 10am-10pm, Sun. 10am-8pm) boasts a helpful and informed staff, a fabulous magazine collection, and Northern California's preeminent calendar of readings by internationally renowned authors.

Technically in the Richmond neighborhood, **Green Apple Books & Music** (506 Clement St., 415/387-2272, www.greenapple-books.com, Sun.-Thurs. 10am-10:30pm, Fri.-Sat. 10am-11:30pm) is worth the trek. Locals head to this fog belt location to get their fill of thousands of titles that include staff picks, new releases, and used nonfiction. Friendly sales staff are on hand to assist with navigating the myriad stacks.

Clothing

Join the countless bargain shoppers who prowl the racks for fabulous forgotten garments, but don't expect to pay $0.25 for that great 1930s bias-cut dress or $0.50 for a cast-off Dior blouse; the merchants in the Haight are experienced used clothiers who know what the good stuff is worth. The same is true at the **Buffalo Exchange** (1555 Haight St., 415/431-7733, www.buffaloexchange.com, daily 11am-8pm), another Haight institution filled with a mix of new and used über-hip clothes.

Originally a vaudeville theater, the capacious **Wasteland** (1660 Haight St., 415/863-3150, www.wastelandclothing.com, Mon.-Sat. 11am-8pm, Sun. noon-7pm) has a traffic-stopping art nouveau facade, a distinctive assortment of vintage hippie and rock-star threads, and a glamour-punk staff.

For more upscale (and unworn) threads, head to **Ambiance** (1458 Haight St., 415/552-5095, www.ambiancesf.com, Mon.-Sat. 10am-7pm, Sun. 11am-7pm). The two-level store is

SAN FRANCISCO BAY AREA

packed with everything from evening dresses to jeans—and tons of customers.

From the grungy, make for the glam at **Piedmont Boutique** (1452 Haight St., 415/864-8075, www.piedmontsf.com, daily 11am-7pm).

The narrow store is a riot of color, filled with feather boas, sequined shorts, fantastic wigs—and those who wear them. This is where San Francisco's drag queens shop. (Tip: Avoid the crowds during Halloween.)

Sports and Recreation

PARKS
Golden Gate Park

The largest park in San Francisco is **Golden Gate Park** (main entrance at Stanyan St. and Fell St., McLaren Lodge Visitors Center at John F. Kennedy Dr., 415/831-2700, www.golden-gate-park.com, daily sunrise-sunset). In addition to popular sights like the Academy of Sciences, the de Young, and the Japanese Tea Garden, Golden Gate Park is San Francisco's unofficial playground. There are three botanical gardens, a children's playground (Martin Luther King Jr. Dr. and Bowling Green Dr.), tennis courts, and a golf course. Stow Lake offers paddleboats for rent (415/752-0347, daily 10am-4pm, $13-17 per hour), and the park even has its own bison paddock (off John F. Kennedy Dr.). On weekends, you will find the park filled with locals roller-skating, biking, hiking, and even Lindy Hopping. Note that the main entrance at John F. Kennedy Drive off Fell Street is closed to motorists every Sunday for pedestrian-friendly fun.

Crissy Field

Crissy Field (1199 E. Beach, Presidio, 415/561-7690, www.crissyfield.org, daily sunrise-sunset), in the Golden Gate National Recreation Area, is a park with a mission. In partnership with the National Park Service,

© DOMINI DRAGOONE

Golden Gate Park is full of quiet, meandering pathways.

ecology programs are the centerpiece. Check the website for a list of classes, seminars, and fun hands-on activities for all ages. Many of these include walks out into the marsh beyond the center and to the landscape of the Presidio and beyond.

Mission Dolores Park

Expect to see lots of locals when you visit **Mission Dolores Park** (Dolores St. and 18th St., 415/831-2700, http://sfrecpark.org/destination/mission-dolores-park, daily sunrise-sunset), usually called Dolores Park and a favorite of Mission district denizens. Bring a beach blanket to sprawl on the lawn, enjoy the views, and do some serious people watching; wear walking shoes and stroll on the paved pedestrian paths; or take your racket and balls and grab a game of tennis up at one of the six courts. On weekends, music festivals and cultural events often spring up at Dolores Park.

McLaren Park

Many people who like to hike prefer it with some semblance of solitude. That can be tough to come by in the ever-crowded Golden Gate Park and Presidio. **McLaren Park** (Mansell St. between Excelsior District and Visitacion Valley, 415/239-7735, www.jennalex.com/projects/fomp/homepage) is something of a hidden gem in the busy City—a crowd-free park with miles of hiking trails, dozens of picnic tables, athletic fields, an indoor pool, and even a nine-hole golf course. You can enjoy a set of tennis, swim some laps, or play a quick round. But most of all, you can walk. Seven miles of trails are asphalt paved, and plenty of undeveloped trails wend off into the brush and trees all around. If you've got the stamina, you can circle the whole park by following its trails. Feel free to bring your canine companion with you to this dog-friendly park. On the other hand, take care walking here if you're a woman alone; McLaren Park is generally quite safe in the daylight hours, but at night it becomes much less safe, so plan to finish up your hiking, picnicking, and playing by sunset.

BEACHES
Ocean Beach

San Francisco boasts of being a city that has everything, and it certainly comes close. This massive urban wonderland even claims several genuine sand beaches within its city limits. No doubt the biggest and most famous of these is **Ocean Beach** (Great Hwy., parking at Sloat Blvd., Golden Gate Park, and the Cliff House, www.parksconservancy.org/visit/park-sites/ocean-beach.html). This 3.5-mile stretch of sand forms the breakwater for the Pacific Ocean along the whole west side of the City. Because it's so large you're likely to find a spot to sit down and maybe even a parking spot along the beach, except perhaps on that rarest of occasions in San Francisco: a sunny, warm day. Don't go out for an ocean swim at Ocean Beach: Extremely dangerous rip currents kill at least one person every year.

Aquatic Park

The beach at **Aquatic Park** (Beach St. and Hyde St., www.nps.gov/safr/planyourvisit/aquaticparkcove.htm) sits right in the middle of the Fisherman's Wharf tourist area. This makes Aquatic Park incredibly convenient for visitors who want to grab a picnic on the Wharf to enjoy down on the beach. The coolest part of Aquatic Park is its history rather than its current presence. It was built in the late 1930s as a bathhouse catering to wealthy San Franciscans, and today, one of the main attractions of Aquatic Park remains swimming: Triathletes and hard-core swimmers brave the frigid waters to swim for miles in the protected cove. More sedate visitors can find a seat and enjoy a cup of coffee, a newspaper, and some people-watching.

Baker Beach

Baker Beach (Golden Gate Point and the Presidio, www.parksconservancy.org/visit/park-sites/baker-beach.html) is best known for its scenery, and that doesn't just mean the lovely views of the Golden Gate Bridge from an unusual angle (from the west and below); Baker is San Francisco's own clothing-optional (that is, nude) beach. But don't worry, plenty of the denizens of Baker Beach wear clothes while flying kites, playing volleyball and Frisbee, and even just strolling on the beach. Baker Beach was the original home of the Burning Man festival before it moved out to the Black Rock Desert of Nevada. Because Baker is much smaller than Ocean Beach, it gets crowded in the summer. Whether you choose to sunbathe nude or not, don't try to swim here. The currents get seriously strong and dangerous because it is so close to the Golden Gate.

SURFING

For some, it may be hard to believe that you can even surf on a trip to San Francisco. **Ocean Beach** (Great Hwy., parking at Sloat Blvd., Golden Gate Park, and the Cliff House, www.parksconservancy.org/visit/park-sites/ocean-beach.html) has a series of beach breaks that can get good in the fall and cause monstrous waves in the winter. Ocean Beach was even the scene of the 2011 Rip Curl Pro Search surf contest, where Kelly Slater won his record, making 11th world title in the sport.

Ocean Beach is not for beginners and, even for accomplished surfers, sometimes it can be difficult to paddle out here. When it's windy or too big at Ocean Beach, surfers head 20 minutes south to the town of Pacifica's **Linda Mar Beach** (Cabrillo Hwy. and Linda Mar Blvd.).

BIKING

In other places, bicycling is a sport or a mode of transportation. In San Francisco, bicycling is a religion (the concept of mountain biking originated here). As a newcomer to biking in the City, it may be wise to start off gently, perhaps with a guided tour that avoids areas with dangerous traffic. The fabulously named **Blazing Saddles** (2715 Hyde St., 415/202-8888, www.blazingsaddles.com) rents bikes and offers guided bicycling tours all over the Bay Area. If you prefer the safety of a group, take the guided tour (daily 10am, 3 hours, reservations required, adults $65, children under 11 $45) through San Francisco and across the Golden Gate Bridge into Marin County. You'll

return to the City by ferry. Blazing Saddles can also supply intrepid cyclists with bike maps of the City and the greater Bay Area. For a sedate introductory ride, you can take the popular self-guided tour of the waterfront. With five Blazing Saddles locations, most in the Fisherman's Wharf area, it's easy to find yourself a cruiser and head out for a spin.

If you're not a serious cyclist, or you're a serious cyclist who's new to the City, take the easy and flat nine-mile ride across the **Golden Gate Bridge** and back. This is a great way to see the bridge and the Bay for the first time, and it takes only an hour or two to complete. Another option is to ride across the bridge and into the town of Sausalito (8 miles) or Tiburon (16 miles), enjoy an afternoon and dinner, and then ride the ferry back into the City (bikes are allowed on board).

If you've got a bit more time and leg strength, consider a scenic ride on the paved paths of **Golden Gate Park** (main entrance at Stanyan St. and Fell St., McLaren Lodge Visitors Center at John F. Kennedy Dr., 415/831-2700, www.golden-gate-park.com) and the **Presidio** (Montgomery St. and Lincoln Blvd., 415/561-4323, www.nps.gov/prsf). A bike makes a perfect mode of transportation to explore the various museums and attractions of these two large parks, and you can spend all day and never have to worry about finding parking.

Looking for some great urban mountain biking? Miles of unpaved roads and trails inside the city limits provide technically challenging rides for adventurous cyclists willing to take a risk or two. Check out the website for **San Francisco Mountain Biking** (www.sfmtb.com) for information about trails, roads, routes, and regulations.

GOLF

A number of golf courses hide in the parks of San Francisco. The premier golf course in the City, the **Presidio Golf Course** (300 Finley Rd. at Arguello St., 50 yards from Arguello Gate, 415/561-4661, www.presidiogolf.com, Mon.-Thurs. $125, Fri.-Sun. $145) was once reserved for the exclusive use of military officers,

TWIN PEAKS

Twin Peaks rises up from the center of San Francisco, and is the second-highest point in the City. Twin Peaks divides the City between north and south, catching the fog bank that rolls in from the Golden Gate and providing a habitat for lots of wild birds and insects, including the endangered Mission Blue Butterfly.

While you barely need to get out of your car to enjoy the stunning 360-degree views of the City from the peaks, the best way to enjoy the view is to take a hike. If you want to scale the less traveled South Peak, start at the pullout on the road below the parking lot. You'll climb a steep set of stairs up to the top of the South Peak in less than 0.2 miles. Stop and marvel at man's industry: the communications tower that's the massive eyesore just over the peak. Carefully cross the road to access the red-rock stairway up to the North Peak. It's only a 0.25 miles, but as with the South Peak, those stairs

seem to go straight up! It's worth it when you look out across the Golden Gate to Mount Tamalpais in the north and Mount Diablo in the east.

If it's the view you're seeking rather than the wildlife and exercise, head to Twin Peaks only on a sunny day. If the fog is in, as so often happens in the summertime, you'll have trouble seeing five feet in front of you. Oh, and don't expect a verdant paradise up there—the grass doesn't stay green long in the spring, so most visitors get to see the dried-out brush that characterizes much of the Bay Area in the summertime and fall.

To get there, drive west up Market Street (eventually turning into Portola Dr.), and turn right onto Twin Peaks Boulevard and past the parade of tour buses to the parking lot past the North Peak. Parking is free and Twin Peaks is open year-round.

government officials, and visiting dignitaries. Since 1995 the 18-hole, par-72 course, driving range, practice putting greens, and clubhouse have been available to the public. Reserve your tee time by phone or online.
Lincoln Park Golf Course (300 34th Ave., 415/221-9911, www.lincolnparkgc.com, Mon.-Thurs. $38, Fri.-Sun. and holidays $42) is an 80-year-old public 18-hole, par-68 course in the Outer Richmond district. It hosts the annual San Francisco City Golf Championships. For tee times at any municipal course, call 415/750-4653.

HIKING

Yes, you can go for a hike inside the city of San Francisco. Most of the parks in the City offer hiking trails to suit various tastes and ability levels. The City also boasts some longer and more interesting trails that present serious hikers with a real challenge.

For an easy nature walk in the Presidio, try the **Lobos Creek Trail** (Lincoln St. at Bowley St., www.bahiker.com/sfhikes/loboscreek.

html, daily dawn-dusk). Less than a mile long, this flat boardwalk trail is wheelchair-accessible and shows off the beginning successes of the ecological restoration of the Presidio. You'll get to see restored sand dunes and native vegetation, which has attracted butterflies and other insects, in turn bringing birds to the trail area. While it's still in the City, this trail gives walkers a glimpse of what the Presidio might have been like 500 years ago. Another easy Presidio hike goes way back into the region's history. The one-mile (one-way) **Lover's Lane** (Funston Ave. and Presidio Blvd., www.nps.gov/prsf/planyourvisit/lovers-lane.htm) once served soldiers stationed at the Presidio who beat down the path into the City proper to visit their sweethearts. Today, you'll have a peaceful tree-shaded walk on a flat semi paved path that passes the former homes of the soldiers, crosses El Polin Creek, and ends at the Presidio Gate.

Want to hike the whole **Bay Area Ridge Trail** (415/561-2595, www.ridgetrail.org)? Prepare to get serious—the whole trail runs more than 335 miles and grows longer annually. It crosses the City of San Francisco from south to north. The easy Presidio section (Arguello Blvd. and Jackson St.) runs 2.7 miles from the Arguello Gate to the foot of the Golden Gate Bridge. If you've been trudging the sidewalks and climbing the hills of the difficult seven-mile section from Stern Grove (Wawona St. and 21st Ave.) to the Presidio's Arguello Gate, you'll be happy to find the gently sloping dirt footpaths through unpopulated forests and meadows of the Presidio. Round out the City section of the trail with the moderate 3.2-mile (one-way) section from Fort Funston (hang glider viewing deck off Fort Funston Rd.) to Stern Grove. If the weather is right, you can watch the hang gliders fly at the fort before pointing your boots north to hike the paved trails through protected glens and residential neighborhoods that most visitors to San Francisco never see.

The **Land's End Trail** (Merrie Way, 415/426-5240, www.parksconservancy.org/visit/parksites/lands-end.html) winds, drops, and rises from the ruins of the Sutro Baths, past the Legion of Honor, and on to the rugged cliffs and beaches where the North American continent ends. At low tide, you can stand out in the wind and see the leftover bits of three ships that all wrecked on the rocks of Point Lobos. Smaller side trails lead down to little beaches, and the views of the Golden Gate are the stuff of legend. The **El Camino Del Mar** trail intersects Land's End, creating a big mostly paved loop for enthusiastic hikers who want to take on a three-plus-mile trek that hits most of the major landmarks of Land's End. Seriously, bring a camera on this hike, even if you have to buy a disposable one. The views from this trail may be some of the most beautiful on earth.

It isn't surprising that Golden Gate Park is riddled with paved pedestrian paths. The surprise is that most of them aren't named, and residents don't go to the park for serious hiking. One exception is the **Golden Gate Park and Ocean Beach Hike** (trailhead at Fell St. and Baker St., www.traillink.com/trail-maps/golden-gate-park-and-ocean-beach.aspx).

Almost seven miles long, this trail runs from the Golden Gate Park Panhandle all the way to the ocean, then down Ocean Beach to the San Francisco Zoo. You'll pass close by the Conservatory of Flowers, the de Young Museum, Stow Lake, Bercut Equitation Field, and several children's play areas.

Probably the closest thing to a true serene backwoods hike in San Francisco can be found at the easy 0.5-mile trail at **Mount Davidson** (Dalewood St., West Portal, daily 6am-10pm, www.bahiker.com/sfhikes/davidson.html), which is the highest point in the City. Park in the adjacent West Portal residential area and wander through the gate and into the woods. Take the main fire road straight up the gentle slope to the top of the mountain, then find the smaller track off to the left that leads to the famous "cross at the top of the mountain." To extend your stay in this pleasant place, either walk down the other side of the mountain or head back to find the smaller branch trails that lead off into the trees.

For a more vigorous and better-known walk, take the moderate one-mile trail at **Glen Canyon** (Bosworth St.). Feel free to bring your canine companion on this trail through an unlikely but lovely little urban canyon. It only takes about half an hour to explore Islais Creek, the nonnative eucalyptus and blackberries, and the attractive if unspectacular views. Take care to avoid the prolific poison oak that spreads throughout the canyon.

The difficult 10.5-mile **California Coastal Trail** (Golden Gate National Recreation Area, www.californiacoastaltrail.info) runs through the city of San Francisco on its way down the state. Originating beneath the Golden Gate Bridge, the trail meanders all the way down the west side of the City. It passes by many major monuments and parks, so you can take a break from hiking to visit Fort Point, the Palace of the Legion of Honor, and the site of the Sutro Baths. You'll get to walk along the famous beaches of San Francisco as well, from Baker Beach to China Beach and on down to Ocean Beach, which account for five miles of the Coastal Trail. You can keep on

GO WILD ON THE FARALLON ISLANDS

On one of those rare clear San Francisco days, you might catch a glimpse of something far off-shore in the distance. It's not a pirate ship or an ocean-based optical illusion. It's the **Farallon Islands,** a series of jagged islets and rocks 28 miles west of the Golden Gate Bridge.

At certain times, humans have attempted to make a living on these harsh rocky outcroppings. In the 1800s, Russians hunted the Farallons' marine mammals for their pelts and blubber. Following the Gold Rush, two rival companies harvested murre eggs on the Farallons to feed nearby San Francisco's growing population.

Now the islands have literally gone to the birds. The islands have been set aside as a National Wildlife Refuge, allowing the region's bird populations to flourish. The Farallons are home to the largest colony of Western gulls in the world and has half the world's Ashy storm petrels.

But this wild archipelago is also known for its robust population of great white sharks that circle the islands looking for seal and sea lion snacks. The exploits of a group of great white shark researchers on the island were detailed in Susan Carey's gripping 2005 book *The Devil's Teeth*.

Nature lovers who want to see the Farallons' wildlife up close can book an all-day boat trip through **San Francisco Whale Tours** (800/979-3370, www.sanfranciscowhaletours.com) or **SF Bay Whale Watching** (415/331-6267, www.sf-baywhalewatching.com). Don't fall overboard.

---

walking all the way down to Fort Funston; the San Francisco portion of the trail terminates at Philip Burton Memorial State Beach. You can enter the trail from just about anywhere and exit where it feels convenient. Get a current trail map to be aware of any partial trail closures.

KAYAKING

For the adventurous, kayaking on San Francisco Bay is a great way to experience the famous waterway on a personal level. **City Kayak** (415/294-1050, www.citykayak.com) has locations at South Beach Harbor (Pier 40, Embarcadero and Townsend St., hours vary by season), with rental equipment available, and at Fisherman's Wharf (Pier 39, Slip A21). Beginners can take guided paddles along the shoreline, getting a new view of familiar sights. More advanced kayakers can take trips out to the Golden Gate and around Alcatraz Island.

WHALE-WATCHING

With day-trip access to the marine sanctuary off the Farallon Islands, whale-watching is a year-round activity in San Francisco. **San Francisco Whale Tours** (Pier 39, Dock B, 800/979-3370, www.sanfranciscowhaletours.

com, daily, $79-89, advance purchase required) offers six-hour trips out to the Farallons almost every Saturday and Sunday, with almost-guaranteed whale sightings on each trip. Shorter whale-watching trips along the coastline run on weekdays, and 90-minute quickie trips out to see slightly smaller local wildlife, including elephant seals and sea lions, also go out daily. Children ages 3-15 are welcome on boat tours (for reduced rates), and kids often love the chance to spot whales, sea lions, and pelicans. Children under age three are not permitted for safety reasons.

YOGA

It's tough to walk two blocks in San Francisco without tripping over a yoga studio or finding people walking the streets with yoga mats tucked under their arms. The best way to find one that has the right kind of classes to keep your practice up while you're on the road is to ask a friend, or your current yogi, which studio they'd recommend in San Francisco. The second-best option is to check out listings in the *Yoga Journal* (www.yogajournal.com/directory). The magazine is based in San Francisco, and the editors not only recommend local studios, they practice in them.

The chain **Hiking Yoga** (1 Ferry Building Plaza, 888/589-2250, www.hikingyoga.com, $20 per hike, 3 hikes $50) has a facility in the Ferry Building. While it's not a traditional yoga class, Hiking Yoga gets you stretching, working out, and hiking around the City all in one 90-minute package. Bonus: Because it's an outdoor hiking thing, you don't need to figure out how to lug a yoga mat along.

SPECTATOR SPORTS

Lovers of the big leagues will find fun in San Francisco and around the Bay Area. The City is home to the National Football League's **San Francisco 49ers** (www.49ers.com). The 49ers play at **Candlestick Park** (490 Jamestown Ave., tickets 415/656-4900, parking 415/656-4949, parking $30), far from the center of the City on Candlestick Point. This doesn't seem to matter to "the Faithful," the loyal fans that have seen the team through their dismal beginnings, rejoiced in their domination of the NFL through the 1980s and 1990s, and continued to cheer as the team "rebuilds" (that is, loses a lot) in the 21st century. Check the website for current single-ticket prices. And be sure to bring a coat to the games—the fog rolls in off the Bay and makes the park chilly and windy. (Note that as of press time, the team is planning to move to a new—and hotly debated—stadium in Santa Clara.)

Major League Baseball's **San Francisco Giants** (http://sanfrancisco.giants.mlb.com), winners of the 2010 World Series, play out the long summer baseball season at **AT&T Park** (24 Willie Mays Plaza, 3rd St. and King St., 415/972-2000). Come out to enjoy the game, the food, and the views at San Francisco's still shiny and new ballpark. Giants games take place on weekdays and weekends, both day and night. It's not hard to snag last-minute tickets to a regular season game. Oh, and be sure to check out the gourmet restaurants that ring the stadium; it wouldn't be San Francisco without top-tier cuisine to complement a midsummer ball game.

Accommodations

San Francisco has plenty of accommodations to suit every taste and most budgets. The most expensive places tend to be in Union Square, SoMa, and the Financial District. Cheaper digs can be had in the neighborhoods surrounding Fisherman's Wharf. You'll find the most character in the smaller boutique hotels, but plenty of big chain hotels have at least one location in town if you prefer a known quantity. In fact, a number of chain motels have moved into historic San Francisco buildings, creating a more unusual experience than you might expect from the likes of a Days Inn.

Be aware that many hotels in San Francisco are 100 percent nonsmoking—you can't even light up on your balcony. If you need a smoking room, you'll have to hunt hard. Be aware that many motels are cracking down on green smoke as well as on cigarettes.

Free parking with a hotel room is rare in the City, existing mostly in motor lodges and chain motels down by the wharf. Overnight garage parking downtown can be excruciatingly expensive. Check with your hotel to see if they have a "parking package" that includes this expense (and possibly offers valet service as well). If you don't plan to leave the City on your trip, consider saving a bundle by skipping the rental car altogether and using public transit. On the other hand, to explore outside the City limits, a car is a necessity.

UNION SQUARE AND NOB HILL

In and around Union Square and Nob Hill, you'll find approximately a zillion hotels. As a rule, those closest to the top of the Hill or to Union Square proper are the most expensive. For a 1-2-block walk away from the center, you get more personality and genuine San Francisco experience for less money and less prestige. There are few inexpensive options in these areas; hostels appear in the direction of the Tenderloin, where safety becomes an issue after dark.

Under $150

While the best bargains aren't in these neighborhoods, you can still find one or two budget-conscious lodgings in the Union Square and Nob Hill area. One of the best deals in town can be had at the **C Golden Gate Hotel** (775 Bush St., 415/392-3702, www.goldengatehotel. com, $115-175). This narrow yellow building has 25 rooms decorated with antiques, giving it a bed-and-breakfast feel. The cheapest option is a room with a shared bathroom down the hall, though there are rooms with their own bathrooms. Centrally located between Union Square and the top of Nob Hill, the Golden Gate serves a fine continental breakfast with fresh croissants.

The **Hotel Bijou** (111 Mason St., 415/771-1200, www.hotelbijou.com, $116-200) might be the most fun of the inexpensive lot. Whimsical decor mimics an old-fashioned movie theater, and in fact a tiny "movie house" downstairs runs double features, free to guests, every night—with only movies shot in San Francisco. The guest rooms are small, clean, and nicely appointed.

Should you find the need for a full-service professional recording studio in your hotel, head straight for **The Mosser** (54 4th St., 800/227-3804, www.themosser.com, $79-189, parking $35). The Mosser's inexpensive guest rooms have European-style shared baths in the hallway and spare Asian-inspired interior decor. Pricier options include bigger guest rooms with private baths; on the other hand, solo travelers can trim their costs by getting a teensy room with a single twin bed. With a rep for cleanliness and pleasant amenities, including morning coffee and comfy bathrobes, this hotel fulfills its goal—to provide visitors to the City with cheap crash space in a great location convenient to sights, shops, and public transportation.

$150-250

C Hotel Rex (562 Sutter St., 800/433-4434,

www.jdvhotels.com/rex, $150-350) is an ideal writer's retreat. The spacious guest rooms all have wooden writing desks and are decorated with the work of local artists. The downstairs Library Bar is a fine place to sip a cocktail or glass of wine while browsing through its library of hardback books. It also screens old movies on Monday nights and hosts live jazz acts on Friday. Along with its literary bent, Hotel Rex is notable for its downtown location just blocks from Union Square.

The **Hotel Monaco** (501 Geary St., 415/292-0100, www.monaco-sf.com, $179-400) shows the vibrant side of San Francisco. Big guest rooms are whimsically decorated with bright colors, while baths are luxurious and feature cushy animal-print bathrobes. Friendly service comes from the staff, who know the hotel and the City and will cheerfully tell you all about both. Chair massage complements the free wine in the large open guest lounge. Be sure to check out the Grand Café and the dining room. In addition, there are onsite spa and fitness facilities for guests. Because the Hotel Monaco is located a couple of blocks from Union Square, you get more, and more fun, for your money.

A San Francisco legend, the **Clift** (495 Geary St., 415/775-4700, www.clifthotel. com, $179-605) has a lobby worth walking into, whether you're a guest of the hotel or not. The high-ceilinged, gray industrial space is entirely devoted to modern art including a Salvador Dalí coffee table. By contrast, the big Philippe Starck-designed guest rooms are almost Spartan in their simplicity, with colors meant to mimic the City skyline. Stop in for a drink at the Redwood Room, done in brown leather and popular with a younger crowd. The Velvet Room serves breakfast and dinner. The Clift is perfectly located for theatergoers, and the Square is an easy walk away.

Over $250

Only half a block down from Union Square, the **Sir Francis Drake** (450 Powell St., 800/795-7129, www.sirfrancisdrake.com, $220-600) has its own history beginning in the late 1920s. Back then, it was the place to stay and play for vaudeville and silent screen stars. Here at the Drake you'll find a bit less opulence in the lobby and a bit more in the guest rooms. The Beefeater doorman (almost always available for a photo), the unique door overhang, and the red-and-gold interior all add to the character of this favorite. Be sure to make it up to the 21st floor's Harry Denton's Starlight Room, where you can take in the city at night while enjoying a cocktail.

The opulence of the lobby at the **Westin St. Francis** (335 Powell St., 415/397-7000, www.westinstfrancis.com, $219-900) matches its elegant address. With more than a century of history as San Francisco's great gathering spot, the St. Francis still garners great prestige. Guest rooms are attractive but small. The cost of a stay pays mainly for the decadent fixtures of the common areas, the four eateries (including Michael Mina's Bourbon Steak), the state-of-the-art gym, spa, top-quality meeting and banquet spaces, and the address on Union Square.

Certain names just mean luxury in the hotel world. The **Fairmont San Francisco** (950 Mason St., 415/772-5000, www.fairmont.com, $329-1,000) is among the best of these. With a rich history, above-and-beyond service, and spectacular views, the Fairmont makes any stay in the City memorable. Check online for package specials or to book a tee time or spa treatment. Be sure to head downstairs for a Mai Tai at the Tonga Room & Hurricane Bar.

Another Nob Hill contender with a top name, the **Ritz-Carlton** (600 Stockton St., 415/296-7465, www.ritzcarlton.com, $450-1,400) provides patrons with ultimate pampering. From the high-thread-count sheets to the five-star dining room and the full-service spa, guests at the Ritz all but drown in sumptuous amenities. Even the "standard" guest rooms are exceptional, but if you've got the bread, spring for the Club Floors, where they'll give you an iPod, a personal concierge, and possibly the kitchen sink if you ask for it.

FINANCIAL DISTRICT AND SOMA

Top business execs make it their, well, business to stay near the towering offices of the Financial District, down by the water on the Embarcadero, or in SoMa. Thus, most of the lodgings in these areas cater to the expense account set. The big-name chain hotels run expensive; book one if you're traveling on an unlimited company credit card. Otherwise, look for smaller boutique and indie accommodations that won't tear your wallet to bits or laugh at your checking account.

$150-250

Upon entering the bright lobby exploding with color, you'll realize the **C Hotel Triton** (342 Grant Ave., 800/800-1299, www.hoteltriton.com, $160-300) is a different kind of hotel. The Triton celebrates San Francisco's independent spirit. The rooms are wallpapered with text from Jack Kerouac's *On the Road,* while copies of Allen Ginsberg's *Howl* take the place of the Gideon Bibles found in most other hotels across the country. There are three specialty suites, including one designed by musician Jerry Garcia and another designed by comedian Kathy Griffin. The third is a Häagen-Dazs "Sweet Suite" that comes stocked with a fridge of the gourmet ice creams. The environmentally friendly practices developed at the Triton are being adopted by sister hotels all over the world. You'll find the guest rooms small but comfortable and well stocked with ecofriendly amenities and bath products. The flat-panel TVs offer a 24-hour yoga channel, and complimentary yoga props can be delivered to your room on request.

For something posh but not overwhelmingly huge, check out **Hotel Griffon** (155 Steuart St., 800/321-2201, www.hotelgriffon.com, $150-449). A boutique business hotel with a prime vacation locale on the Embarcadero, the Griffon offers business and leisure packages to suit any traveler's needs. They're a bit pricier, but the best guest rooms overlook the Bay, with views of the Bay Bridge and Treasure Island.

© STUART THORNTON

the singular Hotel Triton

Le Méridien San Francisco (333 Battery St., 415/296-2900, www.starwoodhotels.com, $229-480) stands tall in the Embarcadero Center, convenient to shopping, dining, and the streetcar and cable car lines to all the favorite downtown destinations. A pedestrian bridge connects the hotel to the Federal Reserve Building if you need to do some serious banking. This expensive luxury hotel pampers guests with Frette sheets, plush robes, marble baths, and stellar views. Expect nightly turndown service and 24-hour room service.

Over $250

It may be part of a chain, but at the recently renovated **Westin San Francisco Market** (50 3rd St., 415/974-6400, www.westinsf.com, $259-509) you'll find plenty of San Francisco charm at your doorstep. Guests stay in pleasant rooms with pretty cityscapes at this large hotel (formerly known as the Argent). Amenities mimic the more expensive SoMa hotels, and seasonal special rates dip down into the genuinely affordable. The attached restaurant,

Ducca, serves breakfast and dinner daily, and the lounge is open until midnight for nightcaps.

Hotel Vitale (8 Mission St., 888/890-8688, www.hotelvitale.com, $309-899) professes to restore guests' vitality with its lovely guest rooms and exclusive spa, complete with rooftop hot soaking tubs and a yoga studio. Many of the good-size guest rooms also have private deep soaking tubs. The Vitale's Americano Restaurant serves Italian fare.

With guest rooms on the 38th to 48th floors of San Francisco's third tallest building, the ◖ **Mandarin Oriental San Francisco** (222 Sansome St., 415/276-9888, www.mandarinoriental.com, $495-6,800) is all about the views. A 2012 room remodel finds the rooms with muted colors so that more of your attention turns to the unparalleled vistas of the city, including the spider web-like cabled Bay Bridge connecting the city to the East Bay and possibly the best view of the Transamerica Pyramid. Even the luxurious beds are raised for prime viewing. Turning your attention inside, you'll find elegant furnishings, a soaking tub, and

view of San Francisco from the Mandarin Oriental

incredible details, including complimentary hotel stationary with your name printed on it. The new Brasserie S&P serves breakfast, lunch, and dinner, while the bar highlights its selection of gins and homemade tonics. With exceptional service, the Mandarin Oriental San Francisco makes everyone feel like a VIP.

For a unique San Francisco hotel experience, book a room at the famous **Hotel Palomar** (12 4th St., 415/348-0302, www.hotelpalomar-sf.com, $268-549). You'll find every amenity imaginable, from extra-long beds for taller guests to in-room spa services and temporary pet goldfish. Be sure to make reservations for dinner at the award-winning Fifth Floor restaurant during your stay. To stay in shape on the road, join a wellness ambassador for a group run on weekday mornings at 7am. Or borrow one of the hotel's complimentary bikes to tool around town.

The **Palace Hotel** (2 New Montgomery St., 415/512-1111, www.sfpalace.com, $279-579) enjoys its reputation as the grande dame of all San Francisco hotels. The original Palace was the dream of William Ralston, who bankrupted himself creating the immense hotel. The rich history of the Palace began when its doors opened in 1875. It was gutted by fires following the 1906 earthquake, rebuilt and reopened in 1909, and refurbished for the new millennium during 1989-1991. In 1919, President Woodrow Wilson negotiated the terms of the Treaty of Versailles over lunch at the Garden Court. Today, guests take pleasure in beautiful bedrooms, exercise and relax in the full-service spa and fitness center, and dine in the Palace's two restaurants. If you're staying at the Palace, having a meal in the exquisite Garden Court dining room is a must, although you may forget to eat as you gaze upward at the stained glass-domed ceiling. If you can't afford to stay here, take one of the hotel's historic tours on Saturdays, Tuesdays, and Thursdays at 10am.

NORTH BEACH AND FISHERMAN'S WHARF

Perhaps it's odd, but the tourist mecca of San Francisco is not a district of a zillion hotels.

Most of the major hostelries sit down nearer to Union Square. But you can stay near the Wharf or in North Beach if you choose; you'll find plenty of chain motels here, plus a few select boutique hotels in all price ranges.

Under $150

The **San Remo Hotel** (2237 Mason St., 800/352-7366, www.sanremohotel.com, $99-129) is one of the best bargains in the City. The blocky old yellow building has been around since just after the 1906 earthquake, offering inexpensive guest rooms to budget-minded travelers. One of the reasons for the rock bottom pricing is the baths—you don't get your own. Four shared baths with shower facilities located in the hallways are available to guests day and night. The guest rooms boast the simplest of furnishings and decorations as well as clean, white-painted walls and ceilings. Some rooms have their own sinks, all have either double beds or two twin beds, and none have telephones or TVs—so this might not be the best choice of lodgings for large media-addicted families. Couples on a romantic vacation can rent the Penthouse, a lovely room for two with lots of windows and a rooftop terrace boasting views of North Beach and the Bay.

$150-250

Hotel Bohème (444 Columbus Ave., 415/433-9111, www.hotelboheme.com, $194-254) offers comfort, history, and culture at a pleasantly low price for San Francisco. The Bohème's long history has included a recent renovation to create an intriguing, comfortable lodging. Guest rooms are small but comfortable, Wi-Fi is free, and the spirit of the 1950s bohemian Beats lives on. The warmly colored and gently lit guest rooms are particularly welcoming to solo travelers and couples, with their retro brass beds covered by postmodern geometric spreads. All guest rooms have private baths, and the double-queen room can sleep up to four people for an additional charge.

The **Washington Square Inn** (1660 Stockton St., 800/388-0220, www.wsisf.com, $191-341) doesn't look like a typical California B&B. With its city-practical architecture and canopy out on the sidewalk, it's more a small, elegant hotel. The inn offers 15 guest rooms with private baths, elegant appointments, and fine linens. Some guest rooms have spa bathtubs, and others have views of Coit Tower and Grace Cathedral. Only the larger guest rooms and junior suites are spacious; the standard guest rooms are "cozy" in the European urban style. Amenities include a generous continental breakfast brought to your room daily, afternoon tea, a flat-screen TV in every guest room, and free Wi-Fi. To stay at the Washington Square Inn is to get a true sense of the beauty and style of San Francisco.

It may be part of a chain, but the **Hyatt at Fisherman's Wharf** (555 North Point St., 415/563-1234, www.fishermanswharf.hyatt.com, $199-599) still merits a visit. The brick facade, unusual for San Francisco, hides an ultramodern lobby and matching guest rooms. Although not too big, guest rooms are elegantly appointed with lots of decadent white linens. Many packages aim at both business travelers and visiting families. Perhaps the best of these is the Park 'N' Play Package, which includes overnight valet parking in the room rate.

For a luxurious stay in the City, save up for a room at **The Argonaut** (495 Jefferson St., 800/790-1415, www.argonauthotel.com, $189-309). With stunning Bay views from its prime Fisherman's Wharf location, in-room spa services, and a yoga channel, The Argonaut is all San Francisco. The rooms feature exposed brick walls and nautical inspired decor. Guest rooms range from cozy standards up to posh suites with separate bedrooms and whirlpool tubs. The SF Maritime National Historic Park's Visitor Center and Interactive Museum is located in the same building as The Argonaut.

Over $250

A great upscale hotel in the heart of San Francisco's visitors' district is the **Best Western Plus Tuscan Inn** (425 North Point St., 800/648-4626, www.tuscaninn.com, $279-459). This luxurious Italian-inspired hotel offers great amenities and prime access to Fisherman's Wharf, Pier 39, Alcatraz, and all the local shopping and dining. The attractive and very modern exterior gives way to earth tones and country-style charm in the common areas. The guest rooms boast bright colors and up-to-date furnishings—much fancier than you might be accustomed to from a Best Western. All guest rooms have private baths. They've also got Internet access, cable TV, and limo service to the Financial District three times daily. Check online for discount rates if you're coming during the middle of the week or booking more than two weeks in advance.

MARINA AND PACIFIC HEIGHTS

These areas are close enough to Fisherman's Wharf to walk there for dinner, and the lodgings are far more affordable than downtown digs.

Under $150

For an unexpected, bucolic park hostel within walking and biking distance of frenetic downtown San Francisco, stop for a night at the **Fisherman's Wharf Hostel** (Fort Mason Bldg. 240, 415/771-7277, www.sfhostels.com/fishermans-wharf, dorm $30, private room $85-105). The hostel sits in Fort Mason, pleasantly far from the problems that plague other SF hostels. The best amenities (aside from the free parking, a free continental breakfast, and no curfews or chores) are the views of the Bay and Alcatraz, and the sweeping lawns and mature trees all around the hostel.

Another one of the many motels lining Lombard Street is the **Lombard Motor Inn** (1475 Lombard St., 415/441-6000, www.lombardmotorinn.com, $86-200). It's got the standard-issue amenities: reasonable-size guest rooms, flat screen TVs, Internet, free parking, and location, location, location. Of course, the location means there's plenty of nighttime noise pouring in through the windows, especially on weekends.

The **Marina Inn** (3110 Octavia St., 800/274-1420, www.marinainn.com, $80-160), built in 1924, exudes old-fashioned San Francisco

charm but boasts pleasant modern amenities. This small family-friendly hotel offers continental breakfast, 24-hour concierge services, and free Wi-Fi. The Inn is within walking distance of major City attractions, including Fisherman's Wharf, Ghirardelli Square, and the cable cars. And if you're feeling a bit scruffy and want to freshen up before your big night on the town, visit the Inn's attached barbershop or salon.

The **Francisco Bay Inn** (1501 Lombard St., 800/410-7007, www.franciscobayinn.com, $80-149) offers good motel lodgings at reasonable-for-San Francisco rates. The stellar location provides easy access to the Golden Gate Bridge, famously crooked Lombard Street, and Fisherman's Wharf. The inn has free Wi-Fi, a free continental breakfast, and, best of all, the Francisco Bay offers free parking—a City rarity worth upwards of $50 per day.

Few frills clutter the clean, comfortable guest rooms at the **Redwood Inn** (1530 Lombard St., 800/221-6621, www.sfredwoodinn.com, $100-120), but if you need a reasonably priced motel room in ever-expensive San Francisco, this is a great place to grab one. From the location on Lombard Street, you can get to points of interest throughout the City.

$150-250

Staying at the ◖ **Marina Motel** (2576 Lombard St., 415/921-9406 or 800/346-6118, www.marinamotel.com, $179-269) feels a bit like you have your own apartment in the fancy Marina district. This European-styled motor lodge features rooms above little garages where you can park your car. More than half of the rooms have small kitchens with a stove, fridge, microwave, and dishes for taking a break from eating out. Though the Marina Motel was built in the 1930s, the rooms are updated with modern amenities including Wi-Fi and TVs with cable. With major attractions like the Exploratorium and the Palace of Fine Arts in walking distance, this reasonably priced motel is a great place to hunker down for a few days and see the nearby sights.

The exterior and interior amenities of the **Hotel Majestic** (1500 Sutter St., 415/441-1100, www.thehotelmajestic.org, $180-210) evoke the grandeur of early-20th-century San Francisco. It is said that one of the former hotel owner's daughters haunts the historic building. The Edwardian-style 1902 building boasts antique furnishings and decorative items from England and France. Cozy guest rooms, junior suites, and one-bedroom suites are available. The Cafe Majestic serves breakfast and dinner, with a focus on local, healthful ingredients.

Pack the car and bring the kids to the **Hotel del Sol** (3100 Webster St., 877/433-5765, www. thehoteldelsol.com, $170-224). This unique hotel-motel embraces its origins as a 1950s motor lodge, with the guest rooms decorated in bright, bold colors with whimsical accents, a heated courtyard pool, palm trees, hammocks, and the ever-popular free parking. Family suites and larger guest rooms have kitchenettes. The Marina locale offers trendy cafés, restaurants, bars, and shopping within walking distance as well as access to major attractions.

Another Pacific Heights jewel, the **Jackson Court** (2198 Jackson St., 415/929-7670, www. jacksoncourt.com, $179-245) presents a lovely brick facade in the exclusive neighborhood. The 10-room inn offers comfortable, uniquely decorated queen rooms and a luscious continental breakfast each morning.

The stately **Queen Anne Hotel** (1590 Sutter St., 800/227-3970, www.queenanne. com, $175-435) brings the elegance of downtown San Francisco out to Pacific Heights. Sumptuous fabrics and rich colors in the guest rooms and common areas add to the feeling of decadence and luxury in this boutique hotel. Small, moderate guest rooms offer attractive accommodations on a budget, while superior rooms and suites are more upscale. Continental breakfast is included, as are a number of high-end services, such as courtesy car service and afternoon tea and sherry.

Over $250

Tucked in with the money-laden mansions of Pacific Heights, **Hotel Drisco** (2901 Pacific Ave., 800/634-7277, www.hoteldrisco.com, $285-575) offers elegance to discerning visitors. Away from the frenzied pace and noise of downtown, at the Drisco you get quiet, comfy guest rooms with overstuffed furniture, breakfast with a latte, and a glass of wine in the evening. Economy rooms have detached baths, and lavish suites have stellar views.

A small, cute inn only a short walk from the Presidio, the **Laurel Inn** (444 Presidio Ave., 800/552-8735, www.jdvhotels.com/laurel_inn, $249-349) provides the perfect place for people with pets or for travelers who want to stay a bit longer in the City. Many of the guest rooms have kitchenettes, and all are comfortable and modern. The **Swank Cocktail & Coffee Club** next door offers a nice place to stop and have a cocktail or a Blue Bottle coffee, and the exclusive boutiques of Pacific Heights beckon visitors looking for a way to part with their cash.

CIVIC CENTER AND HAYES VALLEY

You'll find a few reasonably priced accommodations and classic inns in the Civic Center and Hayes Valley areas.

$100-150

Located in Alamo Square, **The Grove Inn** (890 Grove St., 800/829-0780, www.grovinn. com, $120) offers simple, quiet guest rooms with sunny bay windows, TVs, and phones. A continental breakfast is served every morning. You can walk from the Inn to "postcard row" (ask the innkeepers for directions), take a longer stroll down to the Civic Center, or take public transit or a cab to any of the City's attractions.

Located in Hayes Valley a few blocks from the Opera House, the **Inn at the Opera** (333 Fulton St., 888/298-7198, www.shellhospitality.com/en/Inn-at-the-Opera, $99-179) promises to have guests ready for a swanky night of San Francisco culture. In fact, clothes-pressing services count among the inn's many amenities. French interior styling in the guest rooms and suites once impressed visiting opera stars and now welcomes guests from all over the world. The Inn at the Opera just opened a new restaurant called Plaj, where you can get Scandinavian fare before heading to the opera house.

$150-250

It might seem strange to stay at an inn called **The Parsonage** (198 Haight St., 415/863-3699, www.theparsonage.com, from $220). But this classy Victorian bed-and-breakfast exemplifies the bygone elegance of the City in one of its most colorful neighborhoods. Guest rooms are decorated with antiques, and baths has stunning marble showers. Enjoy pampering, multicourse breakfasts, and brandy and chocolates when you come "home" each night.

Take a step back into an older San Francisco at the **Chateau Tivoli** (1057 Steiner St., 800/228-1647, www.chateautivoli.com, $155-300). The over-the-top colorful exterior matches perfectly with the American Renaissance interior decor. Each unique guest room and suite showcases an exquisite style evocative of the Victorian era. Some furnishings come from the estates of the Vanderbilts and J. Paul Getty. Most guest rooms have private baths, although the two least expensive share a bath.

MISSION AND CASTRO

Accommodations in these neighborhoods are few and tend to run toward modest B&Bs.

$100-150

For a romantic visit to the Castro with your partner, stay at the **Willows Inn Bed & Breakfast** (710 14th St., 800/431-0277, www.willowssf.com, $120-165). The Willows has European-style shared baths and comfortable guest rooms with private sinks and bent willow furnishings, and serves a yummy continental breakfast each morning. Catering to the queer community, the innkeepers at the Willows can help you with nightclubs, restaurants, and festivals in the City and locally in the Castro. One of the best amenities is the friendship and camaraderie you'll find with the other guests and staff at this great Edwardian B&B.

At the **Inn on Castro** (321 Castro St., 415/861-0321, www.innoncastro.com, $135-275), you've got all kinds of choices. You can pick an economy room with a shared bath, a posh private suite, or a self-service apartment. Once ensconced, you can chill out on the cute patio, or go out into the Castro to take in the legendary entertainment and nightlife. The self-catering apartments can sleep up to four and have fully furnished and appointed kitchens. Amenities include LCD TVs with cable, DVD players, and colorful modern art.

GOLDEN GATE PARK AND THE HAIGHT

Accommodations around Golden Gate Park are surprisingly reasonable. Leaning toward Victorian and Edwardian inns, most lodgings are in the middle price range for well above average guest rooms and services. However, getting downtown from the quiet residential spots can be a trek; ask at your inn about car services, cabs, and the nearest bus lines.

Out on the ocean side of the park, motor inns of varying quality cluster on the Great Highway. They've got the advantages of more space, low rates, and free parking, but they range from drab all the way down to seedy; choose carefully.

$100-150

The Summer of Love seems endless to guests at the **Red Victorian Bed, Breakfast, and Art** (1665 Haight St., 415/864-1978, www.redvic.com, $114-220). The Red Vic serves up peace, love, and literature along with breakfast, while community and color (but absolutely no TVs) decorate the guest rooms. Part of the economy of this B&B includes shared, named baths for some guest rooms, although many guest rooms have their own private baths. Enjoy the intellectual, peaceful conversations over breakfast, browse the Peace Arts Gift Shop, and if you can, get in a chat with owner Sami Sunchild. Events from group meditations to tango dancing happen throughout the week down in the Peaceful World Café.

To say the **Seal Rock Inn** (545 Point Lobos

Ave., 888/732-5762, www.sealrockinn.com, $125-177) is near Golden Gate Park pushes even the fluid San Francisco neighborhood boundaries a bit. In fact, this pretty place perches near the tip of Land's End, only a short walk from the Pacific Ocean. All guest rooms at the Seal Rock Inn have ocean views, private baths, free parking, free Wi-Fi, and recent remodels that create a pleasantly modern ambiance. With longer stays in mind, the Seal Rock offers rooms with kitchenettes (two-day minimum stay to use the kitchen part of the room; weird but true). You can call and ask for a fireplace room that faces the Seal Rocks, so you can stay warm and toasty while training your binoculars on a popular mating spot for local sea lions. The restaurant downstairs serves breakfast and lunch; on Sunday you'll be competing with brunch-loving locals for a table.

Way over on the other side of the park, the **Great Highway Inn** (1234 Great Hwy., 800/624-6644, www.greathwy.com, $135-155) sits across the street from Ocean Beach. Actually an old motor-lodge style motel, the Inn features big clean guest rooms, decent beds, road noise, some language problems with the desk when checking in, and a short walk to the Pacific Ocean. Guest rooms have standard-issue floral bedspreads, industrial-strength carpets, and private baths. A better option for travelers with cars, the Great Highway Inn has free parking in an adjacent lot. The motel offers discounted rates to families visiting patients at the nearby UCSF Medical Center.

$150-250

The **Stanyan Park Hotel** (750 Stanyan St., 415/751-1000, www.stanyanpark.com, $155-330) graces the Upper Haight area across the street from Golden Gate Park. This renovated 1904-1905 building, listed on the National Register of Historic Places, shows off its Victorian heritage both inside and out. Guest rooms can be small but are elegantly decorated, and a number of multiple-room suites are available. For a special treat, ask for a room overlooking the park.

SAN FRANCISCO AIRPORT

Because San Francisco Airport (SFO) is actually 13 miles south of the City on the peninsula, there are no airport hotels with a San Francisco zip code. If you're hunting for an urban chic boutique hotel or a funky and unique hostel, the airport is *not* the place to motel-shop. SFO's hotel row has many mid-priced chain motels.

$100-150

Millwood Inn & Suites (1375 El Camino Real, Millbrae, 650/583-3935, www.millwoodinn. com, $112-167) offers contemporary decor and big guest rooms designed for the comfort of both business and vacation travelers. Amenities include free Wi-Fi and satellite TV with an attached DVD player. Gorge on a bigger-than-average free buffet breakfast in the morning. Perhaps best of all, the Millwood Inn offers a complementary airport shuttle—something not all airport motels near SFO do.

$150-250

A generous step up both in price and luxury is the **Bay Landing Hotel** (1550 Bayshore Hwy., Burlingame, 650/259-9000, www.bay-landinghotel.com, $165-185). Updated guest rooms include pretty posted headboards, granite sinks in the baths, tub-shower combos, in-room safes, and free Wi-Fi. Free continental breakfast is served in the lobby, which has a lending library for guests and, frankly, too much decoration.

The **Villa Montes Hotel** (620 El Camino Real, San Bruno, 650/745-0111, http://villa-monteshotel.com, $149-169) offers mid-tier accommodations and amenities on a fairly nice block. Both the exterior and the interior are attractive and modern, complete with slightly wacky lobby decor and an indoor hot tub. Guest rooms have one or two beds, complete with bright white duvets and pillow-top mattresses. Focusing on business travelers, the motel has free in-room Wi-Fi, multiline phones with voice mail, and copy and fax machines for guest use. There is also a free breakfast, and more importantly, a free airport taxi.

Food

One of the main reasons people come to San Francisco from near and far is to eat. Some of the greatest culinary innovation in the world comes out of the kitchens in the City. The only real problem is how to choose which restaurant to eat dinner at tonight.

UNION SQUARE AND NOB HILL
Bakeries and Cafés

With a monopoly on the coffee available in the middle of Union Square, business is brisk at **Emporio Rulli** (333 Post St., Union Square, 415/433-1122, www.rulli.com, daily 7am-7pm, $10-20). This local chain offers frothy coffee, pastries, and upscale sandwiches, plus wine and beer. Expect everything to be over-priced at Rulli. In the summer, sitting at the outdoor tables feels comfortable. In the winter, it's less pleasant, but it's fun to watch the skaters wobble around the tiny outdoor ice rink in the square.

Blue Bottle Café (66 Mint St., 415/495-3394, www.bluebottlecoffee.net, Mon.-Fri. 7am-7pm, Sat.-Sun. 8am-6pm, $5-10), a popular local chain with multiple locations around the city, takes its equipment very seriously. Whether you care about the big copper thing that made your mocha or not, you can get a good cup of joe and a small if somewhat pretentious meal at the Mint Plaza. Other locations include the Ferry Building (1 Ferry Bldg., Suite 7), the Heath Ceramics Factory (2900 18th St.), and a Hayes Valley kiosk (315 Linden St.). Expect a line.

California Cuisine

Make reservations in advance if you want to dine at San Francisco legend **Farallon** (450 Post St., Suite 4, 415/956-6969, www.farallonrestaurant.com, Mon.-Thurs. 5:30pm-9:30pm, Fri.-Sat. 5:30pm-10pm, Sun. 5pm-9:30pm, $30-55). Dark, cave-like rooms are decorated in an under-the-sea theme—complete with the unique Jellyfish Bar. The cuisine, on the other hand, is out of this world. Chef Mark Franz has made Farallon a 10-year fad that just keeps gaining ground. The major culinary theme, seafood, dominates the pricey-but-worth-it menu. Desserts by award-winning pastry chef Emily Luchetti round out what many consider to be the perfect California meal.

Another local mainstay of San Francisco haute cuisine is Wolfgang Puck's **Postrio** (545 Post St., 415/776-7825, www.postrio.com, Mon.-Sat. 6:30am-10am and 11:30am-4pm and 5:30pm-10:30pm, Sun. 11:30am-4pm and 5:30pm-10:30pm, $14-26). Here you'll find everything from Puck's famed pizzas to the best of rarified local sustainable fare. The restaurant has three levels, all of which see their share of celebrities. Not surprisingly, reservations are strongly recommended if you want to dine chez Puck.

Chinese

It may not be in Chinatown, but the dim sum at **Yank Sing** (101 Spear St., 415/781-1111, www.yanksing.com, Mon.-Fri. 11am-3pm, Sat.-Sun. 10am-4pm, $4-11) is second to none. The family owns and operates both this restaurant and its sister location (49 Stevenson St., 415/541-4949), and now the third generation is training to take over. Expect traditional steamed pork buns, shrimp dumplings, egg custard tarts, and such. Note that it's open for lunch only.

French

The famed **Fleur de Lys** (777 Sutter St., 415/673-7779, www.hubertkeller.com, Tues.-Thurs. 6pm-9:30pm, Fri. 5:30pm-10pm, Sat. 5pm-10pm, prix fixe $75-98, reservations strongly recommended) is one of the longest-running and finest dining establishments in San Francisco, and chef Hubert Keller (Keller may be *the* best name in Bay Area dining ever) continues to create delectable and inventive dishes. The dining room is magnificent, with its elaborate tented ceiling, lushly upholstered chairs, and perfect glass accent pieces. But the reason people flock to Fleur de Lys is, and has always been, the food. The absolutely cream-of-the-crop menu isn't really à la carte—instead, you're encouraged to peruse the items and create your own three-, four-, or five-course feast. Vegetarians aren't left out, since Keller creates vegetable-only (and fish-only) dishes with the same love he dedicates to his meats. You'll probably want wine with your meal, which means it's going to cost a bundle. But it's worth the money to splurge at this world-famous spot.

Tucked away in a tiny alley that looks like it might have been transported from Saint-Michel in Paris, **■ Café Claude** (7 Claude Ln., 415/392-3505, www.cafeclaude.com, Mon.-Sat. 11:30am-10:30pm, Sun. 5:30pm-10:30pm, bar until 2am, $18-27) serves classic brasserie cuisine to French expatriates and Americans alike. Much French is spoken here, but the simple food tastes fantastic in any language. Café Claude is open for lunch through dinner, serving an attractive post lunch menu for weary shoppers looking for sustenance at 3 or 4pm. In the evening it can get crowded, but reservations aren't strictly necessary if you're willing to order a classic French cocktail or a glass of wine and enjoy the bustling atmosphere and live music (on weekends) for a few minutes.

Vietnamese

It seemed unlikely that anything worthy could possibly replace Trader Vic's, but **Le Colonial** (20 Cosmo Pl., 415/931-3600, www.lecolonialsf.com, Sun.-Wed. 5:30pm-10pm, Thurs.-Sat. 5:30pm-11pm, $25-32) does it, while paying proper homage to the building's illustrious former occupant. This Vietnamese fusion hot spot takes pride in its tiki lounge, which features live music acts and house DJs six nights a week. Cocktails are big and tropical, and they. But don't skip the food; the lush French-Vietnamese fare blends flavors in a way that seems just perfect for San Francisco.

You'll find all of Southeast Asia in the food at **E&O Trading Company** (314 Sutter St., 415/693-0303, www.eosanfrancisco.com, Mon.-Wed. 11:30am-10pm, Thurs.-Sat. 11:30am-11pm, Sun. 5pm-10pm, $12-26).

This fusion grill serves up small plates like Indonesian corn fritters, mixed in with larger grilled dishes such as black pepper shaking beef. Enjoy the wine list, full bar, and French colonial decor. Reservations are recommended.

FINANCIAL DISTRICT AND SOMA
Bakeries and Cafés

One of the Ferry Building mainstays, the **Acme Bread Company** (1 Ferry Plaza, Suite 15, 415/288-2978, http://acmebread.com, Mon.-Fri. 6:20am-7:30pm, Sat.-Sun. 8am-7pm) remains true to its name. You can buy bread here, but not sandwiches, croissants, or pastries. All the bread that Acme sells is made with fresh organic ingredients in traditional style; the baguettes are traditionally French, so they start to go stale after only 4-6 hours. Eat fast!

For a quick bite, stop in at **The Grove Café** (690 Mission St., 415/957-0558, Mon.-Fri. 7am-11pm, Sat.-Sun. 8am-11pm), in Yerba Buena. This local chain offers fresh soups, salads, and sandwiches as well as coffee and Wi-Fi in an airy and relaxed setting.

Farmers Markets

While farmers markets litter the landscape in just about every California town, the **Ferry Plaza Farmers Market** (1 Ferry Plaza, 415/291-3276, www.ferrybuildingmarketplace.com, Tues. and Thurs. 10am-2pm, Sat. 8am-2pm) is special. At the granddaddy of Bay Area farmers markets, you'll find a wonderful array of produce, cooked foods, and even locally raised meats and locally caught seafood. Expect to see the freshest fruits and veggies from local growers, grass-fed beef from Marin County, and seasonal seafood pulled from the Pacific beyond the Golden Gate. Granted, you'll pay for the privilege of purchasing from this market—if you're seeking bargain produce, you'll be better served at one of the weekly suburban farmers markets. Even locals flock downtown to the Ferry Building on Saturday mornings, especially in the summer when the variety of California's agricultural bounty becomes staggering.

SAN FRANCISCO BAY AREA

© STUART THORNTON

The Ferry Building plays host to the Ferry Plaza Farmers Market.

California Cuisine

From an impossibly small kitchen, chef Dennis Leary turns out some of the biggest flavors in town at **Canteen** (817 Sutter St., 415/928-8870, www.sfcanteen.com, Tues.-Sat. 6pm-10pm, $20-27). Sidle up to the lime-green counter or squeeze into one of the tiny booths to enjoy his eclectic menu—from black cod with couscous to velvety vanilla soufflé. Canteen serves a prix fixe menu on Tuesday and Saturday nights, while an à la carte menu is available on Wednesdays, Thursdays, and Fridays. Reserve early: Seats are in short supply.

Winner of *Esquire Magazine*'s 2011 Restaurant of the Year, **C Michael Mina** (252 California St., 415/397-9222, http://michaelmina.net, Mon.-Thurs. 11:30am-2pm and 5:30pm-10pm, Fri. 11:30am-2pm and 5:30pm-10:30pm, Sun. 5:30pm-10pm, $34-98) finds the celebrity chef using Japanese ingredients and French influences to create bold California entrées. This sleek, upscale restaurant with very attentive service is where Mina showcases his signatures dishes, including his ahi tuna tartare and his Maine lobster pot pie, an inventive take where the lobster, lobster cream sauce, and vegetables are ladled over a flaky pastry crust.

Fifth Floor (12 4th St., 415/348-1555, www.fifthfloorrestaurant.com, Tues.-Sat. 5:30pm-10pm, $28-35) sits on the fifth floor of the Hotel Palomar and has both a casual lounge and a full-scale formal dining room to serve as many diners as possible. New chef David Bazirgan has changed the menu from French to what is described as "New American." An ultra-expensive dinner at Fifth Floor is the perfect excuse to dress to the nines. Don't worry, the dining room decor can take it.

French

The lunch only **Galette 88** (88 Hardie Pl., 415/989-2222, www.galettesf.com, Mon.-Fri. 11:30am-2:30pm, $7.50-10.50) serves sweet and savory crepes, including a vegetarian ratatouille offering. You can wash them down with French ciders, beers, or wine.

Indian

On the more affordable end of the Indian food spectrum you'll find **Chutney** (511 Jones St., 415/931-5541, www.chutneysf.com, daily 11am-midnight, $3-10). With a menu emphasizing curries and masalas—some vegetarian and some meat-laden—Chutney offers a good quick bite, especially late at night.

Italian

Palio d'Asti (640 Sacramento St., 415/395-9800, www.paliodasti.com, Mon.-Fri. 11:30am-2:30pm and 5:30pm-9pm, Sat. 5:30pm-9pm, $15-33) is one of the City's respected elders. The restaurant has been around since just after the 1906 earthquake, and the decor in the dining areas recreates another bygone era in the old country. Try either lunch or dinner, and enjoy the classic Italian menu, which includes wood-fired handmade pizzas as well as homemade pastas and classic Italian entrées. If you're in the City in the fall, be sure to stop in and sample the luscious, expensive, and exceedingly rare Piedmont white truffles.

For fine Italian-influenced cuisine, make a reservation at **Quince** (470 Pacific Ave., 415/775-8500, www.quincerestaurant.com, Mon.-Sat. 5:30pm-10pm, $95-140). Chef-owner Michael Tusk blends culinary aesthetics to create his own unique style of cuisine. It's best to arrive at Quince hungry; the menu is divided into four different courses, or you can try the chef's tasting menu ($140). Once you've had a look at the dishes, made with the finest local and sustainable ingredients, you'll want to try at least one from every course.

Japanese

In these neighborhoods you'll find plenty of sushi restaurants, from the most ultracasual walk-up lunch places to the fanciest fusion joints. **Ame** (St. Regis Hotel, 689 Mission St., 415/284-4040, www.amerestaurant.com, Mon.-Thurs. 6pm-9:30pm, Fri.-Sat. 5:30pm-10pm, Sun. 5:30pm-9:30pm, $35-44) is one of the latter. Appropriately situated in stylish SoMa, this upscale eatery serves a California-Japanese fusion style of seafood. Raw fish fanciers can start with the offerings from the sashimi bar, while folks who prefer their food cooked will find a wealth of options in the appetizers and main courses. The blocky, attractively colored dining room has a modern flair that's in keeping with the up-to-date cuisine coming out of the kitchen. You can either start out or round off your meal with a cocktail from the shiny black bar.

Forget your notions of the plain Jane sushi bar; **Ozumo** (161 Steuart St., 415/882-1333, www.ozumo.com, Mon.-Thurs. 11:30am-2pm and 5:30-10:30pm, Fri. 11:30am-2pm and 5:30pm-11pm, Sat. 5:30pm-11pm, $28-46) takes Japanese cuisine upscale, San Francisco style. Order some classic *nigiri,* a small-plate *izakaya* pub dish, or a big chunk of meat off the traditional *robata* grill. High-quality sake lines the shelves above the bar and along the walls. For non-imbibers, choose from a selection of premium teas. If you're a night owl, enjoy a late dinner on weekends and drinks in the lounge nightly.

Seafood

It's easy to see why the ◖ **Tadich Grill** (240 California St., 415/391-1849, www.tadichgrill.com, Mon.-Fri. 11am-9:30pm, Sat. 11:30am-9:30pm, $15-38), claiming to be the oldest restaurant in the City, has been around for over 150 years. Sit at the long wooden bar, which stretches from the front door back to the kitchen, and enjoy the attentive service by the white-jacketed waitstaff. The food is classic and hearty, and the seafood-heavy menu has 75 entrées including a dozen daily specials. One of the standouts is the restaurant's delectable seafood cioppino, which might just be the best version of this Italian-American stew out there.

Steak

Alexander's Steakhouse (448 Brannan St., 415/495-1111, www.alexanderssteakhouse.com, Mon.-Sat. 5:30pm-10pm, Sun. 5:30pm-9pm, $18-325) describes itself as "where East meets beef." It's true—the presentation at Alexander's looks like something you'd see on *Iron Chef,* and the prices of the *wagyu* beef look like the monthly payment on a small Japanese car. This white-tablecloth steak house that has managed to succeed even in beef-loving SoMa is the very antithesis of a bargain, but the food, including the steaks, is more imaginative than most, and the elegant dining experience will make you feel special as your wallet quietly bleeds out. Console yourself with a cone of cotton candy after dessert—the delicate spun sugar will help make you feel like a kid who blew his allowance at a carnival.

How could you not love a steak house with a name like **Epic Roasthouse** (369 Embarcadero, 415/369-9955, www.epicroast-house.com, Mon.-Tues. 5:30pm-9:30pm, Wed.-Thurs. 11:30am-2:30pm and 5:30pm-9:30pm, Fri. 11:30am-2:30pm and 5:30pm-10pm, Sat. 11am-3pm and 5:30pm-10pm, Sun. 11am-3pm and 5:30pm-9:30pm, $25-55). Come for the wood-fired grass-fed beef; stay for the prime views over San Francisco Bay. Epic Roasthouse sits almost underneath the Bay Bridge, where the lights sparkle and flash over the deep black water at night. On weekends, the steak house offers the hipster City crowd what it wants— an innovative prix fixe brunch menu complete with hair-of-the-dog cocktails ($40) as well as à la carte offerings. Epic!

Vietnamese

Probably the single most famous Asian restaurant in a city filled with eateries of all types is **The Slanted Door** (1 Ferry Plaza, Suite 3, 415/861-8032, http://slanteddoor.com, Mon.-Sat. 11am-2:30pm and 5:30pm-10pm, Sun. 11:30am-3pm and 5:30pm-10pm, $11-45). If all you know of Vietnamese cuisine is rubbery summer rolls and tripe-and-tendon pho, you are in for some seriously tasty reeducation. Owner Charles Phan, along with more than 20 family members and the rest of his staff, pride themselves on welcoming service and top-quality food. Organic local ingredients get used in both traditional and innovative Vietnamese cuisine, creating a unique dining experience. Even experienced foodies remark that they've never had green papaya salad, glass noodles, or shaking beef like this before. The light

afternoon-tea menu (daily 2:30pm-4:30pm) can be the perfect pick-me-up for weary travelers who need some sustenance to get them through the long afternoon until dinner, and Vietnamese coffee is the ultimate Southeast Asian caffeine experience.

CHINATOWN
Chinese Banquets

The "banquet" style of Chinese restaurant may be a bit more familiar to American travelers. Banquet restaurants offer tasty meat, seafood, and veggie dishes along with rice, soups, and appetizers, all served family-style. Tables are often round, with a lazy Susan in the middle to facilitate the passing of communal serving bowls around the table. In the City, most banquet Chinese restaurants have at least a few dishes that will feel familiar to the American palate, and menus often have English translations.

The **R&G Lounge** (631 Kearny St., 415/982-7877, www.rnglounge.com, daily 11:30am-9:30pm, $12-40, reservations suggested) takes traditional Chinese American cuisine to the next level. The menu is divided by colors that represent the five elements, according to Chinese tradition and folklore. In addition to old favorites like moo shu pork, chow mein, and lemon chicken, you'll find spicy Szechuan and Mongolian dishes and an array of house specialties. Salt-and-pepper Dungeness crab, served whole on a plate, is the R&G signature dish, though many of the other seafood dishes are just as special. Expect your seafood to be fresh since it comes right out of the tank in the dining room. California-cuisine mores have made their way into the R&G Lounge in the form of some innovative dishes and haute cuisine presentations. This is a great place to enjoy Chinatown cuisine in an American-friendly setting.

Another great banquet house is **Hunan Home's Restaurant** (622 Jackson St., 415/982-2844, http://hunanhome.ypguides.net, Sun.-Thurs. 11:30am-9:30pm, Fri.-Sat. 11:30am-10pm, $10-15). It is a bit more on the casual side, and it even has another location in suburban Los Altos. You'll find classic items on the menu such as broccoli beef and kung pao chicken, but do take care if something you plan to order has a "spicy" notation next to it. At Hunan Home's, and in fact at most Bay Area Chinese restaurants, they mean *really* spicy.

Dim Sum

The Chinese culinary tradition of dim sum is literally translated as "touch the heart," meaning "order to your heart's content" in Cantonese. In practical terms, it's a light meal—lunch or afternoon tea—composed of small bites of a wide range of dishes. Americans tend to eat dim sum at lunchtime, though it can just as easily be dinner or even Sunday brunch. In a proper dim sum restaurant, you do not order anything or see a menu. Instead, you sip your oolong and sit back as servers push loaded steam trays out of the kitchen one after the other. Servers and trays make their way around the tables; you pick out what you'd like to try as it passes, and enough of that dish for everyone at your table is placed before you.

One of the many great dim sum places in Chinatown is the **Great Eastern** (649 Jackson St., 415/986-2500, http://greateasternrestaurant.net, Mon.-Fri. 10am-midnight, Sat.-Sun. 9am-midnight, $15-25). It's not a standard dim sum place; instead of the steam carts, you'll get a menu and a list. You must write down everything you want on your list and hand it to your waiter, and your choices will be brought out to you, so family style is undoubtedly the way to go here. Reservations are strongly recommended for diners who don't want to wait 30-60 minutes or more for a table. This restaurant jams up fast, right from the moment it opens, especially on weekends. The good news is that most of the folks crowding into Great Eastern are locals. You know what that means.

Another well-known dim sum spot, **Yong Kee** (732 Jackson St., 415/986-3759, www.yongkeecompany.com, Tues.-Sun. 7am-6pm, $10, cash only), offers a completely different dim sum experience. This Cantonese-only hole-in-the-wall caters primarily to locals, but

if you've ever had dim sum or even just Chinese steamed buns before, you'll want to try them here. They're famous for their enormous fresh-made chicken buns *(gai bow)*, which is what the folks lined up at the take-out counter have come for. You can also get a great pork bun, and the rest of the dim sum nibbles are tasty too. Reservations are not taken, but they aren't necessary. Do be aware that Yong Kee isn't a good beginner's dim sum place unless you've got a Cantonese-speaking friend to guide you. But if you're already a fan of the cuisine, you'll love Yong Kee even if you can't understand the menu or the staff.

Tea Shops

Official or not, there's no doubt that the world believes that tea is the national drink of China. While black tea, often oolong, is the staple in California Chinese restaurants, you'll find an astonishing variety of teas if you step into one of Chinatown's small teashops. You can enjoy a hot cup of tea and buy a pound of loose tea to take home with you. Most teashops also sell lovely imported teapots and other implements for proper tea making.

One option is **Blest Tea** (752 Grant Ave., 415/951-8516, http://blesttea.com, tasting $3), which boasts of the healthful qualities of their many varieties of tea. You're welcome to taste what's available for a nominal fee to be sure you're purchasing something you'll really enjoy. If you're lucky enough to visit when the owner is minding the store, ask her lots of questions—she'll tell you everything you ever needed to know about tea.

NORTH BEACH AND FISHERMAN'S WHARF
Bakeries and Cafés

Widely recognized as the first espresso coffeehouse on the West Coast, family-owned **Caffé Trieste** (601 Vallejo St., 415/392-6739, www.caffetrieste.com, Sun.-Thurs. 6:30am-10pm, Fri.-Sat. 6:30am-11pm, cash only) first opened its doors in 1956. It became a hangout for Beat writers in the 1950s and 1960s and was where Francis Ford Coppola penned the screenplay for his classic film *The Godfather* in the 1970s. Sip a cappuccino, munch on Italian pastries and enjoy Saturday afternoon concerts by the Giotta family at this treasured North Beach institution. Now there are six locations from Berkeley to Monterey.

Serving some of the most famous sourdough in the City, the **Boudin Bakery & Café** (Pier 39, Space 5-Q, 415/421-0185, www.boudinbakery.com, Sun.-Thurs. 8am-8pm, Fri.-Sat. 8am-9pm, $6-8) is a Pier 39 institution. Grab a loaf of bread to take with you, or order in one of the Boudin classics. Nothing draws tourists like the fragrant clam chowder in a bread bowl, but if you prefer, you can try another soup, a signature sandwich, or even a fresh salad. For a more upscale dining experience with the same great breads, try **Bistro Boudin** (160 Jefferson St., 415/351-5561, Sun.-Thurs. 11:30am-9:30pm, Fri.-Sat. 11:30am-10pm, $18-30).

Breakfast

Smack-dab in the middle of North Beach, **Mama's on Washington Square** (1701 Stockton St., 415/362-6421, www.mamas-sf.com, Tues.-Sun. 8am-3pm, $8-10) is the perfect place to fuel up on gourmet omelets, freshly baked breads—including a delectable cinnamon brioche—and daily specials like crab Benedict before a day of sightseeing. Arrive early, or be prepared to wait...and wait.

California Cuisine

San Francisco culinary celebrity Gary Danko has a number of restaurants around town, but perhaps the finest is the one that bears his name. **Gary Danko** (800 North Point St., 415/749-2060, www.garydanko.com, daily 5:30pm-10pm, prix fixe $69-102) offers the best of Danko's California cuisine, from the signature horseradish-crusted salmon medallions to the array of delectable fowl dishes. The herbs and veggies come from Danko's own farm in Napa. Make reservations in advance to get a table, and consider dressing up a little for your sojourn in the elegant white-tablecloth dining room.

European

With a culinary style perhaps best described as European fusion, **Luella** (1896 Hyde St., 415/674-4343, www.luellasf.com, Mon.-Sat. 5:30pm-10pm, Sun. 5pm-9pm, $19-29) brings the flavors of Italy, France, and Spain to the City. The tasty original dishes, most with a distinctive splash of California style that complements the European roots, are best enjoyed with a glass of wine from the extensive wine bar. If you're out late or on the run, dinner is served at the wine bar, and a bar menu offers tasty treats after the dining room closes.

French

The **Hyde Street Bistro** (1521 Hyde St., 415/292-4415, www.hydestreetbistrosf.com, Mon. and Wed.-Thurs. 5:30pm-10pm, Fri.-Sat. 5:30pm-10:30pm, $18-30) definitely belongs in San Francisco, what with the cable car clanging by outside the front door and the fog blowing past overhead. But in romance and cuisine, it's all Parisian splendor. A prix fixe menu ($27) offers economy, while the à la carte menu provides a variety of traditional French bistro fare, including snails, chicken liver mousse, and duck confit. This is a perfect place to bring a date for a romantic night out or to celebrate an anniversary.

Greek

In the Greek fishing village of Kokkari, wild game and seafood hold a special place in the local mythology. At **Kokkari Estiatorio** (200 Jackson St., 415/981-0983, www.kokkari.com, Mon.-Thurs. 11:30am-2:30pm and 5:30pm-10pm, Fri. 11:30am-2:30pm and 5:30pm-11pm, Sat. 5pm-11pm, Sun. 5pm-10pm, $22-42), patrons enjoy Mediterranean delicacies made with fresh California ingredients amid rustic elegance, feasting on such classic dishes as zucchini cakes and grilled lamb chops.

Italian

North Beach is San Francisco's own version of Little Italy. Poke around and find one of the local favorite mom-and-pop pizza joints, or try a bigger, more upscale Italian eatery.

At busy **Caffe Delucchi** (500 Columbus Ave., 415/393-4515, www.caffedelucchi.com, Mon.-Wed. 11am-10pm, Thurs. 11am-11pm, Fri.-Sat. 8am-11pm, Sun. 8am-10pm, $12-24), down-home Italian cooking meets fresh San Francisco produce to create affordable, excellent cuisine. You can get hand-tossed pizzas, salads, and entrées for lunch and dinner, plus tasty traditional American breakfast fare with an Italian twist on the weekends. Drinks run to soju cocktails and artisanal Italian and California wines.

Trattoria Contadina (1800 Mason St., 415/982-5728, www.trattoriacontadina.com, Sun.-Thurs. 5pm-9pm, Fri.-Sat. 5pm-9:30pm, $17-27) presents mouthwatering Italian fare in a fun, eclectic dining room. Dozens of framed photos line the walls, and fresh ingredients stock the kitchen in this San Francisco take on the classic Italian trattoria. Kids are welcome, and vegetarians will find good meatless choices on the menu.

A teensy neighborhood place, **L'Osteria del Forno** (519 Columbus Ave., 415/982-1124, www.losteriadelforno.com, Sun.-Mon. and Wed.-Thurs. 11:30am-10pm, Fri.-Sat. 11:30am-10:30pm, $10-18) serves up a small menu to match its small dining room and small tables and small (but full) bar. The delectable northern Italian-style pizzas and pastas paired with artisanal cocktails go a long way toward warming up frozen, fog-drenched visitors from the Wharf and the beach. Locals love L'Osteria, which means it's next to impossible to get a table at lunchtime or dinnertime, and doubly impossible on weekends. Your best bet is to drop by during the off-hours—L'Osteria stays open all afternoon and makes a perfect haven for travelers who find themselves in need of a very late lunch.

Want a genuine world-champion pizza while you're in town? Winner of multiple awards at the 2011 World Championship of Pizza Makers Tony Gemignani can hook you up. **Tony's Pizza Napoletana** (1570 Stockton St., 415/835-9888, www.tonyspizzanapoletana.com, Wed.-Sun. noon-11pm, $15-30) has seven different pizza ovens that cook by wood, coal, gas, or

electric power. You can get a classic American pie loaded with pepperoni, a California-style pie with quail eggs and chorizo, or a Sicilian pizza smothered in meat and garlic. The chef's special Neapolitan-style pizza margherita is a simple-sounding pizza made of perfection. The wood-fired atmosphere of this temple to the pie includes marble-topped tables, dark woods, and white linen napkins stuck into old tomato cans. The long full bar dominates the front dining room—grab a fancy bottle of wine or a cocktail to go with that champion pizza.

Seafood
It's tough to walk down the streets of the Wharf without tripping over at least three big shiny seafood restaurants. You can pick just about any of the big ones and come up with a decent (if touristy) meal. A good way to choose is to stroll past the front doors and take a look at the menus.

It has the look of a big tourist trap, but at the national chain **McCormick and Kuleto's** (900 North Point St., 415/929-1730, www.mccormickandschmicks.com, Sun.-Thurs. 11:30am-10pm, Fri.-Sat. 11:30am-11pm, $20-39), the chefs know how to cook seafood to satisfy even the pickiest foodie. In the grand dining room, with slightly scary light fixtures and stellar views out to the Bay, you'll find an array of fresh fish and a list of innovative preparations.

Steak
A New York stage actress wanted a classic steak house in San Francisco, and so **Harris'** (2100 Van Ness Ave., 415/673-1888, www.harrisrestaurant.com, 5:30pm-close, Sat.-Sun. 5pm-close, $30-80) came to be. The fare runs to traditional steaks and prime rib as well as a bit of upscale, with a Kobe *wagyu* beef and surf-and-turf featuring a whole Maine lobster. Music lovers can catch live jazz in the lounge most evenings.

MARINA AND PACIFIC HEIGHTS
Bakeries and Cafés
Just looking for a quick snack to tide you

over? Drop in at **The Chestnut Bakery** (2359 Chestnut St., 415/567-6777, www.chestnut-bakery.com, Mon. 7am-noon, Tues.-Sat. 7am-6pm, Sun. 8am-5pm). Only a block and a half from Lombard Street, this small, family-owned storefront is a perfect spot for weary travelers to take the weight off their feet and enjoy a cookie, pastry, or one of the bakery's famous cupcakes. If you come in the morning, you'll find scones, croissants, and other favorite breakfast pastries. Be aware that this is a favorite local spot, which means that some items sell out each day.

Italian

A 16 refers to the major road cutting through the Campania region of southern Italy. At **A16** (2355 Chestnut St., 415/771-2216, www.a16sf.com, Mon.-Tues. 5:30pm-10pm, Wed.-Thurs. 11:30am-2:30pm and 5:30pm-10pm, Fri. 11:30am-2:30pm and 5:30pm-11pm, Sat. 5pm-11pm, Sun. 5pm-10pm, $12-28) in San Francisco, you'll find fabulous southern Italian food. Handmade artisanal pizzas, pastas, and entrées tempt the palate with a wealth of hearty flavors. Pasta dishes come in two sizes—a great thing for those with smaller appetites. A wonderful wine list with 500 options complements the food.

For a southern Italian meal with a soft touch, **Capannina** (1809 Union St., 415/409-8001, Sun.-Thurs. 5pm-10pm, Fri.-Sat. 5pm-10:30pm, $16-32) is the place. Soft green walls with marble and glass accents provide a sense of peace. The menu features classic Italian with an emphasis on the fruits of the sea. Many of the ingredients are imported directly from Italy, enhancing the authenticity of each dish. A three-course prix fixe menu is offered 5pm-6pm for $25.

Japanese

With rolls named after rock acts U2 and Elvis, it's no surprise that **Ace Wasabi's** (3339 Steiner St., 415/567-4903, http://acewasabisf.com, Mon.-Thurs. 5:30pm-10:30pm, Fri.-Sat. 5:30pm-11pm, Sun. 5pm-10pm, $6-13 per item) advertises itself as a "rock 'n' roll sushi" joint. Some of the fish here is flown in from

Tokyo's Tsukiji Fish Market, and the menu includes unusual offerings like butterfish nachos.

On the other hand, the **Naked Fish** (2084 Chestnut St., 415/771-1168, www.nakedfish-sushi.com, Mon.-Thurs. 11:30am-2:30pm and 4:30pm-10pm, Fri. 11:30am-2:30pm and 4:30pm-11pm, Sat. noon-3pm and 4:30pm-11pm, Sun. 4:30pm-9:30pm, $5-12 per item) proffers an upscale Japanese dining experience. In a fine dining room or at the sushi bar, taste the sushi, *robata* grill skewers, Hawaiian-style tapas, and spicy appetizers. The sushi roll menu includes some creative twists like baked rolls and others topped with unusual ingredients like beef. Don't skip the sake—Naked Fish has a stellar menu of premium brands, including unfiltered and high-quality bottles rarely found outside of Japan.

If you're in Pacific Heights, give **Kiss Seafood** (1700 Laguna St., 415/474-2866, Tues.-Sat. 5:30pm-8:30pm, $30-60) a try. This tiny restaurant (12 seats in total) boasts some of the freshest fish in town—no mean feat in San Francisco. The lone chef prepares all the fish himself, possibly due to the tiny size of the place. Obviously, reservations are a good idea. When it comes to the menu, anything seafood is recommended, but if you're up for sashimi, you'll be in raw-fish heaven. Round off your meal with a glass of chilled premium sake.

Seafood

Anytime you come to the tiny ■ **Swan Oyster Depot** (1517 Polk St., 415/673-1101, daily 10:30am-5:30pm, $10-25, cash only), there will be a line out the door. With limited stools at a long marble bar, Swan, which opened in 1912, is an old school seafood place that serves fresh seafood salads, seafood cocktails, and clam chowder, the only hot item on the menu. The seafood is fresh—you pass it resting on ice while waiting for your barstool.

Steak

The Marina is a great place to find a big thick steak. One famed San Francisco steak house, **Bobo's** (1450 Lombard St., 415/441-8880, www.boboquivaris.com, daily 5pm-10pm,

$19-70) prides itself on its dry-aged beef and fresh seafood. In season, enjoy whole Dungeness crab. But most of all, enjoy "The Steak," thickly cut and simply prepared to enhance the flavor of the beef.

Another great house of beef is **Izzy's Steak and Chop House** (3345 Steiner St., 415/563-0487, www.izzyssteaks.com, Sun.-Thurs. 5pm-10pm, Fri.-Sat. 5:30pm-10:30pm, $15-30). Here you'll find an array of tasty steak preparations, seafood, and selected nonsteak entrées. Be sure to save room for one of Izzy's classic desserts.

CIVIC CENTER AND HAYES VALLEY
American
Looking for a good old-fashioned American breakfast? Walk on down to **Dottie's True Blue Café** (28 Sixth St., 415/885-2767, http://dotties.biz, Mon. and Wed.-Fri. 7:30am-3pm, Sat.-Sun. 7:30am-4pm, $7-14). The menu is simple: classic egg dishes, light fruit plates, and an honest-to-goodness blue-plate special for breakfast as well as salads, burgers, and sandwiches for lunch. The service is friendly, and the portions are huge. So what's the catch? Everyone in San Francisco knows that there's a great breakfast to be had at Dottie's. Expect lines up to an hour long for a table at this locals' mecca, especially at breakfast on weekend mornings.

California Cuisine
Housed in a former bank, **Nopa** (560 Divisadero St., 415/864-8643, http://nopasf.com, Mon.-Fri. 6pm-1am, Sat.-Sun. 11am-2:30pm and 6pm-1am, $13-28) brings together the neighborhood that the restaurant is named after with a whimsical mural by a local artist, a communal table, and a crowd as diverse as the surrounding area. A creative and inexpensive menu offers soul-satisfying dishes—and keeps tables full into the wee hours. The cocktails are legendary. On weekends Nopa also serves brunch.

French
C Jardinière (300 Grove St., 415/861-5555,

www.jardiniere.com, daily 5 pm-close, $18-40) was the first restaurant opened by local celebrity chef Traci Des Jardins. The bar and dining room blend into one another and feature stunning art deco decor. The ever-changing menu is a masterpiece of French California cuisine, and Des Jardins has long supported the sustainable restaurant movement. Eating at Jardinière is not only a treat for the senses, it is a way to support the best of trends in San Francisco restaurants. Make reservations if you're trying to catch dinner before a show.

Absinthe (398 Hayes St., 415/551-1590, www.absinthe.com, Tues.-Fri. 11:30am-midnight, Sat. 11am-midnight, Sun. 11am-10pm, $15-37) takes its name from the notorious "green fairy" drink made of liquor and wormwood. Absinthe indeed does serve absinthe—including locally made St. George Spirits Absinthe Verte. It also serves upscale French bistro fare, including what may be the best French fries in the City. The French theme carries on into the decor as well—expect the look of a Parisian brasserie or perhaps a café in Nice, with retro-modern furniture and classic prints on the walls. The bar is open until 2am on Thursdays, Fridays, and Saturdays, so if you want drinks or dessert after a show at the Opera or Davies Hall, just walk around the corner.

German
Suppenküche (525 Laguna St., 415/252-9289, www.suppenkuche.com, Mon.-Sat. 5pm-10pm, Sun. 10am-2:30pm and 5pm-10pm, $12.50-20) brings a taste of Bavaria to the Bay Area. The beer list is a great place to start, since you can enjoy a wealth of classic German brews on tap and in bottles, plus a few Belgians thrown in for variety. For dinner, expect German classics with a focus on Bavarian cuisine. Spaetzle, pork, sausage—you name it, they've got it, and it will harden your arteries right up. They now serve a Sunday brunch that's almost as heavy as its dinners. Suppenküche also has a **Biergarten** (424 Octavia St., http://biergartensf.com, Wed.-Sat. 3pm-9pm, Sun. 1pm-7pm) two blocks away.

MISSION AND CASTRO
Bakeries and Cafés

A line snakes into the ☕Tartine Bakery (600 Guerrero St., 415/487-2600, Mon. 8am-7pm, Tues.-Wed. 7:30am-7pm, Thurs.-Fri. 7:30am-8pm, Sat. 8am-8pm, Sun. 9am-8pm, www.tartinebakery.com) almost all day long. You might think that there's an impromptu rock show or a book signing by a prominent author, but the eatery's baked goods, breads, and sandwiches are the stars here. A slab of the transcendent quiche—made with crème fraîche, Niman smoked ham, and organic produce—is an inspired way to start the day, especially if you are planning on burning some serious calories. Meanwhile, there is nothing quite like a piece of Passion Fruit Lime Bavarian Rectangle, a cake that somehow manages to be both rich in flavor and light as air. Sister property **Bar Tartine** (561 Valencia St., www.bartartine.com, Mon.-Thurs. and Sun. 6pm-10pm, Fri.-Sat. 6pm-11pm, $14-25) serves gourmet dinners.

You can also satisfy your sweet tooth at **Bi-Rite Creamery & Bakeshop** (3692 18th St., 415/626-5600, http://biritecreamery.com, Sun.-Thurs. 11am-10pm, Fri.-Sat. 11am-11pm). The ice cream is made by hand with organic milk, cream, and eggs; inventive flavors include honey lavender, salted caramel, and white chocolate raspberry swirl. Pick up a scoop to enjoy at nearby Mission Dolores Park.

California Cuisine

Range (842 Valencia St., 415/282-8283, Mon.-Thurs. 6pm-close, Fri.-Sun. 5:30pm-close, $21-28) may have lost its Michelin Guide star in 2011, but it's no less popular. Consistently rated one of the top Bay Area restaurants, Range serves up expertly crafted cuisine, such as braised pork shoulder with green chile hominy. An inventive cocktail list doesn't hurt either.

Classic American

St. Francis Fountain (2801 24th St., 415/826-4210, www.stfrancisfountainsf.com, Mon.-Sat. 8am-10pm, Sun. 8am-9pm, $8-12) is the City's oldest ice cream parlor, though it now also serves unique diner food. Sure, there's bacon and eggs. But St. Francis also has vegan chorizo egg scrambles and Guinness beer milk shakes. This hipster hotspot also sells quirky 1980s era trading cards from the TV show *Alf* and a special hair metal collection.

French

Frances (3870 17th St., 415/621-3870, Sun.-Thurs. 5pm-10pm, Fri.-Sat. 5pm-10:30pm, $19-27) has been winning rave reviews ever since it opened its doors. The California-inspired French cuisine is locavore-friendly, with an emphasis on sustainable ingredients and local farms. The short-but-sweet menu changes daily and includes such temptations as grilled quail and bacon beignets. Reservations are strongly advised, especially since Frances received its Michelin Guide star.

Italian

Sometimes even the most dedicated culinary explorer needs a break from the endless fancy food of San Francisco. When the time is right for a plain ol' pizza, head for **Little Star Pizza** (400 Valencia St., 415/551-7827, www.littlestarpizza.com, Sun.-Thurs. noon-10pm, Fri.-Sat. noon-11pm, $12-23). A jewel of the Mission district, this pizzeria specializes in Chicago-style deep-dish pies, but also serves thin-crust pizzas for devotees of the New York style. Once you've found the all-black building and taken a seat inside the casual eatery, grab a beer or a cocktail from the bar if you have to wait for a table. Pick one of Little Star's specialty pizzas, or create your own variation from the toppings they offer. Can't get enough of Little Star? They've got a second location in the City (846 Divisadero St., 415/441-1118).

Delfina (3621 18th St., 415/552-4055, www.delfinasf.com, Mon.-Thurs. 5:30pm-10pm, Fri.-Sat. 5:30pm-11pm, Sun. 5pm-10pm, $18-26) gives Italian cuisine a hearty California twist. From the antipasti to the entrées, the dishes speak of local farms and ranches, fresh seasonal produce, and the best Italian American taste that money can buy. With both a charming, warm indoor dining room and an outdoor garden patio, there's plenty of seating at this lovely restaurant.

Mediterranean

La Méditerranée (288 Noe St., 415/431-7210, www.lamednoe.com, Sun.-Thurs. 11am-10pm, Fri.-Sat. 11am-11pm, $9-14) serves delicious Greek and Middle Eastern dishes at reasonable prices. You can get kebabs or baba ghanoush, tabbouleh, baklava, vegetarian dishes, and meatballs. Locals love La Méditerranée for the quality of the food, the quantity provided, and the flexible hours. In warm weather, ask to be seated outside. They now serve brunch with a Middle Eastern twist on weekends.

Mexican

Much of the rich heritage of the Mission district is Hispanic, thus leading to the Mission being *the* place to find a good taco or burrito. For a famous iteration of the classic Mission district burrito joint, join the crowd at **Papalote Mexican Grill** (3409 24th St., 415/970-8815, www.papalote-sf.com, Mon.-Sat. 11am-10pm, Sun. 11am-9pm, $5-12). Build your own plate of tacos or a burrito from a list of classic and specialty ingredients—carne asada, *chile verde,* grilled vegetables, and tofu—whatever makes you happy. What will make you even happier is the price: It's possible to get a filling meal for less than $10.

Farolito Taqueria (2950 24th St., 415/641-0758, www.elfarolitoinc.com, Mon.-Thurs. and Sun. 10am-1:30am, Fri.-Sat. 10am-2:30am, $10) has found favor with the ultra-picky locals who have dozens of taqueria options within a few blocks. It seems that every regular has a different favorite—the burritos, the enchiladas, the quesadillas. Whatever your pleasure, you'll find a tasty version of it at Farolito. A totally casual spot, you order at the counter and sit at picnic-style tables to chow down on the properly greasy Mexican fare. (Don't confuse this Farolito with the taqueria by the same name on Mission Street.)

La Taqueria (2889 Mission St., 415/285-7117, Mon.-Sat. 11am-9pm, Sun. 11am-8pm,

$5-10) is a local Mission favorite for burritos, especially the carne asada.

Seafood

For great seafood in a lower-key atmosphere, locals eschew the tourist traps on the Wharf and head for the **Anchor Oyster Bar** (579 Castro St., 415/431-3990, www.anchoroysterbar.com, Mon.-Fri. 11:30am-10pm, Sat. noon-10pm, Sun. 4pm-9:30pm, $14-39) in the Castro. The raw bar features different ways to have oysters including an oyster soju shot. The dining room serves seafood, including local favorite Dungeness crab. Service is friendly, as befits a neighborhood spot, and it sees fewer large crowds. This doesn't diminish its quality, and it makes for a great spot to get a delicious meal before heading out to the local clubs for a late night out.

Vietnamese

Even casual international food aficionados find that the *banh mi* (Vietnamese sandwiches on French-style baguette bread) at **Dinosaurs** (2275 Market St., 415/503-1421, daily 10am-10pm, $5) makes the grade. Dinosaurs makes good sandwiches, it makes them fast, and it sells them cheap. Diners love the barbecued pork, but the vegan crispy tofu gets mixed reviews. Dinosaurs is a great idea if you don't need a huge meal but want a taste of something you might not be able to get elsewhere.

GOLDEN GATE PARK AND THE HAIGHT
Bakeries and Cafés

The Sunset neighborhood lends itself to a proliferation of cafés. Among the best of these is the **de Young Museum Café** (50 Hagiwara Tea Garden Dr., 415/750-2613, http://deyoung.famsf.org, Tues.-Sun. 9:30am-4:30pm, Fri. 9:30am-8pm, $10-20). Situated inside the museum on the ground floor, with a generous dining room plus outdoor terrace seating, the Café was created with the same care that went into the de Young's galleries. From the day it opened, the focus has been on local sustainable food that's often organic but always affordable. Service is cafeteria-style, but the salads, quiches, and soups are made fresh daily on the premises. Just be sure to get lunch early, or pick an off-hour to eat; the lines at lunchtime can extend for miles.

Visitors to the Presidio can enjoy a quick bite or a leisurely lunch at the **Acre Cafe** (1013 Torney Ave., 415/561-2273, Mon.-Fri. 7am-2:30pm, $10). This simple café serves up fresh food for almost (but not quite) reasonable prices. Open for both breakfast and lunch, it's also a good spot to grab a cup of coffee to enjoy with a morning walk along the paths of the Presidio. Just keep in mind that this is a walk-up style café, so don't expect much by way of customer service. Locals swear by the tuna melt.

One of the prettiest spots in Golden Gate Park is the Japanese Tea Garden. Within the garden is the famous **Tea House** (7 Hagiwara Tea Garden Dr., 415/752-1171, http://japaneseteagardensf.com, Mar.-Oct. daily 9am-6pm, Nov.-Feb. daily 9am-4:45pm, $10-20), where you can purchase a cup of hot tea and a light Japanese meal within the beautiful and inspiring garden.

California Cuisine

One of the most famous restaurant locations on the San Francisco coast is the **Cliff House.** The high-end eatery inhabiting the famed facade is **Sutro's** (1090 Point Lobos Ave., 415/386-3330, www.cliffhouse.com, Mon.-Sat. 11:30am-3:30pm and 5pm-9:30pm, Sun. 11am-3:30pm and 5pm-9:30pm, $25-39). The appetizers and entrées are mainly seafood in somewhat snooty preparations. Although the cuisine is expensive and fancy, in all honesty it's not the best in the City. What *is* amazing are the views from the floor-to-ceiling windows out over the vast expanse of the Pacific Ocean. These views make Sutro's a perfect spot to enjoy a romantic dinner while watching the sun set over the sea.

The Cliff House also houses the more casual **Bistro** (1090 Point Lobos Ave., 415/386-3330, www.cliffhouse.com, Mon.-Sat. 9am-3:30pm and 4:15pm-9:30pm, Sun. 8:30am-3:30pm and 4:15pm-9:30pm, $15-30).

Classic American

For visitors from parts east who long for a taste of home, **The Cheese Steak Shop** (1716 Divisadero St., 415/346-3712, www.cheesesteakshop.com, Mon. and Sat. 10am-9pm, Tues.-Fri. 9am-9pm, Sun. 11am-8pm, $10) provides a welcome respite from the endless California cuisine. Heck, no one can live on bean sprouts all the time. This small franchise serves up hearty cheesesteak sandwiches, Philadelphia style, to order. You can even get a Tastykake, a goodie you won't find in many other places in California.

Japanese

Sushi restaurants are immensely popular in these residential neighborhoods. **Koo** (408 Irving St., 415/731-7077, www.sushikoo.com, Tues.-Thurs. 5:30pm-10pm, Fri.-Sat. 5:30pm-10:30pm, Sun. 5pm-9:30pm, $30-50) is a favorite in the Sunset. While sushi purists are happy with the selection of *nigiri* and sashimi, lovers of fusion and experimentation will enjoy the small plates and unusual rolls created to delight diners. Complementing the Japanese cuisine is a small but scrumptious list of premium sakes. Only the cheap stuff is served hot, as high-quality sake is always chilled.

Thai

Dining in the Haight? If the touristy cafés don't appeal to you, check out the flavorful dishes at **Siam Lotus Thai Cuisine** (1705 Haight St., 415/933-8031, Sun.-Mon. and Wed.-Thurs. noon-4pm and 5pm-9pm, Fri.-Sat. noon-9:30pm, $7-13). You'll find a rainbow of curries, pad thai, and all sorts of Thai meat, poultry, and vegetarian dishes. Look to the lunch specials for bargains, and to the Thai iced tea for a lunchtime pick-me-up. Locals enjoy the casually romantic ambiance at Siam Lotus, and visitors make special trips down to the Haight just to dine here.

Behind its typical storefront exterior, **Marnee Thai** (1243 9th Ave., 415/731-9999, www.marneethaisf.com, daily 11:30am-10pm, $10-20) cooks up some of the best Thai food in San Francisco, with a location convenient to Golden Gate Park. The corn-cake appetizer is a must.

Vietnamese

Thanh Long (4101 Judah St., 415/665-1146, www.anfamily.com, Tues.-Sun. 5pm-9pm, Fri.-Sat. 5pm-10pm, $20-30) was the first family-owned Vietnamese restaurant in San Francisco.

Since the early 1970s, Thanh Long has been serving one of the best preparations of local Dungeness crab in the City: roasted crab with garlic noodles. This isn't a $5 pho joint—expect white tablecloths and higher prices at this stately small restaurant in the outer Sunset neighborhood. Fans include actors Harrison Ford and Danny Glover.

Information and Services

INFORMATION
Tourist Information

The main San Francisco **Visitor Information Center** (900 Market St., 415/391-2000, www.sanfrancisco.travel, May-Oct. Mon.-Fri. 9am-5pm, Sat.-Sun. 9am-3pm, Nov.-Apr. Mon.-Fri. 9am-5pm, Sat. 9am-3pm) can help you even before you arrive. See the website for information about attractions and hotels, and to order a visitors' kit. Once you're in town, you can get a San Francisco book at the Market Street location as well as the usual brochures and a few useful coupons.

If English is not your first language, you'll find materials at the Visitor Information Center in 14 different languages along with multilingual staff.

Newspapers

The major daily newspaper in San Francisco is the *San Francisco Chronicle* (www.sfgate.com). With an appropriately liberal slant on the national political news, a free website, and separate food and wine sections, it's the right paper for its city. The paper's Thursday section "96 Hours" gives information on the coming weekend's entertainment offerings.

San Francisco also has about a zillion alternative papers, free at newsstands all over town. The *San Francisco Bay Guardian* (www.sfbg.com) and the *SF Weekly* (www.sfweekly.com) are the best known and most reputable of these. The alternative rags often have the best up-to-date entertainment information available, so if you're looking for nighttime fun, be sure to pick one up while you're out and about.

SERVICES
Banks and Post Offices

Every major national bank and many regional and international banks have branches in San Francisco. ATMs abound, especially in well-traveled areas like Fisherman's Wharf and Union Square. Ask at your hotel or restaurant for the location of the nearest branch or ATM.

Post offices and mailing centers are common in San Francisco; again, ask the concierge or desk clerk at your hotel for the nearest facility. The **main post office** (1300 Evans Ave., 415/550-5159, www.usps.com, Mon.-Fri. 7am-8:30pm, Sat. 8am-2pm) boasts of its short lines and friendly employees. If you've been shopping for things that don't easily fit into the overhead bin, hit the well-placed post office branch in the basement of Macy's (170 O'Farrell St., 415/552-2330, www.usps.com, Mon.-Sat. 10am-5:30pm, Sun. 11am-5pm). Yes, you read that right—it's open on Sunday.

Internet Access

Need Internet access? You got it! This is San Francisco, after all. Most hotels have Internet access of some kind, the jillion Starbucks locations (sometimes two on the same block) have Wi-Fi for free and plenty of other restaurants and cafés also make it easy to get online.

Luggage and Laundry

If your hotel doesn't have valet service, you can take your dirty linen down to a coin laundry. The most entertaining laundry in the City is **BrainWash Café and Laundromat** (1122

Folsom St., 415/255-4866, www.brainwash. com, Mon.-Thurs. 7am-10pm, Fri.-Sat. 7am-11pm, Sun. 8am-10pm). Enjoy a BrainWash salad or a Burger of Doom with a cold beer and kick back to the sounds of live bands, comedy, and open mics on most nights.

Store your bags through the **Airport Travel Agency** (650/877-0422, daily 7am-11pm, no reservations necessary, $12-25 for 24 hours for most items) on the Departures-Ticketing Level of the International Terminal at the San Francisco Airport, near Gates G91-G102. Fees vary by the size of the object stored. If traveling by bus, rent a locker at the **Greyhound** bus terminal (200 Folsom St., 415/495-1555, www. greyhound.com, daily 5:30am-midnight, $4/ six hours of storage).

Medical and Emergency Services

The **San Francisco Police Department** (766 Vallejo St., 415/315-2400, www.sf-police.org) is headquartered in Chinatown, on Vallejo Street between Powell and Stockton Streets.

San Francisco boasts a large number of full-service hospitals. The **UCSF Medical Center at Mount Zion** (1600 Divisadero St., 415/567-6600, www.ucsfhealth.org) is renowned for its research and advances in cancer treatments and other important medical breakthroughs. The main hospital is at the corner of Divisadero and Geary Streets. Right downtown, **St. Francis Memorial Hospital** (900 Hyde St., 415/353-6000, www.saintfrancismemorial.org), at the corner of Hyde and Bush Streets, has an emergency department.

Getting There and Around

GETTING THERE
Air

San Francisco International Airport (SFO, 800/435-9736, www.flysfo.com) isn't within the City of San Francisco; it is actually about 13 miles south in the town of Millbrae, right on the Bay. You can easily get a taxi ($35) or other ground transportation into the heart of the City from the airport. Both Caltrain and BART are accessible from SFO, and some San Francisco hotels offer complimentary shuttles from the airport as well. You can also rent a car here.

As one of the 30 busiest airports in the world, SFO has long check-in and security lines much of the time and dreadful overcrowding on major travel holidays. On an average day, plan to arrive at the airport about two hours before your domestic flight or three hours before an international flight.

Train and Bus

Amtrak does not run directly into San Francisco. You can ride into San Jose, Oakland, or Emeryville stations, then take a connecting bus into San Francisco.

Greyhound (200 Folsom St., 415/495-1569, www.greyhound.com, daily 5:30am-1am) offers bus service to San Francisco from all over the country.

GETTING AROUND
Car

The **Bay Bridge** (toll $4-6) links I-80 to San Francisco from the east, and the **Golden Gate Bridge** (toll $6) connects Highway 1 from the north. From the south, U.S. 101 and I-280 snake up the peninsula and into the City. Be sure to get a detailed map and good directions to drive into San Francisco—the freeway interchanges, especially surrounding the east side of the Bay Bridge, can be confusing, and the traffic congestion is legendary. For traffic updates and route planning, call **511** (or visit www.511.org).

A car of your own is not necessarily beneficial in San Francisco. The hills are daunting, traffic can be excruciating, and, worst of all, parking prices are absurd. If you plan to spend all of your time in the City, consider dispensing with a car and using cabs and public transit options. Rent a car when you're ready to leave San Francisco, or turn your rental in early if the City is your last stop.

WALKING TOURS

The best way to see San Francisco is to get out and take a walk. You can find dozens of companies offering walking tours of different parts of the City. Here are a few of the best and most interesting.

San Francisco City Guides (415/557-4266, www.sfcityguides.org, free) is a team of enthusiastic San Francisco tour guides who want to show you more about their beloved city. Opt to learn about San Francisco sights like Fort Mason and Fishermen's Wharf or choose a walk where you'll hear about the local locales used by famed director Alfred Hitchcock in his films including *Vertigo*. Visit the website for a complete schedule of the current month's offerings.

One of the most popular walking tour companies in the City is **Foot** (800/979-3370, www.foottours.com, $15-40/person). Foot was founded by stand up comedian Robert Mac, and hires comics to act as guides for their many different tours around San Francisco. If you're a brand-new visitor to the City, pick the two-hour "San Francisco in a Nutshell" tour for a funny look at the basics of San Francisco landmarks and history, or the three-hour "Whole She-bang," a comprehensive if speedy look at Chinatown, Nob Hill, and North Beach. For visitors who are back for the second or third time, check out the more in-depth neighborhood tours that take in Chinatown, the Castro, or the Haight. You can even hit "Nude, Lewd, and Crude," a look at the rise of 18-and-up entertainment in North Beach. Tour departure points vary, so check the website for more information about your specific tour and about packages of more than one tour in a day or two.

For an inside look at the culinary delights of Chinatown, sign up for a spot on **I Can't Believe I Ate My Way Through Chinatown** (650/355-9657, www.wokwiz.com, $90/person). This three-hour bonanza will take you first for a classic Chinese breakfast, then out into the streets of Chinatown for a narrated tour around Chinatown's food markets, apothecaries, and tea shops. You'll finish up with lunch at one of Chef Shirley's favorite hole-in-the-wall dim sum places. For folks who just want the tour and lunch, or the tour alone, check out the standard Wok Wiz Daily Tour ($50/person with lunch, $35/person tour only).

To check out another side of Chinatown, take the **Chinatown Ghost Tour** (877/887-3373, www.sfchinatownghosttours.com, Fri.-Sat. 7:30pm-9:30pm, adults $48, children $24, tour lasts 2 hours). It's hard to find a neighborhood with a richer history rife with ghost stories than San Francisco's Chinatown. The whole thing burned down more than a century ago, and it was rebuilt in exactly the same spot, complete with countless narrow alleyways. This tour will take you into these alleys after the sun sets, when the spirits are said to appear on the streets. You'll start out at Four Seas Restaurant (731 Grant Ave.) and follow your loquacious guide along the avenues and side streets of Chinatown. As you stroll, your guide will tell you the stories of the neighborhood spirits, spooks, and ancestors. The curious get to learn about the deities worshipped by devout Chinese to this day, along with the folklore that permeates what was until recently a closed and secretive culture. Then you head into a former gambling den where a magician will attempt to conjure the soul of a long dead gambler.

If you absolutely must have your car with you, try to get a room at a hotel with a parking lot and either free parking or a parking package for the length of your stay.

CAR RENTAL

All the major car rental agencies have a presence at the **San Francisco Airport** (SFO, 800/435-9736, www.flysfo.com). In addition, most reputable hotels can offer or recommend a car rental. Rates tend to run $90-160 per day and $250-550 per week (including taxes and fees), with discounts for weekly and longer rentals. If you're flying into **Mineta San José Airport** (SJC, www.flysanjose.com) or **Oakland Airport** (OAK, www.flyoakland.com), the cost can drop to $110-250 per week for budget agencies. Premium agencies like Hertz and Avis are much pricier—you'll pay $375-650 for the same car. Off-site locations may offer cheaper rates, in the range of about $375 per week.

DRIVING

Driving in San Francisco can be confusing. Like most major metropolitan centers, one-way streets, alleys, streetcars, taxis, bicycles, and pedestrians all provide impediments to navigation. Touring around the City to see the sights means traffic jams filled with workers on weekdays and travelers on weekends. It means negotiating the legendary steep hills without crashing into the cars behind and in front of you.

PARKING

To call parking in San Francisco a nightmare is to insult nightmares. Every available scrap of land that can be built on has been built on with little left over to create parking for the zillions of cars that pass through on a daily basis. Parking a car in San Francisco can easily cost $50 per day or more. Most downtown and Union Square hotels do not include free parking with your room. Expect to pay $35-45 per night for parking, which may not include in-and-out privileges.

Street parking spots are as rare as unicorns and often require permits (which visitors cannot obtain, as a rule, unless they're friends of Danielle Steel). Parking lots and garages fill up quickly, especially during special events. You're more likely to find parking included at the motels along the edge of the city—Fisherman's Wharf, the Marina, the Richmond, and the Sunset district have the most motor inns with parking included. You definitely don't want to spend your vacation to San Francisco circling the street like a shark hoping to get a parking space.

Muni

The **Muni light rail system** (www.sfmta.com, adults $2, youths and seniors $0.75) has become the butt of jokes among locals because of its reputation for delays. But it can get you where you want to go within San Francisco as

one of Muni's vintage streetcars

© DOMINI DRAGOONE

long as time isn't a concern. A variety of lines snake through the City—those that go down to Fisherman's Wharf use vintage streetcars to heighten the fun for visitors. See the website for a route map, ticket information, and schedules.

To buy tickets, use one of the vending machines placed near some stops. Muni ticket machines are also outside the Caltrain station. See the website for more information about purchasing tickets.

Muni also runs the bus lines, which require the same fares; they can be slightly more reliable than the trains and go all over the City.

BART

Bay Area Rapid Transit (www.bart.gov, $3-10 one-way), or **BART,** is the Bay Area's late-coming answer to major metropolitan underground railways like Chicago's L trains and New York's subway system. Sadly, there's only one arterial line through the City. However, service directly from San Francisco Airport into the City runs daily, as does service to Oakland Airport, the cities of Oakland and Berkeley, plus many other East Bay destinations. BART connects to the Caltrain system and San Francisco Airport in Millbrae. See the website for route maps, schedules (BART usually runs on time), and fare information.

To buy tickets, use the vending machines found in every BART station. If you plan to ride more than once, you can "add money" to a single ticket, and then keep that ticket and reuse it for each ride.

Caltrain

This traditional commuter rail line runs along the peninsula into Silicon Valley, from San Francisco to San Jose, with limited continuing service to Gilroy. **Caltrain** (www.caltrain. com, $3-13 one-way) Baby Bullet trains can get you from San Jose to San Francisco in under an hour during commuting hours. Extra trains are often added for San Francisco Giants, San Francisco 49ers, and San Jose Sharks games.

You must purchase a ticket in advance at the vending machines found in all stations, or get your 10-ride card stamped before you board a train. The main Caltrain station in San Francisco is at the corner of 4th and King Streets, within walking distance of AT&T Park and Moscone Center.

Taxi

You'll find plenty of taxis scooting around all the major tourist areas of the City. Feel free to wave one down or ask your hotel to call you a cab. If you need to call a cab yourself, try **City Wide Dispatch** (415/920-0700).

Marin County

Marin County, in the North Bay, is San Francisco's backyard. Beginning with the Marin Headlands at the terminus of the Golden Gate Bridge, there is a nearly unbroken expanse of wild lands from San Francisco Bay to Tomales Bay. Here you'll find rugged cliffs plunging into the Pacific, towering redwoods, the area's tallest mountain, and verdant pastures home to the Bay Area's celebrated grass-fed beef and award-wining cheese-producing dairy cows.

MARIN HEADLANDS

The Marin Headlands lie north of San Francisco at the north end of the Golden Gate

Bridge. The land here encompasses a wide swath of virgin wilderness, former military structures, and a historic lighthouse.

Once over the bridge, the Alexander Avenue exit offers two options for exploring the Headlands: follow Alexander Avenue to Fort Baker and the Bay Area Discovery Museum, or turn left onto Bunker Road for the Marin Headlands Visitors Center and Nike Missile Site.

Vista Point

Aptly named Vista Point, at the north end of the Golden Gate Bridge, offers views from the

Marin Headlands toward San Francisco. If you dream of walking across the **Golden Gate Bridge** (http://goldengate.org, gates Nov.-mid-Mar. daily 5am-6:30pm, mid-Mar.-Oct. daily 5am-9pm), be sure to bring a warm coat as the wind and fog can really whip through. The bridge is 1.7 miles long, so a round-trip walk will turn into a 3.4-mile excursion. Bikes are allowed daily 24 hours, though after 9pm they must be buzzed through a gate.

To reach Vista Point, take U.S. 101 north across the Golden Gate Bridge. The first exit on the Marin County side is Vista Point; turn right into the parking lot. Note that this small parking lot often fills early.

Fort Baker

Standing at Crissy Field in San Francisco, you may wonder about those charming white buildings across the Bay. They are **Fort Baker** (435 Murray Circle, 415/331-1540, www.nps. gov/goga, daily sunrise-sunset, free), a 335-acre former Army Post established in 1905. With the transfer of many of the Bay Area's military outposts to parkland and civilian use, Fort Baker was handed over to the Golden Gate National Recreation Area and is open to visitors. The location, just east of the Golden Gate Bridge but secluded in a shallow valley, makes it a great destination to enjoy city views and a wind-free beach. The fort is the best example of military architecture from the Endicott Period. It includes many elegant homes with large sweeping porches centered around the oval parade grounds. As with many of the "posts to parks" in the Golden Gate National Recreation Area system, Fort Baker houses a hotel, Cavallo Point Lodge, and a nonprofit called the Institute at the Golden Gate. The Bay Area Discovery Museum is also nearby, along with the tiny Presidio Yacht Club, where all are welcome for a quick drink by the water. But the real attractions are views from or below the bluffs, the sheltered and unpopulated beach, and the graceful architecture.

Bay Area Discovery Museum

The **Bay Area Discovery Museum** (557 McReynolds Rd., Sausalito, 415/339-3900, www.baykidsmuseum.org, Tues.-Fri. 9am-4pm, Sat.-Sun. 10am-5pm, $11) offers kids of all ages a chance to explore the world they live in. The focus is definitely on the younger set; most of the permanent exhibits are geared toward small children, with lots of interactive components and places to play. Kids can check out easy-to-understand displays that describe the natural world, plus lots of Bay Area-specific exhibits. The Discovery Museum also boasts a theater and a café.

Marin Headlands Visitors Center

A great place to start your exploration is at the **Marin Headlands Visitors Center** (Field Rd. and Bunker Rd., 415/331-1540, www.nps. gov/goga, daily 9:30am-4:30pm), located in the old chapel at Fort Barry. The park rangers can give you the current lowdown on the best trails, beaches, and campgrounds in the Headlands.

Point Bonita Lighthouse

The **Point Bonita Lighthouse** (415/331-1540, www.nps.gov/goga, Sat.-Mon. 12:30pm-3:30pm, free) has been protecting the Headlands for over 150 years. It remains an active light station to this day. You need some dedication to visit Point Bonita, since it's only open a few days each week and there's no direct access by car. A 0.5-mile trail with steep sections leads from the trailhead on Field Road. Along the way, you'll pass through a hand-cut tunnel chiseled from the hard rock by the original builders of the lighthouse, then over the dramatic suspension bridge that leads to the building. Point Bonita was the third lighthouse built on the West Coast and was the last staffed lighthouse in California. Despite the presence of the lighthouse, the steamer *City of Rio de Janeiro* struck rocks nearby in 1901, causing the death of its 128 passengers. Today, the squat hexagonal building shelters automatic lights, horns, and signals. For a special treat, call the Marin Headlands Visitors Center to book a spot on a romantic 1.5-hour full-moon tour.

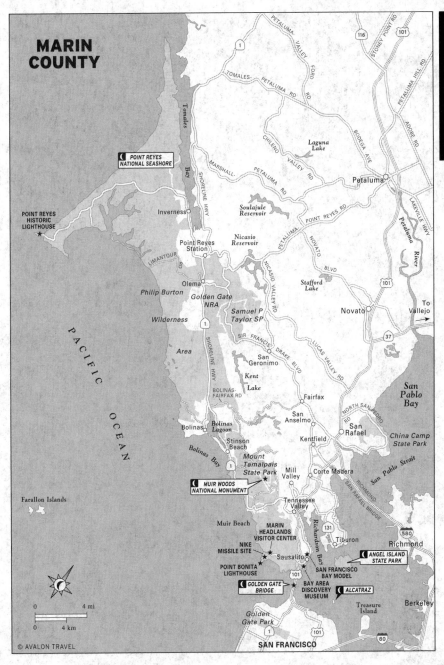

MARIN
COUNTY

POINT REYES
NATIONAL SEASHORE

POINT REYES
HISTORIC
LIGHTHOUSE

Inverness

Point Reyes
Station

Olema

Philip Burton

Golden Gate
NRA

Wilderness

Samuel P
Taylor SP

Area

San
Geronimo

PACIFIC

Kent
Lake

BOLINAS-
FAIRFAX RD

OCEAN

Bolinas

Bolinas
Lagoon

Stinson
Beach

Bolinas Bay

Mount
Tamalpais
State Park

MUIR WOODS
NATIONAL MONUMENT

Farallon Islands

Muir Beach

MARIN
HEADLANDS
VISITOR CENTER

NIKE
MISSILE SITE

POINT BONITA
LIGHTHOUSE

Sausalito

GOLDEN GATE
BRIDGE

SAN FRANCISCO
BAY MODEL

BAY AREA
DISCOVERY
MUSEUM

Tennessee
Valley

Mill
Valley

Corte Madera

Richardson Bay

Tiburon

ANGEL ISLAND
STATE PARK

ALCATRAZ

Richmond

Treasure
Island

Berkeley

Golden
Gate Park

SAN FRANCISCO

PETALUMA
VALLEY
FORD
RD

STONEY POINT RD

TOMALES-
PETALUMA RD

MARSHALL-

Tomales
Bay

SHORELINE HWY

LIMANTOUR RD

SHORELINE HWY

CHILENO
VALLEY RD

PETALUMA
RD

Laguna
Lake

Soulajule
Reservoir

Nicasio
Reservoir

NICASIO VALLEY RD

SIR FRANCIS DRAKE BLVD

Fairfax

San
Anselmo

Kentfield

PETALUMA
RD

POINT REYES RD

Petaluma

BODEGA AVE

ADOBE RD

PETALUMA HILL RD

LAKEVILLE HWY

Petaluma
River

NOVATO

BLVD

Stafford
Lake

Novato

LUCAS VALLEY RD

NORTH SAN PEDRO
RD

San
Rafael

To
Vallejo

San
Pablo
Bay

China Camp
State Park

San Pablo Strait

San Pablo Strait

RICHMOND-
SAN RAFAEL BRIDGE

© AVALON TRAVEL

0   4 mi

0   4 km

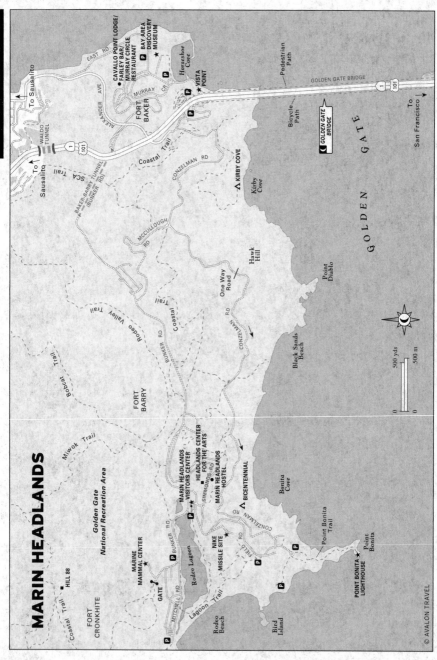

MARIN HEADLANDS

FORT CRONKHITE

Golden Gate
National Recreation Area

Coastal Trail

HILL 88

Miwok Trail

Bobcat Trail

Rodeo Valley Trail

BUNKER RD

Coastal Trail

SCA Trail

To Sausalito

WALDO TUNNEL

To Sausalito

BAKER-BARRY TUNNEL
(BUNKER RD)

Coastal Trail

ALEXANDER AVE

EAST RD

CAVALLO POINT LODGE/
FARLEY BAR/
MURRAY CIRCLE
RESTAURANT

BAY AREA
DISCOVERY
MUSEUM

MURRAY

FORT
BAKER

Horseshoe
Cove

VISTA POINT

CONZELMAN RD

Coastal Trail

MCCULLOUGH RD

KIRBY COVE

Kirby
Cove

Pedestrian Path

GOLDEN GATE BRIDGE

Bicycle Path

GOLDEN GATE
BRIDGE

To
San Francisco

GOLDEN GATE

Hawk
Hill

One Way
Road

CONZELMAN RD

Point
Diablo

Black Sands
Beach

FORT
BARRY

MARIN HEADLANDS
VISITORS CENTER

HEADLANDS CENTER
FOR THE ARTS

MARIN HEADLANDS
HOSTEL

SIMMONDS RD

BICENTENNIAL

CONZELMAN RD

Bonita
Cove

MARINE
MAMMAL CENTER

MITCHELL RD

GATE

Rodeo Lagoon

NIKE
MISSILE SITE

FIELD RD

Point Bonita
Trail

Point
Bonita

POINT BONITA
LIGHTHOUSE

BUNKER RD

Lagoon Trail

Rodeo
Beach

Bird
Island

500 yds

500 m

© AVALON TRAVEL

Marine Mammal Center

Inspired by the ocean's beauty and want to learn more about the animals that live in it? Visit the **Marine Mammal Center** (2000 Bunker Rd., 415/289-7325, www.marine-mammalcenter.org, daily 10am-5pm, free) at Fort Cronkhite in the Marin Headlands. The center is a hospital for sick and injured seals and sea lions. Visitors are free to wander around and look at the educational displays to learn more about what the center does, but the one-hour docent-led **tours** (June-Aug. daily 11am, 1pm, 3pm; Sept.-May Fri. and Mon. 1pm and 3pm, Sat.-Sun. 11am, 1pm, 3pm; adults $7, seniors and ages 5-17 $5, under age 5 free) explain the program in greater depth. Visitors will also get an education on the impact of human activity on marine mammals, and maybe a chance for close encounters with some of the center's patients.

Nike Missile Site

Military history buffs jump at the chance to tour a restored Cold War-era Nike missile base, known in military speak as SF-88. The **Nike Missile Site** (Field Rd. past the Headlands Visitors Center, 415/331-1453, www.nps.gov/goga, Wed.-Fri. 12:30pm-3:30pm and first Sat. each month, free) is the only such restored Nike base in the United States. Volunteers continue the restoration and lead tours every hour at the base, which is overseen by the Golden Gate National Recreation Area. On the tour, you'll get to see the fueling area, the testing and assembly building, and even take a ride on the missile elevator down into the pits that once stored missiles built to defend the United States from the Soviet Union. Because restoration work continues endlessly, the tour changes as new areas become available to visitors.

Hiking

Folks come from all over the world to hike the trails that thread through the Marin Headlands. The landscape is some of the most beautiful in the state, with unparalleled views of the Golden Gate Bridge and the Pacific Ocean.

From the Marin Headlands Visitors Center parking lot (Field Rd. and Bunker Rd.), the **Lagoon Trail** (1.75 miles, easy) encircles Rodeo Lagoon and gives bird-watchers an eagle's-eye view of the egrets, pelicans, and other seabirds that call the lagoon home. The lagoon is also home to the endangered tidewater goby, a small fish. The trailhead is near the restrooms.

An easy spot to get to, **Rodeo Beach** draws many visitors on summer weekends—do not expect solitude on the beach or the trails, or even in the water. Locals come out to surf when the break is going, while beachcombers look for the unique red and green pebbles on the shore. Note that the wind can really howl out here. The Lagoon Trail accesses the beach, but there is also a fairly large parking lot on Bunker Road that is much closer.

At Rodeo Beach is a trailhead for the **Coastal Trail.** To explore some of the battery ruins that pockmark these hills, follow the Coastal Trail (1.5 miles, easy) north to its intersection with Old Bunker Road Trail and return to Bunker Road near the Marine Mammal Center. Or extend this hike by continuing 2.3 miles up the Coastal Trail to the summit of Hill 88 and stellar views. You can loop this trail by linking it with Wolf Ridge Trail to Miwok Trail for a moderate 5.5-mile round-trip hike.

To reach the trailheads and parking lots, follow Bunker Road west to either Rodeo Beach or the Marin Headlands Visitors Center and their adjoining parking lots.

Cycling

If you prefer two wheels to two feet, you'll find the road and trail biking in the Marin Headlands both plentiful and spectacular. From the Tennessee Valley Trailhead, there are many multiuse trails designated for bikers as well as hikers. The **Valley Trail** (4 miles round-trip) takes you down the Tennessee Valley and all the way out to Tennessee Beach. A longer ride runs up the **Miwok Trail** (2 miles) northward. Turn southwest onto the **Coyote Ridge Trail** (0.9 miles), then catch the **Coastal Fire Road** (2 miles) the rest of the way west to Muir Beach. Another fun ride leads from just off U.S.

101 at the Rodeo Avenue exit. Park your car on the side of Rodeo Avenue, then bike down the short **Rodeo Avenue Trail**, which ends in a T intersection after 0.7 miles at **Alta Trail**. Take a left, and access to **Bobcat Trail** is a few yards away. Continue on Bobcat Trail for 2.5 miles straight through the Headlands to the **Miwok Trail** for just 0.5 miles, and you'll find yourself out at Rodeo Beach.

Need to rent a bicycle for your travels? In San Francisco, **Bike and Roll** (899 Columbus Ave., 415/229-2000, www.bikeandroll.com/ sanfrancisco, daily 8am-5pm, tours $60 for 5 hours) offers off-road biking tours of the Marin Headlands, plus bicycle rentals that let you go wherever the spirit moves you.

Accommodations

Lodging options are fairly limited in the Marin Headlands except for one luxurious lodge. Many other luxury-minded travelers choose to stay in Tiburon or Sausalito, while budget-motel seekers head for San Rafael.

Travelers who want budget accommodations indoors often choose the **Marin Headlands Hostel** (Bldg. 941, Fort Barry, 415/331-2777, www.norcalhostels.org/marin, dorm $25-26, private room $72-122). You'll find full kitchen facilities, Internet access, laundry rooms, and a rec room—all the amenities you'd expect from a high-end U.S. hotel. Surprisingly cozy and romantic, the hostel is sheltered in the turn-of-the-20th-century buildings of Fort Barry, creating a unique atmosphere. And, of course, with the Headlands right outside your door and 24-hour access for registered guests, there is no lack of activities or exploration opportunities.

The military personnel who stayed at Fort Baker would be floored by the ☾ **Cavallo Point Lodge** (601 Murray Circle, Fort Baker, Sausalito, 415/339-4700, www.cavallopoint. com, $300-700) that is now on the old installation's grounds. Actually, anyone—military or not—will be impressed with a stay in this luxurious lodge located within the Golden Gate National Parks. Guests can stay in the beautiful historic homes, which were former officers' residences, featuring elegant early-20th-century

Cavallo Point Lodge, in the Marin Headlands

© STUART THORNTON

woodwork, box-beam ceilings, and wraparound porches. For those interested in more modern furnishings, Cavallo Point Lodge also has accommodations in two-story, environmentally friendly buildings. These rooms and suites are situated on a hillside with floor-to-ceiling windows for taking in the strands of fog getting combed through the nearby Golden Gate Bridge. Inside both of the historic and contemporary rooms are luxury amenities including gas fireplaces and large flat screen TVs, while the contemporary rooms also include stone bathroom floors and deep soaking tubs. With the high-end restaurant Murray Circle and the lounge with views Farley Bar on site, and the Bay Area Discovery Museum and the Golden Gate Bridge within walking distance, you may have trouble finding a good reason to leave the grounds of this rejuvenating oasis.

Camping

Camping here requires some planning; lots of other people have the same idea. Be forewarned about pitching a tent, as Marin can be foggy, cold, and windy at any time of year, even in July-August. Bring your warm camping gear if you plan to seek out one of the precious few campsites.

The most popular campground is **Kirby Cove** (877/444-6777, www.recreation.gov, reservations required, $25). Secluded and shaded campsites provide a beautiful respite. Make your reservations well in advance for summer weekends, since this popular campground fills up fast. To get there, follow the one-mile trail from Battery Spencer, the concrete military installation on Conzelman Road.

The **Bicentennial Campground** (Battery Wallace parking lot, 415/331-1540, free) boasts a whopping three campsites easily accessible from the parking lot. Each site can accommodate a maximum of three people, and there's no water available or fires allowed on-site. A nearby picnic area has barbecue grills that campers can use to cook a hot dinner.

Food

End a day of historic hiking with oysters and drinks at Cavallo Point Lodge's **Farley Bar** (601 Murray Circle, Fort Baker, Sausalito, 415/339-4750, www.cavallopoint.com, Sun.-Thurs. 11am-11pm, Fri.-Sat. 11am-midnight, $10-26). Snag a blanket and a seat on the porch to watch the fog roll in over the Golden Gate Bridge. With only 12 drinks on the menu (all $12), the bar boasts one of the most classic and contemporary cocktail menus around. If you find you are not ready to leave after the sun goes down, mosey on inside, where lush leather chairs and sofas are arranged to maximize privacy and where a server is sure to hand you a bar menu with options including steamed mussels and a burger from a cow who once roamed the nearby Marin hills. There's also live music on Monday nights 7:30pm-9:30pm.

Also on-site is the equally excellent **Murray Circle Restaurant** (Cavallo Point Lodge, 601 Murray Circle, Fort Baker, Sausalito, 415/339-4750, www.cavallopoint.com, Mon.-Thurs. 7am-11am, 11:30am-2pm, and 5:30pm-10pm; Fri. 7am-11am, 11:30am-2pm, and 5:30pm-11pm; Sat. 7am-11am, 11:30am-2:30pm, and 5:30pm-11pm; Sun. 7am-11am, 11:30am-2:30pm, and 5:30pm-10pm; $14-30). The long slender dining room is draped in muted greens and golds, creating an effect that perfectly matches the simple elegant style of the historic building. The menu is based on the best Marin produce, seafood, meat, and dairy. Simple dishes are executed with French technique. You'll find raw oysters, bouillabaisse, and alder grilled pork chops.

Information and Services

Aside from the visitors centers and museums, there isn't much in the way of services in the Headlands. Likewise, cell phone reception can be spotty. For a post office, hospital, or bank, you'll have to go to Sausalito or across the bridge to San Francisco.

Getting There and Around

Fort Baker and the Marin Headlands are located just north of the Golden Gate Bridge on Highway 1 and U.S. 101. To get to the

Headlands from San Francisco, take the Alexander Avenue exit, the second exit after you cross the bridge. From the north, Alexander Avenue is the last Sausalito exit. If the visitors center is the first stop on your agenda, turn left onto Bunker Road and go through the one-way tunnel. If you want to hit Fort Barry and the Bonita Lighthouse first, follow Alexander Avenue right and travel under the highway to Conzelman Road, which leads up the hill along the edge of the Headlands. Keep in mind that many of the roads are very narrow and become one-way in places.

Traffic in this area, particularly in the Headlands, can be heavy on beautiful weekend days, so try and plan to get here early and spend the time that other people are stuck in theirs cars exploring the area on foot. Another option is to take bus route 76 of the **Muni** (415/701-2311, www.sfmta.com, Sun. 10am-7pm, $2 one-way). Making stops throughout downtown San Francisco and the north end of the city, this Sunday-only Muni line crosses the Golden Gate and ventures as far as Rodeo Cove in the Headlands. It makes frequent trips, and you can even load bikes on the front.

SAUSALITO

The affluent town of Sausalito wraps around the north end of San Francisco Bay. The main drag runs along the shore, and the concrete boardwalk is perfect for strolling and biking. A former industrial fishing town, Sausalito still has a few old cannery buildings and plenty of docks, most now lined with pleasure boats. Sausalito has a community of people living on 400 houseboats along its northern end.

San Francisco Bay Model

One of the odder attractions you'll find in the North Bay is the **San Francisco Bay Model** (2100 Bridgeway, 415/332-3871, www.spn. usace.army.mil/bmvc, free), which is administered by the U.S. Army Corps of Engineers. It is a scale model of the way the Bay works, complete with currents and tides. Scientists and engineering types love to see how the waters of the Bay move and work.

Accommodations

The Gables Inn (62 Princess St., 415/289-1100, www.gablesinnsausalito.com, $199-425) opened in 1869 and is the oldest B&B in the area. Each of the nine guest rooms is appointed in tasteful earth tones, with white linens and several baths. Although this inn honors its long history, it has also kept up with the times, adding cable TV and Internet access. Genial innkeepers serve a continental breakfast, available for a few hours each morning, and host a wine and cheese soiree each evening.

With a checkered history dating back to 1915, the **Hotel Sausalito** (16 El Portal, 888/442-0700, www.hotelsausalito.com, $165-305) was a speakeasy, a bordello, and a home for the writers and artists of the Beat Generation. Today, this tiny boutique hotel, with its yellow walls and locally built furnishings, evokes the Mediterranean coast. Sink into your cozy room after a day spent walking or biking along the water and a scrumptious dinner out.

The **Casa Madrona Hotel and Spa** (801 Bridgeway, 800/288-0502, www.casamadrona. com, $289-449) is a sprawling collection of structures housing contemporary luxury hotel rooms and suites that satisfy even the pickiest celebrity guest. Poggio, the on-site restaurant, serves award-winning Italian food, and the full-service spa pampers guests with a full menu of body and salon treatments. If you're treating yourself to a room at Casa Madrona, be sure to ask for one with a view overlooking the Bay or the harbor.

For a taste of the life of the richest residents of the area, stay at Sausalito's **Inn Above Tide** (30 El Portal, 800/893-8433, www.innabovetide.com, $330-1,125). Billed as the only hotel in the Bay Area that's actually on the Bay, the inn sits over the edge of the water looking out at the San Francisco skyline. Most guest rooms have private decks that allow guests to take advantage of the sublime views (well, except when it's foggy). Inside the guest rooms, the appointments look like something you'd find in an upscale home rather than a hotel. From the hotel, you can walk downtown to enjoy the shops, spas, and restaurants of Sausalito. Be sure to take advantage of the morning continental breakfast and afternoon wine and cheese though.

Food
Located right on the water, **(Fish.** (350 Harbor Dr., 415/331-3474, www.331fish.com, daily 11:30am-8:30pm, $14-25) is known for serving sustainable seafood. So much so that the California legislature awarded the restaurant a Sustainable North Bay Award. That is just one reason to celebrate Fish. Another reason is its rich Dungeness crab roll drenched in butter. Yet one more is its spicy Saigon salmon sandwich, an explosion of tastes with carrots, jalapenos, cilantro sprigs, and a house made ginger scallion sauce on a delectable roll.

If you're jonesing for some Chinese food, go to **Tommy's Wok Chinese Cuisine** (3001 Bridgeway, 415/332-5818, http://tommyswok. com, Mon.-Thurs. 11:30am-3pm and 4pm-9pm, Fri.-Sat. 11:30am-3pm and 4pm-9:30pm, Sun. 4pm-9pm, $11-18.50). Unlike a typical Chinese restaurant, Tommy's is into the swing of California cuisine fashions. This includes organic free-range chicken, organic tofu, and a heavy emphasis on fresh vegetables—even in the meat dishes. Don't expect to find too many of your sweet syrupy favorites; instead, take a chance on some tasty broccoli or asparagus. They even have lettuce wraps.

Information and Services
To get started, make a stop at the **Sausalito Visitors Center** (780 Bridgeway, 415/332-0505, www.sausalito.org, Tues.-Sun. 11:30am-4pm). Also known as the Ice House, this tiny building, used to store ice in the days before refrigeration technology, has loads of Sausalito materials to browse and purchase. The helpful staff has free maps and tips and sells books, cards, and souvenirs.

In the downtown area are a few cafés with Internet access, and to get cash, there is a **Bank of America** (750 Bridgeway). Sausalito also has a **post office** (150 Harbor Dr., 415/332-0227, www.usps.com,). For a newspaper even more local than the *San Francisco Chronicle,* pick up a copy of the *Marin Independent Journal* (www. marinij.com).

Getting There and Around
Sausalito is just over the Golden Gate Bridge from San Francisco and is easily accessible by bicycle on side roads or by car on U.S. 101. Once in town, navigating by car can be a challenge, as the narrow oceanfront main road gets very crowded on weekends. If you can, park and walk around town, both for your own comfort and to do your part to minimize traffic congestion. Street parking is mostly metered.

If you have the time, a great way to get to Sausalito from San Francisco is by ferry. Two companies make the trip daily, which takes roughly an hour or less. The scenery is beautiful, and it is a great chance to get out on the Bay a lot more cheaply than a bay tour. The **Blue and Gold Fleet** (415/705-8200, www. blueandgoldfleet.com, check website for schedule, adults $10.50, children and seniors $6.25, under age 5 free) makes the trip from Pier 41. Largely serving commuters, the **Golden Gate Ferry** (415/455-2000, http://goldengate.org, see website for schedule, adults $9.75, children and seniors $4.75, under age 5 free) leaves from the Ferry Building, closer to downtown San Francisco. The trip across the Bay is cheaper and a bit faster.

TIBURON
Once a simple fishing town, Tiburon now has some of the most expensive waterfront real estate in the world. The small downtown area that backs onto the marina is popular with the young and affluent crowd as well as longtime yacht owners. Aside from the views, one of the greatest draws to Tiburon is its proximity to Angel Island, the largest in the Bay and one of the most unique state parks around.

(Angel Island State Park
The long history of **Angel Island** (415/435-5390, www.parks.ca.gov, daily 8am-sunset) begins with regular visits (though no permanent settlements) by the Coastal Miwok people. During the Civil War the U.S. Army

© STUART THORNTON

the view from Angel Island's Mount Livermore

created a fort on the island in anticipation of Confederate attacks from the Pacific. The attacks never came, but the Army maintained a base here. Today, many of the 19th-century military buildings remain and can be seen on the tram tour (1 hour, $10-15), on foot, or on a docent-led Segway or Digger electric scooter tour (both 2 hours, $68 pp). If you'd rather get around by pedal power, you can rent bikes ($12.50/hour, $40/day) to explore the island. Later, the Army built a Nike missile base on the island to protect strategically-important San Francisco from possible Soviet attacks. The missile base is not open to the public, but it can be seen from roads and trails.

Angel Island's history also has a shameful side. It served as an immigration station for inbound ships and a concentration camp for the flood of Chinese attempting to escape turmoil in their homeland. While Europeans were waved through with little more than a head-lice check, the Chinese were herded into barracks while government officials scrutinized their papers. After months and sometimes

years of waiting, many were shipped back to China. Today, poetry lines the walls of the barracks, expressing the despair of the immigrants who had hoped for a better life and found little more than prison. Docent-led **tours** (Wed.-Fri. 10am-3pm, Sat.-Sun. 10am-4pm, $5) show this poetry and the buildings of the camps.

Angel Island is a major destination for both casual and serious hikers. Trails of varying difficulty crisscross the island, creating fun for hikers and bikers alike. Adventurous trekkers can scale Mount Livermore via either the **North Ridge Trail** or the **Sunset Trail.** Each runs about 4.5 miles round-trip for a moderate, reasonably steep hike. Stop at the summit's picnic tables and wooden benches for a rest and to watch boats sketch white lines on the blue-green bay. This is also a great place to take in the expanse of the Bay region including the skyscrapers of San Francisco, the lonely rock of Alcatraz, and the Golden Gate Bridge—that is until the pillowy fog comes in to snuff out the views. For the best experience, make a loop, taking one trail up the mountain and the other back down. If you're up for a long paved-road hike, take the **Perimeter Road** (5 miles, moderate) all the way around the island.

While there is no store on the island for supplies, the **Cove Café** (415/435-3392, www. angelisland.com, Mar.-Oct. Mon.-Fri. 10am-3pm, Sat.-Sun. 10am-4pm, $9-15) serves hot sandwiches, wraps, salads, and even a gourmet cheese platter from Cowgirl Creamery. Craving oysters and a beer? Stroll next door to the **Cove Cantina Oyster Bar** (Memorial Day-Sept. Thurs.-Fri. 11am-3pm, Sat.-Sun. 11am-5pm).

CAMPING
Camping (800/444-7275, www.reserveamerica.com, $30) is available at nine primitive sites that fill up quickly (successful campers reserve their campsites six months in advance). The campsites themselves are characterized as "environmental sites"; each is equipped with food lockers (a must), surprisingly nice outhouses, running water, and a barbecue. You must bring your own charcoal or camp stove, as wood fires are strictly prohibited. Three of the sites, the Ridge Sites, sit on the southwest side of the island, known to be fairly windy. The other six sites, the East Bay and Sunrise Sites, face the East Bay. Wherever you end up, plan on walking 0.5-1.75 miles from the ferry to your campsite. Despite the dramatic urban views, camping here is a little like backpacking.

GETTING THERE AND AROUND
Angel Island State Park is located in the middle of San Francisco Bay. To get here, you must either boat in or take one of the ferries that serve the island. The harbor at Tiburon is the easiest place to access Angel Island. The private **Angel Island-Tiburon Ferry** (21 Main St., Tiburon, 415/435-2131, www.angelislandferry. com, adults $13.50, ages 6-12 $11.50, ages 3-5 $3.50, bicycles $1) can get you out to the island in about 10 minutes and runs several times a day. You can also take the **Blue and Gold Fleet** (415/705-8200, www.blueandgoldfleet.com, one-way $14.50-17) to Angel Island if you are departing from either Oakland-Alameda (2990 Main St., Alameda, summer-fall only)

or San Francisco (Pier 41). Be aware, however, that scheduling the ferry can be a little tight. Check website for current schedule.

Ferries have plenty of room for you to bring your own bicycle, or you can rent one (Mar.-Nov. Sat.-Sun., Apr.-Oct. daily, $12.50 per hour, $40 per day) at the main visitors area near the ferry dock. Rentals must always be returned at 4pm. Grab a map from the gift shop. Not all trails are open to bikes, but those that are include the easy five-mile paved Perimeter Road around the island, perfect for newcomers.

Accommodations
It would be difficult to find a place to stay closer to the water than the **C Waters Edge Hotel** (25 Main St., 415/789-5999, www. marinhotels.com, $219-469). This boutique hotel is actually perched on a historic dock over the bay. Most rooms have views of the bay and sights like Angel Island and San Francisco in the distance. They also include luxurious beds and wood burning fireplaces. Another feature that sets Waters Edge apart is that they deliver a full continental breakfast to your room every morning.

Also wonderfully close to the water and attractions of downtown Tiburon, the **Lodge at Tiburon** (1651 Tiburon Blvd., 415/435-3133, www.thelodgeattiburon.com, $229-289) offers the comforts and conveniences of a larger hotel while providing the personal attention and atmosphere of a boutique inn. All the guest rooms are soothing and pretty, but for a special treat, book the Spa Room with a huge raised whirlpool tub set in an alcove overlooking the water. Have dinner or a drink at the attached Tiburon Tavern in the evening, or take a walk downtown to look at the shops.

Food
There are many visitor-friendly restaurants in downtown Tiburon. For a surprisingly good Italian meal, head for **Servino** (9 Main St., 415/435-2676, www.bestservino.com, Mon.-Thurs. 11:30am-3pm and 5pm-10pm, Fri. 11:30am-3pm and 5pm-11pm, Sat. 11:30am-4pm and 5pm-11pm, Sun. 11:30am-4pm and

5pm-10pm, $13-25) on the waterfront. A huge outdoor patio offers diners stunning views of the Bay, Angel Island, and the San Francisco cityscape. Service is as warm and friendly as the classic Italian cuisine. A full bar caters to locals and visitors alike. The menu runs to hearty, somewhat Americanized Italian dishes. You can eat yourself senseless by trying all the courses, or choose just an entrée to keep the meal a bit lighter. The full bar makes a great place to sit should you need to wait for a table, and Servino's hosts live music on Friday nights.

A Tiburon mainstay is **Sam's Anchor Café** (27 Main St., 415/435-4527, www.samscafe.com, Mon.-Thurs. 11am-9:30pm, Fri. 11am-10pm, Sat. 9:30am-10pm, Sun. 9:30am-9:30pm, $15-28). Sitting on the water with a large glassed-in deck, Sam's specializes in seafood, liberally poured glasses of wine, and lounging in the sun on beautiful weekend afternoons. You'll find many locals and visitors catching some rays over oysters on the half shell, fish-and-chips, or a burger. At night, the fare becomes a bit fancier, moving indoors with low lighting. You'll find more elegantly plated dishes, but seafood still reigns, as does the good-time vibe.

Information and Services

To get maps and recommendations, the **Tiburon Chamber of Commerce** (96 Main St., 415/435-5633, 9am-4pm Mon.-Fri.) is a small office, but the staff will be able to answer any questions you may have. The town of Tiburon is small, so don't expect a whole lot in the way of services. There is a **Bank of America** (1601 Tiburon Blvd.), a **Wells Fargo Bank** (1550 Tiburon Blvd.), and a **post office** (6 Beach Rd.).

Getting There and Around

Tiburon is located on a peninsula about eight miles north of the Golden Gate Bridge. From San Francisco, take U.S. 101 north to the Tiburon Boulevard exit. Stay to the right and follow the road along the water for nearly six miles until you reach the small downtown area.

Like Sausalito, Tiburon is very walkable and is a great destination via the ferry from San Francisco. The **Blue and Gold Fleet** (415/705-8200, http://blueandgoldfleet.com, daily, 30 minute-ride, check website for current schedule, adults $10.50, children and seniors $6.25, under age 5 free) runs daily trips to Tiburon from San Francisco's Pier 41.

MILL VALLEY

Situated in the shadow of 2,571-foot Mount Tamalpais, Mill Valley is a great temporary base for an exploration of Marin County's many attractions. Named for a former mill that occupied the area in the 1800s, this upscale city has a walkable downtown with great restaurants, a state-of-the-art music venue, a theater that hosts all sorts of events and the world-renowned Mill Valley Film Festival. There are also recreational opportunities, including the start of the 7.1-mile long Dipsea Trail, which climbs out of the valley and eventually ends at Muir Beach, and nearby Mount Tamalpais, where you can score some of the best views of the Bay Area.

Entertainment and Events

In 2012, the Grateful Dead's Bob Weir helped to open the state of the art **Sweetwater Music Hall** (19 Corte Madera Ave., 415/388-1100, http://sweetwatermusichall.com). Sweetwater is named for Mill Valley's previous music venue, a local legend that hosted performances by Carlos Santana, Jerry Garcia, and Elvis Costello before shutting down in 2007. The latest incarnation hosts rock, blues, funk, and New Orleans acts on a good-sized stage with pristine sound. The mostly middle-aged crowd goes wild on the wooden dance floor, which was salvaged from the original Sweetwater. A café serves up creative small bites like meatloaf sliders.

Mill Valley Beerworks (173 Throckmorton Ave., 415/888-8218, http://millvalleybeerworks.com, daily 5pm-midnight) is a great place to sip a beer after a hike up nearby Mount Tamalpais or following a day of climbing up and down the Dipsea Trail. Beerworks has a rotating menu of seasonally brewed beers made in-house as well as an extensive list of bottled beer from around the world. Sip your suds at the bar or at the long wooden beer garden-like tables with friends.

The **142 Throckmorton Theatre** (142 Throckmorton Ave., 415/383-9600, www.142throckmortontheatre.com) is the place to see all sorts of plays, musicals, and concerts. It's probably best known though for its Tuesday comedy nights, where locals like Robin Williams and Dana Carvey frequently stop in to perform.

Founded in 1978 by the California Film Institute, the **Mill Valley Film Festival** (www. mvff.com) has expanded to an 11-day showcase of films from over 200 filmmakers that occurs every October. The films are shown in Mill Valley and the surrounding area. Heavy-hitting filmmakers and actors, including Sean Penn, Helen Mirren, and Forest Whitaker, have made appearances at the fest. Mill Valley's other big annual event happens the second Sunday of June: The **Dipsea Race** (www.dipsea.org) is the oldest foot race in the nation, with participants running up and down the steep Dipsea Trail.

Accommodations

The place to stay in Mill Valley is hands down the C **Mill Valley Inn** (165 Throckmorton Ave., 415/389-6608, www.marinhotels.com, $200-450). Situated right in Mill Valley's downtown, the Mill Valley Inn has rooms in the modern main building and a historic creek house. Those wanting even more seclusion should opt for one of the two single bedroom cottages shaded by towering redwoods. The rooms in the main building are decorated with repurposed wood furniture and have small balconies overlooking Mill Valley's Throckmorton Street or the small redwood forest behind the inn. Other nice touches include a deluxe continental breakfast and free use of a fleet of mountain bikes for tooling around town or attempting to summit nearby Mount Tamalpais.

Situated on sparkling Richardson Bay, **Acqua Hotel** (555 Redwood Hwy., 415/380-0400, www.marinhotels.com, $149-225) has serene rooms and suites. A night's stay includes a hot breakfast buffet and complimentary use of the hotel's mountain bikes, which can be put to good use on the multi-use trail out front. Though Acqua is walking distance to a couple of restaurants, it is two miles from the downtown section of Mill Valley.

Food

For a small city, Mill Valley has a significant number of notable restaurants. The **Dipsea Café** (200 Shoreline Hwy., 415/381-0298, www.dipseacafe.com, Mon.-Tues. 7am-3pm, Wed.-Sun. 7am-9pm, $9-15) is a great place to fuel up for a day of hiking Mount Tamalpais or the Dipsea Trail. Go hearty with a chicken fried steak and egg platter or opt for a more delicate pear-walnut omelet. With a farm scene painted on the wall and plaid tablecloths, the Dipsea has a country feel. It also serves Greek food after 4pm.

A partnership between celebrity chef Tyler Florence and rocker Sammy Hagar, **El Paseo** (17 Throckmorton Ave., 415/388-0741, www. elpaseomillvalley.com, daily 5:30pm-10pm, $17-68) serves up meaty entrées like veal chops and steak frites.

Bungalow 44 (44 E. Blithedale Ave., 415/381-2500, www.bungalow44.com, Mon.-Tues. 5pm-10pm, Wed.-Thurs. 5pm-10:30pm, Fri.-Sat. 5pm-11pm, Sun. 5pm-9:30pm, $15-30) cooks up salmon and coffee-crusted ribeye on an old fashioned wood burning grill. They also offer vegetarian entrées like roasted stuffed peppers.

Information and Services

Stop into the **Mill Valley Chamber of Commerce** (85 Throckmorton Ave., 415/388-9700, www.millvalley.org, Tues.-Fri. 10am-2pm) on weekdays to learn more about Mill Valley's offerings. Mill Valley also has a **post office** (751 East Blithedale Ave., 415/388-0630, www.usps.com).

Getting There and Around

Mill Valley is easy to get to. Take U.S. 101 north and after going over the Golden Gate Bridge take the East Blithedale/Tiburon

© STUART THORNTON

the towering redwoods of Muir Woods

Boulevard exit. Turn left on East Blithedale and follow the road into downtown Mill Valley.

There is usually parking to be found in Mill Valley, but once here, it's best to leave your car as the downtown is small and everything is walkable.

◖ MUIR WOODS NATIONAL MONUMENT

Established in 1908 and named for naturalist and author John Muir, **Muir Woods National Monument** (Panoramic Hwy., off Hwy. 1, 415/388-2596, www.nps.gov/muwo, daily 8am-sunset, adults $7, under age 15 free) comprises acres of staggeringly beautiful redwood forest nestled in Marin County. More than six miles of trails wind through the redwoods and accompanying Mount Tamalpais area, crossing verdant creeks and the lush forest. These are some of the most stunning—and accessible—redwoods in the Bay Area.

The visitors center is a great place to begin your exploration. The **Muir Woods Visitors Center** (1 Muir Woods Rd., daily 8am-close, closing hours vary) abuts the main parking area and marks the entrance to Muir Woods. In addition to maps, information, and advice about hiking, you'll also find a few amenities. Inside the park, slightly past the visitors center, is the **Muir Woods Trading Company Gift Shop and Cafe** (415/388-7059, www.muir-woodstradingcompany.com, daily 9am-close, closing hours vary) where you can purchase souvenirs and sustenance made from high-quality local ingredients.

Muir Woods is accessed via the long and winding Muir Woods Road. From U.S. 101, take the Stinson Beach/Highway 1 exit. On Highway 1, also named the Shoreline Highway, follow the road under the freeway and proceed until the road splits in a T-junction at the light. Turn left, continuing on Shoreline Highway for 2.5 miles. At the intersection with Panoramic Highway, make a sharp right turn and continue climbing uphill. At the junction of Panoramic Highway and Muir Woods Road, turn left and follow the road 1.5 twisty miles down to the Muir Woods parking lots on the right.

If you're visiting on a holiday or a summer weekend, get to the Muir Woods parking areas early—they fill fast, and afternoon hopefuls often cannot find a spot. Lighted signs on U.S. 101 will alert you to parking conditions at the main parking lot. To avoid the traffic hassle, there is a **Muir Woods Shuttle** (415/455-2000, http://goldengatetransit.org/services/muir-woods.php, summer Sat.-Sun., adults $2, children and seniors $1, children under 6 free) that leaves from various points in southern Marin County, including the Sausalito ferry terminal.

Hiking

Muir Woods boasts many lovely trails that crisscross the gorgeous redwood forest. First-time visitors should follow the wheelchair- and stroller-accessible **Main Trail Loop** (1 mile, easy). Leading from the visitors center on an easy and flat walk through the beautiful redwoods, this trail has an interpretive brochure (pick one up at the visitors center) with numbers along the trail that describe the flora and fauna. Hikers can continue the loop on the **Hillside Trail** for an elevated view of the valley.

One of the first side trails off the Main Trail, the **Ocean View Trail** (3.4 miles, moderate) soon appears to the left. Some advice: Either bring water, or pick up a bottle at the Visitors Center before starting up the trail. The trail climbs through the redwoods for 1.5 miles until its junction with **Lost Trail.** Turn right on Lost Trail and follow it downhill for 0.7 miles to **Fern Creek Trail.** Bear left onto Fern Creek Trail for a lush and verdant return to the Main Trail. Along the way you'll see the much-lauded Kent Tree, a 250-foot-tall Douglas fir.

Alternatively, you can continue on the Main Trail to where Fern Creek Trail starts and hike in the opposite direction to the junction with **Alice Eastwood Camp,** after a brief westward jog on Lost Trail. There you can get a drink of water, use the restrooms, and even have a picnic in this developed area. Follow the **Camp Eastwood Trail** back to the starting point.

It's easier to avoid the crowds by following the Main Trail to its terminus with the **Bootjack Trail** (6.4 miles, moderate). The Bootjack Trail climbs uphill for 1.3 miles before its junction with the **TCC Trail.** Bear left for the TCC Trail and meander through the quiet Douglas firs. At 1.4 miles, the trail meets up with the **Stapleveldt Trail;** turn left again to follow this trail for 0.5 miles to **Ben Johnson Trail,** which continues downhill for one more mile to meet up with the Main Trail.

You may notice signs in this area for the **Dipsea Trail,** which goes from Mill Valley to Muir Beach. This is a strenuous, unshaded 7.1-mile hike, and the only way back is the way you came—but uphill.

Muir Beach

Few coves on the California coast can boast as much beauty as **Muir Beach** (just south of the town of Muir Beach, www.nps.gov/goga, daily sunrise-sunset). From the overlook above Highway 1 to the edge of the ocean beyond the dunes, Muir Beach is a haven for both wildlife and beachcombers. In the wintertime, beach-goers bundle up against the chill and walk the sands of the cove or along the many trails that lead from the beach. If you're lucky, you might find a Monterey pine tree filled with sleepy monarch butterflies, here to overwinter before making their long migration back north in the spring. Springtime brings rare rays of sunshine to Muir Cove, and as the air grows (a little bit) warmer in summer, the north end of the cove attracts another breed of beach life: nudists. If the clothing-optional California lifestyle makes you uncomfortable, stick to the south side, the brackish Redwood Creek lagoon, and the windswept picnic grounds.

Muir Beach is directly off Highway 1. The most direct route is to take U.S. 101 to the Stinson Beach/Highway 1 exit and follow Highway 1 (also called Shoreline Highway) for 6.5 miles to Pacific Way (look for the Pelican Inn). Turn left onto Pacific Way and continue straight to the Muir Beach parking lot. If arriving from Muir Woods, simply continue following Muir Woods Road down to the junction with Highway 1 and turn left onto Pacific Way.

ACCOMMODATIONS AND FOOD

One fine Marin lodging is **The Pelican Inn** (10 Pacific Way, Muir Beach, 415/383-6000, www.pelicaninn.com, $206-289). Inside the Tudor structure, the guest room decor continues the historic ambiance, with big-beam construction, canopy beds, and historic portrait prints. The seven mostly small guest rooms each come with private baths and full English-style breakfast, but no TVs or phones. (There is free Wi-Fi though.)

In addition to quaint bedchambers, you can also get hearty food at the Pelican Inn (Mon.-Fri. 11:30am-3pm and 5:30pm-9pm, Sat.-Sun. 8am-11am, 11:30am-3pm, and 5:30pm-9pm, $16-34). Dark wood and a long trestle table give the proper old English feeling to the dimly lit dining room. The cuisine brings home the flavors of old England, with dishes like beef Wellington, shepherd's pie, and fish-and-chips. True fans of the British Isles will round off the meal with a pint of Guinness.

MOUNT TAMALPAIS STATE PARK

To see the whole Bay Area in a single day, go to **Mount Tamalpais State Park** (801 Panoramic Hwy., Mill Valley, 415/388-2070, www.parks.ca.gov, daily 7am-sunset, day-use parking $8). Known as Mount Tam, this park boasts stellar views of the San Francisco Bay Area—from Mount St. Helena in Napa down to San Francisco and across to the East Bay. The Pacific Ocean peeks from around the corner of the western peninsula, and on a clear day you can just make out the foothills of the Sierra Nevada Mountains to the east. This park is the Bay Area's backyard, with hiking, biking, and camping opportunities widely appreciated for both their beauty and easy access. Ample parking, interpretive walks, and friendly park rangers make a visit to Mount Tam a hit even for less outdoorsy travelers.

In addition to recreation, Mount Tam also

provides the perfect setting for the arts. The **Mountain Theater** (E. Ridgecrest Blvd. at Pan Toll Rd., Mountain Play Association: 415/383-1100, www.mountainplay.org, May-June, ticket prices vary), also known as the Cushing Memorial Amphitheater, built in the 1930s, still hosts plays at its outdoor stone seating. Performances and dates vary; contact the Mountain Play Association for information and tickets. Plan to arrive early, as both parking and seating fill completely well before the show starts. The Mountain Theater also serves as the meeting place for the **Mount Tam Astronomy Program** (E. Ridgecrest Blvd. at Pan Toll Rd., 415/388-2070 or 415/455-5370, www.mttam.net). Held every Saturday April-October near the new and first quarter moon, the group hosts a talk by an astronomer that lasts about 45 minutes, followed by a tour of the night sky and star viewing through telescopes. Bring flashlights.

The **East Peak Visitors Center** (Sat.-Sun. 11am-4pm) is located at the top of Mount Tam, with a small museum and gift shop as well as a picnic area with tables and restrooms and, even, a small refreshment stand. The on-site staff can assist with hiking tips or guided walks. The **Pantoll Ranger Station** (Panoramic Hwy. at Pantoll Rd., 415/388-2070, Fri.-Mon. 9am-5pm), which anchors the western and larger edge of the park, provides hikers with maps and camping information.

Enjoy the views without setting out on the trail at the **Bootjack Picnic Area** (Panoramic Hwy.), which has tables, grills, water, and restrooms. The small parking lot northeast of the Pantoll Ranger Station fills quickly and early in the day.

Hiking

Up on Mount Tam, you can try anything from a leisurely 30-minute interpretive stroll to a strenuous hike up and down one of the many deep ravines. Mount Tam's hiking areas are divided into three major sections: the East Peak, the Pantoll area, and the Rock Springs area. Each of these regions offers a number of beautiful trails, so you'll want to grab a map from the visitors center or online to get a sense of the mountain and its hikes.

For additional hikes, visit the Mount Tamalpais Interpretive Association website (www.mttam.net).

EAST PEAK

The charming, interpretive **Verna Dunshee Trail** (0.75 miles, easy) offers a short, mostly flat walk along a wheelchair-accessible trail. The views are fabulous, and you can get a leaflet at the visitors center that describes many of the things you'll see along the trail. Turn this into a loop hike by continuing on Verna Dunshee counterclockwise; once back at the visitors center, make the climb up to **Gardner Lookout** for stellar views from the top of Mount Tam's East Peak (2,571 ft.).

PANTOLL

The Pantoll Ranger Station is ground zero for some of the best and most challenging hikes in the park. The **Old Mine Trail** (across Panormaic Hwy.) leads up to Mountain Theater via the **Easy Grade Trail** (2 miles, easy-moderate). Eager hikers can continue on the **Rock Springs Trail** to West Point Inn and back via **Old Stage Road** for a more challenging 4.7 miles.

The **Steep Ravine Trail** (3.8 miles, moderate) descends through lush Webb Creek and gorgeous redwoods to meet with the Dipsea Trail. To return to the Pantoll parking area, turn left onto Dipsea Trail and climb the demanding steps back to the **Coastal Fire Road.** Turn left again, then right on the Old Mine Trail for an exhilarating 3.8-mile hike.

The **Dipsea Trail** loop (7.3 miles round-trip, strenuous) is part of the famous Dipsea Race Course (second Sun. in June), a 7.4-mile course renowned for both its beauty and its challenging stairs. The trailhead that begins in Muir Woods, near the parking lot, leads through Mount Tam all the way to Stinson Beach. Hikers can pick up the Dipsea on the Old Mine Trail or at its intersection with the Steep Ravine Trail in Mount Tam, but a common loop is to take the **Matt Davis Trail** (across Panoramic Hwy. from the Pantoll parking area) west all the way to Stinson Beach and then return via the Dipsea Trail to Steep Ravine Trail. This is a long, challenging hike, especially on the way back, so bring water and endurance.

ROCK SPRINGS

Rock Springs is conveniently located near the Mountain Theater, and a variety of trails lead off from this historic venue. Cross Ridgecrest Boulevard and take the **Mountain Theater Fire Trail** to Mountain Theater. Along the top row of the stone seats, admire the vistas while looking for **Rock Springs Trail** (it's a bit hidden). Once you find it, follow Rock Springs Trail all the way to historic West Point Inn. The views here are stunning, and you'll see numerous cyclists flying downhill on Old Stage Road below. Cross this road to pick up Nora Trail, following it until it intersects with **Matt Davis Trail**. Turn right to reach the Bootjack day-use area. Follow the **Bootjack Trail** right (north) to return to the Mountain Theater for a 4.6-mile loop.

Here's your chance to see waterfalls via the lovely **Cataract Trail** (3 miles, easy-moderate). From the trailhead, follow Cataract Trail for a short bit before heading right on **Bernstein Trail.** Shortly, turn left onto **Simmons Trail** and continue to Barth's Retreat, site of a former camp that is now a small picnic area with restrooms. Turn left on **Mickey O'Brien Trail** (a map can be helpful here), returning to an intersection with the Cataract Trail. It's worth the short excursion to follow Cataract Trail to the right through the Laurel Dell picnic area and up to Cataract Falls. Enjoy a picnic at Laurel Dell before returning to Cataract Trail to follow it down to the Rock Springs trailhead.

Cycling

To bike up to the peak of Mount Tam is a mark of local cyclists' strength and endurance. Rather than driving up to the East Peak or the Mountain Home Inn, sturdy cyclists pedal up the paved road to the East Peak. It's a long, hard ride, but for an experienced cyclist the challenge and the views make it more than worthwhile. Just take care, since this road is open to cars, many of which may not realize that bikers frequent the area.

A hard but satisfying trip up the mountain begins at the Lagunitas Trailhead in Ross (15.8 miles, strenuous). From here you take the **Eldridge Grade Fire Road** all the way to East Peak. The scenery is as beautiful as the ride is challenging and technical. To make the trip into a loop, turn onto paved **Ridgecrest Boulevard** for a little over four miles. On the right is the **Rock Springs Lagunitas Fire Road.** Take it all the way back to the trailhead. To reach the peak when you are already up on the mountain, consider parking at the Pantoll Ranger Station and taking **Old Stage Grade** north to either Middle Peak or East Peak (6 miles, moderate). You can make the ride into a longer loop by jumping on **Eldridge Grade** at East Peak, taking it to **Wheeler Trail,** where you will have to walk your bike a short distance and then turn right on **E-Koo Fire Road.** After a couple of miles it will intersect with **Old Railroad Grade** (stay right), which will then meet **Old Stage Grade.** Turn left and head down to the trailhead.

Accommodations

It is quite likely that the **West Point Inn** (100 Old Railroad Grade Fire Rd., Mill Valley, 415/388-9955, www.westpointinn.com, Tues.-Sat., adults $50, children $25) has changed very little since it was built in 1904. The only change is perhaps that guests would take the old train to its doorstep, while today they must hike two miles on a dirt road. The inn has no electricity; instead, it is lit by gaslights and warmed by fires in the large fireplaces in the downstairs lounge and parlor, where guests are encouraged to read, play games, and enjoy each other's company. There are seven guest rooms upstairs and five rustic cabins nearby. All guests must bring their own linens, flashlights, and food, which can be prepared in the communal kitchen. One Sunday a month during the summer, the inn hosts a **pancake breakfast** (9am-1pm, adults $10, children $5) that draws local hikers. The wait can be long, but it is a lot of fun.

Also with terrific views, albeit far less rustic, is **Mountain Home Inn** (810 Panoramic Hwy., 415/381-9000, www.mtnhomeinn. com, $195-345), also built during the heyday of the railroad. You don't have to hike in, however; in fact, the innkeepers would prefer that you relax as much as possible. With 10 guest rooms, many with jetted tubs, wood-burning fireplaces, and private decks, it would be hard to exert yourself. If you do feel like leaving your private hideaway, you can opt for a massage, slip downstairs for a complimentary breakfast, or dine on a three-course prix fixe dinner ($38) in the cozy and warmly lit dining room.

Camping

With spectacular views of the Pacific Ocean it's no wonder that the rustic accommodations at **C Steep Ravine** (800/444-7275, www.reserveamerica.com, cabins $100, campsites $25) stay fully booked. On the steep ravine (the name is no exaggeration) there are seven primitive campsites and 10 cabins. The cabins are considered rustic but each comes equipped with a small wood stove, a table, a sleeping platform, and a grill; the campsites are also spare but each has a table, a fire pit, and a food locker. Restrooms and drinking water are nearby. To book either a cabin or a campsite you need to be on the phone at 8am six months before the date you intend to go. The word is out.

If Steep Ravine is full or you want to camp within hiking distance of the top of the mountain, the **Pantoll Campground** (1393 Panoramic Hwy., 415/388-2070, http://mttam. net/activities/camping.html, $25) has 16 sites with drinking water, firewood, and restrooms nearby. Camping here operates on a first-come, first-served basis, paid for at the ranger station, so get here early. The sites are pleasantly removed from the parking lot, which means that once you have gone to the trouble of hauling in all your gear, you will enjoy the quiet of car-free camping.

Food

Is a gourmet meal at the end of a long hike your idea of the perfect end to the perfect day? Luckily, the **Mountain Home Inn** (810 Panoramic Hwy., 415/381-9000, www.mtnhomeinn.com, Wed.-Sun. 11:30am-3pm and 5:30pm-8:30pm, Mon. 5:30pm-8:30pm, prix fixe dinner $38) opens its kitchen to the public. Enjoy a three-course prix fixe dinner of French-California cuisine overlooking the surrounding mountains and mist-filled valleys. Or, if you are spending the day in the Mount Tam area and don't want to pack a lunch, the Mountain Home Inn also offers grilled sandwiches and fresh salads. The **Wine Bar** (Mountain Home Inn, 810 Panoramic Hwy., 415/381-9000, www.mtnhomeinn.com, Wed.-Sun. 3:30pm-8pm, Mon. 3:30pm-7pm) is open between meals. You can nibble on lighter fare such as a local cheese plate, ceviche, or paella while sipping fantastic local wine on the expansive deck.

Information and Services
For more information, contact the volunteer-run **Mount Tamalpais Interpretive Association** (415/258-2410, www.mttam.net). Because the ongoing California state budget crisis has left the Mount Tam's visitors center and ranger station with limited hours, you may be visiting when both are closed, but the state park did manage to set up free Wi-Fi; if you arrive at the park and need information, you can access the Web just 150-200 feet from the ranger station.

Getting There and Around
Panoramic Highway is a long and winding two-lane road across the Mount Tamalpais area and extending all the way to Stinson Beach.

Once upon a time, well-heeled visitors could take a scenic train ride up to and across Mount Tam. Today, you'll probably want to drive up to one of the parking lots, from which you can explore the trails. Take Highway 1 to the Stinson Beach exit, then follow the fairly good signs up the mountain. Turn right at Panoramic Highway at the top of the hill. Follow the road for five winding miles until you reach the Pantoll Ranger Station. To get to the East Peak Visitors Center, take a right on Pantoll Road, and another right on East Ridgecrest

Boulevard. To access the park from Stinson Beach, take a right on Panorama Highway at the T intersection with Highway 1 just south of town.

Bus access to the park is available via route 61 of the **West Marin Stagecoach** (415/226-0855, www.marintransit.org, daily, $2), providing public transit from Stinson Beach or Mill Valley to Mount Tam, dropping and picking visitors up at the Pantoll Ranger Station.

STINSON BEACH
The primary attraction at **Stinson Beach** (415/868-1922, www.nps.gov/goga, daily 9am-close) is the tiny town's namesake: a broad 3.5-mile-long sandy stretch of coastline with weather that's unusually congenial (for Northern California). Although it's as plagued by fog as anywhere else in the Bay Area, on rare clear days Stinson Beach is the favorite destination for San Franciscans seeking some surf and sunshine.

Sports and Recreation
To get out on the water, swing by **Stinson Beach Surf and Kayak** (3605 Hwy. 1, 415/868-2739, www.stinsonbeachsurfandkayak.com, Fri.-Sun. 10am-6pm, $20-40 per day). The owner, Bill, will set you up with a surfboard, kayak, boogie board, or stand up paddleboard. Wetsuits, which you will certainly need, are available. He also offers surf lessons and is happy to give pointers to novices out on the lagoon about the general etiquette of paddling around wildlife. While he keeps regular store hours on weekends and on holiday Mondays, during the week the shop is "on call." This may mean a bit of planning on your part if you are in Stinson Beach during the week; you can call or page him (415/257-1831) and he'll be happy to help you out.

Accommodations
Given its status as a beach resort town, you will find a few inns and motels to stay the night. The **Sandpiper Inn** (1 Marine Way, 415/868-1632, www.sandpiperstinsonbeach.com, $140-210) has six guest rooms and four cabins, and

you can choose between motel-style accommodations with comfortable queen beds, private baths, and gas fireplaces or the four individual redwood cabins, which offer additional privacy, bed space for families, and full kitchens.

Another nice spot is the **Stinson Beach Motel** (3416 Shoreline Hwy. 1, 415/868-1712, www.stinsonbeachmotel.com, $95-225). It features eight vintage-y beach bungalow-style guest rooms that sleep 2-4 guests each. Some guest rooms have substantial kitchenettes; all have private baths, garden views, flat screen TVs, and blue decor. The motel is a great spot to bring the family for a beach vacation.

Food

A few small restaurants dot the town of Stinson Beach, most of which serve seafood. Among the best is the **Sand Dollar Restaurant** (3458 Hwy. 1, 415/868-0434, www.stinsonbeachrestaurant.com, Mon.-Fri. 11:30am-9pm, Sat.-Sun. 10am-9pm, $10-25). This so-called fish joint actually serves more land-based dishes than seafood, but perhaps the fact that the dining room is constructed out of three old barges makes up the difference. In addition to lunch and dinner, the Sand Dollar serves a popular Sunday brunch.

Getting There

Stinson Beach is an unbelievably beautiful place to get to. First, take the Stinson Beach exit off U.S. 101. Follow the Shoreline Highway (Hwy. 1) as it snakes up the hill past the turnoffs for Tennessee Valley, Muir Woods, and Mount Tamalpais State Park. The road will pass through Green Gulch, where produce is grown for the legendary Greens Restaurant in San Francisco; Muir Beach; and eventually along cliffs high above the Pacific. After about five miles, the highway descends into Stinson Beach. Most of the town is strung along the highway, and signs make it easy to navigate to the beach.

So what's the catch with this idyllic recreation spot? As with so many other places in and near large metropolitan areas in California, it's the traffic. You'll quickly experience this problem if you try to drive into Stinson Beach on a sunny weekend day in summer. With only one lane in each direction and a couple of intersections with stop signs, traffic backups that stretch for miles are all too common. Your best bet is to drive in on a weekday or in the evening when everyone else is leaving the beach.

Fortunately, an alternative to driving is **West Marin Stagecoach**'s (415/226-0855, www.marintransit.org, daily, $2) Route 61, a daily bus that runs from Mill Valley into Stinson Beach.

BOLINAS

Situated alongside the Bolinas Lagoon under the wing of Point Reyes, the unincorporated community of Bolinas is one of the North Bay's most idyllic spots. And the town's reclusive residents want it to stay that way: They've been known to steal any road signs indicating how to get to their community from Highway 1. Bolinas is worth a stop for its beach, tide pools, old timey saloon, and renowned art museum—if you can find it.

Bolinas Museum

The **Bolinas Museum** (48 Wharf Rd., 415/868-0330, www.bolinasmuseum.org, Fri. 1pm-5pm, Sat.-Sun. noon-5pm, summer Wed. 4pm-7pm, free) has a rotating gallery that showcases the work of one coastal Marin artist for two months at a time. It also has a fine arts photography exhibit and a history gallery that illuminates the past of Bolinas and coastal Marin.

Agate Beach Park

Offshore of **Agate Beach Park** (end of Elm St., www.marincounty.org/Depts/PK/Divisions/Parks/Agate-Beach, daily dawn-dusk) is Duxbury Reef, one of the largest shale reefs in North America. Onshore is a coastline dotted with tide pools and bird habitats that are ripe for exploration by wildlife lovers.

Smiley's Schooner Saloon

Built back in 1851, **Smiley's Schooner Saloon** (41 Wharf Rd., 415/868-1311, http://smileys-saloon.com, daily 7:30am-2am) has an Old

West feel, a pool table, and live entertainment Thursdays-Saturdays. It's a good place to soak up the eccentric character of Bolinas.

Getting There and Around
To find Bolinas, drive 4.5 miles north on Highway 1 and turn left onto Olema-Bolinas Road, which may be unmarked. Then drive into town. Once in town, street and beach parking can be a challenge, suggesting Bolinas' secret may be out. The town itself is easily and entertainingly walkable.

POINT REYES NATIONAL SEASHORE
A haven for wilderness buffs, the Point Reyes area boasts acres of unspoiled forest and beach country. Expect cool weather even in the summer, but enjoy the lustrous green foliage and spectacular scenery that result. **Point Reyes National Seashore** (1 Bear Valley Rd., 415/464-5100, www.nps.gov/pore, daily dawn-midnight) stretches for miles between Tomales Bay and the Pacific, north from Stinson Beach to the tip of the land at the end of the bay. Dedicated hikers can trek from the bay to the ocean, or from the beach to land's end. The protected lands shelter a range of wildlife. In the marshes and lagoons, a wide variety of birds—including three different species of pelicans—make their nests. Over a thousand elephant seals call these beaches home, while endangered Myrtle's silverspot butterflies can be found in the dunes and grasslands. The pine forests shade shy deer and larger elk.

There are also a number of ranches, dairy farms, and even an oyster farm that still operate inside the park. Grandfathered in at the time the park was created, these sustainable, generations-old family farms give added character and historical depth to Point Reyes. Another remnant of past times is the historic Point Reyes Lighthouse, which is located on the cliffs of the Point Reyes Headlands, a point of land that is supposed to be the windiest place on the West Coast and the second foggiest spot in North America.

The Point Reyes area includes the tiny towns of Olema, Point Reyes Station, and Inverness.

Visitors Centers
The **Bear Valley Visitors Center** (1 Bear Valley Rd., 415/464-5100, Mon.-Fri. 9am-5pm, Sat.-Sun. 8am-5pm) acts as the central visitors center for Point Reyes National Seashore. In addition to maps, fliers, and interpretive exhibits, you can watch a short video introducing the Point Reyes region. You can also talk to the park rangers, either to ask advice or to obtain beach fire permits and backcountry camping permits.

Two other visitors centers are located at different spots in the vast acreage of Point Reyes. The **Ken Patrick Visitors Center** (Drakes Beach, 415/669-1250, Sat.-Sun. 10am-5pm) sits right on the beach in a building made of weathered redwood. Its small museum focuses on the maritime history of the region, and it acts as the host area for the annual Sand Sculpture event held on the beach every Labor Day Sunday.

Finally, the **Historic Lighthouse and Visitors Center** (415/669-1534, Thurs.-Mon. 10am-4:30pm) is the most difficult of the three to access. You must walk about 0.5 miles up a steep hill from the parking lot to get to this visitors center. You'll find the lighthouse right at your feet once you arrive.

Point Reyes Historic Lighthouse
The jagged rocky shores of Point Reyes make for great sightseeing but incredibly dangerous maritime navigation. In 1870 the first lighthouse was constructed on the headlands. Its first-order Fresnel lens threw light far enough for ships to see and avoid the treacherous granite cliffs. Yet the danger remained, and soon after, a lifesaving station was constructed alongside the light station. It wasn't until the 20th century, when a ship-to-shore radio station and newer lifesaving station were put in place, that the Point Reyes shore truly became safer for ships.

The **Point Reyes Historic Lighthouse** (415/669-1534, www.nps.gov/pore, Thurs.-Mon. 10am-4:30pm) still stands today on the

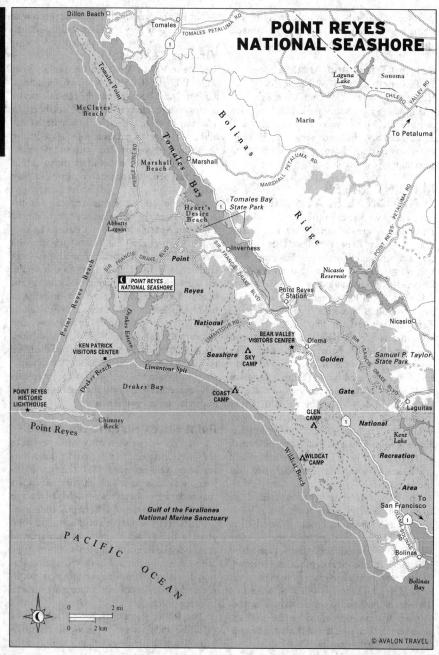

POINT REYES NATIONAL SEASHORE

Dillon Beach

Tomales

TOMALES PETALUMA RD

Laguna Lake

Sonoma

CHILENO VALLEY RD

Tomales Point

McClures Beach

B o l i n a s

Marin

To Petaluma

PIERCE POINT RD

Marshall Beach

Marshall

Tomales Bay

MARSHALL PETALUMA RD

R i d g e

Abbotts Lagoon

Heart's Desire Beach

Tomales Bay State Park

SIR FRANCIS DRAKE BLVD

Inverness

SIR FRANCIS DRAKE BLVD

Point Reyes Beach

POINT REYES NATIONAL SEASHORE

Point

Reyes

Nicasio Reservoir

Point Reyes Station

POINT REYES-PETALUMA RD

Nicasio

National

LIMANTOUR RD

BEAR VALLEY VISITORS CENTER

Olema

SIR FRANCIS DRAKE BLVD

Samuel P. Taylor State Park

KEN PATRICK VISITORS CENTER

Drakes Estero

Seashore

SKY CAMP

Golden

Drakes Beach

Limantour Spit

Drakes Bay

COAST CAMP

Gate

Laguitas

POINT REYES HISTORIC LIGHTHOUSE

GLEN CAMP

National

Chimney Rock

1

Kent Lake

Point Reyes

WILDCAT CAMP

Wildcat Beach

Recreation

Area

To San Francisco

OLEMA-BOLINAS RD

1

Gulf of the Farallones National Marine Sanctuary

Bolinas

Bolinas Bay

P A C I F I C   O C E A N

0   2 mi

0   2 km

the lighthouse at Point Reyes

point past the visitors center, accessed by descending a sometimes treacherous, cold, and windblown flight of over 300 stairs, which often closes to visitors during bad weather for safety reasons. It's worth a visit; the Fresnel lens and original machinery all remain in place, and the adjacent equipment building contains foghorns, air compressors, and other safety implements from decades gone by. Check the website for information about twice-monthly special events when the light is switched on.

Accommodations
OLEMA
The **Point Reyes Seashore Lodge** (10021 Hwy. 1, 415/663-9000, www.pointreyessea-shorelodge.com, $145-295) offers both budget and luxury lodging in its 22 guest rooms and two cottages. Attractive floral patterns mix with clean white walls and attractive wooden accents. All guest rooms have private baths, some with whirlpool tubs, and a couple of suites with special amenities are located away from the main lodge for extra privacy. Outside,

guests can enjoy the attractive gardens with winding brick pathways that roll out to Olema Creek. The Farm House Restaurant, Bar, and Deli adjoin the hotel, providing plenty of food and drink options for the tiny town of Olema.

For something a little quieter, the **Olema Druid's Hall** (9870 Shoreline Hwy./Hwy. 1, 415/663-8727, www.olemadruids.com, $185-385) has only three guest rooms and one cottage. Housed in the 1885 meeting hall of the Druids Association, the inn has a distinct architectural charm, and the surrounding gardens are sculpted with lush flower beds, stands of mature cypresses and pines, and green lawns. Despite the area's reputation for cool nights, you will keep warm with the inn's radiant floor heating while wrapped in the 300-thread-count sheets. Each of the guest rooms is decorated in a style that melds with the Victorian building but is modern enough for any discerning traveler. You can also expect to find a wood-burning fireplace, wireless Internet access, and a minibar. Three of the four offerings also have soaking tubs. All guests can enjoy a complimentary continental breakfast comprised of local ingredients.

POINT REYES STATION
In Point Reyes Station, you can find a guest room and tasty board for a reasonable price at **One Mesa Bed & Breakfast** (1 Mesa Rd., 415/663-8866, www.onemesa.com, $147-230). All three guest rooms have private baths, down comforters, and feather beds, along with included all-day and all-night coffee service. Each guest room is decorated in a different style—most have fireplaces, some have soaking tubs, and all have TVs and VCRs. Guests can make use of the inn's hot tub and enjoy a self-service breakfast on weekdays and a basket of goodies delivered to your door on weekends.

In the heart of Point Reyes Station is the **Point Reyes Station Inn** (11591 Hwy. 1, 415/663-9372, www.pointreyesstationinn.com, $125-225). The five-room inn is light and airy with turn-of-the-20th-century charm. The guest rooms are decorated in heavy antique furnishings that are lightened by the vaulted ceilings, large windows, and glass doors leading to private porches. All but one have fireplaces and private en suite baths. There is a communal hot tub in the garden, and the continental breakfast features eggs from the inn's own chickens and seasonal homegrown fruit.

Lingonberry Farm B&B (12430 Hwy. 1, 415/663-1826, www.lingonberryfarm. com, $145-165) is outfitted in bright, simple Swedish style. Each of the three guest rooms is distinctively decorated in blues, yellows, and crisp whites with trim farm-style furniture and minimalist artwork. All have private baths. Downstairs in the sunny dining area, guests are treated to a breakfast buffet with Swedish and American entrées.

The reason to choose the certified green **Point Reyes Hostel** (1390 Limantour Spit Rd., 415/663-8811, www.norcalhostels.org/ reyes, dorm rooms $24, private rooms $82-120) is for what's next door: Located just off Limantour Road a few miles from the beach, the hostel is steps from fantastic hiking and lush natural scenery. Like most hostels, the accommodations are spare but comfortable. You can pick the überaffordable dorm rooms or opt for one of four private rooms. The hostel has a communal kitchen and three lounge areas, furnished in furniture funky enough to fit in any college-age group house, and there is a place to lock up bicycles.

Located at the west end of Sir Francis Drake Blvd., near the historic Pt. Reyes Lighthouse, the **Drake Beach Café** (1 Drakes Beach, 415/669-1297, www.drakescafe.com, summer Thurs. noon-4pm, Fri.-Sun. 11am-5pm, Mon. noon-4pm, winter and spring Thurs. noon-4pm, Fri.-Sun. 11am-5pm) serves delicious food with an appropriate focus on the local, organic, and sustainable.

INVERNESS

Perhaps the most famous lodging around is **C Manka's Inverness Lodge** (30 Callendar Way, 415/669-1034, www.mankas.com, $285-815). Partially burned down in 2006, the lodge has been rebuilt in the woodsy charm that has made it a favorite of Bay Area weekenders. But Manka's is not so much a lodge as a compound dressed in an oddly ethereal combination of hunting lodge and Arts and Crafts styles. Stay in the lodge, where four upstairs guest rooms are decked out with deep reading chairs, plush beds with tree-limb posts, and antique fixtures. Four similar guest rooms are in the Annex. Two cabins are nearby, and two others are perched on the Inverness Ridge to make the most of the views. All feature large sitting rooms complete with stone fireplaces. Some have private hot tubs or luxurious outdoor showers. Most have private decks overlooking the tree-covered hills. Two more modern lodgings can be found a few miles from the main compound hanging over the edge of Tomales Bay. The Boat House is akin to a small lushly appointed loft with two baths and multiple sleeping spaces. The smaller Boatman's Quarters has equally lovely views of the bay, a private deck, and a fireplace. As you would expect in such a carefully crafted lodge, there is an equally celebrated dining room that features a prix fixe multicourse dinner ($98).

Located in the center of the village of Inverness, **Ten Inverness Way** (10 Inverness Way, 415/669-1648, www.teninvernessway. com, $150-175) shares Manka's love of the Arts and Crafts style but with considerably less ambition. The lodge itself is a 1904 craftsman building, and each of the five guest rooms—named for area hiking trails—is dressed in antiques and colorful quilts that border on country kitsch. Part of the true charm of the place is the way the building's coved ceilings, multi-paned windows, and built-in benches add to the feeling of coziness. In each guest room, you'll also find a queen feather bed and a private bath. In the morning, enjoy coffee, a newspaper, and a full breakfast; evenings see complimentary wine and refreshments with the other guests.

Motel Inverness (12718 Sir Francis Drake Blvd., 415/236-1967, www.motelinverness. com, $99-290) sits handsomely on the bay. Constructed of natural wood with lovely and fanciful flourishes, Motel Inverness is more like a classic lodge than a typical motel. There are guest rooms or more spacious suites available with full kitchens, and all are decorated in light colors with striped bedspreads and minimal fuss. The parking lot abuts the entrance to each room, but the rooms open onto the breathtaking serenity of wetlands bordering the bay. Inside the main lodge is a grand lounge, where you can play pool on the antique pool table, read in front of the great stone fireplace, or relax with a glass of wine on the expansive deck.

Camping

While you would expect the Point Reyes area to abound in camping opportunities, finding a place to pitch a tent is a tall order. The only camping nearby is in the **Point Reyes National Seashore** (www.nps.gov/pore, 415/663-8054, reservations www.recreation.gov, $25), and all are hike-in sites that require reservations months in advance. All campsites have a pit toilet, a water faucet, a picnic table, a charcoal grill, and a food locker.

Sky Camp is the closest to the Bear Valley Visitors Center and is accessed via a trail on Limantour Road. The hike is a moderate 1.4 miles uphill, and the campground includes 11 individual sites and 1 group site. From its location at 1,025 feet, you'll get great views of the Pacific Ocean and Drake's Bay, provided it's not foggy.

Near the end of Limantour Road before the beach is the trailhead for the aptly named **Coast Camp.** While not directly on the beach, the campground is in a quiet valley of coastal scrub and willow trees. It's just 200 yards away from the beach. There are 12 individual campsites and 2 group sites. There are two routes to get here: one that is 1.8 miles uphill along the Laguna and Firelane Trails, and the longer 2.7-mile Coast Trail route, which is flat and considerably easier for carrying camping gear.

The other coastal campground is **Wildcat Camp.** It has five individual sites and three group sites. Like Coast Camp, it is set away from the beach on an open bluff-top meadow. From Bear Valley it is a 5.5-mile hike or an easier but longer 6.7-mile stroll on the Coast Trail.

The most secluded campground is **Glen Camp.** Hidden deep within a valley and protected from ocean winds, the campground is a healthy 4.6 miles from the Bear Valley Trailhead. There are 12 individual sites and no group sites, keeping this a quiet getaway.

Food

OLEMA

Attached to the Point Reyes Seashore Lodge, the **Farm House Restaurant and Bar** (10021 Hwy. 1, 415/663-1264, www.pointreyesseashore.com, Mon.-Thurs. 11:30am-9pm, Fri.-Sun. 11:30am-10pm, $12-29) is the oldest operating business in Olema. In the elegant bright dining room you can enjoy a pleasant range of fresh California cuisine. There is a heavy emphasis on seafood, as you would expect with so many great oyster farms and fishing waters nearby. There are a number of pasta dishes as well as meat-heavy plates such as pork chops, steaks, and roast chicken. You can also get a burger or other classic hot sandwiches if you are looking for a lighter and cheaper meal. There is also a bar menu that features specialty cocktails, locally brewed beer, and oysters prepared half a dozen different ways.

POINT REYES STATION

If you're seeking a rarified organic California meal, you are in the right town. The star of the Point Reyes Station restaurant scene is the **◖ Station House Café** (11180 Hwy. 1, 415/663-1515, www.stationhousecafe.com, Thurs.-Tues. 8am-9pm, $10-17), which is both casual and upscale. Since 1974, long before "organic" and "local" were foodie credos, the Station House Café has been dedicated to serving food with ingredients that reflect the agrarian culture of the area. The restaurant still has the same mission, and the food culture around Point Reyes has gotten even better, making the very reasonably priced California cuisine top-notch. More comfort food than haute cuisine, lots of familiar dishes and fantastic takes on old classics are what you'll find here. Hint: The oyster stew is not to be missed. The dining room is open and unpretentious with large multi-paned windows letting in tons of light.

GRAZING POINT REYES

The Point Reyes food obsession encompasses far more than just restaurants. Local producers take enormous pride in their work, and offer it for sale retail to local cooks and visitors alike. Stopping at one or two local food markets or shops is essential to complete a true Point Reyes experience.

Several oyster farms make their home in Tomales Bay, providing their wares to fine restaurants locally and across the state. The **Hog Island Oyster Co.** (20215 Hwy. 1, 415/663-9218, www.hogislandoysters.com, daily 9am-5pm) is open rain or shine and offers a picnic ground with barbecue grills. (Reservations are required for picnic tables on weekends in summer.) Far from a high-end tourist trap, Hog Island doesn't pretend to be anything other than a working oyster farm. You can buy the goods from a walk-up shack in the midst of warehouses, working buildings, and oyster tanks. If you prefer them raw and completely fresh, a shucker in orange hip-waders stands ready to pry open your jewels then and there. Lemon wedges and a bottle of hot sauce sit carelessly on a folding table that serves as the oyster bar. To take your oysters home, request them packed in ice for a small additional charge.

If you prefer land mammals to shellfish, Point Reyes is like a dream. Both beef and dairy cattle are grazed all over the place – even on legacy-leased parkland. At the **Marin Sun Farms Butcher Shop** (10905 Hwy. 1, Point Reyes Station, 415/663-8997, www.marinsunfarms.com, daily 11am-6pm) you can pick up possibly the best cut of beef you'll ever eat. All Marin Sun Farms cattle are 100 percent grass-fed and humanely (even lovingly) treated. The result is beef that melts like butter and barely requires a knife to cut. Marin Sun also cuts and sells pork, lamb, goat, chicken, and eggs in season; the butcher will be happy to explain meat seasons to you, as well as give you a life history of the meat you're purchasing.

Point Reyes cheeses have become a national phenomenon in top-tier restaurants. To get some of the world's best cheese right from the source, visit the **Cowgirl Creamery** (80 4th St., Point Reyes Station, 415/663-9335, www.cowgirlcreamery.com, Wed.-Sun. 10am-6pm) in Point Reyes Station. It has taken only a little over 10 years for this woman-owned farmhouse cheese factory to become a heavyweight in the artisan cheese world. Though Cowgirl distributes over 200 artisan cheeses from around the world, they deliberately keep their in-house production small – only seven kinds of cheese come from their factory in Point Reyes. They purchase their milk and cream locally, from the nearby Straus Family Creamery. Want to go behind the scenes of this unusual cheesemaking haven? Make a reservation for the weekly tour on Fridays at 11:30am and 3pm.

Finally, for the best fruits and veggies the region has to offer, hit one of the weekly local farmers markets. Point Reyes Station holds its market at **Toby's** (11250 Hwy. 1, 415/663-1223, www.tobysfeedbarn.com, Sat. 9am-1pm). You can also pick up botanical bath products, locally grown and spun wool, and handmade jewelry and crafts.

On the left side of the restaurant is a full bar, where bartenders deftly mix cocktails and pour beer and glasses of wine. There is also an outside patio dripping with wisteria.

Osterina Stellina (11285 Hwy. 1, 415/663-9988, http://osteriastellina.com, daily 11:30am-2:30pm and 5pm-9pm, $24-44) has brought white-tablecloth dining to Point Reyes Station. The Italian eatery has plenty of local items on the menu prepared in a rustic yet elegant Mediterranean fashion. There are thin-crust pizzas, robust pastas with seafood and organic vegetables, and hearty main dishes of pan roasted pork loin and whole roasted local sole. Lunch is a bit more scaled down, but not by much. The wine list is a nice blend of Italian and California wines. Nearly all are available by the glass, but for a price.

Right off Highway 1 along Tomales Bay is the unassuming **Point Reyes Vineyard** (12700 Hwy. 1, 415/663-1011, www.ptreyesvineyard-inn.com, mid-Nov.-May Sat.-Sun. 11am-5pm,

June-mid-Nov. Fri.-Mon. 11am-5pm, and by appointment). This small winery pours some surprisingly tasty vintages. Staff can tell you about the wines as well as direct you to their favorite local restaurants and recreation spots.

If you need a *real* drink (and a bit of local color), slip through the swinging doors of the **Old Western Saloon** (11201 Hwy. 1, 415/663-1661, daily 10am-2am). At this crusty old West Marin haunt you'll see ranchers yukking it up with park rangers, young and old, longtime natives, and recent transplants. It's the place where everyone goes, despite its divey appearance. Live music goes down on Friday and Saturday nights.

Traveling out of Point Reyes Station north along the bay, a stop at **Nick's Cove** (23240 Hwy. 1, 415/663-1033, www.nickscove.com, Mon.-Fri. 11am-9pm, Sat.-Sun. 10am-9pm, $14-29) may be in order. Overlooking the bay in an expansive weathered redwood building, Nick's Cove has recently been revamped. Its combination of charm, relaxed atmosphere, and good-quality classic American food with a slightly modern twist has made this a popular stop for folks passing though the area. The menu is well designed to accommodate all types of diners, from those who want a light nibble with their Bloody Mary to those eager for a high-end meal. They have an impressive selection of raw and cooked oyster platters. Out back is a long deck and a boathouse, perfect to explore with the little ones.

There is no better place to stock a picnic basket than the **Bovine Bakery** (11315 Hwy. 1, 415/663-9420, http://thebovinebakery.wordpress.com, Mon.-Fri. 6:30am-5pm, Sat.-Sun. 7am-5pm), where you can pick up a cup of coffee, loaves of bread, cookies, pizza, quiche, and salads.

Around the corner is **Cowgirl Creamery** (80 4th St., 415/663-9335, www.cowgirlcreamery.com, Wed.-Sun. 10am-6pm), which produces the best cheese in the Bay Area. All of their cheese is made on-site in the French Brie style. Tours of the facility are available Friday mornings by appointment only. At the retail shop inside, you can pick up a stinky but oh-so-good round of Red Hawk, the milder Mount Tam and Pierce Point, or the subtle and seasonal St. Pat's. The store also sells other gourmet treats, from jams to crackers and even pasta and some sandwiches.

The **Tomales Bay Oyster Co.** (15479 Hwy. 1, 415/663-1242, http://tomalesbayoysters.com, Mon.-Fri. 9am-5pm, Sat.-Sun. 8am-6pm) is a low-key affair where you can buy a wide selection of oysters, clams, and mussels in an open air market a few feet from the bay where they are harvested. The smaller oysters tend to be sweeter, but the bigger, meatier ones better lend themselves to barbecuing. And if that is what you have in mind, you're in luck: Tomales Bay Oyster Company is set up with grills and picnic tables ready to host your oyster party. You can bring in whatever other food and drink you see fit, and an afternoon spent here is always a good time.

Dining around the Bay Area, you may have seen **Hog Island** (20215 Hwy. 1, 415/663-9218, www.hogislandoysters.com, daily 9am-5pm) oysters appear on many upscale menus. They are the big boys in the oyster world around here and also have an open-air stand where you can buy and barbecue oysters. While they have excellent oysters, Hog Island gets insanely busy on weekends as many Bay Area folks come to get their raw-oyster fix. Parking can be tricky, and unless you get here really early, you'll have to wait to get a grill and picnic table. To reserve a table, call 415/663-9218 Ext. 255 or email farm@hogislandoysters.com.

INVERNESS

Vladimir's Czechoslovakian Restaurant (12785 Sir Francis Drake Blvd., 415/669-1021, Wed.-Sun. noon-9pm, Tues. 2pm-9pm, prix fixe dinner $27, prix fixe lunch $17, cash only) is a favorite of both locals and visitors. Enter the cool old dining room, complete with stuffed deer heads on the walls, and take a seat. The late Vladimir, who owned the restaurant, could be rude one minute and the next hand you the best pint of beer you ever had. After his death, the restaurant went to his daughter, and the rest of his family still works here, so the atmosphere is the same. The mugs of beer are generous, and the kitchen produces a prix fixe meal of serious Czech food: borscht, rabbit, duck, and all manner of things that might seem heavy or strange to the American palate—but they're delicious. And for those not quite ready to brave Eastern European cuisine, the bar menu offers Americanized concessions such as burgers and quesadillas. Vladimir's is very serious about its no-children policy, which makes it a perfect retreat for romantic couples. Also note that it is cash only.

A great convenient coffee stop is the **Busy Bee Bakery** (12301 Sir Francis Drake Blvd., 415/663-9496, Mon. and Thurs.-Fri. 7:30am-4pm, Sat.-Sun. 8am-5pm). This owner-run shop offers good espresso drinks, delectable homemade (in the back of the shop) pastries, and some lovely photo prints done by the owner.

Priscilla's (12781 Sir Francis Drake Blvd., 415/669-1244, Wed.-Mon. 11am-8pm, $9-16) doses out mainstream fare for very reasonable prices. The charming board-and-bat building also houses a gift store and the post office. The restaurant has an outdoor deck covered just enough to keep you from getting burned while enjoying a sunny afternoon. Both beer and wine are available, and the menu includes salads, hot sandwiches, and fried local oysters.

If you want some of the region's famed oysters, take a beautiful drive out to **Drakes Bay Oyster Co.** (17171 Sir Francis Drake Blvd., 415/669-1149, www.drakesbayoyster.com, daily 8:30am-4:30pm), located in Point Reyes National Seashore. One of the agrarian businesses grandfathered into the park, the farm is located at the edge of Drake's Estero; it's stunning and well worth the drive, and so are the oysters. They may be muddier than their Tomales Bay counterparts, but many argue that they are superior in flavor. This is a small-scale family operation with a few grills and picnic benches. The friendly staff will set you up with enough ice to ensure a spoil-free trip home.

Information and Services

The Point Reyes area tends toward the remote and charmingly rural—there's not much out in the wilderness here. You can get gas only in Point Reyes Station. There are full-service grocery stores in Point Reyes Station (Palace Market) and in Inverness (the aptly named Inverness store). For any other shopping needs, the biggest nearby towns are Novato and Petaluma. The tiny **West Marin Chamber of Commerce** (Point Reyes Station, 415/663-9232, www.pointreyes.org, Fri.-Sun. 11am-4pm) can provide information on the region.

Cell phones do not work in most parts of Point Reyes National Seashore and the adjoining parklands. Check with your inn or hotel for information about Internet access. There is a **post office** (11260 Hwy. 1, 415/663-1305) in the town of Point Reyes Station, and the closest hospital is **Novato Community Hospital** (180 Rowland Way, Novato, 415/209-1300, www.novatocommunity.org).

Getting There and Around

Point Reyes is only about an hour north of San Francisco by car, but getting here can be quite a drive for newcomers. From the Golden Gate Bridge, take U.S. 101 north to just south of San Rafael. Take the Sir Francis Drake Boulevard exit toward San Anselmo. Follow Sir Francis Drake Boulevard west for 20 miles to the small town of Olema and Highway 1. At the intersection with Highway 1, turn right (north) to Point Reyes Station and the Bear Valley Visitors Center.

A slower but more scenic route follows Highway 1 into Point Reyes National Seashore and provides access to the trails near Bolinas in the southern portion of the park. From the Golden Gate Bridge, take U.S. 101 north to the Mill Valley/Stinson Beach exit. Follow the road under the freeway, and when the road splits at the stoplight, turn left onto Shoreline Highway (Hwy. 1). Follow Shoreline Highway, and do not turn right onto Panoramic Highway, for almost 30 miles through Stinson Beach and past Bolinas Lagoon to the coast. From the lagoon, it's 11 miles north to Point Reyes Station. Expect twists, turns, and generally slow going as you approach Point Reyes.

East Bay

The East Bay is unique not only because of its ethnic and economic diversity but for the way its divergent groups come together, making it feel like a true melting pot. In addition to the world-class University of California, Berkeley, the Oakland Museum of California gives the museums across the Bay a run for their money. Big music names are drawn to Berkeley's Greek Theater and Oakland's recently reopened Fox Theatre, and nearly every old neighborhood has a classic movie house showing art-house and foreign flicks, an erudite independent bookstore, and multiple cafés where you can hear patrons arguing over ideas big and small. Since the East Bay is farther form the Pacific, the region often receives sunny days when nearby San Francisco is socked in with fog.

BERKELEY

There's no place quite like Berkeley. While the Haight in San Francisco nurtured the creative side of the 1960s flower children, Berkeley brought out their fire. The town has long been known for its radical, liberal, progressive activism. The youthful urban culture tends to revolve around the University of California, Berkeley. Yet well-heeled foodies also flock to town to sample some of the finest cuisine in Northern California.

University of California, Berkeley

Berkeley is a college town, and fittingly the **University of California, Berkeley** (www.berkeley.edu) offers the most interesting places to go and things to see. If your visit to the area includes your teenagers, think about taking a free guided **campus tour** (510/642-5215, www.berkeley.edu, Mon.-Sat. 10am, Sun. 1pm, by reservation only) to acquaint them with the university and all it has to offer. To get a great view of the campus from above, take an elevator ride up the **Campanile** (Mon.-Fri. 10am-3:45pm, Sat. 10am-4:45pm, Sun. 10am-1:30pm and 3pm-4:45pm, adults $2, seniors and ages 4-17 $1, under age 4 free), formally

called Sather Tower. If you prefer, you can wander around campus on your own, discovering the halls where students live and learn; the newly renovated stadium, which is listed in the National Register of Historic Places; and architectural details such as Sather Gate and South Hall, built in 1873. Or stop in at the **Lawrence Hall of Science** (1 Centennial Dr., 510/642-5132, www.lawrencehallofscience.org, daily 10am-5pm, adults $12, seniors and students $9, ages 3-6 $6, under age 3 free) for a look at the latest exhibits and interactive displays.

Also on campus is the **University of California Botanical Garden** (200 Centennial Dr., 510/643-2755, http://botanicalgarden.berkeley.edu, daily 9am-5pm, adults $10, seniors $8, ages 13-17 $5, ages 5-12 $2, under age 5 free), an immense space with an astounding array of wild plants from around the world. Botany buffs love to spend hours in this place, studying and examining plants outdoors, in the greenhouses, and in the arid house (a habitat for plants requiring extremely hot and dry conditions). Others just come to amble through the peaceful plantings and perhaps stop to sniff a flower or two. You can see over 1,000 different kinds of sunflowers, nearly 2,500 types of cacti, thousands of native California plants, and hundreds of rare and endangered plants collected from around the world.

Entertainment and Events

There's a reasonable variety of evening entertainment to be had in Berkeley. The major regional theater is the **Berkeley Repertory Theatre** (2025 Addison St., 510/647-2949, www.berkeleyrep.org, Tues.-Sun., ticket prices vary). Appropriate to its hometown, the Berkeley Rep puts on several unusual shows from world premieres of edgy new works to totally different takes on old favorites. Recent offerings have included an adaptation of Homer's *Iliad* and the cross-cultural comedy *Chinglish*.

Some of the best entertainment in Berkeley is at the live music venues. The **Starry Plough**

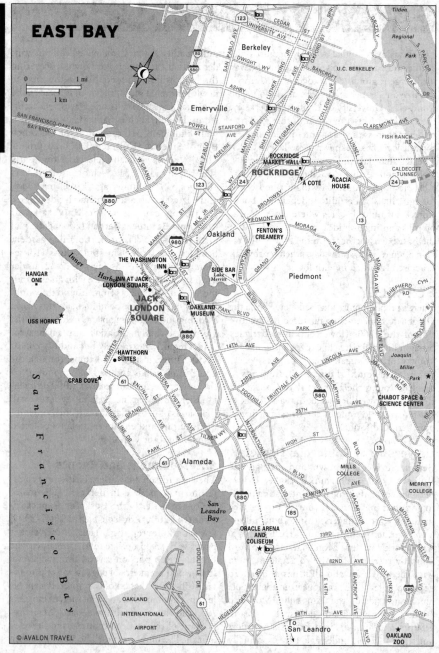

EAST BAY

© AVALON TRAVEL

(3101 Shattuck Ave., 510/841-2082, www. starryploughpub.com, daily 4pm-2am) is an Irish pub with a smallish stage setup. Fabulous Celtic rock groups, folk musicians, and indie bands play here almost every day of the week. Despite lacking a formal dance floor, dedicated fans find ways to create an impromptu space to move to their favorite bands. Every Wednesday night instead of music you'll find the famed Berkeley Poetry Slam—there's nothing like it. Hungry music and spoken-word fans can order a full meal from the kitchen, while the thirsty can quaff a pint or two of Guinness while they sit back and watch the stage.

In Berkeley, the big-name acts come to the **Greek Theater** (2001 Gayley Rd., 800/745-3000, www.apeconcerts.com). This outdoor amphitheater, constructed in the classic Greek style, sits on the UC Berkeley campus. Expect to see top-tier performers playing the Greek, including artists such as Bob Dylan, Wilco, and Gotye, with a view of the bay in the background.

Shopping

Berkeley's citizens grow fierce at the very thought of big chain stores invading their precious downtown area. A few have succeeded, but you'll still find a variety of funky independent shops on **Telegraph Avenue** (between the UC campus and Parker Ave.). One of the best bookstores in the area is **Shakespeare & Co.** (2499 Telegraph Ave., 510/841-8916, http:// shakespeareandcobooks.tumblr.com, Mon.-Thurs. 10am-8pm, Fri.-Sat. 10am-9pm, Sun. 11am-8pm). This new-and-used store definitely has an old-school vibe, complete with the dust and the semi-organized shelves and the musty smell. True bibliophiles can spend hours browsing for treasures.

Moe's Books (2476 Telegraph Ave., 510/849-2087, http://moesbooks.com, daily 10am-10pm) is another Berkeley institution. Also a new-and-used bookstore, Moe's has a newer vibe, including an online retail presence, with lots of hip up-to-date titles. Moe's also attracts literary talent to read and give talks for its regular active reading series. If you drop in on a random Thursday you may get to see Jonathan Lethem, Dave Eggers, or Lawrence Ferlinghetti.

The best Berkeley shopping mall is the revitalized **4th Street** (www.fourthstreetshop. com) between Delaware Street and University Avenue. Here in this once-shady part of town, scores of stores have set up shop and have created a slightly upscale shopping district. You won't find much in the way of large national chains (except for Anthropologie, Apple, and Crate and Barrel), but there are also smaller retailers like Sur La Table and Papyrus. **The Gardener** (1836 4th St., 510/548-4545, www. thegardener.com, Mon.-Sat. 10am-6pm, Sun. 11am-6pm) stocks inspired treasures for your home and garden, including beautifully crafted gardening tools, salad bowls made from unique and reclaimed wood, luscious soaps, and sweet knickknacks to beautify your home. For a bit of whimsy, step into **Castle in the Air** (1805 4th St., 510/204-9801, www.castleintheair. biz, Mon.-Sat. 10am-6pm, Sun. 11am-6pm) for specialty pens, stationery, and notebooks as well as quirky gifts, cards, and art books. **Books Inc.** (1760 4th St., 510/525-7777, Sun.-Thurs. 9:30am-7pm, Fri.-Sat. 9:30am-8pm) is the local independent bookstore with special events and readings many nights.

Sports and Recreation
TILDEN REGIONAL PARK

Tilden Regional Park (Grizzly Peak Blvd., 888/327-2757, www.ebparks.org, daily 5am-10pm) covers the ridge directly above Berkeley. Within its more than 2,000 acres, the park has a celebrated botanical garden, the swimmable Lake Anza and its sandy beaches, an antique carousel, and miniature steam trains, perfect to thrill the little ones. But aside from the attractions, Tilden also offers scores of hiking and mountain biking trails that, except for the breathtaking views of the Bay Area, almost convince you that you are in absolute wilderness. And while this isn't really wilderness, taking a trail map is advisable, as multiple trails crisscross one another, allowing for more adventure but also potential confusion.

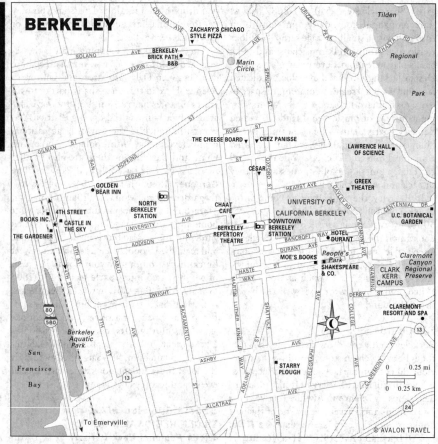

For a simple stroll, consider taking the **Jewel Lake Nature Trail** (1 mile, easy). Located in the Nature Area of the park, generally a quiet area where no dogs are allowed, you'll need to park at the trailhead at the intersection of Central Park Drive and Canon Drive, near the Little Farm and Environmental Education Center. From the parking lot, the trail heads north along Wildcat Creek and out to Jewel Lake. You won't gain much elevation, and although there are exposed patches, the trail is mostly lush and leafy, surrounded by bay laurels, blackberries, and buckeye trees.

For a more rigorous climb, the **Wildcat Peak Loop** (3.5 miles, moderate) leaves from the same trailhead behind the Environmental Education Center. Take **Laurel Canyon Trail** through eucalypti and California bay laurels up through the canyon, which is a gentle grade most of the way. The trail then turns left toward the Rotary Peace Grove and on to Wildcat Peak (1,211 ft.). From the stony vista, you'll be able to see the Golden Gate Bridge, San Pablo Bay, and Mount Diablo, depending on which direction you're facing. To get back down the mountain, take **Wildcat Peak Trail** for about one mile. You'll hit **Jewel Lake Nature Trail.** Turn left, and it will take you back to the trailhead.

If you want to spend some time on the **Bay Area Ridge Trail** (3.5 miles, moderate), a pleasant loop starts at the Quarry Trailhead off Wildcat Canyon Road. Take **Wildcat Canyon Trail** to **Seaview Trail** and turn right. After some time, the trail changes names to **East Bay Skyline National Trail** and **Bay Area Ridge Trail.** At **Big Springs Trail,** take a right back down the mountain. You'll come to a parking lot, but the trail continues on the other side. After nearly one mile, take a left on **Quarry Trail;** it will take you back to the parking lot.

Tilden offers a great many roads and trails for cyclists. The paved roads snaking through the park (Wildcat Canyon Rd., Grizzly Peak Blvd., and South Park Dr.) twist and turn while gaining and losing enough elevation to keep any cyclist busy. As for mountain biking, many of the big trails are shared with hikers. The Bay Area Ridge, Meadows Canyon, and Big Springs Trails are some of the most popular.

WILDCAT CANYON REGIONAL PARK
North of Tilden, the equally large **Wildcat Canyon Regional Park** (5755 Mcbryde Ave., Richmond, 510/544-3092, www.ebparks.org, daily sunrise-sunset) is filled with wide fire roads, all of which are open to cyclists. **Nimitz Way** is a paved trail along the ridgeline that is popular with cyclists young and old. **Harvey Canyon Trail** is a single-track trail also open to cyclists that descends from Nimitz Way down to Wildcat Creek. The only significant restriction for cyclists is that access via the south end of the park is only through the Tilden Nature Area, which allows limited bicycle access. The only route from the south starts at the Little Farm and Environmental Education Center. Bicycles are only permitted on Loop Road, which at Jewel Lake connects with Wildcat Creek Trail.

Wildcat Canyon has fewer trails than Tilden, but it is quieter, and the trails traverse a more challenging topography and allow for longer treks. A healthy loop (7 miles, moderate-strenuous) that allows you to see most of the park and some ridge-top views begins at the Alvarado Trailhead at the north end of the park. Start by taking **Wildcat Creek Trail** to **Harvey Canyon Trail,** which ascends sharply to the ridge. At the top you'll come to the paved **Nimitz Way.** After nearly one mile, continue straight (Nimitz Way veers slightly right) on **San Pablo Ridge Trail** until **Belgium Trail,** and turn left. This trail leads back down to the trailhead.

Accommodations
Offering great value for surprisingly low rates, the **Golden Bear Inn** (1620 San Pablo Ave., 510/525-6770, www.goldenbearinn.com, $100-200) has myriad small unique touches that make it special among budget motels. It's a family-friendly place where parents can rent an inexpensive guest room with two twin beds in a separate bedroom, providing privacy and relaxation for everyone. There is even a cottage available that has two bedrooms, a living room, and a full kitchen for those looking for a longer stay. Cute guest rooms are nicely decorated and have TVs and wireless Internet access. Restaurants and attractions cluster comfortably nearby.

Book a room at the **Berkeley Brick Path Bed & Breakfast** (1805 Marin Ave., 510/524-4277, www.thebrickpath.com, $170-215). The garden is the pride of this inn, and you can stroll down the namesake brick path among the lush greenery and gorgeous flowers, take a seat out on the patio to enjoy your breakfast, or sip an afternoon glass of wine in the gazebo. Each of the three guest rooms has a unique style: one with a brick fireplace, one with a huge whirlpool tub, and the East-West cottage with a full kitchen and private entrance.

The **Hotel Durant** (2600 Durant St., 510/845-8981, www.hoteldurant.com, $160-209) has it all: location, location, views, and location. If you can, get a guest room on the upper floors to take in a view of Oakland, San Francisco, or the Bay. All rooms have free Wi-Fi and coffee makers. From the lobby, you can walk to the university, Telegraph Avenue, and the Elmwood shopping district.

Since 1915, the **Claremont Resort and Spa** (41 Tunnel Rd., 510/843-3000, www.claremontresort.com, $229-359) has catered to rich and famous East Bay visitors. No two of the 279 elegantly furnished guest rooms look quite the same, so you'll have a unique experience even in this large resort hotel. The guest rooms may be plush, but the real focus at the Claremont is fitness and pampering. A full-fledged health club, complete with yoga, Pilates, and spinning classes, takes up part of the huge complex. And the full-service spa, which offers all the current popular body treatments plus aesthetic services, finds favor with visitors and locals alike. The two outdoor pools offer an opportunity to lounge in the East Bay sun.

Food
CASUAL DINING

A downscale ethnic enclave that is well worth a visit is the **Chaat Café** (1902 University Ave., 510/845-1431, www.chaatcafes.com, Sun.-Thurs. 11:30am-9:15pm, Fri.-Sat. 11:30am-9:30pm, $10), which offers spicy Indian cuisine for the right price. This local Bay Area chain serves *chaat* (small plates and appetizers), of course, and you can also get a meaty curry, a tandoori dish, stuffed naan, and more. Although you'll find a few vegetarian specialties on the menu, this particular Indian place sticks more to the meat-eating tradition.

Thin-crust wood-fired pizzas are all the rage among Bay Area foodies, but a trip to the north end of Berkeley to savor **Zachary's Chicago Style Pizza** (1853 Solano Ave., 510/525-5950, www.zacharys.com, Sun.-Thurs. 11am-9:30pm, Fri.-Sat. 11am-10:30pm, $20) is well worth the effort. Their deep-dish cornmeal crust pies come with the standard Italian toppings (pepperoni, sausage, green peppers, mushrooms), or you can opt for the more inventive offerings such as barbecue chicken and Mexican chorizo. But don't worry, all pizzas come slathered in tomato sauce to complete the authentic Chicago style. You can even get a thin-crust pizza, if that is what truly calls to you. Be aware that this small old-school pizzeria fills up quickly, especially on weekend nights. Luckily, if there is a long wait, you can put in your order when you put in your name. Your pizza might make it to your table as you finally sit down to eat.

Another popular place for a pie is **The Cheese Board** (1504 Shattuck Ave., 510/549-3183, http://cheeseboardcollective.coop, Tues.-Sat. 11:30am-3pm and 4:30pm-8pm). A cheese shop and bakery, The Cheese Board serves just one kind of pizza a day, sometimes utilizing unique ingredients like roasted corn, leeks, and limes.

FINE DINING

The very best fine-dining venue, and Alice Waters's baby, is ◖ **Chez Panisse** (1517 Shattuck Ave., restaurant 510/548-5525, café 510/548-5049, www.chezpanisse.com, restaurant prix fixe $85, café $10-30). If you plan to dine in the restaurant at Chez Panisse, you need to make your reservations early and possibly plan your entire trip to Berkeley around the date on which you get a table. You can make a dinner reservation up to one month in advance. And no, we're not exaggerating. The desk takes phone calls 9am-9:30pm Monday-Saturday and a $25 deposit is required. You'll get the chance to enjoy some of the best cuisine that's ever graced a plate in Berkeley or anywhere else. Waters and her successors create French-California dishes at the cutting edge of current trends—Waters doesn't follow trends, she sets them.

Upstairs, the café offers food that's a bit more casual but just as good as the rarified dining room downstairs. It's much easier to get a reservation in the bustling, energetic café than the restaurant, and the casual atmosphere is less intimidating for diners who are new to all this California haute cuisine excess.

Also in north Berkeley, **César** (1515 Shattuck Ave., 510/883-0222, http://cesar-berkeley.com, daily noon-midnight, $30) is a refreshingly modern tapas bar started by three Chez Panisse alumni. As tapas implies, the menu is geared toward small-plate Spanish cuisine, but many of the dishes, such as lamb chops with lentils and steak with caramelized red onions, plus all the *bocadillos* (fresh Spanish-style sandwiches), could stand in for a modest entrée. The bright indoor-outdoor space also lends itself to enjoying one of the many Spanish and California wines or the classic and inventive collection of cocktails.

Information and Services

Newcomers to Berkeley can start at the **Visitors Information Center** (2030 Addison St., 510/549-7040, http://visitberkeley.com, Mon.-Fri. 9am-5pm). You can read about the goings on in Berkeley in the *Daily Californian* (www.dailycal.org). For live entertainment listings and reviews, check out the free *East Bay Express* (www.eastbayexpress.com) published once a week.

As a major metropolitan area, you'll find most services that you need in Berkeley. ATMs for major banks appear on Shattuck and Telegraph Avenues, and near all the major heavily trafficked areas. Just be wary using ATMs, especially after dark. There are two convenient **post offices** (1521 Shattuck Ave.; 2515 Durant Ave., www.usps.com).

For medical assistance, the **Alta Bates Summit Medical Center** (2450 Ashby Ave., 510/204-4444, www.altabatessummit.org) has a 24-hour emergency room.

OAKLAND

Oakland is the biggest city in the East Bay, and although its reputation hasn't always been perfect (and travelers should probably stay in the popular visitor areas), today a great deal of downtown urban renewal has made it a visitor-friendly place with plenty of attractions, accommodations, and good food.

Oakland Museum

The **Oakland Museum of California** (1000 Oak St., 510/318-8400, www.museumca.org, Wed.-Sun. 11am-5pm, adults $12, students and seniors $9, children ages 9-17 $6, children under 8 free, parking $1 per hour) has undergone a renovation that has launched it into the stratosphere of must-see museums. Its uniquely multidisciplinary approach tells California's story through art, history, and science. Within its modernist concrete walls you'll be able to see Thiebaud's and Diebenkorn's take on the urban California landscape, a rare

and authentic Ohlone basket, home furnishings from elite homes of California's early days, and a casting of a once-endemic mastodon. The museum also hosts special theme-based exhibits that compliment its three-pronged approach. You may stumble into one celebrating the social consciousness of street art, a video installation exploring life as a black man in the United States, or retrospectives of the comic-book artist Daniel Clowes or the jewelry maker Margaret de Patta. While it may seem that anything goes at the Oakland Museum, the one caveat is that it must somehow reflect the character of California. Like all good museums, this one has a café, the Blue Oak, which serves wine, espresso, and a selection of salads and sandwiches.

Chabot Space and Science Center

One of the most spectacular sights in the East Bay, **Chabot Space and Science Center** (10000 Skyline Blvd., 510/336-7300, www. chabotspace.org, summer Sun. and Tues.-Thurs. 10am-5pm, Fri.-Sat. 10am-10pm, fall-spring Sun. and Wed.-Thurs. 10am-5pm, Fri.-Sat. 10am-10pm, adults $16, students and seniors $13, youths $12) makes science and space super cool. Up in the Oakland Hills, the Chabot complex includes observatories, a planetarium, a museum, and the Megadome theater, all open to the public (most Bay Area observatory telescopes are private). Unlike the other science museums in the area, which focus mainly on life on earth, Chabot focuses on the life *of* earth and the rest of the universe. You and your family can create your own solar system in an interactive exhibit, ride a space shuttle in the Megadome, and check out Saturn's rings through some of the highest quality telescopes on the West Coast. If your visit runs long, grab a bite to eat and a cup of coffee at the on-site Celestial Café.

Oakland Zoo

For a day with creatures of the land, go to the **Oakland Zoo** (9777 Golf Links Rd., 510/632-9525, www.oaklandzoo.org, summer Mon.-Fri. 10am-4pm, Sat.-Sun. 10am-5:30pm, fall-spring daily 10am-4pm, adults $13.75, youths and seniors $9.75, under age 2 free), where you'll discover an astounding 660 different types of amphibians, mammals, reptiles, and birds living in humane and well-maintained enclosures around the lush and beautiful grounds. There are children's rides, including a carousel, a roller coaster, and a train to keep the excitement high.

Entertainment and Events
BARS
Oakland offers a range of drinking options, from dive bars to fancy establishments where "mixologists" create cocktails with small batch liquors and homemade syrups. But no place in Oakland has been serving spirits or beers longer than **Heinhold's First and Last Chance** (48 Webster St. in Jack London Square, 510/839-6761, http://heinolds.com, Fri.-Sat. noon-12:30am, Sun. noon-Midnight, Mon. 2pm-11pm, Tues.-Thurs. noon-11pm). Surrounded by an ocean of modern development, this small wooden shack was constructed from the wood of a whaling ship in 1883 and still uses its original gaslights for illumination. It's where author Jack London wrote (and drank); it's referenced multiple times in his novel *John Barleycorn.* You'll also notice that the floor and bar tilt at an unusual angle, a result of the 1906 earthquake.

Located downtown in a Victorian building dating to the 1870s, **The Trappist** (460 8th St., 510/238-2900, Sun.-Thurs. noon-midnight, Fri.-Sat. noon-1am) is the place for Belgian beer fans. The rotating menu features 25 beers on tap and 100 bottled beers.

Sidebar (542 Grand Ave., 510/452-9500, http://sidebar-oakland.com, Mon.-Thurs. 11:30am-10pm, Fri. 11:30am-10:30pm, Sat. 4pm-10:30pm) serves delicious throwback cocktails in a sleek bar and restaurant right on Lake Merritt.

LIVE MUSIC
You can find some good live music in Oakland. Perhaps the best-known venue is **Yoshi's** (510 Embarcadero W., 510/238-9200, www.yoshis.

com, Mon.-Thurs. 5:30pm-9pm, Fri.-Sat. 5:30pm-10pm, Sun. 5pm-9pm, shows daily 8pm and 10pm). With a sushi restaurant in one room and the legendary jazz club next door, it's possible to enjoy the sushi without attending the concert, or vice versa. If you're a dinner patron, it's a very good idea to make reservations for the show and claim a seat before you sit down for your meal. Performers at Yoshi's have included Otis Taylor and Kurt Elling.

The renovated **Fox Theater** (1807 Telegraph Ave., 510/302-2250, www.thefoxoakland.com) draws music fans from San Francisco to the East Bay to watch national touring bands in a historic theater. Originally opened in 1928 and closed for nearly 40 years, it was designed in the Moorish style in favor during the decade of the flapper. The theater is now in league with some of the more venerated venues across the Bay like the Fillmore, Warfield, and Great American Music Hall. Recent acts in this relatively intimate venue have included Animal Collective, Melissa Etheridge, and New Order.

Ballroom dancers from all around the Bay Area gather in Oakland on a regular basis to attend the famous **Ye Gaskell Occasional Dance Society** ball (1547 Lakeside Dr., www.gaskellball.com, check website for schedule, $20/ball, $10/dance class). This fabulous fancy-dress event encourages everybody to wear their finest (from any era from 1800 through today, but Victorian is encouraged) to create a picture of beauty swirling around the dance floor. You don't need to be an accomplished dancer to enjoy Gaskell's: Dance classes are offered during the afternoon before the ball, and a quick brush-up takes place before the official opening dance—always a Viennese waltz.

Shopping
Jack London Square (www.jacklondonsquare. com), down on Oakland's surprisingly pretty waterfront, attracts a bustling crowd of visitors and locals who've come to eat, catch a movie, and shop. The absolute best time to shop is during the weekly farmers market (Sun. 9am-2pm). In addition to picking up great local food, including bread, pastries, fruits, and

vegetables, you can enjoy cooking demonstrations, live music, and free yoga on the green.

For more local specialized shops with a neighborhood feel, head to **Rockridge** (College Ave. between Alcatraz Ave. and 51st St.). Foodies will want to explore epicurean **Rockridge Market Hall** (5655 College Ave., 510/250-6000, http://rockridgemarkethall.com, Mon.-Fri. 9am-8pm, Sat. 9am-7pm, Sun. 10am-6pm), where multiple gourmet shops share one roof. Inside the brick building, you'll find a coffee roaster, a bakery, a fresh pasta shop, a fish market, a butcher, wine, and flowers. Every store is known for its adherence to the "eat local" ethos and for its quality. Nearby, bookworms can get their fix at well-regarded and independent **Diesel Bookstore** (5433 College Ave., 510/653-9965, www.diesel-bookstore.com, Mon.-Thurs. 10am-9pm, Fri.-Sat. 10am-10pm, Sun. 10am-6pm).

The **Piedmont Avenue District** is an old Oakland neighborhood with a historic movie theater and mom-and-pop stores. **Phillipa**

Roberts Jewelry (4176 Piedmont Ave., 510/655-0656, www.philipparoberts.com, Mon.-Sat. 10am-6pm, Sun. 11am-5pm) is a charming jewelry and gift store owned and operated by a local jewelry maker. While she stocks an eclectic assortment of housewares and gifts, her handmade jewelry, made largely from silver and semiprecious stones in simple elegant designs, are the real treat. **Spectator Books** (4163 Piedmont Ave., 510/653-7300, www.spectatorbooks.com, Sun.-Thurs. 11am-8pm, Fri. 11am-9pm, Sat. 11am-10pm) specializes in new, used, and rare books. The multiple rooms, stacked high with disheveled books, are a bibliophile's delight.

Sports and Recreation

The jewel of Oakland is **Lake Merritt** (650 Bellevue Ave., 510/238-7275). Here you can take a walk around the lake, play a few holes of golf, rent a kayak for a peaceful paddle, or even get in a set of tennis. For families, **Children's Fairyland** (699 Bellevue Ave., 510/452-2259,

© KARIN LAU/123RF

the marina at Jack London Square

www.fairyland.org, summer Mon.-Fri. 10am-4pm, Sat.-Sun. 10am-5pm, spring-fall Wed.-Sun. 10am-4pm, winter Fri.-Sun. 10am-4pm, $8) provides hours of entertainment and diversion on 10 acres at the edge of the lake.

If you're eager to get out on the water, the **Lake Merritt Boating Center** (568 Bellevue Ave., 510/238-2196, www2.oaklandnet.com, spring-fall Mon.-Fri. 11am-5pm, Sat.-Sun. 10:30am-5pm, summer Mon.-Fri. 10am-6pm, Sat.-Sun. 10:30am-6pm, $12-24 per hour, cash only) has everything from canoes to catamarans, kayaks, and sailboats. On the lake at Lakeside Park off Grand Avenue, it is run by the city, so the prices are fair; the only hitch is that it is cash only.

If you'd rather watch than play, Oakland is home to several professional sports teams of varying reputations and records. The best consistent players are the Major League Baseball **Oakland A's** (510/638-4900, http://oakland.athletics.mlb.com). Part of the American League, the A's have seen their ups and downs, but they almost always put on a good show for their fans. The most notorious team in pro football, the **Oakland Raiders** (800/724-3377, www.raiders.com) calls the East Bay home again after a stint in Los Angeles. If you get tickets to a game, be aware that the home side of the stadium can get rowdy and rough.

All three teams play at the **Oracle Arena and Coliseum** (7000 Coliseum Way, 510/569-2121, www.coliseum.com), a complex with both a covered basketball arena and an open-air stadium that hosts both the A's and the Raiders. Though the vast majority of events and game-goers are perfectly safe, the Coliseum isn't in the best neighborhood, so pay attention as you walk out to your car.

Accommodations

Located in the thick of the Jack London Square District, the **Inn at Jack London Square** (233 Broadway, 510/452-4565, www.innatthesquare.com, $109-139) offers comfortable digs for reasonable rates. In addition to its clean and modestly stylish decor, the hotel has the standard amenities of complimentary Wi-Fi, local shuttle service, and room service. There is also an exercise room and an outdoor pool perfect for relaxing during Oakland's hot summer days. Best of all, the hotel is within easy walking distance of many of the popular eateries, entertainment venues, and other attractions around Oakland's recently revitalized waterfront.

Another option in the Jack London Square area is the **Waterfront Hotel** (10 Washington St., 510/836-3800, www.jdvhotels.com, $159-209), which is unsurprisingly right on Oakland's waterfront. The rooms are decorated with nautical decor, and the west facing ones have views of Oakland's busy harbor. On the premises are an outdoor pool and a restaurant called Miss Pearl's Jam House, which serves Cajun cuisine.

The Washington Inn (495 10th St., 510/452-1776, www.thewashingtoninn.com, $84-149) brings a hint of European elegance to Oakland. Guest rooms are done in clean lines, simple furnishings, and bright white linens with touches of brilliant color. This inn prides itself on pampering its guests, so be sure to take advantage of the extras. The inn's location in the heart of downtown makes it perfect for business and pleasure travelers alike.

Food

A vegan soul food joint? Believe it or not it exists at **Souley Vegan** (301 Broadway St., 510/922-1615, http://souleyvegan.com, Tues.-Sat. 11am-9pm, $10). This popular spot serves southern classics like mustard greens and black eyed peas, but also takes the down home theme to tofu on the barbecued tofu and southern fried tofu menu items.

At the foot of the Oakland Hills, the Piedmont district's main draw is the delightfully retro **Fenton's Creamery** (4226 Piedmont Ave., 510/658-7000, www.fentonscreamery.com, Mon.-Thurs. 11am-11pm, Fri.-Sat. 9am-midnight, Sun. 9am-11pm, $10) which has been serving scoops since 1894. There are scores of flavors including Swiss milk chocolate, rum raisin, black walnut, and pomegranate, sold by the scoop, in classic waffle cones or made up into a sinful sundae. But you can also opt for a burger, grilled ham and cheese, or a Cobb salad. Fenton's also serves breakfast throughout the day.

Near Jack London Square, **Chop Bar** (247 4th St., 510/834-2467, www.oaklandchopbar. com, Mon.-Thurs. 7am-10pm, Fri. 7am-11pm, Sat. 9am-11pm, Sun. 9am-10pm, $12-23) serves breakfast, lunch, and dinner in a cozy, warmly lit space accented in recycled wood and old brass instruments. The food is simple but excellent with an emphasis on artisanal ingredients. The bar has local beer and wines on tap, which is a way to get quality and affordable wines by the glass. Whether you decide to go for a plate of charcuterie with a glass of wine late in the afternoon, or for a sumptuous dinner of oxtail *poutine* or rabbit gallentine, Chop Bar won't disappoint.

In Rockridge is **À Côté** (5478 Collage Ave., 510/655-6469, www.acoterestaurant. com, Sun.-Tues. 5:30pm-10pm, Wed.-Thurs. 5:30pm-11pm, Fri.-Sat. 5:30-midnight, $15-19), which serves small-plate French, Basque, and Italian Mediterranean food. The quality and the price range imply that this is a fine-dining sort of a place, but the communal tables, outdoor patio, and general relaxed atmosphere demonstrate that this is a place where everyone can be comfortable. There are an astounding 40 wines offered by the glass, perfect to pair with each little dish including mussels in Pernod and a lobster mushroom flatbread. Of course, no meal here would be complete without an order of the *pommes frites,* a proud specialty.

Information and Services

Start at the **Oakland Convention and Visitors Bureau** (463 11th St., 510/839-9000, http:// visitoakland.org, Mon.-Fri. 9am-5pm) to get good advice, maps, restaurant recommendations, and traffic tips.

You'll find plenty of banks and ATMs scattered around Oakland; it's a good idea to stick to the ATMs in well-lit visited areas rather than picking a random spot along the freeway at night. The same goes for gas stations and minimarts.

Oakland boasts many **post offices,** including one downtown (1301 Clay St.). Internet access should be easy in a city filled with Starbucks outlets and wired hotels.

For medical attention, head out to **Alameda Hospital** (2070 Clinton Ave., 510/522-3700, www.alamedahospital.org), which has a 24-hour emergency room. In Oakland, **Alta Bates** (350 Hawthorne Ave., 510/655-4000, www.altabatessummit.org) has a summit campus that also has a 24-hour emergency room.

GETTING THERE AND AROUND

Berkeley is north of Oakland along the east side of the San Francisco Bay. If you're driving from San Francisco into the East Bay, take the **Bay Bridge** (westbound toll $4-6). For Berkeley, turn north onto I-580/I-80. Oakland is accessed by via I-80 as well; I-580 borders Oakland to the north, while I-880 parallels I-80 downtown. Avoid driving I-80, I-880, or I-580 during the commuting hours (8am-10am and 4pm-7pm). Be warned that parking in Berkeley and Oakland can be a bona fide nightmare. If you're visiting for the day or for an evening show, consider taking the BART train to avoid the parking hassle.

BART (www.bart.gov, $1.75-5 one-way) is a major form of transit in and around the Bay Area. The Downtown Berkeley station is located underneath Shattuck Avenue in the heart of Berkeley. Other Berkeley stations include North Berkeley, Ashby, and Rockridge. The 12th Street/Oakland City Center station is convenient to downtown Oakland, but there are also trains out to 19th Street and Lake Merritt. BART fares are based on distance (most East Bay destinations $1.75-5 one-way); ticket machines accept cash and debit or credit cards.

Bus service in Oakland and Alameda is run by **AC Transit** (510/891-4706, www. actransit.org, adults $2.10, children and seniors $0.85). Transbay routes connect the East Bay and San Francisco (adults $4.20, children and seniors $2.10).

The **Oakland International Airport** (OAK, 1 Airport Dr., Oakland, 510/563-3300, www.

flyoakland.com) sees less traffic than San Francisco's airport and has shorter security lines and fewer delays. Major airlines include Alaska, Delta, JetBlue, Southwest, and Spirit. From the Oakland airport, you can rent a car, catch a cab or take the **AirBART shuttle** ($3) from the terminals to the BART Coliseum/Airport station. If you fly into San Francisco, you can take BART from the airport across the Bay to Berkeley.

San Jose

Sprawled across the south end of Silicon Valley, San Jose is home to companies like eBay, Cisco, Adobe, IBM, and many others, making it the beating heart of the high-tech industry. Once considered a cultural wasteland, San Jose has worked to change its image, supporting local art and attracting high-end restaurants.

SIGHTS
Rosicrucian Egyptian Museum
Perhaps San Jose's most unusual attraction is the imposing **Rosicrucian Egyptian Museum** (1660 Park Ave., 408/947-3635, www.egyptianmuseum.org, Wed.-Fri. 9am-5pm, Sat.-Sun. 10am-6pm, adults $9, students and seniors $7, children $5). The museum was opened by the Rosicrucian Order in 1928 and has a wonderful collection of ancient Egyptian artifacts, including several mummies—partly unwrapped, a rarity today. Local children and adults love the Rosicrucian's jewels, tomb artifacts, tools, and textiles. The complex also boasts a planetarium, but at the time of writing it is temporarily closed; call for current information on shows and show times.

San Jose Museum of Art
The highly regarded **San Jose Museum of Art** (110 S. Market St., 408/271-6840, www.sjmusart.org, Tues.-Sun. 11am-5pm, also third Thurs. of the month 11am-8pm, adults $8, students and seniors $5, under age 6 free) is right downtown. Housed in a historic sandstone building that was added on to in 1991, the beautiful light-filled museum features modern and contemporary art. Its permanent collection focuses largely on West Coast artists, but major retrospectives of works by the likes of Andy Warhol, Robert Mapplethorpe, and Alexander Calder come through often, giving the museum a broader scope. As a bonus, the museum store offers perhaps the best gift shopping in downtown San Jose. Likewise, the café, with both an indoor lounge and outside sidewalk tables, is a great place to grab a quick bite.

Tech Museum of Innovation
The **Tech Museum of Innovation** (201 S. Market St., 408/294-8324, www.thetech.org, daily 10am-5pm, adults $12, seniors, students and children $9) brings technology of all kinds to kids, families, and science lovers. The interactive displays at the Tech invite touching, letting children explore and learn about medical technology, computers, biology, chemistry, physics, and more using all their senses. Traveling exhibits also make the rounds here and help to flesh out the Tech's somewhat aging displays. Recently, these have included *Mythbusters: The Explosive Exhibition.* The IMAX theater (additional $4) shows films dedicated to science, learning, technology, and adventure.

Winchester Mystery House
For good old-fashioned haunted fun, stop in at the **Winchester Mystery House** (525 S. Winchester Blvd., 408/247-2101, www.winchestermysteryhouse.com, daily 9am-5pm, adults $5-40, seniors $5-37, children $5-30). A San Jose attraction that predates the rise of Silicon Valley, the huge bizarre mansion was built by famous eccentric Sarah Winchester. Kids love the doors that open onto brick walls, stairwells that go nowhere, and oddly shaped rooms, while adults enjoy the story of Sarah and the antiques displayed in many of the rooms. Sarah married into the gun-making

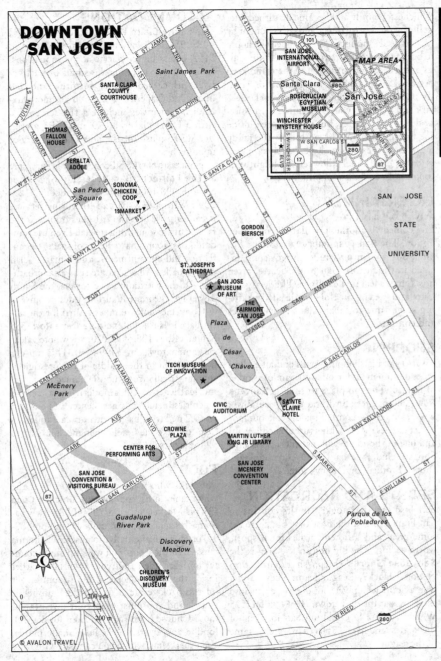

DOWNTOWN SAN JOSE

Saint James Park

SANTA CLARA COUNTY COURTHOUSE

THOMAS FALLON HOUSE

PERALTA ADOBE

San Pedro Square

SONOMA CHICKEN COOP

19MARKET

E SANTA CLARA ST

GORDON BIERSCH

E SAN FERNANDO ST

ST. JOSEPH'S CATHEDRAL

SAN JOSE MUSEUM OF ART

THE FAIRMONT SAN JOSE

Plaza de César Chávez

TECH MUSEUM OF INNOVATION

PASEO DE SAN ANTONIO

CIVIC AUDITORIUM

SAINTE CLAIRE HOTEL

CROWNE PLAZA

MARTIN LUTHER KING JR LIBRARY

CENTER FOR PERFORMING ARTS

SAN JOSE MCENERY CONVENTION CENTER

SAN JOSE CONVENTION & VISITORS BUREAU

McEnery Park

Guadalupe River Park

Discovery Meadow

CHILDREN'S DISCOVERY MUSEUM

Parque de los Pobladores

W SAN CARLOS ST

E SAN CARLOS ST

E WILLIAM ST

W REED ST

S MARKET ST

MAP AREA

SAN JOSE INTERNATIONAL AIRPORT

Santa Clara

San Jose

ROSICRUCIAN EGYPTIAN MUSEUM

WINCHESTER MYSTERY HOUSE

W SAN CARLOS ST

S WINCHESTER BLVD

SAN JOSE STATE UNIVERSITY

0   200 yds
0   200 m

© AVALON TRAVEL

Winchester family and became disturbed later in life by the destruction and death wrought by her husband's products. She designed the house to both facilitate communication with the spirits of the dead and to confound them and keep herself safe. Whether or not ghosts still haunt the mansion is a matter of debate and of faith—visit and make up your own mind. Admission to the grounds is free, but to get a peek inside the house, you must be on one of the many tours. For an extra-spooky experience, take a Friday the 13th or Halloween flashlight tour (book early, as these tours fill up fast).

ENTERTAINMENT AND EVENTS

Live comedy is another popular Silicon Valley option. The **San Jose Improv** (62 S. 2nd St., 408/280-7475, http://sanjose.improv.com), located in the historic San Jose Theatre, often hosts major-league headliners like Margaret Cho and Kevin Nealon while also granting stage time to local talent in showcases and contests.

SHOPPING

A variety of big shopping malls and an endless series of mini malls fan out over San Jose's miles of terrain. The top place to shop is **Santana Row** (Stevens Creek Blvd. and Winchester Blvd., www.santanarow.com). This upscale outdoor center dazzles the eye with its array of chic chain and one-off boutiques, shops, and restaurants. Shops include Sur La Table, Anthropologie, Brooks Brothers, and many more.

SPORTS AND RECREATION

San Jose may be mocked by its cousins in San Francisco and the East Bay, but there are some great and different professional sports worth seeing. The big dog in the area is the **San Jose Sharks** (http://sharks.nhl.com) National Hockey League team. They haven't won a Stanley Cup yet, but everyone gets into the games at the downtown **HP Pavilion** (525 W. Santa Clara St.), making San Jose one of the loudest and liveliest places to watch a game in the league.

ACCOMMODATIONS

The **Sainte Claire Hotel** (302 S. Market St., 408/295-2000, www.thesainteclaire.com, $155) offers big city-style accommodations. Standard guest rooms are small but attractive, with carved wooden furniture and rich linens and draperies. The suites are more luxurious. Amenities include a flat-screen TV with a DVD player, a CD and MP3 player, free Wi-Fi, plush robes, and turndown service upon request.

For a taste of true Silicon Valley luxury, stay at **The Fairmont San Jose** (170 S. Market St., 408/998-1900, www.fairmont.com, $129-209). With a day spa and limousine service, it's no surprise that the 731 guest rooms at the Fairmont are something special. Even the standard guest rooms have plenty of space, elegant fabrics and appointments, and a marble-clad private bath with a separate shower and bathtub. Of the Fairmont's two towers, the South Tower has the more luxurious guest rooms.

Consumer culture takes a turn for the absurd at the **Hotel Valencia Santana Row** (355 Santana Row, 408/551-0010, www.hotelvalencia-santanarow.com, $199-299). This top-tier hotel is right in the middle of the prestigious shopping mall incongruously named for a local musical legend. Ultramodern elegance and amenities include a fitness center and outdoor pool. The lavish baths with upscale toiletries help to make the hotel experience pleasing to all the senses.

FOOD

For folks who want tasty food without the white tablecloths, the **Sonoma Chicken Coop** (31 N. Market St., 408/287-4098, www.sonomachickencoop.com, daily 11am-9pm, $7-12) offers a fun alternative to upscale California cuisine. At the Coop, you walk up to the counter to order, then find your own table either inside the always-packed dining room or out on the back terrace. Your order number is called, and you must grab your own tray of food. Choose from roast chicken (of course), fondue appetizers, duck, homemade pizzas, and other items, which you can pair with tasty side dishes. Plenty of interesting salads make a somewhat lighter meal.

Open seven days a week, **Gordon Biersch** (33 E. San Fernando St., 408/294-6785, www. gordonbiersch.com, Sun.-Wed. 11:30am-11pm, Thurs. 11:30am-midnight, Fri.-Sat. 11:30am-1am, $12-28) is always busy, and the food and beer are tasty. Try the blackened ahi tacos or the Cajun pasta, but don't miss out on one of the handcrafted German-style beers brewed on-site. It has a lively happy hour, particularly if a local sports team is playing on the large overhead TVs in the bar.

Further upscale and up Market Street, **19Market** (19 N. Market St., 408/280-6111, www.19market.com, Mon.-Thurs. 11am-3pm and 5pm-10pm, Fri. 11am-3pm and 5pm-midnight, Sat. 5pm-midnight, $18) serves traditional Vietnamese food with a high polish. The high-end interior features white tablecloths and a bar noteworthy for its inventive cocktails. Happily, the food—such as duck spring rolls and tamarind prawns—matches this sophistication.

INFORMATION AND SERVICES

Before you come to San Jose, visit www.sanjose.org to get all the information you need about the Silicon Valley region and its attractions. Once in town, you can stop in at the **San Jose Convention and Visitors Bureau** (408 Almaden Blvd., 408/295-9600) for maps, brochures, guidebooks, and local advice.

San Jose has its own major daily newspaper that competes for business with its more famous northern neighbor. The *San Jose Mercury News* (www.mercurynews.com) covers national news and wire service stories along with plenty of local events and happenings. The entertainment section can provide some local events info. But when it comes to nightlife, most locals pick up a copy of *San Jose Metro* (www.metroactive.com), a free rag that proclaims itself the hippest of the Silicon Valley entertainment publications.

San Jose has plenty of **post offices,** including a downtown branch (200 South 3rd St.).

Here in the heart of Silicon Valley, it's tough to find a patch of air that doesn't have some Wi-Fi flowing through it. Expect to pay for Internet access at some of the luxury hotels. If that's not to your taste, warchalking is practically an art form here (but you didn't hear that from us).

For medical attention, **Good Samaritan Hospital** (2425 Samaritan Dr., 408/559-2011, www.goodsamsj.org) has 24-hour emergency services.

GETTING THERE AND AROUND

Travelers heading straight for Silicon Valley should skip San Francisco International Airport and fly into **Mineta San Jose International Airport** (SJC, 1667-2077 Airport Blvd., 408/501-0979, www.flysanjose.com) if at all possible. It also has some of the best deals for flying into the Bay Area. This suburban commercial airport has shorter lines, less parking and traffic congestion, and is convenient to downtown San Jose.

Amtrak (800/872-7245, www.amtrak. com) trains come into San Jose, and you can catch either the once-daily Seattle-Los Angeles *Coast Starlight* or the commuter *Capitol Corridor* to Sacramento at the **San Jose-Diridon Station** (65 Cahill St.). See the Amtrak website for information about scheduling and fares.

San Jose-Diridon station is also a hub for **Caltrain** (800/660-4287, www.caltrain.com, $3-13), a commuter train that runs from Gilroy to San Francisco. If you'd like to spend a day or even two in San Francisco but base yourself in Silicon Valley, taking Caltrain is an excellent way to go.

At Diridon station you can even catch the **VTA Light Rail** (408/321-2300, www.vta. org, $2-4), a streetcar network that serves San Jose and some of Silicon Valley as far north as Mountain View.

The VTA also operates Silicon Valley **buses** (408/321-2300, www.vta.org, $2-4), which can get you almost anywhere you need to go if you're patient enough.

As with most of the Bay Area, it's best to avoid San Jose's freeways 7am-9:30am and 4pm-7:30pm Monday-Friday. Arterial U.S. 101 is a dank, dirty stretch of road that's convenient to much of the peninsula. I-280 is much prettier and less convenient, and definitely the easiest, but not the shortest, driving route north to San Francisco. Highway 17 is the fast, treacherous route over the hills from the coast and Santa Cruz; it turns into I-880 in the middle of San Jose and runs past the end of the Bay and then north along the east side of the water all the way to Oakland. Highway 87, sometimes called the Guadalupe Parkway, can provide convenient access to downtown San Jose and the airport.

Parking in San Jose isn't anywhere near as bad as in San Francisco, but you should still be prepared to pay a premium for event parking and enclosed lots at the fancier hotels.

Coastside

Many Bay Area locals escape to the coast south of the City for weekend vacations, enjoying the small-town atmosphere in Half Moon Bay and Pescadero along with the unspoiled beauty of the dozens of miles of undeveloped coastline. Peak seasons for major attractions include October's pumpkin season and winter, when elephant seals return to Año Nuevo.

MOSS BEACH

Midway down the coast between San Francisco and Half Moon Bay on Highway 1, Moss Beach is one of several residential towns that line the coast south of the imposing Devil's Slide. There is little here besides stunning scenery, a few small businesses, and the Fitzgerald Marine Reserve. North of Moss Beach is the lovely Montara, while south is the Half Moon Bay Airport, El Granada, Princeton, and then Half Moon Bay.

Fitzgerald Marine Reserve

For tide-pooling on the coast, the **Fitzgerald Marine Reserve** (200 Nevada Ave., 650/728-3584, http://fitzgeraldreserve.org, daily 8am-close) is the place to go. The 32-acre reserve, which was recently designated a marine protected area, extends from the Montara Lighthouse south to Pillar Point and is considered one of the most diverse intertidal zones in the Bay Area. On its rocky reefs, you can hunt for sea anemones, starfish, eels, and crabs—there's even a small species of red octopus. The reserve is also home to

egrets, herons, an endangered species of butterfly, and a slew of sea lions and harbor seals that enjoy sunning themselves on the beach's outer rocks. Rangers are available to answer any questions and, if need be, to remind you of the strict tide pool etiquette. This includes an unyielding no-dog policy, staying 300 feet from marine mammals, and not removing any plants, animals, shells, or even rocks from the reserve. Persistent ocean spray and blankets of seaweed can keep the reefs slick, so wear shoes with good traction. For the best viewing, come at low tide (tide logs are available at most local bookstores, but for a quick reference, check out www.protides.com) and on weekdays, as this is a popular destination for families. For a more leisurely and drier experience, numerous trails crisscross the windswept bluffs and go through sheltering groves of cypress and eucalyptus trees.

Montara State Beach

Just north of Moss Beach and the Marine Reserve is **Montara State Beach** (2nd St. and Hwy. 1, Montara, www.parks.ca.gov, 650/726-8819, daily 8am-sunset), one of the most beautiful beaches in this area. It is as popular with tide-poolers, surfers, and anglers as it is with picnickers and beachcombers. It is also dog-friendly, which is a big plus as many state beaches have restrictions on canines in the interest of preserving the endangered snowy plover. Thankfully, the beach also remains relatively uncrowded compared to many of the

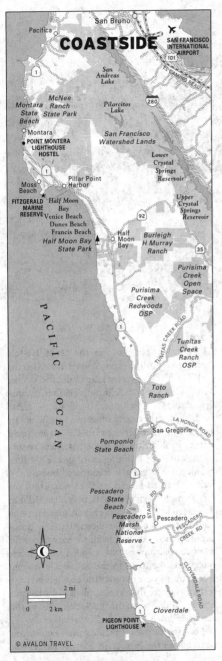

other beaches to the south; it has a tendency to get windy, and there is limited parking.

McNee Ranch State Park

For those who want sweeping views of the coast as well as a heart-pounding hike, **McNee Ranch** (Hwy. 1, across from Montara State Beach, 650/726-8819, www.parks.ca.gov, daily 8am-sunset) fits the bill. The big hike is eight miles up **Montara Mountain,** through dry California chaparral along a series of fire roads. The peak itself is 1,900 feet high (the parking lot is at 100 feet), and it is an arduous but worthwhile climb to the top. Although the trail is unmarked, there are maps at the information board just past the parking lot. Still, it's easy to wing it—just follow the roads uphill. From the top, you can see all the way across the Golden Gate and south past Half Moon Bay. The mountain is also home to the endemic Montara manzanita. Unfortunately, there is no loop trail, so you must return down the mountain. But with the crisscrossing trails, you won't have to come back the same way. Free parking is in a small and poorly marked dirt lot directly across Highway 1 from Montara Beach. An easier option, also free, is to park at the beach, and walk across the road to the trailhead. McNee Ranch is also a popular mountain biking area, and dogs are welcome on leash.

Accommodations

In the neighboring community of Montara, the **Goose and Turrets** (835 George St., Montara, 650/728-5451, www.gooseandturretsbandb. com, $175-230) is a local getaway favorite. A rambling old building houses the inn; inside, decor runs to the eclectic. The Clipper Room is perfect for aviation buffs, and guests who like their space will love the sweeping expanse of hardwood floor in the Hummingbird Room. The food, which includes a full course hot breakfast, and accommodations involve ecologically friendly choices, and the owners are active in local park and community environmental organizations.

For an indulgent hideaway, make a reservation at the **Seal Cove Inn** (221 Cypress Ave.,

SAN FRANCISCO BAY AREA

© STUART THORNTON

Half Moon Bay's Pillar Point Harbor

Moss Beach, 800/995-9987, www.sealcoveinn. com, $235-350). Tucked away in the cypress and pine forest of Moss Beach, this highly regarded 10-room B&B bills itself a "European Sanctuary." Outside, the gabled roof, climbing ivy, and expansive gardens let guests know they have entered the inn's rarified world, as do the interior's warm colors, creamy soft linens, private decks, pre-breakfast coffee, and real wood burning fireplaces.

The **Point Montara Lighthouse Hostel** (16th St. and Hwy. 1, Montara, 650/728-7177, www.norcalhostels.org, dorm $27-30, private room $73-79) offers even better views at a fraction of the price, albeit with a bit less luxury. You can stay in the shared dorm rooms, each with 3-6 beds and either coed or gender-specific. You can also spring for a private room. Either way, you can enjoy use of the shared kitchen, common areas with wood-burning fireplaces, the eclectic garden perched on the cliff, and the private cove beach. Other amenities include Wi-Fi, laundry facilities, an espresso bar, and complimentary linens.

Food

As many people come to the **Moss Beach Distillery** (140 Beach Way, Moss Beach, 650/728-5595, www.mossbeachdistillery.com, Mon.-Thurs. noon-8:30pm, Fri.-Sat. noon-9pm, Sun. 11am-8:30pm, $15-38) for the ghost stories as for the hearty food and terrific ocean views. The Distillery operated as a speakeasy during Prohibition, with the basement rooms in the cliff-side building storing cases of illegal alcohol. It was also frequented by mystery writer Dashiell Hammett. The restaurant offers something of a cross between traditional American food and California cuisine. Portions tend to be large, and service is friendly if occasionally slow during peak times. Folks who want to soak up the old-school speakeasy atmosphere like to sit in the bar, while visitors who want to stare out over the ocean prefer the terrace, where, thankfully, plenty of blankets are on hand to ward off the Pacific chill as the sun goes down.

Looking to pack a picnic lunch before you head out to the Fitzgerald Marine Reserve or

Montara State Beach? Swing by **Gherkin's Sandwich Shop** (171 8th St., Montara, 650/728-2211, daily 8am-8pm, $10) for everything you can imagine between two slices of bread. You'll find oddities like breakfast frittata sandwiches and the Ooey Gooey, with peanut butter, Nutella, and marshmallows. For the less adventurous, there are also classics like BLTs, burgers, and pastrami and swiss cheese. You can also order a variety of sides that include garlic fries and fried pickles, but beware: The sandwiches are huge and can easily be split between two people or saved for a later snack.

You might stumble upon **La Costanera** (8150 Cabrillo Hwy., Montara, 650/728-1600, www.lacostanerarestaurant.com, Tues.-Sun. 5pm-close, $18-36) because of its location. But this place, poised above Montara Beach, is about more than just the view. Skillfully designed with grand sloping picture windows and sunken dining rooms, La Costanera is a sophisticated Peruvian restaurant and the only eatery on this part of the coast to earn a Michelin star two years in a row. There are a variety of ceviches to choose from as well as slow-cooked pork shoulder and lobster gnocchi, all accented in Peruvian sauces and spices. If you only want a quick bite while soaking in the sunset, the bar menu offers hearty plates that could serve as a light dinner.

Getting There and Around

Moss Beach is 23 miles directly south of San Francisco on Highway 1 (Cabrillo Hwy.). From San Francisco, the easiest and most direct—not to mention scenic—route is to follow Highway 1 south all the way to Moss Beach.

Alternatively, if you are coming from I-280 on the peninsula, take Highway 92 west to Half Moon Bay and Highway 1. From Half Moon Bay, Moss Beach is only seven miles north on Highway 1.

HALF MOON BAY

To this day, the coastal city of Half Moon Bay retains its character as an "ag" (agricultural) town. The locals all know each other, even though the majority of residents commute "over the hill" to more lucrative peninsula and Silicon Valley jobs. For those who farm the area, strawberries, artichokes, and Brussels sprouts are the biggest crops, along with flowers, pumpkins, and Christmas trees, making the coast the place to come for holiday festivities. Half Moon Bay enjoys a beautiful natural setting and earns significant income from tourism, especially during the world-famous Pumpkin Festival each October.

Some people know Half Moon Bay for Maverick's, a monster wave that can rise to 80 feet off nearby Pillar Point during the winter months. Maverick's is one of the world's most renowned surf spots and has been chronicled in the 2004 surf documentary *Riding Giants* and the 2012 feature film *Chasing Mavericks*. It is a treacherous wave known for its underwater rocks, great white shark danger, and cold waters. In 1994, it made news around the world for taking the life of big wave surfer Mark Foo.

Onshore from Maverick's is the Pillar Point Harbor and the neighboring town of **Princeton-by-the-Sea,** the other workhorse on the coast. Here, anglers haul in crab, salmon, and herring, and local businesses cater to their needs. This is the place to rent kayaks, go on a chartered fishing trip, and buy fresh fish, sometimes straight off the boat (especially during crab season).

Beaches

The beaches of Half Moon Bay draw visitors from over the hill and farther afield all year long. As with most of the North Pacific region, summer can be a chilly foggy time on the beaches. For the best beach weather, plan your Half Moon Bay trip for September-October. **Half Moon Bay State Beach** (www.parks.ca.gov, parking $10 per day) actually encompasses three discrete beaches stretching four miles down the coast, each with its own access point and parking lot. **Francis Beach** (95 Kelly Ave.) has the most developed amenities, including a good-size campground with grassy areas to pitch tents and enjoy picnics, a visitors center, and indoor hot showers. **Venice Beach** (Venice Blvd., off Hwy. 1) offers outdoor

THE BLUE LADY

With all its history, it's easy to get lost in the ghost stories that haunt San Francisco. Yet two of the most famous Bay Area hauntings aren't anywhere close to Chinatown or Nob Hill. Instead, strange stories and creepy occurrences perch nearer to the perilous cliffs of the Pacific Coast, and lurk in the Santa Cruz Mountain forests.

Just north of Half Moon Bay, the **Moss Beach Distillery** (140 Beach Way, Moss Beach, 650/728-5595, www.mossbeachdistillery.com, Mon.-Thurs. noon-8:30pm, Fri.-Sat. noon-9pm, Sun. 11am-8:30pm, $15-38) has been featured on *Unsolved Mysteries* and written up in countless publications – not for its food, but for its famous ghost: the Blue Lady. Rumor has it that a beautiful young woman walked the cliffs of Moss Beach from her home to the coastside speakeasy (now the Distillery) to meet her lover, a handsome piano player who worked in the bar. The Lady, whose name has never been discovered, perished one night on the cliffs under suspicious circumstances. Some say that her lover had left her, and she threw herself down onto the rocks out of grief; others claim that her seafaring husband came home, discovered his wife's infidelity, and shoved her to eternity. However it happened,

in the middle of the 20th century, odd things started occurring at the Distillery. A storage room with only one door and a barred-over window became stuck from the inside. Eventually, several men bashed it open, only to discover several heavy cases of spirits that had been shoved up against the door to keep it closed. But by whom? No one was in the room, and no one could have gotten out. Many years and a major reconstruction later (the building sits on a slowly eroding cliff that will eventually lie beneath the ocean), an accountant was working late one night in the restaurant's offices. She was startled to hear her printer turn itself on, startled because she was in another office using a different computer and was alone in the building. Upon examination, the printer yielded a single piece of paper with a tiny heart printed on it. The accountant believes this means the ghost likes her.

Today, the Distillery is a favorite with ghost-hunting groups, who often come to spend the night in an old building that gets decidedly creepy after the lights go out. Restaurant patrons rarely have ghostly experiences, unless you count those created by the owner for the entertainment of his customers.

---

showers and flush toilets. **Dunes Beach** (Young Ave., off Hwy. 1) is the southernmost major beach in the chain and the least developed.

Perhaps the most famous beach in the area is one that has no name. At the end of West Point Avenue in Princeton is the Pillar Point Marsh and a long stretch of beach that wraps around the edge of the point. This beach is the launch pad for surfers paddling out to tackle the infamous **Mavericks Break** (Pillar Point Marsh parking lot, past Pillar Point Harbor). Formed by unique underwater topography, the giant waves are the site of the legendary **Mavericks Surf Contest** (http://maverickssurf.com). The competition is always held in winter, when the swells reach their peak, and left until the last minute to ensure that they are the biggest of the year. When perfect conditions present

themselves, the best surfers in the world are given 48 hours' notice to make it to Mavericks to compete. Unfortunately, you can't see the breaks all that well from the beach, but there are dirt trails that crisscross the point, where breathtaking views can be had. Just walk up West Point Avenue past the yellow gate and catch any number of dirt trails heading west toward the bluffs. But for those eyeing the big waves, beware: Mavericks is not a beginner's break, especially in winter, and the giant breakers can be deadly. If you aren't positive you're up to the challenge, don't paddle out.

Entertainment and Events

Locals may complain that there is not a lot going on in Half Moon Bay, but the city boasts one of the best jazz venues and two of the biggest annual events in the Bay Area. Since it opened in 1964, the **Bach Dancing and Dynamite Society** (311 Mirada Rd., Half Moon Bay, 650/726-2020, www.bachddsoc. org) has been a hangout for bohemians and jazz aficionados, hosting the biggest names in jazz—Bill Evans, Dizzy Gillespie, Etta James, and Duke Ellington. Not only is the music fantastic, but the venue, the Douglas Beach House, can't be beat.

In contrast to the Bach's cool vibe, the **Pacific Coast Dream Machines** (Half Moon Bay Airport, 9850 Hwy. 1, www.miramarevents.com) is all muscle and revving engines. This two-day event includes a demolition derby, a flying motorcycle, World War II-era fighter planes, ultra lightweight and antique biplanes, and automobiles from peddle cars to homemade kit cars. The event generally takes place on the last weekend in April, so plan accordingly; whether or not you plan to attend, the traffic congestion is equally legendary.

The biggest annual event in this small agricultural town is the **Half Moon Bay Art & Pumpkin Festival** (www.miramarevents. com). Every October, nearly 250,000 people trek to Half Moon Bay to pay homage to the big orange squash. The festival includes live music, food, artists' booths, contests, activities for kids, an adults lounge area, and a parade. Perhaps the best-publicized event is the pumpkin weigh-off, which takes place before the festivities begin. Farmers bring their tremendous squash in on flatbed trucks from all over the country to determine which is the biggest of all. If anyone breaks the world record of 1,818 pounds, they'll take home an impressive $5,000.

Shopping

Strolling Main Street is another reason folks come to Half Moon Bay. A holdover from the town's agricultural roots is **Half Moon Bay Feed and Fuel** (331 Main St., 650/726-4814, http://halfmoonbay-feedandfuel.com, Mon.-Fri. 8:30am-6pm, Sat. 9am-5pm, Sun. 10am-4pm). Even if you don't need a new saddle or a bale of hay, stopping by the Feed and Fuel

is a fun little detour. There are often baby chicks and bunnies as well as quirky gift items that any Western fanatic or wannabe cowboy would love.

Just on the next block, you can step into a whole other world in **Abode** (417 Main St., 650/726-6060, www.abodehalfmoonbay.com, Sun.-Thurs. 10am-5pm, Fri.-Sat. 10am-6pm). Carefully crafted, Abode almost feels like a treatise on home decorating in which the goal is fluidity between the outside and the inside spaces. There are no bright plastic or enamel wares here, but instead furniture and home accents are all in an earthy palette and are largely made from glass, wood, and other natural materials and designed with artistic quality, craftsmanship, and utility.

Another Half Moon Bay treasure is **Toque Blanche** (604 Main St., 650/726-2898, www. mytoque.com, Mon.-Sat. 10am-6pm, Sun. 10am-5pm), perhaps the best kitchen store in the Bay Area. They have everything from coffeemakers to panini presses, cookie cutters to knives, dinner plates to linens. Some of the bonuses include free cooking demos, super soft French dishtowels, a wall full of different types of salt, and La Chamba Clay Cookware, extremely versatile and attractive Colombian cooking pottery.

To see what Half Moon Bay does best, drop by the **Coastside Farmer's Market** (225 Cabrillo Hwy., 650/726-4895, www.coastsidefarmersmarket.org, May-Dec. Sat. 9am-1pm). There is plenty of local meat, bread, produce, pottery, art, and even wool skeins, spun and dyed by hand. Local bands are always at the market, and there is plenty of street food. The **Half Moon Bay Flower Market** (Main St. and Kelly Ave., 650/712-9439, www.explorer1.com, third Sat. of the month 9am-3pm) is even more of an institution, where local flower growers show off a multitude of blooms and houseplants that range from the domestic to the exotic.

Sports and Recreation

There are plenty of great trails around Half Moon Bay. A local favorite is **Purisima Creek Redwoods** (4.4 miles up Higgins Canyon Rd.,

650/619-1200, www.openspace.org). There are a multitude of trails in this 4,412-acre preserve, and many ascend to Skyline Boulevard for an elevation gain of 1,700 feet. You can take a leisurely stroll through the redwoods, complete with dripping ferns, flowering dogwood, and wood sorrel, along Purisima Creek Trail (3.9 miles, easy-strenuous), until it turns steep and eventually takes you to its literally breathtaking Skyline terminus. If you don't want to crest the ridge of the Santa Cruz Mountains, you can opt for Harkins Ridge Trail (6 miles, moderate), which rises out of the canyon shortly past the trailhead. You'll hike through redwoods, then oaks and chaparral, and back again into firs, pines, and redwoods as you gain 800 feet in elevation over 2.5 miles. To make a loop, cut down Craig Britton Trail, which meets Purisima Creek Trail. To feel like you've conquered a mountain, make the climb to 2,102-foot Bald Knob (9.6 miles, strenuous). From Purisima Creek Trail, take Borden Hatch Mill Trail to Bald Knob Trail, where you will find a flat clearing among the dry madrones, live oaks, and chaparral. You will be rewarded with terrific coastal views.

Fortunately for mountain bikers, nearly all the trails in the preserve are open to cyclists. As you can imagine, the trails are steep and knotted with rocks and tree roots, which makes for an exhausting, exhilarating, or terrifying ride, depending on your experience and attitude.

The most popular trail in Half Moon Bay is the **Coastside Trail** (www.parks.ca.gov). Extending five miles from Miramar Beach to Poplar Beach, this flat, paved trail follows the coast and is filled with joggers, dog walkers, and bikes. There are a multitude of beach-access points along the way, and if you want to go downtown, jump off at Kelly Avenue and take it across Highway 1 to the heart of Half Moon Bay. Beyond the Poplar Beach parking lot, the trail crosses a wooden bridge and turns into a dirt trail. This area is known as the **Wavecrest Open Space** and goes all the way down to the Ritz Carlton. It is much less traveled than the paved Coastside Trail and is a great place to spot herons, egrets, and gray

whales off the coast during their spring migration. Parking is plentiful at Poplar Beach ($2 per hour), at the end of Poplar Street on the south end of town.

For a sedate ocean adventure, take a winter whale-watching cruise or a shallow-water rockfish fishing trip on board the **Queen of Hearts** (Pillar Point Harbor, 510/581-2628, www.fishingboat.com, reservations strongly recommended, $60-90). Whale-watching trips (Jan.-Apr.) cost a bit less than fishing trips on the *Queen of Hearts.* Deep-sea fishing for albacore and salmon (if the season isn't canceled) makes for a more energetic day out on the Pacific, although motion-sickness medication is often recommended.

Bait and Switch Sportfishing (Pillar Point Harbor, 650/726-7133, http://baitandswitch-sportfishing.com, tackle $5-14, 1-day license $12) offers six boats for a wide variety of whale-watching and sport fishing trips, and even trips to watch the Mavericks Surf Contest; call for rates.

One of the coolest ways to see the coast is from the deck of a sea kayak or stand up paddleboard. Many tours with the **Half Moon Bay Kayaking Company** (Pillar Point Harbor, 650/773-6101, www.hmbkayak.com) require no previous kayaking experience. For an easy first paddle, try the Pillar Point tour, the full-moon tour, or the sunset paddle. If you're looking for a wilder ride, sign up for a kayak surfing class—you'll learn how to catch waves safely in specially designed kayaks. The company also offers beginner through advanced classes in closed-deck kayaks. Also the harbor is an ideal place to learn how to stand up paddleboard.

Sea Horse Ranch (1828 Hwy. 1, 650/726-9903, www.seahorseranch.org, daily 8am-5pm, $55 per hour) offers one-hour, 90-minute, and two-hour guided tours that take you along the cliffs and down onto the sands at Half Moon Bay's state beaches. Children over the age of five are welcome, as are riders of all ability levels. The horses here are sedate rental nags who know the routes in their sleep, allowing riders to sit back and enjoy the stunning views and the company of fellow riders.

Accommodations

Half Moon Bay offers several lovely bed-and-breakfasts along with one luxury resort hotel and a hotel of suites right by the harbor among other options.

A stunning property, the **C Ritz-Carlton Half Moon Bay** (1 Miramontes Point Rd., 650/712-7000, www.ritzcarlton.com, $350-3,500) resembles a Scottish castle transported to the California coast. Surrounding the luxury hotel are two emerald green golf courses perched above the Pacific. The sprawling grounds are dotted with always-lit fire pits and chairs to take in the marvelous ocean views. Right out front is Half Moon Bay Coastside Trail, where you can hike for up to seven miles. The hotel also has a spa, restaurant, two fitness rooms, a pool, tennis courts, and a basketball court. New chef Sean Eastwood makes sure that the freshest ingredients from local farms come to your plate at the top-tier restaurant Navio, which also has an extensive 54-page wine list.

Inside, guests enjoy the finest of modern amenities. Bathrooms have marble floors and marble countertops, while many of the posh guest rooms overlook the sea. Another plus is that the hotel's superb staff seems to be as excited to be here as you are.

For a more personal lodging experience, try the **Old Thyme Inn** (779 Main St., 650/726-1616, www.oldthymeinn.com, $159-349), located a few doors down from the Cetrella Bistro. Each uniquely decorated guest room is named after an herb and has luxurious amenities. Downstairs, guests can enjoy the common sitting rooms and the gorgeous garden. Visitors can also take in the original art created by Old Thyme's innkeeper. Each morning the owners serve up a sumptuous breakfast using fresh ingredients.

The **Beach House at Half Moon Bay** (4100 N. Cabrillo Hwy., 650/712-0220 or 800/315-9366, www.beach-house.com/half-moon-bay-hotels.html, $205-415) is situated in an ideal location a few feet from Pillar Point Harbor

© STUART THORNTON

the Ritz-Carlton Half Moon Bay

and the popular Coastside Trail. All the rooms, which are multi-level lofts, have a private patio or balcony to take in the bobbing sailboats and the groaning foghorn. On fog-shrouded days, the Beach House has in-room real wood burning fireplaces and an outdoor hot tub and heated pool on the pool deck to warm up with.

Food

The quality of food in Half Moon Bay is superb. For seafood, go to **C Sam's Chowder House** (4210 N. Cabrillo Hwy., 650/712-0245, www.samschowderhouse.com, Mon.-Fri. 11:30am-9:30pm., Sat. 11am-9:30pm, Sun. 11am-9pm, $12-35), a fusion of an East Coast chowder and lobster shack with West Coast sensibilities and a view of the Pacific. The lobster clambake for two ($60) is a splurge, but it's an excellent introduction to Sam's seafood-heavy menu. Armed with a lobster cracker, bib, and wet nap, attempt to finish the starting bowl of clam chowder followed by a tasty mound that includes a whole lobster, clams, mussels, potatoes, and a spicy Andouille sausage. Many other dinners opt for the buttery lobster roll ($21.95). Owner Paul Shenkman, a veteran restaurateur once associated with nearby Pasta Moon and Cetrella, is a New Jersey native who takes seafood very seriously. The perpetually full parking lot out front points to Shenkman's golden touch.

Open since 1987, **Pasta Moon** (315 Main St., 650/726-5125, www.pastamoon.com, Mon.-Thurs. 11:30am-2:30pm and 5:30pm-9pm, Fri. 11:30am-2:30pm and 5:30pm-9:30pm, Sat. noon-3pm and 5:30pm-9:30pm, Sun. noon-3pm and 5:30pm-9pm, $12-30) is the godmother of fine dining. While managing to be both casual and upscale at once, Pasta Moon serves updated Italian cuisine with an emphasis on fresh, light dishes. Their wood-fired pizzas are particularly good and affordable, as are any of the pasta dishes, made with house-made noodles. The rustic dining room, with a view of the woods and the creek, completes the experience, while the bar and new lounge, humming with live jazz, offers a more casual and urbane evening out.

Cetrella (845 Main St., 650/726-4090, www.cetrella.com, Tues.-Thurs. and Sun. 5:30pm-9:30pm, Fri.-Sat. 5:30pm-10pm, $20-40) also bills itself as a Mediterranean bistro. In truth, the menu includes a range of Mediterranean-themed California cuisine, and the big-beam construction looks like something out of the redwood forests up north. The chef uses local, often organic ingredients to create stunning fare that varies by season. Look for Dungeness crab in winter and artichokes in the spring.

If you think good bread is the secret weapon of a great sandwich, come by the **Garden Deli Café** (356 Main St., 650/726-9507, www.sanbenitohouse.com, $6.60). Located in the historic San Benito House, the deli serves basic sandwiches like turkey, roast beef, and ham that stand out due to the slabs of tasty homemade bread that the ingredients lay between. Get your sandwich to go or eat it in the adjacent courtyard with multi-colored picnic tables.

Information and Services

Visit the **Half Moon Bay Chamber of Commerce** (235 Main St., 650/726-8380, www.halfmoonbaychamber.org, Mon.-Fri. 9am-5pm, Sat.-Sun. 10am-3pm) in the red house just after you turn on Main Street from Highway 92. The chamber also doubles as a visitors center where you can find maps, brochures, and a schedule of events.

Two local publications are the *Half Moon Bay Review* (www.hmbreview.com) and *CoastViews Magazine* (www.coastviewsmag.com). The *Review,* published weekly, provides the best information about live local entertainment. The free *CoastViews* comes out monthly and is available around this region.

The **post office** (500 Stone Pine Rd.) is off Main Street before the bridge heading south. Cell phones work fine in the town of Half Moon Bay, but coverage can be spotty up in the hills above town and out on the undeveloped coastline and beaches along Highway 1.

There is a 24-hour emergency room at the **Seton Coastside Hospital** (600 Marine

Blvd., Moss Beach, 650/563-7100, www.se-toncoastside.org). For less serious health services, the **Coastside Clinic** (Shoreline Station, Suite 100A, 225 S. Hwy. 1, Half Moon Bay, 650/573-3941, www.sanmateomedicalcenter.org) is located just north of the intersection of Kelly Avenue and Highway 1.

Getting There and Around
Half Moon Bay is on Highway 1 about 45 minutes south of San Francisco. From San Francisco, take I-280 south to Highway 92 west to Half Moon Bay and Highway 1. You can also take the scenic route by following Highway 1 directly south from San Francisco all the way to Half Moon Bay.

Parking in downtown Half Moon Bay is usually a fairly easy proposition—except, of course, if you're in town for the Pumpkin Festival, when parking is a nightmare of epic proportions. Your best bet is to stay in town with your car safely stowed in a hotel parking lot before the festival.

PESCADERO
Pescadero is a tiny dot on the map, south of Half Moon Bay and well north of Santa Cruz, with one main street, one side street, and several smallish farms. Despite its tiny size, many Bay Area denizens visit Pescadero for the twisty roads that challenge motorcyclists and bicyclists, fresh produce, its 19th century buildings and, of course, the legendary Duarte's Tavern.

Pescadero State Beach
Pescadero State Beach (Hwy. 1, north of Pescadero Rd., 650/879-2170, www.parks.ca.gov, daily 8am-sunset) is the closest to town. It's a great spot to walk in the sand and stare out at the Pacific, but near-constant winds make it less than ideal for picnics or sunbathing. It does have some facilities, including public restrooms.

Bird lovers flock to **Pescadero Marsh Natural Preserve** (Hwy. 1, www.smcnha.org), located on Highway 1 right across the highway from Pescadero State Beach. This protected

Welcome to Pescadero.

wetland, part of Pescadero State Beach, is home to a variety of avian species, including blue herons, great and snowy egrets, and northern harriers. For the best birding, visit the marsh early in the morning or in late fall or early spring, when migration is in full swing. A footbridge erected in 2011 allows guests to visit the back of the marsh.

San Gregorio State Beach

North of Pescadero, **San Gregorio State Beach** (at the intersection of Hwy. 84 and Hwy. 1, 650/726-8819, www.parks.ca.gov, daily 8am-sunset, $10 per car) stretches farther than it seems. Once you're walking toward the ocean, the small-seeming cove stretches out beyond the cliffs that bound it to create a long stretch of beach perfect for contemplative strolling. San Gregorio is a local favorite in the summer, despite the regular appearance of thick, chilly fog over the sand. Brave beachgoers can even swim and bodysurf here, although you'll quickly get cold if you do so without a wetsuit. Picnic tables and restrooms cluster near the parking lot, although picnicking can be hampered by the wind.

San Gregorio General Store

San Gregorio is a tiny picturesque town of rolling rangeland, neat patches of colorful crops, and century-old homes, including a one-room schoolhouse and an old brothel. Its beating heart is the **San Gregorio General Store** (Hwy. 84 and Stage Rd., 650/726-0565, www.sangregoriostore.com, Mon.-Thurs. 10:30am-6pm, Fri. 10:30am-7pm, Sat. 10am-7pm, Sun. 10am-6pm). Open since 1889, the San Gregorio General Store has an eclectic book section and a variety of cast-iron cookery, oil lamps, and raccoon traps. In the back of the store are coolers stocked with juice, soda, bottled water, and deli sandwiches made in the back kitchen. The real centerpiece is the bar, serving beer, wine, and a large selection of spirits to ranchers and farmers out for a coffee break in the mornings and locals just getting off work. On the weekends the store is packed by mostly out-of-towners, and

the live music keeps things moving. The deep picture windows out front make it a comfy place to watch the afternoon pass by with a cold beer. The San Gregorio General Store lives up to its name: You can even buy stamps or mail a letter at the full-service post office next door.

Pigeon Point Lighthouse

South of Pescadero is 115-foot-high **Pigeon Point Lighthouse** (210 Pigeon Point Rd., at Hwy. 1, 650/879-2120, www.parks.ca.gov, daily 8am-sunset), one of the tallest in the country. First lit in 1872, Pigeon Point is one of the most photographed lighthouses in the United States. Sadly, visitors find the lighthouse itself in a state of disrepair, and recent earthquakes have made climbing to the top unsafe. Yet the monument stands, its hostel still shelters travelers, and visitors still marvel at the incomparable views from the point. Winter guests can look for migrating whales from the rocks beyond the tower.

Año Nuevo State Reserve

Año Nuevo State Reserve (Hwy. 1, south of Pescadero, 650/879-2025, reservations 800/444-4445, www.parks.ca.gov, daily 8am-sunset, $10 per car) is world-famous as the winter home and breeding ground of the once-endangered elephant seals. The reserve also has extensive dunes and marshland. The beaches and wilderness are open year-round. The elephant seals start showing up in December and stay to breed, birth pups, and loll on the beach until early March. Visitors are not allowed down to the elephant seal habitats on their own and must sign up for a guided walking tour. Once you see two giant males crashing into one another in a fight for dominance, you won't want to get too close. Book your tour at least a day or two in advance since the seals are popular with both locals and travelers.

Accommodations

Pescadero has a small but surprisingly good array of lodging options. If budget is a factor,

© STUART THORNTON

the Pigeon Point Lighthouse

try the **Pigeon Point Hostel** (210 Pigeon Point Rd., at Hwy. 1, 650/879-0633, http://norcal-hostels.org/pigeon, dorm $24-30, private room $73-177). This Hostelling International hostel has simple but comfortable accommodations, both private and dorm-style. Amenities include three kitchens, free Wi-Fi, and beach access. But the best amenity of all is the cliff-top hot tub.

At **Costanoa Lodge and Campground** (2001 Rossi Rd., at Hwy. 1, 650/879-1100, www.costanoa.com, campsite $30-65, rooms $180-260), pitch a tent in the campground or rent a whirlpool suite in the lodge. Other options include log-style cabins with shared baths, small tent cabins with shared baths, and private guest rooms. Costanoa's many nature programs educate visitors about the ecology of the San Mateo coast and preservation efforts underway. A small general store offers s'mores fixings and souvenirs, while "comfort stations" provide outdoor fireplaces, private indoor-outdoor showers, baths with heated floors, and saunas that are open daily 24 hours to all guests.

For a little more luxury, the **Pescadero Creek Inn Bed & Breakfast** (393 Stage Rd., 888/307-1898, www.pescaderocreekinn.com, $175-255) is conveniently located in downtown Pescadero, an easy walk from Duarte's, the grocery stores, the local cemetery, and the creek. While the over 100 year-old house isn't completely soundproof, the guest rooms have high ceilings and are prettily appointed; amenities include down feather bed tops. The owner serves a delectable breakfast each morning, and pours his homemade award-winning wines in the afternoon, along with cheese and fruit.

Looking for something unique? The **Pescadero Creekside Barn** (248 Stage Rd., 650/879-0868, www.pescaderolodging.com, $148-165) is nestled in the loft of an old barn. The studio apartment-style space sleeps two and has a TV with a DVD player, a kitchen, and a claw-foot tub. The seclusion and charm make the space perfect for a romantic getaway or a solitary weekend retreat. And Duarte's is located right next door.

Camping

Most of the camping in Pescadero is inland, deep in the redwoods. **Butano State Park** (1500 Cloverdale Rd., 650/879-2040 or 800/444-7275, www.parks.ca.gov, $35) offers 21 drive-in and 18 walk-in campsites. While there are no showers, there are clean restrooms, fire pits, and drinking water. Perhaps the best amenity is the proximity to fantastic hiking in the park. There are quiet strolls through the canopy of redwoods or more athletic treks up dusty ridgelines. The most scenic is the Butano Fire Road that summits at an abandoned airstrip.

Farther inland, past the tiny town of Loma Mar, is **Memorial Park** (9500 Pescadero Creek Rd., 650/879-0238, www.co.sanmateo.ca.us, year-round, $37) with 158 campsites open. Each site accommodates as many as eight people, with a fire pit, picnic tables, and a metal locker to store food and sundries. There is also drinking water, baths with coin-operated showers, and a general store within the park that sells firewood in addition to hot dog buns, ice cream, and soap. While there are fewer hiking trails than at Butano, Memorial boasts an amphitheater and swimming holes in Pescadero Creek.

Food

◖ **Duarte's Tavern** (202 Stage Rd., 650/879-0464, www.duartestavern.com, daily 7am-9pm, $13-25) has been honored by the James Beard Foundation as "An American Classic," and once you walk through the doors you'll see why. The rambling building features sloping floors and age-darkened wooden walls. The food is good, the service friendly, and the coffee plentiful. And while almost everybody comes to Duarte's for a bowl of artichoke soup or a slice of olallieberry pie, it's really the atmosphere that's the biggest draw. Locals of all stripes—farmers, farmhands, ranchers, and park rangers—sit shoulder to shoulder with travelers sharing conversation and a bite to eat, particularly in the dimly lit bar but also in the dining room or at the old-fashioned lunch counter. The greatest assets are the outdated jukebox with classics from Louis Armstrong to the Beach Boys and the excellent Bloody Marys, garnished with a pickled green bean.

If Duarte's is too crowded, venture across the street to the **Pescadero Country Store** (251 Stage Rd., 650/879-0410, Sun.-Thurs. 9am-7pm, Fri.-Sat. 9am-8pm, $11-18). This converted grocery store has a pizza counter serving wood-fired pies, a full-service deli, and a beer and wine bar decorated in a deep blue nautical theme.

If you're heading to Pescadero from Half Moon Bay, stop at **Bob's Vegetable Stand** (Hwy. 1, 5 miles south of Half Moon Bay, 650/712-7740), which has a selection of local produce rivaling any grocery store. Once in Pescadero, **Harley Farms** (205 North St., 650/879-0480, www.harleyfarms.com, farm and shop hours daily 10am-5pm, call for tour information) boasts of being the last working dairy on the San Mateo coast. Its locally famous goat cheese is sold in its farm store. During your stop, you can even assist in the cheese-making process, taking a tour that teaches you how to milk a goat and then create fresh artisanal cheese.

Farther up Pescadero Road at **Phipp's Country Store and Farm** (2700 Pescadero Rd., 650/879-1032, www.phippscountry.com, Apr.-Oct. daily 10am-6pm, Nov.-Mar. daily 10am-5pm), you can pick your own warm-from-the-sun strawberries and olallieberries (spring-summer only). Phipp's also has a quaint country store where they sell homemade jams, jellies, herbal vinegars, and a whole host of heritage beans, grown and dried on the farm.

To round out your picnic, drop by **Arcangeli Grocery** (287 Stage Rd., 650/879-0147, www.normsmarket.com) across the street from Duarte's. All the breads are homemade and delicious, including the Italian artichoke herb bread and the garlic herb sourdough loaf. The pastries—especially the raspberry twists—are also great.

Getting There and Around

Pescadero is 17 miles south of Half Moon Bay. At Pescadero State Beach, Highway 1 intersects Pescadero Road. Turn east on Pescadero Road and drive two miles to the stop sign (the only one in town). Turn left onto Stage Road to find the main drag. Parking is free and generally easy to find on Stage Road or in the Duarte's parking lot. On weekends, you might need to park down the road a ways and walk a block or two.

WINE COUNTRY

Entering California's Wine Country is an unmistakable experience. From the crest of the last hill, sunlight paints golden streaks on endless rows of grapevines that stretch in every direction for as far as the eye can see. Trellises run along both sides of every road, tempting visitors to question the unpicked weeds beneath the vines, the rose bushes capping each row, and the strange motionless fans standing guard high above. A heady aroma of earth and grapes permeates the area. Welcome to the Napa and Sonoma Valleys.

The area's beautiful grapevines are renowned worldwide for producing top-quality vintages and economical varietal table wines. But foodies also know the area as a center for stellar cuisine. Yountville, a tiny upscale town in the middle of Napa Valley, is the favorite haven of celebrity chef Thomas Keller. The food served at his French Laundry restaurant is legendary, as are the prices. Keller's influence helped to usher in a culinary renaissance, and today the lush flavors of local sustainable produce are available throughout the region.

Sonoma Valley has long played second fiddle to Napa in terms of viticultural prestige, but the wines coming out of the area are second to none. The Russian River Valley wineries are often friendlier and less crowded than their Napa counterparts, while the wineries in the southern Carneros region are few and far between. Each offers visitors a more personal experience than Napa and the chance to sample unique and amazing varietals. Sonoma County's craggy coastline and natural beauty provide great recreation opportunities for visitors more fond of the outdoors than the grapes.

© 123RF.COM

HIGHLIGHTS

0   20 mi

0   20 km

Geyserville

Calistoga

A. Rafanelli   Spas

Culinary Institute of America

St. Helena

The Russian River

Santa Rosa

Grgich Hills Winery

Mission San Francisco Solano de Sonoma

Sonoma

Napa

San Rafael

PACIFIC OCEAN

Berkeley

© AVALON TRAVEL

LOOK FOR ❰ TO FIND RECOMMENDED SIGHTS, ACTIVITIES, DINING, AND LODGING.

❰ **Grgich Hills Winery:** Home of the California chardonnay that won the Paris Tasting of 1976, Grgich Hills uses a biodynamic farming process to produce exquisite wines (page 201).

❰ **Culinary Institute of America:** The ancient gray stonework and quietly forested surroundings of the CIA belie the bevy of culinary activity inside. Stop by for cooking classes and demonstrations, to peruse the museum, or to indulge in a meal at the exemplary restaurant or café (page 206).

❰ **Spas:** One truly unique wine country experience is to submerge yourself in a bath of surprisingly soothing warm mud. The quirky Napa County town of **Calistoga** has several spas that offer this treatment (page 213).

❰ **Mission San Francisco Solano de Sonoma:** Sonoma is home to the last California Mission and the centerpiece of Sonoma State Historic Park (page 221).

❰ **The Russian River:** Swim, canoe, or simply float serenely downriver at this center of summer fun (page 237).

❰ **A. Rafanelli:** The best Sonoma reds are produced at this small, unpretentious, and appointment-only winery. Be sure to pick up one of their stunning cabs (page 241).

PLANNING YOUR TIME

Napa and Sonoma form the beating heart of California's great Wine Country. Many visitors plan a weekend in Napa, with weekend trips back to explore Sonoma and the Russian River. If you come during the summer or fall, you'll find a crush in almost every tasting room in the valley; even the smaller boutique labels do big business during the six-month high season (May-Oct.).

Be aware that Highway 29, which runs through the heart of Napa Valley, gets jammed up around St. Helena and can be very slow on weekends. U.S. 101 slows through Santa Rosa during the weekday rush-hour commutes and late in the day on sunny summer weekend afternoons. If you're not up for driving, downtown tasting rooms in the cities of Napa, Sonoma, and Santa Rosa are good alternatives to the slow trek up and down the wine roads.

WINE COUNTRY

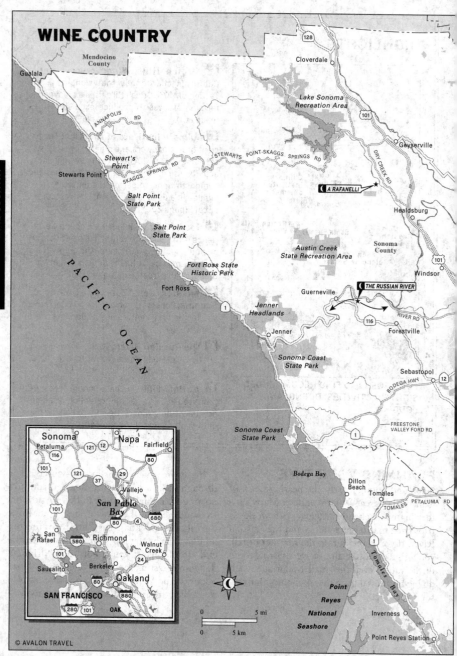

WINE COUNTRY

Mendocino County

Gualala

(128)

Cloverdale

Lake Sonoma
Recreation Area

(101)

ANNAPOLIS   RD

Geyserville

DRY CREEK RD

STEWARTS POINT-SKAGGS SPRINGS RD

Stewart's
Point

SKAGGS   SPRINGS   RD

A RAFANELLI

Stewarts Point

Healdsburg

Salt Point
State Park

(101)

Salt Point
State Park

Austin Creek
State Recreation Area

Sonoma
County

Windsor

Fort Ross State
Historic Park

THE RUSSIAN RIVER

Fort Ross

Guerneville

P A C I F I C

(1)

Jenner
Headlands

RIVER RD

(116)

Forestville

Jenner

O C E A N

Sonoma Coast
State Park

Sebastopol

(12)

BODEGA HWY

FREESTONE
VALLEY FORD RD

Sonoma Coast
State Park

(1)

Bodega Bay

Dillon
Beach

Tomales

PETALUMA   RD

TOMALES

Inset map

Sonoma   Napa   Fairfield

Petaluma   (121) (12)

(116)   (80)

(101)

(121) (37)   (29)

Vallejo

San Pablo
Bay

(101)   (80) (4) (680)

San
Rafael   (580)   Richmond

(101)   Walnut
Creek

Sausalito   Berkeley   (24)

(80)   Oakland

SAN FRANCISCO   (880)

(280) (101)   OAK

Point
Reyes

National

Seashore

Tomales Bay

Inverness

Point Reyes Station

0   5 mi

0   5 km

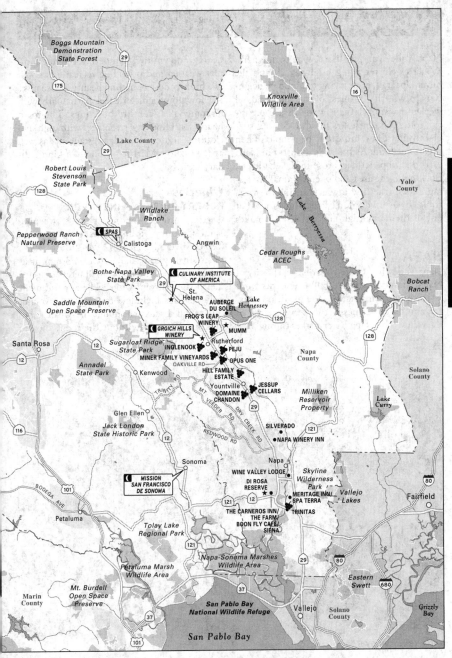

Boggs Mountain Demonstration State Forest

Knoxville Wildlife Area

Lake County

Robert Louis Stevenson State Park

Yolo County

Wildlake Ranch

Pepperwood Ranch Natural Preserve

Cedar Roughs ACEC

Bobcat Ranch

SPAS

Calistoga

Angwin

Bothe-Napa Valley State Park

CULINARY INSTITUTE OF AMERICA

Saddle Mountain Open Space Preserve

St. Helena

AUBERGE DU SOLEIL

Lake Hennessey

Santa Rosa

Sugarloaf Ridge State Park

GRGICH HILLS WINERY

FROG'S LEAP WINERY

MUMM

Napa County

Solano County

Annadel State Park

INGLENOOK

Rutherford

PEJU

MINER FAMILY VINEYARDS

OAKVILLE RD.

OPUS ONE

Kenwood

HILL FAMILY ESTATE

Lake Curry

Jack London State Historic Park

Glen Ellen

Yountville

DOMAINE CHANDON

JESSUP CELLARS

Milliken Reservoir Property

SILVERADO

NAPA WINERY INN

MISSION SAN FRANCISCO DE SONOMA

Sonoma

Napa

WINE VALLEY LODGE

Skyline Wilderness Park

Fairfield

Petaluma

DI ROSA RESERVE

MERITAGE INN/ SPA TERRA

Vallejo Lakes

Tolay Lake Regional Park

THE CARNEROS INN/ THE FARM/ BOON FLY CAFÉ/ SIENA

TRINITAS

Petaluma Marsh Wildlife Area

Napa-Sonoma Marshes Wildlife Area

Mt. Burdell Open Space Preserve

Marin County

Eastern Swett

San Pablo Bay National Wildlife Refuge

Vallejo

Solano County

Grizzly Bay

San Pablo Bay

Napa Valley

Napa Valley can feel like a wine theme park. Wineries cluster along Highway 29 and the Silverado Trail, each trying to outdo its neighbors to win the business of the thousands of weekend visitors. Tasting rooms are plentiful, tours sell out hours in advance, and special events draw hundreds of people. Then there's the food: As the wine industry in Napa exploded, top-tier chefs rose to the challenge, flocking to the area and opening amazing restaurants in the tiny towns that line the wine trails. Even if you don't love wine, a meal at one of the many high-end restaurants makes Napa worth a visit.

NAPA

Napa Valley has a blue-collar heart, the city of Napa, many of whose 80,000 residents work in banking, construction, the medical industry, and other businesses that serve the rest of the valley. The Napa River snakes through the heart of downtown, tempering the hot summer weather and providing recreation as well as a healthy dose of natural beauty. It also gives the downtown a historic feel, particularly with its many 19th-century buildings. The town boasts sparkling new structures with high-end clothiers and cutting-edge restaurants as well as the Oxbow Market—a one-of-a-kind culinary treat.

Wineries

ROBERT SINSKEY VINEYARDS

Getting into the foodie act that's sweeping Wine Country, **Robert Sinskey Vineyards** (6320 Silverado Tr., 707/944-9090, www.robertsinskey.com, daily 10am-4:30pm, tasting $25) offers a menu of small bites alongside their list of current wines. The appointment-only tastings include a tour of the cave and cellar, and discussions about the art of wine-making. With or without the food, the red

Napa Valley vineyards

© GABRIEL SKVOR

DAY TRIPS FROM SAN FRANCISCO

The Napa Valley is less than 100 miles north of San Francisco, making it an ever-popular day-trip destination. If you plan to tour Wine Country, choose one region to explore. Napa and Sonoma are closest to San Francisco, about one hour's drive. Traffic on the winding two-lane roads in these regions can easily become clogged with wine-tasting day-trippers, especially on weekends. To avoid the crowds, try to get an early start or visit on a weekday. Note that most wineries close by 4pm, and some are open only by appointment.

ONE DAY IN NAPA

In downtown Napa, get your bearings at the **Napa General Store** and sample some Napa vintages. Have lunch or just pick up some picnic supplies at **Oxbow Public Market** before hopping back on Highway 29. Drive north to Rutherford and enjoy a tasting at **Grgich Hills,** which offers a relaxed Napa experience. Continue north on Highway 29 to St. Helena and the palatial estate of **Beringer Vineyards.** Many of Beringer's wines are only available here.

After a full day of wine-tasting, give your taste buds a rest with dinner at the **Culinary Institute of America,** where the country's top chefs are trained. The Greystone Restaurant is where that food is served; you can even watch as it's prepared in the open kitchen. From St. Helena, the drive back to San Francisco will take 1.5-2 hours.

Overnight: Spend the night at the aptly named **Zinfandel Inn** and spend a second day exploring Sonoma.

ONE DAY IN SONOMA

From Napa, Highway 121 winds west through the Carneros wine region. Stop off for a bit of bubbly at gorgeous **Domaine Carneros,** where the views and gardens are almost as impressive as the sparkling wines. From Highway 121, Highway 12 twists north into Sonoma. Stretch your legs in Sonoma Plaza and explore the charming downtown area. Stop in at the **Sonoma Mission** for a bit of history, then grab a lunch at **The Girl and the Fig,** housed in the historic Sonoma Hotel.

After lunch it may be time for a massage at the **Garden Spa at MacArthur Place,** or try some Sonoma vintages at the **Charles Creek Vineyard** tasting room right on the square. For more wine-tasting, take Highway 12 north to quaint Glen Ellen and stop in at the **Valley of the Moon,** where the landmark winery will enchant with its stone buildings and unusual sangiovese rosé.

From here, it's a 30-minute drive to downtown Santa Rosa, where you can catch U.S. 101 south to San Francisco, a little over an hour away. You may decide to grab a bite before you head back; if so, try **Jackson's Bar and Oven.**

Overnight: Spend the night at the **Gaige House Inn** in Glen Ellen, or **The Sonoma Hotel** on the plaza in Sonoma.

wines themselves are worth dropping in at this attractive stone-and-wood edifice.

TRINITAS

Situated in a cool cave beneath a hilltop vineyard, the **Trinitas Tasting Room** (875 Bordeaux Way, 707/251-3012, www.trinitascellars.com, daily 11am-7pm, tasting $20-25) functions as the resort wine bar for the Meritage Resort. The bar is open to both hotel guests and passersby, offering tastings of Trinitas wines and bites of cheese, fruit, and tiny gourmet goodies. Seats at the bar make it easy to get comfortable and stay awhile—which quickly becomes desirable when you get your nose inside a glass. Trinitas wines do not tend toward downmarket hotel freebies. These surprisingly balanced, well-crafted wines are more than worth your time, especially if you're serious about your vintages. Expect a small list featuring one or two whites, a rosé, and one or two red wines, all sold at shockingly low per-bottle prices, especially compared to other Napa wines of similar quality. If you happen to be a guest at the inn, wander into the cave at about 5pm for the

WINE COUNTRY

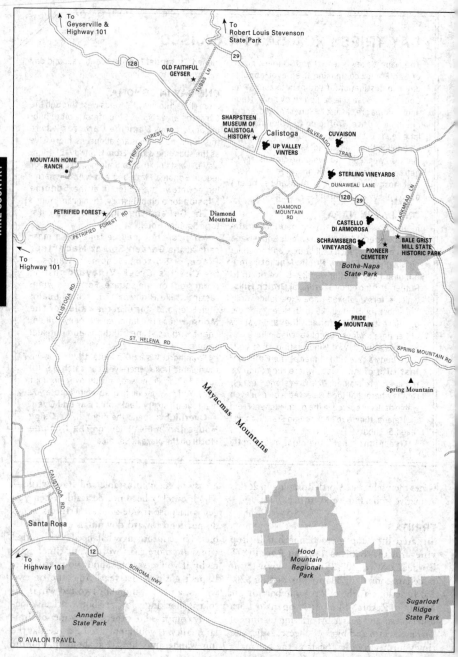

To Geyserville & Highway 101

To Robert Louis Stevenson State Park

128

29

OLD FAITHFUL GEYSER ★

TUBBS LN

SHARPSTEEN MUSEUM OF CALISTOGA HISTORY ★

Calistoga

UP VALLEY VINTERS

SILVERADO

CUVAISON

TRAIL

STERLING VINEYARDS

DUNAWEAL LANE

MOUNTAIN HOME RANCH

PETRIFIED FOREST RD

Diamond Mountain

DIAMOND MOUNTAIN RD

128 29

LARKMEAD LN

PETRIFIED FOREST ★

PETRIFIED FOREST RD

CASTELLO DI ARMOROSA

SCHRAMSBERG VINEYARDS

PIONEER CEMETERY ★

BALE GRIST MILL STATE HISTORIC PARK ★

To Highway 101

CALISTOGA RD

Bothe-Napa State Park

PRIDE MOUNTAIN

ST. HELENA RD

SPRING MOUNTAIN RD

Mayacmas Mountains

Spring Mountain ▲

CALISTOGA RD

Santa Rosa

12

To Highway 101

SONOMA HWY

Hood Mountain Regional Park

Sugarloaf Ridge State Park

Annadel State Park

© AVALON TRAVEL

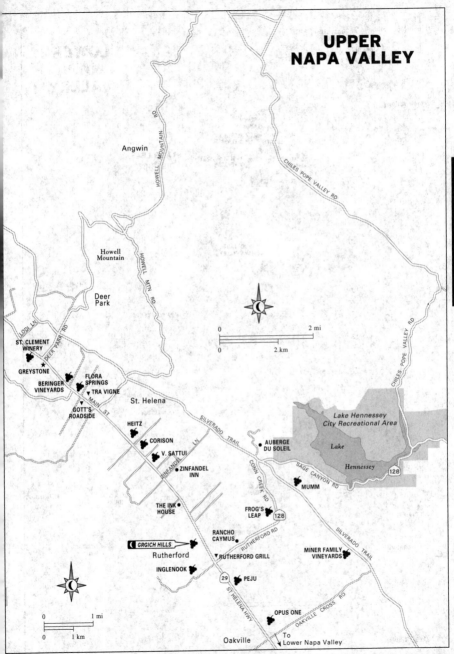

UPPER NAPA VALLEY

Angwin

Howell Mountain

Deer Park

ST. CLEMENT WINERY

GREYSTONE

BERINGER VINEYARDS

FLORA SPRINGS

TRA VIGNE

GOTT'S ROADSIDE

St. Helena

HEITZ

CORISON

V. SATTUI

ZINFANDEL INN

THE INK HOUSE

GRGICH HILLS

Rutherford

RANCHO CAYMUS

RUTHERFORD GRILL

INGLENOOK

PEJU

OPUS ONE

Oakville

To Lower Napa Valley

AUBERGE DU SOLEIL

Lake Hennessey City Recreational Area

Lake Hennessey

MUMM

FROG'S LEAP

MINER FAMILY VINEYARDS

HOWELL MOUNTAIN RD

HOWELL MTN. RD

CHILES POPE VALLEY RD

LODI LN

DEER PARK RD

MAIN ST

SILVERADO TRAIL

ZINFANDEL LN

CONN CREEK RD

SAGE CANYON RD

RUTHERFORD RD

SILVERADO TRAIL

ST HELENA HWY

OAKVILLE CROSS RD

128

128

29

0   2 mi

0   2 km

0   1 mi

0   1 km

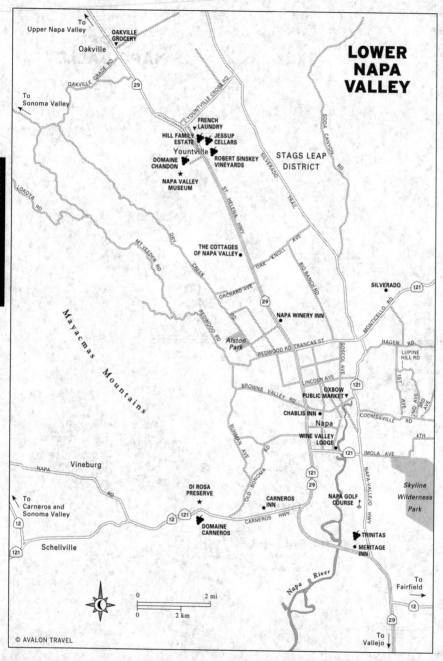

LOWER NAPA VALLEY

To Upper Napa Valley

OAKVILLE GROCERY

Oakville

OAKVILLE GRADE RD

29

To Sonoma Valley

YOUNTVILLE CROSS RD

FRENCH LAUNDRY

HILL FAMILY ESTATE

JESSUP CELLARS

Yountville

DOMAINE CHANDON

ROBERT SINSKEY VINEYARDS

NAPA VALLEY MUSEUM

STAGS LEAP DISTRICT

SODA CANYON RD

SILVERADO TRAIL

ST. HELENA HWY

LOKOYA RD

Mayacmas Mountains

MT VEEDER RD

DRY CREEK RD

REDWOOD RD

THE COTTAGES OF NAPA VALLEY

OAK KNOLL AVE

BIG RANCH RD

ORCHARD AVE

29

SILVERADO

121

MONTICELLO RD

HAGEN RD

LUPINE HILL RD

NAPA WINERY INN

Alston Park

REDWOOD RD   TRANCAS ST

SOSCOL AVE

1ST AVE

2ND AVE

BROWNS VALLEY RD

LINCOLN AVE

121

OXBOW PUBLIC MARKET

COOMBSVILLE RD

CHABLIS INN

Napa

4TH

WINE VALLEY LODGE

121

IMOLA AVE

NAPA VALLEJO HWY

Skyline Wilderness Park

Vineburg

BUHMAN AVE

OLD SONOMA RD

121

29

NAPA RD

DI ROSA PRESERVE

To Carneros and Sonoma Valley

12

121

12

121

CARNEROS INN

CARNEROS HWY

NAPA GOLF COURSE

DOMAINE CARNEROS

TRINITAS

MERITAGE INN

Schellville

Napa River

To Fairfield

12

29

To Vallejo

0   2 mi

0   2 km

© AVALON TRAVEL

WINE COUNTRY

KNOW YOUR GRAPES

California has a few distinctive and easy to find grapes that comprise the basics of winemaking in the state.

Sauvignon Blanc: This pale green grape is used to make both sauvignon blanc and fumé blanc wines in California. Sauvignon blanc grapes grow well in Napa, Sonoma, and warm parts of the state. The California sauvignon blanc wine goes well with salads, fish, vegetarian cuisine, and even spicy ethnic foods. Sauvignon blanc has such a light, fruity, and floral taste it almost seems to float away. The difference between a sauvignon blanc and a fumé blanc is in the winemaking more than the grapes. Fumé blanc wines have a strong odor and the taste of grapefruit. Fumés also pair well with fish dishes and spicy Asian cuisine.

Pinot Noir: Unlike the other red wine grapes, pinot noir grapes do best in a cool coastal climate with limited exposure to high heat. The Anderson Valley and the Monterey coastal growing regions specialize in pinot noir, though many Napa and Sonoma wineries buy grapes from the coast to make their own versions. California vintners make up single-varietal pinot noir wines that taste of cherries, strawberries, and smoke when they're great, and of mold and fish when they're not.

Zinfandel: A good California zinfandel is not what you think it is. For starters, it's not sweet and pale pink. A true zinfandel is a hearty deep red wine. These grapes grow best when tortured by their climate; a few grow near Napa, but most make their homes in Gold Country and the inland Central Coast. Zinfandel was one of the first grapes introduced in California. A few lucky vineyards have "Old Vines" that have been producing these grapes for nearly 100 years. A great zinfandel wine boasts the flavors and smells of blackberry jam and the dusky hues of venous blood. Zinfandel is good with beef, buffalo, and even venison.

Cabernet Sauvignon: If you spend any length of time in Napa or Sonoma, you'll hear the phrase "Cab is King." This always means cabernet sauvignon, a grape from the Bordeaux region of France that creates a deep, dark, strong red wine. The grapes that get intense summer heat make the best wine, which makes them a perfect fit in the scorching Napa Valley. In France, cabernet sauvignon grapes mix with several other varieties to create the famed Bordeaux Blends. In California, especially in Napa, winemakers use cabernet sauvignon on its own to brew some of the most intense single-grape wine in the world. A good dry cab might taste of leather, tobacco, and Bing cherries. Harsh tannins can create a sandpapery feeling in the mouth and an unpleasant tree-bark flavor, making cabernet sauvignon difficult for newcomers to the wine world. Cabs age well, often hitting their peak of flavor and smoothness over a decade after bottling.

free daily tasting of two wines—sometimes Trinitas, sometimes guest vintners.

Sights

At the unique **Di Rosa Preserve** (5200 Sonoma Hwy., 707/226-5991, www.dirosapreserve.org, Nov.-Apr. Wed.-Sun. 10am-4pm, May-Oct. Wed.-Sun. 10am-6pm, $5-15), you'll see the cutting edge of modern California art. With 217 acres, Di Rosa has ample room for three galleries, an outdoor sculpture meadow, and a lake. Take in the festival of color and creativity in the galleries and sculpture garden, or wander the undeveloped portion of the preserve to soak in the colors and shapes of nature.

The **Napa Firefighters Museum** (1201 Main St., 707/259-0609, Wed.-Sat. 11am-4pm, free) makes a perfect 30-60-minute stop right in downtown Napa. The antique fire trucks and fire engines dominate the one-room museum, staffed by volunteers who truly love history and firefighting. But don't let the cool equipment completely overwhelm you; small artifacts and collections of vintage photos tell the story of the Napa Valley and the crucial part played by area firefighting teams and equipment. Flip through

WINE COUNTRY

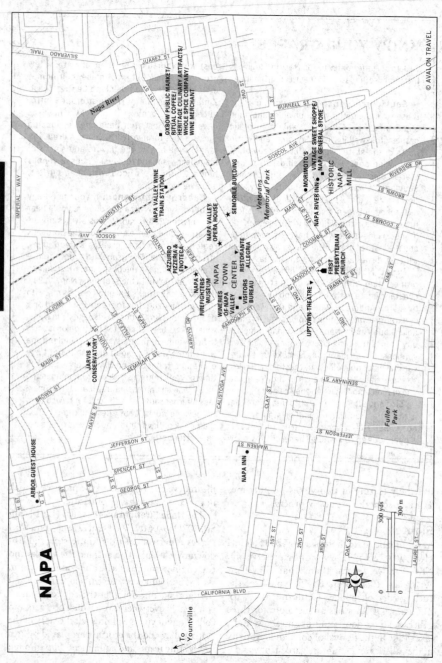

© AVALON TRAVEL

NAPA

Napa River

JUAREZ ST

SILVERADO TRAIL

IMPERIAL WAY

MCKINSTRY ST

CLINTON ST

SOSCOL AVE

OXBOW PUBLIC MARKET/
RITUAL COFFEE/
HERITAGE CULINARY ARTIFACTS/
WHOLE SPICE COMPANY/
WINE MERCHANT

BURNELL ST

NAPA VALLEY WINE
TRAIN STATION

NAPA VALLEY
OPERA HOUSE

SEMORILE BUILDING

Veterans
Memorial Park

SOSCOL AVE

MORIMOTO'S
VINTAGE SWEET SHOPPE/
NAPA GENERAL STORE

HISTORIC
NAPA
MILL

RIVERSIDE DR

NAPA RIVER INN

AZZURRO
PIZZERIA &
ENOTECA

RISTORANTE
ALLEGRIA

NAPA
TOWN
CENTER

NAPA ★
FIREFIGHTERS
MUSEUM

WINERIES
OF NAPA
VALLEY

VISITORS
BUREAU

FIRST
PRESBYTERIAN
CHURCH

UPTOWN THEATRE

YAJOME ST

NAPA ST

ARROYO DR

RANDOLPH ST

COOMBS ST

JARVIS ★
CONSERVATORY

MAIN ST

BROWN ST

HAYES ST

SEMINARY ST

CALISTOGA AVE

CLAY ST

SEMINARY ST

OAK ST

COOMBS ST

BROWN ST

Fuller
Park

JEFFERSON ST

ARBOR GUEST HOUSE

SPENCER ST

GEORGE ST

YORK ST

H ST
G ST
F ST
E ST
D ST
C ST
B ST

WARREN ST

NAPA INN

JEFFERSON ST

1ST ST
2ND ST
3RD ST

OAK ST

LAUREL ST

300 yds

300 m

To
Yountville

CALIFORNIA BLVD

© GABRIEL SKVOR

Napa's Uptown Theatre

poster-size news shots of the many Napa Valley floods, including one that flooded the museum building; examine the collection of old tools; and ask the docents about the incongruous collection of insurance-company plaques.

Live Music

Napa is home to two historic live music venues. Since being reopened in 2010, the **Uptown Theatre** (1350 3rd St., 707/259-0123, www. uptowntheatrenapa.com), which dates back to 1937, has become probably one of the wine country's best music venues. The Uptown even lures Bay Area residents to Napa to see intimate performances by acts including Beck, BB King, and Glen Campbell.

Even older, the **Napa Valley Opera House** (1030 Main St., 707/226-7322, http://nvoh.org) has been around since 1880. It has hosted everyone from early 1900s author Jack London to country music legend Willie Nelson. The Opera House also hosts other events, such as screenings for the **Napa Valley Film Festival** (http://napa-valleyfilmfest.org) in early November.

Spas

Spa Terra (875 Bordeaux Way, 707/251-3000, www.spaterra.com, $65-360) is the jewel of the Meritage Resort's property. The interior of an artificial cave beneath a vineyard seems like an odd choice for a luxury spa, but the gorgeous cavern rooms will make a believer of even the most discerning spa-goer. Begin your pampering with a warm greeting and a required tour of the public areas from your guide. Be sure to show up at least 30 minutes in advance of an appointment—you'll have the run of a tiled hot tub, steam room, and relaxation space both before and after your scheduled treatment. Grab a glass of lemon water, a cool moist cloth for your forehead, and warm out (it's not the least bit chilly in Spa Terra). The menu of treatments includes a full-body scrub using grape-seed extracts, couples massages in two-person rooms, and an espresso-based facial.

Shopping

Downtown Napa strives to be a shopping destination, yet despite some redevelopment efforts, it's still not quite there. The north end of Main Street has some flashy buildings with equally flashy clothiers, but the place to go is the **Historic Napa Mill** (Main St., www. historicnapamill.com), one block down. Formerly the Hatt Warehouse, the mill has since been converted into a lovely shopping and dining center, decorated with rustic touches—weathered redwood, an abundance of trailing vines, and blooming planter boxes and hanging baskets. The historic Napa River Inn is located here, as is the **Vintage Sweet Shoppe** (530 Main St., 707/224-2986, http:// vintagesweetshoppe.com, Sun.-Wed. 10am-6pm, Thurs.-Sat. 8am-10pm), which specializes in chocolate but has enough treats to make anyone's teeth ache. In the same complex, the **Napa General Store** (540 Main St., 707/259-0762, www.napageneralstore.com, daily 8am-6pm) next door offers a bite to eat, a glass of wine, wine-related knickknacks, and other gifts. The store also sells local artwork, including leather crafts and fiber art, all of which has an arty ecological bent.

With so much natural beauty in the Napa Valley, is it any wonder that there are so many artists living here? The **Napa Valley Art Association** (1520 Behrens St., 707/254-2085, www.nvart.org/gallery.html, Sun.-Thurs. 10am-6pm, Fri.-Sat. 10am-9pm) showcases some of the best. The gallery presents pen-and-ink drawings, watercolors, photography, glass jewelry, fiber art, and oil paintings. While there are plenty of lush portraits of vineyards, you'll also find some unusual subjects—jellyfish, abstract aerial photographs, or watery self-portraits. The association plans events that often pair wine-tasting with art shows; check the website before visiting.

Across the River from downtown Napa, the **Oxbow Public Market** (610-644 1st St., 707/226-6529, www.oxbowpublicmarket.com, daily 9am-7pm) is a well-used piece of real estate. Located next to the now-defunct COPIA museum, the Oxbow Public Market has once again breathed life into this "across the tracks" section of Napa. The market is a food lover's delight. Grab a cup of **Ritual Coffee** and browse through the epicurean wares; pick through beautiful cooking- and kitchen-related antiques at the **Heritage Culinary Artifacts;** or get lost in the myriad spices and seasonings at the **Whole Spice Company.** There is also a chocolatier, an olive-oil company, and the venerable **Wine Merchant,** where you can pick up some vino, cheese, and other treats for the road.

Sports and Recreation

Once you're on the trails of **Skyline Wilderness Park** (2201 Imola Ave., 707/252-0481, www.skylinepark.org, summer daily 8am-7pm, winter daily 8am-5pm, $5-6), you may forget you're even in Wine Country. Up at this park, no vineyards encroach on the natural chaparral landscape of Napa's high country. This park includes the Martha Walker Garden—a botanical garden planted with California and Napa native plants in honor of a legendary figure in the local horticultural community. The rest of this 850-acre park is given over to multiple community uses. You'll find campgrounds, hiking trails, horse and bicycle paths, a disc

golf course, and more. Be aware that it gets hot here in the summertime, and not all the campgrounds and trails offer adequate shade to cool off. Even so, the natural beauty of this protected wilderness makes Skyline Park a favorite with both locals and travelers.

Since you're in a land of entertainment options, it seems only natural to enjoy a round of golf during your Wine Country vacation. At the par-72 **Napa Golf Course** (2295 Streblow Dr., 707/255-4333, www.playnapa.com, $38-48), golfers of all levels—even beginners—can enjoy a full 18 holes. More experienced players will enjoy (or curse) the plethora of water features and full-size trees on this course, known locally as a bargain.

Napa River Adventures (Oxbow Public Market, 1147 1st St., 707/259-1833, www.napariveradventures.com, adults $50, children $25) offers 2.5-hour tours of the Napa River, through wetlands and alongside the historic downtown. Float along the river in a lovely small covered motor launch in cushy seats, enjoying the view out the massive wraparound windows. The trip takes you right into the heart of downtown Napa and back to the dock.

Rising in the morning sun over the valley in a brightly colored hot-air balloon is a unique experience. **Balloons Above the Valley** (3425 Solano Ave., 800/464-6824, www.balloon-rides.com, $209-240) offers the full experience: lodging packages that include transportation to the launch site and a champagne brunch after you touch down. On your trip, you'll float serenely over the vineyards of Napa Valley before a gentle descent at a predetermined spot. Be sure to make reservations in advance as trips can fill up quickly, especially during high season (May-Oct.). You must be an early riser too, since most balloon trips depart shortly after dawn. Note that booking online can save you as much as $30.

Accommodations
UNDER $150

The pretty, unassuming **Wine Valley Lodge** (200 S. Coombs St., 707/224-7911, www.winevalleylodge.com, $90-225) welcomes guests

WINE COUNTRY

© GABRIEL SKVOR

the Napa River

with its redbrick and adobe-tile exterior. Inside, guests enjoy serene guest rooms with unobtrusive art, pale yellow walls, and soothing pastel comforters. Guest rooms are a nice size, and you can choose a king bed, two queens, or a suite, depending on your needs. The Wine Valley Lodge also boasts a significant past: In the late 1950s and early 1960s, several movies were filmed in Napa, and various A-list stars, including Rock Hudson, Marilyn Monroe, and even Elvis stayed at the lodge during filming.

$150-250

Outside of town, the newly renovated **Napa Winery Inn** (1998 Trower Ave., 888/522-8999, www.napawineryinn.com, $209-240) is certainly one of the most affordable. Standard amenities include complimentary Wi-Fi, and an outdoor pool sweetens the deal. Pricier guest rooms might boast a fridge, a wet bar, and a kitchenette. The inn also serves a complimentary wine country breakfast.

At the **Chablis Inn** (3360 Solano Ave., 800/443-3490, www.chablisinn.com,

$150-189), the guest rooms include all the usual amenities: a wet bar with a mini fridge, an in-room coffeemaker, a TV with cable, and more. Guest rooms are simply decorated, but the beds are comfortable, the carpets are dark (making it safe to drink just a little bit of red wine in your room), and the address is central to both the attractions of downtown Napa and the famous Highway 29 wine road. Dogs are welcome.

For a different style of historic lodging experience, stay at the **Napa Inn** (1137 Warren St., 800/435-1144, www.napainn.com, $215-295), which comprises two Victorian houses, both painted blue, in historic downtown Napa. You can walk from either to downtown shops and restaurants, and the Wine Train depot is a very short drive. As bed-and-breakfasts go, the Napa Inn is a big one, with more than 10 guest rooms and suites. If you plan to travel with your pet, talk to the inn well in advance to get one of the two pet-friendly guest rooms. Elegant fabrics and lush modern textures moderate the floral and carved-wood decor of the Victorian era. The nicest guest rooms have corner whirlpool tubs and king beds. Breakfast at the Napa Inn is an event, with multiple courses served by candlelight.

For another charming and conveniently located option, consider the **Arbor Guest House** (1436 G St., 707/252-8144, www.arborguesthouse.com, $189-289). The prim white exterior betrays little of the inn's lush Victorian decor. Rich fabric drapes the windows and beds, and polished antiques grace even the smallest corner, while soft lighting and flower-filled vases lend warm touches. There are only five guest rooms, each distinctively decorated; two offer gas fireplaces and two-person jetted tubs for a romantic stay. Guests are invited to a complimentary hot breakfast in the morning and wine and appetizers in the evening.

OVER $250

The **G Napa River Inn** (500 Main St., 877/251-8500, www.napariverinn.com, $250-369) has one of the best locations in Napa—right inside the Historic Napa Mill. You can practically fall out of your guest room and hit the General Store, restaurant, several galleries, the candy store, and at least one other restaurant on the way down. Located steps from the center of Napa's bustling downtown, your guest room might even afford you a view of the Napa River. The interior of this luxury hotel is crammed with high-end antiques and reproductions. Best of all, you can choose from three styles of room decor: Historic Victorian rooms feature canopy beds, floral prints, cushy chairs, and slipper tubs; the nautical rooms, many of which face the river, resemble the inside of a yacht, with wood paneling, porthole-style mirrors, and rope-style accents; and the Wine Country rooms echo the natural wealth of the Napa Valley with floral linens, marble baths, and oak moldings.

The king of Napa lodging is the **Silverado** (1600 Atlas Peak Rd., 707/257-0200, www.silveradoresort.com, $219-559). You'll find the finest in modern amenities and decorations in your room (all guest suites at the Silverado have kitchens and dining rooms), including high-thread-count linens, complimentary Wi-Fi, and a private patio or deck overlooking the grounds. Pale colors with eye-popping jewel-toned accents speak of the best current designers. Outside your guest room, there's so much to do at the Silverado that you'll find it hard to pry yourself away from the grounds to go wine-tasting. Choose from the immense spa with full fitness and salon services, two 18-hole golf courses, two restaurants, 17 tennis courts, 11 pools, and—believe it or not—more.

The Carneros Inn (4048 Sonoma Hwy., 707/299-4900, www.thecarnerosinn.com, $535-750) is an expansive and expensive cottage resort. The immense property, which backs onto real countryside, has three restaurants, a spa, two pools, a fitness center, and even a small market. On arrival, follow the signs to the registration area and then just keep driving—the lobby is at the very top of the resort's hill. Your persistence is rewarded with a charming greeting complete with drinks. The unprepossessing (from the outside) cottages spread out in small clusters for acres, each group surrounding its own garden paths and water features. Inside, the cozy (yes, that does mean "smallish") cottages sparkle with white linens, tile floors, and windows overlooking sizeable private backyards with decks and comfy chaises. But it's the baths that bring Carneros Inn clients back again and again.

The **Meritage Inn** (875 Bordeaux Way, 707/251-1900, www.themeritageresort.com, $200-575) is beside the small Napa Valley airport, convenient to businesspeople and travelers who want easy access to both the Napa Valley and Sonoma-Carneros wine regions. This big motel got a Wine Country makeover—now the grounds, common spaces, and guest rooms have the deep harvest colors and country-elegant style of Tuscany. The lush garden pool is the literal centerpiece of the property, which also includes a wine-tasting room, a fabulous spa, and a refreshingly down-to-earth restaurant. The basic shape of the guest rooms remains true to the Meritage's motel roots, but the Tuscan-style decor and trimmings make a play for elegance, with comfortable beds, deep soaking tubs in the baths, and posh amenities.

Expect a fridge stocked with free water, a coffeemaker, and a complimentary bottle of wine.

Food
CALIFORNIA CUISINE
The FARM (4048 Sonoma Hwy., 707/299-4880, www.thecarnerosinn.com, dinner Wed.-Sun. 5:30pm-10pm, bar/pavilion 4pm-10pm, $31-47) at the Carneros Inn serves up the expected upscale California cuisine, complete with a chef's tasting menu and big white service plates topped with tiny artistic piles of food. So why choose to dine at the determinedly uppercase FARM? The food may be a touch pretentious, but it's cooked perfectly, and the chef has put some imagination into his dishes that really works well. Expect unusual but deftly created flavor combinations, smaller portions appropriate to the number of courses you'll get, and just a touch of molecular gastronomy thrown in for color and interest. The dining room feels more comfortable than many of its ilk, with cushy banquettes and padded chairs. Servers are friendly and good at their jobs, and can help you decipher anything on the menu that might be confusing. Do dress up a little—the FARM has a distinctly upscale vibe. If you want to soak in the atmosphere with a more casual experience, ask about the bar menu; you'll find a burger, flat bread, and even a grilled ham and cheese sandwich for considerably less.

Also at the Carneros Inn, the **Boon Fly Café** (4048 Sonoma Hwy., 707/299-4870, www.the-carnerosinn.com, daily 7am-9pm, $25-40) has classic breakfast dishes and almost down-to-earth salad and sandwich fare. If you're staying at the inn, skip the mediocre service of the café itself and order the Boon Fly menu via room service—the prices are the same in-cottage as in the diner. Eggs are cooked competently, salads are enormous, and the carefully designed down-home dining room is cute. The half-booth banquettes are comfortable to sit in, and lingering over coffee or tea is tolerated. Wine tasters passing through will easily find the Boon Fly—it has a nice big sign on the bright-red barn of a building. Sadly, the Boon Fly does not serve breakfast all day—be sure to arrive and order before 11am if you're dying for an omelet.

CLASSIC AMERICAN
When Napa locals need a diner-style breakfast or lunch, they head to the **Butter Cream Bakery & Diner** (2297 Jefferson St., 707/255-6700, www.buttercreambakery.com, diner daily 5:30am-3pm, bakery Mon.-Sat. 5:30am-6pm, Sun. 5:30am-4:30pm, $10-15). It's not in the ritzy part of downtown, but the brilliant pink- and white-striped building is hard to miss. On the diner side, breakfast is served all day; choose between a small table in the fluorescent-lit linoleum dining room or a stool at the old-school counter. Service is indifferent, but you'll get decently cooked eggs, tasty sandwiches, reasonable portions, and best of all, reasonable prices. Over on the bakery side, mouthwatering turnovers, Danishes, and fruit rings make it easy to get a good breakfast on the go. Dessert pastries, cookies, and cakes tempt even dieters.

ITALIAN
The restaurant at the Meritage Inn, **Siena** (875 Bordeaux Way, 707/251-1950, www.themeritageresort.com, Mon.-Thurs. 6:30am-11am, 11:30am-2pm, 5:30pm-9:30pm, Fri.-Sat. 6:30am-11am, 11:30am-2pm, 5:30pm-10pm, Sun. 8am-1pm, 5pm-9:30pm, $10-30), doesn't serve typical Wine Country cuisine. The food is mostly Italian, much of it hot, hearty, and welcome after a long day of wine-tasting. Choose from fresh salads, pasta dishes, and big entrées, though if you've been in Napa for a while, you may not be able to resist a pizza or a cheeseburger. The waiter can even suggest the right wine or beer to accompany your burger. Desserts also tend toward the dense and filling—consider sharing one among your tablemates. The upholstered booths and dim lighting make a romantic dining experience possible, but the vibe in the dining room manages to stay low-key enough to make jeans-clad diners comfortable.

For simple Italian fare, go to **Azzurro** (1260 Main St., 707/255-5552, www.azzurropizzeria.

com, Mon.-Wed. 11:30am-9:30pm, Thurs.-Sat. 11:30am-10pm, Sun. 11:30am-9:30pm, $12-16). Veterans of Tra Vigne in St. Helena, Michael and Christina Gyetvan opened Azzurro with the intention of bringing their style of Italian food to downtown Napa. A favorite with locals, this trattoria offers wood-fired pizzas in addition to hearty pasta dishes and big rustic salads. The warm and modern interior welcomes diners with wood and stone tables and an open kitchen. Wines by the glass are affordable.

JAPANESE

Sake in Wine Country? Not a bad idea, particularly if it's paired with dinner at **Morimoto's** (610 Main St., 707/252-1600, www.morimotonapa.com, Sun.-Thurs. 11:30am-2:30pm and 5pm-10pm, Fri.-Sat. 11:30am-2:30pm and 5pm-11pm, entrées $29-80, tasting menu $120). Celebrity chef Masaharu Morimoto, who has appeared on the *Iron Chef* TV show, recently relocated to Napa to open this esoteric and sleek Japanese eatery. The elegant interior features steel highlighted by bright yellow accents. The food includes traditional Japanese dishes, all with a unique and modern twist—*gyoza* with bacon cream and duck confit-fried rice are just some of the menu items. There are also a handful of non sequiturs like steak, lobster, and roasted fingerling potatoes. For a full idea of the chef's culinary vision, order the tasting menu.

MARKETS

For a bit of this and a bit of that, venture across the Napa River to the ◖**Oxbow Market** (610-644 1st St., 707/226-6529, www.oxbowpublicmarket.com, daily 9am-7pm). Inside this large open space you can snack on oysters at the **Hog Island Oyster Company**, lunch on tacos from **Pica Pica Maize Kitchen**, or blow your diet at **Kara's Cupcakes.** Hamburgers are just out the side door at **Gott's Roadside,** and around the corner you can find some of the best charcuterie around in delectable take-out sandwiches at the **Fatted Calf** or pizza by the slice at **The Model Bakery.** The bacon *levain,* made with

hunks of bacon and bacon fat from next door, is irresistible.

Perhaps the most acclaimed of these options is the **Kitchen Door** (707/226-6529, www.kitchendoornapa.com, Mon.-Fri. 11am-9pm, Sat.-Sun. 9am-9pm, $10-22). Unlike the market's loud and congested interior, the Kitchen Door has an air of calm. The white-tile wood oven, open seating, and large picture windows draw light in for an illuminating meal. Comfort food comes in all stripes, including some Armenian dishes, rice and noodle bowls, roast chickens, burgers, and sundaes.

Information and Services

The **Napa Valley Welcome Center** (600 Main St., 707/251-5895, www.napavalley.org, daily 9am-5pm), in the middle of downtown Napa, has complimentary maps, guidebooks, and wine-tasting passes. Chat with a friendly local who can direct you to the favorite wineries and restaurants.

A privately run information outpost, the **Napa Tourist Information Center** (1331 1st St., 707/252-1000, www.napatouristinfo.com, Mon.-Thurs. 10am-8pm, Fri.-Sat. 10am-9pm, Sun. 10am-7pm) also has wine-tastings, olive oils tastings, a gift shop, and a limousine service.

For current events, *Wine Country This Week* (www.winecountrythisweek.com) has the best up-to-date information. You can find local news in the daily *Napa Valley Register* (www.napanews.com).

Napa has a **post office** (1351 2nd St., 707/255-0621). The **Queen of the Valley** (1000 Trancas St., 707/252-4411, www.thequeen.org) has both a 24-hour emergency room and trauma center and a by-appointment urgent-care clinic.

Getting There and Around

Napa, in all its bucolic beauty, does not have infrastructure designed for the number of visitors it receives. This is part of its charm—unless you spend your visit sitting in bumper-to-bumper traffic. The best way to experience the valley is to avoid the ever-popular autumn crush

Oxbow Market

and summer weekend afternoons. November and early spring are beautiful seasons to see the valley. But if a summer Saturday spent wine-tasting is impossible to resist, hit the wineries early and stay off the roads from mid-afternoon to early evening. With great restaurants and seductive spas everywhere, you'll easily be able to pass the extra time.

CAR

Considering the number of people that go to Napa, it is not all that easy to get to. Most of the highways in this region are two lanes and frequently go by colloquial names. They are also susceptible to gridlocked traffic thanks to the numerous wine lovers and the occasional race at nearby Infineon Raceway.

Highway 29 is the central conduit that runs north into the valley from the city of Napa. It is also known as the Napa-Vallejo Highway between the two cities, and as the St. Helena Highway from Napa to Calistoga, where it becomes Foothill Boulevard. To reach Highway 29 from San Francisco, take U.S. 101 north across the Golden Gate Bridge to Novato. In Novato, take the exit for Highway 37 east to Napa. Highway 37 skirts the tip of the San Pablo Bay and runs all the way to Vallejo. From Vallejo, take Highway 29 (Sonoma Blvd.) north for seven miles until you reach downtown Napa. Highway 29 will take you as far north as Calistoga.

Highway 37 in Vallejo is especially easy if you're coming from the East Bay, Lake Tahoe, and Sacramento. Highway 37 intersects I-80 at the north end of Vallejo at the exit for Six Flags Discovery Kingdom.

Highway 128 connects the north end of Napa Valley near Rutherford with U.S. 101 in Geyserville. From Geyserville, you can follow this beautiful two-lane road south to Calistoga, where it joins Highway 29.

Coming from **Highway 121** in Sonoma, **Highway 12** east leads directly to Napa. Highway 121 then picks up again at West Imola Avenue and leads east to the **Silverado Trail,** an alternate route north-south in the Napa Valley.

BUS

To avoid the potential headache of driving in Napa, take the **VINE** bus (800/696-6443, http://nctpa.net, adults $1.50-5.50, children $1-2.50), which provides public transportation around Napa Valley, including Napa, Yountville, Oakville, Rutherford, St. Helena, and Calistoga. If you don't want to drive at all, jump aboard the commuter VINE 29 Express, which runs all day Monday-Friday. The Express travels from the El Cerrito BART station in the East Bay and from the Vallejo Ferry Terminal into Napa Valley. Fares are cash-only and require exact change.

NAPA VALLEY WINE TRAIN

If trying to decide which wineries to visit, which restaurants are worth a stop, and how best to avoid weekend traffic sounds exhausting, consider taking the **Napa Valley Wine Train** (1275 McKinstry St., Napa, 800/427-4124, www.winetrain.com, $99-199). The Wine Train offers a relaxing sightseeing experience aboard vintage train cars, where you can sit back and enjoy the food, wine, and views. The train runs from Napa to St. Helena and back, a 36-mile, three-hour, round-trip tour. The least expensive option includes a barbecued lunch and a glass of wine. More amenities at higher prices include a gourmet three-course lunch or dinner, with the option of taking a winery tour along the way. Each package includes seating in a different historic railcar—you might lunch in the 1917 Pullman Car, or take an evening tour of Grgich Hills aboard the 1952 Vista Dome Car. Advance reservations are strongly suggested.

YOUNTVILLE

Named for George Calvert Yount, who planted the first vineyard in Napa Valley, Yountville is the quintessential wine-loving town. There are not even 3,000 residents, but the town has earned widespread fame for its epicurean spirit. You'll find a number of prestigious wineries and champagneries, but it is really restaurateur Thomas Keller who put this postage stamp-size town on the map.

First came the French Laundry, then Bouchon and the Bouchon Bakery, and eventually Ad Hoc. But it's not just a Keller company town; other notable eateries have opened up and keep pace with the big boy. Still, with so many fantastic dining options, you might wish there was more to do in Yountville to extend your stay in order to accommodate as many meals out as possible.

Wineries
DOMAINE CHANDON

One of the premier champagneries in Napa Valley, **Domaine Chandon** (1 California Dr., 888/242-6366, www.chandon.com, daily 10am-5pm, $15-42/tours) offers one of the best tours in Napa—it's a perfect introduction to the process of wine- and champagne-making. Walk out into the vineyards to look at the grapes, head down to the tank- and barrel-filled cellars to learn about the champagne-making process, then proceed into the aging rooms to see the racked bottles, tilted and dusty, aging to the point of drinkability. Finally, you'll adjourn to the tasting room to sample the bubbly concoctions. Chandon also makes still wines, which you can also taste. Reservations are required for tours, and booking in advance is a good idea.

Domaine Chandon also boasts lovely gardens, a stream, and an immense estate. Visitors can walk the open paths among the vineyards, enjoy the delights of the tasting room ($18-25), and make a reservation for dinner at Étoile, the on-site California-French restaurant.

HILL FAMILY ESTATE

Right on Washington Street in downtown Yountville, the **Hill Family Estate** (6512 Washington St., 707/944-9580, www.hillfamilyestate.com, daily 10am-6pm, tasting $10) tasting room and antiques shop offers an elegant tasting and shopping experience. The most affordable item in the room is the tasting glass; you can get two-for-one tasting coupons if you first stop by the Yountville Visitors Center on the next block. Roam among the pricey French antiques as you sip, or stand at the bar to enjoy the company of the Hill family and a small

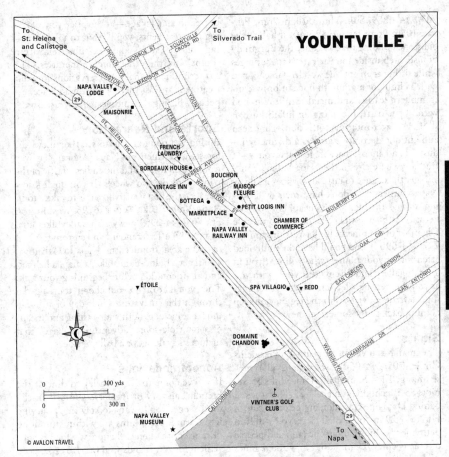

selection of light, balanced red and white wines. The cabernet sauvignons are not made in the typical heavy-handed Napa style, so even tasters with delicate palates will find them drinkable. Ask about the Double Barrel Cab, which is sold in a box that the younger sons of the winery family have blasted with buckshot with their grandfather's double-barrel shotgun.

JESSUP CELLARS

Located in downtown Yountville, the tiny tasting room at **Jessup Cellars** (6740 Washington St., 707/944-8523, www.jessupcellars.com, daily 10am-6pm) offers tastes of incredible boutique red wines that you'll have a hard time finding anyplace else. There are no tours here, no picnic grounds or fancy gardens, but you'll find lush, rich zinfandels and deep, smoky cabernets that are more than worth the sometimes-steep price tag. The tasting room boasts a cute little bar, a few shelves with items for purchase, and staff that love their jobs. If you chat them up, you may find yourself tasting rare Jessup vintages that are not on the usual list.

MASONRIE NAPA VALLEY

Unique tasting room and art gallery **Masonrie Napa Valley** (6711 Washington St.,

707/944-0889, Sun.-Thurs. 10am-7pm, Fri.-Sat. 10am-9pm, tasting $20-40) inhabits the old stone building that was once the Burgundy House. Step inside to taste rare Napa vintages while sitting at an antique wooden table topped with a chunk of mammoth bone or browse ultramodern leather and metal furniture paired with objets d'art, including an inlaid human skull. An ever-rotating collection of modern and antique decorative art has a distinctly industrial and almost macabre feel that you won't find anywhere else in the Napa Valley. You'll also get the chance to taste local wines made by Napa vintners who don't have their own tasting rooms. Tastings aren't cheap, but you can get a two-for-one ticket from the Yountville Chamber of Commerce (6484 Washington St., 707/944-0904), and you'll have the undivided attention of your pourer, who will seat you in a small gallery and discuss the wines with you as you sip. Tasting selections are forever changing, so frequent visitors to the region can keep coming back to try something new.

Sights

The small **Napa Valley Museum** (55 Presidents Circle, 707/944-0500, www.napavalleymuseum.org, Tues.-Sun. 10am-4pm, adults $5, seniors $3.50, children under 17 $2.50) is tucked behind Domaine Chandon on the other side of Highway 29 in Yountville. Here, you will find permanent exhibits about the land and people of Napa Valley. Learn about how the region's geological makeup contributes to winemaking or take in the local art on display.

Spas

An easy walk from anywhere in downtown Yountville, the newly reimagined **Spa Villagio** (6481 Washington St., 800/351-1133, daily 7:30am-9pm, $135-270) has a beautiful space in which to pamper its patrons. You don't need to be a guest at the Villagio Inn to book a treatment at the spa, although you may want to try one of the five Spa Suites—private spaces where singles, couples, and friends can relax before, during, and after their treatments. Be sure to show up an hour early for your massage, facial, or treatment package—at the price you're paying for treatments, you'll want to take advantage of the saunas and hot tubs, relaxation rooms, and the other chichi amenities. The spa recommends making reservations for your treatment at least three weeks in advance, especially during the summer-fall high season.

Sports and Recreation

Biking is a popular way to see the vineyards, forests, and wineries of Napa. You can get away from the highways and the endless traffic of the wine roads on two wheels. If you don't know the area, the best way to bike it is to take a tour. **Napa Valley Bike Tours** (6795 Washington St., 707/944-2953, www.napavalleybiketours.com, $139) offers standard and custom tours all over the area, from central Napa to Calistoga. You'll get a brand-name bike, a map, a helmet, and an orientation before beginning your trek. Then you'll be off on your chosen tour: a pedal through the vineyards, a half-day or full-day tour that includes both wine-tasting and meals, or a multiple-sport "adventure package" that includes kayaking, or a balloon ride.

Accommodations

If you've come to Napa Valley to dine at the French Laundry or immerse yourself in the food scene, you'll want to stay in Yountville if you can. Several inns are within stumbling distance of the French Laundry, which is convenient for gourmands who want to experience a range of wines with the meal.

$100-150

For a motel with a historic twist, book a room at the **Napa Valley Railway Inn** (6523 Washington St., 707/944-2000, www.napavalleyrailwayinn.com, $125-260). The nine guest rooms are converted 100-year-old train cars tightly packed together, making a unique type of hotel. The rooms themselves are funky and narrow but carefully decorated in classic style with rich bedspreads. Some of the perks include the Coffee Caboose, where you can start your day with pastries and coffee, access to the nearby Yountville Fitness Center to burn off any unwanted calories, and a "Napa Valley Travel Packet" ($20), which includes tasting vouchers, maps, bottled water, and Advil.

$150-250

The ◖ **Bordeaux House** (6600 Washington St., 707/944-2855, www.bordeauxhouse.com, $150-250) has it all: a beautiful brick facade, lovely French country interiors, and a location literally three doors down from the French Laundry. The amenities in each individually decorated room will make you feel as though you're staying in a quaint country inn in the south of France. During your stay, take a stroll through the inn's gardens, enjoy a splash in the outdoor spa, and partake of the better-than-continental breakfast in the common area each morning. Perhaps best of all, the location on Washington Street makes a walk from the inn through the best of downtown Yountville an easy prospect.

A French-style inn, the **Maison Fleurie** (6529 Yount St., 800/788-0369, www.foursisters.com, $145-325) offers the best of small-inn style for a more reasonable nightly rate. It is in a perfect location for walking to Bouchon, the Bouchon Bakery, and the many other amazing restaurants, boutiques, and tasting rooms in town. The 13 guest rooms in this "house of flowers" have an attractive but not overwhelming floral decorative theme. The more economical rooms, described as "cozy," are small but attractive. If you've got the budget to splurge, opt for a room in the Bakery Building, where you'll get a fireplace, a jetted spa tub, a king bed, and a private entrance. All guests can enjoy a full breakfast each morning as well as an afternoon wine reception, fresh cookies, and use of the onsite pool and hot tub.

Located next to Bouchon Bakery, wake up to mouthwatering smells at the cozy five rooms **Petit Logis Inn** (6527 Yount St., 877/944-2332, www.petitlogis.com, $210-285). Each of the five rooms has a fireplace, a jetted tub, and a fridge and is decorated in warm creamy colors with an occasional wall mural. Low-key and unpretentious, the inn is best described as "the place to come to pretend you live in Yountville." Unlike many other inns, breakfast is not included but can be arranged for an additional charge at a nearby restaurant.

OVER $250

The **Napa Valley Lodge** (2230 Madison St., 888/944-3545, www.napavalleylodge.com, $300-700), a stunning Mediterranean-style hotel with stucco walls and red tile roofs, loves the sunshine and warmth of the Napa Valley summer. Guests are steeped in the luxury that the Wine Country in general, and Yountville in particular, are known for. Book a spa treatment either in your guest room or out beside the heated pool. Start each day with the complimentary champagne buffet breakfast, or order from the California cuisine room-service menu. Finish each night in the luxury of your guest room—including the Parkside Terrace rooms, with king beds topped with European-style duvets; the Vineyard Courtyard Terrace rooms, with their own patios; and the luxurious King Junior Suite, with a fireplace, two-person soaking tub, and views of the courtyard.

At **The Cottages of Napa Valley** (1012 Darms Lane, 2 miles south of Yountville, 707/252-7810, www.napacottages.com, $395-575), you'll pay a princely sum to gain a home away from home in the heart of Wine Country. Each cottage has its own king bed, outdoor fireplace, kitchenette, and heated bathroom floor. Every morning the quiet staff drops off a basket of fresh pastries from Bouchon Bakery and a pot of great coffee for breakfast to greet you whenever you feel like waking up. Simple yet luxurious country-cottage furnishings feel welcoming and homey, and the staff can help you plan and execute the ultimate Wine Country vacation. They also offer complimentary dinner shuttles into Yountville.

If you're splurging on a no-expenses-spared trip to Napa Valley, enjoy the location and luxury of the **Vintage Inn** (6541 Washington St., 707/944-1112, www.vintageinn.com, $340-740). Guest rooms in the elegant hexagonal buildings feature the softest sheets ever, jetted tubs, wood burning fireplaces, complimentary bottles of wine, and a prettily hidden TV

WINE COUNTRY

and fridge. The French country-meets-Wine Country decor extends to a private patio or deck overlooking the lush gardens. Once you make your way off the property (it's easy to get lost in the landscaping and identical structures of this big resort space), you're at the center of the main drag in Yountville. Walk to wine-tasting rooms, galleries, and of course, the legendary restaurants. But before making reservations for lunch someplace pricey, take a look at the fabulous food offerings at the Vintage Inn. The dining room serves what might be the best complimentary hotel buffet breakfast in California, with buttery French pastries, fresh fruit, and made-to-order omelets. Then, at 3pm, the staff sets out a free full-fledged afternoon tea, complete with finger sandwiches, homemade scones, and organic teas—plus wine, of course. As a sister property of the nearby Villagio, Vintage Inn guests get to use the Villagio's fitness center, tennis courts, and spa.

Food

The tiny town of Yountville boasts perhaps the biggest reputation for culinary excellence in California—a big deal when you consider the offerings of San Francisco and Los Angeles. The reason for this reputation starts and ends with restaurateur Thomas Keller's indisputably amazing **C French Laundry** (6640 Washington St., 707/944-2380, www.frenchlaundry.com, Mon.-Thurs. 5:30pm-9pm, Fri.-Sun. 11am-1pm and 5:30pm-9pm, by reservation only, $270). Once you've obtained that all-important reservation, the fun begins. From the moment you walk in the door of the rambling Victorian, you're treated like royalty. You'll be led to your seat in one of the small dining rooms by one of the many immaculate black-and-white-clad staff. Even if you're new to this level of dining—and most people are— you'll be made to feel more than welcome. The menu, which changes often, offers two main selections: the regular nine-course tasting menu and the vegetarian nine-course tasting menu. You'll have a few either-or choices as you run down each list—usually you'll see two options

for the fish course and two options for the entrée. The waitstaff can help you identify anything you don't recognize or if you're having trouble making a decision. The sommelier is at your beck and call to assist with a wine list that weighs several pounds.

Then the meal begins. From the start, servers ply you with extras—an *amuse-bouche* here, an extra middle course there—and if you mention that someone else has something on their plate that you'd like to try, it appears in front of you as if by magic. Finally, the desserts come, and come, and come. After the fourth separate dessert course, you may want to ask for a white flag to signal your surrender. All together, a meal at the French Laundry can run up to 13 courses and take four hours to eat. Afterward, you might not eat normally for a couple of days, and you'll have spent a good deal of money on a single meal, but it will seem worth it.

If you can't access the French Laundry, try Thomas Keller's other Yountville option, **Bouchon** (6534 Washington St., 707/944-8037, www.bouchonbistro.com, daily 11am-midnight, $18-36). Reservations are still strongly recommended, but you should be able to get one just a week in advance. Bouchon's atmosphere and food scream Parisian bistro. Order traditional favorites such as the *croque madame* or steak frites, or opt for a California-influenced specialty salad or entrée made with local sustainable ingredients.

If you're just looking for a breakfast pastry or a sandwich, walk from Bouchon next door to the **Bouchon Bakery** (6528 Washington St., 707/944-2253, www.bouchonbakery.com, daily 7am-7pm). This ultra-high-end bakery supplies both Bouchon and the French Laundry with pastries and breads and operates a retail storefront. Locals and visitors flock to the bakery at breakfast and lunchtime, so expect a line.

Étoile (1 California Dr., 888/242-6366, www.chandon.com, Thurs.-Mon. 11:30am-2:30pm and 6pm-9pm, $28-42) is another high-end restaurant in Yountville, set inside the tasting facility at the prestigious Domaine Chandon champagnery. Lovely white tablecloths sparkle in the sunlight and overlook

RESERVATIONS FOR THE FRENCH LAUNDRY

Most people familiar with the world of high-end food know that the best restaurant in all of California, and possibly all of the United States, is the French Laundry. Thomas Keller's culinary haven in tiny Yountville has earned the hallowed three-star rating from the Michelin Guide every year since 2006. The restaurant sits inside a charming vintage house; its kitchen garden grows right across the street where anyone can walk down the rows of vegetables and herbs.

Sounds like foodie paradise, right? There's just one problem: getting a table.

The difficulty in getting reservations to the French Laundry is almost as legendary as the French Laundry itself. Rather than expecting to dine at the French Laundry during a planned trip to the Wine Country, savvy travelers expect to plan their whole trip around whatever French Laundry reservation they manage to get.

The bare facts: The French Laundry takes reservations two months in advance. *Precisely* two months. The restaurant accepts reservations by phone, online, and via local concierges. Reservations are accepted for parties for between one and six individuals. Diners can choose between lunch and dinner seatings that offer the same menu. It's easier to get a table for lunch than it is for dinner. Lunch or dinner takes 2.5-4 hours to consume. Budget $500 *per person* for your meal if you plan to drink wine, and $300-350 if you don't. The meals are priced at $275 per person.

The French Laundry starts taking **phone reservations** at 10am daily. Between 9:30 and 9:45am, program their number on your speed dial and begin calling. Continue calling again and again until you get an answer. If you get a continuous busy signal past noon, you'll probably need to try again the next day. And maybe the day after that.

Making **reservations online** works much the same way as on the phone, only it's harder. The French Laundry offers only two tables for each service (lunch and dinner) online per day. Go online at OpenTable (www.opentable.com) at about 8:30am and start trying to snag that table. If you're still trying at 9:30am, it's probably already gone.

Hands down the low-stress way to get a coveted French Laundry table is to hire a concierge to do it for you. The French Laundry lets concierges walk downtown to the restaurant each day to put in bookings for their clients. Call or email a concierge and expect to pay a nominal fee, but if you can afford to dine at the French Laundry, that's pocket change. Give your new best friend a range of dates and times that will suit you, and he or she will do their best to accommodate your request. Do not expect to get your first choice of times; flexible diners will find themselves with a remarkably trouble-free reservation experience.

So is it *really* worth all this rigmarole just to get into one lousy restaurant, then pay a sizeable part of a month's salary for a single meal?

You have to decide for yourself. For many foodies, the gracious welcome at the door, the stunning service throughout the meal, and especially the food that can be found nowhere else are worth both the hassle and the price tag.

Chandon's lush green gardens. The menu at Étoile is inventive even for Napa, and each dish is prepared to utter perfection. Order the chef's tasting menu (4 courses, $90) and add wine pairings (an additional $65) to sample Chandon's wine list.

The other big player in the Yountville restaurant scene is chef Richard Reddington's **Redd** (6480 Washington St., 707/944-2222, www.reddnapavalley.com, Mon.-Sat. 11:30am-2:30pm and 5:30pm-9:30pm, Sun. 11am-2:30pm and 5:30pm-9:30pm, $27-31). Working one time right down the road at Auberge du Soleil, Reddington crafts Wine Country cuisine with shades of Asian, European, and Mexican influences. The menu might include items like sautéed skate or a steak with a bone marrow crust.

Situated in the V Market Place (formerly Vintage 1870), **Bottega** (6525 Washington St.,

707/945-1050, www.botteganapavalley.com, Tues.-Sun. 11:30am-3pm and 5pm-9:30pm, Mon. 5pm-9:30pm, $15-30) is the return to the kitchen for celebrity chef Michael Chiarello. The former host of *Easy Entertaining* on the Food Network has come back to Napa Valley with his flair for Italian cuisine. The exposed brick and bare ceiling beams of the dining room pair nicely with such classic dishes as *tagliarini* with veal and porcini *sugo,* duck served with duck liver mousse, and braised short ribs with spaetzle. The prices, particularly the wine list, are fairly reasonable for the area. While the menu changes with the seasons, try to finish your meal with the ricotta *zeppole*—Italian doughnuts fried to order and topped with praline cream.

Information and Services
Right in the thick of the epicurean madness, the **Yountville Chamber of Commerce** (6484 Washington St., 707/944-0904, http://yountville.com, daily 10am-5pm) also doubles as a visitors center. There are maps available along with always-helpful tips, but swing by to purchase the two-for-one tasting coupons at Hill Family Estate just down the street. There is also a **post office** (6514 Washington St.).

Getting There and Around
Yountville is on Highway 29, just nine miles north of Napa. Downtown Yountville is on the east side of Highway 29, and Washington Street is the main drag, connecting with Highway 29 at the south and north ends of town; to reach the heart of Yountville, exit on California Drive in the south and Madison Street in the north. The Yountville Cross Road will take you from the north end of town to the Silverado Trail.

To reach Yountville by bus, jump aboard the **VINE** (800/696-6443, http://nctpa.net, adults $1.50-5.50, children $1-2.50), a commuter bus service that runs from the East Bay north through Calistoga.

Around town, consider taking the **Yountville Trolley** (707/944-1234, http://nctpa.net, Mon.-Sat. 10am-11pm, Sun. 10am-7pm, free). The trolley runs on a fixed track from Yountville Park along Washington Street to California Drive, conveniently near Domaine Chandon. It may also be a convenient way to get back to your hotel after imbibing too much.

RUTHERFORD AND OAKVILLE
Driving along on Highway 29, you might not even notice the tiny hamlets of Oakville and Rutherford. Neither town has much in the way of a commercial or residential district, and both have tiny populations. Oakville earned a spot on the map in 1903 when the U.S. Department of Agriculture planted an experimental vineyard. Since then, it has garnered distinction as a unique American Viticultural Area (AVA) known for its Bordeaux-style varietals. Oakville is also home to the outstanding Oakville Grocery, opened in 1881.

Rutherford was named for the 1,000 acres given to Thomas Rutherford by his father-in-law, George Yount. The area now has the distinction of growing some of the best cabernet grapes around. Yountville is also home to Grgich Hills, whose chardonnay crashed the Paris Wine Tasting of 1976. Like Oakville, Rutherford is also its own designated AVA.

Wineries
FROG'S LEAP WINERY
With so much outrageous winery architecture in the valley, **Frog's Leap Winery** (8815 Conn Creek Rd., Rutherford, 800/959-4704, www.frogsleap.com, daily 10am-4pm, tasting $20, tours $20) is an understated breath of fresh air. Its historic red barn and modest home and vineyard sit among gardens and vines. This big producer is just west of the Silverado Trail in the flats of Napa Valley; it has been a producer since 1981 and a leader in organic wine production and environmental stewardship. Tasting here is relaxing; sample a flight of four wines on the wraparound porch or inside the vineyard house, accompanied by cheese, crackers, and jam. The highly recommended tour also provides a tasting of four wines, and each tasting is enjoyed somewhere different along the tour—the garden, the red barn, or

in the vineyard, for example. Tours are by appointment only and last about one hour.

MINER FAMILY VINEYARDS
The estate tasting room at **Miner Family Vineyards** (7850 Silverado Trail, Oakville, 800/366-9463, www.minerwines.com, daily 11am-5pm, tasting $25) provides Silverado Trail travelers with a typical taste of the Napa Valley. You'll need to climb a flight of stairs or take the elevator up to the oddly small tasting room that still manages to display an array of upscale souvenirs for sale. The winery mostly makes standard Napa Valley varietal wines such as chardonnay and cabernet sauvignon, with a viognier and a sangiovese thrown in. Most of the wines aren't bad, but they aren't remarkable either—certainly not as remarkable as the prices might indicate. If you've never tasted California wines before, Miner Family might make for a good baseline. If you're an experienced oenophile, you can give this one a pass.

OPUS ONE
Yup, that huge thing on the rise that looks like a missile silo really is a winery. **Opus One** (7900 Hwy. 29, Oakville, 800/292-6787, www.opusonewinery.com, daily 10am-4pm, reservations required, tours $60-85) boasts a reputation as one of the most prestigious, and definitely one of the most expensive, vintners in Napa. The echoing halls inside the facility add to the grandeur of the place, as does the price of a tasting, $40 for a three-ounce pour of a single wine. You're unlikely to find a bottle of Opus One for under $250. If you don't mind the price tag or just can't get enough of the Opus One experience, tours of the estate are also available, and like the tastings, are by appointment only.

◖ GRGICH HILLS WINERY
The tasting room at **Grgich Hills Winery** (1829 St. Helena Hwy., Rutherford, 800/532-3057, www.grgich.com, daily 9:30am-4:30pm, tasting $20) isn't housed in the most elaborate building. The gardens aren't showy, and the working vineyards run right up to the back of the winemaking facility. Active aging barrels crowd the main building and narrow the path to the tasting room's restrooms. If you're looking for a showy Napa Valley experience, this might not be the best place for you. What you will find at Grgich are some of the best wines in the valley, an entirely biodynamic winemaking operation, and the rich history of fine wine from California taking its rightful place alongside or even ahead of the great French vintages. Mike Grgich took his California chardonnay to the Paris Wine Tasting of 1976 and entered it in the white burgundy blind-tasting competition. It won, and French winemakers were incensed; they demanded that the contest be held again, and Grgich's chardonnay won again. That same year, Robert Mondavi's cabernet sauvignon also took top honors in its category at the same contest. The quality of California wines could no longer be ignored, even by the most xenophobic of French wine connoisseurs.

Today, you'll learn about this history when visiting Grgich Hills. You'll also see plenty of information about biodynamic farming, a process that takes organic practices to the next level using all-natural processes and including phenomenon such as the phases of the moon in the growing and harvesting cycles of the vineyards. All Grgich wines are biodynamically grown and made. The best wines might be the descendants of Mike's legendary chardonnay—arguably the best chardonnay made in Napa or anywhere else. But don't ignore the reds; Grgich offers some lovely zinfandels and cabernets. And the Violetta, a dessert wine named for Mike's daughter, is a special treat that's only made in years when the grape conditions are perfect. None of the Grgich wines are cheap, and there's a fee for tasting, but it's more than worth it when you sip these rare, exquisite vintages.

MUMM
You may have already tasted the sparkling wines produced by **Mumm** (8445 Silverado Trail, Rutherford, 800/686-6272, http://mummnapa.com, daily 10am-4:45pm, tasting $7-25). Even for genuine wine aficionados,

© DAN MILLS

Grgich Hills Winery

it's worth spending an hour or two at Mumm Napa, a friendly and surprisingly down-to-earth winery among the often pretentious estates on the Silverado Trail. First, get on the list and take the free tour (10am) of the sample vineyard and the working production facility, and learn from the knowledgeable and articulate tour guides, who will describe the process of making sparkling wine in detailed comprehensible English. All tours wind up in a special treat of a place—the only gallery showing original Ansel Adams prints outside Yosemite Valley. Even if you skip the tour, you can hang out in the gallery as long as you like. Perhaps best of all, after finishing the tour, you'll get a tag that gives you 15 percent off all bottle purchases in the winery.

Tastings happen at tables, with menus and service in restaurant fashion. The prices may look very Napa Valley, but you'll get more wine and service for your money at Mumm. Each pour is three ounces of wine—some of it high-end—and you get three pours per tasting. Good news for designated drivers:

Nonalcoholic gourmet grape sodas or bottled water are complementary as a thank-you for keeping the Silverado Trail safe. If you've brought your dog, you can bring him into the tasting room too; dogs get water, gourmet doggie bones, and plenty of petting from the tasting-room staff.

PEJU

Embodying the ultimate success of the Napa Valley, **Peju** (8466 St. Helena Hwy., Rutherford, 800/446-7358, www.peju.com, daily 10am-6pm, tasting $20) is a 30-year-old family winery that has, through hard work, created great wines that have garnered the attention of international magazines and judging bodies. Today, visitors to Peju see gorgeous sycamore trees, hand-pruned by Tony Peju, running up the drive; a fabulous garden tended by Herta Peju; and solar panels on the roof of the elegant winery building. Inside you'll get tastes of an array of aromatic and award-winning red wines—from the lighter Bordeaux-varietal cabernet franc to the many vintages of classic California cabernet sauvignon. A few whites and perhaps a rosé or a port round out Peju's list.

INGLENOOK

Wine lovers come to enjoy the grand tasting room and museum at **Inglenook** (1991 St. Helena Hwy., Rutherford, 800/782-4266, www.inglenook.com, daily 10am-5pm, reservations required, tasting $50), formerly Rubicon and Niebaum-Coppola. Reservations are required for tastings in the large, elegant tasting room, where you'll find a generous bar area with plenty of staff to help you navigate the wine list. The winemakers take their job seriously, and the results can be spectacular. This estate winery also houses the small Centennial Museum, showcasing old Inglenook wines, zoetropes, and magic lanterns.

RUTHERFORD HILL

If you're planning in advance to visit **Rutherford Hill** (200 Rutherford Hill Rd., Rutherford, 707/963-1871, www.rutherfordhill.com, daily 10am-5pm, tasting $15-30), book a spot on the winery-and-cave tour. The winery is pretty standard for a Napa facility, but the caves impress even experienced wine lovers. Dug back into the hillside, Rutherford's caves provide a natural temperature-controlled space in which to age their array of wines, mostly hearty reds. (If you're looking for a place to hold a special dinner or midsize event, Rutherford rents out space in the caves.) Contrary to the myth perpetuated by the movie *Sideways*, Rutherford produces a fine merlot as well as rich cabernet sauvignons and other tasty varietals.

Accommodations

Courtyards dripping in wisteria, earth-tone stucco, tiled roofs, and rustic stonework draw guests back in time to **Rancho Caymus** (1140 Rutherford Rd., Rutherford, 800/845-1777, www.ranchocaymus.com, $200-370) and Napa Valley's Spanish past. All the rooms have hand-carved walnut beds and fireplaces, while many include a separate sitting area, wood-burning fireplaces, Spanish tiled baths, a refrigerator,

and a private outdoor area. While the decor many be a bit outdated, you can't beat the price in this central part of Napa.

Perched above the valley and located off the Silverado Trail, **Auberge du Soleil** (180 Rutherford Hill Rd., St. Helena, 707/963-1211, www.aubergedusoleil.com, $725-5,200) is the ultimate in Wine Country luxury. Even the most ardent oenophile will be hard-pressed to leave the lush sun-drenched grounds. And why would you leave? The compound features multiple high-end wine-tasting and dining options in addition to a pool, a fitness room, a store, and well-kept gardens accented by modern art. The guest rooms are appointed with Italian sheets, private patios, fireplaces, and TVs in both the living room and the bath. The smallest guest room is 500 square feet, suites can top 1,400 square feet, and the Private Maison is 1,800 square feet. Auberge du Soleil is definitely the place to stay if you have the cash to focus on the inn's amenities and less interest in exploring the area.

Food

The historic **Auberge du Soleil** (180 Rutherford Hill Rd., Rutherford, 800/348-5406, www.aubergedusoleil.com, daily 7am-11am, 11:30am-2:30pm, and 5:30pm-9:30pm, tasting menu $150) has an inn where you can stay the night, but some visitors come just for the food—the charming Mediterranean-style dining room has drawn visitors from all over the world for decades. Sunny yellow tablecloths, a central fireplace, exposed wooden beams, and wall-to-wall picture windows welcome diners. Executive Chef Robert Curry, a legend of the Napa Valley culinary scene, uses the finest local ingredients to create his own take on Mediterranean and California cuisine. Choose one item from each course list on the short but exquisite tasting menu to create a four-course dinner. If you ask, you can also dine à la carte from any of the courses. After all that rich food and fine wine, you might find yourself at the inn's desk, begging to be allowed to stay the night within staggering distance of the restaurant.

© GABRIEL SKVOR

the bistro deck at Auberge du Soleil

One way to experience Auberge du Soleil and Napa Valley luxury without depleting your savings account is to dine in the adjacent ❰ **Bistro & Bar** (daily 11am-11pm, $12-35). Indoors is a bar and small dining area, but outside is a deck where you can take in fine views of Napa Valley and its vineyards braiding the land. Choose from braised short ribs, a charcuterie plate, a salad, a pizza, or the grilled Auberge burger and, of course, from a list of Napa Valley wines to enjoy while you soak up the view.

A long-standing Wine Country favorite is the **Rutherford Grill** (1180 Rutherford Rd., Rutherford, 707/963-1792, www.hillstone. com, Sun.-Thurs. 11:30am-9:30pm, Fri.-Sat. 11:30am-10:30pm, $17-37), which is more casual than many of its Napa Valley peers. Some of the best seats in the house cluster outside the dining room on the wide deck; sheltered by a collection of umbrellas, guests enjoy the pretty gardens with their classic grill fare—cheeseburgers, salads with grilled items, bangers and mash, and a whole array of grilled meats—as well as an extensive and impressive wine list. Perhaps the best part: You can escape from the Rutherford Grill for well under $100 per person.

For a picnic lunch or just a few munchies for the road, stop by the **Oakville Grocery** (7856 St. Helena Hwy., Oakville, 707/944-8802, www.oakvillegrocery.com, daily 7am-6pm). A long-standing Napa Valley institution, the Oakville Grocery has a reputation for stocking only the best food, wine, cheese, and other goodies along Highway 29. Browse the tightly packed shelves or order a hot lunch at the center counter; they serve slow roasted beef and fried chicken sandwiches among other options. To find the building from the northbound highway, look for the large Coca-Cola sign painted on the south side of the building.

Getting There and Around

Oakville is four miles north of Yountville on Highway 29; Rutherford is another two miles north. Both can be easy to miss because of their loose organization and rural character.

The Silverado Trail runs parallel to Highway 29 along this stretch. To reach it from Oakville, take Oakville Road east; in Rutherford, take Rutherford Road (Hwy. 128) east.

ST. HELENA

There are few Northern California towns as picturesque and well-groomed as St. Helena. Bolstered by the lucrative wine industry, St. Helena has the glossy sheen of a reinvented old California farm town. It is filled with fine eateries and quaint expensive shops housed in historic buildings and surrounded block upon block by well-maintained craftsman homes. The Napa campus of the Culinary Institute of America is a major employer in the area, as is the St. Helena Hospital. Highway 29 runs north-south through the center of town, which can give you a quick peek at the sights, but it's not so nice when sitting in traffic on a sunny weekend.

Wineries

BERINGER VINEYARDS

The palatial stone estate buildings of **Beringer Vineyards** (2000 Main St., 707/967-4412, www.beringer.com, June-Oct. daily 10am-6pm, Nov.-May daily 10am-5pm, tasting $20-30) belie the reasonably priced Beringer vintages available in supermarkets across the country. Inside, you'll find an array of wines for tasting, many of which are not readily available outside the tasting room. Outdoors, you can stroll in the beautiful estate gardens that stretch for acres on prime land next to Highway 29. Tours take you into the winemaking facilities and show off the highlights of the vast estate.

CORISON

A rarity among Napa Valley's large-scale producers, **Corison** (987 St. Helena Hwy., 707/963-0826, www.corison.com, daily 10am-5pm, by appointment, tasting $20-40) is the genuine article—a tiny single-proprietor winery producing great wines in small quantities. Technically, Corison takes tasters by appointment only, but in truth they've never turned away a drop-in during regular business hours.

After turning onto a short gravel driveway, you pass a vintage home to reach the small barn that serves as a tasting room. Open the huge white door (it's easier than it looks) and enter the tasting-, barrel-, and stock room. A tiny bar next to the entrance offers tastings from the 3,000 cases the winery produces each year. Expect the attentive staff to talk in loving and knowledgeable terms about the delicious wines they're pouring. Corison's flagship cabernet sauvignon tastes of luscious fruit and perfect balance. The other wines are not distributed—you must buy them here, join the wine club, or long for them from afar.

FLORA SPRINGS

This winery straddles the line between boutiques and big-deal Napa players. You'll find **Flora Springs** (677 S. St. Helena Hwy., 707/967-8032, www.florasprings.com, daily 10am-5pm, tasting $20-55) on a few menus in upscale restaurants and here in the open, airy tasting room that sweeps in a half circle around the bar, with plenty of windows letting in the Napa sunlight. You'll taste a variety of reds and whites, but the cabernet sauvignons are the Flora Springs standouts.

HEITZ

One of the oldest wineries in the valley, **Heitz** (436 St. Helena Hwy., 707/963-3542, www.heitzcellar.com, daily 11am-4:30pm, tasting free) brings sincere elegance to the glitz and glamour of Napa. The high-ceilinged tasting room is dominated by a stone fireplace with comfy chairs. A low bar off to the right sets the stage for an array of Napa Valley cabernet sauvignons. To the happy surprise of many, Heitz's cabernets are well balanced and easy to drink, and though costly, they approach affordable by Napa standards. Most of the grapes used for these wines grow right in the Napa Valley. If you're lucky enough to visit Heitz in February, you can taste the current release of the Martha's Vineyard Cabernet—a vintage grown in the first wine-designated vineyard (the first vineyard to grow grapes for wine rather than eating) in the valley.

WINE COUNTRY

PRIDE MOUNTAIN VINEYARDS

Take advantage of some of Wine Country's scenic drives with a visit to **Pride Mountain Vineyards** (4026 Spring Mountain Rd., 707/963-4949, www.pridewines.com, daily 10am-3:45pm, reservations required, tour and tasting $15, tasting only $10-20), located at the top of a scenic winding road six miles from the turnoff on Highway 29. In addition to the wine, the views are the reward for the effort. Wine-tasting is by appointment only, so once you arrive you'll have the pourer's full attention. It's worth it to take the tour, as you'll see the vineyard and the caves and will be able to taste the wine straight out of the barrel. It's a great education in how wine matures with age.

ST. CLEMENT VINEYARDS

This winery is all about the cabs: While they produce one chardonnay for good measure, the rest of tasting menu at **St. Clement** (2867 Hwy. 29, 866/877-5939, www.stclement.com, daily 11am-5pm, tasting $20-30) features 11 different vintages of cabernet sauvignon. This translates into a fun introduction to the variety and qualities of the grape. But this is not the only reason to visit; St. Clement's elegant two-story Victorian farmhouse is perched on a hill above Highway 29 and is beautifully surrounded by sloping vineyards. The grounds are lush with English gardens and heavy-limbed oaks; in front, tables dot the split-level decks, affording both privacy and a splendid place for a picnic. The winery's deep-blue interior features more modern touches, such as the unique art deco chandeliers. The juxtaposition is unexpected, but it works.

V. SATTUI

A boutique winery that doesn't distribute to retailers, **V. Sattui** (1111 White Lane, 707/963-7774, www.vsattui.com, daily 9am-5pm, tasting $10-15) won the Best Winery award at the California State Fair in 2006, 2007, and 2012—a mighty feat in a state filled with excellent vintners. V. Sattui produces a wide selection of varietals—everything from light-bodied whites to full-flavored cabernet sauvignons.

The dessert madeira is particularly fine—if it's not on the tasting menu, ask your pourer at the bar if they've got a bottle open, and you might just get lucky.

The big tasting room on Highway 29 boasts three spacious bar areas, endless stacks and cases of wine out and ready for purchase, a separate register, and a full deli. The gardens surrounding the facility include a number of picnic tables, and Sattui is a popular lunchtime stop for all-day tasters. But beware: All the recent good press makes even the big Sattui tasting room fill up on weekends in high season (May-Oct.).

Sights

◖ CULINARY INSTITUTE OF AMERICA

The premier institute for training professional chefs in the United States has only three campuses: one in upstate New York, one in Texas, and this one, the **Culinary Institute of America at Greystone** (2555 Main St., 707/967-1010, www.ciachef.edu, restaurant hours Sun.-Thurs. 11:30am-9pm, Fri.-Sat. 11:30am-10pm), with a restaurant, a café, a gourmet shop, one-day cooking classes and demos, a food-history museum, and a stunning set of campus buildings nestled in the forests and vineyards near the town of St. Helena on Highway 29. If Napa is the perfect place to introduce newcomers to the world of high-end food and wine, Greystone takes it to the intermediate and advanced levels. Most people love the De Baun Café and the Spice Islands Marketplace and want to make a reservation to dine in the *Wine Spectator* Greystone Restaurant. Serious foodies or cork dorks should consider signing up in advance to attend a cooking demo or even a seminar at this haven for haute cuisine. Be sure to take a few minutes to wander the charming grounds and marvel at the imposing structures of the campus—made from, of course, gray stonework.

Shopping

As you may be able to tell from the traffic in town, downtown St. Helena is hopping. Quaint and historic storefronts line Highway 29:

Saint Helena's Culinary Institute of America at Greystone

housing galleries, clothiers, jewelers, kitchen stores, and, of course, wine shops, many of which offer wine-tasting. If you are looking to give your palate a rest from the onslaught of wine, two stores in particular are eager to remind you that grapes are not the only crops that grow well here. Over the years, olive trees have begun spreading across the landscape, which makes perfect sense—Napa Valley has an ideal Mediterranean climate for these trees. The resulting olive oil offers one more thing to taste.

The **St. Helena Olive Oil Company** (1351 Main St., 800/939-9880, www.sholiveoil.com, daily 10:30am-5pm) gives you the opportunity to parse out notes of grass, citrus, or pepper in the region's oils. The historic building was once the Bank of Italy and has been redone in perfect Wine Country fashion; an exposed stone wall and the old bank's interior details have been infused with a rustic Mediterranean touch. The selection of at least a dozen different house-made olive oils is terrific, as are the local vinegars and the array of delicious bath and body products. Tasting is encouraged, and it's likely you'll walk away with something.

Out of downtown St. Helena's hubbub, the **Napa Valley Olive Oil Manufacturing Co.** (835 Charter Oak Ave., 707/963-4173, daily 8am-5:30pm) is one of those amazing off-the-beaten-path treasures that travelers feel lucky to find. The tiny, funky old storefront is two blocks off Highway 29 and features a motley collection of plastic-covered picnic tables out front and a faded hand-lettered sign on the door. Inside, take care not to trip over the uneven floor in the cramped, meandering rooms of the shop. Those in the know dart in, grab plainly labeled quart jugs of olive oil, and pay cash for what's obviously a year's supply of the good stuff. You can't taste the oils and vinegars; you'll just have to go on faith that this Italian-owned and operated shop sells the best. The tiny store also has fabulous cheeses and fresh-baked breads, making it a great stop for would-be picnickers who don't mind the less-than-elegant surroundings. Napa Valley Olive Oil Manufacturing Co. has its own bottling facilities, just as the St. Helena

Olive Oil Company does—although here the "facility" consists of the cashier in the back room with a funnel.

Accommodations

The charming small village of St. Helena is right on Highway 29, and its stop signs and traffic signals are often the cause of the endless weekend Wine Country traffic jams. But if you're staying here, you can avoid the worst of the traffic and enjoy the wooded central Napa Valley area.

For the best rates in St. Helena, the **El Bonita Motel** (195 Main St./Hwy. 29, 800/541-3284, www.elbonita.com, $120-280) can't be beat. It is within walking distance of the historic downtown and has a 1950s motel charm. The low-slung 48-room hotel wraps about a patio shaded by oak trees, bordered by a clipped lawn, and filled with tables, chairs, and umbrellas. In the center is a pool, a hot tub, and a sauna, which all guests are encouraged to enjoy. The rooms may not match the indulgence of other Napa inns, but they are clean, comfortable, and pet-friendly, with refrigerators and microwave ovens; some even boast kitchenettes.

At the **Zinfandel Inn** (800 Zinfandel Lane, 707/963-3512, www.zinfandelinn.com, $265-325), you'll find yourself in a two-story English Tudor inn. Lavish stonework adorns the outside of this unique structure. Inside, you'll stay in one of three exquisitely decorated suite-like guest rooms. Each guest room boasts a unique design, complete with antique bedsteads and dressers, feather beds, fireplaces, and tiled whirlpool tubs. All guests enjoy a full breakfast every morning of their stay, plus the rich amenities suited to a Wine Country inn.

A less imposing structure, **The Ink House** (1575 St. Helena Hwy., at Whitehall Lane, 707/963-3890, www.inkhouse.com, $179-300) prides itself on its more casual elegance. A pretty yellow facade looks almost like a wedding cake. Inside, the breakfast room is on the ground floor, all the guest rooms are on the 2nd floor, and the small 3rd-floor solarium is open as a parlor to guests. There are many amenities to enjoy at the Ink House, including a

full gourmet breakfast, an afternoon wine social, complimentary nightcaps, and loaner bicycles. The lounge areas include a pool table and a dartboard; outside, a croquet course and a horseshoe pit afford some gentle recreation. Guest rooms are individually decorated, and each has a view of the surrounding forest and vineyards. Furnishings tend toward American and European antiques, and all the beds are queens.

Food

A highlight of the St. Helena dining scene is the *Wine Spectator* **Greystone Restaurant** (2555 Main St., 707/967-1010, http://ciachef.edu, Sun.-Thurs. 11:30am-9pm, Fri.-Sat. 11:30am-10pm, $21-34, prix fixe $47), better known to its friends as "the restaurant at the CIA," where the world's top aspiring chefs practice their craft. It's easier to get a reservation here than at Thomas Keller's hallowed French Laundry and Bouchon; with several big dining rooms, the CIA can seat large numbers. If you get the right table, you can watch your food being prepared in the open kitchen. The ever-changing menu highlights the best of each season, and the wine list features the best of Napa Valley's vintages; the student chefs plan menus with an eye to wine pairings. There's also a four-course prix fixe menu.

The imposing stone building draped in ivy and surrounded by grapevines is home to **Tra Vigne** (1050 Charter Oak Ave., 707/963-4444, www.travignerestaurant.com, Mon.-Sat. 11:30am-9pm, Sun. 11am-9pm, $18-30). When it opened, Tra Vigne helped bring a modern California culinary sensibility to Napa Valley. Today, it has been overshadowed by the profusion of high-end eateries and celebrity chefs, but its reputation for excellent Italian food is still intact. The warm dining room features white tablecloths, cream walls, plush leather booths, and wooden chairs. The food is equally comfortable, with crisply executed thin-crust pizzas, wood oven-roasted meats, and silky pasta dishes. The extensive wine list includes a number of Italian grappas.

Craving pizza or a low-key meal? **Pizzeria**

Tra Vigne (1016 Main St., 707/967-9999, www.travignerestaurant.com, Sun.-Thurs. 11:30am-9pm, Fri.-Sat. 11:30am-9:30pm, $9-18), next door to Tra Vigne, is considerably more relaxed than its renowned sibling. Inside are long tables opposite the open kitchen, where a huge wood-fired oven sits center stage. The famous thin-crust Italian pizzas lure locals many weekend nights; you can also enjoy hearty plates of pasta or heavy Italian salads. Wash it all down with a pitcher of any number of beers on tap. There are also a number of beers by the bottle in addition to a healthy selection of wine. If you're traveling with kids, Pizzeria Tra Vigne is a great place to stop and relax over a meal. There is even a pool table.

Tired of wine country fare? The **Himalayan Sherpa Kitchen** (1148 Main St., 707/963-4439, http://himalayansherpakitchen.com, Tues.-Sun. 11:30am-3pm and 5pm-9pm, $10-25) serves cuisine from the highest region in the world right in downtown St. Helena. With golden curries, tikka masala dishes, and samosas, the menu resembles the kind of dishes you'd find in an Indian restaurant. The food here is superb, and like the rest of Napa, there is a selection of fine local wines to sip with your meal.

Until recently, **Gott's Roadside** (933 Main St., 707/963-3486, http://gotts.com, summer daily 7am-10pm, winter daily 7am-9pm, $10) was known as Taylor's Refresher, which explains the wooden sign on Highway 29. This classic roadside diner has been around since 1949, but the food has been updated with a modern local-organic sensibility; the burgers, fries, and milkshakes are made with quality ingredients. The Gott brothers, who took over the business in 1999, have added more California-eclectic comfort food like fish tacos, smoked chicken po'boys, and Chinese chicken salad. They have also earned three James Beard awards for bringing fast food up to the quality of well-respected sit-down restaurants.

Information and Services

Pick up maps, information, and discounted wine-tasting vouchers at the **St. Helena Welcome Center** (657 Main St., 707/963-4456, www.sthelena.com, Mon.-Fri. 9am-5pm, Sat.-Sun. 10am-5pm). Thankfully, there is parking in back; turn on Vidovich Lane just north of the visitors center.

For health concerns, the **St. Helena Hospital** (10 Woodland Rd., 707/963-6425, http://sthelenanowaiter.org) has a 24-hour emergency room for quick and reliable service. St. Helena also has a **post office** (1461 Main St., between Pine St. and Adams St.).

Getting There and Around

St. Helena is on Highway 29 in the middle of Napa Valley, eight miles south of Calistoga. To reach the Silverado Trail from St. Helena, take Zinfandel Lane or Pope Street east.

To avoid the constant headache of parking and driving around town, consider hopping aboard **The VINE St. Helena Shuttle** (707/963-3007, http://nctpa.net, Mon.-Fri. 7:45am-5pm, $0.50-1). Unfortunately, the shuttle doesn't run on weekends when traffic congestion is heaviest.

CALISTOGA

Despite their proximity, Calistoga and St. Helena couldn't be more different. While St. Helena leans toward the boutique side of the wine scene and often feels permanently congested, Calistoga has a more laid-back, almost mountain-town crunchiness to it. Located far from the city of Napa, it is one of the most economically diverse towns in the valley, which is reflected in its restaurants, businesses, and hotels. You can browse books, grab great barbecue, or sit at a sidewalk café to enjoy a cheap beer and even forget you are in Wine Country. It is also the land of great and affordable spas, where soaking is treated more as therapy than beauty treatment.

Calistoga gets its unique name from one of its early advocates, Samuel Brannan, who hoped to transform the mineral spring rich region into a spa resort rivaling Saratoga Springs, New York. A drinker, Brannan once tried to proclaim the area the "Saratoga of California" but misspoke and said it would be the "Calistoga of Sarifornia."

Wineries

CASTELLO DI AMOROSA

When you first spy the ramshackle house and its sweetly tended garden near the entrance to **Castello di Amorosa** (4045 Hwy. 29, 707/967-6272, www.castellodiamorosa. com, Mar.-Oct. daily 9:30am-6pm, Nov.-Feb. daily 9:30am-5pm, adults $18, children $8), you might imagine you are stopping in at one of those delightfully rustic north-valley wineries. You couldn't be more wrong. After passing through the gates and ascending a steep hill lined in vineyards and Italian cypress trees, you'll reach the castle at the top. The steep prices for tasting include access to the main floors of the castle; tours, in addition to barrel-tasting, take visitors to the armory and torture chamber. Who knew these were necessities in Wine Country? In terms of wine, Castello di Amorosa produces a number of varietals, such as pinot grigio and muscat, which are overshadowed by their environs. Children are permitted on the tour, however, indicating that the owners are eager to draw in more than just wine lovers. And certainly your kids will oblige, particularly if you give them a sword and call them Lancelot.

CLOS PEGASE

Want some art to ponder while you sample wine? **Clos Pegase** (1060 Dunaweal Lane, 707/942-4981, www.clospegase.com, daily 10:30am-5pm, tasting $20-30) has over 100 art works on its grounds, including sculptor Henry Moore's "Mother Earth" and a painting from Francis Bacon. The entrance is a work of art itself that was designed to resemble a Greek temple. In the tasting room, taste the winery's flagship cabernet sauvignon or their Hommage chardonnay. Clos Pegase also offers 45-minute-long winery tours (11:30am and 2pm, adults $20, students 7-20 $10, 6 and under free) that go into winemaking, architecture, and art while including a visit inside the winery's caves. You can even bring a piece of art from Clos Pegase home with you; most of the wine labels feature an image of artwork that is displayed on the winery's grounds.

CUVAISON

This small winery harks back to the Napa of decades past. The intimate tasting room at **Cuvaison** (4550 Silverado Trail N., 707/942-2468, www.cuvaison.com, daily 10am-5pm, tasting $15-20) doesn't hold busloads of visitors, and the bar might show a few scars, but the tasting room staff know quite a bit about the wine they're pouring, and they want to tell you all about it. This isn't a place for esoteric wine-tasting; you quickly get the feeling that everyone, regardless of their background, is on the same ground and here to have a good time. The quaint building sits on the slope of the mountains bordering Napa Valley and shelters several friendly cats. A picnic area invites a longer stop to enjoy the vineyard views with your lunch and a nice bottle of Cuvaison chardonnay, or just to relax and sip one of their light, tasty reds. Cuvaison also offers a tasting of their exclusive wines underground on their Calistoga Cave Tastings Tour ($25).

SCHRAMSBERG VINEYARDS

At the other end of the Calistoga winery spectrum is **Schramsberg Vineyards** (1400 Schramsberg Rd., 707/942-4558, www.schramsberg.com, tours and tasting 10am-2:30pm, reservations required, $45), founded in 1862 and considered to be one of the best producers of sparkling wine in California. Tastings include four wines, a tour of the 120-year-old caves, and an education in the art of making sparkling wines in the Champagne style. Schramsberg can be visited by appointment only and does not allow pets or children, no matter how small or quiet.

STERLING VINEYARDS

Sterling Vineyards (1111 Dunaweal Lane, 800/726-6136, www.sterlingvineyards.com, Mon.-Fri. 10:30am-4:30pm, Sat.-Sun. 10am-5pm, tasting $25-40) is more appealing for first-timers than for serious wine aficionados. The jewel of the new "Disneyland with wine" culture of Napa, Sterling features a gondola ride and an obligatory tasting tour through the estate rather than a traditional tasting room

© GABRIEL SKVOR

the vineyards at Clos Pegase

experience. It's expensive, and the lines can be long on weekends in high season (May-Oct.).

To be fair, once you've stood in line and bought your tickets, the gondola ride up the mountain to the estate shows off Napa Valley at its best. Take advantage of the time to admire the stellar views of forested hills and endless vineyards. Once up at the estate, you'll be guided around by signs to each tasting venue. Frankly, the wine isn't worth the effort or the high per-bottle price tag, but the estate has some charm, and the views from the deck match those from the gondola.

UP VALLEY VINTNERS

For every winery with a tasting room and tours, there are several smaller boutique vineyards whose wines can only be found and tasted in select restaurants—until now. **Up Valley Vintners** (1371 Lincoln Ave., 707/942-1004, www.upvalleyvintners.com, daily noon-5pm) is a co-op of sorts where smaller winemakers can sell their wine and offer tastings directly to the public. The long and narrow shop features a dark wood bar that extends one-third of the way down. Here you will find locals and travelers happily sitting on bar stools, chatting with the pourer. Past the bar is a retail section where each winery has a profile and plenty of bottles for sale. There is a comfortable lounge area inside and a patio with a table and chairs outside. While all the wines featured come from veteran winemakers of the Calistoga AVA, a real standout is the Dyer cabernet blend. Made from grapes grown on a 2.2-acre vineyard on Diamond Mountain, the blends have a Bordeaux quality and a reputation for excellence, and they are difficult to come by.

Sights
OLD FAITHFUL GEYSER

No, that's not a typo, and you haven't accidentally driven east to Yellowstone. The Napa Valley has its own **Old Faithful Geyser** (1299 Tubbs Lane, 707/942-6463, www.oldfaithfulgeyser.com, summer daily 9am-6pm, winter daily 9am-5pm, adults $10, seniors $7, ages 6-12 $3, under age 6 free). Unlike its more

© GABRIEL SKVOR

Old Faithful Geyser erupts near Calistoga.

famous counterpart, this geothermal geyser is artificial. In the 19th and early 20th centuries, more than 100 wells were drilled into the geothermal springs of the Calistoga area, and many of these created geysers. Old Faithful is one of the few that wasn't eventually capped off, and it's the only one that erupts with clockwork regularity. When you visit the geyser, expect no more than a 40-minute wait to see it erupt 60 feet or higher into the air. A grassy area surrounds the geyser, with benches and chairs scattered around to allow visitors an easy wait for the show. A bamboo garden surrounds the grassy spot (bamboo is one of the few plants that can tolerate the hot mineral water of this area). Also at Old Faithful you'll find an incongruous but cute petting zoo that houses several fainting goats, plus a few sheep and llamas. A coin-operated feeder lets visitors feed and pet the animals—perfect for children who may grow tired of waiting for the geyser to erupt. Note that the water in the pool from which the geyser erupts as well as the geyser itself is very hot. It's not safe to wade in the water or to

stand too close when the geyser goes off. Keep an eye on small children.

PETRIFIED FOREST
The trees of the **Petrified Forest** (4100 Petrified Forest Rd., 707/942-6667, www.petrifiedforest.org, summer daily 9am-7pm, spring and fall daily 9am-6pm, winter daily 9am-5pm, adults $10-16, seniors and students $9-15, children $5) no longer stand—technically this is an archaeological dig that uncovered a forest that existed more than three million years ago. A volcano that no longer exists erupted, blowing over the trees and covering them with ash. During hundreds of thousands of years, the minerals in the ash traded places with the contents of the cells that made up the wood of the trees, petrifying them; now these long-dead trees are made of stone. When you visit the forest, you'll see plenty of upright living trees. Follow your trail map along a 0.5-mile loop to visit the various excavated petrified trees and chunks of trees. You can touch some of the chunks of petrified wood, but most of

the large stone trees are protected by fences to preserve their pristine state. You'll get to see one rare petrified pine tree and a number of petrified coast redwoods, almost all of which have been given names. A fun note: All the trees fell in the same direction and still face that way, showing the direction the blast came from when the volcano erupted. For a few dollars more, you can take an over-one-hour-long walk with a naturalist over ash fall to a view of Mount St. Helena. Inside the visitors center and gift shop, you'll find lots of rocks and minerals, books on geology, and a few rare shards of the petrified trees from this forest.

SHARPSTEEN MUSEUM OF CALISTOGA HISTORY

The **Sharpsteen Museum of Calistoga History** (1311 Washington St., 707/942-5911, www.sharpsteen-museum.org, daily 11am-4pm, $3 donation) takes its name from its founder, Ben Sharpsteen, an Academy Award-winning animator for Disney who had a passion for dioramas. It was through his desire and funding that the immense, exquisitely detailed dioramas depicting the 1860s Calistoga hot springs resort and life in 19th-century Calistoga were built. The other major player in the museum, Sam Brannan, was the first pioneer in Calistoga to build a hot-springs resort using the geothermal springs in the area. At the museum, you'll learn of Brannan's success and subsequent ruin in the resort business as well as his unsuccessful attempt to convert the Napa Valley to Mormonism. Other museum exhibits highlight daily life in 19th-century Napa, complete with artifacts and a nod to the Wappo people, the Native American first residents of this area.

PIONEER CEMETERY

If you're looking for your Napa ancestors or just enjoy prowling through historic graveyards, stop at the **Napa Valley Pioneer Cemetery** (Bothe-Napa Valley State Park, 3801 St. Helena Hwy. N., www.parks.ca.gov, $8), where you'll find the graves of many of Napa's earliest nonnative settlers and some of the more prominent early pioneer families. The cemetery seems to undergo regular maintenance, since paths between plots are kept clear and walkable. But many of the graves are overgrown with vines—some even have full-size oak trees growing through them. The whole area is covered by a dense canopy of forest foliage, making it a pleasantly cool place to visit on hot summer days. You can explore up the hillside, where the paths get more overgrown and some of the tombstones are old wooden planks, their lettering worn away. If you're interested in genealogy, start at the front entrance of the cemetery, where a map and an alphabetical survey of the cemetery are posted. One warning about visiting this cemetery: No, not ghosts, but a lack of parking. There's enough room at the front for one small car; otherwise, you have to park elsewhere and walk carefully along and across Highway 29 to the gate.

Bars

To get a local's perspective on Calistoga and the Wine Country, get a beer or a cocktail at **Susie's Bar** (1365 Lincoln Ave., 707/942-6710, Mon.-Thurs. 10am-2am, Fri.-Sun. 9am-2am, cash only). This dive bar is reached by a long alleyway that opens up into a high ceilinged room with pool tables and brick walls. An unusual feature is a coin-operated grab machine where you can try to pick up stuffed animals or porn DVDs.

On the other end of the spectrum is **Barolo** (1457 Lincoln Ave., 707/942-9900, daily 4:30pm-9:30pm), a wine and cocktail bar, bustling on weekend evenings. Take a seat at the marble bar or a table to have one last glass of wine or a cocktail after a day of relaxing in Calistoga. For those with a growing appetite, Barolo serves up tasty Italian food. The pizza, which has a cracker thin crust, is recommended.

C Spas

To experience a Napa County spa without draining your savings, set up an appointment at **Dr. Wilkinson's Hot Springs Resort** (1507 Lincoln Ave., 707/942-4102, www.

WINE COUNTRY

© STUART THORNTON

the old-school sign at Dr. Wilkinson's Hot Springs Resort

drwilkinson.com, daily 8:30am-5:30pm, $69-179). Tucked into a 1950s motel building, this spa was opened by "Doc" Wilkinson in 1952. Their "The Works" treatment with a 30-minute massage is a two-hour relaxing marathon that includes submersion in a mud bath, a facial mask, a soak in a bubbling mineral whirlpool, a sauna steam, a blanket wrap, and a full body massage. The mud is a mix of sifted volcanic ash from the area and Canadian peat moss cut with local mineral water. It is quite simply a great deal. The spa also offers hour-long facials, hour-long massages, and a hot stone massage. The men and women's spa areas are separate. If you're a guest of the hotel, be sure to take a swim or a soak in one of the three mineral-water pools: There are two outdoor pools and one large spa inside.

At the **Calistoga Hot Springs Spa** (1006 Washington St., 707/942-6269, www.calistogaspa.com, Tues.-Thurs. 8:30am-4:30pm, Fri.-Mon. 8:30am-9pm, $45-138), indulge in a mud bath, a mineral bath, or other typical spa treatments. Also available to the public and guaranteed with a spa reservation is access to Calistoga Hot Springs's four outdoor mineral pools. The lap pool is the coolest at 80°F and is set up for serious swimmers. The 90°F wading pool with fountains offers fun and health benefits for the whole family. Another large soaking pool is set to 100°F and meant primarily for adults. Finally, the enormous octagonal 104°F jetted spa is under a gazebo—the perfect location to relax and enjoy the serenity of spa country.

Two other lovely Calistoga spas, both of which offer full mud and mineral baths as well as spa services, are **Golden Haven** (1713 Lake St., 707/942-8000, www.goldenhaven.com, daily 8am-11pm) and **Indian Springs** (1712 Lincoln Ave., 707/942-4913, www.indianspringscalistoga.com, daily 9am-8pm). In operation since 1862, Indian Springs is the oldest continuously operating pool and spa facility in the state. It offers mud baths, facials, and a dip in an Olympic-sized mineral pool.

Sports and Recreation

Not every bit of open space in the Napa Valley is dedicated to grapes. There are several great state parks where you can indulge in the beauty of the valley and not just what it produces. **Bothe-Napa State Park** (3801 St. Helena Hwy., 707/942-4575, www.parks.ca.gov, daily 8am-sunset) is south of Calistoga on the west side of Highway 29. The park's 2,000-foot elevation provides fantastic views of the valley below and the craggy Mayacamas Mountains beyond, and the nearly 2,000 acres include oak woodlands, coastal redwoods, and occasional open grassland. There are a number of great hikes in the park. **Coyote Peak Trail** climbs to 1,170 feet and forms a 6.5-mile loop with **Upper Ritchey Canyon Trail,** providing great views and a backcountry feel. There is a park swimming pool, but you will have to check with park officials for its operating hours.

Robert Louis Stevenson State Park (Hwy. 29, seven miles north of Calistoga, 707/942-4575, www.parks.ca.gov, daily sunrise-sunset) is named for the author who spent his honeymoon in a tiny cabin here. The park offers fewer amenities than nearby Bothe-Napa State Park, but it does have a trail to the top of Mount St. Helena. The 11.2-mile round-trip hike is strenuous, especially when the trail rises above the lush canopy of bay, Douglas fir, and madrone trees to exposed chaparral. All that huffing and puffing is rewarded at the 4,300-foot summit, where great views of the valley unfold. If it's a clear day, you may even see the San Francisco skyline or Mount Shasta, 192 miles north. The park also has picnic tables for those simply looking for a lovely outdoor place to lunch.

As elsewhere in the valley, biking in Calistoga is a fun and scenic alternative to sitting in congested traffic; it's a great way to get around any time of year. **Calistoga Bikeshop** (1318 Lincoln Ave., 707/942-9687, http://calistogabikeshop.com, $35-85 per day) offers guided tours, self-guided tours, and bike rentals. With cruisers and touring bikes, mountain and road bikes, tandems and trailers, and even electric bikes, this bike shop has everything you need to suit your travel plans. Ask at the shop for directions, maps, and suggestions—from a couple of hours in the vineyards to the most challenging mountain-bike tracks in the area.

Feel like a few rounds of golf? The **Mount St. Helena Golf Course** (2025 Grant St., 707/942-9966, www.napacountyfairgrounds.com, daily 7am-sunset, $12-26) is a charming and inexpensive par-34 nine-hole course; it's the perfect spot for younger or less experienced golfers. The course is flat and straight, with easier lines than many other courses. On the other hand, all those trees along the fairways and the small greens make it interesting for intermediate players.

If you care to take in Calistoga's dramatic scenery from the air, **Calistoga Balloons** (888/995-7700, www.calistogaballoons.com, $219-249) is the only company offering regular flights in the north end of Napa Valley. In addition to the vineyards, wineries, spas, and the charming town of Calistoga, you'll also see Mount St. Helena and the lush forested hills surrounding this lovely area.

Accommodations

A plethora of places to stay cluster at the north end of Napa Valley, where you'll find most of the hotel-and-spa combos plus plenty of mineral-water pools and hot tubs for your pleasure. Calistoga also has some of the best lodging rates around.

UNDER $100

The **Calistoga Inn** (1250 Lincoln Ave., 707/942-4101, www.calistogainn.com, $80-120) has been in continuous operation since 1882, giving guests an old-school hotel experience complete with shared baths and showers, but with sinks in each guest room. The inn provides some of the best bargain accommodations in Napa Valley. Each of the 18 guest rooms is a small cozy haven with a queen bed, simple but charming furnishings, and a view of the town. Amenities include a continental breakfast each morning and an English pub downstairs that serves lunch and dinner. Be sure to make reservations in advance—at these rates, rooms go quickly, especially in summer and fall. Be aware that the pub downstairs has live music four nights a week, so the party can get loud on weekends.

Mountain Home Ranch (3400 Mountain Home Ranch Rd., 707/942-6616, www.mountainhomeranch.com, $70-145) almost feels like summer camp. Set deep in the thickly forested mountains above Calistoga, it has an unpolished charm difficult to find elsewhere. Guests can choose a guest room with a full bath, a rustic cabin, or a cottage with a full bath, a fireplace, and a kitchen. There are two pools, a lake, volleyball and tennis courts, table-tennis tables, a basketball hoop, and a number of hiking trails on the property. There is also a menagerie of barnyard animals to keep any animal-loving kid happy. This being Calistoga, there's also a mineral springs soaking tub. The main house serves a dinner (adults $22, children $16), lunch (adults $17, children $12), and a breakfast of eggs, waffles, and fresh fruit. Needless to say, staying here is a relaxed, funky, and old-fashioned type of family vacation.

$100-150

With these bargain rates, don't expect modern luxury at the **Golden Haven Hot Springs** (1713 Lake St., 707/942-8000, www.goldenhaven. com, $125-229). Still, the rooms are spacious and clean, and all come with complimentary use of the hotel's sundeck, hot tubs, and a swimming pool fed by Calistoga hot springs water. For a few extra dollars, they have rooms with full size spas that can be filled with local mineral water. Golden Haven also has mud baths, massage services, facials, and body wraps for very reasonable prices. Keep your eyes peeled for specials featured on its website.

$150-250

For a weekend of soaking, stay at **C Dr. Wilkinson's Hot Springs Resort** (1507 Lincoln Ave., 707/942-4102, www.drwilkinson.com, $149-300). The main attraction here are the three on-site mineral pools that guests can utilize during their stay. Outdoors, there is an 80°F and 90°F pool, while indoors is a 103°F spa that is large enough to accommodate more than a dozen soakers. To spoil yourself even more, consider booking a treatment in the adjacent spa. The funky 1950s-era resort has multiple lodgings to choose from. Motel rooms are decorated in brown, orange, and beige; bungalows include kitchens; and guest rooms in the restored Victorian do not lack for ruffles and floral patterns. In addition to plush bathrobes, all guest rooms have coffeemakers, cable TV, and hypoallergenic bedding. Dr. Wilkinson's even has freshly laundered bathing suits on loan if you forgot yours. While it's not fancy, the resort staff is friendly, and the pools are worth spending time in.

Equally old-school are the **Hideaway Cottages** (1412 Fair Way, 707/942-4108, www.hideawaycottages.com, $164-350), a collection of 1940s-era bungalows primly decorated in cream with the occasional plaid bedspread. The cottages retain their original details, such as scalloped-edged kitchen cupboards, tile countertops, and charming built-in glass cabinets. Many of the cottages include sitting rooms, full kitchens, and outdoor seating; all are painted crisp white with country-blue trim. The cottages face communal leafy grounds where lawns offer plenty of spots to lounge around the pool and hot tub. In the interest of quiet, no pets or children under age 18 are allowed.

If you're looking for a more traditional bed-and-breakfast experience, you can't miss **The Pink Mansion** (1415 Foothill Blvd., 800/238-7465, www.pinkmansion.com, $225-345), literally: The 1875 mansion is painted unmistakably bright pink from stem to stern, making it a local landmark. Each lush guest room features a unique theme suitable to romance and wine. The more economical guest rooms have queen beds and pretty antique furnishings; the larger suites are spacious enough to dwarf their king beds, and you'll also find fireplaces, whirlpool tubs, and top-tier amenities. You can enjoy the heated indoor pool and spa, a full breakfast each morning, and use of the various TVs and DVD players, plus a movie library, secreted around the house.

The **Roman Spa Hot Springs Resort** (1300 Washington St., 800/914-8957, www. romanspahotsprings.com, $150-650) in the heart of downtown Calistoga has it all: three mineral-water pools, each set at a different temperature (no children under age 4 are allowed in any pool, and the 105°F spa is adults-only), plus saunas to inspire guests to relax and refresh themselves with daily soaks and swims. Guest rooms run the gamut from inexpensive motel-style rooms with floral comforters, whirlpool rooms that include a private two-person mineral bath, to kitchen suites (pots, pans, and dishes provided) that beckon families or groups who plan to stay awhile. The Roman Spa connects to the Calistoga Oasis, which offers an array of spa treatments, including the famous mud baths.

OVER $250

Mount View Hotel and Spa (1457 Lincoln Ave., 800/816-6877, www.mountviewhotel.com, $249-449) is perfectly located on Calistoga's main drag. Guest rooms, suites, and cottages are decorated with tasteful 19th-century antiques and soothing colors inspired by the vines and vintages of the local area. Guest rooms have either two twins, a queen, or a king bed, all feather beds with down comforters. An on-site spa offers facials, body wraps, steam showers, and scrubs. Enjoy the outdoor pool and outdoor spa with mineral waters at your leisure.

Food

Small, homey Calistoga offers a pleasing combination of high-end California cuisine and simple delicious fare. If you need a break from rich, expensive food, a great place to stop for a meal is at the corner of Lincoln Street and Highway 29. ◖ **Buster's Barbecue and Bakery** (1207 Foothill Blvd., 707/942-5605, http://busterssouthernbbq.com, $8-27) brings unpretentious barbecue to Wine Country. You may find lines of mostly locals looking for a good, quick meal at this walk-up eatery at both lunch and dinner. The simple fare includes favorites like barbecue sauce drenched tri tip and pork loin sandwiches served on slabs of garlic toast. You'll also have your pick of traditional sides (baked beans, slaw, potato salad, corn bread) and Southern-style baked goods. The sweet-potato pie is a reputable local favorite. Leave your fancy wine-tasting clothes at home; you might go through half a paper towel roll trying to clean up after having a Buster's barbecue sandwich.

Pacifico Mexican Restaurant (1237 Lincoln Ave., 707/942-4400, Mon.-Thurs. 11am-9pm, Fri. 11am-10pm, Sat. 10am-10pm, Sun. 10am-9pm, $10-20) serves great south-of-the-border fare in a relaxed easygoing atmosphere. The restaurant feels cool, dark, and cavernous; be sure to order a margarita at the full bar. Or, if the weather is nice, take advantage of the outdoor seating along Cedar Street. Staff are very friendly and attentive, and the fajitas are especially good, as is the chile relleno. Try not to fill up on the chips and salsa that appear first—even though the chips are warm, crisp, and fresh, and the house-made salsa is exceptional.

With its high ceilings and stone

© GABRIEL SKVOR

meats grilling outside at Buster's Barbecue and Bakery in Calistoga

fireplace decorated with a mounted elk head, **Brannan's Grill** (1374 Lincoln Ave., 707/942-2233, www.brannanscalistoga.com, Mon.-Thurs. 3pm-9pm, Fri.-Sun. 11:30am-9:30pm, $17-34) feels like an upscale mountain lodge restaurant in Wine Country. Even though it's popular on weekends, settle into a comfortable booth for a meal that could include grilled quail, rack of lamb, seafood, or one of Brannan's tender steaks. Brannan's is also known for its fine cocktails. On some nights, live jazz bands contribute to this popular restaurant's atmosphere.

Information and Services

For discounted wine-tasting vouchers, maps, or tips on the best mud bath, swing by the **Calistoga Visitors Center** (1133 Washington St., 707/942-6333, www.calistogavisitors.org, daily 9am-5pm), located in the heart of downtown Calistoga. You can even grab the *Weekly Calistogan* for a dose of local news and events.

The **post office** (1013 Washington St.) is located one block south of Lincoln Street. A block away, the **Vermeil House Clinic** (913 Washington St., 707/942-6233, Mon.-Fri. 9am-5pm) is affiliated with the St. Helena Hospital and treats nonemergency health concerns.

Getting There and Around

Calistoga is eight miles north of St. Helena on Highway 29. In Calistoga, Highway 29 turns east, becoming Lincoln Avenue. To reach the northern end of the Silverado Trail, follow Lincoln Avenue east through town and turn right to intersect it.

Highway 128 also runs through Calistoga, connecting to U.S. 101 north near Healdsburg. To reach Calistoga from U.S. 101 in Santa Rosa, take the exit for Highway 12 east. Turn left on Farmers Lane, and then turn right on Sonoma Highway (Highway 12). Continue driving east on Highway 12 for 2.4 miles to Calistoga Road. Turn left on Calistoga Road and drive 7.1 miles. Calistoga Road intersects Porter Creek Road, becoming Petrified Forest Road for 4.4 miles. Petrified Forest Road intersects with Foothill Boulevard (Hwy. 128) in Calistoga. Turn right and follow Highway 128 south for one mile to Lincoln Avenue, Calistoga's main drag.

Sonoma Valley

The Sonoma and Carneros wine regions are in the southeast part of Sonoma Valley. The scenery features oak forests and vineyard-covered open spaces. The terminus of El Camino Real is in the small city of Sonoma, which includes the famed Sonoma Mission Inn, historical sights, and a charming town square with plenty of shopping and great places to grab a bite. Wineries cluster in this region, though not as many as in the Russian River Valley; the tasting rooms still have plenty of traffic, but the crowds can be less vicious than in the ultra-popular Napa and Dry Creek Valleys.

Carneros might be described as the "lost" area of Wine Country. The wineries are a bit more spread out than in the Napa and Russian River Valleys, and fewer visitors cram into the tasting rooms. Some prestigious California names make their homes here, and some small boutique vintners quietly produce amazing varietals you won't find outside their tasting rooms.

SONOMA AND CARNEROS
Sonoma Wineries
CHARLES CREEK VINEYARD

Conveniently located on the square in downtown Sonoma, the tasting room at **Charles Creek Vineyard** (483 1st St. W., 707/935-3848, www.charlescreek.com, daily 11am-6pm) beckons visitors with a giant cork cow standing proudly in the middle of the floor. This only-in-Wine-Country objet d'art was won at a charity auction and now entices people to wander into the tasting room to take a closer look. Once inside, it's worth your time to taste the wines. This smaller-production winemaker purchases grapes from Napa and Sonoma to create boutique chardonnays, merlots, and cabernet sauvignons. The winemaker takes care to produce vintages that are easy to drink, especially with food.

RAVENSWOOD WINERY

Ravenswood Winery (18701 Gehricke Rd., 888/669-4679, www.ravenswood-wine.com,

daily 10am-4:30pm, tasting $15) prides itself on making "no wimpy wines." Although the company is now owned by a large conglomerate, Ravenswood wines are still overseen by the original winemaker, Joel Peterson, who began making California zinfandel in 1976. To this day, zinfandel remains the signature varietal under the Ravenswood label. Many of the prized zins come from individual vineyards in Sonoma County, while others are blends of grapes purchased from growers throughout California. When you come to taste, you won't find a stereotypical winery. Unlike many in Napa and Sonoma, Ravenswood sponsors a race car, hosts a bevy of summer barbecues (yep, you can drink zin with ribs), and strives to make tasters of all types feel at home in the winery. Tours and barrel tastings teach newcomers the process of winemaking, while "blend your own" seminars beckon to serious wine connoisseurs. Perhaps best of all, Ravenswood wines are easy on the pocketbook, ranging $13-50 per bottle.

Carneros Wineries
DOMAINE CARNEROS

The Sonoma-Carneros region has perfect conditions for champagne-style grapes, and so the glorious **Domaine Carneros** (1240 Duhig Rd., Napa, 800/716-2788, www.domaine.com, daily 10am-5:45pm, $16-30) makes its estate home here. Visitors rarely fail to be impressed by the grand estate structure, styled in both its architecture and garden setting like the great châteaux of France. Even more impressive are the finely crafted sparkling wines (for legal reasons Domaine Carneros prefers not to use the term *champagne*) and a few still pinot noirs the winery creates using grapes from the Carneros region. The Art of Sparkling Wine Tour ($30) is an excellent opportunity to sample the best wines, tour the grounds, and see how bubbly is made. Domaine Carneros also offers a seated tasting, adding to the overall atmosphere of sophistication and indulgence. If you want to

WINE COUNTRY

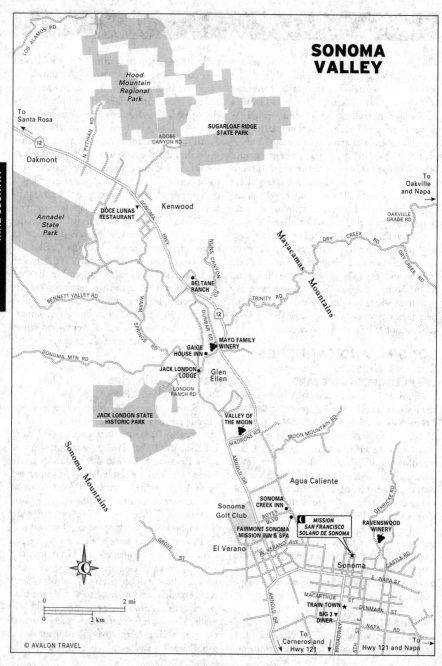

SONOMA VALLEY

To Santa Rosa

Hood Mountain Regional Park

SUGARLOAF RIDGE STATE PARK

ADOBE CANYON RD

LOS ALAMOS RD

N PYTHIAN RD

Oakmont

DÓCE LUNAS RESTAURANT

Kenwood

SONOMA HWY

To Oakville and Napa

OAKVILLE GRADE RD

DRY   CREEK   RD

DRY CREEK RD

Annadel State Park

BENNETT VALLEY RD

WARM   SPRINGS   RD

NUNS CANYON RD

Mayacamas Mountains

BELTANE RANCH

TRINITY RD

DUNBAR RD

SONOMA MTN RD

GAIGE HOUSE INN

MAYO FAMILY WINERY

JACK LONDON LODGE

Glen Ellen

LONDON RANCH RD

JACK LONDON STATE HISTORIC PARK

Sonoma Mountains

VALLEY OF THE MOON

MADRONE RD

MOON MOUNTAIN RD

ARNOLD DR

Agua Caliente

Sonoma Golf Club

SONOMA CREEK INN

BOYES BLVD

GEHRICKE RD

MISSION SAN FRANCISCO SOLANO DE SONOMA

RAVENSWOOD WINERY

FAIRMONT SONOMA MISSION INN & SPA

GROVE   ST

El Verano

W. VERANO AVE

Sonoma

CASTLE RD

E. NAPA ST

MACARTHUR   ST

ARNOLD DR

TRAIN TOWN

BIG 3 DINER

DENMARK   ST

BROADWAY

5TH   ST

NAPA   RD

To Carneros and Hwy 121

To Hwy 121 and Napa

0   2 mi
0   2 km

© AVALON TRAVEL

nibble on something while sipping, select from a cheese or charcuterie plate or a selection of caviar and smoked salmon.

GLORIA FERRER

For a taste of some of the upscale sparkling wines Sonoma can produce, take a long drive through immense estate vineyards to the tasting room at **Gloria Ferrer** (23555 Hwy. 121/ Arnold Dr., Sonoma, 707/996-7256, www. gloriaferrer.com, daily 10am-5pm, glass $2-10). Ferrer also adheres to the popular format for sparkling wineries—there's no traditional tasting. Instead, visitors order one or more full flutes of sparkling wine, then take a seat at an available table either inside the tasting room or out on the patio overlooking the Sonoma Valley. This style of tasting isn't cheap, but the wines here make the cost worth it for any serious sparkling-wine lover. Just be sure that someone is designated as driver—Ferrer doesn't pour stingy flutes.

SCHUG CARNEROS ESTATE

You might recognize the labels at the **Schug Carneros Estate** (602 Bonneau Rd., Sonoma, 800/966-9365, www.schugwinery.com, daily 10am-5pm, tasting $5-10). One of the Carneros region's elders, Walter Schug has made wine that has set the tone for California vintages for many years. The estate itself is worth a visit; the Tudor-esque barn sits in the middle of barns and fields of brilliant-yellow flowering mustard on the valley floor with views of the surrounding mountains all around. Schug's hallmarks are chardonnays and pinot noirs, grapes that grow well in this cooler region, so be sure to try the latest releases of both.

Sights
◖ MISSION SAN FRANCISCO SOLANO DE SONOMA

Mission San Francisco Solano de Sonoma (114 E. Spain St., 707/938-9560, www. parks.ca.gov, daily 10am-5pm, free) is the northernmost of the chain of Spanish missions in California. It is at the corner of the historic plaza in downtown Sonoma—a low,

surprisingly unpretentious block of buildings without much in the way of decoration or crowds. The last mission established, in 1823, and one of the first restored as a historic landmark, in 1926, the Sonoma Mission isn't the prettiest or most elaborate of the 21 missions. But visitors can see museum-style exhibits depicting the life of the later missionaries and Native Americans who lived here, and a unique series of watercolor paintings depicting all of the California missions. Outdoors, guests can rest on benches by the fountain, observe a moment of silence at the Native American mortuary monument, or check out the cactus "wall" that has been growing on the property since the mission era.

It's a little-known fact that California's state flag—the Bear Flag depicting a now-extinct California grizzly bear—first came to be in the tiny rural mission town of Sonoma. To commemorate that historic beginning, the **Bear Flag Monument** (Sonoma Plaza, E. Spain St. and 1st St. E.) was erected. Visit the monument as you stroll the plaza or explore the various sites of the Sonoma State Historic Park.

CORNERSTONE GARDENS

For a break from all the history of Sonoma's main attractions, take a walk in the **Cornerstone Gardens** (23570 Arnold Dr., 707/933-3010, www.cornerstonegardens.com, daily 10am-4pm, free). This unique installation combines an art gallery with the work of the foremost landscape and garden designers in the world. Stroll these unusual gardens, which range from traditional plantings to postmodern multimedia installations, and then finish up your excursion with a crawl through the boutiques, upscale food shops, and wine bars that have recently sprung up around the gardens. Daily wine-tastings and various snacks and nonalcoholic drinks provide welcome refreshment, especially on hot Sonoma summer afternoons.

DEPOT PARK MUSEUM

If you haven't had enough of history in Sonoma, make a stop by the **Depot Park**

© CHRISTIAN BERGMAN

Sonoma's Cornerstone Gardens

Museum (270 1st St. W., 707/938-1762, www. vom.com/depot, Wed.-Sun. 1pm-4:30pm, free) right down the street from the plaza and around the corner from the mission. The museum hosts a small set of exhibits inside a reproduction of the historic Northwestern Pacific Railroad depot, hence the name. Inside are reconstructions of the active depot in the Rand Room, a showcase of the Bear Flag Rebellion, and the life of the indigenous Miwok people.

TRAIN TOWN
Got a train enthusiast in the family? Take them to Sonoma's own **Train Town** (20264 Broadway/Hwy. 12, www.traintown.com, June-Sept. daily 10am-5pm, Sept.-May Fri.-Sun. 10am-5pm, $5.75/train ride). Ride the 15-inch scale train over four miles of track that goes through tunnels, over bridges, and into a mini town with a petting zoo. Or opt for a spin on the roller coaster or the Ferris wheel, or a climb up the clock tower for a magnificent view of the park and beyond.

Spas
The most famous spa in the area is the **Willow Stream Spa** (100 Boyes Blvd., 707/938-9000, www.fairmont.com/sonoma, daily 7:30am-8pm, $95-265). A natural mineral hot spring beneath the Sonoma Mission Inn provides warm water for the indoor and outdoor pools and whirlpools that create the center of the spa's signature Bathing Ritual. Whether you choose a relaxing massage or a challenging yoga class, be sure to arrive at least an hour early to allow time for each step of the ritual, which will relax and focus you for your next treatment or activity. The spa offers an almost bewildering variety of massages, scrubs, wraps, facials, and even more rarified treatments designed to pamper even the most discerning spa-goer. The facilities are surrounded by the inn and a gourmet restaurant, both of which draw visitors from around the world.

At the **Garden Spa at MacArthur Place** (29 E. MacArthur St., 707/933-3193, www.macarthurplace.com/spa.php, daily 9am-8pm, $118-345), you won't just take in the serene beauty of the inn's lush garden; you will be healed, rejuvenated, and beautified. All of the spa's signature treatments are made from the flowers, herbs, and fruit found in the garden, distilled into such luscious effusions as pomegranate body polish, golden passion-flower body wrap, peppermint foot soak, and the red-wine grape-seed bath. The spa also offers a mud-bath soak, a number of different massages, and facial and waxing treatments. Book treatments at least two weeks in advance as space in this fragrant spa fills up fast.

If you're just looking for a lift for your face, visit **The Pampered Pout** (678 Broadway, 707/938-9396, www.thepamperedpout.com, by appointment Tues.-Fri., $80-120). Choose from among nine different 45-50-minute facials to beautify your skin. Esthetician and owner Bridgene Raftery can provide treatments that include a classic European pampering facial, a series of microdermabrasion treatments, and makeup lessons for teens. Specialty facials for teens and men along with eyebrow design round out a complete menu of face-perfect services.

Shopping

There's no more pleasant place to stroll, window shop, or browse for an extravagant trinket than in Sonoma. Around its leafy square are famous structures and state parks, little cafés and eateries, and yes, shops. Lots and lots of shops. Many are on the four main streets bordering the square, but most you will have to hunt for in the nooks and crannies inside the remodeled historic buildings and tiny retail alleyways on each block.

Despite the name, **Large Leather** (481 1st St. W., 707/938-1042, www.largeleather.biz, daily 10am-6pm) is a pint-size store filled with purses, backpacks, belts, wallets, and bracelets. Anything you can think of that is or can be made out of leather can be found here. All items are handcrafted and designed by the owners, Paul Terwilliger and Jessica Zoutendijk.

A different kind of cooking store, **Bram** (493 1st St. W., 707/935-3717, www.bramcookware.com, Thurs.-Mon. 10am-6pm,

Tues. 10am-5pm) is devoted entirely to clay-pot cooking. Dark shelves are stocked with a beautiful selection of deep skillets, stew pots, rondeaux, open casseroles, tagines, rectangular bakers, brams, and roasters. Shoppers will be astounded by the range and diversity of the clay pots available. If you are at a loss for how to use such a beautiful pot, stacks of cookbooks fill the other side of the shop. The extremely knowledgeable staff are eager to share their experiences and preferences.

For handcrafted artistry with a bit more polish, stroll down to **Sonoma Silver Company** (491 1st St. W., 707/933-0999, www.sonomasilver.com, daily 11am-6pm), a slender shop awash in silver rings, pendants, bracelets, and earrings. Multiple local jewelers sell and showcase their work here, but many of the shiny trinkets are made in-house by the company's resident jeweler of 20 years.

You can see other local artwork at the **Fairmont Gallery** (447 1st St. W., 707/996-2667, www.fairmontgallery.com, Thurs.-Sun. noon-5pm). Mostly concentrating in oil paintings and other classic brush-on-canvas fine art, the intimate space, set up in an old A-frame house, is a pleasant reprieve from other bustling shops.

Around the corner from the square is **PK Sonoma** (120 W. Napa St., 707/935-6767, www.pksonoma.com, daily 10am-6pm), where you can buy a spa treatment to take home with you. PK Sonoma's skincare products—including Eye and Lip Silk, made with rose and German chamomile, and Goat's Milk Soap—are made in small batches from locally sourced herbs (lavender is a popular ingredient), giving the store a pleasant farm-to-bath feel. There are even herbal shampoos for your pet.

Accommodations
$150-250

For a charming guest room at reasonable rates within the Sonoma town limits, stay at **Sonoma Creek Inn** (239 Boyes Blvd., 888/712-1289, www.sonomacreekinn.com, $145-199). The whimsical, colorful decor and unique art pieces brighten each guest room and each guest's stay. Amenities include cable TV, free wireless Internet access, and a fridge. Some rooms also have private garden patios. Located a few minutes from downtown Sonoma and convenient to the Carneros wineries, the inn is perfect for travelers who want to spend on wine and dining rather than a motel room.

Right on Sonoma Plaza in the heart of Sonoma, **Les Petites Maisons** (1190 E. Napa St., 800/291-8962, www.lespetitesmaisons. com, $199-359) offers four cute cottages for a homey stay in the Wine Country. Each cottage has its own style, but all have warm colors and comfy furniture to evoke the relaxation needed for a perfect vacation. All the cottages have fully equipped kitchens that allow you to cook your own fresh food after a visit to the fabulous Sonoma farmers markets. Bicycles and gas grills are available by request.

In 1850 one of the first Spanish settlers in the Sonoma area built a home for his family on the town square, and for most of the last century, the **Swiss Hotel** (18 W. Spain St., 707/938-2884, www.swisshotelsonoma.com, $150-240) in the structure has offered beds and meals to travelers. With a renovation in the 1990s the guest rooms have plenty of modern amenities, while the exterior and the public spaces retain the historic feel of the original adobe building. You'll find your guest room light, bright, and airy, with fresh paint and pretty floral comforters. Downstairs, enjoy a meal at the restaurant or have a drink at the historic bar. Step outside to take a walk around the historic plaza.

For the price and the character, the **The Sonoma Hotel** (110 W. Spain St., 800/468-6016, www.sonomahotel.com, $115-248) can't be beat. Built in 1880, the hotel is one of Sonoma's landmark buildings. The interior is decorated in the fashion of the era, with high wood wainscoting, cream-colored walls, polished antiques, and elegant light fixtures. The guest rooms, all with private baths (a rarity in historical digs), are similarly outfitted in trim Victorian fixtures, and many have sloped ceilings, creating a cozy intimate atmosphere.

Not nearly as historic but conveniently located just a few blocks from the square is **El Pueblo Inn** (896 W. Napa St., 707/996-3651, www.elpuebloinn.com, $179-349). In true Spanish style, some guest rooms face a lush central courtyard. The grounds also have a pool and a hot tub. Some rooms boast walls of adobe bricks or lounge areas with fireplaces, but many are standard hotel accommodations—clean and modestly decorated. For the price and location, not to mention views of the garden, it's a good deal. The inn also offers a fitness room, complimentary breakfast, and an in-room safe. Another standout is the down comforters.

OVER $250

Neither historic nor centrally located, the **Fairmont Sonoma Mission Inn & Spa** (100 Boyes Blvd., 707/938-9000, www.fairmont. com/sonoma, $329-640) has another appeal: luxury. Of course, there is the spa, an 18-hole golf course, and the Michelin-starred restaurant, but the guest rooms themselves are enough. Your guest room is the kind of place you'll want to return to after a long day sipping wine or soaking in a mud bath, decorated in smooth Provençal yellows with the occasional brown or red thrown in and featuring four-poster beds with deep mattresses covered in down comforters. Some guest rooms have fireplaces, while others feature marble bathtubs; many overlook gardens. If you can tear yourself away, you may be able to enjoy the other amenities of the hotel or Sonoma.

Food
CALIFORNIA CUISINE

Hot spot **Harvest Moon Café** (487 1st St. W., 707/933-8160, http://harvestmooncafesonoma. com, Mon. and Wed.-Thurs. 5:30pm-9pm, Fri.-Sat. 5:30pm-9:30pm, Sun. 10am-2pm and 5:30pm-9pm, $17-28) has beautiful outdoor patio and a seasonal local-focused menu is the. The menu of this charmingly casual restaurant changes daily to take advantage of the best ingredients available.

Need a hearty breakfast or down-home lunch before you get going on a full day of wine-tasting? Stop in at the **Big 3 Diner** (18140 Hwy. 12, 707/939-2410, www.fairmont.com/

sonoma, daily 7am-9pm, $8-20). The restaurant is part of the Fairmont Sonoma Mission Inn property, which explains both the high prices and the upscale cuisine. But it's good stuff—the kitchen uses high-quality, often organic and local ingredients to create its fancy benedicts and sandwiches. Even locals approve, coming in to be greeted by name by the friendly and efficient staff. If you're staying at the Sonoma Mission Inn, order room service from Big 3 or walk over to the large dining room, outfitted with wooden chairs and tables and a pleasant casual atmosphere.

COFFEE AND TEA

If you just need a cup of coffee and maybe a quick pastry, stop in at the **Barking Dog Coffee Roasters** (201 W. Napa St., 707/996-7446, www.barkingdogcoffee.com, Mon.-Fri. 6am-7pm, Sat.-Sun. 7am-7pm). Barking Dog is where locals go to get their morning mochas. Sip a latte or indulge in a scoop of Caffe Classico gelato or a smoothie, take a seat on a comfy old couch, and maybe even enjoy some live music.

FRENCH

A favorite with the local-sustainable-organic food crowd, ◖ **The Girl and the Fig** (110 W. Spain St., 707/933-3000, www.thegirlandthefig.com, Fri.-Sat. 11:30am-11pm, Sun. 10am-10pm, Mon.-Thurs. 11:30am-10pm, $15-25) is right on Sonoma Plaza. The menu changes often to take advantage of the best local seasonal ingredients; for a special treat, order one of the amazing cheese plates or the three-course Bistro Plat du Jour. If you love the sauces and jams, look for The Girl and the Fig products on-site and at wineries and high-end food shops throughout Wine Country.

PORTUGUESE

It's rare when locals and travelers agree on the best restaurant in any given town. The fact that it's a traditional Portuguese eatery in a sea of California cuisine makes it all the more special. ◖ **LaSalette** (452 1st St. E., 707/938-1927, www.lasalette-restaurant.com,

Mon.-Thurs. 11:30am-2:30pm and 5pm-9pm, Sat.-Sun. 11:30am-9pm, $19-28) has a simple charming atmosphere with a wood-fired oven facing a curving bar that serves drinks and friendly chatter to regulars, along with a full dinner menu. A large outdoor patio is the most popular seating area in summer, although the meandering tile-floored dining room offers plenty of appeal plus a bonus view of the open kitchen. The undisputed star of LaSalette is the food. The unswervingly Portuguese menu features fresh fish and hearty meat dishes plus some good meatless options. Simple yet delectable preparations let the flavors of the principal ingredients shine through. Just ask if you want to make a substitution or leave something out—they're happy to accommodate special requests.

MARKETS

For travelers preparing most of their own meals, or if you're looking for gluten-free grains to take home, the **Fruit Basket** (24101 Arnold Dr., 707/938-4332, daily 7am-6pm) open-air market has a great selection. This isn't a local farm stand—much of the produce is emphatically not local, especially in the winter. But the array of dried beans and grains would put a San Francisco health-food store to shame, making it easy for people with celiac disease and those with food allergies to find great make-it-yourself food options. Despite its suggestive name, the Fruit Basket actually serves as a fully stocked market, selling imported Italian and Mexican foods, dairy products, somewhat superfluous wines, and, of course, fresh fruits and vegetables. The only staple they don't stock is fresh meat. Prices are reasonable, and the market is easy to see and access at the south end of the Sonoma-Carneros wine region.

Information and Services

Before you begin your Sonoma and Carneros wine-tasting adventure, stop in at the **Sonoma Valley Visitors Center** (453 1st St. E., 866/996-1090, www.sonomavalley.com, Mon.-Sat. 9am-5pm, Sun. 10am-5pm). Ask the volunteers for advice on which wineries to visit, and be sure to pick up some complimentary tasting passes.

One of the local papers in the Sonoma Valley is the **Sonoma Index-Tribune** (www.sonomanews.com). Turn to the "Do" and "Shop" sections for visitor information.

For medical attention in Sonoma, head for the **Sonoma Valley Hospital** (347 Andrieux St., 707/935-5000, www.svh.com), which has a full-service emergency room.

Getting There and Around

The town of Sonoma is over the mountains west of the Napa Valley. The main route through the valley is Highway 12, also called the Sonoma Highway. To reach Sonoma from Napa, drive south on Highway 29 and turn west onto Highway 12/121. Turn north on Highway 12 to reach downtown Sonoma.

From the Bay Area, take U.S. 101 north to Highway 37 east. Highway 37 branches sharply north to become Highway 121, then Highway 116 as it winds into the city of Sonoma. Driving south on U.S. 101, you can turn onto Highway 12 south in Santa Rosa and take a scenic journey down into the Sonoma-Carneros wine region.

Parking in downtown Sonoma is easy in the off-season and tougher in the high season (May-Oct.). Expect to hunt for a spot during local events and be prepared to walk several blocks. Most wineries provide ample free parking on their grounds.

For your public transit needs, use the buses run by **Sonoma County Transit** (SCT, 707/576-7433, www.sctransit.com, $1.25-3.45). Several routes serve the Sonoma Valley daily. You can use SCT to get from Sonoma Valley to Santa Rosa, Guerneville, and other parts of the Russian River Valley as well.

It's fitting that in Wine Country, a place at the cutting edge of sustainable agriculture in a state known for its eco-mindedness, you can take a vineyard tour on a Segway. **Sonoma Segway** (524 Broadway, 707/938-2080, www.sonoma-segway.com, tour $99-129, rental $40 per hour) offers a 3.5-hour tour that includes a visit to a local winery, a stop at a local food-based business, and a full visit to historic Sonoma. The tour

starts with a lesson on the Segway, and when you finish you'll get a complimentary bottle of wine if you're of age. If you'd prefer to explore the Sonoma streets and paths on your own, rent a Segway—from two hours and up.

GLEN ELLEN

North of the town of Sonoma, the valley becomes more and more rural. The next hamlet on Highway 12 is Glen Ellen (population 784), surrounded by a couple of regional parks and Jack London State Historic Park, named for one of the town's famous residents (the other big name is Hunter S. Thompson). Downtown Glen Ellen has not caught the Wine Country bug of boutique shops, Michelin-starred restaurants, and over-the-top spas; instead, it still feels like a rural farm town with a few historic structures thrown in for character.

Wineries

MAYO FAMILY WINERY

Breaking from the chardonnay-cab-merlot juggernaut of Sonoma, the **Mayo Family Winery** (13101 Arnold Dr., at Hwy. 12, 707/938-9401, www.mayofamilywinery.com, summer daily 10:30am-6:30pm, winter Thurs.-Mon. 10:30am-6:30pm, tasting $10) produces an array of interesting Italian-style varietals. Here you might taste smoky rich Carignane or barbera, enjoy a fruity white viognier, or savor the chianti-based sangiovese. Mayo Family boasts a big presence in the region, with an on-site tasting room, a small downtown-Sonoma storefront tasting room (1395 Broadway, Sonoma, Tues.-Wed. 4pm-6pm, Thurs.-Mon. 11am-6pm), and up north in Kenwood the prized reserve tasting room (9200 Sonoma Hwy., Kenwood, daily 10:30am-6:30pm, reservations recommended, fee). At the reserve tasting room, your experience includes seven pours of Mayo's best wines, each paired with a small bite of gourmet California cuisine created by chefs on-site. Bon appétit!

VALLEY OF THE MOON

History mixes with the highest winemaking technology California has to offer at **Valley of**

RACEWAY TRAFFIC

Think you can safely ignore Sonoma Raceway's schedule because you don't give a darn about auto or bike racing? Not if you're wise in the ways of event traffic. The turnoff to **Sonoma Raceway** lies roughly at the intersection of Highways 37 and 121. These charming and scenic two-lane roads are great for motoring and sightseeing – unless, of course, you're stuck in bumper-to-bumper race traffic. The absolute worst time to try to drive either of these roads (particularly Hwy. 37 out of Sonoma) is when a major race event has finished. The wretched traffic jams, which truly are more stop than go, can last for hours as people try to exit the racetrack into the unprotected intersection. In the summer, the sweltering heat causes both engines and tempers to overheat, to no good end. So what can you do?

- Check the race schedule (www.racesonoma.com), and avoid the roads in question for at least four hours after the scheduled or estimated end of a big race.

- Plot another route to your next destination, or stick around in Sonoma until well after the traffic is likely to have unsnarled. (Give it about six hours post-race.)

- Escape via Highway 12 east to Napa or west to Santa Rosa. From Santa Rosa, catch Highway 101 south to Marin or San Francisco or north toward the Russian River. If heading to Napa, pick up Highway 37 off of Hwy 101 and then follow it south to Highway 80. Highway 80 will either take you south to the East Bay or east into Sacramento and beyond.

the Moon (777 Madrone Rd., 707/939-4510, www.valleyofthemoonwinery.com, daily 10am-5pm, tasting $5-10), Since the Civil War era, this Sonoma institution has passed through many hands and produced hundreds of wines. The circa-1860s stone buildings house late-model stainless-steel fermentation tanks as well as classic oak barrels. In the tasting room is a small list of boutique wines, from an unusual sangiovese rosé to a classic California cabernet. Valley of the Moon takes pride in its awards, and you'll find that almost every wine you taste has its own list of medals. Check the website for a list of upcoming wine events that show off this great Sonoma landmark at its best.

Sports and Recreation
JACK LONDON STATE HISTORIC PARK
Literary travelers come to Sonoma not just for the fine food and abundant wine but for the chance to visit **Jack London State Historic Park** (2400 London Ranch Rd., 707/938-5216, www.parks.ca.gov, Thurs.-Mon. 9:30am-5pm, $10). Famed author Jack London did in fact live and write in rural Sonoma County at the beginning of the 20th century. Docents offer tours of the park, which include talks on London's life and history. Explore the surviving buildings on London's prized Beauty Ranch or hike up Sonoma Mountain and check out the artificial lake and bathhouse. The pretty stone **House of Happy Walls** (Thurs.-Mon. 10am-5pm), a creation of London's wife, houses a small museum. There's no camping at Jack London State Historic Park, but you can bring a picnic to enjoy on the attractive grounds.

With its vineyards, open spaces, and state parks, the Sonoma Valley begs to be explored on horseback in homage to its pioneering history. The **Triple Creek Horse Outfit** (707/887-8700, www.triplecreekhorseoutfit.com, $60-100) offers guided rides on the 1,850-acre Kunde Ranch that last from one hour up to half a day, taking you beyond what you can see from the windows of your car. To turn it into an epicurean outing, take the popular Picnic Lunch Tour or the Mountain-top Tasting and Ride combo.

SUGARLOAF RIDGE STATE PARK
Mossy waterfalls, hillside grasslands bordered by oaks, exposed rock outcroppings, and even

WINE COUNTRY

© AL STUMPF

Jack London State Historic Park in Glen Ellen

Sonoma Creek's headwaters can be found at **Sugarloaf Ridge State Park** (2605 Adobe Canyon Rd., 707/833-5712, www.parks.ca.gov, daily sunrise-sunset), just outside Kenwood. Despite its beauty, Sugarloaf is rarely visited, so if you're seeking solitude in nature, this may be your place. There are plenty of trails to suit your mood and hiking ability; meander down **Creekside Nature Trail** (1 mile, easy) or take **Canyon Trail** (1.6 miles, easy) to the waterfall, which descends 25 feet through mossy boulders beneath a canopy of redwoods. More athletic hikers can take **Vista Trail Loop** (4.1 miles, moderate-difficult) to the Indian Rock outcropping, which has a lovely view of the canyon below. To hike this trail, take Stern Trail to Bald Mountain Trail and turn right. Eventually, take another right on Vista Trail and cross the mountain, taking another right on Grey Pine Trail. Turn right again on Meadow Trail to return to the parking lot.

The crown jewel of the park, however, is Bald Mountain. Although only 2,729 feet high, the mountain sports views of nearly all of Wine Country as well as the Golden Gate and Sierra Nevada on clear days. The hike to the summit is not that challenging: **Bald Mountain Loop** (6.6 miles, moderate-difficult) begins at Stern Trail, and eventually you take a right turn onto Bald Mountain Trail and follow it to the top. To descend, turn right on Grey Pine Trail, and then make another right onto Meadow Trail.

While the lower part of the park has a lush, heavy canopy, the upper trails are quite exposed and can get hot in the summer and early fall. Be sure to bring sunscreen, a hat, plenty of water, and a map, as the trails can be somewhat confusing.

Sugarloaf is also home to the **Robert Ferguson Observatory** (www.rfo.org), which has three telescopes to take in the night skies. From January to November, the observatory hosts monthly star parties. Check the website for upcoming star parties and night sky classes.

Accommodations

With its wraparound porches and lush gardens, the **Beltane Ranch** (11775 Hwy. 12,

707/996-6501, www.beltaneranch.com, $150-265) looks like it belongs near Savannah, Georgia, rather than Sonoma. But this Valley of the Moon charmer sits in the middle of Wine Country, with five guest rooms and a detached cottage. After a good night's sleep in the pristine country-style guest rooms, guests enjoy a sumptuous breakfast in the dining room or on the porch overlooking the gardens and vineyards beyond. Guests are free to utilize the ranch's tennis court and walking trails.

For a bit of Asian-infused relaxation, stay at one of the best-reviewed inns in Wine Country: the **☾ Gaige House Inn** (13540 Arnold Dr., 800/935-0237, www.gaige.com, $275-575), which offers comfort and luxury built into the design of the guest rooms and common spaces. Special attention is paid to every detail, and each of the 23 guest rooms and suites resemble a spread in an interior-design magazine; suites have baths the size of bedrooms and their own tiny garden spaces. Outdoors is a pool and hot tub, while a breakfast buffet is laid out every morning.

Attached to the redbrick Jack London Saloon and Wolf House Restaurant, the **Jack London Lodge** (13740 Arnold Dr., 707/938-8510, www.jacklondonlodge.com, $120-185) anchors this part of downtown Glen Ellen. The 22-room lodge is modern, with a broad patio, a kidney-shaped pool, and groomed lawns. The inn's interior offers a more Victorian feel with dark wood furniture, rich floral linens, and low lighting, but the history of the building shines through. Vines draping the balcony are a nice touch, as is the hot tub and the creek running through the back of the property. They also rent the **Warm Springs Cottage** ($400-450), a three-bedroom rental in the woods that is located minutes from the main lodge.

Food
At the **Glen Ellen Inn Restaurant** (13670 Arnold Dr., 707/996-6409, www.glenelleninn.com, Thurs.-Tues. 11:30am-9pm, Wed. 5:30pm-9pm, $16-25), French bistro cuisine

meets California gastropub. You'll find this self-described oyster grill and martini bar's dining room inside a cute low building. In addition to the seafood-heavy gourmet menu, the Glen Ellen Inn boasts a full bar and a wine list worthy of its location.

The Fig Café (13690 Arnold Dr., 707/938-2130, www.thegirlandthefig.com, daily 5:30pm-close, brunch Sat.-Sun. 10am-3pm, $11-20) serves the same excellent food as its namesake restaurant in Sonoma but slightly scaled down. The menu leans toward comfort food, with grilled sandwiches, thin-crust pizzas, and a laid-back wine bar. The warm interior and weekend brunch makes it a sure bet.

Information and Services
The small town of Glen Ellen does not have a visitors center, so stock up on maps and tips before you leave Sonoma; the **Sonoma Valley Visitors Center** (453 1st St. E., Sonoma, 866/996-1090, www.sonomavalley.com, Mon.-Sat. 9am-5pm, Sun. 10am-5pm) has information for Glen Ellen. Some of the local inns and hotels can also provide some information.

Likewise, don't expect to find much in the way of wireless Internet access or reliable cellphone reception. If you need to communicate the old-fashioned way, there is a **post office** (13720 Arnold Dr.) next to Jack London Lodge.

Getting There and Around
Glen Ellen is located just off Highway 12, seven miles north of Sonoma. Arnold Drive is the main street through town, and it runs all the way south to Sonoma. To reach Glen Ellen from Santa Rosa, take Highway 12 east through Kenwood for 15.7 miles.

It is also possible to jump over to Glen Ellen from Highway 29 in Oakville. In Oakville, turn west onto Oakville Grade. After 3.2 miles, Oakville Grade becomes Dry Creek Road; the name changes again to Trinity Road in 2.8 miles. Keep to the right on Trinity Road, and in three miles you'll reach Sonoma Highway (Hwy. 12), where you turn left toward Glen Ellen.

Russian River Valley

The Russian River Valley may be the prettiest part of Wine Country. The Russian River runs through it, providing ample water for forests and meadows as well as wide calm spots with sandy banks. Rafting, canoeing, and kayaking opportunities abound on the zippier stretches of the river. If you are visiting for the vino, the area called the Russian River Valley actually encompasses several prestigious American Viticultural Areas, including Dry Creek, Alexander Valley, and, of course, Russian River. Wineries are clustered along three main roads: the Gravenstein Highway (Hwy. 116), River Road, and U.S. 101.

A little to the west of the area's concentrated wine region, you'll reach the river in Guerneville, a noted gay and lesbian resort destination. Even if you're straight (but not narrow), you'll love the kitschy downtown, clothing-optional resorts, and general sense of friendliness and fun that permeates the area.

SANTA ROSA

Santa Rosa is the biggest city in Wine Country and the largest in the North Bay. As such, it is more preoccupied with big-city issues than with wine-tasting. This is a mixed-income area where many people work in building trades and other blue-collar professions. It is also ethnically diverse, with a large Latino population as well as strong Southeast Asian communities. Developed at the turn of the 20th century, the older neighborhoods are filled with charming Craftsman-style bungalows. Downtown boasts some historic buildings, but many did not survive the big earthquakes of 1906 and 1969. Santa Rosa's large size means that there are plenty of things to do with the kids, such as the Charles Shultz and Pacific Air Museums.

Sights
CHARLES M. SCHULZ MUSEUM

Schulz drew the world-famous *Peanuts* comic strip for almost 50 years, and from 1958 until his death in 2000 he lived in Sonoma County.

In honor of Schulz and the *Peanuts* gang, the **Charles M. Schulz Museum** (2301 Hardies Lane, 707/579-4452, www.schulzmuseum. org, Memorial Day-Labor Day Mon.-Fri. 11am-5pm, Sat.-Sun. 10am-5pm, Labor Day-Memorial Day Mon. and Wed.-Fri. 11am-5pm, Sat.-Sun. 10am-5pm, adults $10, seniors and ages 4-18 $5, under age 3 free) opened in 2002. Inside the 27,000-square-foot building, which somehow manages to look like it comes from a four-inch comic strip, you'll find an incredible wealth of multimedia art, original drawings, and changing exhibitions based on the works of Schulz. No matter how many times you visit, you're likely to see something new in the ever-changing exhibits. Plenty of permanent collections provide stability and a base for the museum's theme. The museum owns most of the original *Peanuts* strips, a large collection of Schulz's personal possessions, and an astonishing array of tribute artwork from other comic-strip artists and urban installation designers the world over. Outside the building, the grounds include attractive gardens, the Snoopy Labyrinth, and even the infamous Kite-eating Tree.

Schulz's influence is felt outside the museum property as well. Across the street you can skate at Snoopy's Home Ice (Schulz was an avid hockey player for most of his life). And throughout downtown Santa Rosa, especially in Historic Railroad Square, you'll see colorful sculptures depicting members of the *Peanuts* gang brightening the streets and making people smile.

LUTHER BURBANK HOME AND GARDENS

If you love plants and gardening, don't miss the **Luther Burbank Home and Gardens** (204 Santa Rosa Ave., 707/524-5445, www. lutherburbank.org, gardens year-round daily 8am-dusk, free, tours Apr.-Oct. Tues.-Sun. 10am-4pm, $7). Using hybridization techniques, Luther Burbank personally created

WINE COUNTRY

COURTESY OF THE CHARLES M. SCHULZ MUSEUM AND RESEARCH CENTER

Charles M. Schulz Museum

some of the most popular plants grown in California gardens and landscapes today. You don't have to go to his gardens to see examples of his famous Shasta daisy, an incredibly hardy pure-white daisy hybrid that now blankets vast areas throughout the state. But you will see them in the Luther Burbank gardens in the more than one acre's worth of horticulture, which includes medicinal herbs and showy roses. Check the website for a list of what's in bloom during your visit, as something is sure to be showing its finest flowers every month of the year.

Sports and Recreation

Just as in Napa, one of the popular ways to get a great view of the Russian River Valley is from the basket of a hot-air balloon. Granted, you and your hangover must fall out of bed before dawn for this particular treat—so you might want to make this a first-day adventure before you start wine-tasting. **Wine Country Balloons** (meeting site Kal's Kaffe Mocha, 397 Aviation Blvd., 707/538-7359, www.balloontours.com,

daily, adults $225, seniors $215, children $195) can get you up in the air to start the day high above Wine Country. This big company maintains a whole fleet of balloons that can carry 2-16 passengers. Expect the total time to be 3-4 hours, with 1-1.5 hours in the air.

Accommodations

In the city of Santa Rosa, you'll find all the familiar chain motels. You'll also see a few charming inns and upper-tier hotels that show off the unique aspects of the city that serves as the transition from the Bay Area to true Northern California.

The **Sandman Motel** (3421 Cleveland Ave., 707/544-8570, www.sandmansantarosa.com, $100-140) offers clean, comfortable motel rooms for reasonable prices. The guest rooms are decorated in standard motel style, with dark carpets and floral bedspreads. Amenities include a big heated swimming pool, outdoor whirlpool tub that is heated year-round, coffee and continental breakfast in the lobby each morning, and in-room fridges and

WINE COUNTRY

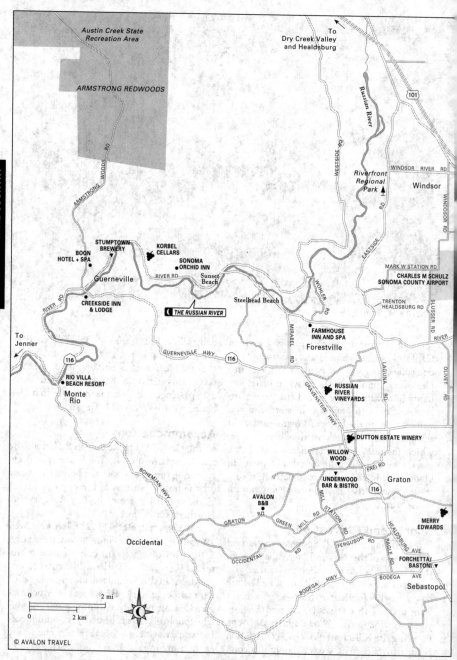

Austin Creek State
Recreation Area

ARMSTRONG REDWOODS

To
Dry Creek Valley
and Healdsburg

Russian River

101

ARMSTRONG WOODS RD

WESTSIDE RD

Riverfront
Regional
Park

Windsor

WINDSOR RIVER RD

WINDSOR RD

EASTSIDE RD

BOON
HOTEL + SPA

STUMPTOWN
BREWERY

KORBEL
CELLARS

SONOMA
ORCHID INN

Guerneville

RIVER RD

Sunset
Beach

Steelhead Beach

MARK W STATION RD

CHARLES M SCHULZ
SONOMA COUNTY AIRPORT

TRENTON
HEALDSBURG RD

SLUSSER RD

RIVER RD

CREEKSIDE INN
& LODGE

◀ THE RUSSIAN RIVER

WOHLER RD

MIRABEL RD

FARMHOUSE
INN AND SPA

Forestville

LAGUNA RD

OLIVET RD

To
Jenner

116

GUERNEVILLE HWY

116

RIO VILLA
BEACH RESORT

Monte
Rio

RUSSIAN
RIVER
VINEYARDS

GRAVENSTEIN HWY

DUTTON ESTATE WINERY

WILLOW
WOOD

FREI RD

Graton

BOHEMIAN HWY

UNDERWOOD
BAR & BISTRO

116

AVALON
B&B

GRATON RD

GREEN HILL RD

MILL STATION RD

HEALDSBURG AVE

MERRY
EDWARDS

BAGLE RD

Occidental

OCCIDENTAL RD

FERGUSON RD

FORCHETTA/
BASTONI

BODEGA AVE

Sebastopol

BODEGA HWY

0   2 mi

0   2 km

© AVALON TRAVEL

RUSSIAN RIVER VALLEY

To
Calistoga and
Napa Valley

MARK WEST SPRINGS RD

SHILOH RD
SKYLINE BLVD
OLD REDWOOD HWY
AIRPORT BLVD
REDWOOD HWY
★ PACIFIC COAST
AIR MUSEUM
LAUGHLIN RD

RD
FULTON RD
■ JOSH ASH & CO

PINER RD
MARLOW RD
CHARLES M.
SCHULZ MUSEUM ★
W STEELE LN
GUERNEVILLE RD
N DUTTON AVE
4TH ST

Santa Rosa
■ LUTHER
BURBANK
HOME &
GARDENS
OCCIDENTAL RD
SEBASTOPOL RD
SEBASTOPOL AVE
PETALUMA HILL RD

12
HEARN AVE
STONY POINT RD
LUDWIG AVE
LLANO RD
101
TODD RD
TODD RD

To
Petaluma

satellite TV. The Sandman is a great place to bring the family.

At the corner of Historic Railroad Square, **Hotel la Rose** (308 Wilson St., 800/527-6738, www.hotellarose.com, $129-189) exemplifies the luxury-hotel concept as it has evolved over the last century. The stone-clad main building rises high over Railroad Square, with more guest rooms available in the more modern carriage house just across the street. Because Hotel la Rose has only 48 guest rooms, you'll see an attention to detail and a level of service that's missing in the larger motels and hotels in the area. The carriage house offers modern decor and amenities, and each large room and suite feels light and bright. In the main building you'll find an older style of elegance, with antique furniture and floral wallpaper appealing to guests who want a taste of what the hotel might have been like back in 1907. A quick trip downstairs takes you to Hotel la Rose's restaurant, Bistro 1907 (Sun.-Wed. 7am-9pm, Thurs.-Sat. 7am-10pm).

At the north end of Santa Rosa, convenient to the major Russian River wine roads, you can stay at the lovely upscale **Vintners Inn** (4350 Barnes Rd., 800/421-2584, http://vintnersinn. com, $265-475). The low, attractive red-tile-roof buildings of the inn and the fabulous John Ash & Co. restaurant are adjacent to a large stretch of vineyard. Every guest room has a king bed, fluffy down bedding, and a patio or balcony overlooking a cute garden-like courtyard. Many guest rooms boast fireplaces and spa tubs, and all feature luxurious appointments. Your stay includes access to the inn's outdoor whirlpool tub and the common den, which has a fireplace. The only downside to the Vintners Inn is its regrettable proximity to a local power station; just try to look in the other direction when admiring the view.

Food

◖ **John Ash & Co.** (4350 Barnes Rd., 707/527-7687, www.vintnersinn.com, Fri. 11:30am-2:30pm and 5pm-9pm, Sat. 5pm-9pm, Sun. 5pm-8:30pm, Mon.-Tues. 5pm-8:30pm, Wed.-Thurs. 11:30am-2:30pm and 5pm-8:30pm,

$15-39) stands out as one of the best high-end California cuisine restaurants in the Russian River region. The large elegant dining room, done up in Mediterranean style, is part of the Vintners Inn, and the only unappetizing thing about it is its location across the street from a power plant. The food runs to pure California cuisine with lots of local and sustainable produce prepared to show off the natural flavors. The menu is fairly short, making it easy to choose from each of the three courses that often highlight seafood, beef, lamb, and seasonal specialties. And, of course, the wine list at John Ash & Co. is something special, with some amazing local vintages that are tough to find anywhere outside the Russian River Valley.

Need something a bit more casual? Get in line for breakfast, brunch, or lunch at the **Omelette Express** (112 4th St., 707/525-1690, http://omeletteexpress.com, Mon.-Fri. 6:30am-3pm, Sat.-Sun. 7am-4pm, $8-12). Owned by local character Don Taylor, who might even be acting as host at the front door on the weekend, this spot is definitely favored by locals. Don calls many of his customers by their first names, but he also welcomes newcomers with enthusiasm. The very casual dining rooms are decorated with the front ends of classic cars, and the menu—no surprise—involves lots of omelets. Portions are huge and come with a side of toast made with homemade bread, so consider splitting one with a friend.

Located in downtown's Railroad Square area, **Jackson's Bar and Oven** (135 4th St., www.jacksonsbarandoven.com, Mon.-Thurs. 11:30am-10pm, Fri.-Sat. 11:30am-11pm, Sun. 11:30am-9pm, $14-22) is a popular spot for tasty cocktails, food, and, no surprise, wine. Dine on Jackson's small bites, salads, sandwiches, and entrées at the curved bar or at a table. Or, even better, order up one of their tasty wood fired pizzas.

Information and Services

The serious local daily newspaper is the **Santa Rosa Press Democrat** (www.pressdemocrat.com). Check the Living and Entertainment sections for visitor information. You can also check out the many Wine Country guides that proliferate in the tasting rooms, motels, and inns of the region.

As a major city, Santa Rosa has plenty of medical services available. If you need help, try **Santa Rosa Memorial Hospital** (1165 Montgomery Ave., 707/546-3210, www.stjosephhealth.org), which has an emergency room.

Getting There and Around

Santa Rosa is 50 miles north of San Francisco on U.S. 101. Be aware that traffic on this major corridor can get congested, particularly during the morning commute and 3pm-7pm Monday-Friday. It also slows on sunny summer afternoons when people go to cool themselves along the Russian River. Fortunately, the side roads that lead to various tasting rooms and recreation spots are seldom crowded.

From U.S. 101, take exit 489 toward downtown Santa Rosa to reach the historic district; downtown is east of the freeway. Wineries are on the west side of town and can be accessed by taking Highway 12 west as well as the U.S. 101 exits for River Road and Guerneville.

Golden Gate Transit (415/455-2000, http://goldengatetransit.org, $10.25) runs buses between San Francisco and Santa Rosa on routes 70, 71, 72, and 80. These routes are geared toward commuters who work in San Francisco, so the southbound buses run in the morning and those going north run in the afternoon.

Pilots can fly into regional **Charles M. Schultz-Sonoma County Airport** (STS, 2290 Airport Blvd., 707/565-7240, www.sonomacountyairport.org).

SEBASTOPOL

Low-key and a bit alternative, Sebastopol is undoubtedly the artistic heart of Sonoma County. The relatively modest digs, low cost of living, liberal politics, natural beauty, and small-town vibe have attracted artists that include heavyweights like Jerry Garcia and Les Claypool of Primus as well as independent painters, sculptors, and ceramists. Downtown Sebastopol contains a number of shops where local artists sell their works, along with bookstores, record stores, and the odd place selling tie-dyed T-shirts. The surrounding farmland was once devoted to orchards, particularly apples, but that has changed over the years; now grapes dominate the Gravensteins. Still, the few remaining orchards give fragrance and beauty to the already scenic country roads, especially during the spring bloom.

Wineries
DUTTON ESTATE
A small winery along the comparatively undiscovered Gravenstein Highway, **Dutton Estate** (8757 Green Valley Rd., 707/829-9463, www. duttonestate.com, daily 10am-4:30pm, tasting $10-15) is in the middle of its own vineyards (don't pick the grapes). Tasters enjoy plenty of personal attention from pourers, along with a small list of white and rosé wines, moving into the red pinots and syrahs that do so well in this area. Dutton's syrahs stand out among the offerings, which can include a few extra pours for those who seem genuinely interested in the wines.

MERRY EDWARDS WINERY
Merry Edwards was the first woman to earn a degree in enology (winemaking) from the prestigious University of California, Davis, program in 1993. After working as a winemaker for numerous Sonoma vintners and developing her own pinot noir grape clone with the help of the facilities and staff at Davis, Merry finally opened her own winery. The **Merry Edwards Winery** (2959 Gravenstein Hwy., 707/823-7466, www.merryedwards.com, daily 9:30am-4:30pm, free tasting) offers tastings in its two glass-walled tasting rooms. Anxious to avoid the overcrowded, under-attended Napa tasting model, each member of Merry Edwards's tasting staff works with only one party of tasters at a time. Instead of forcing your way through a crowd for 12 inches of bar space, you'll be led to a table with comfortable chairs already set with four glasses ready for four different pinot noirs. There are four samples of the same varietal plus a bonus sauvignon blanc served at the end of the tasting. It's easy to spend an hour at Merry

Edwards, soaking up the luxury of a completely different tasting experience. Perhaps most amazingly of all, tasting at Merry Edwards is free. However, you probably won't make it out the door without purchasing at least one bottle of Edwards's stellar wine.

Accommodations
In Sebastopol, the best place to stay is the expensive but lovely **Avalon Bed and Breakfast** (11910 Graton Rd., 707/824-0880, www. avalonluxuryinn.com, $239-329). With only three guest rooms, it offers the ultimate in private and romantic accommodations. All guest rooms have king beds, hot tubs or access to the garden hot tub, fireplaces, air-conditioning, and many luxurious amenities. Because Avalon was purpose-built as a bed-and-breakfast, each guest room is actually a suite with a private entrance and there is plenty of space to spread out to enjoy a longer stay. At breakfast time, you'll be served an organic feast, with produce purchased from a local community-shared agriculture group and loving attention to the details of preparation.

Food
A great break from the endless fancy food is to find a nice ethnic restaurant. In Sebastopol, one of the best is the **Himalayan Tandoori and Curry House** (969 Gravenstein Hwy. S., 707/824-1800, www.himalayanfoodcompany. net, Mon.-Sat. 11am-2pm and 5pm-9pm, Sun. 5pm-9pm, $12-19), which serves up Indian food in the Himalayan style. You'll find vegetable curries and meat tandoori here, both properly spicy, as well as fresh naan, spicy rice pudding, and all sorts of treats. You'll even get a break from the endless river of wine, since there's plenty of beer on the drinks menu.

Walking into downtown's **◖ Forchetta/ Bastoni** (6948 Sebastopol Ave., 707/829-9500, http://forchettabastoni.com) presents a difficult decision. On one side is Southeast Asian street food (*bánh mì* sandwiches, noodle bowls, and curry plates). On the other side is rustic Italian fare in the form of wood-fired pizzas, pastas, and salads, all with the usual California cuisine twist. The twin restaurants are both smartly decorated. The Asian side, Bastoni (Sun.-Thurs. 11:30am-9pm, Fri.-Sat. 11:30am-10pm, $10-16) features skinny communal tables, colorfully worn stools, and cans of chopsticks. Over on the Italian side, Forchetta (Thurs.-Mon. 5pm-9pm, Wed. 6pm-9pm, $17-30), the decor is a bit more urbane with warm wood walls, exposed vents, and simple but artsy glass chandeliers. A full bar takes up most of Bastoni and is filled by happy locals grabbing a quick bite, a drink, or chatting. If you are torn between the two, Bastoni is frequently less busy, but both sides often have space at the chef's tables that face the open kitchens.

The **Underwood Bar and Bistro** (9113 Graton Rd., Graton, 707/823-7023, www.underwoodgraton.com, Tues.-Sat. 11:30am-10pm, Sun. 5pm-10pm, $13-28) serves upscale cuisine in the tiny town of Graton. Plush red velvet and dark wood tables grace the Underwood's dining room, which is recommended by many locals as the best spot in this wine region to sit down to a serious dinner. With a heavy seafood focus, including raw oysters on the half shell, and top-quality meats and produce, Underwood does in fact exemplify Wine Country cuisine. The so-called tapas are actually small plates and appetizers, meant to be shared around the table, but you can share the larger salads and entrées just as easily. The wine list leans heavily toward small local vintners; ask your server to recommend some of the best local wines with dinner. One especially spiffy thing about Underwood: The bar stays open late (10pm-11pm) on Friday-Saturday nights, serving a pared-down but still satisfying late-night menu.

Calling the **Willow Wood** (9020 Graton Rd., Graton, 707/823-0233, www.willowwoodgraton.com, Mon.-Sat. 8am-9pm, Sun. 9am-3pm, $10-25) a deli is somewhat misleading. Sure, they've got a counter, a take-out business, and well-trodden old wooden floors. But really, Willow Wood is an upscale California-Italian restaurant for lunch, featuring souped-up versions of traditional deli sandwiches accompanied by pasta and pickled veggies. Diners sit

on wooden benches to enjoy the large meals, which can also include giant salads and tureens of fresh soup. You can get a beer or a glass of Sonoma wine with your meal, or use the sugar found in the silver alien pod on your table to sweeten the locally beloved hot teas. If you're having trouble making a choice, the open-faced egg salad hot sandwich with bacon and pesto is a favorite.

Information and Services

For maps of the area, souvenirs, newspapers, and wine-tasting coupons, swing by the **Sebastopol Chamber of Commerce Visitors Center** (265 S. Main St., 707/823-3032, www.sebastopol.org, Mon.-Fri. 9am-5pm). Although it's closed on weekends, they do have a 24-hour information kiosk outside.

Published in Sebastopol, the **Sonoma West Times and News** (www.sonomawest.com) covers local happenings and upcoming events; it comes out every Thursday. The **post office** (290 Main St.) is on the same block as the visitors center but on the opposite side of the street.

Getting There and Around

Sebastopol is west of Santa Rosa, accessed by Highways 116 and 12. The heart of downtown Sebastopol is at the intersection of Sebastopol Avenue (Hwy. 12) and Main Street (Hwy. 116). Note that Sebastopol Avenue becomes the Bodega Highway once it hits downtown Sebastopol and extends all the way to, you guessed it, Bodega Bay.

To reach Sebastopol from U.S. 101, take either the exit for Highway 12 west in Santa Rosa or the exit for Highway 116 west at Cotati, eight miles south of Santa Rosa. Highway 116 is the most direct route to continue to the Russian River from Sebastopol.

GUERNEVILLE AND VICINITY

There are only a few wineries in the Guerneville area, but that's OK—people come here to float, canoe, or kayak the gorgeous Russian River that winds through town from Forestville all the way through Monte Rio to the Pacific Ocean at Jenner. In addition to its busy summertime tourist trade, Guerneville is also a very popular gay and lesbian resort area. The rainbow flag flies proudly here, and the friendly community welcomes all.

Wineries
RUSSIAN RIVER VINEYARDS
Ironically, **Russian River Vineyards** (5700 Gravenstein Hwy., Forestville, 707/887-3344, www.russianrivervineyards.com, daily 11am-5pm, tasting $10) really isn't on the Russian River; it is in the coastal hills of nearby Forestville that nurture the Sonoma Coast American Viticultural Area vineyards and wineries. The property doesn't look like a typical high-end winery—the aging wooden buildings seem almost to be falling apart. (Don't worry, the tasting room has recently been shored up.) Sadly, the funky old Victorian house behind the tasting room isn't open for tours—it's part of the private production facility.

The friendly staff help create a classy, small-winery tasting experience. Russian River Vineyards' small list of only red wines reflects the locale—tasters enjoy full-bodied, fruity pinot noirs and interesting varietals from the southern reaches of Europe. The charbono tastes especially good. For lunch, ask for a table in one of the two small dining rooms, divided by the brushed-metal tasting bar. Brunch or light afternoon fare is available every day, as is dinner, which includes a three-course prix fixe option.

KORBEL CELLARS
Champagne grapes like cooler climates, so it makes sense that **Korbel Cellars** (13250 River Rd., Guerneville, 707/824-7000, www.korbel.com, daily 10am-4:30pm, four tastes free, tours daily 11am-3pm, free), the leading producer of California champagne-style sparkling wines, maintains a winery and tasting room on the Sonoma coast. The large, lush estate welcomes visitors with elaborate landscaping and attractive buildings, including a small area serving as a visitors center. Tours of the estate are offered daily. Inside the tasting room, visitors get to sample far more than the ubiquitous Korbel

Brut that appears each New Year's. Korbel makes and sells a wide variety of high-end California champagnes, plus a few boutique still wines and a line of brandies. You can't taste the brandy (that involves a different and harder-to-obtain liquor license), but you can purchase it from the winery store. The facility also has a full-service gourmet deli and picnic grounds for tasters who want to stop for lunch.

The Russian River
Guerneville and its surrounding forest are the center for fun on the river. In summer the water is usually warm and dotted with folks swimming, canoeing, or simply floating tubes serenely downriver amid forested riverbanks and under blue skies. **Burke's Canoe Trips** (8600 River Rd., Forestville, 707/887-1222, www.burkescanoetrips.com, Memorial Day-mid-Oct., $60) rents canoes and kayaks on the Russian River. The put-in is at Burke's beach in Forestville; paddlers then canoe downriver 10 miles to Guerneville, where a courtesy shuttle picks them up. Burke's also offers overnight campsites for tents, trailers, and RVs.

On the north bank, near the small enclave of Monte Rio, **Johnsons Beach & Resort** (16241 1st St., 707/869-2022, www.johnsonsbeach.com, May-Oct. daily 10am-6pm, $30/canoe or kayak for a day) rents canoes, kayaks, pedal boats, and inner tubes for floating the river. There is a safe, kid-friendly section of the riverbank that is roped off for small children; parents and beachcombers can rent beach chairs and umbrellas for use on the small beach. The boathouse sells beer and snacks.

Fly fishers can cast their lines nearby off **Wohler Bridge** (9765 Wohler Rd., Forestville) and **Steelhead Beach** (9000 River Rd., Forestville).

Armstrong Redwoods
An easy five-minute drive from Guerneville on one mostly straight road, **Armstrong Redwoods State Natural Reserve** (17000 Armstrong Woods Rd., Guerneville, 707/869-2015, www.parks.ca.gov, daily 8am-one hour after sunset, $8 per vehicle) often gets

WINE COUNTRY

overlooked, which makes it a bit less crowded than some of the most popular North Coast and Sierra redwood forests. But you can still take a fabulous hike—either a short stroll in the shade of the trees or a multiple-day backcountry adventure. The easiest walk ever to a big tree is the 0.1-mile stagger from the visitors center to the tallest tree in the park, named the Parson Jones Tree. If you saunter another 0.5 miles, you'll reach the Colonel Armstrong Tree, which grows next to the Armstrong Pack Station—your first stop if you're doing heavy-duty hiking. From the Pack Station, another 0.25 miles of moderate hiking leads to the Icicle Tree.

Right next to Armstrong is the **Austin Creek State Recreation Area** (17000 Armstrong Woods Rd., Guerneville, 707/869-2015, www.parks.ca.gov, daily 8am-one hour after sunset, $8 per vehicle). It's rough going on 2.5 miles of steep, narrow, treacherous dirt road to get to the main entrance and parking area; no vehicles over 20 feet long and no trailers of any kind are permitted. But once you're in, some great—and very difficult—hiking awaits you. The eponymous **Austin Creek Trail** (4.7 miles one-way) leads down from the hot meadows into the cool forest fed by Austin Creek. To avoid monotony on this challenging route, create a loop by taking the turn onto **Gilliam Creek Trail** (4 miles one-way). This way you get to see another of the park's cute little creeks as you walk back to the starting point.

Entertainment and Events
BARS
Guerneville wouldn't be a proper gay resort town without at least a couple of good gay bars that create proper nightlife for visitors and locals alike. The most visible and funky-looking of these is the **Rainbow Cattle Company** (16220 Main St., Guerneville, 707/869-0206, www.queersteer.com, daily 6am-2am). Mixing the vibes of a down-home country saloon with a happening San Francisco nightspot, the Rainbow has cold drinks and hot men with equal abandon. Think cocktails in Mason jars, wood paneling, and leather nights. This is just

the kind of queer bar where you can bring your mom or your straight-but-not-narrow friends, and they'll have just as much fun as you will.

It may not look like much from the road, but the **Stumptown Brewery** (15045 River Rd., 707/869-0705, www.stumptown.com, Sun.-Thurs. 11am-midnight, Fri.-Sat. 11am-2am) is the place to hang out on the river. Inside this atypical dive bar is a pool table, Naugahyde barstools, and a worn wooden bar crowded with locals. Out back are the second bar and an outdoor deck with scattered tables overlooking the river. The brewery only makes a few of the beers sold on tap, but they are all great and perfect to enjoy by the pitcher. If you are feeling a little woozy from the beer and sunshine, Stumptown also serves a menu of burgers and grilled sandwiches; the food is a perfect excuse to stay put.

EVENTS
Held at Johnson's Beach in Guerneville, the **Russian River Jazz and Blues Festival** (www.omegaevents.com, 707/869-1595, Sept., $50/day) is a two-day affair with jazz one day and blues the next. The main stage has some pretty big acts, including Buddy Guy, Al Green, and Taj Mahal, but there is plenty of music to groove to throughout the festival grounds. In addition to live acts, food vendors showcase regional fare, local artists hawk their wares, and tents serve glass after glass of wine while sunburned devotees splash around in the river. Much more than just a music festival, this event is the last big bash of the summer season; it takes place at the end of September, just before the weather reliably turns cold. If you plan to stay both days, consider camping here. **Johnson's Beach** (707/869-2011) has designated campsites available on a first-come, first-served basis.

If you in the area in mid-August, you may be able to get tickets for the Stumptown Brewery's annual **Russian River Beer Revival and BBQ Cook Off** (15045 River Rd., 707/869-0705, www.stumptown.com/revival, mid-Aug. Sat. noon-6pm). The event takes place along the river on a grassy field below the restaurant.

Enjoy live music, beer tastings from 30 different breweries, and lots and lots of barbecue. Tickets generally go on sale in June and sell out quickly.

Accommodations

Because it's the major resort town for lovers of Russian River recreation, you'll find a few dozen bed-and-breakfasts and cabin resorts in town. Many of these spots are gay-friendly, some with clothing-optional hot tubs.

UNDER $150

The **Creekside Inn & Lodge** (16180 Neeley Rd., 800/776-6586, www.creeksideinn.com, $90-270) is right along the Russian River outside of downtown Guerneville. The river floods fairly regularly, hence the entire resort perches on stilts that provide pretty views as well as dry carpets. Cabins and cottages at the lodge run short on upscale amenities but long on woodsy kitsch. Every cabin, even the studios, has a full kitchen with a fridge, plenty of space, a comfortable bath, and some of the best complimentary coffee you'll ever get in a hotel room. Choose from economical studios, multiple-bedroom family units, and brand-new eco-cabins that were designed and constructed to have minimal impact on the delicate local environment. The property is large and has a swimming pool for summertime refreshment, but it does not have good river frontage for swimmers. The owners, who know and love their area, will provide good suggestions for local beaches. They'll also make appointments for wine-tasting at their favorite private local wineries; if you're in town for the wine, definitely make use of this service, as you won't necessarily find the best appointment-only tasting rooms on your own.

Riverfront balconies, a private beach, and beautifully landscaped grounds combine to make **Rio Villa Beach Resort** (20292 Hwy. 116, Monte Rio, 877/746-8455, www.riovilla. com, $119-179) an ideal Russian River getaway. With only 11 guest rooms—including some with kitchens—you're guaranteed both privacy with your companion and intimacy with the resort guests as well as the warm owners. A generous continental breakfast is available in the morning, and the Russian River is mere steps away.

$150-250

The ◖ **Sonoma Orchid Inn** (12850 River Rd., Guerneville, 888/877-4466, www.sonomaorchidinn.com, pets welcome, $149-234) experience is made by its amazing owners. They've created beautiful guest rooms with elegant linens and furniture, plus just enough tchotchkes to keep things interesting. The best (and spendiest) rooms have satellite TV with DVRs, DVD players and VCRs, and microwaves and small fridges. On the economy end of the spectrum, the guest rooms are tiny but cute, with private baths and pretty decorations. Best of all, the owners of the Orchid will offer to help you with absolutely anything you need. They not only recommend restaurants and spas, they'll make reservations for you. They've got knowledge about the local wineries, hikes, river spots, and just about everything else in the region. The Orchid makes a perfect inn for visitors who've never been to the area—they're dog friendly, clothing mandatory, and welcoming to travelers of all stripes.

On the road to Armstrong Redwoods, **Boon Hotel + Spa** (14711 Armstrong Woods Rd., Guerneville, 707/869-2721, www.boon-hotels.com, $165-300) is the antithesis of Guerneville's woodsy funkiness. In almost a rebuff to its environs, Boon Hotel + Spa is minimal in the extreme, with white walls devoid of artwork, square armless couches, and beds vast enough to get lost in the fair-trade organic cotton sheets. The slate, chrome, and white palette is offset by bright slashes of red and orange. Many of the 14 guest rooms have freestanding cast-iron fireplaces, private patios, and fridges. True to its name, there is a pool and hot tub (both saltwater, for a little twist) and plenty of facial and massage options to work out the kinks. In the morning, wake up to a pressed pot of locally roasted coffee; in the evening, chill out with a cocktail by the pool.

OVER $250

The **Farmhouse Inn & Spa** (7871 River Rd., Forestville, 707/887-3300, www.farmhouse-inn.com, $345-895) is along River Road in the middle of prime wine-tasting country. The yellow-painted farmhouse is the inn's restaurant and contains the two guest rooms; most of the guest accommodations march up the gently sloped hillside in the form of a row of cottages. The cute little cabins have upscale decor, warm fireplaces, private baths, and precious little space. The most upscale rooms with jetted tubs and private decks are in a barn on the property. The pool area and restaurant aren't big either but make up what they lack in size with charm and an adorable outdoor fireplace area. A gourmet breakfast is available, but reservations are necessary.

Food

River Inn Grill (16141 Main St., Guerneville, 707/869-0481, daily 8am-2pm, $10) is the first eatery you'll see when entering downtown Guerneville. In operation since 1946, this classic diner is the place for breakfast in Guerneville—the heavenly biscuits and gravy is a favorite.

A focal point of downtown Guerneville, **Main Street Station** (16280 Main St., 707/869-0501, www.mainststation.com, summer daily noon-11pm, winter Mon.-Thurs. 4pm-9:30pm, Fri.-Sun. noon-10:30pm, $14-25) offers a big menu filled with homey, casual grub. The mainstay is handmade pizza; you can grab a quick slice for lunch, or bring friends and order a whole pie for dinner. In the evenings, locals and visitors come down to munch sandwiches and pizza, drink beer, and listen to live entertainment on the small stage. Though live folk, jazz, blues, and even comedy happen every single night, this tiny venue gets crowded when a popular act comes to town. Consider making reservations in advance to assure you'll get a seat.

Pat's Restaurant (16236 Main St., 707/869-9905, www.pats-restaurant.com, daily 6am-3pm, $10) is the kind of diner that travelers hope to find. It's homey, casual, and a place locals come to sit at the counter and have breakfast all day long. It sure doesn't look like much from the outside—a small storefront in the middle of downtown Guerneville—but when you peer in the plate-glass windows you'll notice quite a number of diners inside. Classic diner food (eggs, sandwiches, and burgers) is served fresh—the eggs are done perfectly, the hash browns are homemade, and the kitchen actually runs out of favorites like sausage gravy because it's made from scratch daily.

Light, airy, and open, tiny ◖ **Boon Eat + Drink** (16248 Main St., Guerneville, 707/869-0780, www.eatatboon.com, Sun.-Tues. and Thurs. 11am-3pm and 5pm-9pm, Fri.-Sat. 11am-3pm and 5pm-10pm, $12-24) lures diners to line up on the sidewalk in anticipation of local, organic, and sustainable cuisine served with simple elegance. Lunch usually consists of a simple menu of paninis, small plates, and the grass-fed Boon burger. For dinner, hearty main courses combine lamb shank with mint pesto or a flatiron steak with truffle fries. You really can't go wrong here—unless you can't get in.

Information and Services

Off the beaten wine path is the **Russian River Chamber of Commerce and Visitors Center** (16201 1st St., Guerneville, 707/869-9000, http://russianriver.com, daily 10am-5pm) in downtown Guerneville. Here you'll find local staff that can give you serious local recommendations not only for wineries but also for river recreation, restaurants, and other less-traveled local attractions.

Getting There and Around

Guerneville is on Highway 116, alternately named River Road. In downtown Guerneville, Highway 116 is briefly called Main Street. The most direct access is via U.S. 101 north of Santa Rosa; take the River Road/Guerneville exit and follow River Road west for 15 miles to downtown Guerneville.

Alternately, a more scenic and often less crowded route is to take U.S. 101 to Highway 116 near Cotati, south of Santa Rosa. Named the Gravenstein Highway for its route through the apple orchards of Sebastopol, Highway 116 winds about 22 twisty miles through Sebastopol, Graton, and Forestville to emerge onto River Road in Guerneville.

Sonoma County Transit (http://sctransit.com, $2.90) runs a Russian River Express bus, route 20, from downtown Santa Rosa to Guerneville.

HEALDSBURG

A different aspect of the Russian River from Guerneville is at Healdsburg, a small city of 11,000 that is so charming it's easy to forget that people live and work here. The plaza anchors downtown and the wide and slow Russian River, creating the town's natural southern border. Boutiques, chic restaurants, and galleries dot the town, and fresh paint brightens the historic storefronts and planters filled lush with flowers and trailing vines. Healdsburg is also the nexus of three American Viticulture Areas (AVAs): the Russian River AVA, best known for producing pinot noir and chardonnay; Dry Creek AVA, famous for its zinfandel and sauvignon blanc; and the Alexander Valley AVA, which produces predominantly cabernet sauvignon and merlot.

Wineries

A. RAFANELLI

Tasting at **A. Rafanelli** (4685 W. Dry Creek Rd., 707/433-1385, www.arafanelliwinery.com, daily 10am-4pm, by appointment only) feels just about as different from the standard big-business high-end wineries of Wine Country as possible. You can't just walk in, as tastings are by appointment only; there's no marble-covered bar, no chic tasting room. Instead, you walk into the barrel room of the working winery and stand on the concrete floor in the oak- and grape-scented air. The owner-wine-maker will hand out glasses to your group, and you'll begin to taste some of the best red wines produced anywhere in Sonoma County. In a region where the phrase "cab is king" comes up at almost every winery, Rafanelli's cabernet sauvignons are still special. If you can't taste at Rafanelli, look for their zins and cabs at local

Sonoma restaurants, to whom they sell the bulk of their wholesale wines.

ARMIDA

Come to the **Armida** (2201 Westside Rd., 707/433-2222, www.armida.com, daily 11am-5pm) tasting room for the gorgeous scenery and the funky facilities, but stay for the wonderful wines. The driveway meanders up a Russian River hillside to a cluster of geodesic domes set among lovely and sustainable landscaping. Bring a picnic to enjoy on the big deck overlooking the duck pond and the valley beyond. Before you start eating, wander into the tasting room to check out some of the truly tasty Russian River red wines. You'll have your choice of smoky syrahs and jammy zinfandels. The flagship wine, Poizin, is well represented in the wines and logo-wear in the small gift shop that shares space with the tasting bar. Armida sells Poizin in a coffin-shaped box—ask nicely and they might open a bottle for you to taste (and even if they don't, it's still worth buying).

DRY CREEK VINEYARD

It seems odd that a winery named Dry Creek should have sailboats on all its labels, but that's the signature icon on each bottle produced by **Dry Creek Vineyard** (3770 Lambert Bridge Rd., 800/864-9463, www.drycreekvineyard.com, daily 10:30am-4:30pm, tasting $5-10). This midsize winery focuses much effort within its own AVA (Dry Creek, of course), producing many single-vineyard wines from grapes grown within a few miles of the estate. Other wines include grapes from the Russian River Valley AVA. Dry Creek prides itself on both its classic California varietals such as chardonnay, cabernet, and merlot, and on occasionally hopping out of that box and producing something unusual, like a musqué, a chenin blanc, or a Sauternes-style dessert wine. Try as many as you can when you enter the ivy-covered tasting room, styled after a French château.

FERRARI-CARANO

One of the best large wineries in Dry Creek Valley, **Ferrari-Carano** (8761 Dry Creek Rd.,

707/433-6700, www.ferrari-carano.com, daily 10am-5pm, tasting $5-15) provides great standard and reserve wines in an upscale tasting room and winery facility. Upstairs you'll get to taste from Ferrari-Carano's extensive menu of large-production, moderately priced whites and reds. Downstairs, enjoy the elegant lounge area, which includes comfortable seating and a video describing the Ferrari-Carano winemaking process, from grape to glass. Look down into one of the major barrel storage areas, where Ferrari-Carano's wines age right before your eyes. And finally, open the glass doors and enter the reserve tasting room, where for an additional fee you can taste the best of Ferrari-Carano's vintages—smaller runs that are mostly bold assertive reds. Back upstairs you can also browse the larger-than-average gift shop for gourmet edible goodies, wine, kitchen gadgets, and Ferrari-Carano logo-wear.

FOPPIANO

One of the oldest wineries in the Russian River Valley, **Foppiano** (12707 Old Redwood Hwy., 707/433-7272, www.foppiano.com, daily 11am-5pm, tasting $5) dates from 1896. Today, Foppiano is still making a small list of premium red wines. Their signature wine is a legendary petit sirah, unusual for the area. They've also got a great sangiovese, a zin, a cab, and a merlot under the Foppiano label. A second label, Riverside, encompasses a few tasty but exceedingly inexpensive varietals that let drinkers on a budget enjoy Foppiano wines. Inside the farmhouse-style tasting room, enjoy sips of the various vintages, but also be sure to ask for Susan's recipes; the hospitality director and fourth-generation member of the Foppiano family creates and adapts dishes to match the family wines.

FRANCIS FORD COPPOLA WINERY

The legendary director of iconic movies *Apocalypse Now* and *The Godfather* has his own winery in the Healdsburg area. Sure, the **Francis Ford Coppola Winery** (300 Via Archimedes, Geyserville, 707/857-1400, www.franciscoppolawinery.com, daily 11am-6pm) allows you to taste its chardonnays and

syrahs, but also movie buffs can tour the **Movie Gallery**, which is full of film memorabilia including Coppola's Academy Awards and Don Corleone's desk from *The Godfather*. In the summer months, two pools are open to entertain kids while their parents sip wine.

HOP KILN

Bringing truth in advertising to Sonoma, **Hop Kiln** (6050 Westside Rd., 707/433-6491, www. hopkilnwinery.com, daily 10am-5pm) winery is housed in an old hop kiln. Earlier in its history, the Russian River Valley grew more beer-making ingredients than grapes, and this distinctively shaped hop kiln dried the valley's crop each year. Today, you'll find a gift shop inside the main kiln along with an extensive wine-tasting bar that includes typical Wine Country varietals. Hop Kiln also produces unique wines, such as their malbec, grenache, and award-winning pinot noir.

J WINERY

Unlike many wineries that cling to Old World traditions, **J Winery** (11447 Old Redwood Hwy., 888/594-6326, www.jwine.com, daily 11am-5pm, tasting $20-65) loves the cutting edge of the California wine scene. J specializes in California-style sparkling wines. The tasting room is a triumph of modern design, and the tasting experience gives visitors a sample of the best that Wine Country has to offer. Make a reservation at the Bubble Lounge (Thurs.-Sun., reservations required), where, instead of the standard tasting bar and pouring staff, there are tables and waitstaff. Instead of the standard one-ounce pours, you'll enjoy wines specially paired with small bites of high-end California cuisine prepared in J's kitchens by their own team of gourmet chefs. You'll get the chance to taste the sparkly vintages as they are meant to be enjoyed—with an array of often spicy foods.

PORTER CREEK WINERY

Serious cork dorks recommend the tiny tasting room at **Porter Creek Winery** (8735 Westside Rd., 707/433-6321, www.portercreekvineyards. com, daily 10:30am-4:30pm, free tasting), which casual tasters might otherwise miss at a bend on a winding road. Turn onto the dirt driveway, pass the farm-style house (actually the owner's family home), and park in front of a small converted shed—the tasting room. This is old-school Sonoma wine-tasting. Porter Creek has been making its precious few cases of rich red wine each year for the last 30 years or so. You can occasionally find it at local restaurants, but if you like what you taste, buy it here at the winery. Porter Creek's wines are almost all reds, made from grapes grown organically within sight of the tasting room. You might even see the owner-winemaker walking through his vineyards with his family on a sunny afternoon in the off-season.

RAYMOND BURR VINEYARDS

As well as portraying detective Perry Mason on the famous 1960s TV series, Raymond Burr had a second life as a wine connoisseur and orchid lover. Along with his partner, Robert Benevides, he combined these loves to create the **Raymond Burr Vineyards** (8339 West Dry Creek Rd., 888/900-0024, www.raymondburrvineyards.com, daily 11am-5pm). Drive up a bumpy driveway past the greenhouse to reach the parking lot. Wine seekers enter the tiny (by Wine Country standards) tasting room to sip a few of the Burr label vintages and take in some of the actor's memorabilia. Frankly, most of the wines are tasty but not amazing compared to some other Sonoma products, but the staff and the winery's cats are fun and friendly, the views from the tasting room porch out over the valley are stunning, and the tiny bar and small-town experience are reminiscent of an earlier time in the Wine Country.

Flower lovers must come on specific days or make an appointment in advance to tour the greenhouses. Burr and Benevides bred more than 1,000 new orchid varieties, and you can see many of them here on the estate.

WHITE OAK

At **White Oak** (7505 Hwy. 128, 707/433-8429, www.whiteoakwinery.com, daily 10am-5pm, tasting $5), you'll find a wonderful combination of whimsy and wine. This Spanish mission-inspired winery complex is surrounded by green gardens dotted with fun sculptures. Beyond the gardens, estate vineyards grow grapes for Old Vine Zinfandel and other fine wines. Go inside to taste some of the wines—the tasting list is small but prestigious. While white-wine drinkers enjoy the sauvignon blanc and chardonnay, big reds are the specialty of the house. Cabernet sauvignon and zinfandel lovers flock to White Oak for the fabulous regular releases and occasional special library selections. Tours at White Oak provide a look at wine-tasting, describing and illustrating the various components that make up a wine's fragrance.

Sports and Recreation

Newcomers to bicycle touring in the area can choose among several reputable touring companies that will get them on two wheels and pointed in the right direction. **Wine Country Bikes** (61 Front St., 866/922-4537, www.winecountrybikes.com, tour $139 pp, bike rental $35-125 per day) is on the square in downtown Healdsburg. Its Classic Wine Tour starts at 10am and runs until 3:30pm. During your leisurely pedal through the Dry Creek region, you'll stop and taste wine, take walks in vineyards, and learn more about the history of wine in this small, proud AVA. A gourmet picnic lunch is included with the tour. Other tours are longer or more luxurious—check the website for information about multiple-day bike-tour packages that include accommodations. For independent souls who prefer to carve their own routes, Wine Country Bikes also rents road bikes, tandem bikes, and hybrids that you can also take on moderately difficult park trails where biking is permitted.

To become part of the larger bicycling culture in the area, consider participating in the annual **Harvest Century Bicycle Tour** (Healdsburg Chamber of Commerce, 707/433-6935, www.healdsburg.com, July, $85). This event requires some degree of physical fitness, as riders register to ride 20, 30, 60, or 65 miles. The roads are of moderate difficulty, however; while you'll find some inclines, experienced cyclists won't be so tortured as to preclude enjoying the rest of the day with great food, wine, and the companionship of plenty of like-minded souls.

Healdsburg also provides access to water sports on the Russian River. **Russian River Adventures** (20 Healdsburg Ave., 707/433-5599, www.rradventures.info, adults $50, children $25) offers guided paddles down a secluded section of the river in stable, sturdy inflatable canoes. Dogs, children, and even infants are welcome. The trip usually lasts 4-5 hours, with little white water and lots of serene shaded pools. They now provide half-day trips also.

Accommodations

Travelers planning to stay a night in Healdsburg will find that none of the boutique inns and hotels in town come cheap. If you take a room at the **Honor Mansion** (891 Grove St., 707/433-4277, www.honormansion. com, $200-700), you'll probably feel that you are getting your money's worth. Each of the 13 guest rooms and suites has been furnished and decorated with exquisite attention to even the smallest details. Whatever room you choose, you'll be overwhelmed with luxury and want to spend the day in the soft cocoon of your elegant, oversized feather bed. All guest rooms have private baths stocked with high-end toiletries, TVs, CD players, bathrobes, phones, air-conditioning, turn-down service, and more. Naturally, all guest rooms come with a full gourmet breakfast each morning. The Honor Mansion also has a lap pool, a tennis court, a croquet lawn, a bocce pit, and outdoor professional massage service.

On the central town plaza, the **Hotel Healdsburg** (25 Matheson St., 800/889-7188, www.hotelhealdsburg.com, $355-820) is a local icon. The 55-room boutique hotel offers the most upscale amenities, including Frette towels and linens, TVs with DVD players, soaking tubs and walk-in showers, and beautiful decor. Guest rooms have shining wooden floors and furniture, Tibetan throw rugs, and spotless white down comforters. All guest rooms

include free Wi-Fi and a gourmet breakfast, among other amenities, and guests can enjoy the outdoor pool, fitness center, and full-service day spa.

Raford Inn Bed and Breakfast Inn (10630 Wohler Rd., 800/887-9503, www.rafordinn. com, $175-260) offers Healdsburg-level luxury at slightly less stratospheric prices than its nearby competitors. Each of the six guest rooms has a queen bed, air-conditioning, a CD player, and a private bath. Some have fireplaces, oversize showers, and other luxury amenities. All guest rooms have been decorated in attractive minimalist Victorian style that feels historic but doesn't overwhelm the modern guest. Every morning, the Raford serves up a hearty country breakfast—the perfect start to a day of wine-tasting.

Food

In a sea of self-conscious chichi restaurants, the **Healdsburg Charcuterie** (335 Healdsburg Ave., 707/431-7213, http://charcuteriehealdsburg.com, Mon.-Thurs. 11:30am-3pm and 5pm-9pm, Fri. 11:30am-3pm and 5:30pm-9:30pm, Sat. noon-3:30pm and 5:30pm-9:30pm, Sun. noon-3:30pm and 5pm-9pm, $20) makes diners feel at home. With a cute but not annoying pig theme, local art on the walls, and a softly romantic atmosphere, the Charcuterie makes a great option for a romantic but not overwhelming dinner out. The house-cured pork tenderloin sandwich is the house specialty, but vegetarians certainly can find a tasty and well-prepared meal as well. The Charcuterie pours some lovely local vintages and offers wine flights.

The most famous restaurant in Healdsburg is probably **Dry Creek Kitchen** (317 Healdsburg Ave., 707/431-0330, www.charliepalmer.com, Mon.-Thurs. 5:30pm-9:30pm, Fri.-Sat. noon-2:30pm and 5:30pm-10pm, Sun. noon-2:30pm and 5:30pm-9:30pm, $25-39), a chic Charlie Palmer dining room that takes the concept of California cuisine to the next level. Expect to see foam, froth, jus, and coulis splattered across the menu, which can range from upscale but recognizable to totally bizarre. Dry Creek Kitchen serves brunch and lunch on the weekend, offering its own unique take on eggs benedict, sliders, and other standards. This is a great place to check out some Dry Creek AVA vintages.

For an upscale eco-friendly California restaurant without the green propaganda, head to fabulous ☪ **Zin** (344 Center St., 707/473-0946, www.zinrestaurant.com, Mon.-Fri. 11:30am-2pm and 5pm-close, Sat.-Sun. 5pm-close, $16-28), just off the square in downtown Healdsburg. The cavernous dining room takes advantage of its existing antique features for decor, the tables are made with recycled and repurposed materials, and the art on the walls comes from local artists and is for sale. But the real reason to eat lunch or dinner at Zin is undoubtedly the food. The chef creates a menu that fuses upscale Wine Country with Mexican and Southern cuisines, giving Zin a unique twist that sets it apart from a plethora of other upscale restaurants in the region. Most return diners recommend starting with the Mexican beer-battered green beans—fabulous French fries with a guilt-reducing green-vegetable interior. If you've overdosed on haute cuisine, check out the Blue Plate specials for dinner, offering something down-home at a reasonable price each night—think spaghetti with meatballs or chicken and dumplings.

For an independent cup of coffee in Healdsburg, head across the town square to **Flying Goat Coffee** (324 Center St., 707/433-3599, www.flyinggoatcoffee.com, daily 7am-7pm). This attractive West Coast coffeehouse serves above-average lattes, defaults to "no whip" on the mochas, and doesn't make them too sweet either. The relaxed feel and pleasant seating area make it easy to stop and stay awhile.

Oakville Grocery (124 Matheson St., 707/433-3200, www.oakvillegrocery.com, June-Oct. daily 8am-7pm, Nov.-May Sun.-Thurs. 8am-6pm, Fri.-Sat. 8am-7pm), like its cousin in the Napa Valley, sells high-end groceries and local gourmet products to well-heeled customers. It's a great place to pick up gifts for friends back home—they carry fine,

expensive local olive oils, vinegars, soaps, and bath products. You can also get the goods for a proper picnic, with a great selection of cheeses, fresh local breads, an upscale deli counter, a somewhat redundant wine selection, and a few fine nonalcoholic beverages.

A funkier alternative to the Oakville Grocery is the **Jimtown Store** (6706 Hwy. 128, 707/433-1212, www.jimtown.com, Mon. and Wed.-Thurs. 7:30am-4pm, Fri.-Sat. 7:30am-5pm), six miles out of town on a dusty country road. When owners Carrie Brown and her husband, the late John Werner, decided to leave New York City, they landed at this general store, in operation since 1895. The couple brought their gourmet sensibilities and turned the store into a quirky combination of old-fashioned American country store with house-made gourmet jams, jellies, and condiments; penny toys; housewares; best of all, hot lunches. The chalkboard menu presents a tasty assortment of smoked-brisket sandwiches, chili, buttermilk coleslaw, and chorizo and provolone grilled-cheese sandwiches. The benches and picnic tables outside are a great place to unwrap your sandwich, or you can pick up one of their prepared box lunches to go.

Information and Services

Befitting such a desirable destination, the **Healdsburg Chamber of Commerce and Visitors Bureau** (217 Healdsburg Ave., 707/433-6935, www.healdsburg.com, Mon.-Fri. 9am-5pm, Sat. 9am-3pm, Sun. 10am-2pm) is centrally located just off U.S. 101, just as you come into town on Healdsburg Avenue. The friendly staff is happy to load you up with maps, brochures, and helpful tips.

For a bit of local flavor, the **Healdsburg Tribune** (www.sonomawest.com/the_healdsburg_tribune) is published every Thursday. And for health issues, the **Healdsburg District Hospital** (1375 University Ave., 707/431-6500, http://healdsburgdistricthospital.org) has a 24-hour emergency room.

While cell-phone reception is reliable in town, don't expect it to be on Healdsburg's back roads. But unlike the rest of the Russian River Valley region, getting online in Healdsburg is fairly easy. Most hotels and cafés offer access for free or at a price, and the plaza has free Wi-Fi service set up by the city so you can open your laptop and start surfing in the sunshine.

Getting There and Around

Healdsburg is an easy destination, as it is 14 miles north of Santa Rosa on U.S. 101. To reach downtown Healdsburg from U.S. 101, take exit 503, for Central Healdsburg. Healdsburg can also be accessed from Calistoga: Drive north of Calistoga on Highway 128 for 17.4 miles, and at Jimtown, Highway 128 intersects Alexander Valley Road. Continue straight on Alexander Valley Road as Highway 128 turns right, heading north to Geyserville. In 3.3 miles, turn left onto Healdsburg Avenue, which runs to downtown Healdsburg.

NORTH COAST

The rugged North Coast of California is spectacular, its wild beauty in many places unspoiled and almost desolate. The cliffs are forbidding, the beaches are rocky and windswept, and the surf thunders in with formidable authority. This is not the California coast of surfer movies, though hardy souls do ride the chilly Pacific waves as far north as Crescent City.

From Bodega Bay, Highway 1 twists and turns north along hairpin curves that will take your breath away. The Sonoma and Mendocino coasts offer lovely beaches and forests, top-notch cuisine, and a friendly, uncrowded wine region. Along the way, tiny coastal towns—Jenner, Gualala, Point Arena, Mendocino, Fort Bragg—dot the hills and valleys, beckoning travelers with bed-and-breakfasts, organic farms and relaxing respites from the road.

Between the towns are a wealth of coastal access areas to take in the striking meeting of land and sea. Inland, Mendocino's hidden wine region offers the rural and relaxed pace missing from that other famous wine district. Anderson Valley and Hopland can quench your thirst whether it's for beer at the local microbrewery or wine at one of many tasting rooms. Where Highway 1 merges with U.S. 101 is the famous Lost Coast, accessed only via steep narrow roads or by backpacking the famous Lost Coast Trail. This is California at its wildest.

For most travelers, the North Coast means redwood country, and U.S. 101 marks the gateway to those redwoods. The famous, immense coastal sequoias loom along the highway south of the old logging town of Eureka and the hip college outpost of Arcata. A plethora

HIGHLIGHTS

LOOK FOR ◖ TO FIND RECOMMENDED SIGHTS, ACTIVITIES, DINING, AND LODGING.

◖ **The Sea Ranch Chapel:** Embedded with seashells and sea urchins, this tiny place of worship and meditation is wholly unique (page 254).

◖ **Mendocino:** Spend an afternoon or a weekend wandering this arts-filled community and its headlands, which jut out into the Pacific (page 264).

◖ **Avenue of the Giants:** The towering coast redwoods in Humboldt Redwoods State Park are a true must-see. Simply gaze at the silent giants or head to the nearby Eel River for a quick dip (page 290).

◖ **Shelter Cove:** The Lost Coast is a section of the California shoreline like no other – wild and virtually untouched. This tiny town offers one of the best ways to see it with the lovely, relatively accessible **Black Sand Beach** (page 298).

◖ **Arcata Community Forest:** The first city-owned forest in California offers acres of trails winding through second-growth redwoods (page 311).

◖ **Patrick's Point State Park:** Replete with beaches, landmarks, trails, and campgrounds, this is one of the best of the many parks along the North Coast (page 316).

◖ **Prairie Creek Redwoods State Park:** With big trees, impressive wildlife, a long, lonely beach, and one-of-a-kind Fern Canyon, this park is worth a stop (page 321).

◖ **Battery Point Lighthouse:** This lighthouse on an island off Crescent City is only accessible at low tide. If you time it right, you can receive an insightful tour from the lighthouse keeper (page 327).

of state and national parks lure travelers with numerous hiking trails, forested campgrounds, kitschy tourist traps and some of the tallest and oldest trees on the continent. Pitch a tent in Humboldt Redwoods State Park, cruise the Avenue of the Giants, and gaze in wonder at the primordial Founders Grove. Crescent City marks the northern terminus of the California Coast, a seaside town known for fishing, seafood—and for surviving a tsunami.

PLANNING YOUR TIME

If you're planning a road trip to explore the North Coast in depth and want to make stops in more than one destination, plan to spend a full week. Driving is the way to get from place

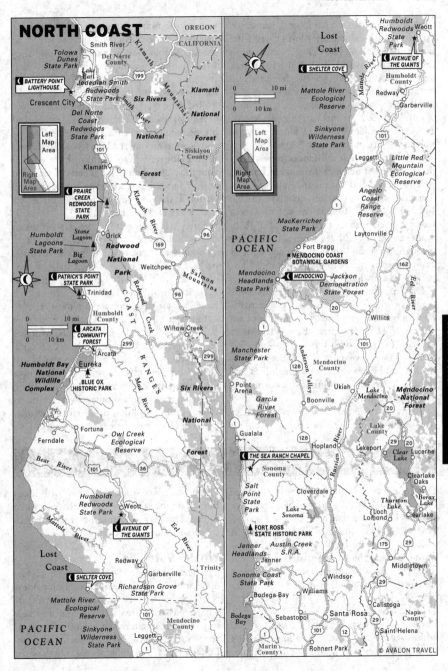

NORTH COAST

OREGON
CALIFORNIA

Smith River
Tolowa Dunes State Park
Del Norte County
Klamath
Lake Earl
Jedediah Smith Redwoods State Park
199
Six Rivers
◀ **BATTERY POINT LIGHTHOUSE**
Crescent City
Smith River
National
Klamath
Del Norte Coast Redwoods State Park
101
National
Siskiyou County
Klamath
Forest
Left Map Area
Right Map Area
◀ **PRAIRE CREEK REDWOODS STATE PARK**
Klamath River
Stone Lagoon
Orick
169
96
Redwood
Humboldt Lagoons State Park
Big Lagoon
National
Weitchpec
Salmon Mountains
◀ **PATRICK'S POINT STATE PARK**
Trinidad
Park
96
Redwood Creek
C O A S T
Humboldt County
0   10 mi
0   10 km
◀ **ARCATA COMMUNITY FOREST**
Willow Creek
299
Arcata
299
R A N G E S
Humboldt Bay National Wildlife Complex
Eureka
BLUE OX HISTORIC PARK
Mud River
Six Rivers
Fortuna
Owl Creek Ecological Reserve
National
Ferndale
Bear River
101
36
Forest
Humboldt Redwoods State Park
Weott
◀ **AVENUE OF THE GIANTS**
Mattole River
Eel River
Redway
Lost Coast
Garberville
Trinity
◀ **SHELTER COVE**
Richardson Grove State Park
Mattole River Ecological Reserve
101
PACIFIC OCEAN
Sinkyone Wilderness State Park
Mendocino County
Leggett
1

Lost Coast
Humboldt Redwoods State Park
Weott
◀ **AVENUE OF THE GIANTS**
Mattole River
Humboldt County
Redway
Garberville
101
Mattole River Ecological Reserve
Sinkyone Wilderness State Park
Little Red Mountain Ecological Reserve
Leggett
Angelo Coast Range Reserve
0   10 mi
0   10 km
Left Map Area
Right Map Area
162
1
MacKerricher State Park
Laytonville
PACIFIC OCEAN
Fort Bragg
■ **MENDOCINO COAST BOTANICAL GARDENS**
Jackson Demonstration State Forest
Eel River
Mendocino Headlands State Park
◀ **MENDOCINO**
20
Willits
1
101
Manchester State Park
128
Mendocino County
Anderson Valley
◀ Point Arena
Ukiah
Mendocino National Forest
Garcia River Forest
Boonville
20
Lake Mendocino
Gualala
128
Hopland
Lake County
Russian River
Lakeport
29
20
Lucerne
Clear Lake
◀ **THE SEA RANCH CHAPEL**
Sonoma County
Clearlake Oaks
Salt Point State Park
Cloverdale
Thurston Lake
Borax Lake
Lake Sonoma
Loch Lomond
Clearlake
▲ **FORT ROSS STATE HISTORIC PARK**
175
29
Jenner Headlands
Austin Creek S.R.A.
Middletown
Jenner
Sonoma Coast State Park
Windsor
29
Bodega Bay
Williams
Calistoga
Bodega Bay
Sebastopol
Santa Rosa
Napa County
1
Marin County
101
Rohnert Park
12
Saint Helena
29

© AVALON TRAVEL

to place, unless you're a hard-core backpacker. Highway 1 winds along the North Coast from Bodega Bay to above Fort Bragg, where it heads east to connect with U.S. 101 at its northern terminus near Leggett. U.S. 101 then heads inland through southern Humboldt County before heading back to the coast at Eureka. North of Eureka, U.S. 101 continues through Arcata, Trinidad, and Crescent City, along with the Redwood National and State Parks.

If you are heading to Mendocino or a section of the coast north of there, take U.S. 101, which is a great deal faster than Highway 1, and then take one of the connector roads from U.S. 101 to Highway 1. One of the best and most scenic connector roads is Highway 128, which heads east off U.S. 101 at Cloverdale and passes through the scenic Anderson Valley, with its many wineries, before joining Highway 1 just south of the town of Mendocino.

Driving times on Highway 1 tends to be longer on the North Coast due to the roadway's twists, turns, and many spectacular ocean vistas. On U.S. 101 north of Leggett, expect to share the road with lumbering—pun intended—logging vehicles. A lot of the roads off U.S. 101 or Highway 1 are worthwhile excursions, but expect adventurous drives through mountainous terrain.

Many Bay Area residents consider Mendocino County ideal for a weekend getaway or romantic retreat. A weekend is about the perfect length of time to spend on the Mendocino coast or in the Anderson Valley wine country. (You might want to extend your trip for a day or two or three...) There are at least 3-4 days' worth of intriguing hikes to take in Redwood National and State Parks.

Along the Lost Coast, the most lodging and dining options can be found in Shelter Cove. If you want to explore the Lost Coast Trail, consider hiking it north to south, with the wind at your back. Spend the night in Ferndale or camp at the Mattole Recreation Site, where the trail begins, so that you can get an early start for the first day of backpacking.

Eureka is the biggest North Coast city, with the most amenities for travelers, so it makes a good base. If you're exploring the redwood parks, consider staying in the smaller towns of Arcata or Trinidad. The campgrounds at Patrick's Point State Park and Prairie Creek State Park are superb places to pitch a tent.

Summer on the North Coast has average daily temperatures in the mid 60s, which is comparable to the temps in southern California during the winter. Expect rain on the North Coast from November to May. The chances of fog or rain are significantly lower in the fall, making it one of the best times to visit. Frequent visitors to the area know this, so many popular hotels book up quickly for fall weekends.

Sonoma Coast

One good way to begin your meanders up the coast is to take U.S. 101 out of San Francisco as far as Petaluma, and then head west toward Highway 1. This stretch of Highway 1 is also called the Shoreline Highway. As you travel toward the coast, you'll leave urban areas behind for a while, passing through some of the most pleasant villages in California.

BODEGA BAY

Bodega Bay is popular for its coastal views, whale-watching, and seafood—but it's most famous as the filming locale of Alfred Hitchcock's *The Birds*. The town of Bodega Bay sits on the eastern side of the harbor, while Bodega Head is a peninsula that shields the bay from the ocean.

Whale-Watching

The best sight you could hope to see is a close-up view of Pacific gray whales migrating home to Alaska with their newborn calves. The whales pass this area January-May on their way from their summer home off Mexico. If you're lucky, you can see them from the shore. **Bodega Head,** a promontory just north of the

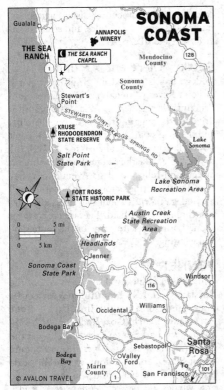

SONOMA COAST

the road and worth the trip. You can even swim at Doran Beach; although it's cold, it's protected from the open ocean waves, so it's much safer than most of the beaches along the coast.

Sonoma Coast State Park

Seventeen miles of coast are within **Sonoma Coast State Park** (707/875-3483, www.parks.ca.gov, day use $8 per vehicle). The park's boundaries extend from Bodega Head at the south up to the Vista Trailhead, four miles north of Jenner. As you drive up Highway 1, you'll see signs for various beaches. Although there are lovely places to walk, fish, and maybe sunbathe on the odd hot day, it is not advisable to swim here. If you go down to the water, bring your binoculars and camera. The cliffs, crags, inlets, whitecaps, mini islands, and rock outcroppings are fascinating in any weather, and their looks change with the shifting tides and fog.

Events

The annual **Bodega Seafood, Art, and Wine Festival** (707/824-8717, www.winecountryfestivals.com, $12-15) combines all the best elements of the Bodega lifestyle. Taking place the last weekend in August, it includes live music in addition to tastings, special dinners, and much more. The proceeds help benefit two worthy organizations: the Bodega Volunteer Fire Department and Stewards of the Coast and Redwoods.

Accommodations

Bodega Bay Lodge (103 Hwy. 1, 707/875-3525 or 888/875-2250, www.bodegabaylodge.com, $300-610) is one of the more luxurious places to stay in the area. The rooms are located in seven separate buildings. If you really want to spoil yourself, secure an ocean club suite, which has a bedroom, private living room, and a private terrace with ocean views. The facility also has a spa, an ocean view pool, a fitness center, a fine restaurant, and a library on its grounds.

Sonoma Coast State Park (707/875-3483, www.parks.ca.gov, day use $8 per vehicle) encompasses several campgrounds along its

bay, is a place to get close to the migration route. To get to this prime spot, travel north on Highway 1 about one mile past the visitors center and turn left onto Eastshore Road; make a right at the stop sign, and then drive three more miles to the parking lot. On weekends, volunteers from **Stewards of the Coast and Redwoods** (707/869-9177, www.stewardsofthecoastandredwoods.org) are available to answer questions. Contact them for organized whale-watching tours or to learn more about their various educational programs.

Doran Regional Park

When you arrive in Bodega Bay, you'll see a sign pointing left for **Doran Regional Park** (201 Doran Beach Rd., 707/875-3540, www.sonoma-county.org, day use $7 per vehicle, camping $28-32). It is less than one mile down

17-mile expanse. Some of these have been ca-sualties (let's hope temporarily) of the ongoing state budget crisis, but as of this writing, you can still get a lovely, sandy spot in the trees in **Bodega Dunes Campground** (2585 Hwy. 1, $35), complete with hot showers and flush toi-lets. To get up-to-date information on closings or re-openings related to Sonoma Coast State Park, call the **district office** (707/865-2391), or stop in at the **Salmon Creek Ranger Station** a little farther north.

Food

Go "wine surfing" at **☪ Gourmet au Bay** (913 Hwy. 1, 707/875-9875, www.gourmetaubay. com, Sun.-Thurs. 11am-7pm, Fri.-Sat. 11am-8pm, tasting $9), where they will pour three wines and lay them out on a miniature surf-board for you to carry out to the deck. Wines are available from a variety of different vint-ners, including major players in the Napa wine scene, small local wineries and the odd French or Australian vintage. Inside, you can sip as you peruse the gift shop, which includes local arti-sanal foods, handmade ceramics and pottery, and an array of toys for wine lovers.

Bodega Bay Lodge's **Duck Club Restaurant** (103 Hwy. 1, 707/875-3525, www.bodegabay-lodge.com, daily 7:30am-11am and 6pm-9pm, $18-36) offers a warm and elegant dining ex-perience featuring hearty American entrées like steak, chicken, and halibut with seasonal vegetables. There's a fireside lounge overlook-ing the bay, and even some outdoor seating for warmer days.

One of the best restaurants in the area is **Terrapin Creek** (1580 Eastshore Dr., 707/875-2700, www.terrapincreekcafe.com, Thurs.-Sun. 11am-2:30pm and 4:30pm-9pm, $22-29), where they make creative use of the abundance of fresh seafood available and cook up tasty pasta, duck, and beef entrées.

Information and Services

The **Sonoma Coast Visitors Center** (850 Hwy. 1, 707/875-3866, Mon.-Sat. 9am-5pm, Sun. 10am-5pm) in Bodega Bay may look small, but it's chock-full of exactly what you came for: maps, brochures, lists, suggestions, trail guides, events schedules, and even live ad-vice from a local expert.

Getting There and Around

Bodega Bay is located on Highway 1 north of Point Reyes National Seashore and west of Petaluma. From the Bay Area, it's a beautiful drive north, hugging the coast, but the cliffs and the road's twists and turns mean taking it slow. A faster way to get here is to take U.S. 101 to Petaluma, take the exit for East Washington Street, and follow Bodega Avenue to Valley Ford Road, cutting across to the coast. You'll hit Bodega Bay just about two miles after you pass through Valley Ford. The latter route takes about 1.5 hours, with some of the route slow and winding.

JENNER

Jenner is on Highway 1 at the mouth of the Russian River. It's a beautiful spot for a quiet honeymoon or a paddle in a kayak. **Goat Rock State Beach** (Goat Rock Rd., 707/875-3483, www.parks.ca.gov, day use $8) is at the mouth of the Russian River inside Sonoma Coast State Park. A colony of Harbor Seals breed and frolic here, and you may also see gray whales, sea otters, elephant seals, and a variety of sea life. Pets are not allowed, and swimming is prohibited.

Accommodations and Food

Both the food and the views are memorable at **☪ River's End** (11048 Hwy. 1, 707/865-2484, www.ilovesunsets.com, summer daily noon-3:30pm and 5pm-8:30pm, winter Thurs.-Mon. noon-3:30pm and 5pm-8:30pm, $19-42). The restaurant is perched above the spot where the Russian River flows into the Pacific, and it's a beautiful sight to behold over, say, oysters or filet mignon. Prices are high, but if you get a window table at sunset, you may forget to think about them.

The **Jenner Inn and Cottages** (10400 Hwy. 1, 707/865-2377 or 800/732-2377, www.jen-nerinn.com, $118-358) has a variety of quiet, beautifully furnished guest rooms mere steps from the river. Some guest rooms have hot tubs and private decks, and breakfast is included.

Fourteen miles north of Jenner proper is the large and luxurious **Timber Cove Inn** (21780 N. Hwy. 1, 707/847-3231 or 800/987-8319, www.timbercoveinn.com, $182-300), with a spacious bar and lounge, an oceanfront patio, guest rooms with spa tubs and fireplaces, and hiking trails nearby.

Information and Services

The small but friendly **Jenner Visitors Center** (10439 Hwy. 1, 707/865-9757, www.stewardsofthecoastandredwoods.org, summer Sun.-Thurs.) is located across the street from the Jenner Inn. The visitors center is staffed by volunteers, so hours can be unpredictable; call ahead to confirm.

Getting There and Around

Jenner is located on Highway 1, right along the ocean. There is no public transportation to get here, but it is a pretty drive from just about anywhere. The fastest route from San Francisco (about 1.75 hours) is to drive up U.S. 101, make a left onto Washington Street in Petaluma. Washington Street becomes Bodega Avenue and then Valley Ford Road before you make a slight left onto Highway 1 and head north toward Jenner. From Sacramento (2.5 hours) or points in the East Bay, take I-80 west and then navigate to Petaluma, where you continue west to Highway 1.

NORTH OF JENNER

As you hug the shore north of Jenner, you'll soon pass through Fort Ross State Historic Park, Salt Point State Park, and Kruse Rhododendron State Reserve.

Fort Ross State Historic Park

There is no historic early American figure named Ross who settled here; believe it or not, "Ross" is short for "Russian," and this park commemorates the history of Russian settlement on the North Coast. A quick rundown of the story: In the 19th century Russians came to the wilds of Alaska and worked with native Alaskans to develop a robust fur trade, killing seals, otters, sea lions, and land mammals for their pelts. The enterprise required sea travel as the hunters chased the animals as far as California. Eventually, a group of fur hunters and traders came ashore on what is now the Sonoma Coast and developed a fortified outpost that became known as **Fort Ross** (19005 Hwy. 1, Jenner, 707/847-3286, www.parks.ca.gov, Sat.-Sun. and holidays sunrise-sunset, visitors center and fort compound Sat.-Sun. and holidays 10am-4:30pm, parking $8). The area gradually became not only a thriving Russian American settlement but also a center for agriculture and shipbuilding and the site of California's first windmills. Learn more at the park's large visitors center, which provides a continuous film and a roomful of exhibits.

You can also walk into the reconstructed fort buildings and see how the settlers lived. (U.S. 101 was originally built through the middle of the fort area, but it was moved to make way for the historic park.) The only original building still standing is the captain's quarters—a large, luxurious house for that time and place. The other buildings, including the large bunkhouse, the chapel, and the two cannon-filled blockhouses, were rebuilt using much of the original lumber used by the Russians. Be aware that a serious visit to the whole fort and the beach beyond entails a level but long walk; wear comfortable shoes and consider bringing a bottle of water.

Unfortunately, this park is one of the casualties of the state's ongoing budget crisis, so since 2011, Reef Campground is closed until further notice, and the park is open for day use only on Saturday-Sunday and holidays. It's still worth a visit, though—just call the **district office** (707/865-2391) before you go to make sure it's open.

Salt Point State Park

Stretching for miles along the Sonoma coastline, **Salt Point State Park** (25050 Hwy. 1, Jenner, 707/847-3221, www.parks.ca.gov, visitors center Apr.-Oct. Sat.-Sun. 10am-3pm, day use $8) provides easy access from U.S. 101 to more than a dozen sandy state beaches. You don't have to visit the visitors center to enjoy this park and its many beaches—just follow the signs along the highway to the turnoffs and parking lots. If you're looking to scuba dive or free dive, head for **Gerstle Cove,** accessible from the visitors center just south of Salt Point proper. The cove was designated one of California's first underwater parks, and divers who can deal with the chilly water have a wonderful time exploring the diverse undersea wildlife.

Kruse Rhododendron State Reserve

For a genteel experience, head east off Highway 1 to the **Kruse Rhododendron State Reserve** (Hwy. 1 near milepost 43, 707/847-3221, www.parks.ca.gov, daily sunrise-sunset, free), where you can meander along the **China Gulf Trail** in the spring, admiring the profusion of pink rhododendron flowers blooming beneath the second-growth redwood forest. If you prefer a picnic, you'll find tables at many of the beaches—just be aware that the North Coast can be quite windy in the summer.

Note that some facilities within this park have been closed due to the ongoing state budget crisis. Call 707/865-2391 before you go, or check the website to make sure the specific area you're headed to is open.

Stewart's Point

Stewart's Point is home to a post office, a small store, and a restaurant—and that's it. **Stewart's Point Store** (32000 S. Hwy. 1, 707/785-2406, www.stewartspoint.net, daily 6am-8pm, hours vary by season) sells groceries, wine, collectible dishes, hand-knitted hats, and Hostess Zingers. They've also got a deli and a bakery on-site. Upstairs, locally grown dinners are served in a historic dancehall (Fri.-Sat. 6:15pm, $10-32).

THE SEA RANCH

The last 10 miles of the Sonoma Coast before entering Mendocino County are the property of The Sea Ranch, a private coastal

community. In the late 1960s, developers purchased a former sheep ranch, planning to build homes that blended into the natural environment. Development was met with opposition from environmental and coastal access groups, which led to the formation of the California Coastal Commission, a state agency that overlooks land use and coastal access on the state's coastline. Sea Ranch was eventually built, but the number of lots was reduced by half, and the development included six points for public access to the ocean, including Gualala Point Regional Park.

Today, the community is known for its distinctive buildings with wood sidings and shingles. One of its structures, Condominium 1, won the American Institute of Architects Gold Medal in 1991 and is now on the National Register of Historic Places. Those hard-fought coastal access points make the Sea Ranch a good place to take a break from driving for a short beach stroll. Visitors who want to linger in this low-key community can spend the night at The Sea Ranch Lodge.

◖ The Sea Ranch Chapel

Looking from the outside like a wooden stingray with a plume on top, The **Sea Ranch Chapel** (mile marker 55.66 Hwy. 1, on the right side of the highway, intersection of Hwy. 1 and Bosun's Reach, www.thesearanchchapel. org, daily sunrise-sunset) is one of the smallest and most creatively designed places of worship that you'll ever see. Designed by architect James Hubble, this tiny building's beautiful interior has polished redwood benches, three stained glass windows, a stone floor with an inserted mosaic, along with embedded local sea shells and sea urchins throughout the structure.

Annapolis Winery

You'll find a pleasant coastal climate and a small list of classic California wines at **Annapolis Winery** (26055 Soda Springs Rd., Annapolis, 707/886-5460, www.annapoliswinery.com, daily noon-5pm, tasting free), a small family-owned winery seven miles east of Sea Ranch. You can usually taste pinot,

© STUART THORNTON

the unique and very tiny Sea Ranch Chapel

cabernet, zinfandel, and port, depending on what they've made this year and what's in stock when you arrive. Take a glass outside to enjoy the views from the estate vineyards out over the forested mountains.

Sports and Recreation

With its front nine holes perched above the Pacific, the **Sea Ranch Golf Links** (42000 Hwy. 1, 707/785-2468, www.searanchgolf. com, Mon.-Thurs. $50, Fri.-Sun. and holidays $60) are like the legendary golf courses at Pebble Beach except without the crowds. Designed by Robert Muir Graves, the course also allows you to putt past redwood trees.

Accommodations and Food

Situated on 52 acres of prime coastal estate, ☾ **Sea Ranch Lodge** (2.5 miles north of Stewart's Point on Hwy. 1, 707/785-2371, http://searanchlodge.com, $249-399) offers 19 rooms, all with simple 1960s throwback decor and ocean vistas that evoke paintings. Hiking trails on the grounds offer a self-guided wildflower walk and a short walk to Black Point Beach. Most rooms are equipped with gas fireplaces for those foggy days on the Sonoma Coast. The walls might be a bit thinner than more modern hotels so earplugs are provided. Guests are also treated to a fine complimentary hot breakfast at the lodge's **Black Point Grill** (2.5 miles north of Stewart's Point on Hwy. 1, 707/785-2371, daily 8am-11am, 11:30am-4:30pm, 5:30pm-9pm, $13-27). Black Point Grill is also open to the public, serving everything from burgers to local seafood in a dining area with large windows facing the sea.

Mendocino Coast

The Mendocino coast is a popular retreat for those who've been introduced to its specific charms. On weekends, Bay Area residents flock north to their favorite hideaways to enjoy windswept beaches, secret coves, and luscious cuisine. This area is ideal for deep-sea anglers, wine aficionados, and fans of luxury spas. Art is especially prominent in the culture; from the 1960s onward, aspiring artists have found supportive communities, sales opportunities, and homes in Mendocino County, and a number of small galleries display local artwork.

Be aware that the most popular inns fill up fast many weekends year-round. Fall-winter is the high season, with the Crab Festival, the Mushroom Festival, and various harvest and after-harvest wine celebrations. If you want to stay someplace specific on the Mendocino Coast, book your room at least a month in advance for weekday stays and six months or more in advance for major festival weekends.

GUALALA

With a population of 585, Gualala ("wa-LA-la") feels like a metropolis along the Highway 1 corridor in this region. While it's not the most charming coastal town, it does have some of the services other places lack.

Since 1961, the **Art in the Redwoods Festival** (46501 Gualala Rd., 707/884-1138, www.gualalaarts.org, mid-Aug., adults $6, under age 17 free) and its parent organization, Gualala Arts, have been going strong. This major event takes place over the course of a long weekend in mid-August and is run by the same people who bring you the Whale and Jazz Festival in Point Arena in April. Now featuring gallery exhibitions, special dinners, a champagne preview, bell ringers, a quilt raffle, and awards for the artists, this festival is a great reason to get the whole family to Gualala for some renewal and inspiration.

Accommodations

When it comes to food and lodging in Gualala, you're not going to hear so many of those Sonoma and Mendocino County adjectives— "luxurious, elegant, pricey"—but you will find choices, which may be welcome.

For the budget-conscious, a good option is **The Surf Motel** (39170 Hwy. 1, 707/884-3571 or 888/451-7873, www.surfinngualala.com, $99-209). Only a few of the more expensive guest rooms have ocean views, but a full hot breakfast and wireless Internet access are included for all guests.

The **Breakers Inn** (39300 Hwy. 1, 707/884-3200, www.breakersinn.com, $185-245) has 28 uniquely decorated rooms named after states and countries. All have decks, spas, and fireplaces.

The **Whale Watch Inn** (35100 Hwy. 1, 800/942-5342, www.whalewatchinn.com, $190-280) specializes in romance. Each of its 18 individually decorated, luxuriously appointed guest rooms has an ocean view and a wood burning stove. Most also have whirlpool tubs. Every morning, a hot breakfast is delivered to your room.

Four miles north of Gualala, the **North Coast Country Inn** (34591 S. Hwy. 1, 707/884-4537, www.northcoastcountryinn.com, $195-225) was once part of a coastal sheep ranch. Six rooms are outfitted with antique furnishings and fireplaces; three also have kitchenettes. Mornings at the North Coast Country Inn begin with a hot breakfast buffet. An antique store and art gallery are also on the inn's grounds.

Camping

Two nearby parks provide good camping options. One is **Gualala River Redwood Park** (46001 Gualala Rd., 707/884-3533, www.gualalapark.com, May-Oct., day use $5 pp, camping $38-45 for 2 people); the other is **Gualala Point Regional Park** (42401 Hwy. 1, 707/785-2377, www.sonoma-county.org, day use $6 per vehicle, camping $28-32), one mile south of the town of Gualala, technically in

hours, which results in tender, flavorful beef brisket, Memphis pulled pork, and St. Louis-style pork ribs.

Locals and visitors rave about the tacos at **Antonio's Tacos** (38820 S. Hwy. 1, 707/884-1789, Mon.-Sat. 8am-7pm, $2-12).

The Gualala **farmers market** (47950 Center St., www.mcfarm.org/gualala, late May-early Nov. Sat. 9:30am-12:30pm) is at the Gualala Community Center. **Surf** (39250 S. Hwy. 1, 707/884-4184, www.surfsuper.com, Sat.-Wed. 7:30am-7pm, Thurs.-Fri. 7:30am-8pm) is a supermarket that also sells flatbread pizzas and sandwiches.

Getting There and Around

Gualala is located 115 miles north of San Francisco on Highway 1, and 60 miles south of Fort Bragg. The **Mendocino Transit Authority** (707/462-1422 or 800/696-4682, www.4mta.org) has a bus line that connects Gualala to Fort Bragg.

POINT ARENA

A small coastal town located 1.5 miles south of its namesake point, Point Arena might be one of the North Coast's best secrets. The town's Main Street is Highway 1, which has a couple of bars, restaurants, markets, and the Arena Theater, which attracts all sorts of cultural events. One mile from the small downtown section is the scenic Point Arena Cove, which has a small fishing pier with rocky beaches on either side. The cove feels like the town's true center, a meeting place where fisherfolk constantly take in the conditions of the ocean. Just north and south of Point Arena on Highway 1 are some great coastal access points.

Sights
POINT ARENA LIGHTHOUSE

Although its magnificent Fresnel lens no longer turns through the night, the **Point Arena Lighthouse** (45500 Lighthouse Rd., 707/882-2777 or 877/725-4448, www.pointarena-lighthouse.com, summer daily 10am-4:30pm, winter daily 10am-3:30pm, adults $7.50, children $1) remains a Coast Guard light and fog

Sonoma County. Both places offer redwoods, the ocean, and the river.

Food
Bones Roadhouse (39080 Hwy. 1, 707/884-1188, www.bonesroadhouse.com, restaurant Mon.-Fri. 11:30am-8 or 9pm, Sat.-Sun. 8am-8 or 9pm, bar 11:30am-10pm, $14-24) advertises its "BBQ, brews and blues." It delivers. This casual barbecue and beer joint at the north end of town cooks its meats on a wood-burning, custom-built smoker for 4-12

the Mendocino coast, north of Fort Bragg

© STUART THORNTON

station. But what makes this beacon special is its history. When the 1906 earthquake hit San Francisco, it jolted the land all the way up the coast, severely damaging the Point Arena Lighthouse. When the structure was rebuilt two years later, engineers devised the aboveground foundation that gives the lighthouse both its distinctive shape and additional structural stability.

Visitors can enjoy the Lighthouse's extensive interpretive museum, which is housed in the fog station beyond the gift shop. Docent-led tours up to the top of the lighthouse are well worth the trip, both for the views of the lighthouse from the top and for the fascinating story of its destruction and rebirth through the 1906 earthquake as told by the knowledgeable staff. Tour groups also have the opportunity to climb right up to the Fresnel lens, taking a rare close look at an astonishing invention that reflected pre-electric light far enough out to sea to protect passing ships. For those who just can't get enough of the lighthouse during daylight hours, consider staying in one of the four former lighthouse keepers' homes (877/725-4448, palight@mcn.org, $125-300, two-night minimum).

ARENA THEATER

If you prefer your entertainment on a screen but still like a little atmosphere, take in a show at the **Arena Theater** (214 Main St., 707/882-3456, www.arenatheater.org). This onetime vaudeville theater was also a movie palace of the old school when it opened in 1929. In the 1990s, the old theater got a restorative facelift that returned it to its art deco glory. Today, you can see all kinds of films at the Arena, from recent box office toppers to new documentaries and unusual independent films. If a film isn't playing, you might find a live musical or theatrical show.

MANCHESTER STATE PARK

Seven miles north of the town of Point Arena, **Manchester State Park** (44500 Kinney Lane, Manchester, 707/937-5804, day use free) is a wild place perfect for a long solitary beach

© STUART THORNTON

the lonely coastline of Manchester State Park

walk. The 3.5-mile-long coast is littered with bleached white driftwood and logs that lie on the dark sand like giant bones as waves crash. Even the water offshore is protected as part of the 3,782-acre Point Arena State Marine Reserve. At the southwestern tip of the park is Arena Rock, a nautical hazard known for sinking at least six ships before the construction of the nearby Point Arena Lighthouse to the south.

Part of the 1,500 acres of onshore parkland was once a dairy ranch. Now, there's beach, dunes, a wetlands trail, and a campground. The drive-in campground ($25, first come, first served) has 41 sites with basic amenities, including fire pits, picnic tables, and pit toilets. Some environmental campsites in the dunes are accessible via a one-mile hike in. The sounds of crashing waves nearby will lull you to sleep.

SCHOONER GULCH STATE BEACH
The area around Point Arena is filled with coastal access points. A local favorite is **Schooner Gulch State Beach** (intersection of Schooner Gulch Rd. and Hwy. 1, three miles south of the town of Point Arena, 707/937-5804, www.parks.ca.gov). From a pullout north of Schooner Gulch Bridge, trails lead to two different beaches. The southern trail leads to **Schooner Gulch Beach,** a wide sandy expanse with rocky headlands and a stream flowing into the sea. But the northern trail leads to a more memorable destination: **Bowling Ball Beach.** At low tide, the ocean recedes to reveal small spherical boulders lined up in rows. Strike! (Unfortunately, the trail to Bowling Ball Beach is prone to closure due to erosion; you may want to call ahead to see if it is open.)

Entertainment and Events
215 Main (215 Main St., 707/882-3215, Mon.-Sat. 2:15pm-2am) is located at—guess where?—215 Main Street. This bar specializes in local wine and beer, with 40 bottles of wine and six beers on tap. There's a heated patio out back. Local dive bar **Sign of the Whale** (194 Main St., 707/882-2259, Mon.-Thurs. 4pm-10pm, Fri.-Sat. 4pm-midnight) is across the street.

© STUART THORNTON

scenic Point Arena Cove

The annual **Whale and Jazz Festival** (707/884-1138, www.gualalaarts.org/whale-jazz) takes place all around Mendocino County in April each year. Some of the nation's finest jazz performers play in a variety of venues, while the whales put on their own show out in the Pacific. Point Arena Lighthouse offers whale-watching from the shore each day, and the wineries and restaurants of the region provide refreshment and relaxation every evening of the festival weekend.

Accommodations

From 1901 to 1957, the ⟨ **Coast Guard House** (695 Arena Cove, 707/882-2442 or 800/524-9320, www.coastguardhouse.com, $165-265) was a working Coast Guard Life-Saving Station. Now the main building, which used to house the enlisted men, hosts overnight guests, who enjoy nice views of Point Arena Cove. Four rooms are available, including a suite with two bedrooms. Two detached cottages on-site offer more privacy. Restaurants are just a short walk away. The friendly and informative innkeepers serve a nice hot breakfast in the main house every morning.

Next door to the Coast Guard House is the **Wharf Master's Inn** (785 Iverson Ave., 707/882-3171 or 800/392-4031, www.wharf-masters.com, $105-550). Every room has a fireplace, a two-person spa, and a private deck. The Wharf Master's House has a kitchen and can accommodate up to eight people.

Food

Arena Market & Café (183 Main St., 707/882-3663, www.arenaorganics.org, summer Mon.-Sat. 7am-7pm, Sun. 8am-6pm, winter Mon.-Fri. 7am-6pm, Sat. 7am-5pm, Sun. 8am-5pm) is a co-op committed to a philosophy of local, sustainable, and organic food, and they do their best to compensate farmers fairly and keep money in the community. This is a medium-size grocery store, so you can stock up on staples or sit at one of the tables in the front of the store and enjoy a bowl of homemade soup or coffee. They're one of the only places in town with Wi-Fi.

The **Uneda Eat Café** (206 Main St., 707/882-3800, www.pangaeacatering.com, Thurs.-Sat. 5pm-8pm, $12-22) preserves the sign of the former owner, who was an Italian butcher: The storefront still says "Uneda Meat Market." Now a dine-in, take-out, and catering operation run by Jill and Rob Hunter, who previously owned the popular Pangaea Restaurant, the menu is decidedly locavore.

Blue on the outside, pink on the inside, **Franny's Cup and Saucer** (213 Main St., 707/882-2500, www.frannyscupandsaucer.com, Wed.-Sat. 8am-4pm) is whimsical and welcoming. The owners, Franny and her mother, Barbara, do all their own baking and they even make truffles and other candies from scratch. It's takeout only, so stop in and pick up a picnic before you go to the lighthouse or one of the parks.

Slightly north of town is **Rollerville Café** (22900 S. Hwy. 1, 707/882-2077, www.rollervillecafe.com, Mon.-Thurs. and Sun. 8am-2pm, Fri.-Sat. 8am-7:30pm, lunch $8-10, dinner $20-24). Dinner may seem a little pricey, but lunch is available all day; breakfast is 8am-11am. This is a small homey place catering to guests at the adjacent timeshare resort as well as locals and travelers.

On the second floor of a two-story building, the **Pier Chowder House & Tap Room** (790 Port Rd., 707/882-3400, www.thepierchowderhouse.com, daily 11am-9pm, $18-25) has an outside deck perfect for taking in the sunset over Point Arena's scenic cove. The menu focuses on seafood. Go for the salmon or rock cod in season; both are caught by local anglers. There is also a long bar with 26 beers on tap.

In the same building as the Pier Chowder House, **Cove Coffee and Tackle** (790 Port Rd., 707/882-2665, $5.50) attracts locals with tasty items like "Nate's Special," an egg sandwich with pesto, cream cheese, sausage, onion, and Swiss cheese. It's a perfect place to go for a morning coffee.

The weekly **Mendocino County Farmer's Market** (214 Main St., 707/964-6718, www.mcfarm.org, Wed. 10:30am-1pm) is in the Point Arena Theater parking lot.

Information and Services

The **Coast Community Library** (225 Main St., 707/882-3114, www.coastcommunitylibrary.org, Mon. and Fri. noon-6pm, Tues. 10am-6pm, Wed. 10am-8pm, Thurs. noon-8pm, Sat. noon-3pm) is a real hub of activity thanks to its central location—the impressive 1928 Point Arena Mercantile Company building—and its free Internet access.

Getting There and Around

Point Arena is located 10 miles north of Gualala on Highway 1, and about 120 miles north of San Francisco.

The **Mendocino Transit Authority** (800/696-4682, www.4mta.org) runs the route 75 bus to connect Point Arena south to Gualala and north to Fort Bragg. The bus usually runs once a day, although schedules are subject to change; contact the transit authority for details.

ELK

The town of Elk used to be called Greenwood, after the family of Caleb Greenwood, who settled here in about 1850. Details of the story vary, but it is widely believed that Caleb was part of a mission to rescue survivors of the Donner Party after their rough winter near Truckee.

Greenwood State Beach

From the mid-19th century until the 1920s, the stretch of shore at **Greenwood State Beach** (Hwy. 1, 707/937-5804, www.parks.ca.gov, visitors center mid-March-Oct. Sat.-Sun. 11am-1pm) was a stop for large ships carrying timber to points of sale in San Francisco and sometimes even China. The visitors center displays photographs and exhibits about Elk's past in the lumber business. It also casts light on the Native American heritage of the area and the natural resources that are still abundant.

A short hike demonstrates what makes this area so special. From the parking lot, follow the trail down toward the ocean. You'll soon come to a fork; to the right is a picnic area. Follow the left fork to another picnic site and then, soon afterward, the beach. Turn left and walk about

© STUART THORNTON

the view from Elk Cove Inn

0.25 miles to reach Greenwood Creek. Shortly past it is a cliff, at which point you have to turn around and walk back up the hill. Even in the short amount of time it takes to do this walk, you'll experience lush woods, sandy cliffs, and dramatic ocean overlooks. In winter, the walk can be dark and blustery and even more intriguing, although it's a pleasure in any season.

Greenwood State Beach is alongside the town of Elk, 10-15 miles north of Point Arena and about 17 miles south of Mendocino.

Accommodations and Food

Perched on a hillside over the stunning Greenwood State Beach cove, the **Elk Cove Inn** (6300 S. Hwy. 1, 800/275-2967, www. elkcoveinn.com, $135-395) offers luxury accommodations, generous hospitality, and superb views of the nearby Pacific, studded with islands and a scattering of offshore rocks. Check-in comes with a complimentary glass of wine or cocktail and a welcome basket filled with goodies including fresh baked cookies. Choose from reasonably priced rooms in the

main house, cozy cabins with an ocean view, or luxurious suites with jetted soaking tubs and private balconies or patios. A private staircase leads down to the beach below, where you can build a campfire or stroll the uncrowded coastline. There's also a full service day spa with a sauna and aromatherapy steam shower. The innkeepers have thought of everything to make your stay top notch, from port wine and chocolates in the rooms to the big morning breakfast buffet of Southern comfort food.

Elk is also home to the luxurious **Griffin House Inn** (5910 S. Hwy. 1, 707/877-3422, www.griffinn.com, $145-325), which offers lovely cottages with oceanfront decks. The lack of TVs and phones in the rooms ensures peace and quiet. Full breakfast can be delivered to your guest room, but there's also a lively dining room.

Housed in a little blue cottage attached to the Griffin House Inn, **Bridget Dolan's Pub & Restaurant** (5910 S. Hwy. 1, 707/877-1820, www.griffinn.com) is a terrific place to hole up with a draft beer on a rainy winter day or fog-laden summer afternoon. The tables are draped in white tablecloths and the small bar is lined with locals. The menu includes burgers, pizzas, and hearty pub fare like cottage pie.

With a perfect location in the center of town and across the street from the ocean, **Queenie's Roadhouse Café** (6061 Hwy. 1, Thurs.-Mon. 8am-3pm, $7-16) is the place to go for hot food and a friendly atmosphere.

The **Beacon Light by the Sea** (7401 S. Hwy. 1, south of Elk, 707/877-3311, Fri.-Sat. 5pm-11pm) is the best bar in the area. Its colorful owner, R. D. Beacon, was born in Elk and has run the Beacon Light since 1971. He claims it's the only place you can get hard liquor for 14 miles in any direction. With 54 different brands of vodka, 20 whiskeys, and 15 tequilas, there's something for every sort of drinker. On clear days, the views stretch all the way to the Point Arena Lighthouse.

ALBION AND LITTLE RIVER

Tiny Albion is along Highway 1 almost 30 miles north of Point Arena and about 8 miles south of Mendocino. Little River is about five miles farther north, also on Highway 1. There is a **post office** (7748 Hwy. 1, Albion, 707/937-5547, www.usps.com, Mon.-Fri. 8:15am-1pm and 2pm-4:30pm), a state park, and several plush places to stay.

Van Damme State Park

The centerpiece of **Van Damme State Park** (Hwy. 1, 3 miles south of Mendocino, 707/937-5804, www.parks.ca.gov, daily 8am-9pm, free) is the **Pygmy Forest,** where you'll see a true biological rarity: Mature yet tiny cypress and pine trees perpetually stunted by a combination of always-wet ground and poor soil-nutrient conditions. To get there, drive along Airport Road to the trail parking lot (opposite the county airport) and follow the wheelchair-accessible loop trail (0.25 miles, easy). You can also get there by hiking along the **Fern Canyon Trail** (7 miles round-trip, difficult).

Kayak Mendocino (707/937-0700, www.kayakmendocino.com, board surfing $30 per hour) launches four Sea Cave Nature Tours (9am, 11:30am, 2pm, and sunset, $50 pp) from Van Damme State Park. No previous experience is necessary; the expert guides provide all the equipment you need and teach you how to paddle your way through the sea caves and around the harbor seals.

Accommodations

Tired of typical cookie cutter motel rooms? There's no place quite like C **The Andiron** (6051 N. Hwy. 1, Little River, 707/937-1543, www.theandiron.com, $109-259). The one- and two-room cabins in a meadow above Highway 1 are filled with curiosities and intentional kitsch. Every room is different. One has a one-of-a-kind camel-shaped bar, while another has a coin-operated vibrating bed. Most have vintage board games, View-Masters, and an eclectic library of books. Standard amenities include small wooden decks and small flat screen TVs. A hot tub under the trees is available for guests. The fun-loving owners throw happy hour parties every weekend, including "Fondue Fridays," when they serve the melted cheese dish along with local beers and wines. The Andiron isn't fancy, but it sure is fun.

The **Albion River Inn** (3790 N. Hwy. 1, 6 miles south of Mendocino, 707/937-1919 or 800/479-7944, www.albionriverinn.com, $195-325) is a gorgeous and serene setting for an away-from-it-all vacation. A full breakfast is included in the room rates, but pets and smoking are not allowed, and there are no TVs.

The **Little River Inn** (7901 N. Hwy. 1, Little River, 707/937-5942 or 888/466-5683, www.littleriverinn.com, $130-375) appeals to coastal vacationers who like a little luxury. It has a nine-hole golf course and two lighted tennis courts, and all its recreation areas overlook the Pacific, which crashes on the shore just across the highway from the inn. The sprawling white Victorian house and barns hide the sprawl of the grounds, which also have a great restaurant and a charming sea-themed bar. Relax even more at the in-house Spa at Little River Inn.

Stevenswood Spa Resort (8211 N. Hwy. 1, Little River, 800/421-2810, www.stevenswood.com, $269-499) is a modern facility with contemporary decor. A classy restaurant and a day spa help you feel relaxed and pampered, as does Van Damme State Park, which surrounds the resort on three sides. Be sure to book one of the outdoor in-ground hot tubs at the spa for a relaxing evening.

Camping

There's camping on the coast at **Van Damme State Park** (Hwy. 1, 707/937-5804, www.parks.ca.gov, reservations 800/444-7275, www.reserveamerica.com, $35), three miles south of Mendocino. The appealing campground offers picnic tables, fire rings, and food lockers, as well as restrooms and hot showers. The park's 1,831 acres include beaches as well as forest, so there's lots of natural beauty to enjoy. Reservations are strongly encouraged.

Food

C**Ledford House Restaurant** (3000 N. Hwy. 1, Albion, 707/937-0282, www.ledfordhouse.com, Wed.-Sun. 5pm-close, $19-30) is beautiful even from a distance; you'll see it on the hill as you drive up Highway 1. With excellent food and nightly jazz performances, it's one of the truly "special occasion" choices in the area.

Tucked into a corner of a convenience store, the **Little River Market Grill & Gourmet Deli** (7746 N. Hwy. 1, Little River, 707/937-5133, Mon.-Fri. 8:30am-6:30pm, Sat.-Sun. 8:30am-7:30pm, $8) is a local's favorite. This better-than-average deli has a surprisingly wide range of options, including burgers, pulled pork sandwiches, and fish tacos. Nice vegetarian options include the tasty pesto veggie and avocado sandwich. This is the place to grab a sandwich for a picnic on the Mendocino Coast.

Stevenswood Spa Resort has a fine on-site restaurant, **The Restaurant at Stevenswood** (8211 N. Hwy. 1, Little River, 707/937-2810, www.stevenswood.com, Thurs.-Tues. 5:30pm-9pm, $22-28).

◧ MENDOCINO

Perched on a headlands surrounded by the Pacific, Mendocino is one of the most picturesque towns on the California coast. Quaint bed-and-breakfasts, art colonies, and local sustainable dining add to its charm, making it a favorite for romantic weekend getaways.

Once a logging town, Mendocino was reborn as an artist community in the 1950s. One of its most striking buildings is the town's Masonic Hall, dating from 1866 and adorned with a redwood statue of Father Time on its roof. Many New Englanders settled in the region in its early years. With its old water towers and historic buildings, it resembles a New England fishing village—so much that it played one in the long-running TV series *Murder, She Wrote.* It was also a stand-in for Monterey in the 1955 James Dean film *East of Eden.*

Mendocino Art Center

The town of Mendocino has long been an inspiration and a gathering place for artists of many varieties, and the **Mendocino Art Center** (45200 Little Lake St., 707/937-5818 or 800/653-3328, www.mendocinoartcenter. org, daily 10am-5pm, donation) is the main institution that gives these diverse artists a community, provides them with opportunities for teaching and learning, and displays the work of contemporary artists for the benefit of both the artists and the general public. Since 1959 the center has offered artist workshops and retreats. Today it has a flourishing schedule of events and classes, five galleries, and a sculpture garden. You can even drop in and make some art of your own. Supervised "open studios" in ceramics, jewelry making, watercolor, sculpture, and drawing take place throughout the year (call for specific schedules, $7-10 per session).

Kelley House Museum

The mission of the lovely, stately **Kelley House Museum** (45007 Albion St., 707/937-5791, www.kelleyhousemuseum.org, summer Thurs.-Tues. 11am-3pm, Oct.-May Fri.-Mon. 11am-3pm, free, tours Sat. 11am, $2) is to preserve the history of Mendocino for future generations. The new addition to the historic house is home to the village archives, which include thousands of photos. In the museum, antique furniture and fixtures grace the rooms. A collection of Victorian clothing, photos, and documents illuminate the story of historic Mendocino, and knowledgeable docents are available to offer more information. Ask about the town's water-rights issues for a great lesson in the untold history of the Mendocino Coast. On weekends, docents lead two-hour walking tours ($10) that detail Mendocino's history.

Mendocino Headlands State Park

No trip to Mendocino is complete without a walk along the rugged coastline of **Mendocino Headlands State Park** (west of town, 707/937-5804, www.parks.ca.gov, daily sunrise-sunset). A series of trails along the seaside cliffs west of town offer views of the area's sea caves and coves. It's a favorite spot for painters and photographers hoping to capture the majesty of the coast. In winter, the park is a great vantage point for viewing migrating gray whales. In town, the **Historic Ford House** (735 Main St., 707/937-5397, www.mendoparks.org, daily 11am-4pm, free, donations encouraged)

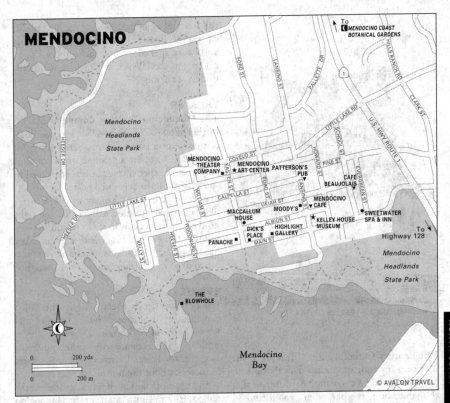

MENDOCINO

Mendocino
Headlands
State Park

Mendocino
Headlands
State Park

Mendocino
Bay

© AVALON TRAVEL

doubles as the Mendocino Headlands State Park Visitor Center.

Point Cabrillo Light Station

Whether you're into scenery or history, nautical or otherwise, you won't want to miss a visit to the **Point Cabrillo Light Station Historic Park** (45300 Lighthouse Rd., 707/937-6122, www.pointcabrillo.org, daily 11am-4pm, $5), north of Mendocino and south of Caspar and Fort Bragg. This beautiful lighthouse has been functioning for more than 100 years since it was built, in part to facilitate the movement of lumber and other supplies south to San Francisco to help rebuild the city after the massive 1906 earthquake. The light station was absorbed into the California State Park system in 2002, and in 2009 became a victim of state budget cuts and saw its services curtailed. The

site is currently being managed by a volunteer organization, the Point Cabrillo Lightkeepers Association. You can take a tour of the famous Fresnel lens, learn about the infamous *Frolic* shipwreck of 1850, and explore the tide-pool aquarium. If you don't want to leave the light station grounds after sundown, consider renting the light keeper's house or two cottages on the grounds for an evening (707/937-5033, www.mendocinovacations.com).

Entertainment and Events
BARS

For a place to hunker down over a pint in Mendocino, head to cozy **Patterson's Pub** (10485 Lansing St., 707/937-4782, www.pattersonspub.com, bar daily 10am-midnight, restaurant daily 11am-11pm). This traditional Irish-style pub is in the former rectory of a

© STUART THORNTON

A wooden statue resides on the top of Mendocino's Masonic Hall.

19th-century Catholic church. It nods to the 21st century with six plasma TVs that screen current games. Order a simple, filling meal at the tables or at the bar, where you'll find 14 beers on tap, a full-fledged wine list, and hard liquor imported from around the world.

So where do the locals go for a drink in heavily visited Mendocino? That would be **Dick's Place** (45080 Main St., 707/937-6010, daily 11:30am-2am), sometimes called Richard's by the Sea. Dick's is an old school, cash-only bar, with a mounted buck head draped in Christmas lights as decor. Dick's is easy to find: Look for the only neon sign on Main Street, in the shape of a martini glass.

LIVE MUSIC

For live music on the Mendocino coast, head to the **Caspar Inn** (14957 Caspar Rd., Caspar, 707/964-5565, www.casparinn.com, Tues.-Sat. 5pm-2am, Sun. 5pm-midnight, cover varies), about five miles north of Mendocino and six miles south of Fort Bragg. The Caspar offers a full bar and a good restaurant menu ($10-22, cash only) in addition to its lineup of bands and other special events, including an open mic night, the "Pool Challenge," and "micro-midget wrestling."

THEATER

The **Mendocino Theater Company** (45200 Little Lake St., 707/937-4477, www.mendocinotheatre.org, shows Thurs.-Sat. 8pm, Sun. 2pm, $10-25) offers a genuine small community-theater experience. All plays are staged in the 81-seat Helen Schoeni Theater for an intimate night of live drama or comedy. The small, old weathered building exudes just the right kind of charm to draw in lovers of quirky community theater. But this little theater company has big goals, and it tends to take on thought-provoking work by contemporary playwrights.

EVENTS

For two weekends every March, the Point Cabrillo Light Station is host to the annual **Whale Festival** (707/937-6123, www.pointcabrillo.org, $5), a chance to get expert guidance as you scan the sea for migrating gray whales headed north for the summer.

In July, musicians of all types descend on the temporarily warmish coast for the **Mendocino Music Festival** (707/937-2044, www.mendocinomusic.com, concert ticket prices vary). For 2.5 weeks, live performances are held at venues around the area. There's always chamber music, orchestral concerts, opera, jazz, and bluegrass, and there's usually world music, blues, singer-songwriters, and dance performances. A centerpiece of the festival is the famed big-band concert. In addition to 13 evenings of music, there are three series of daytime concerts: piano, jazz, and village chamber concerts. No series passes are available; all events require separate tickets.

If restaurants are the heart of the Mendocino food scene, festivals are its soul. **Taste of Mendocino** (http://winecrab.com) comprises a couple of sub festivals: **Mendocino Crab & Wine Days** takes place in January and offers a burst of crab-related events (prices vary);

Mendocino's Point Cabrillo Light Station

in November, the focus is on the wild mushroom season, and you can come to the **Wine & Mushroom Festival** for classes, tastings, and tours (prices vary) to learn to cook or just to eat. Check the website for a plethora of other special events.

Shopping

On the coast, the best place to browse is **Mendocino Village.** Not only are the galleries and boutiques welcoming and fun, the whole downtown area is beautiful. It seems that every shop in the Main Street area has its own garden, and each fills with a riotous cascade of flowers in the summer. Even if you hate to shop, make the trip down to the village just to literally smell the roses.

Panache (45120 Main St., 707/937-0947, www.thepanachegallery.com, daily 10:30am-5pm) displays and sells beautiful works of art in all sorts of media. You'll find paintings, jewelry, sculpture, and art glass. Much of the artistic focus is reminiscent of the sea crashing just outside the large multiple-room gallery.

The wooden furniture and boxes are a special treat: handmade treasures using rare woods are combined and then sanded and polished to silksmooth finishes.

If you love fine woodworking and handcrafted furniture, you will not want to miss the **Highlight Gallery** (45052 Main St., 707/937-3132, www.thehighlightgallery.com, daily 10am-5pm). Although the gallery has branched out in recent years to feature glasswork, ceramics, painting, and sculpture, its roots are in woodwork, which it maintains as a focus.

Sports and Recreation
HIKING

Some of the most popular hiking trails in coastal Mendocino wind through **Russian Gulch State Park** (Hwy. 1, 2 miles north of Mendocino, 707/937-5804, www.parks.ca.gov, $8). Russian Gulch has its own **Fern Canyon Trail** (3 miles round-trip), winding into the second-growth redwood forest filled with lush green ferns. At the four-way junction, turn left to hike another 0.75 miles to the ever-popular waterfall. Be aware that you're likely to be part of a crowd visiting the falls on summer weekends. To the right at the four-way junction you can take a three-mile loop for a total hike of six miles that leads to the top of the attractive little waterfall. If you prefer the shore to the forest, hike west rather than east to take in the lovely wild headlands and see blowholes, grasses, and even trawlers out seeking the day's catch. The biggest attraction is the **Devil's Punchbowl,** a collapsed sea cave 100 feet across and 60 feet deep. There's also a nice beach.

KAYAKING

Kayak and canoe trips are a popular summer activity on the Mendocino Coast. To explore the relatively sedate waters of the Big River estuary, consider renting an outrigger or even a sailing canoe from **Catch a Canoe & Bicycles Too** (44850 Comptche Ukiah Rd., 707/937-0273, www.catchacanoe.com, daily 9am-5pm, boat and bike rentals adults $28 pp for 1-3 hours, ages 6-17 $14 pp; guided tours June-Sept., $65 pp) at the Stanford Inn. The guided tours include an estuary excursion with a naturalist and a ride on an outrigger that utilizes solar energy for power.

SURFING

Big River is a beach break surf spot just south of the town of Mendocino where the Big River flows into the ocean. It's a spot you can check out from Highway 1, and on most days, all levels of surfers can try their hand at surfing the break. More experienced surfers should try **Smuggler's Cove,** located in Mendocino Bay on the south side of Big River. It's a reef break that usually just works during winter swells.

DIVING

A good spot for abalone is **The Blowhole** (end of Main St.), a favorite summer lounging spot for locals. In the water, you'll find abalone and their empty shells; colorful, tiny nudibranchs; and occasionally, overly friendly seals. The kelp beds just off the shore attract divers who don't fear cold water and want to check out the complex ecosystem. Check with the state

Russian Gulch State Park

Department of Fish and Game (888/773-8450, www.dfg.ca.gov) for the rules about taking abalone, which is strictly regulated; most species are endangered and can't be harvested. Game wardens can explain the abalone season opening and closing dates, catch limits, licensing information, and the best spots to dive each year.

SPAS

Of all the reasons people choose to vacation on the Mendocino Coast, the main one seems to be plain old relaxation. The perfect way to do so is to seek out one of the many nearby spas. The **Sweetwater Spa & Inn** (44840 Main St., 800/300-4140, www.sweetwaterspa.com, Sun.-Fri. noon-9pm, Sat. noon-10pm, $15-19/half-hour, $18-23/hour) rents indoor hot tubs by the half-hour and hour. They also have group tub and sauna rates ($10-20). Sweetwater offers a range of massage services ($90-154) at reasonable rates. The rustic buildings and garden setting complete the experience. Appointments are required for massage and private tubs, but walk-ins are welcome to use the communal tub and sauna.

For a massage in the comfort of your own accommodations, make an appointment for a foot rub, herbal facial, full-body massage, or acupuncture with **The Body Works** (707/357-5162, www.massagetime.biz, $125 per hour).

Accommodations
$150-250

The warm and welcoming **(Blackberry Inn** (44951 Larkin Rd., 800/950-7806, www.blackberryinn.biz, $125-225) is in the hills, slightly out of the center of Mendocino. You may be a little confused when you first pull in, since it looks as though you're in a town—a perfectly stylized one from the Old West but without the shooting and the bank robberies. Each of the 16 guest rooms has a different storefront outside, including the bank, the saloon, the barbershop, and the land-grant office. Each is charmingly decorated and beautifully maintained with plush, comfortable bedding cozied up with colonial-style quilts, along with the modern convenience of microwaves, fridges, and free

wireless Internet. The manager-hosts are the nicest you'll find anywhere, and you check in at an office designed to resemble a train station.

(Sweetwater Inn and Spa (44840 Main St., 800/300-4140, www.sweetwaterspa.com, $100-295) harks back to the days when Mendocino was a colony of starving artists rather than a weekend retreat for city dwellers. A redwood water tower was converted into a guest room, joined by a motley connection of detached cottages that guarantee guests great privacy. Every guest room and cottage has its own style—you'll find a spiral staircase in one of the water towers, a two-person tub set in a windowed alcove in the Zen Room, and fireplaces in many of the cottages. The eclectic decor makes each room different, and many return guests request their favorite guest room again. Thick gardens surround the building complex and a path leads back to the Garden Spa. The location, just past downtown on Main Street, is perfect for dining, shopping, and art walks.

The luxurious **Glendeven Inn** (8205 N. Hwy. 1, 707/937-0083 or 800/822-4536, www.glendeven.com, $175-295) is situated in a historic farmhouse with ocean views. The hosts will help you settle in with complimentary wine and hors d'oeuvres in the late afternoon, and wake you in the morning with a three-course made-to-order breakfast, delivered to your room. If you like the food (you will), consider joining them for a five-course **"farm-to-table" dinner** (Wed.-Thurs. and Sat. 6pm, by reservation only, dinner $65, with wine pairings $90).

The **Blue Door Inn** (10481 Howard St., 707/937-4892, www.bluedoorinn.com, $175-275) aims to spoil you. Five sleek, modern rooms come with flat screen TVs and gas fireplaces. The two-course breakfast features homemade pastries and egg dishes.

OVER $250

Up and away from the beaches, sitting amid redwoods, the **Stanford Inn** (44850 Comptche Ukiah Rd., 0.5 miles east of Hwy. 1, 707/937-5615 or 800/331-8884, www.stanfordinn.com, $211-555) is an upscale forest lodge. The location is convenient to hiking and only a short drive down to Mendocino Village and the coast. Guest rooms have beautiful, honey wood-paneled walls, pretty furniture, and puffy down comforters. If you're traveling with a group, consider one of the elegant two-bedroom suites, but be aware that "executive suite" means a junior suite. Other amenities include a wood-burning fireplace, a TV with a DVD player, Internet access, a stereo, a pool, sauna and hot tub, and free use of mountain bikes. Gardens surrounding the resort are perfect for strolling.

The 1882 **MacCallum House** (45020 Albion St., 707/936-0289 or 800/609-0492, www.maccallumhouse.com, $250-400) is the king of luxury on the Mendocino Coast. The facility includes several properties in addition to the main building in Mendocino Village. Choose from private cottages with hot tubs, suites with jetted tubs, and guest rooms with opulent antique appointments. The woodwork gleams and the service pleases. Note that there's a two-night minimum on weekends, and a three-night minimum for most holidays. Room rates include a cooked-to-order breakfast and a $14-per-room credit toward dinner.

The beautifully restored 1909 **Point Cabrillo Head Lightkeeper's House** (45300 Lighthouse Rd., 707/937-5033, www.mendocinovacations.com, 2-night minimum, $833-1,030 for 2 nights) is the home-away-from-home that you'll want to write home about. It's located atop a cliff beside the Pacific, so you can watch for whales, dolphins, and seabirds without leaving the porch. Four bedrooms sleep eight people, with 4.5 baths and a very modern kitchen. Larger groups such as family reunions or wedding parties can also rent two of the cottages nearby.

Food
CONTEMPORARY
One of the most appealing and dependable places to get a good meal any day of the week is the **Mendocino Café** (10451 Lansing St., 707/937-6141, www.mendocinocafe.com, daily 11am-4pm and 5pm-9pm, $14-32). The café

has good, simple, well-prepared food, a small kids menu, a wine list, and a beer list. Enjoy a Thai burrito, a fresh salmon fillet, or a steak in the warm, well-lit dining room. Or sit outside: The café is in the gardens of Mendocino Village, and thanks to a heated patio, you can enjoy outdoor dining any time of day.

FARMER'S MARKET
Mendocino has a weekly **Farmer's Market** (Howard St. and Main St., www.mcfarm.org, May-Oct. Fri. noon-2pm), where you can find seasonal produce, flowers, fish, wine, honey, and more.

FRENCH
◖ **Café Beaujolais** (961 Ukiah St., 707/937-5614, www.cafebeaujolais.com, lunch Wed.-Sun. 11:30am-2:30pm, dinner daily from 5:30pm, $23-35) is a standout French-California restaurant in an area dense with great upscale cuisine. This charming out-of-the-way spot is a few blocks from the center of Mendocino Village in an older creeper-covered home. Despite the white tablecloths and fancy crystal, the atmosphere is casual at lunchtime and gets only slightly more formal at dinner. The giant salads and delectable entrées are made with organic produce, humanely raised meats, and locally caught seafood. Beware: The portions can be enormous, but you can get them half-size just by asking. Having trouble deciding what to order? Ask the waitstaff, who are friendly, helpful, and quite knowledgeable about the menu and wine list—and the attractions of the local area, for that matter. Reservations are available on the website.

VEGETARIAN
Vegetarians and carnivores alike rave about **Ravens Restaurant** (Stanford Inn, 44850 Comptche Ukiah Rd., 0.5 miles east of Hwy. 1, 707/937-5615 or 800/331-8884, www.ravensrestaurant.com, Mon.-Sat. 8am-10:30am and 5:30pm-close, Sun. 8am-noon and 5:30pm-close, $18-23). Inside the lodge, which is surrounded by lush organic gardens, you'll find a big open dining room. Many of the vegetarian

and vegan dishes served use produce from the inn's own organic farm. At breakfast, enjoy delectable vegetarian (or vegan, with tofu) scrambles, omelets, and Florentines, complete with homemade breads and English muffins. At dinner, try one of the unusual salads or a seasonal vegetarian entrée. Even the wine list reflects organic, biodynamic, and sustainable-practice wineries.

Information and Services
Mendocino Village has a **post office** (10500 Ford St., 707/937-5282, www.usps.com, Mon.-Fri. 7:30am-4:30pm). **Moody's Internet Café, Art Gallery, and Coffee Bar** (10450 Lansing St., 707/937-4843, www.moodyscoffeebar. com, daily 6am-8pm) charges $2 per day for wireless Internet access if you bring your own laptop, and an hourly rate ($6) to use its computers.

Getting There and Around
It's simplest to navigate to and within Mendocino with your own vehicle. From U.S. 101 near Cloverdale, take Highway 128 northwest for 60 miles. Highway 128 becomes Highway 1 on the coast; Mendocino is another 10 miles north. A slower, more scenic alternative is to take Highway 1 the whole way from San Francisco to Mendocino; this route takes at least 4.5 hours. Mendocino has a fairly compact downtown area, Mendocino Village, with a concentration of restaurants, shops, and inns just a few blocks from the beach.

The **Mendocino Transit Authority** (800/696-4682, www.4mta.org) operates a dozen bus routes that connect Mendocino and Fort Bragg with larger cities like Santa Rosa and Ukiah, where you can make connections to Amtrak, Greyhound, and airports for access to farther-away points.

FORT BRAGG
A former military outpost and the home to a major logging company, Fort Bragg is the Mendocino Coast's largest city. With chain fast food joints and hotels lining Highway 1 as it passes through town, it doesn't have the immediate charm of its neighbor to the south. But it does offer some great restaurants, interesting downtown shops, and proximity to coastal landmarks, including Glass Beach and MacKerricher State Park.

Skunk Train
One of the famed attractions in Mendocino County is the California Western Railroad, popularly called the **Skunk Train** (depot at end of Laurel St., 866/457-5865, www.skunktrain. com, office winter daily 9am-2pm, summer daily 9am-3pm, adults $49, children $24), perfect for rail buffs and traveling families. The restored steam locomotives pull trains from the coast at Fort Bragg 40 miles through the redwood forest to the town of Willits and back. The adventure lets passengers see the true majesty of the redwoods while giving a hint about life in Northern California before the era of highways. The brightly-painted trains appeal to children, and the historic aspects and scenery call to adults. You can board in either Fort Bragg or Willits, making a round-trip to return to your lodgings for the night. Check the website for rides featuring beer and bratwurst or special events like a Halloween pumpkin patch excursion.

MacKerricher State Park
Three miles north of Fort Bragg, **MacKerricher State Park** (Hwy. 1, 707/964-9112, district office 707/937-5804, www.parks.ca.gov, daily sunrise-10pm, day use free) offers the small duck-filled Cleone Lake, six miles of sandy ocean beaches, four miles of cliffs and crags, and **camping** (reservations 800/444-7275, www.reserveamerica.com, $35). The main attraction for some is a gigantic, almost complete skeleton of a whale near the park entrance. Because there's no day use fee, you can stop in to see the whale even if you don't have time to hang out at the park. If you're lucky, you can also spot live whales and harbor seals frolicking in the ocean. The coast can be rough here, so don't swim or even wade unless it's what the locals call a "flat day"—no big waves and undertow. If the kids want to play in the

water, take them to **Pudding Creek Beach** in the park, about 2.5 miles south of the campground, where they can play in the relatively sheltered area under the trestle bridge. Hikers will enjoy the **Ten Mile Beach Trail** (10 miles round-trip), actually an old logging road that goes from Laguna Point to Ten Mile River.

Glass Beach

The most famous beach in the Mendocino area, **Glass Beach** (Elm St. and Glass Beach Dr.) is not a miracle of nature. The unpleasant origin of this fascinating beach strewn with sea glass was the Fort Bragg city dump. As the ocean rose over the landfill, the heavy glass that had been dumped there stayed put. Years of pounding surf polished and smoothed the broken edges, and now the surf returns our human refuse to the shore. At the tideline, amber, green, and clear sea glass color the shore.

Beachcombers used to collect the smooth coated shards of glass; now that the beach is under the management of MacKerricher State Park, it's against the rules to remove them. But it's still quite a sight. The trail down to Glass Beach is short but steep and treacherous; don't wear sandals—good walking or hiking shoes and attention to safety are a must.

Triangle Tattoo Museum

This is not your grandmother's art museum, so enter at your own risk. For more than 20 years, the **Triangle Tattoo Museum** (356B N. Main St., 707/964-8814, www.triangletattoo.com, daily noon-6pm, free) has displayed the implements of tattooing and photos of their results. To enter, walk up a flight of narrow stairs and stare at the walls, which are completely covered with photos of tattoos. All forms of the art are represented, from those done by indigenous people to those done at carnivals and in prisons. In glass cases upstairs are all types of tattooing devices, some antique. More photos grace the walls of the warren of small rooms in a never-ending collage. The street-side rooms house a working tattoo parlor, and you can find intrepid artists and their canvases working late into the evening. If you're interested, talk to an artist about scheduling an appointment.

Lost Coast Culture Machine

Devotees of contemporary art will want to make a pilgrimage to the **Lost Coast Culture Machine** (190 E. Elm St., 707/961-1600, www. lostcoastculturemachine.org, Wed.-Sun. noon-5pm, donation). Calling itself an "artist-run contemporary art space and handmade paper mill," the venue's exhibitions, presentations, demonstrations, and events vary widely. There's always something interesting going on, and visitors are welcome to drop in.

Pacific Star Winery

The only winery on the Mendocino Coast, **Pacific Star Winery** (33000 N. Hwy. 1, 707/964-1155, www.pacificstarwinery.com, daily 11am-5pm, tasting free) makes the most of its location. Barrels of wine are left out in the salt air to age, incorporating a hint of the Pacific into each vintage. Friendly tasting-room staffers will tell you how much they like their bosses, the winemaker, and which of the winery cats most likes to be picked up. Wines are tasty and reasonably priced, and you can bring your own picnic to enjoy on the nearby bluff, which overlooks the ocean.

Mendocino Coast Botanical Gardens

Stretching 47 acres down to the sea, **Mendocino Coast Botanical Gardens** (18220 N. Hwy. 1, 707/964-4352, www.gardenbythesea.org, Mar.-Oct. daily 9am-5pm, Nov.-Feb. daily 9am-4pm, adults $14, seniors $10, ages 6-17 $5) offer miles of walking through careful plantings and wild landscapes. The garden map is also a seasonal guide, useful for those who aren't sure whether it's rhododendron season or whether the dahlia garden might be in bloom. Butterflies flutter and bees buzz, and good labels teach novice botany enthusiasts the names of the plants they see. Children can pick up their own brochure, called "Quail Trail: A Child's Guide" and enjoy an exploratory adventure designed just for them.

Entertainment and Events

The **Gloriana Musical Theatre** (210 N. Corry St., 707/964-7469, www.gloriana.org) seeks to bring music and theater to young people, so they produce major musicals that appeal to kids, such as *The Aristocats* and *Charlotte's Web*. On the other hand, *Into the Woods* and the *Rock 'N Roll Revue* appeal mostly to people past their second decade. Local performers star in the two major shows and numerous one-off performances that Gloriana puts on each year.

Art is a big deal in the Mendocino Coast. Accordingly, the area hosts a number of art events each year. **Art in the Gardens** (18220 N. Hwy. 1, Fort Bragg, www.gardenbythesea.org, $20 at the door, $15 in advance) takes place each August at the Mendocino Coast Botanical Gardens, for which it is an annual fundraiser. The gardens are decked out with the finest local artwork, food, and wine, and there is music to entertain the crowds who come to eat, drink, view, and purchase art.

Shopping

If you really enjoyed Glass Beach, you may want to stop in at the **Glass Beach Museum and Gift Shop** (17801 N. Hwy. 1, 707/962-0590, www.glassbeachjewelry.com, daily 10am-5pm), 1.1 miles south of Fort Bragg. You can see a wide array of found treasures from over the years, hear stories from Captain Cass, a retired sailor and expert glass scavenger, and also buy sea glass set in pendants and rings.

Vintage clothing enthusiasts will love **If the Shoe Fits** (337 N. Franklin St., 707/964-2580, daily 10am-5pm). Its eclectic collection of used clothing and accessories for men and women usually includes interesting pieces, well-preserved and in good condition.

The place to go on the North Coast to feed your vacation reading habit is—where else?— **The Bookstore** (353 Franklin St., 707/964-6559, daily 10am-5:30pm), a small shop with a well-curated selection of new and used books likely to please discriminating readers. Upstairs is a selection of used records for sale for music lovers.

Sports and Recreation

SPORTFISHING

The Mendocino Coast is an ideal location to watch whales do acrobatics, or to try to land the big one (salmon, halibut, rock cod, or tuna). During Dungeness crab season, you can even go out on a crab boat, learn to set pots, and catch your own delectable delicacy.

Many charters leave out of Noyo Harbor in Fort Bragg. The **Trek II** (Noyo Harbor, 707/964-4550, www.anchorcharterboats.com, daily 7am-8pm, 5-hour fishing trip $80, 2-hour whale-watching $35) offers fishing trips and whale-watching jaunts (Dec.-May). They'll take you rockfishing in summer, crabbing in winter, and chasing after salmon and tuna in season.

The **Noyo Fishing Center** (32440 N. Harbor Dr., Noyo Harbor, 707/964-3000, www.fortbraggfishing.com, half-day fishing trip $65-100, 2-hour whale-watching excursion $35) can take you out salmon fishing or up off the Lost Coast for halibut fishing. They'll help you fish for cod and various deep-sea dwellers in season (May 15-Aug. 15). The crew can even clean and vacuum-pack your catch on the dock before you leave.

HIKING

The hike to take in MacKerricher State Park (Hwy. 1, 707/964-9112, www.parks.ca.gov, visitors center daily 9am-3pm, day use free), three miles north of Fort Bragg, is the **Ten Mile Beach Trail** (10 miles round-trip, moderate), starting at the Laguna Point Parking Area at the north end of Fort Bragg and running five miles up to the Ten Mile River. Most of this path is fairly level and paved. It's an easy walk you can take at your own pace and turn around whenever you want. Street bikes and inline skates are also allowed on this trail.

HORSEBACK RIDING

What better way to enjoy the rugged cliffs, windy beaches, and quiet forests of the coast than on the back of a horse? **Ricochet Ridge Ranch** (24201 N. U.S. 101, 707/964-9669, www.horse-vacation.com) has 10-mile beach trail rides ($50) departing four times a day at 10am, noon, 2pm and 4pm. They also offer longer beach and trail rides, sunset beach rides, and full-fledged riding vacations by reservation (private guided rides $90-310).

SURFING

There are options for surfing in the Fort Bragg area. Just south of town is **Hare Creek** (southwest of the intersection of Hwy. 1 and Hwy. 20, north end of the Hare Creek Bridge), one of the region's most popular spots. North of town is **Virgin Creek** (1.5 miles north of Fort Bragg on Hwy. 1), another well-known break.

The **Lost Surf Shack** (319 N. Franklin St., 707/961-0889, daily 10am-6pm, surfboards $20/day, wetsuits $12.50/day) in downtown Fort Bragg rents surfboards and wetsuits to the surfing inclined.

SPAS

The **Bamboo Garden Spa** (303 N. Main St., Suite C, 707/962-9396, www.bamboogardenspa.com, Tues.-Sat. 10am-8pm, Sun.-Mon. 11am-6:30pm, $80-180) pampers its guests with a wide array of massage, skin, and beauty treatments. Get a 50-minute massage, or try the Balinese Soul Soother or the Vanilla Bean Sugar Scrub.

Accommodations

Stringent zoning laws about development and expansion of businesses in the coastal zone are the main reason you're not likely to find a lot of lodging bargains here; only a few chain hotels have managed to build in Fort Bragg.

UNDER $150

One budget option is the **Surf Motel** (1220 S. Main St., 707/964-5361 or 800/339-5361, www.surfmotelfb.com, $99-275). There's no pool, but the hotel pleases a variety of vacationers by providing a bike-washing station, a fish-cleaning station, an outdoor shower for divers, a garden to stroll through, and an area set aside for horseshoes and barbecues. Your spacious modern guest room comes with breakfast, free wireless Internet access, a microwave,

a fridge, and a blow dryer. If you rent one of the two apartments, you get a whole kitchen and room for four people.

The **Beachcomber Motel** (1111 N. Main St., 707/964-2402, www.thebeachcombermotel.com, $109-259) is clean and decent, offering many rooms with ocean views; pets are allowed in some rooms. Amenities are minimal but acceptable, similar to a low-end chain motel. Expect shampoo and soap in your tiny bath, but little else. Guest rooms are big enough to satisfy, although some visitors find them a bit dark and sparsely furnished. Thin walls and shared patios make noise a problem, and the location at the north end of town makes it a little inconvenient if your goal is to be near downtown Fort Bragg. What really makes the Beachcomber worthwhile, besides its lower-than-B&B prices, is that it's right on Pudding Creek Beach and the popular Ten Mile Beach Trail.

The stately **Grey Whale Inn** (615 N. Main St., 800/382-7244, www.greywhaleinn.com, $135-171) was once a community hospital. The blocky craftsman-style building was erected by the Union Lumber Company in 1915. Today, 13 spacious, simply appointed guest rooms welcome travelers. Whether you get a view of the water or a more pedestrian city view, you'll have a lovely, individually decorated guest room with a private bath and queen or king bed, perhaps covered by an old-fashioned quilt. The inn prides itself on simplicity and friendliness, and its perfect location in downtown Fort Bragg makes visitors feel at home walking to dinner or the beach. It also has a unique feature for an inn: a game room with a pool table and foosball.

$150-250

Weller House (524 Stewart St., 707/964-4415, www.wellerhouse.com, $180-280) is a picture-perfect B&B with elegantly restored Victorian-style guest rooms, ocean views, and sumptuous home cooking. There are even a few gloriously secluded guest rooms for rent up in the old water tower, which is the high point in the whole city of Fort Bragg. If you can't finish writing your novel here, you're just not trying. But that's not all: The manager, Vivien LaMothe, is also a tango dancer, and the third floor of the main building—a gorgeous 1886 mansion listed on the National Register of Historic Places—is, believe it or not, a ballroom (although the original owner, Mr. Weller, manager of the old company store for the mill, was a strict Baptist and used it for Sunday school). The virgin redwood floor, the outstanding acoustics, and the spacious porch where dancers can step out for a breath of air make it a marvelous place for a milonga. Some of the great tango dancers think so too—they come from the Bay Area and far beyond to participate in monthly tango weekends and twice a year tango festivals. Check the website for schedules, celebrity dance teachers, and chamber music concerts. Weller House is one block west of Main Street, in view of the Skunk Train depot, and an easy walk to good restaurants and shopping.

Camping

MacKerricher State Park (Hwy. 1, 707/964-9112, www.parks.ca.gov, reservations 800/444-7275, www.reserveamerica.com, $35), three miles north of Fort Bragg, is also a fine place to spend a night or two as you explore the area. Reservations are recommended April 1-October 15, and they're site-specific. In the winter season, camping is available on a first-come, first-served basis. The park has 107 sites suitable for tents and RVs up to 35 feet in its wooded and pleasant West Pinewood Campground; there are also a group campground and walk-in hike-and-bike sites. Restrooms with flush toilets as well as hot showers are provided, and each campsite has a fire ring, picnic table, and food storage locker.

Food

It used to be that you had to go to the village of Mendocino for a restaurant meal, but lately Fort Bragg has developed a more-than-respectable culinary scene of its own. Many excellent restaurants are available within a few blocks of the town center and beach.

AMERICAN

Upstairs in an old Fort Bragg lumber building, the **◖Mendo Bistro** (301 N. Main St. #J, 707/964-4974, http://mendobistro.com, daily 5pm-9pm, $15-32) has the sort of menu one might expect in a bigger city. One of the best parts of the menu is the "Choice" section, where you choose the style of meat, seafood, or vegetarian option and how it is cooked along with what sauce it is cooked in. The hormone- and antibiotic-free steaks are perfectly cooked and delicious. There are also a great deal of vegetarian offerings on the menu—from an eggplant trio entrée to several meat-free pastas—but the one veggie item to seek out is the Bistro's polenta whether it's the polenta croutons in the Caesar salad or the creamy polenta that comes as a side dish. Before opening Mendo Bistro in 1999, chef Nicholas Petti was a touring musician and onetime member of the seminal alt country band Whiskeytown.

The **North Coast Brewing Company** (444 N. Main St., 707/964-3400, www.northcoast-brewing.com, Wed.-Thurs. and Sun. 4pm-9:30pm, Fri.-Sat. 4pm-10pm, $15-33) opened in 1988, aiming at the then-nascent artisanal beer market. Today, they also serve seafood, steak, and creative salads. Of course, it's best to wash down your beer with a North Coast microbrew. You can taste the magic in their Red Seal Ale, Old Rasputin Russian Imperial Stout, and Scrimshaw Pilsner.

The most popular burger in town is at **Jenny's Giant Burger** (940 N. Main St., 707/964-2235, daily 10:30am-9pm, $2.50-7). This little place has a 1950s hamburger-stand feel, but there's nothing stale about it. The burgers are fresh and antibiotic-free, with garden burger and veggie sandwich options. Jenny's followers are devoted, so it can get crowded, but there are a few outdoor tables, and you can always get your treats to go.

BAKERIES AND CAFES

Despite the often drizzly overcast weather, Mendocino Coast residents and visitors crave ice cream in the summer just like anyone else. **Cowlick's Ice Cream** (250 N. Main St.,

707/962-9271, www.cowlicksicecream.com, daily 11am-9pm) serves delectable handmade ice cream in a variety of flavors. Yes, they really do serve mushroom ice cream during the famous fall Mendo mushroom season. You can get the perennial favorite flavors such as vanilla, chocolate, coffee, and strawberry. If you're lucky, you might also find your favorite seasonal flavor (banana daiquiri, cinnamon, green tea) when you visit. If you're not in downtown Fort Bragg, you can also find this local family-owned chain at the Mendocino Coast Botanical Gardens (18220 N. Hwy. 1); at **Frankie's Ice Cream Parlor** (44951 Ukiah St., Mendocino, 707/937-2436, www.frankiesmendocino.com, daily 11am-9pm) in Mendocino Village; on the Skunk Train; and at **J. D. Redhouse** (212 S. Main St., Willits, 707/459-1214, daily 10am-6pm).

If you're more interested in coffee and pastries than a temporary office space, the **Headlands Coffeehouse** (120 E. Laurel St., 707/964-1987, www.headlandscoffeehouse.com, Mon.-Sat. 7am-10pm, Sun. 7am-7pm) is unquestionably the place to go in Fort Bragg. They have around 15 different self-serve roasts of coffee and food ranging from breakfast burritos to paninis. There is free live music in the evenings and free Internet access. So what's the catch? There are no electrical outlets available for customers, so you can only use your laptop as long as your battery lasts.

If what you're really looking for is a place to spread out and work while having coffee and snacks as a bonus, head to the **Mendocino Cookie Company/Zappa's Coffee** (301 N. Main St., 707/964-0282, www.menodcino-cookies.com, daily 7am-6pm). For a minimal fee they'll let you rent one of their computers, or stay as long as you like in the large atrium area they share with several other businesses, which has free Internet access, plenty of electrical outlets, and elbow room. Oh, and the fresh-baked cookies taste as good as they smell.

BREAKFAST

Egghead's (326 N. Main St., 707/964-5005, www.eggheadsrestaurant.com, daily 7am-2pm,

$6-19) has been serving an enormous menu of breakfast, lunch, and brunch items to satisfy diners for more than 30 years. The menu includes every imaginable omelet combination, cinnamon raisin toast, burritos, Reuben sandwiches, and "flying-monkey potatoes," derived from the *Wizard of Oz* theme that runs through the place.

FARMERS MARKET

Fort Bragg hosts a **farmers market** (Franklin St. between Laurel and Pine, www.mcfarm.org, May-Oct. Wed. 3pm-6pm) that sells lots of good stuff, including wild caught seafood, free range beef, and fresh baked bread.

ITALIAN

Small and almost always packed, the **Piaci Pub & Pizzeria** (120 W. Redwood Ave., 707/961-1133, www.piacipizza.com, Mon.-Wed. 11am-9:30pm, Thurs.-Sat. 11am-10pm, Sun. 4pm-9:30pm, $9-26) has 16 pizzas in three different sizes along with an array of salads, calzones, and focaccia breads with toppings. The pizzas range from traditional pepperoni to more creative options like pesto, chevre, pears, prosciutto, and herbs. Piaci has an extensive list of brews, from Belgian-style beers to hearty ales.

JAPANESE

Taka's Grill (250A N. Main St., 707/964-5204, daily noon-9pm, $12-20) fills up for lunch. Dine in the small indoor area or in the adjacent atrium. The fresh rolls include a flavor-filled mango salmon roll.

MEXICAN

Inside a Fort Bragg strip mall, **Los Gallitos** (130 S. Main St., 707/964-4519, Mon.-Sat. 11am-8pm, Sun. 10am-8pm, $7-16, cash only) doesn't look like much. But you know this is a better-than-average taqueria when the thick fresh tortilla strips and superb salsa hit your table. Everything on the menu, from burritos to tostados is what you'd expect, but the attention to little details like the grilled onions and beans on the very tasty carne asada torta make this place special.

SEAFOOD

With the small fishing and crabbing fleet of Fort Bragg's Noyo Harbor, it's natural that lots of seafood restaurants are clustered nearby. Head down to the harbor where any one of the several casual restaurants and fish markets offer the most authentic, freshest, and simplest preparations of salmon, mussels, and Dungeness crab in season. One spot known for its fish and chips is the **Sea Pal Cove Restaurant** (32390 N. Harbor Dr., 707/964-1300, Wed.-Thurs. noon-5pm, Fri.-Sun. noon-7pm, $6-13, cash only).

THAI

Small and unassuming, but well worth a visit, **Nit's Café** (322 Main St., 707/964-7187, Wed.-Sun. 5:30pm-9pm, $14-26, cash only) specializes in Thai and Asian fusion. Noted for its beautiful presentations of both classic and creative dishes, Nit's gets rave reviews from nearly everyone who tries it.

Information and Services

The **Mendocino Coast Chamber of Commerce and Visitors Center** (217 S. Main St., 707/961-6300, www.mendocinocoast.com, Mon.-Fri. 9am-5pm, Sat. 10am-3pm) has unusually attentive and well-trained staff in addition to all the maps, brochures, and ideas you could possibly want. This operation also serves as the Mendocino County film office, which strongly encourages filmmaking in the area. Come in and get the inside story on where to see the filming locations of *Summer of '42,* in which the bluffs of Fort Bragg play the role of Long Island; *East of Eden; Karate Kid III; Humanoids from the Deep;* and many more. Films have been made around here since the beginning of the silent era, as have television shows. The staff can even direct you to Angela Lansbury's typewriter from *Murder, She Wrote* or to the Skunk Train, which appeared in *The Majestic* with Jim Carrey.

Of all the towns on the Mendocino Coast, Fort Bragg has the most urban atmosphere, complete with supermarkets, big-box stores, and a **post office** (203 N. Franklin St.,

707/964-2302, www.usps.com, Mon.-Fri. 8:30am-5pm).

The **Mendocino Coast District Hospital** (700 River Dr. at Cypress St., 707/961-1234, www.mcdh.org) has the nearest full-service emergency room.

Getting There and Around

Fort Bragg is located on Highway 1; driving here from San Francisco takes about 4 hours. There is no "fast" way to reach Fort Bragg. The road from any direction is narrow and full of curves, at least for an hour or two, so be prepared to make the scenic journey part of the fun. From Willits, take Highway 20 (Fort Bragg-Willits Rd.) west for 30 miles. If ever a road could be described as sun-dappled, this is one. The sun pops in and out among the redwood forest and makes you want to use all the pullouts to take photos. Keep in mind that there is no cell-phone service along this road, so it is not a good place to run out of gas. Allow plenty of time—it takes longer than you'd expect to travel these 30 miles.

As one of the largest towns in the region, Fort Bragg has access to more public transportation. The most enjoyable way to get here is to take the **Skunk Train** (866/457-5865, www.skunktrain.com) from Willits. The **Mendocino Transit Authority** (707/462-1422 or 800/696-4682, www.mta4.org) has a number of bus lines that pass through Fort Bragg, and it also offers **Dial-a-Ride Curb-to-Curb Service** (707/964-1800). The most common way to get to and around Fort Bragg, however, is by car.

Westport

The next town north along Highway 1 is Westport, 16 miles north of Fort Bragg, with its own patch of ocean, a few essential services, and one gem. It's the last settlement before the wild Lost Coast. The motto at the ◀ **Westport Hotel** (3892 Hwy. 1, 707/964-3688 or 877/964-3688, www.westporthotel.us, $140-195) is, "At last, you've found nowhere." The Westport Hotel is marvelous and private, perfect for a honeymoon spent in luxury and comfort. Each of the six guest rooms has one bed and a bath with fixtures that blend perfectly into the historic 1890 house. Some guest rooms have small private balconies overlooking the waves, and all guests have access to the redwood sauna. Fresh scones, fruit, and coffee are delivered to your room in the morning, and a full hot breakfast is served in the dining room.

Inside the Westport Hotel is the **Old Abalone Pub** (3892 Hwy. 1, 707/964-3688 or 877/964-3688, www.westporthotel.us, Thurs.-Mon. 5pm-9pm, afternoon tea Sat. 3pm-5pm, brunch Sun. 10am-2pm, dinner $10-25). Thanks to a large mirror over the bar, everyone in the dining room gets an ocean view—even those seated with their backs to the sea.

Camping is available two miles north of Westport at **Westport-Union Landing State Beach** (Hwy. 1, 707/937-5804, www.parks. ca.gov, $25), with 86 first-come, first-served sites. There are no showers or other amenities, just the cliffs, the waves, the sunsets, and the views.

Mendocino Wine Country

Mendocino's interior valley might not be quite as glamorous as the coast, but it is home to history, art, and liquor. The Anderson Valley is the apex of Mendocino's wine region, although the tiny town of Hopland also has its share of tasting rooms. Ukiah, the county seat, is home to a number of microbreweries and a thriving agricultural industry. Up in determinedly funky Willits, a late-1960s art vibe thrives in the 21st century.

Unlike the chilly windy coast, the interior valleys of Mendocino get hot in the summer. Bring shorts, a swimsuit, and an air-conditioned car if you plan to visit June-September.

ANDERSON VALLEY

The Anderson Valley wine trail, also known as Highway 128, begins in Boonville and continues northwest toward the coast, with most of the wineries clustered between Boonville and Navarro.

Wineries

A big name in the Anderson Valley, **Scharffenberger Cellars** (8501 Hwy. 128, Philo, 707/895-2957, www.scharffenbergercellars.com, daily 11am-5pm, tasting $3) makes wine in Mendocino. The tasting room is elegant and unusually child-friendly.

A broad-ranging winery with a large estate vineyard and event center, **Navarro Vineyards** (5601 Hwy. 128, Philo, 707/895-3686 or 800/537-9463, www.navarrowine.

com, summer daily 9am-6pm, winter daily 9am-5pm, tasting free) offers a range of tasty wines as well as some interesting specialty products such as the non-alcoholic verjus.

In a valley full of great wineries, **Roederer Estate** (4501 Hwy. 128, 707/895-2288, www. roedererestate.com, daily 11am-5pm, tasting $6) sparkles. The California sparkling wines it creates are some of the best you'll taste. The large tasting room features a bar with sweeping views of the estate vineyards and huge cases filled with Roederer's well-deserved awards. Pourers are knowledgeable, and you'll get to taste from magnum bottles—a rarity at any winery. Be sure to ask for a taste of Roederer's rarely seen still wines; you might find something wonderful.

Small boutique wineries are clustered in the Anderson Valley, an area less crowded than Napa or Sonoma. Any of these are worth a visit to seek out gem wines that aren't available in shops. **Esterlina** (1200 Holmes Ranch Rd., Philo, 707/895-2920, www.esterlinavineyards. com, tasting by appointment only, reserve tasting $15 pp, waived with purchase) offers the best view in the valley—come around sunset if you can. Beyond the spectacular vineyard vistas, Esterlina provides tastes of a selection of sparkling and still wines that make it well worth the trip to the top of its hill.

Handley Cellars (3151 Hwy. 128, Philo, 707/895-3876 or 800/733-3151, www.handleycellars.com, May-Oct. daily 10am-6pm,

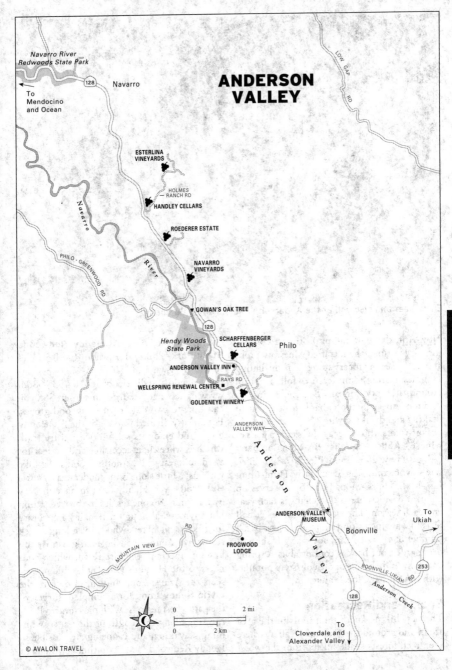

ANDERSON VALLEY

NORTH COAST

© SHANE DOLBIER

Enjoy beer and disc golf at the Anderson Valley Brewing Company.

Nov.-Apr. daily 10am-5pm) offers a complimentary tasting of handcrafted wines you probably won't see in grocery stores. The intriguing Handley tasting room features folk art from around the world for sale. Books on wine are sold too, especially those that focus on women making and drinking wine.

For visitors who prefer a cold beer to a glass of wine, ◖ **Anderson Valley Brewing Company** (17700 Hwy. 253, Boonville, 707/895-2337, www.avbc.com, Apr.-Dec. daily 11am-6pm, Jan.-Mar. Thurs.-Mon. 11am-6pm) serves up an array of microbrews that changes each year and each season. The warehouse-size beer hall feels like a wine tasting room and has a bar, a number of tables, and a good-size gift shop. A beer garden out back is comfortable in spring and fall, and the disc golf course is popular with travelers and locals alike.

Sports and Recreation

The best hiking and biking trails in the area are in and around the Anderson Valley, where evergreen forests shade hikers from the worst of the summer heat. At **Hendy Redwoods State Park** (Philo-Greenwood Rd., 0.5 miles south of Hwy. 128, 707/895-3141 in summer, Mendocino district office 707/937-5804, www.parks.ca.gov, daily 8am-sunset, $8), you can hike to two old-growth redwood groves. For an easy, shaded walk, visit the **Big Hendy** grove and enjoy its self-guided nature trail, which is wheelchair accessible and perfect for a sedate forest walk. Another good short hike with just a little slope is the moderate **Hermit's Hut Trail**—yes, Hendy used to have its very own hermit. No one resides in the tree-stump hut anymore, although it remains a curiosity for hikers. Fit hikers who want a longer trek can weave around the whole park; **Big Hendy Loop** connects to the Fire Road, which connects to the Hermit's Hut Trail, which intersects the Azalea Loop and runs down to the **Little Hendy Loop** for a complete survey of the park's best regions. With the Navarro River running along the length of the park, swimming, kayaking, and canoeing are possible in Hendy Redwoods at certain times of the year.

NORTH COAST BREWERIES

While Napa Valley is known for its wine, California's North Coast is known for its beer. Here local craft beer and microbrews are served in restaurants and line the beer aisles of local supermarkets. One way to get a taste of these beers or to sample their smaller batches is to visit a North Coast brewery or brewpub.

If you're a beer fan, the **Anderson Valley Brewing Company's Tap Room and Brewery** (17700 Hwy. 253, Boonville, 707/895-2337, www.avbc.com, Apr.-Dec. daily 11am-6pm, Jan.-Mar. Thurs.-Mon. 11am-6pm) is well worth a visit. With its high ceilings and copper bar, the taproom feels like an informal tasting room in a winery. They have 20 taps that serve Anderson Valley favorites like Boont Amber Ale, along with 10 taps that feature rotating smaller batch brews including a sour stout. There's more to do at Anderson Valley than just drinking their tasty beers. Brewery tours ($5) are offered every day the taproom is open at 1:30pm and 3pm, while you can also grab a beer and head outdoors to play the brewery's 18-hole disc golf course ($5).

Since opening in 1988, the **North Coast Brewing Company** (455 N. Main St., Fort Bragg, 707/964-2739, www.northcoastbrewing.com, Taproom & Grill Wed.-Thurs. and Sun. 4pm-9:30pm, Fri.-Sat. 4pm-10pm) has expanded so that it takes up all four corners of a Fort Bragg city block with the actual brewery, the brewery shop, and the taproom and grill. Head into the popular taproom to try North Coast favorites including the Red Seal Ale or the more potent Brother Thelonious Belgian Style Abbey Ale.

If you crave sustainable suds, visit the **Eel River Brewing Company's Taproom & Grill** (1777 Alamar Way, Fortuna, 707/725-2739, http://eelriverbrewing.com, daily 11am-11pm), where you can sip organic beer that was made with renewable energy. Drink the Organic IPA or Organic Acai Berry Wheat Ale at the taproom's long wooden bar or head outside to drink in the adjacent beer garden. To tour the brewing facilities in the nearby town of Scotia, contact the company (707/764-1772) during weekday business hours.

The **Lost Coast Brewery & Café** (617 4th St., Eureka, 707/445-4480, www.lostcoast.com, Sun.-Thurs. 11am-10pm, Fri.-Sat. 11am-11pm) feels like a local's bar. The hockey stick-shaped bar and restaurant is filled with people even on weeknights. The brewery's Great White and Lost Coast Pale Ale are the most popular brews, but the smooth Downtown Brown is recommended for darker beer fans.

A few miles inland, the **Mad River Brewing Company Tasting Room** (101 Taylor Way, Blue Lake, 707/668-4151 Ext. 106, www.madriverbrewing.com, Mon.-Fri. 1pm-9pm, Sat. noon-9pm, Sun. noon-8pm) has almost nightly live music to entertain you while you enjoy their Steelhead Extra Pale Ale or Jamaica Red Ale. **Tours** (707/668-4151 Ext. 105, daily 1pm-4pm, free) are also offered daily.

A new craft beer operation that Humboldt County brew fans rave about is the Redwood Curtain Brewing Company. **The Redwood Curtain Brewing Company Tasting Room** (550 S. G St., Arcata, 707/826-7222, www.redwoodcurtainbrewing.com, call or visit website for hours) is the place to try their Imperial Golden Ale or the creative Cerise Coup, which is aged in a French oak chardonnay barrel and then left with cherries for six months. They don't even bottle their beer yet.

Accommodations

Lodging options in and around the Anderson Valley vary widely. In the valley proper you're likely to find funky hotels, cabins, and forest-shaded campgrounds.

The **Anderson Valley Inn** (8480 Hwy. 128, Philo, 707/895-3325, www.avinn.com, $85-180), between Boonville and Philo, makes the perfect spot from which to divide your time between the Anderson Valley and the Mendocino Coast. Six small guest rooms are done up in bright colors, homey bedspreads, and attractive appointments in this small multiple-building inn. A butterfly-filled garden invites guests to sit out on the porches reading the paper and sipping coffee. The two two-bedroom suites have full kitchens and are perfect for travelers looking to stay in the area a bit longer. The friendly owners welcome children and dogs in the suites—both must be attended at all times—and can be very helpful with hints about how best to explore the region. This inn often fills quickly on summer weekends, as it's one of the best-value accommodations in the region. There's a two-night minimum on weekends April-November.

In the middle of Boonville, the quaint **Boonville Hotel** (14050 Hwy. 128, 707/895-2210, www.boonvillehotel.com, $125-350) has a rough weathered exterior that contrasts interestingly with the 15 updated contemporary guest rooms, each of which is bright and airy with earth-tone furniture and an attractive collection of mismatched decorations. If you're traveling with children or pets, request one of the guest rooms set up to accommodate them. Downstairs, you'll find comfortable spacious common areas and a huge garden suitable for strolling. Amenities include a bookshop and a gift shop, a good-size bar, and a dining room. For a relaxing treat, book one of the guest rooms with a balcony, which comes with a hammock set up and ready for napping, or a guest room with an outdoor bathtub for soaking and relaxing.

Camping

Stylish lodgings aren't common in the Anderson Valley, but you can still find a pleasant place to stay near the wineries. For wine and nature lovers on a budget, the campgrounds at **Indian Creek County Park** (Hwy. 128 at mile marker 23.48, 1 mile east of Philo, 707/463-4291, www.co.mendocino.ca.us, $20) and **Hendy Woods State Park** (Philo-Greenwood Rd., 0.5 miles south of Hwy. 128, 8 miles northwest of Boonville, 707/895-3141, www.parks.ca.gov, $20) provide woodsy, shady campsites.

Food

A picnic makes a perfect lunch in the Anderson Valley, and farmers markets and farm stands can supply fresh local ingredients. The **Boonville Farmers Market** (14050 Hwy. 128, Boonville, www.mcfarm.org, May-Oct. Sat. 9:30am-noon) draws a crowd, so be prepared to hunt for parking. For fresh fruit and vegetables every day, try **Gowan's Oak Tree Farm Stand** (6600 Hwy. 128, 2.5 miles north of Philo, 707/895-3353, daily 8am-7pm). The stand belongs to the local Gowan's Oak Tree Farm and sells only in-season local produce and homemade products made with the same fruits and veggies.

For an elegant full-service dining experience, enjoy **Table 128** (14050 Hwy. 128, Boonville, 707/895-2210, www.boonvillehotel.com, by reservation only Apr.-Nov. Thurs.-Mon., Dec.-Mar. Fri.-Sun., $40-50), the restaurant at the Boonville Hotel. Table 128 is family-style and the menu is prix fixe. The food is so fresh and seasonal that the chef won't commit to a menu more than a week in advance, but you can sign up on the website to receive regular menus by email. Reservations are required and must be secured with a credit card for parties of five or more.

Getting There and Around

You can see pretty much all of Anderson Valley from the "wine road," Highway 128. You can get to Highway 128 from U.S. 101 either directly out of Hopland or from Ukiah on Highway 253. From Hopland, take Mountain House Road west for nine miles. Turn right onto Highway 128 and continue north for about 20 miles.

From Ukiah, take U.S. 101 south for three miles. Merge onto Highway 253 and head west for about 17 miles. When you reach Highway 128, turn right. The center of Boonville is less than one mile away.

Many of the major wine-country touring outfits that operate from San Francisco and the Napa Valley also offer trips in the Anderson Valley. **Mendo Wine Tours** (707/937-6700 or 888/805-8687, www.mendowinetours.com, group tours $175 pp, private limo tours $550 for 2 people) is a regional specialist that offers a Lincoln Town Car for small groups and an SUV limo for groups of up to 10.

HOPLAND

Hopland is inland on U.S. 101 about 15 miles south of Ukiah and 28 miles east of the Anderson Valley via Highway 253. Highway 175 leads east to Clear Lake, under 20 miles away.

Solar Living Center

The **Solar Living Center** (13771 S. U.S. 101, 707/472-2450, http://solarliving.org, daily 9am-6pm) is a "12-acre sustainable living demonstration site," showing, among other things, what life might be like without petroleum. The center has exhibits on permaculture, an organic garden, and a demonstration of solar-powered water systems. The **Real Goods** store (707/472-2403) on the property is also a draw for visitors, and the completely recycled restrooms are worth a look even if you don't need one. If your vehicle happens to run on biodiesel, you can fill your tank here.

For more than 15 years, the Solar Living Center has taken a weekend in August to put on "the greenest show on earth," **MoonDance Eco-Fest** (www.solarliving.org). The hundreds of displays, demonstrations, and workshops go far beyond solar power to teach and exemplify the ever-expanding world of permaculture and renewable energy. Keynote speakers each year include top names from the world of ecological activism and science. But it's not all serious business at Eco-Fest; musicians perform on the main stage, and the Saturday Night Moondance features entertainment and DJs for eco-lovers who want to dance deep into the night.

Wineries

To get to the best wineries in Hopland, you don't even need to leave U.S. 101. The highway runs through the center of town, and almost all the tasting rooms are located along it. For those who love wine but not crowds, the tiny wineries and tasting rooms in Hopland are the perfect place to relax, enjoy sipping each vintage, and really chat with the pourer, who just might be the winemaker and owner. **Graziano** (13251 S. U.S. 101, 707/744-8466,

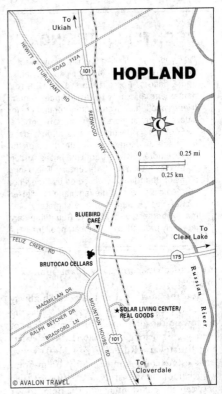

www.grazianofamilyofwines.com, daily 10am-5pm), for example, provides a great small-winery experience.

The star of this mini region is **Brutocao Cellars** (13500 S. U.S. 101, 800/433-3689, www.brutocaocellars.com, daily 10am-5pm, tasting free), whose vineyards crowd the land surrounding the town. It took over the old high school to create its tasting room and restaurant complex. The wide stone-tiled tasting room houses exceptional wines poured by knowledgeable staff. A sizeable gift shop offers gourmet goodies under the Brutocao label, and there are six regulation bocce ball courts if you want to do some lawn bowling with your wine sipping. And if you can't get enough of Brutocao, there is a second tasting room in the Anderson Valley (7000 Hwy. 128, Philo, 800/661-2103, www.

BOONTLING: THE NORTH COAST DIALECT

Take your oddly broken English, throw in some old Scottish and Irish, add a pinch of Spanish and a dash of Pomo, then season with real names and allusions to taste. Speak among friends and family in an isolated community for a dozen years or more. The results: Boontling.

Boontling is a unique and almost dead language developed by the denizens of the then-remote town of Boonville in the Anderson Valley late in the 19th century. The beginnings of Boontling are obscured by time since all the originators of the language are "piked for dusties" – that is, in the cemetery. And many Boonters – speakers of Boontling – are intensely protective of the local lingo. But in the 1960s, Professor Charles C. Adams of Cal State Chico came to town to study the language. He gradually gained the trust of the locals, and was able to write a doctoral thesis, eventually published as a book, *Boontling: An American Lingo*. The book documents the history and acts as a dictionary for the more than 1,000 Boontling terms on record.

So if you find yourself in Anderson Valley drinking "zeese" (coffee) or "aplenty bahl steinber horn" (a really great beer) and hear older folks speaking a language like none you've ever heard, you might just be listening to a rare and endangered conversation in Boontling.

brutocaocellars.com, daily 10am-5pm, tasting free).

Heading north out of town, the highway passes through acres of vineyards spreading out toward the forest in all directions. Many of these grapes belong to **Jeriko** (12141 Hewlett and Sturtevant Rd., 707/744-1140, www.jerikoestate.com, summer daily 10am-5pm, winter noon-5pm, tasting $10). Visitors drive between the chardonnay and the pinot to get to the immense Napa-style tasting room. A glass wall exposes the barrel room with aging wines stacked high, tempting tasters to learn their secrets.

Food

With the closing of the Hopland Inn, Hopland lost some of its best dining and one of its only places to stay. A casual place that most people enjoy is the **Bluebird Café & Catering Company** (13340 S. U.S. 101, 707/744-1633, Mon.-Thurs. 7am-2pm, Fri.-Sun. 7am-7pm, $17-20). Your best bet for a good night's sleep is to stay in Ukiah or Lakeport.

UKIAH

The largest city in Mendocino County, Ukiah is also the county seat. It's known for its wine production.

Sights

SAGELY CITY OF 10,000 BUDDHAS

There's plenty to interest the spiritually curious at the **Sagely City of 10,000 Buddhas** (4951 Bodhi Way, 707/462-0939, www.cttbusa.org, daily 8am-6pm). This active Buddhist college and monastery asks that guests wear modest clothing (avoid short shorts and short skirts, bare chests, and skimpy tank tops) and keep their voices down out of respect for the nuns and monks who make their lives here. The showpiece is the temple, which really does contain 10,000 golden Buddha statues. An extensive gift- and bookshop provides slightly silly souvenirs as well as serious scholarly texts on Buddhism. For a treat, stop in for lunch at the **Jyun Kang Vegetarian Restaurant** (707/468-7966, Wed.-Mon. noon-3pm, $7) on the grounds, which is open to the public.

GRACE HUDSON MUSEUM AND SUN HOUSE

One of the few truly cultural offerings in Ukiah is the **Grace Hudson Museum** (431 S. Main St., 707/467-2836, www.gracehudsonmuseum.org, Wed.-Sat. 10am-4:30pm, Sun. noon-4:30pm, adults $4, seniors and students $3, family $10). This small set of galleries focuses on the life and work of the artist Grace

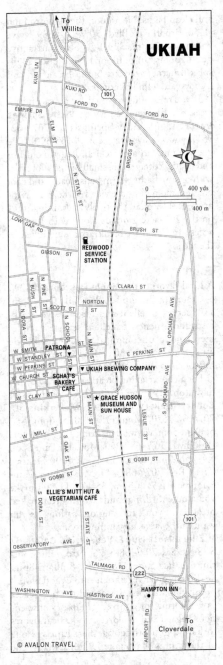

Hudson and her husband, Dr. John Hudson. The life's work of this couple included the study of the Pomo people and other Native American groups. The museum's permanent collection includes many of Grace's paintings, a number of Pomo baskets, and the works of dozens of other California artists. The 1911 craftsman-style **Sun House,** adjacent to the main museum building, was the Hudsons' home, and docent-guided tours are available.

Entertainment and Events

Ukiah Brewing Company (102 S. State St., 707/468-5898, www.ukiahbrewingco.com, kitchen Sun.-Thurs. 11am-9pm, Fri.-Sat. 11am-10pm, bar Mon.-Thurs. 11am-11pm, Fri.-Sun. 11am-1am, $8-11) offers good beer and good entertainment several nights each week. Settle in with a pilsner or amber ale and enjoy the live music and other weekend-evening entertainment. You might even get a chance to sing at the Wednesday open mics.

Sports and Recreation

Lake Mendocino is an artificial lake along the Russian River that is held in place by Coyote Dam. It's just off U.S. 101 north of Ukiah, allowing residents and visitors the chance to powerboat, water-ski, canoe, kayak, fish, and play a round of disc golf. Shockingly uncrowded even on the hottest summer afternoons, this is a great spot to cool off. You can even find a few beaches and lawns on which to spread out a blanket and lie down, and shaded picnic tables where you can enjoy lunch.

You can access the lake from Lake Mendocino Drive, Calpella Drive, and a few other local roads off U.S. 101. Five marinas catering to boaters and two boat ramps are along the shores of the lake. A number of campgrounds also circle the lake—some are boat-in only.

A great place to take a nice cool and shady hike is **Montgomery Woods State Nature Reserve** (Orr Springs Rd., 707/937-5804, www.parks.ca.gov, free), 13 miles west of Ukiah. This remote redwoods park is less crowded than its more accessible and more

NORTH COAST

popular brethren. The quintessential hike at Montgomery runs along **Montgomery Creek** (3 miles, moderate), where you get a chance to see something special and unusual—both the coastal and giant-sequoia species of redwood tree growing in the same park. Montgomery's location and climate make it hospitable to both types, which usually grow hundreds of miles apart.

There is a tranquil and serene (most of the time) historic spa at the edge of Ukiah. Since its establishment in 1854, **Vichy Springs** (2605 Vichy Springs Rd., 707/462-9515, www.vichysprings.com, daily 9am-dusk, treatments $105-195 per hour, baths $50 per day) has been patronized by Mark Twain, Jack London, Ulysses S. Grant, Teddy Roosevelt, and California governor Jerry Brown. The hot springs, mineral-heavy and naturally carbonated, closely resemble the world-famous waters of their namesake at Vichy in France. Services include the baths, a hot pool, and an Olympic-size swimming pool as well as a day spa.

In downtown Ukiah, **Tranquility Day Spa** (203 S. State St., 707/463-2189, http://tranquilitydayspaukiah.com, Mon.-Fri. 10am-5:30pm, Sat. 11am-3pm) caters to the hippie side of this culturally mixed town. Swirling curtains and sandalwood incense pervade the big warehouse space. Tranquility has both salon and spa services for one-stop shopping for a mud mask, a hot-stone massage, a haircut, a Brazilian wax, a reflexology treatment, and even a "Tango Paraffin Bodyfango," with specific services for men, women, and teens.

Accommodations

There are plenty of lodgings in Ukiah, although they tend to be mostly standard chain motels. Out by the airport, the **Fairfield Inn** (1140 Airport Park Blvd., 707/463-3600, www.marriott.com, $99-150) is a good choice. With an elegant lobby, an indoor pool and spa, a small exercise room, and a generous complimentary continental breakfast, it has what you need to be comfortable. The guest rooms are what you'd expect of a decent mid-range chain: floral bedspreads, durable nondescript carpet,

and clean baths. Next door, the **Hampton Inn** (1160 Airport Park Blvd., 707/263-0889, www.hamptoninn.com, $99-149) offers attractive guest rooms, an outdoor heated pool, high-speed Internet access, a buffet breakfast, and a courtyard with koi ponds.

If you're coming to town for a peaceful retreat, the best choice may be **Vichy Springs Resort** (2605 Vichy Springs Rd., 707/462-9515, www.vichysprings.com, $135-390). The guest rooms, in a genteel and rustic old inn and nearby cottages, are small but comfortable, with private baths, warm bedspreads, and cool breezes, and many have views of the mountains or creek. Use of all the pools and hiking trails on the 700-acre grounds along with Internet access and a buffet breakfast are included in the rates.

Food

A local favorite, the **Maple Restaurant** (295 S. State St., 707/462-5221, daily 7am-2pm, $10) serves excellent and inexpensive breakfasts and lunches. Excellent service complements good uncomplicated American-style food. Shockingly good coffee is a final charming touch to this lovely find.

For a cool relaxing breather on a hot Ukiah day, stop in at one of the three locations of **Schat's Bakery Café** (113 W. Perkins St., 707/462-1670, Mon.-Fri. 5:30am-6pm, Sat. 5:30am-5pm, www.schats.com; 1255A Airport Park Blvd., 707/468-5850, Mon.-Fri. 7am-8pm, Sat. 7am-7pm, Sun. 8am-7pm; 1000 Hensley Creek Rd., 707/468-3145, Mon.-Thurs. 7am-8:15pm, Fri. 7am-3pm, $5-12). They'll make you a quick, filling sandwich on fresh-baked bread, and you can hang out as long as you want in the large, airy dining rooms.

Ellie's Mutt Hut & Vegetarian Café (732 S. State St., 707/468-5376, http://elliesmutthutukiahca.com, Mon.-Sat. 6:30am-8pm, $8-15) has great vegetarian entrées and an impressive hot dog list. It's one of the best places in California for a mixed group of conscientious vegans and couldn't-care-less carnivores to have a good time together; Ellie's is one of the things that make Ukiah Ukiah. The atmosphere is hamburger-stand casual, and the food is mostly healthy.

Of the dining options in Ukiah, one of the very best is **Patrona** (130 W. Standley St., 707/462-9181, www.patronarestaurant.com, Mon.-Sat. 11am-5pm and 5:30pm-9pm, Sun. 9am-5pm and 5:30pm-9pm, $13-29), where especially innovative California cuisine is served in a bistro-casual atmosphere by attentive servers. Portions are a good size but not enormous, and the kitchen's attention to detail is impressive. The wine list features all sorts of Mendocino County vintages, plus a good range of European wines. Most wines are available by the bottle only, but the servers will gladly cork an unfinished bottle so you can take it home to enjoy later.

Information and Services

If you need assistance with local lodging, dining, or wine-tasting, try the visitors center at the **Ukiah Valley Conference Center** (200 S. School St., 707/463-6700). Since Ukiah is the county seat, you can find information here about both the city of Ukiah and Mendocino County.

For local flavor, pick up a copy of the **Ukiah Daily Journal** (www.ukiahdailyjournal.com) for the best in up-to-date entertainment and events.

The **Ukiah Valley Medical Center** (275 Hospital Dr., 707/462-3111, www.uvmc.org) has a 24-hour emergency room as part of its full-service facility.

Ukiah has branches of many major banks. You can also find a **post office** (617 S. Orchard Ave., 707/462-3231, www.usps.com). Internet access is available, often for a fee, at many of the chain motels and, of course, at the various Starbucks and other cafés.

Getting There and Around

Ukiah is about 110 miles north of San Francisco (2 hours), a straight shot on U.S. 101. It's also about 60 miles north of Santa Rosa (1 hour) on U.S. 101. From Eureka (3 hours away), take U.S. 101 south for 157 miles. To get to Ukiah from Sacramento (under 3 hours), take I-5 north for 58 miles to exit 578 in Williams, and then get on Highway 20 west. After 79 miles, turn south on U.S. 101 to reach Ukiah in another 6.6 miles.

The **Mendocino Transit Authority** (800/696-4682, www.4mta.org) runs bus service throughout the county, with Ukiah as the hub; you can catch buses here and in Mendocino and Fort Bragg. Private pilots can land at **Ukiah Municipal Airport** (UKI, 1411 S. State St., 707/467-2817, www.cityofukiah.com).

The Redwood Coast

Of all the natural wonders California has to offer, the one that seems to inspire the purest and most unmitigated awe is the giant redwood. *Sequoia sempervirens,* also called coast redwood, grows along the California coast from around Big Sur in the south and into southern Oregon in the north. Coast redwoods hold the records for the tallest trees ever recorded, and are among the world's oldest and all-around most massive living things. The two best places to experience extensive wild groves of these gargantuan treasures are Humboldt Redwoods State Park, in Humboldt County, and Redwood National and State Parks, near

the north end of California around Eureka and Crescent City.

Most of the major park areas along the Redwood Coast can be accessed via U.S. 101 and U.S. 199. Follow the signs to the smaller roads that lead farther from civilization. To get to the redwood parks from the south, drive up U.S. 101 or the much slower but prettier Highway 1. The two roads merge at Leggett, north of Fort Bragg, and continue north as U.S. 101.

People camping in the parks usually pack in their own food and cook at their campsites. To restock, you can drive to Crescent City to find a market or to Eureka for a true supermarket.

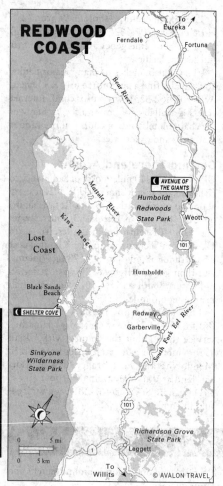

REDWOOD COAST

To Eureka

Ferndale

Fortuna

Bear River

Mattole River

King Range

AVENUE OF THE GIANTS

Humboldt Redwoods State Park

Weott

Lost Coast

101

Humboldt

Black Sands Beach

SHELTER COVE

Redway

Garberville

South Fork Eel River

Sinkyone Wilderness State Park

0   5 mi

0   5 km

101

Richardson Grove State Park

1   Leggett

To Willits

© AVALON TRAVEL

LEGGETT

As Highway 1 heads inland toward Leggett, the ocean views are replaced with redwoods. This part of the road is curvy, winding, and sun-dappled. It's a beautiful drive, so take it slow.

At the junction of Highway 1 and U.S. 101, you'll enter Leggett, famed for the local attraction **Chandelier Drive-Thru Tree** (67402 Drive-Thru Tree Rd., 707/925-6464, www. drivethrutree.com, daily dawn-dusk, $5). The

tree opening is about six feet wide and a little over six feet high. Kids will be thrilled. And, of course, there's a gift shop.

You might slow down as you approach **The Peg House** (69501 U.S. 101, 707/925-6444, http://thepeghouse.net) because of the fake police car situated by the highway. But there's another reason to ease off the gas at this general store and gas station. Believe it or not, The Peg House, which was built with pegs not nails, gets raves for its burgers, tri-tip, and deli sandwiches. Sometimes there is even live music.

GARBERVILLE AND REDWAY

Garberville is the first real town in Humboldt County. Located just three miles northwest is the slightly larger town of Redway, with just a few hundred more residents than Garberville. Known as the "Gateway to the Avenue of the Giants," the two towns can also be considered the gateway to the Lost Coast, since the biggest community along that remote coastline, Shelter Cove, is accessible via a winding 23-mile road from Redway. (Shelter Cove is also the southern terminus of the Lost Coast Trail.) Both towns are good places to get a meal or fill your tank with gas before heading west to the coast or north to the redwoods.

As U.S. 101 continues north, logging trucks hauling massive slabs of lumber become more prevalent, and the roadsides are punctuated with dreadlocked hitchhikers trying to bum a ride.

Richardson Grove State Park

Even if your main destination is a redwood park farther north, save time for a stop at **Richardson Grove State Park** (1600 U.S. 101, 707/247-3318, www.parks.ca.gov, $8), the first of the old-growth redwoods along U.S. 101. This park has special features all its own, like a tree you can walk through and the ninth-tallest coast redwood. The Eel River flows through the park, offering good fishing as well as camping, swimming, and hiking. The visitors center (May-Sept.) in the 1930s Richardson Grove Lodge has cool exhibits and a nature store. Richardson Grove State Park is seven miles south of Garberville.

Mateel Community Center

Located in Redway, the **Mateel Community Center** (59 Rusk Ln., Redway, 707/923-3368, www.mateel.org) brings music, theater, dance, comedy, film, and craft events to southern Humboldt. They also put on local annual events, including Reggae on the River, the Humboldt Hills Hoedown, and the Halloween Boogie. Check the website for a full list of upcoming events.

Accommodations

The place to stay is the **(Benbow Inn** (445 Lake Benbow Dr., 707/923-2124 or 800/355-3301, www.benbowinn.com, $99-575). A swank resort backing onto Lake Benbow, this inn has it all: a gourmet restaurant, a nine-hole golf course, an outdoor swimming pool, and a woodsy atmosphere that blends perfectly with the ancient redwood forest surrounding it. Guest rooms glow with dark polished woods and jewel-toned carpets. Wide king and comfy queen beds beckon guests tired after a long day of hiking in the redwoods or golfing beside the inn.

Several small motels offer reasonable guest rooms, and many have outdoor pools where weary guests can cool off during the heat of summer. The best of these is the **Best Western Humboldt House Inn** (701 Redwood Dr., 707/923-2771, www.bestwestern.com, $140-200). Guest rooms are clean and comfortable, the pool is sparkling and cool, the breakfast is hot, and the location is convenient to restaurants and shops in Garberville. Expect the usual comforts of the Best Western chain. Most guest rooms have two queen beds, great for families and pairs of couples traveling together on a budget.

Camping

Richardson Grove State Park (1600 U.S. 101, 800/444-7275, www.parks.ca.gov, camping $35) has 169 campsites in three campground areas surrounded by redwoods and the Elk River.

You can park your RV year-round at the 112 sites of the posh **Benbow RV Park** (7000 Benbow Dr., 707/923-2777 or 866/236-2697, www.benbowrv.com, $52-60). Premium sites come with complimentary tea and scones at the nearby Benbow Inn.

Food

The restaurant at the **(Benbow Inn** (445 Lake Benbow Dr., 707/923-2124 or 800/355-3301, www.benbowinn.com, daily breakfast, lunch, and dinner, $19-45) matches the lodgings for superiority in the area. It serves upscale California cuisine, with a vegan menu available on request, and features an extensive wine list with many regional wineries represented. The white-tablecloth dining room is exquisite, and the expansive outdoor patio overlooking the water is the perfect place to sit as the temperature cools on a summer evening.

Garberville has several modest eateries that appeal to weary travelers and families with kids. One of these is the **Woodrose Café** (911 Redwood Dr., 707/923-3191, www.woodrosecafe.com, Mon.-Fri. 8am-2pm, Sat.-Sun. 8am-1pm, $9-14). You can get a traditional American-style breakfast and lunch at this small independent eatery, and a lot of the food is organic, local, and healthy, but it doesn't come cheap.

Another good breakfast and lunch stop is the **Eel River Café** (801 Redwood Dr., 707/923-3783, Tues.-Sat. 6am-2pm, $6-12), a diner all the way with black and white checkerboard floors and a long counter with red stools. Try the chicken fried steak with biscuits and gravy.

Need a pick-me-up? You won't find too many Starbucks around here, so enjoy a taste of local Humboldt-roasted coffee instead in Redway. The **Signature Coffee** (3455 Redwood Dr., Redway, 707/923-2661, www.signaturecoffeecompany.com, Mon.-Fri. 7am-5pm) takes pride in its organic product and sustainable practices, and they sell bagged coffee too, so you can stock up for use at the campsite.

There's a supermarket in Garberville, **Ray's Food Place** (875 Redwood Dr., 707/923-2279, www.gorays.com, daily 7am-10pm).

Information and Services

The **Garberville Redway Area Chamber of Commerce** (782 Redwood Dr., 800/923-2613, www.garberville.org, Labor Day-Memorial Day Mon.-Fri. 9am-4pm, Memorial Day-Labor Day Mon.-Fri. 9am-4pm, Sat.-Sun. 10am-4pm) is happy to help visitors get acquainted with the area. There is a convenient **post office** (3400 Redwood Dr., Redway, 707/923-3784, www.usps.com, Mon.-Fri. 8:45am-4:45pm) in nearby Redway. The nearest hospital with an emergency room is **Redwood Memorial Hospital** (3300 Renner Dr., Fortuna, 707/725-3361, www.redwoodmemorial.org).

Getting There and Around

Garberville is located 65 miles south of Eureka and 200 miles north of San Francisco on U.S. 101. From Garberville, take Redwood Drive just three miles to Redway. The best way to get to Humboldt Redwoods State Park from either direction is via U.S. 101. You can also approach the center of the park from Mattole Road from the Lost Coast (Shelter Cove to Mattole). Road signs point to the Avenue of the Giants. Bicycles are not permitted on U.S. 101, but you can ride the Avenue of the Giants and Mattole Road.

The little towns of the Humboldt redwoods region can be short on necessary services such as gas stations. There is a **76 Gas Station** (790 Redwood Dr.) well off the highway.

The **Redwood County Transit** (707/464-6400, www.redwoodtransit.org) bus system offers limited service to Garberville from the north.

HUMBOLDT REDWOODS STATE PARK

Surprisingly, the largest stand of unlogged redwood trees isn't on the coast, and it isn't in the Sierras; it's here in Humboldt, bisected by U.S. 101. Come to this park to hike beneath 300-foot-plus old-growth trees that began their lives centuries before Europeans knew California existed. One highlight of the park is the 10,000-acre Rockefeller Forest, the largest contiguous old growth redwood

forest in the world. Start your visit at the **Humboldt Redwoods State Park Visitors Center** (707/946-2263, www.parks.ca.gov or www.humboldtredwoods.org, Apr.-Oct. daily 9am-5pm, Nov.-Mar. daily 10am-4pm), located along the Avenue of the Giants (Hwy. 254), between the towns of Weott and Myers Flat. It's a nice visitors center, with plenty of information for anyone new to the region or looking for hiking or camping information. You can also enjoy the theater, interpretive museum and gift shop. There is no entrance fee for Humboldt Redwoods State Park and no fee to use the visitors center; the only day-use fee in the park is for the Williams Grove Day Use Area ($8 per vehicle).

While it's more than worth your while to spend a weekend or more in the Humboldt redwoods, you can also enjoy yourself for a few hours just passing through. A drive along the Avenue of the Giants with a stop at the visitors center and a quick nature walk or picnic can give you a quick taste of the lovely southern end of the coastal redwoods region.

◖ Avenue of the Giants

The most famous stretch of redwood trees is the **Avenue of the Giants** (www.avenueofthegiants.net), paralleling U.S. 101 and the Eel River for about 33 miles between Garberville and Fortuna; look for signs on U.S. 101. Visitors come from all over the world to drive this stretch of road and gaze in wonder at the sky-high old-growth redwoods along the way. Campgrounds and hiking trails sprout among the trees off the road. Park your car at various points along the way and get out to walk among the giants. Or walk down to the nearby Eel River for a cool dip.

The Avenue's highest traffic volume is in July-August, when you can expect bumper-to-bumper stop-and-go traffic along the entire road. That's not necessarily a bad thing, as going slow is the best way to see the sights. But if crowds aren't your thing, you might try visiting in spring or fall, or even braving the rains of winter to gain a more secluded redwood experience.

© STUART THORNTON

a drive down the Avenue of the Giants

To enhance your Avenue of the Giants drive, there's an eight-stop audio tour along the route. Pick up an audio tour card at the visitors center or on either side of the drive.

Hiking and Biking

Stop at the Humboldt Redwoods State Park Visitors Center (707/946-2263, www.parks. ca.gov or www.humboldtredwoods.org, Apr.-Oct. daily 9am-5pm, Nov.-Mar. daily 10am-4pm) to pick up a trail map showing the number of hikes accessible on or near this road. Many are very short, so you can make a nice day of combined driving and walking without having to commit to one big trek.

Many visitors start with the **Founder's Grove Nature Loop Trail** (0.6 miles, easy), at mile marker 20.5 on the Avenue of the Giants. This sedate, flat nature trail gives walkers a taste of the big old-growth trees in the park. Sadly, the onetime tallest tree in the world, the Dyerville Giant, fell in 1991 at the age of about 1,600. But it's still doing its part in this astounding ecosystem, decomposing before your eyes on the forest floor and feeding new life in the forest.

Right at the visitors center, you can enjoy the **Gould Grove Nature Trail** (0.6 miles, easy)—a wheelchair-accessible interpretive nature walk with helpful signs describing the denizens of the forest.

If you're looking for a longer walk in the woods, try the lovely **River Trail** (Mattole Rd., 1.1 miles west of Ave. of the Giants, 7 miles round-trip, moderate). It follows the South Fork Eel River, allowing access to yet another ecosystem. Check with the visitors center to be sure that the summer bridges have been installed before trying to hike this trail.

Hard-core hikers who like to go at it all day can get their exercise at Humboldt Redwoods State Park. Start at the **Grasshopper Multiuse Trailhead** (Mattole Rd., 5.1 miles west of Ave. of the Giants) to access the newer **Johnson Camp Trail** (10.5 miles round-trip, difficult) that takes you to the abandoned cabins of railroad tie makers. Or pick another fork from the same trailhead to climb more than 3,000 feet to **Grasshopper Peak** (13.5 miles, difficult). From the peak, you can see 100 miles in any direction, overlooking the whole of the park and beyond.

You can bring your street bike to the park and ride the Avenue of the Giants or Mattole Road. A number of the trails around Humboldt Redwoods State Park are designated multiuse, which means that mountain bikers can make the rigorous climbs and then rip their way back down.

Swimming and Kayaking

The **Eel River**'s forks meander through the Humboldt redwoods, creating lots of great opportunities for cooling off on hot summer days. Check with the park's visitors center for this year's best swimming holes, but you can reliably find good spots at **Eagle Point,** near Hidden Valley Campground; **Gould Bar;** and **Garden Club of America Grove.** In addition to the usual precautions for river swimming, during August-September a poisonous (if ingested) blue-green algae can bloom late in the summer, making swimming in certain parts of the river hazardous.

Events

Humboldt Redwoods State Park is the site of a couple of the best marathons and half-marathons around. It offers flat courses, cool weather, and world-class scenery. If you're looking for an unintimidating place to try your first marathon, or if you need a fast time for a personal record or to qualify for Boston, this is an ideal choice. These events are also less crowded than the famous marathons, and you can camp right in the park where they begin. October has the **Humboldt Redwoods Marathon** (www.redwoodsmarathon.org, $55-65) with a related half-marathon ($50-60) and a 5K ($25). The **Avenue of the Giants Marathon** (www.theave.org, marathon $60, half-marathon $50, 10K $30) is held each May.

Camping

There are few lodging options close to the park. Fortunately, the camping at Humboldt

Redwoods State Park (707/946-2263, www.reserveamerica.com, $35) is good, with three developed car-accessible campgrounds; there are also primitive backcountry campsites ($5). Each developed campground has its own entrance station, and reservations are strongly recommended, as the park is quite popular with weekend campers.

Burlington Campground (707/946-1811, year-round) is adjacent to the visitors center and is a convenient starting point for the marathons and other races that traverse the park in May and October. It's dark and comfortable, engulfed in trees, and has ample restroom facilities and hot showers. **Albee Creek** (Mattole Rd., 5 miles west of Ave. of the Giants, 707/946-2472, mid-May-mid-Oct.) offers some redwood-shaded sites and others in open meadows, which can be nice in the summer if you want to get a little sun. **◖ Hidden Springs Campground** (Ave. of the Giants, 5 miles south of the visitors center, 707/943-3177, early May-Labor Day) is large and popular. Nearby a trail leads to a great Eel River swimming hole. Minimalist campers will enjoy the seclusion of hike-in trail camps at **Johnson** and **Grasshopper Peak.**

Equestrians can also make use of the multiuse trails, and the **Cuneo Creek Horse Camp** (old homestead on Mattole Rd., 8 miles west of Ave. of the Giants, May-mid-Oct., 1 vehicle and 2 horses $35) provides a place for riders who want to spend more than just a day exploring the thousands of acres of forest and meadowland.

Information and Services

Get the best information at the **Humboldt Redwoods State Park Visitors Center** (707/946-2263, www.parks.ca.gov or www.humboldtredwoods.org, Apr.-Oct. daily 9am-5pm, Nov.-Mar. daily 10am-4pm). You can fill your car up in the nearby towns of Piercy, Garberville, Redway, Redcrest, Miranda, and Rio Dell. Markets to stock up on supplies are in Garberville, Redway, Miranda, Phillipsville, Redcrest, Myers Flat, Scotia, and Rio Dell. The nearest hospital with an emergency room is **Redwood Memorial Hospital** (3300 Renner Dr., Fortuna, 707/725-3361, www.redwood-memorial.org).

Getting There
Humboldt Redwoods State Park is 21 miles north of Garberville on U.S. 101. The Avenue of the Giants parallels U.S. 101 and there are several marked exits along the highway to reach the scenic redwood drive.

FERNDALE
Ferndale was built in the 19th century by Scandinavian immigrants who came to California to farm. Little has changed since the immigrants constructed their fanciful ginger-bread Victorian homes and shops. Many cows still munch grass in the dairy pastures that surround the town today.

The main sight in Ferndale is the town itself, which has been designated a historical landmark. Ferndale is all Victorian, all the time: Ask about the building you're in and you'll be told all about its specific architectural style, its construction date, and its original occupants. Main Street's shops, galleries, inns, and restaurants are all set into scrupulously maintained and restored late-19th-century buildings, and even the public restrooms are housed in a small Victorianesque structure.

Architecture buffs can spend hours just strolling around downtown. So it's no surprise that Hollywood has discovered Ferndale as a picturesque setting for a movie: it has starred alongside Jim Carrey in *The Majestic* and Dustin Hoffman in *Outbreak*.

Sights
The **Ferndale History Museum** (515 Shaw St., 707/786-4466, www.ferndale-museum.org, June-Sept. Tues.-Sat. 11am-4pm, Sun. 1pm-4pm, Oct.-Dec. and Feb.-May Wed.-Sat. 11am-4pm, Sun. 1pm-4pm, $1) is a block off Main Street and tells the story of the town. Life-size dioramas depict period life in a Victorian home, and an array of antique artifacts brings history to life. Downstairs, the implements of rural coast history vividly display the reality that farmers and artisans faced in the preindustrial era.

To cruise farther back into the town's history, consider wandering out into the **Ferndale Cemetery** on Bluff Street. Well-tended tombstones and mausoleums wend up the hillside behind the town. Genealogists will love reading the scrupulously maintained epitaphs that tell the human history of the region.

Beaches
Ferndale locals love that they have their own beach just five miles outside of their quaint village. The **Centerville County Park and Beach** (five miles west of Ferndale on Centerville Rd., 707/445-7651, http://co.humboldt.ca.us, daily 5am-midnight, free) stretches for an impressive nine miles and is home to a winter congregation of tundra swans. You are able to drive your four-wheel drive on the sand, ride a horse, or build a big beach bonfire at night here, which is unusual for beaches in California.

Entertainment and Events
Ferndale is a quiet town where the sidewalks roll up early. But for visitors who like to be out and about after 6pm, there are a few decent options. The **Ferndale Repertory Theater** (447 Main St., 707/786-5483 or 800/838-3006, www.ferndale-rep.org, $13-18), the oldest and largest of the North Coast's community theaters, puts on a number of shows each year. Some are wholesome and suitable for the whole family like *Annie*, while others, including *In the Next Room (Or the Vibrator Play)*, feature more adult subject matter. Be sure to check what's on when you're in town. Also check the schedule for special events and performances.

If you want to get a beer or mixed drink in Ferndale, **The Palace** (353 Main St., 707/786-4165, daily 10am-2am) is the local bar with pool tables, shuffleboard, and a jukebox. Late into the night, you can fill the slots at the **Bear River Casino** (11 Bear Paws Way, Loleta, 707/733-9644, www.bearrivercasino.com, daily open 24 hours) in nearby Loleta.

Ferndale has hosted the **Humboldt County Fair** (1250 5th St., www.humboldtcountyfair.

org, adults $8, seniors and students under $8) each August since 1896. For 10 days people from all around the county come to celebrate at the old-fashioned fair, complete with livestock exhibits and horse racing, competitions, a carnival, musical entertainment each night, and a variety of shows for kids and adults on the fairground stages. If you're in the area, come join the fun.

The **Kinetic Sculpture Museum** (580 Main St., 707/733-3841, usually daily 10am-5pm) salutes wacky modernity in all its colorful, weird glory. As the end point of the annual Kinetic Grand Championship sculpture race (www.kineticgrandchampionship.com), Ferndale has the honor of housing a number of these sculptures. The museum is a repository of more than 40 years' worth of artifacts from the great race; docents do not interpret the art, so visitors are free to make what they will of the duckies, froggies, airplanes, and bicycles.

Shopping

A tour of Ferndale's Main Street shops makes for an idyllic morning stroll. The Victorian storefronts house antiques stores, jewelry shops, clothing boutiques, and art galleries. Ferndale is also a surprisingly good place to buy a hat.

The **Golden Gait Mercantile** (421 Main St., 707/786-4891, Mon.-Sat. 10am-5pm) has it all: antiques, candies, gourmet foodstuffs, clothing, hats, souvenirs, and more. Antiques and collectibles tend to be small and reasonably priced. By comparison, **Silva's Fine Jewelry** (400 Ocean Ave., 707/786-4425, www.silvasjewelry.com, daily 8:30am-9pm), on the bottom floor of the Victorian Inn, is not a place for the faint of wallet. But the jewels, both contemporary and antique, are classically gorgeous. Another jewel is the **Blacksmith Shop** (455 Main St., 707/786-4216, www.ferndaleblacksmith.com, daily 9:30am-5:30pm) which displays a striking collection of useful art made by top blacksmiths and glassblowers from around the country. The array of jewelry, furniture, kitchen implements, fireplace tools, and metal things defies description. A gentler warmth comes from the **Golden Bee Candleworks** (451 Main St., 707/786-4508, Wed.-Sat. 10am-5pm, Sun. 11am-4pm),

purveyor of fine products made with honey and beeswax. The candles, soaps, and much more make the whole store smell delicious.

Accommodations

In Ferndale, lodgings tend to be, of course, Victorian-style inns, mostly bed-and-breakfasts. Guests of the **Shaw House Inn** (703 Main St., 707/786-9958 or 800/557-7429, www.shawhouse.com, $125-275) must walk a block or two to get to the heart of downtown Ferndale, but the reward for staying outside the town center is a spacious garden worth a stroll. In the heat of the afternoon, huge shade trees and perfectly positioned garden benches make a lovely spot to sit and read a book, hold a quiet conversation, or just enjoy the serene beauty of garden and town. The interior of the Shaw House has eight guest rooms and three common parlor areas. A lush morning breakfast fortifies shoppers ready to walk up and down Main Street and adventurers preparing to head to the deserted beaches of the Lost Coast or the trails in the nearby redwood forests.

The ◖ **Victorian Inn** (400 Ocean Ave., 707/786-4949 or 888/589-1808, www.victorianvillageinn.com, $115-259) is an imposing structure at the corner of Ocean Avenue and Main Street that also houses Silva's Jewelry. The inn comprises 13 guest rooms, all decorated with antique furnishings, luxurious linens, and pretty knickknacks. For a special treat, rent the Ira Russ Suite, a spacious room with a tower alcove that takes in the town below. In the mornings, a full hot breakfast is served to guests in the downstairs of this historic hotel.

Nothing in Ferndale is far from anything else in Ferndale, and **Hotel Ivanhoe** (315 Main St., 707/786-9000, www.ivanhoe-hotel.com, $95-145) is kitty-corner across from the Victorian Inn. In a town full of history, the Ivanhoe is the oldest extant hostelry. Plaques on the building's exterior describe its rich legacy. Fully refurbished in the 1990s, the four guest rooms are done in rich colors that revive the Western Victorian atmosphere of the original hotel.

If bric-a-brac and scented soaps make your skin itch, an inexpensive not-an-inn lodging

© STUART THORNTON

Ferndale's Victorian Inn

option in Ferndale is the **Redwood Suites** (332 Ocean Ave., 707/786-5000 or 888/589-1863, www.redwoodsuites.com, $95-145). Only a block off Main Street, the property has modern guest rooms that are simple but comfortable. Family suites with full kitchens are available, and the room rates are reasonable.

Food

Tucked into the bottom floor of the Victorian Inn, the **VI Restaurant & Tavern** (400 Ocean Ave., 707/786-4950, http://virestaurant. com, daily 11:30am-9pm, $10-36) feels like a spruced-up Western saloon. Perch yourself at the bar for casual options like fish and chips or sit down at a table for sophisticated dinner entrées like Portuguese paella or antelope short ribs.

Locals come from as far away as Eureka to dine at the restaurant at the **Hotel Ivanhoe** (315 Main St., 707/786-9000, www.ivan-hoe-hotel.com, Wed.-Sun. 5pm-9pm, Wed.-Sun. bar from 4pm, $12-23). It's all about the hearty homemade Italian dishes and friendly personal service. A more casual Italian dining

experience can be had down the street at the **Ferndale Pizza Co.** (607 Main St., 707/786-4345, Tues.-Thurs. 11:30am-9pm, Fri.-Sat. 11:30am-9:30pm, Sun. noon-9pm, $16-21).

If your accommodations don't include breakfast, stop in at the local favorite **Poppa Joe's** (409 Main St., 707/786-4180, Mon.-Fri. 6am-2pm, Sat.-Sun. 6am-noon, $5.50-9). The interior is dim and narrow, but the breakfast and lunch offerings are delicious.

If you need to grab some grub to go, **Valley Grocery** (339 Main St., 707/786-9515, daily 7am-10pm) stocks staples and also maintains a deli; it's a perfect last stop on the way out to a beach picnic. Don't forget to stop at the heavenly candy store **Sweetness and Light** (554 Main St., 707/786-4403 or 800/547-8180, www.sweetnessandlight.com, Mon.-Sat. 10am-5pm, Sun. 11am-4pm).

Information and Services

The *Ferndale Enterprise* (707/786-4611, www.ferndaleenterprise.us, $1) is published once a week on Thursday. The paper also puts out a free souvenir edition once a year just for visitors. Many inns and shops carry the souvenir edition all year long.

If you need medical care, the **Humboldt Medical Group** (528 Washington St., 707/786-4028, www.humboldtmedicalgroup.com) can assist you. Ferndale has a **post office** (536 Main St., 707/786-4642, www.usps.com, Mon.-Fri. 8:30am-5pm, Sat. 10am-noon).

Getting There and Around

Ferndale, like much of the nearby Lost Coast, is not directly accessible from U.S. 101; from U.S. 101 at Fernbridge, follow Highway 211 to Ferndale. Mattole Road leads out of town south toward the Sinkyone Wilderness area, while Centerville Road heads out to the beach. Walking provides the best views and feel of the town.

The Lost Coast

The Lost Coast is one of California's true last undeveloped coastlines. Encompassing northern Mendocino County and southern Humboldt County, this coast is "lost" because the rugged terrain makes it impractical—some might say impossible—to build a highway here. An arduous trek along its wilderness trails is worthwhile to soak up the raw beauty of its rugged beaches.

The King Range National Conservation Area encompasses the northern section of the Lost Coast. Here, King's Peak rises over 4,000 feet from the sea in less than three miles. It's also home to the most popular version of the Lost Coast Trail: a 24-mile backpacking excursion along the region's wild beaches that begins at the mouth of the Mattole River and ends at Shelter Cove's Black Sand Beach.

The Sinkyone Wilderness State Park makes up the southern section of the Lost Coast, which has its own Lost Coast Trail, heading slightly inland on its journey from Bear Harbor to Usal Beach. While the more popular King Range Lost Coast Trail traverses beaches right by the ocean, the 16-mile Sinkyone version is mostly along bluffs with less coastal access.

Situated between the two major sections of the King Range Conservation Area and the Sinkyone Wilderness State Park is the small fishing community of Shelter Cove, which has a few restaurant and lodging options. It's also home to Black Sand Beach and the Cape Mendocino Lighthouse. The few other areas of the Lost Coast accessible by car include Usal Beach and Mattole Beach.

Reaching the Lost Coast involves short detours from U.S. 101. Shelter Cove can be reached by taking Briceland/Shelter Cove Road out of Redway, while Usal Beach is accessible from a dirt road that leaves Highway 1 three miles north of the town of Rockport. The Mattole Recreation Site is found by taking Lighthouse Road off Mattole Road.

MATTOLE ROAD

Mattole Road, a narrow, mostly paved two-lane road, affords views of remote ranchland, unspoiled forests, and a few short miles of barely accessible cliffs and beaches. It's one of the few paved drivable routes that allows you to view the Lost Coast from your car (the other is Shelter Cove Road, farther south). In sunny weather, the vistas are spectacular. This road also serves as access to the even smaller tracks out to the trails and campgrounds of the Sinkyone Wilderness. The most common way to get to Mattole Road is from the Victorian village of Ferndale, where you take a right on Ocean Avenue and follow the signs towards the community of Petrolia.

MATTOLE BEACH

At the northern end of the Lost Coast, **Mattole Beach** (end of Lighthouse Rd., 707/825-2300, www.publiclands.org) is a broad length of sand that's perfect for an easy contemplative stroll. It's also popular for picnicking and fishing. Mattole Beach is also the northern entry point to the Lost Coast Trail, and the start of

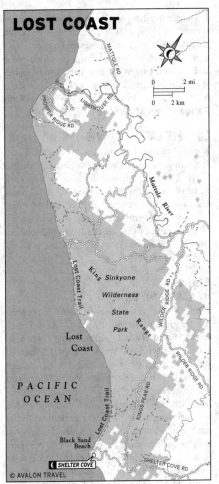

LOST COAST

THE LOST COAST TRAIL

To fully experience one of the country's most remote and rugged coastal areas, backpackers head out on the **Lost Coast Trail.** This 24-mile beach hike stretches from the Mattole River down to Shelter Cove's Black Sand Beach. This is a once-in-a-lifetime experience, hiking alongside primal, mostly wild coastline, interrupted only by the abandoned Punta Gorda Lighthouse and numerous shipwrecks along shore. Waterfalls feather the coastal bluffs, shorebirds fly above the crashing surf, sea lions congregate at the aptly named Sea Lion Gulch, and migrating whales surface along the horizon. On land, you might encounter deer and bears.

This is a strenuous hike, challenging even for experienced hikers. It demands both preparation and stamina. While scenic, the ocean along the trail is also cold, rough, and unforgiving. Use caution, as multiple people have been swept out to sea.

Planning Your Hike

You can hike the trail anytime between spring and fall. Spring is notable for blooming wildflowers. Summer is the most crowded. Fall is the least crowded, and often has the most pleasant weather. During winter, the trail can be impassable due to massive surf or flooding streams.

Allow three days and two nights to complete the trail, hiking around eight miles a day. Be prepared to walk on sand, cobblestones, and boulders. Plan on carrying in everything you'll need (tents, sleeping bags, equipment, food, and water). Carry it all (including any trash) back out to keep the area wild. There are creeks every 1.5-2 miles along the trail, but you need to purify the water before drinking it.

Most people begin the hike at the Mattole River and head south. This is so you are hiking with the winds at your back, rather than in your face. You'll need to park a vehicle at either end of the trail. Parking at the Mattole trailhead is free. There have been vehicle break-ins, so don't leave any valuables in your car. Parking at Black Sand Beach, the southern end of the

a shorter, six-mile round-trip day hike to the **Punta Gorda Lighthouse.** The lighthouse was built in 1911 after the coast and its rocks caused multiple shipwrecks. It was shut down in 1951 due to high maintenance costs.

To reach Mattole Beach from U.S. 101, take the Garberville, Honeydew, or Ferndale exits. Follow the signs to Petrolia on Mattole Road. Turn off Mattole Road onto Lighthouse Road, which is south of the Mattole River Bridge. Follow Lighthouse Road for five miles to the beach.

trail, is also free. The drive between the two trailheads is an hour and 45 minutes. To avoid a half-day of driving between the trailheads, contact **Lost Coast Shuttle** (707/986-7437, www.lostcoastshuttle.com, $200/two people, $25/each additional person), which will drive you from Shelter Cove's Black Sand Beach, where you can leave your car, to the start of the trailhead at Mattole Beach.

In addition to securing transportation, hikers also need a backcountry permit, but these are free as long as you're not an organized group or a commercial enterprise. They also double as fire permits. You can get a permit at a self-service box at one of the trailheads, at the **King Range office** in Whitethorn, or at the **field office** in Arcata (707/986-5400, www.ca.blm.gov/arcata/kingrange).

Bear canisters are mandatory for storing your food and scented items while on the trail so that your camp doesn't attract bears. You can rent bear canisters ($5) just a few miles from the Mattole Trailhead at the **Petrolia General Store** (40 Sherman Rd., Petrolia, 707/629-3455). They're also available in Shelter Cove at **BLM Whitethorn Office** (768 Shelter Cove Rd., 707/986-5400, $5) or in Arcata at the **BLM Arcata Field Office** (1695 Heindon Rd., 707/825-2300, $5).

This is a wilderness hike so there are few signs. You'll mostly just be hiking the beach except for a few spots. Two sections of the trail are impassable at high tides. The first is from Sea Lion Gulch to Randall Creek. The second is from south of Big Flat down to Gitchell Creek. So it's critical to consult a tide chart and manage your time to make sure you pass through these areas of the trail during low tide.

There are no developed campgrounds or facilities along the trail, but dispersed camping is allowed at **Cooksie Creek, Randall Creek, Big Creek, Big Flat Creek, Buck Creek, Shipman Creek** and **Gitchell Creek.**

Dogs are allowed on the trail as long as they are under voice control or on a leash. Dogs should be outfitted with booties so that their paws don't get scraped up by the rocks on the trail.

Before heading to the area, try to get your hands on a copy of Wilderness Press' **Lost Coast Map** (www.wildernesspress.com). You can check on trail conditions by visiting the **U.S. Department of the Interior** website: www.blm.gov/ca (search on "Lost Coast Trail"). More information is also available at the **King Range Information Line** (707/825-2300).

◖ SHELTER COVE

If you're not up for hiking a 24-mile trail, you can still get a taste of the Lost Coast in Shelter Cove, a fishing community with a scattering of restaurants and accommodations. A nine-hole golf course, a small airport, and 40 miles of paved roads and lots are remnants of a large planned community that failed to materialize. But the real highlight of Shelter Cove is its access to the shoreline.

Sights
BLACK SAND BEACH

One of the most beautiful and accessible features of the Lost Coast, the 3.5 mile **Black Sand Beach** (King Range National Conservation Area, www.blm.gov) is named for its unusually dark sand and stones, which contrast with the deep blue ocean water and the towering King Range Mountains in the background. The main beach parking lot has interpretive panels about the region as well as bathrooms and a drinking fountain. It's just north of the town of Shelter Cove; to get there follow Shelter Cove Road, then take a right onto Beach Road, which dead-ends at Black Sand Beach. The long walk across the dark sands to either Horse Creek or Gitchell Creek is relatively easy. This beach also serves as the south end of the Lost Coast Trail.

CAPE MENDOCINO LIGHTHOUSE

At Mal Coombs Park in Shelter Cove, the 43-foot tower of the **Cape Mendocino Lighthouse** (www.lighthousefriends.com, tours Memorial Day-Labor Day daily 10:30am-3:30pm) is quiet and dark. It began life on Cape Mendocino—a 400-foot cliff that marks the westernmost point of California—in 1868. In 1951 the tower was abandoned in favor of a light on a pole, and in 1999 the tower was moved to Shelter Cove, becoming a museum in 2000. When docents are available, you can take a tour of the lighthouse. The original first-order Fresnel lens is now on display in nearby Ferndale.

Sports and Recreation

HIKING

For another great hike, take the **King Crest Trail,** a mountain hike from the southern Saddle Mountain Trailhead to stunning King Peak and on to the North Slide Peak Trailhead. A good solid 10-mile one-day round-trip can be done from either trailhead. To reach Saddle Mountain Trailhead from Shelter Cove, drive up Shelter Cove Road and turn left onto King Peak Road. Bear left on Saddle Mountain Road and turn left on a spur road to the trailhead. Note that only high clearance, four-wheel drive vehicles are recommended.

Also accessible from the Saddle Mountain Trailhead, **Buck Creek Trail** includes an infamous grade, descending more than 3,000 vertical feet on an old logging road to the beach.

An arduous but gorgeous loop trail, the eight-mile **Hidden Valley-Chinquapin-Lost Coast Loop Trail** can be done in one day, or in two days with a stop at water-accessible Nick's Camp. Access it by driving out of Shelter Cove and turning right onto Chemise Mountain Road. The trailhead will be less than a mile on your right.

The many other trails in the Kings Range National Conservation Area near Shelter Cove include **Rattlesnake Ridge, Kinsey Ridge, Spanish Ridge,** and **Lightning.** Before heading to the area, try to get your hands on a copy of Wilderness Press' Lost Coast Map (www.wildernesspress.com).

FISHING

The Lost Coast is a natural fishing haven. The harbor at Shelter Cove offers charter services for ocean fishing. Kevin Riley of **Outcast Sportfishing** (Shelter Cove, 707/986-9842, www.outcastsportfish.com, Apr.-Sept., $225 pp per day) can help plan a charter fishing trip

chasing whatever is in season. The cost includes gear, tackle, and filleting and packaging your fish at the end of the day, but bring your own lunch. Another reputable charter service is **Shelter Cove Sport Fishing** (707/923-1668, www.codking.com, fishing trips $150-225 pp), offering excursions to hunt halibut, albacore, salmon, or rockfish.

If shellfish is your favorite, come to the Shelter Cove area to enjoy the Northern California abalone season. Ask locally for this year's best diving spots, and be sure to obtain a license: The state Department of Fish and Game (888/773-8450, www.dfg.ca.gov) can explain the rules about taking abalone, which is strictly regulated.

SURFING

Big Flat is a legendary surf spot about eight miles north of Shelter Cove on the Lost Coast Trail. While the hike in is challenging, hardcore surfers will find it worth the effort. Local surfers are very protective of this break: Even a writer for *National Geographic Adventure* who wrote about the break, refused to name it for fear of retaliation. He referred to it as "Ghost Point." Be careful. Big Flat is in the middle of nowhere, and a surfer with a broken ankle in 2008 had to be airlifted out of the area.

Accommodations

Shelter Cove offers several nice motels for those who aren't up for roughing it in the wilderness overnight. At the **Shelter Cove Beachcomber Inn** (412 Machi Rd., 707/986-7551, $75-115), each guest room has its own character along with views of the coast or the woods. It's an easy stroll to the airstrip and harbor.

The **Tides Inn of Shelter Cove** (59 Surf Point, 707/986-7900 or 888/998-4337, www.sheltercovetidesinn.com, $165-215) has standard guest rooms as well as luxurious suites. The suites come with fireplaces and full kitchens. All of the guest rooms face the sea, only steps from the inn. The Tides Inn is centrally located within walking distance of the airstrip, local shops, and restaurants.

NORTH COAST

The **Inn of the Lost Coast** (205 Wave Dr., 707/986-7521 or 888/570-9676, www.in-nofthelostcoast.com, $150-250) has an array of large, airy guest rooms and suites with stellar views to suit even luxurious tastes. Ask about discounts for AOPA pilots and AARP members, as well as the AAA discount.

The **Cliff House at Shelter Cove** (141 Wave Dr., 707/986-7344, www.cliffhouseshelter-cove.com, $160-180) is perched atop the bluffs overlooking the black-sand beaches. Only two suites are available; they're perfect for a romantic vacation or family getaway. Each has a full kitchen, living room, bedroom, gas fireplace, and satellite TV.

Camping

For many, staying on the Lost Coast near Shelter Cove means camping in the wilderness near the trails. If you're planning to camp in the backcountry, you need a permit. Permits are free and can be obtained from self-service boxes at the trailheads, or by visiting the local office of the **Bureau of Land Management** (BLM, 768 Shelter Cove Rd., Whitethorn, 707/986-5400, www.ca.blm.gov). Bear canisters are mandatory; if you don't have one, you can rent one ($5) with a major credit card at the **Petrolia General Store** (40 Sherman Rd., Petrolia, 707/629-3455).

If you prefer a developed campground in the area around Shelter Cove with amenities like restrooms, grills, fire rings, picnic tables, bear boxes, and potable water, there are a number of sites in the King Range National Conservation Area (no permit required). Campgrounds are open year-round. Reservations are not available but the odds of getting a site are pretty good, given the small number of people who come here, even in high season. Some of the larger BLM camping areas (707/986-5400, www.ca.blm.gov) in the King Range are **Wailaki** (Chemise Mountain Rd., 13 sites, $8), **Nadelos** (Chemise Mountain Rd., tents only, 8 sites, $8), **Tolkan** (King Peak Rd., 5 RV sites, 4 tent sites, $8), and **Horse Mountain** (King Peak Rd., 9 sites, no water, $5). Trailers and RVs (up to 24 feet) are allowed at most sites except Nadelos.

If you are driving an RV, it's wise to check road conditions beforehand.

For more developed camping in Shelter Cove, the nearby **Shelter Cove RV Campground** (492 Machi Rd., Whitethorn, 707/986-7474, RVs $46, tents $36) is just feet away from the airport and has views of the ocean. They have a deli and store (summer daily 8am-6pm, winter daily 9am-5pm, grill summer daily 8am-5pm, winter daily 9am-4pm) on-site so you don't have to bring all your own food.

Food

For a delicious seafood meal, visit the glass-fronted A-frame **Chart Room** (210 Wave Dr., 707/986-9696, www.chartroom.cc, Sat.-Wed. 5pm-9pm, $20-25). Seafood and hearty meat and pasta dishes are available along with vegetarian fare, sandwiches, and soups. The Chart Room also has beer, wine, and cocktails that you can drink on the deck. Be sure to check out the nautical and aeronautical gift shop.

The hearty menu at the **Cove Restaurant** (10 Seal Ct., 707/986-1197, www.sheltercov-eoceanfrontinn.com, Thurs.-Sun. 5pm-9pm, $13-30), heavy on the seafood, is perfect after a hard day of hiking, fishing, or beachcombing, especially with the Cove's views of the coast.

Enjoy a slice of pizza or a whole pie at **Fish Tank Pizzeria** (205 Wave Dr., 707/986-7672, Wed.-Sun. 4pm-9pm). Go for coffee, breakfast, or a sandwich at the **Fish Tank Espresso Gallery** (205 Wave Dr., 707/986-7850, Sun.-Thurs. 7am-2pm, Fri.-Sat. 7am-2pm and 5pm-9pm). The Espresso Gallery also serves sushi on Friday nights.

Information and Services

Don't expect much information or services in remote Shelter Cove. For an overview of the community, visit www.sheltercoveca.info and www.sheltercove-lostcoast.com. There's a **post office** (498 Shelter Cove Rd., Whitethorn, 707/986-7532, www.usps.com) on the road to Shelter Cove. There are no medical facilities in Shelter Cove, but emergency services are coordinated through the **Shelter Cove Fire Department** (9126 Shelter Cove Rd.,

© STUART THORNTON

wild Usal Beach

Whitethorn, 707/986-7507, www.sheltercove-ca.gov). The nearest hospital with an emergency room is **Redwood Memorial Hospital** (3300 Renner Dr., Fortuna, 707/725-3361, www.redwoodmemorial.org).

Getting There and Around
To reach Shelter Cove from U.S. 101 North, take the second Garberville exit. After exiting, look for the Shelter Cove signs and turn west on Briceland Road, which becomes Shelter Cove Road. Though it is just 23 miles on Shelter Cove Road, it takes an hour because it's windy and goes down to one lane at one section.

Pilots can fly into the **Shelter Cove Airport** (707/986-7447, www.sheltercove-ca.gov/airport/airport.htm) if weather conditions cooperate.

SINKYONE WILDERNESS STATE PARK
Encompassing the southern section of the Lost Coast, the **Sinkyone Wilderness State Park** (707/986-7711, www.parks.ca.gov) is a wild region of steep coastal mountains and surf-pounded beaches spotted with wildlife, including bears and elk. The Roosevelt Elk had disappeared from the region until a herd from Prairie Creek State Park was reintroduced here. With their impressive antlers, the elk bulls usually weigh 700-1,100 pounds and can be quite a sight to see in the wild.

Though not as popular as the Lost Coast Trail connecting Black Sand Beach to the Mattole River up north, the Sinkyone Wilderness has a 16-mile **Lost Coast Trail** that starts at Bear Harbor, south of Needle Rock, and ends at Usal Beach. This trail, which takes backpackers 2-3 days, has more climbing than the more popular beach trail to the north. The rigorous hike is mostly on bluffs above the coastline. It passes through virgin redwood groves and mixed forest with beach access at **Wheeler Beach.**

Needle Rock
The easiest accessible spot in the northern Sinkyone is **Needle Rock,** the former sight of a small settlement and the current location of a park visitor center. The area's namesake rock is nearby on a black sand beach. Visitors can camp at five creekside environmental campsites (first come, first served, $5) as well as an old barn (first come, first served, $30). Camping is done by self-registration. To reach Needle Rock, head off U.S. 101 at the Garberville exit and take Redwood Road to Redway. Drive Briceland Road in Redway until it becomes Mendocino County Road 435. The road dead-ends into the state park. The last 3.5 miles are unpaved, steep, and narrow.

Needle Rock's visitors center was once a ranch house. Now it is staffed by a volunteer year-round. The visitors center has information on the region's history and various artifacts. You can also purchase maps and firewood here.

Usal Beach
Located at the southern tip of Sinkyone Wilderness State Park, **Usal Beach** is a remote, two-mile black sand beach under cliffs bristling with massive trees. It's accessible to adventurous

coastal explorers via a steep, unpaved six-mile dirt road that is not for the faint-hearted or the squeamish. Passenger cars can make the drive until the winter rainy season, when four-wheel drive becomes necessary. To find it, drive about an hour north of Fort Bragg on Highway 1 and then turn left on an unmarked road at mile marker 90.88.

When you reach the beach, you can fish from shore or beachcomb the sandy expanse.

Watch sea lions torpedo through the ocean and pelicans splash into the water looking for food. Facilities include 35 primitive drive-in campsites (first come, first served, $25) with picnic tables, fire pits, and pit toilets. The rangers come here to collect the camping fees on some days, but otherwise you self register to camp. Be aware that although firearms are not allowed in the park, locals sometimes shoot guns at night here.

Eureka and Vicinity

The town of Eureka began as a seaward access point to the remote gold mines of the Trinity area. Almost immediately, settlers realized the value of the redwood trees surrounding them and started building a logging industry as well. By the late 19th century, people were getting rich and some building lovely Victorian homes as well as commercial buildings downtown. Today, lumber is still a major industry in Eureka, but because of the Victorian charm and lumber-baron history that pervade the town, tourism is another industry. Come to wander the five-block-long boardwalk on Humboldt Bay and the charming downtown shopping area or to enjoy the art sprouting up all over, including colorful murals on the sides of buildings and sculptures along the city streets. (If you drive through Eureka on U.S. 101, you'll definitely miss the best aspects of the city.) Outdoors enthusiasts can fish and hike, while history buffs can explore museums, Victorian mansions, and even a working historic mill.

SIGHTS
Blue Ox Millworks and Historic Park

Even in a town that thrives on the history of lumber, the **Blue Ox Millworks and Historic Park** (1 X St., 707/444-3437 or 800/248-4259, www.blueoxmill.com, tours Mon.-Fri. 9am-5pm, Sat. 9am-4pm, adults $7.50, over age 64 $6.50, ages 6-12 $3.50) is special. Blue Ox has a working lumber mill, an upscale wood and cabinetry shop, a ceramics studio, a blacksmith forge, an old-fashioned print shop, a shipbuilding yard, a school, a rose garden, and a historic park. It also has the world's largest collection of human-powered woodworking tools made by the historic Barnes Equipment Company. The Blue Ox owners, Eric and Viviana Hollenbeck, didn't intend to start an immense historical enterprise; they just couldn't afford new power tools for their shop, so they rescued and rehabilitated 19th-century human-powered jigsaws, routers, and other woodworking tools. Today, the rambling buildings are filled with purchased, donated, and rehabbed tools of all kinds, which craftspeople use to create ornate custom items for homes and historic buildings across the country. The school teaches high school students about things like digging their own clay, making pottery, and hand-setting type to print their own yearbooks. Newer workshops feature a glassblowing kiln and a darkroom where students can learn "historic" (that is, nondigital) photography methods, making their own photosensitive paper and developing black-and-white and sepia prints "just the way they did at Gettysburg." Visitors to the Blue Ox learn about the real lives and times of craftspeople of the late 1800s and early 1900s as they tour the facilities and examine the equipment. If you ask, you might be allowed to touch and even work a piece of wood of your own. Also, be sure to stop in at the gift shop—a converted lumberjack

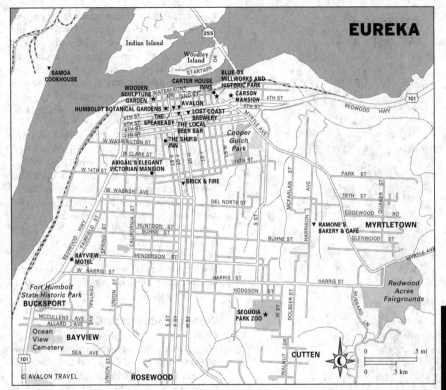

EUREKA

barracks—to check out the ceramics and woodwork the students have for sale.

Carson Mansion

Gables, turrets, cupolas, and pillars: the **Carson Mansion** (143 M St., www.ingomar. org, view only from the outside) has all these architectural flourishes. The three-story, 18-room, elaborate Victorian mansion was built by William Carson in 1884 and 1885 after he struck it rich in the lumber business. Almost demolished in the 1940s, it was purchased and renovated by local businesses that formed the Ingomar Club, which now uses it for private dinner parties. It's touted as one of the most photographed buildings in the country, but you'll have be satisfied with a picture from the street; the building and grounds are not open to the public.

Clarke Historical Museum

The privately-owned **Clarke Historical Museum** (240 E St., 707/443-1947, www. clarkemuseum.org, Wed.-Thurs. 11am-4pm, Fri.-Sat. 11am-6pm, adults $3, under age 5 free) is dedicated to preserving the history of Eureka and the surrounding area. Changing exhibitions illuminate the Native American history of the area as well as the gold rush and logging eras. The Nealis Hall annex displays one of the best collections of Native American artifacts in the state.

Fort Humboldt State Historic Park

Established in 1853 to protect white settlers—particularly gold miners—from the local Native Americans, the original Fort Humboldt lasted only 17 years as a military

EUREKA VICINITY

Trinidad

PACIFIC OCEAN

CENTRAL AVE

MURRAY RD

OLD RAILROAD GRADE RD

101

299

Humboldt Bay NWR

Arcata

ARCATA COMMUNITY FOREST

Arcata Bay

BASE RD

NEW NAVY

101

Eureka

101

South Bay

Eel River Wildlife Area

Humboldt Bay NWR

Headwaters Forest Ecological Reserve

211   101   Fortuna

© AVALON TRAVEL

industry, along with examples of the type and size of redwood trees loggers were cutting and removing from 19th-century forests. Finally, you can spend a few minutes enjoying the tranquil historic garden, where master gardeners maintain the type of garden fort residents kept here 150 years ago.

Sequoia Park Zoo

The **Sequoia Park Zoo** (3414 W St., 707/441-4263, www.sequoiaparkzoo.net, summer daily 10am-5pm, winter Tues.-Sun. 10am-5pm, adults $6, seniors $5, ages 3-12 $4) might seem small, but its mission is a big one: It seeks not only to entertain visitors but also to preserve local species and educate the public about their needs. The "Secrets of the Forest" exhibit recreates the ecology of the Northern California forest while allowing visitors to see the multifarious species that live here. Be sure to say hi to Bill the Chimpanzee.

Wooden Sculpture Garden

Conveniently located downtown in the shopping district, the **Wooden Sculpture Garden of Romano Gabriel** (315 2nd St., www.eurekaheritage.org) is behind a glass wall for all to see. Romano Gabriel was a furniture maker, carpenter, and gardener who immigrated from Mura, Italy to Eureka in 1913, creating the bright colorful artworks over many years and placing them in his front yard. The Eureka Heritage Society now preserves and maintains this sculpture garden for all to enjoy.

Humboldt Botanical Gardens

Staff and local volunteers have worked for years to create **Humboldt Botanical Gardens** (College of the Redwoods, 7351 Tompkins Hill Rd., 707/442-5139, www.hbgf.org, summer Wed.-Sat. 10am-2pm and first Sun. of the month 11am-3pm, adults $5, under age 12 free), a celebration of the ecosystems of Humboldt County. The 44-acre site includes native plants, ornamental plants, and plants that grow in riparian regions.

installation. Today, **Fort Humboldt State Historic Park** (3431 Fort Ave., 707/445-6567, www.parks.ca.gov, daily 8am-5pm) gives visitors a glimpse into the lives of 19th-century soldiers and loggers. In its early days, it was home to a young Ulysses S. Grant. The original fort hospital now serves as a museum. A sedate but fairly long walking tour takes you through recreations of historic fort buildings, then out to the logging display, where you'll find several "steam donkeys," a piece of equipment that revolutionized the logging

© STUART THORNTON

Eureka's most photographed building: the Carson Mansion

ENTERTAINMENT AND EVENTS
Bars

The biggest and most popular restaurant and bar in Eureka is definitely the **Lost Coast Brewery & Café** (617 4th St., 707/445-4480, www.lostcoast.com, Sun.-Thurs. 11am-10pm, Fri.-Sat. 11am-11pm). The tall cream-and-green building is perched off by itself on the main drag, easy to spot as you pass through town. The brewery draws crowds, especially on weekends, and makes popular microbrews including Great White and Downtown Brown, which are on tap here. Come for tasty brewpub-style food, and try one or more of the delicious beers.

As the name suggests, **The Local Beer Bar** (517 F St., 707/497-6320, Mon.-Thurs. 4pm-10pm, Fri.-Sat. 4pm-11pm, Sun. 2pm-8pm) is all about local beers. Chalkboard painted skateboards behind the bar announce the rotating 22 beers on tap, which always include Humboldt brews like Redwood Curtain and Mad River as well as rarities such as barrel-aged and sour beers. This great little beer hall has

modern, creative touches like a bar made out of keg coolers, tabletops made from road signs, and local art decorating the walls.

Located in Opera Alley, **The Speakeasy** (411 Opera Alley, 707/444-2244, Sun.-Thurs. 4pm-11pm, Fri.-Sat. 4pm-1:30am) is the place to go in Eureka for tasty cocktails. This dark, narrow bar, which sometimes has live music, serves up Southern-style drinks, including a great mint julep.

For a solid dive-bar experience, spend an evening at **The Shanty** (213 3rd St., 707/444-2053, daily noon-2am). Hang out indoors and listen to the inspired mix of tunes from the jukebox, or the occasional live musicians. Head outdoors to play ping-pong or pool or smoke a cigarette. The extended happy hour (Mon.-Fri. 4pm-7pm, Sat.-Sun. noon-4pm) offers top-shelf beers and liquors and rock-bottom prices.

Live Music

A restored theater in downtown Eureka, the **Arkley Center for the Performing Arts** (412 G St., 707/442-1956, www.arkleycenter.com) is the home of the Eureka Symphony and North Coast Dance. The elegant venue, which has chandeliers hanging from its ceilings, also hosts rock, country, and jazz acts. Walking around downtown Eureka, you can't miss the Arkley due to the striking mural of musicians and dancers on the back of the building.

Theater

Eureka's **North Coast Repertory Theater** (300 5th St., 707/442-6278, www.ncrt.net, $15-20, cash only) performs a mix of musicals, comedies, and the occasional Shakespeare or heavy-duty drama. Many performances benefit local charities.

Events

Music lovers flock to Eureka each year for a number of big music festivals. **Blues by the Bay** (Halvorsen Park, 707/445-3378, www. bluesbythebay.org, all-weekend pass $75-95, individual events $25-55) is one of the largest. Held at Halvorsen Park on Humboldt Bay, the two-day festival in early September features many of the finest blues musicians alive playing in a spectacular setting. Accompanying the wailing blues are art, food, and microbrew booths.

Another big event is the **Redwood Coast Jazz Festival** (various venues around town, 707/445-3378, www.redwoodjazz.org, all-event pass $25-85, individual events $10-50). For four days in March, music lovers can enjoy every style of jazz imaginable, including Dixieland, zydeco, and big band. The festival also features dance contests and silent-movie screenings.

SHOPPING

The Eureka antiques scene is the largest California antiques market north of the Bay Area. In Old Town and downtown, seekers find treasures from the lumber baron-era and Victorian delights, from tiny porcelain figurines to huge pieces of furniture. **Annex 39** (610 F St., 707/443-1323, Mon.-Fri. noon-5:30pm, Sat. by appointment) specializes in vintage linens and laundry products and also

has a great selection of art deco and mid-century modern pieces. **Heritage Antique & Coins** (521 4th St., 707/444-2908, Tues.-Sat. 10am-5pm) is a coin shop that also carries jewelry and Native American artifacts. Generalists will love rooting through the huge **Antiques and Goodies** (1128 3rd St., 707/442-0445, www.antiquesandgoodies.com, Wed.-Sat. 10am-5pm and by appointment) and **Old Town Antiques** (318 F St., 707/442-3235, Mon.-Sat. 10:30am-5:30pm).

For an afternoon of shopping in Eureka, head down toward the water to 2nd Street. Most of the buildings here are historic, and you might find an unassuming brass plaque describing the famous brothel that once inhabited what is now a toy store. Literature lovers have a nice selection of independent bookstores: **Eureka Books** (426 2nd St., 707/444-9593, www.eurekabooksellers.com, daily 10am-6pm) has a big airy room in which to browse a selection of new and used books. **Booklegger** (402 2nd St., at E St., 707/445-1344, Mon.-Sat. 10am-5:30pm, Sun. 11am-4pm), just down the street, is a small but well-organized new-and-used bookshop that specializes in antique books.

Galleries and gift shops abound, highlighting various aspects of California culture. The **Sewell Gallery Fine Art** (423 F St., 707/269-0617, www.sewellgallery.com, Tues.-Sat. 10am-6pm, Sun. noon-5pm) showcases the visual artworks of 50 regional artists from painters to glass makers. **Many Hands Gallery** (438 2nd St., 877/445-0455, www.manyhandsgallery.net, Mon.-Sat. 9:30am-9pm, Sun. 10am-6pm) represents approximately 100 local artisans and also displays work from national and international artists cooperatives, fair-trade organizations, and commercial importers. The offerings are eclectic, representing many cultural, spiritual, and religious traditions from around the globe. Don't get the idea that this place is sanctimonious, though; you'll find plenty of humor and whimsy, and prices range from 10 cents to $10,000.

SPORTS AND RECREATION
Fishing

Eureka is a serious fishing destination. Oodles

of both ocean and river fishing opportunities abound all over the region, and several fishing tournaments are held each year. Anywhere in California, you must have a valid state fishing license to fish in either the ocean or the rivers. Check with your charter service or guide to be sure they provide a day license with your trip. If they don't, you will have to get your own.

For deep-sea fishing, **Celtic Charter Service** (Woodley Island Marina, Dock D, 707/442-7115, www.shellbacksportfishing.com, fishing mid-May-Sept., crabbing Nov., salmon and rockfish trips $140 pp, halibut fishing $160 pp, albacore $200 pp, crabbing $65 pp) offers excursions leaving daily at 6:30am and returning at 2pm-3pm. Prices vary, as different fishing methods allow for different numbers of people on the boat. The company rents out tackle and sells day licenses as well. **Full Throttle Sportfishing** (Woodley Island Marina, 707/498-7473, www.fullthrottlesportfishing.com, $150-250) supplies all needed tackle and can take you out to fish for salmon, rockfish, tuna, or halibut. Trips last all day, and most leave at 6:30am. If you're launching your own boat, public launches are the **Samoa Boat Ramp** (New Navy Base Rd., daily 5am-midnight) and the **Fields Landing Boat Ramp** (Railroad Ave.), both managed by Humboldt County Public Works (1106 2nd St., 707/445-7491, http://co.humboldt.ca.us, Mon.-Fri. 8am-noon and 1pm-5pm).

Eureka also has good spots for pier fishing. In town, try the K Street Pier, the pier at the east end of Commercial Street, or the pier at the end of Del Norte Street. Farther north, the north jetty (Hwy. 255, across Samoa Bridge) also has a public pier open for fishing.

Bird-Watching

The national, state, and county parks lacing the Eureka area create ideal bird-watching conditions. The **Humboldt Bay National Wildlife Refuge Complex** (1020 Ranch Rd., Loleta, 707/733-5406, www.fws.gov/humboldtbay) encompasses several wildlife-refuge sites where visitors are welcome. At the Salmon Creek Unit, you'll find the **Richard J. Guadagno**

Headquarters and Visitors Center (daily 8am-5pm), which is an excellent starting place for a number of wildlife walks. To get to the visitors center from U.S. 101, take the exit for Hookton heading north and turn left onto Eel River Drive. Take the first right onto Ranch Road, and you'll find the visitors center parking lot.

Hiking and Biking

Not only is there a vast system of trails in the state and national parks, the city of Eureka maintains a number of multiuse biking and hiking trails as well. Most familiar is the Old Town Boardwalk, part of the **Waterfront Trail** that comprises disconnected sections along Humboldt Bay. **Sequoia Park Trail** begins at the Sequoia Park Zoo and wends through redwood forests, past a duck pond, and through a meadow. This trail is paved and friendly for strollers and wheelchairs. The unpaved **Elk River Trail** (end of Hilfiker Lane) stretches for one mile through wild meadows along the coast. **Cooper Gulch Trail** is a more sedate stroll than a strenuous hike, circling the Cooper Gulch park playing fields.

Kayaking, Rafting, and Stand Up Paddleboarding

The water is cold, but getting out on it in a kayak can be exhilarating. If you're new to the sport or just want a guided trip of the area, guided paddles, lessons, rentals, and kayak fishing trips are available through **Humboats Kayak Adventures** (Woodley Island Marina, 707/443-5157, www.humboats.com, canoe and kayak rentals $25-75, 2-hour full-moon kayak tour $50). Guides lead a huge variety of tours, from serene paddles in the harbor suitable for children to 30-mile-plus trips designed for experienced kayakers.

River rafters and kayakers have great opportunities for rapids fun on the inland Klamath and Trinity Rivers. **Bigfoot Rafting Company** (Willow Creek, 530/629-2263 or 800/722-2223, www.bigfootrafting.com, adults $69-89, youth $59-79) leads half-day, full-day, and multiday trips on both rivers as well as on the

NORTH COAST

Cal-Salmon and the Smith Rivers. Experts can take inflatable kayaks down the Class IV rapids, and newcomers can find a gentle paddle with just enough white water to make things interesting.

You can also explore Humboldt Bay from the top of a stand up paddleboard. **All Out SUP** (5339 Meyers Ave., 707/616-0532, www. alloutsup.com, $75 pp) teaches beginners the basics before embarking on a tour around Woodley Island.

ACCOMMODATIONS

With such a wealth of Victorian houses, Eureka is a natural location for classic bed-and-breakfast accommodations. Chain motels are also available in abundance, many of them quite cheap. But for a real taste of the town, try one of the charming inns.

Under $150

Originally built by one of the town's founders, **Abigail's Elegant Victorian Mansion** (1406 C St., 707/444-3144, www.eureka-california. com, $89-170) offers an authentic Victorian experience. The owners have taken pains to learn the history of the house and the town and have added appropriate decor to create a truly Victorian mansion, right down to the vintage books in the elegant library. The inn also retains many of the large home's original fixtures. Anyone with an interest in Victoriana need only ask for a tour, and the owners will gladly take an hour or more to describe the artifacts in each room. Each of the five guest rooms comes with its own story and an astonishing collection of antiques. All guest rooms have private baths, although they might be across the hall. While you're not encouraged to bring small children to this romantic inn, families and groups traveling together can request combined rooms with additional beds. Abigail's recently instituted "economic stimulus pricing," which means it lowered all the room rates. In order to make that possible, they no longer serve breakfast, but it's still a lovely place to stay.

If B&Bs just aren't your style, get a room at the **Bayview Motel** (2844 Fairfield St., 707/442-1673 or 866/725-6813, www.bay-viewmotel.com, $110-175). This hilltop motel has lovely views of Humboldt Bay from many of the guest rooms and from the grounds. Guest rooms are spacious and decorated in slightly more elegant colors and fabrics than at the average chain motel. You'll find wonderful whirlpool suites, free Wi-Fi, cable TV, wet bars, and coffeemakers. If you're traveling with the family, you can rent a double suite—two rooms with an adjoining door and separate baths. Although not right in downtown Eureka, it's an easy drive from the Bayview for dinner, shopping, and strolling by the harbor.

$150-250

The Ship's Inn (821 D St., 707/443-7583 or 877/443-7583, www.shipsinn.net, $140-180) is a newish B&B in an oldish, recently restored Victorian home on the east side of town. Few guest rooms and a friendly innkeeper make a stay at this inn delightfully like staying in a friend's grand home. Breakfast is particularly good, and the small garden is the perfect place to sit out in the afternoon reading a good book. Each of the three guest rooms has its own decoration and theme; the Captain's Quarters take the inn's name to heart with a blue-and-gold nautical design, while the other guest rooms tend more toward classic Victorian floral. Unlike many B&Bs, you'll find TVs in every room, along with fireplaces, plush robes, and private baths.

The ◖ **Carter House Inns** (301 L St., 800/404-1390, www.carterhouse.com, $179-495) have a range of accommodations in a cluster of butter-yellow Victorian buildings near the Carson Mansion. The main building has 23 rooms with knotty pine furniture and carpeted floors. A number of the deluxe rooms and suites in the main house have gas fireplaces and soaking tubs. Across the street, a reproduction of a Victorian mansion has six rooms, including a family suite with two bedrooms, while **The Bell Cottage** has three rooms and a full common kitchen. If you really want to splurge, rent **The Carter Cottage,** which has two bathrooms, a back deck with a fountain, a soaking tub, and a large den and kitchen area. No matter where you choose to stay, you'll be treated to a hot breakfast and an afternoon wine and appetizer hour. You can also dine or snack in the inn's renowned Restaurant 301. Warning: You may never want to leave.

FOOD
American
The ◖ **Samoa Cookhouse** (511 Vance Rd., Samoa, 707/442-1659, www.samoacookhouse.net, summer daily 7am-9pm, winter daily 7am-8pm, $16) is a historic Eureka institution. Red-checked tablecloths cover long, rough tables to recreate the atmosphere of a logging-camp dining hall. The all-you-can-eat meals are served family-style from huge serving platters. Diners sit on benches and pass the hearty fare down in turn. Think big hunks of roast beef, mountains of mashed potatoes, and piles of cooked vegetables. This is the place to bring your biggest appetite. After dinner, browse the small Historic Logging Museum and gift shop.

Restaurant 301 (301 L St., 800/404-1390, www.carterhouse.com, daily 6pm-9pm, $24-35) at the Carter House Inns seems like a top-shelf San Francisco or Los Angeles eatery lost on the distant North Coast. The chef creates an ever-changing menu of delectable delicacies, with tasting menus that give diners the best chance to experience this great restaurant. On the succession of plates served at a relaxed pace, you'll find everything from exotic duck dishes to simple local seafood preparations to items from the restaurant's own on-site kitchen garden. For a special treat, try the wine flights suggested with the menus. Restaurant 301 is known for their extensive wine list with over 3,400 selections.

Another high-end Eureka restaurant that impresses even the most discriminating Bay Area-trained palates is **Avalon** (239 G St., 707/445-0500, www.avaloneureka.com, Tues.-Sun. 5pm-9pm, $20-28), a restaurant that speaks to the hearts of eco-conscious carnivores with sustainably sourced steaks, mixed grills, and game meats prominent on the menu.

The **Surfside Burger Shack** (445 5th St., 707/268-1295, Mon.-Sat. 11am-9pm, Sun. 11am-8pm, $5.50-8) is nowhere near the ocean. It's actually right on a busy Eureka street. But the shack does have surfing decor and darn good burgers made from grass-fed Humboldt cows. The classic cheeseburger hits the spot, but the shack also gets creative with the beef. For example, the "Surfside Sunrise" is a burger topped with cheese, bacon, an egg, and maple syrup.

Bakeries
Ramone's Bakery & Café (209 E St., 707/445-2923, Mon.-Fri. 7am-6pm, Sat. 8am-5pm, Sun. 8am-4pm; 2297 Harrison Ave., 707/442-1336, Mon.-Sat. 6:30am-9pm, Sun. 7:30am-7pm) is a genuine local North Coast chain. All locations (including one in Arcata and one in McKinleyville) sell fresh from-scratch baked goods and candies. Come in the morning to enjoy a fresh cup of coffee roasted in-house and a Danish or a scone, indulge in an afternoon pastry, or even get a whole tart, cake, or loaf of fresh-baked bread to take out for an afternoon picnic.

Italian
Brick & Fire Bistro (1630 F St., 707/268-8959, www.brickandfirebistro.com, Mon. and Wed.-Thurs. 11:30am-8:30pm, Fri. 11:30am-9pm, Sat. 5pm-9pm, Sun. 5pm-8:30pm, $14-22) updates Italian classics with a menu that includes fire-roasted polenta lasagna and pizzas with ingredients like locally smoked salmon and quail eggs.

INFORMATION AND SERVICES
The **Humboldt County Convention and Visitors Bureau** does not operate a public visitors center, but if you need something, drop by the business office (1034 2nd St., 800/346-3482, www.redwoods.info, Mon.-Fri. 9am-5pm) and they'll do their best to help you.

The website is an ideal place to do research on vacation plans anywhere in the Redwood Coast region, and you can call the travel hotline (800/346-3482) for information.

The **Eureka Chamber of Commerce** (2112 Broadway, 707/442-3738, www.eurekachamber.com, Mon.-Fri. 8:30am-5pm) runs a helpful facility, with plenty of literature about things to do in town and beyond.

The *Times-Standard* (www.times-standard.com) covers both national and local news and includes information about events in the North Coast region. You can pick up a copy at many businesses around the region. Check the entertainment section for the latest hot spots and live events during your stay.

As the big urban area on the North Coast, Eureka and Arcata have the major services travelers may need. You'll find branches of major banks, complete with ATMs, which are also available at supermarkets, pharmacies, and other businesses.

Naturally, you'll find **post offices** (337 W. Clark St., 707/442-1768, Mon.-Fri. 8:30am-5pm, Sat. noon-3pm; 514 H St., 707/442-0856, Mon.-Fri. 8:30am-5pm).

Eureka has a full-service hospital, **St. Joseph Hospital** (2700 Dolbeer St., 707/445-8121, www.stjosepheureka.org), with an emergency room and an urgent care center for less serious issues.

GETTING THERE AND AROUND

Eureka is on U.S. 101, easily accessed by car from north or south. From Crescent City, Eureka is less than an hour's drive south on U.S. 101.

In Eureka, driving is the only option if you're not staying downtown, especially if you want to head out to Woodley Island. You can easily visit the 2nd Street shops and restaurants on foot. Parking downtown is metered or free on the streets, and not too difficult to find except on holiday or event weekends.

Bus service in and around Eureka is operated by the **Humboldt Transit Authority** (HTA, www.hta.org, adults $1.40, children and seniors $1.10). The HTA's **Eureka Transit System** (ETS) runs within town limits, and the **Redwood Transit System** (RTS, www.redwoodtransit.org, adults $2.75, children and seniors $2.50) can take you around the area, from Eureka north to Crescent City, south to Ferndale, and east to Willow Creek.

Eureka has a small commercial airport, **Arcata-Eureka Airport** (ACV, 3561 Boeing Ave., McKinleyville, 707/839-5401, http://co.humboldt.ca.us/aviation), that serves the North Coast region. You can fly in and out on Horizon Air (a division of Alaska) or United Airlines. Expect flights to be expensive but convenient.

Arcata

Located on the northern shore of barbell-shaped Humboldt Bay, Arcata has a distinctly different feel than its southern neighbor. The hippie daughter of blue-collar Eureka, Arcata is home to Humboldt State University. Students make up almost half of the city's population, and the town has become known for its liberal politics; at one point the city council was made up mostly of Green Party members. This progressive atmosphere feels a world away from most of the other small towns in the region.

With about half the population of Eureka, Arcata has a small town atmosphere. The heart of Arcata is the Arcata Plaza, a town park with a William McKinley statue, a couple of palm trees, and a grassy lawn. Here you'll almost always find folks hanging out, playing music, and smoking non-tobacco cigarettes. Circling the plaza are independent restaurants, bars, coffee shops, and stores selling items like shirts made out of hemp. (A local law limits chains and franchises downtown.)

Arcata has a lively arts and music scene along with a handful of restaurants that you might expect in a bigger city. It makes a great home base for exploring the wild North Coast.

SIGHTS
C Arcata Community Forest
The first city-owned forest in California, the 2,134-acre **Arcata Community Forest** (east ends of 11th St., 14th St., and California St., 707/822-5951, www.cityofarcata.org) has trails winding through second-growth redwoods, open for hiking, mountain biking, and horseback riding. Just east of the city's downtown and behind Humboldt State University, the forest is an ideal place to stroll between the silent giants, many of which are cloaked in moss, and take in stumps the size of compact cars and vibrant green waist-high ferns. The park also has a section with picnic tables and a playground.

Arcata Marsh and Wildlife Sanctuary
Believe it or not, one of Arcata's most popular places to take a hike is in a section of their wastewater treatment facility. The **Arcata Marsh Interpretive Center** (569 S. G St., 707/826-2359, www.cityofarcata.org, Tues.-Sun. 9am-5pm, Mon. 1pm-5pm) is an information station with a small museum that explains how the city transformed an industrial wasteland into a 307-acre wildlife sanctuary using Arcata's wastewater. You can also hike the sanctuary's five miles of hiking and biking paths, or try to spot some of the 270 bird species that now use the marsh as a migratory stop.

ENTERTAINMENT AND EVENTS
Bars
A strip of dive bars lines the edge of Arcata Plaza on 9th Street. The best of the bunch, **The Alibi** (744 9th St., 707/822-3731, www.thealibi.com, daily 8am-2am), dates back to the 1920s. The Alibi serves cheap, well-crafted cocktails, including a wide range of Bloody Marys. It also has an extensive breakfast, lunch, and dinner menu with 28 specialty burgers and entrées from burger steaks to organic tofu cutlets.

A few feet away, **Everett's Club** (784 9th St., 707/822-2291, Tues. 3pm-5pm and 9pm-1am, Wed.-Thurs. 6pm-2am, Fri. 2pm-2am, Sat. 8am-2am, Sun. 4pm-5pm and 9pm-1am) is a place where you can drink with the locals while big game heads mounted on the walls stare down at you. Out back is a small patio for the smoking crowd.

Humboldt Brews (856 10th St., 707/826-2739, www.humboldtbrews.com, daily noon-11pm except music nights when it stays open until 2am) serves 25 beers on tap, as well as food. This popular hangout also has a pool table and an adjacent room that serves as a concert space.

Live Music
Music legends play at Humboldt State University's **John Van Duzer Theatre** (1 Harpst St., 707/826-4411, www.humboldt.edu, check website for schedule). Elvis Costello, Ziggy Marley, and Alison Krauss have all graced its stage. Up and coming acts visit campus as well, typically performing at **The Depot** (University Center, 1 Harpst St., 707/826-4411).

Humboldt Brews (856 10th St., 707/826-2739, www.humboldtbrews.com, daily noon-11pm except music nights when it stays open until 2am) hosts mid-sized national jam bands, indie acts, and reggae outfits.

Funk bands fill up the dance floor at **Jambalaya** (915 H St., 707/822-4766, www.jambalayaarcata.com, Mon.-Fri. 9am-2am, Sat.-Sun. 10pm-2am), a few feet away from Arcata Plaza. The kitchen serves up New Orleans-style po'boys.

Festivals and Events
Arcata Plaza is the starting line of the **Kinetic Grand Championship** (Memorial Day weekend, http://kineticgrandchampionship.com), a three-day, 42-mile race featuring human-powered art sculptures that continues on to Eureka and Ferndale.

Also in the plaza is June's annual **Arcata Main Street Oyster Festival** (www.oysterfestival.net), which celebrates the local Kumamoto oyster with—you guessed it—oysters. There's also live music and flowing micro-brewed beer.

Cinema

Dating back to 1938, the art deco **Arcata Theatre Lounge** (1036 G St., 707/822-1220, www.arcatatheatre.com) screens movies, hosts concerts, and hosts events like "Sci-Fi Pint and Pizza Night," where they show old science fiction movies. The theater seats have been replaced by circular tables and chairs, and the full bar serves food as well as drinks, making it a perfect place for a night out.

A few blocks away, the 1914 **Minor Theatre** (1001 H St., 707/822-3456, www.catheatres.com) is one of the oldest still operating movie theaters in the country, showing independent movies as well as Hollywood films.

SPORTS AND RECREATION

Both the **Arcata Community Forest** (east ends of 11th St., 14th St. and California St., 707/822-5951, www.cityofarcata.org) and the **Arcata Marsh and Wildlife Sanctuary** (569 S. G St., 707/826-2359, www.cityofarcata.org) have miles of hiking trails. The **Redwood Canopy Tour** (786/200-4260, www.northcoastadventurecenters.com, $75 for 2-3 hours) offers a more adventurous approach to the Community Forest: ascending 70-100 feet into the redwood canopy and then using a zip line to travel among the treetops.

The famous 18-hole **Redwood Curtain Disc Golf Course** (accessible from Humboldt State University's Redwood Science Lab, though parking is only available in the lot after 5pm, www.parinfinity.org) winds its way through massive redwood trees. On the second hole, the tee is located atop a 10-foot high redwood stump. Sunday mornings at 11:11am, random double matches take place.

For local sports action, get a ticket to see the **Humboldt Crabs** (Arcata Ball Park, F St. and 9th St., 707/826-2333, http://humboldtcrabs.com), the oldest continually-operated collegiate summer baseball team in the country.

SHOPPING

There are shops located around Arcata Plaza and along H Street, which has a number of unique stores. Head into **Pacific Paradise** (1087 H St., 707/822-7143, Mon.-Sat. 10am-7pm, Sun. 10:30am-6:30pm) to stock up on Humboldt County essentials like golf discs, hoodies, tie-dyes, and smoking equipment.

Across the street, the **Tin Can Mailman Used & Rare Books Store** (1000 H St., 707/822-1307, www.tincanbooks.com, Mon.-Sat. 10am-7pm, Sun. 11am-6pm) crams together two full floors full of used books. If you'd rather get the latest fiction or memoir, head over to **Northtown Books** (957 H St., 707/822-2834, www.northtownbooks.com, Mon.-Thurs. and Sat. 10am-7pm, Fri. 10am-9pm, Sun. noon-5pm). They also have an extensive magazine collection.

Solutions (858 G St., 707/822-6972) is right on the plaza and the place to pick up hemp clothing, organic bedding, and eco-goods.

A few blocks from the plaza, **Holly Yashi** (1300 9th St., 707/822-5132, www.hollyyashi.com, Mon.-Sat. 10am-6pm) specializes in niobium jewelry. Niobium is a metal that gains streaks of color after being dipped in an electrically charged bath. You can watch artists at work crafting the jewelry in the attached studio.

ACCOMMODATIONS

Downtown lodging options are surprisingly limited. The **Hotel Arcata** (708 9th St., 707/826-0217, www.hotelarcata.com, $88-159) is nothing fancy, but it has a superb location right on the plaza. The rooms are small, but all the bathrooms have claw foot tubs outfitted with showerheads. The bottom floor of the hotel is home to the popular Tomo Japanese Restaurant as well as a gift shop and beauty salon.

The Lady Anne Bed and Breakfast (902 14th St., 707/822-2797, http://ladyanneinn.com, $115-220) has a little more character, with five rooms in an old Victorian from 1888. All have private bathrooms and most include gas-burning woodstoves. A music room is decorated with all sorts of instruments including a piano, an accordion, and a bass guitar that guests are allowed to play. Like all good B&Bs, the Lady Anne serves a full, hot breakfast.

© STUART THORNTON

Arcata Plaza

A few miles from the Plaza, the **Best Western Arcata Inn** (4827 Valley West Blvd., 707/826-0313, http://bestwesterncalifornia.com, $109) is a well-regarded chain motel option in the area. The rooms have satellite TV and Wi-Fi, and there's a swimming pool and hot tub on the grounds.

FOOD

For a small city, Arcata has a lot of worthwhile dining options. Many of the restaurants are committed to using ingredients from local Humboldt farms and ranches.

American

Almost everything served up or sat on in **Luke's Joint** (887 H St., 707/826-0415, www.lukesjointarcata.com, daily 9am-8pm, $7-13) is made in Humboldt County. The produce hails from local farms and the furniture is made by local companies. Luckily, this small eatery has more to recommend it than its dedication to the local economy. Luke's serves big, tasty hot sandwiches, wraps, and salads for breakfast,

lunch, and dinner. Be sure to review the section of the menu titled "Sublime Swine," which has a series of smoked pork shoulder sandwiches and tacos.

French

◖**Renata's Creperie and Espresso** (1030 G St., 707/825-8783, Tues.-Thurs. and Sun. 8am-3pm, Fri.-Sat. 8am-3pm and 5pm-9pm, $4-12) is the best place to start the day. Their organic buckwheat crepes are artfully decorated with drizzled sauces and well-placed garnishes, and deliver on their promising looks with sweet and savory fillings. Renata's is also open for dinner on Friday and Saturday nights.

Italian

Named for a region in Central Italy, **Abruzzi** (780 7th St., 707/826-2345, www.abruzziarcata.com, daily 5pm-9pm, $12-40) is the place to go for fine dining around the plaza. The menu includes free-range chicken dishes, seafood offerings, and classic pastas like Bolognese, primavera, and alfredo.

Japanese

A local institution for almost 30 years, ◖**Tomo Japanese Restaurant** (708 9th St., 707/822-1414, www.tomoarcata.com, Mon.-Sat. 11:30am-2pm and 5pm-9pm, Sun. 5pm-9pm, $10-22) serves sushi rolls and other entrées that are as eclectic as its hometown. Get a spicy tofu roll or a truly unique locally smoked albacore roll. Like any great sushi bar, Tomo has a list of sakes, but there's also a full bar.

Markets

Stop in **Wildberries Marketplace** (747 13th St., 707/822-0095, www.wildberries.com, daily 6am-midnight) to stock up for a picnic in the redwoods. Alongside the aisles of health foods, there's a café, juice bar, and coffee shop. Wildberries also hosts its own farmer's market (www.humfarm.org, Tues. 3:30pm-6:30pm).

The Arcata Plaza also hosts a Saturday **farmer's market** (www.humfarm.org, mid-Apr.-mid-Nov. Sat. 9am-2pm) that includes live music.

NORTH COAST

INFORMATION AND SERVICES

The **California Welcome Center** (1635 Heindon Rd., 707/822-3619, www.arcatachamber.com, daily 11am-5pm) has information on Arcata as well as the rest of California. There's also Internet access if you need to go online.

Though based in Eureka, the daily *Times-Standard* (www.times-standard.com) also covers Arcata. *The Lumberjack* (http://thelumberjack.org) is the Humboldt State University student newspaper.

Arcata has a **post office** (799 H St., 707/822-3370, www.usps.com) located right off the plaza.

The **Mad River Community Hospital** (3800 Janes Rd., 707/822-3621, http://madriverhospital.com) has an emergency room and urgent care department.

GETTING THERE AND AROUND

Arcata is eight miles north of Eureka on U.S. 101. Once there, it's easiest to just park your car and walk around the small city.

If you grow weary of walking, the **Arcata & Mad River Transit System** (www.arcatatransit.org, adults $1.50, children and seniors $1) runs a fleet of red and yellow buses that travel all over Arcata.

Nearby McKinleyville has a small commercial airport, **Arcata-Eureka Airport** (ACV, 3561 Boeing Ave., McKinleyville, 707/839-5401, http://co.humboldt.ca.us/aviation), that serves the North Coast region. You can fly in and out on United Airlines. Expect flights to be expensive but convenient.

Trinidad and Vicinity

With a population of just 360 people, Trinidad is one of the smallest incorporated cities in California; it's also one of the most beautiful. Perched on a bluff over boat-studded Trinidad Bay, Trinidad has a wealth of natural assets, including scenic headlands and wild beaches on either side of town. It also has a long history: The town was named by two Spanish Navy men who came to the area on Trinity Sunday in 1775. Located right off U.S. 101, Trinidad is worth a visit, whether it's for a stop to stretch your legs or a tranquil weekend getaway.

SIGHTS
Trinidad Memorial Lighthouse

Not an actual lighthouse but a replica of the one on nearby Trinidad Head, **Trinidad Memorial Lighthouse** (Trinity St. and Edwards St.) is the local photo opportunity. It was built by the Trinidad Civic Club in 1949 with prize money from the "Build a Better Community Contest." The small red and white building sits on a bluff above the bay where boats bob in the water. A marble slab and a series of plaques list those individuals who have been lost at sea. To the left of the lighthouse is the old Trinidad fog bell.

Trinidad Head

A rocky promontory north of the bay, the 380-foot-high **Trinidad Head** (end of Edwards St.) affords great views of the area's beaches, bay, and town. A one-mile-long loop trail on the headlands goes under canopies of vegetation and then out to a series of clear spots with benches. A large stone cross on the west end of Trinidad Head marks where Spanish seamen initially erected a wooden cross. Below the cross is a small wooden deck where you can glimpse the top of the Trinidad Head Lighthouse. The squat lighthouse on a 175-foot-high cliff was activated in 1871. In 1914, the lighthouse made news when, according to the lighthouse keeper, a huge wave extinguished the light.

Trinidad State Beach

Below the bluffs of Trinidad Head, **Trinidad State Beach** (end of Edwards St.,

Trinidad Memorial Lighthouse

707/677-3570, www.parks.ca.gov, daily sunrise-sunset, free) runs north for a half-mile. Spruce-tufted Pewetole Island and a scattering of scenic coastal islets lie offshore. It's a great place for a contemplative walk.

Humboldt State University Marine Laboratory

Students come to the **HSU Marine Laboratory** (570 Ewing St., 707/826-3671, www.humboldt.edu, tours by appointment only, self-guided tours $1 pp, guided tours $2 pp) to learn about the area's coastal critters. A tour of the lab includes looks at invertebrates from nearby intertidal zones.

SPORTS AND RECREATION
Kayaking and Whale-Watching

Protected Trinidad Bay is an ideal spot for a scenic sea kayaking excursion. **Humboats Kayak Adventures** (707/443-5157, www.humboats.com, $75/three-hour tour) runs guided whale-watching tours in the spring and early summer when gray whales migrate right through

the protected harbor area. In the summer and fall, Humboats offers a kayak-based tour of Trinidad's headlands.

Sportfishing

If you'd rather have the satisfaction of catching your own fresh seafood, head out to sea with one of two Trinidad-based fishing outfits. Fish for rockfish, salmon, or Dungeness crab with **Trinidad Bay Charters** (707/499-8878, www.trinidadbaycharters.net) or **Patrick's Point Charters** (707/445-4106, www.patrickspointcharters.com, $100/half-day).

Surfing

South of Trinidad are some of Humboldt County's best known surf spots. **Moonstone Beach** (three miles south of Trinidad on Scenic Dr.) is a popular surf break where the Little River pours into Trinidad Bay. Up the road a half a mile, **Camel Rock** (about 2.3 miles south of Trinidad on Scenic Dr.) has right breaks that peel inside of a distinct, double-humped offshore rock.

ACCOMMODATIONS

The only lodging in Trinidad proper is the **Trinidad Bay Bed and Breakfast** (560 Edward St., 707/677-0840, www.trinidadbaybnb.com, $230-350), right across the street from the Trinidad Memorial Lighthouse. Each of the four rooms has a view of Trinidad Bay; two rooms have private entrances, and all have private bathrooms. A hot three-course breakfast is served every morning.

Between the main section of Trinidad and Patrick's Point State Park, **The Lost Whale Bed & Breakfast Inn** (3452 Patrick's Point Dr., 707/677-3425, http://lostwhaleinn.com, $270-315) has five rooms with great views of the Pacific and four with garden views. Two rooms have lofts to accommodate up to four people. There's a private trail to the beach below, an ocean-view hot tub, and a wood-burning sauna. A seven-course breakfast buffet is served every morning.

For those who want to rough it a bit, **The Emerald Forest** (753 Patrick's Point Dr., 707/677-3554, www.cabinsintheredwoods.com, $149-289) has a variety of rustic cabins for rent. The higher-end cabins have full kitchens and amenities like wood-burning stoves. RV and tent campsites are also available ($33-45), although the ones at nearby Patrick's Point State Park are more spacious.

FOOD

Stock up on delicious, locally smoked seafood at ◖ **Katy's Smokehouse** (740 Edwards St., 707/677-0151, www.katyssmokehouse.com, daily 9am-6pm). There are smoked oysters and salmon jerky, but you can't go wrong with the smoked king salmon. It's not a sit-down restaurant, so you'll need to get your order to go. It's great to bring on a camping trip to the nearby parks—just don't leave it out, or you'll end up feeding it to the bears.

The friendly, spunky staff at the **Beachcomber Café** (363 Trinity St., 707/677-0106, http://trinidadbeachcomber.blogspot.com, Mon.-Fri. 7am-4pm, Sat.-Sun. 8am-4pm) serve up coffee, cookies, paninis, and bagels. It also has free Wi-Fi with a purchase.

The original café that was opened in the current spot of the **Seascape Restaurant** (1 Bay St., 707/677-3762, daily 7am-8pm, $9-17) was blown away by a massive storm in 1959. While the Seascape might not blow you away, it has a great location on Trinidad Bay. It serves seafood sandwiches, burgers, and fish and chips, and something called a "Grilled Smokey" that's little more than salmon cream cheese spread between two toasted pieces of sourdough bread. Also of interest is a breakfast entrée of scrambled eggs topped with clam chowder.

Just north of Trinidad, the **Larrupin Café** (1658 Patrick's Point Dr., 707/677-0230, www.larrupin.com, Fri.-Wed. 5pm-9pm, $20-30) mesquite barbecues everything from tofu kebabs to creole prawns. They are also known for their mustard dill and red sauces, which you can purchase to take home.

INFORMATION AND SERVICES

To plan a trip to Trinidad, visit the **Official Trinidad Visitor Chamber of Commerce** website (www.trinidadcalif.com), which has lots of great information about the small community.

Trinidad is a small city, so don't expect too many services. However, there is a **post office** (357 Main St., 707/677-3117, www.usps.com). Most major services can be found in nearby Arcata.

GETTING THERE AND AROUND

Trinidad is 15 miles north of Arcata on U.S. 101. Take the 728 exit off the highway.

The **Redwood Transit System** (707/443-0826, www.redwoodtransit.org, adults $2.75, children and seniors $2.50) has buses that connect from Arcata and Eureka to Trinidad.

◖ PATRICK'S POINT STATE PARK

Patrick's Point State Park (4150 Patrick's Point Dr., 707/677-3570, www.parks.ca.gov, day use $8) is a rambling coastal park 25 miles north of Eureka, replete with beaches, historic landmarks, trails, and campgrounds. It's not the biggest of the many parks along the North Coast, but it is one of the best. The climate remains cool year-round, making it perfect for hiking and exploring, if not for ocean swimming. There's a native plant garden, a visitors center, and three campgrounds ($35), plus a recreated Yurok Village. Because Patrick's Point is small in comparison to the other parks, it's easy to get around. Request a map at the gate and follow the signs along the tiny and often nameless park roads.

Sights

Prominent among the local landmarks is the place the park was named after: **Patrick's Point,** which offers panoramic Pacific views and can be reached by a brief hike from a convenient parking lot. Adjacent to Patrick's Point in a picturesque cove is **Wedding Rock,** a promontory sticking out into the ocean like an upturned thumb. People really do hike the narrow trail out to the rock to get married; you might even see a bride and groom stumbling

along holding hands on their way back from the ceremony.

The most fascinating area in the park is **Sumeg Village,** a recreation of a native Yurok village based on an actual archaeological find east of here. Visitors can crawl through the perfectly round hobbit-like hole-doors into semi-subterranean homes, meeting places, and storage buildings. Or check out the native plant garden, a collection of local plants the Yurok people used for food, basketry, and medicine. Today, the local Yurok people use Sumeg Village as a gathering place for education and celebrations, and they request that visitors tread lightly and do not disturb this tranquil area.

Those who want to dip a toe in the ocean rather than just gaze at it from afar will be glad to know that Patrick's Point has a number of accessible beaches. The steep trail leading down to **Agate Beach** deters few visitors. This wide stretch of coarse sand bordered by cliffs shot through with shining quartz veins is perfect for lounging, playing, and beachcombing. The

© STUART THORNTON

Sumeg Village in Patrick's Point State Park

semiprecious stones for which it is named really do appear here. The best time to find good agates is in the winter, after a storm.

Hiking

Only six miles of trails thread their way through Patrick's Point. Choose from the **Rim Trail** (four miles round-trip), which will take you along the cliffs for a view of the sea and if you're lucky a view of migrating whales. Tree-lovers might prefer the **Octopus Tree Trail**, which provides a great view of an old-growth Sitka spruce grove.

Camping

The three campgrounds at Patrick's Point (information 707/677-3570, reservations 800/444-7275, www.reserveamerica.com, $35) have a total of 124 sites. It can be difficult to determine the difference between **Agate Beach, Abalone,** and **Penn Creek,** so be sure to get good directions from the park rangers when you arrive. Most campsites are pleasantly shaded by the groves of trees; all include a picnic table, fire pit, and food storage cupboard, and you'll find running water, restrooms, and showers nearby.

Information and Services

You can get a map and information at the **Patrick's Point State Park Visitors Center** (707/677-1945, summer daily 9am-5pm, winter usually daily 10am-4pm), immediately to the right when you get to the entry gate. Information about nature walks and campfire programs is posted on the bulletin board.

Getting There and Around

Patrick's Point State Park is located on the coast, 25 miles north of Eureka and 15 miles south of Orick on U.S. 101.

Redwood National and State Parks

The lands of Redwood National and State Parks (www.nps.gov/redw, day use and camping free) meander along the coast and include three state parks—Prairie Creek Redwoods, Del Norte Coast Redwoods, and Jedediah Smith. This complex of parkland encompasses most of California's northern redwood forests. The main landmass of Redwood National Park is just south of Prairie Creek State Park along U.S. 101, stretching east from the coast and the highway. To get to the park from the south, drive along Bald Hills Road.

REDWOOD NATIONAL PARK
Thomas H. Kuchel Visitors Center

If you're new to the Redwood National and State Parks, the **Thomas H. Kuchel Visitors Center** (U.S. 101, west of Orick, 707/465-7765, spring-fall daily 9am-5pm, winter daily 9am-4pm) is a large facility with a ranger station, clean restrooms, and a path to the shore. You can get maps, advice, permits for backcountry camping, and books. In the summer, rangers run patio talks and coast walks that provide a great introduction to the area for children and adults. You can also have a picnic at one of the tables outside the visitors center, or you can walk a short distance to Redwood Creek.

Trees of Mystery

Generations of kids have enjoyed spotting the gigantic wooden sculptures of Paul Bunyan and his blue ox, Babe, from U.S. 101. The **Trees of Mystery** (15500 U.S. 101 N., 707/482-2251 or 800/638-3389, www.treesofmystery.net, June-Aug. daily 8:30am-6:30pm, Sept.-May daily 9:30am-4:30pm, adults $15, seniors $11, ages 7-12 $8) doesn't disappoint as a great place to take a break from the road to let the family out for some good cheesy fun. Visitors can enjoy the original Mystery Hike, the SkyTrail gondola ride through the old-growth redwoods, and the palatial gift shop. Perhaps best of all, at the left end of the gift shop is a little-known gem: the Native American museum. A

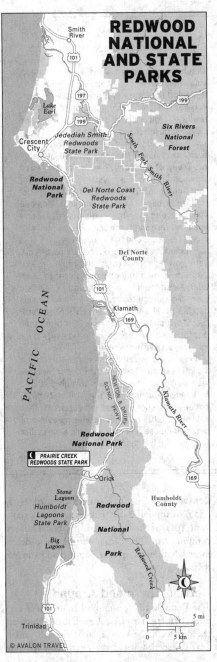

REDWOOD NATIONAL AND STATE PARKS

large collection of artifacts from ethnic groups across the country and indigenous to the redwood forests grace several crowded galleries. The restrooms here are large and well-maintained, which makes Trees of Mystery a nice stop en route.

Hiking

One of the easiest, most popular ways to get close to the trees is to walk the **Lady Bird Johnson Trail** (Bald Hills Rd., 1.4 miles, easy). This nearly level loop provides an intimate view of the redwood and fir forests that define this region. It's not far from the **Thomas H. Kuchel Visitors Center** (U.S. 101, west of Orick, 707/465-7765, summer daily 9am-5pm, winter daily 9am-4pm), and the staff there can direct you to the trailhead and provide a simple map. Another easy-access trail is **Trillium Falls** (Davison Rd. at Elk Meadow, 2.8 miles, easy). You may not see elk or trillium flowers, but the redwood trees along this cool, dark trail are striking, and the small waterfall is a nice treasure in the woods. This little hike is lovely any time of year but best in spring, when the water volume over the falls is at its peak.

The **Lost Man Creek Trail** (east of Elk Meadow, 1 mile off U.S. 101, 0.5-22 miles, easy-difficult) has it all. The first 0.5 miles is perfect for wheelchair users and families with small children. But as the trail rolls along, the grades get steeper and more challenging. You can customize the length of this out-and-back trail by turning around at any time. If you reach the Lost Man Creek picnic grounds, your total round-trip distance is 22 miles with more than 3,000 feet of elevation gain and several stream crossings.

Another fabulous long hike is the **Redwood Creek Trail** (Bald Hills Rd. spur off U.S. 101, difficult), which follows Redwood Creek for eight miles to the **Tall Trees Grove.** If you have someone willing to act as a shuttle driver, you can pick up the **Tall Trees Trail** and walk another 6 miles (a total of 14 miles) to the **Dolason Prairie Trail,** which takes you back out to Bald Hills Road.

TOURIST TRAPS

the Trees of Mystery's Paul Bunyan statue

As you wend your way up U.S. 101 through the verdant forests filled with rare trees, you'll become aware of something besides parks and trails luring visitors to pull over and rest awhile. You'll know them by the collections of chainsaw carvings, the kitschy hand-painted signs, and the cheap, shiny toys out front. Whether you've found a Redwood Sculpture Emporium, a Drive-Thru Tree, or a Mystery Spot, hang on to your wallet when you stop at one of the Redwood Coast's tourist traps.

The granddaddy of all tourist traps — it's even an example of the concept in Wikipedia — is the **Trees of Mystery.** Trees of Mystery has it all: wood sculptures, a "mystery" visual-trickery trail, and a gondola ride. But most of all, it's got a gift shop the size of a supermarket selling souvenirs beyond your imagination (unless you've imagined varnished redwood slices painted with images of Jesus and the Virgin Mary).

The various Drive-Thru Trees are usually privately-owned tourist traps, and you'll pay $10-20 to drive on a tiny one-way street through a large mutilated tree. The novelty of finding trees big enough to create drive-thru tunnels catches the attention of many out-of-state visitors. And families on long road trips often shell out for the drive-thru trees to sidetrack their kids for just five more minutes.

Finally, you can't miss the roadside redwood sculpture stands. They dot the sides of the highway, selling wooden animals lovingly sculpted by chainsaw artists. You'll also find T-shirts, coffee mugs, shot glasses, and dozens of other souvenirs. Little animal figurines made out of petrified moose and elk turds are a particular favorite with the children.

Accommodations and Camping

If you want to sleep indoors but still stay close to the national park, your best bet is the **Green Valley Motel** (120784 U.S. 101, Orick, 707/488-2341, $44) in nearby Orick.

There are no designated campgrounds in Redwood National Park, but free backcountry camping is allowed; permits may be necessary in certain areas. The **Elam Camp** and the **44 Camp** are both hike-in primitive campgrounds along the Dolason Prairie Trail.

Contact the **Crescent City Information Center** (1111 2nd St., Crescent City, 707/465-7335, spring-fall daily 9am-5pm, winter daily 9am-4pm) if you're planning a backcountry camping trip. The center can help you determine whether you need a permit and issue one if you do.

Getting There and Around

The Redwood National and State Parks line U.S. 101 from Prairie Creek Redwoods in the south all the way up to Jedediah Smith near Crescent City at the northern end. The

© STUART THORNTON

lush Fern Canyon, in Prairie Creek Redwoods State Park

Thomas H. Kuchel Visitors Center at the south end of the park is located 40 miles north of Eureka on U.S. 101.

◖ PRAIRIE CREEK REDWOODS STATE PARK

In addition to the silent majesty of the redwoods, **Prairie Creek Redwoods State Park** (Newton B. Drury Dr., 25 miles south of Crescent City, 707/465-7347, campground 707/488-2171, www.parks.ca.gov, day use $8) has miles of wild beach, roaming wildlife, and a popular hike through a one-of-a-kind fern draped canyon. The 14,000 acres of Prairie Creek offer a sampler platter of the best natural elements of the North Coast.

For wildlife enthusiasts, one of the many reasons to visit Prairie Creek is a chance to view a herd of **Roosevelt elk.** This subspecies of elk can stand up to five feet high and can weigh close to 1,000 pounds. These big guys usually hang out at—where else?—the Elk Prairie, a stretch of open grassland along the highway. The best times to see the elk are early morning and around sunset. August to October is the elk mating season, when the calls of the bulls fill the air. The elk do roam all over the park, but there's a good chance you might see some in the prairie located off the southern end of the Newton B. Drury Drive. The park asks that you stay in the viewing area and let the elk enjoy grazing in peace.

Prairie Creek Visitors Center

Just beyond the entrance off U.S. 101, the **Prairie Creek Visitors Center** (Newton B. Drury Dr., 707/488-2039, usually daily 9am-5pm) includes a small interpretive museum describing the history of the California redwood forests. A tiny bookshop adjoins the museum, well stocked with books describing the history, nature, and culture of the area. Many ranger-led programs originate at the visitors center, and permits are available for backcountry camping in the park.

Newton B. Drury Scenic Drive

A gorgeous scenic road through the redwoods,

Newton B. Drury Scenic Drive, off U.S. 101 about five miles south of Klamath, features old-growth trees lining the roads, a close-up view of the redwood forest ecosystem, and a grove or trailhead every hundred yards or so. The turn off is at the **Big Tree Wayside,** where you can walk up to the 304-foot-high **Big Tree.** It's life was almost cut short by a homesteader who wanted to cut it down to use the stump as a dance floor. Follow the short, five-minute loop trail near the Big Tree to see the other giants in the area.

Gold Bluffs Beach

Gold Bluffs Beach (Davison Rd., three miles north of Orick off U.S. 101) is truly wild. Lonely waves pound the shore, a spikey graph of Sitka spruce top the nearby bluffs, and herds of Roosevelt elk frequently roam the wide salt-and-pepper colored sands. Prospectors found gold flakes here in 1850, giving the beach its name. But, unsurprisingly, the region was too remote and rugged to maintain a lucrative mining operation. You can access Gold Bluffs Beach by taking Davison Road. No trailers are allowed on Davison Road.

Hiking

Perhaps the single most famous hiking trail along the redwood coast is **Fern Canyon** (Davison Rd., Prairie Creek Redwoods State Park), near Gold Bluffs Beach. This hike runs through a narrow canyon carved by Home Creek. Five-fingered ferns, sword ferns, and delicate lady ferns cascade down the steep canyon walls. Droplets from seeping water sources keep the plants alive. The unusual setting was used as a dramatic backdrop in the films *Return of the Jedi* and *Jurassic Park 2.*

To get to the trailhead, take U.S. 101 three miles north of the town of Orick and then, at the Prairie Creek visitors center, turn west onto Davison Road (no trailers allowed) and travel two more miles. This rough dirt road takes you through the campground and ends at the trailhead 1.5 miles later.

A short one-mile loop trail climbs out of the canyon, surrounded by the park's trees, their limbs sleeved in green mosses. You can extend this hike into a longer (6.5 miles, moderate) loop by starting at the same place; when the trail intersects with James Irvine Trail, bear right and follow that spur. Bear right again onto **Clintonia Trail** and walk through a redwood grove to Miners Ridge Trail. Bear right onto Miners Ridge, an old logging road, and follow it down to the ocean. Walk 1.5 miles along Gold Bluffs Beach to complete the loop.

Miners Ridge and **James Irvine Loop** (12 miles, moderate) covers some of the same ground but starts from the visitors center instead of the Fern Canyon trailhead, avoiding the rough dirt terrain of Davison Road. Start out on **James Irvine Trail** and bear right when you can, following the trail all the way until it joins Fern Canyon Trail. Turn left when you get to the coast and walk along Gold Bluffs Beach for 1.5 miles. Then make a left onto the Clintonia Trail and head back toward the visitors center.

If you're starting at the visitors center but don't want to do the entire 12-mile loop, you can cut this hike roughly in half. When you get to the Clintonia Trail on your way out to the coast, make a left instead of continuing on the James Irvine Trail. This will take you over to Miners Ridge, where you make another left to loop back to the starting point, for a total of about six miles. This is a pleasant hike with plenty of great trees; the drawback is that you don't get to see Fern Canyon.

If you're hiking the **California Coastal Trail** (www.californiacoastaltrail.info), you can do a leg here at Prairie Creek. The Coastal Trail runs along the northern coast of this park. Another way to get to the campground is via the **Ossagon Creek Trail** (north end of Newton B. Drury Dr., 2 miles round-trip, moderate). It's not long, but the steep grade makes it a tough haul in spots, and the stunning trees along the way make it worth the effort.

Camping

The **Elk Prairie Campground** (127011 Newton B. Drury Dr., Orick, campground 707/488-2171, reservations 800/444-7275, www.

reserveamerica.com, vehicles $35, hikers and cyclists $5) has 75 sites for tents or RVs and a full range of comfortable camping amenities. You can get a shower and purchase wood for your fire ring. Several campsites are wheelchair-accessible, so be sure to ask for one if you need it when you reserve your site. A big campfire area is north of the campground, an easy walk for campers interested in the evening programs put on by rangers and volunteers.

For a sand camping experience, head out to **Gold Bluffs Beach Campground** (Davison Rd., 3 miles north of Orick, www.nps.gov/redw, no reservations, $35/regular sites, $20/environmental sites). There are 26 sites for tents or RVs and 3 environmental sites. Amenities include flush toilets, water, solar showers, and wide ocean views. The surf can be quite dangerous here, so be extremely careful if you go in the water.

Backcountry camping is allowed in Prairie Creek, but only in two designated camping areas, Ossagon Creek and Miners Ridge (3 sites each, $5). Permits are available at the campground kiosk or the Prairie Creek visitors center (Newton B. Drury Dr., 707/488-2171, usually daily 9am-5pm).

Getting There

Prairie Creek Redwoods is located 50 miles north of Eureka and 25 miles south of Crescent City on U.S. 101. Newton B. Drury Drive traverses the park and can be accessed from U.S. 101 north or south.

DEL NORTE COAST REDWOODS STATE PARK

South of Crescent City, **Del Norte Coast Redwoods State Park** (Mill Creek Campground Rd., off U.S. 101, 707/465-7335, www.parks.ca.gov, $8) encompasses a variety of ecosystems, including eight miles of wild coastline, second-growth redwood forest, and virgin old-growth forests. One of the largest in this system of parks, Del Norte is a great place to get lost in the backcountry with just your knapsack and your fishing rod, exploring meandering branches of Mill Creek.

Hiking

Guided tours, nature trails, and wheelchair-accessible trails and campgrounds are all available at Del Norte. You'll want to dress in layers to hike as it can get down into the 40s even in summer. There are several rewarding yet gentle and short excursions that start and end in the Mill Creek Campground.

The **Trestle Loop Trail** (1 mile, easy) begins across from the campfire center in the campground. Notice the trestles and other artifacts along the way; the loop follows the route of a defunct railroad from the logging era. It's okay to eat the berries along this path; just keep in mind that bears and other animals like them as much as you do, so the more abundant the food, the more likely you'll have company. If you want more after this brief walk, take the nearby **Nature Loop Trail** (1 mile, easy), which begins near the campground entrance gate. This trail features interpretive signage to help you learn about the varieties of impressive trees you'll be passing.

These coastal parks are a cherished destination for serious hikers as well as sightseers, so it is possible to get a great workout along with the scenery. The northern section of the great **California Coastal Trail** (CCT, www.californiacoastaltrail.info) runs right through Del Norte Coast Redwoods State Park. The trail has been under development since 1972 and is ultimately envisioned as a 1,200-mile pathway along beaches and forests all the way from the Oregon border to the Mexican border. Not all of it will be completed for some time to come, but the parts available for use in Del Norte offer a great illustration of what the project is meant to be. The Coastal Trail is reasonably well marked; look for signs with the CCT logo.

The "last chance" section of the California Coastal Trail (Enderts Beach-Damnation Creek, 14 miles, strenuous) makes a challenging day hike. To reach the trailhead, turn west from U.S. 101 onto Enderts Beach Road in Del Norte, three miles south of Crescent City. Drive 2.3 miles to the end of the road, where the trail begins.

The trail follows the historic route of U.S.

101 south to Enderts Beach. You'll walk through fields of wildflowers and groves of trees twisted by the wind and saltwater. Eventually, the trail climbs about 900 feet to an overlook with a great view of Enderts Beach. At just over two miles, the trail enters Del Norte Coast Redwoods State Park, where it meanders through Anson Grove's redwood, fir, and Sitka spruce trees. At 4.5 miles, cross Damnation Creek on a footbridge, and at 6.1 miles, cross the Damnation Creek Trail. (For a longer hike, take the four-mile round-trip side excursion down to the beach and back.) After seven miles, a flight of steps leads up to milepost 15.6 on U.S. 101. At this point, you can turn around and return the way you came, making for a gloriously varied day hike of about 14 miles round-trip.

One alternative is to make this a point-to-point hike, either by dropping a car off at one end to get you back at the end of the day, or by having one group of hikers start at each end of the trail and exchange keys at a central meeting point.

If you've made arrangements for a lift back at the end of the day, you can continue on to the DeMartin section of the Coastal Trail. From here, descend through a lush grove of ferns and take a bridge over a tributary of Wilson Creek, enjoying views of the rocky coast far below. The wildflowers continue as you enter Redwood National Park and wander through the grasslands of DeMartin Prairie. The southern trailhead (where you pick up your vehicle if you're doing the trail one-way north-south) is at the Wilson Creek Picnic Area on the east side of U.S. 101 at the north end of DeMartin Bridge.

Camping

The **Mill Creek campground** (U.S. 101, 7 miles south of Crescent City, 800/444-7275, www. reserveamerica.com, May 1-Sept. 7, vehicles $35, hikers and cyclists $5) is in an attractive setting along Mill Creek. There are 145 sites for RVs and tents, and facilities include restrooms and fire pits. Feel free to bring your camper to the Mill Creek campground; it has spots for RVs and a dump station on-site. Call

in advance to reserve a spot and to be sure that your camper does not exceed the park's length limit. There are no designated backcountry campsites in Del Norte, and backcountry camping is not allowed.

Information and Services

Del Norte State Park has no visitors center, but you can get information from the **Crescent City Information Center** (1111 2nd St., Crescent City, 707/465-7335, spring-fall daily 9am-5pm, winter daily 9am-4pm). Minimal restroom facilities are available at the Del Norte campgrounds, and the park has an RV dump station but no RV hookups.

Getting There

Del Norte Coast Redwoods is located seven miles south of Crescent City on U.S. 101. The park entrance is on Hamilton Road, east of U.S. 101.

JEDEDIAH SMITH REDWOODS STATE PARK

The best redwood grove in the old growth of **Jedediah Smith Redwoods State Park** (U.S. 199, 9 miles east of Crescent City, 707/465-7335, www.parks.ca.gov, $8 per vehicle) is the **Stout Memorial Grove.** This bunch of coastal redwood trees is, as advertised, stout—although the grove was named for a person, not for the size of the trees. These old giants make humans feel small as they wander in the grove. These are some of the biggest and oldest trees on the North Coast and were somehow spared the loggers' saws. Another great thing about this grove is the lack of visitors, since its far-north latitude makes it harder to reach than some of the other big redwood groves in California.

Visitors Centers

There are two visitors centers in Jedediah Smith, about five minutes apart. Both offer similar information and include materials about all of the nearby parks. One is the **Jedediah Smith Visitors Center** (U.S. 101, Hiouchi, 707/458-3496, summer daily

SAVE THE REDWOODS

The stereotype of a tree-hugging conservationist usually brings to mind dirty, long-haired college students living on tarp-covered platforms and tying themselves to trees. Many visitors (and heck, residents) of California might imagine that it was a bunch of dreadlocked hippies and starving artists that saved the huge swaths of redwoods lining the North Coast region.

Nothing could be further from the truth. The California redwoods were saved by some very rich people.

Powerful rich white men poured their power, political connections, and, in some cases, millions of their own dollars into a group called the **Save the Redwoods League** (www.savetheredwoods.org). The three founders were a U.C. professor named John Merriam and fellow conservationists Madison Grant and Henry F. Osborn. After surveying the destruction of the forests surrounding brand-new U.S. 101 in 1917, the three men decided that something had to be done. And thus the League was born.

For over 90 years, the Save the Redwoods League has aggressively pursued the conservation of redwood forests in California. Using high-level political connections, the League successfully lobbied the U.S. government to create Redwood National Park and to expand the territory protected by Sequoia National Park. The league is also a major player at the state level, creating and expanding state parks all over the landscape.

So how did they get hold of all those groves? They bought them. Large donations plus the resources of League members have given the League the ability to buy thousands of acres of redwood forest, then donate them to various parks. They're still doing it to this very day, and in the 21st century the League has made several major purchases to expand Sequoia National Park, Redwood National Park, and several state parks.

Got some spare change in your ashtray? You can donate to Save the Redwoods and help the group preserve and expand California's fabulous redwoods. Donate your life savings, and they might even name a grove after you! (No promises though.)

9am-5pm, mid Sept.-mid May closed) and the other is the **Hiouchi Information Center** (U.S. 199, Hiouchi, 707/458-3294, summer daily 9am-5pm, fall-spring hours vary).

Hiking

The trails running through the trees make for wonderfully cool and shady summer hiking. Many trails run along the river and the creeks, offering a variety of ecosystems and plenty of lush scenery to enjoy. Wherever you hike, stay on the established trails. Wandering into the forest, you can trample the delicate and shallow redwood root systems, unintentionally damaging the trees you're here to visit.

The **Simpson Reed Trail** (U.S. 199, 6 miles east of Crescent City, 1 mile, easy) takes you from U.S. 199 down to the banks of the Smith River.

To get a good view of the Smith River, hike the **Hiouchi Trail** (2 miles, moderate). From the Hiouchi Information Center and campgrounds on U.S. 199, cross the Summer Footbridge and then follow the river north. The Hiouchi Trail then meets the Hatton Loop Trail and leads away from the river and into the forest.

If you're looking for a longer and more aggressive trek, try the **Mill Creek Trail** (7.5 miles round-trip, difficult). A good place to start is at the Summer Footbridge. The trail then follows the creek down to the unpaved Howland Hill Road.

If it's redwoods you're looking for, take the **Boy Scout Tree Trail** (5.2 miles, moderate). To get to the trailhead, you have to drive a rugged unpaved road for a couple of miles, but there are plenty of impressive trees to enjoy. The trail is usually quiet, with few hikers, and the gargantuan forest will make you feel truly tiny. About three miles into the trail, you'll come to a fork. If you've got time, take both forks: first the left, which takes you to the small, mossy, and very green Fern Falls, and then the right, which takes you to the eponymous Boy Scout Tree, one of the impressively huge redwoods.

Boating and Swimming

You'll find two boat launches in the park: one at Society Hole and one adjacent to the Summer Footbridge, which is only open in winter. Down by the River Beach Trail, you'll find **River Beach** (immediately west of the Hiouchi Information Center), a popular spot for swimming in the river. Swimming is allowed throughout the park, but be very careful—rivers and creeks move unpredictably, and you might not notice deep holes until you're on them. Enjoy the cool water, but keep a close eye on children and other loved ones to ensure a safe time.

Fishing

With the Smith River and numerous feeder creeks running through Jed Smith, it's not surprising that fishing is one of the most popular activities. Chilly winter fishing draws a surprising number of anglers to vie for king salmon up to 30 pounds and steelhead up to 20 pounds. Seasons for both species run October-February. In the summer you can cast into the river to catch cutthroat trout.

Camping

The ◖ **Jedediah Smith Campground** (U.S. 199, Hiouchi, 800/444-7275, www.reserveamerica.com, vehicles $35, hike-in or cycle-in primitive sites $5) is beautifully situated on the banks of Smith River, with most sites near the River Beach Trail (immediately west of the Hiouchi Information Center). There are 106 RV and tent sites. Facilities include plenty of restrooms, fire pits, and coin-operated showers. Reservations are advised, especially for summer and holiday weekends. The campground is open year-round, but reservations are accepted only Memorial Day-Labor Day. Jedediah Smith has no designated backcountry campsites, and camping outside the developed campgrounds is not allowed. If you're backpacking, check at one of the visitors centers for help in finding the nearest place to camp overnight.

Getting There

Jedediah Smith Redwoods State Park (U.S. 199, 9 miles east of Crescent City, 707/458-3018, www.parks.ca.gov, $8 per vehicle) is northeast of Crescent City along the Smith River, next door to the immense Smith River National Recreation Area (U.S. 199 west of Hiouchi). You can get there by taking U.S. 199 nine miles east of Crescent City.

Crescent City

The northernmost city on the California coast perches on the bay that provides its name. Cool and windswept, Crescent City is a perfect place to put on a parka, stuff your hands deep into your pockets, and wander along a wide, beautiful beach. The small city also has a vibrant surf scene centered around South Beach, which frequently has good waves for longboarders.

Crescent City is also known for surviving tsunamis. In 1964, a tsunami caused by an Alaskan earthquake wiped out 29 city blocks and killed 11 people. It was the most severe tsunami on the U.S. West Coast in modern history. In 2011, the devastating earthquake in Japan resulted in a tsunami that laid waste to the city's harbor. The old rusted warning sirens on the tops of the city's utility poles still work; when they sound, there's a chance of massive waves coming to shore.

Due to the depressed logging and fishing economy, Crescent City's downtown has its fair share of shuttered businesses. But if you're looking for an inexpensive hotel room to use as a base to explore the nearby redwoods or the area's impressive beaches, a night or two in Crescent City will fit the bill.

SIGHTS
Point St. George

Wild, lonely, beautiful **Point St. George** (end

of Washington Blvd.) epitomizes the glory of the North Coast of California. Walk out onto the cliffs to take in the deep blue sea, wild salt- and flower-scented air and craggy cliffs and beaches. On a clear day, you can see all the way to Oregon. Short steep trails lead across wild beach prairie land down to broad, flat, nearly deserted beaches. In spring-summer wildflow- ers bloom on the cliffs, and swallows nest in the cluster of buildings on the point. On rare and special clear days, you can almost make out the **St. George Reef Lighthouse** alone on its perch far out in the Pacific.

◖ Battery Point Lighthouse

Located on an island just north of Crescent City Harbor, the **Battery Point Lighthouse** (end of A St., 707/464-3089, daily Apr.-Sept., daily tides permitting, 10am-4pm, Oct.-Mar. Sat.-Sun. tides permitting 10am-4pm, adults $3, children 8-15 $1) is only accessible at low tide, when a rocky spit littered with tide pools emerges, serving as a walkway for visitors. The 1856 lighthouse's current keepers reside on the island in one-month shifts; they also lead tours. You'll see a Fresnel lens and a working clock that was used by Battery Point's first lighthouse keeper. After viewing the two resi- dential floors of the building, the docent leads any adventurous visitors up a metal ladder through a small hole into the lantern room, where you'll be able to feel the heat of the still working light just feet away. On a clear day, you'll also be able to see the pencil-like outline of the St. George Reef Lighthouse in the distance. St. George is situated on a small, wave-washed rock seven miles from shore, and its dangerous location resulted in the deaths of four keepers who worked there.

Ocean World

Are the kids bored with all the gorgeous scen- ery? A great family respite is **Ocean World** (304 U.S. 101 S., 707/464-4900, www.ocean- worldonline.com, summer daily 9am-9pm, winter daily 10am-6pm, adults $10, children $6). Tours of the small sea park depart about every 15 minutes and last about 40 minutes.

Featured attractions are the shark petting tank, the 500,000-gallon aquarium, and the sea lion show. After the tour, take a stroll through the immense souvenir shop, which sells gifts of all sizes, shapes, and descriptions, many with nau- tical themes.

Del Norte County Historical Society Museum

The **Del Norte County Historical Society Museum** (577 H St., 707/464-3922, www. delnortehistory.org, Apr.-Sept. Mon.-Sat. 10am-4pm, Oct.-Mar. by appointment, free) provides an educational respite from the chilly sea breezes. The Historical Society maintains this small museum that features the local his- tory of both the Native Americans who were once the only inhabitants of Del Norte County and the encroaching white settlers. Featured ex- hibits include the wreck of the *Brother Jonathan* at Point St. George, the story of the 1964 tsu- nami, and artifacts of the local Yurok and Tolowa people.

ENTERTAINMENT AND EVENTS

If you're looking for varied and rocking nightlife, Crescent City is not your town, but a few options exist for insomniacs. Most of the action after 9pm is at **Elk Valley Casino** (2500 Howland Hill Rd., 707/464-1020 or 888/574-2744, www.elkvalleycasino.com, daily 24 hours) at the eastern edge of town. Elk Valley is a bit more upscale than other local Native American casinos, with genuine aluminum-siding walls, poker and blackjack tables, a VIP card room, and a small non- smoking slots area. The on-site restaurant is the **Full House Bar & Grill** (Sun.-Thurs. 7am-10pm, Fri.-Sat. 7am-11pm, $7-29); a late-night food menu (daily 7am-2am) is available from the bar.

The **Tsunami Lanes Bowling Center** (760 L St., 707/464-4323, www.tsunamilanes.com, Mon.-Fri. noon-10pm, Sat. noon-midnight, adults $3 per game, seniors and children $2) is a straight-up bowling alley, serving beer and greasy fries to all comers late into the evening.

© STUART THORNTON

Crescent City's Battery Point Lighthouse

Theater

The **Del Norte Association for Cultural Awareness** (Crescent Elk Auditorium, 994 G St., 707/464-1336, www.dnaca.net) hosts several live musical acts and other performances each year and provides a community arts calendar. Check this year's schedule for upcoming shows.

Cinema

If all else fails, you can take in a first-run movie at the **Crescent City Cinemas** (375 M St., 707/570-8438, www.catheatres.com). Or even better, take in a movie in an old-fashioned drive-through theater at **Red's Crescent Drive-In Theatre** (four miles north of Crescent City on Elk Valley Crossroads, 707/464-1813, $12/vehicle).

Events

For almost 50 years, the Yurok people have held a festival to honor a creature most precious to them: the mighty salmon. The **Klamath Salmon Festival** (www.yuroktribe.org) takes place in August each year and includes a parade, live music, games, and, of course, salmon dinners served all day.

Each August since the early 1980s, the **Crescent City Triathlon** (707/465-3995, www.crescentcitytriathlon.com, adults $30-50, children $20-25) has challenged participants of all ages. This triathlon is a 5K run, a 500-yard swim, and a 12-mile bike ride (c'mon—you can do that). There's also a duathlon, which involves a run, a bike ride, and then another run; and there's a triathlon for kids that varies in intensity by age group, making it possible for anyone ages 5-12 to join the fun.

SPORTS AND RECREATION
Beaches

The sands of Crescent City are a beachcomber's paradise. Wide, flat, sandy expanses invite strolling, running, and just sitting to contemplate the broad crashing Pacific. **South Beach** (Hwy. 1 between Anchor Way and Sand Mine Rd.), as advertised, is located at the south end of town. Long, wide, and flat, it's perfect for a romantic stroll, as long as you're bundled up. The adventurous and chill-resistant can try surfing and boogie boarding. Farther south, **Crescent Beach** (Enderts Rd.) is two miles south of town. It's a wide, sandy beach. Down a half-mile dirt trail, **Enderts Beach** (Enderts Rd.) is a superb beach nestled along the coast south of Crescent City. This pocket beach has a creek flowing into the ocean and an onshore rock arch.

It might look tempting on rare sunny days, but swimming from the beaches of Crescent City is not for the faint of heart. The water is icy cold, the shores are rocky, and as elsewhere in Northern California, undertow and rip currents can be dangerous. No lifeguards patrol these beaches, so you are on your own.

Bird-Watching

Birders flock to Crescent City because the diverse climates and habitats nourish a huge variety of avian residents. The parks and preserves have become destinations for enthusiasts looking for "lifers" hard to find anyplace else. Right in town, check out **Battery Point Lighthouse Park** and **Point St. George.** For a rare view of an Aleutian goose or a peregrine falcon, journey to **Tolowa Dunes State Park** (1375 Elk Valley Rd., 707/465-2145, www.parks.ca.gov, daily sunrise-sunset, free), specifically the shores of Lake Earl and Kellog Beach. South of town, **Enderts Beach** is home to another large bird habitat.

Fishing and Whale-Watching

Anglers on the North Coast can choose between excellent deep-sea fishing and exciting river trips. The Pacific yields ling cod, snapper, and salmon, while the rivers are famous for chinook (king) salmon, steelhead, and cutthroat trout. Mammal-loving travelers can choose whale-watching over fishing. The *Tally Ho II* (1685 Del Mar Rd., at the harbor, 707/464-1236) is available for a variety of deep-sea fishing trips (May-Oct., half-day trip $100 pp), whale-watching (Feb.-Mar., 3-hour trip $50), or a combination of the two.

Enderts Beach

River fishers have a wealth of guides to choose from. **Ken Cunningham Guide Service** (50 Hunter Creek, Klamath, 707/391-7144, www.salmonslayer.net, $200-250) will take you on a full-day fishing trip; the price includes bait, tackle, and the boat. **North Coast Fishing Adventures** (1657 Childrens Ave., McKinleyville, 707/498-4087 or 707/839-8127, www.norcalriverfishing.com, $200 pp, minimum $400 per day) covers the Klamath and Smith Rivers as well as smaller waterways.

Hiking

The redwood forests that nearly meet the wide sandy beaches make the Crescent City area a fabulous place to hike. The hikes at **Point St. George** aren't strenuous and provide stunning views of the coastline and surrounding landscape. **Tolowa Dunes State Park** (1375 Elk Valley Rd., 707/465-2145, www.parks.ca.gov, daily sunrise-sunset, free), north of Point St. George, offers miles of trails winding through forests, across beaches, and meandering along the shores of Lake Earl.

Horseback Riding

The rugged land surrounding Crescent City looks even prettier from the back of a horse. Casual riders enjoy a guided riding adventure through redwoods or along the ocean with **Crescent Trail Rides** (2002 Moorehead Rd., 707/951-5407, www.crescenttrailrides.com, 1.5 hours $60, 4 hours $160). Under the same management, **Fort Dick Stable** (2002 Moorehead Rd., 707/951-5407, www.fortdickstable.com) offers boarding and riding lessons.

A great place to ride is **Tolowa Dunes State Park** (1375 Elk Valley Rd., 707/465-2145, www.parks.ca.gov, daily sunrise-sunset, free), which maintains 20 miles of trails accessible to horses. Serious equestrians with their own mounts can ride in to a campsite with corrals at the north end of the park off Lower Lake Road.

Surfing

While Crescent City is a long way from the legendary Southern California surf scene, the northernmost coastal city in California has a collection of surf breaks. Pioneering big wave surfer Greg Noll even lives in Crescent City. Just south of the harbor you'll find the most popular break in town, **South Beach** (Hwy. 1 between Anchor Way and Sand Mine Rd.), with peeling waves perfect for longboarders and beginners. It was once home to the Annual Noll Longboard Classic. North of town, **Point St. George** (end of Washington Blvd.) has a reef and point break that comes alive during winter. Run over to **South Beach Outfitters** (128 Anchor Way, 707/464-2963 or 877/330-7873, http://southbeachoutfitters.com, summer daily 10am-5pm, winter Wed.-Sun. 10am-5pm, board rental $25, wetsuit rental $10) to rent a board and wetsuit.

ACCOMMODATIONS

Lodgings in Crescent City are affordable even during the midsummer high season and can be surprisingly comfortable.

The aptly named **Curly Redwood Lodge** (701 U.S. 101 S., 707/464-2137, www.curlyredwoodlodge.com, $70-95) is constructed of a single rare curly redwood tree. You'll get to see the lovely color and grain of the tree in your large, simply decorated guest room. A 1950s feel pervades this friendly unpretentious motel even though it offers free Wi-Fi and is upgrading to flat screen TVs in every room. Right on U.S. 101, you can walk to South Beach or the Crescent City Harbor.

Few frills decorate the family-owned **Pacific Inn** (220 M. St., 707/464-9553 or 800/977-9553, $52-73), but the guest rooms are clean, inexpensive, and comfortable. Its central downtown location makes for easy access to restaurants, museums, and points of interest.

The **Lighthouse Inn** (681 U.S. 101 S., 707/464-3993 or 877/464-3993, www.lighthouse101.com, $89-145) has an elegant but whimsical lobby filled with dolphins and dollhouses to welcome guests, and the enthusiastic staff can help with restaurant recommendations and sights. Stylish appointments and bold colors grace each guest room. Corner suites with oversize whirlpool tubs make a perfect romantic retreat for couples at a reasonable nightly rate, while standard double rooms are downright cheap, given their comfort.

The **Anchor Beach Inn** (880 U.S. 101 S., 800/837-4116, www.anchorbeachinn.com, $59-118), at the south end of town, offers great access to South Beach, the harbor, and several good seafood restaurants. The ocean views overlook a wide swath of asphalt RV park, but the guest rooms have attractive decor and are clean and well maintained; continental breakfast and Internet access are included.

The best lodging location in town may be the █ **Cottage by the Sea** (205 S. A St., 707/951-1448 or 877/642-2254, www.vrbo.com, $135). Downtown and right on the coast, both the honeymoon cottage and the house overlook the Battery Point Lighthouse. At this nontraditional B&B, the owner cooks breakfast on request. Special rates are available for stays of at least three days.

FOOD

Not surprisingly, seafood is standard fare in Crescent City, but family restaurants and one or two ethnic eateries add some appealing variety.

American

Enjoy an impressive variety of fresh and healthy food at **The Good Harvest Cafe** (575 U.S. 101 S., 707/465-6028, Mon.-Sat. 7:30am-9pm, Sun. 8am-8pm, $10-35). It serves the best breakfast in town, with vegetarian options like tofu rancheros and veggie frittata. Steak and lobster dinner is at the high end of the dinner menu, which also includes burgers, pasta, vegetarian entrées, and big salads. Kitschy Native American decorations abound inside and out.

Fishermans Restaurant (700 U.S. 101 S., 707/465-3474, daily 6am-9pm, $11-26) is a casual place to grab a bite. You can walk in wearing jeans and sandy sneakers. The diverse dinner menu includes fresh local seafood offerings. Breakfasts feature biscuits and gravy, pancakes, and thick juicy bacon, all delicious—and big enough—to sustain you through a long day of hauling nets.

Coffee Shops and Markets

The **Java Hut** (437 U.S. 101 N., 707/465-4439, daily 5am-10pm, $5) is a drive-through and walk-up coffee stand that serves a wide array of coffee drinks. Beware of long lines of locals during the morning hours.

The small, family-owned, award-winning **Rumiano Cheese Co.** (511 9th St., 707/465-1535 or 866/328-2433, www.rumianocheese.com, June-Dec. Mon.-Fri. 9am-5pm, Sat. 9am-3pm, Jan.-May Mon.-Fri. 9am-5pm) has been part of Crescent City since 1921. Come to the tasting room for the cheese and stay for, well, more cheese. The dry jack cheese is a particular favorite, though lots of varieties are available.

Like many California towns, Crescent City runs a **farmers market** (Del Norte County Fairgrounds, 451 U.S. 101 N., 707/460-3537, June-Oct. Sat. 9am-1pm). While the harvest season is more restricted here than points south, veggie lovers can still choose from an array of fresh local produce all summer long.

Seafood

Northwood's Restaurant (675 U.S. 101 S., 707/465-5656, daily 6am-9pm, $8-20) prides itself on serving the freshest fish available, and in Crescent City that can mean the fillet you're eating for dinner was caught that very morning by a local fishing boat. The varied menu also includes imported exotic fish plus a number of land-based entrées to appeal to every palate.

For better seafood still at a reasonable price, the best bet is **The Chart Room** (130 Anchor Way, 707/464-5993, www.chartroomcrescentcity.com, summer Mon. 11am-4pm, Tues.-Sun. 6:30am-8pm, winter Thurs.-Sun. 7am-7pm, $10-23). It's very casual, the food is excellent, and it's right on the ocean, so you can watch sea lions cavort on the pier while you eat. If anyone in your party is not a seafood lover, the lasagna is excellent.

Thai

A Thai restaurant in Crescent City? Believe it. The **Thai House** (105 N. St., 707/464-2427, Sun.-Thurs. 11am-9pm, Fri.-Sat. 11am-10pm,

$10-15) does passable Thai food including curries and pad Thai.

INFORMATION AND SERVICES

The **Crescent City and Del Norte County Chamber of Commerce Visitors Center** (1001 Front St., 707/464-3174 or 800/343-8300, www.exploredelnorte.com, Mon.-Fri. 10am-4pm) is a good place to visit when you arrive. You'll find knowledgeable staffers who can advise you on "secret" local sights as well as the bigger attractions advertised in the myriad brochures lining the walls.

Also in town is the **Crescent City Information Center** (1111 2nd St., 707/465-7335, spring-fall daily 9am-5pm, winter daily 9am-4pm) run by Redwood National and State Parks. This friendly place has maps, souvenirs, and rangers who can chat about hiking, camping, and exploring the parks.

The Daily Triplicate (707/464-2141, www.triplicate.com), the local newspaper of Crescent City, is published Tuesday, Thursday, and Saturday. You can pick up a Del Norte County Map and a copy of *101 Things to Do in Del Norte/Southern Oregon* (www.101things.com) at the visitors center and many local businesses.

GETTING THERE AND AROUND

The main routes in and out of town are U.S. 101 and U.S. 199. Both are well maintained but are twisty in spots, so take care, especially at night. From San Francisco, the drive to Crescent City is about 350 miles (6.5 hours). It is 85 miles (under two hours) from Eureka north to Crescent City on U.S. 101. Traffic isn't a big issue in Crescent City, and parking is free and easy to find throughout town.

Jack McNamara Field (CEC, 5 miles northwest of town, 707/464-7288, www.fly-cec.com) is also called Del Norte County Airport and is the only airport in Crescent City. United Express has daily nonstop flights to San Francisco and Sacramento.

Redwood Coast Transit (RCT, 707/464-6400, www.redwoodcoasttransit.org, adults $0.75, senior and disabled $0.50, punch passes $10) handles bus travel in and around Crescent City. Make sure to have exact change handy. Four in-town routes and a coastal bus from Smith River to Arcata provide ample public-transit options for travelers without cars. Pick up a schedule at the visitors center (1001 Front St.) or local stores for current fares and times.

MONTEREY BAY

A half-moon-shaped indentation on California's Central Coast, Monterey Bay is at the heart of the state's marine ecosystems. This wild and rugged coastline provides ample opportunities to enjoy and explore the largest marine sanctuary in the country. Dive into the pristine waters off Monterey to explore the bay's swaying kelp forests. Board a whale-watching boat to spot gray whales sounding outside the harbor. Or ride the waves at world-renowned surf breaks.

This area has become a favorite getaway for locals as much as visitors. It's easy to see why. Small cities and towns dot the coastline, each with its fair share of notable attractions. The Santa Cruz Boardwalk is a seaside amusement park that offers roller coasters and bumper cars alongside a family-friendly stretch of sand. The Monterey Bay Aquarium artfully presents close-up views of local sea creatures, from cuddly sea otters to sleek sharks and surreal glowing jellyfish. Historic Cannery Row, immortalized by John Steinbeck in his novel of the same name, now offers seaside dining and shopping. Victorian architecture, small-town charm, and butterfly migrations are the draws at Pacific Grove. Exclusive coastal community Pebble Beach offers luxurious amenities alongside some of the most-photographed coastal scenery in the state. Carmel-by-the-Sea, founded by artists, is an idyllic village gently descending to a white-sand beach. And inland Carmel Valley offers a sunny escape from encroaching seaside fog, as well as a burgeoning wine industry with enough tasting rooms to fill a long, relaxing afternoon.

© SHANE DOLBIER

HIGHLIGHTS

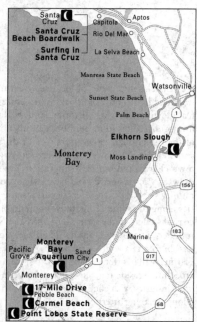

LOOK FOR (TO FIND RECOMMENDED SIGHTS, ACTIVITIES, DINING, AND LODGING.

PLANNING YOUR TIME

If you're coming to this part of the state for a weekend, pick an area and explore it in depth. Don't try to get everywhere in only two days. For a relaxed weekend without much travel, focus your trip on Santa Cruz or the Monterey Peninsula. If you've got more than a couple of days, start in either Santa Cruz or Monterey and work your way down or up the coast on Highway 1. In five days, you could easily hit major attractions including the Santa Cruz Boardwalk and Monterey Bay Aquarium, have a few great meals, and even find time to relax on a beach or in the woods.

Highway 1 connects the region from Santa Cruz southward to Carmel. At rush hour in the mornings and afternoons, the Santa Cruz section of Highway 1 can be jammed. Heading south from Santa Cruz, Highway 1 becomes a two-lane road near Moss Landing, about midway to Monterey, which can cause backups on busy weekends or if an accident occurs. The Highway 1 traffic generally lightens up around Monterey, although there can be slow spots heading north out of Monterey or south near Carmel during busy summer weekends and on summer weekday afternoons. Mountainous Highway 17, connecting the Bay Area city of

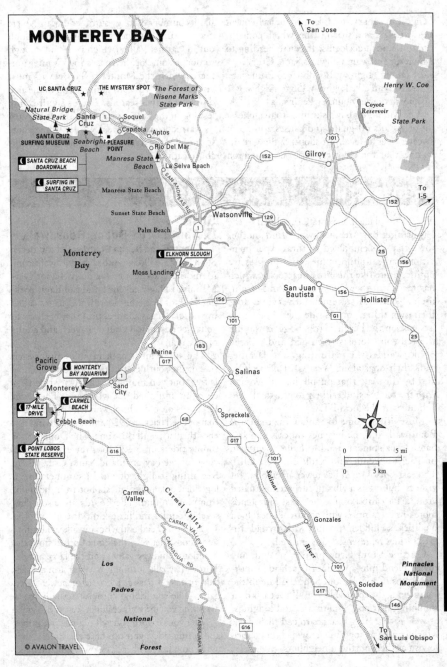

MONTEREY BAY

To San Jose

UC SANTA CRUZ ★   ★ THE MYSTERY SPOT

Natural Bridge State Park

The Forest of Nisene Marks State Park

Henry W. Coe

Coyote Reservoir

State Park

Santa Cruz   Soquel
SANTA CRUZ SURFING MUSEUM
Capitola   Aptos
Seabright Beach ■ PLEASURE POINT   Rio Del Mar
◖ SANTA CRUZ BEACH BOARDWALK
Manresa State Beach   La Selva Beach
◖ SURFING IN SANTA CRUZ

Manresa State Beach

Sunset State Beach

Palm Beach

101

152   Gilroy

To I-5

152

Monterey Bay

◖ ELKHORN SLOUGH

Moss Landing

Watsonville   129

25

156

San Juan Bautista   156   Hollister

G1

25

156

101

183

Marina
G17

Salinas

Pacific Grove
◖ MONTEREY BAY AQUARIUM
1
Monterey ★   Sand City
◖ 17-MILE DRIVE   ◖ CARMEL BEACH
Pebble Beach   68   Spreckels

G17

101

Carmel Valley   *Carmel Valley*

CARMEL VALLEY RD

◖ POINT LOBOS STATE RESERVE

G16

CACHAGUA RD

Los

Padres

Gonzales

Salinas   River

101

Pinnacles National Monument

National

G17   Soledad

146

To San Luis Obispo

Forest

TASSAJARA RD

G16

0   5 mi
0   5 km

© AVALON TRAVEL

San Jose to Santa Cruz, is known for its frequent heavy traffic and sharp turns, which contribute to frequent accidents. If you're heading to Monterey and want to bypass Santa Cruz, consider taking Highway 101 down to Prunedale, where you can take Highway 156 to Highway 1 just north of the Monterey Peninsula.

The Monterey Bay's summer fog catches a lot of visitors off guard and causes a jump in sweater sales at local gift shops. Santa Cruz is warmer than the Monterey Peninsula, but it too has its number of foggy summer days. If you're craving sun, consider spending an afternoon out in Carmel Valley, which is inland enough to dodge some of the coast's fog. While summer is when the Monterey Bay sees its most visitors, it is worth considering a trip to the area during the other seasons. There's significantly less fog in the fall, which often brings the area its warmest temperatures. Winter brings rainstorms, but the days without rain offer remarkably clear skies.

Santa Cruz

There's no place like Santa Cruz. Even in the left-leaning Bay Area, you won't find another town that has embraced cultural experimentation, radical philosophies, and progressive politics quite like this little beach city, which has made out-there ideas into a kind of municipal cultural statement. Everyone does their own thing: surfers ride the waves, nudists laze on the beaches, tree-huggers wander the redwood forests, tattooed and pierced punks wander the main drag, and families walk their dogs along West Cliff Drive. Oh, and by the way, that purple-haired woman with the tongue stud is likely to be a dedicated volunteer at the local PTA.

Most visitors come to Santa Cruz to hit the Boardwalk and the beaches. Locals and UC Santa Cruz students tend to hang downtown on Pacific Avenue and stroll on West Cliff. The east side of town has fewer attractions for visitors, but offers a vibrant surf scene situated around Pleasure Point. The West Side tends more toward families with children. Local food qualifies as a hidden treasure, with myriad ethnic cuisines represented and enjoyed.

Outside Santa Cruz proper, several tiny towns blend into appealing beachside suburbia. Aptos, Capitola, and Soquel all lie to the south along the coast. They've all got their own shopping districts, restaurants, and lodgings, as well as charming beaches to call their own, which can be as foggy, as crowded, or as nice to visit as their northern neighbors.

SIGHTS
◖ Santa Cruz Beach Boardwalk

The **Santa Cruz Beach Boardwalk** (400 Beach St., 831/423-5590, www.beachboardwalk.com, Memorial Day-Labor Day daily, Labor Day-Memorial Day weekends and holidays, parking $12), or just "the Boardwalk" as it's called by the locals, has a rare appeal that beckons to young children, too-cool teenagers, and adults of all ages.

The amusement park rambles along each side of the south end of the Boardwalk; entry is free, but you must buy either per-ride tickets or an unlimited ride wristband. The Giant Dipper is an old school wooden roller coaster that opened back in 1924 and is still giving riders a thrill after all this time. The Double Shot shoots riders up a 125-foot tower with great views of the bay or inland Santa Cruz before freefalling straight down. In summertime, a log ride cools down guests hot from hours of tromping around. The Boardwalk also offers several toddler and little-kid rides.

At the other end of the Boardwalk, avid gamesters choose between the lure of prizes from the traditional midway games and the large arcade. Throw baseballs at things, try your arm at skee-ball, or take a pass at a classic or newer video game. The traditional carousel actually has a brass ring you (or your children) can try to grab.

After you've worn yourself out playing games and riding rides, you can take the stairs down to the broad, sandy beach below the Boardwalk.

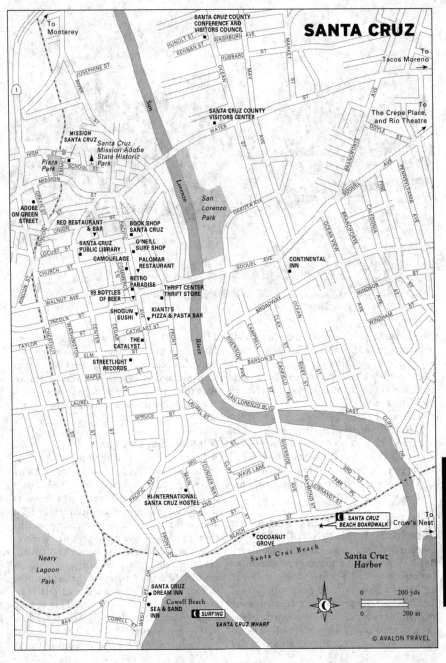

SANTA CRUZ

To Monterey

SANTA CRUZ COUNTY CONFERENCE AND VISITORS COUNCIL

To Tacos Moreno

To The Crepe Place, and Rio Theatre

SANTA CRUZ COUNTY VISITORS CENTER

MISSION SANTA CRUZ

Santa Cruz Mission Adobe State Historic Park

Plaza Park

San Lorenzo Park

ADOBE ON GREEN STREET

RED RESTAURANT & BAR

BOOK SHOP SANTA CRUZ

SANTA CRUZ PUBLIC LIBRARY

O'NEILL SURF SHOP

CAMOUFLAGE

PALOMAR RESTAURANT

CONTINENTAL INN

RETRO PARADISE

99 BOTTLES OF BEER

THRIFT CENTER THRIFT STORE

SHOGUN SUSHI

KIANTI'S PIZZA & PASTA BAR

THE CATALYST

STREETLIGHT RECORDS

HI-INTERNATIONAL SANTA CRUZ HOSTEL

SANTA CRUZ BEACH BOARDWALK

Crow's Nest

To Crow's Nest

COCOANUT GROVE

Neary Lagoon Park

Santa Cruz Beach

Santa Cruz Harbor

SANTA CRUZ DREAM INN

Cowell Beach

SEA & SAND INN

SURFING

SANTA CRUZ WHARF

0   200 yds

0   200 m

© AVALON TRAVEL

MONTEREY BAY

© STUART THORNTON

Santa Cruz Beach Boardwalk

It's a great place to flop down and sun yourself, or brave a dip in the cool Pacific surf. Granted, it gets a bit crowded in the summertime. But you've got all the services you could ever want right here at the Boardwalk, plus the sand and the water (and the occasional strand of kelp). What could be more perfect?

During the summer, the Boardwalk puts on free Friday night concerts on the beach featuring retro acts like hair metal band Warrant and 1980s New Wave band A Flock of Seagulls. See the website for a complete schedule of upcoming acts.

Monterey Bay National Marine Sanctuary Exploration Center

Opened in the summer of 2012, the **Monterey Bay National Marine Sanctuary Exploration Center** (35 Pacific St., 831/421-9993, http://montereybay.noaa.gov, Wed.-Sun. 10am-5pm, free) is Santa Cruz's newest attraction. Just feet away from the Santa Cruz Boardwalk and the Santa Cruz Wharf, the two-story building introduces visitors to the nearby Monterey Bay National Marine Sanctuary. Among the exhibits is an intertidal touch pool, a water-filled tank that recreates the Monterey Submarine Canyon, and an interactive weather station with real-time weather, surf, and buoy reports. A theater screens footage from a remote operated vehicle in the bay.

Mission Santa Cruz

Believe it or not, weird and funky Santa Cruz started out as a Mission town. **Mission Santa Cruz** (130 Emmet St., 831/426-5686, Tues.-Sat. 10am-4pm, Sun. 10am-2pm) was one of the later California missions, dedicated in 1791. Today, the attractive white building with its classic red-tiled roof welcomes parishioners to the active Holy Cross church and fourth-grade students from around the Bay Area to the historic museum areas of the old mission. In fact, the building you can visit today, like many others in the mission chain, is not the original complex built by the Spanish fathers in the 18th century. Instead it's a replica that was built in the 1930s. After you finish your tour of the complex and grounds, be sure to stop in at the Galeria, which houses the mission gift shop and a stunning collection of religious vestments—something you won't see in many other California missions.

Long Marine Laboratory

While the Monterey Bay Aquarium down the road in Monterey provides the best look into the nearby bay, the **Long Marine Laboratory** (Delaware Ave., 831/459-3800, http://seymourcenter.ucsc.edu, Tues.-Sat. 10am-5pm, Sun. noon-5pm, adults $6, children $4) is a worthwhile stop for people interested in sea creatures and marine issues. The large, attractive gray building complex at the end of Delaware Avenue sits right on the edge of the cliff overlooking the ocean—convenient for the research done primarily by students and faculty of UCSC. Your visit will be to the **Seymour Marine Discovery Center**—the part of the lab that's open to the public. You'll be greeted outside the door by a full blue whale skeleton that's lit up at night. Inside, instead of a standard

© STUART THORNTON

Santa Cruz Surfing Museum

aquarium setup, you'll find a marine laboratory similar to those used by scientists elsewhere in the complex. The aquariums showcase fascinating creatures including monkeyface eels and speckled sanddabs, while displays highlight environmental issues like shark finning. Kids particularly love the touch tanks, while curious adults enjoy checking out the seasonal tank that contains the wildlife that's swimming around outside in the bay *right now*.

If you've never been to Long/Seymour before, the best way to introduce yourself to the lab is to take a tour. Tours run at 1pm, 2pm, and 3pm each day; sign up an hour in advance to be sure of getting a slot.

University of California at Santa Cruz

The **University of California at Santa Cruz** (1156 High St., 831/459-0111, www.ucsc.edu) might be the single most beautiful college campus in the country. Set up in the hills above downtown Santa Cruz, the classrooms and dorms sit underneath groves of coast redwood trees, amongst tangles of ferns and vines and woodland creatures. Call 831/459-4118 for a tour of the campus (groups of six or more, reservations required). Or just find a parking lot and wander out into the woods like the students do, looking for a perfect circle of trees to sit and meditate within.

Santa Cruz Surfing Museum

Just feet away from Santa Cruz's most well-known surf spot, Steamer Lane, the tiny **Santa Cruz Surfing Museum** (1701 West Cliff Dr., 831/420-6289, www.santacruzsurfingmuseum.org, Wed.-Mon. 10am-5pm, donations appreciated) is housed within a still operating lighthouse. Run by the Santa Cruz Surfing Club Preservation Society, the one-room museum has pictures of Santa Cruz's surfing culture from the 1930s to the present. One haunting display on shark attacks includes a surfboard with bite marks from a local great white shark.

Wilder Ranch State Park

North of Santa Cruz's city limits, the land on

MONTEREY BAY

SURF CITY

There's a plaque outside the Santa Cruz Surfing Museum that explains how three Hawaiian princes introduced surfing to California in 1885. Apparently, they rode redwood planks from a nearby lumber mill on waves at the mouth of the San Lorenzo River in Santa Cruz.

While Santa Cruz's claim as being the birthplace of surfing on the mainland is not disputed, the popular surfing town calling itself "Surf City" has raised the hackles of southern California's Huntington Beach, which also likes to have its tourist T-shirts adorned with "Surf City." In 2006, Huntington Beach was awarded exclusive use of the title "Surf City" by the U.S. Patent and Trademark Office and went after Santa Cruz beachwear stores that sold T-shirts with the words "Santa Cruz" and "Surf City."

Despite Huntington Beach's aggressive legal action, the residents of Santa Cruz might have the last laugh. In 2009, *Surfer Magazine* proclaimed that Santa Cruz is "The Real Surf City, USA" in a piece about the top 10 surf towns. To Huntington Beach's chagrin, it didn't even make the magazine's top 10 list.

both sides of Highway 1 suddenly gives way to farmland perched atop coastal terraces. The best place to get a feel for this mostly undeveloped stretch of coastline is to visit **Wilder Ranch State Park** (1401 Coast Rd., 831/426-0505, www.parks.ca.gov, daily 8am-sunset, $10). The park allows visitors to step back in time and discover what it was like to live on a ranch over 100 years ago at their many living history demonstrations. For those who would rather check out the park's natural beauty in the present, the 2.5-mile-long **Old Cove Landing Trail** is a flat easy hike out to the coastline, which is pocketed with sea caves and usually decorated with wildlife from elegant cormorants to harbor seals lazing on the coastal shelves.

The Forest of Nisene Marks State Park

Take a walk at **The Forest of Nisene Marks State Park** (four miles north of Aptos on Aptos Creek Rd., 831/763-7062, www.parks.ca.gov, daily sunrise-sunset), once the site of serious logging operations, but now shaded by second-growth redwoods. Mountain bikers can ride up the fire road through the center of the park, while hikers can head out on over 30 miles of hiking trails that take off from the roadway. One popular hike is the **Loma Prieta Grade Trail** (six miles round-trip), which follows an old railway bed up to the remnants of a lumber camp. Another point of interest within the park is the epicenter of the 1989 Loma Prieta earthquake, which interrupted television coverage of the World Series and caused the collapse of a section of San Francisco's Bay Bridge.

The Mystery Spot

Klamath has the Trees of Mystery, Leggett has its drive-through tree, and Santa Cruz has its own kitschy tourist trap: **The Mystery Spot** (465 Mystery Spot Rd., 831/423-8897, www.mysteryspot.com, winter Mon.-Fri. 10am-4pm, Sat.-Sun. 10am-5pm, $5/door, $6/advance online, children under 3 free, $5/parking per vehicle). It's a tiny piece of land just outside of Santa Cruz where gravity fails. Balls can roll uphill and people can stand off the side of a wall. It may be an area of spatial distortion where the laws of physics don't apply...or it may be a collection of optical illusions. Regardless, it has a sweet gift shop that sells the near iconic Mystery Spot bumper sticker and other necessities like thong underwear.

ENTERTAINMENT AND EVENTS
Bars and Clubs

Lovers of libations should grab a drink at **Red Restaurant & Bar** (1003 Cedar St., 831/425-1913, www.redsantacruz.com, daily 3pm-1pm), located upstairs in the historic Santa Cruz Hotel Building. Creative cocktails include signature creations like the "Jean Grey," a mix of house-infused Earl Grey organic gin, lemon, and simple syrup. With its dark wood paneling and burgundy bar stools, Red feels like an old speakeasy. It also serves a comprehensive late night menu until 1am for those who need some food to soak up their alcohol.

The Crepe Place (1134 Soquel Ave., 831/429-6994, http://thecrepeplace.com, Mon.-Thurs. 11am-midnight, Sat.-Sun. 9am-midnight) has recently emerged as a hangout for the hipster crowd, who are drawn in by the high-profile indie rock acts and popular Bay Area bands that perform in its intimate front room.

Live Music

The Catalyst (1011 Pacific Ave., advance tickets 866/384-3060, door tickets 831/423-1338, www.catalystclub.com), right downtown on Pacific Avenue, hosts a variety of reggae, rap, and punk acts from Snoop Dogg to Agent Orange. Be sure to check the calendar when you buy tickets—some shows are 21 and over only. The main concert hall is a standing-room-only space, while the balconies offer seating. The bar sits downstairs adjacent to the concert space. The vibe tends to be low-key, but it depends on the night and the event. The more retro acts draw an older crowd. The Catalyst also hosts free jazz music in The Atrium on most Mondays. You can buy tickets online or by phone; purchasing in advance is recommended, especially for national acts.

The **Crow's Nest** (2218 East Cliff Dr., 831/476-4560, www.crowsnest-santacruz.com, $3-8) is as a venue for all kinds of live musical acts. You might see a jazz-fusion group one night and a Southern rock band the next. Lots of funk bands play the Nest—it's just appropriate to the Santa Cruz ethos. Check the website for a performance calendar, but it's a good bet that you'll get live musical entertainment here every night Wednesday-Saturday.

A former 1940s movie house, the **Rio Theatre** (1205 Soquel Ave., 831/423-8209, www.riotheatre.com) has been hosting everything from film festivals to performances by national touring acts like Yo La Tengo and Hot Tuna. Check the theater's website for a full list of upcoming events.

Comedy

For a good laugh in Santa Cruz, the **Crow's Nest** (2218 East Cliff Dr., 831/476-4560, www.crowsnest-santacruz.com, comedy Sun. 9pm, $7) hosts a weekly stand-up comedy show. Because the show runs on Sunday nights, the Crow's Nest takes advantage of the opportunity to hire big-name comics who have been in San Francisco or San Jose for weekend engagements. This lets folks see headliners in a more casual setting for a fraction of the cost of the big-city clubs. The Crow's Nest, with its great views out over the Pacific, also has a full bar and restaurant. You can enjoy drinks and dinner while you get your giggle on.

Theater

If you prefer historic theater to modern, UCSC puts on an annual summer Shakespeare festival: **Shakespeare Santa Cruz** (1156 High St., 831/459-2159, http://shakespearesantacruz.org, $15-50). This five-week festival usually runs in the second half of July through August. There are two venues, both on the UCSC campus, one indoor at the Theatre Arts Mainstage and the other out in the redwood forests in the Festival Glen. Each year the festival puts up at least two Shakespeare plays—2012 selections included *Twelfth Night* and *Henry IV*—plus at least one other production (often a more contemporary play). At the outdoor glen, audience members are encouraged to bring their own picnics. This can make for the perfect romantic date, or a fun outing for the whole family.

SHOPPING

For a small city, Santa Cruz has a bustling downtown, centered on Pacific Avenue. The quirky performance artists on the sidewalk might make you think you're in Berkeley or San Francisco. It's a good idea to park in one of the structures a block or two off Pacific Avenue and walk from there. At the north end, shoppers peruse antiques, boutique clothing, and kitchenware. Down at the seedier south end of the mall, visitors can get shiny new body jewelry, a great new tattoo, or a silicone sex toy. In the middle, you can grab a cappuccino, a cocktail, or a bite to eat in one of the many independent eateries.

Book Shop Santa Cruz (1520 Pacific Ave., 831/423-0900, www.bookshopsantacruz.com, Sun.-Thurs. 9am-10pm, Fri.-Sat. 9am-11pm) is a superb independent bookstore that hosts regular readings by literary heavy hitters like Jonathan Franzen and Daniel Handler.

Santa Cruz's Jack O'Neill is credited with making cold-water surfing possible with the invention of the wetsuit. His **O'Neill Surf Shop** (110 Cooper St., 831/469-4377, Sun.-Thurs. 10am-8pm, Fri.-Sat. 10am-9pm) specializes in surfboards, brand name clothing, and, of course, wetsuits. If your trip to California has gotten you hooked on riding the waves, and you just have to invest in your own equipment, O'Neill can be a good place to start. You can also buy a T-shirt or some sweats here—handy if you didn't pack quite right for Central Coast summer fog. There's also another location in Capitola (1115 41st Ave., 831/475-4151, Mon.-Fri. 9am-8pm, Sat.-Sun. 8am-8pm).

If you're wanting to buy clothes in Santa Cruz, chances are you're looking for a secondhand store. This town has plenty of 'em. One of the largest of these sits only a block off Pacific Avenue—the aptly if redundantly named **Thrift Center Thrift Store** (504 Front St., 831/429-6975, Mon.-Sat. 9am-8pm, Sun. 10am-6pm). This big, somewhat dirty retail space offers a wide array of cheap secondhand clothes. You'll need to hunt a bit to find that one perfect vintage item, but isn't that the fun of thrift shopping?

Camouflage (1329 Pacific Ave., 831/423-7613, www.shopcamoflauge.com, Mon.-Thurs. 11am-8pm, Fri.-Sat. 11am-10pm, Sun. 11am-7pm) is an independent, family-owned and women-friendly adult store. The first room contains mostly lingerie and less-shocking items. Dare to walk through the narrow black-curtained passage and you'll find the *other* room, which is filled with grown-up toys designed to please women of every taste and proclivity.

Stop in to **Streetlight Records** (939 Pacific Ave., 831/421-9200, www.streetlightrecords.com, Sun.-Mon. noon-8pm, Tues.-Thurs. 11am-9pm, Fri.-Sat. 11am-10pm) to pick up the latest music for your drive down the coast. With records and turntables making a serious comeback, Streetlight is also the place in Santa Cruz to find new and used vinyl.

SPORTS AND RECREATION
Beaches

At the tip of the West Side, **Natural Bridges State Park** (2531 West Cliff Dr., 831/423-4609, www.parks.ca.gov, daily 8am-sunset, $10) used to have three coastal arches right offshore. Even though there is only one arch remaining, this picturesque state park has a beach that doesn't stretch wide, but falls back deep, crossed by a creek that feeds out into the sea. An inconsistent break makes surfing at Natural Bridges fun on occasion, while the near-constant winds that sweep the sands bring out windsurfers nearly every weekend. Hardy sun-worshippers brave the breezes, bringing out their beach blankets, umbrellas, and sunscreen on rare sunny days (usually in late spring and fall). Back from the beach, a wooded picnic area has tables and grills for small and larger parties. Even farther back, the park has a monarch butterfly preserve, where the migrating insects take over the eucalyptus grove during the fall and winter months. Rangers offer guided tours of the tide pools that range out to the West Side of the beach. You can access these by a somewhat scrambling short hike (0.25-0.5 miles) on the rocks cliffs. These odd little holes filled with sea life aren't like most tide pools—many are nearly perfect round depressions in the sandstone cliffs worn away by harder stones as the tides move tirelessly back and forth. Just don't touch the residents of these pools, since human hands can hurt delicate tide pool creatures.

At **Cowell's Beach** (350 West Cliff Dr.), lots of beginning surfers have rode their first waves. This West Side beach sits right at a crook in the coastline that joins with underwater features to create a reliable small break that lures new surfers by the dozens.

At the south end of Santa Cruz, down by the harbor, beachgoers flock to **Seabright**

© STUART THORNTON

the last remaining natural bridge at Santa Cruz's Natural Bridges State Park

Beach (East Cliff Dr. at Seabright Ave., 831/427-4868, www.santacruzstateparks.org, daily 6am-10pm, free) all summer long. This miles-long stretch of sand, protected by the cliffs from the worst of the winds, is a favorite retreat for sunbathers and loungers. While there's little in the way of snack bars, permanent volleyball courts, or facilities, you can still have a great time at Seabright. There is a lot of soft sand to lie in, plenty of room to play football or set up your own volleyball net, and, of course, easy access to the chilly Pacific Ocean. There's no surfing here—Seabright has a shore break that delights skim-boarders, but makes wave riding impossible.

Down in Capitola, one of the favorite sandy spots is **New Brighton State Beach** (1500 Park Ave., Capitola, 831/464-6330, www.parks.ca.gov). This forest-backed beach has everything: a strip of sand that's perfect for lounging and cold-water swimming, a forest-shaded campground for both tent and RV campers, hiking trails, and ranger-led nature programs. If you plan to camp, call in advance to make reservations at this popular state park, or just come for the day and set up your spot out on the sand. New Brighton can get crowded on rare sunny summer days, but it's nothing like the wall-to-wall people of the popular Southern California beaches. There's also an old cement ship down the beach that can be accessed by walking out on a pier.

◖ Surfing

The coastline of Santa Cruz has more than its share of great surf breaks. The water is cold, demanding full wetsuits year-round, and the shoreline is rough and rocky—nothing at all like the flat sandy beaches of SoCal. But that doesn't deter the hordes of locals who ply the waves every day they can. The surfing culture pervades the town—if you walk the cliff, you'll likely pass the *To Honor Surfing* sculpture. Santa Cruz loves this statue, and it's often dressed up and always gets a costume for Halloween.

If you're a beginner, the best place to start surfing Santa Cruz is **Cowell's** (stairs at West

Cliff and Cowell's Beach). The waves rarely get huge here, and they typically provide long, mellow rides, perfect for surfers just getting their balance. Because the Cowell's break is acknowledged as the newbie spot, the often-sizeable crowd tends to be polite to newcomers and tourists.

For more advanced surfers looking for smaller crowds in the water, **Manresa State Beach** (San Andreas Rd., Aptos, 831/761-1795, www.parks.ca.gov) is a nice beach break south of Santa Cruz. Manresa is several minutes' drive toward Aptos. During summer, it's a great place to surf and then recline on the beach.

Visitors who know their surfing lore will want to surf the more famous spots along the Santa Cruz shore. **Pleasure Point** (between 32nd Ave. and 41st Ave.) encompasses a number of different breaks. You may have heard of The Hook (steps at 41st Ave.), a well-known experienced longboarder's paradise. But don't mistake The Hook for a beginner's break; the locals feel protective of the waves here and aren't always friendly towards inexperienced tourists. The break at 36th and East Cliff (steps at 36th Ave.) can be a better place to go on weekdays—on the weekends, the intense crowding makes catching your own wave a challenge. Up at 30th and East Cliff (steps at 36th Ave.), you'll find shortboarders catching larger, long peeling sets if there is a swell in the water.

The most famous break in all of Santa Cruz can also be the most hostile to newcomers. **Steamer Lane** (West Cliff between Cowell's and the Lighthouse) has a fiercely protective crew of locals. But if you're experienced and there's a swell coming in, Steamer Lane can have some of the best waves on the California coast.

Yes, you can learn to surf in Santa Cruz despite the distinct local flavor at some of the breaks. Check out either **Club Ed** (831/464-0177, www.club-ed.com) or the **Richard Schmidt School Inc.** (849 Almar Ave., 831/423-0928, www.richardschmidt.com) to sign up for lessons. Who knows, maybe one day the locals will mistake you for one of their own!

Stand Up Paddleboarding

The latest water sport craze has definitely hit Santa Cruz. Stand up paddleboarders vie for waves with surfers at Pleasure Point and can also be found in the Santa Cruz waters with less wave action. **Covewater Paddle Surf** (726 Water St., 831/600-7230, www.covewater.com, 2-hour lesson/$59) conducts beginner stand up paddleboarding (SUP) classes in the relatively calm waters of the Santa Cruz Harbor. They also offer yoga classes where the SUPs function like giant floating yoga mats.

Hiking and Biking

To walk or bike where the locals do, just head out to **West Cliff Drive.** This winding street with a full-fledged sidewalk trail running its length on the ocean side is the town's favorite walking, dog-walking, jogging, skating, scootering, and biking route. You can start at Natural Bridges (the west end of West Cliff) and go for miles. The *To Honor Surfing* statue lies several miles down the road, as do plenty of fabulous views. Bring your camera if you're strolling West Cliff on a clear day—you won't be able to resist taking photos of the sea, cliffs, and sunset. Just be sure to watch for your fellow path-users. What with the bicyclists and skaters and such, it can get a bit treacherous if you don't watch where you're going.

Spas

It's hard to beat a soak in some hot water after a day of surfing Santa Cruz's breaks or walking the city's vibrant downtown area. The **Tea House Spa** (112 Elm St., 831/426-9700, www.teahousespa.com, daily 11am-midnight, $12/hour pp) is a half block off Pacific Avenue and offers private hot tubs with a view of a bamboo garden. It's not a fancy facility, but the tubs will warm you up and mellow you out.

ACCOMMODATIONS
Under $150

Staying at a hostel in Santa Cruz just feels right. And the **Hostelling International Santa Cruz Hostel** (321 Main St., 831/423-8304, www.hi-santacruz.org, $29 dorm, $55 private room,

$150 cottage) offers the area's only real budget lodging. These historic renovated cottages are just two blocks from the Santa Cruz Boardwalk. It's clean, cheap, friendly, and also close to Cowell's Beach. You'll find a spot to store your surfboard or bike for free, and car parking is $2 per day. The big homelike kitchen is open for guest use and might even be hiding some extra free food in its cupboards. Expect all the usual hostel-style amenities, a nice garden out back, an outdoor deck, free linens, laundry facilities, and a free Internet kiosk. Just be aware that there is an 11pm curfew.

$150-250

For a room overlooking the ocean, stay at the **Sea & Sand Inn** (201 West Cliff Dr., 831/427-3400, www.santacruzmotels.com, $199-449). Every room in the house comes with an ocean view (hence the high price for what is really a pretty basic motel room), and suites with hot tubs and private patios make for a wonderful seaside vacation. Rooms and suites do have nicer-than-average decor with pretty furniture, private baths, and free Internet access. There's also a grassy lawn and small deck overlooking Cowell's Beach.

The four-room **Adobe on Green Street** (103 Green St., 831/469-9866, www.adobeongreen. com, $189) offers lovely bed-and-breakfast accommodations close to the heart of downtown Santa Cruz. The location, within walking distance of downtown, lets you soak in the unique local atmosphere to your heart's content. A unifying decorative scheme runs through all four-guest rooms—a dark and minimalist Spanish Mission style befitting Santa Cruz's history as a mission town. Each room has a queen bed, a private bathroom (two have whirlpool tubs), a small TV with DVD player, and lots of other amenities that can make you comfortable even over a long stay. An expansive continental spread is set out in the dining room each morning 8am-11am. Expect yummy local pastries, organic and soy yogurts, eggs, coffee, and juice. In keeping with the Santa Cruz ethos, the Adobe runs on solar power. The owner of the adobe is also the founder of the Santa Cruz

Food Tour, a 1.8-mile stroll to five tasting locations. More information can be found at www. santacruzfoodtour.com.

Located amongst a strip of motels on Ocean Street, the **Continental Inn** (414 Ocean St., 831/429-1221, www.continentalinnsantacruz. com, $220) doesn't look like much from the outside. But, inside, most of the rooms have hardwood floors and all include a fridge and microwave. It is also a short walk to Santa Cruz's downtown.

Over $250

The ◖ **Santa Cruz Dream Inn** (175 West Cliff Dr., 831/426-4330, www.dreaminnsantacruz. com, $309) is in a location that cannot be beat. Perched over Cowell's Beach and the Santa Cruz Wharf, the Dream Inn has 165 rooms, all with striking ocean views and either a private balcony or a shared common patio. The rooms have a retro chic feel that matches perfectly with the vibrant colors of the nearby Santa Cruz Boardwalk.

On a sunny day, it would be difficult to ever leave the Dream Inn's sun deck, which is located right on Cowell's Beach. You can take in the action of surfers, stand up paddleboarders, and volleyball players from the comforts of the deck's heated swimming pool or large, multi-person hot tub. Or you could just relax on a couch or reclining chair while sipping a cocktail from the poolside bar.

If hunger strikes, the Dream Inn's Aquarius Restaurant serves tasty fare for breakfast, lunch, and dinner. They also offer signature cocktails like the "Cold Water Classic," which is named after an annual Santa Cruz surf contest.

FOOD
California Cuisine

At **Cafe Cruz** (2621 41st Ave., Soquel, 831/476-3801, www.cafecruz.com, Mon.-Sat. 11:30am-2:30pm and 5:30pm-close, Sun. 5:30pm-close, $16-30), the menu runs toward homey American favorites done up with a California twist (ribs, rotisserie chicken, bowls of pasta, and crunchy fresh salads). Cafe Cruz purchases the freshest local produce, meats, seafood, and

Shadowbrook

even drinks they can find. You can munch locally caught fish with goat cheese from Half Moon Bay and an organic soda from Monterey. The attractive white-tablecloth dining room welcomes casual and elegant diners alike, and if you choose wisely you can get an upscale meal for medium-scale prices.

The Santa Cruz region boasts one serious upscale eatery. Dining at **Shadowbrook** (1750 Wharf Rd., Capitola, 831/475-1511, www. shadowbrook-capitola.com, Mon.-Fri. 5pm-8:45pm, Sat. 4:30pm-9:30pm, Sun. 4:30pm-8:45pm, $25) begins with taking a cable car down to the dining area. The cliffside location has perhaps the most impressive views and atmosphere of any restaurant in the area. Shadowbrook makes for a perfect spot to stage the ultimate romantic date, complete with candlelight and fine chocolate desserts.

Coffee and Bakeries

For a casual sandwich or pastry, head to **Kelly's French Bakery** (402 Ingalls St., 831/423-9059, www.kellysfrenchbakery.com, Sat.-Thurs. 7am-7pm, Fri. 7am-8pm, $10). This popular bakery makes its home in an old industrial warehouse-style space, and its domed shape constructed out of corrugated metal looks like anything but a restaurant. It's got both indoor and outdoor seating, and serves full breakfasts and luncheon sandwiches. You can order to stay in or to go, and pick up a breakfast or sweet pastry, some bread, or a cake.

French

In Aptos, **Cafe Sparrow** (8042 Soquel Dr., Aptos, 831/688-6238, www.cafesparrow. com, Mon.-Fri. 11:30am-2pm and 5:30pm-close, Sat. 5:30pm-close, Sun. 9am-2pm and 5:30pm-close, $20) serves country French cuisine that's consistently tasty. Whatever you order, it will be fantastic. The seafood is noteworthy as are the steaks. Cafe Sparrow's kitchen prepares all the dishes with fresh ingredients, and the chef (who can sometimes be seen out in the dining room checking on customer satisfaction with the food) thinks up innovative preparations and creates tasty sauces. He's also willing to accommodate special requests and dietary restrictions with good cheer. For dessert, treat yourself to the profiteroles, which can be created with either ice cream or pastry cream.

Italian

Right on bustling Pacific Avenue, **Kianti's Pizza & Pasta Bar** (1100 Pacific Ave., 831/469-4400, www.kiantis.com, Mon.-Fri. 11am-10pm, Sat.-Sun. 10am-10pm, $13-21) draws in crowds with individual and family-sized servings of pastas, pizzas and salads. Pizzas toppings range from traditional Italian ingredients to more creative options (one pie is covered with seasoned beef, lettuce, tomato, avocado, and tortilla chips).

Japanese

When locals who love their sushi get that craving for raw fish, they head for **Shogun Sushi** (1123 Pacific Ave., 831/469-4477, Mon.-Wed. 11:30am-2:20pm, 5pm-9pm, Thurs.-Sat. 11:30am-2:20pm, 5pm-10pm, $14). Right on Pacific Avenue, Shogun serves big fresh slabs of *nigiri*. They also have an interesting collection of sushi rolls including the "Saketemp Roll," which is a large, multi-colored combination of shrimp tempura, cucumber, avocado, green onion, mayo, and smoked salmon. The fish served here is some of the freshest you'll find in this seacoast city. Their meats and other dishes also please diners with fresh ingredients and tasty preparations. Do be aware that there's often a wait for a table in the evenings, especially on weekends.

Mexican

Santa Cruz has some great taquerias, but **Tacos Moreno** (1053 Water St., 831/429-6095, http:// tacosmoreno.com, $6) may be the best. Around lunch, locals line up outside the nondescript eatery. Tacos Moreno serves just the basics: burritos, tacos, quesadillas, and beverages to wash them down. The standout item is the al pastor burrito supreme with crispy barbecued pork, cheese, sour cream, and guacamole among other savory ingredients.

South American

Cafe Brasil (1410 Mission St., 831/429-1855, www.cafebrasil.us, daily 8am-2:45pm, $10-20) serves up the Brazilian fare its name promises. Painted jungle green with bright yellow and blue trim, you can't miss this totally Santa Cruz breakfast and lunch joint. In the morning, the fare runs to omelets and ethnic specialties including a dish with two eggs topping a piece of steak. Lunch includes pressed sandwiches, meat and tofu dishes, and Brazilian house specials. A juice bar provides rich but healthy meal accompaniments that can also act as light meals on their own. To try something different, get an acai bowl—acai is a South American fruit with a robust cherry-like flavor.

INFORMATION AND SERVICES
Tourist Information

While it can be fun to explore Santa Cruz just by using your innate sense of direction and the bizarre, those who want a bit more structure to their travels can hit the **Santa Cruz County Visitors Center** (303 Water St., Suite 100, 800/833-3494, www.santacruz.org) for maps, advice, and information.

Media and Communications

Santa Cruz publishes its own daily newspaper, the *Santa Cruz Sentinel* (www.santacruzsentinel.com). You'll get your daily dose of national wire service news and current events, local news, plus some good stuff for visitors. The *Sentinel* has a Food section, a Sunday Travel section, and plenty of up-to-date entertainment information.

The small city also has two free weekly newspapers filled with upcoming events: *Santa Cruz Weekly* (www.santacruzweekly.com) and *Good Times* (www.gtweekly.com).

You can get your mail on at the **post office** (850 Front St., 831/426-0144) near the Mall.

Santa Cruz is wired. You'll definitely be able to access the Internet in a variety of cafés and hotels. There are Starbucks locations here, and the many indie cafés often compete with their own (sometimes free) Wi-Fi.

MONTEREY BAY

Santa Cruz has plenty of banks and ATMs (including some ATMs on the arcade at the Boardwalk). Bank branches congregate downtown near Pacific Avenue. The West Side is mostly residential, so you'll find a few ATMs in supermarkets and gas stations, but little else.

Medical Services

Despite its rep as a funky bohemian beach town, Santa Cruz's dense population dictates that it have at least one full-fledged hospital of its own. You can get medical treatment and care at **Dominican Hospital** (1555 Soquel Ave., 831/462-7700, www.dominicanhospital.org).

GETTING THERE AND AROUND

Visitors planning to drive or bike around Santa Cruz should get themselves a good map, either before they arrive or at the visitor's center in town. Navigating the winding, occasionally broken-up streets of this oddly shaped town isn't for the faint of heart. Highway 1, which becomes Mission Street on the West Side, acts as the main artery through Santa Cruz and down to Capitola, Soquel, Aptos, and coastal points farther south. You'll find that Highway 1 at the interchange with Highway 17, and sometimes several miles to the south, is a parking lot most of the time. No, you probably haven't come upon a major accident or a special event. It's just like that all the time, and will be until the construction widening the highway to deal with the heavy traffic is complete.

Car

If you're driving to Santa Cruz from Silicon Valley, you've got two choices of roads. Most drivers take fast, dangerous Highway 17. This narrow road doesn't have any switchbacks and is the main truck route "over the hill." Most locals take this 50-mile-per hour corridor fast—probably faster than they should.

Each year, several people die in accidents on Highway 17. So if you're new to the road, keep to the right and take it slow, no matter what the traffic to the left of you is doing. Check traffic reports before you head out; Highway 17 is known to be one of the worst commuting roads in all of the Bay Area, and the weekend beach traffic in the summer jams up fast in both directions too.

For a more leisurely drive, you can opt for two-lane Highway 9. The tight curves and endless switchbacks will keep you at a reasonable speed; use the turnouts to let the locals pass, please. On Highway 9, your biggest obstacles tend to be groups of bicyclists and motorcyclists, both of whom adore the slopes and curves of this technical driving road. The good news is that you'll get an up-close-and-personal view of the gorgeously forested Santa Cruz Mountains, complete with views of the valley to the north and ocean vistas to the south.

Parking

Parking in Santa Cruz can be its own special sort of horror. Downtown, head straight for the parking structures one block away from Pacific Avenue on either side. They're much easier to deal with than trying to find street parking. The same goes for the beach and Boardwalk areas. At the Boardwalk, just pay the fee to park in the big parking lot adjacent to the attractions. You'll save an hour and a possible car break-in or theft trying to find street parking in the sketchy neighborhoods that surround the Boardwalk.

Bus

In town, the buses are run by the **Santa Cruz METRO** (831/425-8600 www.scmtd.com, adults $2/single ride, passes available). With routes running all around Santa Cruz County, you can probably find a way to get nearly anywhere you'd want to go on the METRO.

Moss Landing

Located in the center of the Monterey Bay, 25 miles south of Santa Cruz and 15 miles north of Monterey, Moss Landing is a picturesque, working fishing village—if you can ignore the rising smokestacks of the towering Moss Landing Power Plant. The main drag, Moss Landing Road, has a scattering of antique stores and art galleries, and the Moss Landing Harbor is home to a fleet of fishing vessels. To the south of the harbor's mouth, Salinas River State Beach offers miles of wild, undeveloped shoreline. North of the inlet, Zmudowski State Beach is popular with local surfers during the winter months. Offshore, the Monterey Submarine Canyon is one of North America's largest submarine canyons. It's the reason that the Moss Landing Marine Laboratories and Monterey Bay Aquarium Research Institute have local addresses. The **Moss Landing Chamber of Commerce** website (www.mosslandingchamber.com) offers visitor information.

SIGHTS
◖ Elkhorn Slough

Elkhorn Slough is the second largest section of tidal salt marsh in California after the San Francisco Bay. The estuary hosts an amazing amount of wildlife that includes marine mammals and over 340 bird species, which makes it one of the state's best birding spots. The best way to explore the slough is by kayak, where you can view rafts of lounging sea otters and a barking rookery of California sea lions from water level. Located in Moss Landing's North Harbor, which connects to the slough, **Monterey Bay Kayaks** (2390 Hwy. 1, 831/373-5357, www.montereybaykayaks.com, $50-120 for 2-5-hour tours) has kayak rentals as well as a range of guided tours from a three-hour paddle up the slough to monthly full moon tours. While paddling a kayak is the recommended way to view the slough, the **Elkhorn Slough Safari**

Kayaking Moss Landing's Elkhorn Slough is a highlight for nature lovers.

© STUART THORNTON

MONTEREY BAY

(831/633-5555, www.elkhornslough.com) is a possibility for those who wish to take a tour of the estuary by boat.

ENTERTAINMENT AND EVENTS
Bars
The **Moss Landing Inn** (7902 Hwy. 1, 831/633-9803, http://wenchilada.com, Mon.-Thurs. noon-1am, Fri.-Sun. 11:30am-1am or 2am) is not a place to spend the night but rather a dive bar where you can spend a few hours getting acquainted with the local characters. It's connected to The Whole Enchilada restaurant, and sometimes offers live music on weekends.

Festivals and Events
The success of reality TV shows like *Antiques Roadshow* and *American Pickers* have people scouring yard sales and antique shops for collectibles. On the last Sunday of July, Moss Landing is flooded with these enthusiasts for the annual **Moss Landing Antique Street Fair** (831/633-4501, www.mosslandingchamber. com). The giant outdoor antique market has over 200 booths selling collectibles, while other booths nearby serve local foods like fried fish and artichokes.

SHOPPING
Moss Landing it known for antique stores like the **Cottage By the Sea** (7981 E. Moss Landing Rd., 831/633-9909, Wed.-Mon. 11am-5pm) and **Hamlin Antiques** (8071 Moss Landing Rd., 831/633-3664, Thurs.-Tues. noon-5pm). It's also home to a growing arts community. Across the road from the Haute Enchilada Café, **Galeria Dos** (7902 Moss Landing Rd., 831/633-5843, www. hauteenchilada.com, daily 11am-5pm) has multiple rooms filled with sculptures, watercolors, woodworks, and ceramic items. Housed in the former post office, the aptly named **Old Post Office Gallery** (7981 Moss Landing Rd., 831/632-0488, Tues.-Sun. 11am-5pm) features visual arts including lots of landscape paintings.

SPORTS AND RECREATION
Beaches
Just north and south of Moss Landing's Harbor, **Moss Landing State Beach** (Jetty Rd., 831/649-2836, www.parks.ca.gov) and **Zmudowski State Beach** (20 miles north of Monterey on Hwy. 1, take Struve Rd. and turn onto Giberson Rd., 831/649-2836, www. parks.ca.gov) stretch for miles. They're mostly enjoyed by locals who fish, surf, or ride horses on the beach.

Whale-Watching
For a glimpse of marine mammals in the wild, from gray whales to orcas, catch a ride with **Sanctuary Cruises** (7881 Sandholt Rd., 831/917-1042, www.sanctuarycruises. com, adults $50, children 12 and under $40). Running on biodiesel, the 43-foot ocean vessel *Sanctuary* takes passengers out daily for 4-5-hour cruises. **Blue Ocean Whale Watch** (7881 Sandholt Rd., 831/600-5103, www.blueocean-whalewatch.com, adults $48, seniors $40, children 12 and under $38) also heads out into the bay for four-hour whale-watching expeditions.

Fishing
If you're interested in catching your own seafood, consider heading out with **Westwind Charter Sport Fishing & Excursions** (7881 Sandholt Rd., 831/392-7867, https://westwind-charter.com, $115 pp). Depending on what's in season, you can catch salmon, rock cod, halibut, or Dungeness crab.

ACCOMMODATIONS AND CAMPING
With its nautical decor, the **C Captain's Inn** (8122 Moss Landing Rd., 831/633-5550, www. captainsinn.com, $140-275) is the perfect place to spend an evening in the fishing village. The Captain's Inn offers rooms in two buildings: a historic structure that was once the site of the Pacific Coast Steamship Company and the Boathouse, where every room has a superb view of the nearby tidal marsh. The Boathouse rooms are recommended for animal lovers and nautical enthusiasts. Wildlife enthusiasts might

© STUART THORNTON

Phil's Fish Market is known for its cioppino.

be able to catch a glimpse of marine mammals or birds in the nearby tidal marsh, while maritime fans can climb into bed sets crafted out of boats or boat parts.

Seeking solitude and miles of nearly empty coastline? The **Monterey Dunes Company** (407 Moss Landing Rd., 831/633-4883 or 800/553-8637, www.montereydunes.com, $345-690) rents 2-4-bedroom homes on the beach south of Moss Landing. Guests also have access to the development's tennis courts, swimming pool, saunas, and hot tub.

The **Moss Landing KOA Express** (7905 Sandholt Rd., 831/633-6800 or 800/562-3390, $68-75) has almost 50 RV sites right in the Moss Landing Harbor area.

FOOD

As a harbor town, Moss Landing is probably best known for its seafood restaurants. The most popular is (**Phil's Fish Market** (7600 Sandholt Rd., 831/633-2152, www.philsfish-market.com, Sun.-Thurs. 10am-8pm, Fri.-Sat. 10am-9pm, $20), known for its cioppino, a hearty Italian American seafood stew that includes clams, mussels, fish, Dungeness crab, prawns, and scallops. A heaping bowl comes with a green salad and garlic bread. A bluegrass band plays on some nights.

The Whole Enchilada (7902 Hwy. 1, 831/633-6038, http://wenchilada.com, daily 11:30am-9pm, $10-24) does seafood with a Mexican slant. Dine on seafood enchiladas, Mexican-style cioppino or chile relleno stuffed with crab, shrimp, and cheese in the brightly colored dining room or outdoor patio.

Part art gallery, part eatery, fanciful **Haute Enchilada Café & Galleries** (7902 Moss Landing Rd., 831/633-5843, www.hauteen-chilada.com, daily 10am-8pm, $17) is bursting with color. Try the calamari steak or veggie polenta lasagna.

MONTEREY BAY

Monterey

The best days in Monterey are picture perfect: It's no wonder that so many artists have been inspired to paint this land- and seascape. The blue of the ocean calls you to wander the twisting coastline, taking in the boats, kayaks, and otters playing along the bay.

Monterey has a past as a fishing town. Native Americans were the first to fish the bay, and fishing became an industry with the arrival of Euro-American settlers in the 19th century. Author John Steinbeck immortalized this unglamorous industry in his novel *Cannery Row*. Its blue-collar past is still evident in its architecture, even though the cannery workers have been replaced by visiting tourists.

Monterey is the "big city" on the well-populated southern tip of the wide-mouthed Monterey Bay. There are actually two main sections of Monterey: the old, downtown area and "New Monterey," which includes Cannery Row and the Monterey Aquarium. The old downtown is situated around Alvarado Street and includes the historic adobes that make up the Monterey State Historic Park. "New Monterey" bustles with tourists during the summer. The six blocks of Cannery Row retain much of the sardine-cannery look described in Steinbeck's novel, though the buildings have been spruced up a bit (and in some cases, completely rebuilt) since the 1940s. The canneries are long gone, and today the Row is packed with businesses, including the must-see Monterey Bay Aquarium, seafood restaurants, shops, galleries, and wine tasting rooms. The Aquarium is constantly packed with visitors, especially on summer weekends. One way to get from one section to the other is to walk the Monterey Bay Coastal Recreation Trail, a paved path that runs right along a stretch of coastline.

SIGHTS
Cannery Row

Cannery Row (www.canneryrow.com) did once look and feel as John Steinbeck described it in his famed novel of the same name. In the 1930s and 1940s, fishing boats docked here and offloaded their catches straight into the huge warehouse-like cannery buildings. Low-wage workers processed the fish and put it into cans, ready to ship across the country and around the world. But overfishing took its toll, and by the late 1950s, Cannery Row was deserted; some buildings actually fell into the ocean.

A slow renaissance began in the 1960s, driven by new interest in preserving the historic integrity of the area, as well as a few savvy entrepreneurs who understood the value of beachfront property. Today, what was once a workingman's wharf is now an enclave of boutique hotels, big seafood restaurants, and souvenir stores selling T-shirts adorned with sea otters. All that is left of the old canneries are the exteriors of some buildings: the ones with corrugated metal siding and crossovers that connected them to the nearby railway. Cannery Row is anchored at one end by the aquarium and runs for several blocks, which include a beach, then leads into the Monterey Harbor area.

◖ Monterey Bay Aquarium

The first aquarium of its kind in the country, the **Monterey Bay Aquarium** (886 Cannery Row, 831/648-4800, www.montereybayaquarium.org, daily 10am-6pm, adults $32.95, children $19.95) is still unique in many ways. From the very beginning, the aquarium's mission has been conservation, and they're not shy about it. They have taken custodianship of the Pacific coastline and waters in Monterey County down to Big Sur, and take an active role in the saving and conservation of at-risk wildlife in the area. Many of the animals in the aquarium's tanks were rescued, and those that survive may eventually be returned to the wild. All the exhibits you'll see in this mammoth complex contain only local sea life. If you fear that the tight focus might make the tanks dull, you needn't worry. The exhibits and shows put on by the residents of Monterey Bay delight children and adults alike.

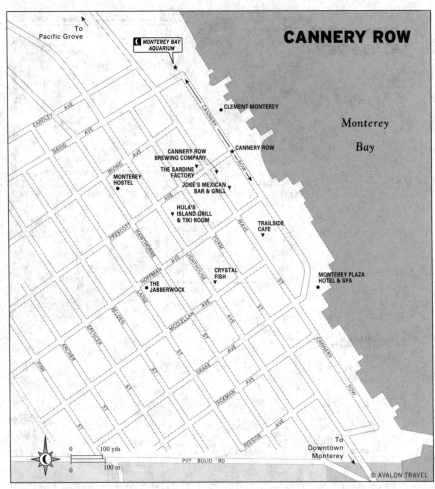

CANNERY ROW

To Pacific Grove

MONTEREY BAY AQUARIUM

CLEMENT MONTEREY

Monterey

Bay

CANNERY ROW BREWING COMPANY

CANNERY ROW

THE SARDINE FACTORY

MONTEREY HOSTEL

JOSE'S MEXICAN BAR & GRILL

HULA'S ISLAND GRILL & TIKI ROOM

TRAILSIDE CAFE

CRYSTAL FISH

MONTEREY PLAZA HOTEL & SPA

THE JABBERWOCK

EARDLEY AVE
DAVID AVE
IRVING AVE
PRESCOTT
HAWTHORNE
HOFFMAN
LAINE
BELDEN
SPENCER
ARCHER
PINE ST
LIGHTHOUSE AVE
FOAM ST
WAVE ST
CANNERY ROW
McCLELLAN AVE
DRAKE AVE
DICKMAN AVE
REESIDE AVE
PVT BOLIO RD

To Downtown Monterey

0   100 yds
0   100 m

© AVALON TRAVEL

The aquarium displays a dazzling array of species. When you come to visit, a good first step is to look up the feeding schedules for the tanks you're most interested in. The critters always put on the best show at feeding time, and it's smart to show up several minutes in advance of feeding to get a good spot near the glass.

The living, breathing **Kelp Forest** is just like the kelp beds outside in the Bay proper—except this one is 28 feet tall. Between the swaying strands of kelp, leopard sharks glide over the aquarium floor and warty sea cucumbers

and starfish adorn rocks. Try to time your visit for either the 11:30am or 4pm feeding time, when the fish in the tank put on quite a show.

The deep-water tank in the **Open Sea** exhibit area always draws a crowd. Inside its depths, hammerhead sharks and an odd-looking enormous sunfish coexist. The aquarium has even had one of the ocean's most notorious predators in this tank: the great white shark. The aquarium has great whites infrequently, but if one is on display, it's definitely worth looking at this sleek and amazing fish up close.

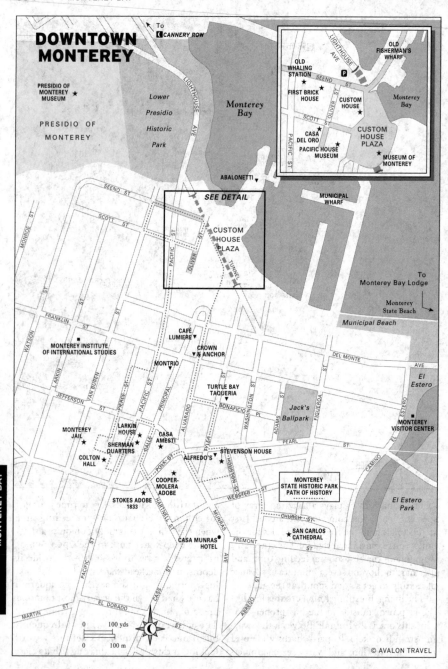

DOWNTOWN MONTEREY

To CANNERY ROW

Detail inset (SEE DETAIL):

- OLD WHALING STATION
- OLD FISHERMAN'S WHARF
- FIRST BRICK HOUSE
- CUSTOM HOUSE
- CASA DEL ORO
- PACIFIC HOUSE MUSEUM
- CUSTOM HOUSE PLAZA
- MUSEUM OF MONTEREY
- LIGHTHOUSE AVE
- SEENO ST
- SCOTT ST
- OLIVER ST
- PACIFIC ST
- Monterey Bay

Main map labels:

- PRESIDIO OF MONTEREY MUSEUM
- PRESIDIO OF MONTEREY
- Lower Presidio Historic Park
- Monterey Bay
- LIGHTHOUSE AVE
- ABALONETTI
- SEE DETAIL
- CUSTOM HOUSE PLAZA
- MUNICIPAL WHARF
- TUNNEL
- To Monterey Bay Lodge
- Monterey State Beach
- Municipal Beach
- MONROE ST
- SCOTT ST
- SEENO ST
- PACIFIC ST
- OLIVER ST
- FRANKLIN ST
- WATSON ST
- LARKIN ST
- VAN BUREN ST
- JEFFERSON ST
- MONTEREY INSTITUTE OF INTERNATIONAL STUDIES
- CAFÉ LUMIERE
- CROWN & ANCHOR
- MONTRIO
- PIERCE ST
- PACIFIC ST
- PRINCIPAL
- DEL MONTE AVE
- El Estero
- TURTLE BAY TAQUERIA
- ALVARADO
- BONAFICIO
- WASHINGTON
- PL
- ADAMS ST
- Jack's Ballpark
- FIGUEROA ST
- ESTERO ST
- MONTEREY VISITOR CENTER
- MONTEREY JAIL
- LARKIN HOUSE
- SHERMAN QUARTERS
- CASA AMESTI
- COLTON HALL
- GALLE ST
- POLK ST
- ALFREDO'S
- STEVENSON HOUSE
- TYLER ST
- HOUSTON ST
- PEARL ST
- CAMINO
- COOPER-MOLERA ADOBE
- WEBSTER ST
- MONTEREY STATE HISTORIC PARK PATH OF HISTORY
- El Estero Park
- STOKES ADOBE 1833
- HARTNELL ST
- MUNRAS AVE
- CHURCH ST
- CASA MUNRAS HOTEL
- FREMONT ST
- SAN CARLOS CATHEDRAL
- PACIFIC ST
- CASS ST
- MARTIN ST
- EL DORADO ST
- ABREGO ST

0   100 yds
0   100 m

© AVALON TRAVEL

STEINBECK

John Ernst Steinbeck was born in Salinas, California in 1902 and grew up in its tiny, isolated agricultural community. He somehow managed to escape life as a farmer, a sardine fisherman, or a fish canner, and ended up living the glamorous life of a writer for his too-short 66 years.

Steinbeck's experiences in the Salinas Valley farming community and in the fishing town of Monterey informed many of his novels. The best known of these is *Cannery Row*, but *Tortilla Flat* is also set in working-class Monterey (though no one knows exactly where the fictional "Tortilla Flat" neighborhood was supposed to be). The Pulitzer Prize-winning novel *The Grapes of Wrath* takes more of its inspiration from the Salinas Valley. Steinbeck used the Valley as a model for farming in the Dust Bowl – the wretched, impoverished era that was the Great Depression.

In fact, Steinbeck was fascinated by the plight of working men and women; his novels and stories generally depict ordinary folks going through tough and terrible times. Steinbeck lived and worked through the Great Depression – thus it's not surprising that many of his stories do *not* feature happy Hollywood endings. Steinbeck was a realist in almost all of his novels, portraying the good, the bad, and the ugly of human life and society. His work gained almost immediate respect: In addition to his Pulitzer, Steinbeck also won the Nobel Prize for Literature in 1962. Almost every American high school student from the 1950s onward has read at least one of Steinbeck's novels or short stories; his body of work forms part of the enduring American literary canon.

As the birthplace of California's most illustrious literary son in the 20th century, Salinas became equally famous for spawning the author and inspiring his work. You'll find a variety of Steinbeck maps online (www.mty-county.com) that offer self-guided tours of the regions made famous by his various novels. Poor Steinbeck's name is taken in vain all over now-commercial Cannery Row – even the cheesy Wax Museum tries to draw customers in by claiming kinship with the legendary author. More serious scholars of Steinbeck prefer the **National Steinbeck Center** (1 Main St., Salinas, 831/796-3833, www.steinbeck.org, daily 10am-5pm, $11) and the **Steinbeck House** (132 Central Ave., Salinas, 831/424-2735, www.steinbeckhouse.com, summer tours 1pm-3pm), both in the still-agricultural town of Salinas. And if the museums aren't enough, plan to be in Monterey County in early August for the annual **Steinbeck Festival** (www.steinbeck.org), a big shindig put on by the Steinbeck Center in order to celebrate the great man's life and works in fine style.

The **Wild About Otters** exhibit gives visitors a personal view of rescued otters. The adorable, furry marine mammals come right up to the glass to interact with curious children and enchanted adults. You can watch aquarists feed and train the otters daily at noon, 2pm, and 4pm.

One of the aquarium's most popular exhibits is its **Jellies** display. Here the lighting illuminates the delicate-looking crystal jellies and the comet-like lion's mane jellyfish.

It is easy to spend all day at the aquarium. If you get hungry, try for a table at the full-service restaurant and bar, complete with white tablecloths and a view of the bay. A self-service café offers sandwiches, salads, and ethnic dishes. You'll hardly be able to escape the souvenirs as a different gift shop sits in a corner of almost every exhibit hall.

If you possibly can, plan your visit to the Monterey Bay Aquarium on a weekday rather than a weekend. The aquarium is a wildly popular weekend destination. Especially in the summer, the crowds can be forbidding. Weekdays can be less crushing (though you'll run into school groups during much of the year), and the off-season is almost always a better time to visit. The aquarium has facilities for wheelchair access to almost all exhibits.

Be sure to pick up one of the aquarium's

Monterey State Historic Park has some of California's oldest buildings.

© STUART THORNTON

Seafood Watch booklets, which reveals what are the most environmentally friendly kinds of seafood to eat on the West Coast.

Monterey State Historic Park

Monterey State Historic Park (20 Custom House Plaza, 831/649-7118, www.parks.ca.gov, gardens May-Sept. daily 9am-5pm, Oct.-Apr. daily 10am-4pm, free) pays homage to the long and colorful history of the city of Monterey. This busy port town acted as the capital of California when it was under Spanish rule, and then later when the area became part of United States territory. Today, this park provides a peek into Monterey as it was in the middle of the 19th century—a busy place filled with dock workers, fishermen, bureaucrats, and soldiers. And yet it blends into the modern town of Monterey as well, and modern stores, galleries, and restaurants sit next to 150-year-old adobe structures. Guided tours ($5) of several of the museums and adobes are offered most days; a walking tour of Old Monterey (Fri.-Sun. 10:30am, 12:30pm, 2pm) meets at the Pacific House.

It's tough to see everything in just one visit to Old Monterey. If you only get to one spot on your first trip, make it the **Custom House** (Fri.-Sun. 10am-4pm, $3). It's California State Historic Landmark Number 1, and the oldest government building known to still stand in the state. You can spend some time wandering the adobe building, checking out the artifacts on display, or even just looking out the upstairs window towards the sea. Also on the plaza is the **Pacific House Museum** (Fri.-Sun. 10am-4pm, $3). The first floor shows a range of Monterey's history from the Native Californians to the American Period, while the second floor has a plethora of Native American artifacts.

There are 10 other buildings that comprise the park; most were built with adobe and/or brick between 1834 and 1847. These include: the **Casa del Oro;** the **Cooper-Molera Adobe** (525 Polk St., guided tours Fri.-Sun. 10:30am and 1:30pm); the **First Brick House;** the **Larkin House** (464 Calle Principal, guided tours Fri.-Sun. noon and 3pm); the **Old**

Whaling Station; the **Pacific House;** the **Sherman Quarters;** and the **Stevenson House** (530 Houston St., open Sat. and the 4th Sun. of every month, 1pm-4pm), the former residence of Robert Louis Stevenson.

Famous artists, writers, and military men have stayed in some of these spots, most of which have long histories playing several different roles. Look down as you walk to see if you're stepping on antique whalebone sidewalks. And be sure to take a few minutes to admire the many beautiful gardens surrounding the adobes, which are lovingly maintained by local groups.

Museum of Monterey

Formerly the Maritime Museum of Monterey, the **Museum of Monterey** (5 Custom House Plaza, 831/372-2608, www.museumofmonterey.org, Tues.-Sat. 10am-5pm, Sun. noon-5pm, $10) has expanded its focus to include more of the coastal city's history. The large modern facilities have an upstairs devoted mostly to maritime artifacts, including the original Fresnel lens from the Point Sur Light Station and a model of 1940s Cannery Row. The downstairs now rotates art exhibits including a colorful display on the 1967 Monterey Pop Festival, which was up for most of 2012.

Fisherman's Wharf

Monterey's **Fisherman's Wharf** (1 Old Fisherman's Wharf, www.montereywharf.com, daily, hours vary) comes on like a smaller version of San Francisco's popular tourist attraction of the same name. Where tons of sardines were once shipped out of Monterey Harbor, you'll now find a collection of seafood restaurants, touristy gift shops, and whale-watching boats. Most of the wharf's seafood restaurants offer free shots of their competing clam chowders to those walking by. It might be enough to stave off your hunger until the next meal.

Dennis the Menace Park

Originally envisioned by Hank Ketcham, the creator of the comic strip, **Dennis the Menace Park** (777 Pearl St., 831/646-3860, 10am-dusk daily) opened in 1956. Ketcham was heavily involved in the design process; he moved to the area after World War II, and lived here until his death in 2001. There's a nine-foot climbing wall, suspension bridge, long green curvy slide attached to brightly colored jungle gyms, real black locomotive, and a whole lot more, as well as a bronze sculpture of the little menace near the entrance.

ENTERTAINMENT AND EVENTS
Live Music

After a long hiatus, downtown Monterey's historic **Golden State Theatre** (417 Alvarado St., box office 831/321-4571, www.goldenstatetheatre.com) is hosting live music again. The theater dates back to 1926 and was designed to look like a Moorish castle. Performers in its ornate main room have included music legends like Patti Smith and John Prine. Smaller touring acts and local bands often play in the lobby.

Bars and Clubs

Descending down into **The Crown and Anchor** (150 W. Franklin St., 831/649-6496, www.crownandanchor.net, daily 11am-2am) feels a bit like entering a ship's hold. Along with the maritime theme, The Crown and Anchor serves up 20 international beers on tap. Sip indoors or on the popular outdoor patio.

Another good bet for a beer or cocktail is the **Cannery Row Brewing Company** (95 Prescott Ave., 831/643-2722, www.canneryrowbrewingcompany.com), just a block up from bustling Cannery Row. They pour 75 beers on tap, ranging from hefeweizens to barleywine. Expect good happy hour deals on food and beer 3pm-6pm.

A distinct stone building just a couple blocks off Alvarado Street, **Alfredo's** (266 Pearl St., 831/375-0655, Sun.-Thurs. 10am-midnight, Fri.-Sat. 10am-2am, cash only) is a cozy dive bar with dim lighting, a gas fireplace, cheap drinks and a good jukebox.

Festivals and Events

The Monterey region hosts numerous festivals

and special events each year. Whether your pleasure is fine food or funky music, you'll probably be able to plan a trip around some sort of multi-day festival with dozens of events and performances scheduled during Monterey's busy year.

In keeping with the Central Coast's obsession with food and wine, the annual **Monterey Wine Festival** (800/422-0251, www.monterey-wine.com, mid-June) celebrates wine with a generous helping of food on the side. A number of tasting events mark this two-day festival. Check the website for this year's venues, ticket prices, and event dates and times. This festival offers the perfect opportunity to introduce yourself to Monterey and Carmel wineries, many of which have not yet hit the "big time" in major wine magazines. The Wine Festival is just one of many similar events held each year in the region, so if you can't make it you'll have plenty of other opportunities to enjoy all the best edibles and drinkables the Central Coast has to offer.

One of the biggest music festivals in California is the **Monterey Jazz Festival** (2004 Fairground Rd., 831/373-3366, www. montereyjazzfestival.org, Sept.). As the site of the longest-running jazz festival on earth, Monterey attracts 500 artists from around the world to play on its eight stages. Held each September—a month that offers the best chance for beautiful weather on the Monterey Bay—this long weekend of amazing music can leave you happy for the whole year. The event is held at the Monterey County Fairgrounds, which lets visitors enjoy all the different concerts without having to drive from venue to venue. Recent acts to grace the Monterey Jazz Festival's stages include Tony Bennett, Herbie Hancock, and Trombone Shorty. Camping is not permitted at the fairgrounds, but you can camp nearby, or get a room in one of the Monterey lodgings that partner with the festival to provide reasonably priced lodgings for attendees.

SPORTS AND RECREATION

The Monterey Bay is the premier Northern California locale for a number of water sports, especially scuba diving.

Scuba Diving

Any native Northern Californian knows that there's only one really great place in the region to get certified in scuba diving—the Monterey Bay. Even if you go to a dive school up in the Bay Area, they'll take you down to Monterey for your open-water dive. Accordingly, dozens of dive schools cluster in and around the town of Monterey (check Carmel and Santa Cruz as well, if you prefer).

A local's favorite, **Bamboo Reef** (614 Lighthouse Ave., 831/372-1685, www.bambooreef.com) offers SCUBA lessons and rents equipment just a few blocks from popular dive spots, including Breakwater Cove.

Another of your many dive shop options is the **Aquarius Dive Shop** (2040 Del Monte Ave., 831/375-1933, www.aquariusdivers.com). Aquarius offers everything you need to go diving out in Monterey Bay, including air and nitrox fills, equipment rental, certification courses, and help booking a trip on a local dive boat. Aquarius works with five boats to create great trips for divers of all interests and ability levels. Call or check the website for current local dive conditions as well.

Kayaking and Stand Up Paddleboarding

With all the focus on sustainable tourism in Monterey, coupled with the lovely recreation area formed by Monterey Bay, it's no wonder that sea kayaking is popular here. Monterey's coastline is as scenic a spot as any to learn to stand up paddleboard (SUP). Whether you want to try paddling for the first time or you're an expert who hasn't brought your own gear out to California, you'll find a local outfit ready and willing to hook you up.

Adventures by the Sea (299 Cannery Row, 831/372-1807, www.adventuresbythesea.com, summer daily 9am-8pm, winter daily 9am-58pm, tours $60 pp, rentals $30/day) rents kayaks for whole days to let you choose your own route in and around the magnificent Monterey Bay kelp forest. If you're not confident enough to go off on your own, Adventures offers tours from Cannery Row. Your guide can tell you all

SEA SANCTUARY

The Monterey Bay is in a federally protected marine area known as the **Monterey Bay National Marine Sanctuary** (MBNMS). Designated as a sanctuary in 1992, the protected waters stretch far past the confines of Monterey Bay to a northern boundary seven miles north of the Golden Gate Bridge and a southern boundary of Cambria in San Luis Obispo.

MBNMS holds many marine treasures including the Monterey Bay Submarine Canyon, which is right offshore of the fishing village of Moss Landing. The canyon is similar in size to the Grand Canyon and has a rim to floor depth of 5,577 feet.

In 2009, MBNMS expanded to include another fascinating underwater geographical feature: the Davidson Seamount. Located 80 miles southwest of Monterey, the undersea mountain rises an impressive 7,480 feet, yet its summit is still 4,101 feet below the ocean's surface.

The sanctuary was created for resource protection, education, public use, and research. The MBNMS is the reason so many marine research facilities including the Long Marine Laboratory, the Monterey Bay Marine Laboratory, and the Moss Landing Marine Laboratories dot the Monterey Bay's shoreline.

about the wildlife you're seeing: harbor seals, sea otters, pelicans, seagulls, and maybe even a whale in the wintertime! The tour lasts about 2.5 hours and the available tandem sit-on-top kayaks make it a great experience for school-age children. Adventures by the Sea also run a tour of Stillwater Cove at Pebble Beach. Reservations are recommended for all tours, but during the summer the Cannery Row tour leaves regularly at 10am and 2pm, so you can stop by on a whim and see if there's a spot available.

Right on Monterey Beach, **Monterey Bay Kayaks** (693 Del Monte Ave., 831/373-5357, www.montereybaykayaks.com, tours $50-60 pp) specializes in tours of central Monterey. (There's also a branch up in Moss Landing on the Elkhorn Slough.) You can choose between open-deck and closed-deck tour groups, beginning tours perfect for kids, or long paddles designed for more experienced sea kayakers. Check the website for specific tour prices, times, and reservation information. If you prefer to rent a kayak and explore the bay on your own, Monterey Bay Kayaks can help you with this too. If you really get into it, you can also sign up for closed-deck sea kayaking classes to learn about safety, rescue techniques, tides, currents, and paddling techniques.

Hiking

If you want to explore Monterey's coastline without the possibility of getting wet, head out on the **Monterey Bay Coastal Recreation Trail** (831/646-3866, www.monterey.org). The 18-mile paved path stretches from Pacific Grove to the south all the way to the North Monterey County town of Castroville. The best section is from Monterey Harbor down to Pacific Grove's Lovers Point Park.

Jack's Peak County Park (25020 Jacks Peak Park Rd., 831/775-4895, www.co.monterey.ca.us, daily 10am-close) is home to the highest point on the Monterey Peninsula. Its 0.8-mile-long **Skyline Trail** passes through a rare Monterey pine forest and offers glimpses of fossils from the Miocene epoch found nearby before reaching the summit, which offers an overview of the whole peninsula.

The home a U.S. Army post from 1917 to 1994, the dunes north of Monterey are a part of one of California's newest parks, **Fort Ord Dunes State Park** (831/649-2836, www.parks.ca.gov, 8am-half hour after sunset, free). Walk along a four-mile road past remnants of the military past or head down to the remote beach for a stroll. To reach Fort Ord Dunes State Park from Monterey, head north on Highway 1 and exit the Lightfighter Drive exit. Turn left onto 2nd Avenue and then take another left on Divarty Street. Take a right on 1st Avenue and follow the signs to the park entrance at the 8th Street Bridge over Highway 1.

Fishing and Whale-Watching

Whales pass quite near the shores of Monterey year-round. While you can sometimes even see them from the beaches, any number of boats can take you out for a closer look at the great beasts as they travel along their own special routes north and south. The area hosts many humpbacks, blue whales, and gray whales, plus the occasional killer whale, Minke whale, fin whale, and pod of dolphins. Bring your own binoculars for a better view, but the experienced boat captains will do all they can to get you as close as possible to the whales and dolphins. Most tours last 2-3 hours and leave from Fisherman's Wharf, which is easy to get to and has ample parking. If you prefer not to rise with the sun, pick a tour that leaves in the afternoon.

Monterey Bay Whale Watch (84 Fisherman's Wharf, 831/375-4658, www.montereybay-whalewatch.com) leaves right from an easy-to-find red building on Fisherman's Wharf and runs tours in every season. (Call or check the website for schedules.) You must make a reservation in advance, even for regularly scheduled tours. Afternoon tours are available. **Monterey Whale Watching** (96 Fisherman's Wharf, 800/979-3370, www.baywatchcruises.com) prides itself on its knowledgeable guides/marine biologists and its comfortable, spacious cruising vessels. The *Princess Monterey* offers morning and afternoon tours, and you can buy tickets online or by phone.

If you'd rather catch fish than watch mammals, **Randy's Fishing Trips** (Fisherman's Wharf, 800/979-3370, www.randysfishing-trips.com) can take you out for salmon, halibut, albacore, mackerel, rock cod, flatfish, and even squid and Dungeness crab in season. They can also take you out for a whale-watching trip if that's your preference. Trips can be scheduled for the morning or afternoon. You can bring your own food—catering is not provided—including a small cooler for your drinks. If you don't have a California fishing license, you can purchase a one-day license at the shop before your trip. While you can try to walk up to the bright teal-painted shop at Fisherman's Wharf, it's best to get tickets for your trip in advance; either call or buy online from Randy's website.

Golf

Yes, you can play golf outside of Pebble Beach! And it's often much cheaper to play here than to head for the hallowed courses of that gated community.

The public **Monterey Pines Golf Course** (1250 Garden Rd., 831/656-2167, $16-38, cart $15) offers 18 holes for a comparatively tiny green fee. It's a short par-69 course that has three levels of tee to make the game fun for players of all levels. Monterey Pines was originally built as a private Navy course for the pleasure of the officers at the major naval installation north of town. Today, it is open to all who want to play. Call ahead for tee times.

A bit more pricy but still not Poppy Hills or Pebble Beach, **Del Monte Golf Course** (1300 Sylvan Rd., 831/373-2700, www.pebblebeach.com, $40-110, cart $25) is part of that legendary set of courses. This historic 18-hole, par-72 course, along with two other courses, still plays host to the Pebble Beach Invitational each year. You won't get the ocean views of Pebble Beach, but you will be treated to lovely green mountains surrounding the course as you play through. The property includes a full-service pro shop and the Del Monte Bar & Grill. You can check available tee times online, then call to book your preferred time.

Motor Sports

If you're feeling the need for speed, you can get lots of it at the **Mazda Raceway Laguna Seca** (1021 Monterey-Salinas Hwy., 831/242-8201, www.laguna-seca.com), one of the country's premier road-racing venues. Here you can see historic auto races, superbikes, speed festivals, and an array of Grand Prix events. The major racing season runs May-October. In addition to the big events, Laguna Seca hosts innumerable auto clubs and small sports car and stock car races. If you've always wanted to learn to drive or ride racecar-style, check the schedule to see if one of the track classes is happening during your visit. These often happen in the middle of the week, and are a near daily event in the off-season.

Be sure to check the website for parking directions specific to the event you plan to attend—this is a big facility. You can camp here, and certainly you'll find plenty of concessions during big races.

Gym

If you have been indulging in the Monterey Peninsula's fine dining scene, work off some of your added pounds at the **Monterey Sports Center** (301 E. Franklin St., 831/646-3730, www.monterey.org, Mon.-Fri. 5:30am-9:30pm, Sat. 7am-6pm, Sun. 8:30am-6pm, seniors $6, adult $8.50, 6-17 years old $5, under 5 $3.25). This clean, city-run facility has a weight training center, a cardio fitness room, two indoor pools, a new sauna facility and a waterslide. They also offer over 100 group exercise options very week, from aqua Zumba to Pilates, for an added fee.

ACCOMMODATIONS
Under $150

The **Monterey Hostel** (778 Hawthorne St., 831/649-0375, http://montereyhostel.org, $28/bunk, $79/private room, $99/family room with five beds) offers inexpensive accommodations within walking distance of the major attractions of Monterey. This hostel has a men's dorm room, women's dorm room, private rooms, a five-person family room, and a coed dorm room with 16 beds—earplugs not included. There's no laundry facility on-site, but there are full enclosure bike lockers. The hostel has some unexpected perks including a free pancake breakfast every morning and an ice cream social on Sundays. Linens are included with your bed, and there are comfy, casual common spaces with couches and musical instruments. And then there's that location...You can walk to the aquarium and Cannery Row, stroll the Monterey Bay Coastal Trail, or drive over to Carmel to see a different set of sights.

$150-250

A cute, small, budget motel, the **Monterey Bay Lodge** (55 Camino Aguajito, 831/372-8057, www.montereybaylodge.com, $149-189) brings a bit of the Côte d'Azur to the equally beautiful coastal town of Monterey. With small rooms decorated in classic yellows and blues, a sparkling pool with a fountain in the shallow end, and an on-site restaurant serving breakfast and lunch, the Lodge makes a perfect base for budget-minded families traveling in the Monterey region.

Centrally located in old Monterey, hacienda-inspired ◖**Casa Munras Hotel** (700 Munras Ave., 800/222-2446, www.hotelcasamunras. com, $160-194) blends in well with the historic adobes nearby. In addition to its well-appointed but basic rooms, the hotel has a spa, restaurant, and outdoor heated pool on its grounds. It's in walking distance of the restaurants and stores lining Alvarado Street.

Be sure to call in advance to get a room at **The Jabberwock** (598 Laine St., 831/372-4777, www.jabberwockinn.com, $169-309), a favorite with frequent visitors to Monterey. This Alice in Wonderland-themed B&B is both whimsical and elegant. Be sure to take the owners up on their daily wine and appetizer reception in the afternoon—they are gold mines of information about the area, and will be happy to recommend restaurants and activities for all tastes. Though located up a steep hill, the Jabberwock is within walking distance of Cannery Row and all its adjacent attractions (it's worth the extra exercise to avoid the cost or hassle of parking in the tourist lots).

Over $250

Monterey's newest fine lodging, **The Clement Monterey** (750 Cannery Row, 831/375-4500, www.ichotelsgroup.com, $335-844) is just steps away from the Monterey Aquarium and has sweeping views of the bay. Even the standard rooms here have marble bathrooms with soaking tubs.

Want to stay right on Cannery Row in a room overlooking the bay? You'll pay handsomely at the **Monterey Plaza Hotel & Spa** (400 Cannery Row, 831/646-1700, www. montereyplazahotel.com, $300-549), but it's worth it. This on-the-water luxury hotel has it all: restaurant, coffee shop, spa, private beach, room service, and upscale guest room goodies. Rooms range from "budget" garden and Cannery Row-facing accommodations to ocean-view rooms with private balconies and huge suites that mimic posh private apartments. They also offer a complimentary shuttle to locations in Monterey and nearby Pacific Grove.

CAMPING

It's a little known secret that there is one campground on the Monterey Peninsula. A mile up a hill from downtown Monterey, the 50-acre **Veterans Memorial Park** (Via Del Rey and Veterans Dr., 831/646-3865, www.monterey. org, $27/single vehicle, $32/two vehicles) has 40 first come, first served campsites with views of the Monterey Bay below.

FOOD

The organic and sustainable food movements have caught hold on the Central Coast. The Monterey Bay Seafood Watch program (www. montereybayaquarium.org) is the definitive resource for sustainable seafood, while the Salinas Valley inland hosts a number of organic farms.

American

For coffee, espresso, and home-baked beignets, head to the **Trailside Café** (550 Wave St., 831/649-8600, www.trailsidecafe.com, Mon.-Fri. 8am-3pm, Sat.-Sun. 8am-4pm, $10-15). This Cannery Row restaurant serves breakfast and lunch on a heated patio overlooking the bay and the nearby Monterey Bay Coastal Trail.

Connected to the Osio Cinemas, Monterey's art-house movie theater, **Café Lumiere** (365 Calle Principal, 831/920-2451, daily 7am-10pm) is where Monterey's old Sicilian anglers hang out in the morning while sipping coffee drinks and munching on pastries. Lumiere has daily lunch specials that tend to be a good deal for their price. This coffee shop offers free Wi-Fi to its customers.

Inside an old brick firehouse, **Montrio** (414 Calle Principal, 831/648-8880, www.montrio.com, daily 5pm-close, $15-20) is another entry in elegantly casual Monterey dining. The menu boasts a wide range of small bites and appetizers alongside meat and seafood entrées. Montrio has some inspired cocktails to sip with your meal including the "Beta Vulgaris," a refreshing concoction that utilizes roasted beet juice.

1833 (500 Hartnell St., 831/643-1837, www.restuarant1833.com, Mon.-Thurs. 5:30pm-10pm, Fri.-Sat. 5:30pm-1am, $25) is housed in one of Monterey's most historic buildings, an adobe from—guess when?—1833 that is supposed to be haunted. But now the multi-room building has been gussied up for a big city crowd. At a lit white onyx bar, patrons can try interesting intoxicants including a homemade coffee liquor and an herbal limoncello made from Meyer lemons harvested from an isolated ridge in nearby Big Sur. This place is brimming with culinary creativity. Even if you don't feel like dropping money on rotating entrées like pan roasted mahi mahi, try the bacon cheddar biscuit with maple chili butter, the definitive meeting of sweet and savory. For those who truly want to explore the unique menu, the nightly $65 "1833 Experience" is a filling five-course introduction.

Markets

The primary farmers market in the county, the **Monterey Farmers Market** (Alvarado St. between Del Monte and Pearl, www.oldmonterey. org, winter Tues. 4pm-7pm, summer Tues. 4pm-8pm) takes over downtown Monterey with fresh produce vendors, restaurant stalls, jewelry booths, and live music every Tuesday afternoon.

Mexican

Brightly colored **Turtle Bay Taqueria** (431 Tyler St., 831/333-1500, www.turtlebay.tv, Mon.-Thurs. 11am-7:30pm, Fri.-Sat. 11am-8:30pm, $9) blares salsa music while serving up a healthy, seafood-heavy menu. This isn't a typical Mexican food joint: The hearty burrito wraps include items like calamari and locally caught sanddabs (when in season) over beans, rice, cabbage, and salsa. The sopa de lima, a Mexican style chicken soup, hits the right spot on cold days when Monterey is socked in with fog.

Jose's Mexican Bar & Grill (638 Wave St., 831/655-4419, daily 11am-10pm, $8-15) is a great place to take a break from the summer crowds on Cannery Row, which is just a block away. Located in a homey red building, this family-owned eatery pleases with tasty margaritas and hearty Mexican fare. The fajitas never disappoint, and you'll probably have some leftover for another meal. Jose's also has an underground bar that frequently hosts bands on weekends.

Seafood

On weekends, there is typically a line out the door at ◖ **Monterey's Fish House** (2114 Del Monte Ave., 831/373-4647, Mon.-Fri. 11:30am-2:30pm and 5pm-9:30pm, $18-30), one of the peninsula's most popular most seafood restaurants. Once you get inside, you can expect attentive service and fresh seafood including snapper, albacore tuna, and calamari fished right out of the nearby bay. Nods to Monterey's Italian fishermen include Sicilian calamari and cioppino (Italian seafood stew).

Out on Fisherman's Wharf, **Abalonetti** (57 Fisherman's Wharf, 831/373-1851, www.abalonettimonterey.com, $16) serves up fresh Monterey Bay calamari in the standard fried variety and the surprisingly good buffalo style, with tentacles and rings drenched in the tangy sauce usually reserved for chicken wings.

For a South Pacific spin on seafood, head to **Hula's Island Grill & Tiki Room** (622 Lighthouse Ave., 831/655-4852, www.hulas-tiki.com, Tues.-Sat. 11:30am-close, Sun.-Mon. 4pm-close, $13-25). With surfing movies playing on the TVs and tasty tiki drinks, it's a fun place to hang out. In addition to fresh fish and a range of tacos, the menu has land-based fare like Jamaican jerk chicken.

COURTESY OF HULA'S ISLAND GRILL

Hula's Island Grill & Tiki Room

Sushi

Fresh seafood and creative rolls make **Crystal Fish** (514 Lighthouse Ave., 831/649-3474, Mon.-Thurs. 11:30am-2pm and 5pm-9pm, Fri. 11:30am-2pm and 5pm-10pm, Sat.-Sun. 1pm-9pm, $8-27) the Monterey go-to for sushi. There's not a lot of ambience, but there are a lot of rolls, including fresh salmon, tuna, eel, octopus, and calamari, accentuated by sauces like creamy avocado, mango, wasabi, and miso. Unusual ingredients include lemon slices, asparagus, and eggplant.

INFORMATION AND SERVICES

In Monterey, the **El Estero Visitors Center** (401 Camino El Estero, 888/221-1010, www. seemonterey.com) is the local outlet of the Monterey County Convention and Visitors Bureau. The **Monterey Peninsula Chamber of Commerce** (380 Alvarado St., 831/648-5360) can also provide helpful information.

The local daily newspaper is the *Monterey County Herald* (www.montereyherald.com). Meanwhile, the *Monterey County Weekly* (www.montereycountyweekly.com) is a popular free weekly with a comprehensive listing of the area's arts and entertainment events.

Monterey has two convenient **post offices** (565 Hartnell St.; 686 Lighthouse Ave.).

For medical needs, the **Community Hospital of the Monterey Peninsula** (CHOMP, 23625 Holman Hwy., 831/425-4667, www.chomp. org) provides emergency services to the area.

GETTING THERE AND AROUND

Most visitors drive into Monterey via scenic Highway 1. Inland, U.S. 101 allows access into Salinas from the north and south. From Salinas, Highway 68 travels west into Monterey.

For a more leisurely ride, **Amtrak's Coast Starlight train** (11 Station Place, Salinas, daily 8am-10pm) travels through Salinas.

The **Greyhound** bus station (19 W. Gabilan, Salinas, 831/424-4418, www.greyhound. com, daily 5am-11:30pm) offers service into Monterey.

Once in Monterey, take advantage of the free **WAVE** bus (Waterfront Area Visitor Express, 831/899-2555, www.monterey.org, Memorial Day weekend-Labor Day daily 10am-8pm) that loops between downtown Monterey and the Aquarium.

Pacific Grove

Sandwiched between historic Monterey and exclusive Pebble Beach, and close to major attractions like the Monterey Bay Aquarium, Pacific Grove makes a fine base for exploring the peninsula. It's also worth a visit for its colorful turn of the 20th century Victorian homes and its striking strand of coastline. The town has chosen "America's Last Hometown" as its nickname; it may make you nostalgic for small town living. Founded in 1875 as a Methodist summer retreat, this quiet city is not the place to go for a night of carousing. But Pacific Grove's downtown is perfect for a relaxing afternoon. Stroll past the canary yellow, purple, and green Victorian homes and cottages on Lighthouse Avenue (To avoid confusion, it's worth noting

that there's a different Lighthouse Avenue in adjacent Monterey).

For those who don't want to pay the entrance fee to drive Pebble Beach's 17-Mile Drive, Pacific Grove's "Poor Man's 17-Mile Drive" winds around a piece of coastal real estate between Lover's Point Park and Asilomar Beach that's almost as striking. Start on Ocean View Boulevard by Lover's Point and continue onto Sunset Drive to get the full experience. In the springtime, flowering ice plant right along the road adds a riot of color to the landscape.

SIGHTS
Lover's Point Park

It is no surprise that the aptly named **Lover's**

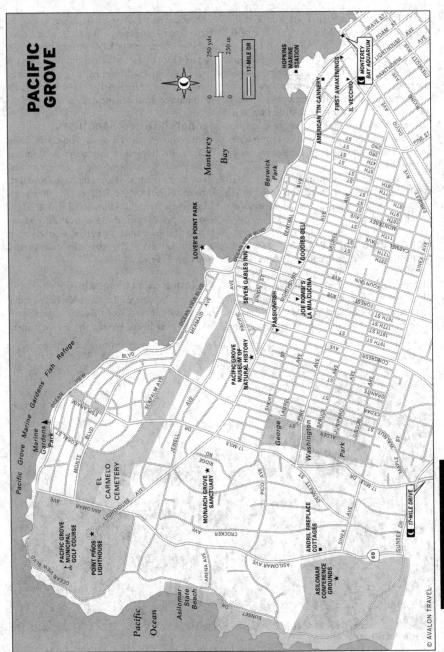

PACIFIC GROVE

Monterey Bay

Pacific Ocean

250 yds

250 m

— : 17-MILE DR

Pacific Gardens Marine Gardens Fish Refuge

Marine Gardens Park

Berwick Park

Pacific Grove Marine Gardens Fish Refuge

HOPKINS MARINE STATION

AMERICAN TIN CANNERY

FIRST AWAKENINGS

IL VECCHIO

MONTEREY BAY AQUARIUM

WAVE ST

FOAM ST

LIGHTHOUSE AVE

HAWTHORNE AVE

PRESCOTT AVE

DAVID AVE

PINE ST

1ST ST
2ND ST
3RD ST
4TH ST
5TH ST
6TH ST
7TH ST
8TH ST
9TH ST
10TH ST
11TH ST
12TH ST
13TH ST

EARDLEY AVE

MONTEREY AVE

CARMEL AVE

SINEX AVE

CENTRAL AVE

LIGHTHOUSE AVE

LAUREL AVE

FOUNTAIN AVE

FOREST AVE

CONGRESS AVE

GRANITE ST

CEDAR ST

GIBSON AVE

WALNUT ST

LOVER'S POINT PARK

OCEANVIEW BLVD

SEVEN GABLES INN

PASSIONFISH

GOODIES DELI

JOE ROMBI'S LA MIA CUCINA

UNION ST

PACIFIC GROVE MUSEUM OF NATURAL HISTORY

PACIFIC AVE

MERMAID AVE

OCEAN VIEW BLVD

SERPALM AVE

ESPLANADE

MONTE BLVD

CORAL ST

ASILOMAR AVE

EL CARMELO CEMETERY

PACIFIC GROVE MUNICIPAL GOLF COURSE

POINT PIÑOS LIGHTHOUSE

OCEAN VIEW BLVD

LIGHTHOUSE AVE

JEWELL AVE

17-MILE DR

RIDGE RD

MONARCH GROVE SANCTUARY

George Washington Park

SHORT ST

LAUREL AVE

PINE AVE

ALDER ST

SPRUCE ST

JUNIPERO AVE

DENNETT ST

PICO AVE

CROCKER AVE

ANDRIL FIREPLACE COTTAGES

ASILOMAR AVE

ARENA AVE

SUNSET DR

Asilomar State Beach

ASILOMAR CONFERENCE GROUNDS

SINEX AVE

MAPLE ST

17-MILE DR

17-MILE DRIVE

68

© AVALON TRAVEL

MONTEREY BAY

Point Park (Ocean View Blvd. and 17th St., 831/648-3100, www.ci.pg.ca.us) is one of the area's most popular wedding sites. A finger of land with a jumble of rocks at its northernmost point, Lover's Point offers expansive views of the interior section of the Monterey Bay.

The park also has a sheltered pocket beach, which is ideal for a dip or wading on Pacific Grove's infrequent hot days. Also a kelp forest right offshore is a superb spot for snorkelers to get a feel for Monterey Bay's impressive underwater ecosystem.

During summer months, there is an old-fashioned hamburger stand above the beach and a vendor that rents kayaks, bikes, and snorkeling equipment.

Point Pinos Lighthouse

Surrounded by a golf course, **Point Pinos Lighthouse** (80 Asilomar Ave. between Lighthouse Ave. and Del Monte Ave., 831/648-3176, www.ci.pg.ca.us, Thurs.-Mon. 1pm-4pm, adults $2, children $1) has the distinction of being the oldest continuously operating lighthouse on the West Coast. It was one of the first eight lighthouses built on the West Coast, starting operations in 1855. Point Pinos is also notable for the two female lighthouse keepers who served there during its long history. The light was automated in 1975, but it is still an active aid to local marine navigation.

Monarch Grove Sanctuary

Pacific Grove is also known as "Butterfly Town U.S.A." An impressive migration of Monarch butterflies descends on the town each year. Tucked in a residential area, the small **Monarch Grove Sanctuary** (Ridge Rd. between Lighthouse Ave. and Short St., 831/648-5716, www.ci.pg.ca.us, free) offers strands of eucalyptus and pine trees which are cloaked with colorful insects during the migration period (October-February).

Asilomar State Beach

One of the Monterey Peninsula's most popular beaches, **Asilomar State Beach** (take the 68 West exit off Hwy. 1 and turn left on Sunset

Lover's Point Park

© STUART THORNTON

MONTEREY BAY

Dr., 831/646-6440, www.parks.ca.gov) draws beachgoers, walkers, and surfers. The beach itself is a narrow one-mile-long strip of coastline with a boardwalk trail on the dunes behind it. You can keep walking on the trail into nearby Pebble Beach, an easy, cost-free way to get a taste of that exclusive community.

Pacific Grove Museum of Natural History

The **Pacific Grove Museum of Natural History** (165 Forest Ave., 831/648-5716, www. pgmuseum.org, Tues.-Sun. 10am-5pm, $3 suggested donation) is easy to find. Just look for the life-size gray whale sculpture outside. Inside is an exhibit of marine mammal artifacts, a bird collection with 409 mounted birds, and an installation on an annual Pacific Grove visitor: the monarch butterfly.

ENTERTAINMENT AND EVENTS

If you want a wild night out on the town, you're not going to get it in Pacific Grove. But there are a couple of family-friendly annual events in P.G., which has the nickname of "America's Last Hometown." Recalling another era, Pacific Grove's **Good Old Days** (www.pacificgrove.org) is a weekend of good clean fun every April that includes a parade, a quilt show, pony rides, and live entertainment.

For over 70 years, the kids of Pacific Grove have been getting dressed up like butterflies at the **Butterfly Parade and Bazaar** (www. pacificgrove.org), which welcomes the wintering monarch butterflies to the area every fall.

SPORTS AND RECREATION
Scuba Diving and Snorkeling

Some of the best scuba diving and snorkeling spots on the Monterey Peninsula lie off Pacific Grove. **Lover's Point Park** (Ocean View Blvd. and 17th St., 831/648-3100, www.ci.pg.ca.us) has a protected cove and kelp forest right off its shores. The cove's protected sandy beach makes an easy entry point for scuba divers and snorkelers who want to explore the kelp forest. Just a few blocks away is **Otter Cove** (intersection

of Ocean View Blvd. and Sea Palm Ave.), a dive spot that is best during calm ocean days. One of the highlights is a pinnacle that rises from 50 feet to just 18 feet below the surface. If you need equipment, visit **Bamboo Reef** (614 Lighthouse Ave., 831/372-1685, www.bambooreef.com) or **Aquarius Dive Shop** (2040 Del Monte Ave., 831/375-1933, www.aquariusdivers.com) in nearby Monterey.

Surfing

During the summer and fall, clean swells produce fun waves at **Asilomar State Beach** (take the 68 West exit off Hwy. 1 and turn left on Sunset Dr., 831/646-6440, www.parks.ca.gov), making it one of the peninsula's most popular surf spots. Winter produces big, often dangerous swells, so stay out of the water during that time of the year. **Sunshine Freestyle Surf & Sport** (443 Lighthouse Ave., Monterey, 831/375-5015, www.sunshinefreestyle.com) rents boards and wetsuits in nearby Monterey.

Golf

The **Pacific Grove Golf Links** (77 Asilomar Blvd., 831/648-5775, www.pggolflinks.com, daily sunrise-sunset, Mon.-Thurs. $46, Fri.-Sun. and holidays $52) doesn't have the acclaim of the nearby Pebble Beach courses, but it's located on a similar, gorgeous length of coastline just a few miles away.

ACCOMMODATIONS
$150-250

Staying overnight at the **Asilomar Conference Grounds** (804 Crocker Ave., 831/372-8016, www.visitasilomar.com, $170-277) can feel a bit like going back to summer camp. There are lots of common areas on the 107 acres including the Phoebe Apperson Hearst Social Hall, where visitors can relax by a roaring fire or play pool at one of two billiards tables. Breakfast, which comes with an overnight stay, is served in what feels like a camp mess hall.

There is a real range of accommodations here from historic rooms to family cottages to modern rooms with a view of nearby Asilomar Beach. The rooms with an ocean view and a fireplace are definitely recommended for those who don't mind spending a little more money. Note that all the rooms here lack TVs and telephones. It's an incentive for you to head outdoors.

The frequently overlooked state park-owned lodging hosts a multitude of conferences, so expect to see corporate types with laminated conference badges walking through the forests of Monterey pine, Monterey cypress, and coast live oaks alongside the roaming herds of semi-wild deer.

Over $250

The most striking bed-and-breakfast on the coast of Pacific Grove, the **Seven Gables Inn** (555 Ocean View Blvd., 831/372-4341, www.sevengablesinn.com, $259-349) is perched just feet away from Lover's Point. Decorated with antique furniture and artwork, the Seven Gables Inn is for those who want to step back in time and experience ornate Victorian and Edwardian style lodging. Impressively, every single room has superb ocean views.

Right across the street from the Asilomar Conference Grounds, the **Andril Fireplace Cottages** (569 Asilomar Ave., 831/375-0994, www.andrilcottages.com, $220-595) offers a cluster of cabins surrounded by pine forest. Most of the 1-5-bedroom structures have their own kitchens, private decks and, as the name promises, fireplaces. Outdoors are a whirlpool tub, ping-pong table, and some barbecue grills.

FOOD
American

Stop into **Goodies Deli** (518 Lighthouse Ave., 831/655-3663, http://goodiesdeli.blogspot.com, Mon.-Sat. 9:30am-4pm, $8) for a hearty sandwich. Thirty-two options include classics like Philly cheese steaks and BLTs, as well as alternative choices like hot tofu and teriyaki chicken. The dining area is a bit sterile, so grab your sandwich to go for a picnic at nearby Lover's Point.

Breakfast

Located in one end of the cavernous American Tin Cannery shopping mall, **First Awakenings** (125 Oceanview Blvd., 831/372-1125, www.firstawakenings.net, daily 7am-2pm, $10) serves up oversized versions of classic breakfast fare including huevos rancheros, eggs benedict, crepes, and omelets. On sunny days, you can dine outside on the large patio, surrounded by the sounds of nearby Monterey Bay.

French

Spoil yourself at **Fifi's Bistro Café** (1188 Forest Ave., 831/372-5325, www.fifisbistrocafe.com, Mon.-Sat. 11:30am-3pm and 5pm-9pm, Sun. 10am-3pm and 5pm-9pm, $16-30). Decadent dinner entrées include goat cheese-stuffed chicken breast and duck in a Grand Marnier sauce. There's also an extensive wine list. And, oh yeah, Fifi's has the best French onion soup on the peninsula.

Italian

Travel to Italy without leaving the peninsula at **Joe Rombi's La Mia Cucina** (208 17 St., 831/373-2416, http://joerombi.com, Wed.-Sat. 5pm-close, $21-29). The professional, well-dressed waitstaff serves dishes like hand-rolled ravioli and eggplant Parmesan. Don't miss the arancini (fried rice balls) appetizer!

Il Vecchio (110 Central Ave., 831/324-4282, Tues.-Sat. 5pm-9:30pm, Sun.-Mon. 5pm-10pm, $13-22) is a new Pacific Grove favorite, but the name Il Vecchio, meaning "the old," refers to traditional Italian fare like gnocchi with pesto and Italian sausages with white cannellini beans. Popular Tuesday night family dinners (5pm-6:30pm, adults $15, children $8) offer a changing all-you-can-eat four-course dinner.

Seafood

The Monterey Peninsula is known for its seafood, and **Passionfish** (701 Lighthouse Ave., 831/655-3311, www.passionfish.net, Sun.-Thurs 5pm-9pm, Fri.-Sat. 5pm-10pm, $26) is one of the region's most highly regarded seafood restaurants. The menu here changes daily but may feature ocean dwelling delicacies like sea scallops in a tomato truffle butter or shrimp in a black pepper rum sauce. Passionfish also has an impressive 400-item wine list.

SHOPPING

A canning factory no more, the **American Tin Cannery** (125 Oceanview Blvd., 831/372-1442, www.americanincannery.com, daily 10am-6pm) is an indoor mall with discount outlets for national brands including Bass, Pendleton, and Nine West. You can also take a break from shopping at an indoor black light miniature golf course.

INFORMATION AND SERVICES

To pick up pamphlets on Pacific Grove's sights and lodging options, stop in at the **Pacific Grove Tourist Information Center**

(100 Central Ave., 831/324-4668, www.pacificgrove.org, Mon.-Fri. 9am-5pm, Sat.-Sun. 10am-5pm). Pacific Grove has its own banks, restaurants, and a **post office** (680 Lighthouse Ave., 831/373-2271, www.usps.com, Mon.-Fri. 9am-4pm, Sat. 10am-1pm). For medical needs, the **Community Hospital of the Monterey Peninsula** (CHOMP, 23625 Holman Hwy., 831/425-4667, www.chomp.org) is actually located closer to Pacific Grove than Monterey. It provides emergency services to the area.

GETTING THERE AND AROUND

Most visitors drive into Pacific Grove via the scenic Highway 1. From Highway 1, take the Highway 68 west exit to downtown Pacific Grove.

Pebble Beach

Located between Pacific Grove and Carmel, the gated community of Pebble Beach lays claim to some of the Monterey Peninsula's best, highest-priced real estate. Pebble Beach is famous for the scenic 17-Mile Drive and its collection of high-end resorts, restaurants, spas, and golf courses, owned by the Pebble Beach Company, a partnership that includes golf legend Arnold Palmer and film legend Clint Eastwood. In February, Pebble Beach hosts the annual AT&T Pebble Beach National Pro-Am, a charity golf tournament that pairs professional golfers with celebrities.

SIGHTS
17-Mile Drive

The best way to take in the stunning scenery of Pebble Beach is the **17-Mile Drive**. But don't get too excited yet—long ago, the all-powerful Pebble Beach Corporation realized that the local scenery is also a precious commodity, and began charging a toll ($9.50/vehicle). The good news is that when you pay the fee at the gatehouse, you receive a map of the drive that describes the parks and sights that you will pass along the winding coastal

road: the much-photographed Lone Cypress, the beaches of Spanish Bay, and Pebble Beach's golf course, resort, and housing complex. If you're in a hurry, you can get from one end of the 17-Mile Drive to the other in 20 minutes. But go slowly and stop often to enjoy the natural beauty of the area (and get your money's worth). There are plenty of turnouts where you can stop to take photos of the iconic cypress trees and stunning coastline. You can picnic at many of the beaches, most of which have basic restroom facilities and ample parking lots. The only food and gas to be had are at the Inn at Spanish Bay and the Lodge at Pebble Beach.

ENTERTAINMENT AND EVENTS

If you dream of watching Bill Murray or Kevin Costner play golf—and who doesn't?—plan a trip to Pebble Beach in February for the **AT&T Pebble Beach National Pro-Am** (www.pebblebeach.com). This almost weeklong tournament pairing pro golfers with Hollywood celebrities is the biggest annual event in Pebble Beach and arguably the whole Monterey Peninsula.

MONTEREY BAY

SPORTS AND RECREATION
Biking

Traveling the **17-Mile Drive** by bike means you don't have to pay the $9.50 vehicle admission fee. It's also a great bike route. Cyclists can enjoy the smells and sounds of the spectacular coastline in a way that car passengers just can't. Expect fairly flat terrain with lots of twists and turns, and a ride that runs...about 17 miles. Foggy conditions can make this ride a bit slick in the summer, but spring and fall weather are perfect for pedaling.

Golf

There's no place for golfing quite like Pebble Beach. Golf has been a major pastime here since the late 19th century; today avid golfers come from around the world to tee off inside the gated community. You can play courses trodden by the likes of Tiger Woods and Jack Nicholson, pause a moment before you putt to take in the sight of the stunning Pacific Ocean, and pay $300 or more for a single round of golf.

One of the Pebble Beach Resort courses, **Spyglass Hill** (1700 17-Mile Dr., 800/654-9300, www.pebblebeach.com, 18-hole Par 72) gets its name from the Robert Louis Stevenson Novel *Treasure Island*. Don't be fooled—the holes on this beautiful course may be named for characters in an adventure novel, but that doesn't mean they're easy. Spyglass Hill boasts some of the most challenging play in this golf course-laden region. Expect a few bogeys, and tee off from the Championship level at your own (ego's) risk.

Another favorite with the Pebble Beach crowd is the famed **Poppy Hills Golf Course** (3200 Lopez Rd., 831/622-8239, www.poppyhillsgolf.com, 18-hole Par 72). Though it's not managed by the same company, Poppy Hills shares amenities with Pebble Beach golf courses. Expect the same level of care and devotion to the maintenance of the course and your experience as a player.

ACCOMMODATIONS AND FOOD

You need to drop some serious money to stay in Pebble Beach. Expect luxury amenities at **The Lodge at Pebble Beach** (1700 17-Mile Dr., 831/647-7500 or 800/654-9300, www.pebblebeach.com, $715-2,425), located by the 18th hole of the Pebble Beach Golf Links. Most rooms and suites have wood burning fireplaces as well as private patios or balconies. Some of the high-end rooms have their own spas.

Like The Lodge at Pebble Beach, **The Inn at Spanish Bay** (2700 17-Mile Dr., 831/647-7500 or 800/654-9300, www.pebblebeach.com, $615-2,425) has rooms with fireplaces and decks or patios. There's also a fitness center and tennis pavilion on-site.

To experience the luxury of Pebble Beach without dropping your savings on a night's stay, enjoy dinner in the exclusive community then head back to a less expensive lodging in nearby Pacific Grove or Monterey. The Hawaiian fusion cuisine of celebrity chef Roy Yamaguchi is center stage at **Roy's at Pebble Beach** (The Inn at Spanish Bay, 2700 17-Mile Dr., 831/647-7423, daily 6:30am-10pm, $26-78). Island-inspired dishes include seafood and sushi, all with an Asian flair.

At **The Tap Room** (The Lodge at Pebble Beach, 1700 17-Mile Dr., 831/625-8535, daily 11am-11:30pm, $17-52), burgers, bratwurst, and potato skins share the menu with Wagyu beef filet mignons and fresh Maine lobsters.

GETTING THERE

There are several gates to get into Pebble Beach including three in Pacific Grove and one in Carmel. Admission to Pebble Beach is $9.50 if you aren't staying here. You can get the fee waived if you are going in to dine at a Pebble Beach restaurant.

Carmel-by-the-Sea

There are no addresses in Carmel-by-the-Sea (frequently referred to as simply Carmel). There are lots of trees and no street lights, and street signs are wooden posts with names written perpendicularly, to be read while walking along the sidewalk, rather than driving down the street. There's little to do at night. These are a few clues as to how this village facing the Pacific Ocean maintains its lost-in-time charm.

Formerly a Bohemian enclave where local poets George Sterling and Robinson Jeffers hung out with literary heavyweights, including Jack London and Mary Austin, Carmel-by-the-Sea is now a popular vacation spot for the well moneyed, the artistic, and the romantic. People come to enjoy the small coastal town's almost European charm: strolling its sidewalks, peering into the windows of upscale shops and art galleries, which showcase the work of sculptors, plein air painters, and photographers. Between the galleries are some of the region's most revered restaurants. The main thoroughfare, Ocean Avenue, slopes down to Carmel Beach, one of the finest on the Monterey Peninsula.

The old world charms of Carmel can make it a little confusing for drivers. Because there are no addresses, locations are sometimes given via directions, for example: on 7th between San Carlos and Delores; or the northwest corner of Ocean Avenue. You get used to it. The town is compact, laid out on a plain grid system, so you're better off getting out of your car and walking anyway. Expect to share everything from Carmel's sidewalks to its restaurants with our furry canine friends. Carmel is very pro-pup.

SIGHTS
◖ Carmel Beach

Found at the end of Carmel-by-the-Sea's Ocean Avenue, **Carmel Beach** (Ocean Ave., 831/624-4909, daily 6am-10pm) is one of the Monterey Bay region's best beaches. Under a bluff dotted with twisted skeletal cypress trees, it's a long white sandy beach that borders a usually clear blue-green Pacific. In the distance to the South, Point Lobos juts out from the land like a pointing finger, while just north of the beach, the green-as-billiard-table-felt golf courses cloak the grounds of nearby Pebble Beach.

Like most of Carmel, Carmel Beach is very dog friendly. On any given day, all sorts of canines fetch, sniff, and run on the white sand.

For surfers, Carmel Beach is one of the Monterey area's most consistent breaks. It's also the annual site of the Sunshine Freestyle Surfabout, the only surf contest in Monterey County.

Carmel Mission
San Carlos Borromeo de Carmelo Mission

(3080 Rio Rd., 831/624-1271, www.carmel-mission.org, daily 9:30am-5pm, adults $6.50, children $2) was Father Junípero Serra's personal favorite among his California mission churches. He lived, worked, and eventually died here, and visitors today can see a replica of his cell. A working Catholic parish remains part of the complex, so please be respectful when taking the self-guided tour. The rambling buildings and courtyard gardens show some wear, but enough restoration work has gone into the church and living quarters to make them attractive and eminently visitable. The Carmel Mission has a small memorial museum in a building off the second courtyard, but don't make the mistake of thinking that this small and outdated space is the only historical display. In fact, the "museum" runs through many of the buildings, showing a small slice of the lives of the 18th- and 19th-century friars. The highlight of the complex is the church with its gilded altar front, its shrine to the Virgin Mary, the grave of Father Serra, and ancillary chapel dedicated to the memory of Father Serra. Round out your visit by walking out into the gardens to admire the flowers and fountains and to read the grave markers in the small cemetery.

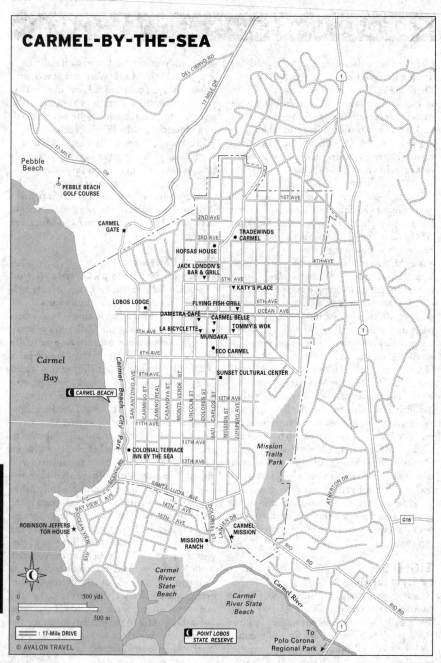

CARMEL-BY-THE-SEA

Pebble
Beach

PEBBLE BEACH
GOLF COURSE

17-MILE DR

DEL CIERVO RD

CARMEL
GATE

1ST AVE

2ND AVE

3RD AVE   TRADEWINDS
CARMEL

HOFSAS HOUSE

4TH AVE

JACK LONDON'S
BAR & GRILL
5TH AVE

▼ KATY'S PLACE

LOBOS LODGE   FLYING FISH GRILL   6TH AVE

DAMETRA CAFÉ   OCEAN AVE

CARMEL BELLE
LA BICYCLETTE ▼   ▼ TOMMY'S WOK

MUNDAKA

7TH AVE

8TH AVE   ● ECO CARMEL

Carmel

Bay

9TH AVE   SUNSET CULTURAL CENTER

CARMEL BEACH

SAN ANTONIO AVE

CARMELO ST

CAMINO REAL

CASANOVA ST

MONTE VERDE ST

LINCOLN ST

DOLORES ST

SAN CARLOS ST

MISSION ST

JUNIPERO AVE

10TH AVE

Carmel Beach City Park

11TH AVE

SCENIC RD

12TH AVE

COLONIAL TERRACE
INN BY THE SEA
13TH AVE

Mission
Trails
Park

ATHERTON DR

SANTA LUCIA AVE

BAY VIEW AVE

14TH
AVE

DOLORES ST

LASUEN DR

G16

OCEAN VIEW AVE

15TH
AVE

CARMEL
MISSION

RIO RD

ROBINSON JEFFERS
TOR HOUSE ★

MISSION
RANCH

RIO RD

Carmel River

Carmel
River
State
Beach

Carmel
River State
Beach

0   500 yds

0   500 m

To
Polo Corona
Regional Park

══ : 17-Mile DRIVE

POINT LOBOS
STATE RESERVE

© AVALON TRAVEL

© STUART THORNTON

Monterey cypress trees frame Carmel Beach.

Tor House

Local poet Robinson Jeffers penned nature poems to the uncompromising beauty of Carmel Point and nearby Big Sur. He built this rugged-looking castle on the Carmel coast in 1919. He named it **Tor House** (26304 Ocean View Ave., 831/624-1813, www.torhouse.org, tours Fri.-Sat. 10am-3pm, $10), after its rocky setting, and added the majestic Hawk Tower a year later. The granite stone structure exists today as an example of the Carmel ethos that Jeffers embodied and as a monument to his work and poetry.

◖ Point Lobos State Reserve

Said to be the inspiration behind the setting of Robert Louis Stevenson's *Treasure Island,* **Point Lobos State Reserve** (three miles south of Carmel, 831/624-4909, www.parks. ca.gov, $10/vehicle) is a wonderland of coves, hills, and jumbled rocks. The reserve's Cypress Grove Trail winds through a forest of antler-like Monterey cypress trees that are cloaked in a striking red algae. Point Lobos also offers

a lesson on the region's fishing history in the Whaler's Cabin, a small wooden structure that was built by Chinese fishermen in the 1850s. Half of the reserve is underwater, and it is open for scuba divers who want to explore the 70-foot-high kelp forests located just offshore. The parking lots in Point Lobos tend to fill up on crowded weekends, but the reserve allows people to park on nearby Highway 1 and walk in to visit the park during these times.

ENTERTAINMENT AND EVENTS

The events and entertainment in Carmel tend to center around either art or food. This town loves its haute culture, so you won't find too many sports bars or generic movie theaters here. Instead, enjoy classical music, a wealth of live theater, and a glass of wine in the mild evenings.

Live Music

Classical music aficionados will appreciate the dulcet tones of the musicians who perform

MONTEREY BAY

for **Chamber Music Monterey Bay** (831/625-2212, www.chambermusicmontereybay.org). This society brings talented ensembles and soloists in from around the world to perform on the lovely Central Coast. One night you might find a local string quartet, and on another night you'll get to see and hear a chamber ensemble. (String quartets definitely rule the small stage and intimate theater.) Far from banning young music fans from the **Sunset Cultural Center** (San Carlos St. at Ninth Ave., 831/620-2048, www.sunsetcenter.org), Chamber Music Monterey Bay reserves up-front seats at all its shows for children and their adult companions.

The Sunset Cultural Center also hosts concerts by acts including multicultural bluesman Taj Mahal and Fleetwood Mac guitarist Lindsey Buckingham.

Bars and Clubs

Carmel's once nearly non-existent nightlife gained a pulse with the opening of **Mundaka** (San Carlos St. and Seventh Ave., 831/624-7400, www.mundakacarmel.com, daily 5:30pm-close) in 2009. This Spanish style tapas bar attracts Carmel's younger crowd (i.e., pre-senior citizen) with live music and DJs every night of the week except Sunday. Many shirts have been ruined here by drinking wine from one of Mundaka's porrons, glass wine pitchers with a spout that allows you to pour wine into your mouth from above your head.

With its all dark wood, fancy ceiling, and quiet elegance, **Jack London's Bar & Grill** (Dolores St. and Fifth Ave., 831/624-2336, www.jacklondons.com, daily 11am-close) has a full menu of fancier-than-average bar food and a wine list that would do a high-end restaurant proud. The bar serves food until 10pm on weekdays and 11pm on weekends. But it's also got big-screen TVs tuned to the games of the day and live music each Friday and Saturday. If you've brought your favorite canine companion, you'll find a welcoming seat outside on the patio, where the full menu is served.

Theater

Despite its small size, Carmel has a handful of live theater groups. In a town that defines itself by its love of art, theater arts don't get left out. Don't hesitate to ask the locals what's playing where when you're in town.

The **Pacific Repertory Theater** (831/622-0100, www.pacrep.org, adults $10-38, students $10-20, children $7) is the only professional theater company on the Monterey-Carmel Peninsula. Its shows go up all over the region, most often in the **Golden Bough Playhouse** (Monte Verde St. and Eighth Ave.), the company's home theater. Other regular venues include the **The Forest Theater** (Mountain View St. and Santa Rita St.), and the **Circle Theater** (Casanova St. between Eighth and Ninth Aves.) within the Golden Bough complex. The company puts on dramas, comedies, and musicals both new and classic. You might see a work of Shakespeare or a classic like *Fiddler on the Roof* or maybe enjoy your favorite songs from *The Fantasticks,* or sing along to the newer tunes of *Hairspray!* Check the website for upcoming shows, and buy tickets online or over the phone to guarantee you'll get seats while you're in town.

Each fall, PacRep puts up the **Carmel Shakespeare Festival** (www.pacrep.org), a short showing of Shakespeare that's good enough to draw the notice of Bay Area theater snobs. Check the website for information on this year's shows and the venues.

Festivals and Events

In a town famed for art galleries, one of the biggest events of the year is the **Carmel Art Festival** (Devendorf Park at Mission St., www.carmelartfestival.org, May). This four-day event celebrates visual arts in all media with shows by internationally acclaimed artists at galleries, parks, and other venues all across town. This wonderful festival also sponsors here-and-now contests, including the prestigious plein air (outdoor painting). Visitors get a rare opportunity to witness the artists outdoors, engaging in their creative process as they use the Carmel scenery for inspiration. Round out your festival experience by bidding on paintings at the end-of-event auction. You can get a genuine bargain on original artwork while supporting both the artists and the festival. Perhaps best of all, the Carmel Art Festival is a great place to bring your family—a wealth of children's activities help even the youngest festival goers become budding artists.

For a more classical experience, one of the most prestigious festivals in Northern California is the **Carmel Bach Festival** (www.bachfestival.org). For 15 days each July, Carmel-by-the-Sea and its surrounding towns host dozens of classical concerts. Naturally the works of J. S. Bach are featured, but you can also hear renditions of Mozart, Vivaldi, Handel, and other heavyweights of Bach's era. Choose between big concerts in major venues or intimate performances in smaller spaces with only a small audience between you and the beautiful music. Concerts and recitals take place literally every day of the week—budget-conscious music lovers can just as easily enjoy the festival in the middle of the week as on the weekends.

The **Carmel Art & Film Festival** (http://carmelartandfilm.com) lures movie debuts and movie stars to Carmel in October. Local resident (and former mayor) Clint Eastwood singles out one film each year for the Clint Eastwood Filmmakers Award at this four-day arts celebration.

During the summer, the **Forest Theater** (Mountain View St. and Santa Rita St., 831/626-1681, www.foresttheaterguild.org, $7) puts on its popular **Films in the Forest** series. Under the stars and trees, movie lovers can take in classics like *Singin' in the Rain* or more recent releases like *War Horse*. It's okay to bring in a bottle of wine or some snacks to sample during the flicks. Be sure to also pack a blanket to soften the blow of the theater's wooden bench seats. Visit the Forest Theater website for the summer film schedule.

SHOPPING
It is easy to spend an afternoon poking into Carmel's many art galleries from the classical mythical sculptures on display at **Dawson Cole Fine Art** (Lincoln St. and 6th, 831/624-8200, www.dawsoncolefineart.com, Mon.-Sat. 10am-6pm, Sun. 10am-5:30pm) to the playful paintings of a blue dog on display at **Rodrigue Studio Carmel** (Dolores St. between Ocean and 7th, 831/626-4444, http://georgerodrigue.com, Mon.-Sat. 10am-5pm, Sun. noon-5pm).

When your head starts spinning from all the art, head to **Carmel Plaza** (Ocean Ave. and Mission St., 831/624-1385, www.carmelplaza.com, Mon.-Sat. 10am-6pm, Sun. 11am-5pm), which offers lots of ways to part with your money. This outdoor mall has luxury fashion shops like Louis Vuitton as well as the hip clothing chain Anthropologie. But don't miss locally-owned establishment The Cheese Store, which sells delicacies like cave-aged Gruyere cheese that you can pair with a local wine.

Worth a browse is the eclectic **Carmel Bay Company** (Ocean Ave. and Lincoln Ave., 831/624-3868, www.carmelbaycompany.com, daily 10am-5pm), which features copper armoires and a fascinating collection of vintage photograph prints.

For the environment lover in your life, pick up natural milk-based paint or books like *The Gorgeously Green Diet* at **Eco Carmel** (San Carlos St. and 7th Ave., 831/624-1222, www.ecocarmel.com, Mon.-Sat. 10am-6pm, Sun. 11am-5pm). If you carry your purchases out without a bag, you get a 25-cent token that you can donate to one of three rotating non-profits.

SPORTS AND RECREATION
Surfing
Carmel Beach (Ocean Ave., 831/624-4909, daily 6am-10pm) has some of the area's most consistent beach breaks. Contact **Carmel Surf Lessons** (831/915-4065, www.carmelsurf-lessons.com) if you want to try and learn to surf at Carmel Beach. To rent a board, head to Monterey's **Sunshine Freestyle Surf & Sport** (443 Lighthouse Ave., Monterey, 831/375-5015, www.sunshinefreestyle.com).

ACCOMMODATIONS
$150-250
Lobos Lodge (Monte Verde and Ocean Aves., 831/624-3874, www.loboslodge.com,

$125-265) sits right in the midst of downtown Carmel-by-the-Sea, making it a perfect spot from which to dine, shop, and admire the endless array of art in this upscale town. Each of the 30 rooms and suites offers a gas fireplace, a sofa and table, a bed in an alcove, and enough space to stroll about and enjoy the quiet romantic setting. All but two of the rooms have a patio or balcony where you can enjoy the product of a local vineyard outside.

The Bavarian-inspired, locally-owned **Hofsas House** (San Carlos St. between 3rd and 4th Aves., 831/624-2745, www.hofsashouse.com, $145-400) offers surprisingly spacious rooms in a quiet semi-residential neighborhood within easy walking distance of downtown Carmel. If you have a crew, Hofsas House has family suites for rent with two bedrooms and two bathrooms. If you can, get an ocean-view room with a patio or balcony and spend some time sitting outside looking over the town of Carmel out toward the serene (from a distance) Pacific waters.

Located in a neighborhood just a block from Carmel Beach, **Colonial Terrace Inn By The Sea** (San Antonio Ave between 12th and 13th Aves., 831/624-2741, www.thecolonial-terrace.com, $219-349) is the best place in the small town to fall asleep with the white noise of breaking waves. In addition to superb ocean views from the property, Colonial Terrace has a nice brick courtyard surrounded by blooming flowers to enjoy on the area's warmer days.

Outside of downtown Carmel, **Mission Ranch** (26270 Dolores St., 831/624-6436, www.missionranchcarmel.com, $165-325) is a sprawling old ranch complex with views of sheep-filled pastures and Point Lobos in the distance. If you get a glimpse of Mission Ranch's owner, it might just make your day. It's none other than Hollywood icon and former Carmel-by-the-Sea mayor Clint Eastwood. On the grounds is a restaurant with a nightly sing-a-long piano bar that is popular with Carmel's silver-haired crowd.

Over $250
◖ **Tradewinds Carmel** (Mission and 3rd Ave., 831/624-2776, www.tradewinds.com, $250-550) brings a touch of the Far East to California. Inspired by the initial proprietor's time spent in Japan, the 28 serene hotel rooms are decorated with Asian antiquities and live orchids. Outside, the grounds feature a water fountain that passes through bamboo shoots and horsetails along with a Buddha meditation garden, where an oversized Buddha head overlooks a trio of cascading pools.

FOOD
Breakfast
Katy's Place (Mission and 6th Ave., 831/624-0199, www.katysplacecarmel.com, daily 7am-2pm, $10-20), serves gigantic classic breakfasts, like Denver omelets and biscuits and gravy, inside or outside on a redwood shaded deck. The longtime local's favorite also has some unique eggs benedict combinations including the "Benedict Romanoff," which has sliced smoked salmon and caviar.

◖ **Carmel Belle** (Doud Craft Studios, Ocean Ave. and San Carlos St., 831/624-1600, www.carmelbelle.com, daily 8am-5pm, $9.50) is a little eatery with a big attention to detail. In the open section of an indoor mall, Carmel Belle serves up creative fare for breakfast and lunch, including an open-faced breakfast sandwich featuring a slab of toasted bread topped with a poached egg, strips of thick bacon, a bed of arugula, and wedges of fresh avocado that you can pile on top. Meanwhile its slow-cooked Berkshire pork sandwich with red onion-currant chutney is a perfect example of what can happen when savory meets sweet.

Chinese
For an authentic hole-in-the-wall locals' dining experience, seek out **Tommy's Wok** (San Carlos St. between Ocean and 7th Ave., 831/624-8518, Tues.-Sun. 11:30am-2:30pm and 4:30pm-9:30pm, $10-20). You can dine in or take out items like the Mu Shu Pork.

French
If the international feel of Carmel-by-the-Sea has put you in the mood for European food,

have dinner at the quaint French eatery **La Bicyclette** (Dolores St. at 7th Ave., 831/622-9899, www.labicycletterestaurant.com, daily 8am-11am, 11:30am-10pm, $28-36). The three-course dinner menu changes nightly, but often features steak and rabbit.

Mediterranean

While **Dametra Café** (Ocean Ave. at Lincoln St., 831/622-7766, www.dametracafe.com, $18) has a wide ranging international menu that includes an all-American cheeseburger and Italian dishes like spaghetti ala Bolognese, it's best to go with the lively restaurant's signature Mediterranean food. The Greek chicken kebab entrée is a revelation with two chicken and vegetable kebabs drizzled with a distinct aioli sauce over yellow rice and a Greek salad.

Seafood

The **Flying Fish Grill** (Mission St. between Ocean and 7th Aves., 831/625-1962, http://flyingfishgrill.com, daily 5pm-10pm, $20-34) serves Japanese-style seafood with a California twist in the Carmel Plaza open-air shopping mall. Entrées include rare peppered ahi and black bean halibut.

INFORMATION AND SERVICES

You'll find the **Carmel Visitors Center** (San Carlos between 5th and 6th Aves., 831/624-2522, www.carmelcalifornia.org, daily 10am-5pm) right in the midst of downtown Carmel-by-the-Sea.

For more information about the town and current events, pick up a copy of the weekly **Carmel Pine Cone** (www.pineconearchive.com), the local newspaper.

The nearest major medical center to Carmel-by-the-Sea and the Carmel Valley is in nearby Monterey. For minor issues, head for the **Community Hospital of Monterey** (23625 Holman Hwy., Monterey, 831/624-5311, www.chomp.org).

GETTING THERE AND AROUND

If you've made it to Monterey by car, getting to Carmel is a piece of cake. The quick and free way to get to Carmel from the north or the south is via Highway 1. From Highway 1, take Ocean Avenue into the middle of downtown Carmel. A more expensive but more beautiful route is via Pebble Beach's 17-Mile Drive.

As you read the addresses in Carmel-by-the-Sea and begin to explore the neighborhoods, you'll realize something interesting. There are no street addresses. (Some years ago Carmel residents voted not to enact door-to-door mail delivery, thus there is no need for numeric addresses on buildings.) So you'll need to pay close attention to the street names and the block you're on. Just to make things even more fun, street signs can be difficult to see in the mature foliage and a dearth of streetlights can make them nearly impossible to find at night. If you can, show up during the day to get the lay of the land before trying to navigate after dark.

MONTEREY BAY

Carmel Valley

When the Carmel coastline gets socked in with summer fog, locals flock inland to the reliably sunny Carmel Valley. But locals aren't the only people making their way to this corridor between the Santa Lucia Mountains. Carmel Valley is becoming known as a burgeoning but still unassuming wine region due to its tasty cabernet sauvignons, merlots, and other reds.

The landscape changes quickly as you leave the coast: You'll see the mountains rising above you, as well as farms, ranches, and orchards. Thirteen miles east of Highway 1 is the unincorporated Carmel Valley Village. In this small strip of businesses hugging Carmel Valley Road are a collection of wineries, tasting rooms, restaurants, and even an Old West saloon.

SIGHTS
Earthbound Farms

One of the largest purveyors of organic produce in the United States, Earthbound Farms began at the **Earthbound Farms Farm Stand** (7250 Carmel Valley Rd., 831/625-6219, www.ebfarm.com, Mon.-Sat. 8am-6:30pm, Sun. 9am-6pm). This 2.5-acre farm and roadside stand offers visitors easy access to its smallish facility in the Carmel Valley. Drive up to the farm stand and browse a variety of organic fruits, veggies, and flowers. Outdoors, you can ramble into the fields, checking out the chamomile labyrinth and the kids' garden (yes, your kids can look *and* touch). Select and harvest your own fresh herbs from the cut-your-own-herb garden, or leave the cooking to the experts and purchase delicious prepared organic dishes at the farm stand. If you're interested in a more in-depth guided tour of the farm, check the website for a schedule of walks, which will take you, a group, and an expert guide—perhaps a chef or local famous foodie—out into the fields for a look at what's growing and how to use it.

WINERIES

Its tiny size necessarily limits the number of vineyards and wineries that can set up shop in the Carmel Valley. But this small, charming wine region makes for a perfect wine-tasting day trip from Carmel, Monterey, or even Big Sur. Small crowds, light traffic, and meaningful tasting experiences categorize this area, which still has many family-owned wineries. You'll get personal attention and delicious wines, all in a gorgeous green setting.

The **Bernardus Winery** (5 W. Carmel Valley Rd., 800/223-2533, www.bernardus.com/winery, daily 11am-5pm, tasting $5-10) sits on a vineyard estate that also hosts a connected luxurious lodge and gourmet restaurant. Bernardus creates a small list of wines. The grapes growing all around you go into the pride of the winery: the Bordeaux-style blended red Marinus Vineyard wine. Other varietals (chardonnay, pinot noir, and sauvignon blanc) come from cool coastal vineyards. If you're interested and lucky, you might also get to sip some small-batch vintages of single-vineyard wines that are available only in the tasting room.

The biggest name in the Carmel Valley is **Chateau Julien** (8940 Carmel Valley Rd., 831/624-2600, www.chateaujulien.com, Mon.-Fri. 8am-5pm, Sat.-Sun. 11am-5pm). The European-styled white estate building with the round turret is visible from the road. The light, airy tasting room is crowded with barrels, wine cases, souvenirs, and tasting glasses. When you enter, you'll be offered sips from the wide selection of chardonnays, cabernets, syrahs, merlots, and more. If you're lucky, you might find yourself tasting a rare Reserve blended red or a 10-year-old port. For a treat, call ahead and reserve a spot on the twice-daily complimentary vineyard and winery tours. These tours conclude with a special tasting outside on the flagstone patio when weather permits.

On the other end of the spectrum, tiny **Parsonage Village Vineyard** (19 E. Carmel Valley Rd., 831/659-7322, www.parsonagewine.com, Fri.-Mon. 11am-5pm, tasting $5) often doesn't make it onto Carmel Valley wine maps—which is a shame, because some of

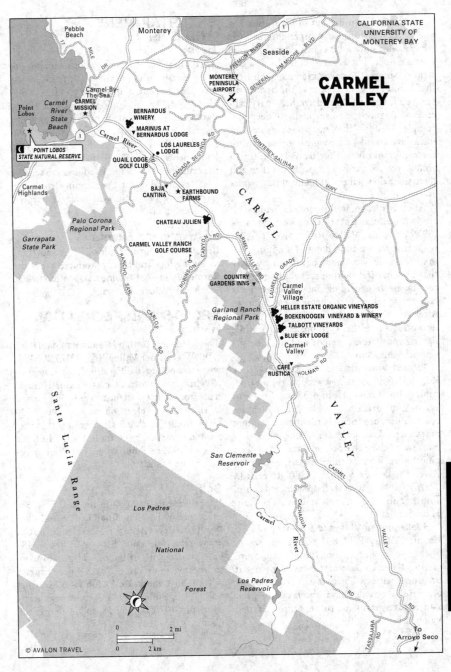

CALIFORNIA STATE UNIVERSITY OF MONTEREY BAY

Pebble Beach

Monterey

Seaside

CARMEL VALLEY

MONTEREY PENINSULA AIRPORT

Carmel-By-The-Sea

CARMEL MISSION

Point Lobos

Carmel River State Beach

BERNARDUS WINERY

MARINUS AT BERNARDUS LODGE

POINT LOBOS STATE NATURAL RESERVE

Carmel River

LOS LAURELES LODGE

QUAIL LODGE GOLF CLUB

Carmel Highlands

BAJA CANTINA ★ EARTHBOUND FARMS

C A R M E L

Palo Corona Regional Park

CHATEAU JULIEN

Garrapata State Park

CARMEL VALLEY RANCH GOLF COURSE

COUNTRY GARDENS INNS

Carmel Valley Village

Garland Ranch Regional Park

HELLER ESTATE ORGANIC VINEYARDS

BOEKENOOGEN VINEYARD & WINERY

TALBOTT VINEYARDS

BLUE SKY LODGE

Carmel Valley

CAFÉ RUSTICA

V A L L E Y

S a n t a   L u c i a   R a n g e

San Clemente Reservoir

Los Padres

Carmel River

National

Forest

Los Padres Reservoir

To Arroyo Seco

0   2 mi

0   2 km

© AVALON TRAVEL

CANADA SECUNDA RD

ROBINSON CANYON RD

CARMEL VALLEY RD

RANCHO SAN CARLOS RD

LAURELES GRADE

HOLMAN RD

CACHAGUA RD

CARMEL VALLEY RD

TASSAJARA RD

MONTEREY-SALINAS HWY

FREMONT BLVD

GENERAL JIM MOORE BLVD

17 MILE DR

the best syrah coming out of California (arguably) comes from this unpretentious little winery with only a nine-acre estate vineyard to work with. The tasting room sits in a tiny strip of shops, the space glowing with light that bounces off the copper of the bar. At the bar, you'll taste wonderful syrahs, hearty cabernet sauvignons, and surprisingly deep and complex blends—the Snosrap (that's Parsons spelled backwards) table wine is inexpensive for the region and incredibly tasty. If you find a vintage you love at Parsonage, buy it then and there since they sell out of many of their wines every year.

Another smaller, well-regarded Carmel winery is the **Heller Estate Organic Vineyards** (69 W. Carmel Valley Rd., 831/659-6220, www.hellerestate.com, daily 11am-5pm, tasting $7). Heller is a completely organic winery that uses natural methods, including predatory wasps, to get rid of vineyard insect pests rather than resorting to chemical-laden sprays. After visiting the tasting room, sit with a bottle outdoors in Heller's sculpture garden while sipping your latest purchase and enjoying the Carmel Valley sun.

Talbott Vineyards (53 W. Carmel Valley Rd., 831/659-3500, www.talbottvineyards. com, Mon.-Thurs. 11am-4:30pm, Fri.-Sun. 11am-5pm) utilizes two vineyards 18 miles apart to produce their chardonnays and pinot noirs. At the Carmel Valley tasting room, they pour six of their chardonnays and six of their pinot noirs. There's another tasting room on River Road near Salinas (1380 River Rd., 831/675-0942, www.talbottvineyards.com, Thurs. and Mon. 11am-4:30pm, Fri.-Sun. 11am-5pm).

Boekenoogen Vineyard & Winery (24 W. Carmel Valley Rd., 831/659-4215, www. boekenoogenwines.com, daily 11am-5pm, tasting $5-10) was a cattle ranch before it became a winery. Their tasting room offers pinot noirs, chardonnays, and syrahs, as well as a garden patio for those sunny Carmel Valley afternoons.

ENTERTAINMENT AND EVENTS
Bars
While many of Carmel Valley's ranches are being transformed into vineyards, **The Running Iron Restaurant and Saloon** (24 E. Carmel Valley Rd., 831/659-4633, Mon.-Fri. 11am-2am, Sat. 10am-2am, Sun. 9am-2am) keeps the region's cowboy past alive. This watering hole's Old West style includes branding irons and other cowboy paraphernalia hanging from the ceiling and the walls. In addition to serving beer, wine, and liquor, the Running Iron offers an extensive food menu with seafood, burgers, and even pizza.

Festivals and Events
In June, the Carmel Valley Village shows off its local wines and locally produced art at the **Carmel Valley Art & Wine Celebration** (www. carmelvalleychamber.com).

SPORTS AND RECREATION
Hiking
The 4,462-acre **Garland Ranch Regional Park** (700 W. Carmel Valley Rd., 831/372-3196, www.mprpd.org, daily sunrise-sunset, free) allows hikers to take in all sorts of natural ecosystems from oak woodlands to redwood forests. With the park's elevation ranging 200-2,000 feet above sea level, it is also a great place to get a workout especially on trails like the 1.6-mile hike to La Mesa Pond, where you climb to superb views of the valley.

Golf
If you want to play golf in the sun, head out to Carmel Valley. The **Quail Lodge Golf Club** (8000 Valley Greens Dr., 831/620-8866, www.quaillodge.com, $100-150) has an 18-hole course with 10 lakes and an academy to improve your game. Two 18-hole courses at **Rancho Canada Golf Club** (4860 Carmel Valley Rd., 800/536-9459, www.ranchocanada.com, $10-70) wind back and forth over the Carmel Valley River.

Spas

Following an exhausting day of wine-tasting in Carmel Valley, unwind at **Refuge Spa** (27300 Rancho Carlos Rd., 831/620-7360, www.refuge.com, daily 10am-10pm, $39). Sprawled over two acres under the Santa Lucia Mountains, this adult water park includes warm waterfalls tumbling into soaking pools and two kinds of cold plunge pools: one that is comparable to the body shocking temperature of a mountain stream in the Sierras, and the other close to the chilling temp of the nearby Pacific Ocean. Don't miss the eucalyptus steam room, where a potent minty cloud of steam will purge all of your body's impurities.

ACCOMMODATIONS

For folks who come to Carmel Valley to taste wine, hike in the woods, and enjoy the less expensive golf courses, **Country Garden Inns** (102 W. Carmel Valley Rd., 831/659-5361, www.countrygardeninns.com, $181-199) offers a perfect spot to rest and relax. Actually composed of two inns, the Acacia and the Hidden Valley, Country Garden's small B&Bs offer violet and taupe French Country-style charm in the guest rooms, as well as a pool, a self-serve breakfast bar, and strolling gardens outdoors. Rooms run from romantic king-bed studios up to big family suites and most sleep at least four people (with daybeds in the window nooks).

Hosting on and off since 1915, the former ranch at **Los Laureles Lodge** (313 W. Carmel Valley Rd., 831/659-2233, www.loslaureles. com, $130-285, three-bedroom house $650) can put you up in a guest room, a honeymoon cottage, or a three-bedroom house. Enjoy the property's restaurant, saloon, and, most of all, its swimming pool and adjacent pool bar.

There's plenty of space to take Carmel Valley's frequent sunshine at the **Blue Sky Lodge** (10 Flight Rd., 831/659-2256, www. blueskylodge.com, $139-169). It has an outdoor heated pool and spa, and some rooms have patios. Others have fully equipped kitchens.

FOOD

For a taste of Wine Country cuisine in the Carmel Valley, reserve a table at **Marinus at Bernardus Lodge** (415 W. Carmel Valley Rd., 831/658-3595, www.bernardus.com, Wed.-Sun. 6pm-9pm, $85). The exquisite California cuisine features the produce, fish, and meat of local producers. Choose a three-, four-, or five-course meal, or go for broke and get the chef's tasting menu.

The frequently sunny Carmel Valley is a great place to dine al fresco. With a large outdoor dining area, **Café Rustica** (10 Delfino Pl., 831/659-4444, www.caferusticacarmel. com, Tues.-Sun. 11am-2:30pm and 5pm-9pm, $16-25) is known for its nightly fish specials and herb roasted half chicken.

Sip margaritas on the large wooden deck at **Baja Cantina** (7166 Carmel Valley Rd., 831/625-2252, www.carmelcantina.com, Mon.-Fri. 11:30am-close, Sat.-Sun. 11am-close, $13-20). Inside, catch a sports game on one of the big screen TVs or enjoy the car memorabilia covering the walls. The menu includes hearty Americanized Mexican cuisine like rosemary chicken burritos and wild mushroom and spinach enchiladas.

The creative menu at **Lokal** (13762 Center St., 831/659-5886, Wed. 8am-3pm, Thurs.-Fri. 8am-8pm and 5:30pm-10:45pm, Sat. 9am-2:30pm and 5:30pm-10:45pm, Sun. 9am-2:30pm, $13-24) takes advantage of the valley's farms and wines. The ever-changing menu by chef Brendan Jones utilizes fresh, locally sourced ingredients in creations like a crab hot-dog or an intensely tasty crispy pork belly laid atop a steamed bun. The wine list leans heavily towards bottles produced just miles away. Sit at a candle-lit table or the long bar made from the 1967 Monterey Pop Festival's stage.

INFORMATION AND SERVICES

Call or visit the website of the **Carmel Valley Chamber of Commerce** (831/659-4000, http://carmelvalleychamber.com) for basic information before arriving. Most services are available in nearby Carmel-by-the-Sea, but the unincorporated community of Carmel Valley has a **post office** (11 Via Contenta, 831/659-8839, www.usps.com) and a **Safeway** (104 Midvalley, 831/624-4600, daily 24 hours). The nearest major medical center to Carmel Valley is in nearby Monterey. For minor issues, head for the **Community Hospital of Monterey** (23625 Holman Hwy, Monterey, 831/624-5311, www.chomp.org).

GETTING THERE AND AROUND

To get to the Carmel Valley, take Highway 1 to Carmel Valley Road, which is a major intersection with a stop light. Take Carmel Valley Road east for 13 miles to the Carmel Valley Village, where most of the area's restaurants and wineries are located.

BIG SUR AND THE CENTRAL COAST

California natives will tell you that the words "Big Sur" mean a lot of different things. Is Big Sur a state park with a lot of redwoods? Is it a small city tucked in an undeveloped section of California? Is it a valley, a river, a scenic drive? Or is Big Sur really a state of mind? "Big Sur" has been all of the above and more.

Big Sur's 90 miles of rugged coastline begin just south of Carmel on the Monterey Peninsula, and stretch south all the way to San Simeon. Here, the mountains rise up suddenly, and drop just as dramatically into the sea. Highway 1 twists and turns like a two-lane snake, trying to keep up with the land- and seacape.

Big Sur is wild—a place where vertical cliffs drop straight into the ocean, redwood trees tickle the sky, and hiking trails lead to spouting waterfalls and secluded beaches. In fact, the miles and miles of hiking trails in this region outnumber the paved roads. With resorts like Ventana and Post Ranch, Big Sur offers retreats where visitors can experience this wild, indisputable natural beauty while pampering themselves with luxurious relaxation.

Continuing south, the road evens out, and the coastline gets less extreme, becoming the host to a string of some of California's best beach towns, each with its own allure. San Simeon is home to one of California's biggest attractions: the magnificent Hearst Castle, a monument to the incredible wealth of newspaper magnate William Randolph Hearst. Just a few miles south, Cambria has a pleasant downtown and Moonstone Beach, where you can pick up pieces of the gemstone right off the sand. Cayucos is an old-fashioned beach

HIGHLIGHTS

◖ **Big Sur Coast Highway:** One of the most scenic drives in the world, Big Sur's Highway 1 passes redwood forests, crystal-clear streams and rivers, while offering breathtaking, ever-present views of the coast (page 386).

◖ **Pfeiffer Beach:** With rock formations off-shore and purple sand, Pfeiffer Beach is one of Big Sur's most picturesque spots. (page 389).

◖ **Pfeiffer Big Sur State Park:** Marvel at towering redwoods and dip in the cleansing Big Sur River at this developed state park, which also has one of the area's finest campgrounds (page 393).

◖ **Hearst Castle:** Newspaper magnate William Randolph Hearst's 56-bedroom manse is the closest thing that the United States has to a castle (page 407).

◖ **Morro Rock:** The 576-foot-high "Gibraltar of the Pacific" is one of the great photo-ops of the Central Coast (page 416).

◖ **Montana de Oro State Park:** This underrated natural treasure is comprised of 8,000 mostly undeveloped acres of coves, peaks, and canyons (page 416).

◖ **Madonna Inn:** The rooms, restaurants, bars – and even the bathroom – are worth a look at this monument to kitsch (page 422).

LOOK FOR ◖ TO FIND RECOMMENDED SIGHTS, ACTIVITIES, DINING, AND LODGING.

town with its own strand of sand and a pier that dates all the way back to the late 1800s. Morro Bay boasts an almost 600-foot domed rock formation that can be seen from the town's Embarcadero, which has a string of restaurants, hotels, and tourist shops. Just out of Morro Bay is one of the best coastal state parks in all of California: Montana de Oro.

It's worth detouring a few miles inland to visit college town San Luis Obispo, with its vibrant weekly farmer's market, a California mission, and the kitschy but cool Madonna Inn, and nearby Paso Robles' thermal springs and up-and-coming wineries. Heading back to the coast again, Pismo Beach feels like a hip vacation spot—from 50 years ago.

PLANNING YOUR TIME

The busy season for Big Sur and the Central Coast is during the summer months. This is also when there can be frequent coastal fog. Away from the coast, the Big Sur Valley can

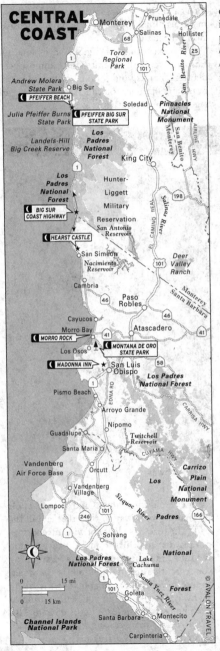

CENTRAL COAST

offer some relief from the fog. Similarly, a trip inland to Paso Robles usually offers higher temperatures. In Big Sur and the Central Coast reservations are essential for hotels and campsites during the summer. The fall is the ideal time for a trip to the area, with warmer temperatures and fewer crowds.

Highway 1, the road in and out of Big Sur, is a twisting, sometimes two-lane highway, with frequent construction and closures. Check the California Department of Transportation website (www.dot.ca.gov) for information about closures and possible delays. If you are driving slower than most traffic on Highway 1, pull over into a pullout and allow the traffic to pass. The roadway also connects the Central Coast towns south of Big Sur. Highway 1 passes right by San Simeon, Cambria, Cayucos, Morro Bay, San Luis Obispo, and Pismo Beach. Ample exit signs tell drivers when to turn off the highway. South of Cambria, Highway 46 over the hills connects Highway 1 to Paso Robles. Farther south, Highway 1 and U.S. 101 come together at San Luis Obispo. If you're heading to San Luis Obispo and aren't interested in a leisurely coastal drive, U.S. 101 will get you there quicker.

A lot of people drive through Big Sur in a day, taking Highway 1 from Carmel to San Simeon and pulling off at the road's many turnouts to take in the views. Outdoors enthusiasts who want to get off the highway and *really* experience Big Sur will need at least a couple of days. The Big Sur Valley (26 miles south of Carmel) is a good place to stay if you want both a great outdoors experience and amenities such as restaurants and lodging. The valley is also home to Pfeiffer Big Sur State Park, with has over 200 campsites. The south coast of Big Sur toward San Simeon has significantly fewer amenities; there are a few campgrounds and the Treebones Resort. On the Central Coast south of Big Sur, pick a town as a base and plan to spend a few days exploring the area sights. In a weekend, you can visit Hearst Castle, hike Montana de Oro, and get in some beach time.

A trip to Big Sur involves planning. It's a

good idea to secure supplies and gas before entering Big Sur (at Carmel in the north or Cambria in the south). While Big Sur does have a few markets, you will pay higher prices for a smaller selection of goods. Definitely fill up your tank before heading into Big Sur. While there are a few gas stations on the 90-mile stretch of coastline, you will pay a premium for a gallon of gas. Gas stations in Big Sur have made headlines for having the most expensive gas in the nation.

The towns south of Big Sur have more infrastructure, with amenities including supermarkets, banks, and a range of lodging and restaurant options. You can also get gas here at regular state gas station prices.

Big Sur

Big Sur welcomes many types of visitors. Nature-lovers come to camp and hike the pristine wilderness areas, to don thick wetsuits and surf often-deserted beaches, and even to hunt for jade in rocky coves. On the other hand, some of the wealthiest people from California and beyond visit to relax at unbelievably posh hotels and spas with dazzling views of the ocean. Whether you prefer a low-cost camping trip or a luxury resort, Big Sur offers its beauty and charm to all. Part of that charm is Big Sur's determination to remain peacefully apart from the Information Age (this means that your cell phones may not work in many parts of Big Sur).

SIGHTS
◖ Big Sur Coast Highway
Even if you're not up to tackling the endless hiking trails and deep wilderness backcountry of Big Sur, you can still get a good sense of the glory of this region just by driving through it. The **Big Sur Coast Highway,** a 90-mile stretch of Highway 1, is quite simply one of the most picturesque roads in the country. A two-lane road, Highway 1 twists and turns with Big Sur's jagged coastline, running along precipitous cliffs and rocky beaches, through dense redwood forest, over historic bridges, and past innumerable parks. In the winter, you might spot migrating whales offshore spouting fountains of air and water, while spring finds yucca plants feathering the hillsides and wildflowers coloring the landscape. Construction on this stretch of road was completed in the 1930s, connecting Cambria to Carmel. You can start

© GABRIEL SKVOR

the twists and turns of the Big Sur Coast Highway

out at either of these towns and spend a whole day making your way to the other end of the road. The road has plenty of wide turnouts set into picturesque cliffs to make it easy to stop to admire the glittering ocean and stunning wooded cliffs running right out to the water. Be sure to bring a camera on your trip along Highway 1—you'll find yourself wanting to take photos every mile for hours on end. Also be aware that there can be frequent highway delays due to road construction.

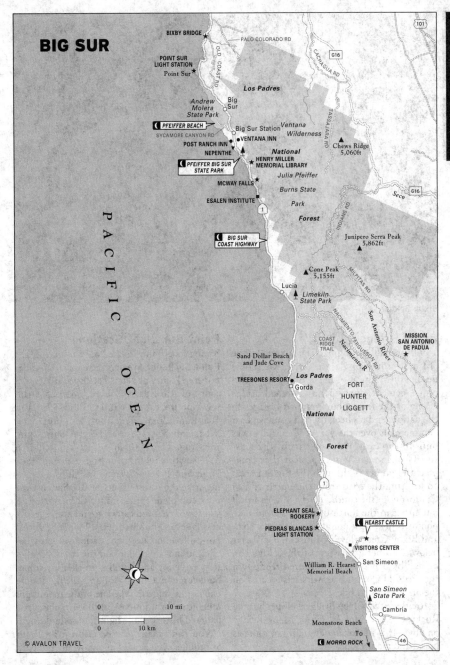

BIG SUR

BIXBY BRIDGE ★
PALO COLORADO RD
POINT SUR
LIGHT STATION ★
Point Sur

Los Padres

*Andrew
Molera
State Park*
Big
Sur
☾ PFEIFFER BEACH
SYCAMORE CANYON RD
Big Sur Station ○
● VENTANA INN
POST RANCH INN ▲
NEPENTHE ▲
☾ PFEIFFER BIG SUR
STATE PARK
■
*Ventana
Wilderness*

National
HENRY MILLER
MEMORIAL LIBRARY

MCWAY FALLS ■
Julia Pfeiffer

ESALEN INSTITUTE ■
Burns State

Park
Forest

☾ BIG SUR
COAST HIGHWAY

Lucia ○
▲ *Limekiln
State Park*

*Cone Peak
5,155ft* ▲

COAST
RIDGE
TRAIL

*Sand Dollar Beach
and Jade Cove*
Los Padres
TREEBONES RESORT ●
○ Gorda

National

Forest

CACHAGUA RD G16
TASSAJARA RD

▲ *Chews Ridge
5,060ft*

Seco G16

INDIANS RD

*Junipero Serra Peak
5,862ft* ▲

MILPITAS RD

NACIMIENTO FERGUSSON RD

San Antonio River

MISSION
SAN ANTONIO
DE PADUA ★

FORT
HUNTER
LIGGETT

Nacimiento R.

ELEPHANT SEAL
ROOKERY ★
☾ HEARST CASTLE ★
★
PIEDRAS BLANCAS
LIGHT STATION ★
■ VISITORS CENTER

*William R. Hearst
Memorial Beach* ○ San Simeon

▲ *San Simeon
State Park*

○ Cambria

Moonstone Beach
To
☾ MORRO ROCK ↓ 46

P A C I F I C

O C E A N

0   10 mi
0   10 km

© AVALON TRAVEL

1

Bixby Bridge

© GABRIEL SKVOR

Bixby Bridge

You'll probably recognize the **Bixby Bridge** (13 miles south of Carmel) when you come upon it on Highway 1 in Big Sur. The picturesque, cement, open-spandrel arched bridge is one of the most photographed bridges in the nation, and it's been used in countless car commercials over the years. The bridge was built in the early 1930s as part of the massive Government Works project that completed Highway 1 through the Big Sur area, connecting the road from the north end of California to the south. Today, you can pull out either to the north of the bridge to take photos or just look out at the attractive span and Bixby Creek flowing into the Pacific far below. Another great view of the bridge can be had by driving a few hundred feet down the dirt Old Coast Road, which is located on the bridge's north side.

Are there two Bixby Bridges? Nope, but the Rocky Creek Bridge (north of Bixby Bridge on Hwy. 1) is similar in design, if not quite as grand and picturesque.

Point Sur Light Station

Sitting lonely and isolated out on its cliff, the **Point Sur Light Station** (Hwy. 1, 0.25 miles north of Point Sur Naval Facility and 19 miles south of Rio Rd. in Carmel, 831/625-4419, www.pointsur.org, winter tours Sat.-Sun. 10am and 2pm, Wed. 1pm, plus Apr.-Oct. Wed. and Sat. 10am and 2pm, Sun. 2pm, July-Aug. Thurs. 10am, adults $10, children $5) crowns the 361-foot-high volcanic rock Point Sur. It keeps watch over ships navigating near the rocky waters of Big Sur. It's the only complete 19th-century light station in California that you can visit, and even here access is severely limited. First lit in 1889, this now fully automated light station still provides navigational aid to ships off the coast; families stopped living and working in the tiny stone-built compound in 1974. But is the lighthouse truly uninhabited? Take one of the moonlight tours (call for information) to learn about the haunted history of the light station buildings.

You can't make a reservation for a Point Sur tour, so you should just show up and park

the Point Sur Light Station

your car off Highway 1 on the west side by the farm gate. Your guide will meet you there and lead you up the paved road 0.5 miles to the light station. Once there, you'll climb the stairs up to the light, explore the restored keepers' homes and service buildings, and walk out to the cliff edge. Expect to see a great variety of wildlife, from brilliant wildflowers in the spring to gray whales in the winter to flocks of pelicans flying in formation at any time of year. Be sure to dress in layers; it can be sunny and hot or foggy and cold, winter or summertime, and sometimes both on the same tour! Tours last three hours and require more than a mile of walking, with a bit of slope, and more than 100 stairs.

The farm gate is locked and there's no access to the light station without a tour group. Tour schedules can vary from year to year and season to season; it's a good idea to call ahead before showing up. If you need special assistance for your tour or have questions about accessibility, call 831/667-0528 as far in advance as possible of your visit to make arrangements. No strollers, food, pets, or smoking are allowed on light station property.

Big Sur Station

If you haven't yet stopped at one of the larger state parks in the area and hit the visitors center, pull in at **Big Sur Station** (Hwy. 1, 0.33 miles south of Pfeiffer Big Sur, 831/667-2315, Wed.-Sun. 9am-4pm). The ranger station offers maps and brochures for all the major parks and trails of Big Sur, plus a minimal bookshop. This is also where the trailhead for the popular backcountry **Pine Ridge Trail** is located. You can get a free backcountry fire permit as well as pay for Pine Ridge Trailhead parking here.

◖ Pfeiffer Beach

Big Sur has plenty of striking meetings of land and sea, but **Pfeiffer Beach** (end of Sycamore Canyon Rd., http://campone.com, daily 9am-8pm, $5) is definitely one of the coastline's most picturesque spots. This frequently windswept beach has two looming rock formations right where the beach meets

© STUART THORNTON

the imposing rocks of Pfeiffer Beach

the surf, and both of these rocks have holes that look like doorways, allowing waves and sunlight to pass through.

For newcomers getting to Pfeiffer Beach is a bit tricky. It is located at the end of the second paved right south of the Big Sur Station. Motorists (no motor homes, please) must then travel down a narrow, windy, two-mile road before reaching the entrance booth and the beach's parking lot. It's part of the adventure.

Big Sur Spirit Garden

A favorite among art-lovers, the **Big Sur Spirit Garden** (Hwy. 1, Loma Vista, 831/238-1056, www.bigsurspiritgarden.com, daily 9am-6pm) changes a little almost every day. The "garden" part includes a variety of exotic plants, while the "spirit" part devotes itself to modern and postmodern Fair Trade art from as nearby as a few miles and as far away as India. The artwork tends toward brightly colored small sculptures done in a childlike, exuberant style. The Spirit Garden offers educational programs, community celebrations, musical events, and more.

The most interesting feature of the garden is its "Spirit Nests," which are like giant birds nests made of tree branches. Call ahead for information on upcoming events.

Henry Miller Memorial Library

A number of authors have done time in Big Sur, soaking in the remote wilderness and sea air to gather inspiration for their work. Henry Miller lived and wrote in Big Sur for 18 years, and his 1957 novel *Big Sur and the Oranges of Hieronymus Bosch* describes his time here. Today, the **Henry Miller Memorial Library** (Hwy. 1, 0.25 miles south of Nepenthe Restaurant, 831/667-2574, www.henrymiller. org, Wed.-Mon. 11am-6pm) celebrates the life and work of Miller and his brethren in this quirky community center/museum/coffee shop/gathering place. The library is easy to find as you drive either north or south on Highway 1—look for the hand-painted sign and funky fence decorations. What you won't find is a typical lending library or slicked-up museum. Instead, inside is a well-curated bookstore featuring the works of Miller as well as other authors like Jack Kerouac and Richard Brautigan, along with a crew of employees who are always worth striking up a conversation with. Over the last few years, the library has become an important arts and music center for the Central Coast. The small redwood-shaded lawn has hosted concerts by some of music's biggest names, including Arcade Fire, the Red Hot Chili Peppers, and Philip Glass, to a crowd of just 300 lucky souls. Also, during the summer months, the library hosts an international short film series every Thursday night free of charge. Check the library's website for a list of upcoming events. Who knows? You might find out that one of your favorite groups—or soon to be favorite bands—is performing at the library while you are in Big Sur.

Nacimiento-Fergusson Road

The only road that traverses Big Sur's Santa Lucia Mountains, the **Nacimiento-Fergusson Road** (4 miles south of the town of Lucia and 35 miles north of Hearst Castle) offers spectacular coastal views to those who are willing to wind up this twisty, paved, 1.5-lane road. Simply drive a few miles up to see an eyeful of the expansive Pacific Ocean or to get above Big Sur's summer fog. The road connects Highway 1 to U.S. 101, but passes through Fort Hunter Liggett army base on its journey. The road is frequently closed during the winter months.

Sand Dollar Beach

Located on Big Sur's less developed southern end, **Sand Dollar Beach** (60 miles south of Rio Rd. in Carmel and 30 miles north of Hearst Castle, http://campone.com, daily 9am-8pm, $5) is one of the longest accessible strands of beach in Big Sur. After hiking down a staircase, you arrive at this half moon-shaped beach tucked under cliffs that keep the wind down. Though frequently rock strewn, the beach is a great place to plop down for a picnic or an afternoon in the sun. Out front, a series of uncrowded beach breaks offer waves for surfers even during the flatter summer months.

Salmon Creek Falls

One of the southern portion of Big Sur's best natural attractions is **Salmon Creek Falls** (8 miles south of Gorda or 3.5 miles north of Ragged Point on Hwy. 1). Flowing year round, a pair of waterfalls pour down rocks over 100 feet high and their streams join halfway down. To get a great perspective of the falls, take an easy 10-minute walk over a primitive trail littered with rocks from the highway. The unmarked parking area is a pullout in the middle of a hairpin turn on Highway 1.

HIKING

The main reason to come to Big Sur is to get out of your vehicle and hike its beaches and forests. There are lots of hiking opportunities here from short walks under a canopy of redwood trees to multi-day backpacking trips into Big Sur's wilderness interior.

Garrapata State Park

Garrapata State Park (located on Hwy. 1, 6.7 miles south of Rio Rd. in Carmel and 18 miles north of the Big Sur Valley, 831/624-4909, www.parks.ca.gov) has most of the features that make Big Sur such a famed destination for outdoor enthusiasts: redwood trees, rocky headlands, pocket beaches, and ocean vistas from steep hills and mountains. Garrapata, which means "tick" in Spanish, includes Garrapata Beach, northern Big Sur's finest beach, and two miles of coastline. The two-mile round-trip **Soberanes Point Trail** to the west of the highway is a mild hike up and around the park's rocky headlands. Stroll along the beach, scramble up the cliffs for a better view of the ocean, or check out the seals, sea otters, and sea lions near Soberanes Point. In the wintertime, grab a pair of binoculars to look for migrating gray whales passing quite close to shore here.

For a more invigorating hike, connect the **Soberanes Canyon Trail** with the **Rocky Ridge Trail,** making a 4.5-mile loop. In Soberanes Canyon, you'll get a taste of a small redwood forest before climbing up to the outstanding coast views offered by Rocky Ridge, which is 1,700 feet high. In the spring months, the trail

© STUART THORNTON

Sand Dollar Beach

is littered with a profusion of wildflowers. A bench on the coastal side of Rocky Ridge offers a great place to catch your breath and take in the scenery. This is the same landscape that inspired nature poet Robinson Jeffers to pen his popular poem, "The Place For No Story."

Expect little in the way of facilities here—you'll park in a wide spot on Highway 1, and if you're lucky you might find a pit toilet open for use.

Andrew Molera State Park

At 4,800 acres, **Andrew Molera State Park** (Hwy. 1, 20 miles south of Carmel, 831/667-2315, www.parks.ca.gov, day use $10) is a great place to immerse yourself in Big Sur's coastal beauty. Once home to small camps of Esselen Native Americans, then a Spanish land grant, this chunk of Big Sur eventually became the Molera ranch. The land was used to grow crops and ranch animals, and as a hunting and fishing retreat for family and friends. It is also where the park's namesake, Andrew Molera, ran a successful dairy operation making Monterey

Jack cheese. In 1965, Molera's sister Frances sold the land to the Nature Conservancy, and when she died three years later the ranch was sold to the California State Park system as per her will.

Today, the **Cooper Cabin,** which is off the Trail Camp Beach Trail, is a remnant from the park's past. The redwood structure built in 1861 is the oldest building standing on the Big Sur coast. The **Molera Ranch House Museum** (831/667-2956, http://bigsurhistory.org, Sat.-Sun. 11am-3pm) displays stories of the life and times of Big Sur's human pioneers and artists as well as the wildlife and plants of the region. Take the road toward the horse tours to get to the ranch house.

The park has numerous hiking trails that run down to the beach and up into the forest along the river—many are open to biking and horseback riding as well. Most of the park trails lie to the west of the highway. The beach is a one-mile walk down the easy, multi-use **Trail Camp Beach Trail.** From there, climb on out on the **Headlands Trail,** a 0.25-mile loop, for

the view of Pico Blanco Mountain from Andrew Molera State Park

a beautiful view from the headlands of the Big Sur River emptying into the sea. If you prefer to get a better look at the river, take the flat, moderate **Bobcat Trail** (5.5 miles round-trip) and perhaps a few of its ancillary loops. You'll walk right along the riverbanks, enjoying the local microhabitats. Just be sure to look out for bicycles and the occasional horse and rider. For an even longer and more difficult trek up the mountains and down to the beach, take the eight-mile **Ridge Bluff Loop.** You'll start at the parking lot on the Creamery Meadow Beach Trail, then make a left onto the long and fairly steep Ridge Trail to get a sense of the local ecosystem. Then turn right onto the Panorama Trail, which runs down to the coastal scrublands, and finally out to the Bluffs Trail, which takes you back to Creamery Meadow.

A fairly short but steep hike that is never crowded is the **East Molera Trail,** which is located on the east side of Highway 1. From the main parking lot, walk to the white barn and take the tunnel under the road that leads to the trail. The trail is a steep series of switchbacks that climb up to a saddle with coast views to the west and a glimpse of the imposing, pyramid-shaped Pico Blanco Mountain to the east.

At the park entrance, you'll find bathrooms but no drinkable water and no food concessions. If you're camping here, be sure to bring plenty of your own water for washing dishes as well as drinking. If you're hiking for the day, pack in bottled water and snacks.

Pfeiffer Big Sur State Park

The most developed park in Big Sur is **Pfeiffer Big Sur State Park** (Hwy. 1, 26 miles south of Carmel, 831/667-2315, www.parks.ca.gov, day use $10). It's got the Big Sur Lodge, a restaurant and café, a shop, an amphitheater, a somewhat incongruous softball field, plenty of hiking-only trails, and lovely redwood-shaded campsites. This park isn't situated by the beach; it's up in the coastal redwoods forest, with a network of roads that can be driven or biked up into the trees and along the Big Sur River.

Pfeiffer Big Sur has the tiny **Ernest Ewoldsen Memorial Nature Center,** which features stuffed examples of local wildlife. It's open seasonally; call the park for days and hours. Another historic exhibit is the **Homestead Cabin,** located off the Big Sur Gorge Trail, once the home of part of the Pfeiffer family—the first European immigrants to settle in Big Sur.

No bikes or horses are allowed on trails in this park, which makes it quite peaceful for hikers. For a starter walk, take the popular **Pfeiffer Falls Trail,** a 1.5-mile round-trip stroll. You'll find stairs on the steep sections and footbridges across the creek, then a lovely platform at the base of the 60-foot waterfall where you can rest and relax midway through your hike. But even better than the seasonal waterfall at the trail's end are the impressive redwoods along the way, including some that have been hollowed out by previous fires, creating cave-like trunks that you can peer into. For a longer, more difficult, and interesting hike that leaves the park and goes into the adjoining Ventana Wilderness, start at the Homestead Cabin and head to the **Mount Manuel Trail** (10 miles round-trip, difficult). From the Y-intersection with the Oak Grove Trail, it's four miles of sturdy hiking to Mount Manuel, a 3,379-foot peak that looms high over the Big Sur Valley.

Need to cool off after hiking? Scramble out to the entirely undeveloped **Big Sur River Gorge,** where the river slows and creates pools that are great for swimming. Relax and enjoy the water, but don't try to dive here.

This is one of the few Big Sur parks to offer a full array of services. Before you head out into the woods, stop at the **Big Sur Lodge** restaurant and store complex to get a meal and some water, and to load up on snacks and sweatshirts. Between the towering trees and the summer fogs, it can get quite chilly and somewhat damp on the trails.

Julia Pfeiffer Burns State Park

One of Big Sur's best postcard perfect views can be attained at **Julia Pfeiffer Burns State Park** (Hwy. 1, 37 miles south of Carmel and 12 miles south of Pfeiffer Big Sur State Park, 831/667-2315, www.parks.ca.gov). To get here,

the **Overlook Trail** runs only 0.66 miles round-trip, along a level wheelchair-friendly boardwalk. Stroll under Highway 1, past the Pelton wheelhouse, and out to the observation deck and the stunning view of **McWay Falls.** The 80-foot-high waterfall cascades year-round off a cliff and onto the beach of a remote cove, where the water wets the sand and trickles out into the sea. The water of the cove gleams bright cerulean blue against the just-off-white sand of the beach—it looks more like the South Pacific than Northern California. Anyone with an ounce of love for the ocean will want to build a hut right there beside the waterfall. But you can't—in fact, the reason you'll look down on a pristine and empty stretch of sand is that there's no way down to the cove that is even remotely safe.

The tiny Pelton wheel exhibit off the Overlook Trail isn't much unless you're a huge fan of hydraulic engineering history. It does have an interpretive exhibit (including the old Pelton wheel itself) describing what a Pelton wheel is and what it does.

If you're up for a longer hike after taking in the falls, go back the other way to pick up the **Ewoldsen Trail** (4.5 miles round-trip, moderate-difficult). This trek takes you through McWay Canyon, where you'll see the creek and surrounding lush greenery as you walk. Some of Big Sur's finest redwoods are located here. Then you'll loop away from the water and climb up into the hills. One part of the trail is perched on a ridgeline, where there is little vegetation growing on the steep hillside below. This is the site of a 1983 landslide that closed the highway below for a whole year. Be sure to bring water, as this hike can take several hours.

If you want to spend all day at Julia Pfeiffer Burns State Park, drive north from the park entrance to the Partington Cove pullout and park along the side of the highway. On the east side of the highway, start out along the **Tanbark Trail** (6.4 miles round-trip, difficult). You'll head through redwood groves and up steep switchbacks to the top of the coastal ridge. Be sure to bring your camera to record the stunning views before you head back down

McWay Falls at Julia Pfeiffer Burns State Park

the fire road to your car. The west side of the road is where you pick up the two-mile round-trip **Partington Cove Trail,** an underrated walk that goes to a striking, narrow coastal inlet. It begins as a steep dirt road until it reaches the bottom where the trail traverses a bridge over Partington Creek and through a 60-foot-long tunnel blasted into the rock. The trail arrives at a cove, where John Partington used to ship out the tanbark trees that he had harvested in the canyon above.

Jade Cove Recreation Area

It's easy to miss **Jade Cove Recreation Area** (Hwy. 1, two miles south of Sand Dollar Beach) as you barrel down Highway 1 towards San Simeon. A road sign marks the area, but there's not much in the way of a formal parking lot or anything else to denote the treasures of this jagged, rough part of the Big Sur coastline. Park in the dirt/gravel strip off the road and head past the fence. It's fun to read the unusual signs along the narrow, beaten path that seems to lead to the edge of a cliff. The signs explain that you cannot bring in mining equipment, or take away rocks or minerals obtained from behind the high-tide line. If you're into aerial sports, you can hang-glide off the cliffs here.

Once you get to the edge of the cliff, the short trail gets rough. It's only 0.25 miles, but it's almost straight down a rocky, slippery cliff. Don't try to climb down if you're not in reasonable physical condition, and even if you are, don't be afraid to use your hands to steady yourself. At the bottom, you'll find huge boulders and smaller rocks and very little sand. You may also see a small herd of locals dressed in wetsuits and scuba gear. But most of all, you'll find the most amazing minerals in the boulders and rocks. Reach out and touch a multi-ton boulder shot through with jade. Search the smaller rocks beneath your feet for chunks of sea-polished jade. If you're a hard-core rock nut, you can join the locals in scuba diving for jewelry-quality jade. As long as you find it in the water or below the high-tide line, it's legal for you to take whatever you find here. Be aware that there is also lots of serpentine here.

Serpentine has a similar green color to jade but has no real value.

Jade Cove has no water, no restrooms, no visitor's center, and no services of any kind.

SPORTS AND RECREATION
Horseback Riding

You can take a guided horseback ride into the forests or out onto the beaches of Andrew Molera State Park with **Molera Horseback Tours** (831/625-5486, http://molerahorseback-tours.com, $40-70). Tours of 1-2.5 hours depart each day starting at 9am—call ahead to guarantee your spot, or take a chance and just show up at the stables 15 minutes ahead of the ride you want to take. If you prefer, call to book a private guided ride for yourself and your party. Each ride takes you from the modest corral area along multi-use trails through forests or meadows, or along the Big Sur River, and down to Molera Beach. You'll guide your horse along the solid sands as you admire the beauty of the wild Pacific Ocean.

Molera Horseback Tours are suitable for children over six and riders of all ability levels; you'll be matched to the right horse for you. All rides go down to the beach. Tours can be seasonal, so call ahead if you want to ride in the fall or winter. Guides share their knowledge of the Big Sur region and wildlife, and welcome questions about the plants you're seeing as you walk your horse down the trail. Early-morning and sunset rides tend to be the prettiest and most popular.

Backpacking

If you long for the lonely peace of backcountry camping, the **Ventana Wilderness** (www.ventanawild.org) area is ideal for you. This area comprises the peaks of the Santa Lucia Mountains and the dense growth of the northern reaches of the Los Padres National Forest. It has 167,323 acres of steep V-shaped canyons and mountains that rise to over 5,000 feet. You'll find many trails beyond the popular day hikes of the state parks, especially as Big Sur stretches down to the south. One of the most popular hikes is the 10-mile-long climb on the **Pine Ridge Trail** (Big Sur Station, 0.25 miles south of Pfeiffer Big Sur State Park) to **Sykes Hot Springs,** a cluster of warm mineral pools at a backcountry camp situated on the Big Sur River. The trail leaves from the Big Sur Station, where you should secure a campfire permit and a parking pass before heading out. Farther south, the **Vicente Flat Trail** (4 miles south of Lucia on Hwy. 1, across from the Kirk Creek Campground, 10 miles roundtrip) heads up towards Cone Peak, the jagged mountain rising in the distance, while gaining sweeping views of the coast. You can do this one as a grueling up and back day hike to the Vincente Flat Camp or backpack it. Check the Ventana Wilderness Alliance website (www.ventanawild.org) in advance to find reports on the conditions of the trails you've decided to tackle, and stop in at Big Sur Station to get the latest news on the backcountry areas.

Fishing

No harbors offer deep-sea charters around Big Sur, but if your idea of the perfect outdoor vacation includes a rod and reel, you can choose between shore and river fishing. Steelhead run up the Big Sur River to spawn each year, and a limited fishing season follows them up the river into **Pfeiffer Big Sur State Park** and other accessible areas. Check with Fernwood Resort (831/667-2422, www.fernwoodbigsur.com) and the other lodges around Highway 1 for the best spots this season.

The numerous creeks that feed into and out of the Big Sur River also play home to their fair share of fish. The California Department of Fish and Game (www.dfg.ca.gov) can give you specific locations for legal fishing, season information, and rules and regulations.

If you prefer the fish from the ocean, you can cast off several of the beaches for the rockfish that scurry about in the near-shore reefs. **Garrapata State Beach** has a good fishing area, as do the beaches at **Sand Dollar.**

Scuba Diving

There's not much for beginner divers in Big Sur. Expect cold water and an exposure to the ocean's swells and surges. Temperatures range in the mid 50s in the shallows, dipping into the 40s as you dive deeper down. Visibility is 20-30 feet, though rough conditions can diminish this significantly; the best season for clear water is September-November.

The biggest and most interesting dive locale here is the **Julia Pfeiffer Burns State Park** (Hwy. 1, 12 miles south of Pfeiffer Big Sur, 831/667-2315, www.parks.ca.gov, daily sunrise-sunset). You'll need to acquire a special permit at Big Sur Station and prove your experience to dive at this protected underwater park. The park, along with the rest of the coast of Big Sur, is part of the Monterey Bay National Marine Sanctuary. You enter the water from the shore, which gives you the chance to check out all the ecosystems, beginning with the busy life of the beach sands, then heading out to the rocky reefs, and then into the lush green kelp forests.

Divers at access-hostile **Jade Cove** (Hwy. 1, two miles south of Sand Dollar Beach) aren't usually interested in cute, colorful nudibranchs or even majestic gray whales. Jade Cove divers come to stalk the wily jade pebbles and rocks that cluster in this special spot. The semi-precious stone striates the coastline right here, and storms tear clumps of jade out of the cliffs and into the sea. Much of it settles just off the shore of the tiny cove, and divers hope to find jewelry-quality stones to sell for a huge profit.

If you're looking for a guided scuba dive of the Big Sur region, contact **Adventure Sports Unlimited** (303 Potrero St., #15, Santa Cruz, 831/458-3648, www.asudoit.com).

Bird-Watching

Many visitors come to Big Sur just to see the birds. The Big Sur coast is home to innumerable species, from the tiniest bushtits up to grand pelicans and beyond. The most famous avian residents of this area are no doubt the rare and endangered California condors. Once upon a time, condors were all but extinct, with only a few left alive in captivity and conservationists struggling to help them

breed. Today, more than 70 birds soar above the trails and beaches of Big Sur. You might even see one swooping down low over your car as you drive down Highway 1! (You'll know it if this happens—a condor's wingspan can exceed nine feet.)

The **Ventana Wilderness Society** (VWS, www.ventanaws.org) watches over many of the endangered and protected avian species in Big Sur. As part of their mission to raise awareness of the condors and many other birds, the VWS offers bird-watching expeditions. Check their website for schedules and prices.

One of the hot spots of VWS conservation efforts and tours is Andrew Molera State Park. You can head out on your own to take a look around for some of the most interesting species in the Big Sur area. But wherever you choose to hike, be it beach or forest, you're likely to see a variety of feathered friends fluttering about.

Spas

The Spa at Ventana (831/667-4222, www.ventanainn.com, daily 9am-7pm, $140-575) offers a large menu of spa treatments to both hotel guests and visitors. You'll love the serene atmosphere of the treatment and waiting areas. Greenery and weathered wood create a unique space that helps to put you in a tranquil state of mind, ready for your body to follow your mind into a state of relaxation. Indulge in a soothing massage, purifying body treatment, or rejuvenating or beautifying facial. Take your spa experience a step further in true Big Sur fashion with an astrological reading, essence portrait, or shamanic revealing. If you're a hotel guest, you can choose to have your spa treatment in the comfort of your own room or out on your private deck.

Just across the highway from the Ventana, the **Post Ranch Inn's Spa** (47900 Hwy. 1, 831/667-2200, massage $150/hour) is another ultra-high-end resort spa. But it is only open to those who are spending the evening at the spendy resort. Shaded by redwoods, the relaxing spa offers massages and facials along with more unique treatments including Big Sur jade stone therapy and craniosacral therapy.

CALIFORNIA CONDORS

With wings spanning 10 feet from tip to tip, the California condors soaring over the Big Sur coastline are some of the area's most impressive natural treasures. But, in 1987, there was only one bird left in the wild, which was taken in captivity as part of a captive breeding program. The condors' population had plummeted due to its susceptibility to lead poisoning along with deaths caused by electric power lines, habitat loss, and their being shot by indiscriminate humans.

Now the reintroduction of the high flying California condor, the largest flying bird in North America, to Big Sur and the Central Coast is truly one of conservation's greatest success stories. In 1997, the Monterey County-based non-profit the Ventana Wildlife Society (VWS) began releasing the giant birds back into the wild. Currently, 70 wild condors soar above Big Sur and the surrounding area, and in 2006, a pair of condors were found nesting in the hollowed-out section of a redwood tree.

The species recovery in the Big Sur area means that you might be able to spot a California condor flying overhead while visiting the rugged coastal region. Look for a tracking tag on the condor's wing to determine that you are actually looking at a California condor and not just a big turkey vulture. Or take a two-hour tour with the **Ventana Wildlife Society** (831/455-9514, tours the second Sun. of every month, $50/person), which uses radio telemetry to track the released birds. Or visit the **VWS Discovery Center** (in Andrew Molera State Park, Hwy. 1, 22 miles south of Carmel, 831/624-1202, www.ventanaws.org, Memorial Day-Labor Day Sat.-Sun. 9am-4pm), where there's an exhibit that details the near extinction of the condor and the attempts to restore its population.

ENTERTAINMENT AND EVENTS
Live Music

Over the last few years, Big Sur has become an unexpected hotbed for big music concerts.

More than just a place to down a beer and observe the local characters, **Fernwood Tavern** (Hwy. 1, 831/667-2422, www.fernwoodbigsur.com, Sun.-Thurs. noon-midnight, Fri.-Sat. noon-1am) also has live music, erecting a large concert stage in their campground for performances by acts like Conor Oberst, Beach House, and the Mother Hips. Most of the big name acts swing through Big Sur in the summer and fall. Even when Big Sur isn't hosting nationally known touring bands, Fernwood has a wide range of regional acts on Saturday nights. You might hear country, folk, or even indie rock from the small stage. Most live music happens on weekends, especially Saturday nights, starting at 9pm. Even without the music, the tavern can get lively in the evenings, with locals drinking from the full bar, eating, and hanging out on the back deck under the redwoods. Check the bar's website for current events.

Down the road, the **Henry Miller Memorial Library** (0.25 miles south of Nepenthe Restaurant, 831/667-2574, www.henrymiller.org) has had some internationally known acts perform on its stage—bands like Arcade Fire, the Red Hot Chili Peppers, and the Fleet Foxes, who typically fill arenas. Check their website for upcoming events.

Bars

The primary watering hole in Big Sur is **Fernwood Tavern** (Hwy. 1, 831/667-2422, www.fernwoodbigsur.com, Sun.-Thurs. noon-midnight, Fri.-Sat. noon-1am). Enjoy a beer or cocktail inside or out back on a deck under the redwoods.

The newest place to grab a beer in Big Sur is the **Big Sur Taphouse** (47250 Highway 1, 831/667-2225, www.bigsurtaphouse.com, Mon.-Thurs. noon-10pm, Fri. noon-midnight, Sat. 10am-midnight, Sun. 10am-10pm). The Taphouse has 10 rotating beers on tap, with a heavy emphasis on West Coast microbrews. They also serve better than average bar food, including tacos and pork sliders.

© STUART THORNTON

the Infinity Jade Pool at Big Sur's Post Ranch

Festivals and Events

Each year, the Pacific Valley School hosts the fundraising **Big Sur Jade Festival** (www.bigsurjadeco.com, Oct.). Come out to see the artists, craftspeople, jewelry makers, and rock hunters displaying their wares in the early fall. The school is located across Highway 1 from Sand Dollar Beach. Munch snacks as your feet tap to the live music playing as part of the festival. Check the website for the exact dates and information about this year's festival.

Throughout the summer months, Big Sur cultural mecca the Henry Miller Memorial Library (0.25 miles south of Nepenthe Restaurant, 831/667-2574, www.henrymiller.org) hosts the **Big Sur International Short Film Screening Series,** where free films from all over the globe are shown every Thursday night. Check the website for the schedule.

ACCOMMODATIONS
$100-150

Along Highway 1 in the valley of Big Sur, you'll find a couple of small motels. One of the

more popular of these is the **Fernwood Resort** (Hwy. 1, 831/667-2422, www.fernwoodbigsur.com, $110). The low sprawl of buildings includes a 12-room motel, a small convenience store, a restaurant, and a bar that is a gathering place for locals and a frequent host of live music. Farther down the small road, you'll find the campgrounds, which include a number of tent cabins as well as tent and RV sites. The motel units are located on either side of the restaurant/bar/convenience store. Rooms have queen beds and attached private bathrooms, but no TVs. If you tend to get chilly in the winter (or the summer fog), ask for a room with a gas stove. Two rooms have a two-person hot tub sitting just outside on the back deck. In the summertime, book in advance to be sure of getting a room, especially on weekends.

When locals speak of Deetjen's, they could be referring to the inn, the restaurant, or the family that created both. But they all do speak of Deetjen's, which operates as a non-profit organization dedicated to offering visitors to the Big Sur region great hospitality for reasonable rates. To stay at **Deetjen's Big Sur Inn** (48865 Hwy. 1, 831/667-2377, www.Deetjen's.com, $80-250) is to become a small part of Big Sur's history and culture. It doesn't look like a spot where legions of famous writers, artists, and Hollywood stars have laid their precious heads, but Deetjen's can indeed boast a guest register that many hostelries in Beverly Hills would kill for. The motley collection of buildings also welcomed transient artists, San Francisco bohemians, and the occasional criminal looking for a spot to sleep as they traversed the coast on bicycles or even on foot.

Your guest room at Deetjen's will be unique, still decorated with the art and collectibles chosen and arranged by Grandpa Deetjen many moons ago. The inn prides itself on its rustic historic construction—expect thin weathered walls, funky cabin construction, no outdoor locks on the doors, and an altogether one-of-a-kind experience. Five rooms have shared baths, but you can request a room with private bath when you make reservations. Deetjen's prefers to offer a serene environment, and to that end does not permit children under 12 unless you rent both rooms of a two-room building. Deetjen's has no TVs or stereos, no phones in guest rooms, and no cell phone service. One of the primary sources of entertainment is the rooms' guest journals, which have occupied the evenings of those who have stayed here for years. A pay phone is available for emergencies, but other than that you're truly cut off from the outside world. Decide for yourself whether this sounds terrifying or wonderful.

$150-250

If you want to stay inside one of the parks but tents just aren't your style, book a room at the **Big Sur Lodge** (47225 Hwy. 1, 800/424-4787, www.bigsurlodge.com, $204-306) in Pfeiffer Big Sur State Park. The best part about the lodge is that you can leave your room and walk a few feet to start hiking on Pfeiffer Big Sur's trails. The lodge is keeping with the land's historic past as a place for visitors to spend an evening. In the early 1900s, the park was a resort owned by the pioneering Pfeiffer family.

Deetjen's Big Sur Inn

(Other area attractions, including Julia Pfeiffer Burns State Park and Pfeiffer Beach, are named for the clan.) Though the amenities have been updated, the Big Sur Lodge still evokes the classic woodsy vacation cabin. Set in the redwood forest along an array of paths and small roads, the rustically appointed rooms feature quilts, understated decor, and simple but clean bathrooms. There is one accommodation that can sleep six and others with kitchenettes. You can stock your kitchen at the on-site grocery store, or just get a meal at the lodge's restaurant or café.

The lodge has a swimming pool for the sunny summer and fall days in the Big Sur forest. But the real attraction is its right-outside-your-door access to the Pfeiffer Big Sur trails. You can just leave your car outside your room and hike the day away inside the park. Or take a short drive to one of the other state parks and enjoy their charms for free with proof of occupancy at Big Sur Lodge.

Despite the forbidding name, **Ragged Point Inn** (19019 Hwy. 1, 805/927-4502, http://raggedpointinn.net, $200-300) takes advantage of its location to create an anything-but-ragged hotel experience for its guests. If you've come to Big Sur to bask in the grandeur of the Pacific Ocean, this is your hotel at the southern end of the Big Sur coast. The Ragged Point Inn perches on one of Big Sur's famous cliffs, offering stellar views from the purpose-built glass walls and private balconies or patios of almost every room in the house. Budget-friendly rooms still have plenty of space, a comfy king or two double beds, and those unreal ocean views. If you've got a bit more cash to burn, go for a luxury room, with optimal views, soaring interior spaces, plush amenities, and romantic two-person spa bathtubs. Outside your room, enjoy a meal in the full-service restaurant or get picnic supplies from the snack bar or the mini-mart, fill up for a day trip at the on-site gas station, or peruse the works of local artists in the gift shop or jewelry gallery. A special treat is the hotel's own hiking trail, which makes a 350-foot descent past a waterfall to Ragged Point's private beach.

Over $250

One of Big Sur's two luxury resorts, **Ventana** (48123 Hwy. 1, 831/667-2331, www.ventanainn.com, $500-1,400) is a place where the panoramic views begin on the way to the parking lot. Picture home-baked pastries, fresh yogurt, in-season fruit, and organic coffee that can be delivered to your room in the morning or eaten in the dining room. And that's just the beginning of an unbelievable day at the Ventana. Next, don your plush spa robe and rubber slippers (all you are required to wear on the grounds of the hotel and spa) and head for the Japanese bathhouse. Choose from two bathhouses, one at each end of the property. Both are clothing-optional and gender segregated, and the upper house has glass and open-air windows that let you look out to the ocean. Two swimming pools offer a cooler hydro-respite from your busy life; the lower pool is clothing-optional, and the upper pool perches on a high spot for enthralling views. Even daily complimentary yoga classes can be yours for the asking.

The guest rooms range from the "modest" standard rooms with king beds, tasteful exposed cedar walls and ceilings, and attractive green and earth tone appointments, all the way up through generous and gorgeous suites to full-sized multi-bedroom houses. You can also take an evening stroll down to the Restaurant at Ventana Inn—the only spot on the property where you need to wear more than your robe and flip-flops. If you're headed to the Spa at Ventana Inn for a treatment, you can go comfy and casual.

Even though a night at **C** **Post Ranch** (47900 Hwy. 1, 800/524-4787, www.post-ranchinn.com, $625-2,500) can total more than some people's monthly paycheck, an evening staring at the smear of stars over the vast blue Pacific from one of the stainless steel hot water soaking tubs on the deck of Post Ranch's ocean facing rooms can temporarily cause all life's worries to ebb away. Though it may be difficult to leave the resort's well-appointed units, it is a singular experience to soak in Post Ranch's Infinity Jade Pool, an ocean facing

ESALEN: AN ADVANCED CALIFORNIA EXPERIENCE

The Esalen Institute is known throughout California as the home of Esalen massage technique, a forerunner and cutting-edge player in ecological living, and a space to retreat from the world and build a new and better sense of self. Visitors journey from all over the state and beyond to sink into the haven that's sometimes called "The New Age Harvard."

One of the biggest draws of the Institute sits down a rocky path right on the edge of the cliffs overlooking the ocean. The bathhouse includes a motley collection of mineral-fed hot tubs looking out over the ocean – you can choose the Quiet Side or the indoors Silent Side to sink into the water and contemplate the Pacific Ocean's limitless expanse, meditate on a perfect sunset or arrangement of stars, or (on the Quiet Side) get to know your fellow bathers.

Who will be naked. Regardless of gender, marital status, or the presence of others.

Esalen's bathhouse area is "clothing optional"; its philosophy puts the essence of nature above the sovereignty of humanity, and it encourages openness and sharing among its guests – to the point of chatting nude with total strangers in a smallish hot tub. You'll also find a distinct lack of attendants to help you find your way around. Once you've parked and been given directions, it's up to you to find your way down to the cliffs. You'll have to find your own towel, ferret out a cubby for your clothes in the changing rooms, grab a shower, then wander out to find your favorite of the hot tubs. Be sure

you go all the way outside past the individual clawfoot tubs to the glorious shallow cement tubs that sit right out on the edge of the cliff with the surf crashing just below.

In addition to the nudity and new-age culture of Esalen, you'll learn that this isn't a day spa. You'll need to make an appointment for a massage (at $165 a pop), which grants you access to the hot tubs for an hour before and an hour after your 75-minute treatment session. If you just want to sit in the mineral water, you'll need to stay up late. Very late. Inexpensive ($20) open access to the Esalen tubs begins on a first-come, first-served basis at 1am and ends at 3am. Many locals consider the sleep deprivation well worth it to get the chance to enjoy the healing mineral waters and the stunning astronomical shows.

If you're not comfortable with your own nudity or that of others, you don't approve of the all-inclusive spiritual philosophy, or you find it impossible to lower your voice or stop talking for more than 10 minutes, Esalen is not for you. If you've never done anything like this before, think hard about how you'll really feel once you're in the changing area with its naked hippies wandering about.

But if this description of a California experience sounds just fabulous to you, make your reservations now! The **Esalen Institute** (55000 Hwy. 1, 831/667-3000, www.esalen.org) accepts reservations by phone if necessary. Go to the website for more information.

warm pool made from chunks of the green ornamental stone.

On a 1,200-foot-high ridgeline, all the rooms at this luxury resort have striking views, whether it's of the ocean or the jagged peaks of the nearby Ventana Wilderness. The units also blend in well with the natural environment, including the seven tree houses, which are perched 10 feet off the ground.

A night at Post Ranch also includes an impressive breakfast with made-to-order omelets and French toast as well as a spread of pastries, fruit, and yogurt served in the Sierra Mar

Restaurant with its stellar ocean views. All in all, a night at Post Ranch is a big expense, but it is a memorable one if you have the funds or recently won the lottery.

CAMPING

Many visitors to Big Sur want to experience the unspoiled beauty of the landscape daily. To accommodate true outdoors lovers, many of the parks and lodges in the area have overnight campgrounds. You'll find all types of camping here, from full-service, RV-accessible areas to environmental tent campsites to wilderness backpacking. You can camp in a state park or out behind one of the small resort motels near a restaurant and a store and possibly the cool refreshing Big Sur River. Pick the option that best suits you and your family's needs.

In summer months, especially on weekends, campers without reservations coming to Big Sur are frequently turned away from the full campgrounds. A backup option—for the desperate—is to try and secure one of the 12 first come, first served tent campsites at **Bottcher's Gap** (11 miles south of Carmel's Rio Rd., take Palo Colorado Rd. eight miles inland, 805/434-1996, http://campone.com, $12). There are little amenities and it can get hot up there, but at 2,100 feet, the camp has some good views of the Big Sur backcountry.

Andrew Molera State Park

Andrew Molera State Park (Hwy. 1, 20 miles south of Carmel, 831/667-2315, www.parks.ca.gov, $25/night) offers 24 walk-in, tent-only campsites located 0.25-0.5 miles from the parking lot via a level, well-maintained trail. You'll pitch your tent in a pretty meadow near the Big Sur River, in a site that includes a picnic table and a fire ring. No reservations are taken, so come early in summertime to get one of the prime spots under a tree. While you're camping, look out for bobcats, foxes, deer, raccoons (stow your food securely!), and any number of birds. From the camping area, it's a one-mile easy hike to the beach.

Fernwood Resort

The **Fernwood Resort** (47200 Hwy. 1, 831/667-2422, www.fernwoodbigsur.com $45/tent site, $50/campsite with electric hookup, $75/tent cabin, $100/adventure tent) offers a range of camping options. There are 66 campsites located around the Big Sur River, some with electric hookups for RVs. Fernwood also has tent cabins, which are small canvas-constructed spaces with room for four in a double and two twins. You can pull your car right up to the back of your cabin. Bring your own linens or sleeping bags, pillows, and towels to make up the inside of your tent cabin. Splitting

the difference between camping and a motel room are the rustic "Adventure Tents," canvas tents draped over a solid floor whose biggest comfort are the fully made queen beds and wood stoves with wood provided. There's also electricity courtesy of an extension cord run into the tent. All camping options have easy access to the river, where you can swim, inner tube, and hike. Hot showers and bathrooms are a short walk away. Also, you will be stumbling distance from Big Sur's most popular watering hole, the Fernwood Bar.

While checking into your camping spot at Fernwood's Big Sur kiosk, be sure to check out the albino redwood located across the dirt road from the booth.

Pfeiffer Big Sur State Park

The biggest and most developed campground in Big Sur sits at **Pfeiffer Big Sur State Park** (Hwy. 1, 800/444-7275, www.parks.ca.gov, www.reserveamerica.com, $35/standard campsite, $50/riverside campsite). With 218 individual sites, each of which can take two vehicles and eight people or an RV (32 feet or shorter, trailers 27 feet max, dump station on-site), there's enough room for almost everybody here—except during a crowded summer weekend. During those times, a grocery store and laundry facilities operate within the campground for those who don't want to hike down to the lodge, and plenty of flush toilets and hot showers are scattered throughout the campground. In the evenings, walk down to the Campfire Center for entertaining and educational programs.

Pfeiffer Big Sur fills up fast in the summertime, especially on weekends. Advance reservations are highly recommended.

Julia Pfeiffer Burns State Park

With over 200 drive-in campsites, Pfeiffer Big Sur State Park is where most campers in the area go. But **Julia Pfeiffer Burns State Park** (Hwy. 1, 37 miles south of Carmel and 12 miles south of Pfeiffer Big Sur State Park, 831/667-2315 or 800/444-7275, www.parks.ca.gov, www.reserveamerica.com, $30) has two walk-in environmental campsites perched over the ocean behind the stunning McWay Waterfall. It's a short 0.33-mile walk to these two sites, which have fire pits, picnic tables, and a shared pit toilet, but there is no running water here. Obviously these two sites book up far in advance—particularly in the summer months—but it is worth checking in at Pfeiffer Big Sur State Park to see if there have been any cancellations.

Kirk Creek Campground

A popular U.S. Forest Service campground on the south coast of Big Sur, **Kirk Creek Campground** (50 miles south of Monterey on Hwy. 1 or 65 miles north of San Luis Obispo on Hwy. 1, 805/434-1996, www.recreation.gov, $22) has a great location on a bluff above the ocean. Right across the highway is the trailhead for the Vicente Flat Trail and the scenic mountain Nacimiento-Fergusson Road. The sites have picnic tables and campfire rings with grills, while the grounds have toilets and drinking water.

Plaskett Creek Campground

If you really want to get your fill of Sand Dollar Beach, consider camping at **Plaskett Creek Campground** (55 miles south of Monterey on Hwy. 1 or 60 miles north of San Luis Obispo, 805/434-1996, www.recreation.gov, $22), which is located right across the highway from Big Sur's largest beach. The sites here are in a grassy area under Monterey pine and cypress trees. There are picnic tables and a campfire ring with a grill at every site along with a flush toilet and drinking water in the campground.

Treebones Resort

For the ultimate high-end California green lodging-cum-camping experience, book a yurt (a circular structure made with a wood frame covered by cloth) at the **Treebones Resort** (71895 Hwy. 1, 877/424-4787, www.treebonesresort.com). The resort got its name from the locals' description of this scrap of land, which was once a wood recycling plant with sun-bleached logs lying about—"tree

bones." Yurts ($189-250) at Treebones tend to be spacious and charming, with polished wood floors, queen beds, seating areas, and outdoor decks for lounging. There are also five walk-in campsites ($85 for two people, breakfast and use of the facilities included). For a real different experience, camp in the human nest ($110), a bundle of wood off the ground outfitted with a futon mattress. In the central lodge, you'll find nice hot showers and usually clean restroom facilities. Being away from any real town, Treebones has a couple of onsite dining options: the Wild Coast Restaurant and the Wild Coast Sushi Bar. Check the website for a list of items to bring and the FAQ about the resort facilities to make your stay more fun. There are also four family yurts, though children under six are not allowed.

FOOD

As you traverse the famed Highway 1 through Big Sur, you'll quickly realize that a ready meal isn't something to take for granted. You'll see no In-N-Out Burgers, Starbucks, or Safeways lining the road here. While you can find groceries, they tend to appear in small markets attached to motels. Pick up staple supplies in Cambria or Carmel before you enter the area if you don't plan to leave again for a few days to avoid paying premiums at the mini-marts.

Casual Dining

The **Redwood Grill** (Hwy. 1, 831/667-2129, www.fernwoodbigsur.com, daily 11:30am-9pm, $10-15) at Fernwood Resort looks and feels like a grill in the woods ought to. Even in the middle of the afternoon, the aging, wood-paneled interior is dimly lit and strewn with casual tables and chairs. Walk up to the counter to order burritos, burgers, or wraps, then on to the bar to grab a soda or a beer.

One of Big Sur's most popular attractions is actually ◖ **Nepenthe** (48510 Hwy. 1, 831/667-2345, www.nepenthebigsur.com, daily 11:30am-10pm, $15-42). The restaurant is on the site of a spot where Rita Hayworth and Orson Welles owned a cabin until 1947, when they sold the piece of real estate to the family that started Nepenthe. The deck offers views on par with some of those you might attain on one of Big Sur's great hikes. At sunset, order up a basket of fries with Nepenthe's signature Ambrosia dipping sauce and wash them down with a potent South Coast margarita. During dinner, there is glazed duck and an eight-ounce filet mignon, but the best bet is the restaurant's most popular item: the Ambrosiaburger, a ground steak burger drenched in that tasty Ambrosia sauce. If you find yourself in Big Sur in late October, be sure to check out Nepenthe's annual Bal Masque Halloween party, Big Sur's biggest party.

Outside, the seasonal **Café Kevah** (breakfast and lunch Presidents Weekend-New Year's Day, weather permitting, $10-12) on the patio at Nepenthe offers a similar sampling at slightly lower prices. Drape your arms over the wrought-iron railing and stare out into the mesmerizing blue-gray of the Pacific below and beyond you, and you just might forget the Benedict or sandwich on your plate.

The **Big Sur Bakery** (47540 Hwy. 1, 831/667-0520, www.bigsurbakery.com, bakery opens daily at 8am, restaurant Mon. 11am-2pm, Tues.-Fri. 11am-2pm and 5:30pm-close, Sat.-Sun. 10:30am-2:30pm and 5:30pm-close, $15-32) might sound like a casual, walk-up eating establishment, and the bakery part of it is. You can stop in from 8am every day to grab a fresh-baked scone, a homemade jelly donut, or a flaky croissant sandwich to save for lunch later on. But on the dining room side, an elegant surprise awaits diners who've spent the day hiking the redwoods and strolling the beaches. Be sure to make reservations or you're unlikely to get a table, and you'd miss out on the creative wood-fired pizzas, wood-grilled meats, and seafood. At brunch, they serve the unique wood-fired bacon and three-egg breakfast pizza.

Easing into the day is easy at **Deetjen's** (48865 Hwy. 1, 831/667-2378, www.Deetjen's. com, daily breakfast and dinner, $10-32). Amongst fanciful knick knacks and cabinets displaying fine china, fill up on Deetjen's popular eggs Benedict dishes or the equally worthy Deetjen's dip, a turkey and avocado sandwich that comes with some hollandaise dipping sauce. In the evening, things get darker and more romantic as entrées, including the spicy seafood paella and a roasted, smoked bacon wrapped pork tenderloin, are served to your candle-lit table.

If it's a warm afternoon, get a table on the sunny back deck of the **Big Sur River Inn Restaurant** (46480 Hwy. 1, 831/667-2700, http://bigsurriverinn.com, $14). On summer Sundays, bands perform on the crowded deck, and you can take your libation out back to one of the chairs situated right in the middle of the cool Big Sur River. This restaurant serves sandwiches, burgers, and fish and chips for lunch along with steak, ribs, and seafood at dinner. The bar is known for its popular spicy Bloody Mary cocktails.

An unassuming local's spot, **Ripplewood Restaurant** (47047 Highway 1, 831/667-2242, www.ripplewoodresort.com, daily 8am-2pm, $8-16) serves breakfast and lunch. Sit inside or outside next to flowering plants while enjoying chorizo and eggs or an omelet named after one of Big Sur's natural sights. Lunch includes a range of sandwiches, burgers, salads, and Mexican choices.

Fine Dining

You don't need to be a guest at the gorgeous Ventana to enjoy a fine gourmet dinner at **The Restaurant at Ventana** (Hwy. 1, 831/667-4242, www.ventanainn.com, daily 11:30am-4:30pm and 6pm-9pm, $36-50). The spacious dining room boasts a warm wood fire, an open kitchen, and comfortable banquettes with plenty of throw pillows to lounge against as you peruse the menu. If you're visiting for lunch or an early supper on a sunny day, be sure to request a table outside so you can enjoy the stunning views with your meal. The inside dining room has great views from the bay windows too, along with pristine white tablecloths and pretty light wooden furniture. Even with such a setting as the restaurant has, the real star at this restaurant is the cuisine. The chef offers a daily-changing spread of haute California cuisine dishes, many of which feature organic or homegrown produce and local meats. You can choose an à la carte main course entrée or go for the five-round prix fixe.

The **Sierra Mar** (47900 Hwy. 1, 831/667-2800, www.postranchinn.com, daily 12:15pm-9pm, lunch $40, dinner $110) restaurant at the Post Ranch Inn offers a decadent four-course prix fixe dinner menu every night and a less formal three-course lunch every day. With floor to ceiling glass windows overlooking the plunging ridgeline and the Pacific below, it's a good idea to schedule dinner here during sunset. The daily menu rotates but some courses have included farm-raised abalone in a cherry tomato-basil brown butter and a 42-hour braised tender, succulent short rib.

Markets

With no supermarkets or chain mini-marts in the entire Big Sur region, the local markets do a booming business. You can stock up on staples such as bread, lunchmeat, eggs, milk, marshmallows, and graham crackers at various local stores.

The best of these is the **Big Sur Deli** (47520 Hwy. 1, 831/667-2225, www.bigsurdeli.com, daily 7am-8pm, $7.25), which offers basic goods. It is also the spot to grab a sandwich or burrito to bring on a picnic or take back to your campsite. With Big Sur's remoteness causing some high food prices, the deli is a deal for hungry locals and tourists alike. The possibilities include fresh roasted turkey sandwiches and grande meat burritos with beans, rice, salsa, and cheese. There are also rotating specialties available behind the counter like tamale pie and shepherd's pie.

Also good is the **River Inn Big Sur General Store** (46840 Hwy. 1, 831/667-2700, daily 7:30am-9pm), which has basic snacks as well as a burrito and fruit smoothie bar.

INFORMATION AND SERVICES

There is no comprehensive visitor's center in Big Sur anymore. It's a good idea to visit the **Big Sur Chamber of Commerce**'s website

(www.bigsurcalifornia.org) before visiting the area. On the site, there is up-to-date information about hikes as well as links to lodging and restaurants.

The **Big Sur Station** (0.33 miles south of Pfeiffer Big Sur State Park, 831/667-2315) covers general information, especially on the backcountry. Be sure to pick up an *El Sur Grande,* a newspaper-looking publication put out by the Big Sur Chamber of Commerce with a map and guide to local businesses.

Be aware that your cell phone may not work in all of Big Sur, especially out in the undeveloped reaches of forest and on Highway 1 away from the valley of Big Sur.

For health matters, the **Big Sur Health Center** (46896 Hwy. 1, Big Sur, 831/667-2580, Mon.-Fri. 10am-1pm and 2pm-5pm) can take care of minor medical needs, and provides an ambulance service and limited emergency care. The nearest full-service hospital is the **Community Hospital of the Monterey Peninsula** (23625 Holman Hwy., Monterey, 831/625-4775, www.chomp.org).

GETTING THERE AND AROUND

"Highway 1" sounds like a major freeway to many visitors, and down south it does get big and flat and straight. But along Big Sur, Highway 1 is a narrow, twisting, two-laned, cliff-carved track that's breathtaking both because of its beauty and because of its dangers. Once you get five miles or so south of Carmel, expect to slow down—in some spots north of the town of Big Sur you'll be driving really slow around hairpin turns carved into vertical cliffs. Be sure to use the roadside turnouts to let locals pass. If you're coming up from the south, Highway 1 is fairly wide and friendly up from Cambria, only narrowing into its more hazardous form as the cliffs get higher and the woods thicker.

Plan to spend several hours driving from Carmel to Cambria, partly to negotiate the difficult road and partly to make use of the many convenient turnouts to take photos of the unending spectacular scenery. Most of the major parks in the Big Sur region spring right off Highway 1, making it easy to spend a couple of days meandering along the road, stopping at Julia Pfeiffer or Andrew Molera to hike for a few hours or have a picnic on the beach. Also there is frequent roadwork on Highway 1.

Cambria and Vicinity

When it comes to this area, there is only one true sight. Cambria owes much of its prosperity to the immense tourist trap on the hill: Hearst Castle. Located about seven miles north in San Simeon, Hearst Castle, quite frankly, *is* San Simeon; the town grew up around it to support the overwhelming needs of its megalomaniacal owner and never-ending construction.

◖ HEARST CASTLE

There's nothing else in California quite like **Hearst Castle** (Hwy. 1 and Hearst Castle Rd., 800/444-4445, www.hearstcastle.org, tours daily 8:20am-3:20pm, $25). Newspaper magnate William Randolph Hearst conceived of the idea of a grand mansion in the Mediterranean style, on the land his parents bought along the central California coast. His memories of camping on the hills above the Pacific led him to choose the spot on which the castle now stands. He hired Julia Morgan, the first female civil engineering graduate from UC Berkeley, to design and build the house for him. She did a brilliant job with every detail, despite the ever-changing wishes of her employer. By way of decoration, Hearst assisted in the relocation of hundreds of European medieval and Renaissance antiquities, from tiny tchotchkes to whole gilded ceilings. William Randolph also adored exotic animals, and created one of the largest private zoos in the nation on his thousands of Central Coast acres. Though most of the zoo is gone now, you can still see the occasional zebra grazing peacefully along Highway 1 to the south of the castle, acting as heralds to the exotic nature of Hearst Castle ahead.

The visitor's center is a lavish affair with a gift shop, restaurant, café, ticket booth, and movie theater. Here you can see the much-touted film *Hearst Castle–Building the Dream,* which will give you an overview of the construction and history of the marvelous edifice, and of William Randolph Hearst's empire. After buying your ticket, board the shuttle that takes you up the hill to your tour. (No private cars are allowed on the roads up to the castle proper.) There are five tours to choose from, each focusing on different spaces and aspects of the castle.

The **Grand Rooms Museum Tour** is recommended for first-time visitors. It begins in the castle's assembly room, which is draped in Flemish tapestries, before heading into the dining room, billiard room, and impressive movie theater, where you'll watch a few old Hearst newsreels. Then the guide lets you loose to take in the stunning outdoor Neptune Pool and the indoor gold and blue decorated pool. Another way to see the castle is on the **Evening Museum Tour,** a seasonal evening tour with volunteers dressed in 1930s fashion who welcome guests as if you arrived at one of Hearst's legendary parties.

Expect to walk for at least an hour on whichever tour you choose, and to climb up and down many stairs. Even the most jaded traveler can't help but be amazed by the beauty and opulence that drips from every room in the house. Lovers of European art and antiques will want to stay forever.

The park recommends that visitors buy tour tickets at least a few days in advance, and even further ahead for Tour 5 and on summer weekends. For visitors with limited mobility, a special wheelchair-accessible tour is available. Strollers are not permitted. The restrooms and food concessions all cluster in the visitors center—but no food, drink, or chewing gum is allowed on any tour.

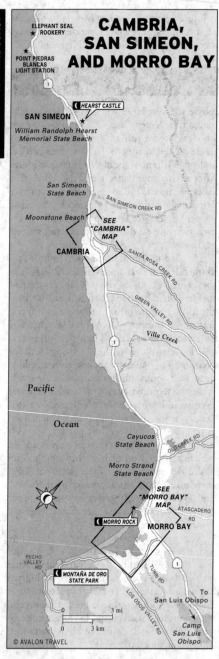

Historic San Simeon

The tiny town of San Simeon was founded primarily to support the construction efforts up the hill at Hearst Castle. The town dock provided a place for ships to unload tons of marble, piles of antiques, and dozens of workers. The general store and post office acted as a central gathering place for the community, and today you can still walk up the weathered wooden steps and make a purchase. Around the corner at the building's other door, you can buy a book of stamps or mail a letter at the tiny but operational post office.

The **William Randolph Hearst Memorial State Beach** (750 Hearst Castle Rd., San Simeon, 805/927-2020, www.parks.ca.gov, daily dawn-dusk) sits in San Simeon's cute little cove and encompasses the remaining structure of the old pier. You can lie on the beach or have a picnic up on the lawn above the sand.

CAMBRIA

Once you're through with the castle tours, a few attractions in the lower elevations beckon as well. Cambria began as, and to a certain extent still is, an artists' colony. The windswept hills and sparkling ocean provide plenty of inspiration for painters, writers, sculptors, glassblowers, and more. The small beach town becomes surprisingly spacious when you start exploring it. Plenty of visitors come here to ply Moonstone Beach, peruse the charming downtown area, and just drink in the laid-back, art-town feel.

Sights
NITT WITT RIDGE

While William Randolph Hearst built one of the most expensive homes ever seen in California, local eccentric Arthur Harold Beal (a.k.a. Captain Nit Wit or Der Tinkerpaw) got busy building the cheapest "castle" he could. **Nitt Witt Ridge** (881 Hillcrest Dr., 805/927-2690, tours by appointment) is the result of five decades of scavenging trash and using it as building supplies to create a multi-story home like no other on the coast. The rambling structure is made of abalone shells, used car rims, and toilet seats, among other found materials.

© STUART THORNTON, USED WITH PERMISSION FROM CALIFORNIA STATE PARKS/HEARST CASTLE ®

Hearst Castle

Today, you can make an appointment with owners Michael and Stacey O'Malley to take a tour of the property. (Please don't just drop in.) It's weird, it's funky, and it's fun—an oddly iconic experience of the Central Coast.

CAMBRIA CEMETERY

"Artsy" isn't a word that's usually associated with graveyards, but in Cambria it fits. The **Cambria Cemetery** (6005 Bridge St., 805/927-5158, www.cambriacemetery.com, daily 9am-4pm) reflects the artistic bent of the town's residents in its tombstone decor. Unlike many cemeteries, at Cambria the family and friends of the deceased are allowed to place all manner of personal objects at their loved ones' graves. You'll see painted tombstones, beautiful panes of stained glass, unusual wind chimes, and many other unique expressions of love, devotion, and art as you wander the 12 wooded acres.

MOONSTONE BEACH

Known for its namesake, a shimmering gemstone littered on its shore, **Moonstone Beach** (Moonstone Beach Dr.) is a scenic pebbly slice of coastline with craggly rocks offshore. Huts constructed from driftwood can be found on some sections of the beach, and there is plenty more than just moonstones to find washed up on the shoreline. There is also a wooden boardwalk that runs along the top of the bluffs above the beach to take in the scenery and watch moonstone collectors wander about below with buckets in the tideline.

PIEDRAS BLANCAS LIGHT STATION

First illuminated in 1875, the **Piedras Blancas Light Station** (meet at the Piedras Blancas Motel, 1.5 miles north of the light station on Hwy. 1, 805/927-7361, www.piedrasblancas. gov, tours mid-June-Sept. Mon.-Sat. 9:45am-11:45am, Sept.-mid-June Tues., Thurs., and Sat. 9:45am-11:45am, adults $10, children 6-17 $5, children five and under free) and its adjacent grounds can be accessed with a two-hour tour. The name "piedras blancas" means "white rocks" in Spanish. In 1948, a nearby earthquake caused a crack in the lighthouse

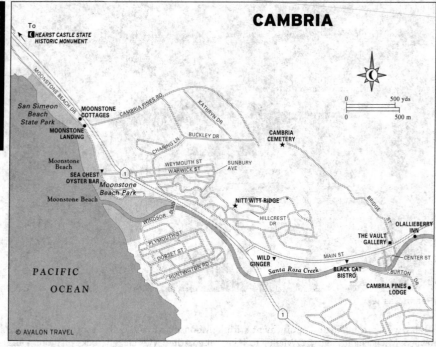

CAMBRIA

tower and the removal of a first order Fresnel lens, which was replaced with an automatic aero-beacon. Since 2001, the lighthouse has been run by the Bureau of Land Management.

PIEDRAS BLANCAS ELEPHANT SEAL ROOKERY

Stopping at the **Piedras Blancas Elephant Seal Rookery** (seven miles north of San Simeon on Hwy. 1, 805/924-1628, www.elephantseal.org, free) is like watching a nature documentary in real time. On this sliver of beach, up to 17,000 elephant seals rest, breed, give birth, or fight one another for the love of a mate. The rookery is right off Highway 1: Turn into the large gravel parking lot and follow the boardwalks north or south to viewing areas where informative plaques give background on the elephant seals, and volunteer docents are available to answer questions (daily 10am-4pm). The beaches themselves

are off limits to humans; they're covered in the large marine mammals. In the fall, most adult seals head out to sea, returning in early to mid December. Most of the seal births occur between the end of December and the middle of February.

Nightlife

If a day of touring Hearst Castle has you hankering for a beer, Cambria has two wildly different options. **Mozzi's** (2262 Main St., 805/927-4767, http://mozzissaloon.com, Mon.-Fri. 1pm-midnight, Sat.-Sun. 11am-2am) is a saloon with pool tables and a blaring jukebox. Meanwhile, the **Cambria Ale House** (2084 Main St., 805/395-1295, Mon.-Thurs. 1pm-9pm, Fri.-Sat. noon-10pm, Sun. 1pm-8pm) is a tiny beer bar with a rotating selection of six unique microbrews on tap and a fridge stocked with bottle beers that you can purchase to go. On most nights you can sit down on a couch

© STUART THORNTON

Cambria's quirky Nitt Witt Ridge

or at the small bar to take in some music by the area's singer/songwriters.

Accommodations

Located next to a church, the **Bridge Street Inn-HI Cambria** (4314 Bridge St., 805/927-7653, http://bridgestreetinncambria.com, $28-80) used to be the pastor's house. Now it's a clean, cozy hostel with a dorm room and four private rooms. The kitchen has a cast iron kitchenware collection, and there's a volleyball court out front. Part of Bridge Street's appeal is its enthusiastic young owner Brandon Follett, who sometimes books live bands to play in the hostel. Even if there's no band scheduled to play, it doesn't take much to entice Brandon to grab his acoustic guitar and play an eclectic song for his guests.

Many of the accommodations in Cambria sit along the small town's very own Hotel Row, a.k.a. Moonstone Beach Drive. One of these is the **Moonstone Landing** (6240 Moonstone Beach Dr., 805/927-0012, www.moonstone-landing.com, $150-295), which provides inexpensive partial-view rooms with the decor and amenities of a mid-tier chain motel, as well as oceanfront luxury rooms featuring porches with ocean views, soaking tubs, and gas fireplaces.

The Burton Inn (4022 Burton Dr., 805/927-5125, www.burtoninn.com, $150-350) offers apartment-sized accommodations, some decorated in an ornate English style and others with a casual beach feel. The tall-ceilinged family suites have multiple bedrooms that can sleep six while promoting both togetherness and privacy.

One of the cuter and more interesting lodgings on Moonstone Beach Drive, **Moonstone Cottages** (6580 Moonstone Beach Dr., 805/927-1366, http://moonstonecottages.com, $259-329) offers peace and luxury along with proximity to the sea. Expect your cottage to include a fireplace, a marble bathroom with a whirlpool tub, a flat-screen TV with a DVD player, Internet access, and a view of the ocean.

For a great selection of anything from economical standard rooms up to rustic cabins with king beds and a fireplace, pick the

© STUART THORNTON

a driftwood hut on Moonstone Beach

Cambria Pines Lodge (2905 Burton Dr., 800/445-6868, www.cambriapineslodge.com, $139-300). All rooms have plenty of creature comforts, including TVs, private bathrooms, and, in some cases, fireplaces. There's also a nice garden area with flowering plants, benches, and sculptures.

A favorite even among the many inns of Cambria, the **Olallieberry Inn** (2476 Main St., 888/927-3222, www.olallieberry.com, $150-225) sits in a charming 19th-century Greek Revival home and adjacent cottage. Each of the nine rooms features its own quaint Victorian-inspired decor with comfortable beds and attractive appointments. A full daily breakfast (complete with olallieberry jam) rounds out the comfortable personal experience.

Her Castle Homestay Bed and Breakfast Inn (1978 Londonderry Ln., 805/924-1719, www.HerCastle.cc, $120-160) is a bit different from your average B&B, with only two rooms available and lots of personal attention from the owners. When you make your reservations, you can ask about a half-day wine tour or dinner

reservations. The Her Castle can be the perfect hideaway for two couples traveling together who desire the privacy of "their own house."

Food

The best place to fuel up for a Hearst Castle tour is easily **◖ Sebastian's Store** (442 Slo San Simeon Rd., San Simeon, 805/927-3307, Weds.-Sun. 11am-4pm, $11). Housed in a building that also has the Hearst Ranch Winery Tasting Room and the tiny San Simeon U.S. Post Office, this popular but small eatery serves up tender, juicy beef from the nearby Hearst Ranch in their burgers, French dips, and unique creations like the "Hot Beef Ortega Melt" with beef, melted pepper jack cheese, melted cheddar cheese, Ortega chilies, and jalapenos. This is a popular place, and the sandwiches take a few minutes so don't stop in right before your scheduled Hearst Castle tour.

The **Main Street Grill** (603 Main St., 805/927-3194, http://firestonegrill.com, daily 11am-8pm, $4-18) is a popular eatery housed in a cavernous building located on the way into

© DEBORAH SCARBOROUGH

Black Cat Bistro

Cambria. The tri-tip steak sandwich—tri tip drenched in barbecue sauce and placed on a French roll dipped in butter—is the favorite here, even though the ABC burger, with avocado, bacon, and cheese topping the meat, puts most burger joints to shame.

If the smell of the salt air on Moonstone Beach leaves you longing for a seafood dinner, head for the **Sea Chest Oyster Bar** (6216 Moonstone Beach Dr., 805/927-4514, daily 5:30pm-9pm, $20-30, cash only). No reservations are accepted, so expect a long line out the door at opening time, and prepare to get here early (or wait a long while) for one of the window-side tables. The seafood tends to be fresh, with a good selection of raw oysters, and the atmosphere is tourist friendly.

Perhaps the most famous, restaurant in Cambria is the ◖ **Black Cat Bistro** (1602 Main St., 805/927-1600, www.blackcatbistro. com, Thurs.-Mon. 5pm-close, $18-30). Inside the homey interior, you can't go wrong with the mini crab rellenos appetizer: crab stuffed inside crispy fried lipstick peppers in a tasty

but not overpowering duo of sauces. Also the chipotle shrimp pasta entrée is a winner due to its shrimp, pasta, cherry tomatoes, and roasted corn drenched in a light chipotle cream sauce.

Part of an expansive but still totally local family business, **Linn's Restaurant** (2277 Main St., 805/927-0371, www.linnsfruitbin. com, daily 8am-9pm, $14-32) serves tasty, unpretentious American favorites in a casual, family-friendly atmosphere. If you love the olallieberry pie with your meal, you can purchase a ready-to-bake pie, jam, or even vinegar at Linn's café, gourmet shop, or their original farm stand while you're in Cambria.

In ubiquitously high-priced Cambria, one of the best food bargains in town is **Wild Ginger** (2380 Main St., 805/927-1001, www. wildgingercambria.com, Mon.-Wed. and Fri.-Sat. 11am-2:30pm and 5pm-9pm, Sun. 5pm-9pm, $15). This tiny pan-Asian café serves delicious fresh food at its few tables including Vietnamese caramelized prawns and eggplant curry. Wild Ginger also carries an array of take-out fare displayed in a glass case crammed into the back of the dining room. Come early for the best selection of dishes.

Information and Services

Stop by the **Cambria Chamber of Commerce** (767 Main St., 805/927-3624, http://cambria-chamber.org) to get basic information about the area.

The nearest hospital to Cambria is the **Twin Cities Hospital** (1100 Las Tablas Rd., Templeton, 805/434-3500), well east of the coast town. It sits near U.S. 101, just south of the junction of state Highway 46 and U.S. 101.

Getting There and Around

Most Californians making a weekend getaway to Cambria from either Northern California or Southern California. You can drive the Pacific Coast Highway (Highway 1) right into Cambria—this is the prettiest but not the fastest way to get here. For a quicker route, take U.S. 101 to the Paso Robles area and then turn west onto Highway 46, which brings you right to the town of Cambria.

If you prefer to travel by rail, you can take **Amtrak's *Coast Starlight*** (www.amtrak.com) to either the Paso Robles or the San Luis Obispo (SLO) stations, and make arrangements to rent a car (easiest from SLO) or get alternative transportation out to the coast.

CAYUCOS

Just 13 miles south of Cambria along Highway 1, Cayucos is one of California's best little beach towns. There are no real attractions here except for the small strip of a beach between open hillsides and the Pacific. But there are a good number of nice restaurants and places to stay, so it makes a pleasant, less touristy place to spend the night while visiting the area attractions, including Hearst Castle (which is just 30 miles north).

Cayucos is named after the native Chumash word for kayak or canoe. One of the early proponents of the town was Captain James Cass, who with a business partner built the pier, along with a store and a warehouse in the late 1800s. Today, the long narrow pier still stands, while the warehouse is the town's community center and home of the Cayucos Art Society Gallery.

Recreation

The major attraction of Cayucos is **Cayucos State Beach** (Cayucos Dr., 805/781-5930, www.parks.ca.gov) and the pier, which was built way back in 1875 by Captain James Cass. The beach has volleyball courts, swing sets, and lifeguard stands, which are staffed during the summer months. The ocean here can be calmer than at other beaches nearby, making the beach a good place for swimmers or beginning surfers. The pier is lit at night for night fishing.

Just a few feet from the beach, **Good Clean Fun** (136 Ocean Front Lane, 805/995-1993, http://goodcleanfunusa.com, daily 9am-6pm) rents surfboards, wetsuits, bodyboards, SUPs, and kayaks. They also have surf lessons, a surf camp, kayak tours, and kayak fishing outings.

Nightlife

The **Old Cayucos Tavern** (130 North Ocean Ave., 805/995-3209, daily 10am-2am) is a classic Western saloon, with a poker room in the back and a bar up front. In the barroom, over 10 beers are available on tap and topless cowgirl paintings adorn the walls. There are also two pool tables and a shuffleboard table for those who want to play games without the fear of losing their money in the card room. Live bands perform on weekends.

If you would rather sample some local wines, the **Full Moon Wine Bar and Bistro** (10 North Ocean Ave., #212, 805/995-0095, www.fullmoontastingroom.com, Thurs.-Sat. 4pm-10pm, Sun.-Mon. 1pm-8pm) has a heavy selection of wines from nearby Paso Robles, Monterey, and Santa Barbara, as well as Europe. Full Moon serves soups, salads, dips, tapas, sandwiches, and deserts with an ocean view.

Shopping

Cayucos is known for its antiques. **Rich Man Poor Man Antiques Mall** (146 N. Ocean Ave., 805/995-3631, daily 10am-5pm) has over 80 dealers selling every thing from furniture to estate jewelry. Just down the street, **Remember When** (152 N. Ocean Ave., 805/995-1232, daily 10am-5pm) is home to antiques and collectibles.

Accommodations

The **C Cass House Inn and Restaurant** (222 North Ocean Ave., 805/995-3669, http://casshouseinn.com, $225-325) offers five comfortable rooms in the old house of Captain James Cass, who basically founded Cayucos. Although the building was built in 1867, the rooms have modern, even luxurious amenities, including Anichini bed and bath linens, Wi-Fi, flat screen TVs, and Tivoli radios. Cass House is just a block from the beach, so crashing waves will lull you to sleep. The tasty breakfast includes bacon cured on-site and fresh-pressed orange juice.

Another fine bed-and-breakfast option is the **Cayucos Sunset Inn Bed and Breakfast** (95 South Ocean Ave., 805/995-2500 or 877/805-1076, www.cayucossunsetinn.com, $229-349). Each of the five two-room suites has private balconies, soaking tubs, and fireplaces. The

© STUART THORNTON

Cass House Inn in Cayucos

innkeepers provide breakfast in the morning, milk and cookies delivered to your room every evening, and other thoughtful gestures.

The **Seaside Motel** (42 South Ocean Ave., 805/995-3809 or 800/549-0900, www.seasidemotel.com, $110-160) has brightly colored, uniquely decorated rooms. Some are themed like the birdhouse and sunflower rooms, while others have kitchenettes. All rooms have flat screen TVs and Internet. Suites are available for larger groups.

Food

Rudell's Smokehouse (101 D St., 805/995-5028, www.smokerjim.com, daily 11am-6pm, $4-11) is nothing more than a little shack in spitting distance from the beach. But this little place serves some of the tastiest fish tacos you'll ever eat, including salmon and albacore variations. The seafood is smoked and the unexpected but welcome presence of chopped apples gives the fixings a sweet crunch.

A more formal option, the **Cass House Restaurant** (222 North Ocean Ave., 805/995-3669, http://casshouseinn.com, Thurs.-Mon. 5pm-8:30pm, $68/four-course meal) occupies a room in the bottom floor of the historic house. The menu changes daily. Everything is seasonally inspired, locally sourced, and made in-house, even the butter.

Hoppe's Garden Bistro and Wine Shop (78 North Ocean Ave., 805/995-1006, Wed.-Sun. 11am-2pm and 5pm-close, $14-60) serves French-inspired cuisine inside or outside in its garden. Dinner entrées include meat options like roasted pheasant, vegetarian offerings like grilled polenta, and a range of seafood dishes like sautéed abalone.

Located in a two-story red building on Cayucos' main drag, the **Brown Butter Cookie Company** (98 N. Ocean Ave., 805/995-2076, www.brownbuttercookies.com, daily 9am-6pm) bakes and sells original cookie creations on-site. Sample the delectable original brown butter sea salt cookie and other creative recipes, including coconut lime and cocoa mint. You'll have a hard time leaving without a full bag of cookies.

Cayucos has its own **farmer's market** (Cayucos Vet's Hall parking lot, 10 Cayucos Dr., 805/296-2056, Fri. 10am-12:30pm) from June to August.

Information and Services

Cayucos has a few basic services including its own **bank** (107 N. Ocean Ave., 805/995-3671) with an ATM and **post office** (97 Ash Ave., Mon.-Fri. 9am-4pm).

Getting There

Cayucos is right off Highway 1. It is 13 miles south of Cambria and 8 miles north of Morro Bay.

Morro Bay

The picturesque Central Coast fishing village of Morro Bay is dominated by Morro Rock, a 576-foot-high volcanic plug that looms over the harbor. In 1542, Juan Rodriguez Cabrillo, who was the first European explorer to navigate the California coast, named the landmark Morro Rock, because he thought it appeared to resemble a moor's turban. The rock was an island until the 1930s, when a road was built connecting it to the mainland. The area around the rock is accessible, but the rock itself is off limits because it is home to a group of endangered peregrine falcons.

With a view of the rock, the small city's Embarcadero is a string of tourist shops, restaurants, and hotels strung along Morro Bay, a large estuary that includes the harbor, the Morro Bay State Marine Recreational Management Area, and the Morro Bay State Marine Reserve. Uphill from the water, more restaurants, bars, and stores are located in Morro Bay's Olde Towne section.

Having natural attractions, including the stunning Montana de Oro State Park just miles out of town, and with a nice waterfront focus, Morro Bay is a worthy destination or detour for a weekend, even though a lot of the area's lodging books up during the high season's weekends.

SIGHTS
◀ Morro Rock

It would be difficult to come to the town of Morro Bay and not see **Morro Rock** (www.slostateparks.com). The 576-foot-high volcanic plug, which has been called the "Gibraltar of the Pacific," dominates the town's scenery whether you are walking along the bayside Embarcadero or beachcombing on the sandy coastline just north of the prominent geologic feature. It's worthwhile to get close and stare up at the volcanic plug but resist any urges to try and climb it because it's a state preserve and a home for nesting peregrine falcons.

◀ Montana de Oro State Park

Seeking a serious nature fix on the Central Coast? Head for sprawling 8,000-acre **Montana de Oro State Park** (seven miles south of Los Osos on Pecho Rd., 805/528-0513, www.parks.ca.gov). Its seven miles of coastline, with coves, tide pools, sand dunes, and almost 50 miles of hiking trails, is just the fix you need.

A great way to get a feel for the park's immense size is to hike up the two-mile **Valencia Peak Trail** (four miles round-trip). In springtime, the trail sides are decorated with blooming wildflowers and the 1,347-foot-high summit offers commanding views of Montana de Oro's pocketed coastline and Morro Rock jutting out in the distance. From this vantage point, during the right time of year, the park's Sticky Monkey Flower, wild mustard, and California poppies dust the hillsides in gold. The hike is steep and exposed, so make sure to bring plenty of water on warm days.

For a feel of the coast, park right in front of **Spooner's Cove** and walk out on its wide, coarse grained beach. On the cove's north end, Islay Creek drains into the ocean. There's also a picturesque arch across the creek in the rock face on the north side.

The **Spooner Ranch House Museum** informs visitors of the parkland's early

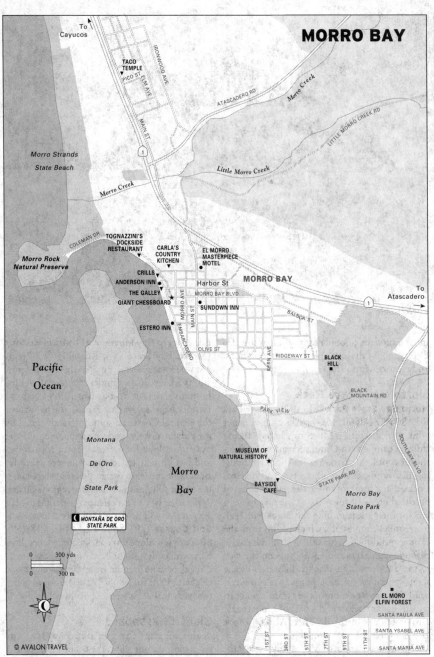

MORRO BAY

To Cayucos

TACO TEMPLE

PICO ST
ELM AVE
IRONWOOD AVE
MAIN ST

ATASCADERO RD

Morro Creek

LITTLE MORRO CREEK RD

Morro Strands State Beach

1

Little Morro Creek

Morro Creek

COLEMAN DR

Morro Rock Natural Preserve

TOGNAZZINI'S DOCKSIDE RESTAURANT

CARLA'S COUNTRY KITCHEN

EL MORRO MASTERPIECE MOTEL

CRILLS
ANDERSON INN
THE GALLEY
GIANT CHESSBOARD

Harbor St

MORRO BAY

MORRO BAY BLVD

SUNDOWN INN

MORRO AVE
MAIN ST
EMBARCADERO

1

To Atascadero

BALBOA ST

ESTERO INN

OLIVE ST

KERN AVE
RIDGEWAY ST

BLACK HILL

BLACK MOUNTAIN RD

Pacific Ocean

PARK VIEW

SOUTH BAY BLVD

Montana

De Oro

State Park

Morro Bay

MUSEUM OF NATURAL HISTORY

STATE PARK RD

BAYSIDE CAFÉ

Morro Bay State Park

MONTAÑA DE ORO STATE PARK

0   300 yds
0   300 m

EL MORO ELFIN FOREST

SANTA PAULA AVE

SANTA YSABEL AVE

1ST ST
3RD ST
5TH ST
7TH ST
9TH ST
11TH ST

SANTA MARIA AVE

© AVALON TRAVEL

© STUART THORNTON

Morro Rock

inhabitants, the Spooner family. There are also displays about the area's plants, mountain lions, and raptors within the small facility.

Morro Bay State Park

Morro Bay State Park (Morro Bay State Park Rd., 805/772-2560, www.parks.ca.gov) is not your typical state park. Sure, it has hiking trails, a campground, and recreational opportunities. But this park also has its own natural history museum, golf course, and marina. Located just south of town, the park is situated on the shores of Morro Bay. One way to get a feel for the park is to hike the **Black Hill Trail** (three miles round-trip), which begins from the campground road. This 600-foot climb passes through chaparral and eucalyptus on the way to the 640-foot-high Black Hill, a part of the same system of volcanic plugs that produced nearby Morro Rock. From the summit, you can see the estuary below and a part of Montana de Oro State Park in the distance. Also on Black Hill is a forest of Monterey pine.

One unique aspect of Morro Bay State Park

is the **Morro Bay Museum of Natural History** (Morro Bay State Park Rd., 805/772-2694, www.slostateparks.com, daily 10am-5pm, adults $3, age 16 and under free). Small but informative, the Morro Bay Museum of Natural History has displays that explain the habitats of the Central Coast and some interactive exhibits for kids. An observation deck hanging off the museum allows for a great view of Morro Bay and has binoculars so that you spot wildlife. Beside the museum is a garden that shows how the native Chumash utilized the region's plants.

Another way to experience the park is to play a round of golf at the **Morro Bay State Park Golf Course** (201 State Park Rd., 805/782-8060, www.slocountyparks.com, weekdays $43, weekends $48) or head out on the water in a kayak or canoe rented from the **Kayak Shack** (10 State Park Rd., 805/772-8796, www.morrobaykayakshack.com, $12-16/hour).

Giant Chessboard

Within the city's Centennial Parkway is Morro Bay's most unique sight: the **Giant Chessboard**

the view from Valencia Peak in Montana de Oro State Park

(Centennial Pkwy., 805/772-6278). It's a 16-foot-by-16-foot chessboard with waist-high chess pieces that can weigh as much as 30 pounds each. The four picnic tables adjoining the Giant Chessboard have built-in chessboards where the local chess fiends play. You can reserve the giant board for a small fee through the Morro Bay Recreation and Parks Department.

ENTERTAINMENT AND EVENTS
Bars

With old gas and oil cans hanging from the ceiling, the **The Fuel Dock** (900 Main St., 805/772-8478, daily noon-2am) lives up to its name. Behind the bar is a good selection of liquors and beer to lube people up. The front room has a stage that hosts live bands on weekends, while the back room has a couple of pool tables.

Nearby **Legends Bar** (899 Main St., 805/772-2525, daily 11am-2am) has a pool table, shuffleboard, jukebox, and a giant moose head.

Down on the Embarcadero, **The Libertine Pub** (801 Embarcadero, 805/772-0700, Mon.-Fri. 3pm-midnight, Sat.-Sun. noon-midnight) is the place for the discerning beer drinker. They have 20 beers on tap, which are updated on a chalkboard, and a selection of over 80 bottled beers.

Festivals and Events

Strong winds kick up on the Central Coast in the spring. The **Morro Bay Parade and Kite Festival** (800/231-0592, www.morrobay.org) takes advantage of these gales with pro kite fliers twirling and flipping their kites in the sky. The festival also offers kite-flying lessons.

For over 30 years, the **Morro Bay Harbor Festival** (800/366-6043, www.mbhf.com) has showcased the best of the region, including wines, seafood, live music, and a clam chowder contest.

SPORTS AND RECREATION

With beaches, a bay, and hiking trails, there are lots of recreational opportunities in Morro Bay

NINE SISTERS

One of the distinctive features of San Luis Obispo County are the nine ancient volcanic peaks known as the Nine Sisters of the Morros. These extend from the prominent 576-foot **Morro Rock** of Morro Bay 14 miles south to the 775-foot **Islay Hill,** which is located in the City of San Luis Obispo.

The Nine Sisters' highest peak is the 1,559-foot **Bishop Peak.** The top portion is a part of the 360-acre Bishop Peak Natural Reserve and a popular spot for hikers and rock climbers.

The Nine Sisters also make for unique animal and plant habitats. Morro Rock is a nesting place for peregrine falcons, while **Hollister Peak** hosts a colony of black-shouldered kites.

and the surrounding area. One different way to take in the bay's sea life is to take a 45-minute tour of Morro Bay in a 21-passenger submarine with windows run by **Sub Sea Tours** (699 Embarcadero #9, 805/772-9463, www.subseatours.com, adults $14, seniors and students $11, children $7).

Beaches

There are several beaches in and around Morro Bay. Popular with surfers and beachcombers, **Morro Rock Beach** (west end of Embarcadero, 805/772-6200, www.morro-bay.ca.us) lies within city limits, just north of Morro Rock. **The Morro Bay Sandspit** (www.slostateparks.com) is a four-mile-long line of dunes and beach that separates Morro Bay from the ocean. The northernmost mile is within city limits, while the southern portion is located in Montana de Oro State Park. You can access this area by walking in from the state park or by paddling across Morro Harbor to the land south of the harbor mouth.

Just north of town is **Morro Strand State Beach** (two miles south of Cayucos on Hwy. 1, 805/772-2560, www.parks.ca.gov). The strand is three miles of beach that is popular with anglers, windsurfers, and kite fliers.

Surfing

Morro Rock Beach (west end of Embarcadero, 805/772-6200, www.morro-bay.ca.us) has a consistent beach break. It's a unique experience to be able to stare up at a giant rock while waiting for waves. **Wavelengths Surf Shop** (998 Embarcadero, 805/772-3904, board rental $20/day, wetsuit rental $10/day) is on the Embarcadero on the way to the beach. It rents boards and wetsuits.

Kayaking and Stand Up Paddleboarding

The protected and scenic waters of Morro Bay are great for paddling around whether you're in a kayak or on a stand up paddleboard (SUP). **Central Coast Stand Up Paddling** (501 Embarcadero, 805/395-0410, www.centralcoastsup.com, Mon.-Tues. and Thurs. 10am-5pm, Fri.-Sat. 9am-6pm, Sun. 9am-5pm) and **Kayak Horizons** (551 Embarcadero, 805/772-6444, www.kayakhorizons.com, daily 9am-5pm) both rent kayaks and stand up paddleboards from the Embarcadero. From Morro Bay State Park, you can secure a canoe or kayak from **Kayak Shack** (10 State Park Rd., 805/772-8796, www.morrobaykayakshack.com) and paddle around the bay from there.

ACCOMMODATIONS
Under $150

The **Sundown Inn** (640 Main St., 805/772-3229 or 800/696-6928, http://sundowninn.com, $139-149) is a well-priced motel in walking distance to Morro Bay's downtown and waterfront areas. The rooms have refrigerators, microwaves, and, here's something different, coin-operated vibrating beds.

$150-250

The ◖ **El Morro Masterpiece Motel** (1206 Main St., 805/772-5633, www.masterpiece-motels.com, $149-269) is a great place to stay for art enthusiasts and quirky motel lovers. Each room is decorated with framed prints from master painters, and the hallways also have prints of paintings from Henri Matisse, Vincent Van Gogh, and Norman Rockwell. There's also a large indoor spa pool decorated like a Roman bathhouse that further differentiates this motel from other cookie cutter lodging options.

All eight rooms at the **Estero Inn** (501 Embarcadero, 805/772-1500, www.esteroinn. com, $159-279) are suites with microwaves and refrigerators. Located right on the bay, the Estero Inn also has continental breakfasts for their guests.

Over $250

The family run **Anderson Inn** (897 Embarcadero, 805/772-3434, www.andersoninnmorrobay.com, $239-349) is an eight-room boutique hotel located right on Morro Bay's busy Embarcadero. Three of the rooms are perched right over the estuary with stunning views of the nearby rock. Those premium rooms also include fireplaces and jetted tubs.

CAMPING

Located a couple of miles outside of downtown Morro Bay, the **Morro Bay State Park Campground** (Morro Bay State Park Rd., 800/444-7275, www.parks.ca.gov, tent site $35, RVs $50) has 140 campsites with many shaded by eucalyptus and pine trees. Right across the street is the Morro Bay estuary.

Six miles southwest of Morro Bay, **Montana de Oro State Park** (seven miles south of Los Osos on Pecho Rd., 800/444-7275, www. parks.ca.gov, $25) has more primitive camping facilities. There are walk-in environmental campsites and a primitive campground behind the Spooner Ranch House that has pit toilets.

FOOD
American

The giant parking lot outside **Carla's Country Kitchen** (213 Beach St., 805/772-9051, $9) attests to the popularity of this breakfast and lunch spot. With blue-and-white-checkered tablecloths, Carla's serves heaping portions of breakfast classics, including scrambles and omelets, along with sandwiches and burgers. The "Pooney" scramble is a tasty mess of spinach, cheeses, eggs, bacon, and mushrooms, though the accompanying biscuits—which looked amazing—were a bit dry.

Within Morro Bay State Park, the **Bayside Café** (10 State Park Rd., 805/772-1465, www. baysidecafe.com, Mon.-Wed. 11am-3pm, Thurs.-Sun. 11am-8:30 or 9pm, $8-25) is—true to its name—right by the bay. The lunch menu skews towards burgers and fish and chips, while dinner features fancier fare including lobster scampi.

Mexican

Taco Temple (2680 N. Main St., 805/772-4965, Mon.-Sat. 11am-9pm, Sun. 11am-8:30pm, $5-22) is housed in a big multi-colored building east of Highway 1. Inside, people worship the Temple's crab cake and fish tacos. They also have unusual offerings like sweet potato enchiladas and calamari tacos.

Seafood

Seafood is the way to go when dining in the fishing village of Morro Bay. An unassuming fish house with views of the fishing boats and the bay, 🍷 **Tognazzini's Dockside Restaurant** (1245 Embarcadero, 805/772-8100, www.bonniemarietta.com, summer Sun.-Thurs. 11am-9pm, Fri.-Sat. 11am-10pm, winter Sun.-Thurs. 11am-8pm, Fri.-Sat. 11am-9pm, $18-27) has an extensive seafood menu as well as art pieces depicting sultry mermaids hanging on the wall. Entrées include albacore kebabs and wild salmon in a unique tequila marinade. If you're an oyster lover, you simply can't go wrong with Dockside's barbecued oysters appetizer, which features the shellfish swimming in a garlic butter studded with scallions. Behind the main restaurant is the **Dockside Too Fish Market** (summer daily 10am-8pm, winter Sun.-Thurs. 10am-6pm, Fri.-Sat. 10am-8pm), a local's favorite with beer, seafood, and live music.

A more upscale seafood option is **The Galley Seafood Bar & Grill** (899 Embarcadero,

805/772-7777, http://galleymorrobay.com, daily 11am-2:30pm and 5pm-close, $18-46). It serves seafood with light sauces. Popular items include the fresh fish and pan seared scallops.

INFORMATION AND SERVICES

For the lowdown on Morro Bay, stop by the **Morro Bay Chamber of Commerce and Visitors Center** (845 Embarcadero, Suite D, 805/772-4467 or 800/231-0592, www.morrobay.org, daily 9am-5pm).

Morro Bay is big enough to have supermarkets and banks. It also has a **post office** (898 Napa Ave., www.usps.com, Mon.-Fri. 9am-5pm, Sat. 9am-1pm).

The closest hospital with emergency services is **French Hospital Medical Center** (1911 Johnson Ave., 805/543-5353, www.frenchmedicalcenter.org).

GETTING THERE AND AROUND

From U.S. 101, take Highway 41 West and then head south on Highway 1 to the Morro Bay exits. If you are driving on Highway 1 from the north or south, just look for the Morro Bay exits.

San Luis Obispo

Eleven miles inland from the coast, San Luis Obispo (SLO) is a worthy home base to explore nearby Montana de Oro State Park and Morro Bay. Founded in 1772 by Junipero Serra, SLO is one of California's oldest communities. Despite this, the presence of the nearby California Polytechnic State University gives the small city a youthful, vibrant feel.

Higuera Street is a one-way, three-lane street lined with restaurants, clothing stores, and bars. A half block away, restaurant decks are perched over the small San Luis Obispo Creek, a critical habitat for migrating steelhead.

In front of the Mission San Luis Obispo de Tolosa is a plaza overlooking the creek with grassy lawn sections, plenty of benches, and a fountain with sculptures of bears, a fish, and one of the area's first human residents.

SIGHTS
Mission San Luis Obispo de Tolosa

Founded by Junipero Serra way back in 1772, **Mission San Luis Obispo de Tolosa** (751 Palm St., 805/781-8220, www.missionsanluisobispo.org, summer daily 9am-5pm, winter daily 9am-4pm) was the fifth in the chain of 21 California missions. The church itself is narrow and long with exposed wooden beams on the ceiling. On the grounds, there is a small **museum**

(805/543-6850, summer daily 9am-5pm, winter daily 9am-4pm, suggested donation $3) with artifacts from the Native Chumash people and exhibits on the mission and its missionaries. A nice garden and the Mission Plaza out front of the mission complex are a nice place to spend the afternoon on a warm day.

◖ Madonna Inn

A kitschy attraction worth seeing even if you aren't spending an evening there, the **Madonna Inn** (10 Madonna Rd., 805/543-3000, www.madonnainn.com) is a sprawling complex right off U.S. 101 that includes a café, a steakhouse, a bar, a dance floor, a wine cellar, and a collection of 110 themed rooms like "The Caveman," a unit with a solid rock wall and a waterfall shower.

Obviously, the rooms are for overnight guests, but there is still a lot to take in if you pull over for a peek. The **Copper Café & Pastry Shop** has copper plated tables and a copper plated circular bar, while the **Gold Rush Steak House** is a garish explosion of giant fake flowers and rose-colored furniture. It might remind you of a room in your grandmother or great aunt's home—on steroids.

Men have the unique pleasure of being able to use the famous rock waterfall urinal in the men's room.

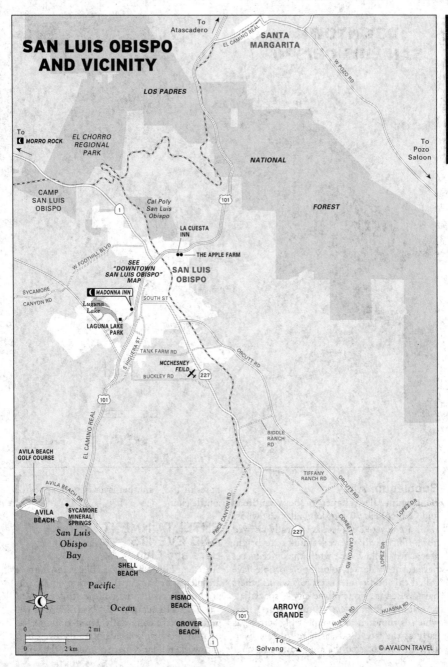

SAN LUIS OBISPO AND VICINITY

To Atascadero

EL CAMINO REAL

SANTA MARGARITA

W POZO RD

LOS PADRES

To Pozo Saloon

To MORRO ROCK

EL CHORRO REGIONAL PARK

NATIONAL

FOREST

CAMP SAN LUIS OBISPO

1

101

Cal Poly San Luis Obispo

LA CUESTA INN

W FOOTHILL BLVD

THE APPLE FARM

SEE "DOWNTOWN SAN LUIS OBISPO" MAP

SAN LUIS OBISPO

SYCAMORE CANYON RD

MADONNA INN

SOUTH ST

Luguna Lake

LAGUNA LAKE PARK

S HIGUERA ST

TANK FARM RD

ORCUTT RD

MCCHESNEY FEILD

101

BUCKLEY RD

227

EL CAMINO REAL

BIDDLE RANCH RD

AVILA BEACH GOLF COURSE

TIFFANY RANCH RD

ORCUTT RD

AVILA BEACH DR

AVILA BEACH

SYCAMORE MINERAL SPRINGS

PRICE CANYON RD

227

LOPEZ DR

San Luis Obispo Bay

CORBETT CANYON RD

LOPEZ DR

SHELL BEACH

Pacific Ocean

ARROYO GRANDE

PISMO BEACH

101

HUASNA RD

HUASNA RD

0   2 mi

GROVER BEACH

0   2 km

1

To Solvang

© AVALON TRAVEL

DOWNTOWN SAN LUIS OBISPO

Bubblegum Alley

Bubblegum Alley (Higuera St. between Broad and Garden) is a 70-foot-long alleyway whose walls are covered in pieces of already chewed gum. The newly chewed chunks are bright green, red, yellow, etc., while the older pieces have turned a darker color. Some people have called this oddity an "eyesore," while others have touted it as one of the city's "special attractions." Regardless, Bubblegum Alley, which is rumored to have possibly started as early as the late 1950s, is here to stay. Even after firemen blasted the alleyway with water

hoses in 1985, another layer of gum appeared a little later.

ENTERTAINMENT AND EVENTS
Bars and Clubs

Since San Luis Obispo is a college town, there are plenty of bars in the downtown area. A popular spot with the college students, **Mo/Tav** (725 Higuera St., 805/541-8733, www.motherstavern.com, daily 11am-1:30am) has two-for-one-drink nights, karaoke evenings, and weekend dance parties. Across the street

the pool deck at the Madonna Inn

is another popular drinking establishment called the **Frog & Peach Pub** (728 Higuera St., 805/595-3764, daily noon-2am). It has live music almost seven nights a week along with a back deck, where you can have a drink on a warmer evening.

The **Black Sheep Bar & Grill** (1117 Chorro St., 805/544-7433, www.blacksheepslo.com, daily 11am-2am) has a cozy pub feel on un-crowded nights. This brick-walled, wood-floored tavern has a fireplace and a back patio. It also serves a burger basted in a Guinness beer reduction sauce.

Creekside Brewing Company (1040 Broad St., 805/542-9804, www.creeksidebrewing.com, Sun.-Wed. 11am-midnight, Thurs.-Sat. 11am-1:30am) is a small brewpub that serves a menu of 5-6 house-made beers. You can sip brews like their popular IPA on a deck hanging over the creek or in the cavernous downstairs bar.

Live Music
SLO Brewing Company (1119 Garden St., 805/543-1843, www.slobrewingco.com,

Tues.-Sun. 11:30am-2am, Mon. 3pm-2am) is a brewery, restaurant, bar, and music venue. Upstairs are pool tables and the dining area, while downstairs is a stage that has hosted acts like The Strokes, Green Day, and Snoop Dogg. Check the website for a list of upcoming acts.

Another venue for live music, the **Performing Arts Center** (1 Grand Ave., 805/756-7222, www.pacslo.org), which is located on the California Polytechnic State University campus, also has live theater events, lectures, and comedy performances.

East of San Luis Obispo, the **Pozo Saloon** (90 West Pozo Rd., Pozo, 805/438-4225, www.pozosaloon.com) is a historic watering hole from 1858 that somehow pulls in acts like Willie Nelson, Dwight Yoakam, Snoop Dogg, and The Black Crowes to perform on its outdoor stage.

Cinema
The **Palm Theatre** (817 Palm St., 805/541-5161, www.thepalmtheatre.com) has the unique distinction of being the first solar-powered

movie theater in the country. The Palm frequently screens independent, foreign, and art-house films.

The **Fremont Theatre** (1035 Monterey St., 805/541-2141, http://themovieexperience2. blogspot.com) is an art deco movie house from 1942 that shows new films as well as classic movies.

Festivals and Events

The **San Luis Obispo Farmers' Market** (Higuera St. between Osos and Nipomo Sts., www.slocountyfarmers.org, http://down-townslo.com, Thurs. 6:10pm-9pm) is a true phenomenon. One of the largest farmers' markets in the state, this weekly gathering has the goods of 70 farmers and lots of live music.

Every March, the **San Luis Obispo International Film Festival** (817 Palm St. and 1035 Monterey St., 805/546-3456, http:// slofilmfest.org) screens a range of films at the city's Palm Theatre and Fremont Theatre along with other county spots including Paso Robles and Avila Beach. The five-day fest draws film folks like Josh Brolin and John Waters.

Festival Mozaic (various locations, 805/781-3009 or 877/881-8899, www.festivalmozaic. com) has a winter concert series and a summer music festival. It features chamber music, orchestra performances, and educational events in venues including Mission San Luis Obispo de Tolosa and the Hearst Castle.

ACCOMMODATIONS
$100-150

A superb value, the **C Peach Tree Inn** (2001 Monterey St., 800/227-6396, http://peachtree-inn.com, $69-150) has nice rooms, a friendly staff, and a complimentary breakfast. The finest rooms at the Peach Tree are the Creekside Rooms, which each have their own brick patio. Next to the lobby is a large common room with a back deck and rocking chairs for enjoying San Luis Obispo's frequently pleasant weather. The Peach Tree is located on the Old SLO Trolley route and is an easy one-mile walk to San Luis Obispo's downtown.

Just across the street from the Peach Tree, the

La Cuesta Inn (2074 Monterey St., 805/543-2777, www.lacuestainn.com, $119-169) has reasonably priced rooms right near U.S. 101. This privately owned hotel has a pool, hot tub, and a deluxe continental breakfast.

Also in this cluster of accommodations is the **Apple Farm Inn** (2015 Monterey St., 805/544-2040 or 800/255-2040, www.applefarm.com, $129-269), which has more upscale rooms in their inn ($189-269) and less expensive rooms in the surrounding Trellis Court ($129-189). The inn rooms are twice the size of the Trellis Court rooms and are decorated like traditional bed-and-breakfast offerings. But all the court rooms have gas fireplaces. On the grounds is a heated pool, soaking tub, and the Apple Farm Restaurant & Bakery.

$150-250

The **C Sycamore Mineral Springs Resort** (1215 Avila Beach Dr., 805/595-7302, www. sycamoresprings.com, $129-279) is located on 100 acres in a tranquil canyon with mineral springs bubbling beneath it. The collection of accommodations here range from cozy rooms with a queen bed to a two-story guesthouse with three bedrooms and three bathrooms.

Up on stilts, the Sycamore Mineral Springs Resort's West Meadows Suites include a living room with a gas fireplace and a bedroom with a four-poster king bed. The best feature of the suites are their back decks, which include large soaking tubs that can be filled with fresh mineral water from below at whatever temperature you desire.

Being 10 miles from San Luis Obispo, Sycamore Canyon might not be ideal if your plan is to maximize your time in the historic city's downtown. But, if you want a rejuvenating stay in a nice natural setting, the mineral springs resort has plenty of amenities on its grounds, including a yoga dome, a labyrinth, a wellness center, a restaurant, some hillside hot tubs fed by sulfur mineral springs, and hiking options including the Bob Jones Trail, a paved walkway that goes two miles from the resort to the coastal community of Avila Beach.

If you ever wanted to know how it feels

to spend the night in a cave or in a room inspired by the European country of Portugal, you should plop down some money to spend a whole evening at the **Madonna Inn** (10 Madonna Rd., 805/543-3000, www.madonnainn.com, $189-459). An under-hyped asset on Madonna Inn's 2,200 acres is its pool deck with a large heated pool, two hot tubs, a poolside bar, and a view of an artificially-made cascade tumbling down the hillside.

FOOD

San Luis Obispo restaurants clearly take advantage of their location near farms and wineries. Even the higher-end establishments aren't that fancy due to the big college presence.

Being inside **Franks Famous Hot Dogs** (950 California Blvd., 805/541-3488, daily 6:30am-9pm, $2-5) feels a bit like you've time traveled back to the 1950s. College students from nearby Cal Poly sit in the red and white booths snacking on Franks' daily handmade burgers, fries, or steamed hot dogs. Whether you get a chili cheese dog or a monster burger, the super low prices recall another era. It's rumored that they have a great breakfast burrito as well.

Though it's located in a neighborhood a few blocks from downtown, **High Street Deli** (350 High St., 805/541-4738, www.highstdeli.com, daily 9am-5:30pm, $6-8.50) is worth seeking out if you are a sandwich enthusiast. The "California Turkey" is a heated slab of tastiness with roasted turkey, an Ortega chile, slices of avocado, and more on toasted sourdough slices. They also sell Italian subs, hot pastramis, and meatloaf sandwiches. After ordering, hunker down on a stool at one of the barrel tables to eat these creations while they're still warm.

Hearty homestyle food can be had at the **Apple Farm Restaurant** (2015 Monterey St., 805/544-6100, www.applefarm.com, daily 7am-9pm, $12-24). In a colorful dining room decorated with produce signs, breakfast, lunch, and dinner is served daily. The mornings feature omelets and chicken fried steak, while dinner stretches out into steak and seafood entrées.

On a nice day, **Novo** (726 Higuera St., 805/543-3986, www.novorestaurant.com, Mon.-Sat. 11am-close, Sun. 10am-2pm, $16-32) has a collection of decks overlooking San Luis Obispo Creek for dining and drinking. Novo serves tapas including fresh shrimp avocado spring rolls and full-on entrées like lavender lamb chops. International flavors creep into the menu on items like pork *carnitas sopes,* Thai curries, and a stir-fried noodle dish.

Another worthy place for dinner or lunch is the Rachael Ray-approved **Blue Sky Café** (1121 Broad St., 805/545-5401, www.bigskycafe.com, Mon.-Thurs. 7am-9pm, Fri. 7am-10pm, Sat. 8am-10pm, Sun. 8am-9pm, $9-22). There are plenty of options for carnivores, but Blue Sky has some vegetarian entrées, including one that is a plate of local vegetables served in a variety of preparations.

The menu items at **Koberl at Blue** (998 Monterey St., 805/783-1135, www.epkoberl.com, restaurant daily 5pm-10pm, bar Sun.-Wed. 4pm-midnight, Thurs.-Sun. 4pm-2am, $23-48) are designed to be paired with a glass of wine. So whether you get the tempura fried oyster appetizer or the sautéed veal liver entrée be sure to order wine whether it's a Paso Robles cabernet or a Bordeaux from France.

Luna Red (1023 Chorro St., 805/540-5243, www.lunaredslo.com, Mon.-Sat. 11am-close, $15-32) is in an enviable location between Mission Plaza and bustling Higuera Street. With ample outdoor patio seating, Luna Red serves what it calls "an amalgamation of world cuisines." This claim is supported with a menu that includes sashimi, ceviche, lamb kebabs, and a hummus platter.

INFORMATION AND SERVICES

Information about sights and lodging in San Luis Obispo County can be attained at the **San Luis Obispo Chamber of Commerce Visitor's Center** (895 Monterey St., 805/781-2777, www.slochamber.org, Sun.-Wed. 10am-5pm, Thurs.-Sat. 10am-7pm).

San Luis Obispo has its own daily newspaper

dining at Novo

© STEVE MILLER

called **The Tribune** (www.sanluisobispo.com) and its own free weekly newspaper **New Times** (www.newtimesslo.com).

San Luis Obispo is a city with most basic services. There are two **post offices** (893 Marsh St., 805/543-5353; 1655 Dalidio Dr., 805/543-2605).

In case of emergencies, San Luis Obispo is home to two hospitals: **Sierra Vista Regional Medical Center** (1010 Murray Ave., 805/546-7600, www.sierravistaregional.com) and **French Hospital Medical Center** (1911 Johnson Ave., 805/543-5353, www.french-medicalcenter.org).

GETTING THERE AND AROUND

Both Highway 1 and U.S. 101 funnel into San Luis Obispo to the north. Coming from the south, use the Highway 1/U.S. 101 combined freeway into town.

There's also an **Amtrak** station in San Luis Obispo (1011 Railroad Ave., www.amtrak.com), where the *Coast Starlight* train stops.

Paso Robles

As an up-and-coming wine-growing region, Paso Robles has become a familiar destination and appellation for state residents as well as a popular side trip from nearby Cambria. Huge crowds do not descend on Paso every weekend as they do in the more popular wine regions and you can still find room at the tasting bars, engage with knowledgeable tasting room staff, meet the occasional winemaker tending bar, and enjoy a friendly country atmosphere both in town and on the wine roads. For the best tasting experience, visit the Paso region over the weekend—many of the smaller winery tasting rooms are open only Thursday-Monday or even only Friday-Sunday. Most tasting fees are waived with a wine purchase.

WINERIES

The wine industry is growing by leaps and bounds in and all around Paso. The Paso Robles region now boasts more than 200 wineries, over 100 of which have tasting rooms open to the public. The hills outside of town are braided with rows of vines. For the purposes of this book, the sprawled landscape is divided into four easily navigable parts: Highway 46

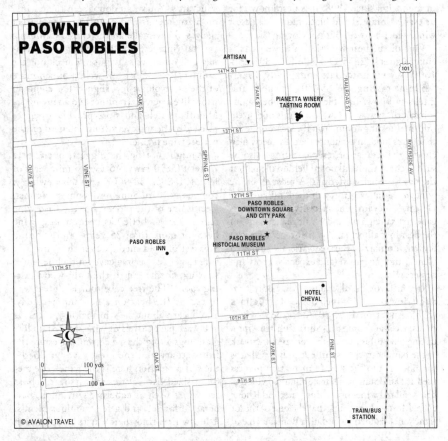

DOWNTOWN PASO ROBLES

ARTISAN
14TH ST
PIANETTA WINERY TASTING ROOM
13TH ST
12TH ST
PASO ROBLES DOWNTOWN SQUARE AND CITY PARK
PASO ROBLES INN
PASO ROBLES HISTOCIAL MUSEUM
11TH ST
HOTEL CHEVAL
10TH ST
9TH ST
TRAIN/BUS STATION
OAK ST
VINE ST
OLIVE ST
SPRING ST
PARK ST
RAILROAD ST
RIVERSIDE AV
PINE ST
PARK ST
0   100 yds
0   100 m
© AVALON TRAVEL
101

West, Highway 46 East (which does not directly connect to Hwy. 46 West), Downtown Paso Robles, and Remote—the area to the north of town on several roads branching away from U.S. 101.

Highway 46 West

The densest concentration of wineries cluster along Highway 46 West and the little roads that spring off that main thoroughfare. Many intrepid wine tasters never make it past this short and easy-to-travel stretch, which locals refer to as the Westside.

Rotta Winery (250 Winery Rd., 805/237-0510, www.rottawinery.com, daily 10:30am-5:30pm, tasting fee $5) has been making wine in the region since 1908. It is best known for its estate zinfandel and black monukka desert wine, which is sweet but not cloying.

One of the best wineries in these parts is **Hunt Cellars** (2875 Oakdale Rd., 805/237-1600, www.huntcellars.com, daily 10am-5:30pm, tasting fee $5-10). Friendly and intensely knowledgeable staff members pour some of the best wines in Paso at this mid-sized, informal tasting room. You'll enter a building that looks more like a house than a winery, then choose the regular or reserve tasting. Also be sure to check the chalkboard behind the bar for the day's specialty offerings. Almost all of the wines at Hunt are grown in the family-owned Destiny Vineyard. The specialty of the house is cabernet sauvignon, and Hunt makes some of the best in California. You'll also get to taste a few chardonnays, other red varietals, some red blends, and the famed (and expensive) port and dessert wines.

If you favor small wineries that only produce tiny runs of wine, **Dark Star Cellars** (2985 Anderson Rd., 805/237-2389, www. darkstarcellars.com, Fri.-Sun. 10:30am-5pm, tasting fee $10) is perfect for you. Be sure to ask at the bar about the "synthetic gravity" that is so important to the slow fermentation process used at Dark Star. You'll taste about 10 vintages here—all red wines of the Bordeaux and Rhone tribe. Most visitors think that the best of the lot is the much-lauded Ricordati, a Bordeaux blend

that wins international awards year after year. Perhaps the nicest surprise of all comes when you've picked your favorites; prices at Dark Star range up to about $35 a bottle, and many are under $30.

Highway 46 East

It's not as crowded as 46 West, but Highway 46 East has plenty of great wineries. You might even recognize one or two names out in the Eastside.

One of the biggest winemakers to maintain a tasting room in the Paso region is **Cellar 360 Paso Robles** (7000 Hwy. 46 E., 805/226-7133, www.meridianvineyards.com, Thurs.-Sun. 10am-5pm, tasting fee $5) at Meridian Vineyards. You've no doubt seen these wines on many menus and countless supermarket shelves. They make all the classic California varietal vintages, with bestsellers in chardonnay and cabernet sauvignon. Check out the Limited Release list for, well, a bunch more of the same plus a few slightly less common wines like a gewurztraminer and a sangiovese. Meridian's deli and store provide a perfect place to gather up everything you need for the perfect wine picnic.

It might not be the biggest, but **Eberle Winery** (3810 Hwy. 46 E., 3.5 miles east of U.S. 101, 805/238-9607, www.eberlewinery. com, daily 10am-5pm, until 6pm in summer, free) is one of the pioneers of the Paso wine region. Gary Eberle has been making wine here for more than 25 years, and winning a passel of gold medals over that time. Be sure to get a spot on a cave tour while you're visiting, then head to the light-wood tasting room. The free cave tour is a great way to escape the heat on a hot summer's day. You'll learn about the winemaking process as you walk past barrels of wine stacked up like giant logs along the cave's walls. Despite the fun statuary and the great caves at Eberle, the star attraction here is the wine. The medium-sized list features mostly hearty, bold red wines such as cabernet sauvignon, barbera, zinfandel, and a few fabulous blends. A few whites find their way to the bar, such

© STUART THORNTON

vineyards at Eberle Winery

as the Paso favorite viognier and the lesser-known roussanne. Taste as many as you possibly can—and you'll be surprised at how many bottles you'll want to walk away with. With most vintages selling for $15-25, you might be able to afford a few extras.

Downtown Paso Robles

Many wineries have set up tasting rooms right in the middle of downtown Paso.

At **Orchid Hill Vineyard** (1140 Pine St., 805/237-7525, www.orchidhillwine.com, daily noon-6pm, tasting fee $5) offers a small list of varietals, which includes viogniers, syrah, sangiovese, and zinfandel. Visitors also spend some time gaping at the walls, which bear the original artwork of local artists.

The Pianetta Winery's vineyards are 14 miles north of town, but the **Pianetta Winery Tasting Room** (829 13th St., 805/226-4005, www.pianettawinery.com, Sun.-Thurs. noon-6pm, Sat.-Sun. 11am-7pm, tasting fee $5) is right in the heart of Paso Robles. The Pianetta Winery is known for its cabernet sauvignons.

Remote Wineries

Even if you don't love wine, it's worth the trip up to **Adelaida Cellars** (5805 Adelaida Rd., 800/676-1232, www.adelaida.com, daily 10am-5pm, tasting fee $10). You'll get stunning views of Adelaida's mountain vineyards and down to the valley below. Adelaida wines are made mostly with grapes grown on the estate vineyards, and the results can be fabulous. Adelaida takes advantage of its high elevation and difficult soil to raise grapes that produce small lots of top-tier boutique wines. Their signature wine is their pinot noir. The winery produces vintages under four labels; the Reserve and Adelaida labels run toward the higher end, while the SLO and Schoolhouse labels provide tasty and affordable table wines suitable for everyday drinking.

A local producer with prestigious founders and backers, **Tablas Creek Vineyard** (9339 Adelaida Rd., 805/237-1231, www.tablascreek.com, daily 10am-5pm) specializes in Rhone and Chateauneuf-du-Pape varietals and blends. Taste from the longish list of current commercial and winery-only vintages. Tablas Creek takes its winemaking seriously, maintaining its own grapevine nursery, keeping its vineyards organic, and using only its own yeasts created on-site. If such practices interest you, call in advance to get a spot on the vineyard and winery tours (daily 10:30am and 2pm). End your survey of this showplace with a visit to the dark bar and bright artwork of the tasting room. You'll find many uncommon-for-California blends and varietals here, and the Tablas Creek bar staff can help you expand your palate and your knowledge of wine.

Halter Ranch Vineyard (8910 Adelaida Rd., 805/226-9455, www.halterranch.com, daily 11am-5pm, tasting fee $10) sits on a 1,000-acre ranch property once owned by a pioneer of the Paso Robles area. In 2000, the ranch was bought by a Swiss emigrant who planted almost 280 acres of grapes from the Bordeaux and Rhone varietal families. All the vineyards are farmed using organic and sustainable methods, which combine with the limestone-rich soil and unique climate to help create intensely flavorful wines. The ranch is fronted by a charming white Victorian farmhouse, and tours (call in advance) take you around both this house and the other historic buildings on the property, as well as the two winemaking facility structures. This newish winery has a small list from which to taste and purchase; its flagship vintages are syrah and cabernet sauvignon, but the less expensive ranch red and ranch white blends are also good buys.

Wine Festivals and Events

Consider coming to town during one of the several wine-oriented festivals held in and around Paso Robles. The biggest is the **Paso Robles Wine Festival** (www.pasowine.com, $55-125), which happens the third weekend of May each year. The central event of the festival, the Outdoor Wine Tasting, happens on Saturday in Paso's downtown city park. More than 80 wineries bring out their wares, making it fabulously easy to find your favorites and learn about some new vintners in the region.

In addition to the central tasting, most Paso wineries keep their tasting room doors open, offering tours, special tastings, food pairings, winemakers, and more. Buy your tickets for the wine festival well in advance.

In the fall, the **Harvest Wine Tour Weekend** (www.pasowine.com) celebrates the changing foliage of the grapevines and the frantic rush to bring in the grapes and start the juices fermenting. Nearly 100 wineries throughout Paso put on events during the third weekend of October. Check with your favorites to learn what's coming this year. You might want to sign up early for a cooking class, or just show up to join in on some messy but fun grape stomping. If you're lucky, you might even get to take a tour of a winemaking facility in full furor, and learn a bit about how your favorite vintages are made. As with the spring Wine Festival, it's a good idea to book your room and make your plans early for the Harvest Tour—the event has become quite popular with wine aficionados across the state and beyond.

Wine Tours

If you prefer not to do your own driving on your wine-tasting excursions (something to consider if everyone in your party enjoys wine), take one of the many available wine tours. **The Wine Wranglers** (866/238-6400, http://thewinewrangler.com, $90-120 depending on pick-up location) offers daily group tours, plus customized individual tours for a higher fee. Experienced guides will take you to some of the biggest and best wineries in the region. Group tour guests ride in the comfort of a small luxury bus; buses pick up tasters from Cambria, San Luis Obispo, Morro Bay, Pismo Beach, Paso Robles itself, and a number of other towns in the county. A picnic lunch in one of the vineyards is included, as are all tasting fees at the wineries you visit. If you know the region, feel free to request a stop at your favorite winery!

To taste at your own pace, contact **The Wine Line** (805/610-8267, www.hoponthewineline. com, starts at $60), where a chauffeured van will drop you off and pick you up at your choice of 60 wineries.

SIGHTS

It's not the biggest or most diverse, but you'll have fun exploring the **Charles Paddock Zoo** (9100 Morro Rd., Atascadero, 805/461-5080, www.charlespaddockzoo.org, daily 10am-4pm, adults $5, children $4). Plan an hour or two to make a leisurely tour of the funky prehensile-tailed porcupines and the famous slender-tailed meerkats. You can also visit the aviary to enjoy the twitters and squawks of more than a dozen varieties of common and exotic birds. The Zoo makes a fun destination if you've brought your kids to the largely adult playground that is Paso Robles.

A good spot for younger kids is the **Paso Robles Children's Museum at the Volunteer Firehouse** (623 13th St., 805/238-7432, www.pasokids.org, Sun. and Thurs.-Fri. 11am-4pm, Wed. and Sat. 10am-4pm, adults $7, children $6). As much a playground as a museum, the space offers themed interactive exhibits with a slight educational bent for toddlers and elementary school-aged children. Kids can draw, paint, climb, jump, play, and learn in one of the few spots in Paso Robles dedicated entirely to the younger set.

The **Paso Robles Pioneer Museum** (2010 Riverside Ave., 805/239-4556, www.pasoroblespioneermuseum.org, Thurs.-Sun. 1pm-4pm, free, donations welcome) celebrates the settlement of San Luis Obispo County. Exhibits have a distinctly Western Americana flavor and include some larger displays of carriages, farm equipment, and even an old one-room schoolhouse.

SPORTS AND RECREATION

Harris Stage Lines (5995 N. River Rd., 805/237-1860, www.harrisstagelines.com) doesn't offer the typical sedate trail rides. Instead of climbing up onto the back of a horse, you'll get into a refurbished historic coach or wagon and go for a ride like they did in the 19th century. Harris has a restored stagecoach, a chuck wagon, and even a couple of Hollywood-built Roman-style chariots. Call in advance to arrange the perfect outing for your party. If you're really into the historic vehicle

scene, you can even book a private driving lesson. Riding lessons are also available.

The craze for floating above vineyards in a balloon basket has made it as far as Paso Robles. This wine region sits in a pretty valley that's perfect for a romantic ballooning jaunt. **Let's Go Ballooning!** (meet at Rio Seco Winery, 4295 Union Rd., 805/458-1530, www.sloballoon.com, $189/person) can take you on a one-hour ride up over the Paso wine country any day of the week. You'll meet early at the Rio Seco Winery and spend 2-3 hours with your pilot, preparing and learning about how to ride safely.

Several minutes' drive from downtown Paso, the **River Oaks Hot Springs & Spa** (800 Clubhouse Dr., 805/238-4600, www.riveroakshotsprings.com, Tues.-Sun. 9am-9pm, $12-16/hour) sits on country club land over one of the local sulfur-heavy mineral springs. You'll smell the sulfur even as you drive up and walk from the parking lot to the spacious lobby. An attendant will show you the facilities and guide you to your room. A popular and reasonably priced option here is an hour of relaxation and healing in one of the outdoor or indoor open-air hot tubs. You can use the faucets to set your own perfect temperature, and gaze out into the thick gardens that screen the spas from the adjacent golf course. For a more thoroughly relaxing experience, pick a massage or facial treatment to go with your hot tub (or alone, if you don't care for sulfur water). Check the website for package specials (many of which include wine served in the privacy of your hot tub room) and aesthetic treatment options.

ACCOMMODATIONS

Accommodations around Paso Robles tend toward upscale wine-themed B&Bs. While in downtown Paso Robles, there are a couple of unique hotels.

$150-250

The **Orchard Hill Farm Bed & Breakfast** (5415 Vineyard Dr., 805/239-9680, www.orchardhillbb.com, $230-285) has an English country feel. The attractive manor house offers luxurious rooms with top-tier amenities, a gourmet breakfast, balconies off each room, and attractive grounds for walking and lounging.

The **Canyon Villa** (1455 Kiler Canyon Rd., 805/238-3362, www.thecanyonvilla. com, $235-285) is built in the Mediterranean style that suits this area as well. The decor of the four guest rooms continues the Italianate theme, while the oversized spa tubs, posh linens, private balconies, and gas fireplace create a feeling of lush comfort.

Over $250

A half block from Paso Robles' town square, the **Hotel Cheval** (1021 Pine St., 805/226-9995, www.hotelcheval.com, $300-475) is a boutique hotel with 16 rooms overlooking a courtyard with two outdoor word-burning fireplaces. Also on the grounds is the Pony Club, a wine and champagne bar that frequently hosts live music.

Even before Paso Robles was known for its wineries, the inland town was a destination for people who wanted to soak in its hot mineral waters. The **Paso Robles Inn** (1103 Spring St., 800/676-1713, http://pasoroblesinn.com, $251-409) taps into Paso's naturally occurring springs. Its deluxe spa rooms have a private mineral tub in the room or on their deck. Outside, there are gardens, a heated pool, and spa on the property, which dates back to 1891.

Out in the wooded region between Paso and the coast, the **Chanticleer Vineyard Bed and Breakfast** (1250 Paint Horse Pl., 805/226-0600, www.chanticleervineyardbb.com, $255) offers relaxed vacationing. Each of the three rooms includes an iPod dock, organic spa toiletries, a fresh, seasonal breakfast, vineyard views, and access to the house stock of cute fuzzy animals.

FOOD

Getting back to the heavily Mexican influence of Paso's agricultural roots, grab a taco or two at **Papi's** (840 13th St., 805/239-3720, daily 11am-9pm, $10). Prices may be a bit higher than some taquerias in honor of Paso's new tourist status, but the casual atmosphere and tasty tortas make up for it.

It's not the fanciest place in town, but the food at ◖ **Panolivo** (1344 Park St, 805/239-3366, www.panolivo.com, daily 7:30am-8:30pm, $17-28) might be the tastiest truly traditional French cuisine in town. Panolivo serves breakfast, lunch, and dinner every day. Panolivo's breakfast sandwich with cheese, ham, and a chives and parmesan egg omelet is a great way to start the day. For dinner, Panolivo serves a range from a lobster ravioli dish to bouef bourguignon.

At **Artisan** (1401 Park St., 805/237-8084, www.artisanpasorobles.com, Mon.-Thurs. 11am-2:30pm and 5pm-9pm, Fri.-Sat. 11am-2:30pm and 5pm-10pm, Sun. 10am-2:30pm and 2:30pm-5pm, $10-30), old school American cookery gets a California wine country makeover. The white tablecloths and numerous wine glasses hint at the fancy cuisine to come. At dinner, entrées include tea smoked duck breast and local rabbit, but don't miss the jalapeno cornbread with honey butter appetizer.

PRACTICALITIES

The closest thing to a visitors center is the **Paso Robles Chamber of Commerce** (1225 Park St., 805/238-0506, www.pasorobleschamber.com, Mon.-Fri. 8:30am-4:30pm, Sat.-Sun. 10am-2pm). Pick up a guide to Paso Robles, or specific dining, lodging, and winery information.

For medical attention, the nearest hospital is **Twin Cities Community Hospital** (1100 La Tablas Rd., 805/434-3500, www.twincitieshospital.com) in nearby Templeton.

The two best ways to get to Paso Robles are by car and by train. Drivers can take U.S. 101 from the north or the south directly to town. Once in Paso Robles, take Highway 46 east or west for the main wine road.

On the rails, the **Amtrak Coast Starlight** (www.amtrak.com) stops right in Paso. Avoid driving altogether by taking the train into town, then renting a limo or getting on with a wine tour.

Pismo Beach

Walking around Pismo Beach, it feels like you've stepped back in time to a southern California beach town from 50 years ago. With its long running, sandy beach studded with lifeguard stands and volleyball courts, the coastline in front of this community could be in Los Angeles County or Orange County. The main attraction—besides the surf and sand—is the 1,200-foot-long Pismo Pier. On either side of the pier, surfers ride peaky waves. Meanwhile, anglers dangle their fishing poles off the side, hoping to land a perch or smelt.

Formerly known as the "Clam Capital of the World," Pismo used to be the best place to gather the famous Pismo Clam, an edible bivalve that can be found on sandy beaches from Half Moon Bay to Baja California. Nowadays due to over-farming and the fact that sea otters have been munching on lots of the tasty bivalves, the clam population is so low that there is basically no clamming going on anymore in Pismo.

The town's one-way Pomeroy Avenue is like Main Street. It is lined with beachwear shops, candy stores, and fish and chips restaurants.

Getting to Pismo Beach is easy. Exit right off U.S. 101. While there may be no must-see attractions in Pismo, the town makes a good stop-over between San Francisco and Los Angeles. It's close to Morro Bay, Hearst Castle, and Montana de Oro State Park—and it's an ideal place to enjoy the simple pleasures of the beach.

SIGHTS
Pismo Pier

The first **Pismo Pier** (end of Pomeroy Ave.) was built for shipping back in 1881. Though that pier and another were destroyed by storms, the third version, built in 1985 and 1986, still

© STUART THORNTON

Pismo Beach

stands today. Walking out on the pier is a great way to get an eyeful of the far ranging Pismo Beach and the Oceano Dunes to the south. A small concession shack on the pier sells snacks and rents bodyboards and fishing rods.

Oceano Dunes

It's a rare treat to be able to actually drive on one of California's beaches, and that is possible, as long as you have the right vehicle, at the **Oceano Dunes State Vehicular Recreation Area** (three miles south of Pismo Beach off Hwy. 1, 805/473-7220, www.parks.ca.gov, day use 6am-11pm, $5/day per vehicle). There are 3,600 acres of dunes, beach, wetlands, lakes, and riparian areas to explore by four-wheel drive, dune buggy, four wheeler, or foot. In the 1930s and 1940s, the dunes were home to the "Dunites," a collective of mystics, nudists, writers, and artists who believed that the dunes were a center for creative energy. Be careful if you decide to drive on the beach without the proper vehicle. Getting your car stuck in the sand can make for a long afternoon. You can also rent ATVs for the dunes at **B.J.'s ATV Rentals** (197 Grand Ave., Grover Beach, 805/481-5411, www.bjsatvrentals.com) and **Arnie's ATV Rentals** (311 Pier Ave., Oceano, 805/474-6060, http://pismoatvrentals.com).

If you want to explore the dunes but you don't have the proper vehicle, the **Oceano Dunes Preserve Trail** (two or more miles round-trip) allows hikers to experience the region without fear of getting run over.

Pismo Beach Monarch Butterfly Grove

Sure, beachgoers and anglers flock to Pismo Beach, but the coastal community's most popular visitors are the thousands of monarch butterflies that take over a forest of eucalyptus and pine trees in the **Pismo Beach Monarch Butterfly Grove** (Hwy. 1 at the southernmost end of the City of Pismo Beach, 800/443-7778, www.monarchbutterfly.org) between November and February. During this time, docents and volunteers are onsite to answer questions 10am-4pm.

Dinosaur Caves Park

Not your usual city park, **Dinosaur Caves Park** (corner of Cliff St. and Shell Beach Rd., 805/773-4657, www.pismobeach.org, daily sunrise-sunset, free) offers 11 acres of serious play for the wee ones, with concrete dolphins, an orca, and best of all a friendly-looking dinosaur and three cracked dinosaur eggs.

ENTERTAINMENT AND EVENTS

Harry's Night Club & Beach Bar (690 Cypress St., 805/773-1010, www.qualitysites.com, daily 10am-2am) has live bands every night of the week except for Thursday, which is karaoke night. Expect most of the acts to be classic rock cover bands. Harry's also has big screen TVs for taking in sporting events and three pool tables for those who'd like to shoot a game or two.

The **Pismo Beach Clam Festival** (805/773-4382, www.pismochamber.com) honors the beach town's clamming past every fall with a clam chowder cook-off and a clam dig. The fest also highlights other aspects of Pismo with surf lessons, live music, and a wine walk.

In June, one of California's largest car shows takes over downtown Pismo and the pier during the **Classic at Pismo Beach Car Show** (866/450-7469, http://thepismobeachclassic.com). Over 1,000 show vehicles are displayed at this free event.

SHOPPING

There is shopping to be done in Pismo Beach. To save money on some big name clothing brands, head to the **Pismo Beach Premium Outlets** (333 Five Cities Dr., 805/773-4661, www.premiumoutlets.com, Mon.-Sat. 10am-9pm, Sun. 10am-7pm), where Levi's, Lane Bryant, PacSun, and others have outlet stores.

SPORTS AND RECREATION
Fishing

Anglers can try their luck at trying to snag a big one off the Pismo Pier. The pier is the most heavily fished and second-most productive pier on the Central Coast. If you didn't bring a rod, you can rent one from the small shack on the pier. No license is required for fishing off the pier.

If you'd rather head out into deeper waters, contact **Patriot Sportfishing** (805/595-7200, www.patriotsportfishing.com, adults $82/full-day, children under 12 $52/full-day) out of nearby Avila Beach. Their specialty is rock cod fishing.

Surfing

On either side of the Pismo Pier, waves consistently break for surfers. One of the best aspects of surfing the pier is that the surf is less susceptible to getting destroyed by the winds that wreck waves at other local breaks. Rent a board from **Pismo Beach Surf Shop** (470 Price St., 805/773-2089, www.pismobeachsurfshop.com, $18-35/half-day, $35-50/full-day).

Kiteboarding and Stand Up Paddleboarding

One way to experience the ocean at Pismo is to ride on a board powered by wind or paddle. **California Kiteboarding** (695 Price St., Suite 103, 805/550-3768, www.pismobeachkiteboarding.com) offers lessons on how to kiteboard ($240/three hours) and how to stand up paddleboard ($85/two-hour private lesson, $65/two-hour group lesson).

Horseback Riding

Exploring the coastline just south of Pismo Beach by horseback is possible through the **Pacific Dunes RV Resort and Riding Stables** (1205 Silver Spur Pl., Oceano, 805/489-7787 or 888/908-7787, $50). Their one-hour rides go between dunes and out to the beach.

ACCOMMODATIONS

Pismo Beach's best lodging options are located on bluffs north of the pier and the small downtown area.

Every room at the moderately priced **Kon Tiki Inn** (1621 Price St., 805/773-4833, www.kontikiinn.com, $170-200) has a sweeping view of the ocean as well as a patio or balcony. In front of the large hotel, there is a heated pool, hot tubs, and a staircase to the beach below.

One perk of staying at the Kon Tiki is that guests get full use of the adjacent Pismo Beach Athletic Club, which offers Zumba classes and has an indoor lap pool.

The exteriors of the buildings at the **Cottage Inn By the Sea** (2351 Price St., www.cottage-inn.com, $99-359) are meant to conjure up images of the English countryside. All of the rooms have gas fireplaces, a fridge, and a microwave. The Cottage Inn also has a heated pool and hot tub. Past the small pool deck is a spot on the bluffs over the beach with chairs and tables set up. It's a perfect location to take in the sunset or the stars with the Pismo Pier in the distance.

For families or even couples who want to stretch out a bit, the ◖ **Pismo Lighthouse Suites** (2411 Price St., 805/773-2411, www.pismolighthousesuites.com, $229-429) all have two rooms and two bathrooms, which is a rare hotel luxury. In addition, the suites have nautical decor, like lamps designed to resemble lighthouses and paintings of sea scenes, while the oceanfront suites each include a balcony or patio to take in the fine views of the Pacific or Pismo Beach. Kids will love the family play deck that has a small mini golf course, ping pong tables, a badminton course, and a giant chess and checkers set. In addition, there's a heated pool, a spa, and beach access.

CAMPING

Pismo State Beach has two campground options. The **Oceano Campground** (555 Pier Ave., Oceano, 800/444-7275, www.parks.ca.gov, tent sites $35, RVs $50) is ideal for birders. It is adjacent to a migratory bird habitat surrounding a lagoon. Also in the park is the **North Beach Campground** (Hwy. 1, Pismo Beach, 800/444-7275, www.parks.ca.gov, tent sites $35) that is in close proximity to the Pismo Beach Monarch Butterfly Grove.

FOOD
Italian

Guiseppe's Cucina Italiana (891 Price St., 805/773-2870, www.giuseppesrestaurant.com, Mon.-Thurs. 11:30am-3pm and 4:30pm-10pm, Fri. 11:30am-3pm and 4:30pm-11pm, Sat. 4:30pm-11pm, Sun. 4:30pm-10pm, $12-32) began as the senior project of a Cal Poly student. Now, almost 25 years later, the restaurant is still highlighting the cuisine of the Pugliese region of Italy with pastas, meat dishes, and wood-fired pizzas, including one topped with clams.

Markets

Like most California coastal towns, Pismo Beach has its own weekly **farmer's market** (Pismo Pier, 805/773-4382, www.pismochamber.com, Wed. 3pm-6pm) on Wednesday afternoons.

Mexican

By the string of hotels on Price Street, the sleek, stylish **◖ Ventana Grill** (2575 Price St., 805/773-0000, http://ventanagrill.com, Mon.-Thurs. 11:30am-9pm, Fri.-Sat. 11:30am-10pm, Sun. 10am-9pm, $14-39) serves up tasty California-Mexican dishes with ocean views. Menu items include entrées like tequila lime chicken, Alaskan halibut ceviche, and crab encrusted mahi mahi. Ventana also has some darn good margaritas in unique flavors like prickly pear and pineapple.

Away from the tourist strip in Shell Beach, **Zorro's Café & Cantina** (927 Shell Beach Rd., 805/773-9676, daily 7:30am-9pm, $10-18) serves Mexican and American style breakfast, lunch, and dinners. Breakfast has unique offerings like chile relleno and eggs, while dinner has more typical items including fajitas and burritos.

Seafood

On most days a line snakes out of the brightly colored **◖ Splash Café** (197 Pomeroy Ave., 805/773-4653, www.splashcafe.com, Sun.-Thurs. 8am-8:30pm, Fri.-Sat. 8am-9pm, $5-10). People are willing to wait for a taste of the eatery's popular clam chowder. It's not health food, but the rich, buttery clam chowder (served in a cup, bowl, or bread bowl) utilizes three different types of clams and hits the spot

on a chilly day or after spending some time in the nearby Pacific. They also serve fish tacos, burgers, and fried seafood.

For a more sophisticated menu and better views, dine at **Steamers of Pismo** (1601 Price St., 805/773-4711, www.steamerspismobeach.com, Mon.-Thurs. 11:30am-3pm and 4:30pm-9pm, Fri. 11:30am-3pm and 4:30pm-10pm, Sat. 11:30am-3pm and 4pm-10pm, Sun. 11:30am-3pm and 4pm-9pm, $16-33). The menu has deep fried seafood and chips platters along with shrimp jambalya and chorizo and clam linguine. Steamers' happy hour (Sun.-Thurs. 3pm-7pm, Fri.-Sat. 3pm-6pm) offers a sampler of steamed clams, a fish taco, and a cocktail for the price of a dinner entrée.

It's not a good idea to wear your best clothes to the **Cracked Crab** (751 Price St., 805/773-2722, www.crackedcrab.com, Sun.-Thurs. 11am-9pm, Fri.-Sat. 11am-10pm, $12-53). The signature dish is a bucket for two of three kinds of shellfish steamed with Cajun sausage, red potatoes, and corn. You are given a mallet, a crab cracker, and a bib. If that sounds like too much work, order a seafood sandwich or another entrée like grilled albacore.

INFORMATION AND SERVICES

There's a **California Welcome Center Pismo Beach** (333 Five Cities Dr., Suite 100, 805/773-7924, www.visitcwc.com, Mon.-Sat. 10am-9pm, Sun. 10am-7pm) located at the Pismo Premium Outlets. In the center of Pismo Beach, the **Pismo Beach Chamber of Commerce Visitor Information Center** (581 Dolliver St., 805/773-4382 or 800/443-7778, www.pismochamber.com, Mon.-Fri. 10am-5pm, Sat. 10am-2pm) has pamphlets, maps, and information. There are a few banks in Pismo Beach along with a **post office** (100 Crest Dr., 805/481-5971, www.usps.com, Mon.-Fri. 9am-5:30pm, Sat. 9am-2pm). The nearby **Arroyo Grande Community Hospital** (345 South Halcyon Rd., 805/489-4261, www.arroyograndehospital.org) has services for emergencies.

SANTA BARBARA AND VENTURA

The California coast changes dramatically at Point Conception, which sticks out like an elbow into the Pacific. It's where the west-facing coastline tilts to face south, and the colder waters of the Pacific collide with the distinctly warmer Santa Barbara current. This is also where the more rugged Northern and Central coastline gives way to the Southern California beaches of the popular imagination.

As Highway 1 moves south into Santa Barbara County, you reach the Gaviota Coast. Its popular state parks and beaches are the last major holdout of wilderness along the Pacific before the coastline succumbs to development and Southern California sprawl. Places like idyllic Refugio State Beach offer escape from civilization to droves of visitors from Santa Barbara and farther south.

One of California's most picturesque cities, Santa Barbara is where Southern California begins. You'll notice a plethora of palm trees and chic, healthy residents. It's famous for its pleasant Mediterranean climate and Spanish Colonial Revival architecture. After a 1925 earthquake, the city rebuilt itself in the style of the Santa Barbara Mission, arguably the most beautiful of the California missions, with white stucco surfaces, red-tiled roofs, arches, and courtyards.

South of Santa Barbara, the city of Ventura has a grittier, more urban feel than Santa Barbara. It's charming and walkable, with a historic downtown and popular beach boardwalk, but its biggest attraction is its reliable surf break.

Offshore, the Channel Islands hover on the horizon like ghosts of the California coast's former self. Commonly reached by boat, these

SANTA BARBARA

HIGHLIGHTS

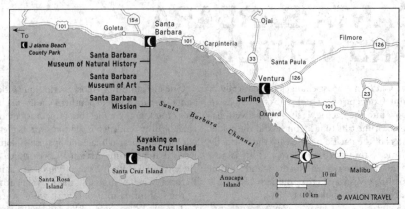

LOOK FOR ◖ TO FIND RECOMMENDED SIGHTS, ACTIVITIES, DINING, AND LODGING.

◖ **Santa Barbara Museum of Natural History:** This extensive museum includes a planetarium and a sea center. Impressive exhibits include a giant blue whale skeleton and a pygmy mammoth specimen. (page 444).

◖ **Santa Barbara Mission:** Graceful architecture, serene surroundings, and an informative museum make this the "Queen of the Missions" (page 445).

◖ **Santa Barbara Museum of Art:** This underrated gem houses fascinating temporary exhibits and an impressive permanent collection that includes French impressionist master-pieces (page 446).

◖ **Surfing:** Surfers of all abilities flock to the consistent waves of Ventura's **C Street** (page 466) and Santa Barbara's **Rincon** (page 450), which offers some of California's best winter waves.

◖ **Jalama Beach County Park:** With great surfing, fishing, camping, and beachcombing, this stretch of remote, undeveloped coastline is perfect for getting away from it all (page 461).

◖ **Kayaking on Santa Cruz Island:** There is no better way to experience the sea caves of the Channel Islands than by kayak (page 471).

isolated islands (Anacapa, Santa Cruz, Santa Rosa, San Miguel, and Santa Barbara) offer visitors a glimpse of the wild, undeveloped coastline of over 100 years ago, as well as amazing recreational opportunities and encounters with rare endemic animal species.

PLANNING YOUR TIME

It's possible to explore this section of the Santa Barbara and Ventura coast in a weekend. Both Santa Barbara and Ventura make fine bases of operations to enjoy this region, though accommodations in the former can be quite pricey.

With U.S. 101 stringing Ventura, Santa Barbara, and the sections of the Gaviota Coast together, the region is easy to travel around in. For the most part, the City of Santa Barbara has ample signs directing you to its downtown and other sites, including the Santa Barbara Mission.

Those wanting to travel out to more remote places like the Channel Islands National Park and remote sections of the Gaviota Coast, particularly Jalama Beach County Park, should add a few days to their stay in the region. Getting out to the Channel Islands involves getting a space on a boat or plane. In addition, boats travel to some islands only every few days. It is nice to secure a hotel in Ventura or Santa Barbara after a camping expedition on the islands to ease yourself back into civilization before heading on to your next destination.

Santa Barbara

It's been called the American Riviera, with weather, community, and sun-drenched beaches reminiscent of the Mediterranean coast. In truth, Santa Barbara is all California.

Nestled between the Pacific Ocean and the mountains, its copious sunshine, wide roads, warm sandy beaches, and challenging mountain trails inspire physical activity and healthy living. Along the waterfront, a paved path allows anyone on two feet, two wheels, or anything else that moves to enjoy the coastline alongside grassy areas with palm trees gently swaying in the breeze. At least five weekly area farmers markets make healthy produce abundant and accessible.

Santa Barbara is also where beach culture meets high culture. You'll find lots of museums, outdoor shopping areas, great restaurants, and four-star resorts. And a growing young wine region thrives. But the pace of life slows down enough to make it a favorite escape for Southern California locals as well. It's not surprising that many of these refugees from Los Angeles decide to stay and become Santa Barbara residents.

SIGHTS
Santa Barbara Maritime Museum
It's only fitting that the **Santa Barbara Maritime Museum** (113 Harbor Way, Suite 190, 805/962-8404, www.sbmm.org, Thurs.-Tues. 10am-5pm, until 6pm Memorial Day-Labor Day, adults $7, children and seniors $4, free for military personnel in uniform) sits right on the working harbor. It began as a Government Works Project during the Depression. For more than 50 years, the station was used by the U.S. Navy as a training facility. After being sold back to the city of Santa Barbara in 1995, construction began on the museum, which opened in 2000. A dozen

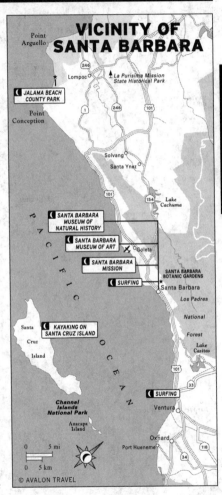

different exhibits, including ones on shipwrecks, commercial fishing, and surfing, show off the history of the California coast's relationship to the sea. The Munger Theater screens

SANTA BARBARA

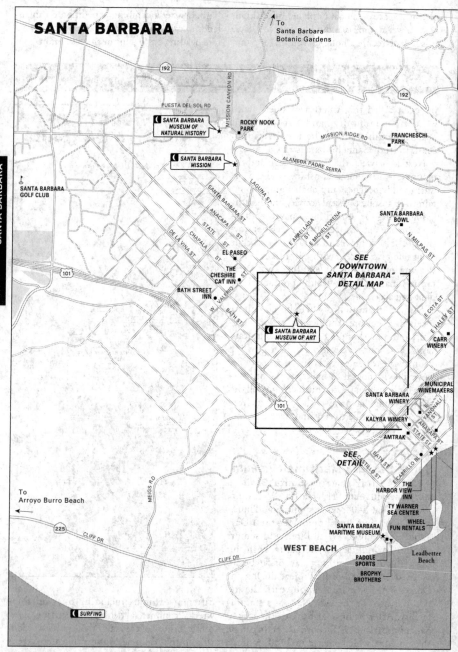

SANTA BARBARA

To
Santa Barbara
Botanic Gardens

192

PUESTA DEL SOL RD

☾ SANTA BARBARA MUSEUM OF NATURAL HISTORY ★

ROCKY NOOK PARK

MISSION RIDGE RD

FRANCHESCHI PARK

192

ALAMEDA PADRE SERRA

☾ SANTA BARBARA MISSION ★

LAGUNA ST

SANTA BARBARA ST

SANTA BARBARA GOLF CLUB

ANACAPA ST

STATE ST

E ARRELLAGA ST

E MICHELTORENA ST

SANTA BARBARA BOWL

N MILPAS ST

DE LA VINA ST

CHAPALA ST

EL PASEO

THE CHESHIRE CAT INN ●

101

BATH STREET INN ●

W VALERIO ST

BATH ST

VALERIO ST

SEE "DOWNTOWN SANTA BARBARA" DETAIL MAP

E COTA ST

E HALEY ST

CARR WINERY

☾ SANTA BARBARA MUSEUM OF ART ★

101

SANTA BARBARA WINERY ■

KALYRA WINERY ■

AMTRAK ■

MUNICIPAL WINEMAKERS ■

E YANONALI ST

ANACAPA ST

STATE ST

SEE DETAIL

BATH ST

CASTILLO ST

E CABRILLO BL

THE HARBOR VIEW INN

To
Arroyo Burro Beach

MEIGS RD

225

CLIFF DR

CLIFF DR

TY WARNER SEA CENTER

WHEEL FUN RENTALS

SANTA BARBARA MARITIME MUSEUM ★

WEST BEACH

Leadbetter Beach

PADDLE SPORTS

BROPHY BROTHERS

☾ SURFING

SANTA BARBARA

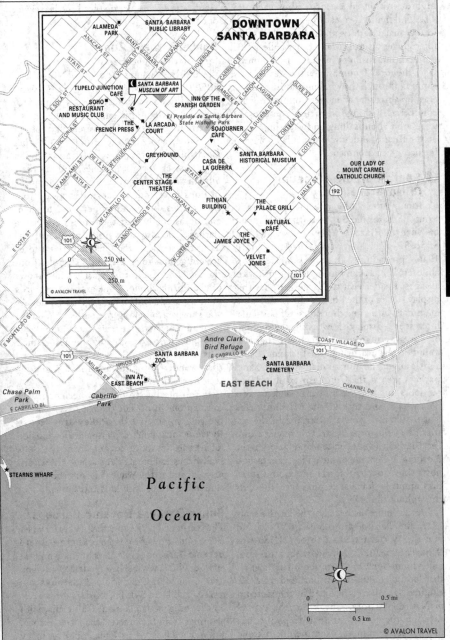

high-definition educational films each day. The Children's Area features hands-on exhibits that make learning about the sea lots of fun for younger visitors. Many other galleries tell the maritime history of California, beginning with the local Chumash Native Americans, running through the whaling and fur-hunting eras, up through the modern oil drilling and commercial fishing industries. You can also learn a bit about sailing and yachting, safety on the Pacific, and how you can help preserve the ocean's environment.

C Santa Barbara Museum of Natural History

Continuing the outdoors theme that pervades Santa Barbara, the **Santa Barbara Museum of Natural History** (2559 Puesta del Sol, 805/682-4711, www.sbnature.org, daily 10am-5pm, adults $11, seniors and teens $8, children $7) has exhibits to delight visitors of all ages. Inside, visit the large galleries that display stories of the life and times of insects, mammals, birds, and dinosaurs. Of particular interest is a display showcasing the remains of a pygmy mammoth specimen that was found on the nearby Channel Islands. Learn a little about the human history of the Santa Barbara area at the Chumash exhibit. Head outdoors to circle the immense skeleton of a blue whale, and to hike the Mission Creek Nature Trail. If you're interested in the nature of worlds other than this one, go into the **Gladwin Planetarium** and wander the Astronomy Center exhibits. The Planetarium hosts shows portraying the moon and stars, plus monthly Star Parties and special events throughout the year.

If you're more interested in the Earth's array of sea life, head down to Stearns Wharf and visit the **Ty Warner Sea Center** (211 Stearns Wharf, 805/962-2526, www.sbnature.org, daily 10am-5pm, multi-museum passes at either location, adults $8, seniors and teens $7, children $5), which is operated by the Museum of Natural History. Check out the tunnel through the 1,500-gallon tide pool tank, touch a sea cucumber, examine microscopic sea creatures, and get involved in the science of oceanography.

Santa Barbara Zoo

It's not the biggest zoo in the state, but the **Santa Barbara Zoo** (500 Ninos Dr., 805/962-5339, www.sbzoo.org, daily 10am-5pm, adults $14, children and seniors $10) is a cool little municipal zoo. It shelters its critters in enclosures that resemble those of the San Diego Zoo, including a multi-species habitat that mimics an African savannah with giraffes, tortoises, cranes, and meerkats all hanging out together. Granted, the pride of lions next door are corralled away from the giraffes, but you can get close to them and occasionally hear them roar. The Santa Barbara Zoo also takes pride in its local, endangered species—the Channel Island foxes are indigenous to an area only 20 miles from the zoo. The "California Trail" exhibit shows off California condors, one of the rarest birds in the state and still an endangered species. As you slowly stroll along the paths, you'll also see giant anteaters, huge elephants, monkeys, and snow leopards. One of the best-named kids' exhibits ever, "Eeeww!" showcases reptiles, wonderfully slimy amphibians, and insects at children's eye level.

If you need a stroller or wheelchair, you can rent one just inside the zoo. Also close to the gate you'll find the **Ridley-Tree House Restaurant,** which offers plenty of outside tables and a walk-up arrangement that sells sandwiches and burgers. Also there's Mexican-inspired fare at **The Wave.** The gift shop offers cute souvenirs for both kids and adults.

Santa Barbara Botanic Gardens

The year-round perfect weather makes for a perfect spot to grow the gorgeous **Santa Barbara Botanic Gardens** (1212 Mission Canyon Rd., 805/682-4726, www.sbbg.org, daily 9am-5pm, until 6pm Mar.-Oct., adults $8, seniors and teens $6, children $4). The gardens focus solely on the indigenous plants of California, with plantings from the deserts, chaparral, arroyo, and more. The gardens spread out over many acres and cross several hiking trails. Check out the small stand of coastal redwoods, the centerpiece of the park, which remains shaded and cool even when the sun beats down in the heat of summertime. Another proud garden shows off the beauty of native California lilacs. The mission of the gardens encompasses conservation of not only the California wilderness areas, but the water and soil in developed areas as well. Visit the Home Demonstration Garden for an example of beautiful landscaping using California natives that are suited to the climate and conditions, and thus need less irrigation and chemical fertilizers.

Guided tours are offered on Saturdays and Sundays at 11am and 2pm with your admission ticket—join the standard tour or call ahead to arrange a private tour. You can take your own self-guided tour with a map and the advice of the docents. The shop offers books and garden-themed gifts, while the nursery sells native Californian plants. The garden does not include a restaurant or snack bar.

◖ Santa Barbara Mission

It's easy to see why the **Santa Barbara Mission** (2201 Laguna St., 805/682-4713, http://santabarbaramission.org, daily 9am-4:30pm, self-guided tours adults $5, seniors $4, children $1, children 6 and under free, docent-guided tours Thurs.-Fri. 11am, Sat. 10:30am, adults $8, children free) is referred to as the "Queen of the Missions." It is larger, more beautiful, and more impressive than many of the other missions. It is also second to none for its art displays and graceful architecture, all of which are complemented by the serene local climate and scenery. Unlike many of the California missions, the church at Santa Barbara remained in service after the secularization of the mission chain in the 19th century. When you visit, you'll find the collection of buildings, artwork, and even the ruins of the water system in better shape than at many other missions in the state. The self-guided tour includes a walk through the mission's striking courtyard with its blooming flowers and towering palm trees and entrance

© STUART THORNTON

the striking Santa Barbara Mission

to the mission museum, which has among other displays a photo of the church after an earthquake in 1925 toppled its towers and a collection of Chumash artifacts. The original purpose of the mission was to transform the native Chumash into Christians. The mission's cemetery is the final resting place of more than 4,000 of these Chumash people.

◀ Santa Barbara Museum of Art

The two-floor **Santa Barbara Museum of Art** (1130 State St., 805/963-4364, www.sbma.net, Tues.-Sun. 11am-5pm, adults $9, seniors, students with ID, and children $6) has an impressive art collection that would make some larger cities envious. Wander the spacious, well-curated museum and take in some paintings from the museum's collection of Monets, which is the largest collection of the French impressionist's paintings in the West. Also the museum has ancient works like a bronze head of Alexander from Roman times and a collection of Asian artifacts including a 17th- or 18th-century Tibetan prayer wheel. There are interesting temporary exhibitions on display as well.

WINERIES

The wines of Santa Barbara County have been receiving favorable reviews and write-ups in the national media. The area is predominantly known for pinot noir and chardonnay, but with the diversity of microclimates, there are over 50 grape varietals planted here. This means you can find traditional varieties like cabernet sauvignon, merlot, sauvignon blanc, and syrah, but also sangiovese, dolcetto, viognier, cabernet franc, malbec, and others.

Santa Barbara

Not all wine-tasting is done surrounded by vineyards. On the **Urban Wine Trail** (www. urbanwinetrailsb.com) you can sample some of the county's best wines without even seeing a vine. Near Lower State Street, a block from the beach, you can walk to six tasting rooms. Visiting others that are part of the trail will require a little driving. Recently passed legislation means that some, but not all, wineries

can now offer wines by the glass in addition to wine-tasting, so if you sample something you like, you can purchase a glass to enjoy on the spot or a bottle to take with you.

Kalyra Winery (212 State St., 805/965-8606, www.kalyrawinery.com, Mon.-Fri. noon-7pm, Sat.-Sun. noon-8pm) is famous for having been featured in the 2004 movie *Sideways*. This tasting room wasn't in the film, but you can still sample the California and Australian wines made by Mike Brown, an Aussie and an avid surfer. There's a tiki room setting here. Kalyra started out making sweet wines, and still offers quite a few, but has a broad portfolio.

Once you're done at Kalyra Winery, walk a block down Yanonali Street to **Santa Barbara Winery** (202 Anacapa St., 805/963-3633, www.sbwinery.com, daily 10am-5pm), the oldest winery in the county, started in 1962. The chardonnay is delightful and truly expresses a Santa Barbara character with its bright citrus notes. Other varieties include pinot noir, sangiovese, and sauvignon blanc. If you are looking to sample a diverse array of wines, this is your best stop. The tasting bar is just a few feet from the barrel room, and there's a good-size gift shop.

Municipal Winemakers (22 Anacapa St., 805/931-6864, www.municipalwinemakers.com, Sun.-Wed. 11am-6pm, Thurs.-Sat. 11am-11pm, tasting $10) is in an unpretentious small space with an even smaller deck. Inside are rough wood ceilings and plain walls, with a four-top table and standing room at the bar. This is a weekend venture for owner Dave Potter, who will answer your questions and pour his wines. The offerings are Rhone-style wines, including Grenache, syrah, and a sparkling shiraz.

Carr Winery (414 N. Salsipuedes St., 805/965-7985, www.carrwinery.com, Sun.-Wed. 11am-6pm, Thurs.-Sat. 11am-8pm, tasting $10) focuses on small lots of syrah, Grenache, cabernet franc, and pinot noir. The tasting room is in a World War II Quonset hut, with a bar up front and tables in the back. The wine bar features live music on Fridays and house wines on tap.

Santa Maria Valley

Detour to the Santa Maria Valley to sample wines in the region made famous by the movie *Sideways*. Running roughly parallel to U.S. 101, **Foxen Canyon Road** is a back road hugging the foothills, with multiple wineries along the way.

From the south, take the Alisos Canyon Road turnoff from U.S. 101, about 25 miles north of the Highway 1-U.S. 101 split. Take Alisos Canyon Road 6.5 miles and turn left onto Foxen Canyon Road. Foxen Winery is about 5.5 miles down the road. Foxen Canyon Road eventually turns into East Betteravia Road and connects back to U.S. 101.

From the north, take the East Betteravia Road exit from U.S. 101, and head east about three miles until it turns into Foxen Canyon Road. From this point, Tepusquet Road, where Kenneth Volk is located, is about 10 miles away.

Foxen Winery now has two tasting rooms: the solar powered **Foxen** (7600 Foxen Canyon Rd., 805/937-4251, daily 11am-4pm, tasting $10) and the rustic, shack-like **Foxen 7200** (7200 Foxen Canyon Rd., 805/937-4251, daily 11am-4pm, tasting $10). The newer Foxen at the 7600 location is where you can sample burgundy, Rhones and the underappreciated chenin blanc. Head to Foxen 7200 for Bordeaux or Tuscan varieties. Foxen's long-standing reputation goes back six generations, and its 10 acres are the only dry-farmed vineyard in the area, meaning that irrigation is not used.

Set in an old barn, **Rancho Sisquoc** (6600 Foxen Canyon Rd., 805/934-4332, www.ranchosisquoc.com, Mon.-Thurs. 10am-4pm, Fri.-Sun. 10am-5pm, tasting $8) makes a beautiful spot for a picnic. The wood-sided tasting room is rustic but comfortable, and the surrounding setting—a vast field with low hills in the distance—is perfect for some quiet, wine-enhanced relaxation.

Located on a little road off Foxen Canyon Road, award-winning **Kenneth Volk Vineyards** (5230 Tepusquet Rd., 805/938-7896, www.volkwines.com, daily 10:30am-4:30pm, tasting $10) offers all the strange wines you've never tried. In addition to the standard offerings like chardonnay, pinot noir, viognier, cabernet sauvignon, and merlot, Kenneth Volk is a champion of heirloom varieties: funky, wonderfully oddball wines like the Portuguese grape wine touriga and the jasmine aroma white wine torrantes. You won't regret the long trek to get to the tranquil property along the Tepusquet Creek, surrounded by oak and sycamore trees.

At the southern end of Foxen Canyon is another cluster of wineries, not too far from Los Olivos. One of the oldest wineries in the county, **Zaca Mesa Winery** (6905 Foxen Canyon Rd., Los Olivos, 805/688-9339, www.zacamesa.com, daily 10am-4pm, Memorial Day-Labor Day Fri.-Sat. open until 5pm, tasting $10) is the kind of winery tasters love to discover. A mid-sized producer with a mid-sized facility and tasting room, Zaca quietly makes some of the best Central Coast wines to be found anywhere in the region. The first vineyards on the property were planted in the early 1970s, long before anyone else saw Santa Barbara as a place with potential for great winemaking. In 1978, Zaca Mesa planted the first syrah in Santa Barbara County. Zaca makes many of the Rhone varietals that grow so well in the climate of the Central Coast, such as viognier, roussanne, and syrah. Classics lovers will enjoy the chardonnay, and adventurous types shouldn't skip the syrahs and the Z Cuvee. After or while imbibing, play a game of chess on the winery's life-size chessboard or take a stroll on their hiking trail.

ENTERTAINMENT AND EVENTS

A wealthy town with close ties to cosmopolitan Los Angeles, Santa Barbara offers visitors a wealth of live cultural displays, from a symphony and opera to a near-endless parade of festivals. The students of UCSB add a lively bit of zest to the town's after-dark scene.

Bars and Clubs

The proximity of UCSB to downtown Santa Barbara guarantees a livelier nighttime scene than you'll find elsewhere on the Central

Coast. Check with the locals to discover the ever-changing hot spots. Bars cluster on State Street and beyond, and plenty of hip clubs dot the landscape here.

The best place to start an evening out on the town is at **Joe's Café** (536 State St., 805/966-4638, www.joescafesb.com, daily 7:30am-11pm). This steakhouse and bar is known for the stiffest drinks in town. Don't expect a fancy cocktail menu. Just go with the classics in this historic establishment with a throwback feel due to its checkered tablecloths, tin paneled ceiling, and framed black and white photos of mostly old men adorning the walls.

Tonic (634 State St., 805/897-1800, www.tonicsb.com, Thurs.-Sat. 8pm-1:30am) has a hipster feel, complete with exposed brick walls and a long glass bar. Top-flight DJs spin a mostly hip-hop or house groove, with the occasional mash-up for variety. Tonic also hosts college nights and ladies nights. Two lounges provide a respite from the partiers at the main bar and on the dance floor. To cool down, go outside to the huge outdoor patio, which has its own funky octagonal bar.

If you prefer to dance and drink to live bands, head over to **Velvet Jones** (423 State St., 805/965-8676, www.velvet-jones.com, daily 9pm-2am). Artists as big as the Foo Fighters have performed at the venue in the last few years. Beware that on Wednesdays the bar hosts an 18 and up electronic music dance night. Check the calendar at the website for upcoming events and shows.

Located in an upstairs suite, **Soho** (1221 State St., Suite 205, 805/962-7776, http://sohosb.com, doors open at daily 5pm) has hosted big time touring acts including Jimmy Cliff, Donavon, and Built to Spill. It has live music seven nights a week. With its brick walls, Soho is going for a sophisticated New York City-type of feel. Make reservations to have an organic dinner at the venue before taking in the evening's entertainment.

For a traditional Irish bar experience in downtown Santa Barbara, head to **The James Joyce** (513 State St., 805/962-2688, www.sb-jamesjoyce.com, daily noon-1:30am). Peanut shells litter the floor as locals sip Guinness at the bar or play competitive games of darts in the backroom. The James Joyce has live entertainment six days a week including Irish music on Sundays.

Live Music

Founded in 1873, the **Lobero Theater** (33 E. Canon Perdido St., 805/963-0761, www.lobero.com) is the oldest continuously operating theater in the state. While it used to host entertainers like Tallulah Bankhead and Bela Lugosi, it now welcomes jazz acts like Pat Metheney and Diane Reeves along with indie rock darling Jenny Lewis and jam band Chris Robinson Brotherhood. The medium-sized theater has only one level, and it's filled with cushy red velvet seats—perfect for a music-filled night out on the town. Check the website for the shows coming up during your visit. Also be sure to look into the annual film festival. You can buy tickets online, by phone, or at the box office during your stay.

Classical Music

The **Santa Barbara Symphony** (Granada Theatre, 1214 State St., 805/898-9386, www.thesymphony.org) aspires to compete with its brethren in Los Angeles and San Francisco. The symphony orchestra puts up seasons that pay homage to the greatest composers the world has ever seen, plus the works of less-known but equally talented artists. Whether you prefer Mozart or Mahler, you can listen to it at the concert hall at the Granada Theatre. Every seat has a great view of the stage, and the acoustics were designed with music in mind, making for an overall great symphony experience.

Opera Santa Barbara (OSB, Granada Theatre, 1214 State St., www.operasb.com) has put up such classics as *Aida, Don Pasquale* and *Madame Butterfly.* In fine tradition, OSB enjoys a focus on the classics and little-known works of the Italian masters. Operas are staged at the Granada Theatre.

Dance

At the **Center Stage Theater** (751 Paseo

Nuevo, 805/963-0408, www.centerstagetheater.org) look for everything from plays with a formerly incarcerated cast to improv comedy performances. Center Stage focuses on dance, offering more ballet and modern dance performances than it does plays. A handful of local groups including the Lit Moon Theatre and Out of the Box Theater Company has made the Center Stage their home.

SHOPPING

If you're looking for a fairly standard shopping expedition in Santa Barbara, go to **State Street.** From end to end, this busy main drag hosts a near-unbelievable array of mall-style stores, plus a few independent boutiques for variety. You'll find lots of lovely women's apparel, plenty of housewares stores, and all the usual stuff you'd expect to find in a major urban shopping center. Also explore the **Paseo Nuevo Shopping Center** (651 Paseo Nuevo, 805/963-7147, www.paseonuevoshopping.com, Mon.-Fri. 10am-9pm, Sat. 10am-8pm, Sun. 11am-6pm), a series of pathways off State Street that has clothing stores, including Nordstrom and Macy's, along with chain eateries like Chipotle and California Pizza Kitchen.

Also right off State Street is **La Arcada Court** (1114 State St., 805/966-6634, www.laarcadasantabarbara.com), a collection of shops, restaurants, specialty stores, and art galleries. Along the tile-lined walkways, playful human-like sculptures appear in front of some of the shops.

BEACHES

There's nothing easier than finding a beach in Santa Barbara. Just follow State Street to its end, and you'll be at the coastline.

East Beach

Named because it is east of Stearns Wharf, **East Beach** (1400 Cabrillo Blvd., www.santabarbaraca.gov, daily sunrise-10pm) is all soft sand and wide beach, with a dozen volleyball nets in the sand close to the zoo (if you look closely you can see the giraffes and lions). It has all the amenities a sun worshipper could hope

for: a full beach house, a snack bar, a play area for children, and a path for biking and in-line skating. The beachfront has picnic facilities and a full-service restaurant at the East Beach Grill. The **Cabrillo Pavilion Bathhouse** (1119 East Cabrillo Blvd.), built in 1927, offers showers, lockers, a weight room, a single rentable beach wheelchair, and volleyball rental.

West Beach

On the west side of Stearns Wharf, **West Beach** (Cabrillo Blvd. and Chapala St., between Stearns Wharf and the harbor, daily sunrise-10pm) has 11 acres of picturesque sand for sunbathing, swimming, kayaking, windsurfing, and beach volleyball. There are also large palm trees, a wide walkway, and a bike path, making it a popular tourist spot. Outrigger canoes also launch from this beach.

Leadbetter Beach

Considered by many to be the best beach in Santa Barbara, **Leadbetter Beach** (Shoreline Dr. and Loma Alta Dr., daily sunrise-10pm) divides the area's south-facing beaches from the west-facing ones. It's a long, flat beach with a large grassy area. Sheer cliffs rise from the sand, and trees dot the point. The beach, which is also bounded by the harbor and the breakwater, is ideal for swimming because it's fairly protected, unlike the other flat beaches.

Many catamaran sailors and windsurfers launch from this beach, and you'll occasionally see surfers riding the waves. The grassy picnic areas have barbecue sites that can be reserved for more privacy, but otherwise there is a lot of room. The beach and the park can get packed during the many races and sporting events held here. There are restrooms, a small restaurant, and outdoor showers. Directly across the street is Santa Barbara City College. If you enter the stadium and walk up the many steps, you'll get some terrific views of the harbor, plus a workout.

Arroyo Burro Beach

To the north of town, **Arroyo Burro Beach** (Cliff Dr., 805/687-3714, www.sbparks.org, daily 8am-sunset), also known as Hendry's, is a favorite for locals and dog owners. To the right as you face the water, past Arroyo Burro Slough, dogs are allowed off-leash to dash across the packed sand and frolic and fetch out in the gentle surf. Arroyo Burro is rockier than the downtown beaches, making it less friendly to games and sunbathers. But the rocks and shells make for great beachcombing, and you might find a slightly smaller crowd on sunny weekend days. You'll find a snack bar, restrooms, outdoor showers, and a medium-sized pay parking lot for your convenience. At peak times, when the parking lot is full, there's no other parking around.

It's flanked by large cliffs, one of which is home to the **Douglas Family Preserve.** The 70-acre, eucalyptus-studded, dog-friendly preserve is popular with locals, but few visitors ever hear about it. The parcel was planned to become housing, but a grassroots campaign raised awareness of the potentially destructive development, and fund-raising efforts to purchase it were bolstered when actor Michael Douglas made a substantial donation, allowing the parcel to remain undeveloped. He then named it after his father, actor Kirk Douglas.

Goleta Beach

At the base of the University of California, Santa Barbara campus, **Goleta Beach Park** (5986 Sandspit Rd., daily sunrise-10pm) is popular for its picnic tables, barbecue pits, horseshoes, multiple restrooms, and fishing opportunities. The grassy area is partially shaded by trees, and there's also a small jungle gym for the kids. The pier is popular for fishing, and the low breaks make it an easy entry for kayakers. You can also launch small boats from the pier on weekends, when a crane lowers boats into the water (there is no launch ramp directly into the water). On the mountain-facing side along the bike path are a few platforms for viewing birds in the slough behind the beach.

Butterfly Beach

Butterfly Beach (Channel Dr., across from the Four Seasons Hotel, Montecito, daily sunrise-10pm) is accessed by a handful of steps leading to the narrow beach. Many people come here hoping to catch a glimpse of a celebrity from nearby Montecito, but chances are that won't happen. Butterfly is the most west-facing beach in Santa Barbara, meaning that you can actually see the sun set over the Pacific here. To find it, take U.S. 101 to Olive Mill Road in Montecito (a few minutes south of Santa Barbara). At the stop sign, turn toward the ocean (away from the mountains) and follow it 0.25 miles along the coast; Butterfly Beach is on the left. The beach is packed most weekends and often weekdays too, and parking is limited. Park on either side of the street along the beach, or drive up Butterfly Road and park in the nearby neighborhoods. Bring your lunch, water, and sunscreen—there are no public facilities at this beach. Dogs roam freely here.

Carpinteria State Beach

Carpinteria State Beach (5361 6th St., Carpinteria, 805/968-1033, daily 7am-sunset, day-use $10, camping $35-65) has designated itself the "world's safest beach." Whether that's true or not, this beautiful, wide, flat beach is definitely a favorite for locals and visitors alike. With plenty of campgrounds, picnic tables, outdoor showers, RV hookups, telephones, and a short walk to Linden Avenue's restaurants, shops, and grocery store, you'll have everything you need within walking distance. Parts of the campgrounds are tree-lined but right next to the train tracks; passing trains might wake up light sleepers. There is a great sense of community among the campers here.

SPORTS AND RECREATION

With the year-round balmy weather, it's nearly impossible to resist the temptation to get outside and do something energetic and fun in Santa Barbara. From golf to sea kayaking, you've got plenty of options for recreation here.

◖ Surfing

The trick to surfing Santa Barbara is to know that during the summer months the Channel

Islands block the south swells that would hit the county. But, during fall and winter, the big north and northwest swells wrap around Point Conception and transform places like Rincon into legendary surf breaks.

Leadbetter Point (Shoreline Park, just north of the Santa Barbara Harbor) is a slow, mushy wave perfect for beginners and longboarders. The locals are reasonably welcoming, and the small right break makes for easy and fun rides.

For a bit more of a challenge, paddle out to the barrels at **Sandspit** (Santa Barbara Harbor). The harbor's breakwater creates hollow right breaks for adventurous surfers. Be careful though: Sandspit's backwash has been known to toss surfers onto the breakwater.

Known as the "Queen of the Coast," **Rincon** (U.S. 101 at Bates Rd. on the Ventura County/ Santa Barbara County line) is considered California's best right point break. If you catch a wave outside, there's a chance you can score a memorable-for-life 300-yard-long ride. You might also see three-time world champion and revered surfer Tom Curren in the lineup. But, if it's firing, you'll also most likely be sharing the break with lots of other surfers. The time to investigate Rincon is during the winter.

Looking for surfing lessons? Check out the **Santa Barbara Surf School** (805/745-8877, www.santabarbarasurfschool.com). The instructors have decades of surfing experience and pride themselves on being able to get beginners up and riding in a single lesson. They also offer five-day surf camps in the summer.

Kayaking and Stand Up Paddleboarding

One of the best ways to see the Santa Barbara Harbor and Bay is under your own power in a kayak or stand up paddleboard. A number of rental and touring companies offer lessons, guided paddles, and good advice for exploring the region. **Channel Islands Outfitters** (117B Harbor Way, 805/617-3425, www.channelislandso.com, daily 7am-7pm) has everything you need to paddle the waters of Santa Barbara and Ventura. You can rent a sea kayak or a stand up paddleboard to take your own ride around

the harbor or out into the bay. Channel Islands also offers a Santa Barbara Harbor kayak tour and a Goleta Point stand up paddleboard tour. They have more adventurous sea kayak tours around the nearby Channel Islands. Whether you choose a lesson or a tour, reservations in advance are recommended, especially for summer weekends.

The **Santa Barbara Sailing Center** (133 Harbor Way, 805/350-9090, http://sbsail.com) also provides kayak rentals and stand up paddleboard rentals, as well as sea kayaking tours.

Sailing

At the **Santa Barbara Sailing Center** (133 Harbor Way, 805/350-9090, http://sbsail.com), you can learn to sail, charter a sailboat, or rent a power boat. The sailing center also offers sailing excursions aboard the 50-foot *Double Dolphin* sailing catamaran.

Fishing and Whale-Watching

Santa Barbara's prime location on the coast makes it a great spot for deep-sea fishing and whale-watching. With its proximity to the feeding grounds of the blue and humpback whales, Santa Barbara is one of the best spots to go whale-watching in the state.

If you're looking for a whale-watching expedition, birding expedition, or a dinner cruise, check out the **Condor Express** (301 W. Cabrillo Blvd., 805/882-0088, www.condorexpress.com). In the summertime, they can take you out to the Channel Islands to see the blue and humpback whales feed; in the winter, the captain sails into the path of migrating gray whales. The boat is a 72-foot catamaran with posh amenities and lots of outdoor deck space that can seat almost 127 people. Whale-watching cruises depart almost daily all year long; call to purchase tickets in advance.

If you want to go fishing, give **WaveWalker Charters** (691 Camino Campana, 805/964-2046, www.wavewalker.com) a call. This private six-passenger charter boat rents for $960 for a three-quarters day—expensive unless you bring five friends along to split the cost! Bait and all tackle are included with the charter, but a fishing license is not. Call for more information about what you can fish for when.

Golf

It might not get the most press of the many golf destinations in California, but with its year-round mild weather and resort atmosphere, Santa Barbara is a great place to play a few holes. There are six public courses within an hour of downtown Santa Barbara—everything from a popular municipal course to championship courses with views of the ocean from the greens.

It's still a golf course, but **Glen Annie** (405 Glen Annie Rd., 805/968-6400, www.glenanniegolf.com, $57-72, carts $13) has worked with Audubon International to create wildlife habitats on its land. Who knows what you might see when you're out walking the lush, green, 18-hole, par-72 course? Well, you'll definitely get great views of the town of Santa Barbara, the ocean, and the Channel Islands on this hilly course. The Frog Bar & Grill, the on-site restaurant, draws any number of non-golfers up to Glen Annie for lunch. Set in a castle-like structure, the Frog serves California cuisine dishes that are a far cry from most clubhouse fare. So come for the golf, but stay for the unusual and delicious fare.

If you're already interested in exploring Santa Barbara's wine country, consider reserving a tee time at **La Purisima Golf Course** (3455 Hwy. 246, Lompoc, 805/735-8395, $29-79). This golf course, built in 1986, gets high praise for its design and difficulty level—even if you're an expert golfer, "La Piranha" will test your skills. The par-72 course is a 45-minute drive from downtown Santa Barbara, but many locals think it's worth the trip. In addition to the 18 holes, you can access the grass driving range, the short-game practice area, and the pro shop. A number of PGA and LPGA golf pros are on hand to help you improve your game.

The **Sandpiper** (7925 Hollister Ave., 805/968-1541, www.sandpipergolf.com, $74-159, cart $16) boasts some of the most amazing views you'll find in all of Santa Barbara. They're so great because they're right up close, and on several holes your ball is in danger of falling into the world's largest water trap. And hey, there's a great championship-rated 74.5, 18-hole, par-72 golf course out there on that picturesque beach too! Take advantage of the pro shop and on-site restaurant, but do be aware of the semi-formal, denim-free dress code Sandpiper enforces. It's not cheap, but a long walk on the beach with a great golf game in the middle of it seems well worth it to an endless stream of golfers who rank Sandpiper as one of their favorite courses.

Spas

Folks who can afford to live in Santa Barbara tend to be able to afford many of the finer things in life, including massages, facials, and luxe skin treatments. You'll find a wide array of day spas and medical spas in town.

If you prefer a slightly more natural spa experience, book a treatment at **Le Reve** (21 W. Gutierrez, 805/564-2977, www.le-reve.com). Using biodynamic skin care products and pure essential oils, Le Reve makes good on the advertising that bills it as an "aromatherapy spa." Choose from an original array of body treatments, massage, hand and foot pampering, facials, and various aesthetic treatments. If you're up for several hours of relaxation, check out the spa packages that combine facials with massage and body treatments.

Cielo Spa and Boutique (1725 State St., Ste. C, 805/687-8979, www.cielospasb.com) prides itself on its warm, nurturing environment. Step inside and admire the scents and the soft lighting and the natural, New Agey decor. Contemplate the colorful live orchids, feel soothed by the flickering candlelight, and get lost in the tranquil atmosphere. The menu of services has an almost Northern Californian flare, with signature champagne treatments and a focus on organics and natural lotions and potions. Check into the luxury packages that combine massages, facials, and more for a full day in the spa.

SOLVANG

Founded in 1911 as a Danish retreat, Solvang makes a fun side trip. It's ripe with Scandinavian heritage as well as a theme-park atmosphere not lacking in kitsch. In the 1950s, far earlier than other themed communities, Solvang decided to promote itself via a focus on Danish architecture, food, and style, which still holds a certain charm over 50 years later. You'll still hear the muted strains of Danish spoken on occasion, and you'll notice storks displayed above many of the stores in town as a traditional symbol of good luck.

Solvang draws nearly two million visitors each year. During peak summer times and holidays, people clog the brick sidewalks. Try to visit during off-season, when meandering the lovely shops can still be enjoyed. It's at its best in the fall and early spring when the hills are verdant green and the trees in town are beautiful.

The **Elverhøj Museum** (1624 Elverhoj Way, 805/686-1211, www.elverhoj.org, Wed.-Thurs. 1pm-4pm, Fri.-Sun. noon-4pm, $3 donation) features exhibits of traditional folk art from Denmark, including paper-cutting and lace-making, wood clogs, and the rustic tools used to create them. It also offers a comprehensive history of the area with nostalgic photos of the early settlers.

The small **Hans Christian Andersen Museum** (1680 Mission Dr., 805/688-2052, www.solvangca.com, daily 10am-5pm, free) chronicles his life, work, and impact on literature. Displays include first editions of his books from the 1830s in Danish and English.

Contact the **Solvang Visitor Information Center** (1639 Copenhagen Dr., 805/688-6144, www.solvangusa.com) for more advice on a Solvang visit.

GETTING THERE

If you're heading from Santa Barbara north to Solvang, you have two choices. You can drive the back route, Highway 154, also known as the San Marcos Pass Road, and arrive in Solvang in about 30 minutes. This is a two-lane road, with only a few places to pass slower drivers, but it has some stunning views of the coast as you climb into the hills. You pass Cachuma Lake, then turn west on Highway 246 to Solvang. The other option is to take U.S. 101, which affords plenty of coastal driving before you head north into the Gaviota Pass to reach Solvang. This route is longer, about 45 minutes' drive time. Highway 246 is known as Mission Drive in the town, and it connects both to U.S. 101 and Highway 154, which connects to Santa Barbara in the south and U.S. 101 farther north.

ACCOMMODATIONS

If you want a posh beachside room in Santa Barbara, you'd better be prepared to pay for it. Actually almost all of Santa Barbara's hotels charge a premium rate. On the other hand, there are a couple of charming and reasonably priced accommodations near downtown and other attractions.

$150-250

A lovely little boutique hotel in a quiet residential neighborhood near the beach, the **Franciscan Inn** (109 Bath St., 805/963-8845, www.franciscaninn.com, $155-325) looks just like a Spanish Colonial Revival hacienda, with pale, adobe-style walls and a traditional red-tiled roof. Guest rooms offer everything from cute, economical, double-bed rooms to luxurious multiple-room suites. The decor ranges from classic to modern. The largest suite sleeps seven comfortably; smaller rooms can sleep four if they're friendly. The amenities add to the charm of the place; you can grab an item from their full continental breakfast and a cup of coffee in the morning, or a warm cookie in the afternoon. Take a swim in the heated pool, soak in the whirlpool tub, check your email with the free Wi-Fi, or even throw in a load of laundry at the on-site coin-op machines. Stearns Wharf and downtown are a short walk away.

The **Bath Street Inn** (1720 Bath St., 805/682-9680, www.bathstreetinn.com, $165-295) specializes in small-town charm and hospitality. It's large for a B&B, with eight rooms in the Queen Anne main house and another four in the more modern summerhouse. Each room has its own unique color scheme and style. Certainly you'll find some traditional floral Victorian decor, but many of the rooms are done up with elegant stripes rather than cloying blooms. Some rooms have king beds, others queens, and several have two-person whirlpool tubs. Despite the vintage trappings, the Bath Street Inn features a few modern amenities including free Wi-Fi. But the inn has not entered the DVD era yet. All rooms have a TV and VCR, and the common area has an extensive videotape collection of movies. Early each morning, a sumptuous home-cooked breakfast is served downstairs. Choose between sharing your meal with your fellow guests in the dining room, or escaping to the sunny garden patio for a bit of privacy.

It's a chain now, but the **Holiday Inn Express at the Hotel Virginia** (17 W. Haley St., 805/963-9757, www.hotelvirginia.com, $170-275) has lots of history in Santa Barbara. Sitting near the main drag, the Hotel Virginia has welcomed guests who come to take the waters and enjoy the scenery of Santa Barbara since 1916. Ten years ago it was renovated to bring it up to code and to spiff up the older guest rooms. Today it is run by the folks at Holiday Inn Express, but they elected not to eradicate the historic charm and atmosphere of the Virginia. When you walk into the lobby, you'll step onto a red-tiled floor and gaze upon a bright, multihued blue fountain. Some of the rooms retain the hotel's historic past with exposed brick walls. The smallish bathrooms feature prized showerheads, and the beds have both cotton and feather pillows to choose from. If you choose to stay in your room for a while, you can make yourself coffee to sip while watching your LCD flat-screen. The restaurants and shops of State Street are steps from the lobby, and the beach isn't too much farther.

If you're in Santa Barbara to soak up the sun on the sandy beaches, book a room at the **Inn at East Beach** (1029 Orilla Del Mar, 805/965-0546, www.innateastbeach.com, $160-325).

Unsurprisingly, it's just a block from East Beach, and a nice walk along the waterfront boardwalk will take you to Stearns Wharf and to downtown. Guests will find sizeable rooms done up in blue carpets and comforters with pine furniture and a strange plethora of telephones. The inn prides itself on its attractive swimming pool and courtyard area, and you can feel free to bring down a bottle of wine and enjoy the balmy evenings with fellow guests. If you're planning a longer stay, get a kitchen suite so you can cook your own meals and take advantage of the inn's guest laundry facilities. The Inn at East Beach also serves a complimentary extended continental breakfast.

Over $250

If you're willing to pay a premium rate for your room, the **Cheshire Cat Inn** (36 W. Valerio St., 805/569-1610, www.cheshirecat.com, $219-409) can provide you with true luxury B&B accommodations. Each room has an *Alice in Wonderland* name, but the decor doesn't really match the theme—instead of whimsical and childish, you'll find comfortable Victorian elegance. Guest rooms are spread out through two Victorian homes, the coach house, and two private cottages. Some suites feel like well-appointed apartments complete with a dining room table, soaking tub, and a bookshelf stocked with a few hardbacks. Relax in the evening in the spacious octagonal outdoor spa, or order a massage in the privacy of your own room. Each morning, come downstairs and enjoy a breakfast. In addition to the fine facilities, the Cheshire Cat's warm innkeepers will make you feel immediately at home.

For a taste of Santa Barbara's posh side, stay at the **Inn of the Spanish Garden** (915 Garden St., 805/564-4700, www.spanishgardeninn.com, $349-505). This small boutique hotel gets it right from the first glimpse; the building in the historic Presidio neighborhood has the characteristic whitewashed adobe exterior with a red-tiled roof, arched doorways, and wooden balconies. Courtyards seem filled with lush greenery and tiled fountains, while the swimming pool promises relief from the

the rooftop pool at Santa Barbara's Canary Hotel

© STUART THORNTON

heat. Inside, guest rooms and suites whisper luxury with their white linens, earth-toned accents, and rich, dark wooden furniture. Enjoy the benefits of your own gas fireplace, deep soaking bathtub, French press coffee maker, plush bathrobes, and honor bar. The complimentary continental breakfast can be delivered right to your door upon request. Also upon appointment, you can arrange for a massage or facial in the comfort of your room. The Spanish Inn sits only three blocks from State Street, and within walking distance of a number of theaters and historic Santa Barbara attractions.

Are you ready and willing to pay premium prices for a luxury beachfront resort hotel room? If so, check out the **Harbor View Inn** (28 W. Cabrillo Blvd., 800/755-0222, www. harborviewinnsb.com, $325-795). This stunning Spanish Colonial-style property sits right across the street from the flat white sands of West Beach and steps from Stearns Wharf. Blooming flowers and bright ceramic tiles create beautiful outdoor spaces everywhere on the property. The pool is a focal point of the resort,

with long hours and food and beverage service. The pool deck also features a kids' pool, hot tub, and a view of the nearby Pacific. Inside your lovely guest room, soft lighting and orange-and-red tones create a feeling of warmth. Suites offer palatial spaces and extra amenities. Every room also has a porch or balcony. If you want to enjoy a tasty meal without leaving the resort property, choose between room service and the on-site oceanfront restaurant Eladio's. Eladio's is best known for its breakfasts, but serves three meals each day and has a good list of wines that is heavy on the local vintages.

The newest Santa Barbara luxury lodging establishment is the stylish, playful ◀ **Canary Hotel** (31 West Carrillo St., 805/884-0300, www.canarysantabarbara.com, $295-675). Worth splurging on, the elegant rooms have wooden floors, extremely comfortable, canopied beds, and giant flat screen TVs. (The rooms also have unexpected amenities like a pair of binoculars for sightseeing and bird-watching as well as a giant candle to set the mood for romantic evenings.) While it may be difficult to leave such comforts, the hotel has a rooftop pool and lounge on its sixth floor that offers stunning views of the Santa Ynez Mountains and the red-tiled roofs of the beautiful coastal city. Downstairs, the hotel restaurant and bar Coast serves breakfast, lunch, dinner and a recommended happy hour menu from 4pm-7pm Monday-Friday.

FOOD
Breakfast
The **Tupelo Junction Café** (1218 State St., 805/899-3100, www.tupelojunction.com, Tues.-Sat. 8am-2pm and 5pm-9pm, Sun.-Mon. 8am-2pm, $14) serves breakfast, lunch, and dinner, but it is the breakfast that shouldn't be missed. The attractive waitstaff and sleek but not fancy interior will remind you that you're in Santa Barbara, even though at this Southern meets Southern California restaurant, your juice or mimosa will be served in a mason jar. The collision between cuisines takes place on morning menu items including a breakfast wrap with Southern elements like Andouille sausage mixed into what is basically a California Mexican style breakfast burrito with a tasty avocado salsa. Don't miss the half biscuit covered in a spicy red sausage gravy that is served as a breakfast appetizer.

Cafés
Whether you're a vegetarian or not, you'll find something delicious at the **Sojourner Café** (134 E. Canon Perdido St., 805/965-7922, www.sojournercafe.com, Sun.-Wed. 11am-10pm, Thurs.-Sat. 11am-11pm, $11). In fact, a select few dishes include a bit of lean poultry or fish in amongst the veggies. Sojourner features healthful dishes made with ingredients that showcase local organic and sustainable farms. Lots of the cuisine has ethnic flavors, from familiar Mexico to exotic India. Daily specials use ingredients that are fresh and in-season, including some seafood. Then again, Sojourner also serves a classic root beer float and chocolate milkshakes as well as a big selection of house-baked confections to go along

with their health food. Sojourner displays the work of local artists on a rotating schedule, and the walls are painted with images of fruits and vegetables. If you fall in love with the wall art over your table, inquire with your server about purchasing it.

Also boasting a healthy menu is the **Natural Café** (508 State St., 805/962-9494, www.naturalcafe.com, daily 11am-9pm, $8). The Santa Barbara location is part of a small chain, but Natural Café feels right at home on State Street. The mostly vegetarian menu includes items like tofu hot dogs and an array of salads, but makes room for healthy carnivore options like turkey burgers and chicken sandwiches.

California Cuisine
Of the many and varied high-end California cuisine restaurants that crowd Santa Barbara, **Bouchon** (9 W. Victoria St., 805/730-1160, www.bouchonsantabarbara.com, daily 5pm-10pm, $28) might be the best. Though it's no relation to the bistro of the same name in Yountville, Bouchon prides itself on both creative cuisine and top-notch service every night. You'll pay a premium to dine here, but it's worth it for a special night out. Your server will be your guide, helping you make selections from the menu, recommending wine pairings with each course, and answering any questions you might have about the restaurant or the food. California-style dishes are prepared with local and organic ingredients whenever possible, and the menu changes often based on what's available. The wine list is a special treat. It consists entirely of wines from Santa Barbara County. Servers have favorites and they're generally great. The presentation of the food matches its quality. The dining room features romantic low lighting, smallish tables, interesting artwork, and an outdoor patio that's perfect for balmy summer nights.

A bit less fancy, **Opal** (1325 State St., 805/966-9676, http://opalrestaurantandbar.com, Sun. 5pm-10pm, Mon.-Thurs. 11:30am-2:30pm and 5pm-10pm, Fri.-Sat. 11:30am-2:30pm and 5pm-11pm, $15) is a favorite of

Santa Barbara locals. Matter of fact, Opal's menu points out that items including the pesto sautéed bay scallop salad and the chile crusted filet mignon are locals' favorites. In addition to their eclectic offerings, most with an Asian twist, the stylish eatery serves up gourmet pizzas from a wood-burning oven and fine cocktails from a small bar.

Coffee

A long narrow coffee shop right on State Street, **The French Press** (1101 State St., 805/963-2721, Mon.-Fri. 6am-7pm, Sat. 7am-7pm, Sun. 8am-7pm) is lined with hipsters and couples getting caffeinated and using the free Wi-Fi. The very popular café has a small seating area out front on State Street and out back on Figueroa Street. As its name suggests, the French Press does serve individually prepared French press coffee and espresso along with other beverages that'll leave your body buzzing. Also on the drink menu is the Magic Bowl, a steamed milk, chamomile, and honey mixture.

Creole

The Palace Grill (8 E. Cota St., 805/963-5000, www.palacegrill.com, daily 11:30am-3pm and 5:30-10pm, Fri.-Sat. until 11pm, $20-40) boasts of being one of Santa Barbara's most popular restaurants and a little piece of old New Orleans in sunny California. The atmosphere gets lively in the evenings, so this isn't the place to come for a quiet meal. Live entertainers delight the crowds several nights each week, and every once in awhile a restaurant-wide sing-along breaks out. The food is pure Louisiana bayou; look for classically prepared etouffes, jambalaya, and gumbo ya-ya. The seafood is fresh, the steaks are aged to perfection, and much of the fresh finned fish and meat is served blackened and spiced in Cajun style. Even the appetizers and desserts drip Creole and Cajun flavors. Start off with a house specialty cocktail or a glass of California wine. While you dine, be sure to take a moment to appreciate the particularly fine service that is a staple of the Palace's reputation.

Mexican

Have you ever wanted to know what true, authentic Mexican food might taste like? ◖ La **Super-Rica Taqueria** (622 N. Milpas St., 805/963-4940, Sun.-Thurs. 11am-9pm, Fri.-Sat. 11am-9:30pm, $5) can hook you up. Of course, you must be prepared to stand in line with dozens of locals and even commuters up from Los Angeles and the occasional Hollywood celeb who think La Super-Rica's got some of the best down-home Mexican cuisine in all of SoCal. This was Julia Child's favorite taco stand, and it's been reviewed by the *New York Times.*

Folks don't come for the ambiance—it's a taqueria in what feels like a beach shack. You also need to adjust your concept of Mexican food; if you're looking for a fast-food burrito supreme with chips and salsa, you'll definitely be disappointed. (Actually, there's no burrito on the menu.) But if you're ready for the real deal, you've found it. The corn tortillas are made fresh for every order, the meat is slow cooked and seasoned to perfection, and the house special is a grilled pork-stuffed pasilla chile. Vegetarians can choose from a few delicious meat-free dishes including the rajas, a standout item of sautéed strips of pasilla peppers, sautéed onions, melted cheese, and herbs on a bed of two fresh corn tortillas.

Middle Eastern

For a Middle Eastern feast, go to **Zaytoon** (209 E. Canon Perdido St., 805/963-1293, www.zaytoon.com, Mon.-Tues. 11:30am-11pm, Wed.-Sat. 11:30am-midnight, Sun. 5pm-11pm, $18). This restaurant and hookah bar appeals to a crowd that wants to enjoy an evening out with a group of friends, to share a hookah around the table, and to ogle talented belly dancers shimmying amongst the tables. While the interior dining room is attractive, with potted palms and gauzy fabric draped from the ceiling, it's not the best place to sit at Zaytoon. Instead, try to get a table out on the garden patio, a large, softly lit space almost completely enveloped by a living green jungle. It is out here that you can order up your own hookah. The menu has most standard Middle Eastern favorites, such as baba ghanouj, hummus, falafel, Greek salad, shawarma, and kebabs of many kinds.

Seafood

It takes something special to make Santa Barbara residents take notice of a seafood restaurant, and **◖ Brophy Brothers** (119 Harbor Way, 805/966-4418, www.brophybros.com, Sun.-Thurs. 11am-10pm Fri.-Sat. 11am-11pm, $23) has it. Look for a small list of fresh fish done up California style with upscale preparations. The delectable menu goes heavy on locally caught seafood. At the clam bar, you can order some fresh steamed clams or oysters, a bowl of the house clam chowder, or a tasty seafood salad. With a prime location looking out over the masts of the sailboats in the harbor, it's no surprise that Brophy Brothers gets crowded at both lunch and dinnertime, especially on weekends in the summertime. There's also a location in Ventura Harbor.

If you were wondering: Yes, they do mean *that* **Endless Summer** (113 Harbor Way, 805/564-4666, www.endlesssummerbarcafe. net, daily 11:30am-close, $10). When they decided to create a new restaurant in the harbor area, the owners went to Bruce Johnson, a Santa Barbara resident and acknowledged creator of the "real" surfing movie genre, and asked him if he would mind having a restaurant named for his most famous film. Bruce thought it was a fine idea, and not only gave the project his blessing, he quickly became a regular in the dining room. Photos of Bruce, other famous surfers, and lots of surfing paraphernalia—including framed movie posters from *The Endless Summer* and *The Endless Summer II* films—deck the walls of this harbor-side bar and café. The menu has plenty of salads and sandwiches, includes a tasty Cajun-seared ahi appetizer with a terrific wasabi dipping sauce, and the restaurant also serves from the menu of the Waterfront Grill downstairs. Service is friendly, and the atmosphere tends towards casual local hangout. Many patrons know each other and the staff, and the bar gets crowded as the evening wears on.

INFORMATION AND SERVICES

The **Santa Barbara Conference and Visitors Bureau** (1601 Anacapa St., 805/966-9222, www.santabarbaraca.com) maintains an informative website and center. The **Outdoor Santa Barbara Visitors Center** (113 Harbor Way, Waterfront Center, 4th Fl., 805/884-1475, daily 11am-5pm) provides information about Channel Islands National Park, the Channel Islands National Marine Sanctuary, the Los Padres National Forest, and the City of Santa Barbara.

As a major metropolitan city, Santa Barbara publishes its own daily newspaper, the *Santa Barbara News Press* (www.newspress.com). Look for it in shops, on newsstands, and in your hotel or inn. Check the *Scene and Life* sections for information about entertainment, events, and attractions. Also the *Santa Barbara Independent* (www.independent.com) is the local free weekly that has a comprehensive events calendar.

The major hospital in town is **Santa Barbara Cottage Hospital** (400 W. Pueblo St., 805/682-7111, www.sbch.org), which includes a full-service emergency room.

GETTING THERE AND AROUND

To reach Santa Barbara by air, fly into the **Santa Barbara Municipal Airport** (500 Fowler Rd., 805/967-7111, www.flysba.com). A number of major commercial airlines fly into Santa Barbara, including United, Alaska/Horizon, Frontier, and American Airlines.

A more beautiful and peaceful way to get to Santa Barbara is by train. The **Amtrak Coast Starlight** (www.amtrak.com) runs into town daily. From Los Angeles or San Francisco's east bay, connect to other trains that run into California from points east.

Santa Barbara is located on U.S. 101, also known as the Pacific Coast Highway and El Camino Real in this neck of the woods. To head out to the Santa Ynez Valley and other local wine regions, take CA Highway 154 east. If staying in Santa Barbara proper, expect fairly standard city driving, complete with traffic jams during weekday business hours and on beach access roads on the weekends. Parking can be challenging, especially at the beach on sunny summer weekends. Expect to pay a premium for a good-to-mediocre spot, or to walk for several blocks. If possible, take the local public streetcar from the downtown area to the beach and leave your car elsewhere.

Santa Barbara has its own transit authority. The **MTD Santa Barbara** (805/963-3364, www.sbmtd.gov, regular fare: local service $1.75, waterfront service $0.25) runs both the local bus service and the Waterfront Shuttle and Downtown-Waterfront lines. Have exact change to pay your fare when boarding the bus or shuttle; if transferring buses, ask the driver for a free transfer pass.

The Gaviota Coast

In some ways, the Gaviota Coast is Southern California's last major stand against the encroachment of urbanization. It acts as a soothing balm to residents from Santa Barbara south to the sprawling metropolis of Los Angeles, escaping civilization for a weekend in nature. This stretch of coastline (between Goleta's Coal Oil Point to Vandenberg Air Force Base's Point Arguello and beyond to remote Point Sal) is unpopulated and only lightly touched by development.

It wasn't always this way. Before European settlers arrived, it was one of the most densely populated regions of native California. The Chumash lived here and harvested sustenance from the Santa Barbara Channel using canoes. Then the missionaries came and attempted major agricultural projects in now nearly unpopulated places including Jalama and Honda Canyon. After the mission system collapsed, the area was divided up by Mexican land grants before large ranches started popping up. Some large ranching operations, such as the Hollister Ranch, still exist today.

It's a great place for a day trip from Santa Barbara—it's only 20 miles to the first park, El Capitan State Beach—for a day of relaxing on a beach, hiking, surfing, or stand up paddle boarding. Even though this is a rural stretch of coastline, the area's three state parks—El Capitan State Beach, Refugio State Beach, and Gaviota State Park—are typically crowded during the summer months. It's also a great place to camp for the night.

Pockets of the Gaviota Coast are protected by the presence of El Capitan State Beach, Refugio State Beach, Gaviota State Park, and the impressive Jalama Beach County Park. But there's still a push by local conservation groups, including the Gaviota Conservancy, to designate this area a National Shoreline.

EL CAPITAN STATE BEACH

Closest to Santa Barbara, **El Capitan State Beach** (10 Refugio Rd., Goleta, 805/986-1033, www.parks.ca.gov, $10) offers a narrow, rocky beach with tide pools and the largest campground of the three Gaviota Coast state parks.

On February 26, 1776, the Anza expedition camped in the region that would later become El Capitan State Beach. A day earlier, Father Pedro Font wrote in his journal: "the people of the expedition, some of whom have never seen the ocean, have much to admire."

There is still much to admire here: a nice but narrow strand of beach for sunbathing, surf fishing, a few infrequent waves offshore for surfers, and stands of sycamore and oak trees offering shade along El Capitán Creek. A stairway provides access from the bluffs to the beach area. Amenities include RV hookups, pay showers, restrooms, hiking and biking trails, a fabulous beach, a seasonal general store, and an outdoor arena. Many of the camping sites offer an ocean view.

Camping

El Capitan State Beach (10 Refugio Beach Rd., Goleta, 800/444-7275, www.reserveamerica.com, $45) is the largest of the state park campgrounds on the Gaviota Coast. It has 123 campsites strung along multiple loops in the shade or sun depending on your preference—if you get here early enough. The sites offer a little more privacy than Refugio or Gaviota, and there is a walkway and stairs accessing the rocky beach below.

For the inexperienced camper, **El Capitan Canyon** (11560 Calle Real, 866/352-2729, www.elcapitancanyon.com, canvas safari tents from $155, cabins $225-795) offers several ways to ease into the outdoors. On 300 acres of land that includes private hiking trails and a spa, El Capitan Canyon is also a place for more experienced outdoor enthusiasts to pamper themselves. The accommodations here—some are far from camping—begin with canvas safari tents and yurts that include beds and furniture but have no running water, even though there are bathhouses nearby. The cedar cabins are available in a range of options from a bunk cabin that is perfect for families to the property's priciest offering, the Safari Cabin, a two-bedroom suite with a loft and an ocean view. Most of the other cabins are like small wooden studio apartments complete with kitchenettes and, in some cases, deep soaking tubs. In front of each is a picnic table and fire pit for communing with nature.

On the grounds, the **Canyon Market** serves a nice selection of breakfast, lunch, and dinner options. They also will deliver BBQ kits to your cabin so you can prepare your meal on an open fire. These kits start at $60 for hamburgers, hot dogs, and veggie burgers, so expect more than Oscar Meyer wieners and Costco patties.

El Capitan Canyon's cabins appeal to couples seeking a restful, romantic retreat as well as families with children. Kids will love the heated pool and a short hike to a llama and goat enclosure.

REFUGIO STATE BEACH

If Gaviota State Park is the region's hiking hotspot, **Refugio State Beach** (10 Refugio Beach Rd., Goleta, 805/968-1033, www.parks.ca.gov, $10) is the best place for a beach day on the Gaviota Coast. This thin but long finger of beach is lined with scenic palm trees. Here, brave children plunge into the chilly but not cold waters and scream while their parents look on taking in the comforts of the frequent sun.

The land on which Refugio is based used to be a cattle ranch in the late 1700s called Nuestra Senora del Refugio. In 1798, Jose Maria Ortega took over the ranch and started to do a little smuggling on the side, trading with stocked foreign ships, which was forbidden by the ruling Spanish. These activities piqued the interest of the Monterey pirate Hippolyte de Bouchard, who traveled down hoping to score some of the smuggled goods in 1818. Even though Refugio's residents hid themselves and the loot, Bouchard took it upon himself to burn the ranch house and smuggling station before departing.

Now the only ominous presence offshore are the hazy oilrigs in the distance that look like ghostly pirate ships. As for Refugio, the waters are way less scary. This is a well-protected cove for sea kayaking or stand up paddleboarding. There are also beginning and advanced kayak tours, which include kayak usage, provided by Refugio's park rangers.

Camping
Refugio State Beach (10 Refugio Beach Rd., Goleta, 800/444-7275, www.reserveamerica. com, $45) has 67 campsites to crash out at after a day at the nearby beach, which is just feet away from some sites. In the summer, the sites, which are fairly close together, can feel a bit crowded, but this is a scenic campground shaded by trees.

GAVIOTA STATE PARK

Of the Gaviota Coast's three state parks, **Gaviota State Park** (10 Refugio Beach Rd., Goleta, 805/968-1033, www.parks.ca.gov, $10) is the place to head for hiking. The park has multiple trails leading into its 2,000 acres of oak woodland and chaparral backcountry. One of these is the 0.7-mile hike up to the **Gaviota Hot Springs.** If you get lost easily, this mostly unsigned trail is going to be a challenge. The

Gaviota State Park

trailhead is actually about 2.5 miles north of the state park's main entrance on the exit off U.S. 101 to Highway 1 heading to Lompoc. Take an immediate right at the exit and then another right to an unmarked parking area. From there, it doesn't get any easier. Take the unmarked trail about a half a mile up and when the main trail veers left go straight on what looks like a spur trail. A few hundred yards up is a warm—not hot—pool behind a little artificially-made dam and under a palm tree. It's a nice pool to relax in during the few times when it is not overrun.

More adventurous hikers, can continue on the main path up to **Gaviota Peak,** a 2,458-foot peak that offers one of the best views of the Gaviota Coast. It's a strenuous three-mile hike one-way.

Besides the hiking trails, Gaviota State Park has a nice little beach area under the shadow of an 811-foot-high train trestle. Just west of the beach is a fishing pier, where on crowded days, the plethora of upright fishing poles stand like bristles off the wooden structure.

Camping

Gaviota State Park (10 Refugio Beach Rd., Goleta, 800/444-7275, www.reserveamerica. com, $45) has 39 campsites in a small loop by Gaviota Creek just 100 yards from the beach. These sites are mostly open to the elements, including the wind that roars through Gaviota Pass and the heat, because there is little tree cover to block the sun.

◖ JALAMA BEACH COUNTY PARK

The western portion of Santa Barbara County around Point Conception is mile after mile of desolate beach, uncrowded waves, and mostly uninhabited coastal bluffs. The best place to experience a truly wild patch of the Gaviota Coast is to head out to **Jalama Beach County Park** (9999 Jalama Rd., Lompoc, 805/736-3504, www.sbparks.org, day use $10). It is the only public beach between Gaviota State Beach and the beach at the tiny town of Surf, a stretch of more than 48 miles.

On this section of coast, there have been

THE UFOS OF THE GAVIOTA COAST

During a night camping at Jalama Beach County Park or another spot on the Gaviota Coast, you may look up and see a strange flying object overhead. Most likely it's not an alien craft searching for humans to probe but an unmanned satellite or test missile launched from the Vandenberg Air Force Base.

Encompassing over 99,000 acres of land on the elbow of the California coast by Point Conception, Vandenberg was initially an Army base called Camp Cooke. In 1965, the Air Force took over the sprawling base and began launching test missiles as a reaction to Russia's Sputnik launch in 1957. The base has the distinction of being the place where the first polar orbiting satellite was sent into space in 1959.

Vandenberg was also designed to be the West Coast space shuttle launch and landing site. But the site's technical problems and the space program's decision to consolidate shuttle operations at Cape Canaveral in Florida caused the closure of the shuttle program at Vandenberg in 1989.

If you see a UFO in the sky while in the west section of Santa Barbara County, check out Vandenberg's launch schedule at www.vandenberg.af.mil to see if it's a missile being tested or a satellite being sent into space. If it's not listed, you have seen a true unidentified flying object.

remote location, Jalama is a park with some unexpected amenities including a playground, a horseshoes pit, a basketball court, flushing toilets, and the well-stocked **Jalama Beach Store and Grill**. The little store has almost all you could need, including canned goods, firewood, cold beer, cigars, and, even, DVD rentals. Meanwhile, the grill serves breakfast, lunch, and dinner including their patented—seriously the patent hangs by the pickup window—Jalama Burger, a tasty third-pounder that'll make burger fans drool.

While the park's facilities are impressive for its remote location, the coastline here is the draw. Surfers can ride waves right out front, while anglers cast off the beach for perch and rockfish. For the adventurous, from Jalama, it's a six-mile beach hike to the east to Point Conception, one of California's best-known maritime landmarks. Check to make sure it's low tide before heading out.

Jalama draws families camping to renew their ties far from cell phone service in their first-come, first-served sites; surfers hoping to score uncrowded waves; anglers hoping to reel in a few fish; and beachgoers who like their beaches in an undeveloped state.

Camping

Jalama Beach County Park (9999 Jalama Rd., Lompoc, 805/736-3504, www.sbparks. org, tent camping $20-40, RV camping with hookups $35-40) has 117 first-come, first-served campsites. There are 12 spots whose sites blend into the beach out front and a row of RV-friendly sites on a bluff with a view of the park below. The amenities here are surprisingly good, including clean bathrooms with flushing toilets, fire pits, picnic tables, and an outdoor shower for washing off after any ocean recreation. Be aware that the spring and early summer winds in this area can be quite fierce.

The park also offers seven popular cabins for rent (805/686-5050, $100-200) for those who want to experience the region's beauty without roughing it.

some serious shipwrecks. In 1854, the steamship Yankee Blade hit some rocks and sank, killing 415 people. Later, in 1923, the largest peacetime loss of U.S. Navy ships occurred when seven destroyers ran aground and 23 people perished nearby at Honda Point.

As you wind around on the 14.5-mile-long Jalama Road towards the park, you'll know you are on the way to someplace special, if you are into out-of-the-way treasures. Despite its

Ventura

Ventura is short for San Buenaventura, which means the "city of good fortune." There is much that is good about Ventura, including its weather (daytime temperatures average 70 degrees), consistent waves for surfers, and a historic downtown that includes a restored mission.

Despite being so close to Los Angeles, Ventura has retained its seaside charm. Downtown Ventura is compact and easy to walk around; it is three blocks from the beach and still feels somehow unfettered by "progress," with buildings that date to the 1800s (a long time by California standards). In recent years, the city has encouraged the growth of an impressive arts scene and a thriving restaurant landscape. But it's still a bit scruffier than nearby Santa Barbara, with a sizeable homeless population for its relatively small size.

A few blocks from Main Street is Surfer's Point, a coastal area also known as "C" Street. A ribbon of pavement by the ocean, the Omer Rains Bike Trail almost always hosts a collection of walkers, runners, and cyclists.

Farther away, the Ventura Harbor has a cluster of restaurants, bars, and hotels located around the harbor, which is the gateway to the nearby Channel Islands National Park.

SIGHTS
Mission San Buenaventura
Referred to as the "mission by the sea," **Mission San Buenaventura** (211 E. Main St., 805/643-4318, www.sanbuenaventuramission.org, self-guided tours daily 10am-5pm, adults $4, seniors $3, children $1) sits right on Ventura's Main Street and just blocks from the beach.

SANTA BARBARA

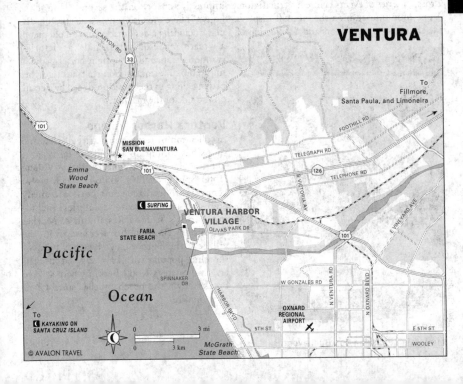

The church is just one of six missions that was personally dedicated by Junípero Serra, the founder of California's mission system.

A seven-mile-long aqueduct was built to the mission to feed it water from the Ventura River. Because of its abundant water, Mission San Buenaventura became known for its lush orchards and gardens.

Not that living at this mission was without hardships. In 1812, a series of earthquakes and the resulting tidal wave forced the mission's padres and the native people scrambling inland. Later, pirate Hippolyte de Bouchard's threat to pillage the mission again led to the mission's residents temporarily relocating.

Construction on the current day mission began in earnest in 1792 after a fire burned the first church building. Today, the mission is a peaceful remnant of California's past with beautiful high ceilings and walls decorated with paintings of Jesus at various "Stations of the Cross," a series of events before his crucifixion. A one-room museum on the grounds displays the church's original doors and a collection of native Chumash artifacts. Between the museum and the church is a scenic garden with a tile fountain, an old olive press, and a shrine.

Olivas Adobe Historical Park

For a peek into California's 1800s rancho period, take a docent-led tour of **Olivas Adobe Historical Park** (4200 Olivas Park Rd., 805/658-4728, www.olivasadobe.org, guided tours Sat.-Sun. 11am-4pm, adults $5, family $10, seniors $3), owned by the City of Ventura. Constructed in 1847, the main house on the 4,693-acre Rancho San Miguel was home to Raymundo Olivas, his wife Theodora, their 21 children, and their employees.

The 45-minute tour illuminates what life was like during the ranch period, from how the adobe walls were constructed to how bread was baked in outdoor baking ovens. Stops include a bedroom where the eight Olivas daughters somehow managed to live together and an impressive chapel on the second floor of the house. There are also some curiosities on display, including a desk made from an old piano, a wreath made of human hair, a Victorian era mousetrap, and an upright barrel piano, a music box-like contraption that has figurines playing along to the music produced by a crank on the side of the machine.

Ventura Harbor Village

A collection of restaurants, art galleries, and shops has sprung up around the fairly large Ventura Harbor. The **Ventura Harbor Village** (1583 Spinnaker Dr., 805/642-8538, www.venturaharborvillage.com) hosts a comedy club and popular seafood eateries, including Andria's Seafood Restaurant & Market and Brophy Brothers. Just feet away from the village is the Harbor Cove Beach, a piece of shoreline popular with kayakers and kite fliers, and Surfer's Knoll Beach, where a wave breaks down the beach by the Santa Clara river mouth.

a fountain at Mission San Buenaventura

ENTERTAINMENT AND EVENTS
Bars and Clubs
Winchester's Grill and Saloon (632 E. Main St., 805/653-7446, www.winchestersventura.com, Mon.-Fri. 4pm-1am, Sat.-Sun. 11am-11pm) is the place to go if you want something poured from a tap. Behind the 40-foot mahogany bar, bartenders serve up 36 beers, three ciders, and a root beer from Winchester's many taps. You can enjoy your beverage inside or on one of two heated patios. It can get loud and a little rowdy; people seem to step inside and become cowboys.

Live Music
The Majestic Ventura Theater (26 S. Chestnut St., 805/653-0721, www.venturatheater.net) gets a variety of pretty big national acts, including music icons Alice Cooper and Snoop Dogg—yup, Snoop Dogg is an icon now—along with newer acts like The Dirty Heads and Dengue Fever. The 1,200-person-capacity Mission-style theater opened in 1928 as a movie house; decades later it was converted into a concert venue. The old chandeliers still hang in the auditorium, and other remnants of the 1920s decor remain.

Festivals and Events
In the summer, Ventura's art studios and other venues open their doors for a weekend during the **Westside ArtWalk** (http://westsideartwalk.org). Some places that participate include the Museum of Ventura County and the Ventura Visitor's Center. Other participating venues include restaurants, salons, antiques shops, unique boutiques, and coffee shops—most any place with walls.

The **Ventura County Fair** (10 W. Harbor Blvd., 805/648-3376, www.venturacountyfair.org) goes down every summer within the Ventura County Fairgrounds, which is right by the city's main coastal recreation area. Expect the usual attractions: Ferris wheel, cotton candy, and livestock exhibits. Live nightly entertainment often features 1980s acts like Bret Michaels and Joan Jett.

SHOPPING
Art Galleries
Ventura's strong arts scene has been overshadowed by Los Angeles, but that is beginning to change. **Red Brick Gallery** (315 E. Main St., 805/643-6400, www.redbrickart.com, Mon.-Thurs. 11am-6pm, Fri.-Sat. 10am-7pm, Sun. 11am-5pm) offers shows that rotate every six weeks. The gallery, lined with exposed redbrick walls, it represents about 150 artists, working in paint, wood, glass, photography, and jewelry.

Specialty Stores
A veteran of Ventura Harbor Village for over 20 years, **Harbor Wind & Kite Co.** (1575 Spinnaker Dr., Suite 107B, 805/654-0900, www.harborwindkite.com, Sun.-Thurs. 10am-6pm, Fri.-Sat. 10am-7pm) has kites literally hanging everywhere, as well as every conceivable type of kite and kite accessory.

Thrift Stores
Ventura has long been known for a plethora of inexpensive thrift stores, but in recent years many have been converted into restaurants or bars. Still, there are bargains to be had. Try **Treasure Chest Thrift Shop** (328 E. Main St., 805/653-0555, daily 10am-7:30pm) or **The Arc Foundation of Ventura County Thrift Store** (265 E. Main St., 805/650-8611, Mon.-Sat. 9am-6pm, Sun. 10am-5pm).

Outlet Malls
If the many thrift stores in downtown Ventura aren't satisfying your shopping impulses, head to the **Camarillo Premium Outlets** (740 E. Ventura Blvd., off Los Posas Ave., 805/445-8520, www.premiumoutlets.com, Mon.-Sat. 10am-9pm, Sun. 10am-8pm, holiday hours vary). Actually in the town of Camarillo, east of Ventura's southern neighbor Oxnard, there are 160 outlet stores peddling reduced price brand name merchandise from Banana Republic and J. Crew.

BEACHES
San Buenaventura State Beach
San Buenaventura State Beach (San Pedro

St. off U.S. 101, 805/968-1033, www.parks. ca.gov, day-use $10) has an impressive two miles of beach, dune, and ocean. It also includes the 1,700-foot Ventura Pier, home to Eric Ericsson's Seafood Restaurant and Beach House Tacos. The historic pier was built way back in 1872. This is a safer place to swim than some area beaches. It doesn't get the breakers that roll into the nearby point. Cyclists can take advantage of trails connecting with other nearby beaches, and sports enthusiasts converge on the beach for occasional triathlons and volleyball tournaments. Facilities include a snack bar, an equipment rental shop, and an essential for the 21st-century beach bum—Wi-Fi, although to pick up the signal, you need to be within about 200 feet of the lifeguard tower.

Emma Wood State Beach

Bordering the estuary north of the Ventura River, **Emma Wood State Beach** (W. Main St. and Park Access Rd., 805/968-1033, www. parks.ca.gov, day-use $10) includes the remnants of a World War II artillery site. There are no facilities, but a few minutes' walk leads to the campgrounds (one for RVs and one group camp; first-come, first-served in winter, reservations required spring-fall). At the far eastern side of the parking lot is a small path leading out to the beach that goes under the train tracks. To the right are views up the coast to the Rincon. The beach itself has many rocks—some nearly the size of footballs—strewn about. It is a great spot for windsurfing, as the winds come off Rincon Point just up from the mouth of the Ventura River to create ideal windy conditions. There's a 0.5-mile trail leading through the reeds and underbrush at the far end of the parking lot; although you can hear the surf and the highway, you can't see anything, and you'll feel like you're on safari until you reach the beach where the Ventura River ends.

Harbor Cove Beach

Families flock to **Harbor Cove Beach** (1900 Spinnaker Dr., daily dawn-dusk), located directly across from the Channel Islands Visitors Center at the end of Spinnaker Drive. The harbor's breakwaters provide children and less confident swimmers with relative safety from the ocean currents. The wind can kick up at times, but when it's calm it's practically perfect. There's plenty of free parking, lifeguards during peak seasons, restrooms, and foot showers. Food and other amenities can be found across the street at Ventura Harbor Village.

Faria Beach

Farther north, the Ventura County-run **Faria Beach** (4350 W. U.S. 101, at State Beach exit, 805/654-3951, daily dawn-dusk) is available for tent camping and has 15 RV hookups. The campground has a playground and horseshoe pits, barbecues, and shower facilities but is quite small. It's also very crowded with campers, trucks, and people during nice weather because of its proximity to the water. You might find you have more companions than you care for, but it's a long, flat beach, so you can spread out.

SPORTS AND RECREATION
◖ Surfing

Ventura is definitely a surf town. The series of point breaks referred to as California Street, **"C Street"** for short, is the best place for consistent right breaks. There are three distinct zones along this mile-long stretch of beach. At the point is the Pipe, with some pretty fast short breaks. Moving down the beach is the Stables, which continues with the right breaks, with an even low shoulder, and then C-Street, breaking both right and left. The waves get mushier and easier for beginners the closer you get to Ventura Pier. There is a pay parking lot right in front of the break across the street from the Ventura County Fairgrounds (10 W. Harbor Blvd.). South of downtown Ventura, **Ventura Harbor** has waves that refract off the harbor's jetties.

SURF CLASSES
Surfclass (805/200-8674, www.surfclass.com, two-hour session $90) meets at various beaches

© STUART THORNTON

Ventura's C Street surf break

around Ventura, depending on weather and swells. They teach everyone from novice landlubbers to rusty shredders. The two-hour class rates are quite reasonable, and they limit class size for individual attention. They will also teach you surf etiquette and lingo.

Ventura Surf School (461 W. Channel Islands Blvd., 805/218-1484, www.venturasurf-school.com, private two-hour lesson $125, two or more $80 pp, four or more $75 pp) can also teach you to surf, and they offer a weeklong surf camp and kids-only classes. Beginner lessons are at Mondos Beach.

SURF RENTALS

If you just need gear, swing by **Seaward Surf and Sport** (1082 S. Seaward Ave., 805/648-4742, www.seawardsurf.com, winter daily 10am-7pm, summer daily 9am-9pm, surfboard rental $15-50), which is the place to go to buy or rent most anything for the water (including body boards and wetsuits). It is a half a block from the beach, so you can head straight to the water.

All sorts of gear, including long boards and boogie boards, are available at **Beach Break Surf Shop** (1557 Spinnaker Dr., Suite 108, 805/650-6641, www.beachbreaksurfshop.com, daily 10am-6pm, all-day wetsuit rental $20). It's already at the harbor, so you can pick up your gear, cross the street, and hit the beach.

Whale-Watching

December-March is the ideal time to see Pacific gray whales pass through the channel off the coast of Ventura. Late June-late August has the narrow window for both blue and humpback whales as they feed offshore near the islands. **Island Packers Cruises** (1691 Spinnaker Dr., Suite 105B, 805/642-1393, www.islandpackers.com, $25-75) has operated whale-watching cruises for years and is the most experienced. It also runs harbor cruises with a variety of options, including dinner cruises and group charters. Most whale-watching trips last about three hours. Remember that whale-watching is weather-dependent, so cancellations can occur.

Biking

The eight-mile-long, paved **Omer Rains Trail** heads along Ventura's beachfront from San Buenaventura State Beach past the Ventura Pier and Surfer's Point to Emma Wood State Beach. **The Ventura River Trail** (Main St. and Peking St., www.ventura-usa.com) follows the Ventura River inland from Main Street just over six miles one-way, ending at Foster Park. From here it joins the **Ojai Trail,** a two-lane bike path that follows Highway 33 into Ojai (16 miles one-way). If you want to pedal it, **Wheel Fun Rentals** (850 Harbor Blvd., 805/765-5795, www.wheelfunrentals.com) rents out beach cruisers, surreys, mountain bikes, and low riding chopper bikes.

FOOD
American

With brick walls and beer-making vats behind the bar, the **Anacapa Brewing Company** (472 East Main St., 805/643-2337, http://anacapabrewing.com, Sun.-Wed. 11:30am-9pm, Thurs.-Sat. 11:30am-midnight, $14) looks like a brew pub should. Regulars sit at a long bar drinking the brewery's Pierpoint IPA, which goes down easy, while families eat burgers, salads, and pizzas at booths and tables. The menu also has a few unexpected entrées like the fried chicken and waffle plate.

Farmers Markets

Downtown Ventura County's Farmer's Market (Santa Clara St. and Palm St., www.vccfarmersmarkets.com, Sat. 8:30am-noon) has produce stands along with vendors selling tamales and pot stickers.

If you miss that one, there's still the **Midtown Ventura Market** (front west parking lot at Pacific View Mall, E. Main St. and Pacific View Dr., www.vccfarmersmarkets.com, Wed. 9am-1pm) on Wednesdays.

Italian

Bolstered by a popular wood bar, **Café Fiore** (66 California St., 805/653-1266, www.fiorerestaurant.net, Mon.-Thurs. 11:30am-3pm and 5pm-10pm, Fri.-Sat. 11:30am-3pm and 5pm-11pm, Sun. 11:30am-3pm and 5pm-9pm, $16-32) is a hotspot for Ventura professionals grabbing a cocktail or meal after work. The food includes Italian favorites like cioppino, osso buco, and chicken parmesan, served in a sleek, high-ceilinged room decorated with furnishings that recall the interior of a Cost Plus World Market. Expect to wait a while for service on crowded nights and during happy hour.

Mexican

Not in the most scenic section of Ventura, the **Cuernavaca Taqueria** (1117 N. Ventura Ave., 805/653-8052, Mon.-Fri. 10am-8:30pm, Sat.-Sun. 9am-7:30pm, $8) is worth traveling to for its tasty street-style tacos alone. This is a typical taqueria with an unassuming interior and soccer blaring on the television, but the tacos are a step above most other taquerias. The al pastor taco finds marinated pork shavings under chunks of pineapple on a tortilla bed. The al pastor taco alone was enough to inspire an intrepid food writer from the *L.A. Weekly* to make the trek to the taqueria and write a glowing review about the al pastor; the review now hangs on its wall.

Seafood

Right on the Ventura Harbor, **Andria's Seafood Restaurant & Market** (1449 Spinnaker Dr., 805/654-0546, www.andriasseafood.com, Sun.-Thurs. 11am-9pm, Fri.-Sat. 11am-10pm, $11) is a local's favorite for fresh seafood. With plastic trays and dinghy furniture, Andria's feels like an old school cafeteria, but the seafood is good. A lot of the menu features fried fare—the fish and chips is recommended—but there are also items like a scallop stir fry. It's a good place to get a casual seafood dinner without breaking the bank.

Vegetarian

Mary's Secret Garden (100 S. Fir St., 805/641-3663, www.maryssecretgarden.com, Tues.-Thurs. 4pm-9:30pm, Fri.-Sat. 11am-9:30pm, $13) isn't just for vegetarians, it's for anyone who enjoys healthy dining. The prices are a bit steep—$9 for a small hummus plate!—but the food is organic, vegan, and full of flavor. The secret burger, a veggie burger that can be ordered with fake bacon and avocado, evokes shades of its beefy counterpart but has its own tasty thing happening.

ACCOMMODATIONS
Under $150

The **Bella Maggiore Inn** (67 South California St., 805/652-0277, $75-180) has a great location a few blocks from the beach and just a block off Ventura's Main Street. Some of the rooms are no larger than a college dorm room but there is a lobby with couches and Italian chandeliers. Even better is a courtyard with a fountain and dining area surrounded by the vine-draped sides of the building. The moderate room prices also include a hot breakfast in the morning.

Calling the **Best Western Plus Inn of Ventura** (708 E. Thompson Blvd., 805/643-3101, http://bestwesterncalifornia.com, $90-180) an inn might be a stretch. It's more like a motel. But all the rooms have a fridge and microwave, while a heated pool and small hot tub are outside. It's also close to downtown Ventura and the beach.

$150-250

If you are traveling to the Channel Islands National Park out of Ventura Harbor, the **Four Points By Sheraton Ventura Harbor Resort** (1050 Schooner Dr., 805/658-1212, www.fourpoints.com, $145-175) is a great place to lay your head before an early morning boat ride or to relax after a few days camping on the islands. The rooms are clean and comfortable with balconies and patios. With a gym, tennis court, pool, and basketball court, there is a wide array of recreational opportunities available at the resort. For folks who have hiked all over the Channel Islands, Four Points has a hot tub in a glass dome to ease your aching muscles.

A few hundred yards from the Ventura Pier and right by the beach, the **Crowne Plaza Ventura Beach** (450 East Harbor Blvd.,

800/842-0800, www.cpventura.com, $139-239) has rooms with ocean view balconies if you get a room on the fifth floor or higher. It also offers pet-friendly rooms for $50 more.

Also on the coast—specifically right back from San Buenaventura State Beach—**The Pierpont Inn & Spa** (550 Sanjon Rd., 805/643-6144, www.pierpontinn.com, $119-299) is situated on some nice manicured grounds with grassy areas and flowers. The historic property, which goes back to 1910, has guest rooms, suites, cottages, and a bungalow. In addition, there's a full service spa on the grounds.

INFORMATION AND SERVICES

The **Ventura Visitor's Center** (101 California St., 805/648-2075, www.ventura-usa.com, Mon.-Fri. 8:30am-5pm, Sat. 9am-5pm, Sun. 10am-4pm) occupies a big space in downtown Ventura and offers a lot of information including a historic walking tour guide of the city.

Community Memorial Hospital (147 N. Brent St., 805/652-5011, www.cmhshealth.org) has the only emergency room in the area.

GETTING THERE AND AROUND

Ventura is 1.5 hours north of **LAX** (1 World Way, Los Angeles, 310/646-5252, www.lawa.org). To get to Ventura from LAX without a vehicle, contact the **Ventura County Airporter** (805/650-6600, www.venturashuttle.com), a bus that goes back and forth between the places.

While Ventura's Greyhound station closed a few years back, **Amtrak** (Harbor Blvd. and Figueroa St., 800/872-7245, www.amtrak.com) still comes to town.

With a car, Ventura exits are right off U.S. 101. The city is 34 miles south of Santa Barbara on U.S. 101 and 65 miles north of Los Angeles on the highway.

Travel Ventura in a cab by calling **Gold Coast Cab** (805/444-6969, www.goldcoastcab.com).

Channel Islands National Park

Channel Islands National Park sweeps visitors back in time to a past when coastal California was undeveloped. Only accessible by boat or plane, Channel Islands National Park is in the top 20 least crowded national parks due to its remote location. Those few who get to the five islands are treated to uncrowded trails, isolated beaches, and an extensive marine sanctuary. It's a place to experience the state in its purest, most natural form. Kelp forests offshore sway in the ocean's surge as pumpkin-colored garibaldi (the California state fish) swim past rocks dotted with multi-colored sea urchins. Onshore, rare species, including the island fox and the Santa Cruz Island scrub jay, roam freely.

The islands have been federally protected for just over 30 years. Long before they were a national park they were ranch lands, and archaeological evidence suggests that the islands were inhabited as long as 12,000 years ago. Santa Cruz Island, in particular, was prime grazing land in the 1800s for cattle and sheep, which were safe from the predators found on the mainland. Santa Cruz was also home to a winery, the remnants of which are still visible.

The most traveled to of the park's islands are **Anacapa,** a dramatic 5-mile spine jutting out from the sea, and **Santa Cruz Island,** California's largest island at 24 miles long and up to 6 miles wide. Sailing to the islands can take 3-4 hours, and motorboats make the trip even faster, yet exploring the islands isn't common. San Miguel, the farthest west, is not a short trip, nor is the small rock island of Santa Barbara. But Anacapa, Santa Cruz, and to a lesser degree Santa Rosa can be visited as day trips, although only Santa Cruz and Anacapa trips are available year-round. There can be tough weather conditions, and it's often very windy since there's little shelter.

Inexpensive day trips allow visitors to explore, hike, kayak, snorkel, camp, and scuba

Santa Cruz Island

© KARE TRABANT

dive at the islands. Multiday trips allow for extended camping excursions into the islands' interiors and for visiting several of the islands.

SANTA CRUZ ISLAND

Santa Cruz is the largest of the islands, and by far the most popular island to visit, in part because it most closely resembles the mainland and, frankly, it is the most hospitable. There are more old buildings on this island than the others, and there is a day camp near Scorpion Bay where you can pitch a tent, store your food in metal lockers, and explore on foot. There are trees here as well as old dried-out creeks and former grasslands that are often barren depending on the amount of winter rainfall. At the center of the island, the thick, dense vegetation feels almost prehistoric. This is also the only place in the world to see endemic species such as the Channel Islands fox and island scrub jay, and large beautiful ravens make their homes here.

The environmental organization The Nature Conservancy owns 76 percent of the scorpion-shaped Santa Cruz Island, while the National Park Service possesses and maintains the remaining 24 percent of the island. The two primary points of entry onto Santa Cruz are **Scorpion Anchorage** and **Prisoners Harbor.** The island has a range of hiking trails, snorkeling opportunities, two campgrounds, and an abundance of amazing sea caves that can be explored by sea kayak.

Travel time is 90 minutes, and travelers offload onto a short pier directly connected to shore, though shore landings from a skiff are possible depending on conditions.

Scorpion Ranch Complex

Believe it or not, Santa Cruz Island hosted an extensive ranching operation in the mid 1800s up until the 1980s. The **Scorpion Ranch Complex** gives park visitors a glimpse into this isolated way of life. The ranch area is home to various farming equipment and wooden ranch structures in various states of decay. The small visitor center has displays on threatened species, conservation, and the native Chumash people in one room and a model ranch kitchen in the other room.

Sports and Recreation
HIKING

A quick introduction to Santa Cruz's cliff top coastal views and, on clear days, views to the mainland can be found on the moderate two-mile-long **Cavern Point Loop.** If you have more time, the more strenuous 7.5 mile round-trip **Smugglers Cove Trail** is really an old ranch road that cuts across the island's eastern interior to arrive at a south-facing beach. Even if you don't find the elusive Santa Cruz Island scrub jay on the 4.5-mile **Scorpion Canyon Loop,** you'll be treated to a hike up one of the island's unique canyons and then a bunch of stunning coastal views.

KAYAKING

Santa Cruz island is pocketed with some of the world's most incredible and largest sea caves, and the best way to explore them is by kayak. Sea kayaking Santa Crux is no less than an amazing experience. The easiest way to find some sea caves is to paddle northwest (left) out of Scorpion Anchorage. Entering some of these cathedral-sized caves will take your breath away quicker than any artificially-made architectural treasure. In some of the deeper caves, the ocean surge creates a deep railroad-like rumble. Meanwhile, almost all have starfish decorating their walls and a sublime green glow. Outside of the caves, sea lions and seals periscope their heads out of the water between mats of kelp. Next door to Island Packers, the boat concession that gets most visitors to Santa Cruz and the other islands, is the **Channel Islands Kayak Center** (805/984-5995, www.cikayak.com, single kayaks $35, double kayaks $55), where you can rent kayaks for excursions or sign up for island cave tours or a history and wildlife tour. You must reserve a space for your kayak first through Island Packers.

SNORKELING AND SCUBA DIVING

Right east and west of the Scorpion Anchorage Pier are kelp beds that are terrific for snorkeling

kayaking off Santa Cruz Island

© STUART THORNTON

and Scuba diving. Diving trips need to be scheduled from Ventura Harbor. Options include the **Peace Dive Boat** (1691 Spinnaker Dr., G Dock, Ventura Harbor, 805/650-3483, www.peaceboat.com, $105-525 trips) and **Cal Boat Diving** (805/486-1166, http://calboatdiving.com, $105-125 trips, $45-65 gear rentals).

Camping

The most popular campground on Santa Cruz Island is the **Scorpion Ranch Campground** (877/444-6777, www.recreation.gov, $15), a 0.5-1-mile walk in from where the boast drops you off at Scorpion Anchorage. The lower campground has 22 sites in a eucalyptus-shaded canyon, while the upper loop has three regular sites and six group sites in a meadow. The upper loop is a nice spot but it's twice as far to lug your camping gear. The campgrounds have a picnic table and food storage box at every site. There are also pit toilets and water available.

There's also camping out of Prisoners Harbor if you hike the strenuous 3.5 miles to the **Del Norte Backcountry Campsite** (877/444-6777, www.recreation.gov, $15). This remote spot in an oak grove 700 feet high has picnic tables and a pit toilet.

ANACAPA ISLAND

There are sheer cliffs almost all the way around Anacapa Island, giving it the most dramatic appearance in the Channel Island chain. The spine of the island is a stunning volcanic formation which curves and bends toward Santa Cruz Island. The vegetation is sparse and low, and there are few trees. The island is home to about 130 sea caves as well as the largest brown pelican rookery in the country. In actuality, Anacapa is three islets inaccessible to each other except by boat.

Anacapa is the closest island to the mainland, just 12 miles off the southern California city of Oxnard (travel time to the island is under an hour). Almost all trips to Anacapa arrive at East Anacapa, where there is a campground, ranger station, and a lighthouse. Off the tip of East Anacapa is one of the Channel

THE CHANNEL ISLANDS' SPECIAL SPECIES

© STUART THORNTON

SANTA BARBARA

an island fox

Where are you going to find the Santa Cruz Island scrub jay, the island fox, or the island night lizard? The answer is only in the Channel Islands.

Due to its remote location, the five islands of Channel Islands National Park have 23 endemic terrestrial animals and 11 land birds that are now island-only subspecies or races. These animals have evolved and changed from their counterparts on the mainland to adapt to the islands' unique natural habitat.

The island scrub jay has the smallest range of any North American bird species: the 96-square-mile Santa Cruz Island. It is a brighter blue, has a bigger bill, and is larger than its mainland counterpart.

Meanwhile, the island fox is the largest of the Channel Islands' native mammals. But the animal is a third smaller than its relatives on the continent.

This doesn't mean that these special species are entirely safe even on the isolated Channel Islands. In the 20th century, habitat destruction, predation by feral cats, and a 1959 wildfire led to the extinction of an endemic subspecies of song sparrow on Santa Barbara Island.

Luckily, the island fox population has recovered since hitting a low of 100 animals on San Miguel, Santa Rosa, and Santa Cruz Islands in 1999. A captive breeding program has now stabilized the animal's numbers, and if you camp in Santa Cruz Island's Scorpion Ranch Campground, be prepared to hide your food from the clever animals.

Islands' most notable features: the 40-foot-high Arch Rock.

Sports and Recreation

With 130 sea caves on its small coastline, Anacapa is ripe for exploration by sea kayak. Access to the water is only available from East Anacapa's Landing Cove and West Anacapa's Frenchys Cove due to the islands' rugged cliffs. To secure a kayak for Anacapa or a kayak tour of the waters around Anacapa Island, contact the **Channel Islands Kayak Center** (3600 S. Harbor Blvd., Suite 2-108, Ventura Harbor, 805/984-5995, www.ci-kayak.com, single kayaks $35, double kayaks $55) before heading out. You must first secure a space for your kayak by calling Island Packers (805/642-1393), the concession that takes people out to the island.

There are only two hiking trails on Anacapa: the 1.5-mile round-trip **Inspiration Point Loop** and the 0.5-mile **Lighthouse Trail.** The Inspiration Point Loop takes you past a painter's palette of colorful wildflowers in the spring, while the short walk to the lighthouse allows you to look at the last permanent lighthouse that was built on the West Coast.

Camping

The **Anacapa Campground** (877/444-6777, www.recreation.gov, $15) is reachable by a 0.5-mile hike on East Anacapa that includes 154 stairs. This primitive camping area has seven sites with pit toilets and picnic tables.

SANTA ROSA ISLAND

The second largest island in Channel Islands National Park after Santa Cruz, the rugged, windy Santa Rosa Island is less visited than Anacapa and Santa Cruz. The 53,000-acre island has a mountainous spine inland that rises to 1,574 feet at Soledad Peak. The vistas from the tops of some of the plateaus are beautiful, with views of neighboring Santa Cruz Island and the mainland coastline in the distance. There are also some beautiful white-sand beaches as well as coastal lagoons and places that seem virtually untouched. It is also home

to a rare subspecies of Torrey pine that is considered one of the rarest pines in the world.

On the island, the remains of a pygmy mammoth—a mini mammoth just 4-6 feet tall!—were discovered in 1994. Santa Rosa also has protected archaeological sites from the native Chumash.

Travel time is about three hours by boat; you'll need to climb a 20-foot steel-rung ladder to reach flat land.

Sports and Recreation

Due to the frequent high winds, sea kayaking, snorkeling, diving, and swimming are only recommended for those with significant experience. But for those who want to explore dry land, Santa Rosa has a handful of hikes for hikers who don't mind sweating. The strenuous 12-mile **East Point Trail** takes in the rare Torrey pine forest and some unrestricted beaches. The 13-mile **Lobo Canyon Trail** goes to a water-sculpted canyon that looks like it could be in the southwest. There are also easier outings including exploring **Water Canyon Beach,** as long as it isn't too windy out.

Camping

Camping on Santa Rosa can be done at the **Water Canyon Campground** (877/444-6777, www.recreation.gov, $15), a 1.5-mile flat hike in. There are 15 sites with picnic tables and pit toilets.

Also you can do backcountry camping (805/658-5711, free) right on the beach mid August-December.

SAN MIGUEL ISLAND

Being the westernmost of the park's islands means that San Miguel Island is frequently hit with extreme weather and wind. It is a remote and desolate place, but offers stark beauty and more species of birds, plants, and animals here than on the other islands. For hearty park visitors, San Miguel has a stunningly beautiful beach at Cuyler Harbor and an alien-looking caliche forest; caliche are sand castings of ancient vegetation.

The island has an archaeological site of the

Chumash that contains some of the oldest remnants of humans in North America. Also, there is the possibility that Spanish explorer Juan Rodriguez Cabrillo died on the remote island. Though there is no concrete evidence, a memorial to Cabrillo stands on a bluff over Cuyler Harbor.

Travel time is about four hours. A skiff will usually run you to shore, but it depends on the weather conditions, which can be hit-and-miss.

Sports and Recreation

San Miguel has a few hiking options though some hikes can only be undertaken with a park ranger as a guide. Visitors are free to explore the two-mile **Cuyler Harbor Beach** on their own. To visit the **Caliche Forest,** a ranger will need to be contacted and accompany you on the strenuous five-mile hike. The 16-mile round-trip ranger-led **Point Bennett** takes in-shape hikers to a collection of over 30,000 seals and sea lions.

Due to fierce weather, sea kayaking, snorkeling, diving, and swimming are extremely limited on San Miguel.

Camping

The nine primitive sites of the **San Miguel Campground** (877/444-6777, www.recreation.gov, $15) can be reached by a steep one-mile hike uphill. There are picnic tables and pit toilets.

SANTA BARBARA ISLAND

The one-square-mile Santa Barbara Island is the smallest of the park's islands, little more than a small rock in the lonely Pacific, virtually impossible to see from the mainland. It's also the southernmost island. Santa Barbara is home to impressive seabird colonies, including one of the world's largest colonies of Xantus's murrelets. There is also a sea lion rookery on the island.

Secluded and lonely, it's a rare stop. Travel time is just over three hours; once here, you have to climb a steel-rung ladder from a skiff, then laboriously trudge up a 0.25-mile set of steps to reach the top.

Sports and Recreation

The island has three hiking trails, including the moderate two-mile **Arch Point Trail,** the strenuous five-mile **Elephant Seal Cove Trail,** and a moderate four-mile hike to the **Sea Lion Rookery.**

From a sea kayak, paddlers will be able to see a handful or arches and lots of sea lions. Access is only from Landing Cove.

Being the southernmost island, the waters off Santa Barbara Island are a little warmer for snorkeling. Though there is good visibility offshore, there have been sightings of great white sharks feeding on sea lions in the area. Access is only from Landing Cove.

Camping

The **Santa Barbara Island Campground** (877/444-6777, www.recreation.gov, $15) has 10 primitive sites with pit toilets and picnic tables that can be reached after a steep 0.5-mile hike.

INFORMATION

In preparation for a trip to the islands, visit the **Channel Islands National Park Visitors Center** (1901 Spinnaker Dr., 805/658-5730, www.nps.gov, daily 8:30am-5pm) in Ventura Harbor Village, where you'll find a bookstore, display of marine life, exhibits, and a 25-minute introductory film on the islands.

GETTING THERE

The most popular way to get to the Channel Islands National Park is by hopping onboard a boat run by **Island Packers Cruises** (1691 Spinnaker Dr., Suite 105B, Ventura Harbor, 805/642-1393, www.islandpackers.com). Even the boat ride out to the islands is an adventure with porpoises frequently racing beside the boats. There's also a snack bar onboard selling what one crewmember called "college food," which is candy bars, beer, and salted snacks.

Trips to **Anacapa** (daily, adults $56, ages 3-12 $39, over age 54 $51), the closest island, take an average of 45 minutes.

The most common landing at **Santa Cruz** (May-Oct. daily, Nov.-Apr. Tues. and Fri.-Sun., adults $56, ages 3-12 $39, over age 54 $51) is Scorpion Cove, with a crossing time of 90 minutes.

Santa Rosa trips (adults $78, ages 3-12 $62, over age 54 $70) take 2.5-3 hours and include stops at Santa Cruz.

San Miguel day trips (adults $100, ages 3-12 $80, over age 54 $90) are uncommon due to the 3-4-hour travel time. But there are a few days each year when you can do it, typically in September-October.

If the high seas aren't your thing, go by air via **Channel Islands Aviation** (805/987-1301, www.flycia.com).

LOS ANGELES AND ORANGE COUNTY

Los Angeles is the California that the rest of the world envisions. It's true that palm trees line sunny boulevards and the Pacific Ocean starts to warm to a swimmable temperature here, and that traffic is always a mess. But celebrities don't crowd every sidewalk signing autographs, and movies aren't filming on every corner.

Instead, L.A. combines the glitz, crowds, and speed of the big city with an easier, friendlier feel in its suburbs. A soft haze often envelops the warm beaches, which draw lightly-clad crowds vying to see and be seen while children play in the water. Power shoppers pound the sparkling pavement lining the ultra-urban city streets. Tourists can catch a premiere at the Chinese Theatre, try their feet on a surfboard at Huntington Beach, and view the prehistoric relics at the La Brea Tar Pits.

For visitors who want a deeper look into the Los Angeles Basin, excellent museums dot the landscape, as do theaters, comedy clubs, and live-music venues. L.A. boasts the best nightlife in California, with options that appeal to star-watchers, hard-core dancers, and cutting-edge music lovers alike.

Out in the suburbs of Orange County lies the single most recognizable tourist attraction in California: Disneyland. Even the most jaded native residents tend to soften at the bright colors, cheerful music, sweet smells, and sense of fun that permeate the House of Mouse.

PLANNING YOUR TIME
When you get into Los Angeles, you'll understand quickly that you'll need to pick and choose your itinerary. The vast urban sprawl is

© 123RF.COM

LOS ANGELES

HIGHLIGHTS

LOOK FOR **(** TO FIND RECOMMENDED SIGHTS, ACTIVITIES, DINING, AND LODGING.

(Griffith Park: This large urban park in the Santa Monica Mountains is home to the iconic Hollywood sign and the Griffith Observatory (page 488).

(Hollywood Walk of Fame: Walk all over your favorite stars – they're embedded in the ground beneath your feet (page 490).

(Grauman's Chinese Theatre: Take in a movie premiere, step into the footprints of movie stars, or grab a photo-op with one of the costumed superheroes hanging out in front of this Hollywood icon (page 491).

(Los Angeles County Museum of Art: You can easily spend a full day taking in this diverse array of exhibits, showcasing art from the ancient to the ultramodern (page 494).

(The Getty Center: The art collections alone would make this sprawling museum complex worth a visit. The soaring architecture, beautiful grounds, and remarkable views of the skyline make it a must. And except for paid parking, it's entirely free (page 495).

(Santa Monica Pier: Ride the scrambler, take in the view from the solar-powered Ferris wheel, or dine on a hot dog on a stick at this hundred-year-old amusement park by the sea (page 497).

(Venice Boardwalk: It's hard not to be amused when walking down this paved coastal path in L.A.'s most free-spirited beach community, crowded with street performers, bodybuilders, and self-identified freaks (page 498).

(California Adventure: Tour a Disneyfied version of the golden state at the newest theme park in the **Disneyland Resort,** which includes the Pixar-inspired Cars Land (page 539).

(The *Queen Mary*: Take a tour, spend the evening, or stay the night on this huge art deco ocean liner docked in the Long Beach Harbor. Decide for yourself whether it's truly haunted (page 548).

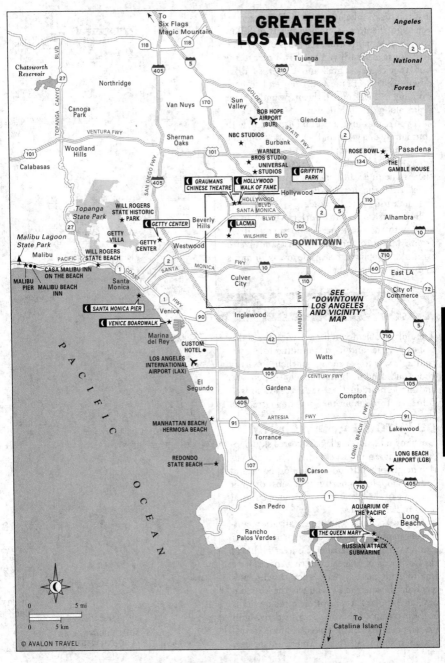

GREATER LOS ANGELES

LOS ANGELES

© AVALON TRAVEL

just too big to take in unless you've got several weeks in the area. Your best bet is to follow your own heart to whatever types of activities are your favorites. If you're a first-timer to the Los Angeles area, a great initial tour is a drive down Wilshire Boulevard from end to end, stopping to check out all the many and various sights along the 15-mile way.

If you're planning a trip to Disneyland with your family or a group of friends, stick with the Mouse as your main plan. Many people spend several days exploring the parks, never leaving the Anaheim area. Plenty of restaurants and hotels circle the theme park area, making staying and eating here a breeze.

Sun-worshippers and surfers will want to stick with the coastline. It's possible to drive from Malibu to San Juan Capistrano over a weekend, stopping at beachside towns for meals and to spend the night.

Sights

The only problem you'll have with the sights of Los Angeles and its surrounding towns are finding a way to see enough of them to satisfy you. You'll find museums, streets, ancient art, and modern production studios ready to welcome you throughout the sprawling cityscape.

DOWNTOWN AND VICINITY

Downtown L.A. has tall, glass-coated skyscrapers creating an urban skyline, sports arenas, rich neighborhoods, poor neighborhoods, and endless shopping opportunities. Most of all, it has some of the best and most unique cultural icons in L.A. County.

After years of talk about revitalization, ambitious architectural projects, such as architect Frank Gehry's Walt Disney Concert Hall and the Cathedral of Our Lady of the Angels, have finally made good on hopes for Downtown's renewal. Elsewhere in Downtown, the Museum of Contemporary Art features works by titans of 20th-century art. Koreatown is thriving in the 21st century. Little Tokyo is home to restaurants, shops, an Asian American theater,

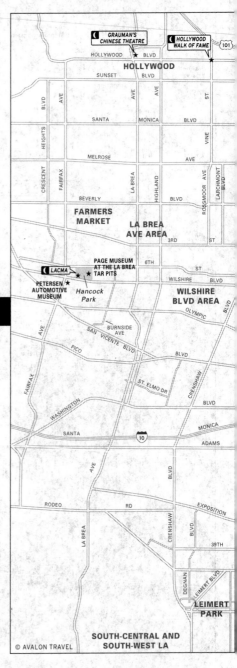

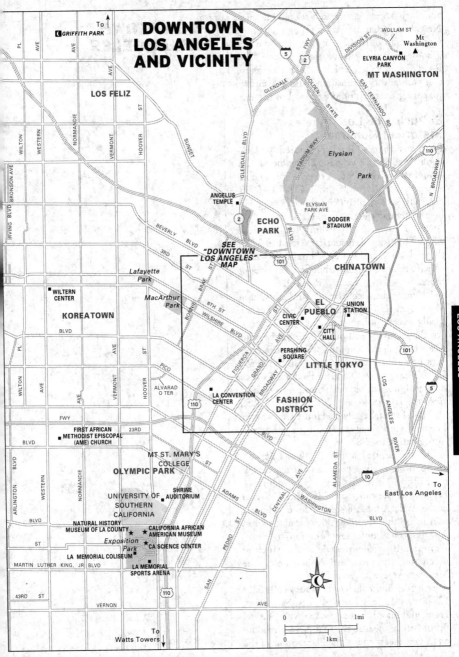

DOWNTOWN LOS ANGELES AND VICINITY

LOS ANGELES

and the Japanese American National Museum. Neighboring Chinatown, although much less vibrant than other Chinatowns, has spawned a booming gallery scene along Chung King Road. Even kids get a kick out of the museums and parkland of Exposition Park. Downtown makes a great start for any trip to Los Angeles.

El Pueblo de Los Angeles Historical Monument

For a city that is famously berated for lacking a sense of its own past, **El Pueblo de Los Angeles** (Olvera St. between Spring and Alameda Sts., 213/625-3800, 213/485-6855, or 213/628-1274, http://elpueblo.lacity.org, visitors center daily 10am-3pm) is a veritable crash course in history. Just a short distance from where Spanish colonists first settled in 1781, the park's 44 acres house 27 buildings—11 of which are open to the public as businesses or museums—dating from 1818 to 1926.

Facing a central courtyard, Our Lady Queen of the Angels Catholic Church still hosts a steady stream of baptisms and other services. On the southern end of the courtyard stands a cluster of historic buildings, the most prominent being Pico House, a hotel built in 1869-1870. The restored Old Plaza Firehouse, which dates to 1884, exhibits firefighting memorabilia from the late 19th-early 20th centuries. And on Main Street, Sepulveda House serves as the Pueblo's visitors center and features period furniture dating to 1887.

Off the central square is **Olvera Street,** an open-air market packed with mariachis, clothing shops, crafts stalls, and taquerias. Hidden in the midst of this tourist market is the Avila Adobe, a squat adobe structure said to be the oldest standing house in Los Angeles. The home now functions as a museum detailing the lifestyle of the Mexican ranchero culture that thrived here before the Mexican-American War.

Free 50-minute docent-led **tours** (213/628-1274, www.lasangelitas.org, Tues.-Sat. 10am, 11am, and noon) start at the Las Angelitas del Pueblo office, next to the Old Plaza Firehouse on the southeast end of the Plaza. Some of the

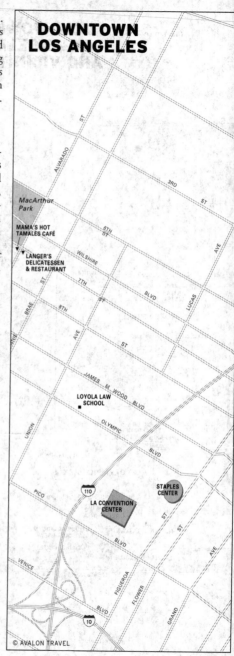

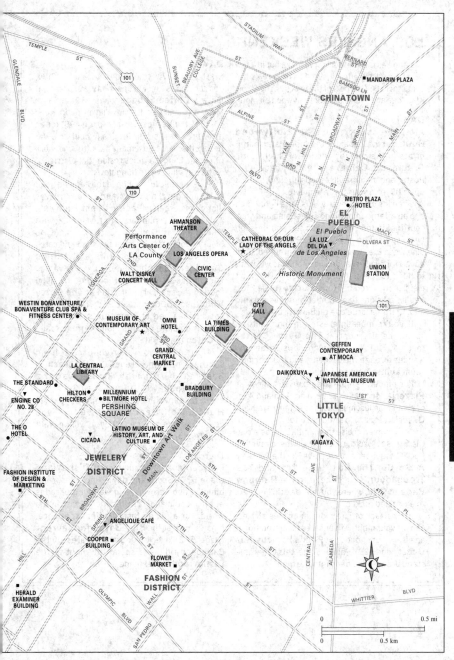

LOS ANGELES

LOS ANGELES WEEKEND

Los Angeles is notoriously sprawling, but in a few days, it's possible to hit some of the area's top spots, including the best of the beaches, the Magic Kingdom, and even a dash of Hollywood glamour.

DAY 1

After breakfast, drive to **Hollywood Boulevard.** Check out the movie-star handprints in the cement outside of the historic **Grauman's Chinese Theatre** (page 491). Poster and memorabilia shops abound, so pick up a still from your favorite movie.

Then it's off to Beverly Hills for a light lunch and an afternoon of window-shopping and star-spotting. Try one of L.A.'s top see-and-be-seen lunch spots, **The Ivy** (page 529), where celebs dine when they want to get photographed. (Call ahead for a reservation.) Fashionistas will want to head to the glamorous designer shopping district anchored by **Rodeo Drive** (page 510). You'll find signs to a number of public parking lots; there's a large one on Beverly Drive.

If you're more interested in high culture, spend the afternoon at **The Getty Center** (page 495). Take in dizzying views of the city, wander through the gardens, and tour the museum's outstanding art collections.

For dinner, sample the luxurious slices at **Pizzeria Mozza** (page 528) on Highland Avenue, or some luscious pasta at sister restaurant **Osteria Mozza,** located next door.

After dinner, cruise the nightlife scene along the **Sunset Strip,** (page 504), where revelers flock to legendary music clubs like the **Whisky A Go Go**, **The Roxy Theatre**, and **The Troubadour.** Or just head to the **Rainbow Bar and Grill,** where you may be drinking next to a grizzled rocker.

If an attack of late-night munchies strikes, cap off your night with another local tradition – an after-hours hot dog at **Pink's Famous Hot Dogs** (page 528). Rain or shine, this venerable stand draws a line deep into the night.

DAY 2

Start your day with orange pancakes or huevos rancheros and European-style espresso at **Cora's Coffee Shoppe** (page 530) in Santa Monica, a local favorite with a lovely patio. Head south to the **Venice Canals** (page 499) for an after-breakfast stroll. Originally built as a Venetian-themed amusement park, this network of canals is now a quiet residential district of waterways lined with bungalows.

Pack a picnic lunch, hop in the car, and head north for dazzling views and ocean breezes along the gorgeous **Pacific Coast Highway.** The highway connects Santa Monica with Malibu and its beautiful beaches, giving you plenty of opportunity to hit the sand and catch some rays. Try to catch a wave at **Malibu Surfriders Beach** (page 512). If you've had your fill of sunshine, spend your time in Malibu touring the small art collection at **The Getty Villa** (page 500) instead. End your day with seaside seafood at **Neptune's Net** (page 531), or go more romantic (and more upscale) at **Catch** (page 531).

Alternately, you may choose to head south to one of the Orange County beaches. Beachcombers might choose **Laguna Beach** (page 566), while surfers will want to experience the beach breaks at **Huntington Beach** (page 564). If you spend the night in the O.C., you will be well-situated for Day 3.

DAY 3

Let your inner child run free at **Disneyland** (page 537). Spend the day riding rides, rambling through crowds, and watching parades at the most lovingly crafted theme park in the world. For a full on Disney-riffic experience, enjoy a meal at the **Blue Bayou Restaurant** (page 542) overlooking the Pirates of the Caribbean ride, and spend the night at the **Disneyland Hotel** (page 540).

best times to visit are during festive annual celebrations like the Blessing of the Animals, around Easter, and, of course, Cinco de Mayo.

Cathedral of Our Lady of the Angels

Standing on a hillside next to the Hollywood Freeway (U.S. 101), the colossal concrete **Cathedral of Our Lady of the Angels** (555 W. Temple St., 213/680-5200, www.olacathedral. org, Mon.-Fri. 6:30am-6pm, Sat. 9am-6pm, Sun. 7am-6pm, open later for special events, tours Mon.-Fri. 1pm, free)—the first Roman Catholic cathedral to be built in the United States in 25 years and the third largest cathedral in the world—has been a vital part of the revitalization effort in L.A.'s beleaguered Downtown. It replaced the Cathedral of Saint Vibiana, which was damaged in the 1994 Northridge earthquake. Since its 2002 opening, the cathedral, which serves as much more than a place of worship, has attracted millions of visitors for free guided tours and such events as Christmas and Chinese New Year.

Every aspect of Spanish architect Rafael Moneo's design is monumental: the 25-ton bronze doors, 27,000 square feet of clerestory windows of translucent alabaster, and the 156-foot-high campanile topped with a 25-foot-tall cross. The cathedral, with seating for 3,000, is merely one part of a larger complex that houses the archbishop's residence, a conference center, and an expansive public courtyard. Critics of the lavish, nearly $190 million price tag dubbed the cathedral the "Taj Mahony" after Cardinal Roger Mahony, who oversaw the project. Others questioned the archdiocese's plan to counter operating expenses by offering crypts in the cathedral's underground mausoleum to wealthy patrons willing to donate $50,000 or more for such a privileged resting place.

The construction of a massive cathedral in the 21st century could have easily been a major anachronism. But the building's sleek design suggests a more forward-looking posture for the Catholic Church. The cathedral is proving to be a monument not just for the more than four million Catholics in L.A.; with events like music recitals, wine tastings, and art exhibitions, it welcomes the city as a whole.

Union Station

When **Union Station** (800 N. Alameda St., Amtrak 800/872-7245, www.amtrak.com, 24 hours daily) opened in 1939, 1.5 million people supposedly passed through its doors in the first three days, all wanting to witness what is now considered the last of the nation's great rail stations. Architects John and Donald Parkinson's design—an elegant mixture of Spanish mission and modern styles, incorporating vaulted arches, marble floors, and a 135-foot clock tower—was a fitting monument to the soaring aspirations of a burgeoning Los Angeles.

The station's immediate public success masked a decades-long political struggle over its construction. Civic planners first floated the idea of a unified terminal as early as 1911 but encountered stiff opposition from the major railroads, all of which feared the increased competition that a consolidated terminal would bring. After an entrenched campaign for public opinion, a site was finally approved by voters in 1926.

During the 1940s, Union Station thrived as a hub for both civilian and military traffic, and its stucco facade became a familiar backdrop in scores of classic films. But with the ascendancy of the automobile, the station fell into decline. By the 1970s the terminal was more often populated by pigeons than people.

Since the 1990s, however, the station has experienced a modest renaissance. Today, as the hub for the city's commuter rail network, it houses L.A.'s first modern subway line, which runs from Union Station to the mid-Wilshire and Hollywood districts. In 2003, the Metro Gold Line linked Downtown L.A. to Pasadena, with a future goal of extending east to Montclair. It will also be a major hub of the planned California High Speed Rail System. But even if your travel plans aren't locomotive, the station offers a rare glimpse of a more glamorous era of transport.

LOS ANGELES

MOCA

The **Museum of Contemporary Art, Los Angeles** (250 S. Grand Ave., 213/626-6222, www.moca.org, Mon. and Fri. 11am-5pm, Thurs. 11am-8pm, Sat.-Sun. 11am-6pm, adults $12, students and seniors $7, under age 12 free) is better known to its friends as MOCA. Here you'll see an array of artwork created between 1940 and yesterday afternoon. Highlights of the permanent collections include pop art and abstract expressionism from Europe and the United States. MOCA has two other locations in the area: The **Geffen Contemporary at MOCA** (152 N. Central Ave.) and the **MOCA Pacific Design Center** (8687 Melrose Ave., West Hollywood).

Downtown Art Walk

The dramatic sculptures and fountains adorning two blocks on Hope Street (300-500 Hope St.) include Alexander Calder's enormous *Four Arches* (1974) beside the Bank of America Plaza and Nancy Graves's whimsical *Sequi* (1986) near the Wells Fargo Center. A free, self-guided, public **Downtown Art Walk** (213/617-4929, http://downtownartwalk.org, second Thurs. of month, hours vary by gallery but usually noon-9pm) on the second Thursday evening of each month centers predominantly on the galleries in the area bounded by Spring, Main, 2nd, and 9th Streets, but it spreads out to the Calder and Graves pieces on Hope Street.

Los Angeles Central Library

The **Central Library** (630 W. 5th St., 213/228-7000, www.lapl.org, Mon., Wed., and Fri.-Sat. 10am-5:30pm, Tues. and Thurs. 10am-8pm) brings a bit of studious quiet to the business and bustle of Downtown. It is the third largest public library in the United States. The exterior's Egyptian influence owes much to the discovery of King Tut's tomb in 1922, the year the library was designed. Enter at Flower Street to visit the Maguire Gardens.

Bradbury Building

One of several historic L.A. structures featured in the movies *Chinatown* (1974), *Blade Runner* (1982), and *The Artist* (2011), the 1893 **Bradbury Building** (304 S. Broadway, lobby open daily 9am-5pm) is an office building that wows filmmakers with its light-filled Victorian court that includes wrought-iron staircases, marble stairs and open cage elevators. On Saturdays mornings, 2.5-hour docent-led tours (213/626-1893, www.laconservancy.org, Sat. 10am, reservations required, $10), run by the Los Angeles Conservancy, take visitors through Downtown to sights including the Bradbury Building.

Japanese American National Museum

The **Japanese American National Museum** (369 E. 1st St., 213/625-0414, www.janm.org, Tues., Wed., Fri.-Sun. 11am-5pm, Thurs. noon-8pm, adults $9, students and seniors $5, under age 5 free) focuses on the experience of Japanese people coming to and living in the United States. Japanese immigrants came by the thousands to California—one of the easiest and most pleasant places in the United States to get to from Japan. From the beginning they had a hard time of it, facing unending prejudice, exclusion, fear, and outright hatred. Despite this, the immigrants persisted, even after the horrific treatment of the Japanese American population by the U.S. government during World War II. Today, sushi bars are almost as common as diners in urban centers, and whole nurseries are devoted to bonsai gardening thrive. But the influence of Japanese culture reaches far beyond these everyday reminders; it has become integral to the unique mix of California culture. This museum shows the Japanese American experience in vivid detail, with photos and artifacts telling much of the story. You'll also find galleries sheltering temporary exhibitions like a recent one on origami art.

Fashion Institute of Design and Marketing

Have you come to L.A. for the fabulous designer clothes, but your credit cards are screaming in agony? Is your all-time favorite TV show *Project Runway?* Then L.A. has the perfect museum for you. **The Fashion Institute of Design and Marketing Museum and Galleries** (FIDM, 919 S. Grand Ave., Suite 250, 213/623-5821, http://fidmmuseum.org, Tues.-Sat. 10am-5pm, free) are open to the public, giving costume buffs and clotheshorses a window into high fashion, Hollywood costume design, and the world of a fashion design school. Check the website for current and upcoming exhibitions at the museum. Each winter around award season, the museum shows off a collection of costumes from the previous year's movies, highlighting the film honored with the Oscar for Best Costume Design. Through the rest of the year, FIDM pulls from its collection of more than 10,000 costumes and textiles to create exhibits based on style, era, movie genre, and whatever else the curators dream up. Parking is available in the underground garage for a fee. When you enter the building, tell the folks at the security desk that you're headed for the museum. A small but fun museum shop offers student work, unique accessories, and more.

Also housed in the FIDM building is the **Annette Green Perfume Museum** (Mon.-Sat. 10am-5pm, free). This is the world's first museum dedicated to scent and the role of perfume in society.

Natural History Museum of Los Angeles County

If you'd like your kids to have some fun with an educational purpose, take them to the **Natural History Museum of Los Angeles County** (900 Exposition Blvd., 213/763-3466, www.nhm.org, daily 9:30am-5pm, adults $12, students and seniors $9, teens $8, children $5, parking $8). This huge museum features many amazing galleries; some are transformed into examples of mammal habitats, while others display artifacts of various peoples indigenous to the western hemisphere. The Discovery Center welcomes children with a wide array of live animals and insects, plus hands-on displays that let kids learn by touching as well as looking. Dinosaur lovers can spend a whole day examining the museum's collection of fossils and models, which includes a trio of different aged T. rex specimens. Be sure to visit the megamouth shark as you walk through; it's the second specimen of the species ever recorded. Rock nuts flock to the Natural History Museum to see the fabulous gem and mineral display, complete with gold and a vault filled with rare precious stones. If you're interested in the natural history and culture of California, be sure to spend some time in the Lando Hall of California History.

The Natural History Museum sits within the larger Exposition Park complex. The **Natural History Museum Grill** (daily 10am-4pm) is the museum café. All exhibits are accessible for both wheelchairs and strollers, but ask at the ticket booths if you need special assistance to tour the museum. Do be aware that the surrounding neighborhood can be rough, so don't plan to explore the area around the museum on foot.

California Science Center

Another gem of Exposition Park, the exhibits at the **California Science Center** (700 Exposition Park Dr., 323/724-3623, www.californiasciencecenter.org, daily 10am-5pm, admission free, parking $10) focus on the notable achievements and gathered knowledge of humankind. Some of the best traveling scientific exhibits stop here, and permanent exhibits start before you even enter the building with the outdoor Science Plaza. Once inside, you'll find galleries dedicated to air and space technology, life as we know it, and human creativity. The new "Ecosystems" exhibit showcases 11 different natural environments including a living kelp forest and a polar ice wall. The last of NASA's space shuttles, the *Endeavour* is the newest and biggest feature at the Science Center, To see the shuttle, as well as take in an exhibit featuring the shuttle program's images and artifacts, reserve a timed entry by calling 213/744-2019 or by visiting www.californiasciencecenter.org.

Many people come to the California Science Center for the **IMAX theater** (daily, adults $8.25, seniors, teens, and students $6, children $4), which shows educational films on its tremendous seven-story screen. Your IMAX tickets also get you onto the rideable attractions of the Science Court.

LOS FELIZ AND SILVER LAKE

East of Hollywood, northwest of Downtown, Los Feliz, doggedly pronounced by most locals as "Los FEEL-is," is home to an eclectic mix of retired professionals, Armenian immigrants, and movie-industry hipsters lured by the bohemian vibe, mid-century modern architecture, and the neighborhood's proximity to Griffith Park. Despite the fact that gentrification brought waves of wealthier and more fashionable residents, this enclave and its neighbor to the southeast, Silver Lake, have so far managed to retain their unique, laid-back flavor.

◖ Griffith Park

Griffith Park (Los Feliz Blvd., Zoo Dr., or Griffith Park, 323/913-4688, www.laparks.org, daily 5am-10:30pm, free) is the largest municipal park with an urban wilderness area in the country. It has an endless array of attractions and amenities to suit every style of visitor. If you love the stars, visit the recently renovated **Griffith Observatory** (2800 East Observatory Rd., 213/473-0800, www.griffithobs.org, Tues.-Fri. noon-10pm, Sat.-Sun. 10am-10pm, free), where free telescopes are available and experienced demonstrators help visitors gaze at the stars—the ones in the sky, that is. Or take in a film about the earth or sky in the aluminum-domed **Samuel Oschin Planetarium** (in Griffith Observatory, visit www.griffithobservatory.org for show times, $3-7).

Golfers can choose among two 18-hole courses, one 9-hole course, and a 9-hole, par-three course located on the parklands. A swimming pool cools visitors in the summer. You'll find a baseball field, basketball and tennis courts, children's playgrounds, and endless miles of hiking and horseback riding trails threading their way far into the backcountry of the park.

If you prefer a more structured park experience, try the **L.A. Zoo and Botanical Gardens** (5333 Zoo Dr., 323/644-4200, www.lazoo.org, daily 10am-5pm, adults $16, seniors $13, children $11, free parking). If the weather is poor (yes, it does rain in L.A.), step inside the **Museum of the American West** at the Autry National Center (4700 Western Heritage Way, 323/667-2000, www.theautry.org, Tues.-Sat. 10am-4pm, Sun. 11am-5pm, adults $10, students and seniors $6, children $4).

Kids love riding the trains of the operating miniature railroad at both the **Travel Town Railroad** (5200 Zoo Dr., 323/662-9678, www.griffithparktrainrides.com, Mon.-Fri. 10am-3:15pm, Sat.-Sun. 10am-4:15pm, $2.50) from the **Travel Town Museum** (5200 Zoo Dr., 323/662-5874, http://traveltown.org, Mon.-Fri. 10am-4pm, Sat.-Sun. 10am-6pm) and the **Griffith Park & Southern Railroad** (4400 Crystal Springs Dr., 323/664-6903, www.griffithparktrainrides.com, Mon.-Fri. 10am-4:15pm, Sat.-Sun. 10am-4:30pm, $2.50).

Griffith Park has played host to many production companies over the years, with its land and buildings providing backdrops for many major films. Scenes from *Rebel Without a Cause* were filmed here, as were parts of the first two *Back to the Future* movies. Its use is appropriate to the park's rich history. Much of the land that now makes up the 4,210-acre park was donated by miner and philanthropist Griffith J. Griffith (really). It has changed much over the years, but remains one of Los Angeles's great prizes.

The **Hollywood Sign** sits on Mount Lee, which is part of the park and indelibly part of the mystique of Hollywood. A strenuous five-mile hike will lead you to an overlook just above and behind the sign. To get there, drive to the top of Beachwood Drive, park and follow the Hollyridge Trail.

Hollyhock House

Hollyhock House (4800 Hollywood Blvd., 323/644-6269, www.hollyhockhouse.net, docent-led tours Fri.-Sun. 12:30pm, 1:30pm, 2:30pm, and 3:30pm, adults $7, seniors $3, children $2) was the first L.A. home designed by Frank Lloyd Wright. Finished in 1923, it was built for Aline Barnsdall, a patron of the arts, and is located in what is now **Barnsdall Art Park.** Hollyhocks, Barnsdall's favorite flower, are an elemental theme in the decor.

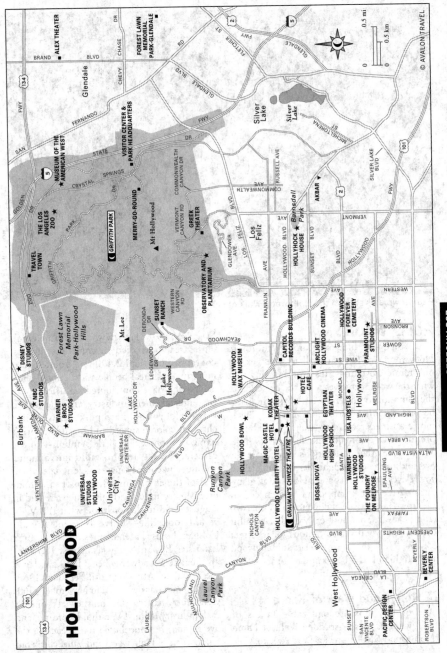

HOLLYWOOD

LOS ANGELES

© STUART THORNTON

Paul Newman's star on the Hollywood Walk of Fame

HOLLYWOOD

You won't find blocks of movie studios in Hollywood, and few stars walk its streets except on premiere evenings. It's an odd irony that what the world perceives to be the epicenter of the film industry has little left of that industry beyond its tourist destinations. The only "real" movie business remaining are the blockbuster premieres at the major movie theaters here. Most of the other destinations range from the oversold to the downright kitschy. But still, if you've ever had a soft spot for Hollywood glamour or American camp, come and check out the crowds and bustle of downtown Tinseltown (and be aware that no local would *ever* call it that). Hollywood is also famous for its street corners. While the most stuff sits at Hollywood and Highland, the best-known corner is certainly Hollywood and Vine.

【 Hollywood Walk of Fame

One of the most recognizable facets of Hollywood is its star-studded **Walk of Fame** (Hollywood Blvd. from La Brea Ave. to Vine St., 323/469-8311, www.walkoffame.com). This area, portrayed in countless movies, contains more than 2,400 five-pointed stars honoring both real people and fictional characters who have contributed significantly to the entertainment industry and the legend that is Hollywood. Each pink star is set in a charcoal-colored square and has its honoree's name in bronze. The little symbols—movie camera, TV set, record, radio microphone, and tragedy-comedy masks—designate which part of the entertainment industry the honoree is recognized for. Eight stars were laid in August 1958 to demonstrate what the Walk would look like—Olive Borden, Ronald Colman, Louise Fazenda, Preston Foster, Burt Lancaster, Edward Sedgwick, Ernest Torrance, and Joanne Woodward. Legal battles delayed the actual construction until February 1960, and the walk was dedicated in November 1960. Gene Autry has five stars on the walk, one for each industry (film, TV, radio, recording, and live theater) he contributed to. At each of the four corners of Hollywood and Vine, check out

© STUART THORNTON

Grauman's Chinese Theatre

the four moons that honor the three Apollo 11 astronauts—Neil Armstrong, Michael Collins, and Edwin E. "Buzz" Aldrin Jr. Also look for your favorite cartoon characters: Kermit the Frog, Mickey Mouse, and Bugs Bunny are all honored on the Walk of Fame.

You don't need to pay to get into anything, just get out on the sidewalk and start to stroll; the complete walk is about 3.5 miles. You'll be looking down at the stars, so watch out for other pedestrians crowding the sidewalks in this visitor-dense area. At the edges of the Walk of Fame, you'll find blank stars waiting to be filled by up-and-comers making their mark on Tinseltown. If you desperately need to find a specific star and want help doing so, you can take a guided tour of the Walk, but really, it's a waste of money—careful reading and an online map (www.hollywoodusa.co.uk) will find you everyone's star you need to see.

Hollywood Wax Museum

It immortalizes your favorite stars, all right. If you want to see the Hollywood heavyweights all dressed up in costume and completely unable to run away, visit the **Hollywood Wax Museum** (6767 Hollywood Blvd., 323/462-5991, www.hollywoodwaxmuseum.com, daily 10am-midnight, adults $16, seniors $14, children $9). You can't miss it, since the brilliant sign lights up a good chunk of Hollywood Boulevard, especially at night. Inside, you'll see everyone from Lucille Ball to Captain Jack Sparrow. The shtick of this wax museum is, of course, movies. The exhibits are re-creations of the sets of all sorts of films, and as you pass through you'll be right in the action (if staring at eerie, life-size wax likenesses of real people can be called action). You can even get a glimpse of stars on the red carpet at an awards show-style set.

The Hollywood Wax Museum first opened to amazed crowds in February 1965. To this day, it remains inexplicably popular with visitors and locals alike.

If you need yet another cotton-candy museum experience, right across the street is the **Guinness World of Records Museum** (6780 Hollywood Blvd., 323/463-6433, www.ripley-attractions.com, daily 10am-midnight, adults $17, children $9). Here you'll find exhibits describing the records related in the book of the same name.

C Grauman's Chinese Theatre

You can't miss the **Grauman's Chinese Theatre** (6801 Hollywood Blvd., 323/461-3331, www.chinesetheatres.com) on Hollywood Boulevard. With its elaborate 90-foot-tall Chinese temple gateway and unending crowd of visitors, the Chinese Theatre may be the most visited and recognizable movie theater in the world. Along with the throngs of tourists out front, there are usually elaborately costumed movie characters from Captain Jack Sparrow to Spiderman shaking hands with fans and posing for pictures. Inside the courtyard you'll find handprints and footprints of legendary Hollywood stars. Be sure to stop and admire the bells, dogs, and other Chinese artifacts in the courtyard—most are the genuine article, imported from China by special permit in the 1920s. The theater

FILM FESTIVALS

Home of Hollywood and many of the world's most famous movie stars, Los Angeles is an ideal place to go to the movies. It's even better when you can attend a film festival.

There seems to be an endless array of film festivals in the Los Angeles area, but here are a few notable fests. Co-founded by actor Danny Glover, the **Pan African Film and Arts Festival** (http://discoverblackheritage.com) takes place in February and highlights the works of people of African descent from all over the world.

Movies including Pixar's *Brave* have debuted at the **Los Angeles Film Festival** (www.lafilmfest.com). The LAFF happens in June and includes the screening of 100 films.

Outfest (www.outfest.org) is the oldest continuous film festival in Los Angeles, and it highlights LBGT-oriented movies in July.

The **Downtown Film Festival L.A.** (www.dffla.com), which also goes down in July, is for filmgoers who enjoy under-the-radar indie cinema.

The non-profit American Film Institute played some of 2011's biggest pictures of the year including *The Artist* at its November 2011 **AFI Fest** (www.afi.com). Come to see what are sure to be some of the year's most talked about movies.

a glimpse of the stars at a premiere, be aware that most of these are private events.

Egyptian Theater

Even before Grauman's Chinese, Hollywood had the **Egyptian Theater** (6712 Hollywood Blvd., 323/466-3456, www.americancinematheque.com, adults $11, students and seniors $9). Built under the auspices of the legendary Sid Grauman, the Egyptian was the first of the grandiose movie houses in Hollywood proper and a follower of those in Downtown Los Angeles. King Tut's tomb had been discovered in 1922, and the glorified Egyptian styling of the theater followed the trend for all things Egyptian that came after. The massive courtyard and the stage both boasted columns, sphinxes, and other Egyptian-esque decor. The first movie to premiere at the Egyptian was *Robin Hood*, in 1922, followed nine months later by the premiere of *The Ten Commandments*. In the 1920s, the showing of a film was preceded by an elaborate live "prologue," featuring real actors in costume on a stage before the screen (the early ancestry of the *Rocky Horror Picture Show*). The Egyptian's stage was second to none, and the prologue of *The Ten Commandments* was billed as the most elaborate to date.

After a haul through the 1950s as a reserved-seat, long-run movie house, the Egyptian fell into disrepair and eventually closed. A massive renovation completed in 1998 restored it to its former glory. Today, you can get tickets to an array of old-time films, or take a morning tour to get a glimpse at the history of this magnificent old theater. Expect to pay $5-20 for parking in one of the nearby lots.

Hollywood Forever Cemetery

The final resting place of such Hollywood legends as Rudolph Valentino, Marion Davies, and Douglas Fairbanks, the **Hollywood Forever Cemetery** (6000 Santa Monica Blvd., 323/469-1181, www.hollywoodforever.com, daily 8am-5pm) has received a dramatic makeover and now offers live funeral webcasts. During the summer, the cemetery screens films

was built by Sid Grauman and opened in all its splendor on May 18, 1927, with the premiere of *The King of Kings*. For the first time, stars swanned up the red carpet to the cheers (and eventual riot) of the throng of thousands of fans gathered outside. The next day, the public was allowed into the now hallowed theater.

The studios hold premieres at the Chinese Theatre all the time. Check the website for showtimes and ticket information. The Chinese Theatre has only one screen but seats over 1,000 people per showing. While you're welcome to crowd the sidewalk to try to catch and holds concerts by national touring acts on its Fairbanks Lawn. Visit their website for a list of upcoming events.

Paramount Studios

Paramount Studios (5555 Melrose Ave., 323/956-5000, www.paramountstudios.com, tours $48-150) is the only major movie studio still operating in Hollywood proper. The wrought-iron gates that greet visitors were erected to deter adoring Rudolph Valentino fans in the 1920s. Tours ranging from 2-4.5 hours are available. Visit the website or call the studio for tour information.

Mulholland Drive

As you drive north out of central Hollywood into the residential part of the neighborhood, you will find folks on street corners hawking maps of stars' homes on **Mulholland Drive** (entrance west of U.S. 101 via Barham Blvd. exit) and its surrounding neighborhoods. Whether you choose to pay up to $10 for a photocopied sheet of dubious information is up to you. What's certain is that you can drive the famed road yourself. When you reach the ridge, you'll see why so many of the intensely wealthy in Los Angeles choose to make their homes here. From the ridgeline, on clear days you can see down into the Los Angeles Basin and the coast to the west, and the fertile land of the San Fernando Valley to the east. Whether you care about movie-star homes or not, the view itself is worth the trip, especially if it has rained recently and the smog is down. You won't see the facade of Britney Spears's multimillion-dollar hideaway facing the street, but a few homes do face the road—most boasting mid-century modern architecture. If you can see them, they probably don't belong to movie stars, who guard their privacy from the endless intrusion of paparazzi and fans.

LA BREA, FAIRFAX, AND MIRACLE MILE

This midtown district can seem a bit of a mishmash, lacking an overarching identity of its own. And yet the area's streets are among the best known and most heavily trafficked in Los Angeles.

Lined with fabric emporiums, antiques dealers, and contemporary furniture design shops, Beverly Boulevard and La Brea Avenue north of Wilshire Boulevard are increasingly trendy haunts for interior decorators. Along bustling and pedestrian-friendly Fairfax Avenue, kosher bakeries and signs in Hebrew announce the presence of the neighborhood's sizable Jewish population. Around the corner on 3rd Street, the Farmers Market is one of L.A.'s historic gathering places. And farther south, Wilshire Boulevard is home to some of the city's many museums, including the Los Angeles County Museum of Art.

La Brea Tar Pits

Even if you've never been within 1,000 miles of California before, you've probably heard of the **La Brea Tar Pits** and the wonders found within them. But where once tour groups made their stinky way around crude fences protecting them from the pits, now paved paths lead around the most accessible pits, and others (mostly those that are in active excavation) are accessible by guided tour only. Nothing can stop the smell of the tar, or the slow bubbling of the shallow miasma of water that covers the tar.

If what interests you most are the fossilized contents of the tar pits, head for the beautiful **Page Museum** (5801 Wilshire Blvd., 323/857-6300, www.tarpits.org, daily 9:30am-5pm, adults $11, students and seniors $8, children $5, parking $7-9). The Page contains the bones of many of the untold thousands of animals that became trapped in the sticky tar and met their fate there. The museum's reasonably small size and easy-to-understand interpretive signs make it great for kids and good for a shorter stop for grown-ups. You'll see some amazing skeletal remains, including sloths the size of Clydesdale horses. Genuine mammoths died and were fossilized in the tar pits, as were the tiniest of mice and about a zillion dire wolves. One of the coolest things for science geeks is the big windowed cage housing the paleontologists at work. You can watch them cleaning, examining, sorting, and cataloging bones from the most recent excavations.

◖ Los Angeles County Museum of Art

Travelers who desperately need a break from the endless, shiny, and mindless entertainments of L.A. can find respite and solace in the **Los Angeles County Museum of Art** (5905 Wilshire Blvd., 323/857-6000, www.lacma. org, Mon.-Tues. and Thurs. 11am-5pm, Fri. 11am-8pm, Sat.-Sun. 10am-7pm, adults $15, seniors and students with ID $10, under age 18 free), the largest art museum in the western United States. Better known to its friends as LACMA, this museum complex prides itself on a diverse array of collections and exhibitions of art from around the world, from the ancient to the most ultramodern. With nine full-size buildings filled with galleries, don't expect to get through the whole thing in an hour, or even a full day. You'll see all forms of art here, from classic painting and sculpture to all sorts of decorative arts (that is, ceramics, jewelry, metalwork, and more). All major cultural groups are represented, so you can check out Islamic, Southeast Asian, European, and Californian art, plus more. Specialties of LACMA include Japanese art and artifacts in the beautifully designed Pavilion for Japanese Art and the costumes and textiles of the Doris Stein Research Center. Several galleries of LACMA West are dedicated to art and craft for children. Perhaps best of all, some of the world's most prestigious traveling exhibitions come to LACMA; past exhibitions have included the works of Salvador Dalí and a new take on Tutankhamen.

You'll do a lot of walking from gallery to gallery and building to building at LACMA. Inquire at one of the two welcome centers for wheelchairs. Not all the buildings are connected; you must walk outside to get to the Japanese Pavilion and LACMA West. The complex is equipped with two full-service museum cafés, an ATM, and a gift and bookshop. And finally, if you're in need of some fine rental artwork, LACMA can hook you up.

If you prefer automotive artistry to more conventional forms, head across the street from LACMA to the **Petersen Automotive Museum** (6060 Wilshire Blvd., 323/930-2277, www.petersen.org, Tues.-Sun. 10am-6pm, adults $10, seniors $8, children $3, students or active military with ID $5, parking $2-8).

Farmers Market

Begun in 1934 as a tailgate co-op for a handful of fruit farmers, the **Farmers Market** (6333 W. 3rd St., 323/933-9211 or 866/993-9211, www. farmersmarketla.com, Mon.-Fri. 9am-9pm, Sat. 9am-8pm, Sun. 10am-7pm) quickly became an institution for Angelenos who flocked here to buy produce, flowers, and candy, or just to cool their cars and have a chat.

The market was built by entrepreneurs Roger Dahlhjelm and Fred Beck, who leased the land at 3rd Street and Fairfax Avenue from oil tycoon Arthur Fremont Gilmore; it quickly grew beyond its initial wooden produce stalls into a bustling arcade. A whitewashed clock tower went up in 1941, signaling the market's growing importance as an ersatz village square for local residents. During the 1940s and 1950s, the tables at Magee's and Du-par's were crowded with regulars, and over the years the site has hosted circus acts, parades, petting zoos, and Gilmore's "Gas-a-teria," reputedly the world's first self-service gas station.

Today, the market remains a favorite locale for people-watching and, along with the adjacent shopping center, The Grove, now has over 30 restaurants and 50 shops hawking everything from hot sauce to stickers. Gourmands will find fresh fruit, chocolate truffles, sushi, gumbo, Mexican cuisine, and a plethora of other foods. There are even annual events, such as a vintage auto show in early June, free summer concerts every Thursday and Friday, and a fall festival.

BEVERLY HILLS AND WEST HOLLYWOOD

Although the truly wealthy live above Hollywood on Mulholland Drive, in Bel Air, or on the beach at Malibu, there's still plenty of money floating around in Beverly Hills.

Some of the world's best and most expensive shops sit on the streets of Beverly Hills. You'll also find more-than-adequate high-end culture in the area, which bleeds into West L.A. The division seems almost seamless now, compared to the tremendous class gash that used to exist between Beverly Hills and the infamous Sunset Strip.

Sunset Strip

A much shorter but equally famous stretch of road, the **Sunset Strip** really is part of Sunset Boulevard—specifically the part that runs 1.5 miles through West Hollywood from the edge of Hollywood to the Beverly Hills city limits. The Strip exemplifies all that's grandiose and tacky about the L.A. entertainment industry. Few other places, even in California, boast about the number and glaring overstatement of their billboards. You'll also find many of the Strip's legendary rock clubs, such as **The Roxy** and the **Whisky a Go Go** and the infamous after-hours hangout **The Rainbow Bar & Grill**. Decades worth of up-and-coming rock acts first made their names on the Strip and lived at the "Riot Hyatt."

If you last visited the Strip more than a decade ago, you might fear bringing your children to what was once a distinctly seedy neck of the woods. Then again, old-timers might be horrified now by the gentrification of the Strip. Today, a woman alone can stroll the street in comfort in daylight. At night, especially on weekends, no one's alone on the Strip. Don't plan to drive quickly or park on the street after dark; the crowds get big, complete with celebrity hounds hoping for a glimpse of their favorite star out for a night on the town.

WESTWOOD

Designed around the campus of UCLA and the Westwood Village commercial district, this community situated between Santa Monica and Beverly Hills won national recognition in the 1930s as a model of innovative suburban planning. And while the generic faces of nondescript offices and apartment blocks have since encroached on the area, especially to the west,

recent slow-growth initiatives have preserved the heart of Westwood as one of L.A.'s most pleasant neighborhoods.

University of California, Los Angeles

From its original quad of 10 buildings, the campus of the **University of California, Los Angeles** (UCLA, bounded by Hilgard Ave., Sunset Blvd., Le Conte Ave., and Gayley Ave., tours 310/825-8764, www.ucla.edu) has become the largest in the University of California system, with more than 400 buildings set on and around the 419 beautifully-kept acres with a student population of nearly 40,000. Today its facilities include one of the top medical centers in the country, a library of more than eight million volumes, and a number of renowned performance venues, including Royce Hall and Schoenberg Hall.

Running from the south edge of the UCLA campus along Westwood Boulevard toward Wilshire Boulevard, the Westwood Village shopping district caters to a lively mix of students and local residents with a clutch of bookstores, record shops, and cafés. The district also boasts the highest density of movie theaters in the country, with a number of restored landmarks.

◖ The Getty Center

Located on a hilltop above the mansions of Brentwood and the 405 freeway, **The Getty Center** (1200 Getty Center Dr., 310/440-7300, www.getty.edu, Tues.-Thurs. and Sun. 10am-5:30pm, Fri.-Sat. 10am-9pm, admission free, parking $15) is famous for art and culture in Los Angeles. Donated by the family of J. Paul Getty to the people of Los Angeles, this museum features European art, sculpture, manuscripts, and European and American photos. The magnificent works are set in fabulous modern buildings with soaring architecture, and you're guaranteed to find something beautiful to catch your eye and feed your imagination. The spacious galleries have comfy sofas to let you sit back and take in the paintings and drawings. Be sure to take a stroll outdoors to

LOS ANGELES

© STUART THORNTON

the artful architecture of the Getty Center

admire the sculpture collections on the lawns as well as the exterior architecture.

On a clear day, the views from the Getty, which sweep from Downtown L.A. clear west to the Pacific, are remarkable. But the museum pavilions themselves are also stunning. Richard Meier's striking design is multi-textured, with exterior grids of metal and unfinished Italian travertine marble, similar to that used by the Romans to build the Colosseum. The blockish buildings have fountains, glass windows several stories high, and an open plan that permits intimate vistas of the city below. There is also a central garden to stroll through and a cactus garden perched on a south-facing promontory with a view of the city below.

Pierce Brothers Westwood Village Memorial Park

Not known as well as L.A.'s Hollywood Forever Cemetery or Forest Lawn, the **Pierce Brothers Westwood Village Memorial Park** (1218 Glendon Ave., 310/474-1579, www.pbwvmortuary.com) is the final resting place of some of the world's most popular entertainers and musicians. Under the shadows of the towering high rises of Wilshire Boulevard, this small cemetery is the home of Marilyn Monroe's crypt, which is frequently decorated with lipstick marks from her enduring legion of fans. Westwood Village Memorial Park is home to other entertainment icons including Rat Packer Dean Martin, author Truman Capote, eclectic musician Frank Zappa, and *The Odd Couple* Walter Matthau and Jack Lemmon.

SANTA MONICA, VENICE, AND MALIBU

When many people from around the world think of "L.A.," what they're really picturing are the beach communities skirting the coastline to the west of Los Angeles proper. Some of the most famous and most expensive real estate in the world sits on this stretch of sand and earth. Of the communities that call the northern coast of L.A. County home, the focal points are Malibu to the north, Santa Monica, and then Venice to the south.

Malibu doesn't look like a town or a city in the conventional sense. If you're searching for the historic downtown or the town center, give up; there isn't one. Instead, the "town" of Malibu stretches for more than 20 miles, hugging the beach the whole way. A few huge homes perch precariously on the mountains rising up over the coastline, also part of Malibu. Many beach-loving superstars make their homes here, and the price of a beach house can easily exceed $20 million.

A few more liberal and social stars prefer to purchase from among the closely packed dwellings of Venice Beach. A bastion of true California liberal-mindedness and the home of several famous landmarks, Venice might be the perfect (if expensive) place to take a movie-style L.A. beach vacation.

Santa Monica comes as close to a community of moderate means as you'll find in this region. With its fun-but-not-fancy pier, its inexpensive off-beach motels, and a huge variety of delicious and inexpensive dining options, Santa Monica is a great choice for a family vacation.

Santa Monica Pier

For the ultimate in SoCal beach kitsch, you can't miss the **Santa Monica Pier** (Ocean Ave. at Colorado Ave., 310/458-8901, www.santa-monicapier.org). As you walk the rather long stretch of concrete out over the water, you'll see an amazing array of carnival-style food stands, an arcade, a small amusement park, a trapeze school, and restaurants leading out to the fishing area at the tip of the pier. There's even an aquarium located under the pier! The main attraction is **Pacific Park** (310/260-8744, www.pacpark.com, Sun.-Thurs. 11am-11pm,

© STUART THORNTON

Santa Monica Pier

Fri.-Sat. 11am-12:30am, rides priced individually, $3-5 per ride, all-ride pass $16-22, parking $6-12). This park features a roller coaster, a scrambler, and the world's first solar-powered Ferris wheel. Several rides are geared for the younger set, and a 20-game midway provides fun for all ages. Beneath the pier lies a sandy beach with a decent surf break—one of the major attractions of the area in the summer.

You can drive onto the first half of the pier. Parking lots sit both on and beneath it, although your chances aren't great if you're trying for a spot on a summer weekend. Many hotels and restaurants are within walking distance of the pier, as is the Third Street Promenade shopping district.

ⓒ Venice Boardwalk

If the Santa Monica Pier doesn't provide you with enough chaos and kitsch, head on down to the **Venice Boardwalk** (Ocean Front Walk at Venice Blvd., www.venicebeach.com) for a nearly unlimited supply of both year-round. Locals refer to the Boardwalk as "The Zoo"

and tend to shun the area, especially in the frantic summer months. As you shamble down the tourist-laden path, you'll pass an astonishing array of tacky souvenir stores, tattoo and piercing parlors, walk-up food stands, and more. On the beach side of the path, dozens of artists create sculptures and hawk their wares. You can watch sculptors create amazing works of art out of sand, or purchase a piece of locally made jewelry. This area has more than its share of L.A.'s colorful characters—turbans, feather boas, and roller skates are not uncommon. The beach side includes the infamous **Muscle Beach** (two blocks north of Venice Blvd., www.musclebeach.net), an easily distinguished chunk of sand filled with modern workout equipment and encircled by a barrier.

The wide, flat beach adjacent to the Boardwalk gets incredibly crowded in the summer. Parking can be nightmarish in this district of car-free walking streets. Expect to park far from the beach and the Boardwalk and to pay for the privilege. The beach at Venice is lifeguard-protected and has restroom and

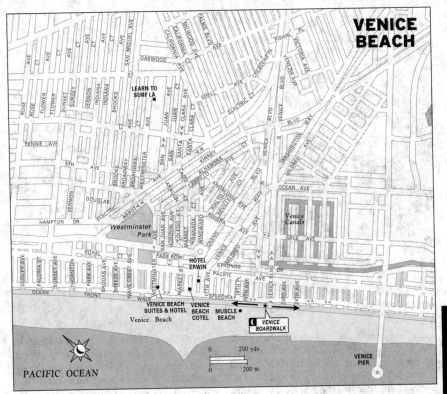

shower facilities built on the sand. You can get all the junk food you can stomach from the Boardwalk stands.

Venice Canals

If you've grown tired of the frenzied Boardwalk (or the idea of those crowds make you break out in hives), consider taking a much more sedate walk along the paths of the **Venice Canals** (generally bounded by Washington Blvd., Strongs Dr., S. Venice Blvd., and Ocean Ave.). Venice locals seek out the canals when they want to take a stroll or walk their dogs (Venice is a very dog-oriented town) and enjoy the serenity and peace of the quiet waterways. The home gardens and city-maintained landscaping add a lush layer of greenery to the narrow canals. Taking these paths gets you deep into the neighborhood and close to the impressive

20th-century Southern California architecture of Venice. Many of the people who own homes on the canals launch small boats and put on an annual boat parade for the holidays. As you wander this area, marvel at the history of the canals, modeled after those in this beach town's European namesake city. Also, admire the tenacity with which the city saved these last few from the landfill that removed their brethren from the landscape.

Will Rogers State Historic Park

Did you grow up loving the films and culture of the early Hollywood western? If so, one of the best sights in Santa Monica for you is **Will Rogers State Historic Park** (1501 Will Rogers Park Rd., Pacific Palisades, 310/454-8212, www.parks.ca.gov, grounds open daily 8am-sunset, tours Thurs.-Fri. on the hour

Venice Boardwalk's vendor stalls

© STUART THORNTON

11am-3pm, Sat.-Sun. on the hour 10am-4pm, free, $12 for parking). This 186-acre ranch with its sprawling 31-room house was the home and retreat of Will Rogers and his family. Rogers's widow, Betty, donated the property to the state on her death in 1944. Today, you can tour the large home and check out some of the facilities of the active working ranch that still exist on the property. Or take a walk around the regulation-size polo field that was Will's joy. If you share Will's love of horses, visit the stables to take a lesson or go out for a ride out on the local range. Travelers who prefer their own two feet can take a three-mile hike to Inspiration Point or a longer trek on the Backbone Trail out into the Santa Monica Mountains.

Malibu Pier

There are few true "sights" along the long thin stretch of sand that is Malibu. One of those worth checking out is the **Malibu Pier** (23000 Pacific Coast Hwy., 888/310-7437, www.malibupiersportfishing.com). The pier gets busy in the summer and lonely in the winter, though the die-hard surfers plying the adjacent three-point break stick around year-round. A few pier anglers also brave the so-called chilly weather of the Malibu off-season, but you'll feel a sense of some solitude when you walk out across the planks. Some attractions out on the pier include interpretive signs describing the history of Malibu, sport fishing and whale-watching charters, restaurants, and food stands. In the near future, a surf museum is scheduled to open on the structure. If you'd prefer to ride the waves yourself, you can rent surf and boogie boards as well as other beach toys on the pier.

The Getty Villa

Even driving up to **The Getty Villa** (17985 Pacific Coast Hwy., Pacific Palisades, 310/440-7300, www.getty.edu, Wed.-Mon. 10am-5pm, free but reservations are required, parking $15) on its Roman-inspired stone driveway will send your mind back to ancient times. The two-floor villa is modeled after a Roman country house that was buried by the AD 79

Malibu's Getty Villa is an underrated gem.

eruption of Mount Vesuvius. The villa's architecture and surrounding gardens is a replica of the type of world the 1,200 works of art inside were produced in. The museum features amazingly intact statues and jewelry from the ancient Greeks, Romans, and Etruscans. Stare at the larger than life "Marbury Hall Zeus" from around AD 100 or a Greek sculpture of the same god that was submerged in the sea causing it to look like coral. Tickets are free, but you have to reserve them in advance if you want to enjoy this exclusive, intimate, and dazzling experience.

PASADENA

If Venice Beach is the liberal haven of L.A., rockers love the Sunset Strip, and gay people flock to West Hollywood, Pasadena is the elder statesman of Los Angeles neighborhoods and towns. Once a resort-like haven for the very wealthy, Pasadena gently decayed, then was recreated as a charming upper-middle-class residential town. Dotted throughout Pasadena you can still see fabulous examples of the craftsman architecture that was prevalent throughout Southern California in the early 20th century. This older city also lays claim to one of the best known and most attended parades (and ensuing college football games) in the United States, the Rose Parade on New Year's Day.

The Huntington

Some of the most beautiful botanical gardens in the world grow in Pasadena. **The Huntington** (1151 Oxford Rd., San Marino, 626/405-2100, www.huntington. org, Memorial Day-Labor Day Wed.-Mon. 10:30am-4:30pm, Labor Day-Memorial Day Wed.-Thurs. and Mon. noon-4:30pm, Sat.-Sun. 10:30am-4:30pm, adults Mon.-Fri. $20, adults Sat.-Sun. $23, seniors Mon.-Fri. $15, seniors Sat.-Sun. $18, students Mon.-Fri. $12, students Sat.-Sun. $13, children $6) also includes an amazing library filled with rare and ancient books and manuscripts. Literary travelers and locals come to the Huntington to view and worship the Gutenberg Bible and a manuscript of *The Canterbury Tales*. Art lovers come to view works by Van der Weyden, Gainsborough, Hopper, and more. And everyone comes to explore the 120 acres of gardens, the most popular part of the complex.

More than a dozen different gardens beckon, including the Desert Garden, the Japanese Garden, and the Rose Garden. It takes more than one tour to get a real sense of all that grows here; pick your favorite area and enjoy a peaceful respite from the endless chaos of the L.A. area. Admission to the center includes a docent-led garden tour. Check the website for a look at what will be in bloom when you're in town.

Some of the best museum café food in the state can be had at the **Rose Garden Tea Room and Café** (Tea Room reservations 626/683-8131, no reservations needed for café, Mon. and Wed.-Fri. noon-4:30pm, Sat.-Sun. 10:45am-4:30pm, adults $28, ages 4-8 $15, ages 2-3 $7.50). You can get a scrumptious buffet-style high tea when the museum is open. For a more traditional snack or light lunch, the walk-up café offers salads, sandwiches, and hot soups.

The Gamble House

Where Northern California prides itself on its Victorian architecture, major construction didn't get underway quite as fast in the southern part of the state. Here many of the wealthy residents, such as the Gambles (of Procter & Gamble), built homes in the early 20th century. **The Gamble House** (4 Westmoreland Pl., 626/793-3334, www.gamblehouse.org, Thurs.-Sun. noon-3pm, adults $10, seniors and students with ID $7, under age 12 free) was designed and decorated by legendary SoCal architects Greene and Greene in the American craftsman or American arts and crafts style. The only way to get inside is to take a tour (schedules vary by season). To buy tickets, go to the side of the main mansion and into the garage, built in the same style as the house, that now acts as a bookstore and ticket office.

Inside the house, you'll be led from room to room as the docent describes the construction and decor in detail. The craftsman aesthetic attempted to answer the overly ornate and precious Victorian style with long, clean lines and botanical motifs. The Greenes took this philosophy to heart in the construction of the Gamble house—you'll learn how they created this masterpiece as you view each unique room. You'll also see how the Gambles lived inside the house and hear some of their stories, even that of the house's possible haunting by Aunt Julia. The only places in the mansion that you won't see are two upstairs servants' rooms, now the home of two lucky architecture students who live in the house each school year.

Norton Simon Museum

Believe it or not, much of the nearly two millennia of art displayed at the **Norton Simon Museum** (411 W. Colorado Blvd., 626/449-6840, www.nortonsimon.org, Wed.-Thurs. and Sat.-Mon. noon-6pm, Fri. noon-9pm, adults $10, seniors $7, students and children free) were once part of a private collection. Wealthy industrialist Norton Simon collected the thousands of works of art over 30 years. He particularly loved the European Renaissance, the works of South and Southeast Asia, and 20th-century sculpture. Several of his most famous Auguste Rodin sculptures decorate the walkway up to the main entrance to the museum. You can visit the lovely modern building housing large, airy galleries to study the beautiful works of fine art. Be sure to head outside to walk through the sculpture gardens in the courtyards behind the building. You can purchase books and reproductions in the museum store or grab a bite to eat at the simple, walk-up Garden Café.

Rose Bowl Stadium

The **Rose Bowl Stadium** (1001 Rose Bowl Dr., 626/577-3101, www.rosebowlstadium.com, office Mon.-Fri. 8:30am-5:30pm), true to its name, is the home to the famed granddaddy of the bowl games and to the UCLA college football team. Built in 1922, this huge elliptical bowl at first had an open side. It was closed only a few years later, and now seats almost (but not quite) 100,000 people—perfect for the Super Bowl as well as the flea markets and endless parade of college games. In addition to the endless vista of seats, you'll find plenty of restrooms and concessions scattered throughout the stadium—far more than the average college football team's home turf.

You can visit the Rose Bowl anytime, although you might need a ticket during an event, and you'll definitely need to plan in advance to attend the Rose Bowl game. Check the online calendar to find a fun event to attend for the best sense of this National Historic Landmark.

Entertainment and Events

NIGHTLIFE
Bars

Whatever your taste in bars, whether it tends toward hipster dives, old-school watering holes, or beautiful lounges, L.A. will be able to offer its version.

Golden Gopher (417 W. 8th St., 213/614-8001, http://213nightlife.com, Sat.-Mon. 8pm-2am, Tues.-Fri. 5pm-2am), which started the Downtown nightlife scene, draws hipsters from all over L.A. For those who don't know the meaning of excess, a liquor store on the premises—allowed by a very, very old liquor license—sells bottles of booze and craft beers to go.

The soaring two-story **Broadway Bar** (830 S. Broadway, 213/614-9909, http://213nightlife.com, Tues.-Fri. 5pm-2am, Sat. 8pm-2am, available for private parties and special events Sun.-Mon.) looks straight out of the 1920s, with a polished circular bar, gilt walls, spacious balconies, and a crowd that could be coming from the opera or a local punk show.

Featured in films like *L.A. Confidential,* the historic **Formosa Café** (7156 Santa Monica Blvd., 323/850-9050, Mon.-Fri. 4pm-2am, Sat.-Sun. 6pm-2am) is a landmark that has changed little since 1925. Chinese decor embellishes the dimly lit main bar, and two large patios pack in young hipsters.

A spot for old-school cocktails is **Musso & Frank Grill** (6667 Hollywood Blvd., 323/467-7788, www.mussoandfrank.com, Tues.-Sat. 11am-11pm). Caught in a Hollywood time warp, this L.A. institution—with its hushed lighting, wood-paneled walls, and gruff, red-jacketed barkeeps—has been serving expert martinis and steaks since 1919.

Across from the Chateau Marmot on Hollywood's Sunset Strip, **The Den of Hollywood** (8226 W. Sunset Blvd., 323/656-0336, www.denofhollywood.com, Mon.-Fri. 5pm-2am, Sat. 3pm-2am, Sun. 11am-2am) has an outside fire pit, while inside there is a collection of board games including Rock

'Em, Sock 'Em Robots. Some nights have DJs and karaoke.

At **The Village Idiot** (7383 Melrose Ave., 323/655-3331, www.villageidiotla.com, Mon.-Fri. 11:30am-2am, Sat.-Sun. 10am-2am), the gastro-pub craze has finally hit the left coast, and the beautiful set has taken notice. Besides the eye candy, the food is pretty delicious too. It's a perfect place for a late-afternoon drink.

With beautiful ocean views, glittering mosaics, marble floors, and romantic piano music, **Casa del Mar Lobby Lounge** (1910 Ocean Way, Santa Monica, 310/581-5533, www.hotelcasadelmar.com, Sun.-Thurs. 10:30am-midnight, Fri.-Sat. 10:30am-1:30am) is a dramatic real-life sandcastle on Santa Monica Beach and offers perhaps the most elegant cocktail experience in the city.

Also in Santa Monica, **Ye Olde King's Head** (116 Santa Monica Blvd., Santa Monica, 310/451-1402, www.yeoldekingshead.com, daily 10am-2am) is a totally different experience. Stretching down a long half a block, Ye Olde King's Head is a British pub, restaurant, and gift shop. Crowded on most nights, the pub is home to dart games and a wide range of imbibing patrons visiting from far and near.

Clubs

Want to know which of the many dance and nightclubs in the L.A. area is the hottest or hippest or most popular with the stars this week? You'll need to ask the locals or read the alternative weekly papers when you arrive, since these things change almost weekly.

Know that clubs in L.A. get crowded on weekend nights and that bouncers take joy in selecting only the chicest hipsters in line to allow into the sacred spaces beyond the doors. Women have a slight edge, but in the top L.A. clubs, this can mean little to nothing. Being young and beautiful helps, of course, as does being dressed in the latest designer fashions and knowing a celebrity or the club's owner.

So put on your finest and fanciest clubbing outfit, head out, and go for it!

For serious rockers looking for something a little bit heavier, there's the **Key Club** (9039 W. Sunset Blvd., West Hollywood, 310/274-5800, www.keyclub.com, daily 7pm-2am, from $12, depending on the band). The Key Club caters to the heavy metal-and-dining crowd (yes, there is definitely such a thing in L.A.), with a full stage that hosts live bands and a full-service restaurant. This club feels like a warren, what with the stage and dance room, the casual and (in theory) quieter room down the hall, and The Plush Lounge VIP suite upstairs. Of course, you'll find more than one full bar inside this multipurpose club.

The **Three Clubs Cocktail Lounge** (1123 Vine St., Hollywood, 323/462-6441, www.threeclubs.com, daily 6pm-1:45am, no cover) acts both as a locals' watering hole and a reasonably priced nightclub catering mostly to the collegiate set. Expect to find the dance floor of the rear club crowded and sweaty, with fairly generic modern dance mixes blaring out over the crush of writhing bodies. Two bars serve up drinks to the masses, and drinks are a bit cheaper here than in the hotter spots. But if you're a lone female, be aware that Three Clubs has no decent parking, and you may have to walk several blocks along Hollywood Boulevard long after dark. Consider bringing a friend or two along with you to up your safety quotient.

Made popular by artists like Girl Talk, mashups are created by draping the vocals of one song over the music of another song. **Bootie LA** (http://bootiemashup.com) puts on bootleg mashup dance parties twice a month in Los Angeles at venues including **The Echoplex** (1154 Glendale Blvd., Los Angeles).

Gay and Lesbian

An alternative to glammed-up West Hollywood gay bars, **Akbar** (4356 Sunset Blvd., Silver Lake, 323/665-6810, www.akbarsilverlake.com, Mon. 7pm-2am, Tues.-Sun. 4pm-2am) pulls in a gay-friendly crowd with its cozy Moroccan-themed decor, neighborhood vibe, and friendly, unpretentious bartenders.

Sleek, glamorous, and candlelit, **The Abbey Food and Bar** (692 N. Robertson Blvd., West Hollywood, 310/289-8410, www.abbeyfoodandbar.com, daily 9am-2am) is a popular bar with a great outdoor patio and pillow-strewn private cabanas—all of which are usually jam-packed. Savvy bartenders mix 22 different specialty martinis in flavors that include chocolate banana and creamsicle.

Every Thursday night, **Avalon Hollywood** (1735 Vine St., Hollywood, 323/462-8900, http://avalonhollywood.com, Thurs. 9:30pm-3am, Fri. 9:30pm-5am, Sat. 9:30pm-8am) hosts **TigerHeat,** which is said to be the West Coast's largest gay event. In 2008, Lady GaGa performed a few songs at the event, while Britney Spears and Elton John have made appearances on other nights.

Live Music

Los Angeles has long been one of the biggest destinations for struggling young rockers to come out, live cheap, and struggle to grab a spot on stage to take their shot at that all-important record contract. The clubs in the Sunset district, particularly those on the Sunset Strip, incubated some of the biggest rock acts of all time long before anybody knew who they were. The top three clubs drip rock history from their very walls. You might want to hold your nose when you first walk into the **Whisky a Go Go** (8901 Sunset Blvd., West Hollywood, 310/652-4202, www.whiskyagogo.com, cover from $10). Despite a stench almost as memorable as its sound, throngs of music fans pack into the Whisky every night of the week. Truth be told, the Whisky doesn't draw many big name acts that often anymore. Most nights you'll get a lineup of new bands—sometimes as many as seven in one evening. The Whisky also hosts many cover and tribute bands that pay homage to the elders that once played here, such as Led Zeppelin and The Doors.

Almost next door to the Whisky you'll find **The Roxy Theatre** (9009 Sunset Blvd., West Hollywood, 310/278-9457, http://theroxyonsunset.com, cover charge varies). A comparative newcomer to the scene, The Roxy opened in 1973 with Neil Young performing. The second(ish) generation of heavy-duty rock acts made their name here (think Guns N' Roses, Jane's Addiction, and Pearl Jam). Today you'll find the newer mid level acts gracing the stage. Most shows feature 3-5 bands. The big black-box theater has an open dance floor, comfy-ish booths (if you can get one), and bare-bones food service during shows. Street parking is nearly nonexistent, and nearby lots will cost $5-15 or more, so think about taking public transit or a cab to the show. You'll find the performance calendar on the website, and tickets are available through major ticket agents. For one of the best after-hours parties on the Strip, try to get into **On the Rox,** located directly above The Roxy. Or stagger next door to the **Rainbow Bar & Grill** (9015 Sunset Blvd., West Hollywood, 310/278-4232, www.rainbowbarandgrill.com, daily 11am-2am).

It's not on the Strip, but its reputation is just as big and bad as its brethren. **The Troubadour** (9081 Santa Monica Blvd., West Hollywood, 310/276-6168, www.troubadour.com, ticket prices vary) opened its doors in 1957. Over its more than 50 years, Bob Dylan jammed, totally unknown comic Steve Martin sang, Tom Waits was discovered, Billy Joel opened for somebody else, Metallica headlined for the very first time, and countless A-list bands have recorded in and even about The Troubadour. Today, it's known for hosting amateur acts and cult favorites (Langhorne Slim, White Denim) and even secret shows by mainstream hit-makers like Coldplay. You can check the events calendar in advance to find your favorite bands and then buy tickets online. If you've decided on a whim to hit tonight's show, you can buy tickets at the on-site box office on the day of the show only, as long as the show isn't sold out.

With less history under its belt, **The Echo** (1822 W. Sunset Blvd., Echo Park, 213/413-8200, www.attheecho.com) is where a lot of the up-and-coming national indie acts who come to the city are performing. In the Echo Park neighborhood, The Echo has an occasional legend like Jonathan Richman perform

in between younger acts including Woods and Beachwood Sparks.

Comedy

Not far behind the live music scene, L.A.'s live comedy scene is second only to Manhattan's as a way to see the brightest current stars and the most impressive young new talent. More than a dozen major live comedy clubs make their home in the smog belt. Pick your favorite, sit back, and laugh (or groan) the night away.

Located in the former Ciro's Nightclub on the Strip, **The Comedy Store** (8433 Sunset Blvd., West Hollywood, 323/650-6268, www.thecomedystore.com, age 21 and older, $15-20) is owned by 1980s comedian Pauly Shore's mother, Mitzi. With three separate rooms, you'll find a show going on at The Store every night of the week; most start at 9pm or later, but you can check the website's calendar for both early and late shows. In all three rooms you'll often find a showcase featuring more than a dozen stand-up comics all performing one after another, and leaving space for possible celebrity drop-ins. Local sketch and improv groups also have regular gigs at The Store. Once upon a time, legendary comics got their start here. Imagine being among the first people ever to see Yakov Smirnoff perform, or getting to see Steve Martin or Whoopi Goldberg 10 feet from your table for less than $20. That's the level of talent you'll find performing here on a nightly basis. You can buy tickets online for bigger shows, and at the door for no sellouts and The Belly Room. If you'd rather perform than watch the action, sign up for the comedy open mics on Sundays and Mondays at 7pm.

It seems unlikely that a major comedy club would make its home in peaceful, suburban Pasadena, but that's where you'll find the **Ice House Comedy Club** (24 N. Mentor Ave., off Colorado Blvd., 626/577-1894, www.icehousecomedy.com, show times vary Thurs.-Sun., cover varies). With shows running nightly and a double-header most Saturday nights, anyone who wants a laugh will enjoy an evening at the Ice House. Comedians who've performed here recently include Rob Schneider and Alex Reymundo. Also 50 live comedy albums have been recorded here for the likes of Lily Tomlin and George Lopez. You'll also find a focus on female comics and a regular Latino comedy showcase here. If you actually favor a lower-budget, newer-comic evening, hit the Ice House **Annex**, the smaller ancillary room right next door to the main club.

THE ARTS
Theater
Even with all the hoopla over film in L.A., there's still plenty of room for live theatrical entertainment in and around Tinseltown.

The most notable annual event at the **Kodak Theatre** (6801 Hollywood Blvd., 323/308-6300, www.kodaktheatre.com, box office Mon.-Sat. 10am-6pm, Sun. 10am-4pm) is the Academy Awards, often called the Oscars. But for the rest of the year, the Kodak hosts live shows of various types. Many other awards shows make their homes here, and the stage is often graced by major performers such as Eddie Izzard, Ricky Gervais, and Cirque du Soleil. Also look for classical music concerts and vocal music performances.

Some theatergoers prefer outdoor entertainment to indoor, and the **Ford Theater** (2580 Cahuenga Blvd. E., 323/461-3673, www.fordamphitheater.org, box office Tues.-Sun. noon-5pm and two hours before evening performances, ticket prices vary) certainly takes advantage of Hollywood's temperate climate to bring the shows outdoors. Every sort of theatrical event imaginable can find a stage at the Ford, from hip hop dance to spoken word. Lots of musical acts play the Ford—think jazz, folk, world music, and beyond. Children's shows come to the Ford, and the theater even puts up the occasional film-based multimedia production. Check the events calendar to see what's up during your visit.

The **Ahmanson Theater** (135 N. Grand Ave., 213/628-2772, www.centertheatregroup.org, box office Tues.-Sun. noon-6pm and two hours before performances, ticket prices vary) specializes in big, Broadway-style productions. You might see a grandiose musical,

heart-wrenching drama, or gut-busting comedy here. Expect to find the names of many familiar shows on the schedule from popular modern productions like *War Horse* to classics including *Mary Poppins*. With hundreds of seats (all of them expensive), there's usually enough room to provide entertainment even for last-minute visitors.

Well-known television actors including Jason Alexander and Neil Patrick Harris frequently act in the productions at the **Geffen Playhouse** (10886 Le Conte Ave., 310/208-5454, www.geffenplayhouse.com, ticket prices vary). Some shows developed here move on to Broadway.

Classical Music
Although L.A. is better known for its rock than its classical music offerings, you can still find plenty of high-culture concerts as well. If you love the grandiose, get a ticket for a show at the **Los Angeles Opera** (135 N. Grand Ave., 213/972-8001, www.losangelesopera.com, box office Tues.-Sat. 10am-6pm, Sun. 10am-6pm, prices vary). The L.A. Opera has only existed since 1986, but in that time it has grown to be one of the largest opera companies in the United States, gaining national recognition for the quality of its work. The dazzling performances held in the Dorothy Chandler Pavilion at the Music Center of Los Angeles County have included such masterworks of the genre as *Don Giovanni* and *Madame Butterfly*. Each season includes six or more different operas. Grammy winning singer Placido Domingo has been the opera's general director since 2003.

If you prefer your musicians in black and white, take in a show by the **Los Angeles Philharmonic** (111 S. Grand Ave., 323/850-2000 or 800/745-3000, www.laphil.com, box office Tues.-Sun. noon-6pm and two hours before and until 30 minutes after each performance begins, $43-160), better known to its friends as the L.A. Phil. The philharmonic performs primarily at the **Walt Disney Concert Hall** (111 S. Grand Ave.). Concerts can range from classics by famed composers like Tchaikovsky, Bach, and Beethoven to the world music of Asha Bhosle or jazz by Bobby McFerrin. Guest performers can be the modern virtuosi of classical music—Midori plays here on occasion. Whatever style of music you choose to listen to, conductor Esa-Pekka Salonen or one of his guests will lead you on a wonderful aural journey.

With its art deco band shell set against canyon chaparral, the **Hollywood Bowl** (2301 N. Highland Ave., 323/850-2000 or 800/745-3000, www.hollywoodbowl.com, box office Tues.-Sun. noon-6pm) has long been a romantic setting for outdoor summer concerts by the L.A. Philharmonic and other artists.

If you're interested in supporting the work of amateur musicians or just seeing a chamber concert in a more intimate setting, consider getting tickets to the **Los Angeles Doctors Symphony** (323/209-4826, www.ladso.org, $15-20). This lovely community orchestra has been performing regularly since its inception in 1953 and most recently performed concerts at the **Wilshire Ebell Theatre** (743 S. Lucerne Blvd., just off Wilshire Blvd., 323/939-1128, www.ebell.com, box office Mon.-Fri. 10am-5pm). Many, though by no means all, of the musicians you'll hear are members of the medical profession. They play everything from Mozart and Schubert to traditional music of various cultures, depending on the concert venue and the event. Check the website for the annual schedule, programs, and ticket information. If they're playing when you're in town, it's definitely worth your time to support the musical culture of Los Angeles.

Cinema

Movie premieres are a big deal in L.A. for obvious reasons. Crowds throng the streets outside of the Chinese Theatre and the Egyptian, where the stars tromp down the red carpets to enjoy the sight of themselves on the big screen. Even the standard AMC and other theater chains get packed on opening nights, so come early or buy tickets online to assure yourself of seats to your favorite star's latest release.

The current favorite movie house for star sightings is the **ArcLight Hollywood Cinema** (6360 W. Sunset Blvd., Hollywood, 323/464-1478, www.arclightcinemas.com, adults $14-16, seniors $12-14.50, children $10.50-11.50, add $3.50 pp for 3-D movies). Perhaps this is due to the ArcLight's 21-and-older-only screenings of major blockbuster movies, which allow patrons to purchase beer and wine at the café and bring their drinks into the theater with them. But most of all, the ArcLight complex offers the best visual and sound technologies, all-reserved seating, and the updated geodesic Cinerama Dome theater. Do be sure to make reservations in advance (you can buy tickets online or at the theater) if you want great seats to the latest films. The ArcLight also shows a few art-house flicks and even the occasional "retrospective" (code for old) movie in its hallowed theaters. Ask for parking validation for a discount on the adjacent parking structure. You'll need it, since due to the ArcLight's status as a Hollywood favorite, you'll pay above even the usual high L.A. movie theater rates to see a film here.

Shopping

In Los Angeles, shopping qualifies as a major source of entertainment for locals and visitors alike. Don't worry about being materialistic or a spendthrift here—that's what you're *supposed* to be. If it exists anywhere on earth, you can probably buy it somewhere in L.A., whether "it" is a Smart car, a bunch of flowers, an indie CD, or a pair of pants that cost as much as a Smart car. Different areas and towns have their own unique shopping feel, so decide what kind of retail experience you want and then pick the right spot to find it.

DOWNTOWN AND VICINITY
Flower District

If you have even the slightest love of plants and flowers, you can't miss the world-famous **L.A. Flower District** (700 block of Wall St.,

213/622-196, www.laflowerdistrict.com, Mon. and Wed. 8am-noon, Tues. and Thurs. 6am-11am, Fri. 8am-2pm, Sat. 6am-2pm). Sometimes called "America's Flower Market," this vast sea of color and beauty is a triumph of American multicultural entrepreneurial spirit. The first flower cultivators in Los Angeles were Japanese Americans, and today many growers are of Hispanic descent—perhaps especially fitting for an industry that creates products in all colors of the rainbow. When you visit this vast sea of beauty, you'll find a fun cacophony of different languages being spoken as floral retailers vie for the best products available on any given day. But never fear: Anyone can come and stroll the narrow aisles of the various markets, and you'll find plenty of premade bouquets with which to impress your sweetie. Or better yet, find someone who can create a custom arrangement for you, since just about every kind of cut flower, potted plant, and exotic species can be purchased here. You can take away a bouquet filled with flowers you've never even seen before.

Among other major events, the Flower District supplies the unbelievable needs of the Rose Parade each New Year's. Literally millions of flowers go into the creation of the stunning floats (which must incorporate flowers to qualify for most of the awards in the parade). It's hard to image the work necessary to fill the orders for the floats, but the denizens of the flower market do it every year.

One caution: While the flower market itself is safe for visitors, the area to the south is not. Get good directions before you come, and don't plan to wander the neighborhood on foot.

Jewelry District

If you're looking for the bleeding edge of style when you shop for jewelry, you can't do much better than the Los Angeles **Jewelry District** (bounded by 5th St., 8th St., Broadway, and Olive St., www.lajd.net). With more than 3,000 wholesalers, even the most avid lover of sparkly stones and glittering gold will get his or her fill here. Do be a little bit careful if you're a woman alone, especially at dusk or later, as

this isn't the cleanest part of Downtown L.A. But you can shop in reasonable peace here, and even in some confidence that you won't get ripped off as long as you do some preliminary research. The district website provides information on vendor ratings and a map to help you get around more easily. From wholesale dealers of unset gems to professional gem setters who'll create a beautiful piece from the stones you've bought, you can find just about anything you ever dreamed of here.

Chung King Road

A mix of modern art galleries and fun touristy gift shops line the 900 block of **Chung King Road**, a one-block stretch of Chinatown. Interior decorators often browse the eclectic selection here. It might be quiet during the day but become alive during art opening evenings.

Kinokuniya

The Little Tokyo bookstore **Kinokuniya** (123 Astronaut E. Onizuka St., 213/687-4480, www.kinokuniya.com) carries both Japanese- and English-language merchandise, including a wide selection of manga (Japanese comic books), cookbooks, glossy home-decor and art books, fashion magazines, and stationery.

LOS FELIZ AND SILVER LAKE

The shopping options in Los Feliz and Silver Lake reflect the neighborhoods' penchant for variety, with everything from secondhand resale stores to sophisticated boutiques.

Sunset Junction

Artsy, hip boutiques, cafés, and restaurants line **Sunset Junction** (Sunset Blvd. from Santa Monica Blvd. to Maltman Ave.), a colorful stretch of Sunset Boulevard concentrated around where Sunset meets Santa Monica Boulevard (or, rather, where Santa Monica Boulevard ends). Weekend mornings bring floods of neighborhood locals down from the hills. This strip is also home to the **Silver Lake Certified Farmer's Market** (213/484-4002, Tues. 2pm-7:30pm, Sat. 8am-1:30pm).

© LINDSAY GEORGE

Skylight Books

Skylight Books

The fiercely independent Skylight Books (1818 N. Vermont Ave., 323/660-1175, www.skylightbooks.com, daily 10am-10pm) in Los Feliz features alternative literature, literary fiction, Los Angeles-themed books, and an extensive film section. They often have autographed copies of books by authors who have recently spoken here.

HOLLYWOOD
Hollywood and Highland Center

At the center of the efforts to revitalize Hollywood, located next to the Chinese Theatre and connected to the Kodak Theatre, **Hollywood and Highland Center** (6801 Hollywood Blvd., 323/467-6412 or 323/817-0200, www.hollywoodandhighland.com, Mon.-Sat. 10am-10pm, Sun. 10am, parking $2-10) flaunts outlandish architecture that's modeled after the set of the 1916 film *Intolerance*. Stroll amid the eateries and boutiques that surround the open-air Babylon Court.

Amoeba Music

Encompassing an entire city block and two floors, **Amoeba Music** (6400 Sunset Blvd., 323/245-6400, www.amoeba.com, Mon.-Sat. 10:30am-11pm, Sun. 11am-9pm) is the world's largest independent music store. There are smaller Amoeba Music stores—which are still huge—in the San Francisco Bay Area, but this is the place in L.A. to find that rare record or used CD. Amoeba also hosts free performances by acts of all sizes, which have included the Flaming Lips and Elvis Costello in the past.

LA BREA, FAIRFAX, AND MIRACLE MILE
West 3rd Street

The stretch of charming and eclectic shops on **West 3rd Street** between Fairfax Avenue and La Cienega Boulevard encompasses one-of-a-kind clothing boutiques, home stores, and bath-and-body shops. At one end you'll find the Farmer's Market and The Grove shopping center; at the other, the Beverly Center.

Among the various home and clothing stores on West 3rd Street, you'll find **Traveler's Bookcase** (8375 W. 3rd St., 323/655-0575, www.travelbooks.com, Mon. 11am-7pm, Tues.-Sat. 10am-7pm, Sun. noon-6pm). Both armchair travelers and true globetrotters browse the extensive selection of guidebooks at this comfortable and friendly bookstore. Travel-oriented literature rounds out the stock.

BEVERLY HILLS AND WEST HOLLYWOOD
Rodeo Drive

If you're reading this book, you probably don't have enough money to go on a serious spree in the shops of **Rodeo Drive.** The hottest stars and other big spenders come here to purchase the best and most expensive goods the world has to offer.

Have you ever bought a $1,500 pair of pants? Walk into **Chanel** (400 N. Rodeo Dr., Beverly Hills, 310/278-5500, www.chanel.com, Mon.-Sat. 10am-6pm, Sun. noon-5pm) and you'll be able to. You'll see original artwork, catalogs, and the very edgiest high-end clothes in existence, and salespeople who will look down their noses at you if your outfit cost less than four figures. Head upstairs for racks of on-sale clothing from last season, although you'll quickly learn that "on sale" is a relative concept. If you're lucky, you might even get dissed by one or more of the über-rich women wearing fur hats and carrying yippy little dogs (they're unaware of the irony). Hunt the racks for the classic tweedy Coco Chanel dress—you will find it. Or if you prefer another designer, head outside and find one; all the big leaguers, from Dior to Michael Kors, maintain storefronts on Rodeo Drive.

Although Rodeo Drive is most famous for its designer apparel, many other retailers offer a vast array of expensive things, including sunglasses, jewelry, and housewares. If you're looking for, or just want to look at, the perfect diamond ring, walk past the guards into the huge hallowed halls of **Tiffany's** (210 N. Rodeo Dr., Beverly Hills, 310/273-8880, www.tiffany.com, Mon.-Sat. 10am-7pm, Sun. 11am-5pm).

The store has three floors of the most exquisite necklaces, bracelets, rings, watches, and accessories you'll ever find anywhere. This storefront compares easily to its sister store in Manhattan. You'll find the sales help here a bit friendlier than in the clothing stores, since even the middle class of L.A. comes to Tiffany's to purchase special-occasion jewelry.

The wealthy who want to fall asleep with their skin soothed by the softest sheets around go to **Frette** (459 N. Rodeo Dr., Beverly Hills, 310/273-8540 or 800/353-7388, www.frette.com, Mon.-Sat. 10am-6pm, Sun. noon-5pm) to make their purchases. This store doesn't get as crowded as many others on Rodeo Drive, and much of Frette's business is with high-end hotels. But the doors of this open, airy retail store remain defiantly open, beckoning shoppers who love luxury. Salespeople encourage you to pet the merchandise, comparing one set of sheets to another and imagining the feel of the plushy bath sheets after your next shower.

Melrose Avenue

Melrose Avenue (between San Vicente Blvd. and La Brea Ave.) is really two shopping districts. High-end fashion and design showrooms dominate the western end, near La Cienega Boulevard; head east past Fairfax Avenue for tattoo parlors and used clothing.

If you miss 1960s mod, 1970s grooviness, 1980s power-dressing, or even last year's haute couture, drop by **Decades** (8214 1/2 Melrose Ave., 323/655-0223, www.decadesinc.com, Mon.-Sat. 11:30am-6pm, or by appointment) and browse among the prime vintage Courrèges, Hermès, and Pucci castoffs.

If you adore the clothes from *Sex and the City* and *Friends,* stop in at **Ron Robinson at Fred Segal** (8118 Melrose Ave., 323/651-1800, www.ronrobinson.com, Mon.-Sat. 10am-7pm, Sun. noon-6pm), a deluxe department store that has everything from the ridiculously trendy to the severely tasteful.

Futuristic specs from **I.a.Eyeworks** (7407 Melrose Ave., 323/653-8255 or 800/348-3337, ext. 4, www.laeyeworks.com, Mon.-Fri. 10am-7pm, Sat. 10am-6pm, Sun. noon-5pm, they start removing inventory about 30 minutes before closing time) have appeared in films like *The Matrix* and *Blade Runner,* and celebs like Jennifer Aniston and Wesley Snipes are fans of the store's lightweight, trend-defining frames.

The buyers at **Wasteland** (7428 Melrose Ave., 323/653-3028, www.wastelandclothing. com, Mon.-Thurs. 11am-8pm, Fri.-Sat. 11am-9pm, Sun. noon-8pm) carefully pick out merchandise for their club-hopping clientele, so everything at this secondhand store has style. The selection covers a wide range, from Gucci to Gap.

Book Soup

Located on the strip of Sunset Boulevard more famous for nightlife than shopping, the indie bookstore **Book Soup** (8818 Sunset Blvd., 310/659-3110, www.booksoup.com, Mon.-Sat. 9am-10pm, Sun. 9am-7pm) crams every nook and cranny of its space, but the film section is particularly strong. Check out the schedule of high-profile readings, or pick up a signed edition.

SANTA MONICA, VENICE, AND MALIBU

Shopping down by the beaches can be as much fun as anyplace else in the L.A. area. Santa Monica offers the best bet for an entertaining retail experience, since Venice Beach and Malibu tend more toward strip malls.

Third Street Promenade

Looking for the place where middle-class locals come to shop in the L.A. area? Head for the **Third Street Promenade** (3rd St., Santa Monica, 310/393-8355, http://thirdstreet-promenade.org). Much of 3rd Street in Santa Monica is closed to auto traffic to make it easier to walk along the Promenade. This long vertical outdoor mall features all your favorite chain stores for clothing, shoes, jewelry, housewares, computers, and just about anything else you can think of. You'll find people plying the Promenade day and night, seven days a week. If your goal is a serious retail spree, come out to the Promenade on a weekday during daylight hours to avoid the bigger crushes of people that pile into the area on weekends. On the other hand, if you're looking for a fun social outing, the Promenade gets popular with a younger crowd at night. You can hit one of the movie theaters, stop in at a bar, or just stroll the pedestrian walks enjoying the mild night air and the street performers who work the area. The Promenade is within easy walking distance of the Santa Monica Pier and the adjacent beach.

The Promenade's shops tend toward classic mall fare. You'll find a tremendous three-story Gap offering classic clothes to the masses. The high-end Anthropologie and Armani Exchange can get you looking fine for the remainder of your L.A. vacation and beyond. If you need a new computer or a shiny iPod or iPhone to get you back home in style and entertained, a huge Apple Store can hook you up. There's also a gargantuan Barnes & Noble to pick up some more vacation reading. If you're looking to catch the latest flick, choose from four different movie theaters. On Wednesdays and Saturdays, you can get the freshest and tastiest fruits and vegetables from the legendary farmers market at the Promenade.

PASADENA
Old Town Pasadena

Once a quaint downtown area serving a small but wealthy community, **Old Town Pasadena** (Colorado Blvd., 626/356-9725, www.oldpasadena.org) today is essentially a street-based shopping mall, with upscale chain stores inhabiting classic art deco and mid-century modern buildings.

Off the main strip along Colorado Boulevard, one block down Raymond Avenue, is **Distant Lands** (20 S. Raymond Ave., 626/449-3220 or 800/310-3220, www.distantlands.com, Mon.-Thurs. 10:30am-8pm, Fri.-Sat. 10:30am-9pm, Sun. 11am-6pm), a one-stop shop for travelers that has guidebooks, maps, travel accessories, clothing, and luggage. Even if you're not planning a special trip, the store's ambience is conducive to armchair travel.

LOS ANGELES

Sports and Recreation

You'll find an endless array of ways to get outside and have fun in the L.A. area. Among the most popular recreation options are those that get you out onto the beach or into the Pacific Ocean.

BEACHES

If you're in SoCal for the first time, it's almost a given that one of your destinations is a genuine California beach. You've got plenty to choose from in the L.A. area. From north of Malibu down to Manhattan Beach and Hermosa Beach, you'll find a seemingly endless stretch of public beaches. Unlike their Northern California counterparts, most of these have lots of visitor amenities, such as snack bars, boardwalks, showers, beach toy rental shacks, surf schools, and permanent sports courts. Believe it or not, those listed here are just a drop in the bucket; if none of these beaches do it for you, you can choose from dozens of others that stretch in a nearly unbroken line from one end of the county to the other.

Not all L.A. beaches are created equal. With very few exceptions, you won't always find clean, clear water to swim in, since pollution is a major issue on the L.A. coast. Also keep in mind that Los Angeles County is not a tropical zone. The water does warm up in the summer, but not into the 80s like you find in Hawaii. Happily, it's also not in the icy 50s and 60s, as in the northern reaches of the state. Expect to cool off significantly when you dive into the surf, and if you plan to be out in the water for an extended period, get yourself a wetsuit to prevent chills that can turn into hypothermia.

Leo Carrillo State Park

Just 28 miles north of Santa Monica, **Leo Carrillo State Park** (28 miles northwest of Santa Monica on Pacific Coast Hwy., 310/457-8143, www.parks.ca.gov, daily 8am-10pm) feels like a Central Coast beach though it is right outside of Los Angeles city limits. Here you can explore the park's natural coastal features,

including tide pools and caves. A point break offshore draws surfers when the right swell hits. Also dogs are allowed on a beach at the northern end of the park.

Zuma Beach

If you're a fan of David Hasselhoff or Pamela Anderson, be informed that **Zuma Beach** (30000 Pacific Coast Hwy. in Malibu, 19 miles north of Santa Monica, surf report 310/457-9701, http://beaches.lacounty.gov, parking $3-10) is where a lot of the TV show *Baywatch* was filmed. This popular surf and boogie-boarding break, complete with a nice big stretch of clean white sand, fills up fast on summer weekends but isn't as crowded on weekdays. Grab a spot on the west side of the Pacific Coast Highway (Hwy. 1) for free parking, or pay for one of the more than 2,000 spots in the beach parking lot. Zuma has all the amenities you need for a full day out at the beach, from restrooms and showers to a kid-friendly snack bar and a beachside boardwalk.

Water lovers can ride the waves or just take a swim in the cool and (unusual for the L.A. area) crystal-clear Pacific waters. Zuma has lifeguards during daylight hours, and for landlubbers, it's got beach volleyball courts set up and a playground for the kids. Perhaps best of all, this beach doesn't fill up with litter-happy visitors; it's actually a locals' favorite for weekend R&R.

Malibu Beach

In a sea of mansions fronting the beach, **Malibu Lagoon State Beach** (23200 Pacific Coast Hwy., 310/457-8143, www.parks.ca.gov, daily 8am-sunset) and its ancillary **Malibu Surfriders Beach,** which was the epicenter of the 1960s surf culture, offer public access to the great northern L.A. location. Running alongside the **Malibu Pier** (23000 Pacific Coast Hwy., 310/456-8031 or 888/310-7437, www.malibupiersportfishing.com), this pretty stretch of sugar-like sand offers a wealth of activities as well as pure California relaxation. This beach offers a number of unusual attractions, including both the **Adamson House** (23200 Pacific Coast Hwy., 310/456-8432, www.adamson-house.org, Wed.-Sat. 11am-2pm, adults $7, ages 6-16 $2, under age 5 free) and the adjoining **Malibu Lagoon Museum.** You can take a guided tour that goes through the museum and out to the wetlands, butterfly trees, tide pools, and flower gardens. Malibu Creek runs into the ocean here, creating a unique wetlands ecosystem that's well worth exploring. In 2012, a controversial move was made by the state to drain and reshape the lagoon.

If a beach party is more your style, you can rent beach toys at the pier and stake your spot on the sand. Surfers work the break here year-round; be careful of your fellow riders.

At the intersection that leads to the museum, you can also drive down to the main parking lot. It's likely to fill up fast in the summer, so get here early for a spot.

Will Rogers State Beach

If you're a film buff and a beach bum, you must take a day out of your travel schedule to hang out on the **Will Rogers State Beach** (17000 Pacific Coast Hwy., Pacific Palisades, 310/305-9503, http://beaches.co.la.ca.us, parking $4-12), yet another fabulous full-service L.A. beach with a number of movies filmed here. Even if you don't care about that, you'll love the nearly two miles of sandy beach, easy to get to from the parking lot, studded with volleyball courts, playground equipment, restrooms, and picnic tables. The bike path running along the land side of the sand runs for 22 miles or so south. Out in the water, you can swim, skin-dive, and surf. A mild right point break offers a good learning ground for beginners. Lifeguards protect the shores during the day in summer, and the locals think their lifeguards are some of the best looking in the county. Just be sure to pay attention to the flags and signs, since pollution can be a problem at Will Rogers due to storm drains emptying into the ocean.

Bring cash to pay for parking, but be happy that with more than 1,750 spots, you'll probably find one that's legal and reasonably secure.

Santa Monica State Beach

If you're looking for "The Beach" in Santa Monica, well, it's hard to miss. The waterside edge of town is lined by **Santa Monica State Beach** (Pacific Coast Hwy., 310/458-8573, http://santa-monica.org, parking from $7), which is operated by the city of Santa Monica. For 3.5 miles, the fine sand gets raked daily beneath the sun that shines over the beach more than 300 days each year. Flop down in the sand to enjoy the warm sunshine, take a dip in the endless waves of the Pacific, stroll along the boardwalk, or stand at the edge of the water and peer out to see if you can catch sight of a pod of dolphins frolicking in the surf. If you don't mind crowds, hang out on the sand right near the pier. The best people-watching runs south of the pier area and on toward Venice Beach. For a bit more elbow room, head north of the pier to the less populated end of the beach.

Due to its location right "in" town and adjacent to and beneath the Santa Monica Pier, you'll find a near-endless array of services at the beach. On the pier and just across from the beach, you can get snacks and meals, rent surf and boogie boards, hit the arcade, and go shopping. Parking varies, depending on which part of the beach you head for. The north end has spotty parking, the pier area can get really crowded but has more options, and the south probably has the best bet for a good spot.

SURFING

The northern section of Los Angeles has some of the region's best surf breaks including County Line, which is on the L.A./Ventura county line, and Zuma, a series of beach breaks along the beach of the same name. But L.A.'s premiere surf spot is Malibu, one of the world's most famous waves. This is where the 1960s surf culture took hold due to legends like Miki Dora, an iconic Malibu-based surfer. It's also the setting of the 1978 cult surf film *Big Wednesday*. Malibu is known for its crowds, but if you are able to score one of those long peeling rights off the cobblestone point, all in the world will be all right.

If you've left your board at home but come to Malibu as waves are peeling off the point, run to the **Malibu Surf Shack** (22935 Pacific Coast Hwy., 310/456-8508, www.malibusurf-shack.com, daily 10am-6pm, $20-40 per day) to rent a board.

The southern section located right off the city offers places to surf, but not with the same quality as the breaks up around Malibu. Venice Beach has waves that typically close out, while Hermosa Beach and Manhattan Beach sometimes have decent waves.

Surf Lessons

If you've never surfed before, your best bet is to sign up for a lesson or two with a reputable surf school. Most schools can get you standing up on your longboard on the very first lesson. One of these, **Learn to Surf LA** (641 Westminster Ave., Suite 5, Venice, 310/663-2479, www.learntosurfla.com, $75-120), has lessons on the beach near the Santa Monica Pier (near lifeguard tower No. 18), Manhattan Beach's 45th Street Lifeguard Tower, and Venice Beach's Navy Street Lifeguard Tower. You can take a private lesson, a semiprivate lesson with friends, or join a regularly scheduled group. Each lesson lasts almost two hours and includes all equipment (you'll get a full wetsuit in addition to a board), shore instruction and practice, and plenty of time in the water. No, the brightly-colored foam longboards you'll learn on aren't the coolest or most stylish, but they're perfect for new surfers looking for a stable ride on smaller waves. Learn to Surf LA offers lessons for both kids and adults, and this can be a great activity for the whole family to tackle together. Intermediate and advanced surfers can also find great fun with this school, which has advanced instructors capable of helping you improve your skills.

STAND UP PADDLEBOARDING

There has been friction between stand up paddleboarders and surfers at breaks including Malibu. Still, if you want to try out the latest water sports craze, contact **Poseidon Stand Up Paddle Surfing** (1654 Ocean Ave., Santa Monica, 310/694-8228, www.poseidonstandup.com) for rentals or lessons in Santa Monica, Marina del Rey, and Malibu.

HANG GLIDING

You can pick the kind of ground you want to soar over in L.A.: the ocean or the inland mountains and valleys. If you prefer to see the water slipping past beneath you, head for **Dockweiler State Beach Training Park** (12661 Vista del Mar, El Segundo, Wed.-Sun. 11am-sunset). For a higher-altitude adventure, head to the San Fernando Valley and up to **Sylmar Flight Park** (12600 Gridley St., Sylmar, 818/362-9978, daily 8am-sunset). For a good school and rental facility, call **Windsports Soaring Center** (12623 Gridley St., Sylmar, 818/367-2430, http://windsports.com, reservations office Tues.-Fri. 10am-6pm, $85-229). You can go tandem with an instructor at Sylmar Flight Park (recommended for first-time gliders) or get bold and try a solo ride, which starts at an altitude of five feet out on the beach at Dockweiler. Windsports provides all the equipment and training you need, so all you have to bring are a good pair of athletic shoes, a bottle of water, and, of course, a camera.

SPAS

Inside the Westin Bonaventure Hotel in Downtown L.A., enjoy some good pampering at the **Bonaventure Club and Spa** (404 S. Figueroa St., 213/629-0900, www.bonaventu-reclub.com, daily 11am-11pm, from $28). With a focus on beauty as well as health and relaxation, the Bonaventure Club features a number of heavy-duty facials, as well as dermabrasion and collagen treatments. You'll also find a full nail and waxing salon along with an array of massages and body scrubs. The Bonaventure isn't the poshest spa around, but you'll get decent service. The locker rooms, sauna, and other facilities are clean, and the spa is open later than most to accommodate busy travelers. Book in advance if you want a specific treatment at a specific time of day, but you're likely to find a same-day appointment if you aren't too picky about exactly which treatment you want.

For a taste of Beverly Hills luxury, try **Thibiant Beverly Hills** (449 N. Canon Dr., 310/278-7565, www.thibiantspa.com), where you can blast yourself clean with a deluge shower, and then have your body slathered with mud, milk, seaweed, or papaya.

Over in Santa Monica, **Exhale** (Fairmont Miramar Hotel and Bungalows, 101 Wilshire Blvd., 310/319-3193, www.exhalespa.com, Mon., Wed. and Fri. 6:30am-9pm, Tues. and Thurs. 6am-9pm, Sat. 8am-9pm, Sun. 8am-8pm) explores the mind-body connection with fusion yoga classes, massage, and ayurvedic therapy. If you don't want to get that deep, you can also just have your nails done.

SPECTATOR SPORTS

Befitting a major American city, Los Angeles boasts a nearly full complement of professional sports teams. L.A. no longer has a National Football League team, but once it had two. Oops!

The **L.A. Kings** (213/742-7100 or 888/546-4752, http://kings.nhl.com, $34-465) are no joke now after winning the 2012 Stanley Cup. They play lightning-fast NHL ice hockey in Downtown L.A. at the Staples Center (1111 S. Figueroa St., 213/742-7100, www.staples-center.com).

As great legends of the National Basketball Association, the individual players and the organization as a whole of the **Los Angeles Lakers** (310/426-6031 or 866/381-8924, www.nba.com) have well and truly earned their places. Although Magic Johnson no longer dunks for the Lakers, Kobe Bryant carries on the star torch for the still-winning team.

Major League Baseball takes advantage of the perfect climate in L.A. to host some of the most beautiful outdoor summer games anywhere in the country. The **Los Angeles Dodgers** (1000 Elysian Park Ave., Los Angeles, 323/224-1507, http://losangeles.dodgers.mlb.com, $12-120) make their home in this hospitable climate, playing often and well throughout the long baseball season. Just one thing: Don't refer to **Dodger Stadium** (1000 Elysian Park Ave.) as "Chavez Ravine" unless you really mean it. That old-field designation has become a derogatory term used primarily by San Francisco Giants fans.

Accommodations

From the cheapest roach-ridden shack motels to the most chichi Beverly Hills hotel, Los Angeles has an endless variety of lodgings to suit every taste and budget.

DOWNTOWN AND VICINITY

If you want to stay overnight in Downtown L.A., plan to pay for the privilege. As expected, most hostelries here run to high-rise towers catering more to businesspeople than the leisure set. Still, if you need a room near the heart of L.A. for less than a month's mortgage, you can find one if you look hard enough. But be aware that once you get into the Jewelry District and farther toward the Flower Market, the neighborhood goes from high-end to sketchy to downright terrifying. If you need a truly cheap room, avoid these areas and head instead for Pasadena or the San Fernando Valley.

Under $150

You won't miss the sign for the **Metro Plaza Hotel** (711 N. Main St., 213/680-0200 or 800/223-2223, http://metroplazahoteldowntownla.com, $95-145). The low-rise hotel with its white facade and big, oddly constructed front marquee sits near Union Station, convenient for rail travelers and public-transit riders. Inside, you'll find your guest room looks like any average, reasonably clean motel room. The bedspreads are floral, the carpets light blue, and the space ample. A complimentary continental breakfast comes with your room, and the Metro Plaza has an on-site fitness center. But the true gems here are the location, central to transportation to all the major L.A. attractions, and the lower-than-average price point for the region.

Can you imagine staying at a cute B&B

only a mile from the towering skyscrapers of Downtown Los Angeles? The **Inn at 657** (657 and 663 W. 23rd St., 213/741-2200, www.patsysinn657.com, $135-225) is two side-by-side buildings with one-bedroom guest accommodations and two-bedroom suites, each individually decorated. You'll find a comfortable antique bed in a room scattered with lovely fabrics and pretty antiques. Each morning, you'll head downstairs to the long, dark table set with fine china for a full breakfast complete with fruit, hot food, great coffee, and fresh juice. The inn has a massage therapist on retainer, a nail salon they love just down the street, Wi-Fi, and a moderate-cost laundry service. You're within easy distance of the Staples Center, the Downtown shopping areas, and the rest of the attractions of Los Angeles.

$150-250

With its red-tiled floor, painted furniture, and lushly landscaped poolside bar, the **Figueroa Hotel** (939 S. Figueroa St., 213/627-8971 or 800/421-9092, www.figueroahotel.com, $150-265) is a Spanish-Moroccan oasis in the heart of Downtown.

The **O Hotel** (819 S. Flower St., 213/623-9904 or 855/782-9286, www.ohotelgroup.com, $138-230), formerly known as The Orchid Hotel, is an upscale property that takes the modern urban chic hotel concept and does it L.A.-style. True to its original name, orchids are a major theme of this hotel, and you'll find plants in the common areas. A boutique establishment, the O has only 67 guest rooms. You'll find tapas, fish, burgers, and poultry at the on-site restaurant, plus a full bar. The health spa offers both fitness facilities and massage along with other spa services. Perhaps best of all for travelers who come to L.A. for its retail possibilities, you won't need the services of the 24-hour concierge desk to find the Macy's Plaza center just across the street from the hotel.

With **The Standard** (550 S. Flower St., 213/892-8080, www.standardhotels.com, $200-375), hipster hotelier André Balazs, of the Chateau Marmont, and the Mercer, transformed the former home of Superior Oil into a mecca for the see-and-be-seen crowd. From its upside-down sign to the minimal aesthetic in the guest rooms, the hotel gives off an ironic-chic vibe. If you're sharing a room, be sure you and your roommate are comfortable with the fishbowl-like showers: The only thing between the showerer and the rest of the room is clear glass. The rooftop bar has spectacular views of the Downtown cityscape along with unique features like waterbed pods to sit in. The bar was in the 2005 film *Kiss Kiss, Bang Bang*.

Over $250

If you're longing for a taste of true L.A. style, get a room at the **Omni Los Angeles at California Plaza** (251 S. Olive St., 213/617-3300 or 888/444-6664, www.omnihotels.com, $290). From the grand exterior to the elegant lobby and on up to your guest room, the light colors, live plants, and lovely accents will make you feel rich, even if it's just for one night. Your guest room or suite will have plush mattresses and your choice of pillows, stylish decor, plushy towels and robes, and all the right amenities to make your stay perfect. If you're in town for business, you can get a guest room complete with a fax machine, copier, and office supplies. On the other hand, if you're on vacation with your family, you can get a suite specially decorated to delight your children—with a closing door to an adult bedroom to delight you. You can dine at this magnificent hotel, choosing between the **Noé Restaurant** (Sun.-Thurs. 5pm-10pm, Fri.-Sat. 5pm-11pm) and the **Grand Café** (Mon.-Fri. 6:30am-3pm, Sat.-Sun. 7am-3pm). Take a swim in the lap pool or a run on the exercise equipment in the large fitness room. Relax with a massage, hot river rock treatment, or facial at the Spa at Omni. Whatever your pleasure, you'll find it here.

If you're yearning to stay someplace with a movie history, book a room at the **Westin Bonaventure Hotel and Suites** (404 S. Figueroa St., 213/624-1000, www.starwood-hotels.com, $180-2,500). The climactic scene of the Clint Eastwood thriller *In the Line of Fire* was filmed in one of the unusual elevators in the glass-enclosed, four leaf clover-shaped high-rise building. This hotel complex has every single thing you'd ever need: shops, restaurants, a day spa, a concierge, and plenty of nice guest rooms. You'll find your room comfortable and convenient, complete with fancy beds and clean spacious baths. Views range from fairly innocuous L.A. streets to panoramic cityscapes. The most fun restaurant and lounge to visit at the Bonaventure is without doubt the **Bona Vista Lounge** (daily 5pm-1am), which slowly rotates through 360 degrees at the top of the building.

The **Hilton Checkers** (535 S. Grand Ave., 213/624-0000 or 800/445-8667, www.hiltoncheckers.com, $330-1,500) is an intimate Downtown boutique hotel. The elegant guest rooms feature marble-floored baths, and there's a classy fusion restaurant and a great rooftop pool on-site.

Since 1923, the **Millennium Biltmore Hotel** (506 S. Grand Ave., 213/624-1011 or 800/245-8673, www.millenniumhotels.com, $200-5,000), the grande dame of L.A. hotels, has hosted many dignitaries and heads of state. Guest rooms are impressive, but majestic public spaces—the Rendezvous Court, the Crystal Ballroom, and the Gallery Bar—really dazzle. They also have a Roman-style indoor swimming pool.

HOLLYWOOD

If you're star-struck, a serious partier, or a rock music aficionado, you'll want to do more than just visit Hollywood—you'll want to stay the night within staggering distance of the hottest clubs or the hippest music venues. Heck, you might even luck out and find yourself sleeping in the same room where Axl Rose once vomited or David Lee Roth broke all the furniture.

Under $150

Reputed to be one of the best hostels in the state, the **USA Hostels-Hollywood** (1624 Schrader Blvd., 323/462-3777 or 800/524-6783, www.usahostels.com, $38-43 dorm, $112 private room) still offers the same great prices you'll find at seedier, more bare-bones hostels. OK, so the exterior doesn't look like much. But in this case, it's what's inside that counts. You can choose between dorm rooms and private guest rooms, but even the larger dorm rooms have baths attached—a nice convenience that's unusual in the hostel world. (You'll also find several common baths in the hallways, helping to diminish the morning shower rush.) Another great boon is the daily all-you-can-make pancake breakfast, which is included with your room along with all the coffee or tea you can drink. Add that to the $6 barbecue nights on Monday, Wednesday, and Friday, and you've got a great start on seriously diminished food costs for this trip. This smaller hostel also goes a long way to fostering a sense of community among its visitors, offering a standard array of area walking tours and a beach shuttle, plus free comedy nights, movie nights, and open mic nights. If you need to make contact with friends back home, hook up to the free Wi-Fi with your own laptop or use one of the complimentary Internet kiosks.

The **Hollywood Celebrity Hotel** (1775 Orchid Ave., 323/850-6464 or 800/222-7017, www.hotelcelebrity.com, $140-209) is a nice budget motel that aspires to Hollywood's famed luxury. Guest rooms have satin comforters, Hollywood-flavored black-and-white artwork, and a modern aesthetic in the furnishings and accents. Amenities include free-wired high-speed Internet, valet laundry service, a fitness room, and steam rooms. In the morning, come down to the lobby for a complimentary continental breakfast, and in the evenings take advantage of otherwise hard-to-come-by passes to the **Magic Castle** (7001 Franklin Ave., Hollywood, 323/851-3313, www.magiccastle.com). Leave your car in the gated, off-street parking lot.

$150-250

If you've got a little bit more cash, you'll find more lodging options in Hollywood. One good spot is the **Magic Castle Hotel** (7025 Franklin Ave., 323/851-0800 or 800/741-4915, www.magiccastlehotel.com, $180-350), named for the world-renowned magic club next door. It boasts the best customer service of any

L.A.-area hostelry. You'll have to make that judgment for yourself, but if one of your goals for your visit to the area is to find a way into the exclusive **Magic Castle** (7001 Franklin Ave., Hollywood, 323/851-3313, www.magiccastle.com), their ancillary hotel has your ticket waiting at the desk, though there is a door charge. If you're just looking for a nice place to relax between days filled with touring, you'll definitely get that here. Sparkling light guest rooms with cushy white comforters and spare, clean decor offer a haven of tranquility. A courtyard pool invites lounging day and night, and you can even enjoy a midnight swim here without breaking the hotel rules (so long as you don't wake the other guests). All suites at the Magic Castle have their own kitchens. But be sure to enjoy the little luxurious touches, such as high-end coffee, baked goodies in the free continental breakfast, plushy robes, and nightly turndown service.

The **Hollywood Hills Hotel** (1999 N. Sycamore Ave., check-in at the Magic Castle Hotel, 7025 Franklin Ave., at the base of the hill, 323/874-5089 or 800/741-4915, www.hollywoodhillshotel.com, $190-400, parking $8 per day) is not to be confused with the Best Western Hollywood Hills. The Hollywood Hills Hotel offers truth in advertising, set up in the Hollywood Hills, offering lovely views of the L.A. skyline on rare smog-free days. The view of the resort itself can be almost as grand, with its Chinese styling and attractive greenery. All guest rooms here, even the studios, have fully equipped kitchens for travelers seeking to save money on meals. The style of these suites is somewhere between a standard motel and a more upscale resort. You'll find floral comforters, warm-toned walls, and attractive if sparse artistic touches. Best of all, the guest rooms facing out over the city have huge windows to help you enjoy the view from the comfort of your bed. On-site, you'll find a cool Chinese pagoda, a prettily landscaped swimming pool, and a grand California-Asian restaurant, **Yamashiro** (323/466-5125, www.yamashirorestaurant.com, Mon.-Thurs. 5:30pm-9:30pm, Fri. 5:30pm-10:30pm, Sat.

5pm-10:30pm, Sun. 4:30pm-9:30pm, valet parking $8).

For a nice-priced guest room in the Hollywood vicinity, stay at the **Hollywood Orchid Suites** (1753 Orchid Ave., 323/874-9678 or 800/537-3052, www.orchidsuites.com, $160-190). The Orchid's location couldn't be better; it's in the Hollywood and Highland Center, right behind the Chinese Theatre, next door to the Kodak Theatre, and around the corner from Hollywood Boulevard and the Walk of Fame. If you're a film lover or star seeker on a moderate budget, it's tough to do better than this—especially with the free parking and proximity to public transit. Guest rooms are actually suites, with plenty of space and an eye toward sleeping your large family or several friends all in the same suite. All suites but the juniors have full kitchens. Don't expect tons of luxury in the furnishings or the decor; it all looks like last decade's motel stuff, although you'll get a coffeemaker, free Wi-Fi, and other better-than-average perks. The rectangular pool offers cooling refreshment in the summer, perfect after a long day of stalking Brad or Britney.

BEVERLY HILLS AND WEST HOLLYWOOD

Most travelers don't come to Beverly Hills looking to stay in a youth hostel. In a town whose name equals wealth, the point is to dive headfirst into the lap of luxury. Although you might have to save up to get a room near Rodeo Drive, if you choose wisely, you might just get a sense of how the 1 percent lives for just one or two nights.

For budget accommodations in the general vicinity, look to the chain motels in the West Hollywood area, which serves as L.A.'s gay mecca. Lodgings here fall between the Ramada and Beverly Hills-priced unique upscale hotels.

$150-250

The **Hotel Beverly Terrace** (469 N. Doheny Dr., Beverly Hills, 310/274-8141 or 800/842-6401, www.hotelbeverlyterrace.com, $200-260) is a rare affordable alternative in the area.

This spruced-up, retro-cool motor hotel enjoys a great spot on the border of Beverly Hills and West Hollywood.

Over $250

A newcomer to the Beverly Hills luxury hotel scene, **The Mosaic Hotel** (125 Spalding Dr., Beverly Hills, 310/278-0303 or 800/463-4466, www.mosaichotel.com, $250-700) offers a laid-back, urban vibe in both its chill common areas and its comfortable guest accommodations. Guest rooms are furnished in contemporary fabrics, with soothing light colors blending into attractive wall art and fluffy white down comforters. Mattresses are topped with feather beds, and the baths sparkle and sooth with Frette towels and Bulgari bath products. If you've got the cash to spring for a suite, you'll be treated to something that feels like your own elegant apartment, with a living room with 42-inch plasma TV, a sofa, and an armchair. Downstairs, a hip bar and small dining room offer top-shelf cocktails and tasty California cuisine. Friendly, helpful staff will serve you tidbits in the bar and can help with any travel or room needs.

The most famous of all the grand hotels of Beverly Hills, the **Beverly Wilshire** (9500 Wilshire Blvd., Beverly Hills, 310/275-5200, www.fourseasons.com, from $500) is now a Four Seasons property. But never fear: The recent multimillion-dollar renovation didn't scour away all the classic charm of this historic hotel. Nor did it lower the price of the privilege of sleeping inside these hallowed walls. Even the plainest of guest rooms here features exquisite appointments such as 42-inch plasma TVs, elegant linens, attractive artwork, and even live plants. Of course, guests with greater resources can rent a suite; the presidential suite resembles nothing so much as a European palace, complete with Corinthian columns. With an in-house spa, a dining room, room service, and every other service you could want, folks who can afford it consider a stay at the Beverly Wilshire well worth the expense.

In West Hollywood, the **Sunset Tower Hotel** (8358 Sunset Blvd., West Hollywood, 323/654-7100, www.sunsettowerhotel.com, $300-2,500) might look familiar to recent visitors to Disney's California Adventure. Indeed, its architecture inspired the "Tower of Terror" ride at the amusement park. But there's no terror in the Sunset Tower today. Instead, you'll find a gorgeous art deco exterior and a fully renovated modern interior. Guest accommodations range from smallish standard queen guest rooms with smooth linens and attractive appointments up to luxurious suites with panoramic views and limestone baths. All guest rooms include flat-screen TVs, 24-hour room service, and free Wi-Fi.

With architecture like a French castle, **Chateau Marmont** (8221 Sunset Blvd., West Hollywood, 323/656-1010 or 800/242-8328, www.chateaumarmont.com, $425-4,500) looks out on the city from its perch above the Sunset Strip. It has long attracted the in crowd, from Garbo to Leo. It is also where writers from F. Scott Fitzgerald to Hunter S. Thompson have holed up to produce work. The design is eccentric and eclectic, from vintage 1940s suites to Bauhaus bungalows. The hotel was front and center in Sofia Coppola's 2010 film *Somewhere.*

The **Le Montrose Suite** (900 Hammond St., West Hollywood, 310/855-1115 or 800/776-0666, www.lemontrose.com, $209-329) will give you a taste of the kind of luxury celebrities expect in their accommodations, especially in trendy, gay-friendly West Hollywood. The atmosphere and decor are almost desperately modern, from the silver discs behind the front desk to the neo-patchwork bedspreads in the guest rooms. Happily, you'll find lots of plush comfort in among the primary colors and plain geometric shapes in your guest room. A Berber carpet snuggles your feet, a high-end entertainment system sees to your every audio-visual and gaming need, and a gas fireplace provides just the right romantic atmosphere for an evening spent indoors. Outside your posh suite, you can take a dip in the rooftop saltwater swimming pool and whirlpool, play a set on the lighted tennis courts, or get in a good workout inside the fitness center. Hotel guests alone can enjoy the gourmet delicacies of the private dining room or order from 24-hour room service. If you're dying for some great clubbing or a seat at a show while you're in town, just ask the concierge, who can provide the assistance you need.

WESTWOOD
Over $250
A few fancy hotels rise off of Westwood's Wilshire Boulevard. Close to attractions including the Getty Museum and UCLA, the **Hotel Palomar Los Angeles-Westwood** (10740 Wilshire Blvd., 310/475-8711, www.hotelpalomar-lawestwood.com, $250-500) is a great place to lay your head if you don't mind throwing down some money. (Actually, you might be able to score a deal at the hotel on weekends, because weekdays the Palomar is filled with business travelers.) In this boutique luxury hotel, the red glowing elevator and red accents in the rooms are inspired by the lipstick of nearby Hollywood starlets. The hotel's spa suites feature luxurious soaking tubs along with striking views of the sprawling city laid out below. The Hotel Palomar is also just a half-mile from the restaurants, bars, and stores of Westwood Village.

SANTA MONICA, VENICE, AND MALIBU
Arguably, the best place to stay in Los Angeles is down by the beach. It seems ironic that you can camp in a park for $25 in exclusive Malibu, and you can pay over $1,000 for a resort room in so-called "working-class" Santa Monica. But whether you choose either of those or a spot in Venice Beach, you'll get some of the best atmosphere is the region.

Under $150
For a bed indoors for cheap, your options near the beach run to youth hostels. The huge **HI-Santa Monica** (1436 2nd St., Santa Monica, 310/393-9913, www.hilosangeles.org, $46-150) offers 260 beds in a building constructed specifically to house the hostel and which recently underwent a $2 million renovation. You'll be

right in the thick of downtown Santa Monica in a good neighborhood, within walking distance of the Santa Monica Pier, the Third Street Promenade, and the beach. Plenty of great cheap restaurants cluster in the area, or you can make use of the hostel's open kitchen. This ritzy hostel offers tons of amenities for the price, including a computer room, a TV room, a movie room, excursions, wheelchair access, sheets with the bed price, and even a complimentary continental breakfast every morning. If you prefer to find your own way around L.A., the local public transit system runs right outside the door.

The **Venice Beach Cotel** (25 Windward Ave., Venice, 310/399-7649 or 888/718-8287, www.venicebeachcotel.com, $30-80 winter, $40-150) claims to be "a hostel with hotel standards." You can make your own judgments on its amenities, which include women's-only and coed dorms with and without in-room baths, private rooms, and private rooms with baths. Rooms get maid service daily (a rarity in the hostelling world), along with clean towels and linens. Also the hostel has a computer room, and a kickback lounge welcomes guests and encourages them to socialize. But the best part of the Cotel is undoubtedly its location *on* the Boardwalk right across from Muscle Beach. Fall out of your bunk and into the warm sands of Venice's beach every morning. The fabulous restaurants of Washington Street are reached by an easy walk, and the canals sit just a block or two away. Reserve well in advance for summer.

$150-250
The reasonably priced (for what it is) and fantastically fun **Custom Hotel** (8639 Lincoln Blvd., Westchester, 310/645-0400, www.customhotel.com, $150-220), is south of Venice near LAX. The in-room Wi-Fi is free, as are the views of the city. You'll find the staff incredibly friendly and helpful, ready to help with anything from valet parking to dinner reservations. Fear not if you're seeking food and drink and would rather not leave the hotel: Custom Hotel has six social lounges, each with its own concept, including the VIP lounge—inspired LAX

Lounge; the Transonic gaming lounge; the Axis Annex art gallery; and the Duty Free vending machine room. There are places throughout the hotel to relax while gathering with others to share ideas. Want a little more? Try out **DECK 33 Bar Restaurant,** featuring Pacific Rim-influenced cuisine and overlooking the sun deck and pool, or **Hanger 39,** the event space on the lobby floor with its own entrance and bar. Less unique but crucial, the Custom offers complimentary shuttle buses to nearby LAX.

The **Venice Beach Suites & Hotel** (1305 Ocean Front Walk, 310/396-4559 or 888/877-7602, www.venicebeachsuites.com, $150-300) is a surprisingly lovely and affordable little Venice hotel. It sits right on the beach, but it's far enough from the Boardwalk to acquire a touch of peace and quiet. You can also stroll over to Washington Boulevard to grab a meal or a cup of coffee, or just wander out of the lobby and straight onto the beach. Inside, the guest rooms and suites all have full kitchens so you can cook for yourself—perfect for budget-conscious travelers and folks staying in Venice for several days. The kitchen is also great for simply coming in from the beach for a quick lunch with ice-cold drinks. The guest room decor is cuter than that of an average motel; you might find exposed brick walls and polished hardwood floors stocked with rattan furniture and cute accessories. Check the website for weeklong rental deals.

If you're looking for a moderate-priced motel near the beach, look to the 1950s-era motor inns of Santa Monica. One of these that manages to be cute and kitschy is the **Bayside Hotel** (2001 Ocean Ave., Santa Monica, 310/396-6000 or 800/525-4447, www.baysidehotel.com, $210-290). The hotel is not right on the beach, but you can walk in there in about two minutes. If you crave elegance along with speedy check-in and checkout, the Bayside isn't for you. But if you're seeking a fun stay in a place that looks like it ought to be in a Gidget movie, the Bayside may be just right.

For a charming hotel experience only a block from the ever-energetic Boardwalk, stay at the **Inn at Venice Beach** (327 Washington Blvd.,

800/828-0688, www.innatvenicebeach.com, $160-350, parking $7 per day). The charming orange-and-brown exterior, complete with a lovely bricked interior courtyard-cum-café, makes all guests feel welcome. Inside, you might be surprised by the brightly colored modern furniture and decor. Common spaces are done in a postmodern blocky style, while the guest rooms pop with brilliant yellows and vibrant accents. The two-story boutique hotel offers 45 guest rooms, and its location on Washington Street makes it a perfect base from which to enjoy the best restaurants of Venice. Start each day with a complimentary continental breakfast, either in the dining room or outside in the Courtyard Café. If you need to stay connected, the inn has complimentary Wi-Fi throughout.

If you want to bring your family to stay in legendary Malibu, one of the best hotels is the **Casa Malibu Inn on the Beach** (22752 Pacific Coast Hwy., 310/456-2219 or 800/831-0858, $170-500). This pleasant and kid-friendly property sits right on the beach. Actually it claims to be the only hotel in all of Los Angeles County with its own private beach. Many of the guest rooms have ocean views; some also have gas fireplaces for cozy cool winter evenings. Some of the gleaming white baths have bathtubs, perfect for a relaxing soak after a long day out on the beach. Head down to the lobby of this unpretentious 1950s-era building for a genuinely fresh continental breakfast each morning. From there, you can stagger right out onto the sand to pick out a prime spot before the crowds descend. You can take one of the hotel's beach chairs with you, and you don't even have to worry about parking.

Yes, you really can stay at the **Hotel California** (1670 Ocean Ave., Santa Monica, 310/393-2363 or 866/571-0000, $219-329). Appropriately decorated with classic longboards and electric guitars, this moderate hotel sits a short block from the beach and next to the Santa Monica Pier. You'll be in the perfect spot to enjoy all the best of Santa Monica without ever having to get into a car or worry about finding parking. Inside the hotel, you'll

Hotel Erwin

find hardwood floors and matching bedsteads, calming pale yellow walls, and white comforters and linens. Choose between a classic guest room and a suite with a jetted tub. Outside, enjoy the lush greenery of the oddly named Spanish Courtyard, which looks more like something from the tropics than from Europe. Other perks include free Wi-Fi, a mini fridge, and a smoke-free hotel experience.

Over $250

There's probably no hotel in Venice Beach that is a better reflection of the edgy beach town's attitude than **Hotel Erwin** (1697 Pacific Ave., 310/452-1111, www.hotelerwin. com, $250-600). Situated just feet from the Venice Beach Boardwalk and Muscle Beach, Hotel Erwin has graffiti art adorning the outside wall by its entrance and in some of its rooms. The rooms all have balconies and playful decor including lamps resembling the barbells used by the weightlifters at nearby Muscle Beach. Sitting atop the hotel is High, a rooftop bar that allows you to take in all

the action of the bustling boardwalk while sipping a cocktail. The staff here is laid-back, very genial, and accommodating.

In Malibu, if you've got silly amounts of cash to spare, stay at the **Malibu Beach Inn** (22878 Pacific Coast Hwy., Malibu, 310/456-6444 or 800/462-5428, www.malibubeachinn. com, $425-1,200). This ocean-side villa offers all the very best furnishings and amenities. Every guest room has a view of the ocean, and the boutique hotel sits on "Billionaire's Beach," an exclusive stretch of sand that's difficult to access unless you're a guest of one of its properties. Your guest room will be done in rare woods, gleaming stone, and the most stylish modern linens and accents. A plasma TV, plush robes, and comfy beds tempt some visitors to stay inside, but equally tempting are the balconies with their own entertainment in the form of endless surf, glorious sunsets, and balmy breezes. The more affordable guest rooms are a bit small but just as attractively turned out as the over-the-top suites. When lunch and dinnertime come, go downstairs to the airy, elegant, on-site Carbon Beach Club ($31-50) to enjoy delicious cuisine in an upscale beach atmosphere.

One of the best-known resort hotels at the beach in L.A. has long been **Shutters on the Beach** (1 Pico Blvd., Santa Monica, 310/458-0030, www.shuttersonthebeach. com, $595-6,000). Make no mistake: You'll pay handsomely for the privilege of laying your head on one of Shutters' hallowed pillows. On the other hand, the gorgeous airy guest rooms will make you feel like you're home, or at least staying at the home you'd have if you could hire a famous designer to decorate for you. Even the most modest guest rooms have not only the comfortable beds, white linens, plasma TVs, and oversize bathtubs of a luxury hotel, but also a comfortable clutter of pretty ornaments on tables and shelves. If you can pry yourself out of your private space, head down to the famed lobby for a drink and a people-watching session. Get a reservation for the elegant One Pico or grab a more casual sandwich or salad at beachside Coast.

The impressive multilevel resort edifice sits right on the beach, so there's no need to find a premium parking spot to enjoy a day in the sand. If you long for more formal relaxation, book a massage at the ONE Spa. Art lovers can spend hours just wandering the halls of the hotel, examining the works of many famous modern photographers and painters.

PASADENA

Pasadena lodgings run to the old standard national chains plus a few funky 1950s-era motor lodges and the occasional upscale B&B. If you're planning to stay in Pasadena over the New Year, book early: The town fills up for the legendary Rose Parade. If your aim is to get yourself a guest room from which you can watch the Rose Parade, book earlier still; while you can get the perfect view from a room of your own, such places are at a premium during parade season.

Under $150

The top pick of the quaint motor inns is the **Saga Motor Hotel** (1633 E. Colorado Blvd., 626/795-0431 or 800/793-7242, www.the-sagamotorhotel.com, $80-135). Outside it's all 1950s, including the structure of the low buildings. The ambiance extends to the door of your guest room, which includes a doorknob and an actual metal key to open it with. But inside your room, the decor gets a lot more contemporary. The big space has either a king or two double beds, clean if worn carpeting and linens, and a nice bath with a surprisingly good bathtub and nice hot showers. Location-wise, the Saga is right on the Rose Parade route on broad Colorado Boulevard, but it's not right downtown or in Old Town. Sadly, the service is spotty at best, but few people expect concierges at motor hotels.

Of the main chain motels, the best inexpensive one might be the **Comfort Inn** (2462 E. Colorado Blvd., 626/405-0811, www.comfortinn.com, $85-92). You'll find comfortable amenities in pleasant standard motel rooms, along with a good set of views of the Rose Parade. Expect room prices to skyrocket for the parade.

$150-250

Once upon a time, Pasadena was the resort haven of wealthy East Coasters. To revisit this wealthy past, stay at **The Bissell House Bed & Breakfast** (201 Orange Grove Ave., 626/441-3535 or 800/441-3530, www.bissellhouse.com, $160-260) on "Millionaire's Row." The tall mint-green Victorian surrounded by the deeper green of lush mature landscaping opens its doors to well-heeled travelers who want a luxurious place to stay while they're in the L.A. area. It is named for one of its residents, Anna Bissell McCay, heiress to the original Bissell vacuum-cleaner fortune. Each of the five guest rooms and two suites has a unique decorating scheme, yet each shares a European floral theme that binds the inn together into a coherent whole. Guest rooms have comfy beds, a luxurious bath (most have claw-foot tubs), and lots of wonderful amenities, and the property has a swimming pool with a hot tub and lots of lovely plants scattered about. Your room rate includes a full breakfast each morning, served at the long table in the downstairs dining room.

Food

You'll find a wide variety of cuisine all over Los Angeles and its surrounding towns. Whatever kind of food you prefer, from fresh sushi to Armenian, you can probably find it in a cool little hole-in-the-wall somewhere in L.A. Local recommendations often make for the best dining experiences, but even just walking down the right street can yield a tasty meal.

DOWNTOWN AND VICINITY

Sure, you can find plenty of bland tourist-friendly restaurants serving American and Americanized food in the Downtown area—but why would you, when one of Downtown L.A.'s greatest strengths is its ethnic diversity and the great range of cuisine that goes along with it? An endless array of fabulous holes-in-the-wall awaits you. Getting local recommendations is the best way to find the current hot spots, or you can choose from among this tiny sampling of what's available.

Classic American

If you're just looking for a good pastrami sandwich, you can get it at **Langer's Delicatessen and Restaurant** (704 S. Alvarado St., 213/483-8050, www.langersdeli.com, Mon.-Sat. 8am-4pm, $12-25). Operating continuously since 1947, the house specialty at Langer's is a hot pastrami sandwich that some say is the best in the world (yes, that includes New York City). Whether you're willing to go that far or not, Langer's serves both hot and cold dishes in the traditional Jewish deli style to satisfy any appetite level or specific craving. Granted, it's still California, so you can get fresh avocado on your tongue sandwich if you really want to. You'll also find a vast breakfast menu and plenty of desserts (noodle kugel, anyone?). If you don't have time to sit down for lunch, order in advance and pick up your meal curbside. If you can dine in, be sure to take a few minutes to gaze at the photos on the walls; the family you'll see has run this deli since it opened in the postwar era.

Located in an old firehouse building, **Engine Co. No. 28** (644 S. Figueroa St., 213/624-6996, www.engineco.com, Mon.-Fri. 7:30am-midnight, Sat.-Sun. 11am-midnight, $14-40) is decked out in classic wood paneling, leather, and brass. Meatloaf and chili are the big sellers.

French

A surprisingly cute little brick-fronted café, the **Angelique Café** (840 S. Spring St., 213/623-8698, www.angeliquebistro.com, Tues.-Fri. 11:30am-3pm and 5pm-10pm, Sat.-Sun. 8am-3pm and 5pm-10pm, $11-20) offers a relaxed French atmosphere and good French-style food. The original chef-owner came from France and brought his recipes and his dining aesthetic with him. The large menu has an array of both French and American dishes, heavy on the salads and more traditional hot fare. If you come for breakfast, you can choose from a list of omelets and crepes plus a few American egg dishes, or the more traditional continental breakfast of pastry and coffee. Angelique's small green-and-yellow dining room is open for breakfast and lunch only. If it's a nice day, grab a table outside on the wrought iron-fenced patio, which has almost as many tables as the inside dining room.

Greek

Originally a Greek import company in the 1960s, the **Papa Cristos Taverna** (2771 W. Pico Blvd., 323/737-2970, www.papacristos.com, Tues.-Sat. 9:30am-8pm, Sun. 9am-4pm, $7-18) restaurant opened in the 1990s. The import shop still supplies the local Greek community with hard-to-come-by delicacies, which also become ingredients in the cuisine at the Taverna. Dishes are traditionally Greek, from the salads to the kebabs to the baba ghanouj. After you're finished with your meal, wander the aisles of the store to pick up a few unusual Greek delicacies to take with you.

Italian

It seems odd to name a high-end restaurant

after a decidedly low-end bug, but that's what the owners of █ **Cicada Restaurant** (617 S. Olive St., 213/488-9488, www.cicadarestaurant.com, Wed.-Fri. 5:30pm-9pm, $21-95) did. Set in the 1920s Oviatt building, decorated in high French art deco style, the beautiful restaurant glitters with some of its original Lalique glass panels—be sure to check out the elevator doors on your way in or out. The palatial dining room features huge round tables for large parties and balcony seating for intimate duos. The immense space lets Cicada place its tables farther apart than in most restaurants, giving diners a sense of privacy and romance that can be hard to come by.

As for the food, calling it "Italian" isn't quite right, since the cuisine here fuses Italian concepts with California ingredients, techniques, and presentations. Expect a varied seasonal menu of inventive dishes, including pastas and meats in the Italian style with distinct California flavors. Be sure to save room for Cicada's beloved desserts, which many diners declare to be their favorite part of the meal.

Japanese

There are lots of ramen places in Little Tokyo, but busy, noisy █ **Daikokuya** (327 E. 1st St., 213/626-1680, www.daikoku-ten.com, Mon.-Thurs. 11am-midnight, Fri.-Sat. 11am-1am, Sun. 11am-11pm, under $10) is among the very best, hailed by no less an authority than Pulitzer Prize-winning food writer Jonathan Gold. The steaming bowls of hearty pork broth and noodles satisfy even the brawniest appetite.

For a serious authentic Japanese cuisine experience, visit █ **Kagaya** (418 E. 2nd St., 213/617-1016, Tues.-Sat. 6pm-10:30pm, Sun. 6pm-10pm, $40-128). Even L.A. denizens who've eaten at shabu-shabu places in Japan come back to Kagaya again and again. They make reservations in advance, because the dining room is small and the quality of the food makes it popular even on weeknights. The term *shabu-shabu* refers to paper-thin slices of beef and vegetable that you dip and swish into a pot of boiling *daishi* (broth), then dunk in *ponzu* or other house-made sauces before eating. The

shabu-shabu is but one course in the meal you'll get at Kagaya, since all meals include several appetizers (varieties change daily), shabu-shabu with beef and seafood, udon noodles, and dessert. You can pay a premium for Wagyu beef if you choose, but the king crab legs in season are part of the regular price of dinner. Even the regular beef here isn't cheap, but the quality makes it worth the price. Sit at the counter if you want to watch all your food be prepared before your eyes.

Korean

One of the largest Asian neighborhoods in Los Angeles is Koreatown. It's only fitting that a city with such a large Korean population has plenty of good Korean restaurants. One of these is **Chunju Han-il Kwan** (3450 W. 6th St., 213/480-1799, Mon.-Sat. 11am-11pm, Sun. 11am-10pm, $10-15). This is an authentic Korean restaurant that caters primarily to the expat Korean community. You won't find English menus here, but you will find helpful waitstaff who can guide you through the process of ordering. If your server tells you a dish is very spicy, she means it, but that doesn't mean you won't love it anyway. The menu is eclectic to say the least—you can get a hot dog, octopus, fish soup, Korean stew (thickened with American cheese), kimchi, and much more. Many patrons crave the veggie side dishes that come with the entrées. Don't worry about your standard of dress when you dine here, since this casual restaurant resides in a strip mall and has gas burners on the tables.

Markets

In operation since 1917, the **Grand Central Market** (317 S. Broadway, 213/624-2378, www.grandcentralsquare.com, daily 9am-6pm) houses dozens of food vendors. Most sell hot prepared foods, but you'll also find stalls selling spices and Latino pantry goods. A $10 or more purchase and validation will get you an hour's free parking at the garage (308 South Hill St.).

Mexican

Everyone in L.A. (and most of the rest of

FOLLOW THAT FOOD TRUCK!

Some of Los Angeles' most interesting – and tasty – food is not coming from upscale restaurants with tables draped in white linens. Rather, a lot of the city's best culinary creations are being served out of food trucks. Here gourmet chefs can follow their dreams with little overhead, and the result is some of the L.A. food scene's most blogged about bites. There is even an **LA Street Food Fest** (http://lastreetfoodfest.com) held in the Rose Bowl annually due to the rise of this foodie phenomenon.

Websites including **Find LA Food Trucks** (www.findlafoodtrucks.com) and **Trux Map** (www.foodtrucksmap.com) have sprung up to help you find some of your roving favorites.

One of the early food truck favorites that is still going strong is **Kogi BBQ** (twitter @ko-gibbbq, http://kogibbq.com). Kogi serves a hybrid of Mexican and Korean food with items that include kimchi quesadillas and short rib tacos.

The owner of **The Grilled Cheese Truck** (twitter @grlldcheesetruk, http://thegrilledcheesetruck.com) was inspired to start a truck selling grilled cheeses after he entered the Annual Grilled Cheese Invitational in the Rose Bowl and realized how many people loved this basic sandwich. His famous item is the cheesy mac and rib, which has barbecued pork tucked into the grilled cheese.

Sure, **Frysmith** (twitter @frysmith, http://eatfrysmith.com) has chili cheese fries. But this truck also has kimchi fries and rajas fries that include marinated steak on top.

Happy hunting!

California, for that matter) knows that the best tamales come from the kitchens of Mexican grandmothers and get sold on the streets from carts or trucks. If you're not a local and don't feel able to find the best little sidewalk tamale cart, your best option is ◖ **Mama's Hot Tamales Café** (2122 W. 7th St., 213/487-7474, www.mamashottamales.com, daily 11am-3:30pm, $6-10). Open pretty much for lunch only, Mama's serves salads, appetizers, burritos, tostadas, and other simple Latin American dishes. But if you know what's right, you'll order the house namesake: a homemade tamale.

Located on Olvera Street, **La Luz del Dia** (1 W. Olvera St., 213/628-7495, www.luzdeldia.com, Mon. 10am-3:30pm, Tues.-Thurs. 10am-8pm, Fri.-Sat. 10am-9pm, Sun. 8:30am-9pm, $7-10) has been dishing up simple, spicy Mexican food since 1959. Get a beer, a combination plate with delicious homemade corn tortillas, and watch the tourists go by.

LOS FELIZ AND SILVER LAKE
Coffee and Tea
The baristas at **Intelligentsia** (3922 Sunset Blvd., 323/663-6173, www.intelligentsiacoffee.com, Sun.-Wed. 6am-8pm, Thurs.-Sat. 6am-11pm) are true artisans, pulling shots and steaming milk with cultish reverence. Many of the beans are direct-trade and shade-grown. Linger on the lovely patio, paved with gorgeous blue tiles imported from Nicaragua.

Contemporary
French fries in origami bags. Toasters on every table. Dishes with names like Mac Daddy and Cheese. Everything plays into the love-it-or-leave-it hip factor at **Fred 62** (1850 N. Vermont Ave., 323/667-0062, www.fred62.com, daily 24 hours, $7-15), where the booths feel like old Chevy backseats and everyone's a garage-band star. The hip eatery hosts many celebrities and was featured in a recent Prince video.

Mexican
Not every taco stand wins awards from the James Beard Foundation. ◖ **Yuca's** (2056 Hillhurst Ave., 323/662-1214, www.yucasla.com, Mon.-Sat. 11am-6pm, $5) received the honor in 2005, but it simply confirmed what Los Feliz locals have known for decades: This shack serves truly memorable (and cheap) tacos and burritos. Vegetarians beware: Even the beans are made with pork fat.

Thai

Routinely topping critics' lists of the best Thai restaurants in Los Angeles, elegant **Jitlada** (5233 W. Sunset Blvd., 323/663-3104, www.jitladala.com, Tues.-Sun. 11am-3pm and 5pm-10:30pm, $10-30) specializes in the cuisine of southern Thailand, which is rarely seen on U.S. menus. *L.A. Weekly* food writer Jonathan Gold proclaimed that Jitlada offered "the spiciest food you can eat in Los Angeles at the moment."

HOLLYWOOD

Hollywood's got just as many tasty treats tucked away in strip malls as other areas of Los Angeles. If you want to rub elbows with rock stars, you're likely to find yourself at a big, slightly raunchy bar and grill. For a chance at glimpsing stars of the silver screen, look for up-scale California cuisine or perhaps a high-end sushi bar. If all you need is tasty sustenance, you can choose from a range of restaurants.

Brazilian

Need food really, really, *really* late? **Bossa Nova** (7181 W. Sunset Blvd., 323/436-7999, www.bossafood.com, Sun.-Wed. 11am-3:30am, Thurs.-Sat. 11am-4am, $10-20) can hook you up. A big menu of inexpensive entrées can satisfy any appetite from lunch to way past dinnertime at Bossa. Some of the dishes bear the spicy flavors of the owners' home country of Brazil, but you'll also find a ton of pastas, plenty of salads, and classic Italian-American build-your-own pizzas. Check out the desserts for some South American specialties if you need sweets after a long night out at the clubs. Not near the Sunset Strip? Bossa Nova has two other L.A. locations: one on Robertson Boulevard and one in West L.A. If you've made it back to your hotel room and aren't inclined to leave again, Bossa delivers.

Breakfast

If you're a flapjack fan, a trip to Hollywood should include a breakfast at ◖ **The Griddle Café** (7916 Sunset Blvd., 323/874-0377, www.thegriddlecafe.com, Mon.-Fri. 7am-4pm, Sat.-Sun. 8am-4pm, $11). This hectic, loud breakfast joint serves up creations like a "Red Velvet" pancake and a pancake with brown sugar baked bananas in a buttermilk batter. For those who prefer savory to sweet, The Griddle has delicious breakfast tacos and a cobb omelet with all the fixins of a cobb salad except the lettuce. With the Director's Guild of America building next door, The Griddle Café is also a place where you may spot a celebrity.

Classic American

If you've ever owned a rock album—any rock album—it's worth your time to stop in for a meal at ◖ **The Rainbow Bar & Grill** (9015 W. Sunset Blvd., 310/278-4232, www.rainbowbarandgrill.com, daily 11am-2pm, $15). You'll find a lack of fancy sauces and an amazing myriad of rock-and-roll memorabilia, including farmed photos of rockers Alice Cooper, Dion, and Slash in this dark (but no longer smoky) restaurant. To the surprise of some intrepid diners, the hallowed haven, in which countless rockers have been serviced by innumerable groupies, does serve a darn tasty cheeseburger. If you show up for lunch on a weekday, you're likely to have the cavernous space almost to yourself to enjoy your salad and make your slow way along the walls checking out the endless parade of photos, guitars, newspaper snippets, and other cool stuff. In the even dimmer bar area, you can play a for-real game of authentic table Ms. Pac-Man as you sip your favorite cocktail or quaff a beer.

Nighttime is a whole different story. The crowds start trickling into the Rainbow as the sun goes down. By the time the shows let out at the Roxy and the Whisky, your chances of finding a booth diminish significantly. The good news is that the rockers still gather here after playing shows in the neighborhood. Lemmy of Motorhead is known to hang out in the Rainbow Room almost every night when his band is not touring. You never know who you'll bump into as you weave your way through the main dining room and outdoor patio to get your next drink. The back rooms also open up late, and you'll find dancing, drinking, smoking (*sh!*), and fun upstairs in a warren-like space that includes either two or three separate bar-and-club spaces on any given night, depending on whose tales you believe.

If you prefer to combine your love of live acts and your need for food, head for the **Hotel Café** (1623 1/2 N. Cahuenga Blvd., 323/461-2040, www.hotelcafe.com, daily 7pm-close, 21 and over, $10-30). Food choices run to the casual here—paninis, salads, and desserts, but the restaurant has a beer list, a wine list, and a full bar. The restaurant opens early; it's easiest to secure a table if you show up before the show starts. After 7pm, prepare for things to get loud. If you do love yourself some new-to-the-scene music, stick around.

On the more casual end of the spectrum, **Pink's Famous Hot Dogs** (709 N. La Brea Ave., 323/931-4223, www.pinkshollywood. com, Sun.-Thurs. 9:30am-2am, Fri.-Sat. 9:30am-3am, $3.50-7) is hot dog heaven. Frankophiles line up at this roadside stand (lit up like a Las Vegas show club into the wee hours of the morning) for variations on a sausage in a bun that range from the basic chili dog to the more elaborate Martha Stewart Dog. It has been at the same location since 1939.

California Cuisine

It seems right somehow that the spot in L.A. that combines live music with upscale cuisine is on Melrose Avenue. At ◖**The Foundry on Melrose** (7465 Melrose Ave., 323/651-0915, www.thefoundryonmelrose.com, Mon.-Wed. 6pm-11pm, Thurs.-Sat. 6pm-1am, Sun. 5:30pm-11pm, $25-30), expect to find elegance and art in a style that improbably marries arts and crafts, art deco, and modern industrial. The art extends to the plates, where the chef creates elaborate presentations of an array of ingredients. The dinner menu is small, seasonal, and utterly haute California. You might even see an occasional celebrity dining here, though you'll also remark on the refreshing lack of oh-so-trendy 'tude at this restaurant. At the big curving black bar, you can get a lighter (and less pricey) meal from the bar menu. If you prefer an alfresco dining

experience, ask for a table out on the patio (yes, that's an olive tree dangling its streamers in your soup). The third room at the Foundry shelters a small piano bar and a mix of music, from Lunes Latinos on Monday to Bluesy Tuesday and Suds and Songs Sunday.

Italian

The warm but clamorous dining room at ◖**Pizzeria Mozza** (641 N. Highland Ave., 323/297-0101, www.pizzeriamozza.com, daily noon-midnight, $8-24) has been packed since chef Nancy Silverton, founder of La Brea Bakery, opened the doors in 2006. The wood-fired oven turns out rustic, blistered pizzas with luxurious toppings. Reservations are tough to get, but bar seats are available for walk-ins.

As smashingly popular (and as raucous) as Pizzeria Mozza is the chef's Italian restaurant next door, **Osteria Mozza** (6602 Melrose Ave., 323/297-0100, www.osteriamozza.com, daily noon-midnight, $10-40). Serving more than just pizza, the Osteria offers a fuller menu of luscious pastas and adventurous meat dishes. Check out the "mozzarella bar menu," an assortment of appetizer-size dishes featuring bufala, burrata, and ricotta.

LA BREA, FAIRFAX, AND MIRACLE MILE
California Cuisine

Pairing meat and potatoes with a retro-clubby dining room, **Jar** (8225 Beverly Blvd., 323/655-6566, www.thejar.com, Sun.-Thurs. 5:30pm-9:30pm, Fri.-Sat. 5:30pm-10:30pm, $10-65) puts a Southern California spin on the traditional steak house. Meats and grilled fishes are served à la carte with your choice of sauce, and the side orders serve two. Jar is also known for its Sunday brunch—try the Lobster Benedict.

Deli

Midnight snackers unhinge their jaws on the hulking corned beef sandwiches at **Canter's Deli** (419 N. Fairfax Ave., 323/651-2030, www. cantersdeli.com, daily 24 hours, $12-18), in the heart of the Jewish Fairfax district. This venerable 24-hour deli also boasts its share of star sightings, so watch for noshing rock stars in the wee hours of the morning.

Lunch doesn't get much better than the high-end bounty in the deli cases at **Joan's on Third** (8350 W. 3rd St., 323/655-2285, www.joansonthird.com, Mon.-Sat. 8am-8pm, Sun. 8am-6pm, $10-15). Mix and match fine sandwiches, roasted vegetables, and artisanal cheeses. There are also sidewalk tables, and a breakfast kitchen serving organic eggs and French toast.

BEVERLY HILLS AND WEST HOLLYWOOD

Between Beverly Hills and West L.A. you'll find an eclectic choice of restaurants. Unsurprisingly, Beverly Hills tends toward high-end eateries serving European and haute California cuisine. On the other hand, West L.A. boasts a wide array of international restaurants. You'll have to try a few to pick your favorites, since every local has their own take on the area's best eats.

Brazilian

There's nothing like a good steak dinner, Brazilian style. At **Fogo de Chao** (133 N. La Cienega Blvd., Beverly Hills, 310/289-7755, www.fogodechao.com, Mon.-Thurs. 11:30am-2pm and 5pm-10pm, Fri. 11:30am-2pm and 5pm-10:30pm, Sat. 4:30pm-10:30pm, Sun. 4pm-9:30pm, lunch $36, dinner $58), be prepared for an interactive dining experience. The meat is slow-roasted, then skewered and cut right onto your plate by ever-moving servers. Be sure to use the red-and-green token on your table; if you don't turn it over to the red side occasionally, you will be continuously bombarded with the 15 different kinds of meat the restaurant offers. The fixed-price meal includes endless trips to the salad bar, fresh-cut veggies, and traditional Brazilian side dishes (fried bananas are a starch here, not a dessert). The extensive wine list includes plenty of both California and European vintages, plus a wider-than-average selection of ports and dessert wines. While the food is fabulous, you'll get the most out of a meal here with a lively group that will enjoy the service as much as the spicy flavors.

Classic American

The Ivy (113 N. Robertson Blvd., 310/274-8303, Mon.-Sat. 8am-11pm, Sun. 8am-10pm, $10-43) is an industry institution: a sun-dappled, cottage-like space where the A-list goes as much to be seen and photographed as to eat. Dishes like chopped salad and soft-shell crab punctuate the new American menu. Call ahead for a prized spot on the sidewalk patio.

Coffee and Tea

A grand afternoon tea in stately Beverly Hills just seems like the right thing to do at least once. You can get some of the best tea in L.A. at ◖ **The Living Room in The Peninsula Hotel** (9882 Santa Monica Blvd., Beverly Hills, 310/975-2736, www.peninsula.com, seatings daily noon, 2:30pm and 5pm, $18-45). The Peninsula has three restaurants, but for tea head to the elegant Living Room and grab a comfy chair near the fireplace. Sit back and enjoy the delicate harp music while admiring the elegant and tasteful furnishings in this posh space. If you skipped lunch or plan to miss dinner, go with the heartier Royal Tea or Imperial Tea. Lighter eaters prefer the Full Tea or the Light Tea. All come with tea sandwiches, scones, pastries, and, of course, a pot of tea. The loose-leaf teas are Peninsula originals; many are flavored. For an extra fee, you can add a glass of champagne to complete your high tea experience.

The dress is business casual. Don't show up in jeans, flip-flops, and a T-shirt.

Italian

If you're looking for upscale Italian cuisine in a classy environment, enjoy lunch or dinner at **Il Pastaio Restaurant** (400 N. Canon Dr., Beverly Hills, 310/205-5444, www.giacominodrago.com, Mon.-Thurs. 11:30am-11pm, Fri.-Sat. 11:30am-midnight, Sun. 11:30am-10pm, $15-30). The bright dining room offers a sunny luncheon experience, and the white tablecloths and shiny glassware lend an elegance to dinner, served reasonably late into the evening even on weekdays. Boasting a large menu for a high-end restaurant, Il Pastaio offers a wide variety of salads, risotto, and pasta dishes as well as some overpriced antipasti and a smaller list of entrées. Preparations and dishes evoke authentic Italy, so you might see osso buco or fettuccine bolognese on the menu. The blue-painted bar offers a tasteful selection of California and Italian vintages, and serious wine lovers will be pleased to see the Italian selections broken out by region.

Happily located right on the Strip, the **Vivoli Cafe & Trattoria** (7994 Sunset Blvd., West Hollywood, 323/656-5050, www.vivolicafe. com, Tues.-Sun. 11am-2pm and 5pm-10pm, $15-30) offers a copious menu of Italian cuisine. Expect white tablecloths, wooden chairs, and friendly service at this locals' favorite. The broad menu focuses on seafood and a surprising variety of salads, but you can also get your favorite cheese-heavy pasta dishes or hearty, meaty entrées. Don't forget dessert—"leave the gun, take the cannoli."

SANTA MONICA, VENICE, AND MALIBU

Yes, there's lots of junky beach food to be found in Santa Monica and Venice Beach, but there are also an amazing number of gems hiding in these towns.

Barbecue

As is right and proper in California, you have to go to the seedier part of town to get the best authentic Southern barbecue. **Baby Blues BBQ** (444 Lincoln Blvd., Venice, 310/396-7675, www.babybluesvenice.com, daily 11:30am-10pm, $10-32) disobeys the haute Venice rule of AWOL (Always West of Lincoln), sitting right on Lincoln Boulevard with its grubby sidewalks and elderly strip malls. This disreputable street corner location (it's really not that bad) does not dissuade locals, who line up at lunchtime to grab a plate of ribs or chicken. The menu pays little attention to cholesterol or carb counters. Choose from sausages, pulled pork, beer-braised brisket, barbecued chicken, and pork or beef ribs, all covered in homemade sauces and spice rubs. The cooks know their business, and regional specialties from different parts of the South are created with specific intent and understanding of the cuisine. Fixin's (side dishes) include Baby Blues's famed hot cornbread, baked beans, slaw, mac and cheese, and other appropriate stuff.

Caribbean

How can you not love a restaurant called **Cha Cha Chicken** (1906 Ocean Ave., Santa Monica, 310/581-1684, www.chachachicken. com, Mon.-Thurs. 11am-9:45pm, Sat. 10am-10pm, Sun. 10am-9pm, $7-12)? It looks just like it sounds—a slightly decrepit but brightly painted shack only a short walk from the Santa Monica Pier and the Third Street Promenade. You can't miss it even if you're driving quickly down Ocean Avenue. The best place to get a table is definitely the palm tree-strewn patio area outdoors. It's the perfect atmosphere to enjoy the wonderful and inexpensive Caribbean dishes that come from the fragrant kitchen. The jerk dishes bring a tangy sweetness to the table, while the *ropa vieja* heats up the plate, and the funky enchiladas put a whole new spin on a Mexican classic. Salads, sandwiches, and wraps are popular with lighter eaters and the lunch crowd. Quaff an imported Jamaican soda or a seasonal *agua fresca* with your meal, since Cha Cha Chicken doesn't have a liquor license.

Contemporary

Cora's Coffee Shoppe (1802 Ocean Ave., Santa Monica, 310/451-9562, www.corascoffee. com, daily 7am-3pm, $12) doesn't look like much: It's a tiny building with a smallish, old fashioned diner sign. But don't be fooled by the unpretentious exterior. The small, exquisite restaurant inside is something of a locals' secret hiding in plain sight, serving breakfast and lunch to diners who are more than willing to pack into the tiny spaces that Cora's calls dining rooms. In addition to the two tiny marble-topped tables and miniature marble counter inside, a small patio area off to one side offers a warm and pleasant atmosphere screened by latticework and venerable bougainvillea vines.

What's best about Cora's is simply the food. The chefs, crammed into the tiny kitchen, use high-end and sometimes organic ingredients to create breakfast and lunch dishes from typical fare like omelets and oatmeal to unexpected items including a hamburger salad and a BLT done up with a smear of goat cheese. The espresso drinks are reminiscent of European coffees—dark, bitter, and served in cups the size of bowls. Perhaps it's the coffee that keeps the staff moving so fast, endlessly serving and busing and serving some more to keep up with the steady flow of diners, many of whom the waiters seem to know quite well.

Another unpretentious eatery with great food is **Blue Plate** (1415 Montana Ave., Santa Monica, 310/260-8877, www.blueplatesanta-monica.com, daily 8am-9pm, $12). This sleek diner with a clean blue and white decor serves the basics: salads, sandwiches, and wraps. While the cuisine is not as creative as Cora's, Blue Plate's menu items are healthy and tasty. There is also an expanded menu for dinner that includes tacos, seafood, and steak. Be aware that this is a small, loud place and that you might be inches away from another table.

Italian

The **C&O Trattoria** (31 Washington Blvd., Marina del Rey, 310/823-9491, www.cotrattoria.com, Mon.-Thurs. 11:30am-10pm, Fri.-Sat. 8am-11pm, Sun. 8am-10pm, $13-23) manages to live up to its hype and then some. Sit outside in the big outdoor dining room, enjoying the mild weather and the soft pastel frescoes on the exterior walls surrounding the courtyard. C&O is known for its self-described gargantuan portions, which are best shared family-style among a group of diners. Be sure to start off with the addictive little garlic rolls. Next, seriously consider the pasta list, which includes some truly creative and delectable preparations. The rigatoni al forno is a standout out item. If you need help deciding on dishes, be sure to ask your friendly, knowledgeable server, who will be attentive but not overzealous. While C&O

has a nice wine list, it's worth trying out the house chianti, where you get to serve yourself on an honor system.

Mexican

Located on Venice's hip Abbot Kinney Boulevard, **Casalinda** (1357 Abbot Kinney Blvd., Venice, 310/664-1177, Sun.-Thurs. 11:30am-9:30pm, Fri.-Sat. 11:30am-10pm, $9.50) offers up classic taqueria fare with slightly steeper prices. There are tacos and burritos as well as more unique items like octopus ceviche. The tortas, which are Mexican sandwiches, are a tasty combination of ripe slabs of avocado, crema fresca, onions, tomatoes, a black bean paste and your choice of chicken, pork, steak, or for the adventurous, tongue.

Seafood

Neptune's Net (42505 Pacific Coast Hwy., Malibu, 310/457-3095, www.neptunesnet.com, summer Mon.-Thurs. 10:30am-8pm, Fri. 10:30am-9pm, Sat.-Sun. 10am-8:30pm, winter Mon.-Fri. and 10:30am-7pm, Sat.-Sun. 10am-7pm, $12) in Malibu catches all kinds of seafood to serve to hungry diners. Situated on the Malibu coastline adjacent to the county line surf break, you'll often find sandy and salt-encrusted local surfers satisfying their enormous appetites after hours out on the waves or bikers downing a beer after a ride on the twisting highway. Even Midwestern visitors who are put off by the endless raw and rare fish eaten in California will feel comfortable dining in this casual palace of fried seafood. One of the Net's most satisfying options is the shrimp tacos: crispy fried shrimp on tortillas topped with a pineapple salsa. The large menu includes a seemingly endless variety of other combinations, à la carte options, and side dishes.

Catch (1910 Ocean Way, Santa Monica, 310/581-7714, www.hotelcasadelmar.com, daily 7am-3pm and 5:30pm-10pm, $16-45) in the Casa del Mar hotel looks out on spectacular ocean views. The menu offers choices from land and sea, including grilled octopus, a Dungeness crab salad, Carlsbad mussels, and filet mignon.

LOS ANGELES

© STUART THORNTON

Neptune's Net's tasty shrimp tacos

Thai

If your tastes run to the exotically spicy and romantic, walk across Pacific Avenue from Venice Beach into Marina Del Ray and to the **Siamese Garden** (301 Washington Blvd., Marina Del Rey, 310/821-0098, http://siamese-garden.net, Mon.-Thurs. 5pm-10pm, Fri.-Sat. 4pm-11pm, Sun. 4pm-10pm, $10-30). A favorite of local couples looking for a romantic evening out, Siamese Garden boasts outdoor tables set in an overhanging lantern-lit garden, complete with glimpses of the Venice Canals through the foliage and fencing. In the kitchen, Siamese Garden prides itself on creating delightful dishes with only the freshest and best produce and ingredients available. The wide menu offers all of your favorite Thai classics, such as coconut soup, pad thai, and a rainbow of curries. Mint, lemongrass, peanut sauce, basil, and hot chilies crowd the menu with their strong and distinct flavors. Vegetarians have a great selection of tasty dishes, while carnivores can enjoy plenty of good beef, poultry, and seafood. For dessert, try one of the fun sticky rice

and fruit dishes. To accompany your meal, you can get a rich Thai iced tea (ask to see one before you order if you've never had it before) or a light Thai beer.

PASADENA
Afghan

For a delicious and upscale dining experience, have lunch or dinner at **Azeen's Afghani Restaurant** (110 E. Union St., 626/683-3310, www.azeensafghanirestaurant.com, Mon.-Fri. 11am-2pm and 5:30pm-9:30pm, Sat.-Sun. 5:30pm-9:30pm, $16-22). Inside you'll find white tablecloths, black furniture, and unusual paintings. On the menu, the offerings take you into another world—one largely mysterious to Westerners. Trade routes, invasions, religion, ethnicity, and lots and lots of sand all contribute to the way Afghanistan and its cuisine have evolved. Vegetarians, be aware that while you will find some limited options, Afghan food tends heavily toward meat. Kebabs of all kinds are a regional specialty, and the country's proximity to India brings with it a love for truly spicy (and incredibly flavorful) dishes. At Azeen's, you can get kebabs, spicy lamb dishes, dumplings, and traditional desserts.

Asian

If you're just dying for Thai or Vietnamese food, one of the better spots in Pasadena is **Daisy Mint** (1218 E. Colorado Blvd., 626/792-2999, www.daisymint.com, daily 11am-3pm and 5pm-9pm, $10-30). The tiny green dining room's exposed brick and original artwork speak of SoCal, while the menu items tend to come from Southeast Asia and beyond. You'll find the aforementioned Thai and Vietnamese, plus Korean and uniquely Californian Asian-fusion dishes here. Some of the fun special touches of the house include a variety of steamed rice that you can choose to accompany your meal, and a large selection of unusual and fragrant teas. Pick whatever you think will go best with your satay, curry, seafood, or soup. Reservations are recommended on weekend evenings.

Barbecue

If you're looking for some down-home Southern food, head straight for **Big Mama's Rib Shack** (1453 N. Lake Ave., 626/797-1792, www.bigmamas-ribshack.com, Tues.-Thurs. 11:30am-9pm, Fri.-Sat. 11:30am-10pm, Sun. noon-8pm, $10-30). While Big Mama never brewed up the sauce at this Pasadena kitchen, she was a Southern restaurateur who made her way from Georgia across the country to California over her long life. Today, her legacy lives on in the big ol' menu at Big Mama's, which boasts traditional Southern cuisine plus a number of creole and Cajun dishes that speak to a strong New Orleans influence. Whether your poison is a po'boy or good gumbo, you can get it in hearty portions at Big Mama's. Fish lovers will find oysters and catfish, but strict vegetarians will find their dining options limited. And Big Mama's isn't a diet-friendly establishment since few salads balance out the weight of the fried chicken, smothered ribs, and velvet cake.

California Cuisine

For an upscale meal without having to fight the crowds on the west side or Downtown, check out **Bistro 45** (45 S. Mentor Ave., 626/795-2478, www.bistro45.com, Tues.-Thurs. 5pm-9pm, Fri.-Sat. 5pm-10pm, Sun. 5pm-8:30pm, $22-36). This nationally lauded restaurant has beautiful dining rooms: one light and bright with hardwood floors and peach walls with beautiful glass lantern fixtures, and one semi-outdoor space done in gray-blues with distinctive woven chairs and classic French prints. The cuisine is grounded in the French tradition but includes a hearty twist of California in the preparation. Menus change seasonally (or more often), and offer lots of fresh seafood as well as high-end meat and veggie-based dishes. For lunch, lighter appetites can be satisfied with fancy salads, but don't expect much of a midday price break on the bigger entrées. The wine list shifts seasonally to complement the food, and Bistro 45 boasts a full bar with a list of signature martini-esque cocktails.

Greek

For a quick and reasonably healthy lunch in downtown Pasadena, try **Pita! Pita!** (927 E. Colorado Blvd., Suite 101, 626/356-0106, Sun.-Thurs. 7am-9pm, Fri.-Sat. 8am-10pm, $5-10). This walk-up Greek place offers tasty meals with lots of fresh veggies that fill you up without emptying your wallet in the process. If you eat in, you can find your own seat on the uncovered tables in the narrow dining room with its worn tile floor. Fill up your own cup with soda or water while you wait for your pita wrap or falafel and hummus plate. If you're in a hurry, order your food to go. The pita wrap sandwiches are big and a bit juicy, but properly wrapped, they can be reasonably sidewalk-friendly.

Information and Services

TOURS

If you don't feel up to driving around Los Angeles on your own (and no one will blame you if you don't), dozens of tour operators would love to do the driving for you and let you sit back and enjoy the sights and sounds of Southern California. You can choose between driving tours, walking tours, and even helicopter tours that take you up to get a bird's-eye view of the city, beaches, and the wide Pacific Ocean.

Walking Tours

In among the dozens of cheesy "walking tour" operators who will charge you to walk you over the stars on Hollywood Boulevard (which you can do yourself for free), one organization can give you a better, more in-depth look into the true history of the Los Angeles area. The **Los Angeles Conservancy** (213/623-2489, www. laconservancy.org, tours Sat. mornings, adults $10, children $5) offers more than a dozen different walking tours that explore the architectural history of different parts of Los Angeles in depth. You can pick a style-themed tour, such as Art Deco or Modern Skyline, or a specific street, area, or major structure, such as Union Station, the Broadway Theaters, or the Biltmore Hotel. Check the website for tour schedules and for a few self-guided tours you can take on your own if you can't make your chosen guided tour. While children are welcome on Conservancy tours, the nature of the entertainment focuses much more on adult visitors; consider leaving the kids elsewhere so they are not bored to bits by all the talk of moldings and archways.

Bus Tours

For bus tours, you can't beat the weight of history provided by **Starline Tours** (800/959-3131, www.starlinetours.com, adults $40-140, children $30-125), which has been in the business of showing L.A. and Hollywood to visitors since 1935. Take a tour of Movie Stars Homes (which actually covers many famous star-studded spots around the region), Hollywood, or try the Grand Tour of Los Angeles (which can be narrated in many languages) for a start. Starline can pick you up at almost any hotel in L.A. Your tour vehicle will be either an air-conditioned minibus, a full-size bus, or a topless "Fun Bus" with a second open-air deck that lets visitors breathe the native smog of L.A. unhindered. Fun Tours also allow passengers to jump on and off at various sights and attractions as they please. Expect your tour to last 2-6 hours, depending on which route you choose. Once you're on board, sit back, relax, and enjoy the sights and stories of Los Angeles.

INFORMATION
Visitor Information

New to L.A.? Make one of your first stops one of the two visitors centers. The **Los Angeles Convention and Visitors Bureau** (www. discoverlosangeles.com) maintains Visitor Information Centers adjacent to a Metro station in Hollywood at **Hollywood and Highland Visitors Center** (6801 Hollywood Blvd., 323/467-6412). There are self-serve visitor information centers at the Los Angeles Convention Center and the Port of Los Angeles (Berth 93). L.A. has also created a Mobile Visitors Center, so just look to the streets for the brightly decorated Honda Element. The denizens of this van can give you maps, brochures, information, and advice about visiting the greater L.A. area.

If you're an advance planner, you can take advantage of the Visitors Bureau website to grab half-price tickets to all sorts of shows all around L.A. Visit the website on Tuesday about a week in advance of the date you want to see a show; you'll see all available tickets posted. These tickets are also offered at the bricks-and-mortar Visitor Information Center in town.

Media and Communications

Los Angeles is home to one of the country's

major daily newspapers, the *Los Angeles Times* (www.latimes.com). Pick one up at any newsstand anywhere in the city for a healthy dose of national news, regional current events, and even some good up-to-the-minute restaurant and nightlife information. The Food section comes out once a week, and the Travel section is included with the Sunday edition.

Every Thursday, the free alt weekly *L.A.Weekly* (www.laweekly.com) hits newsstands all over the city. Currently owned by Village Voice Media, the publication's main focus is on arts and cultural events.

You'll find Wi-Fi at nearly every hotel, a café with Internet access on nearly every corner, and the need to pay a fee for that access in some places. Expect to pay $10-20 per day to connect your laptop to the Internet.

All those Hollywood agents would probably spontaneously combust if they ever lost signal on their cell phones. You'll get coverage pretty much everywhere in L.A., regardless of your provider, with the possible exception of a few minutes going over a mountain pass.

SERVICES
Post Offices

Each separate municipality in the L.A. region has at least one **post office** (www.usps.com); options inc include Downtown (750 W. 7th St., Suite 33), Hollywood (1615 Wilcox Ave.), and Beverly Hills (8383 Wilshire Blvd., Suite 106).

Medical Services

The greater L.A. area offers some of the best medical care options in the world. People come from all over to get novel treatments and plastic surgery in the hospitals frequented by the stars. If you need immediate assistance, **Los Angeles County+USC Medical Center** (1200 N. State St., emergency 911, 323/409-1000, www.ladhs.org) can fix you up no matter what's wrong with you.

Getting There and Around

AIR

L.A. is one of the most commercial airport-dense metropolitan areas in the country. Wherever you're coming from and whichever part of L.A. you're headed for, you can get there by air. **Los Angeles International Airport** (LAX, 1 World Way, Los Angeles, 310/646-5252, www.lawa.org), known as LAX, has the most flights to and from the most destinations of any area airport. LAX is also the most crowded of the L.A. airports, with the longest security and check-in lines. If you can find a way around flying into LAX, do so. One option is to fly into other airports in the area, including **Bob Hope Airport** (BUR, 2627 N. Hollywood Way, Burbank, 818/840-8840, www.burbankairport.com) and the **Long Beach Airport** (4100 Donald Douglas Dr., Long Beach, 562/570-2600, www.lgb.org). It may be a slightly longer drive to your final destination, but it can be well worth it. If you must use LAX, be sure to arrive a minimum of two hours ahead of your domestic flight time for your flight out, and consider three hours on busy holidays.

TRAIN AND BUS

Amtrak (800/872-7245, www.amtrak.com) has an active rail hub in Los Angeles. Most trains come in to **Union Station** (800 N. Alameda St., 323/466-3876), which has been owned by the Los Angeles Metropolitan Transportation Authority (MTA, www.metro.net) since 2011. From Union Station, you can get to the Bay Area, Redding, and eventually Seattle on the *Coast Starlight* train, or you can take the *Pacific Surfliner* down the coast to San Diego. The *San Joaquin* runs out to Sacramento via the Bay Area. To get to and from L.A. from the East, the *Southwest Chief* comes in from Chicago, Kansas City, and Albuquerque. The famed *Sunset Limited* runs from Jacksonville, Florida, to New Orleans, El Paso, and then Los Angeles.

From Union Station, which also acts as a

Metro hub, you can take Metro Rail to various parts of Los Angeles. Against fairly significant odds in the region that invented car culture, Los Angeles has created a functional and useful public transit system. The **Metro** (www.metro.net, cash fare $1.50, day pass $5) runs both the subway Metro Rail system and a network of buses throughout the L.A. metropolitan area. You can pay on board a bus if you have exact change. Otherwise, purchase a ticket or a day pass from the ticket vending machines at all Metro Rail Stations.

Some buses run 24 hours. The Metro Rail lines start running as early as 4:30am and don't stop until as late as 1:30am. See the website (www.metro.net) for route maps, timetables, and fare details.

CAR

Los Angeles is crisscrossed with freeways, providing numerous yet congested access points into the city. From the north and south, I-5 provides the most direct access to downtown L.A. From I-5, U.S. 101 south leads directly into Hollywood; from here, Santa Monica Boulevard can take you west to Beverly Hills. Connecting from I-5 to I-210 will take you east to Pasadena. The best way to reach Santa Monica, Venice, and Malibu is via Highway 1, also known as the Pacific Coast Highway. I-10 can get you there from the east, but it will be a long, tedious, and trafficked drive.

Think you're up to the challenge of driving the world-infamous L.A. freeway system? Consider carefully. It's not as much fun as you might think. Traffic can be awful all the time. (If you believe you'll miss the jam on I-405 just because it's 8pm, you're flat wrong. I-405 often stays jammed up.) Local drivers accustomed to the conditions don't bother being polite, so expect to be cut off constantly and to deal with drivers paying attention to everything in the world but the road. And finally, if you're planning to use the traffic reports or local advice, there's a catch. Most road signs use numbers. But locals, including the radio traffic reporters, use names. There's no visible name-to-number translation on most maps, and just to make things even more fun, the names change (sometimes into one another) depending on where you are. Public transit is an increasingly viable and definitely preferable alternative.

Parking

Parking in Los Angeles can be as much of a bear as driving. And it can cost you quite a lot of money. You will find parking lots and structures included with many hotel rooms—L.A. is actually better than San Francisco about that. But parking on the street can be difficult or impossible, parking lots in sketchy areas (like the Flower and Jewelry Districts) can be dangerous, and parking structures at popular attractions can be expensive.

Taxis

Taxis aren't cheap, but they're quick, easy, and numerous. And in some cases, when you add up gas and parking fees, you'll find that the cab ride isn't that much more expensive than driving yourself.

To call a cab, try: **Yellow Cab** (877/733-3305, L.A., LAX, Beverly Hills, Hollywood) and **City Cab** (888/248-9222, San Fernando Valley, Hollywood, and LAX), which now has a small fleet of green, environmentally-friendly vehicles. Or check out www.taxicabsla.org for a complete list of providers and phone numbers.

Disneyland Resort

The "Happiest Place on Earth" lures millions of visitors of all ages each year with promises of fun and fantasy. During high seasons, waves of humanity flow through **Disneyland Resort** (1313 N. Harbor Blvd., Anaheim, 714/781-4623, http://disneyland.disney.go.com, daily 9am-midnight, ticket prices vary, one-day over age 9 $87, ages 3-9 $81, one-day Hopper Ticket for entry to both parks, over age 9 $125, ages 3-9 $119), moving slowly from Land to Land and ride to ride. The park is well set up to handle the often-immense crowds. Everything from foot-traffic control to ample restrooms makes even a Christmastime trip to Disneyland a happy time for the whole family. Despite the undeniable cheese factor, even the most cynical and jaded resident Californians can't quite keep their cantankerous scowls once they're ensconced inside Uncle Walt's dream. It really *is* a happy place.

Disney's rides, put together by the park's "Imagineers," are better than those at any other amusement park in the state—perhaps better than any in the world. The technology of the rides isn't more advanced than other parks, but it's the attention to detail that makes a Disneyland ride experience so enthralling. Even the spaces where you stand in line match the theme of the ride you're waiting for, from the archaeological relics of Indiana Jones to the tombstones of the Haunted Mansion. If you've got several days in the park, try them all, but if you don't, pick from the best of the best in each Land.

ORIENTATION

The Disneyland Resort is a massive kingdom that stretches from Harbor Boulevard on the east to Walnut Street on the west and from Ball Road to the north to Katella Avenue to the south and includes two amusement parks, three hotels, and an outdoor shopping and entertainment complex. The Disneyland-affiliated hotels (Disneyland Hotel, Paradise Pier Hotel, and the Grand Californian) all cluster on the western side of the complex, between Walnut Street and Disneyland Drive (West St.). The area between Disneyland Drive and Harbor Boulevard is shared by the actual Disneyland amusement park in the northern section and the California Adventure amusement park in the southern section, with Downtown Disney between them in the central-west section. There is no admission fee for Downtown Disney. You can reach the amusement park entrances via Downtown Disney (although visitors going to Disneyland or California Adventure should park in the paid lots, rather than the Downtown Disney self-park lot, which is only free for the first three hours) or from the walk-in entrance (for those taking public transportation or being dropped off) on Harbor Boulevard. There are also trams from the parking lot to the entrance.

DISNEYLAND

Your first stop inside the park should be one of the information kiosks near the front entrance gates. Here you can get a map, a schedule of the day's events, and the inside scoop on what's going on in the park during your visit.

New Orleans Square

In New Orleans Square, the unquestioned favorite ride for the 21st century is the revamped **Pirates of the Caribbean.** If you haven't visited Disneyland in a few years, you'll notice some major changes to this old favorite. Beginning in the dim swamp overlooked by the Blue Bayou Restaurant, the ride's classic scenes inside have been revamped to tie in more closely to the movies. Look for Jack Sparrow to pop up among your other favorite disreputable characters engaged in all sorts of debauchery. Lines for Pirates can get long, so consider grabbing a Fastpass for this one if you don't want to wait. Even if you don't Fastpass, the line for Pirates moves fast. Pirates is suitable for younger children as well as teens and adults.

For a taste of truly classic Disney, line up in the graveyard for a tour of the **Haunted**

Mansion. Next to Pirates, this ride hasn't changed much in the last 40 years. It hasn't needed to. The sedate motion makes the Haunted Mansion suitable for younger children, but beware: The ghosties and ghoulies that amuse adults can be intense for little kids.

Adventureland

Adventureland sits next to the New Orleans Square area. **Indiana Jones** is arguably one of the best rides in all of Disneyland, and the details make it stunning. As you stand in the line, check out the signs, equipment, and artifacts in mock-dusty tunnels winding toward the ride. The ride itself, in a roller-coaster style variant of an all-terrain vehicle, jostles and jolts you through a landscape that Indy himself might dash through, pursued by booby traps and villains. Hang on to your hat—literally! Use the pouches provided in your seat to secure your unattached things, or they will get jostled out of this exciting ride. This one isn't the best for tiny tots, but the big kids love it, and everyone might want a Fastpass for the endlessly popular attraction.

On the other end of the spectrum, you'll either love the **Tiki Room** or you'll hate it. Up a tree, literally, you'll take a seat and enjoy some classic pseudo-Polynesian tiki entertainment. Even the smallest children love the bright colors and cheerful songs in the Tiki Room, though some adults can't quite hack the cheesiness here.

Frontierland

Take a ride on a Wild West train on the **Big Thunder Mountain Railroad.** This older roller coaster whisks passengers away on a brief but fun thrill ride through a "dangerous, decrepit" mountain's mine shafts. As you stand in line, be sure to read the names of the locomotives as the trains come rushing by.

Fantasyland

The favorite of many Disneyland visitors, Fantasyland rides tend to cater to the younger set. And for many Disneyphiles, the ultimate expression of Uncle Walt's dream is **it's a small world.** Toddlers adore this ride, which introduces their favorite Disney characters and the famous (some would say infamous) song. You can almost feel the fairy dust sprinkling down on you as you tour this magical miniature kingdom. (Warning: If ultra-cutesiness makes you gag, you might want to skip this one.)

Kids who are just a little bit older might prefer the crazy fun of **Mr. Toad's Wild Ride.** Even though it's not really a roller coaster, this ride makes for big fun for children and adults alike. What's cool about Mr. Toad's is the wacky scenery you'll get to see along the ride, from a sedate library to the gates of hell.

If it's a faster thrill you're seeking, head for one of the most recognizable landmarks at Disneyland. The **Matterhorn Bobsleds** roller coaster looks like a miniature version of its namesake in the Swiss Alps. Inside, you board a sled-style coaster car and plunge down the mountain on a twisted track that takes you past rivers, glaciers, and the Abominable Snowman.

Tomorrowland

In order to keep up with the realities of the future, many of the rides in this section of the 50-year-old park have been updated or even replaced over the years. An enhanced version of the classic 3-D film musical **Captain EO,** starring Michael Jackson is back. Fans of all ages can experience the magic of this innovative film.

Another classic that has been given a makeover to connect it to a Disney blockbuster movie is the **Finding Nemo Submarine Voyage.** On this ride, you and fellow guests board a submarine and descend into an artificial pool. Under the water, you'll find yourself in the brightly colored world of Nemo and his frantic father, filled with an astonishing array of sea life. Help your kids count the number of familiar fish!

Finally, for bigger visitors, the best thrill ride of the main park sits inside a space-age building. **Space Mountain** is a fast roller coaster that whizzes through an almost entirely darkened world. All you'll see are the stars overhead. You will hear your screams and those of your fellow passengers as your "spaceship" swerves and

HERE AT DISNEY, WE HAVE A FEW RULES

Think that anything goes at the Happiest Place on Earth? Think again. Uncle Walt had distinct ideas about what his dream theme park would look like, and that vision extended to the dress and manners of his guests. When the park opened in 1950, among the many other restrictions, no man sporting facial hair was allowed into Disneyland. The rules on dress and coiffure have relaxed a bit since the opening, but you still need to mind your manners when you enter the Magic Kingdom.

- Adults may not wear costumes of any kind except on Halloween.

- No shirt, no shoes, no Disneyland.

- If you must use the F word, do it quietly. If staff catches you cussing or cursing in a way that disturbs others, you can be asked to desist or leave.

- The happiest of happiness is strictly prohibited inside the Magic Kingdom. If you're caught having sex on park grounds, not only will you be thrown out, you'll be banned from Disneyland for life (at least that's the rumor).

- Ditto for any illicit substances.

plunges along tracks you cannot see. Despite its age, Space Mountain remains one of the more popular rides in the park. Consider getting a Fastpass to keep out of sometimes-long lines.

CALIFORNIA ADVENTURE

Disney's **California Adventure** (http://disneyland.disney.go.com, daily 8am-11pm, ticket prices vary, one-day over age 9 $87, ages 3-9 $81, one-day Hopper Ticket for entry to both parks, over age 9 $125, ages 3-9 $119) celebrates much of what makes California special. If Disney is your only stop on this trip but you'd like to get a sense of the state as a whole, California Adventure can give you a little taste. (For my money, though, you'd do better to extend your vacation and spend some time exploring California in all its real non-Disneyfied glory.)

Like Disneyland proper, California Adventure is divided into themed areas. Rides in California Adventure tend toward the thrills of other major amusement parks but include the great Disney touches that make the Mouse special.

You'll find two information booths just inside the main park entrance, one off to the left as you walk through the turnstile and one at the opening to Sunshine Plaza. Here's where you'll get your park guide, *Time Guide,* and

more information about what's going on in the park that day.

Hollywood Land

Celebrating SoCal's famed film industry, the Backlot holds the ultimate thrill ride inside: **The Twilight Zone Tower of Terror.** Enter the creepy "old hotel," go through the "service area," and take your place inside an elevator straight out of your worst nightmares. This ride aims for teens and adults rather than little kids, and it's not a good one for folks who fear heights or don't do well with free-fall rides.

Less extreme but also fun, **Monsters, Inc. Mike & Sully to the Rescue!** invites guests into the action of the movie of the same name. You'll help the heroes as they chase the intrepid Boo. This ride jostles you around a bit but can be suitable for smaller kids as well as bigger ones.

A Bug's Land

Want to live like a bug? Get a sample of the world of tiny insects on **It's Tough to Be a Bug!** This big-group, 3-D, multisensory ride offers fun for little kids and adults alike. You'll fly through the air, scuttle through the grass, and get a good idea of what life is like on six little legs. But beware: When they say this ride engages *all your senses,* they mean it.

For the littlest California Adventurers, **Flik's Fun Fair** offers almost half a dozen rides geared toward toddlers and little children. They can ride pint-size hot-air balloons known as Flik's Flyers, climb aboard a bug-themed train, or run around under a gigantic faucet to cool down after hours of hot fun.

Paradise Pier

Paradise Pier mimics the Santa Monica Pier and other waterfront attractions like it, with thrill rides and an old-fashioned midway. Most of the extreme rides cluster in the Paradise Pier area. It seems reasonable that along with everything else, Disney does the best roller coasters in the business. They prove it with **California Screamin'**, a high-tech roller coaster designed after the classic wooden coasters of carnivals past. This extra-long ride includes drops, twists, a full loop, and plenty of time and screaming fun. California Screamin' has a four-foot height requirement and is just as popular with nostalgic adults as with kids. **Toy Story Mania!** magnifies the midway mayhem as passengers of all ages use Spring-Action Shooters to take aim at targets in a 4-D ride inspired by Disney-Pixar's *Toy Story*.

Condor Flats

Want a bird's-eye view of California? Get on board **Soarin' Over California.** This combination ride and show puts you and dozens of other guests on the world's biggest "glider" and sets you off over the hills and valleys of California. You'll feel the wind in your hair as you see the vineyards, mountains, and beaches of this diverse state.

Grizzly Peak

Get Disney's version of a wilderness experience at Grizzly Peak. Enjoy a white water raft ride through a landscape inspired by the Sierra Nevada foothills on the **Grizzly River Run.** Kids can earn badges in tracking and wolf howling on the **Redwood Creek Challenge Trail.**

Cars Land

California Adventure's latest expansion is a section of the park inspired by the hit 2006 film *Cars*. Float on larger than life tires on the **Luigi's Flying Tires** ride or be serenaded by Mater as you ride in a tractor on **Mater's Junkyard Jamboree.** The **Radiator Springs Racers** finds six-person vehicles passing locations and characters from *Cars* before culminating in a real-life race with a car of other park visitors.

Parades and Shows

Watch your favorite Pixar characters come to life in the **Pixar Play Parade.** Other regular shows in California Adventure are **Disney Junior–Live on Stage!** and **Disney's Aladdin–A Musical Spectacular.** Both of these shows hark back to favorite children's activities and movies. Your kids can sing along with favorite songs and characters while you take a load off your feet and relax for a while. Check your park guide and *Time Guide* for more information about these and other live shows throughout California Adventure.

DOWNTOWN DISNEY

You don't need an admission ticket to take a stroll through the shops of the Downtown Disney District. In addition to the mammoth World of Disney Store, you'll find RIDEMAKERZ, a Build-a-Bear workshop, and a LEGO Imagination Center. For adults, the House of Blues Store, Sephora, and the Sunglass Icon boutique beckon. You can also have a bite to eat or take in some jazz or a new release movie at Downtown Disney.

ACCOMMODATIONS

The best way to get fully Disneyfied is to stay at one of the park's hotels. Several sit just beside or across the street from the park.

Disney Hotels

For the most iconic Disney resort experience, you must stay at the **Disneyland Hotel** (1150 Magic Way, Anaheim, 714/956-6425 or 714/778-6600, http://disneyland.disney.go.com, $468-772). This nearly 1,000-room high-rise monument to brand-specific family entertainment has everything a vacationing Brady-esque bunch could want: themed swimming pools, themed play areas, and even character-themed guest rooms that allow the kids to fully immerse themselves in the Mouse experience. Adults and families on a budget can also get rooms with either a king or two queen beds and more traditional motel fabrics and appointments. The monorail stops inside the hotel, offering guests the easiest way into the park proper without having to deal with parking or even walking.

It's easy to find the **Paradise Pier Hotel** (1717 S. Disneyland Dr., Anaheim, 714/956-6425 or 714/999-0990, http://disneyland.disney.go.com, $305-532); it's that high-rise thing just outside the parks on the California Adventure side. This hotel boasts what passes for affordable lodgings within walking distance of California Adventure, Downtown Disney, and Disneyland's main gate. Rooms are cute, colorful, and clean; many have two double or queen beds to accommodate families or couples traveling together on a tighter budget. You'll find a (possibly refreshing) lack of Mickeys in the standard guest accommodations at the Paradise, which has the feel of a beach resort motel. After a day of wandering the park, relax by the rooftop pool.

The **Grand Californian Hotel and Spa** (1600 S. Disneyland Dr., Anaheim, 714/956-6425 or 714/635-2300, http://disneyland.disney.go.com, $485-1,058) is inside California Adventure, attempting to mimic the famous Ahwahnee Lodge in Yosemite. While it doesn't quite succeed (much of what makes the Ahwahnee so great is its views), the big-beam construction and soaring common spaces do feel reminiscent of a great luxury lodge. The hotel is surrounded by gardens and has restaurants, a day spa, and shops attached on the ground floors; it can also get you right out into Downtown Disney and thence to the parks proper. Guest rooms at the Californian offer more luxury than the other Disney resorts, with dark woods and faux-craftsman detailing creating an attractive atmosphere. You can get anything from a standard guest room that sleeps two up to spacious family suites with bunk beds that can easily handle six people. As with all Disney resorts, you can purchase tickets and a meal plan along with your hotel room (in fact, if you book via the website, they'll try to force you to do it that way).

Outside the Parks

The massive park complex is ringed with motels, both popular chains and more interesting independents. **The Anabella** (1030 W. Katella Ave., Anaheim, 714/905-1050 or 800/863-4888, www.anabellahotel.com, $110-260) offers a touch of class along with a three-block walk to the parks. The elegant marble-clad lobby seems like it belongs closer to Downtown L.A. than Downtown Disney. Guest rooms are furnished with an eye toward modern, stylish decor (occasionally at the expense of practicality). Adults looking for an overnight escape from the endless parade of kid-oriented entertainment and attractions will find a welcome respite at the Anabella. A decent restaurant, nail salon, and minimart are on the hotel property, and a fairly lousy diner is right next door. You can get limited room service at the Anabella, and you can leave your car in their parking lot to avoid the expense of parking at Disneyland.

Another nice out-of-park hotel within walking distance of Disneyland is the **Desert Palms Hotel & Suites** (631 W. Katella Ave., 714/535-1133 or 888/788-0466, www.desertpalmshotel.com, $80-300). Its spacious and elegant lobby welcomes visitors, the pool and spa provide fun for children and adults alike, and the many amenities make travelers comfortable. Regular guest rooms have one king or two queen beds, a TV, a phone, Internet access, and not a ton of room to walk around after all your luggage is crowded in with the furniture. Bedspreads catch the eye with their bright, multicolored palm design; the rest of the decor is neutral by comparison. Guests with more discretionary income can choose from a number of suites, some designed to delight children and others aimed at couples on a romantic getaway.

Away from the Disneyland complex and

surrounding area, the accommodations in Orange County run to chain motels with little character or distinctiveness, but the good news is that you can find a decent room for a reasonable price.

The **Hyatt Regency Orange County** (11999 Harbor Blvd., Garden Grove, 714/750-1234 or 800/492-8804, http://orangecounty.hyatt.com, $170-270) in Garden Grove is about 2.5 miles (10 minutes' drive on Harbor Blvd.) south of the park. The attractive guest rooms are decorated in the latest style inside a tall glass-fronted tower. White linens emphasize the cleanliness of beds and baths, while bright yellows and deep blues provide classy artistic touches. In the sun-drenched atrium, enjoy a cocktail or sit back and read a good book in the attractive atmosphere. Grab a chaise longue by the pool or take a refreshing dip. If you're bringing your family, consider renting one of the "family-friendly suites" that have separate bedrooms with bunk beds and fun decor geared toward younger guests.

Near John Wayne Airport, the **Best Western Orange County Airport** (2700 Hotel Terr., Santa Ana, 714/432-8888 or 800/432-0053, www.bestwestern-oc.com, $109-149) offers everything you expect of the popular national chain, including floral and wine-colored decor in the comfortable guest rooms, a pool and hot tub, and a free shuttle to and from the airport. Down in the lobby you'll find a complimentary "cook-to-serve" breakfast each morning (that is, prepackaged heat-and-eat items plus cold cereals, bagels, and coffee).

FOOD
Disneyland
One of the few things the Mouse doesn't do too well is haute cuisine. For a truly good or healthy meal, get a hand stamp and go outside the park. But if you're stuck inside and you absolutely need sustenance, you can get it. The best areas of the park to grab a bite are Main Street, New Orleans, and Frontierland—they offer the most variety in concessions—but you can find at least a snack almost anywhere in the park.

For a sit-down restaurant meal inside the park, make reservations in advance for a table at the **Blue Bayou Restaurant** (New Orleans Square, 714/781-3463, over $36 pp). The best part about this restaurant is its setting in the dimly lit swamp overlooking the Pirates of the Caribbean ride. Appropriately, the Bayou has a reputation for being haunted. The Cajunish cuisine matches the junglelike setting, although if you're looking for authenticity, you'd do better to look elsewhere. You will get large portions, and tasty sweet desserts make a fine finish to your meal. Watch your silverware, though—the alleged ghosts in this restaurant like to mess around with diners' tableware.

If you need to grab a quicker bite, *don't* do it at the French Market restaurant in the New Orleans area. It sells what appears to be day-old (or more) food from the Bayou that has been sitting under heat lamps for a good long time.

California Adventure
If you need a snack break in California Adventure, you'll find most of the food clustered in the Golden State area. Take a tour of the **Boudin Bakery,** then taste the delectable products of these places in the nearby restaurants. For a Mexican feast, try **Cocina Cucamonga Mexican Grill** (under $15 pp). For more traditional American fare, enjoy the food at the **Pacific Wharf Cafe** (under $15 pp), a Boudin Bakery restaurant, or the **Taste Pilots' Grill** (under $15 pp).

Unlike Disneyland proper, in California Adventure, responsible adults can quaff their thirst with a variety of alcoholic beverages. If you're just dying for a cold beer, get one at **Bayside Brews.** Or, if you love the endless variety of high-quality wines produced in the Golden State, head for the **Golden Vine Winery,** where you can learn the basics of wine creation and production. Have a glass and a pseudo-Italian meal at the sit-down **Wine Country Trattoria at the Golden Vine Winery** (714/781-3463, $15-36).

Downtown Disney
Downtown Disney is outside the amusement

parks and offers additional dining options. National chains like **House of Blues** (1530 S. Disneyland Dr., Anaheim, 714/778-2583, www.houseofblues.com, daily 11am-1:30am, $15-28) and **Rainforest Café** (1515 S. Disneyland Dr., Anaheim, 714/772-0413, www.rainforestcafe.com, Sun.-Thurs. 8am-11pm, Fri.-Sat. 8am-midnight, $11-18) serve typical menu staples like sandwiches, burgers, pasta, and steak and seafood entrées, with House of Blues putting a Southern spin on these items and adding live-music shows, while kid-friendly Rainforest Café puts on tropical touches like coconut and mango. **ESPN Zone** (1545 Disneyland Dr., Anaheim, 714/300-3776, www.espnzone.com, Sun.-Thurs. 11am-11pm, Fri.-Sat. 11am-midnight) has similar offerings, but due to numerous closures across the country, the Downtown Disney spot is now just one of two locations of this "sports bar on steroids" concept restaurant. The other is in Los Angeles (1011 S. Figueroa St., 213/765-7070).

There are also more individual restaurants, but even these feel a little like chains. The most distinctive of them, **Ralph Brennan's Jazz Kitchen** (1590 S. Disneyland Dr., Anaheim, 714/776-5200, www.rbjazzkitchen.com, daily 8am-10pm, $18-30), is meant to replicate the experience of eating in New Orleans's French Quarter. The Cajun menu hits all the staples, including jambalaya, beignets, and various blackened meats and seafood.

The Patina Restaurant Group runs **Catal Restaurant** (1580 Disneyland Dr., Anaheim, 714/774-4442, www.patinagroup.com, daily 8am-3pm and 5pm-10pm, $13-42), with Mediterranean fare; **Naples Ristorante** (1550 Disneyland Dr., Anaheim, 714/776-6200, www.patinagroup.com, Sun.-Thurs. 11am-10pm, Fri.-Sat. 11am-11pm, $15-46) for Italian food; and **Tortilla Joe's** (1510 Disneyland Dr., Anaheim, 714/535-5000, www.patinagroup.com, Sun.-Thurs. 11am-10pm, Fri.-Sat. 11am-11pm, $15-21) for Mexican food.

Finally, **La Brea Bakery** (1556 Disneyland Dr., Anaheim, 714/490-0233, www.labreabakery.com, Sun.-Thurs. 8am-11pm, Fri.-Sat. 8am-midnight) is the Disney outpost of an L.A. favorite. This bakery, founded by Nancy Silverton of the highly touted Campanile restaurant in L.A., supplies numerous markets and restaurants with crusty European-style loaves. The morning scones, sandwiches, and fancy cookies here are superb.

PRACTICALITIES
Tickets

There are as many varied ticket prices and plans as there are themes in the park. A single-day theme park ticket will run you $87, ages 3-9 $81. A variety of other combinations and passes are available online (http://disneyland.disney.go.com).

To buy tickets, go to one of the many kiosks in the central gathering spot that serves as the main entrance to both Disneyland proper and California Adventure. Bring your credit card, since a day at Disney is not cheap. After you've got tickets in hand (or if you've bought them online ahead of time), proceed to the turnstiles for the main park. You'll see the Disneyland Railroad terminal and the large grassy hill with the flowers planted to resemble Mickey's famous face. Pass through, and head under the railroad trestle to get to Main Street and the park center. You can exit and reenter the park on the days your tickets are valid for.

The already expensive regular one-day Disneyland ticket doesn't include California Adventure. If you're interested in checking out California Adventure as well as Disneyland proper, your best bet is to buy a **Park Hopper** pass (one-day $119-125, two-day $188-200), which lets you move back and forth between the two parks at will for a slight discount. If you're planning to spend several days touring the Houses of Mouse, buy multiday passes in advance online to save a few more bucks per day. It'll help you feel a little bit better about the wads of cash you'll undoubtedly drop on junk food, giant silly hats, stuffed animals, and an endless array of Disney apparel.

The magical **Fastpasses** are free with park admission and might seem like magic after awhile. The newest and most popular rides offer Fastpass kiosks near the entrances. Feed your ticket into one of the machines and it will spit out both your ticket and a Fastpass with your specified time to take the ride. Come back during your window and enter the always-much-shorter Fastpass line, designated by a sign at the entrance. If you're with a crowd, be sure you all get your Fastpasses at the same time, so you all get the same time window to ride the ride.

Information

Each park has information booths near the park entrance.

For visitor information about Disneyland and the surrounding area, contact the online and phone only **Anaheim Visitor Center** (714/817-9733, www.anaheim411.com).

Need a dose of hard news? Get a copy of the *Los Angeles Times* (www.latimes.com) Orange County Edition.

The O.C. has plenty of Internet access, although you'll find few people crouched over laptops inside Disneyland. Look to your hotel, or find a Starbucks outside the park to hook up to the world.

Services

Check your park map or look for signs to the restrooms available in each Land of the park. Restrooms have ample space, so you'll rarely find lines even on the most crowded days.

If mobility is a problem for you or for a small child in your family, consider renting (no, they're not free) a stroller, wheelchair, or scooter. Ask for directions to the rental counter when you enter the park.

Cell phones work inside Disneyland, which is actually a fabulous thing. It's already loud and raucous in the parks, and the ability to use cell phones to connect with lost family or party members at Disneyland is one of *the* finest advances in modern technology in a long, long time.

Disneyland offers its own minor medical facilities, which can dispense first aid for scrapes, cuts, and mild heat exhaustion. They can also call an ambulance if something nastier has occurred. The **West Anaheim Medical Center**

(3033 W. Orange Ave., Anaheim, 714/827-3000, www.westanaheimmedctr.com) is a full-service hospital with an emergency room.

If you need to stow your bags or hit the restroom before plunging into the fray, banks of lockers and restrooms sit in the main entrance area.

Getting There

The nearest airport to Disneyland, serving all of Orange County, is **John Wayne Airport** (SNA, 18601 Airport Way, Santa Ana, 949/252-5200, www.ocair.com). It's much easier to fly into and out of John Wayne than LAX, though it can be more expensive. John Wayne's terminal has plenty of rental car agencies, and many shuttle services that can get you where you need to go—especially to the House of Mouse.

If you have to fly into LAX for scheduling or budget reasons, you can catch a shuttle straight from the airport to your Disneyland hotel. Among the many companies offering and arranging such transportation, the one with the best name is **MouseSavers** (www.mousesavers.com). Working with various shuttle and van companies, MouseSavers can get you a ride in a van or a bus from LAX or John Wayne to your destination at or near Disneyland.

Disneyland is located on Disneyland Drive in Anaheim and is most accessible from I-5 south where it crosses Ball Road (stay in the left three lanes for parking). The parking lot (1313 S. Disneyland Dr.) costs $15 for a car or motorcycle, $20 for an oversize vehicle such as a motor home or tractor without the trailer, and $25 for buses and tractor-trailer rigs.

If you're coming to the park from elsewhere in Southern California, consider leaving the car (avoiding the parking fees) and taking public transit instead. **Anaheim Resort Transit** (ART, 1280 Anaheim Blvd., Anaheim, 714/563-5287, www.rideart.org) can take you to and from the Amtrak station and all around central Anaheim for $4 per day. You can buy passes via the website or at conveniently located kiosks.

Getting Around

Disney's California Adventure sits across the

main Disney entry plaza from Disneyland. You can enter from the main parking lots, from Downtown Disney, or you can hop over from Disneyland. Need a tram for the long-distance walk in or out of the park? The **Lion King Tram Route** can get you to and from the main parking areas. The **Mickey & Friends Tram Route** takes you toward Downtown Disney and the resort hotels.

INLAND ORANGE COUNTY

The lure of the inland O.C., a primarily residential area, tends to be dominated by the Mouse. But if you just have to get away from the overwhelming cutesy happiness for a while, a few other entertaining attractions lurk in the shadows.

Knott's Berry Farm

Believe it or not, other amusement parks make their home in Orange County. For a taste of history along with some ultra-modern thrill rides and plenty of cooling waterslides, head for **Knott's Berry Farm** (8039 Beach Blvd., Buena Park, 714/220-5200, www.knotts.com, park hours vary, adults $40-58, seniors and children $26-30, parking $15). This park's unusual name stems from its agricultural past. The fertile land beneath the roller coasters really was a berry farm decades ago. The Knott family grew strawberries, raspberries, boysenberries, and more here, then made the fruits of their labors into preserves. Knott's jams retain their popularity in supermarkets across the country to this day.

Today, instead of berry vines you'll find twisting tracks at this thrill-oriented park. From the tall landmark GhostRider wooden coaster to the 30-story vertical drop ride to the screaming Silver Bullet suspended coaster, even the most hard-core ride lover will get excited by Knott's. For the younger crowd, Camp Snoopy offers an array of pint-sized rides and attractions, plus Snoopy and all the characters they love from the Peanuts comics and TV shows.

In the heat of the summer, many park visitors adjourn from the coasters to **Knott's Soak City** (Memorial Day-Labor Day daily, May-Sept. weekends, adults $28-34, seniors and children $24, parking $15-20). The full-sized water park has 22 rides, a kid pool and water playground, and plenty of space to spread out and enjoy the O.C. sunshine after cooling off on the waterslides. You can score significant savings on admission tickets at both the amusement park and water park by purchasing tickets online.

Discovery Science Center

If you'd like your kids to spend at least one day in the O.C. doing something educational, take them to the **Discovery Science Center** (2500 N. Main St., Santa Ana, 714/542-2823, www.discoverycube.org, daily 10am-5pm, adults $15, children and seniors $13, parking $4). The star attraction, the interactive DinoQuest, lets kids get inside the lost world of dinosaurs. Way inside! You can also take a quick nap on a bed of nails, create your own clouds and tornadoes, and experience the buffeting of a hurricane inside a wind tunnel. The Discovery Science Center combines interactive play with scientific learning to create a fun day.

Accommodations

Away from the Disney resorts, the accommodations in inland Orange County run to chain motels. The good news is that you can find a decent room for a reasonable price almost everywhere you go in the O.C. The less-good news is that you won't find much of anything in the way of character or distinction in any of them.

The **Days Inn Buena Park/Knotts Berry Farm** (7121 Beach Blvd., Buena Park, 714/670-7280, www.daysinn.com, $100-130) used to be a Red Roof Inn. The latest incarnation offers a clean bed and bathroom near Knott's and Disney. Amenities include a heated pool and a spa, free Wi-Fi, and a fitness center. Medium-sized motel rooms feature a standard motel setup with a variety of bed configurations, dark carpets, and floral bedspreads.

At the **Best Western Orange County Airport** (2700 Hotel Terrace, Santa Ana, 714/432-8888, www.bestwestern-oc.com,

ALTERNATIVES TO THE MOUSE

The longtime Hollywood-centric alternative to Disneyland is the **Universal Studios Hollywood** (100 Universal City Plaza, Los Angeles, 800/864-8377, www.universalstudios. com, hours vary, adults $80, children under 48 inches tall $72, parking $10-15) theme park. Kids adore this park, which puts them right into the action of their old favorite movies. Flee the carnivorous dinosaurs of *Jurassic Park*, take a rafting adventure on the pseudo-set of *Waterworld*, or quiver in terror of an ancient curse in *Revenge of the Mummy*. Also experience the shape-shifting Transformers in a new ride based on the movies and the Hasbro toy. If you're the parent rather than the child, you may find some of the effects on the rides pretty cheesy. On the other hand, you may be thrown back to your childhood with memories of your favorite TV shows and movies. One of the major attractions recreates the nightmare world of *Terminator 2: Judgment Day*—in 3-D.

If you're more interested in how the movies are made than the rides made from them, take the Studio Tour. You'll get an extreme close-up of the sets of major blockbuster films like *War of the Worlds*. The *King Kong* set (along with the famed New York set and a number of others) was destroyed in an accidental fire in 2008, but replaced in July 2010 with King Kong: 360 3-D. Better yet, you can get tickets to be part of the studio audience of TV shows currently taping at the Audiences Unlimited Ticket Booth. If you're a serious movie buff, consider getting a VIP pass—you'll get a six-hour tour that takes you onto working sound stages, into the current prop warehouse, and through a variety of working build shops that service films and programs currently filming.

You can enjoy a meal, store your heavier things in a locker, and buy a near-infinite number of souvenirs at Universal Studios. If you need a little help getting yourself or your child around, rent a wheelchair or stroller. Pretty much every ride and show is wheelchair-accessible—ask at the ticket booth for more information about how to get around easily or if you need assisted-listening devices and TTD phones.

For yet another amusement park adventure, hit **Six Flags Magic Mountain** (Magic Mountain Parkway, Valencia, 661/255-4100, www. sixflags.com, hours vary, adults $65, children $40). This park provides good fun for the whole family—even the snarky teenagers who hate almost everything. Magic Mountain has long been the extreme alternative to the Mouse, offering a wide array of thrill rides. You'll need a strong stomach to deal with the g-forces of the major-league roller coasters and the death-defying drops including the new Lex Luthor: Drop of Doom, where you plummet 400 feet at speeds up to 85 mph. For the younger set, plenty of rides offer a less intense but equally fun amusement-park experience. Both littler and bigger kids enjoy interacting with the classic Warner Brothers characters, especially in Bugs Bunny World, and a kids' show features Bugs, Donald, and others. Other than that, Magic Mountain has little in the way of staged entertainment—this park is all about the rides. The park is divided into areas, just like most other major theme parks—get a map at the entrance to help maneuver around and pick your favorite rides.

You'll find services, souvenirs, and snacks galore throughout the park. The food offerings run to burgers, pizza, and international fast food. The highest concentration of snack shacks sits in the Colossus County Fair area—others are evenly distributed throughout the other areas. You can also by tchotchkes in any area, but most of the shopping centers around Cyclone Bay. All major services can be found at the park, including many ATM machines, a first-aid station, ample restrooms, and disability assistance. The Guest Relations office at Six Flags Plaza can help you with just about anything you need.

$100-150) you'll find everything you expect of the popular national chain, including floral and wine-colored decor in your comfortable guest room, a pool and hot tub, and a free shuttle to and from John Wayne Airport. Down in the lobby, you'll find a complimentary "cook-to-serve" breakfast each morning (that is, pre-packaged heat-and-eat items plus cold cereals, bagels, and coffee).

In Garden Grove, stay at the **Hyatt Regency Orange County** (11999 Harbor Blvd., Garden Grove, 714/750-1234, http://orangecounty.hyatt.com, $170-395). The attractive rooms are decorated in the latest style inside a tall glass-fronted tower. White linens emphasize the cleanliness of beds and bathrooms, while bright yellows and deep blues provide classy artistic touches. In the sun-drenched atrium, enjoy a cocktail or sit back and read a good book in the attractive atmosphere. Grab a chaise lounge by one of the two pools or take a refreshing dip. Or grab a beer at the onsite OC Brewhouse. If you're bringing your family, consider renting one of the "family-friendly suites" that have separate bedrooms with bunk beds and fun decor geared toward younger guests.

If your major destination is Knott's Berry Farm, consider staying at the **Knott's Berry Farm Resort Hotel** (7675 Crescent Ave., Buena Park, 714/995-1111, www.knotts.com, $155-222). This high-rise resort includes all the extras and amenities you'd expect from a corporate hotel. You can lounge by the pool and spa, work out at the fitness center, and have dinner in one of the on-site restaurants, the Amber Waves dining room. Get a drink at the Sports Bar after a long day out at the park or seeing the sights of O.C. Your comfortable room will greet you each night; choose one queen, two queens, or a king bed. Also, for kids, there are Snoopy-themed rooms available. Check the Internet for a variety of specials and discount rates.

Food

Want to keep the kids—and yourself—entertained during dinner? Check out one of the dinner-and-a-show restaurants, both near Disney and Knott's Berry Farm at Buena Park. At the famous **Medieval Times** (7662 Beach Blvd., Buena Park, 866/543-9637, www.medievaltimes.com, adults $58, children 12 and under $36), you'll enter a castle-shaped building, take your seat, and watch as gallant knights battle for the title of First Knight. You'll see live jousts (there's a big courtyard in this restaurant!), swordfights, and ladies in gowns parading for your pleasure. Your meal, served on a pewter-styled plate, provides hearty if not particularly healthy or high-quality sustenance. Vegetarian and kids' meal options are available upon request.

If you prefer pirates to knights, the O.C. can hook you up. Practically next door to the castle, buckle your swash at the **Pirate's Dinner Adventure** (7600 Beach Blvd., 714/690-1497, www.piratesdinneradventure.com, adults $58, children 3-11 $39). Combining dinner theater, the current pirate craze, and a touch of Cirque du Soleil, everyone in your family will find something to watch at dinner with the Pirates. Even if the cheesy acting and the swordfights don't do it for you, the aerobatics that form an integral part of this show can be great fun to marvel at. A four-course meal includes both chicken and meat (or fish), plus salad and dessert. It's not the best food, but hopefully you'll be too busy enjoying the show to care. Check for special holiday shows in season.

If you're looking for a bite to eat sans pirates and knights, **Casa De Soto Restaurant** (8562 Garden Grove Blvd., Garden Grove, 714/530-4200, www.casadesoto.com, daily 11:30am-9pm, $10) offers standard Mexican fare in three festive rooms.

Thasos Greek Island Grill (3940 S. Bristol St., Santa Ana, 714/708-3000, www.greekislandgrille.com, Sun.-Wed. 10:30am-9pm, Thurs.-Sat. 10:30am-9:30pm, $10) serves Mediterranean specialties including soulvlaki, gyros, and moussaka.

Information and Services

For the 411 on the O.C., visit the **Anaheim Visitor Center** (714/991-4636, www.

anaheim411.com), inside the Jolly Roger Hotel at the corner of Katella and Harbor. You can also mail a letter or package here.

Need a dose of hard news? Need a does of hard news? Get it in a copy of the **Los Angeles Times** (www.latimes.com), Orange County Edition.

The O.C. has plenty of Internet access, though you'll find few people crouched over laptops inside Disneyland. Look to your hotel, or find a Starbucks outside the park to hook up to the world.

The **West Anaheim Medical Center** (3033 W. Orange Ave., Anaheim, 714/827-3000, www.westanaheimmedctr.com) is a full-service hospital with an emergency room.

South Bay

The Los Angeles coastline passes the Palos Verde Peninsula, stretching farther south to Long Beach, where haunted ships and sunny coasts await.

SIGHTS
◖ The *Queen Mary*
The major visitor attraction of Long Beach is **The *Queen Mary*** (1126 Queens Hwy., Long Beach, 562/435-3511 or 877/342-0738, www. queenmary.com, daily 10am-6pm, adults $25, seniors and military $22, children $15, parking $5-12), one of the most famous ships ever to ply the high seas. This great ship, once a magnificent pleasure cruise liner, now sits at permanent anchor (it has been gutted and is no longer seaworthy) in Long Beach Harbor. The *Queen Mary* acts as a hotel (877/342-0738, $140-400), a museum, an entertainment center with several restaurants and bars, and a gathering place for both locals and visitors. You can book a stateroom and stay aboard, come for dinner, or just buy a regular ticket and take a self-guided tour. The museum exhibits describe the history of the ship, which took its maiden voyage in 1936, with special emphasis on its tour of duty as a troop transport during World War II. You can explore many of the decks at the bow, including the engine room that still boasts much of its massive machinery, the art gallery, and the various upper exterior decks where vacationers once relaxed on their way to Europe.

But it's not just the extensive museum and the attractive hotel that make the *Queen Mary* famous today. The ship is also one of the most famously haunted places in California. Over its decades of service, a number of unfortunate souls lost their lives aboard the *Queen Mary,* and it is rumored that several of them have stuck with the ship ever since their tragic deaths. If you're most interested in the ghost stories of the *Queen Mary,* book a spot on one of the Attractions at Night, which include the **Paranormal Ship Walk** (877/342-0738, Tues.-Thurs. 8pm), which takes you to the hottest haunted spots, and **Dining With the Spirits** (Fri.-Sat. 7pm), a combination of dinner and a two-hour haunted tour. For more serious ghost hunters, **Paranormal Investigation** tours happen on Fridays. Appropriately, the investigations begin at midnight. During the day, the 35-minute long **Ghosts and Legends Tour** (Sun.-Thurs. 11am-6pm, Fri.-Sat. 11am-7pm) is available. The "tour" is like a haunted house for kids complete with smoke machines and flashing lights.

The *Queen Mary* offers a large pay parking lot near the ship's berth. You'll walk from the parking area up to a square with a ticket booth and several shops and a snack bar. Purchase your general-admission ticket to get on board the ship. It's also a good idea to buy any guided tour tickets at this point. Night tours can fill up in advance, so consider calling ahead to reserve a spot.

Russian Attack Submarine
Berthed right next to the luxurious *Queen Mary* you'll find a much smaller and more lethal little boat, the **Russian Attack Submarine** (562/432-0424 or 877/342-0738,

© STUART THORNTON

The *Queen Mary*

www.queenmary.com, daily 10am-6pm, adults $11, seniors, military, and children $10, or included in the *Queen Mary*'s First Class Passage package, adults $45, children $34). Code-named "The Scorpion," it helped the Soviet Union spy on the United States for more than 20 years during the Cold War. Your admission includes a brief history film and the opportunity to explore the innards of the submarine. Squeeze through the tiny spaces and learn how members of the Soviet Navy lived and worked aboard this attack submarine, which has a history that's still shrouded in secrecy.

Aquarium of the Pacific

Even the locals enjoy the exhibits at **Aquarium of the Pacific** (100 Aquarium Way, 562/590-3100, www.aquariumofpacific.org, daily 9am-6pm, adults $26, seniors $23, children $15). The large aquarium hosts animal and plant life native to the Pacific Ocean, from the local residents of SoCal's sea up to the North Pacific and down to the tropics. While the big modern building isn't much to look at from the outside, it's what's inside that's beautiful. Aquarium of the Pacific has far more than the average number of touch-friendly tanks. Kids and adults all love the unusual feel of sea stars, urchins, and rays. More exciting, you can dip your fingers into the Shark Lagoon and "pet" a few of the more than 150 sharks the aquarium cares for. If you prefer tamer and more colorful denizens of the air, spend time in the loud Lorikeet Forest. Overall, there are 11,000 ocean animals representing 500 species on view.

BEACHES
Manhattan Beach

Manhattan Beach (The Strand, 310/305-9503, http://beaches.lacounty.gov) is about 12 miles south of Santa Monica. The route along surface streets, with some stretches of coast-side driving, will take about 30 minutes. The beach is centered around the fishing pier that is essentially an extension of Manhattan Beach Boulevard beyond The Strand, a popular paved path.

Hermosa Beach

Hermosa Beach (Hermosa Beach Blvd. at 33rd St., 310/305-9503, http://beaches.lacounty. gov) lies about two miles south of Manhattan Beach. Administered by Los Angeles County Beaches and Harbors, both Hermosa and Manhattan Beaches offer volleyball nets, pristine sand, and wave breaks that surfers love. A paved path is packed with bikers, runners, and in-line skaters.

Redondo Beach

Sitting next to the Redondo Beach Pier, **Redondo State Beach** (400-1700 Esplanade, 310/305-9503, surf report 310/399-8471, http://beaches.lacounty.gov, usually daily sunrise-sunset, parking $5-12 depending on beach and season) gets really crowded in the summer, so if rubbing elbows with your fellow sun worshippers doesn't work for you, Redondo isn't your best bet. On the other hand, the lack of surfers makes swimming a prime activity here, complete with lifeguards during daytime. You'll also find the usual volleyball and other beach games, the bike path (which is lit at night), and the restaurants of the pier. The beach features restrooms and showers, and a large multilevel pay parking structure at the pier offers ample space to stow your car for the day.

ENTERTAINMENT AND EVENTS

The beach cities of Hermosa Beach, Manhattan Beach, and Redondo Beach are littered with bars. They range from sports bars to faux Irish pubs to dive bars like Hermosa Beach's **Poop Deck** (1272 The Strand, Hermosa Beach, 310/376-3223). There are also plenty of bars with outdoor decks where you can enjoy a cocktail or beer after a day at the beach.

It might be shocking that you could catch a comedy act by some of the world's biggest comedians in the coastal town of Hermosa Beach. **The Comedy & Magic Club** (1018 Hermosa Ave., Hermosa Beach, 310/372-1193, http://comedyandmagicclub.com, performances Tues.-Sun.) hosts a set of comedy every Sunday night by *The Tonight Show*'s Jay Leno. The

small venue, which holds just 250 people, also has had big-time comedians including Jerry Seinfeld, Ray Romano, and Bob Saget onstage to do their bits. The small club doubles as a comedy museum with memorabilia including Seinfeld's puffy shirt and Kevin James' uniform from his show *King of Queens*.

ACCOMMODATIONS
Manhattan Beach

For a cute near-the-sand motel in Manhattan Beach, stay at the **Sea View Inn at the Beach** (3400 Highland Ave., 310/545-1504, www.theseaviewinn.com, $130-325). Only two blocks from the sands of the beach, this is a great place to hole up if you're in town for some surfing, volleyball, or sunbathing along the shore. (You'll avoid the traditional summer beach parking nightmare by leaving your car at the motel.) Just grab a boogie board and some beach chairs from the lobby and head out. Inside, guest room appointments are prettier and more coordinated than those of most moderate motels. Guest rooms are done in light blues and whites, with matching prints on the walls and possibly even a live plant to add a homelike touch. The complex of blocky, mid-century modern buildings has its own small swimming pool as well, set in a small, plant-strewn courtyard. Just around the corner, you'll find an array of restaurants, shops, bars, and clubs.

Hermosa Beach

For a full beach experience, stay at the 🄲 **Beach House at Hermosa Beach** (1300 The Strand, 310/374-3001 or 888/895-4559, www.beach-house.com, $229-349). Located right on The Strand, a paved coastal path popular with bikers and runners, every room at the Beach House has a patio or deck to take in all the nearby beach action. The "loft suite" has a cushy king bed with Frette sheets, a big bath with a separate tub and shower, two TVs, a stereo, a stove top, and a gas fireplace. The casual, upscale decor makes visitors feel at home, but you'll probably want to spend more time out on the porch or balcony on sunny days. Guests get a free continental breakfast, the use of the outdoor spa, and access to the on-site gym. If you prefer an outdoor workout, enjoy The Strand for a walk, run, or bike ride.

Redondo Beach

Of the three Best Westerns that make up much of Redondo Beach's hospitality, the **Best Western Sunrise** (400 N. Harbor Dr., 310/376-0746 or 800/334-7384, www.bestwestern-sunrise.com, $190-240) is the best of the lot, with guest rooms overlooking Redondo's King Harbor and the location within walking distance of the pier and its restaurants and bars. Guest rooms are clean and comfortable, and the decor is cute and modern, with earth-tone bedspreads and light wood furniture. You'll get all the standard amenities you'd expect at a Best Western, plus a nice pool and spa, a gym, free Wi-Fi, and a complimentary breakfast.

Long Beach

(The Varden (335 Pacific Ave., 562/432-8950, www.thevardenhotel.com, $119-159) offers the type of tiny, clean, and modern rooms you'd expect to find in Europe. If you don't mind your bathroom being a foot or two from your bed, the sleek little rooms in this hotel, which dates back to 1929, are a great deal. The oldest operating hotel in Long Beach, The Varden is named after an eccentric circus performer named Dolly Varden, who is rumored to have hoarded jewels on the premises. The staff is very friendly and helpful, and coffee, ice, and fresh fruit are available to guests 24 hours a day. It's also one block from Pine Street, which is lined with restaurants and bars.

Looking for something completely different? Check in to the **Boat and Bed** (Dock 5A, Rainbow Harbor, 562/436-3111 or 800/436-2574, www.boatandbed.com, $200-325, overnight parking $24 unless you get the $10 discount parking pass from Dockside). You won't get a regular old hotel room; instead, you'll get one of four yachts. The yachts run 38-54 feet and can sleep four or more people each ($25 pp charge after the first two). The amenities include TVs with DVD players, stereos, kitchen facilities, wet bars, and ample seating. The boats are in walking distance

from the harbor's restaurants and the aquarium. No, you can't actually take your floating accommodations out for a spin; these yachts are permanent residents of Rainbow Harbor.

FOOD
Manhattan Beach

Have you come to Los Angeles to seek genuine home-style Mexican food? You can find it at **Sion's Mexican Restaurant** (235 N. Sepulveda Blvd., 310/372-4504, Mon. 9am-2pm, Tues.-Sat. 8am-9pm, Sun. 8am-3pm, $10). Expect nothing fancy, but everything fresh—from tacos to salsa—in this utterly casual and family-owned hole-in-the-wall.

Hermosa Beach

(Hot's Kitchen (844 Hermosa Ave., 310/318-2939, www.hotskitchen.com, daily 11am-10pm, $4.50) has a taco menu you have to see to believe. The over 50 tacos offered include wildly inventive takes on the taco like a shrimp tempura with unagi sauce number and a duck confit offering with grits, braised greens, and a maple glaze. Sure, most southern California taquerias serve tacos at half the price of those at Hot's Kitchen, but almost every single taco served in this hip reclaimed wood restaurant—with a great beer selection I might add—are a singular culinary creation.

Redondo Beach

The **Green Temple Vegetarian Restaurant** (1700 S. Catalina Ave., 310/944-4525, www.greentemple.net, Tues.-Thurs. 11am-4pm and 5pm-9pm, Fri.-Sat. 11am-4pm and 5pm-10pm, Sun. 9am-4pm and 5pm-9pm, $10-20) strives for Southern California Zen in both its cuisine and its dining room. The vegetarian menu includes a broccoli pine nut casserole and a shepherd's pie made with crumbled veggie burger instead of ground beef.

Long Beach

Combining elegance, fine continental-California cuisine, and great ghost stories, **Sir Winston's Restaurant and Lounge** (1126 Queens Hwy., 562/499-1657, www.queensmary.

com, daily 5pm-10pm, $30-50) floats gently on board the *Queen Mary*. For the most beautiful dining experience, request a window table and make reservations for sunset. And dress in your finest; Sir Winston's requests that diners adhere to their semiformal dress code.

A locals' favorite down where the shops and cafés cluster, **Natraj Cuisine of India** (5262 E. 2nd St., 562/930-0930, http://lbnatraj.webs. com, Sun.-Thurs. 11am-2:30pm and 5pm-10pm, Fri.-Sat. 11am-2:30pm and 5pm-11pm, $10-30) offers good food for reasonable (by L.A. standards) prices. Come by for the all-you-can-eat lunch buffet Monday-Saturday to sample a variety of properly spiced meat and vegetarian dishes created in classic Indian tradition.

INFORMATION AND SERVICES

For information, maps, brochures, and advice about Long Beach and the surrounding areas, visit the **Long Beach Convention and Visitors Bureau** (301 E. Ocean Blvd., Suite 1900, 562/436-3645 or 800/452-7829, www. visitlongbeach.com, Mon.-Fri. 8am-5pm).

Long Beach has a **post office** (300 Long Beach Blvd., 562/628-1303 or 800/275-8777).

For medical attention, visit the emergency room at the **Long Beach Memorial Medical Center** (2801 Atlantic Ave., Long Beach, 562/933-2000, www.memorialcare.org).

GETTING THERE

While you can get to the coast easily enough from LAX, the **Long Beach International Airport** (LGB, 4100 Donald Douglas Dr., 562/570-2600, www.lgb.org) is both closer to Long Beach and less crowded than LAX.

I-710, which runs north-south, is known as the Long Beach Freeway. Along the coast, the Pacific Coast Highway (Hwy. 1) can get you from one beach town to the next.

Parking in Long Beach and the other beach towns is just as bad as parking anywhere else in L.A. Prepare to pay for the privilege of stuffing your car someplace for the day. Beach parking on summer weekends is the worst, but on weekdays and in the off-season you can occasionally find a decent space down near the beach for reasonable rates.

Catalina Island

For a slice of Greece in Southern California, take a ferry or a helicopter out to Catalina Island (Catalina Island Chamber of Commerce, 310/510-1520, www.catalinachamber.com). You can see Catalina from the shore of Long Beach on a clear day, but for a better view, you've got to get onto the island. The port town of Avalon welcomes visitors with plenty of European-inspired hotels, restaurants, and shops. But the main draw of Catalina lies outside the walls of its buildings. With its Mediterranean summer climate, Catalina draws hikers, horseback riders, and ecotourists. Most of all, it beckons to water lovers of all kinds, from scuba divers and snorkelers to kayakers and anglers.

The climate on Catalina tends toward the temperate, with beautiful, warm, sunny summer days that make getting out into the ocean

a pleasure. Even in the winter, you'll find pleasantly warmish days and cool nights. But every once in a while, when the Santa Ana winds come billowing down from the mainland, life in Avalon harbor gets exciting. Storms and winds can whip up the seas, which then come crashing up onto and over the beaches and walkways of Avalon. When you see the yellow sandbags, be aware that the locals are serious. Even on a nonflooding morning, the Pacific can completely engulf the harbor-side beaches, hit the retaining walls, and spray dozens of feet into the air. If you're lucky enough to be around, take a walk down toward the waterside and enjoy the show.

SIGHTS
The Casino Theatre and Ballroom

No, it's not that kind of casino. The **Casino**

Catalina Island's Casino Theatre and Ballroom

Theatre and Ballroom (1 Casino Way, 310/510-7428, www.visitcatalinaisland.com) at Avalon harks back to the older Italian meaning of the word, "a gathering place." The round white art deco building, which opened in 1929, acts as a community gathering place and home for all sorts of different activities, including the Catalina Island Jazz Festival. The Avalon Theatre, home to a Page organ, is located on the main level and plays first run movies. Be sure to check out the murals by John Gabriel Beckman, of Grauman's Chinese Theatre fame, inside the theatre.

Wrigley Memorial and Botanical Garden

Upcountry, the coolest place to visit may be the **Wrigley Memorial and Botanical Garden** (Avalon Canyon Rd., 1.5 miles west of town, 310/510-2897, www.catalinaconservancy.org, daily 8am-5pm, adults $7, seniors and veterans with ID $5, ages 5-12 and students with ID $3, under age 5 and active military and their families free), operated by the Catalina Island Conservancy. Stroll through serene gardens planted with flowers, trees, and shrubs that are native to California or even unique to Catalina. You'll see a number of endangered species among the plants that grow nowhere else in the world. The temperate climate on Catalina lends itself to hardy, drought-tolerant species that still manage to produce beautiful colors and fragrances. Just don't eat (or let your kids eat) the wild tomatoes—they're incredibly poisonous. Also, don't bother with the Catalina cherries. They're not deadly, but they don't taste very good.

At the center of the garden you can't miss the Wrigley Memorial, a 130-foot-tall edifice dedicated to the memory of chewing-gum magnate William Wrigley Jr. Wrigley adored Santa Catalina Island and used his sticky fortune to make many improvements to it; most notably, he funded the building of the Avalon Casino. The monument is made and decorated with mostly local materials; the crushed stone on the facade comes from the island, as do the blue flagstones, the red roof tiles, and the brightly

© STUART THORNTON

LOS ANGELES

Catalina Island's Wrigley Memorial

colored decorative ceramic tiles. All the local-centric construction makes a perfect center-piece to the gardens.

For a more thorough look at the history, culture, and diverse natural abundance of Catalina, visit the **Nature Center at Avalon Canyon** (1202 Avalon Canyon Rd., 310/510-0954, www.catalinaconservancy.org, summer daily 10am-4pm, winter Fri.-Wed. 10am-4pm, free) just down the road from the botanical garden. Here you can learn more about the native plants, indigenous people, and the ocean channel and its islands, of which Catalina is the most visited.

Catalina Island Museum

Another take on the history of Catalina is displayed at the **Catalina Island Museum** (The Casino, 1 Casino Way, Avalon, 310/510-2414, www.catalinamuseum.org, daily 10am-5pm, adults $5, seniors $4, ages 6-15 $2, under age 6 free). Located on the ground floor of the landmark Casino, this small museum makes for a great 15-30-minute culture stop in the middle

of a beach vacation. Learn about William Wrigley Jr.'s development of the island and the World War II history of Catalina in revolving exhibits. You'll find a good-size collection of Native American artifacts from the island's original inhabitants, plus a huge collection of historic photos. Look for Hollywood stars enjoying Catalina's natural beauty and luxurious resort amenities among the photographic history of the island. Purchase reproductions of tiles, photos, and more in the museum store, and check the website for museum activities geared to kids and adults.

SPORTS AND RECREATION

Outdoor recreation is the main reason most people venture across the channel to Catalina. On land or in the water, you'll find the activities that are right for you.

Scuba and Snorkeling

If you want to get out into the water on your own, you'll find plenty of places to kick off from shore. The most popular spot is the **Avalon Underwater Park** (Casino Point). This protected area at the north end of town has buoys and markers to help you find your way around the reefs and keep safe. Not only will you see the famous bright-orange garibaldi fish, you'll get the opportunity to meet gobies, jellyfish, anemones, spiny lobsters, and plenty of other sea life. Out at the deeper edge of the park, nearly half a dozen wrecked ships await your examination. Snorkeling and scuba tour groups come here, as do locals and visitors who rent equipment from local shops and shacks or bring their own. Expect big crowds on summer weekends.

If you prefer to take a guided tour, a number of companies offer snorkeling, scuba, kayaking, and combinations all around the island. **Catalina Snorkel & Scuba** (310/510-8558, www.catalinasnorkelscuba.com) is located right on Lover's Cove a short walk from the ferry terminal and offers guided snorkel tours of the Lover's Cove Marine Reserve that include all equipment with the fees. This clear-water preserve sits just southeast of the boat terminal and includes a life-filled kelp forest. If you're a certified scuba diver, you can book a two-hour guided tour of Avalon Underwater Park. If you want to become a scuba diver, Catalina Snorkel & Scuba offers certification classes as well as intro tours that give you a taste of the world underwater. Catalina Snorkel & Scuba also offers equipment rental for snorkelers and divers who want to take off on their own.

Another company to try is **Snorkel Catalina** (107 Pebbly Beach Rd., Avalon, 562/547-4185 or 877/218-9156, www.snorkelingcatalina. com). This company specializes in deeper-water excursions farther away from shore, taking guests out on a custom pontoon boat all year long. If your purpose in coming to Catalina is to see dolphins and sea lions, Snorkel Catalina can make it happen for you. Standard tours run 1-2 hours and let you check out the prettiest fish, sleekest seals, and friendliest dolphins around the island.

If it's hardcore scuba you're interested in, take a walk out to **Catalina Divers Supply** (800/353-0330, www.catalinadiverssupply. com, daily 8am-5pm). The little green shack out toward the end of the pier offers everything from certification and referral classes to guided shore dives at the Avalon Marine Preserves to charter trips on the 46-foot *Scuba Cat*. You'll see things that just aren't visible from the surface with a snorkel. The company highly recommends making reservations for any of their tours and trips.

Kayaking

Kayaking is one of the most popular ways to see otherwise unreachable parts of Catalina. Rent a kayak, or if you're not confident in your own navigation abilities, take a tour with a reputable company. **Descanso Beach Ocean Sports/Catalina Island Kayak & Snorkel** (310/510-1226, www.kayakcatalinaisland. com, $48-96 half-day-full-day) offers several kayak tours to different parts of the island. You don't need previous river or sea kayaking experience to take these tours, since double sit-on-top kayaks make the trip easy and safe even for total beginners and small kids. But if you

are a rescue-certified sea kayaker, the folks at Descanso Beach also have an array of lean, sleek, enclosed ocean kayaks for advanced paddlers. This company offers regular year-round trips to Frog Rock (2 hours), Fox Canyon (3 hours, includes a nature walk), and Willow Cove (half-day excursion with snorkeling and hiking). All trips start at Descanso Beach Club, north of Avalon and the Casino.

Another kayak tour provider, **Wet Spot Rentals** (off Pebbly Beach Rd. across the bay from the Casino, 310/510-2229, www.catalinakayaks.com, $35-75 half-day-full-day) specializes in a full-day land and sea tour that includes both kayaking and an auto tour into the Catalina backcountry. After a van trip and nature tour at the airport on top of the hill, you'll travel down to the less-traveled windward side of the island. You'll get a rare opportunity to kayak on the other side of the island from Avalon, exploring the coves and cliffs around Little Harbor. A brief portage and hike takes you to a waterfall. This fabulous, nearly whole-island tour takes all day, and lunch, water, and all equipment, including sit-on-top beginner kayaks, are provided. Wet Spot also offers several shorter kayak expeditions; they're a great operator if you want to combine kayaking with snorkeling the reefs of the leeward (Avalon) side of the island.

These operators also rent kayaks to individuals (you'll have to prove yourself capable to rent an enclosed sea kayak). They also have an array of snorkel equipment, and you can take a kayak out for some fabulous fish watching and even skin diving.

Rafting

For an adventurous ocean tour, head out with **Catalina Ocean Rafting** (103 Pebbly Beach Rd., 310/510-0211 or 800/990-7238, www. catalinaoceanrafting.com, adults $78-140, ages 5-11 and military $67-109, ages 12-18 get the lower rate when accompanied by two paying adults). From Avalon harbor you'll head out on 1.25-hour, half-day, or full-day trip on a powered inflatable raft. The small maneuverable craft can take you right up to cliffs and into sea caves, around Eagle Rock and Ribbon Rock, and into reef areas perfect for snorkeling (equipment is provided with your tour). You'll get to harbors beyond Avalon and enjoy lunch, drinks, and snacks as part of your trip. A raft tour is a great way for adventurous newcomers to get the lay of the land and sea before striking off on their own.

Swimming

In the summer, the waters of Catalina can reach more than 70°F—perfect for taking a long, lazy swim in the salty waters of the Pacific. Bring your family out to any one of the charming beaches in the sunny coves for a lazy day on the beach and in the water. The most crowded spots will be at the Avalon Underwater Park, the harbor, and other coves near Avalon. For a more deserted beach, try the windward side of the island; just be aware that it may be, well, windy. Keep a close eye on your children and even adult friends wherever you swim. Catalina's beaches, like most of the California coastline, are subject to dangerous rip currents.

Wildlife-Watching

If you're not keen on swimming in the ocean, but you want a peek at the famous Catalina garibaldi (a bright-orange fish), take a semi-submersible or glass-bottom boat tour. The **Undersea Tour** (310/510-8687 or 800/626-7489, www.visitcatalinaisland.com, Mon.-Fri. noon, 1pm, 2pm, and 3:30pm, Sat.-Sun. 11am, noon, 1pm, 2pm, and 3pm, adults $36, seniors $33, children $27) takes you a few feet underwater for 45 minutes in a comfy cabin to watch the abundant array of aquatic life around Avalon. For a special (and budget-conscious) treat, book a nighttime Undersea Tour to check out a whole different variety of sea species. Every seat on the boat has a great view of the water, and kids love the colorful fish and mysterious bat rays that glide gracefully by.

In the summer, take another boat trip out at night to see one of the legends of Catalina. A **Flying Fish Boat Trip** (310/510-8687 or 800/626-1496, www.visitcatalinaisland.com, adults $28, seniors $26, children $22) lights up the air just over the waterline, making visible

Avalon Harbor

© STUART THORNTON

LOS ANGELES

the famous Catalina flying fish as they leap out, putting on a unique show.

Biking

Even most of the locals on Catalina eschew cars in favor of smaller, lighter forms of transportation. A great way to get around and beyond Avalon is on a bicycle. You can bring your own aboard the ferries that travel to and from the airport. If you don't have one, you can rent a bicycle right on the island at **Brown's Bikes** (underneath Holly Hill House, 100 yards from the ferry dock, 310/510-0986, www.catalinabiking.com, daily 9am-5pm, $8-18 per hour, $20-45 per day). If you're looking for a simple, one-speed cruiser to putter around downtown Avalon and down to the beach, you can get one for $8 per hour or $20 per day. With no gas to buy, it's the ultimate in affordable transportation. Brown's also has 6- and 21-speeds, tandems, an array of mountain bikes, and electric bicycles. You'll also get a map of the bikeable roads and trails in Avalon and around the island.

Mountain bikers, this island's for you: An array of trails from easy to steep and difficult take you up into the hills, providing views and thrills galore. Street bikers will find that Avalon is bike-friendly; the road that runs along the shore on either side of the town is paved, mostly level, and zoned for bicycles. If you've got the legs for it, you can obtain a permit from the Catalina Conservancy to ride farther afield. Call or email Brown's Bikes for more information on biking outside Avalon.

Golf

As most of Catalina Island is devoted to wildlife preservation, you won't find a wealth of golf courses here. But if you just can't abide the notion of going for a trip without exercising your clubs, get yourself a tee time at the 9-hole **Catalina Island Golf Course** (1 Country Club Dr., Avalon, 310/510-0530, www.visit-catalinaisland.com, $35-85), which has 9- or 18-hole rounds, discounts for seniors, and higher rates on weekends. You'll be walking on greens built in 1892, used for the Bobby Jones Invitational Tournament from the 1930s through the 1950s, and more recently played on by up-and-coming SoCal junior players such as Craig Stadler and Tiger Woods as they built their skills. Heck, even if you don't play, it's worth walking the course on a sunny day just to enjoy the unbelievable views out to the Casino, the town of Avalon, and the clutch of sailboats bobbing in the harbor. The full-service pro shop provides rental equipment and golf carts as well as a set of **tennis courts** you can rent by the hour.

If your taste in golf runs a little less serious, head for **Golf Gardens** (10 Island Plaza, 310/510-1200, www.balboapavilion.com, hours vary, adults $7, children $4), a miniature golf course one block inland from the fountain just past the Discovery Tours Plaza and across the street from the City Library. This is a great break for kids tired of sightseeing and ecotouring. This cute 18-hole course has a tropical feel, complete with palm trees and good putting challenges.

Spas

You've got a surprising number of massage and spa options right in and around Avalon. If you prefer your massage in the privacy of your hotel room or condo, call **Catalina Sea Spa** (310/510-8920, www.catalinamassage-bymichelle.net, massage $85-135,), formerly known as Massage by Michelle. The therapists love to work with couples looking for a relaxing day or evening of romance, and they are trained in a variety of massage techniques and spa therapies, including heated stones and Thai massage. Book a simple Swedish massage or a full spa package with facials, body scrubs, and massages for one or two people. Check the website for a full list of available treatments. Be sure to book in advance to get the date and time you want. Studio sessions are also available.

Whether you're looking for a divine romantic experience with your sweetie or a solo day of spa-induced respite from your busy life, you'll find it at **The Spa at Catalina** (888 Country

Club Rd., Avalon, 310/510-9255, www.catalinaspa.com, $55-319). This full-service day spa offers all sorts of massage and treatment packages, from a simple half-hour of bodywork up to nearly three hours of head-to-toe bliss. The spa has dual rooms (many complete with private baths for two) to serve couples or pairs of friends who want to enjoy their treatments together. Choose from the many packages that focus on facials and scalp treatments using lavender, peppermint, and other delicious essential oils. You can also breathe deep and detox with a body wrap or heated stone massage. The spa sits in Falls Canyon outside downtown Avalon; ask about getting a free shuttle from your hotel to the spa at the Best Western Canyon Hotel when you book your treatments. It's best to make reservations at least a couple of days in advance; even in winter, same-day appointment availability is rare.

Decide for yourself whether the treatments you receive in downtown Avalon live up to the name **A Touch of Heaven** (205 Crescent Ave., 310/510-1633, www.atouchofheavendayspa.com, daily 9am-5pm, $45-240) at the back of the Metropole Market Place. This day spa echoes the European flavor of the town surrounding it; you'll find an extensive menu of Euro-style facials, from the intense relaxation of a LaStone Facial to the aesthetically focused glycolic-lactic acid peel and facial. Also look for a few unusual treatments, including raindrop therapy and ear candling, as well as practitioners of both Eastern and Western massage modalities. The spa also offers massage for children, and well-behaved young people are welcome to enjoy the treatments here.

Tours

One of the main forms of entertainment on the island is touring. You can take a bus tour, a Jeep tour, a glass-bottom boat tour, and more. The Catalina Island Conservancy offers **Jeep Eco-Tours** (310/510-2595, www.catalinaconservancy.org, up to 6 people $549 chartered half-day, $889 chartered full-day, non-chartered two-hour tour $70 pp, non-chartered three-hour tour $109 pp) out in the wilds of

Catalina. You can go much farther on these tours than you can by yourself—out into the wilderness to see the bison, the wild horses, plant species unique to the island, and more. Be sure to bring your camera, both for close-ups and for views out toward the sea. On the full-day trips, you'll get lunch, drinks, and snacks, while on the half-day trip you'll get snacks and drinks.

For a sedate view of Catalina's more settled areas as well as it's road-viewable wilderness, try an **Inland Motor Tour** (800/626-7489, www.visitcatalinaisland.com, year-round daily, from $77). This 3.5-hour tour aboard a restored 1950s cruising bus takes you away from the coastline and into the island's interior via old stagecoach routes. Along the way you'll see Middle Ranch, the magnificent Arabian horses and Old West mementos of El Rancho Escondido, and the Airport in the Sky Nature Center. A shorter version of this tour is the **Skyline Drive** (310/510-8687 or 800/626-1496, daily year-round, adults $47, seniors $42, children $36), a two-hour trip that takes you up from Avalon to the Airport in the Sky Nature Center along a route cluttered with spectacular vistas of island and ocean.

If you want a guided walking tour of Avalon, try **Catalina Adventure Tours** (877/510-2888, www.catalinaadventuretours.com, adults $22, seniors $18, children $14) for a 90-minute look at Avalon's attractions, past, and architecture. The one-hour tour by **Icons of Avalon** (310/502-6131, www.iconsofavalon.com, $30) is followed by 30 minutes of wine-tasting. Of course, this tour is for those age 21 and older. They also offer Ghost Tour of Avalon (www.ghosttoursofcatalina.com, adults $15, children $12). And for the more independent-minded visitor, try **GPS Walking Tours** (310/510-8687, www.visitcatalinaisland.com, $15 per device). Each device can guide 4-6 people, an ideal money saver for families.

The newest way to see the island is by zipping down its hillsides. The **Catalina Zip Line Eco Tour** (800/626-1496, www.visitcatalinaisland.com, Mon.-Fri. 9am-4pm, Sat.-Sun. 7am-6pm, $109-120) is a two-hour tour by zip line that drops from 440 feet to 60 feet above sea level.

ACCOMMODATIONS

You'll find plenty of charming inns and hotels on Catalina; most sit in or near Avalon. You can also camp on Catalina, and ecotourists often prefer to immerse themselves in the natural world of the island by sleeping and eating outdoors.

Under $150

The **Hotel Atwater** (125 Sumner Ave., 800/322-3434, www.visitcatalinaisland.com, spring-fall, $140-390) has bright, cheerful guest rooms for reasonable rates. Take in the history of a budget hotel that's been hosting guests since the 1920s. Clean, light-colored economy rooms provide the best value for your buck, while the more upscale suites cost more and offer prettier decor and better amenities. Whichever type of room you book, you'll have a TV, air-conditioning, and more. You'll find storage for your diving gear and bikes, and a rinse-off area outside for divers, snorkelers, and swimmers. The Atwater usually closes each winter; call ahead to confirm availability.

For inexpensive indoor accommodations, your best bet is the **Hermosa Hotel & Cottages** (131 Metropole St., 310/510-1010 or 877/453-1313, www.hermosahotel.com, $100-175). This simple budget hotel has guest rooms that now have their own bathrooms. (Be aware of a two-night minimum for stays involving a Saturday night in the high season.) The cottages have private baths, and some have kitchens and TVs. "Family units" can sleep up to nine in the main building and have kitchens—perfect for larger families or groups of friends traveling together on a budget. The 100-plus-year-old building sits only about a block from the harbor beaches and a short walk from the Casino, shops, and restaurants.

$150-250

Want to stay right on the waterfront? Book a room at the bright yellow **Hotel Mac Rae** (409 Crescent Ave., 310/510-0246 or 800/698-2266, www.hotelmacrae.com, $160-260). This bit of Catalina history has been in the Mac Rae family for four generations, and they've been running the hostelry since 1920. The Mediterranean flavor of Avalon follows you into the guest rooms and common spaces of the Mac Rae. Relax with a drink in the bright brick courtyard. You can choose one of the premium guest rooms that looks right out into the harbor, or a more economical courtyard-view room. Grab a complimentary continental breakfast downstairs, and either eat in the courtyard or take your coffee and your pastries back to your pretty Côte d'Azur-styled guest room for more privacy. Catching the afternoon ferry but want to enjoy one last morning in the warm Catalina water? The Mac Rae has luggage storage and even a public shower for use after you check out.

For a European hotel experience in Avalon, stay at the **Hotel Metropole** (205 Crescent Ave., 310/510-1884, www.hotel-metropole. com, $200-1,050). The comfortably cluttered and warmly decorated guest rooms feel like home almost immediately. You'll find gas fireplaces in some guest rooms and oversize two-person whirlpool bathtubs in a few pretty tiled baths. The beds feel great after a long day of ocean swimming or the ferry ride over from Long Beach. The little extras are nice too, from the nightly turndown service to the L'Occitane toiletries. You can also use the Wi-Fi service in your room. The Metropole is built in a modern style with a pretty gray paint job. On the roof you'll find a whirlpool tub with glass walls enclosing its deck, letting you look out over the rooftops into the harbor. The lower-end guest rooms don't have much in the way of ocean views, so for a window on the water, you have to pay premium rates for an oceanfront room or suites ($500-800). You can walk half a block down the street to the ocean. For extra pampering, make an appointment at the day spa located on the bottom floor of the hotel appropriately named A Touch of Heaven (205 Crescent Ave., 310/510-1633, www.atouchofheavendayspa. com, daily 9am-5pm, $40-240). Just outside by the back elevator, start a shopping jaunt in the little Metropole center, where you can grab a cup of coffee, or walk down Crescent Avenue for a meal.

The **Villa Portofino** (111 Crescent Ave., 310/510-0555 or 888/510-0555, www.hotel-villaportofino.com, rooms $125-550) offers Mediterranean elegance on the Avalon waterfront. The bright-white exterior with red tile roofs invites you inside this 34-room boutique hotel. Guest rooms range from small standard rooms up through immense, lush, individually named suites with fireplaces, soaking tubs, and richly colored furnishings. Amenities include a complimentary continental breakfast, free Wi-Fi, free beach chairs and towels, and an on-site restaurant, Ristorante Villa Portofino (101 Crescent Ave., 310/510-2009, www.ristorante-villaportofino.com, $15-36). The Portofino's location is perfect—right on the main drag running along the harbor-side beach. There's also a rooftop sun deck with chairs and a great view of the harbor.

Over $250

A striking, clean, white-and-yellow building just feet from one of Avalon's most popular beaches, the **Pavilion Hotel** (513 Crescent Ave., 877/778-8322, www.visitcatalinaisland.com, $300-800) boasts a nice private patio very close to downtown's action. The rooms are clean and modern but not luxury caliber, though there is a nice courtyard with a tropical garden and fire pit to hang out in.

CAMPING

Camping is the best way to get away from Avalon and stay on other parts of the island. It's also a great way to get to know the precious Catalina wilderness in an up-close-and-personal way. Check the island's visitors website (www.visitcatalinaisland.com) for a list and descriptions of all the major campgrounds around the island. Also be sure to read the regulations, which are more stringent than at some other camping areas and are strictly enforced. Permits are required for all campsites. Also check out the equipment rentals; if you don't want to

bring your own tent and gear, you can rent it at the Two Harbors campground (310/510-8368).

You have a choice of more than half a dozen campgrounds, some on the coast and some up the mountains in the interior. One of the largest and most developed campgrounds sits just outside the tiny town of **Two Harbors** (310/510-8368, www.visitcatalinaisland.com, adults $21, children $12, tent cabins $50). Book online to avoid the $25 "administration fee" for reservations phoned in. You can go to the website and see a photo gallery of the campgrounds and check out a map of the campsites before you make a reservation. You can bring your own tent and equipment, rent it, or book one of the tent cabins at this site. The tent cabins come with cots and mattresses, sunshades, and a camp stove and lantern in addition to the usual barbecue grill, fire ring, and picnic table. All campers have access to showers, restroom facilities, and lockers to keep valuables safe while you're out exploring the area.

If you're looking to camp on the beach, check out the **Little Harbor** (310/510-8368, www.visitcatalinaisland.com, summer adults $18, children $9, winter adults $16, children $8, tent cabins $50) campground. Located seven miles from the town of Little Harbor, the sandy campsites make a perfect place to sleep if your aim is snorkeling, kayaking (Wet Spot Rentals, 310/510-2229), and playing away from all the casual island visitors. You'll find potable water, showers, and toilets here. The best way to get to the Little Harbor campground is to take the Safari Bus, so be sure to book seats and space for your gear when you book your campsite.

Perhaps the coolest way to stay on Catalina is to bring or rent a kayak and paddle into one of the **boat-in campsites** (310/510-8368, www.campingcatalinaisland.com, adults $12-16, children $6-8). These 11 primitive campsites can't be accessed by land at all—you must bring and moor your own boat. You'll get a wholly natural experience at any of these beautiful remote locations, with no running water, showers, or toilet facilities, or shade structures. Whatever you want and need, you must pack into your boat with you. A ranger checks each campsite daily, so you're not completely cut off from the outside world. However, take precautions such as bringing a two-way radio and an above-average first-aid kit just in case an emergency crops up.

FOOD

To be honest, the culinary presence on Catalina isn't much to write home about. While there's certainly no lack of restaurants in Avalon, the trend toward delicious cuisine at both the high and low ends hasn't made it across the channel to the island yet. You might consider getting a guest room or a condo with a kitchen and cooking a few of your own meals to save a bit of cash while you're here. Still, a traveler has to go out to eat sometimes. Here are a few places to try.

Classic American

All the locals recommend that tourists try **Steve's Steakhouse** (417 Crescent Ave., 310/510-0333, www.stevessteakhouse.com, summer daily 11:30am-2pm and 5pm-9pm, winter daily 5pm-9pm, $15-33). Steve's offers a wide array of classic steak house fare with plenty of seafood options thrown in as a nod to the water lapping the harbor beach just outside. The burgers also hit the spot after a day of hiking and swimming. Generous portions of meat or fish are accompanied by traditional steak-house sides, and the desserts up the ante with some tasty sweetness (the mud pie's not half bad).

El Galleon (411 Crescent Ave., 310/510-1188, www.catalinahotspots.com, Sun.-Thurs. 11am-8pm, Fri.-Sat. 11am-9pm, $10-30) is probably a better place to get a drink than have dinner. El Galleon's decor is a busy improbable mix of maritime items and Mardi Gras paraphernalia. The large menu speaks to hearty American diners with lots of aged steaks, chicken dishes, and fresh fish. Lighter eaters can peruse the selection of salads, soups, and seafood appetizers. For a major feast, take a look at the prix fixe menu, which, when available, offers a hearty four-course dinner (about $70 pp). The dessert menu offers a few unusual treats, plus a wide array of sweet and strong coffee drinks to round off your evening. Better yet, order one of El Galleon's 18-ounce cocktails or one of their German beers on tap and watch the bar's nightly karaoke, which kicks off at 9pm.

A more refined dining experience can be had at the **Avalon Grille** (423 Crescent Ave., 310/510-7494, www.visitcatalinaisland.com, daily 11:30am-3pm and 5pm-10pm, $22-60). There are the typical seafood and meat offerings along with some surprises including an entrée of grilled wild boar pork chops and buffalo ribs. Eat them inside under twirling ceiling fans or in tables under a canopy beside the restaurant.

Coffee

Most coffee shops in Avalon don't offer Wi-Fi. The **Café Metropole** (205 Crescent Ave., 310/510-9095, www.cafemetropole.com, daily 11am-close) has Internet availability with a purchase of a coffee or one of its daily iced teas. The café also serves up an inviting selection of sandwiches and vegetarian fare.

Italian

The **Ristorante Villa Portofino** (101 Crescent Ave., 310/510-2009, www.ristorantevillaportofino.com, summer Sun.-Thurs. 5pm-10pm, Fri.-Sat. 5pm-11pm, winter Weds.-Sun. 5pm-9pm, $15-36), attached to the Villa Portofino hotel, serves tasty pasta and protein dishes with a distinct Italian flare—and you'll get a fabulous harbor view with your cannelloni or calamari. In homage to the locale, the menu here runs to seafood, with some classic and a few inventive preparations. The pastas bring homey comfort food to Catalina, and the hot appetizer menu is well worth a look. For dessert, the Ristorante offers a goodly selection of Italian favorites, such as cannoli and *panna cotta*. In the summer, see if you can get a table on the patio to enjoy the balmy island breezes—you'll feel almost as though you're really on the Mediterranean coast of Italy.

Mexican

Looking for an unpretentious taco? You can get one at the **Catalina Cantina** (313 Crescent

Ave., 310/510-0100, Sun.-Thurs. 11am-9:30pm, Fri.-Sat. 11am-10pm, $15-25) or its fast-food walk-up neighbor, the **Topless Taco.** Serving a mix of American diner fare (think burgers and fries, wings, and fish-and-chips) and Americanized Mexican staples (burritos, fajitas, combo plates), the Catalina Cantina offers tasty food for decent prices. Better still, if you come in the evening, cool off with one of the Cantina's buckets o' liquor. Rum punch, margaritas, something called the Blue Shark, and more come in either normal human-size glasses or in a 24-ounce bowl that they really hope you'll share with friends.

Seafood

Part local's bar and part no-frills seafood restaurant, (**The Lobster Trap** (128 Catalina St., 310/510-8585, www.catalinalobstertrap.com, daily 11am-late, $14-41) serves up stuffed lobster, lobster salad, and lobster tacos. (It is strange though that the local lobster costs more than the imported Maine and Atlantic lobster on the menu.) Plastic lobsters and plastic fish decorate the wall, and some diners can eat their seafood, pasta, poultry, or steak on a raised platform that looks like a boat.

INFORMATION AND SERVICES

If you are camping in a remote location, talk to the rangers at the Two Harbors station before leaving to learn how best to contact them or the police in an emergency. Bring a two-way radio, since cell signals may be unreliable or nonexistent.

For medical assistance, go to the **Catalina Island Medical Center** (100 Falls Canyon Rd., 310/510-0700, www.catalinaislandmedicalcenter.org).

The major local daily newspaper on Catalina is the *Los Angeles Times* (www.latimes.com). Your hotel might have copies. A good website for visitors is www.visitcatalinaisland.com.

If you're looking for kitschy souvenirs and re-production ceramic tiles, you can find them in downtown Avalon in the area sometimes called the **South Coast Plaza.**

GETTING THERE AND AROUND

There are two ways to get to Catalina: by boat and by air.

Boat

Most folks take the ferry over from the mainland coast. The **Catalina Express** (310/519-1212, www.catalinaexpress.com, round-trip adults $73, seniors $66, ages 2-11 $57, under age 2 $5, bikes and surfboards $7) serves as the major carrier, with multiple departures every day, even in the off-season. During the summer high season, you can choose to leave from Long Beach, San Pedro, and Dana Point. Most ferries dock at Avalon, but you can arrange to travel directly to Two Harbors from San Pedro if you prefer. You can bring your bike, your luggage, and your camping gear aboard for a comfortable hour-long ride on one of eight ferries. Bars on both levels offer snacks and drinks, and TVs help make the cruise go by a little faster. On the way it's worth looking out the window, however: You might spot seals or sea lions, different varieties of pelicans, or even a pod of dolphins playing in the swells. Catalina Express also offers plenty of return cruises to the mainland each day.

An alternate ferry service, the **Catalina Flyer** (Balboa Pavilion, 400 Main St., Newport Beach, 800/831-7744, www.catalinainfo.com, round-trip adults $69, seniors $64, ages 3-12 $52, under age 3 $5, parking $15-25) offers one trip out and one trip back each day. The Flyer operates primarily March-November.

Air

You can also get to Catalina by air. There is a helicopter pad just northwest of Avalon harbor. **Island Express Helicopter Service** (1175 Queens Hwy. S., Long Beach, 800/228-2566, www.islandexpress.com, daily 8:30am-sunset, round-trip $211 pp) can fly you from Long Beach or San Pedro to Catalina in about 15 minutes. You can get a cab into town from the helipad. Island Express also offers aerial tours of the island and various travel packages. Or if you prefer to fly your own small plane to

Catalina, the **Airport in the Sky** (310/510-2495, www.catalina.com, mid-Apr.-mid-Oct. 8am-7pm, mid-Oct.-mid-Apr. 8am-4:30pm) offers general aviators a 3,250-foot runway, $10 parking, and a $25 landing fee—there is no gas, though, so fuel up for a round trip before you head out. The Catalina Island Conservancy's **Wildlands Express/Airport Shuttle** (310/510-0143, adults $26, ages 5-11 $21, under age 5 free) is one way to make it the 10 miles or so from the airport to Avalon and back again. Reservations are required, so call ahead.

Car

On Catalina, cars just aren't the fashionable way to get around. Even the locals tend to eschew full cars since they aren't practical in the tiny town of Avalon. Instead, locals and visitors in the know prefer to drive golf carts. Walk from the ferry dock down toward town, and you'll see any number of rental services, complete with herds of carts out and ready for use. The cost runs $40-60 per hour for a 4-6 passenger cart with a $40-60 deposit. A couple of easy-to-find companies include **Island Rentals** (125 Pebbly Beach Rd., 310/510-1456) underneath the Holly Hill House near the ferry dock and **Cartopia** (615 Crescent Ave., 310/510-2493).

You can also grab a taxi if you need to get somewhere in a hurry, especially with your luggage. Taxis hover near the ferry dock when the ferries are due in each day, and it's customary to share your ride with as many people as can fit into the car (which is often a minivan). To get a cab back to the ferry or the helipad when it's time to leave, call **Catalina Transportation Services** (310/510-0025, www.catalinatransportationservices.com, rates vary) for a taxi, shuttle, charter, or trolley. It takes only about 10 minutes for a taxi to get to just about anywhere in town.

Bus

Public transit on Catalina includes the **Safari Bus** (310/510-2800, adults $10-32, children $10-26, depending on destination), which runs from Avalon to Two Harbors each day. The bus stops at the southeast corner of Island Plaza in Avalon. You can buy tickets at Visitors Services and the Discovery Tours booth on the Pleasure Pier. Alternately, the **Avalon Trolley** (310/510-0025 or 310/510-0342, mid-June-mid-Sept. daily, mid-Sept.-mid-June Sat.-Sun., holidays, and cruise ship days, $2/one way, $7/day pass) runs in and around Avalon, hitting most of the major sightseeing and outdoor adventuring spots near town. With two lines that converge inland, you can get where you need to go for a reasonable fare without having to hoof it. The trolley runs approximately every 30-40 minutes, with the entire route taking about an hour.

LOS ANGELES

Orange County Coast

The Orange County coast begins at Huntington Beach and stretches south across a collection of sunny scenic beaches until ending at San Juan Capistrano. Along the way, Newport Beach, Huntington Beach, Laguna Beach, and Dana Point provide surf, sun, and sand galore. These resort-oriented towns offer great vacationing potential to all comers.

Surfers from around the world are familiar with coastal Orange County. Surfwear companies including Quiksilver, Volcom, and Hurley have their headquarters here, while the editorial offices of *Surfer Magazine* and *Surfing Magazine* are based in the county. If you've ever seen a surf mag or surf movie, you've seen surfers ripping Orange County surf breaks like Salt Creek and Trestles.

HUNTINGTON BEACH

The main reason to come to the west edge of Orange County is to hit the beach. The good news is that the coast of the O.C. is rife with wide, flat, sandy beaches. The bad news is that the beaches still get crowded in the summer. If you want a prime spot, come early in the morning and try to avoid having to park a car if you possibly can.

Beaches

Huntington City Beach (Pacific Coast Hwy. from Beach Blvd. to Seapoint St., beach headquarters 103 Pacific Coast Hwy., 714/536-5281, www.huntingtonbeachca.gov, beach daily 5am-10pm, office Mon.-Fri. 8am-5pm) runs the length of the south end of town, petering out toward the oil industry facilities at the north end. This famous beach hosts major sporting events such as the X Games and the U.S. Open of Surfing. But even the average beachgoer can enjoy all sorts of activities on a daily basis, since Huntington City Beach includes a cement walkway for biking, in-line skating, jogging, and walking. On the sand, get up a game of Frisbee or take advantage of the beach volleyball courts. Out in the water,

catch a wave on either side of the pier or make use of prevailing winds for a thrilling kite-surfing run. Nonriders can boogie board, bodysurf, and skim board closer to the shore. Anglers and lovers prefer the Huntington Beach Pier, which leads out over the water. While dogs aren't allowed on the main portion of Huntington City Beach, the beach offers a dog-friendly section at the north end where dogs can be let off-leash, and you'll even see the occasional surfer riding tandem with a four-legged friend.

This beach offers plenty of services and amenities. In high season, lifeguards keep watch over surfers and swimmers. A number of concession stands make their homes along Huntington City Beach, so you can buy drinks and snacks or rent a wetsuit and surfboard. Buildings with restrooms and outdoor showers also rise from the sand at regular intervals, though lines do form during the most crowded summer weekends and holidays.

Accommodations

You can have your beachfront room at the **Sun 'N Sands Motel** (1102 Pacific Coast Hwy., 714/536-2543, www.sunnsands.com, $130-190). At this tiny place (17 guest rooms) you can expect standard motel-room decor in your king or double-queen guest room, plus an adequate private bath, a TV with movie channels, and Wi-Fi access. But the main attraction lies across the treacherous Pacific Coast Highway: long, sweet Huntington Beach. *Be careful* crossing the highway to get to the sand. Find a traffic light and a crosswalk rather than risking life and limb for the minor convenience of jaywalking.

For something more upscale, book a room at the new **Shorebreak Hotel** (500 Pacific Coast Hwy., 714/861-4470, www.shorebreak-hotel.com, $314-860). Some rooms have private balconies that look out over the beach and pier, while everyone can enjoy the hotel's courtyard with fire pits, its onsite restaurant, and fitness center.

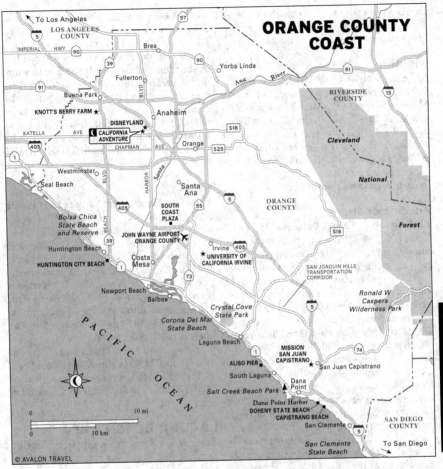

© AVALON TRAVEL

Food

For a quick bite to eat, stop off at the **Bodhi Tree Vegetarian Cafe** (501 Main St., Suite E, 714/969-9500, www.bodhitreehb.com, Wed.-Mon. 11am-10pm, $8-16) for vegetarian soups, salads, and sandwiches.

Sugar Shack Café (213 Main St., 714/536-0355, www.hbsugarshack.com, Thurs.-Tues. 5am-4pm, Wed. 5am-8pm, $10) is a great place for breakfast, serving breakfast burritos and omelets.

NEWPORT BEACH
Beaches

Most of the activity in **Newport Beach** (1200 Newport Center Dr., Suite 120 800/942-6278, www.visitnewportbeach.com) centers around Newport Pier (McFadden Pl.) and Main Street on the Balboa Peninsula. Some folks like to hark back to the old days of individual beach houses and long, lazy summer vacations.

Newport Beach's **The Wedge** (east end of Balboa Peninsula) is the world's most famous bodysurfing spot. On south swells, the wave here jacks up off the adjacent rock jetty and creates monsters up to 30 feet high that break almost right on the beach. Beginners beware, but anyone can spectate from the beach.

Nightlife

A legendary Newport Beach area dive bar, the **Goat Hill Tavern** (1830 Newport Blvd., Costa Mesa, 949/548-8428, Mon.-Fri. noon-2am, Sat.-Sun. 11am-2am) is a beer shack with an impressive 141 beers on tap. The beers are all available as pitchers that you can drink under broken bikes, license plates, and photos hanging off the bar's walls and ceiling. There is an "outside patio" available for smokers.

Accommodations

The **Crystal Cove Beach Cottages** (35 Crystal Cove, 800/444-7275, www.crystalcovebeach-cottages.org, dorm $33-98, cabins $125-191) can help recreate the feeling of another time. Right out on the sands of historic Crystal Cove south of downtown Newport Beach, this collection of cabins offer a delightful and serene beach vacation experience to all who stay here. Ten or so of the cabins are individual rentals where you get the whole house to yourself. The other 10 or so "dorm cottages" offer by-the-room accommodations (linens included, room doors lock) that give even solo budget travelers the opportunity to experience life on a Southern California beach. Another four cottages were restored with disabled guests in mind. Maid service is minimal, with towels changed every four days and trash taken out daily. None of the cottages have TVs or any type of digital entertainment. And all the cottages include a common refrigerator and microwave, but no full kitchen, so you'll need to make plans to eat out—perhaps at the adjacent **Beachcomber Cafe** (15 Crystal Cove, 949/376-6900, www.thebeachcombercafe.com, daily 7am-9:30pm), where items like a breakfast order of filet mignon chilaquiles or a dinner seafood pot pie are served.

The **Island Hotel Newport Beach** (690 Newport Center Dr., 866/554-4620, www.the-islandhotel.com, $200-360) offers perhaps the ultimate O.C. experience. It's a luxury high-rise hotel situated in a giant shopping mall within a few minutes' drive of the beach. No, really. On the bright side, the tropical-themed guest rooms really do have both luxury and comfort in abundance. Expect cushy beds with white linens, attractive private baths, big TVs, views over the mall (and if you're lucky, out to the ocean beyond the city), and all the best amenities. One of the best of these goodies rests within the room service menu; it's called the "Grab and Go Menu" and it's a selection of gourmet box lunches.

Food

The Island Hotel's **Palm Terrace Restaurant** (690 Newport Center Dr., 866/554-4619, www.theislandhotel.com, Mon.-Fri. 6:30am-2pm and 6pm-10pm, Sat.-Sun. 7am-2pm and 6pm-10pm, $10-35) offers stylish small bites and sophisticated entrées in a picturesque setting. For something French, colorful **Pescadou Bistro** (3325 Newport Blvd., 949/675-6990, www.pescadoubistro.com, Tues.-Sun. 5:30pm-close, $20-35) will fit the bill. Meanwhile, **Eat Chow** (211 62nd St., 949/423-7080, www.eatchownow.com, Mon.-Thurs. 8am-9pm, Fri. 8am-10pm, Sat. 7am-10pm, Sun. 7am-9pm, $9-18) is a local's favorite with items that include breakfast carnitas tacos and a shredded redeye burrito.

LAGUNA BEACH AREA

The coastline moving south from Laguna Beach through San Clemente has some of the nicest sand in the county. You'll find more than a dozen separate beaches here, though many connect to one another—you just have to choose your favorite. The area has also become known for its art galleries, upscale dining, and the mission at San Juan Capistrano, which now attracts human visitors as well as swallows.

Mission San Juan Capistrano

One of the most famous and beloved of all the California missions is **Mission San Juan Capistrano** (26801 Oretga Hwy., 949/234-1300, www.missionsjc.com, daily 8:30am-5pm, adults $9, seniors $8, ages 4-11 $6, under age 3 free). The lovely little town of San Juan Capistrano hosts flocks of swallows, which return every year at about the same time in the spring to fanfare and celebration by the whole town. These celebrations began during the mission's heyday in the 18th century, and may have been started by Native Americans centuries before that. Swallows are extremely loyal to their nesting grounds.

Today, thanks in part to the famous birds, this mission has a beautiful new Catholic church on-site, extensive gardens and land, and an audio tour of the museum, which was created from the old mission church and buildings. In late fall and early spring, monarch butterflies flutter about in the flower gardens and out by the fountain in the courtyard. Inside the original church, artifacts from the early time of the mission tell the story of its rise and fall. This was the only mission church where Father Junípero Serra, founder of the chain of missions in California, presided over Sunday services. The graveyard outside continues that narrative, as do the bells and other buildings of the compound. If you love stories of times past, you could spend hours wandering Mission San Juan Capistrano, with or without the audio tour. The complex includes adequate restrooms for visitors, plus plenty of garden and courtyard benches for rest, relaxation, and quiet meditation and reflection.

Regrettably, when you exit the mission into the charming town of San Juan Capistrano and stroll back to look at the historic buildings, you'll be standing next to a Starbucks. But if you turn the corner, you'll find yourself on the town's main street, which positively drips Spanish colonial history. Each old adobe building boasts a brass plaque describing its history and use over the years. In names and decor, the swallow is a major theme in the town, which nestles in a tiny valley only minutes from the sea.

Beaches

In Laguna, **Heisler Park** and **Main Beach Park** (Pacific Coast Hwy., www.lagunabeachinfo. com) offer protected waterways, with tide pools and plenty of water-based playground equipment. The two parks are connected, so you can walk from one to the other. Both display works of local art in the form of benches and sculptures. Hang out on a bench, pick a spot on the sand to lounge about, or take a swim in the cool Pacific. If you're into scuba diving, you can dive several reefs right off the beach. You'll find all the facilities and amenities you need at Heisler and Main Beach Parks, including picnic tables, lawns, and restrooms. Use the charcoal grills provided rather than bringing your own. You can park on the street if you find a spot, but be aware that the meters get checked all the time, so feed them well.

At the southern tip of the O.C., Dana Point has a harbor (34551 Puerto Pl., 949/923-2280, www.ocparks.com) that has become a recreation marina that draws visitors and locals from all around. It also has several beaches nearby. One of the prettiest is **Capistrano Beach** (35005 Beach Rd., 949/923-2280 or 949/923-2283, www.ocparks.com, daily 6am-10pm, parking $1-2 per hour). You can relax on the soft sand or paddle out and catch a wave. Paths make biking, in-line skating, and walking popular pastimes, while others prefer a rousing game of volleyball out on the sand. You'll find a metered parking lot adjacent to the beach, plus showers and restrooms available.

Also in Dana Point, **Doheny State Beach** (25300 Dana Point Harbor Dr., 949/496-6172, www.parks.ca.gov, daily 6am-10pm, $15) is popular with surfers and anglers. The northern end of Doheny has a lawn along with volleyballs courts, while the southern side has a popular campground with 121 campsites.

Another fine area beach is **Salt Creek Beach** (33333 S. Pacific Coast Hwy., 949/923-2280, www.ocparks.com), a renowned surf break and great place to spend a day in the sun. There's a grassy area above the beach in case you don't want to get sandy.

Surfing and Stand Up Paddleboarding

Salt Creek Beach (33333 S. Pacific Coast Hwy., 949/923-2280, www.ocparks.com) is known for its point break that produces peeling lefts and its feisty shore break.

Though the construction of the Dana Point Harbor in 1966 destroyed one of Southern California's most famous surf spots, it has created a placid area ideal for stand up paddleboarding (SUP). To experience the phenomenon firsthand, rent an SUP or purchase one from the **Paddle Surf Warehouse** (342000 Pacific Coast Hwy., 949/488-8041, www.paddlesurfwarehouse.com, Wed.-Sun. 9:30am-5:30pm, SUP rental half day $40, SUP rental two days $120).

One of California's most revered surf spots is situated in San Clemente, just south of Dana Point. It is called **Trestles,** and it is a series of world-class breaks that includes Uppers and Lowers. On any given day, Trestles is home to some of Southern California's finest surfers, who rip the waves apart. The breaks are also where an annual pro surf contest is held every year. Trestles is a 20-minute walk from the San Onofre State Beach parking lot under Highway 5 and over a train track.

Accommodations

For travelers looking to escape the endless crowds of the Newport-Huntington Beach scene, options beckon from farther south on the O.C. coast. The **Blue Lantern Inn** (34343 Street of the Blue Lantern, Dana Point, 800/950-1236, www.bluelanterninn.com, $235-520) crowns the bluffs over the Dana Point Harbor. This attractive contemporary inn offers beachfront elegance, from the exterior to the downstairs restaurant to the guest rooms. Each of the 29 guest rooms boasts soothing colors, charming appointments, and lush amenities, including a spa tub in every bath, gas fireplaces, and honest-to-goodness free drinks in the mini fridge. Seventeen of the rooms feature patios or balconies with impressive views of the harbor and the Pacific. The inn also offers complimentary bike usage, a hot breakfast, and an afternoon wine and appetizers spread.

Food

In San Clemente, **(South of Nick's** (110 N. El Camino Real, San Clemente, 949/481-4545,

view of Dana Point Harbor from the Blue Lantern Inn

© STUART THORNTON

http://thenickco.com, daily from 11am, $10-38) offers a menu with an upscale Mexican twist. The seafood and meat entrées come with creative sauces like a tequila Serrano cream and sweet chipotle. The fresh-made guacamole and chips may be the best you'll ever have. The bar keeps up with the kitchen's creativity by serving up regular margaritas as well as coconut and cucumber versions. Big brother restaurant **Nick's Laguna Beach** (440 South Coast Highway, 949/376-8595, www.thenickco.com, Mon.-Thurs. 11am-11pm, Fri. 11pm-midnight, Sat. 7:30am-midnight, Sun. 7:30am-11pm, $12-29) serves creative takes on American comfort food, including a fried deviled eggs appetizer, as well as standards like a burgers, boneless buttermilk fried chicken.

Also in Laguna Beach, **Eva's Caribbean Kitchen** (31732 South Coast Highway, 949/499-6311, www.evascaribbeankitchen.com, Tues.-Sun. 5pm-close, $21-36) serves up classic island cuisine from conch fritter appetizers to jerk chicken entrées. The impressive seven-page rum list is worthwhile reading.

At **Sapphire Laguna** (1200 South Coast Highway, Laguna Beach, 949/715-9888, www.sapphirellc.com, Mon.-Thurs. 11am-10:30pm, Fri. 11am-11pm, Sat. 10am-11pm, Sun. 10am-10:30pm, $24-37), chef Azmin Ghahreman knows no international boundaries. His international seasonal cuisine might include a Greek octopus salad, Morrocan couscous, a half jidori chicken or Hawaiian-style steamed mahimahi.

INFORMATION AND SERVICES

Need assistance on arriving on the O.C. coast? A good place to get it is the **Huntington Beach Marketing and Visitors Bureau** (301 Main St., Suite 208, 714/969-3492 or 800/729-6232, www.surfcityusa.com, Mon.-Fri. 9am-5pm), which also has a visitor information kiosk (Pacific Coast Hwy. and Main St., times vary according to season).

The major newspaper on the O.C. coast is the Orange County edition of the *Los Angeles Times,* which you can pick up at any newsstand.

Each town on the coast has at least one **post office,** including those in Huntington Beach (6671 Warner Ave., 800/275-8777) and in Newport Beach on the inland tip of the bay (1133 Camelback St., 949/640-4663), or down by the ocean (204 Main St., 949/675-1805).

If you need medical care while you're visiting the beach, **Hoag Hospital** (1 Hoag Dr., Newport Beach, 949/764-4624, www.hoaghospital.org) can probably fix whatever's broken.

GETTING THERE

John Wayne Airport (SNA, 18601 Airport Way, Santa Ana, 949/252-5200, www.ocair.com) is the closest airport to the main beaches of the Orange County coast. It's much easier to fly into and out of John Wayne than LAX, though it can be more expensive. John Wayne's terminal has plenty of rental car agencies.

The Orange County Transportation Authority (OCTA, 550 S. Main St., Orange, 714/560-6282, www.octa.net, $1.50 fare, $4 day pass) runs buses along the O.C. coast. The appropriately numbered Route 1 bus runs right along the Pacific Coast Highway (Hwy. 1) from Long Beach down to San Clemente and back. Other routes can get you to and from inland O.C. destinations, including Anaheim. Regular bus fares are payable in cash on the bus with exact change. You can also buy a day pass from the bus driver.

The one true highway on the O.C. coast is the Pacific Coast Highway, often called "the PCH" for short and officially designated Highway 1. You can get to the PCH from I-405 near Seal Beach, or catch I-710 to Long Beach and then drive south from there. From Disneyland, take I-5 to Highway 55, which takes you into Newport Beach. If you stay on I-5 going south, you'll eventually find yourself in San Juan Capistrano.

Parking along the beaches of the O.C. on a sunny summer day has been compared to one of Dante's circles of hell. You're far better off staying near the beach and walking out to your perfect spot in the sand. Other options include public transit and pay parking.

SAN DIEGO

San Diego is the ideal destination for anyone whose idea of the perfect California vacation is a day (or a week, or a month) lying on a white sand beach, sipping cocktails and looking out over the Pacific Ocean. Resort hotels and restaurants perch along the seaside, beckoning visitors to what is often thought to be the friendliest big city in California.

Even though San Diego's physical area seems small compared to other parts of California, it can't be beat for density of things to see. From a world-famous zoo to dozens of museums to the thick layer of military and mission history, San Diego offers education, enlightenment, and fun to visitors with all different interests.

Animal lovers flock to the San Diego Zoo and Sea World, while water spirits dive into the Pacific Ocean to catch a wave or examine a variety of sea life in their natural habitat. Travelers who want a little more of the trappings of city life will enjoy the bar and club scene, as well as a thriving theater community.

Across the bay, the long, blue Coronado Bridge connects San Diegans to Coronado, an island-like enclave that beckons beach bums and film aficionados alike to the grandly historic (and reputedly haunted) Hotel del Coronado, where the Marilyn Monroe film *Some Like It Hot* was filmed.

North of San Diego proper, the towns of La Jolla, Del Mar, Encinitas, and Oceanside offer a more relaxed pace for exploring. Snorkel the azure water of La Jolla Cove or vie for a piece of that pristine sand with the beach crowd. Splurge some of that vacation cash on a horse race at the Del Mar Racetrack, or get an

HIGHLIGHTS

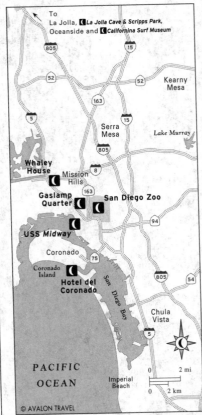

To La Jolla, **(** La Jolla Cave & Scripps Park, Oceanside and **(** Californina Surf Museum

Kearny Mesa

Serra Mesa

Lake Murray

Whaley House

Mission Hills

Gaslamp Quarter **(**

San Diego Zoo

USS *Midway*

Coronado

Coronado Island

Hotel del Coronado

San Diego Bay

Chula Vista

PACIFIC OCEAN

Imperial Beach

0   2 mi

0   2 km

© AVALON TRAVEL

LOOK FOR **(** TO FIND RECOMMENDED SIGHTS, ACTIVITIES, DINING, AND LODGING.

(Gaslamp Quarter: This former red light district is now the hub of San Diego's downtown, filled with restaurants, bars, and shops (page 574).

(USS *Midway*: This aircraft carrier, once the largest ship in the world, served during the Cold War, Vietnam, and Desert Storm. Docents, many of them veterans, vividly recall what life was like onboard (page 577).

(San Diego Zoo: The most popular tourist attraction in Balboa Park is home to all sorts of animals, including giant pandas (page 578).

(Whaley House: Skeptics doubt this 1857 home is really haunted. It may not be filled with ghosts, but it's definitely full of history (page 581).

(Hotel del Coronado: You don't have to stay at the luxurious Hotel del Coronado to enjoy this San Diego landmark. The Del has a historical museum, a shopping center, a range of restaurants, and a relaxing beach right out front (page 584).

(La Jolla Cove and Scripps Park: Snorkel or scuba dive offshore, kayak through sea caves, or just relax on the sand at this scenic spot (page 586).

(California Surf Museum: Up in North County, this museum offers homage to the pioneers of the coastal sport with exhibits and regularly occurring summer events (page 588).

up-close and personal interaction with the exotic animals at the Wild Animal Park.

PLANNING YOUR TIME

Compared to other parts of California, San Diego's major attractions sit relatively close together, and it's easy to get from one place to another in a reasonable amount of time. San Diego County has arguably the best beaches in the state. If your travel goals are focused on sand and surf, consider staying in Mission Bay or Point Loma, or farther afield in the North County coastal area. On the other hand, if you're in town to see the zoo or take in some museums, you'll be spending time in Balboa Park, which abuts the Old Town and

SAN DIEGO

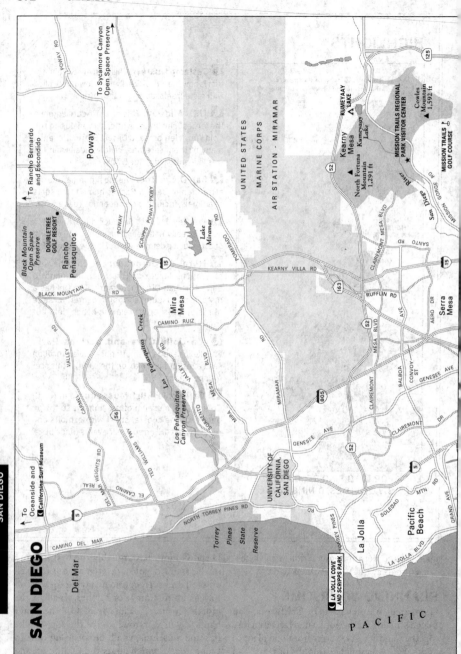

SAN DIEGO

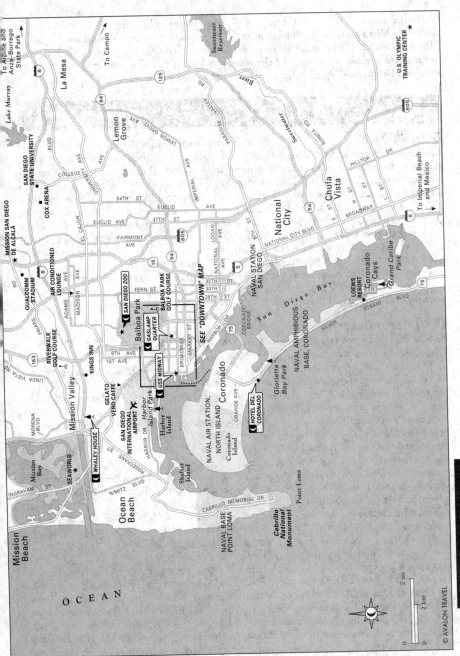

© AVALON TRAVEL

downtown areas. If you're starting a tour of California Missions, head for Old Town first. Military history and Navy buffs will be content to spend their whole trip within the city limits of San Diego, dividing their time between the Harbor and Point Loma. If you've got an extra couple of hours and you haven't been out there yet, take the bridge over to Coronado to gawk at the ridiculous exuberance of the Hotel del Coronado.

Sights

DOWNTOWN

The downtown area of San Diego isn't as big and intimidating as its cousins in San Francisco and Los Angeles. Instead, you'll find a smaller, homier area that feels safe to walk in—even if you're a lone woman after dark. The Gaslamp Quarter highlights downtown, offering hundreds of restaurants, dozens of bars and clubs, and a rich history. The area near the airport has a range of hotels and skirts the harbor of San Diego Bay with its museums and ships and ship-museums. The rest of downtown stretches out toward Old Town and Balboa Park.

◖ Gaslamp Quarter

Perhaps the best known area of downtown San Diego, the **Gaslamp Quarter** (Fourth, Fifth, and Sixth Sts. and Broadway, www.gaslamp. org) exudes atmosphere, whether you visit during the day or night. Of course, the Gaslamp Quarter has exuded atmosphere since its earliest inception in the 19th century. The Fifth Street Pier led sailors right to the area, where saloons and brothels flourished. Ida Bailey—a famous lady of the evening—moved in and cemented the area (then called Stingaree) as a red-light district. Famous Wild West lawman Wyatt Earp ran three gambling halls in the region. After decades of thriving debauchery, a police raid in 1912 heralded the end of the Gaslamp Quarter's popularity. Throughout the first two-thirds of the 1900s, the area decayed, becoming a low-rent district filled with porn theaters and liquor stores. In the mid-1970s, the Gaslamp Quarter Association came to be, and the renewal of this downtown area began.

Today, the Gaslamp Quarter bustles with foot traffic, both locals and tourists. People crowd into the popular and sometimes quirky restaurants, dance like mad at the many bars and clubs, and spend their cash in the shops and boutiques. (But only tourists insist on taking photos under the Gaslamp Quarter sign.) Ghosts reputedly haunt several buildings here; check into a ghost tour or explore on your own to try to see or feel a spook. In general, the Gaslamp Quarter is quite safe, though you will see a scattering of homeless people wandering and sometimes sleeping on the sidewalks. In the evenings, the gas lamp-shaped streetlights illuminate the sidewalks and the historic architecture of some of the structures, especially along Fifth Street.

Maritime Museum of San Diego

Once you're on the downtown waterfront, it's easy to spot the **Maritime Museum of San Diego** (1492 N. Harbor Dr., 619/234-9153, www.sdmaritime.org, daily 9am-8pm, adults $15, seniors, students and military $12, children $8): Just look for the tall masts with sails. This museum features a collection of floating historic ships, many of which still sail on a regular basis. The gem of the collection, the famous *Star of India* has been plying the high seas for almost 150 years. Other genuine historic ships include the *Medea,* the *Berkeley,* and a Soviet submarine. Another ship that makes regular passenger cruises is the *Californian*—the state's Official Tall Ship. (Yes, California has such a thing!)

Come any day to tour the various ships at dock—onboard you'll find a wealth of exhibits depicting the maritime history of San Diego, war at sea in centuries past, the story of the ship you're on, and more. This museum makes a perfect outing for anyone who loves naval history, sailing, ships in general, or even just being

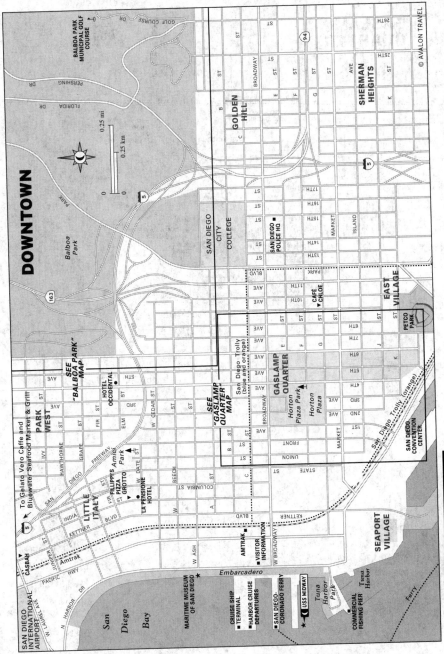

DOWNTOWN

SAN DIEGO

0 0.25 mi
0 0.25 km

BALBOA PARK MUNICIPAL GOLF COURSE

GOLF COURSE DR
PERSHING DR
FLORIDA DR

Balboa Park

PARK

SEE "BALBOA PARK" MAP

To Gelato Vero Caffe and Bluewater Seafood Market & Grill

CASBAH

SAN DIEGO INTERNATIONAL AIRPORT

N HARBOR DR
W LAUREL AVE
PACIFIC HWY
Amtrak

LITTLE ITALY

FILIPPI'S PIZZA GROTTO
LA PENSIONE HOTEL

PARK WEST

HOTEL OCCIDENTAL

GOLDEN HILL

SAN DIEGO CITY COLLEGE

SAN DIEGO POLICE HQ

SHERMAN HEIGHTS

CAFÉ CHLOE

EAST VILLAGE

PETCO PARK

GASLAMP QUARTER

SEE "GASLAMP QUARTER" MAP

San Diego Trolly (blue and orange)

Horton Plaza Park
Horton Plaza

San Diego Trolly (orange)

SAN DIEGO CONVENTION CENTER

San Diego Bay

MARITIME MUSEUM OF SAN DIEGO

Embarcadero

CRUISE SHIP TERMINAL
HARBOR CRUISE DEPARTURES
SAN DIEGO-CORONADO FERRY

USS MIDWAY

VISITOR INFORMATION
AMTRAK

SEAPORT VILLAGE

Tuna Harbor Park
Tuna Harbor

COMMERCIAL FISHING PIER

Ferry

© AVALON TRAVEL

SAN DIEGO

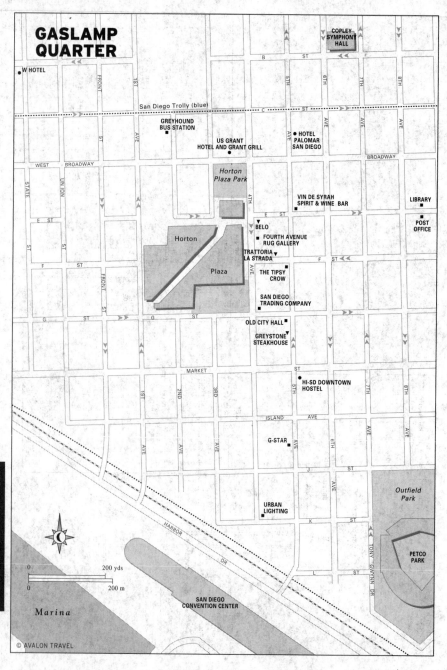

GASLAMP QUARTER

W HOTEL

San Diego Trolly (blue)

GREYHOUND
BUS STATION

US GRANT
HOTEL AND GRANT GRILL

HOTEL
PALOMAR
SAN DIEGO

COPLEY
SYMPHONY
HALL

*Horton
Plaza Park*

VIN DE SYRAH
SPIRIT & WINE BAR

LIBRARY

POST
OFFICE

BELO

FOURTH AVENUE
RUG GALLERY

TRATTORIA
LA STRADA

Horton

Plaza

THE TIPSY
CROW

SAN DIEGO
TRADING COMPANY

OLD CITY HALL

GREYSTONE
STEAKHOUSE

MARKET

HI-SD DOWNTOWN
HOSTEL

ISLAND

G-STAR

*Outfield
Park*

URBAN
LIGHTING

PETCO
PARK

0   200 yds
0   200 m

Marina

SAN DIEGO
CONVENTION CENTER

© AVALON TRAVEL

SAN DIEGO

© STUART THORNTON

a fighter plane on the deck of the USS *Midway*

out on the water. The museum recommends that you make reservations in advance for their historic ship cruises.

◖ USS *Midway*

Once the largest ship in the world, the **USS Midway** (910 N. Harbor Dr., 619/544-9600, www.midway.org, daily 10am-4pm, adults $18, seniors and students $15, children and retired military $10) is now docked along San Diego's Navy Pier. This carrier, which dates to the period just after World War II, served as an active part of the U.S. Navy through Desert Storm in 1991. Onboard, you'll get to roam throughout the ship, checking out everything from the enlisted mess to the dreaded brig as you climb narrow metal steps from deck to deck. Up top, the flight deck includes military planes and helicopters including the F-14 Tomcat, the co-star of the 1980s movie *Top Gun*. One of the best parts of a trip to the *Midway* is the opportunity to talk to the docents, many of whom are veterans who served aboard the ship during the Cold War, Vietnam, or Desert Storm. Consider

taking one of the docent-guided tours if you're interested in the realities of life aboard an aircraft carrier. The self-guided audio tour also makes a good introduction to the ship, after which you can check out the flight simulators, linger near the exciting aircraft, or head to the café and gift shop at the stern. Parts of the ship are wheelchair accessible and there are restrooms onboard.

BALBOA PARK AND HILLCREST

The Balboa Park you see today was created for the 1915 Panama-California World Exposition. The Spanish Revival architecture is set amid immense, almost tropical, greenery and welcomes visitors with a wealth of museums, halls, exhibitions, gardens, and open spaces. Stop at the **Balboa Park Visitors Center** (1549 El Prado, 619/239-0512, www.balboapark.org, daily 9:30am-4:30pm) for a park map and to plan your visit—there won't be time to see it all!

Hillcrest, immediately northwest of the park, was once a gentrified residential area. Today, a

SAN DIEGO

SAN DIEGO WEEKEND

While you might not see everything in San Diego within a couple of days, you can see some of the city's best sights and even have a little time to kick back at the beach.

DAY 1

Fortify yourself for a full day of sightseeing at the Hillcrest neighborhood's **Hash House A Go Go** (page 618), where the portions are enormous and tasty. Then head out into nearby **Balboa Park** (page 577), a sprawling urban park with everything from an art museum to a cactus garden. Be sure to visit the world famous **San Diego Zoo** (page 578), home to lots of exotic animals including giant pandas.

From Balboa Park, drive out to Point Loma. This peninsula has the **Cabrillo National Monument** (page 583), which marks where the Spanish explorer first landed on the West Coast, and the **Old Point Loma Lighthouse** (page 584), one of the oldest lighthouses in the state.

For sunset, drive up to the top of the 822-foot-high **Mount Soledad** (page 585), which offers 360 degree views of the city. While there, take in the sobering veteran's memorial.

Treat yourself to dinner at the elegant **Grant Grill** (page 616) in the elegant **US Grant Hotel** (page 607). If you still have energy, head out into the surrounding **Gaslamp Quarter** (page 574) for a post dinner cocktail. If you are adventurous, try to find your way into the **Vin de Syrah Spirit & Wine Parlor** (page 594).

DAY 2

Start the morning right with a tasty French American breakfast in downtown's **Café Chloe** (page 617). Take a few minutes to sip your coffee and read some of the restaurant's magazines or watch people pass by on the sidewalk heading to work.

Get in you car and head out to **La Jolla Cove** (page 586). Snorkel in the offshore marine reserve and then soak up some of Southern California's famous sun on the cove's small, scenic beach.

Then dry out by going out to the island-like Coronado for a sunset cocktail at the historic **Hotel del Coronado** (page 584). When hunger strikes, beeline to the **Blue Water Seafood Market & Grill** (page 617) located north of downtown for fish tacos. End the evening with a trip to Old Town for a night tour of the **Whaley House** (page 581), considered to be the most haunted house in America.

---

touch of shabbiness has met with hip urban renewal to create a mixed neighborhood that still shelters many older residents while providing entertainment and energy to a younger crowd. Hillcrest beckons to the San Diego gay community as well, with clubs and bars creating a hip queer nightlife scene.

◖ San Diego Zoo

The jewel of San Diego's vast interconnected wildlife park system, the **San Diego Zoo** (2920 Zoo Dr., 619/231-1515, www.sandiegozoo.org, summer daily 9am-9pm, rest of the year daily 9am-5pm, adults $42, children $32) lives up to its reputation and then some. The 100-acre zoo actually doubles as the state's largest botanical garden. The zoo grows lovely plants from around the globe that serve as shelter, hiding places, and food for the hundreds of exotic animals that inhabit state-of-the-art enclosures. You'll see perennial zoo favorites including elephants, lions, polar bears, and you'll also meet a host of other famous and exotic species, such as meerkats, one-foot-tall deer, pythons, and parrots. For the comfort of the human visitors, ample restrooms, benches, concessions, and gift shops scatter through the zoo.

To get the best zoo experience possible, stroll its meandering paved walkways, stopping whenever and wherever you feel a need to watch the birds and beasts as they sleep, eat, and play. Some of the paths can be steep—if you're visiting with kids or folks who have trouble walking, keep that in mind when you plan. The map provided by the zoo can help with good walking routes for your party's endurance

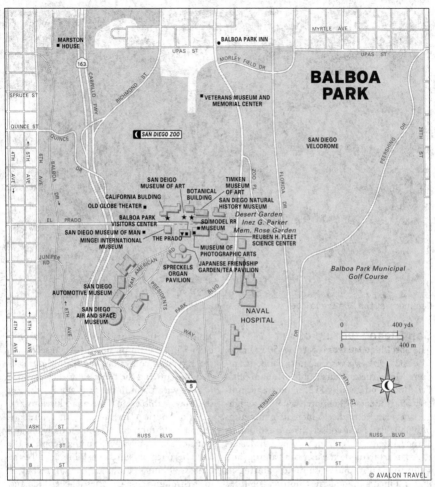

BALBOA PARK

MARSTON HOUSE

BALBOA PARK INN

MYRTLE AVE

UPAS ST

UPAS ST

MORLEY FIELD DR

163

CARRILLO FWY

RICHMOND ST

SPRUCE ST

VETERANS MUSEUM AND MEMORIAL CENTER

QUINCE ST

QUINCE ST

SAN DIEGO ZOO

SAN DIEGO VELODROME

PERSHING DR

28TH ST

4TH AVE

5TH AVE

6TH AVE

BALBOA DR

ZOO PL

TIMKEN MUSEUM OF ART

SAN DEIGO MUSEUM OF ART

FLORIDA DR

BOTANICAL BULDING

SAN DIEGO NATURAL HISTORY MUSEUM

CALIFORNIA BULIDING

OLD GLOBE THEATER

Desert Garden

EL PRADO

BALBOA PARK VISITORS CENTER

SD MODEL RR MUSEUM

Inez G. Parker Mem. Rose Garden

SAN DIEGO MUSEUM OF MAN

MINGEI INTERNATIONAL MUSEUM

THE PRADO

REUBEN H. FLEET SCIENCE CENTER

JUNIPER RD

MUSEUM OF PHOTOGRAPHIC ARTS

Balboa Park Municipal Golf Course

SPRECKELS ORGAN PAVILION

JAPANESE FRIENDSHIP GARDEN/TEA PAVILION

SAN AMERICAN RD

PRESIDENTS WAY

PARK BLVD

SAN DIEGO AUTOMOTIVE MUSEUM

NAVAL HOSPITAL

SAN DIEGO AIR AND SPACE MUSEUM

4TH AVE

5TH AVE

8TH AVE

PERSHING DR

28TH ST

0   400 yds

0   400 m

5

ASH ST

A ST

RUSS BLVD

RUSS BLVD

A ST

B ST

B ST

© AVALON TRAVEL

SAN DIEGO

levels. If you can't do it all, pick the paths that take you to your primary points of interest—be those pandas, birds, or big kitty-cats. For another great way to enhance your experience, pick up one or more of the fliers that describe the park's extensive flora in detail. Plant lovers love playing Spot the Acacia as they enjoy the animals.

If walking the whole zoo just isn't for you, consider one of the bus rides. The Guided Bus Tour takes you to many of the highlights of the zoo, letting dozens of animals show off

for you as you snap photos from the coveted upper deck of the two-story bus. Friendly and knowledgeable docents drive the buses and describe each of the animals and their habitats as you pass. If you just want to get from one section of the zoo to another, jump on an Express Bus. For a special treat, take the Skyfari from the front of the park to the rear, where the polar bears play in their pond. You'll get a lovely view of the whole of Balboa Park out to the sea as you traverse the length of the zoo in less than 10 minutes.

© STUART THORNTON

flamingos at the San Diego Zoo

SAN DIEGO

San Diego Museum of Art

The **San Diego Museum of Art** (1450 El Prado, 619/232-7931, www.sdmart.org, Sun. 10am-5pm, Mon.-Tues., Thurs., and Sat. 10am-5pm, Fri. 10am-9pm, adults $12, seniors and military $9, students $8, children $4.50) is a highlight, even among the 15 incredible museums of Balboa Park. The collections and exhibitions at the Museum of Art range from Old Masters to Asian art to modern American painting and sculpture. From photography to painting in unusual media to modern sculpture, you'll see many media as you stroll through the galleries admiring the art of centuries. For a deeper experience, take one of docent tours that run a few times each day. Check the website for the latest special exhibitions and upcoming fun museum events.

San Diego Museum of Man

Rather than focusing solely on the arts and achievements of humankind, the **San Diego Museum of Man** (1350 El Prado, 619/239-2001, www.museumofman.org, daily 10am-4:30pm, adults $12.50, seniors $10, students $8, children $5) hones in on humans themselves. In the Egyptian collection, you'll find mummified humans and the possessions they planned to take with them to the next world, while in the Maya exhibit you'll see reproductions and relics of South American daily life. The museum also features exhibits on the daily life and times of the Kumeyaay, the native people of the San Diego region. Further exhibits describe the process of human evolution and physiology. A tour through these galleries teaches kids and adults alike about their own history, growth, development, and lifestyles. The museum website highlights special events and traveling exhibitions from skateboarding culture in Native America to instruments of torture.

Palm Canyon

For a peaceful break from the endless educational opportunities of Balboa Park, take a walk through **Palm Canyon** (1549 El Prado, location 34 on the Balboa Park map, daily). The canyon offers visitors an intense look at various varieties of that ubiquitous California icon: the palm tree. With 58 species of palms creating a cool, shady space, the Canyon is a perfect place to slow down and enjoy a break on a hot summer day. The Mexican fan palms at the center of the garden have lived here almost 100 years. The groomed paths connect the canyon to the Old Cactus Garden; the Alcazar Garden also sits adjacent to the palms, and a tram stop nearby makes access a breeze.

Japanese Friendship Garden

Cultural centers form an important element of Balboa Park. The **Japanese Friendship Garden** (2125 Park Blvd., 619/232-2721, www. niwa.org, daily 10am-4pm, adults $4, senior, students, and military $3, children under 6 free) began as a teahouse during the 1915-1916 Exposition, and grew over the years to include many elements of a traditional Japanese formal garden. You can enjoy the tranquility of the Zen garden, koi pond, and wisteria arbor, or take tea and noodle soup at the **Tea Pavilion** (2215 Pan American Way, 619/231-0048). This is the perfect place to enjoy a quiet walk hand-in-hand with your sweetie. For variety, the garden displays temporary exhibitions that mesh with the Japanese cultural traditions exemplified here. Check the website for one-day classes in Japanese arts, usually held on weekends.

Botanical Building

To experience flora indoors, visit the striking **Botanical Building** (1549 El Prado, Fri.-Wed. 10am-4pm, free). Inside the lattice structure are 2,100 plants including ferns and orchids. Of special interest is a carnivorous plant bog with pitcher plants and Venus flytraps and a "touch and smell garden" with fragrant lemon mint and chocolate.

Other Museums and Gardens

Balboa Park is filled with a number of other worthy museums, and meandering paths lead to even more botanical areas and gardens. It's impossible to see everything in one day, but a repeat visit could include the **Air and Space Museum** (2001 Pan American Plaza, 619/234-8291, www.aerospacemuseum.org, adults $17.50, seniors and students $14.50, children $7) for a history through human flight; the **Reuben H. Fleet Science Center** (1875 El Prado, 619/238-1233, www.rhfleet.org, Mon.-Thurs. 9:30am-5pm, Fri. 9:30am-9pm, Sat. 9:30am-8pm, Sun. 9:30am-6pm, $8), where young ones can explore the interactive science exhibits; and the **Natural History Museum** (1788 El Prado, 619/232-3821, www.sdnhm. org, Sun.-Fri. 10am-5pm, Sat. 9am-5pm, adults $17, seniors $15, student, military, and children over 13 $12, children $11), which houses a vast collection of fossils and other artifacts presenting San Diego's geologic history.

OLD TOWN

San Diego is the oldest European-settled "town" in California. The Old Town area encompasses the first Spanish settlements of what would eventually become California, 19th-century homes and businesses, parks, and modern shops and restaurants. Old Town is the perfect place to get started on a historic tour of California, a ghost-hunting visit to San Diego, or a good sightseeing trip.

◖ Whaley House

Billed as the most haunted house in all of the United States, the **Whaley House** (2476 San Diego Ave., 619/297-7511, www.whaleyhouse. org, Sun.-Wed. 10am-5pm, Thurs.-Sat. 10am-9:30pm, summer daily 10am-9:30pm, adults daytime $6, children daytime $4, adults evening $10, children evening $5) was built by Thomas Whaley in 1856. Over the century it was inhabited, many members of the Whaley family lived and died inside the brick-constructed Greek Revival mansion. The house was also leased out as a home, and used as a courthouse, general store, and billiards hall, among other things. Before Whaley built the house on the corner of San Diego Avenue and Harney Street, the spot was used for at least one public hanging on record.

Reportedly, the haunting of the Whaley House began almost as soon as the Whaleys first moved in. Thomas Whaley believed that the specter of a criminal hanged on the land was the source of loud, ominous footfalls that rattled the floorboards of his new home late at night. More recently, visitors have spotted many different ghosts inside the house, which has been featured on the Travel Channel's *America's Most Haunted*. Children and adults have seen male shades, female spirits, and even the vision of a spaniel dog that matches the description of Thomas Whaley's family pet. If you love a good ghost story and long to see the spirits of the Whaley House yourself, consider coming to visit at night, or even calling ahead and booking a private tour (two people minimum) after 10pm.

Even if you don't believe all the ghost stories, the Whaley House Museum contains enough concrete lore pertaining to the house and its various incarnations to entertain history buffs for hours. Self-guided tours are enhanced by the wandering docents, who can answer questions about the artifacts inside the house as well as the house itself. And should you feel an unexpected chill or see an inexplicable shadow as you wander through a room, well, the staff is used to that sort of thing and will be happy to help you out with the experience!

Old Town San Diego

The **Old Town San Diego State Historic Park** (corner of San Diego Ave. and Twigg St., 619/220-5422, www.parks.ca.gov, daily 10am-5pm, free) makes a great place to start exploring the history of California's first town. The visitors center sits in a house first built in 1853 as a family home and set of local offices by attorney James Robinson. Another major home, the McCoy House, was built in 1869, excavated and reconstructed over the years 1995-2000. Move on to the early 19th-century Mexican pueblos, including La Casa de Machado y Stewart; this adobe structure contains many artifacts that would have been part of the daily life of San Diego citizens in 1821-1872. Out and about in the park, you can enjoy period music, pet the burros, and observe the park staff engaging in activities folks might have done 150 years ago.

Wednesdays and Saturdays are living history days, and the park hosts many events over the course of each year. If you're more into the afterlife of the residents of Old San Diego, you can visit the El Campo Santo Cemetery—the oldest cemetery in the city. The park also includes a number of known haunted sites, including the Robinson-Rose House, Casa de Bandini, and La Casa de Estudillo.

Presidio Park

One of the early Mexican settlements in San Diego was a military installation, now **Presidio Park** (2811 Jackson St., 619/692-4918). Inside the park, the **Junípero Serra Museum** (2727 Presidio Dr., 619/232-6203, daily 10am-4pm, adults $6, seniors and students $4, children $3) sits on the spot where Father Junipero Serra and Captain Gaspar de Portola established the Presidio fort. Its collections include housewares, artifacts, and a cannon from the Mexican occupation through the early California period of San Diego through 1929. If you prefer nature with your history, take a stroll along the more than two miles of trails winding through the acres of gardens and wild areas of the park. Palm Canyon features lawns surrounded by stately old palm trees. The Arbor has a more formal garden feel, complete with pillars and flowers. It's hard to believe as you wander the charming parkland that you're on the site of a former military base.

Mission San Diego del Alcala

The first mission erected in California was **Mission San Diego del Alcala** (10818 San Diego Mission Rd., www.missionsandiego.com, daily 9am-4:45pm). It was blessed by Father Junipero Serra in 1769, making it the first Christian church in California. Ironically, it was also the poorest Mission for most of its heyday. Native Americans raided and burned it, the harsh soil resisted cultivation, and eventually the Mexican independence from Spain rendered the church a secular building. Time and renovation came to the Mission, and it was re-established as a sacred space. It still operates as an active Catholic church today; if you visit, please respect the Mission as a house of worship even as you appreciate its significance as a museum. The church you see is actually the fifth church built on this site, erected and fortified against California's infamous earthquakes. One of the bells in the tower is original (dating to 1801). Inside, you'll see evidence of the life of the Franciscan monks who operated the Mission until 1834, and of the native Kumeyaay people who lived here before the Europeans came and whose lives were changed forever by their arrival.

POINT LOMA

Point Loma is at once one of the most beautiful and one of the most important pieces of land in the San Diego region. From the tip of the point, you can see everywhere, from the Cuyamaca Mountains to the land and seas of Mexico, and down into the safe harbor of the San Diego Bay. This fabulous view also meant a perfect place to build a defense for the harbor and the settlements beyond. Accordingly, Point Loma has served more than 200 years as a military installation. From owl limpets to soldiers' graves, there are innumerable unique items to see in the area.

Fort Rosecrans Military Reserve

San Diego has historically maintained an extensive military presence, regardless of whose rule the land fell under. Even today, a large U.S. Navy installation remains here, guarding the Pacific shores. Fort Rosecrans began as a Spanish Presidio that was fortified against imminent British threat in the late 1700s. Then called Fort Guijarro, it lasted as an active Spanish military base only 40 years, after which it began to decay. After the creation of California as a state, the U.S. government refurbished the fort to protect the San Diego harbor once more. It was rechristened Fort Rosencrans, and parts of it are still used to this day for Army Reserve activities.

Today, when you visit the parklands of Cabrillo National Monument, you can see remnants of old buildings belonging to the fort, many used during the two World Wars.

But the highlight of any visit to the fort is the **Fort Rosecrans National Cemetery** (1880 Cabrillo Memorial Dr., 619/553-2084, visitation hours Mon.-Fri. 8am-4:30pm, Sat.-Sun. 9:30am-5pm). In addition to the haunting rows of stark white tombstones marching in dressed line across green lawns, you'll find graves here from combatants who fought wars of the California Republic. Wander the grounds to view graves old and recent, as well as monuments to fallen soldiers from little-known battles long past and to near forgotten tragedies like the 1905 boiler explosion on the USS *Bennington*.

Cabrillo National Monument

Cabrillo National Monument (1800 Cabrillo Memorial Dr., 619/557-5450, www.nps.gov, daily 9am-5pm, $5/vehicle, $3 bike-in, $3/ walk-in) celebrates the initial encounter of San Diego Bay by Spanish Explorer Juan Rodriguez Cabrillo in the mid-16th century. This was the first landing of the Spanish— indeed of any Europeans—on the West Coast of North America. Today, a large statue of Cabrillo stands within the monument lands, overlooking the San Diego Bay. At the visitors center, you can learn more about the history of Cabrillo's life and explorations.

The wildlife and the scenery are other great reasons to visit the national monument. Views from the high places here are second to none. Turning around, you can see the harbor, the San Diego cityscape, the Pacific Ocean, and all the way south to Mexico. Be sure to bring your camera! For a micro-view of San Diego's seas, check the tide tables and head down to the tide pools on the west side of Point Loma. Here you'll find a myriad of sea life waiting for discovery. Just be sure that you and your children look with your eyes, not your fingers—many tide pool creatures can be injured or even killed by a mere touch from a human.

The parkland of Cabrillo offers hiking trails through the southern coastal scrub ecosystem so precious and unique to this part of the state. Enjoy the wildlife and lovely plants, and come in spring for the best profusion of wildflowers.

Old Point Loma Lighthouse

Among the oldest lighthouses in California, the **Old Point Loma Lighthouse** (1800 Cabrillo Memorial Dr., 619/557-5450, daily 9am-5pm) began its watch over the San Diego Bay in 1855. Unfortunately, the light was often dimmed by pernicious fog, and a new lighthouse went into operation in a better location in 1891. Luckily for visitors today, the old lighthouse remained unmolested. Come in to peruse the exhibits, or sign up for a ranger-led tour and talk that goes into detail about the history of the lighthouse. You'll see the restoration of the lighthouse by the National Park Service to its original mid-19th-century glory. Perhaps the most interesting stories you'll hear during your visit are of the lighthouse-keepers and their families. Several descendants of the original keepers have provided family stories to round out the human history of the lighthouse. Old Point Loma Lighthouse is part of the Cabrillo National Monument (and covered in its admission fee), perfectly located for a day out exploring the early history of California's statehood.

CORONADO
◖ Hotel del Coronado

When it opened in 1888, the **Hotel del Coronado** (1500 Orange Ave., 800/468-3533, www.hoteldel.com) was the largest hotel resort in the world. Since then, it has hosted a parade of presidents and movie stars. The Del, as its called by some, has also had its influence on popular culture. It's where author L. Frank Baum wrote some of *The Wonderful Wizard of Oz*, while the Stephen King story *1408*, which later became a film, was partially inspired by a supposed haunting in the hotel. But the Del might be best known as the setting of the 1959 comedy *Some Like It Hot* starring Marilyn Monroe, Tony Curtis, and Jack Lemmon.

Today, even though it's not the largest resort in the world, the Del's stately red shingle-roofed buildings still sprawl over a couple of blocks. Even if you are not staying over at the hotel, it's worth a visit to imagine the glamour of days gone by. You can also wander around the historical buildings, go shopping in its shops, dine in its restaurants, grab a drink in one of its bars, or just sit on the beach out front.

MISSION BAY

Mission Bay offers serene waters untroubled by the sometimes-pounding Pacific surf. It's a perfect place to center your family vacation, take in the natural wonders of Mission Bay Park, or head for the colorful fun of Sea World. The Mission Bay area also has three beach communities that feel far removed from the downtown's tall buildings. While the main attractions here are the wide expanses of beach, these towns are worth a visit for people who love little beach communities. The farthest south of these is **Ocean Beach,** which was flooded with hippies during the 1960s. Centered around Newport Avenue, which is lined with cigar shaped palm trees, Ocean Beach today seems to have retained a bit of its countercultural feel.

On the north side of the San Diego River estuary is **Mission Beach.** The community is still home to Belmont Park, a beachfront amusement park.

Between La Jolla and Mission Beach is **Pacific Beach.** During summer days, the three-mile-long boardwalk and beach are filled with sunbathers, runners, and surfers. On Pacific Beach's Crystal Pier are a hotel and a bait shop.

Mission Bay Park

The acres of **Mission Bay Park** (Mission Blvd., 619/276-8200, www.sandiego.gov) are not a natural wonder. The over 4,000 acres include the largest artificially-made aquatic park in the country. The land and sea of the popular recreation area were once a tidal marsh—the primary outlet of the San Diego River. In the 1940s, the marsh was dredged and the beaches and land formations you see today were created. Among them are 19 miles of charming sandy beach perfect for sunbathing, sandcastle making, beach volleyball, and more—and 14 miles of bike paths. Half of the designated parkland is actually off the shore, in the abundant calm waterways. Swim in one of the eight designated, lifeguard-protected areas throughout the park, or take a deeper dive out into the channel to kite surf or water-ski. In the non-swimming, non-skiing areas, you can string out a line and go fishing. Despite the manmade nature of this park, it has several areas that have become significant wildlife preserves. You can go birding at Perez Cove, Telecote Creek, Fiesta Island, or a number of other spots throughout the park.

SeaWorld San Diego

With a charming mix of rides and sea-life attraction, **SeaWorld San Diego** (500 SeaWorld Dr., 800/257-4268, www.seaworld.com, hours vary, adults $63-73, children $55-65) makes a fun destination for families. SeaWorld is navigable in half a day, even when taking the time to include some rides and shows. Kids love meeting Shamu and his brothers and sisters in the killer whale pool just inside the park entrance. Also in SeaWorld you'll meet sharks, endangered sea turtles, dolphins, and other denizens of the deep. On hot days, the river ride and splash-down roller coaster cool off overheated park visitors. Plenty of food concessions (including a coffee stand) revive weary families, getting them ready for more animal shows and action-packed rides. If you want to have breakfast or dinner with Shamu at the restaurant looking out into the killer whale tank, advance reservations are recommended.

While SeaWorld offers great fun for small children, the laboriously cute decor, rollercoaster-style rides, and trained animal acts can get a bit tiresome for more sophisticated or outdoor-oriented adult travelers. The food in the park also caters to the younger set, and tends to be higher on fat content than quality. Frankly, better adult-oriented wild animal experiences are available in the San Diego area at both the zoo and the Wild Animal Park. But, if you go, buy your tickets online to save some significant money.

Belmont Park

Belmont Park (3146 Mission Blvd., 858/228-9317, www.belmontpark.com), is a Mission Beach amusement park that was initially built in the 1920s. The only remnant of the original park is the **Giant Dipper** rollercoaster and the **Mission Beach Plunge,** a pool that is now part of the **Wave House Athletic Club** (3115 Ocean Front Walk, 858/228-9300, www.wavehouse-athleticclub.com).

LA JOLLA

North of San Diego, La Jolla (which means "The Jewel") is a well-to-do neighborhood filled with high-end boutiques, exemplary restaurants, and a coastline awash in scenic beauty.

Mt. Soledad Veterans Memorial

A great way to get a grip on the layout of San Diego is to drive to the top of 822-foot-high Mount Soledad and take in its amazing 360 degree panoramic view of the city. The land is part of the **Mt. Soledad Veterans Memorial** (6905 La Jolla Scenic Dr., 858/459-2314, www.soledadmemorial.com), where six walls at the peak have 3,000 granite plaques honoring U.S. veterans from the Revolutionary War up to the recent Iraq War. The highest point of the small mountain above the walls and plaques is a large concrete cross that caused a national controversy in 2011 about religious symbols being displayed on government land. Whatever your view on that issue is, your view of San Diego will be superb and can include the city's downtown, Scripps Pier, and on clear days, the Coronado Islands off the coast of Baja Mexico.

Sunny Jim's Cave

Of the seven sea caves in the La Jolla cliffs, **Sunny Jim's Cave** (1325 Coast Blvd., Mon.-Fri. 10am-5pm, Sat.-Sun. 10am-5:30pm, adults $4, children $3) is unique. You don't need a kayak or scuba gear to get down into this cave; an artificially-made tunnel created 100 years ago lets visitors into the cavern via a reliable land route. You'll purchase admission at the weathered, shingle-fronted Cave Store, then climb carefully down the 145 steps to the cavern proper. You'll see a sizeable sea cave of sandstone, carved over the millennia by the Pacific into the cliffside. You can look from inside the

LA JOLLA

Point La Jolla **◖ SCRIPPS PARK**

◖ LA JOLLA COVE

*Ellen Browning
Scripps Park*

BROCKTON VILLA ▼

Goldfish
Point

■ **SUNNY JIM'S
CAVE**

*La Jolla
Bay*

**GEORGE'S
AT THE COVE** •

Shell Beach ■

LA VALENCIA •
LA JOLLA INN •

● **JEWELS BY
THE SEA**

**CHILDREN'S
POOL** ★

**LA JOLLA
VISITOR
CENTER** ■

**AJA
RUGS** ■

Wipeout Beach

PROSPECT

CAVE ST

PROSPECT PL

COAST BLVD

GIRARD AVE

HERSCHEL AVE

IVANHOE AVE

PROSPECT ST

**PACIFIC
OCEAN**

0   200 yds
0   200 m

**MUSEUM OF
CONTEMPORARY ART
SAN DIEGO** ★

EADS
ST

FAY
AVE

SILVERADO

DRURY
LN

KLINE
ST

SILVER ST

BISHOPS
LN

EADS
AVE

ST

DRAPER
AVE

COAST
BLVD

PROSPECT

LA
JOLLA
BLVD

RAVINA ST

PEARL

TORREY PINES RD

BLUEBIRD
LN

VIRGINIA
WAY

OLIVET
ST

CABRILLO
AVE

■ **GIRARD AVENUE
COLLECTION**

FAY
AVE

Nicholson
Point

Whispering
Sands Beach

To
Bird Rock and
Pacific Beach
▼

© AVALON TRAVEL

cave out towards the ocean—an interesting and perhaps just a little bit eerie view.

But how did the tunnel get built? Gustav Schultz, a retiree and painter, hired laborers to hand-dig the tunnel in 1903 as a tourist attraction. The cave was later named "Sunny Jim's" after a cartoon breakfast cereal mascot by L. Frank Baum, the author of *The Wonderful Wizard of Oz*. (No, I am not making this up.) Schultz painted local landscapes in the Cave Store until his death in 1912.

◖ La Jolla Cove and Scripps Park

One of the most photographed beaches in the state, **La Jolla Cove** (1100 Coast Rd.) differs from other San Diego beaches. The small cove sits sandwiched between two sandstone cliffs, and the coarse sand feels more like the rough pebbles of the northern part of the state than the silky-soft stretches of the south. There's also a cave at the west end of the beach that delights children. Visitors snap pictures of the picturesque scenery, swim in the warm water, and

Mt. Soledad Veterans Memorial

© STUART THORNTON

trek up to **Ellen Browning Scripps Park** (Coast Blvd., www.sandiego.gov, 4am-8pm) for a picnic or a game of soccer on the manicured lawn. La Jolla Cove is famous for its sparkling clear water, and at low tide scuba divers and snorkelers enjoy the local marine life in the offshore **La Jolla Underwater Park Ecological Reserve,** which is full of silver sardines, bright orange garibaldi navigating between swaying kelp. You may even catch a glimpse of a leopard shark. Lifeguards stay on duty year-round from 9am until sunset during the high season and from 10am in wintertime. Up at Scripps Park, landlovers enjoy walking on the boardwalk along the cliffs overlooking the vast Pacific, playing on the lawns, and admiring the oddly grown trees scattered around providing shade. The park has restrooms and showers. Parking for either the beach or the park can be tough, especially in the summer. Consider parking in a pay lot downtown and hoofing it down to the beach.

Birch Aquarium
The **Birch Aquarium at Scripps** (2300 Expedition Way, 858/534-3474, http://aquarium.ucsd.edu, daily 9am-5pm, adults $14, seniors $10, youth 3-17 $9.50) is run by the University of California at San Diego. Both children and adults love the Scripps Institute's research and displays in this state-of-the-art aquarium complex. For a classic beginning, view sea life from oceans the world over along the Hall of Fishes. This area includes coral reef displays from Mexico and the Caribbean, a kelp forest similar to the ones right off the La Jolla coast, and the fabulous and fascinating Shark Reef. The sea horse display highlights the unique fish, while the more somber climate change exhibit includes a fictional weather forecast from 2050.

Museum of Contemporary Art San Diego–La Jolla
The **MCASD La Jolla** (700 Prospect St., 858/454-3541, www.mcasd.org, Thurs.-Tues. 11am-5pm, general admission $10, free for those 25 and under) is one of two MCASD campuses in the area. (The other is in

SAN DIEGO

one of La Jolla's sea caves

downtown San Diego.) At the La Jolla site, perfectly located on Prospect Street for easy access, you'll see works of art in all media created from 1950 to the present. MCASD takes particular pride in its collections of Pop and Minimalist art from the 1960s and 1970s, as well as a selection of pieces from artists working in the San Diego and Tijuana areas. Step outside to view the site-specific installations of the **Edwards Sculpture Garden.** If you love the new, unique, and misunderstood arts of the modern era, the MCASD La Jolla is a must-see. And if all that art makes you hungry, be sure to stop at the museum café for a quick bite.

NORTH COUNTY

As you drive north up the Pacific Coast Highway from downtown San Diego, you begin to see where all the legends about California beaches and surfing came from. The sun shines down over desert plants, pale sands, little surf towns, the mountains to the east, and the glittering blue sea to the west. If you want a movie-style California beach vacation, you

can't do better than a weekend (or a whole week or two!) in Encinitas, Del Mar, Carlsbad, or Oceanside. At the same time, the north end of San Diego County offers some great sights and activities, from the Wild Animal Park to Mission San Luis Rey.

◖ California Surf Museum

It's impossible to think of California without thinking of surfing or the state's surf culture at some point. And at the legendary **California Surf Museum** (223 N. Coast Hwy., Oceanside, 760/721-6876, www.surfmuseum.org, daily 10am-4pm, adults $5, students, military, and seniors $3, children under 12 free), you can admire, appreciate, and learn about the ancient sport and art of surfing. While surfing's origins may be in the South Pacific islands, the unusual sport began to catch on at the warm beaches of Southern California, catching on big once surf movies began to appear in theaters. From the silly Frankie Avalon and bongo drum fluff pieces to the semi-documentary *Endless Summer,* surf movies inspired thousands of

© STUART THORNTON

the California Surf Museum

boys and young men to get out and try to catch a wave. With the novel *Gidget* and subsequent movies, what had been an almost all-male endeavor caught on with girls, too. Surfing became a part of the California version of the 1960s and 1970s hippie movement—earning the respect of the young and the animosity of the older generation. Today, there's no such thing as an "average" surfer. You might find a 10-year-old out tearing it up and a 70-year-old hanging ten, both at the same break.

At the small but interesting Surf Museum, you'll see and pay homage to all that has gone into the California surf scene over its many decades. One exhibit on the history of board shaping shows the progression of the surfboard from the wooden Hawaiian models to the lightweight foam boards used today. Among the boards showcased is world champion surfer Andy Iron's thruster, which is a modern surfboard with three fins. Also on display in another exhibit is the shark bitten board of Bethany Hamilton, a pro surfer who lost her left arm in 2003 after being attacked by a shark while surfing. In the summer, the museum screens surf films weekly; check the website for current exhibitions and events at the museum.

San Diego Wild Animal Park

The San Diego Zoo doesn't keep too many large animals in the confines of its limited site. To see and experience the life and times of giraffes, lions, elephants, and other natives of spacious grasslands in Africa and Asia, visit the wildly popular **San Diego Wild Animal Park** (15500 San Pasqual Valley Rd., Escondido, www.sandiegozoo.org, daily 9am-4pm or later, adults $42, children $32, parking $10). Deliberately set well away from the center of urban San Diego, this huge park gives a variety of animals the space they crave to live more naturally. You could spend days in the Wild Animal Park and not see all the diverse species that live here. Walking trails offer miles of adventure through different areas of the park, such as Condor Ridge, Lion Camp, Gorilla Forest, and the African Outpost. If you're not up for a day of hardcore hiking, consider

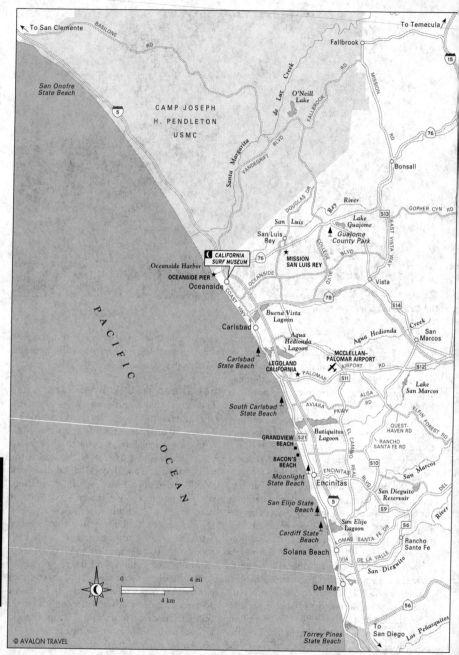

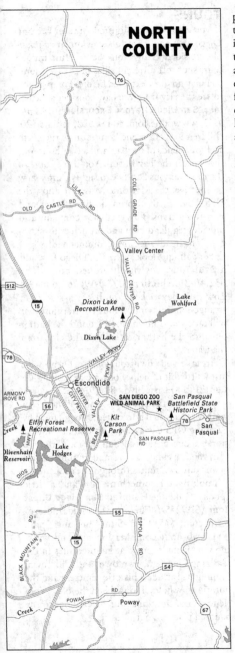

NORTH COUNTY

paying extra for one of the "Safari" tours that take guests out into different areas of the park in colorful vehicles. On Safaris, docents tell their groups about the wildlife (both animal and vegetable) as they come upon it. You can experience the thrill of seeing a cheetah run full-speed, the simple pleasure of the grazers enjoying an afternoon munching grasses and leaves, or the vista of the full park from the air by zip line or from the ground by Segway.

The Wild Animal Park caters both to families and to adults without children seeking a more grown-up experience. Check your map for the location of playgrounds and family-themed attractions. On the website, you can find out which tours and dates are best for an adults-only day at the park. Ample food, restrooms, and concessions cluster around the entrance area, but services get thinner as you get farther out into the park.

Mission San Luis Rey

Sometimes referred to as the "King of the Missions," **Mission San Luis Rey** (4050 Mission Ave., Oceanside, 760/757-3651, www.sanluisrey.org, self-guided tours Mon.-Fri. 9:30am-5pm, Sat.-Sun. 10am-5pm, adults $5, seniors $4, children $3) certainly is the biggest of the California missions. It is also one of the most lavishly restored. You can visit the stately formal gardens, complete with manicured lawns, roses, antique sculptures, and ruins of structural elements of the mission buildings. Or take a tour of the museum and church, both of which contain the history of Mission San Luis Rey through interpretive panels and many artifacts. Out in front of the mission, a unique experience awaits as you explore the ruins of the Lavanderia. This large open space contains the remains of the area where Native Americans washed their clothes and themselves outside of the mission grounds. Take the stairs down to seek out the remains of the gargoyles that once sprayed water for laundry. The cemetery is one of the largest and best maintained in the mission system, with memorials dating from the earliest days of this 1798-founded Franciscan church.

SAN DIEGO

San Diego Botanic Garden

Plant and garden lovers come from around the world to visit the **San Diego Botanic Garden** (230 Quail Gardens Dr., Encinitas, 760/436-3036, www.qbgardens.org, daily 9am-5pm, adults $12, seniors and students $8, children $6), formerly called Quail Botanical Gardens. The plants in this 30-plus-acre spread come from around the world too, as the botanic garden plays home to sub-gardens highlighting rare plant species from almost every continent. Paths meander through the dozens of sub-gardens, inviting visitors to take their time and enjoy the multihued beauty surrounding them on all sides. No visit to the Botanic Garden is complete without viewing the famous Bamboo Garden and the new Undersea Succulent Garden filled with rare succulents. The Rainforest Garden has its own waterfall, and the Subtropical Fruit Garden boasts plump offerings that don't grow elsewhere even in California.

A coffee cart offers minimal refreshments, or you can bring your own picnic to enjoy in the designated picnic areas on the grounds. Restrooms hide delicately amongst the plants, and the visitors center and gift shop sit at the center of the gardens. Knowing that kids often get bored when presented with endless plants, the grounds host the West Coast's largest interactive children's garden.

LEGOLAND

Kids have built castles and spaceships for decades with the toy building game Legos. Now let your little builders see Legos on a grand scale at **LEGOLAND** (1 LEGOLAND Dr., Carlsbad, 760/918-5346, http://california.legoland.com, hours vary, adults from $60, children from $52). Peer at dinosaurs built from LEGO bricks on **Coastersaurus,** a roller coaster that reaches the relatively benign speed of 21 miles per hour. Or wander through **DUPLO Village,** where you can gaze at safari animals made from—guess what?—LEGO bricks. Don't worry; there are plenty of shops here to purchase the latest LEGO toys.

TOURS

If you've only got a limited time in the San Diego area and want to see as much as possible, consider taking a tour. Several fun, unique tours show off different sides of the city, some you may not have explored before. For instance, to see the city from the bay, consider a harbor tour. **San Diego Harbor Excursion** (619/234-4111, www.sdhe.com, adults $22, seniors $20, children $11) offers one-hour tours of the north and south ends of the bay, and a two-hour tour that covers the bay in full. You'll see some of the most famous San Diego sights from a new perspective: the Maritime Museum ships, the USS *Midway,* the Coronado Bay Bridge, and Fort Rosencrans. This excursion company also provides regular dinner and brunch cruises; reservations in advance are recommended!

For a unique look at the San Diego Bay, add a **Seal Tour** (www.trolleytours.com, adults $32.40-36, children $17.10-19) to your Old Town Trolley ticket. You'll get a ride on a strange-looking amphibious contraption that will take you from the road around the harbor out into the harbor to look at the city from the water.

To take your own tour of San Diego with just a little bit of help, book a cute talking **Go Car** (2100 Kettner Blvd., 800/914-6227, www.gocartours.com, daily 9am-5pm, $49/hour). In your Go Car, you'll be directed through town by a talking GPS navigation unit that also knows stories about the sights of San Diego. With a Go Car, you can either take a standard tour, or program your own routes through the area.

Looking for something fun and a little spooky? Take the **Haunted San Diego Ghost Tour** (619/255-6170, www.hauntedsandiego-tours.com, $35, Wed.-Sun. 7pm and 9pm). This two-hour combination bus and walking tour includes stops at haunted sites in the Gaslamp Quarter, downtown, and Old Town. Highlights include a historic cemetery and the notorious Whaley House. For the best experience, take the 9pm tour to experience the haunted places in darkness.

TEMECULA WINE-TASTING

Wine? In Southern California? Yes, indeed! It's not Napa or Sonoma, but if you want to sample all the wine the state has to offer, don't miss out on the terrific vintages available in SoCal.

The major wine-producing region is the Temecula Valley. An hour north of San Diego, off I-15, this small, hot valley hosts 35 wineries. Most tasting rooms cluster along Rancho California Road, but it's also worth exploring farther into the valley for hidden gems. The **Temecula Valley Winegrowers Association** (www.temeculawines.org) offers a tasting map.

With vineyards first planted in 1974, **Hart Family Winery** (41300 Avenida Biona, 951/676-6300, www.hartfamilywinery.com, daily 9am-4:30pm, $5) produces only 5,000 cases of wine each year. Low production allows for intense attention to detail and quality in every single bottle. Despite the small total case number, you can try a number of varietals. Try the fruity white viognier, the stunning syrah, and less famous varietals like Grenache Rose and Tempranillo.

Built on an 11-acre estate in the style of a French chateau, **Churon Winery** (33233 Rancho California Rd., 951/694-9071, www.innatchuronwinery.com, daily 10am-4:30pm, $10) also operates as a high-end inn — so you can enjoy the wines all night long! Their list encompasses many French-styled reds and classic California whites plus a few select dessert sweets (including sherry).

Elegant **Falkner Winery** (40620 Calle Contento, 951/676-8231, www.falknerwinery.com, daily 10am-5pm, $8) takes particular pride in producing different wines from the average California vintner. Try the wonderful blended reds, made in the traditions of Tuscany and Bordeaux. For wine drinkers who like a little sweet with their savory, Falkner offers a number of not-quite-dry wines that are *not* as syrupy as a standard dessert wine. Enjoy a Mediterranean lunch at the on-site restaurant, Pinnacles and tour the winery on weekends.

From the colorful frescoes decorating the tasting room to the posh GrapeSeed Spa, **South Coast Winery & Resort** (34843 Rancho California Rd., 951/587-9463, www.wineresort.com, daily 10am-6pm, $10) caters to luxury-loving travelers. You can book a private villa or reserve a table at the Tuscan-style Vineyard Rose restaurant. Try wines from four different South Coast labels, from the splashy and moderately priced Elevation wines to the elegant Carter Estate Reserve vintages. The inclusive $40 winery tour concludes with a private wine-and-cheese tasting.

A large extended family owns and runs most every aspect of the **Wilson Creek Winery & Vineyards** (35960 Rancho California Rd., 951/699-9463, www.wilsoncreekwinery.com, daily 10am-5pm, $10). One of the Wilson mainstays is Almond Champagne, a truly special occasion beverage. Other sweet wines might include Muscat Canelli, Angelica cream sherry, and chocolate port. More traditional wine lovers will enjoy the hefty cabernet, zinfandel, and petit sirah. If jazz is your vice, check the website for the annual calendar of concerts.

A tiny family operation, **Palumbo Family Vineyards & Winery** (40150 Barksdale Circle, 951/676-7900, www.palumbofamilyvineyards.com, Fri.-Tues. 11am-5pm) takes pride in growing every grape that goes into each bottle. With 13 acres of vineyards, the winery produces 2,500 cases of wine each year. A season's release might include five wines — mostly reds with a token viognier or other hot-weather white for variety. Nicholas Palumbo is a chef as well as winemaker, and has been known to entertain private parties.

Entertainment and Events

NIGHTLIFE
Bars and Clubs

The Gaslamp Quarter is the hottest part of downtown San Diego for the young and energetic nighttime crowd. Consider just walking around Fourth Street and seeing what bar or club suits you for the evening.

For a dance club experience, stop by **Belo** (919 Fourth Ave., 619/231-9200, www.belo-sandiego.com, Thurs.-Sat. 9pm-2am). Belo hosts foam fests, DJs, and the occasional hip hop act. Internationally renowned DJs including Deadmau5 and Paul Oakenfold have performed in the club's "Green Room."

Getting into the ultra hip **◖ Vin De Syrah Spirit & Wine Parlor** (901 5th Ave., 619/234-4166, www.syrahwineparlor.com, Tues.-Wed. and Sun. 4pm-midnight, Thurs.-Sat. 4pm-2am) is an adventure. Go down a graffiti covered staircase to a subterranean area with an unmarked vegetation covered door. That's the entrance. Inside sip creative cocktails or wine—there's a whole page of French wines offered here—while taking in the bar's eclectic decor that includes wine vines, lots of mirrors, and umbrellas hanging from the roof.

Formerly the The Bitter End, **The Tipsy Crow** (770 Fifth St., 619/338-9300, http://thetipsycrow.com, Mon.-Fri. 3pm-2am, Sat.-Sun. noon-2am) offers three different bar experiences in a building that dates back to 1874. "The Nest" is a place to lounge while sipping drinks including The Tipsy Crow's signature cocktail the "Salty Dog," which is simply freshly squeezed grapefruit juice and vodka in a glass with a salted rim. Or drink craft beers in "The Main" at the large room's 40-foot mahogany bar. If you seek entertainment, head downstairs to "The Underground," where there is frequent live entertainment including bands and comedians.

A local's favorite, **Hamilton's Tavern** (1521 30th Ave., 619/238-5460, http://hamiltonstavern.com, Mon.-Fri. 3pm-2am, Sat.-Sun. 1pm-2am, $10) is located in a neighborhood near Balboa Park. Like a dive bar with impeccable tastes, the tavern serves a range of 26 craft beers on tap and a surprisingly creative bar food menu with items including chicken wings in a mole sauce and a grilled cheese with brie, honey, apples, and walnuts.

Gay and Lesbian

With a young, hip scene and a significant gay presence, nightlife in Hillcrest is happening most every night of the week.

The Brass Rail (3796 Fifth Ave., 619/298-2233, www.thebrassrailsd.com, Mon. and Wed. 8pm-2am, Fri.-Sat. 4pm-2am, Sun. 10am-8pm) is one of San Diego's oldest gay venues. Offerings include drag shows, DJs, and happy hours.

Urban Mo's (308 University Ave., 619/491-0400, www.urbanmos.com, daily 9am-2am) describes itself as a "hetero friendly gay restaurant." It has everything from line dancing nights to all-you-can-eat spaghetti nights.

Live Music

San Diego enjoys its music, and you'll find plenty of opportunities to hear live classical, jazz, rock, and more throughout town. You'll have no trouble finding everything from tiny dive bars with mini-stages up to huge multi-day music festivals. Whether you prefer mellow jazz, danceable blues, or hard-hitting rock, odds are it's playing live. Check web guides to the Gaslamp (www.gaslamp.org) and Hillcrest (http://gothere.com) for listings of who's hosting what when you're in town.

Since 1989, **The Casbah** (2501 Kettner Blvd., 619/232-4355, www.casbahmusic.com, most nights 8:30pm-2am) has been snagging some of the biggest acts in indie and alt rock. Bands from Death Cab for Cutie to the Arcade Fire have performed in the club to just over 200 people.

The music venue chain **House of Blues** (1055 Fifth Ave., 619/299-2583, www.house-ofblues.com) has shows by national touring acts of all types. The revered San Diego music venue The Casbah even books some performances here.

Though it's a half hour north of San Diego proper, Solano Beach's **Belly Up Tavern** (143 S. Cedros Ave., Solano Beach, 859/481-8140, www.bellyup.com, hours vary) regularly scores legends including Willie Nelson and Toots & the Maytals. They also have up-and-comers and indie favorites.

If you're in Point Loma for the evening, head to Humphrey's for live music any time of year. **Humphrey's Backstage Music** (2241 Shelter Island Blvd., 619/224-3577, www.humphreysbackstagelive.com) offers a lounge-style venue with live music or DJs spinning danceable tunes or playing charming smooth jazz to drink and converse by. Check the website for this month's schedule. If you're around in the summer season, buy tickets in advance for the local favorite concert series, **Humphreys Concerts by the Bay** (www.humphreysconcerts.com). National acts come out to play against the backdrop of the marinas of Shelter Island as the sun sets over San Diego Bay. The outdoor venue takes advantage of the evening climate, so you can bask in the warm air under the stars as you listen to the tunes of your favorite rock band or folk singer.

Comedy

A Greek restaurant by day, **The Comedy Palace** (8878 Clairemont Mesa Blvd., 858/573-9067, www.thecomedypalace.com, comedy performances Thurs.-Sat., $20-25) serves up comedy Thursday, Friday, and Saturday nights. The weekend comics have frequently appeared on TV.

CASINO GAMBLING

If your first love is a night donating money to the local Native American tribe, a number of casinos outside the city proper can hook you up.

A few miles east of San Diego, two casinos offer a good time. **Club Sycuan** (5469 Casino Way, El Cajon, 800/279-2826, www.sycuan. com) sits in the suburb of El Cajon. This casino and resort offers fun for all comers, with a hotel, several restaurants (including a buffet), a golf course, tennis courts, and gaming floors. At Club Sycuan, you'll find thousands of slot machines, plus an array of table games including blackjack, pai gow poker, mini-baccarat, roulette, and craps. You can also enjoy the tension of the Bingo Palace and the smoke-free atmosphere of the Poker Room. Vegas-style stage acts entertain weary gamers and golfers in the evening. There's also a complimentary shuttle to Club Sycuan from different parts of San Diego.

Nope, that's not a Back East boarding school. That big, classically styled building east of La Jolla is actually the **Barona Valley Ranch Resort and Casino** (1932 Wildcat Canyon Rd., Lakeside, 619/443-2300, www.barona.com). This upscale resort brings a touch of class to the Las Vegas-style casino. Stay in the large, posh hotel (that's the big building), eat dinner at the Steakhouse or the Buffet and grab lunch at the noodle house, pamper yourself in the day spa or out at the pool, or play around at the Barona Creek Golf Club. Finally, hit the casino for plenty of up-to-date loose slots plus 70 table games, including craps, roulette, cash baccarat, and much more. You can also hang out in the poker room, or play the ponies at the off-track betting parlor.

While no casinos grace the North County coastline, if you're vacationing in Del Mar or Encinitas, gaming possibilities lurk only a few miles east. You'll find part of the ever-popular **Harrah's** (777 Harrah's Rincon Way, Valley Center, 877/777-2457, www.harrahsrincon.com) chain off Highway 76 northeast of Oceanside. The typical Harrah's tower rises high over the tiny town of Valley Center, offering over 600 hotel rooms, eight different eateries (including an oyster bar, a buffet, and a coffee house), and a full-service spa. The gaming rooms offer hundreds of slots, a World Series of Poker room, and plenty of table games, including craps, roulette bingo, and blackjack. To cool off in the heat of summer, rent a cabana or pull up a chaise lounge at the gorgeous two-tiered pool.

SAN DIEGO

Yet another large, blocky, luxurious casino, the **Pala Casino Resort and Spa** (11154 Hwy. 76, Pala, 877/946-7252, www.palacasino.com) dominates the landscape on hot, dry Highway 76 east of Oceanside. The dining options are especially fine here: there's Mama's Cucina Italia, which offers entertainment with your meal; a casual Asian meal at Noodles; all-you-can-eat at the Choice Buffet; or elegance at The Oak Room. Entertainment also comes big at the Pala, with two large theaters (one indoor, one outdoor), a lounge, and an event center. In the casino proper, you'll find the largest array of new slot machines in the area, plus more than 80 table games. A high-limit room offers fun for high rollers, and a smoke-free room provides relief for sensitive noses who still want to play.

THE ARTS
Theater

Live theater lives well in San Diego. Most every area and district has at least a theater or two, and several big houses garner national acclaim for world-class productions. If you're in San Diego for more than one night, it will be worth your while to take in a show at the Old Globe, the La Jolla Playhouse, or one of the innumerable repertory theaters.

The **Old Globe** (Copley Plaza, Balboa Park, 619/234-5623, www.oldglobe.org, box office Tues.-Sun. noon-6pm or end of show), one of the most famous theater complexes in California, sits in the middle of Balboa Park. Originally constructed to produce abbreviated Shakespeare plays for the 1935 California Pacific International Exposition, the magnificent Old Globe was remodeled to permanence in 1937. It has been producing a full season ever since, growing to add two auxiliary theaters: the Cassius Carter Centre Stage and the Lowell Davis Festival Stage. The Old Globe, restored to its original magnificence after a fire in 1978, seats almost 600 people, and has produced world premieres of plays such as *Into the Woods* and *The Full Monty* that go on to become Broadway spectaculars and worldwide hits. If you can get a ticket to something new at the Old Globe, you may find yourself seeing history being made. Today the Globe puts on 15 plays and musicals a year.

The Old Globe theaters are reminiscent of the complex at the legendary Ashland Shakespeare festival. The huge outdoor Lowell Davis facility can seat almost 700 spectators and puts up shows during the summer and fall festival season. The smaller Cassius Carter Stage presents theater in the round, in an intimate black-box-style setting. See the website for a list of the shows playing at each theater, as well as for ticket sales and seating charts. At the Copley Theater complex, enjoy a snack and a drink at Lady Carolyn's Pub or browse for souvenirs at the gift shop.

For a night of high budget, fabulous Broadway theater or an adventurous off-center world premiere, check out a show at the **La Jolla Playhouse** (La Jolla Village Dr. and Gilman Dr., 858/550-1010, www.lajollaplayhouse.com, box office Sun.-Mon. noon-7pm, Tues.-Wed. noon-7:30pm, Thurs.-Sat. noon-8pm, shows Tues.-Wed. 7:30pm, Thurs.-Fri. 8pm, Sat. 2pm and 8pm, Sun. 2pm and 7pm). This top-tier theater company produces big musicals, small experimental plays, historical dramas, and everything in between. Check the website for this year's main season schedule. In late 2012, the playhouse was presenting the world premiere of a musical based off the Flaming Lips album *Yoshimi Battles the Pink Robots*. The Playhouse actually encompasses a building complex with three separate theaters. Originally created by an ensemble of Hollywood actors, the Playhouse delights in showing off both well-known popular shows and great world premieres. Look for originality in sets and costuming, as well as top-notch acting.

For a charming night out on the North Coast, grab a seat at the **North Coast Repertory Theater** (987 Lomas Santa Fe Dr., Solano Beach, 858/481-1055, http://north-coastrep.org, box office daily noon-4pm, performance days noon-curtain, shows Wed.-Sun.). The North Coast Rep produces about eight shows each year, including musicals, dramas, comedies, and family favorites. With ticket prices at around $20 per show, a laid-back evening of good repertory theater isn't hard to obtain. The theater at Lomas Santa Fe Plaza is located conveniently near I-5 and the Del Mar Racetrack, for easy access after a day's sightseeing.

Classical Music

The **Organ Concerts in Balboa Park** (www.sosorgan.com) provide a unique, free live music experience that all visitors and locals can enjoy. Every week of the year for almost a century, the Spreckels Organ has serenaded the park with beautiful music. Concerts happen on Sundays 2pm-3pm, and on Monday nights at 7:30pm in the summertime. Come out, take a seat on a park bench, and relax as the music washes over you.

If you love opera, be sure to get tickets to the **San Diego Opera** (box office 619/533-7000, www.sdopera.com, Mon.-Fri. 8:30am-4:30pm) during your visit. Originally created to produce San Francisco Opera productions in the 1950s, the San Diego Opera quickly grew into an independent production company to rival even its famed neighbor to the north. In addition to the regular season filled with original productions of famous operas, you'll find the San Diego Opera hosting international stars at special concerts and presenting a variety of musicals to the San Diego community.

All regular Opera performances take place at the **Civic Theatre** (Third Ave. and B St.). You'll find several parking structures and surface lots nearby—parking usually starts at $10 and goes up on concert nights. The MTS trolley stops right behind the Theatre entrance, and is a great option if you're staying anywhere near the trolley line or are taking the train into the Santa Fe station. If you're coming from the North County for a night of culture, check the Opera's website for information about the San Diego Opera Caravan, a pay bus service to and from Carlsbad to the Civic Theatre.

Cinema

You'll find plenty of first-run multi-screen cineplexes scattered throughout the San Diego area. But if you're looking for a fun vintage movie-going experience, try the **Ken Cinema** (4061 Adams Ave., 619/283-3227, www.landmarktheatres.com). Built in 1912, this single-screen theater now specializes in running independent, foreign films and restored classics. Happily, the seats are not the same vintage as the rest of the theater—new, comfortable theater chairs were installed in 2004. There's no parking lot, so you'll have to try your luck on the street with the locals who come to the Ken regularly to see something other than the standard new Hollywood fare.

If you're in La Jolla and looking for fun and unusual film entertainment, head up to the **La Jolla Village Cinemas** (8879 Villa La Jolla Dr., 858/453-7622, www.landmarktheatres.com). This four-screener shows a variety of different styles of movie, from independent to foreign to popular. Enjoy better-than-average concessions, plus an array of good food and drink centered right around the theater. If you're looking for a midnight movie experience, call and see if they're running something while you're in town.

The best deal in town is the throwback **South Bay Drive-In Theatre** (2170 Coronado Ave., 619/423-2727, www.southbaydrivein.com, adults $7, children 5-9 $1, cash only), where you can catch a double feature of the latest movies for just $7 a person. You also get to view them from the comforts of your own car.

FESTIVALS AND EVENTS

Summer is event season in San Diego. If you're visiting between June and October, you can hardly help tripping over some fun congregation of folks. Check the web or the tourist bureau for tickets to your favorite events and for information about what's going on in the area during your visit.

Adams Avenue Street Fair

Unfortunately, San Diego's massive annual music festival Street Scene called it quits after its 2009 installment. But the smaller **Adams Avenue Street Fair** (http://adamsaveonline.

com, Sept.) is just as much fun. For those who need a music fix, 90 music acts perform on seven stages. There are also carnival rides, vendors, and booths at this long-running street fair, one of the largest in California.

LGBT Pride Parade and Festival

There's nothing sexier than loving yourself. To celebrate being yourself, each year San Diego hosts its own San Diego **LGBT Pride Parade and Festival** (www.sdpride.org, June). Smaller than the mammoth festival in San Francisco, San Diego Pride is still one of the city's biggest annual celebrations. The weekend is packed with events and attractions, from a 10K run to a Ferris wheel. No matter who you are or what you're into, there's something for you here. You'll find almost a dozen stages, each offering a different style of music from hip-hop to acoustic to Latino to lavender. One of the biggest events is the Saturday Pride Parade featuring creative floats, music, and wildly celebratory people. If you love baseball and queer life, plan ahead and purchase tickets to the Padres Pride event called "Out in the Park."

The parade and festival take place in Balboa Park, spilling out to the Hillcrest neighborhood especially in the evening, and out to Petco Park for the Padres baseball event. Check the website for information about park-and-ride services, parking, bicycle parking, public transit, and more. You can purchase tickets in advance, or at the festival. There's no smoking at the festival. If you need wheelchair assistance, contact the festival organizers in advance.

San Diego Bay Fair

For an event that's unique to San Diego and totally noisy, you can't beat the **San Diego Bay Fair** (www.sandiegobayfair.org, Sept.), formerly known as the Thunderboat Regatta. For one weekend each September, Mission Bay revs up and gets loud, hosting a supercharged power-boat-racing event. You can see drag boat racing, Formula One, cracker box inboards, and much more. Stands are set up on beaches around the bay to allow the most people the best views of the races — be sure to buy your tickets in advance to get a good seat. The excitement at this event is contagious, and the tension is real. Be sure to bring earplugs and extra money for parking if you want a space anywhere near the bay. (Alternately, check the website and the local resorts for deals on hotel rooms within walking distance of race-viewing areas.) Kids of all ages are welcome — check the schedule for this year's family-oriented events.

San Diego County Fair

The **San Diego County Fair** (2260 Jimmy Durant Blvd., Del Mar, 858/755-1161, www.sdfair.com, June-July) runs for several weeks every summer and boasts being one of the very best in the state. Naturally it's held at the famed Del Mar County Fairgrounds, which were purposely built for this celebration of San Diego agriculture.

Shopping

Shopping in San Diego runs primarily to malls and shopping centers that offer a good, if selective, experience. Downtown, wander the Gaslamp Quarter for San Diego-grown clothing or hit the immense Horton Plaza for stores you know. Old Town is fun for unique Mexican souvenirs and is a short jump from Mission Valley where the mall is king. Farther north, La Jolla provides a more relaxed, upscale experience.

DOWNTOWN
Gaslamp Quarter

As you stroll the streets of the Gaslamp Quarter you'll find many stores are local chains, like the **San Diego Trading Company** (376 Fifth Ave., 619/696-9581, www.sandiegotradingcompany.com, Mon.-Thurs. 9am-9:30pm, Fri.-Sat. 9am-10pm, Sun. 9am-7pm) or surfing/resort wear purveyors such as **Quiksilver Boardriders Club** (402 Fifth Ave., 619/234-3125, www.

quiksilver.com, Sun.-Thurs. 10am-8pm, Fri.-Sat. 10am-9pm).

In casual California, it makes sense to find several stores devoted to the sale of jeans. **G-Star** (470 Fifth Ave., 619/238-7088, www.g-star.com, Mon.-Sat. 11am-8pm, Sun. 11am-7pm) offers fun, eclectic men's and women's wear made mostly from denim. Their motto is "luxury denim for the streets." You'll find familiar jeans, jackets, and accessories inside the chain **Lucky Brand Jeans** (621 Fifth Ave., 619/230-9260, www.luckybrandjeans.com, Mon.-Sat. 11am-10pm, Sun. 11am-9pm).

Specialty items of obvious types are available at **Urban Lighting** (301 Fourth Ave., 619/232-6064, www.urbanlighting.net, Mon.-Fri. 9am-5pm, Sat. 10am-4pm), and **Fourth Avenue Rug Gallery** (827 Fourth Ave., 619/234-8700, www.armanfinerugs.com, Mon.-Sat. 11am-8pm).

Horton Plaza

Looking for a big mall to gather all your favorite shops together into one place? Visit **Westfield Horton Plaza** (324 Horton Plaza, San Diego, 619/239-8180, www.westfield.com, Mon.-Fri. 10am-9pm, Sat. 10am-8pm, Sun. 11am-6pm). With all the standard Westfield mall amenities, including day spas, salons, and plenty of food options, you'll feel right at home here.

Many of your favorite midrange to upscale chain boutiques make a home at Horton Plaza. Shop at Baby Gap, Bebe, Guess, and Victoria's Secret, among others. Horton Plaza also offers an immense array of jewelry shops, accessory stores, and leather boutiques. For shoes, you'll find everything from Vans to Foot Locker.

OLD TOWN
Bazaar Del Mundo

A perfect way to experience shopping in Mexico without making the trek down to Tijuana is to visit Old Town's famed **Bazaar del Mundo** (4133 Taylor St., 619/296-3161, Sun.-Mon. 10am-5:30pm, Tues.-Thurs. 10am-9pm, Fri.-Sat. 9am-9pm). Easily accessed from I-5 and I-8, this cheerful and colorful shopping center brings the best of Mexico across the border.

From the familiar figures in the **Laurel Burch Gallerita** to the unusual and often elegant imports of **Artes de Mexico,** you'll find perfect gifts for everyone on your list (and for yourself, of course). When you come down to the Bazaar, come hungry! Some of the best and most visitor-friendly Mexican food is served here.

Fashion Valley

Another big urban mall, **Fashion Valley** (7007 Friars Rd., 619/688-9113, www.simon.com, Mon.-Sat. 10am-9pm, Sun. 11am-7pm) has plenty of the shopping experience you desire. A bit higher end than Horton Plaza, Fashion Valley focuses more on the home and offers some designer boutiques.

Appropriately, fashions for men, women, and children of all ages abound at Fashion Valley. Kids can grow up here, going from Gymboree to GapKids and on up to The Limited Too. Gentlemen have a number of options for all parts of life, from the casual times at J. Crew and Old Navy to more formal situations in Bernini, Gucci, and After Hours Formal Wear.

Not surprisingly, women have the most clothing options here at the mall. The mature crowd prefers Ann Taylor and Talbots, while the teens and twenties shoppers flock to Abercrombie & Fitch and Forever 21. For inexpensive and sporting shoes, run to Foot Locker or Shiek Shoes. Fancy sunglasses peek out the windows at Occhiala da Sole and thousands of watches keep the time inside Tourneau.

LA JOLLA

Shopping in La Jolla feels a little like a spending spree in the sophisticated areas of Los Angeles. This upscale suburb prides itself on its walking-and-shopping, much of which is centered around Prospect Street. Be sure to veer off onto the side streets, which hide some true gems!

Prospect La Jolla

Big name and upscale chain stores rent space on Prospect, as do locally owned one-of-a-kind boutiques. You can go lingerie shopping at **Victoria's Secret** (1111 Prospect St., 858/459-0688, www.victoriassecret.com, Mon.-Thurs.

10am-7pm, Fri.-Sat. 10am-8pm, Sun. 11am-6pm). Look for monochromatic women's wear at **White House/Black Market** (7927 Girard Ave., 858/459-2565, www.whitehouseblackmarket.com, Mon.-Thurs. 10am-9pm, Fri.-Sat. 10am-9:30pm, Sun. 10am-7:30pm), or a matching men's tuxedo at **Imperial Taylor and Formal Wear** (7744 Fay Ave., 858/459-8891, Mon.-Fri. 9:30am-4:30pm, Sat. 10:30am-1pm). Dozens more apparel stores, from the casual to the highest of high-end cluster in La Jolla.

Naturally, only the funkiest or fanciest jewels will do to complement the lovely clothing sold in La Jolla (a town whose name translates as "The Jewel"). You can browse in jewelry stores, from reasonably priced costume jewelry all the way up to designer diamonds. For local fine jewelry, visit **Jewels by the Sea** (1237 Prospect St. B, 858/459-5166, Mon. and Weds.-Sat. noon-6pm, Sun. 1pm-6pm).

Elegant antique stores cluster in La Jolla, beckoning wealthy patrons to furnish and decorate their homes with the beautiful artifacts of the past. Pick up a great new piece for your collection at shops such as **AJA Rugs** (955 Prospect St. E, 858/459-0333, Mon.-Sat. 10am-7pm, Sun. 11am-6pm) or the **Girard Avenue Collection** (7505 Girard Ave., 858/459-7765, Mon.-Sat. 10:30am-5:30pm, Sun. 10:30am-4pm).

Sports and Recreation

San Diego has more than its share of sunny days year-round, so get outside! With dozens of miles of beaches, zoos, parks, trails, and endless opportunities for recreation, even the most dedicated couch potatoes can find something great to do under the famed California sun.

BEACHES

If you come to San Diego, you must go to the beach. It's an imperative. From Encinitas and Del Mar down almost to the Mexican border, the California coast shows off its best. The San Diego beaches all seem to be 100 yards wide, perfectly flat, 100 percent pale, soft, sugar sand, and run as far in either direction as the eye can see. A few rocks appear in spots, but they're few and far between (especially in comparison to the rugged northern coastline). Bring your towel, umbrella, sunscreen, swimsuit, and surfboard. And if it's a weekend in the summertime, come early in the morning to stake a prime spot in the sand.

For a list of beaches maintained by the City of San Diego, check out this website: www.sandiego.gov.

Ocean Beach

Small for a San Diego beach, **Ocean Beach** (1950 Abbot St., Ocean Beach, daily 24 hours) is a one-mile stretch of sand broken up by several rock jetties. It beckons locals and visitors alike with its lifeguard-protected waters, multiuse areas, and famous Dog Beach. On Dog Beach, at the north end of Ocean Beach, dogs are allowed off-leash all day, every day. (Please clean up after your dog!) Farther south, you'll find designated areas for fishing, surfing, and swimming. Check with the lifeguards to figure out which is which. Be aware that rip currents can be strong at Ocean Beach, and take care when you're out in the water. At the south end of the beach, you can take a walk out on the Ocean Beach pier; some people even bring a pole to spend some quiet time fishing out on the pier.

If you need a restroom or showers, head for the main lifeguard station at Abbot Street, which has both. Lifeguards stay on duty from 9am until dusk daily. Amazingly ample parking can be found at three lots that range from the south to the north end of the beach. (The smallest lot is the one by the lifeguard station; go north or south for better parking opportunities.)

Black's Beach

Locals' favorite **Black's Beach** (north of downtown La Jolla and south of Torrey Pines State Beach) has found fame as a surf break. A deep-water canyon offshore acts as a wave magnet pulling in any swell from a westerly direction. But pause a second before grabbing your board and clambering down the 300-foot cliffs: Black's doubles as a well-known nude beach.

The main difficulty with Black's Beach is getting here. As an unofficial beach without a permanent lifeguard station, you won't find any parking lots; you'll have to do the best you can on the street. No well-built or easily climbed stairways lead down to Black's, so you can either scramble down the cliff paths, or take your chances with the tides and enter from an adjacent beach to the north or south. Finally, lifeguards are stationed here in the summer months only and the waters are unregulated, so be extremely careful of your fellow surfers and swimmers!

Coronado Main Beach
The can't-miss Hotel del Coronado marks the **Coronado Main Beach** (Ocean Blvd.). Anyone can walk through the outdoor common areas of the Del to get out to this charming sandy beach. This beach is not a surfing beach, but rather a place to relax. Yet another fabulous sun-drenched chunk of coastline, the Coronado Main Beach gets ultra-crowded in the summertime, so come early if you want a prime spot of your own. Do pay attention to the signs and flags—a nasty breakwater of large boulders hides under the water just in front of the Del at high tide. Also take a look at the odd-shaped dunes; from the air, they spell out "Coronado."

Del Mar City Beach
Running along the length of downtown Del Mar, **Del Mar City Beach** (15th St. and Coast Blvd. to the Rivermouth) is touted as one of the best beaches in an area, famous for its welcoming sands. With the exception of easy parking, this huge strip of coastline has it all. The soft sand invites sunbathers, who can spend all day soaking up rays. The ocean beckons, the cool Pacific making a perfect counterpoint to hot San Diego summer days. A decent surf break near the center of City Beach beckons to new

and experienced wave riders alike. (You can even take surf lessons here.) Dogs are allowed on a section of the beach north of 29th Street. Lifeguards protect the shores, complete with the towers that mark all guarded San Diego county beaches. Be sure to pay attention to the colored flags on the beach. Blue means swimming is okay, and a red flag means out front is a surfing area.

Once you find a place on the street to park (bring quarters for the meters), getting onto the beach is easy. The area is flat and simple to access, and in some places boardwalks and paths make beach access even simpler. Just off the beach, the **Powerhouse Community Center** offers restrooms, restaurants and a stage.

SURFING AND STAND UP PADDLEBOARDING
With its endless sunshine and magnificent breaks, San Diego offers some of the best surfing in California. The temperate water (averaging 65-70°F in the summer), allows surfing year-round down here, although wetsuits can be a good idea in winter. San Diego is also an ideal place to learn how to stand up paddleboard (SUP). One of the main reasons is that if you fall off the board the water is warmer than it is in the rest of California! The calm waters of Mission Bay are ideal for beginners, while the waves at La Jolla Shores are usually not too big for those who want to try riding a wave on an SUP.

Surf Breaks
San Diego boasts plenty of classic Southern California surfing. In La Jolla, **Black's Beach** is the best beach break in the county. But access to the spot involves hiking down the twisting path of a 300-foot-high cliff face. **Del Mar City Beach** (15th St. and Coast Blvd. to the Rivermouth, Del Mar), in addition to being a great sandy spot to hang out, offers fine beginning and intermediate waves. There's also a reef that produces waves at 15th Street. **Mission Beach** boasts year-round waves as well as lifeguards, restroom facilities, and about a zillion tourists and sun

worshippers in the summertime. If you're serious about surfing, check out **Windansea Beach** (6800 Neptune Pl.), which has a heavy shore break and a rockier coastline with a reef that produces one of the region's most revered waves. You will find dense crowds of fellow surfers, so this isn't the best spot for beginners to try out their boards. On the other hand, the small, consistent waves at **La Jolla Shores** (8200 Camino del Oro, La Jolla), also called Scripps, bore the hardcore masters, but are perfect for novice surfers. Just stick within the lifeguard-designated surfing areas to avoid the swimmers and scuba divers sharing the water here. North of Del Mar, **Cardiff Reef** is a great spot for longboarding, while **Swami's** is a legendary right point break in Encinitas located in front of a gold-domed temple.

Surf Lessons and Rentals

Never ridden a wave before? Check out one of San Diego's many surf schools. You'll go to a small-wave beach, learn the basics on dry land, and then paddle out for the first time. Most schools promise to get you up and riding (if only for a few seconds) the very first time! Or if you've come to Southern California specifically to surf, check with the schools about multi-day, all-inclusive (lodging too!) "surf camps" that get you surfing all day, every day. Most of the surf schools rent and sell boards, leashes, wetsuits, and board care equipment—everything you need for your first surf set-up, and repair and replacement equipment if you're an expert.

Competitive surfer Rick Gehris started **Surfari** (3740 Mission Blvd., 858/337-3287, www.surfarisurf.com, $55/day group lesson, $85/day private lesson, start times 9am, 11am, 1pm, 3pm), which operates at Mission Beach. Each 2.5-hour lesson includes land instruction, interactive in-the-water instruction, and an hour afterward on your own to play. Regular group lessons happen almost every day of the year. For a more intense learning experience, book a discounted three-day lesson series.

The **San Diego Surfing Academy** (800/447-7873, www.surfingacademy.com, $100/group lesson, $150/three-hour private lesson) runs year-round at the north end of South Carlsbad State Beach Campgrounds. You must make an appointment to take lessons with the SDSA, but the quality of instruction makes it worth the bother. All equipment is included in the fee. With two-hour group classes and by-the-hour private lessons, this safety-oriented school makes certain you'll know what you're doing out there in the surf. If you want to take your surfing to the next level, look into SDSA's customized surf camps.

The first women-centered surf school in the world, **Surf Diva** (2160 Avenida de la Playa, La Jolla, 858/454-8273, www.surfdiva.com, $90/hour private lessons, $170/two-day clinic, $390/weeklong clinic, $25/1.5-hour SUP rentals) creates an estrogen-friendly, supportive atmosphere for girls ages five and up to learn the ins and outs of the waves at La Jolla Shores. They are branching out with SUP rentals and lessons, as well as classes for the whole family (including males!). Book a private lesson, or take a 2-5-day clinic to get serious about the sport. Lessons at Surf Diva make a fun and creative kickoff for a bachelorette party.

OEX Dive & Kayak (858/454-6195, www.oexcalifornia.com, rentals start at $25) rents SUPs from three locations: La Jolla, Mission Bay, and Sunset Beach.

BOATING

In Mission Bay and San Diego Bay, the calm waters make great fun of all forms of boating, from paddle-boating to waterskiing to sailing. Kayaking is a special local favorite pastime, especially for would-be explorers of the famous La Jolla Caves. If you plan to exit the bays for the open ocean, be sure you're either competent to navigate a watercraft on the open sea, or have somebody with you who can do it. Watch the weather reports, and pay attention to local experts.

Power Boating and Waterskiing

On the calm waters of the two bays, you can water-ski and wakeboard, dash around on a Jet Ski, or just cruise offshore in a speedboat. **Seaforth Boat Rentals** (888/834-2628, www.seaforthboatrentals.com, $40-900) has five locations: in Mission Bay, downtown San Diego, Harbor Island, Coronado, and the Coronado Marriott. If you're planning to cruise, rent one of the large speedboats, which range up to over 50 feet and have plenty of room for passengers, coolers, and snacks. If you've got an athletic crew with you, reserve a ski boat. For a more motorcycle-like on-the-water experience, pick up a modern, powerful Jet Ski that rides 2-3 people.

Another multi-boat rental outfit with several locations in and around San Diego is **Action Sport Rentals** (858/581-5939, www.action-sportrentals.com, $85-185). Rent yourself a three-seater Jet Ski or 6-12-passenger speedboat and tool around the bays. For a bigger party, Action offers 13-passenger power pontoon boats. If you want to water-ski or wakeboard but don't have anyone to drive the boat, reserve some time with Action's professional driver. You'll get rides on whatever type of toy (wakeboard, skis, kneeboard, tube) you want behind their competitive-class ski boat.

Sailing

Whether you want a quiet putter around the bay or an exhilarating adventure on the open ocean, you can get just the sailing experience you want in San Diego. **Seaforth Boat Rentals** (888/834-2628, www.seaforthboatrentals.com) offers 16-54-feet rental sailboats. You can also book a sailing lesson, or even hire a captain to take care of the practicalities while you and your party enjoy a glass of wine and a meal or snack on the water.

Kayaking

With so many calm, protected bays, plus an array of exciting sea caves, it's no wonder that San Diego boasts some of the best sea kayaking in the state. Whether you've got your own boat or you plan to rent or take a tour, the most popular spots to paddle are the La Jolla Caves, part of the larger **La Jolla Cove Ecological Reserve** (1100 Coast Blvd., www.sandiego.gov). **La Jolla Kayak** (2199 Avenida de la Playa, 858/459-1114, www.lajollakayak.

com, single kayaks start at $45, double kayaks start at $59) does a two-hour tour of the caves and underwater park of La Jolla.

SNORKELING AND SCUBA DIVING

The reefs and wrecks off San Diego offer amazing sights, clear waters, and brightly colored sea life—whether you want a guided tour or go off on your own.

A great place to enjoy a calm snorkel with your family is the **La Jolla Cove.** Make a reservation with a professional outfit such as **Scuba San Diego, Inc.** (619/260-1880, www.scubasandiego.com) to take a guided tour of the La Jolla Cove Ecological Reserve. They also offer an exciting night dive; a Scuba Adventure trip for new divers who are not yet certified; and a dive trip to Wreck Alley, where eight shipwrecks rest on the ocean floor, including an almost-400-foot-long destroyer. Or bring your own (or rent some) equipment and kick off the shore on your own (with at least one friend, of course).

FISHING

Any number of charter companies offer half- to full-day deep sea fishing trips for everything from rock cod to yellow fin tuna and mahi-mahi, depending on the season. Most companies include both Mexican and California fishing licenses with your charter as needed, as well as rental or included tackle and fish cleaning and filleting services. The tuna season (for fishing well offshore for large tuna) runs from early summer through the fall most years.

Leaving right out of the San Diego harbor, **H&M Landing** (2803 Emerson St., 619/222-1144, www.hmlanding.com, half-day adults $40-46, tackle $9.50) offers half-, three-quarter-, full-day, and evening trips year-round. Shorter trips ply the Point Loma kelp beds, while longer trips can head out to the Coronado Islands or farther into the open water.

Seaforth Sportfishing (1717 Quivira Rd., 619/224-3383, www.seaforthlanding.com, half-day adults $44, tackle extra) offers half-day through multi-day trips to fish for most of the major species fishable in the San Diego area. You can even catch a barracuda! Seaforth's year-round half-day trips last five hours (morning or afternoon), allow the catching of more than half a dozen types of fish, and are perfect for families with children or new anglers. Three-quarter day trips really last all day (eight hours) and can range down as far as the Coronado Islands in Mexico. The Overnight Mexico and Multi-Day Tuna trips are best for more experienced fishers who don't suffer from too much seasickness, and are looking to reel in a bigger catch. On any Seaforth trip, expect a full galley with snacks, meals, and beverage service.

Point Loma Sportfishing (1403 Scott St., 619/223-1627, www.pointlomasportfishing. com, adults half-day $45, tackle extra) offers 18 boats and an extensive list of fishing options. With Point Loma, hardcore anglers can book a two-week cruise that ranges more than 1,000 miles from San Diego, going after enormous deep-water tuna and other major-league sport fish. On the other hand, several of Point Loma's boats offer sedate, family- and beginner-friendly half-day (6 hours) and three-quarter-day (8-10 hours) trips for rockfish, sea bass, barracuda, and yellowtail near the San Diego and northern Mexico coastlines. Private charter boats are available for parties of 5-25.

For small groups looking to fish together, **Action Sport Rentals** (2580 Ingraham St., 619/226-2929, www.danalanding.com) at Dana Landing maintains a fleet of six-passenger fishing boats that can handle half-day to two-day fishing trips. Action Sport Rentals offers bay-safe skiffs, tackle, and bait year-round. You'll also find a launch here if you've brought your own boat.

WHALE-WATCHING

If you prefer to catch marine life with your camera rather than a hook and line, consider taking a whale-watching cruise out from the San Diego coastline. Most of the sportfishing outfits also offer whale-watching trips and charters in season (winter through mid-spring). **Hornblower Cruises** (1066 N. Harbor Dr., 619/686-8700, www.hornblower.com) offers daily nature cruises at 9:30am and 1:30pm year-round. This nearly four-hour adventure is great for families, and includes a kid-friendly marine habitat video; seal, sea lion, and dolphin viewing; and guaranteed whale spotting. Hornblower offers one of the most comfortable, tourist-friendly sea experiences, with a snack bar, indoor decks with panel windows for good viewing, and a yacht highly rated for its stability.

AIR SPORTS

With a strong military history and endlessly fabulous weather, it's no wonder that aviation-based sports are a big deal in San Diego.

Flying and Skydiving

Yes, you really can go to "war" during your otherwise tranquil vacation in San Diego. **Barnstorming Adventures** (800/759-5667, www.barnstorming.com, $220-430 per person, depending on type of flight) offers the rare opportunity to fly an air combat mission in a light plane designed for dogfighting. For a more peaceful aviation experience, book a scenic flight for one or two people in an old-fashioned biplane.

If you prefer jumping out of planes to riding in them, head up north to **Skydive Elsinore** (20701 Cereal St., Lake Elsinore, 951/245-9939, www.skydiveelsinore.com). This full-service skydiving school and outfitter can take you on a great jump, regardless of your experience level. Beginners can take a tandem jump after a brief introductory lesson, or go more intensive with a full-fledged skydiving course culminating with a solo jump. If you're a more experienced jumper, take a look at the website for your diving options.

Gliding

For perhaps the most unusual views of northern San Diego County you can get, go **Sky Sailing** (31930 Hwy. 79, Warner Springs, 760/782-0404, www.skysailing.com, daily, scenic trips from $80/person). In a silent glider or "sail plane," you'll catch thermal updrafts, see Palomar Mountain and Warner Springs Ranch, and feel the wonder of birdlike flight. If you're interested in sightseeing, make a weekday reservation or just drop by on the weekend for a flight flown by an FAA-certified pilot. If it's actually flying a glider yourself that lights your fire, book a lesson or rent a glider of your own. (Hand-controlled gliders are available for pilots with special needs.) And if you've got a strong stomach and great faith in your ability to survive, ask about the Sensational Aerobatic Rides.

If you prefer the notion of gliding off a sea cliff into the air above the Pacific Ocean, your destination is the **Torrey Pines Glider Port** (2800 Torrey Pines Scenic Dr., 858/452-9858, La Jolla, $150/paragliding, $200/hang gliding). Here you can book a tandem flight on either a hang glider or a paraglider with only 20 minutes of pre-flight instruction. The specialty of the house is paragliding, and you can sign up for lessons and get certified to paraglide all on your own.

GOLF
With fabulous sunny weather year-round, San Diego and its surrounding countryside are a golfer's dream. Wherever you go, you'll find a course or two awaiting you, from easy nine-holers up to U.S. Open hosts. If you're new to the area, consider calling **Showtime Golf** (866/661-2334 Ext. 1, www.showtimegolf. com). This golf service provider can get you advance or last-minute tee times, book you into local tournaments, and answer all your questions about the vast range of golfing options in the San Diego area.

If you know anything about golf in San Diego and La Jolla, you know that the One True Golf Course here is **Torrey Pines** (11480 N. Torrey Pines Rd., La Jolla, 858/452-3226, www.torreypinesgolfcourse.com). Home of the 2008 U.S. Open, the Torrey Pines Golf Course has two championship 18-hole courses located on coastal cliffs with views of the ocean. Plan to book well in advance for a tee time at this gorgeous course.

HIKING
In addition to walks on the beach, the **Torrey Pines State Reserve** (12600 North Torrey Pines Rd., 858/755-2063, www.torreypine. org, daily 8am-sunset, $10) offers some unusually beautiful wilderness trails. Be sure to look for *Pinus torreyana*—the rarest species of pine tree in the United States. The shortest walk is the **High Point Trail,** only 100 yards up to views of the whole reserve, from the ocean to the lagoon to the forest and back. For an easy, under-one-hour walk, take the **Guy Fleming Trail** for a level 0.66 miles through forest, wildflower patches, and views of the ocean. For a longer walk, leave the visitors center by the road, then take the **North Fork Trail** west to the **Broken Hill Trail,** which will bring you right down to the beach stairway and a great view of Flat Rock.

SPECTATOR SPORTS
San Diego Chargers
Are you ready for some football, without the snow, sleet, or freezing rain of the back east outdoor stadiums? Then grab tickets to **Qualcomm Stadium** (entrance on Friars Rd., www.sandiego.gov) in the Mission Valley neighborhood. The **San Diego Chargers** (www.chargers.com) are a good team in the AFC West, and they tend to make the playoffs most recent years until 2010. If you're driving in, plan to arrive at the parking lot at least two hours early since the lot often fills up and even closes an hour before kickoff. Also, try to avoid going in or out via Highway 15, which is the most congested route to the stadium. A better way to get here might be the Mission Trolley System (MTS), which has special event bus service to the stadium, as well as regular stops at Qualcomm on the Blue and Green trolley lines. The NTCD system also provides express bus service to all home games.

Once you've made it into the stadium, you'll find ample food, drink, restrooms, souvenirs, ID bracelets for your kids, and first aid and other services throughout. Alcohol sales are limited and end at the close of the third quarter. For a more posh NFL experience, check whether tickets are available at the club level, which has squishier seats and a waitstaff.

San Diego Padres

While you're in San Diego, why not take yourself and your family out to a baseball game? The **San Diego Padres** (http://sandiego.padres. mlb.com) play throughout the regular season (and hopefully into the World Series) at **Petco Park** (100 Park Blvd., 619/795-5000) in downtown San Diego. Few rainouts mar the Padres' home season, and in addition to the game, you can view Balboa Park, the cityscape, and San Diego Bay from the lovely and spacious modern stadium. Sit back with a brew or a soda, enjoy the extra legroom, and bask in the perfect spring baseball weather of San Diego.

Petco Park is well situated for fans that prefer to avoid the inevitable parking nightmares and take public transit in to the game. The MTS trolleys and buses have multiple stops within a block or two of the ballpark, and the Coaster rail line offers extra trains on game nights for fans coming in from the North County towns. If you're staying in the Gaslamp Quarter, consider just walking over to the stadium from your lodgings. If you must drive, prepare to pay $8-15 for downtown lot parking and $20 for a slot right by the park.

Del Mar Racetrack and Fairgrounds

In horseracing season, you'll find significant crowds descending on the tiny town of Del Mar and the famous **Del Mar Fairgrounds** (2260 Jimmy Durante Blvd., Del Mar, 858/755-1161, www.delmarfairgrounds.com), where some of the finest thoroughbreds ever to grace a track have raced to victory. The track was built in the late 1930s, with Bing Crosby supplying both

funds and fame to create the glorious equestrian facilities that continue to delight race and horse fans to this day. The various structures at the Fairgrounds are built in the style of various California missions, and careful attention to detail has created possibly the most beautiful permanent indoor-outdoor exhibition facilities in the state.

Races usually run July-early September. Wagering rules can be found at the track or on the Fairgrounds website, as can information about the off-season telecast racing series. Come out and join in the excitement of live thoroughbred racing in one of the most hospitable climates in the world! Show up on Friday afternoons to enjoy the **Del Mar Summer Concert Series,** which includes a free pass to see acts like Jimmy Cliff and Cake by just attending one of the last races of the day at the facility.

If you prefer a different style of equestrian event, come to Del Mar a little bit earlier in the year for the **Del Mar National Horse Show** (www.delmarnational.com). This event lasts three weeks each spring, with a full week each devoted to Western events, dressage, and hunter/jumper activities. Be sure to book your room and buy tickets in advance, as this is one of the most popular horse shows in the western United States each year.

Any number of other events take place at the Fairgrounds every month of the year. Check the website for a calendar of upcoming events, plus ticket information. Ample pay parking surrounds the Fairgrounds, or if you're taking the train, grab a free shuttle from the Coaster straight to the racetrack.

Accommodations

DOWNTOWN

Acres of hotels cluster throughout downtown San Diego. Whether you need a budget hostel or want a high-end luxury resort, you'll find it. Many mid-tier and upscale chains offer bed and board downtown—all you have to do is walk around to find the Sheraton, Hilton, or Holiday Inn. For a more interesting lodging experience, look to the smaller chains and the independents.

Under $100

Looking for budget accommodations in the heart of San Diego? For a start, call the **HI-San Diego** (521 Market St., 800/909-4776, www.sandiegohostels.org, $30-170). Located perfectly right in the middle of the Gaslamp Quarter, you can get just about anywhere from this almost-elegant youth hostel. (Bring your HI card for lower rates!) Inside, you'll find private and double rooms, as well as dorm rooms that sleep 4-10 people in single beds. The amenities include all standard hostel fare: coin-op laundry, an open kitchen, a common room with a TV, and a garden area. Plan to bring or buy a lock for the lockers provided in the dorm rooms. The hostel's packed events calendar includes free walking tours of Balboa Park and the downtown area. Between the food and nightlife of the Gaslamp and the endless stream of interesting people and activities, the HI-San Diego is the perfect resting place for young people visiting San Diego.

Looking for a Mediterranean-style student hotel for a whole week? Try the **Hotel Occidental** (410 Elm St., 619/232-1336, www.hoteloccidental-sandiego.com, $175-300/week), where the minimum stay is for seven nights. Located only a block and a half from the entrance to Balboa Park, you can visit the zoo and museums, or head downtown to the Gaslamp Quarter. Don't expect tons of in-room luxury here—smaller rooms share baths, and even some of the larger rooms have only a half-bath, with shower facilities down the hall.

Decor feels European (in the Ikea sense when it comes to furniture), with lots of clean lines and plain linens and small, ingeniously used spaces. Hotel-wide amenities include free Wi-Fi and private kitchenettes that let you keep some of your own food rather than depending on restaurants for every meal.

$100-150

With enough rooms for a medium-sized motel, but the feel of a small inn, **La Pensione Hotel** (606 W. Date St., 800/232-4683, www.lapensionehotel.com, $100-200) prides itself on offering the best value in the best location in downtown San Diego. The exterior blends the look of a Mediterranean home with the Spanish Colonial Revival style of Southern California. Renovated in 2011, a standard room has one queen-sized bed, unusual photographic wall art, and a clean bathroom. The upgraded Argento Collection rooms have premium features, including platform beds and velvety wool carpets. The hotel is located in Little Italy, within easy walking distance of great restaurants and cafés, and only blocks from the Gaslamp Quarter. The staff can help you with taxis and public transit, making it possible to avoid driving.

La Pensione does not have as many off-street parking spots as they do rooms, so parking is first come, first served during the high season. And if you're bringing your kids, be aware that trundle beds and such are not available, and the hotel requests that only two people stay in any one room.

Over $250

If you want to stay in *the* classic San Diego hotel and you've got the money to do it, book a room at the **US Grant Hotel** (326 Broadway, 619/232-3121, www.starwoodhotels.com, $280-500). Built in 1910, the US Grant has anchored the Gaslamp Quarter for 100 years. Inside, you'll be showered with luxury, from the elegant lobby to the in-house spa to the gorgeous guest rooms (which include luxurious showers). Even the standard guest rooms have plush linens, nine-foot ceilings, original artwork, and the many amenities that mark the US Grant worth the cost of admission. You've got all the restaurant options of the Gaslamp within staggering distance, or you can stay in the hotel and dine at the upscale California-style Grant Grill. Whether your interests are surfing or golfing, the concierges can help you with arrangements for activities around the city.

For a fun hotel stay downtown, hit the exclusive **W Hotel San Diego** (421 W. B St., 619/398-3100, www.starwoodhotels.com, $190-500). This swanky, ultra-modern hotel has the perfect location—convenient to the airport, walking distance to the harbor, and a short jaunt to the fabulous restaurants in the Gaslamp Quarter. Upper-level guest rooms offer views of city and the bay. Rooms feature cushy beds with featherbeds and down comforters, and are done in an almost-industrial, urban-chic style that echoes the grander decor of the entrance, lobby, and bars. Despite the hard lines and cool blue-and-silver color scheme, touches of whimsy abound. (Be sure to take a moment to read the labels on your toiletries—it's worth the time.) But best of all, the service here is exceptional, even in this tourist-friendly region. Just call down, and anything you want will be at your doorstep, probably in about 15 minutes. You'll find every amenity you could dream of, from 24-hour room service to first-aid kits to Wi-Fi to condoms—but beware, none of these are complimentary. For a fun night out without the hassle of a car or a cab, head up to The Rooftop Bar, the W's bar created with real sand and fruity umbrella drinks to mimic an actual SoCal beach scene.

For a great view of downtown and the bay beyond, book a room on one of the top floors at **Hotel Palomar San Diego** (1047 S. 5th Ave., 619/515-3000 or 888/288-6601, www.hotelpalomar-sandiego.com, $250-900). With lots of windows, these elegant, modern rooms also have wood floors and stone wash basins in the bathroom. Onsite is a heated rooftop

Hotel Palomar San Diego

swimming pool, spa, and the Saltbox, a "gastro-lounge" serving creative plates and tasty cocktails. The friendly staff at the Hotel Palomar host a daily wine tasting 5pm-6pm and allow guests to borrow their on-site surfboards and bikes to enjoy San Diego's glorious outdoors.

BALBOA PARK AND HILLCREST

Lodgings right by the park aren't plentiful. For a better selection, check out downtown and Old Town, which are within easy public transit and driving distance to the wonders of Balboa Park and the fun of Hillcrest.

$100-150

Looking to stay at an inn that evokes the true spirit of San Diego? Try the Spanish-Colonial Revival-style **Balboa Park Inn** (3402 Park Blvd., 619/298-0823, www.balboaparkinn.com, $100-250). This funky boutique hotel offers 26 unique rooms and suites with names like Harlequin and Emma's Diary, each beautiful in its own decorative style. Smaller rooms just offer a simple bed-and-bath setup, while the more numerous suites offer multiple rooms, kitchens, decks, and often more than one bed. Balboa Park Inn is the perfect place for families looking for moderate prices and the attractions of Balboa Park. Situated just north of the park, you can walk from the inn just two blocks to the San Diego Zoo. The quiet neighborhood isn't much for nightlife, but offers peace for visitors who long for a good night's sleep.

Another small, stylish charmer is the **Hillcrest Inn** (3754 5th Ave., 800/258-2280, www.hillcrestinn.net, $120-150). Situated in the up-and-coming Hillcrest neighborhood within a few minutes' drive of Balboa Park, this small hotel offers entirely acceptable rooms at reasonable prices. While amenities aren't luxe, you will get a TV, refrigerator, microwave, and clean private bathroom, as well as access to the hotel's outdoor spa. Around the Hillcrest area, you'll find the center of San Diego's gay culture, plus easy access to downtown and the Gaslamp Quarter. If you can snag an unmetered on-street parking spot, take it, since

parking at the inn costs extra. Luckily, lots of restaurants, shops, parks, bars, and clubs are within easy walking distance of the inn, so you may only need to park once.

OLD TOWN

You'll find a massive cluster of national chain motels in Old Town, so this is a great place to land if you need a place to stay on short notice. However, if you want something a little less generic but still reasonably priced, Old Town can hook you up with that too.

Under $100

For thrift, exterior charm, and location, location, location, you can't beat the **Old Town Inn** (4444 Pacific Hwy., 619/260-8024, www.oldtown-inn.com, $90-135). Built to resemble a rancho with a low profile and narrow columns, this motel sits across the street from the Old Town Transit Center, so you can catch a bus or trolley and get virtually anywhere in San Diego County from here. The white-painted, red-tile-roofed exterior of the motel gives way to plain motel rooms inside, with muted pastels, dark carpets, and floral bedspreads. If you plan to cook your own meals, go for a deluxe room, which includes a two-burner stove, refrigerator, and microwave. This family-friendly motel allows kids 12 and under to stay for free, has a heated pool, and offers a free daily continental breakfast.

$100-150

The **Kings Inn** (1333 Hotel Circle S., 619/297-2231, www.kingsinnsandiego.com, $89-169) offers spacious, nonsmoking motel rooms at affordable prices. Guest rooms are done in florals with jewel-colored carpets and light walls, with either one king or two queen beds. Outside, take a dip in the cute apostrophe-shaped pool or accompanying spa. The location is convenient to sightseeing and transportation, and attached are two family restaurants that provide room service to the motel. The Amigo Spot serves authentic Mexican cuisine, and the Waffle Spot has (surprise) waffles, as well as Mexican and American egg breakfast dishes and a kids' menu.

The **Padre Trail Inn** (4200 Taylor St., 619/297-3291, www.padretrailinn.com, $109-199) has upscale furniture and brand-name toiletries, so you'll feel just a little bit pampered in your pleasant room here. Spend a few hours lounging by the side of the pool, or dive right into sightseeing in Old Town. The exterior matches the locale—a Spanish Revival hacienda was the inspiration for the Padre Trail Inn.

$150-250

For a cheerful modern stay in San Diego that feels almost like home, stay in the **Sommerset Suites Hotel** (606 Washington St., 800/962-9665, www.sommersetsuites.com, $189-319). Light, bright bedrooms offer a touch of class in this 80-unit, all-suite, non-smoking motel, and each room offers a full kitchen. Enjoy free Wi-Fi in your room or down by the pool, where you can take a refreshing dip on a hot day or a hot spa soak on a cool evening. Technically the Sommerset is in the Uptown neighborhood adjacent to Old Town, but it's easy to reach shopping and dining in Old Town, or all the major attractions in San Diego.

Though Craftsman architecture holds sway in much of Southern California, the Victorians had their say too. To immerse yourself in the Victorian era in San Diego, stay at **A Victorian Heritage Park Inn** (2470 Heritage Park Row, 800/995-2470, www.heritageparkinn.com, $125-300). This B&B has a dozen amazing guest rooms, each with a unique decorative scheme that complements the classic Queen Anne lines of the mansion itself. Expect to be pampered with featherbeds, private baths (many with claw foot or whirlpool tubs), antique canopy and poster beds, and glorious views out the windows. A traditional afternoon tea is served downstairs each day, complete with finger sandwiches. Surrounding the inn you'll find the Victorian Heritage Park of San Diego, a small cluster of immaculately restored 19th-century homes and gardens set in almost eight acres of space, complete with cobble-stoned streets and views of downtown and the ocean to the west.

POINT LOMA

While your kids will love the proximity to SeaWorld, you'll love the almost European stylings of the classic ocean-side resorts on Point Loma and Shelter Island. You're still within easy driving range of all major San Diego attractions, without the crowds and the downtown feel. If you own your own boat and plan to bring it to San Diego, consider one of the resorts on Shelter Island—most have private marinas that rent slips.

Under $100

For the cheapest accommodations near the beach, book a bed or a family room in the **◖ HI-San Diego, Point Loma Hostel** (3790 Udall St., 619/223-800/909-4776, www.sandiegohostels.org, $20-40/dorm bed, $58-80/private room, $60-104/family room). A short drive or a longish two-mile-walk from famous Ocean Beach, this charming bright-red hostel sits in the midst of a residential area of Point Loma. The proprietors encourage bicycling exploration of San Diego by providing ample bike racks for secure storage. Or if you prefer, the bus stop is only a block away from the hostel, making it easy to get to the zoo, Old Town, the beaches, or wherever else you want to go. Inside, you'll find 4-10-bed dorms and private or family rooms that include linens, Internet access, and storage lockers. Cook in the common kitchen and eat in the living room or play ping-pong out on the courtyard. The owners love to see families, as well as budget-minded singles here at the hostel, and this is a great place to stay for a truly inexpensive family beach vacation.

For folks who want a budget bed with more privacy than a hostel can afford, the **Dolphin Motel** (2912 Garrison St., 619/758-1404, www.dolphin-motel.com, $55-100) offers comfortable rooms at reasonable rates. The white walls match the pristine white bedspreads, daring you to find fault with the cleanliness at this budget motel. Pick a room with a queen bed and a single or a slightly larger room that has a queen bed and a double. While the rooms aren't huge, you'll get a comfortable bed for the duration of your stay. Best of all, you're only a short walk from the sea, and the fishing, kayaking, and other water sports of San Diego are easily accessible (some only across the street). Enjoy a pastry and a morning cup of coffee on the house out in the attractive little courtyard. Or get your own food and sit out on the balcony, enjoying the calm air of Point Loma. The motel is right across from the sport fishing landing.

$150-250

A Shelter Island charmer, **The Bay Club Hotel and Marina** (2131 Shelter Island Dr., 800/672-0800, www.bayclubhotel.com, $180-220) provides bay and harbor views, comfortable rooms, and charming amenities. Outside your room, you'll find a funky geometric swimming pool with matching spa, a fitness center, and a brown-and-white bar and grill with a 1950s-style tropical resort feel. In the morning, there's a complimentary breakfast buffet for guests. Be sure to stop at the desk before heading out into town to grab discount passes to various attractions. Bringing your boat to San Diego? Call the Bay Club to make arrangements to rent a slip in the private marina, which is convenient to the bay, the open ocean, and an on-water fuel station.

The exterior of the **Kona Kai Resort** (1551 Shelter Island Dr., 619/221-8000 or 800/566-2524, www.resortkonakai.com, $189-209) evokes the legendary Hotel del Coronado. But on the property, you'll find a sense of peace and tranquility that feels more like a Hawaiian resort out away from the city. With a fitness center, a pool, and a full-service spa, you won't lack for pampering and amenities as you bask in the Shelter Island sunshine. Inside, your room will fulfill all your oceanside vacation ideals with soft neutral tones on the walls, and colorful and green accents creating a tropical paradise. Befitting a tropical resort, the Kona Kai has its own private beach by the marina. If you plan to take a seagoing adventure, you can moor your personal or rental boat at the private marina (slips up to 200 feet), or you can head over to SeaWorld or downtown for

land-lubbing activities. Even if you get seasick, it might be worth a stroll down to the marina to check out the mega-yacht docking area and get a glimpse at how the other 1 percent live.

Over $250

Consider staying across the bay from downtown San Diego, on Shelter Island at **Humphrey's Half Moon Inn & Suites** (2303 Shelter Island Dr., 800/542-7400, www.halfmooninn.com, $290-600, parking $10). This resort property looks out over the bay towards the city skyline. It has its own private marina and a lush tropical garden (heavy on the palm trees, of course). Your large, home-styled room might look out into the greenery or over the great blue bay. If you're in the mood for luxury, add an "enhancement," such as champagne and strawberries or an in-room massage, to your room reservation. If you're feeling lazy, spend a day by the pool, enjoying fruity rum drinks from the poolside bar. On the other hand, energetic travelers can take a boat out onto the water, head into town to check out the attractions, or take a bike ride around Shelter Island. Come evening, you can dine at the on-site gourmet restaurant, then dance the night away to live music at the hotel's own club. In the summertime, get tickets to one of the famed outdoor concerts held on the resort property.

CORONADO

While the Hotel del Coronado dominates the Coronado scenery and certainly makes for a fun place to stay, the island town also offers an array of other accommodations. You can find a good place to lay your head for a reasonable rate here, or go over the top at the Del or one of the other big beach resorts.

Under $150

For an inexpensive stay on Coronado Island, visit the **El Rancho Motel** (370 Orange Ave., 619/435-2251, www.elranchocoronado.com, $99-120). A few blocks from the Del, the beaches, and the downtown area of Coronado, the El Rancho lets you enjoy the high life without the high prices. Each unit of the El Rancho has its own air-conditioning, TV, fridge, and microwave, plus a comfortable bed and a pleasant tiled bathroom. You'll feel right at home in the small lodge-like motel with its white exterior and mostly matching interior. Be sure to ask the innkeeper (who lives on-site at the motel) about the best food, shopping, and good beach spots on the island.

$150-250

If you can't quite afford a stay at the Del this time, the next best thing might be the **Glorietta Bay Inn** (1630 Glorietta Blvd., 619/435-3101, www.gloriettabayinn.com, $209-350). Literally across the street from the Del, the stately white mansion was the dream home of John D. Spreckels, who in the latter half of the 19th century owned the Del and most of the rest of San Diego in the bargain. Today, the lovely structure oozes charm, even as the less-glamorous motel buildings behind it offer spacious budget accommodations. For a premium, you can book a room inside the mansion proper; each of these is uniquely decorated and includes upscale services and amenities. The "Inn Rooms" behind the mansion are spacious, with adequate amenities and cheerful tropical-resort decor. If you're bringing your family for several days of beach time, the Inn Suites offer a full kitchen and a living room as well as one or two bedrooms, making them an ideal base of operations. No matter which building you stay in, a free continental breakfast is served each morning in the mansion's breakfast room. Grab a pastry and your coffee and enjoy exploring the mansion common rooms, which boast photos commemorating the history of the house and the Spreckels family. Then jog across the street to gape at the Del or just pass through onto Coronado Beach.

At **Villa Capri By the Sea** (1417 Orange Ave., 800/231-3954, www.villacapribythesea. com, $150) you get all the benefits of staying right at the hot center of Coronado (that is, near the Del), without the costs or the ghosts. Bring your whole family or several friends— the suites sleep up to six people, and include a full kitchen with all pots and pans necessary

for cooking great meals. Yet you can still walk across the street to enjoy the restaurants and shops of the Del, and to get out onto Coronado Beach. Inside, the living rooms are dimly lit but comfortable, the kitchens are light and homey, and the bright bedrooms look perfect for a sunny beach vacation. On the hottest days, you'll appreciate your own oasis of air-conditioning, cable TV, and Wi-Fi after hours out on the sand playing with on-loan beach toys. Check the website for special Internet rates.

Over $250

 Hotel del Coronado (1500 Orange Ave., 800/468-3533, www.hoteldel.com, $325-1,300) dominates the landscape of Coronado Island. Even in Southern California, the Del, as it's called by its friends and neighbors, wins a prize for grandiosity. The white-painted, red-roofed mammoth sprawls for acres from the beach to the road, taking up a couple of blocks all its own. Inside, the Del is at once a historical museum, shopping mall, food court, and, oh yeah, it's a hotel too! Famously haunted, the Del offers almost 700 rooms, plus another 70-plus individual cottages at Beach Village. Your best bet to catch a ghost in action is to book a room in the Victorian Building. For a more modern hotel experience, stay in the Ocean Towers or California Cabanas. Room sizes and decor vary, from smaller Victorian-decorated guest rooms to expansive resort-themed suites. Pick what you (and your budget) like best! If you want a view, be aware that ocean-facing rooms cost extra.

The best thing about staying at the Del is that you almost never have to leave. You can fall out of the hotel onto Coronado Beach, grabbing a spot early on this oft-crowded strip of sand in the summertime. In the winter, the hotel puts up an improbable ice rink out on the "back porch." You can pick from among several restaurant (or room service) for meals, and even shop for a new bikini in the downstairs of the main building.

MISSION BAY

The perfect location to find a room if you're traveling with your family to SeaWorld or

the grand Hotel del Coronado

planning a wild-water vacation off the shore, Mission Bay offers plenty of inexpensive chain and independent motels. If you're looking for luxury, you can also check in to one of the upscale resorts along the beach.

Under $150

Mission Bay Motel (4221 Mission Blvd., 866/649-5828, www.missionbaymotel.com, $140-170) offers clean, comfortable accommodations at the right price near the beach and Mission Bay Aquatic Park. This cheerful, white-and-blue-painted, low-built motor hotel has small, white-painted and pastel-decorated rooms, and makes a perfect base from which to enjoy the many sights and sun-drenched beaches of San Diego. You can choose from rock bottom priced singles (which actually sleep two people) up to multi-bed rooms with kitchenettes that can accommodate the whole family. The residential Pacific Beach neighborhood offers affordable local restaurants, a beach a block away, and car or public transit access to the rest of the San Diego area.

$150-250

Almost affordable rates seem a surprise at oceanside **The Dana on Mission Bay** (1710 W. Mission Bay Dr., 800/445-3339, www.thedana. com, $160-430). It's so close to SeaWorld that you can walk to the park, and it has its own private marina for serious sea-lovers. Pick from two blocks of rooms—the Marina Cove section offers less expense rooms without views of the ocean; you might look over the garden or the pool. Inside, Marina Cove rooms are fairly small, with brightly colored, tropical-themed decor. The Waters Edge premium rooms have wonderful views out over the Pacific and a subtler, elegant design scheme. Rent a personal watercraft or a boat directly from The Dana and take a spin on Mission Bay. Or stay on the 10-acre resort property and splash in one of the two large swimming pools.

If your reason for coming to San Diego is to loll about on the beach sipping fruity cocktails, the **Bahia Resort** (998 W. Mission Bay Dr., 800/576-4229, www.bahiahotel.com, $229-600) is the perfect place to drop your suitcase and change into your swimsuit. Set right on the beach in Mission Bay, you can stumble out of your hotel room onto a strip of sun-warmed sugar sand. If you prefer your water a bit more contained, the charming Moroccan decor surrounding the large pool and tremendous (30-person) spa is for you. For the ultimate in splendid relaxation, order from the café and waiters will deliver right to you at poolside. Inside, the understated guest rooms are done in a variety of styles. Enjoy the comfort of the plush beds, the overstuffed furniture, and the homey touches prevalent especially in the larger apartment-like suites. The hotel restaurant, Café Bahia, offers tasty traditional breakfast, lunch, and dinner with just a touch of Middle Eastern flavor. For a treat, eat outdoors!

Sleep over the ocean at the **Crystal Pier Hotel** (4500 Ocean Blvd., 800/748-5894, www.crystalpier.com, $175-525). These cottages and suites are perched right on Pacific Beach's Crystal Pier above the crashing surf. Each place has a fully equipped kitchenette, parking space, and private deck over the beach.

SAN DIEGO

Over $250

San Diego seems littered with gorgeous high-end resort hotels, and the Mission Bay area is no exception. One of the nicest of these is the **Catamaran Resort** (3999 Mission Blvd., 800/422-8386, www.catamaranresort.com, $309-600). Garden rooms and studios, which have one or two beds, stylish decor, and top-tier amenities (plus full kitchens in the studios), can have surprisingly reasonable rates. The premier rooms—bayfront rooms and suites—have grand views of the ocean, some with direct access right down to the Catamaran's beach. A great reason to stay at the Catamaran, the private beach runs to a private pier with a water-sports rental facility that can hook you up whether you prefer high-powered, wind-powered, or human-powered watercraft. (Windsurfing is a favored activity on Mission Bay.) For younger guests, the Catamaran Kids Club keeps children occupied and happy while their parents enjoy the sea, the spa, or the private comforts of their hotel room. Also on-site you'll find the Atoll Restaurant, which serves three meals a day and a sumptuous champagne brunch on Sunday mornings and early afternoons.

LA JOLLA

If you want to stay in ritzy La Jolla, be prepared to bust out your credit card. This uptown burg doesn't come cheap. While a few motels offer decent rooms for under $200, you'll find the best locations and rooms well over that price point. If you simply must stay in La Jolla on a budget, a few major chain motels lurk around near downtown.

$100-150

One of the few pleasant lower-budget La Jolla accommodations is the **Sands of La Jolla** (5417 La Jolla Blvd., 800/643-0530, www.sandsoflajolla.com, $99-189). It's not located in the center of the action, which helps the price point stay a little bit lower, but you can still use a car to reach the beaches, the La Jolla Cove, and the top attractions in San Diego proper. Inside, you'll find pleasant motel rooms furnished with light woods and sunny yellow wall and window treatments. Deluxe rooms and suites offer full kitchenettes, and all rooms have refrigerators, microwaves, and toaster ovens to help you save money by buying some of your own food from the store rather than eating at a pricey restaurant. This nice little motel also offers family-friendly, multi-bed rooms and suites for great beach vacations.

$150-250

Perfectly located and reasonably priced (for La Jolla), the **La Jolla Inn** (1110 Prospect St., 888/855-7829, www.lajollainn.com, $169-199) sits comfortably between the main shopping drag and the sloping sidewalk down to the beach. The brick facade with dark blue awnings stands out in an area of wood and adobe-style construction. Inside, you'll think you've found a boutique hotel on the Mediterranean, with small bright rooms that feature natural wood furniture and colorful homemade quilts. Upper rooms also offer the best art ever: a view out over the Pacific. All guests get to take advantage of the free continental breakfast and the afternoon snack (served at 2pm—perfect for a quick break from the beach). Be sure to take advantage of the pay underground parking as this area gets crowded in high season.

Over $250

In La Jolla, upscale accommodations abound. One of the most charming is the C **Estancia La Jolla Hotel and Spa** (9700 Torrey Pines Rd., 858/550-1000, www.estancialajolla.com, $300-400). Built on an historic Mexican rancho, the traditional arrangement of buildings and courtyards gleam with restoration and vitality. (When driving in, look for the resort name on a standard cross-street sign.) Palm trees and succulents grace the landscape. Inside, spacious guest rooms in neutral tones are accented with bright oranges, yellows, and greens. Beds offer an extra-comfy night's sleep, made even better by a visit to the spa or a day spent lounging under a cabana by the vast swimming pool, sipping drinks from the poolside bar. The hotel offers many of the amenities of a full-scale resort, including a restaurant and wine bar. As you stroll the groomed paths through the endless gardens dotted with native plants, you'll also find the main lobby and the main sitting room, complete with huge stone fireplace and all the help you need from friendly concierges at the desk.

The candy-colored **La Valencia Hotel** (1132 Prospect St., 858/454-0771, www.lavalencia. com, $285-3,500) has it all: ocean views, high-end restaurants, sumptuous guest rooms, and a great downtown location. Guest rooms, suites, and villas are decorated tastefully in earth tones with splashes of bright color. Living plants provide both oxygen and a homey sense of elegance both in the rooms and throughout the resort. Downstairs, take advantage of the state-of-the-art workout room, then cool off in the large sparkling blue pool. You can walk to the cliffside boardwalk or down to the beach from the La Valencia, and enjoy the shopping and restaurants of Prospect Street.

The Lodge at Torrey Pines (11480 N. Torrey Pines Rd., 858/453-4420, www. lodgetorreypines.com, $400-600) offers luxury, service, amenities, and access to the amazing Torrey Pines Golf Course. You'll be struck by the classic Southern California Craftsman architecture—the exterior of the lodge is a work of art in itself. The Craftsman elegance continues into the rooms, with designer fabrics, tasteful appointments, gorgeous marble bathrooms, and views of the golf course and ocean. If you plan to play golf, check the golf packages and arrange your tee time through the hotel. Non-golfers have a number of great recreation options too. Book an appointment at the full-service spa, rent one of the charming cabanas down at the beach, or take a guided hike at the state reserve. If traveling with family, there are numerous kids' activities and amenities available at the resort.

NORTH COUNTY

If your one major purpose in coming to the San Diego area is to lounge on a white-sand beach, consider booking a stay north of the city proper. Some of the best beaches cluster in the North County area. Accordingly, you'll find everything from modest motels to fancy resorts available in the area.

Under $150

For a good, modest motel that's clean and reasonably close to the beach and everything else, stay at the **Moonlight Beach Motel** (233 Second St., Encinitas, 800/323-1259, www.moonlight-beachmotel.com, $130-175). Cheerful budget motel rooms greet guests with floral bedspreads and light-painted walls. Most rooms have a kitchenette, complete with refrigerator and microwave, making it easy to store and chill beach drinks and snacks in your room. Rooms are clean enough to feel comfortable sleeping in, but not so fancy that you'll be horrified if a little bit of sand makes it onto the carpet. The motel sits near both U.S. 101 and I-5, making it a perfect base from which to get anywhere in the San Diego area. If you prefer to stay close by, you're only a few blocks from Moonlight Beach. Go surfing, play a game of volleyball, or just relax into the sand for a day. (From the motel on a busy summer weekend day, walk to the beach if you can to avoid the parking nightmare down closer to the sand.)

$150-250

Built in the charming Spanish Colonial Revival style, **Les Artistes** (944 Camino Del Mar, Del Mar, 858/755-4646, www.lesartistesinn.com, $175-295) offers something different from the standard chain motel experience. Each room is named for and decorated in the style of a particular artist or style, from the French countryside of Monet to the peace of Zen. Despite its unique and fun style, this is a budget motel; the rooms are small and you won't be able to trip over your doorsill and fall into the ocean. But the beach and downtown Del Mar with its restaurants and shops are only a few blocks away. And you can bring your family (several rooms have multiple beds), including your beloved pet, to Les Artistes and receive a warm welcome. Don't bring your cigarettes, however, as Les Artistes is entirely non-smoking.

If you want a beach house of your own rather

SAN DIEGO

than a motel room that's part of a huge block, book a daily or weekly bungalow or suite at the **Wave Crest Resort** (1400 Ocean Ave., Del Mar, 858/755-0100, www.wavecrestresort.com, $200-500). Here you'll get a studio, one-bedroom, or two-bedroom private unit. These are condo-style accommodations, so you'll get nice furnishings but no daily maid service. Even if you go for a more economical garden-facing unit, you'll enjoy the view of the meticulous landscaping that makes the whole complex lovely. For a modest extra fee, your unit will face the near-enough-to-touch Pacific Ocean. Take a quick walk to Seagrove Park and down to the beach beyond. Perhaps the only downside, which can also be an upside, is its proximity to the rail line and the highways. They provide both easy transportation and noise.

Over $250

For a classic luxury resort experience, complete with a golf course, multiple swimming pools, ocean views, and almost every service you can dream up, stay at the **Four Seasons Aviara** (7100 Four Seasons Point, Aviara, 760/603-6800, www.fourseasons.com, $352-525). You'll find everything in your guest room exactly as you'd expect from a Four Seasons hotel, from the L'Occitane toiletries to the specially made comfy beds to the tasteful tropical decor. Downstairs, the lobby and common areas shine with marble floors and columns. You can indulge at the various independently owned shops, including a wonderful little jewelry store that specializes in unique colored gems, many of which are mined in San Diego County. The concierge and desk staff is as friendly and helpful as possible at all times—you can get whatever you want whenever you want, pretty much.

On the Four Seasons property you can play 18 holes of golf and a set of tennis, splash with the kids in the family swimming pool, or get serious in the adults-only pool. Round out your day with a treatment from the hotel spa. In the evening, dine at one of the three on-site restaurants. If you've come with your family, you can get the kids involved in a number of activities tailored for the younger set, and escape and enjoy some of the more adult aspects of the resort.

For another tip-top resort experience, book a room at the newly reopened **L'Auberge Del Mar** (1540 Camino Del Mar, Del Mar, 800/245-9757, www.laubergedelmar.com, $375-720). Enjoy the elegant guest rooms, posh spa, upscale dining, and superior amenities, all with glorious views overlooking the ocean. Enjoy floating around in the leisure pool or getting a workout in the lap pool. For guaranteed access to the tennis courts, book a court and a time in advance.

Food

San Diego doesn't have the celebrated culinary culture of San Francisco or the Wine Country, but you can still get a good meal in this town. Due to San Diego's proximity to the border and the ocean, you'll easily find delicious Mexican food and fresh seafood. In places like the Gaslamp Quarter, Hillcrest, and La Jolla, you can find great food just by wandering down the main drag and reading menus as you go.

DOWNTOWN

Downtown San Diego offers an astonishing array of dining choices, from comfortable American fare to wonderful French café food and a surprisingly diverse Italian option, and on to upscale California cuisine.

California Cuisine

A local legend, the **⟨ Grant Grill** (326 Broadway, 619/744-2077, www.grantgrill.com, daily breakfast, lunch, and dinner, $24-45) has been serving upscale cuisine since 1951. The wonderful ambiance of the posh dining room makes even the most casual of diners feel wealthy and "part of the crowd." The Grant Grill, part of the US Grant hotel, serves breakfast, lunch, and dinner every day, and offers a full-service lounge with live music and a lobby where you can enjoy top-end aperitifs and digestifs. At lunch and dinner, you'll find the fanciest of California-style cuisine on the menu. For dinner, choose from the à la carte menu, or enjoy a full five-course tasting menu that's something of a bargain. For an extra fee, you can add wine pairings to each course of the tasting menu.

While the Grant Grill is clearly aware of current culinary trends, it also honors its storied past. It still serves the mock turtle soup that was a hit during its early days and a superbly smooth Manhattan made with old-fashioned bitters that are blended and aged in oak for 100 days.

If you're female, coming into the Grant Grill makes you a part of history. In the 1950s and 1960s, the Grill was an exclusive and exclusionary men's club. In 1969, a group of local businesswomen staged a sit-in, and the Grant Grill was forced to move into the modern era.

French

C Café Chloe (721 9the Ave., 619/232-3242, www.cafechloe.com, Mon.-Fri. 7:30am-10pm, Sat. 8:30am-10:30pm, Sun. 8:30am-9:30pm, $15-25) transports diners and coffee sippers to a Parisian café. While Chloe's intimate café feel and attentive service should be noted, it's the food here that truly stands out. The breakfasts, including a dish with eggs, peppers, onions, and prosciutto, are a tasty way to begin the day while sipping coffee. Later on, the dinner menu changes according to what's freshest in the meat and vegetable departments and could include entrées like spiced duck breast or wild salmon in a pinot noir sauce. While dining, stare at the passersby from one of the café's sidewalk seats or flip through a magazine from the restaurant's magazine rack.

Italian

Looking for some comfortable, warm Italian food without high prices or pretenses? Go where the locals go: **Filippi's Pizza Grotto** (1747 India St., 619/232-5094, www.

realcheesepizza.com, Tues.-Thurs. 11am-10:30pm, Fri.-Sat. 11am-11:30pm, Sun.-Mon. 11am-10pm, $10-15). Walk through the tempting Italian market at the front into the dimly lit restaurant at the rear of the building. Enjoy the classic atmosphere, complete with red-and-white checkered tablecloths. Order a pizza, some lasagna, or a giant meatball sandwich. Pastas come with classic and uncomplicated marinara and the pizza might be the best in all of San Diego. Best of all, Filippi's serves late into the evening—until almost midnight on weekends. You'll definitely have to jostle with the local crowd for a seat on Friday and Saturday nights. You can find Filippi's locations in other parts of San Diego County—but the original is this Little Italy location.

Steak and Seafood

A couple miles north of San Diego's downtown, the Mission Hills neighborhood has one popular locals' eatery worth seeking out if you want some great seafood. The **C Blue Water Seafood Market & Grill** (3667 India St., 619/497-0914, http://bluewaterseafoodsandiego.com, Mon.-Thurs. 11am-9pm, Fri. 11am-10pm, Sat. 11:30am-10pm, Sun. 11:30am-9pm, $4-25) has a simple concept done really well. First, you pick what fresh seafood you want. Then you choose what kind of marinade you'd like it cooked in. Finally, you select it as a sandwich, salad, plate, or taco. Expect to wait in a long line out the door if you come during busy hours.

Looking for a rich slab of beef after a long day playing outside? Head for the **Greystone Steakhouse** (658 Fifth Ave., 619/232-0225, www.greystonesteakhouse.com, daily dinner only, $30-48) in the heart of the Gaslamp Quarter. This upscale eatery makes a great start to a night out on the town with your sweetie. The white tablecloths light up the dim interior, where the dining area surrounds a staircase leading down into the belly of the restaurant. Or if you prefer, get a table on the small patio out front so you can people-watch as the Gaslamp heats up with the evening crowd. The menu includes all your favorite steakhouse standards—great cuts of beef, lobster and tuna, and an array of yummy sides. You'll also find some interesting California-style entrées and appetizers. Portions are big, so consider splitting an entrée with your dinner partner so you can both enjoy an appetizer and some dessert. The wine list focuses on California wines and includes a good selection of local vintages, and the full bar offers pre-dinner cosmos and martinis. The service can be a bit slow during the dinner hours, but it's friendly and helpful.

BALBOA PARK AND HILLCREST

The fun and funky Hillcrest neighborhood offers an array of dining options, from ethnic to upscale to down-home. To pick your own favorite, wander up and down India Street and read the menus in the windows. Most every restaurant on India wins local approval.

American

If you're looking for a hearty breakfast or a unique American dinner, the local Hillcrest favorite hangout is **Hash House A Go Go** (3628 5th Ave., 619/298-4646, www.hashhouse-agogo.com, Mon. 7:30am-2pm, Tues.-Thurs. 7:30am-2pm and 5:30pm-9pm, Fri. 7:30am-2pm and 5:30pm-9:30pm, Sat.-Sun. 7:30am-2:30pm and 5:30pm-9:30pm, breakfast and lunch $8-17, dinner $15-39). The Hash House puts its own spin on casual American food, including an array of fresh local ingredients that take the oversized dishes up a notch. You'll dine in a modern atmosphere with an industrial-urban decorative scheme, complete with brushed-metal tabletops. For breakfast, the obvious choice is of course hash, which is served in a skillet, though you've got dozens of other options including French toast that's as thick as a phone book. Lunch and dinner feature especially wonderful salads, plus plenty of great entrées from duck mac and cheese to burgers stuffed with mashed potatoes, bacon, and cheddar cheese. You won't go hungry here.

If you want a quiet dinner, try the **Crest Café** (425 Robinson Ave., 619/295-2510, www.crestcafe.net, daily 7am-midnight, $8-16). This colorful, cheerful diner welcomes a more sedate crowd with a bright dining room and three wonderful meals per day. In amongst the traditional diner fare, you'll find a few upscale dishes, such as lemon-ricotta pancakes and orange marmalade-stuffed French toast. You'll also see a wide array of Mexican-inspired entrées, alongside diner dishes that have been made over with an eye towards modern health consciousness. Dinner includes comfort food favorites like turkey meatloaf and chicken potpie. Open till midnight, the Crest is the perfect place to stop and grab a late-night snack after (or during) a night out in Hillcrest.

If you're in Balboa Park, chances are you're visiting the museums or the zoo. At the zoo, grab a bite at **Albert's Restaurant** (Gorilla Tropics at the San Diego Zoo, 619/685-3200, www.sandiegozoo.org, $11-29). This sit-down eatery serves lunch year-round and dinner during the summer nights when the zoo stays open late. Sit indoors to escape the heat, or out on the patio to enjoy the view of the gardens surrounding the animal enclosures. Relax with a drink at the bar, order a simple salad or sandwich, or enjoy a hearty steak dinner.

A modest palace dedicated to all things pork, ◀ **Carnitas' Snack Shack** (2632 University Ave., 619/294-7675, http://carnitassnackshack.com, Wed.-Mon. noon-midnight, $9) can be found by looking for the pig atop its roof or the line spilling down the sidewalk in front of this small eatery. The menu changes daily and is written up on a chalkboard, but needless to say the fare is pig-heavy. The shack pork sandwich includes pork schnitzel, pulled pork, and bacon, while the juicy carnitas tacos are about the best you'll find anywhere. There is a small shaded place to eat on the side of the building, but if there's a long line, it might be better to get your food to go. And don't forget to double up on your cholesterol medication.

Cafés

If you need a quick bite before a show at one of the Old Globe Theaters, the closest eats can be had at **Lady Carolyn's Pub** (1363 Old Globe Way, 619/231-1941, ext. 2751, Tues.-Fri.

Carnitas' Snack Shack

from 7pm, Sat.-Sun. from 1pm). This walk-up snack bar offers soups in sourdough bowls, salads, wine, and Irish coffees. Open every day a show goes up (until the theater shuts its doors), Lady Carolyn's can get crowded on weekends. Dine early if you can.

Coffee and Tea

Round out your Balboa Park experience with a cup of tea and a meal at the **Tea Pavilion** (2215 Pan American Plaza, 619/231-0048, www.balboapark.org, Mon. 10:30am-3pm, Tues.-Sun. 10:30am-4pm). As advertised, the specialty of the house is tea. You'll find a great cuppa, whether you favor herbal, green, or black teas. You can also get a bowl of noodles, some sushi, or a quick snack. To take some of the Japanese experience home with you, wander into the market section to peruse the unusual imported food and drink.

If all that tromping around through the park has tired you out, perk up with a drink from **Daniel's Coffee Cart** (1549 El Prado, www. balboapark.org, Tues.-Sun. 8am-5:30pm, Mon. 8am-4:30pm). You'll find all your favorite espresso drinks, plain ol' coffee, tea, and pastries.

A favorite Hillcrest coffee shop is **Gelato Vero Caffe** (3753 India St., 619/295-9269, Mon.-Thurs. 6am-midnight, Fri. 6am-1am, Sat. 7am-1am, Sun. 7am-midnight, $10), which serves the workday-morning caffeine-jonesing crowd *and* the late-night dessert and coffee hounds. The gelato is all made in-house, and the owners and fans assert that you won't find any better this side of Italy. The small café has little seating in the main room; if you want to sit down and enjoy your coffee or gelato and there doesn't seem to be room, hit the stairway off to the side out the door of the café to find the upper deck and inside cottage seating.

OLD TOWN

Old Town is more about the history, shopping, and sights than it is about dining. Most locals head downtown for a meal. But if you really want to eat here, Mexican food is your best bet.

In Old Town's little corner of Mexico, Bazaar

del Mundo, you can find some great South-of-the-Border eats in a variety of styles and price ranges. Join the party at **Casa Guadalajara** (4105 Taylor St., 619/295-5111, www.casaguadalajara.com, Mon.-Thurs. 11am-10pm, Fri. 11am-11pm, Sat. 7am-11pm, Sun. 7am-10pm, happy hour Mon.-Fri. 4pm-7pm, $10-14). From the moment you see the low, whitewashed, adobe-style building with the red-tiled roof, you'll start to feel the Mexican atmosphere. Inside, enjoy the music of strolling mariachis as you sip a margarita and dine on excellent regional Mexican cuisine. The seafood-heavy menu features Mexican classics as well as the chef's unique creations. Be sure to check out the daily specials!

POINT LOMA

Out on Point Loma, the food is all about the fish—not a surprise, considering that this spit of land sits out in the water, surrounded on three sides by bay and ocean. Whatever style you like your fish cooked (or uncooked) in, Point Loma can serve it to you.

Japanese

In the world of high-end seafood, the Japanese are famed for creating some of the best dishes on Earth. For some amazing sushi, go to **Umi Sushi** (2806 Shelter Island Dr., 619/226-1135, www.umisushisandiego.com, Mon.-Sat. 11:30am-2:30pm and 5pm-10pm, $4-11). If you love your rolls, choose from three-dozen on the menu, plus plenty of *nigiri*, sashimi, specialty platters, and "sushi boats." For folks who love Japanese food but quail at the thought of raw fish, Umi offers hot entrées, noodle dishes, salads, and more. Sit up at the sushi bar to see your food put together, or pick a table out in the classically Japanese-styled dining room.

Mediterranean

Weary of fish and looking for a respite from the endless seafood of Point Loma? Grab a bite of something completely different at the **Fairouz Cafe and Gallery** (3166 Midway Dr., 619/225-0308, www.alnashashibi.com, Sun.-Thurs. 11am-9pm, Fri.-Sat. 11am-10pm, $15-20). The bright, cheerful dining room features the original artwork of Al Nashashibi, a painter with roots in Jerusalem. (Yes, you can purchase works you see while dining; inquire with your server.) As for the food, you'll find meat and vegetarian entrées in the Middle Eastern tradition, with lots of lamb and chicken, plus several Greek specialties, such as stuffed grape leaves. At lunchtime, look to the appetizers and salads for lighter fare.

Steak and Seafood

For the best of the land out by the sea, visit ◖ **Island Prime** (880 Harbor Island Dr., 619/298-6802, www.cohnrestaurants.com, daily lunch from 11am and dinner from 5pm, $28-52). This huge house of steak and fish seats more than 600 on a top evening. Ask in advance for a window seat or a table out on the deck overlooking the harbor and the San Diego skyline. On the deck, you might find yourself by one of the fires, feeling as though you were dining at your own private beach house (well, except for the crowd, of course). The simple decor makes use of the wooden architectural features of the building. If you're boating on the San Diego waters, dock-and-dine at the neighboring Sunroad Marina. The menu boasts shellfish, finned fish, and plenty of hearty meats in a classic steakhouse-meets-California style. Start (or finish) your meal with a martini or another fabulous cocktail.

For a lighter meal, head for the C-Level cocktail lounge. In addition to the high-octane libations, the lounge serves a light dinner menu—that really isn't all that light. Whichever you choose, you'll find a pleasant trend towards local and organic ingredients in Prime's dishes.

One of the best things about dining in San Diego is the opportunity to enjoy a fabulous meal while looking out over the harbor or the ocean. That's just what you'll get at **Humphreys by the Bay** (2241 Shelter Island Blvd., 619/224-3577, www.humphreysbythebay.com, Sun.-Thurs. 7am-2pm and 5:30pm-9pm, Fri.-Sat. 7am-2pm and 5:30pm-10pm, $21-29). The white tablecloths on the candlelit

DINNER CRUISES

An unforgettable way to dine in this coastside community is to take a dinner cruise in the calm waters of San Diego Bay. While you shouldn't expect the food on these cruises to be the best for the price, the atmosphere and scenery make up for any culinary deficiencies. Be forewarned that the drinks tend to be a bit weak as well; if you love a strong cocktail, plan to hit one of the many downtown bars before or after your cruise.

The juggernaut of the dinner and event cruise industry in California, **Hornblower** (1066 N. Harbor Dr., 619/686-8715, www.hornblower.com, daily boarding 6:30pm, $73) offers a popular three-hour dinner cruise every night. Pick up a glass of complimentary champagne as you walk down the gangplank onto the yacht. Enjoy your three-course dinner (or more, if you pay extra) as the sun drops below the horizon.

Take a constitutional stroll on the deck and return for dessert, or make for the entertainment deck and dance the evening away as the yacht slowly makes its way around the bay. If you prefer a daytime cruise, book passage for a Sunday champagne brunch.

San Diego Harbor Excursion (1050 N. Harbor Dr., 619/234-4111, www.sdhe.com, Mon.-Fri. $66.50, Sat. $76.50, Sun. brunch $59.50) also offers nightly dinner cruises and Sunday champagne brunches out on the bay. With an array of options, including vegetarian entrées and a children's dinner package at a reduced rate, San Diego Harbor Excursion offers a fun cruise and a tasty meal. Be sure to reserve your place at the table a few days in advance for Friday and Saturday nights and for Sunday brunches in summertime.

tables look right out over the Humphreys Marina and off towards the San Diego city skyline. This hotel-based restaurant serves three meals a day, plus brunch on Sundays. On the dinner menu, seafood reigns, though various land-based entrées get their due as well. Or combine the two for an extravagant meal that makes for the best of everything. At lunchtime, upscale sandwiches and salads make the most of lighter midday standards. Whichever you choose, lunch or dinner, don't miss the awesome seafood soups! The breakfast menu includes all the egg-based standards, fresh fruits, and pastries, and a few scrumptious surprises. Sunday brunches are buffet-style, with plenty of made and carved-to-order specialties.

If what you really want is the freshest slab of fish to be found on Point Loma, eat at the aptly named **Point Loma Seafoods** (2805 Emerson St., 619/223-1109, www.pointlomaseafoods.com, Mon.-Sat. 9am-8pm, Sun. 10am-8pm, $5-14). Much of the fish sold here, either as a hot meal to eat right here or chilled in paper ready to cook, comes straight off the fishing boats in the harbor. Shellfish, including local spiny lobster, is fresh, top quality, and sold only

in season—making Point Loma Seafood the perfect place for a seafood lunch. Hot food and sandwiches come with slaw and fries—perfect accompaniments for fish. The cold foods include seafood salads plus a small array of sushi and sashimi. The atmosphere is the antithesis of upscale, which make it perfect for many visitors looking for reasonable prices and truly great fish.

CORONADO

To find your own food in Coronado, stroll down Orange Avenue. While you'll definitely find your fellow tourists here, you'll also find a large number of restaurants in a bunch of different styles and ethnicities that are worth trying out.

American

If you're a night owl and find yourself looking for nourishment after hours, you can find it at the **Night & Day Café** (847 Orange Ave., 619/522-2912, www.thenightanddaycafe.net, Mon. 6am-2pm, Tues. and Sun. 6am-10pm, Wed.-Thurs. 6am-2am, Fri.-Sat. 24 hours, $10). This small, hole-in-the-wall diner will make you feel right at home. You'll find a wide range of pancakes, omelets, burgers, and lots of Mexican food from huevos rancheros to churros.

French

With the opulence of the Del overseeing the town, a night out for French cuisine seems appropriate here. You'll do well at **Chez Loma French Bistro** (1132 Loma Ave., 619/435-0661, www.chezloma.com, daily 5pm-9pm, $23-36). You can walk to this charming restaurant that's located in the historic Carez Hizar House—a white-frame house that leads into warm, red dining rooms. The cuisine tends toward the classic French brasserie style, with the occasional hint of California color in some of the dishes. The wine list is worth a visit all on its own; it's not immense, but it shows off the best of California and France, including a large selection of flights (samples of three different wines all in one type). The food and the ambiance have caught the attention of local foodies, and Chez Loma has been highly reviewed and presented with a number of regional restaurant awards.

Steak and Seafood

For good food in a fanciful atmosphere, get a table at **Peohe's** (1201 First St., 619/437-4474, www.peohes.com, Mon.-Sat. 11:30am-2:30pm and 5pm-close, Sun. 4:30pm-close, $24-56). It offers a cute tropical atmosphere, great views of San Diego Bay, and tasty offerings from land and sea. The menu is friendly to tourists new to the fresh California fish concept, while still offering pros at the game some interesting new preparations. If you prefer to keep your fish off the grill, order from the sushi bar. To go with your meal, enjoy a festive cocktail. The Volcano is the house special, and it serves two with near-lethal potency. Finally, Peohe's prides itself on its huge and tasty homemade desserts. If you possibly can, round out your meal with a Hot Chocolate Lava cake.

Thai

If your preference is hot and casual, eat at **Swaddee Thai Restaurant** (1001 C St.,

619/435-8110, Mon.-Sat. 11am-3pm and 5pm-10pm, Sun. 5pm-10pm, $13-25). Off the main tourist drag, Swadee's tasty Thai cuisine appeals to locals, and is something of a hidden gem. They have typical Thai fare like Pad Thai as well as tasty green and red curry dishes.

MISSION BAY

Locals and visitors alike flock to Mission Bay for a day's entertainment. As the sun sets, the need for food kicks in. Along Mission Bay, you'll find an array of ethnic eats to please any palate.

Burgers

Regularly proclaimed one of the best burger joints in the country, **Hodad's** (5010 Newport Ave., Ocean Beach, 619/224-4623, www.hodadies.com, Sun.-Thurs. 11am-9pm, Fri.-Sat. 11am-10pm, $5-10) has been serving burgers in San Diego's Ocean Beach neighborhood since 1969. Today a line still snakes out the door at mealtimes as people attempt to get inside the license plate-decorated shack to munch down delicious burgers, including the worth-the-wait single bacon cheeseburger with its perfectly crispy bacon.

Italian

Luigi's at the Beach (3210 Mission Blvd., 858/488-2818, Sun.-Thurs. 11am-11pm, Fri.-Sat. 11am-midnight, $11-30) is the place to go for Italian food at Mission Bay. Sit outside for the best people-watching, or inside for a loud, bright, tasty meal. The house red wine or one of the 28 beers on tap accompanies the inexpensive cuisine perfectly—including the pizza, which includes creations like seafood alfredo and Philly steak pies. Speaking of Luigi's pizza, you'll want to order a single slice unless you're part of a large crowd. A whole Luigi's pie barely fits on a four-top. Luigi's can get loud and rowdy, especially on game day, as many locals bring their posse for pizza and the game on the big-screen.

Seafood

At the boastfully named **World Famous** (711

COURTESY OF GEORGE'S AT THE COVE

Ocean Terrace at George's at the Cove

Pacific Beach Dr., 858/272-3100, daily 7am-midnight, $10-55) in Pacific Beach enjoy breakfast, lunch, or dinner with a view. Fish, purchased fresh daily, is the specialty of the house here, and preparations range from classic American to a variety of ethnic stylings that might be called "fusion" if this were San Francisco. Grab a drink at the bar and take a seat either indoors in the Vegas-inspired dining room or outdoors on the seaside patio. The wine list features some of the best-known California vintners.

LA JOLLA

For a good selection of food in La Jolla, stroll or drive down Prospect Street. You'll find an array of high-class California cuisine, plus coffee shops and more casual dining options.

California Cuisine

◖ **George's at the Cove** (1250 Prospect St., 858/454-4244, www.georgesatthecove.com, daily 11am-3:45pm and 5pm-9:45pm) is a La Jolla institution. The complex actually

includes three separate restaurants. The favorite, **Ocean Terrace** (daily lunch and dinner, $15-20) offers casual outdoor seating on the roof of the building year-round, with unpretentious and delicious cuisine. Enjoy seafood as you look out over La Jolla Cove, or choose a simple salad or sandwich for a lighter meal. Downstairs, you'll find the ultra-urban **California Modern** (daily dinner, $35-40). The industrial design of the dining room precedes the chic, if sometimes a bit overwrought, dishes you'll find on the menu here. Windows offer views of the Cove, while cushioned seats make diners along the wall comfortable as they settle in for a multi-course dinner. Finally, if you're really looking for a cocktail out on the balcony, **George's Bar** (daily lunch and dinner, $15-20) has just what you're looking for. You can order from the Ocean Terrace menu, or just sip your drinks as you enjoy the warm evening air.

Seafood

Looking for good seafood and a fabulous view

to go with it? Have a meal at **Brockton Villa** (1235 Coast Blvd., 858/454-7393, http://brocktonvilla.com, daily 8am-9pm, $15-34), which is open for breakfast, lunch, and dinner. Here you can enjoy classic American dishes with a California twist, plus plenty of fish, of course. The casual atmosphere of this beach bungalow blends perfectly with the sugar sand beaches of the San Diego area. Wooden tables, funky mismatched chairs, and the bright white paint inside evoke a sense of the casual resort atmosphere of historic La Jolla. For fun, read the menu for information on the quirky history of the bungalow, which dates from the late 1800s.

NORTH COUNTY

Each town ranging up the Pacific Coast Highway to Del Mar and Carlsbad has a main drag filled with restaurants. You'll find ethnic enclaves, homey diners, and more.

California Cuisine

Looking for elegant yet casual beach town dining? Try the famed **Arterra** (11966 El Camino Real, Del Mar, 858/369-6032, www.arterrarestaurant.com, Mon.-Fri. 6:30am-10:30am, 11:30am-2pm, and 4pm-9:30pm, Sat. 7am-11:30am and 4pm-9:30pm, Sun. 7am-11:30am, $20-39). Improbably located inside the San Diego Marriott Del Mar, Arterra offers anything but standard chain hotel fare. Start with a drink and perhaps a seafood appetizer in the modern, comfortable outdoor lounge. Once you're seated for dinner inside the plush, red-splashed dining room, you'll find great service and top cuisine created from the freshest local and organic ingredients around. The tasting menus (with or without wine pairing) are a popular option, letting you sample the greatest variety of dishes. Get adventurous and try something new, since there's plenty of cutting-edge cuisine on the menu. And don't forget the wine; the list includes many boutique California charmers that pair wonderfully with the cuisine. If your preference is for uncooked fish, go for something from the surprisingly good sushi bar.

Italian

On the almost Mediterranean-feeling north coast of San Diego County, sunny Italian food somehow seems appropriate. Some of the best just off the beach is served in Encinitas at ▨ **Via Italia Trattoria** (569 S. Pacific Coast Hwy., Encinitas, 760/479-9757, www.viaitaliapizzeria.com, daily noon-10pm, $12-30). This Italian-owned and -operated casual restaurant feels like a real trattoria on the coast of Italy. You can get a budget-friendly yet fabulously delicious thin-crust pizza, a dish of steaming pasta with your choice of traditional sauce, or an upscale seafood entrée. The food is fresh, cooked just right, and delectable. Whatever you order from the large menu, you'll enjoy eating it in the casual dining room. Or if you just want a quick drink and an appetizer, take a seat at the bar.

For haute cuisine with an Italian flair, make the drive out to the Four Seasons Aviara and have dinner at **Vivace** (7100 Aviara Resort Dr., Carlsbad, 760/448-1234, www.vivace-restaurant.com, Mon.-Sat. 6pm-9:30pm, Sun. 11:30am-3pm, $23-50). A perfect restaurant for a romantic night out, Vivace offers contemporary Italian cuisine in several courses. Attentive, knowledgeable servers can help you with both the menu and the wine list, which provides great menu-matching selections from California, Italy, and other wine regions of Europe. As you sip your wine, you can admire the elegant tropical-themed decor throughout the several interconnected dining spaces. (Be sure to look down; the floor is gorgeous!) Be sure to plan at least an hour and a half so that you can enjoy the whole dining experience, right through dessert and coffee.

Mexican

A favorite of local surfers after a day in the waves, ▨ **Juanita's Taco Shop** (290 N. Coast Hwy., Encinitas, 760/943-9612, Mon.-Thurs and Sun. 7am-midnight, Fri.-Sat. 7am-3am, $5) doesn't look like much from the outside. Under metal bars, the windows of this small taqueria are plastered with surf stickers, while inside, an ocean mural covers the walls and ceiling of the small dining area. But here it's the tasty Mexican food that counts. You can't go wrong with the juicy carnitas burrito. It might be the best meal that you've had for under $5 on your whole trip.

Sushi
◖ **The Fish Joint** (514 S. Coast Hwy., Oceanside, 760/450-0646, Sun.-Thurs. noon-9pm, Fri.-Sat. noon-9:30pm, $15) is not your typical sushi restaurant. Your sushi will probably be made by a tattooed surfer as punk music blares overhead. There's sake here, but there are also a handful of microbrews on tap. The rolls at The Fish Joint are creative and include offerings like the local favorite "Chronic Roll," spicy tuna, crab, and avocado tempura flash fried and topped with spicy mayo and spicy citrus sauce.

Information and Services

INFORMATION
Tourist Information
The San Diego Convention and Visitor's Bureau operates two visitors centers, each of which can help you with everything from flight information to restaurant coupons to hotel reservations. Downtown, head for the **International Visitor Information Center** (1140 North Harbor Dr., 619/236-1212, www.sandiego.org, Oct.-May daily 9am-4pm, June-Sept. daily 9am-5pm). In La Jolla, make use of the **La Jolla Visitor Center** (7966 Herschel Ave., 619/236-1212, www.sandiego.org, Sept.-Oct. and Apr.-May Mon.-Fri. 11am-5pm, Sat. 10am-6pm, Sun. 10am-4pm, Nov.-Mar. Mon.-Thurs. 11am-4pm, Fri. 11am-5pm, Sat. 10am-5pm, Sun. 10am-4pm, June-Aug. Mon.-Sat. 10am-6pm, Sun. 10am-5pm). To get a feel for the town before you arrive, check out the SDCVB website at www.sandiego.org. Friendly folks can answer emails and phone calls about most anything pertaining to San Diego County.

Media and Communications
As a well-traveled tourism destination, San Diego has a wide range of publications you can pick up to help you plan the details of your visit. The daily newspaper is the *San Diego Union-Tribune* (www.utsandiego.com).

San Diego also has two free alternative weekly newspapers: the *San Diego CityBeat* (www.sdcitybeat.com) and the *San Diego Reader* (www.sandiegoreader.com).

Some stores and hotels carry *San Diego Magazine* (www.sandiegomagazine.com), a glossy monthly publication focused on the culture and lifestyle of the region. While this isn't a tourist-centered magazine, you can still find good information about what's hot *right now,* especially in the dining and shopping scenes.

It's pretty easy to get online in San Diego. Most hotels have either wireless or cabled high-speed Internet access in rooms, though it isn't always free. Business-oriented accommodations also often maintain several public-access computers for guests. You can also find Wi-Fi in many coffee houses, both chain and independent, plus public libraries and some bookshops. As of this writing, San Diego does not have free municipal wireless service.

SERVICES
Banks and Post Offices
Banking in San Diego is easy—like most big cities, ATM machines abound not only at bank branches, but in restaurants, bars, and minimarts as well. You'll find branches of most of the major American banks here, including Wells Fargo, Bank of America, Washington Mutual, and many more.

You'll find plenty of U.S. Post Office branches scattered throughout San Diego. If you need to ship your shopping home, you'll find a downtown **post office** (51 Horton Plaza), convenient to the mall and much of downtown. South of Balboa Park, there is another post office (815 E St.). In La Jolla, there's a branch (720 Silver St.) only a few blocks from Prospect. Each town in the North County has its own post office, of course, including in Encinitas (1150 Garden View Rd.).

Medical Services

With UC San Diego in town, the number of major medical centers in and around San Diego is higher than the average. If you must get sick on vacation, San Diego isn't the worst place to do it. In town, the **UCSD Medical Center- Hillcrest** (200 West Arbor Dr., 619/543-6222) offers emergency and clinic services, as does **Scripps Mercy Hospital** (4077 Fifth Ave., 619/294-8111, www.scripps.org). The **Kaiser Permanente Medical Center** (4647 Zion Ave., 619/528-5000) includes a full-service, 24-hour emergency room. La Jolla also has a heavy load

of hospitals, with **Scripps Green Hospital** (10666 N. Torrey Pines Rd., 858/554-9100) and **Scripps Memorial Hospital** (9888 Genesee Ave., 858/626-4123).

In the North County area, the only trauma center is within the **Palomar Medical Center** (555 East Valley Pkwy., 760/739-3000) in Escondido. You can get regular hospital services at the **Scripps Memorial Hospital** (354 Santa Fe Dr., 760/633-6501) in Encinitas.

Most of the beaches in San Diego County maintain a lifeguard presence in the summertime, and many have lifeguards patrolling in the winter as well. Look for the light blue towers on the beach to find the nearest available lifeguards, or for permanent buildings bearing a large red cross.

Getting There and Around

If you're coming to San Diego from Los Angeles, you'll be relieved by the easing of traffic. If you're coming from anyplace else, you may be horrified by the packed highways. In the grand scheme of California transit, San Diego isn't the worst place to try to get around. The highway network makes some sense, there's almost adequate in-town public transit, and the rail and air travel centers bustle with activity.

If you prefer human-powered transportation, San Diego's fabulous weather, generally safe streets, and miles of mostly along-the-coast paths make bicycling and walking eminently possible as your major mode of transportation.

GETTING THERE
Air

The major-league **San Diego International Airport** (3665 N. Harbor Dr., 619/400-2404, www.san.org), a.k.a. Lindbergh Field, is stuffed right along San Diego Bay, convenient to downtown, Coronado, and almost every major San Diego attraction. Short-term parking sits adjacent to the terminals and costs $1 per hour on average. Long-term lots surround the airport; check the airport website for specifics. A

60-minute maximum, free "cell phone lot" lets drivers wait for incoming passengers without having to drive endlessly around the airport.

If you're flying a light plane in, the most convenient general aviation airports to downtown San Diego are Brown Field (8,000-foot runway) and Montgomery Field (4,600-foot runway). Eight additional general aviation airports are scattered throughout the county. For information, check www.miramarairshow.com.

Train

To get to San Diego by train from the north or the east, find your way aboard the **Amtrak Pacific Surfliner** (www.amtrak.com), a train that runs a dozen times a day from Paso Robles along the Pacific Coast down to San Diego. Boarding is easy from most major California destinations in the area, including San Luis Obispo, Santa Barbara, Los Angeles, and Anaheim. Check into transfers from the *Coast Starlight* and the *Capitol Corridor* routes as well. Amtrak services the **Santa Fe station** (1050 Kettner Blvd.) and the **Old Town Transit Center** (4005 Taylor St.).

For a reliable local commuter train, jump on board **The Coaster** (www.sdcommute.

com, Mon.-Sat., adults $4-5.50 one-way, senior and people with disabilities $2-2.75 one-way, children under 6 free). The Coaster runs from Oceanside into downtown San Diego and back a dozen times a day Monday-Friday, with six trains running Saturdays, plus special event and holiday service. Purchase tickets from the vending machines in every train station. In the North County, NCTD Coaster Connecter bus routes can connect to the train station. In San Diego proper, catch the trolley or the bus from either the Old Town Transit Center or the Santa Fe station.

Car

Most visitors drive into San Diego via the heavily traveled I-5 from the north or south. I-805 runs parallel to I-5 at La Jolla and leads south into Mission Valley. To drive between the North County and San Diego, take I-15, which runs north-south farther inland. Be sure to avoid rush hour, as the back up on I-15 can become extensive after Poway. Both I-805 and I-15 cross I-8, which runs east-west through Mission Valley. The smaller yet surprisingly pretty Route 163 runs north-south from I-5 in Balboa Park north to I-15 in Miramar.

GETTING AROUND
Car

This is Southern California. Most people drive here whether they need to or not. Happily, this is *not* the Los Angeles Basin, so traffic sometimes relaxes into a bearable state.

Parking is the hardest at the beaches in the summertime. Everyone else in the state seems to be trying to find a parking spot close to the sand between June and September. If you possibly can, find another way to get from your accommodations to the beach, be it bicycle, public transit, or your own two feet. If you must drive, check out the parking situation ahead of time (most beaches' websites offer parking information) and plan ahead. Bring cash for pay parking, come early in the morning, and be prepared to walk up to a mile from your parking spot down to the beach itself.

In the various downtown areas, you'll find fairly average city parking issues. Happily, San Diego's major attractions and event venues tend to be accompanied by large parking structures. Just be prepared to pay a premium if you're doing something popular.

Bus and Trolley

In downtown San Diego, Coronado, and La Jolla, the **MTS** (www.sdcommute.com, bus ticket $1-5, trolley ticket $1.25-6) operates both an extensive bus system and trolley routes. The North County is served by the North County Transit District, or NCTD. If you plan to make serious use of the trolleys and buses, use the vending machines at trolley stations to get a day pass—a regular day pass is a bargain at $5, and two-, three-, and four-day passes can save you even more money. Day passes work on NCTD Breeze buses as well as most MTS routes.

See the website for more information about schedules, routes, and fares for both the MTS and NCTD services. If you plan to pay your fare for buses or trolleys on-board, have exact change available. The vending machines are more forgiving, as many take $1 and $5 bills and make change.

If you don't have a car with you, or just want to avoid driving for a while, hop onto the **Old Town Trolley** (www.trolleytours.com, adults $32.40-36, children $16.20-18) for a great look at the highlights of San Diego without the headaches of parking and traffic. The trolley can take you in a loop through downtown (including the Gaslamp Quarter), Old Town, out over the bridge to the Del on Coronado, and around the San Diego Bay Harbor. You can get on and off the trolley at any time to visit a museum, go shopping, or grab a bite to eat. Another trolley will appear to take you on your way. As long as you stay onboard, the driver will narrate, pointing out the sights as you pass them, and make stops at the biggest and most important. While the Old Town Trolley is way too expensive to use in place of public transportation, it's a great way to get out and see the highlights of the city in a day. Check the website for discounted online tickets.

SAN DIEGO

BACKGROUND

The Land

GEOGRAPHY

California's geographic profile is as diverse as its population. At nearly 159,000 square miles, California is the third-largest state in the United States, stretching 770 miles from the Oregon state line to its southern border with Mexico. California includes the **Sierra Nevada** mountain range, numerous national parks and monuments, coastal and giant redwoods, volcanoes, and the tallest mountain in the continental United States, **Mount Whitney,** at 14,505 feet. In addition, two major tectonic plates—the north-moving Pacific and south-moving North American Plate—give California a reputation for shaking things up a bit.

Mountain Ranges

The California coast is characterized by craggy cliffs, rocky beaches, and enormous coast redwoods *(Sequoia sempervirens)* that reach heights up to 380 feet. The coast is bounded by the aptly named Coast Range, ruggedly steep mountains formed 30 million years ago when part of the Pacific Plate jammed, folded, and compressed to form the Coast Range and Transverse Range. In addition to the Coast Range, there are two other significant high-elevation regions in the state. In the north, the Cascade Mountains evolved through volcanic activity 10 million years ago when the Juan de Fuca Plate, earth's smallest tectonic

© 123RF.COM

plate caught between the North American and Pacific Plates, collided with the North American Plate and was forced under the larger plate. Magma from the melting plate raised a series of mountains, including California's two active volcanoes—Mount Lassen and Mount Shasta. Mount Lassen (10,462 feet) last blew its top in 1915; today, the surrounding park offers a glimpse into the earth's formation. Majestic Mount Shasta, along I-5 north of Redding, has not erupted in quite some time. At 14,179 feet, Mount Shasta's extreme height creates its own weather system.

To the east is the Sierra Nevada, stretching 400 miles north-south and forming the eastern spine of the state. Its peaks and valleys include Mount Whitney, Lake Tahoe, Yosemite, and the giant sequoias (Sequoiadendron giganteum) in Sequoia and Kings Canyon National Parks. The Sierra Nevada formed 60 million years ago when magma seeped up between the Pacific and North American Plates. It created a massive pool of granite that slowly cooled to form a batholith, a massive dome-shaped formation of intrusive igneous rock. For the past 12 million years the formation has been pushing upward.

Earthquakes and Faults

Earthquakes occur when the tectonic plates that compose the earth's crust shift along faults, the boundaries between the plates—and California's seat on the Pacific Ring of Fire is well established. The North American Plate and Pacific Plate came together about 150 million years ago, causing compression and folding of the earth's crust that created the Sierra Nevada; it eventually eroded to fill with sediments what would become the Central Valley. About 30 million years ago a ridge of the Pacific Plate became jammed and caused the folding and compression that formed the Coast and Transverse Ranges. More importantly, the contact caused the Pacific Plate to change direction and move northward, forming the San Andreas Fault. This infamous strike-slip fault, where two tectonic plates move horizontally, the North American Plate moving mostly southward and the Pacific Plate moving mostly northward, runs along the North Coast, near San Francisco, and east of Los Angeles before branching off into Mexico and the Pacific Ocean.

The plates frequently catch as they move past each other, storing energy and causing tension to build. When the plates jolt past one another, they release this energy in the form of an earthquake. Earthquakes along numerous faults happen daily, 10,000-37,000 times each year. Most register less than magnitude 3 and go unnoticed by Californians used to the shake, rattle, and roll. However, there have been several significant earthquakes in California history. The **1906 San Francisco earthquake** had a magnitude of 7.7-8.3 and involved the "rupturing" of the northern 300 miles of the San Andreas Fault from San Juan Bautista to Cape Mendocino. The **1989 Loma Prieta earthquake,** with an epicenter near Loma Prieta Peak in the Santa Cruz Mountains, was small by comparison at magnitude 6.9 and with only 25 miles of ruptured fault. California's stringent building codes, developed in the wake of deadly and destructive earthquakes, include an extensive seismic retrofit program that has brought older buildings, overpasses, bridges, and other structures up to stringent standards.

CLIMATE

Vast in size and varied in geography, California also has a vastly varied climate, from boiling heat in the Central Valley to subarctic temperatures at mountain summits.

Along the North Coast, the weather stays fairly constant: chilly, windy, and foggy. Summer days rarely reach 80°F, and winter rainstorms can pound the area. San Francisco shares its cool and foggy climate with temperatures in the 50s and 60s well into summer. South on the peninsula or across the Bay in Marin County and the East Bay, the temperature may rise 20-30°F, and the fog often makes way for sun.

North of San Francisco, the Wine Country is graced with milder weather and warm summers, perfect for growing grapes.

The Central Coast is a bit warmer than the

San Francisco Bay Area, but still, expect cool temperatures and fog in summer. A chilly wind accompanies the rain in the winter, often closing mountain roads and highways, including Highway 1.

From the Los Angeles Basin down to San Diego and up the coast to Santa Barbara, temperatures are mild all year long. Expect fog on the beaches during the summer, cool days in the wintertime, and hotter temperatures in the inland valleys and Disneyland. For the best summertime beach weather in the state, head for San Diego.

ENVIRONMENTAL ISSUES

Californians face several major environmental issues. The state battles drought, and water for crops, farms, and human consumption is always in short supply. Conservation measures can include limiting development and urban sprawl, restricting water usage, and designating set periods for personal and recreational use, such as watering lawns.

Water pollution is also an issue. Most tap water is safe to drink, but swimming in California's plentiful bays, lakes, and rivers as well as the Pacific Ocean requires more caution. Pollution may cause *E. coli* outbreaks at beaches, affecting wildlife and beachgoers alike. Fishing is no longer permitted in San Francisco Bay due to high mercury levels in the Bay's fish.

Many of the state's grand oak trees have succumbed to sudden oak death, a disease that spreads through spores to eventually kill live oaks, black oaks, and tanoaks. To control its spread, travelers are advised to clean all camping equipment thoroughly and to buy and burn local firewood rather than importing it from elsewhere.

Flora and Fauna

FLORA
Redwoods

A visit to California's famous redwoods should be on every traveler's list. The **coast redwood** (*Sequoia sempervirens*) grows along the North Coast as far south as Big Sur. Coast redwoods are characterized by their towering height, flaky red bark, and moist understory. Among the tallest trees on earth, they are also some of the oldest, with some individuals almost 2,000 years old. Coast redwoods occupy a narrow strip of coastal California, growing less than 50 miles inland to collect moisture from the ocean and fog. Their tannin-rich bark is crucial to their ability to survive wildfires and regenerate afterward. The best places to marvel at the giants are within the Redwood National and State Parks, Muir Woods, and Big Basin State Park.

The **giant sequoia** (*Sequoiadendron giganteum*) grows farther inland in a 260-mile belt at 3,000-8,900 feet elevation in the Sierra Nevada mountain range. Giant sequoias are the largest trees by volume on earth; they can grow to heights of 280 feet with a diameter up to 26

coast redwoods

© 123RF.COM

feet and can live for thousands of years. Giant sequoias share the ruddy bark of the coast sequoia as well as its fire-resistant qualities. The best places to see giant sequoias up close are at Sequoia and Kings Canyon National Parks, Calaveras Big Trees, and the Mariposa Grove at Yosemite National Park.

Oaks

California is home to many native oaks. The most common are the **valley oak, black oak, live oak,** and **coastal live oak.** The deciduous valley oak *(Quercus lobata)* commonly grows on slopes, valleys, and wooded foothills in the Central Valley. The black oak, also deciduous, grows throughout the foothills of the Coast Range and Sierra Nevada; it is unfortunately one of the victims of sudden oak death. The live oak habitat is in the Central Valley, while the coastal live oak occupies the Coast Range. The acorns of all these oaks were an important food supply for California's Native American population and continue to be an important food source for wildlife.

Wildflowers

California's state flower is the **California poppy** *(Eschscholzia californica).* The pretty little perennial grows just about everywhere, even on the sides of the busiest highways. The flowers of most California poppies are bright orange, but they also appear occasionally in white, cream, and an even deeper red-orange.

FAUNA
Mountain Lions

Mountain lions *(Felis concolor)* are an example of powerful and potentially deadly beauty. Their solitary territorial hunting habits make them elusive, but human contact has increased as more homes are built in mountain lion habitat throughout California. Many parks in or near mountain lion territory post signs with warnings and advice: Do not run if you come across a mountain lion; instead make noise and raise and wave your arms so that you look bigger. The California Fish and Game Department (www.dfg.ca.gov) offers a downloadable brochure on encounters and other tips.

Black Bears

Don't take the name **black bear** *(Ursus americanus)* too literally. The black bear can actually have brown and even cinnamon-colored fur, sometimes with a white patch on the chest. The black bear is pretty common throughout North America, including in the forests of Northern California south to Sonoma County, the Sierra Nevada, and the Transverse Range. They are also frequently spotted on the North Coast's Lost Coast Trail. While the black bear can appear cuddly from a distance, distance is exactly what should separate bears and humans—at least 25 feet or more. These are wild animals; do not attempt to feed or approach them, and never come between a mama bear and her cubs. Bears can run up to 30 mph, and they can definitely outrun you. Campers should use bear-proof food lockers at campgrounds or a bear canister in the backcountry; never keep food or any scented products (toothpaste, energy bars, hair products) in a tent or in view inside a car. Bears can be crafty and destructive—some have broken into cars and shredded the interiors looking for food. Bears are mostly nocturnal but can be seen out during the day, and they do not always hibernate in winter.

Whales

The massive, majestic **gray whale** *(Eschrichtius robustus)* was once endangered, but its numbers have rebound with international protection. The gray whale measures about 40 feet long and has mottled shades of gray with black fins; its habitat is inshore ocean waters, so there is a chance to get a glimpse of them from headlands up and down the coast. Gray whales generally migrate south along the coast November-January, and closer to shore February-June when they migrate northward. Mendocino County is a perfect place to watch the water for a glimpse of whales breaching.

Perhaps a more recognizable behemoth is the **humpback whale** *(Megaptera novaeangliae).* At 45-55 feet long, the humpback is the only large

© STUART THORNTON

A sea otter lounges in the water at the Elkhorn Slough.

whale to breach regularly, then roll and crash back into the water, providing one of the best shows in nature; the whale also rolls from side to side on the surface, slapping its long flippers. Humpbacks generally stay a little farther from shore, so it may be necessary to take a whale-watching cruise to catch a glimpse of them, but their 20-foot spouts can help landlubbers spot them from shore. Look for humpbacks April-early December off the coast near Big Sur, particularly at Julia Pfeiffer Burns State Park.

The **blue whale** (*Balaenoptera musculus*) is the largest animal on earth. At 70-90 feet long, the blue whale even exceeds dinosaurs in size. With a blue-gray top and a yellowish bottom, the blue whale has a heart the size of a small car, two blowholes, but alas does not breach. They can be seen June-November off the California coast, especially at Monterey and north of Point Reyes.

California Sea Lions

Watching a beach full of **California sea lions** (*Zalophus californianus*) sunning themselves and noisily honking away can be a pleasure. Sea lions are migratory, so they come and go at will, especially in the fall when they head to the Channel Islands for breeding. If you have a serious hankering to see California sea lions, try Pier 39 near Fisherman's Wharf or on the coast at Seal Rocks, both in San Francisco.

Sea Otters

Much higher on the cuteness scale is the **sea otter** (*Enhydra lutris*), which can be spotted just off shore in shallow kelp beds. Once near extinction, the endearing playful sea otter has survived; now there are more than 2,000 in California waters. It can be a bit mesmerizing to witness a sea otter roll on its back in the water and use a rock to break open mollusks for lunch. Sea otter habitat runs mainly from Monterey Bay to Big Sur, but they have also been spotted in the waters near Mendocino.

Birds

California has a wide range of habitat with accessible food and water that makes it perfect for hundreds of bird species to nest, raise their young, or just stop over and rest during long migrations. Nearly 600 species have been spotted in California, so it may be just the place for a bird-watcher's vacation.

Among the most regal of California's bird species are raptors. The **red-tailed hawk** *(Buteo jamaicensis)* is found throughout California and is frequently sighted perched in trees along the North Coast highway, in the Central Valley, and even in urban areas such as San Francisco. The red-tailed hawk features a light underbelly with a dark band and a distinctive red tail that gives the bird its name.

Although not as common as it once was, **Swainson's hawk** *(Buteo swainsoni)* has been an indicator species in California's environment. The Swainson's hawk population has declined due to loss of habitat and excessive pesticide use in agricultural lands in the Central Valley; its main diet consists of the locusts and grasshoppers that feed on these crops, passing the contaminants on to the birds. These hawks are smaller than the red-tailed hawk, with dark brown coloring and some white underparts either on the chest or under the tail.

With wings spanning 10 feet from tip to tip, the **California condor** *(Gymnogyps californianus)* is the largest flying bird in North America. In the recent past, the condors' population had plummeted due to its susceptibility to lead poisoning, along with deaths caused by electric power lines, habitat loss, and gunshots from indiscriminate humans. In 1987, there was only one California condor left in the wild; it was taken into captivity as part of a breeding program. In 1997, the Monterey County-based non-profit the Ventana Wildlife Society (VWS) began releasing the giant birds back into the wild. Currently, 70 wild condors soar above California's Central Coast. The species' recovery is one of conservation's great success stories.

Reptiles
Several varieties of **rattlesnakes** are indigenous to the state. The Pacific Northwest rattler makes its home in Northern California, while more than half a dozen

© JOE BURNETT

A California condor soars over the Big Sur coastline.

different rattlesnake varieties live in Southern California, including the western diamond-back and the Mojave rattlesnake.

If you spot California's most infamous native reptile, keep your distance. All rattlesnakes are venomous, although death by snakebite is extremely rare in California. Most parks with known rattlesnake populations post signs alerting hikers to their presence; hikers should stay on marked trails and avoid tromping off into meadows or brush. Pay attention when hiking, especially when negotiating rocks and woodpiles, and never put a foot or a hand down in a spot you can't see first. Wear long pants and heavy hiking boots for protection from snakes as well as insects, other critters, and unfriendly plants you might encounter.

Butterflies

California's vast population of wildflowers attracts an array of gorgeous butterflies. The **monarch butterfly** *(Danaus plexippus)* is emblematic of the state. These large orange-and-black butterflies have a migratory pattern that's reminiscent of birds. Starting in August, they begin migrating south to cluster in groves of eucalyptus trees. As they crowd together and close up their wings to hibernate, their dull outer wing color camouflages them as clumps of dried leaves, thus protecting them from predators. In spring, the butterflies begin to wake up, fluttering lazily in the groves for a while before flying north to seek out milkweed on which to lay their eggs. Pacific Grove, Santa Cruz, and Pismo Beach are great places to visit these California "butterfly trees."

History

THE FIRST RESIDENTS

The diverse ecology of California allowed Native Americans to adapt to the land in various ways. Communities settled from the border of present-day Oregon south through the mountain ranges and valleys, along the coast, into the Sierra Nevada, and in the arid lands that stretch into Mexico. These groups include the Maidu, Miwok, Yurok, and Pomo. More than 100 Native American languages were spoken in California, and each language had several dialects, all of which were identified with geographic areas. There are about two dozen distinct Native American groups in the Del Norte-Humboldt-Mendocino area alone. The following is an overview of the groups most commonly encountered when traveling around the state.

Yurok

The Yurok people are the largest Native American population in California, and they continue to live along the Klamath River and the Humboldt County coast near Redwood National Park, north of Eureka and south of Crescent City. Spanish explorers arriving in 1775 were the Yurok's first contact with Europeans. Fur traders and trappers from the Hudson's Bay Company arrived in about 1827, but it wasn't until gold miners arrived in 1850 that the Yurok faced disease and destruction that diminished their population by 75 percent. Researchers put the 1770 population at 2,500-3,100, which dropped to 669-700 by 1910. Today, there are more than 5,000 Yurok living in California and about 6,000 in the United States overall.

Pomo

The name for the Pomo people and their language first meant "those who live at the red earth hole," possibly referring to the magnesite used for red beads or the reddish earth and clay mined in the area. It was also once the name of a village near the present-day community of Pomo in Potter Valley. The Pomo territory was large, bounded by the Pacific Ocean to the west and extending inland to Clear Lake in Lake County. Today, the territory includes present-day Santa Rosa and much of the Sonoma County wine country.

In 1800 there were 10,000-18,000 Pomo

living in approximately 70 communities that spoke seven Pomo languages. But as the Pomo interacted and traded with the Russians at Fort Ross, added pressure came from the Spanish missionaries and American settlers pressing in from the south and east. European encroachment may have been the reason Pomo villages became more centralized and why many Pomo retreated to remote areas to band together in defense.

The Pomo suffered not only from lifestyle changes and loss of territory but from diseases for which they had no immunity. Missionaries, traders, and settlers brought with them measles, smallpox, and other diseases that devastated indigenous populations. In 1850 miners began settling in the Russian River Valley, and the Lake Sonoma Valley was homesteaded. As a result, the U.S. government forced the Pomo off their land and onto reservations. Historians believe there were 3,500-5,000 Pomo in 1851, but only 777-1,200 by 1910. There were nearly 5,000 Pomo by the early 1990s.

Miwok

Before contact with white settlers in 1769, the Miwok people lived in small bands in separate parts of California. The Plains and Sierra Miwok lived on the Sacramento-San Joaquin Delta, parts of the San Joaquin and Sacramento Valleys, and the foothills and western slopes of the Sierra Nevada. The Coast Miwok—including the Bodega Bay Miwok and the Marin Miwok—lived in what is now Marin and southern Sonoma Counties. Lake Miwok people were found in the Clear Lake Basin of Lake County. The Bay Miwok were in present-day Contra Costa County. Miwok domesticated dogs and grew tobacco but otherwise depended on hunting, fishing, and gathering for food. Miwok in the Sierra exploited the California black oak for acorns, and it is believed that they cultivated the tree in parts of what is now Yosemite National Park.

Like so many indigenous people in California, the Miwok suffered after explorers, missionaries, miners, and settlers arrived. Historians estimate there were at least 11,000

Miwok in 1770, but in all four regions there were only about 671 Miwok in 1910 and 491 in 1930. Today, there are about 3,500 Miwok.

Ohlone

The Ohlone people once occupied what is now San Francisco, Berkeley, Oakland, Silicon Valley, Santa Cruz, Monterey, and the lower Salinas Valley. The Ohlone (a Miwok word meaning "western people") lived in permanent villages, only moving temporarily to gather seasonal foods such as acorns and berries. The Ohlone formed an association of about 50 different communities with an average of 200 members each. The villages interacted through trade, marriages, and ceremonies. Basket weaving, ceremonial dancing, piercings and tattoos, and general ornamentation indicated status within the community and were all part of Ohlone life. Like other Native Americans in the region, the Ohlone depended on hunting, fishing, gathering, and agrarian skills such as burning off old growth each year to get a better yield from seeds.

The Ohlone culture remained fairly stable until the first Spanish missionaries arrived to spread Christianity and to expand Spanish territorial claims. Spanish explorer Sebastián Vizcaíno reached present-day Monterey in December 1602, and the Rumsen group of Ohlone were the first they encountered. Father Junípero Serra's missionaries built seven missions on Ohlone land, and most of the Ohlone people were brought to the missions to live and work. For the next 60 years, the Ohlone suffered, as did most indigenous people at the missions. Along with the culture shock of subjugation came the diseases for which they had no immunity—measles, smallpox, syphilis, and others. It wasn't until 1834 that the California missions were abolished and the Mexican government redistributed the mission land holdings.

The Ohlone lost the vast majority of their population between 1780 and 1850 because of disease, social upheaval from European incursion, and low birth rates. Estimates are that there were 7,000-26,000 Ohlone when Spanish soldiers and missionaries arrived, and about 3,000 in 1800 and 864-1,000 by 1852. There are 1,500-2,000 Ohlone people today.

Yokuts

The Yokut people have inhabited the Central Valley for at least 8,000 years; they may even have been the first people to settle here. The Yokuts live in the San Joaquin Valley from the Sacramento-San Joaquin River Delta south to Bakersfield and east to the Sierra Foothills. Sequoia and Kings Canyon National Parks are included in this area, as are the cities of Fresno and Modesto. Like other Native Americans, the Yokuts developed water transportation, harvesting abundant tule reeds to work them into canoes.

Spanish explorers entered the valley in 1772 and found 63 different Yokut groups scattered up and down the Central Valley. Many of the Yokuts were taken to the various missions, where they suffered from European subjugation and diseases. Later, as miners entered the region, the Yokut people were forced from their lands. There may have been as many as 4,500 Yokuts when the Spaniards arrived, but the last full-blooded member of the Southern Yokuts is said to have died in 1960. Yokut descendants today live on the Tule River Reservation near Porterville and at the Santa Rosa Rancheria near Lemoore.

Paiute

The Paiute people are grouped by their language—despite location, political connection, or even genetic similarity. For the Northern Paiutes and the Southern Paiutes, that language is the Numic branch of the Uto-Aztecan family of Native American languages. The Northern Paiutes live in the Great Basin; the Southern Paiutes lived in the Mojave Desert on the edge of present-day Death Valley National Park. Between the Northern Paiutes and the Southern Paiutes are the Mono Lake Northern Paiutes and the Owens Valley Paiutes.

The Northern Paiute lifestyle was well adapted to the harsh environment of the Great Basin. Each band occupied a territory usually centered around a lake or other water source that also provided fish and waterfowl. Food drives to capture rabbits and pronghorn were communal and often involved nearby bands. Piñon nuts were gathered and stored for winter, and grass seeds and roots were part of the diet. Because of their remoteness, the Northern Paiutes may have completely avoided the hardships of the mission period. Their first contact with European Americans may have occurred in 1820, but sustained contact did not happen until the 1840s; several violent confrontations over land and other conflicts occurred in this period. In the end, smallpox did more to decimate the Northern Paiutes than warfare. The Northern Paiutes established colonies that were joined by Shoshone and Washoe people and eventually received recognition by the federal government.

The Southern Paiutes were not as fortunate as the Northern Paiutes. The first contact with Europeans came in 1776, when the priests Silvestre Vélez de Escalante and Francisco Atanasio Domínguez met them while seeking an overland route to the California missions. The Southern Paiutes suffered slave raids by the Navajo and Ute before Europeans arrived, and the raids increased afterward. In 1851, Mormon settlers arrived and occupied local water sources, and the slave raids ended. Settlers and their agrarian practices such as cattle herding drove away game and limited the Southern Paiutes' ability to gather food, disrupting their traditional lifestyle.

Chumash

The Chumash lived on land from Malibu up to Paso Robles, but they also traveled out to the northern Channel Islands. Before the Mission Period, they had over 20,000 people living in 150 independent villages scattered along the coast.

The Chumash were a maritime culture that built large wooden canoes called tomols to fish and travel among their coastal enclaves. They are also known for their cave paintings in places like Santa Barbara's Painted Cave State Historic Park.

During the Mission Period, five missions were built in Chumash territory. Shortly after the foundation of these missions, European diseases wiped out a large number of the Chumash. By 1831, there were less than 3,000 Chumash on this section of the California coast.

Today, there is a band of Chumash living on a reservation in Santa Barbara's Santa Ynez Valley.

EXPLORATION

Juan Rodríguez Cabrillo, a Portuguese explorer and adventurer, was commissioned in 1542 by the Viceroy of New Spain (Mexico) to sail into what is now San Diego Bay. He continued north as far as Point Reyes before heading to Catalina Island in late November 1542 to winter and make repairs to his ship. On Christmas Eve, Cabrillo tripped, splintering his shin, and the injury developed gangrene. He died on January 3, 1543, and is buried on Catalina. The rest of his party arrived in Barra de Navidad on April 14, 1543. Having found no wealth, advanced Native American civilization or agriculture, or northwest passage, Portuguese interest in exploring California lapsed for more than 200 years.

English explorer **Francis Drake** claimed a chunk of the Northern California coast in 1579. It is thought that Drake landed somewhere along Point Reyes to make extensive repairs to his only surviving ship, *The Golden Hind.* Drakes Bay, just east of Point Reyes, is marked as the spot of his landing, but the actual location is disputed. Drake eventually left California and completed the second recorded circumnavigation of the world (Ferdinand Magellan's was the first).

THE MISSION PERIOD

In the mid-1700s, Spain pushed for colonization of Alta California, rushing to occupy North America before the British beat them to it. The effort was overly ambitious and underfunded, but missionaries started to sweep into present-day California.

The priest **Junípero Serra** is credited with influencing the early development of California. A Franciscan monk, Serra took an active role in bringing Christianity and European diseases to Native American people from San Diego north to Sonoma County. The Franciscan order built a string of missions; each was intended to act as a self-sufficient parish that grew its own food, maintained its own buildings, and took care of its own people. However, mission structures were limited by a lack of suitable building materials and skilled labor. Later, the forced labor of Native Americans was used to cut and haul timbers and to make adobe bricks. By the time the missions were operating, they claimed about 15 percent of the land in California, or about one million acres per mission.

Spanish soldiers used subjugation to control indigenous people, pulling them from their villages and lands to the missions. Presidios (royal forts) were built near some of the missions to establish land claims, intimidate indigenous people, and carry out the overall goal of finding wealth in the New World. The presidios housed the Spanish soldiers that accompanied the missionaries. The cities of San Francisco, Santa Barbara, San Jose, and later Santa Cruz grew from the establishment of these missions and the presidios.

In 1821, Mexico gained independence from Spain along with control of Alta California and the missions. The Franciscans resisted giving up the land and free labor, and Native Americans continued to be treated as slaves. From 1824 to 1834 the Mexican government handed out 51 land grants to colonists for land that had belonged to Native Americans and was held by nearby missions. From 1834 to 1836 the Mexican government revoked the power of the Franciscans to use Native American labor and to redistribute the vast mission land holdings.

In the 20th century, interest in the history of the missions was rekindled, and funds were invested to restore many of the churches and complexes. Today, many of the missions have been restored as Catholic parishes, with visitors centers and museum displays of various levels of quality and polish. Some have been restored as state parks.

THE BEAR FLAG REVOLT

Mexico gained independence in 1821, claiming the Spanish lands that would become California and the U.S. Southwest. Hostilities between U.S. and Mexican troops began in April 1846 when a number of U.S. Army troops in the future state of Texas were attacked and killed. The first major battle of the Mexican-American War was fought the following month, and Congress responded with a declaration of war.

Rumors of possible Mexican military action against newly arrived settlers in California led a group of 30 settlers to seize the small Sonoma garrison in 1846. The uprising became known as the Bear Flag Revolt after a hastily designed flag depicting a grizzly bear and a five-point star was raised over Sonoma as the revolutionaries declared independence from Mexico. John A. Sutter, who had received a land grant near present-day Sacramento, and his men joined and supplied the revolt.

Captain John C. Frémont, who was leading a U.S. Army Corps of Topographical Engineers Exploratory Force, returned to Northern California when he received word that war with Mexico was imminent and that a revolt had occurred. The Bear Flag Revolt was short-lived; Frémont took over the rebellion and replaced the Bear Flag with the U.S. flag. Without orders and without knowing about the declaration of war, Frémont went on to the San Francisco Presidio to spike, or disable, the canons there. More U.S. ships, marines, and sailors arrived and took control of California ports up and down the coast. Frémont's forces grew into the California Battalion, whose members were used mainly to garrison and keep order in the rapidly surrendering towns.

THE GOLD RUSH

James Marshall was a carpenter employed by **John Sutter** to build a sawmill in Coloma near Placerville. Marshall made a glittery discovery on January 24, 1848, in a nearby stream: gold. Soon news spread to Sacramento and San Francisco that chunks of gold were on the riverbeds for the taking, and the Gold Rush was on. Thousands of people streamed into Northern California seeking gold. After panning streams and water-blasting hillsides for gold, the famous hard-rock mines of California began construction. Although panning continued, by the 1860s most of the rough men had taken jobs working in the dangerous mines. The most productive region was a swath of land nearly 200 miles long, roughly from El Dorado south to Mariposa, known as the Mother Lode or Gold Country. Mining towns such as Sonora, Volcano, Placerville, Sutter's Creek, and Nevada City swelled to huge proportions, only to shrink back into obscurity as the mines eventually closed one by one. Today, Highway 49 winds from one historic Gold Rush town to the next, and gold mining has mostly given way to tourism.

As American and European men came to California to seek their fortunes in gold, a few wives and children joined them, but the number of families in the average mining town was small. A few lone women joined in the rush to the gold fields in the oldest profession, serving the population of single male miners and laborers with female companionship.

Another major group of immigrants came to California from China—not to mine but to labor and serve the white miners. Most were forced to pass through the wretched immigration facilities on Angel Island in the middle of San Francisco Bay before being allowed onto the mainland; others were summarily shipped back to China. San Francisco's Chinatown became a hub for the immigrants, a place where their language was spoken and their culture understood. Thousands headed east, becoming low-level laborers in the industry surrounding the mines or workers on the railroads continuously being built to connect Gold Country to the rest of the country.

The dramatic population boom caused by the Gold Rush ensured that California would be on the fast track to admission into the United States, bypassing the territorial phase.

California became a state in 1850—it had gone from a Mexican province to the 31st U.S. state in little more than four years.

THE RAILROADS

California's population swelled to more than 250,000 within three years of the Gold Rush. To avoid the grueling cross-country trip, Eastern industrialists pushed for a railroad to open the West. While politicians argued, **Theodore D. Judah** got to work. Judah came to California from New York at the bidding of the promoters of the Sacramento Valley Railroad. The route linked the Embarcadero along the Sacramento River to Folsom, the jumping-off point to the gold fields. When the Sacramento Valley Railroad project ended in 1856, Judah became a passionate advocate for a transcontinental railroad. He lobbied in Washington D.C. and in 1861 convinced a group of merchants—men who would become known as the Big Four—to incorporate the Central Pacific Railroad in Sacramento.

The Big Four were **Leland Stanford, Charles Crocker, Collis Huntington,** and **Mark Hopkins,** and they were instrumental in developing the state railroad system from 1861 to 1900. Stanford operated a general store for miners before becoming an American tycoon, industrialist, politician, and the founder of Stanford University. Crocker founded a small independent iron forge, invested in the railroad venture, and eventually gained a controlling interest in Wells Fargo Bank before buying the rest of the bank for his son. Huntington was a Sacramento merchant who later went on to build other railroads. Hopkins was another Sacramento merchant who formed a partnership with Huntington before joining him in investing in the transcontinental railroad.

In mid-1862 President Abraham Lincoln signed the Pacific Railroad Act, giving the Central Pacific Railroad the go-ahead to build the railroad east from Sacramento and the Union Pacific Railroad to build west from Omaha. The government used land grants and government loans to fund the project. Workers for the two companies met May 10, 1869, at Promontory Summit, Utah, to complete the nation's first transcontinental railroad with a ceremonial golden spike.

THE GREAT DEPRESSION

The stock market crash of 1929 led to the Great Depression. Many property owners lost their farms and homes, and unemployment in California hit 28 percent in 1932; by 1935, about 20 percent of all Californians were on public relief.

The Great Depression transformed the nation. Beyond the economic agony was an optimism that moved people to migrate to California. Settling primarily in the Central Valley, these Midwest transplants preserved their ways and retained identities separate from other Californians. The Midwest migrant plight was captured in **John Steinbeck**'s 1939 novel *The Grapes of Wrath.* Steinbeck, a Salinas native, gathered information by viewing first-hand the deplorable living and labor conditions under which Okie families existed. The novel was widely read and was turned into a movie in 1940. Government agencies banned the book from public schools, and libraries and large landowners campaigned to have it banned elsewhere. That effort lost steam, however, when Steinbeck won the 1940 Pulitzer Prize.

Even during the worst economic depression in U.S. history, Californians continued to build and move forward. The San Francisco-Oakland Bay Bridge was completed in 1936 and the Golden Gate Bridge in 1937, connecting the land around San Francisco Bay and putting people to work. The 1939 Golden Gate International Exposition on Treasure Island in San Francisco Bay helped show the Great Depression the door.

WORLD WAR II

During World War II, San Francisco became home to the liberty ships, a fleet of like-design ships built quickly to help supply the war effort. Some liberty ships, known as the Mothball Fleet, are now tied together farther up Carquinez Strait and can be seen while driving south on I-680 near one of the state's first capitals, Benicia.

Unfortunately, California was also home to a deplorable chapter in the war—the internment camps for Japanese people and Japanese Americans. In reaction to the attack on Pearl Harbor, President Franklin Roosevelt signed Executive Order 9066 in 1942, creating "military exclusion zones" for people of Japanese ancestry. Approximately 110,000 Japanese Americans were uprooted and sent to war relocation camps in desolate areas such as Manzanar, in the dry basin of the eastern Sierras; Tulelake, in the remote northeast corner of the state; and as far away as North Dakota and Oklahoma.

In San Francisco, the immigration station on Angel Island became a deportation center in addition to interring Japanese prisoners of war. Today, examples of their carved inscriptions on the prison walls remain as part of the museum in the old barracks building.

THE 1960S

Few places in the country felt the impact of the radical changes of the 1960s more than California. It's arguable that the peace and free-love movements began here, probably on the campus of the indomitable **University of California, Berkeley.** Certainly Berkeley helped to shape and foster the culture of hippies, peaceniks, and radical politics. The college campus was the home of the Black Panthers, anti-Vietnam War sit-ins, and numerous protests for many progressive causes.

If Berkeley was the de facto home of 1960s political movements, then San Francisco was the base of its social and cultural phenomena. Free concerts in Golden Gate Park and the growing fame of the hippie community taking over a neighborhood called Haight-Ashbury drew young people from across the country. Many found themselves living on Haight Street for months and experimenting with the mind-altering chemicals emblematic of the era. The music scene became the stuff of legend. The Grateful Dead—one of the most famous and longest-lasting of the 1960s rock bands—hailed from the Bay Area.

THE DOT-COM ERA

The spectacular growth of the electronics industry started in Silicon Valley, south of San Francisco. Many firms settled in the area of Palo Alto, Santa Clara, Sunnyvale, and San Jose, producing innovations such as personal computers, video games, and networking systems at an incredible pace. All these firms were based in the Santa Clara Valley, dubbed Silicon Valley after the material used to produce integrated circuits. Hewlett-Packard and Varian Associates were among the early companies that grew here. Even today, the tenant list is impressive: Facebook, YouTube, LinkedIn, Adobe Systems, Apple, Cisco Systems, Intel, Oracle Corporation, SanDisk, and Symantec.

The demand for skilled technical professionals was so great in the high-tech industry that firms had difficulty filling openings and began lobbying to have visa restrictions eased so they could recruit professionals from abroad. Later, however, the dot-com financial bubble that formed in the mid-1990s burst, and tech-industry stock values plummeted in April 2000; many tech companies went into bankruptcy or were sold for a fraction of their worth, and jobs evaporated overnight. Within a few years, it seemed that many of the coveted high-tech jobs were "off-shored" (sent to India for 10 percent of the U.S. labor cost) or "on-shored" by recruiting among newcomers from China and India.

Despite the dot-com bust, Silicon Valley continues to be the technological hub of the state. Among metropolitan areas, Silicon Valley has the highest concentration of tech workers, with nearly 286 out of every 1,000 private-sector jobs. And the money is good too—the San Jose-Sunnyvale-Santa Clara metropolitan area has the most millionaires and billionaires per capita in the United States.

Government and Economy

GOVERNMENT

California is often viewed as a place where liberalism has run amok. It's true that California is home to what many consider liberal views: political protests and free speech, legalized medical marijuana use, environmental activism, and gay and lesbian rights. These beliefs are not incorporated as a whole throughout the state, however. Major metropolitan areas, such as San Francisco, and areas along the coast have become havens for artists, musicians, and those seeking alternatives to mainstream America. Populations in the Central Valley and the Sierra Nevada Foothills often show more conservative leanings at the polls.

California is overwhelmingly Democratic, but when it comes to politics, not everything is predictable. In 2008 California voters approved Proposition 8, which outlawed same-sex marriage equality, by 52.2 percent to 47.8 percent; voters in some counties approved the ban by more than 75 percent. A ballot measure to legalize marijuana use was defeated that same year. Yet Californians also voted for Barack Obama as president the same year by a definitive majority, 61 percent to 37 percent. Obama took the state again in the 2012 election with 53 percent of the votes.

ECONOMY

California boasts the eighth-largest economy in the world, although the ongoing global economic downturn may put a dent in that ranking in the years to come. Still, California's contribution to the United States outpaces even its immense size and population; it continues to be the country's number-one economy.

California's number-one economic sector is farming. The Central Valley's agricultural juggernaut supplies the world with crops that include grapefruit, grass-fed beef, rice, corn, and tomatoes. Sweet strawberries and spiky artichokes grow in abundance in the cooler Central Coast region. As the fog gets colder and drippier in Marin, ranchers take advantage of the naturally growing grasses for herds of cattle. Agriculture, including fruit, vegetables, nuts, dairy, and wine production, help make California the world's fifth-largest supplier of food and agriculture commodities.

Today, organic farms and ranches are proliferating across the state. In addition to the giant factory farms prevalent in the Central Valley, you'll also see an increasing number of small farms and ranches growing crops using organic, sustainable, and even biodynamic practices. Most of these farmers sell directly to consumers by way of farmers markets and farm stands—almost every town or county in California has a weekly farmers market in the summer, and many last year-round.

And then there's the wine. It seems like every square inch of free agricultural land has a grapevine growing on it. The vineyards that were once seen primarily in Napa and Sonoma can now be found on the slopes of the Sierra Foothills, on the northern Mendocino coast, and in Carmel Valley and Paso Robles. It's actually the wine industry that's leading the charge beyond mere organic and into biodynamic growing practices—using sheep to graze and maintain vineyards weeds, providing natural fertilizer, harvesting grapes, and pruning vines.

ESSENTIALS

Getting There

FLYING INTO SAN FRANCISCO

San Francisco's major airport is **San Francisco International Airport** (SFO, U.S. 101, San Mateo, 800/435-9736, www.flysfo.com), located approximately 13 miles south of the City. Plan to arrive at the airport up to three hours before your flight leaves. Airport lines, especially on weekends and holidays, are notoriously long, and planes can be grounded due to fog.

To avoid the SFO crowds, consider booking a flight into one of the Bay Area's less crowded airports. **Oakland International Airport** (OAK, 1 Airport Dr., Oakland, 510/563-3300, www.flyoakland.com) serves the East Bay with access to San Francisco via the Bay Bridge and commuter trains. **San Jose International Airport** (SJC, Airport Blvd., San Jose, 408/392-3600, www.sjc.org) is south of San Francisco in the heart of Silicon Valley. These airports are quite a bit smaller than SFO, but service is brisk from many U.S. destinations.

Several public and private transportation options can get you into San Francisco. **Bay Area Rapid Transit** (BART, www.bart.gov, one-way ticket to any downtown station $8.10) connects directly with SFO's international terminal, providing a simple and relatively fast (under one hour) trip to downtown San Francisco. The BART station is an easy walk or a free shuttle ride from any point in the airport. **Caltrain**

© 123RF.COM

(www.caltrain.com, tickets $2.75-12.75) is a good option if you are staying farther south on the peninsula. To access Caltrain from the airport, you must first take BART to the Millbrae stop, where the two lines meet. This station is designed for folks jumping from one line to the other. Caltrain tickets range in price depending on your destination.

Shuttle vans are another cost-effective option for door-to-door service, although these make several stops along the way. From the airport to downtown San Francisco, the average one-way fare is $17-25 per person. Shuttle vans congregate on the second level of SFO above the baggage claim area for domestic flights, and on the third level for international flights. Advance reservations guarantee a seat, but these aren't required and don't necessarily speed the process. Some companies to try include **Quake City Shuttle** (415/255-4899, www.quakecityshuttle.com) and **SuperShuttle** (800/258-3826, www.supershuttle.com).

For **taxis**, the average fare to downtown San Francisco is around $40.

FLYING INTO LOS ANGELES

The greater Los Angeles area is thick with airports. **Los Angeles International Airport** (LAX, 1 World Way, 310/646-5252, www.lawa.org) serves the greater Los Angeles area, and is located about 10 miles south of the city of Santa Monica. If you're coming in from another country or from across the continent, you're likely to find your flight coming into this endlessly crowded hub. If you're flying home from LAX, plan plenty of time to get through security and the check-in lines—up to three hours for a domestic flight on a holiday weekend.

To miss the major crowds, consider flying into one of the many suburban airports. **John Wayne Airport** (SNA, 18601 Airport Way, Santa Ana, 949/252-5200, www.ocair.com) serves Disneyland perfectly, and the **Long Beach Airport** (LGB, 4100 Donald Douglas Dr., 562/570-2600, www.lgb.org) is convenient to the beaches. **Ontario Airport** (ONT, 1923 E. Avion Dr., Ontario, 909/937-2700, www.lawa.

org) is farther out but a good option for travelers planning to divide their time between Los Angeles, Palm Springs, and the deserts.

In Los Angeles, free shuttle buses provide service to the Los Angeles County Metropolitan Transportation Authority **Metro Rail** (323/466-3876, www.mta.net), accessible at the Green Line Aviation Station. Metro Rail trains connect Long Beach, Hollywood, North Hollywood, Downtown Los Angeles, and Pasadena. Passengers should wait under the blue "LAX Shuttle Airline Connection" signs outside the lower-level terminals and board the "G" shuttle. Passengers may also take the "C" shuttle to the **Metro Bus Center** (323/466-3876, www.mta.net), which connects to buses that serve the entire L.A. area. Information about bus service is provided via telephones on the Information Display Board inside each terminal.

Shuttle services are also available if you want to share a ride. **Prime Time Shuttle** (800/733-8267, www.primetimeshuttle.com) and **SuperShuttle** (800/258-3826, www.supershuttle.com) are authorized to serve the entire Los Angeles area out of LAX. These vans can be found on the lower arrivals deck in front of each terminal, under the orange "Shared Ride Vans" signs. Average fares for two people are about $32 to Downtown Los Angeles, $34 to West Hollywood, and $30 to Santa Monica.

Taxis can be found on the lower arrivals level islands in front of each terminal, below the yellow "Taxi" signs. Only licensed taxis are allowed into the airport; they have standard rates of about $40 to downtown and $30 to West Los Angeles.

REGIONAL AIRPORTS

Domestic flights can be an economical and faster option when traversing between major cities within the state. San Francisco International Airport (SFO, www.flysfo.com), Oakland International Airport (OAK, www.flyoakland.com), and San Jose International Airport (SJC, www.sjc.org) connect with several smaller regional airports. These include the **Monterey Regional Airport** (MRY, www.

© 123RF.COM

traffic on the Golden Gate Bridge

montereyairport.com), the **Santa Barbara Airport** (SBA, www.flysba.com), the **San Luis Obispo County Regional Airport** (SLO, www.sloairport.com), and the **Arcata-Eureka Airport** (ACV, http://co.humboldt.ca.us). **Southwest Airlines** (www.southwest.com) provides affordable flights among the larger airports, while **United Airlines** (www.united.com) has regular flights to regional airports. Geared toward commuters, flights are generally frequent but a bit pricy.

TRAIN

Several long-distance **Amtrak** (www.amtrak.com) trains rumble through California daily. There are eight train routes that serve the region: The *California Zephyr* runs from Chicago and Denver to Emeryville; the *Coast Starlight* travels down the West Coast from Seattle and Portland as far as Los Angeles; the *Pacific Surfliner* will get you to the Central Coast. There is no train depot in San Francisco; the closest station is in Emeryville in the East Bay. Fortunately, comfortable coach buses ferry travelers to and from the Emeryville Amtrak station with many stops in downtown San Francisco.

CAR

California is great for road trips. Scenic coastal routes such as Highway 1 and U.S. 101 are often destinations in themselves. **Highway 1,** also known as the Pacific Coast Highway, follows the North Coast from Leggett to San Luis Obispo on the Central Coast and points south. Running parallel and intertwining with Highway 1 for much of its length, **U.S. 101** stretches north-south from Crescent City on the North Coast through the Central Coast, meeting Highway 1 in San Luis Obispo.

Road closures are not uncommon in winter. Highway 1 along the coast can shut down due to flooding or landslides. I-5 through the Central Valley can either close or be subject to hazardous driving conditions resulting from tule fog, which can reduce visibility to only a few feet.

Traffic jams, accidents, mudslides, fires, and snow can affect highways and interstates at any time. Before heading out on your adventure, check road conditions online at the **California Department of Transportation** (Caltrans, www.dot.ca.gov). The **Thomas Guide Road Atlas** (www.thomasguidebooks.com, $14) is a reliable and detailed map and road guide and a great insurance policy against getting lost.

Common-sense maintenance consciousness is required on the road. If the car gets hot or overheats, stop for a while to cool it off. Never open the radiator cap if the engine is steaming. After it has sat, squeeze the top radiator hose to see if there's any pressure in it; if there isn't, it's safe to open. Never pour water into a hot radiator—you could crack your block. If you start to smell rubber, your tires are overheating, and that's a good way to have a blowout. Stop and let them cool off. In winter in the high country, a can of silicone lubricant such as WD-40 will unfreeze door locks, dry off humid wiring, and keep your hinges in shape.

Car and RV Rental

Most car-rental companies are located at each

of the major California airports. To reserve a car in advance, contact **Budget Rent A Car** (800/527-0700, www.budget.com), **Dollar Rent A Car** (800/800-4000, www.dollar.com), **Enterprise** (800/261-7331, www.enterprise.com), or **Hertz** (800/654-3131, www.hertz.com).

To rent a car, drivers in California must be at least 21 years of age and have a valid driver's license. California law also requires that all vehicles carry liability insurance. You can purchase insurance with your rental car, but it generally costs an additional $10 per day, which can add up quickly. Most private auto insurance will also cover rental cars. Before buying rental insurance, check your car insurance policy to see if rental-car coverage is included.

The average cost of a rental car is $40 per day or $210 per week; however, rates vary greatly based on the time of year and distance traveled. Weekend and summer rentals cost significantly more. Generally, it is more expensive to rent from car rental agencies at an airport. To avoid excessive rates, first plan travel to areas where a car is not required, then rent a car from an agency branch in town to further explore more rural areas. Rental agencies occasionally allow vehicle drop-off at a different location from where it was picked up for an additional fee.

Another option is to rent an RV. You won't have to worry about camping or lodging options, and many facilities, particularly farther north, accommodate RVs. However, RVs are difficult to maneuver and park, limiting your access to metropolitan areas. They are also expensive, both in terms of gas and the rental rates. Rates during the summer average $1,300 per week and $570 for three days, the standard minimal rental. **Cruise America** (800/671-8042, www.cruiseamerica.com) has branches in San Francisco, San Jose, San Luis Obispo, Los Angeles, Costa Mesa, Oceanside, and San Diego. **El Monte RV** (800/337-2214, www.elmonterv.com) operates out of San Francisco, Paso Robles, Los Angeles, Newport Beach, and San Diego among other places.

BUS

A very affordable way to get around California is on **Greyhound** (800/231-2222, www.greyhound.com). The San Francisco Station (200 Folsom St., 415/495-1569) is a hub for Greyhound bus lines. They also have stations all along the coast from Crescent City down to San Diego. Greyhound routes generally follow the major highways, traveling U.S. 101. Most counties and municipalities have bus service with routes to outlying areas.

Visas and Officialdom

PASSPORTS AND VISAS

Visiting from another country, you must have a valid passport and a visa to enter the United States. If you hold a current passport from one of the following countries, you may qualify for the Visa Waiver Program: Andorra, Australia, Austria, Belgium, Brunei, Czech Republic, Denmark, Estonia, Finland, France, Germany, Greece, Hungary, Iceland, Ireland, Italy, Japan, Latvia, Liechtenstein, Lithuania, Luxembourg, Malta, Monaco, the Netherlands, New Zealand, Norway, Portugal, San Marino, Singapore, Slovakia, Slovenia, South Korea, Spain, Sweden, Switzerland, Taiwan, and the United Kingdom. To qualify, you must apply online with the Electronic System for Travel Authorization and hold a return plane or cruise ticket to your country of origin dated less than 90 days from your date of entry. Holders of Canadian passports don't need visas or visa waivers.

In most other countries, the local U.S. embassy should be able to provide a tourist visa. The average fee for a visa is US$160. While a visa may be processed as quickly as 24 hours on request, plan at least a couple of weeks, as there can be unexpected delays, particularly during the busy summer season (June-Aug.).

EMBASSIES

San Francisco and Los Angeles are home to embassies and consulates from many countries around the globe. If you should lose your passport or find yourself in some other trouble while visiting California, contact your country's offices for assistance. To find an embassy, check online at www.state.gov, which lists the websites for all foreign embassies in the United States. A representative will be able to direct you to the nearest embassy or consulate.

CUSTOMS

Before you enter the United States from another country by sea or by air, you'll be required to fill out a customs form. Check with the U.S. embassy in your country or the **Customs and Border Protection website** (www.cbp.gov) for an updated list of items you must declare.

If you require medication administered by injection, you must pack your syringes in a checked bag; syringes are not permitted in carry-ons coming into the United States.

Also, pack documentation describing your need for any narcotic medications you've brought with you. Failure to produce documentation for narcotics on request can result in severe penalties in the United States.

If you're driving into California along I-5 or another major highway, prepare to stop at Agricultural Inspection Stations a few miles inside the state line. You don't need to present a passport, a visa, or even a driver's license; instead, you must be prepared to present all your fruits and vegetables. California's largest economic sector is agriculture, and a number of the major crops grown here are sensitive to pests and diseases. In an effort to prevent known pests from entering the state and endangering crops, travelers are asked to identify all produce they're carrying in from other states or from Mexico. If you've got produce, especially homegrown or from a farm stand, it could be infected by a known problem pest or disease. Expect it to be confiscated on the spot.

You'll also be asked about fruits and veggies on your U.S. Customs form, which you'll be asked to fill out on the airplane or ship before you reach the United States.

Tips for Travelers

CONDUCT AND CUSTOMS

The legal **drinking age** in California is 21. Expect to have your ID checked if you look under age 30, especially in bars and clubs, but also in restaurants and wineries. Most California bars and clubs close at 2am; you'll find the occasional after-hours nightspot in San Francisco.

Smoking has been banned in many places throughout California. Don't expect to find a smoking section in any restaurant or an ashtray in any bar. Smoking is illegal in all bars and clubs, but your new favorite watering hole might have an outdoor patio where smokers can huddle. Taking the ban one step further, many hotels, motels, and inns throughout California are strictly nonsmoking, and you'll be subject to fees of hundreds of dollars if your room smells of smoke when you leave.

There's no smoking in any public building, and even some of the state parks don't allow cigarettes. There's often good reason for this; the fire danger in California is extreme in the summer, and one carelessly thrown butt can cause a genuine catastrophe.

ACCESS FOR TRAVELERS WITH DISABILITIES

Most California attractions, hotels, and restaurants are accessible for travelers with disabilities. State law requires that public transportation must accommodate the special needs of travelers with disabilities and that public spaces and businesses have adequate restroom facilities and equal access. This includes national parks and historic structures, many of which have been refitted with ramps and wider doors. Many hiking trails are also accessible to wheelchairs, and most campgrounds designate specific campsites that meet the Americans with Disabilities Act standards. The state of California also provides a free telephone TDD-to-voice relay service; just dial 711.

If you are traveling with a disability, there are many resources to help you plan your trip. **Access Northern California** (http://accessnca.org) is a nonprofit organization that offers general travel tips, including recommendations on accommodations, parks and trails, transportation, and travel equipment. **Access-Able** (http://access-able.com) is another travel resource, as is **Gimp-on-the-Go** (www.gimponthego.com). The message board on the **American Foundation for the Blind** (www.afb.org) website is a good forum to discuss travel strategies for the visually impaired. For a comprehensive guide to wheelchair accessible beaches, rivers, and shorelines from Santa Cruz to Marin County, including the East Bay and Wine Country, contact the **California Coastal Conservancy** (510/286-1015, www. scc.ca.gov), which publishes a free and downloadable guide. **Wheelchair Getaways** in San Francisco (800/638-1912, www.wheelchair-getaways.com, $95-110 per day), Los Angeles (800/638-1912), and San Diego (877/388-4883) rent wheelchair-accessible vans and offer pickup and drop-off service from airports ($100-300). Likewise, **Avis Access** (888/879-4273, www.avis.com) rents cars, scooters, and other products to make traveling with a disability easier; click on the "Services" link on their website.

TRAVELING WITH CHILDREN

Many spots in California are ideal destinations for families with children of all ages. Amusement parks, interactive museums, zoos, parks, beaches, and playgrounds all make for family-friendly fun. On the other hand, there are a few spots in the Golden State that beckon more to adults than to children. Frankly, there aren't many family activities in Wine Country. This adult playground is all about alcoholic beverages and high-end dining. Similarly, the North Coast's focus on original art and romantic B&Bs brings out couples looking for weekend getaways rather than families. In fact, before you book a room at a B&B that you expect to share with your kids, check to be sure that the inn can accommodate extra people in the guest rooms and whether they allow guests under age 16.

WOMEN TRAVELING ALONE

California is a pretty friendly place for women traveling alone. Most of the major outdoor attractions are incredibly safe, and even many of the urban areas boast pleasant neighborhoods that welcome lone female travelers. But you'll need to take some basic precautions and pay attention to your surroundings, just as you would in any unfamiliar place. Carry your car keys in your hand when walking out to your car. Don't sit in your parked car in a lonely parking lot at night; just get in, turn on the engine, and drive away. When you're walking down a city street, be alert and keep an eye on your surroundings and on anyone who might be following you. In rural areas, don't go tromping into unlit wooded areas or out into grassy fields alone at night without a flashlight; many of California's critters are nocturnal. Of course, this caution applies to men as well; mountain lions and rattlesnakes don't tend to discriminate.

SENIOR TRAVELERS

California makes an ideal destination for older or retired folks looking to relax and have a great time. You'll find senior discounts nearly every place you go, including restaurants, golf courses, major attractions, and even some hotels, although the minimum age can range 50-65. Just ask, and be prepared to produce ID if you look young or are requesting a senior discount. You can often get additional discounts on rental cars, hotels, and tour packages as a member of **AARP** (888/687-2277, www. aarp.org). If you're not a member, its website can also offer helpful travel tips and advice. **Elderhostel** (800/454-5768, www.roadscholar. org) is another great resource for senior travelers. Dedicated to providing educational opportunities for older travelers, Elderhostel provides

COASTING CALIFORNIA WITH THE KIDS

Driving the California coast is a classic family road trip, with a range of attractions for kids to enjoy.

SAN FRANCISCO AND THE BAY AREA

With its interactive exhibits, San Francisco's **Exploratorium** allows kids experience science firsthand. Both the **San Francisco Zoo** and **Oakland Zoo** have all sorts of animals to meet. Kids will also want to take a spin on **Pier 39**'s **San Francisco Carousel,** painted with images of the City by the Bay.

WINE COUNTRY

Wine Country is better known for romance than a family attractions, but there are a few. Santa Rosa's **Charles M. Schulz Museum** is for fans of the *Peanuts* comic strip. Kids love Calistoga's **Old Faithful Geyser,** which also has an adjacent petting zoo. Even some wineries are kid-friendly. **Castello di Amorosa** looks like a fairy-tale castle and serves juice to visitors under 21. **Francis Ford Coppola Winery** entices parents with movie memorabilia; kids can enjoy the property's two pools on warm summer days.

NORTH COAST

South of Crescent City, the **Trees of Mystery** will fascinate the little ones with a near-50-foot statue of Paul Bunyan and the **Skytrail,** a gondola ride above the redwood forest. With low ceilings and porthole entryways, the buildings of **Patrick's Point State Park**'s **Sumeg Village** are a fun place for kids to learn about Native American history. Just south of Trinidad, **Moonstone Beach** is a family favorite.

MONTEREY BAY

The **Santa Cruz Beach Boardwalk** offers nonstop amusement. Families flock to **Monterey Bay Aquarium** to see cute sea otters and scary sharks up close. If your kids just want to play, you can't beat Monterey's **Dennis the Menace Park,** which has all sorts of slides, bridges, and swing sets.

BIG SUR AND THE CENTRAL COAST

Pismo Beach's **Dinosaur Caves Park** has fun stuff like concrete dolphins, a play ship, a dinosaur statue, and three dinosaur eggs. To see underwater sea life without donning snorkeling gear, hitch a ride with Morro Bay's **Sub Sea Tours,** where families ride in a mini submarine.

SANTA BARBARA AND VENTURA

The **Santa Barbara Zoo** has a popular kid's exhibit called "Eeeww!," which focuses on all sorts of slithery species. Just west of Santa Barbara, **Refugio State Beach** has a protected cove calm enough for kids to wade in and the park store is available for a round of ice cream.

LOS ANGELES AND ORANGE COUNTY

Families crowd the **Santa Monica Pier** for its amusement park, arcade and aquarium. In Long Beach, the **Aquarium of the Pacific** wows kids with live penguins, sea otters, and sharks. You may have also heard of an Orange County attraction that's become popular with families: a place called **Disneyland.** This amusement park is apparently home to an anthropomorphic mouse.

SAN DIEGO

The **San Diego Zoo** has everything from scurrying spiders to giant pandas. In Escondido, the **San Diego Wild Animal Park** is run by the same folks but has the animals spread out over more land. One way to view the animals is by safari. To see water creatures, head to **SeaWorld,** which has rides, shows, and exhibits, in addition to dolphins and whales. Up in Carlsbad, **LEGOLAND** is a whole amusement park dedicated to the popular plastic building blocks.

package trips to beautiful and interesting destinations. Called "Educational Adventures," these trips are generally 3-9 days long and emphasis history, natural history, art, music, or a combination thereof.

GAY AND LESBIAN TRAVELERS

California is known for its thriving gay and lesbian communities. In fact, the Golden State is a golden place for gay travel—especially in the bigger cities and even in some of the smaller towns around the state. As with much of the country, the farther you venture into rural and agricultural regions, the less likely you are to experience the liberal acceptance the state is known for. The **International Gay and Lesbian Travel Association** (www.iglta.org) has a directory of gay- and lesbian-friendly tour operators, accommodations, and destinations.

San Francisco has the biggest and arguably best **Gay Pride Festival** (www.sfpride.org) in the nation, usually held on Market Street on the last weekend in June. Year-round, the Castro District offers fun of all kinds, from theater to clubs to shopping, mostly targeted at gay men but with a few places sprinkled in for lesbians. If the Castro is your primary destination, you can even find a place to stay in the middle of the action.

West Hollywood in Los Angeles has its own upscale gay culture. Just like the rest of L.A.'s clubs, the gay clubs are havens of the see-and-be-seen crowd.

Santa Cruz on the Central Coast is a quirky town specially known for its lesbian-friendly culture. A relaxed vibe informs everything from underground clubs to unofficial nude beaches to live-action role-playing games in the middle of downtown. Even the lingerie and adult toy shops tend to be woman-owned and operated.

San Diego also has its own **San Diego Pride Festival and Parade** (www.sdpride.org), which is one of the largest on the West Coast and happens every July.

Health and Safety

MEDICAL SERVICES

For an emergency anywhere in California, **dial 911.** Inside hotels and resorts, check your emergency number as soon as you get to your guest room. In urban and suburban areas, full-service hospitals and medical centers abound, but in more remote regions, help can be more than an hour away.

If you're planning a **backcountry expedition,** follow all rules and guidelines for obtaining **wilderness permits** and for self-registration at trailheads. These are for your safety, letting the rangers know roughly where you plan to be and when to expect you back. National and state park visitors centers can advise in more detail on any health or wilderness alerts in the area. It is also advisable to let someone outside your party know your route and expected date of return.

Being out in the elements can present its own set of challenges. Despite California's relatively mild climate, **heat exhaustion** and **heat stroke** can affect anyone during the hot summer months, particularly during a long strenuous hike in the sun. Common symptoms include nausea, lightheadedness, headache, or muscle cramps. **Dehydration** and loss of electrolytes are the common causes of heat exhaustion. If you or anyone in your group develops any of these symptoms, get out of the sun immediately, stop all physical activity, and drink plenty of water. Heat exhaustion can be severe, and if untreated can lead to heat stroke, in which the body's core temperature reaches 105°F. Fainting, seizures, confusion, and rapid heartbeat and breathing can indicate the situation has moved beyond heat exhaustion. If you suspect this, call 911 immediately.

Similar precautions hold true for **hypothermia,** which is caused by prolonged exposure to cold water or weather. For many in California, this can happen on a hike or backpacking trip without sufficient rain gear, or by staying too long in the ocean or another cold body of water without a wetsuit. Symptoms include shivering, weak pulse, drowsiness, confusion, slurred speech, or stumbling. To treat hypothermia, immediately remove the wet clothing, cover the person with blankets, and feed him or her hot liquids. If symptoms don't improve, call 911.

WILDERNESS SAFETY

Many places are still wild in California, making it important to use precautions with regard to wildlife. While California no longer has any grizzly bears, **black bears** thrive and are often seen in the mountains foraging for food in the spring, summer, and fall. Black bears certainly don't have the size or reputation of grizzlies, but there is good reason to exercise caution. Never get between a bear and her cub, and if a bear sees you, identify yourself as human by waving your hands above your head, speaking in a calm voice, and backing away slowly. If a bear charges, do not run. One of the best precautions against an unwanted bear encounter is to keep a clean camp; store all food in airtight, bear-proof containers; and strictly follow any guidelines given by the park or rangers.

Even more common than bears are **mountain lions,** which can be found in the Coast Range, as well as grasslands and forests. Because of their solitary nature, it is unlikely you will see one, even on long trips in the backcountry. Still, there are a couple things to remember. If you come across a kill, probably a large partly eaten deer, leave immediately. And if you see a mountain lion and it sees you, identify yourself as human, making your body appear as big as possible, just as with a bear. And remember: Never run. As with any cat, large or small, running triggers its hunting instincts. If a mountain lion should attack, fight back; cats don't like to get hurt.

The other treacherous critter in the backcountry is the **rattlesnake.** They can be found in summer in generally hot and dry areas from the coast to the Sierra Nevada. When hiking in this type of terrain—many parks will indicate if rattlesnakes are a problem in the area—keep your eyes on the ground and an ear out for the telltale rattle. Snakes like to warn you to keep away. The only time this is not the case is with baby rattlesnakes that have not yet developed their rattles. Unfortunately, they have developed their fangs and venom, which is particularly potent. Should you get bitten, immediately try to suck out the venom with your mouth and then spit it out. Use a piece of cloth as a tourniquet on your upper arm or leg to reduce the blood flow to the bite. This will lessen the chance of the venom spreading. Next, get immediate medical help.

Mosquitoes can be found throughout the state. At higher elevations they can be worse, prompting many hikers and backpackers to don head nets and apply potent repellents, usually DEET. The high season for mosquitoes is late spring-early summer.

Ticks live in many of the forests and grasslands throughout the state, except at higher elevations. Tick season generally runs late fall-early summer. If you are hiking through brushy areas, wear pants and long-sleeve shirts. Ticks like to crawl to warm moist places (armpits are a favorite) on their host. If a tick is engorged, it can be difficult to remove. There are two main types of ticks found in California: dog ticks and deer ticks. Dog ticks are larger, brown, and have a gold spot on their backs, while deer ticks are small, tear-shaped, and black. Deer ticks are known to carry Lyme disease. While Lyme disease is relatively rare in California—there are more cases in the northernmost part of the state—it is very serious. If you get bitten by a deer tick and the bite leaves a red ring, seek medical attention. Lyme disease can be successfully treated with early rounds of antibiotics.

There is only one major variety of plant in California that can cause an adverse reaction in humans if you touch the leaves or stems: **poison oak,** a common shrub that inhabits forests throughout the state. Poison oak has a characteristic three-leaf configuration, with scalloped leaves that are shiny green in

© 123RF.COM

Warning: beach crossing!

the spring and then turn yellow, orange, and red in late summer-fall. In fall, the leaves drop, leaving a cluster of innocuous-looking branches. The oil in poison oak is present year-round in both the leaves and branches. Your best protection is to wear long sleeves and long pants when hiking, no matter how hot it is. A product called Tecnu is available at most California drugstores—slather it on before you go hiking to protect yourself from poison oak. If your skin comes into contact with poison oak, expect a nasty rash known for its itchiness and irritation. Poison oak is also extremely transferable, so avoid touching your eyes, face, or other parts of your body to prevent spreading the rash. Calamine lotion can help, and in extreme cases a doctor can administer cortisone to help decrease the inflammation.

CRIME AND SAFETY PRECAUTIONS

The outdoors are not the only place that harbors danger. In both rural and urban areas, theft can be a problem. When parking at a trailhead or in a park or at a beach, don't leave any valuables in the car. If you must, place them out of sight, either in a locked glove box or in the trunk. The same holds true for urban areas. Furthermore, avoid keeping your wallet, camera, and other expensive items, including lots of cash, easily accessible in backpacks; keep them within your sight at all times. Certain urban neighborhoods are best avoided at night. If you find yourself in these areas after dark, consider taking a cab to avoid walking blocks and blocks to get to your car or to wait for public transportation. In case of a theft or any other emergency, call 911.

Information and Services

MONEY

California businesses use the U.S. dollar ($). Most businesses also accept the major credit cards Visa, MasterCard, Discover, and American Express. ATM and debit cards work at many stores and restaurants, and ATMs are available throughout the region. In more remote areas, such as the North Coast, some business may only accept cash, so don't depend entirely on your plastic.

You can change currency at any international airport in the state. Currency exchange points also crop up in downtown San Francisco and at some of the major business hotels in urban areas.

California is not a particularly expensive place to travel, but keeping an eye on your budget is still important. San Francisco and the Wine Country are the priciest regions for visitors, especially with the amount of high-quality food and luxury accommodations. Advance reservations for hotels and marquee restaurants in these areas are recommended.

Banks

As with anywhere, traveling with a huge amount of cash is not recommended, which may make frequent trips to the bank necessary. Fortunately, most destinations have at least one major bank. Usually Bank of America or Wells Fargo can be found on the main drags through towns. Banking hours tend to be Monday-Friday 8am-5pm, Saturday 9am-noon. Never count on a bank being open on Sundays or on federal holidays. If you need cash when the banks are closed, there is generally a 24-hour ATM available. Furthermore, many cash-only businesses have an ATM on-site for those who don't have enough cash ready in their wallets. The unfortunate downside to this convenience is a fee of $2-4 per transaction. This also applies to ATMs at banks at which you don't have an account.

Tax

Sales tax in California varies by city and county, but the average rate is around 8.5 percent. All goods are taxable with the exception of food not eaten on the premises. For example, your bill at a restaurant will include tax, but your bill at a grocery store will not. The hotel tax is another unexpected added expense to traveling in California. Most cities have enacted a tax on hotel rooms largely to make up for budget shortfalls. As you would expect, these taxes are higher in areas more popular with visitors. In Wine County you can expect to add an additional 12-14 percent onto your hotel bill, while in San Francisco the tax tops 15 percent. Some areas like Eureka have a lower hotel tax of 10 percent.

Tipping

Tipping is expected and appreciated, and a 15 percent tip for restaurants is about the norm. When ordering in bars, tip the bartender or waitstaff $1 per drink. For taxis, plan to tip 15-20 percent of the fare, or simply round up the cost to the nearest dollar. Cafés and coffee shops often have tip jars out. There is no consensus on what is appropriate when purchasing a $3 beverage. Often $0.50 is enough, depending on the quality and service.

COMMUNICATIONS AND MEDIA

With the exception of rural and wilderness areas, California is fairly well connected. Cell phone reception is good except in places far from any large town. Likewise, you can find Internet access just about anywhere. The bigger cities are well wired, but even in small towns you can log on either at a library or in a café with a computer in the back. Be prepared to pay a per-minute usage fee or purchase a drink.

The main newspapers in California are the *San Francisco Chronicle* and the *Los Angeles Times.* Of course, there are other regional papers that may offer some international news in addition to the local color. As for radio, there are some news stations on the FM dial, and in most regions you can count on finding a National Public Radio (NPR, www.npr.org) affiliate. While they will all offer some NPR news coverage, some will be more geared toward music and local concerns.

Because of California's size both geographically and in terms of population, you will have to contend with multiple area codes—the numbers that prefix the seven-digit phone number—throughout the state. The 800 or 866 area codes are toll-free numbers. Any time you are dialing out of the area, you must dial a 1 plus the area code followed by the seven-digit number.

To mail a letter, find a blue post office box, which are found on the main streets of any town. Postage rates vary by destination. You can purchase stamps at the local post office, where you can also mail packages. Stamps can also be bought at some ATMs and online at www.usps.com, which can also give you the location and hours of the nearest post office. Post offices are generally open Monday-Friday, with limited hours on Saturday. They are always closed on Sunday and federal holidays.

MAPS AND VISITOR INFORMATION

When visiting California, you might be tempted to stop in at one of several Golden State Welcome Centers scattered throughout the state. In all honesty, these visitors centers aren't that great. If you're in an area that doesn't have its own visitors center, the State Welcome Center might be a useful place to pick up maps and brochures. Check www.visitcwc.com to find a local Welcome Center wherever you're visiting. Otherwise, stick with local, regional, and national park visitors centers, which tend to be staffed by volunteers or rangers who feel a real passion for their locale.

If you are looking for maps, almost all gas stations and drugstores sell maps both of the place you're in and of the whole state. **California State Automobile Association** (CSAA, www.csaa.com) offers free maps to auto club members.

Many local and regional visitors centers also offer maps, but you'll need to pay a few dollars for the bigger and better ones. But if all you need is a wine-tasting map in a known wine region, you can probably get one for free along with a few tasting coupons at the nearest regional visitors center. Basic national park maps come with your admission payment. State park maps can be free or cost a few dollars at the visitors centers.

The state's **California Travel and Tourism Commission** (916/444-4429, www.visitcalifornia.com) also provides helpful and free tips, information, and downloadable maps and guides.

California is in the Pacific time zone (PST and PDT) and observes daylight saving time March-November.

Internet Resources

It should come as no surprise that the California travel industry leads the way in the use of the Internet as a marketing, communications, and sales tool. The overwhelming majority of destinations have their own websites—even tiny towns in the middle of nowhere proudly tout their attractions on the Web.

California Department of Transportation
www.dot.ca.gov/hq/roadinfo/statemap.htm
Check here for state map and highway information before planning a coastal road trip.

Visit California
www.visitcalifornia.com
Before your visit, visit the official tourism site of the state of California.

California Outdoor and Recreational Information
www.caoutdoors.com

This recreation-focused website includes links to maps, local newspapers, festivals, and events as well as a wide variety of recreational activities throughout the state.

California State Parks
www.parks.ca.gov

The official website lists hours, accessibility, activities, camping areas, fees, and more information for all parks in the state system.

State of California
www.ca.gov/tourism/greatoutdoors.html

This website offers outdoor resources for California state and government organizations. Check for information about fishing and hunting licenses, backcountry permits, boating regulations, and more.

SFGate
www.sfgate.com

This website affiliated with the *San Francisco Chronicle* offers information on activities, festivals, and events in the city by the bay.

WineCountry
www.winecountry.com

This tourism website offers information on all of California's wine regions, including Napa, Sonoma, Mendocino, Carmel Valley, Paso Robles, Santa Barbara, and Temecula.

LATourist
www.latourist.com

This informative tourist website is dedicated to the City of Angels.

Los Angeles Convention and Visitors Bureau
www.lacvb.com

It's the official website of the Los Angeles Convention and Visitors Bureau.

Disneyland
http:/disneyland.disney.go.com

Find information on all things Disney here.

Index

List of Maps

www.moon.com

DESTINATIONS | ACTIVITIES | BLOGS | MAPS | BOOKS

MOON.COM is ready to help plan your next trip! Filled with fresh trip ideas and strategies, author interviews, informative travel blogs, a detailed map library, and descriptions of all the Moon guidebooks, Moon.com is all you need to get out and explore the world—or even places in your own backyard. While at Moon.com, sign up for our monthly e-newsletter for updates on new releases, travel tips, and expert advice from our on-the-go Moon authors. As always, when you travel with Moon, expect an experience that is uncommon and truly unique.

KEEP UP WITH MOON ON FACEBOOK AND TWITTER
JOIN THE MOON PHOTO GROUP ON FLICKR